AF819986

General Intelligence & Reasoning Test

VERBAL & NON-VERBAL REASONING

SSC (CGL, CHSL, MTS, CPO, GD), **Railway** (NTPC, Group D, ALP)
CUET, Police (Constable, SI) & All Other
Competitive Exams...

No. 1 Best Selling Book of Reasoning for all ***One Day Exams*** in India

General Intelligence & Reasoning Test

VERBAL & NON-VERBAL REASONING

SSC (CGL, CHSL, MTS, CPO, GD), **Railway** (NTPC, Group D, ALP) **CUET, Police** (Constable, SI) & All Other Competitive Exams...

Author

RK Jha

Suported by

Varun Bali & Team Members

arihant

SUCCESS AND NOTHING LESS

arihant
SUCCESS AND NOTHING LESS

ARIHANT PUBLICATIONS (INDIA) LIMITED

Administrative & Production Offices

Regd. Office
'Ramchhaya' 4577/15, Agarwal Road, Darya Ganj, New Delhi -110002
Tele: 011- 47630600, 43518550

Head Office
Kalindi, TP Nagar, Meerut (UP) - 250002
Tel: 0121-7156203, 7156204

Sales & Support Offices
Agra, Ahmedabad, Bengaluru, Bareilly, Chennai, Delhi, Guwahati, Hyderabad, Jaipur, Jhansi, Kolkata, Lucknow, Nagpur & Pune.

PRICE ₹ 260.00

PO No : TXT-XX-XXXXXXX-X-XX

Published by Arihant Publications (India) Ltd.

For further information about the books published by Arihant, log on to www.arihantbooks.com or e-mail at info@arihantbooks.com

PREFACE

Reasoning is the process of thinking in logical way in order to form the conclusion or judgement from information. Reasoning basically tests candidates logical thinking and skill to draw inferences. Importance of reasoning is increasingly moving centre stage in general competitive or entrance examinations. The questions that are asked in different examinations are not easy to solve and one cannot solve these problems without having a proper practice, once you know the basic concepts behind problems, you can solve them in least time.

The book '**General Intelligence & Reasoning Test**' will certainly help the candidates to become familiar with the concepts and approaches, which are used to solve the various reasoning problems. The book covers all the three types of reasoning comprehensively i.e. Verbal, Analytical and Non-Verbal Reasoning divided into chapters. Each chapter is further divided into types of questions asked in competitive exams. Each section also contains previous year questions upto January 2025 asked in different competitive exams like SSC (CGL, CPO, 10+2, MTS), Railway (NTPC, Group D, ALP), CUET & State Recruitment Exams.

Latest trends and level of difficulty of questions being asked in various competitive exams have been incorporated in this book. The questions and their accurate solutions will help the candidates to practice more in minimum time.

Features of Book

- Complete coverage of **Verbal, Non-verbal & Analytical Reasoning**.
- **Typewise distribution** of Synopsis and Questions with Concept Map.
- Coverage of all types questions in **Exam Approach Examples.**
- **3000+ Lattest PYQs** coverage upto January 2025 (Typewise).
- MRC (Most Repeating Concept) Marking in Exercise of Every Chapter.
- Coverage of **Trending Concept** and **Helping Tips** in Examples.
- **Detailed Explanation** of all questions with **Smart Approach.**

I am thankful to **Arihant Publications (India) Limited** for giving me the opportunity to write such a book, which covers complete syllabus of almost all competitive exams; SSC, Railway, State Police Recruitments, etc.

I am also very thankful to **Mohd. Shahid Saifi** and **Content Expert Team** (Nikhil Sharma, Ranjan Kumar and Manju Dahiya) for their sincere efforts for the compilation of this book.

I am very sure that this book will add a new dimension to the preparation of **Reasoning Test** for various competitive examinations and prove a great help in cracking the examination.

RK Jha

CONTENTS

Verbal Reasoning

1. Analogy 1-16
2. Classification 17-26
3. English Alphabet Test 27-33
4. Word Formation 34-39
5. Arrangement of Words 40-45
6. Coding-Decoding 46-60
7. Series Test 61-72
8. Conditional Number/Letter/Symbol 73-81
9. Direction and Distance 82-92
10. Blood Relation 93-104
11. Ranking Arrangement Test 105-112
12. Sitting Arrangement 113-124
13. Puzzle Test 125-134
14. Clock and Calendar 135-146
15. Mathematical Operations 147-156
16. Mathematical Reasoning 157-165
17. Inserting the Missing Characters 166-174
18. Mathematical Statements and Conclusions (Inequality) 175-181
19. Decision Making 182-189
20. Cube, Cuboid and Dice 190-203
21. Venn Diagram 204-213

Analytical Reasoning

22. Syllogism 214-228
23. Statement and Conclusions 229-237
24. Statement and Arguments 238-244
25. Statement and Assumptions 245-251
26. Statement and Courses of Action 252-257
27. Assertion and Reason 258-262
28. Cause and Effect 263-268

Non-verbal Reasoning

1. Figure Analogy 269-274
2. Figure Classification 275-280
3. Figure Series 281-287
4. Figure Completion 288-293
5. Figure Formation 294-297
6. Embedded Figures 298-301
7. Counting of Figures 302-310
8. Mirror and Water Images 311-316
9. Paper Folding and Cutting 317-322
10. Figure Matrix 323-328

CHAPTER

01 Analogy

Analogy

Analogy means similarity of an element with an another element on the basis of their properties, shape, type, features and characteristics etc. Questions asked in this chapter required selection of appropriate words/letters/numbers from the options based on a particular relationship between the given pair of words/letters/numbers.

Word Analogy

In word analogy, similarity is found out by finding the certain relationship between words or words pair. The relationship can be based on synonyms, antonyms, countries and their capitals, currencies, languages, rivers, sports, national symbols, equipment and measurement etc.

e.g. Diet : Dietician : : High Blood Sugar : ?

(a) Oncologist (b) Urologist

(c) Dermatologist (d) Diabetologist

Sol. (d) As, Diet is suggested by Dietician. Similarly, High Blood Sugar is controlled by Diabetologist.

Letter Analogy

In letter analogy, the similar letter/letter-pair can be find out by establishing relationship between given letter/letter-pair. The relationship can be based on number of letters and mathematical operations on them, forward and reverse order of letters according to the English alphabet, opposite letters, sum of the position of letters in the alphabet, increasing and decreasing the number of letters, mathematical operations between letters etc.

e.g. SAME : WDOF : : GOAL : ?

(a) KRCM (b) KRBM (c) KSCM (d) JRCM

Sol. (a) As,

S	A	M	E
+4↓	+3↓	+2↓	+1↓
W	D	O	F

Similarly,

G	O	A	L
+4↓	+3↓	+2↓	+1↓
K	R	C	M

Number Analogy

In number analogy, the similar number/number-pair can be find out by establishing a mathematics relationship between other number/number-pair. The relationship can be based on the order of numbers, order of their squares and cubes, numbers and number groups and mathematical operations on them (addition, subtraction, multiplication, division etc.), order of prime numbers etc.

e.g. 7 : 32 : : 28 : ?

(a) 126 (b) 136

(c) 116 (d) 128

Sol. (c) As, 7 : 32

$\Rightarrow$ $(7 \times 4) + 4 = 28 + 4 = 32$

Similarly, 28 : ?

$\Rightarrow$ $(28 \times 4) + 4 = 112 + 4 = \boxed{116}$

Mixed Analogy

In mixed analogy, the relationship are established between given group of letters/numbers. The candidates are asked to find out the correct group from the given alternatives which shares the same relationship as it is between the given group of letters/numbers.

e.g. RAT : 18120 : : GOD : ?

(a) 7174 (b) 7164

(c) 7154 (d) 7144

Sol. (c) As,

R	A	T	
↓	↓	↓	
18	1	20	(Positional value)

Similarly,

G	O	D	
↓	↓	↓	
7	15	4	(Positional value)

Score Booster

More than one answer can be possible in number analogy. So, keep in mind the options and find the relation of similarly/ symmetry.

In letter analogy, when we find out the relation between more than two letter in a question, then we can find the answer by knowing the relation of any one letter through the options.

Important Facts/Information related to Analogy

1. **Basic Relationship** In this type of relationship, the relation which exists between the two elements of the first pair, the same relation exists between the two elements of the second pair also.

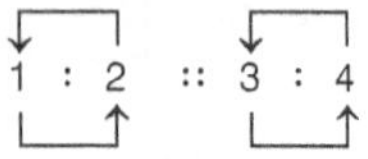

Here, in 1 : 2 :: 3 : 4, the type of relationship that will exists between 1 to 2 or 2 to 1 will be the same type of relationship that will exist between 3 to 4 or 4 to 3.

2. **Developed Relationship** In this type of relationship, the first element of the first pair is related to the first element of the second pair in the same way as the second element of the first pair is related to the second element of the second pair.

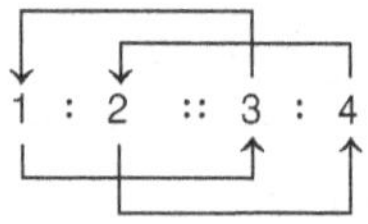

Here, some relationships are given, which are useful for solving questions based on word analogy.

I. Country : Capital

Some important examples based on this relationship are as follows

Iraq	:	Baghdad	Australia	:	Canberra
Russia	:	Mascow	Greece	:	Athens
Bhutan	:	Thimpu	Germany	:	Berlin

II. Country : Currency

Some important examples based on this relationship are as follows

China	:	Yuan	Greece	:	Euro
India	:	Rupee	UK	:	Pound
Kuwait	:	Dinar	USA	:	Dollar

III. State : Capital

Some important examples based on this relationship are as follows

West Bengal	:	Kolkata
Rajasthan	:	Jaipur
Bihar	:	Patna

IV. Instrument : Measurement

Some important examples based on this relationship are as follows

Seismograph	:	Earthquake
Thermometer	:	Temperature
Speedometer	:	Speed
Barometer	:	Pressure
Balance	:	Mass

V. Quantity : Unit

Some important examples based on this relationship are as follows

Power	:	Watt
Time	:	Second
Force	:	Newton
Current	:	Ampere
Pressure	:	Pascal

VI. Word : Synonym

Some important examples based on this relationship are as follows

Abduct	:	Kidnap
Dearth	:	Scarcity
Substitute	:	Replace

VII. Word : Antonym

Some important examples based on this relationship are as follows

Chaos	:	Peace
Gentle	:	Harsh
Notice	:	Ignore
Cruel	:	Kind

VIII. Animals/Things : Keeping place

Some important examples based on this relationship are as follows

Grains	:	Granary
Animals	:	Zoo
Birds	:	Aviary
Aeroplane	:	Hangar

Other Important Relations of Word Analogy

- Country : Continent
- Country : Parliament
- Country : National Emblem
- Country : National Animal
- Country : National Flower
- Country : River
- Country : Tribe
- Country : Port
- Country : Place
- City : Industry
- Country : Government Documents
- Country : National Monuments
- Country : News agency
- Country : Intelligence Agency
- Country : Newspaper
- Country : National Game
- Country : Natural Site
- State : High court
- Product : Raw Material
- Product : Worker
- Person : Workplace
- Person : Tool
- Tool : Work
- Person : Place
- Animals : Group
- Science : Field of Study
- Revolution : Production Sector
- Animal : Sound
- Animal : Young one
- Religion : Place of Worship
- Religion : Religious Books
- Flag : Meaning
- Symbol : Meaning
- Buildings : Place
- City : Founder
- Dynasty : Founder
- Person : Tomb
- Sports : Complex
- Invention : Inventor
- Sports : Awards
- Individuals : Related Games
- Union Territory : Capital

Exam Approach Examples

Based on Word Analogy

Example 1 **'Musician' is related to 'Piano', in the same way as 'Farmer' is related to.....**

(a) Bullock (b) Plough (c) Field (d) Cultivation

Sol. *(b)* As, 'Musician' plays 'Piano' for music. Similarly, 'Farmer' uses 'Plough' for farming.

Directions (Ex. Nos. 2-6) *In each of the following questions, select the related word from the given alternatives.*

Example 2 **Colour : Red :: Profession : ?** ***SSC MTS 2019***

(a) Lawyer (b) Court
(c) School (d) Black

Sol. *(a)* As, Red is a colour. Similarly, Lawyer is a profession.

Example 3 **Pig : Piglets : : Deer : ?**

(a) Pup
(b) Foal
(c) Fawn
(d) Calf ***SSC CGL (Tier-I) 2024***

Sol. *(c)* As, the young one of 'Pig' is called 'Piglets'.

Similarly, the young one of 'Deer' is called 'Fawn'.

> **Helping Tips**
> To solve such type of questions one should be wellversed with English vocabalary and topics of general science. One should also have the knowledge in certain topics of general awareness such as country, capital, currencies, rivers, animals and their places of dwelling etc.

Example 4 **Damage : Repair : : Whisper : ?** ***UP Police SI 2021***

(a) Hiss (b) Murmur
(c) Hint (d) Shout

Sol. *(d)* As, 'Repair' is opposite word of 'Damage'. Similarly, 'Shout' is opposite word of 'Whisper'. Hence, option (d) is correct answer.

Example 5 **Mosquito : Malaria : : Rat : ?** ***Haryana CET Group D 2023***

(a) Rabies (b) Typhoid
(c) Plague (d) Dengue

Sol. *(c)* As, 'Malaria' is a disease caused by the bite of a 'Mosquito'. Similarly, 'Plague' is the specific disease associated with Rats.

Example 6 **Virat Kohli : Cricket : : Saina Nehwal : Badminton : : Viswanathan Anand : ?** ***SSC MTS 2022***

(a) Basketball (b) Chess
(c) Tennis (d) Football

Sol. *(b)* As, 'Virat Kohli' plays 'Cricket' and 'Saina Nehwal' plays 'Badminton'. Similarly, 'Viswanathan Anand' plays 'Chess'.

Example 7 **Select the word-pair in which the two words bear the same relationship to each other as similar to the words of the given pair bear.** ***Rajasthan Police Constable 2022***

Insomnia : Sleep

(a) Bacteria : Vaccine (b) Parasite : Malaria
(c) Stammer : Speech (d) Dementia : Walking

Sol. *(c)* As, Insomnia is a sleep disorder that can make it difficult to fall a sleep. Similarly, Stammer is a speech disorder involving frequency problem with normal fluency and flow of speech.

Example 8 **A group of three interrelated word is given. Choose a word from the given alternatives that is similar to the given words and hence belongs to the same groups.** ***DSSSB DASS 2019***

Camel : Cat : Goat

(a) Donkey (b) Hen
(c) Owl (d) Snake

Sol. *(a)* As, Camel, Cat, Goat and Donkey belong to the class of mammals.

Example 9 **Select the option in which the words do not share the same relationship as that shared by the given group of words.**

Patient : Surgeon : Surgery ***RRB NTPC 2021***

(a) Chalk : Teacher : Students (b) Cloth : Tailor : Stitch
(c) Vegetables : Chef : Cook (d) Clay : Potter : Pottery

Sol. *(a)* As, Patient, Surgeon and Surgery is related to each other, in the same way all options share the same relationship except option (a) Chalk, Teacher and Students.

Based on Letter Analogy

Example 10 **GAMU is related to JDPX in a certain way based on the English alphabetical order. In the same way LHTC is related to OKWF. To which of the following is BRLQ related following the same logic?** ***SSC (10+2) 2023***

(a) EUOT (b) DTNS
(c) ETOS (d) CTOU

Sol. *(a)* As,

G A M U
+3↓ +3↓ +3↓ +3↓
J D P X

and

L H T C
+3↓ +3↓ +3↓ +3↓
O K W F

Similarly,

B R L Q
+3↓ +3↓ +3↓ +3↓
E U O T

Example 11 **Select the option that is related to the third letter-cluster in the same way as the second letter-cluster is related to the first letter-cluster.**

JST : HPX :: PWJ : ? ***CUET (UG) Section III 2022***

(a) NTN (b) MSR (c) MTN (d) NSP

Sol. *(a)* As, J S T (−2, −3, +4) → H P X

Similarly, P W J (−2, −3, +4) → N T N

Directions (Ex. Nos. 12 and 13) *In the given analogy, choose the word which will replace the question mark* (?).

Example 12 NEGI : MVTR : : SING : ? *NTA CUET (UG) 2024*

(a) TRNS (b) TRNT
(c) FRMT (d) HRMT

Sol. *(d)* As, N E G I → M V T R (Opposite letters)

Similarly, S I N G → H R M T (Opposite letters)

Example 13 MEK : NVP : : GYT : TBG : : JWH : ? *SSC CGL (Tier-I) 2024*

(a) QDS (b) QDT
(c) PCR (d) PCS

Sol. *(a)* As, M E K → N V P (Opposite place letter)

and G Y T → T B G (Opposite place letter)

Similarly, J W H → Q D S (Opposite place letter)

Trending Concept

Questions based on two/three pair of letters/letter groups are being repeatedly asked in SSC (CGL, CHSL, CPO) examination. They are very important for upcoming examination.

Example 14 Select the pair of letter- clusters which follows the same pattern as that followed by the two sets of pair of letter-clusters given below. Both pairs of letter-clusters follow the same pattern. *SSC CHSL (Tier-I) 2023*

CGJ : HLO

KPS : PUX

(a) FKL : KPQ (b) WXY : GEF
(c) DEF : ABC (d) HGK : SQP

Sol. *(a)* As, C G J (+5, +5, +5) → H L O

and K P S (+5, +5, +5) → P U X

Similarly, F K L (+5, +5, +5) → K P Q

Based on Number Analogy

Example 15 24 is related to 8 following a certain logic. Following the same logic, 54 is related to 20. Which of the following numbers is related to 18 using the same logic? *SSC CPO 2024*

(a) 12 (b) 42
(c) 63 (d) 26

Sol. *(c)* As, 24 : 8 ($2 \times 4 = 8$)

and 54 : 20 ($5 \times 4 = 20$)

Similarly, 63 : 18 ($6 \times 3 = 18$)

Directions (Ex. Nos. 16 and 17) *Select the option that is related to the third number in the same way as the second number is related to the first number.*

Example 16 5 : 150 : : 8 : ? *CUET (UG) Section III 2023*

(a) 864 (b) 576
(c) 262 (d) 186

Sol. *(b)* As, 5 : 150

$\Rightarrow \quad 5^2 \times (5 + 1) = 25 \times 6 = 150$

Similarly, 8 : ?

$\Rightarrow \quad 8^2 \times (8 + 1) = 64 \times 9 = \boxed{576}$

Example 17 13 : 1331: : 17 : ? *CUET (UG) Section III 2022*

(a) 2642 (b) 1453
(c) 3375 (d) 1829

Sol. *(c)* As, in 13 : 1331

$\Rightarrow \quad (13 - 2)^3 = (11)^3 = 1331$

In the similar way, in 17 : ?

$\Rightarrow \quad (17 - 2)^3 = (15)^3 = \boxed{3375}$

Directions (Ex. Nos. 18 and 19) *Select the set in which the numbers are related in the same way as are the numbers of the following sets.*

Example 18 (3, 16, 6), (4, 22, 6) ***SSC CGL (Tier-I) 2022***

(a) (9, 10, 11)
(b) (7, 43, 6)
(c) (9, 70, 8)
(d) (12, 50, 5)

Sol. *(c)* As, (3, 16, 6)

$\Rightarrow \quad (3 \times 6) - 2 = 18 - 2 = 16$

and (4, 22, 6) $\Rightarrow (4 \times 6) - 2 = 24 - 2 = 22$

Similarly, from option (c) (9,70,8)

$\Rightarrow \quad (9 \times 8) - 2 = 72 - 2 = 70$

Example 19 (9, 343, 2)
(12, 729, 3) ***SSC CGL (Tier-I) 2022***

(a) (12, 125, 7)
(b) (13, 4, 89)
(c) (98, 49, 92)
(d) (12, 66, 20)

Sol. *(a)* As, (9, 343, 2) $\Rightarrow 9 - 2 = 7$

$\Rightarrow \quad (7)^3 = 343$

and (12, 729, 3)

$\Rightarrow \quad 12 - 3 = 9 \Rightarrow (9)^3 = 729$

Similarly, (12, 125, 7) $\Rightarrow 12 - 7 = 5 \Rightarrow (5)^3 = 125$

Trending Concept

These types of questions (Ex-18 and 19), based on triplets are currently in trend. They are very important, specially for SSC CGL & CHSL exams.

Example 20 In the following number-pairs, the second number is obtained by applying certain mathematical operations to the first number. Which numbers should replace X and Y so that the pattern followed by the two numbers on the left side of : : is same as that on the right side of : : ? ***IB 2024***

X : 729 : : 13 : Y

(a) X = 27 , Y = 1440
(b) X = 11, Y = 2132
(c) X = 9, Y = 1320
(d) X = 9, Y = 2197

Sol. *(d)* Here, in each number pair, second number is the cube of first number, then

X : 729 : : 13 : Y

$X = \sqrt[3]{729} = \boxed{9}$

and $Y = (13)^3 = \boxed{2197}$

Based on Mixed Analogy

Directions (Ex. Nos. 21-23) *Replace the question mark with an option that follows the same logic applied in the first pair.*

Example 21 WEST : 75 : : EAST : ? ***UP Police SI 2021***

(a) 63 (b) 56 (c) 48 (d) 53

Sol. *(d)* As,

W E S T
↓ ↓ ↓ ↓
23 + 5 + 19 + 20 = 67 ⇒ 67 + 8 = 75

Similarly,

E A S T
↓ ↓ ↓ ↓
5 + 1 + 19 + 20 = 45 ⇒ 45 + 8 = $\boxed{53}$

Example 22 WELL : 13 : : LEAN : ? ***UP Police SI 2021***

(a) 16 (b) 12 (c) 32 (d) 8

Sol. *(d)* As,

W E L L
↓ ↓ ↓ ↓
23 + 5 + 12 + 12 = 52

$\Rightarrow \quad \frac{52}{4} = 13$

Similarly,

L E A N
↓ ↓ ↓ ↓
12 + 5 + 1 + 14 = 32

$\Rightarrow \quad \frac{32}{4} = \boxed{8}$

Example 23 NICE : 13182422 :: PRICE : ?

(a) 119128422 (b) 119182422
(c) 111982224 (d) 119128242

Sol. *(b)* As,

N I C E ⟶ 13 18 24 22
(Opposite letter place value)

Similarly,

P R I C E ⟶ $\boxed{11\ 9\ 18\ 24\ 22}$
(Opposite letter place value)

Chapter Challenge

Based on Word Analogy

1. 'Big' is related to 'Small' in the same way as 'Thick' is related to *DSSSB 2024*
(a) Broad (b) Long (c) Thin (d) Tear

2. 'Manipur' is related to 'Imphal' in the same way as 'Nagaland' is related to *RRB NTPC 2021*
(a) Gangtok (b) Shillong
(c) Aizawl (d) Kohima

3. 'Taj Mahal' is related to 'India' in the same way as 'Statue of Liberty' is related to *SSC Steno 2023*
(a) Africa (b) USA
(c) England (d) Australia

4. 'Light' is related to 'Darkness' in the same way as Transparent' is related to *RRB NTPC 2021*
(a) Glass (b) Paper
(c) Opaque (d) Translucent

5. 'Valuable' is related to 'Precious' in the same way as 'Dry' is related to *SSC CGL 2020*
(a) Farm (b) Arid (c) Rough (d) Wet

6. 'Pedal' is related to 'Bicycle' in the same way as 'Oar' is related to *SSC CPO 2023*
(a) Car (b) Television
(c) Canoe (d) Motor cycle

7. 'Supply' is related to 'Demand' in the same way as 'Production' is related to *RRB NTPC 2021*
(a) Factory (b) Inventory
(c) Income (d) Consumption

8. 'Flourine' is related to 'Halogen' in the same way as 'Helium' is related to *SSC Steno 2020*
(a) Inert gas (b) Gas
(c) Radioactive (d) Metal

Directions (Q. Nos. 9-35) *In each of the following questions, there is a certain relationship between two given words on one side of (::) and one word is given on another side (::) while another word is to be found from the given alternatives, having the same relation with this word as the words of the given pair bear. Choose the correct alternative.*

9. Axe : Woodcutter : : Stethoscope : ? *DSSSB Lab Asst. 2024*
(a) Tailor (b) Chef
(c) Sculptor (d) Doctor

10. Lion : Den : : Rabbit : (?) *UP Police Constable 2024*
(a) Trench (b) Burrow (c) Hole (d) Pit

11. Before : After : : Enjoy : .... *Haryana CET 2023*
(a) Sad (b) Happy
(c) Suffer (d) Pain

12. Library: Books : : School : ? *UP Police Constable 2020*
(a) Newspaper (b) Students
(c) Buildings (d) Laboratory

13. Lawyer : Court : : Beautician : ? *RRB NTPC 2020*
(a) House (b) Ship (c) Class (d) Parlour

14. Moo : Cow : : Neigh : ? *SSC MTS 2020*
(a) Owl (b) Wolf (c) Horse (d) Bear

15. Knife : Cut : : Ladle : ? *SSC CGL (Tier-I) 2022*
(a) Chop (b) Serve
(c) Slice (d) Spread

16. Grip : Hold : : Imbibe : ? *UP Police ASI 2021*
(a) Repel (b) Absorb
(c) Bore (d) Annoy

17. Gravity : Discovery : : Telephone : ? *RRB NTPC 2021*
(a) Explore (b) Invention
(c) Experiment (d) Construct

18. Pig : Piglet : : Lion : ? *UP Police SI 2021*
(a) Puppy (b) Calf (c) Kitten (d) Cub

19. Telescope : Distant Objects : : Microscope : ? *SSC CGL (Tier-I) 2022*
(a) Big objects (b) Tiny objects
(c) Very large objects (d) Heavy objects

20. Frog : Jump : : Snake : ? *DSSSB Lab Asst. 2024*
(a) Swim (b) Drag (c) Jump (d) Run

21. Hongkong : China : : Vatican : ? *SSC (MTS) 2013*
(a) France (b) Mexico
(c) Canada (d) Rome

22. Mammal : Man : : Reptile : ? *SSC (10 + 2) 2022*
(a) Butterfly (b) Lizard
(c) Rat (d) Whale

23. Ant : Antling : : Deer : ? *SSC CGL (Tier-I) 2022*
(a) Pup (b) Fawn
(c) Cub (d) Foal

24. Nairobi : Kenya : : Oslo : ? *SSC (10+2) 2022*
(a) Cuba (b) Thailand
(c) Norway (d) Denmark

25. Amplify : Magnify : : Hinder : ? *UP Police ASI 2021*
(a) Encourage (b) Obstruct
(c) Assist (d) Comfort

26. Sleep : Insomnia : : Memory : ? *UP Police Constable 2020*
(a) Haemophilia (b) Alzheimer's
(c) Diabetes (d) Ischemia

27. Jordan : Amman : : Qatar : ? *Delhi Police Constable 2020*
(a) Manila (b) Colombo
(c) Doha (d) Kabul

28. Ballet : Choreographer : : Clothes : ? *SSC CPO 2020*
(a) Tailor (b) Printer
(c) Shopkeeper (d) Producer

29. Radiology : Radiations : : Seismology : ? *RPF SI 2019*
(a) Earthquake (b) Famine
(c) Weather (d) Rainfall

30. Hen : Pullet : : Kangaroo : .... *Haryana CET 2023*
(a) Calf (b) Pup (c) Joey (d) Cube

31. Vitamin A : Retinol : : Vitamin C : ? *Haryana CET 2023*
(a) Calciterol (b) Niacin
(c) Tocopherol (d) Ascorbic acid

32. Cardiology : Heart : : Mycology : ..... *Haryana CET 2023*
(a) Shells (b) Skull (c) Fungi (d) Diseases

33. Pediatrics : Children : : Neurology : ? *RRB NTPC 2020*
(a) Heart (b) Eyes (c) Brain (d) Veins

34. Museum : Curator : : Prison : ? *UPSSSC Forest Guard 2022*
(a) Manager (b) Monitor (c) Warden (d) Jailor

35. Japan : Green Pheasant : : India : ? *RRB JE 2019*
(a) Parrot (b) Emu (c) Peacock (d) Sparrow

Directions (Q. Nos. 36-45) *Select the word pair in which the two words are related in the same way as the two words in the following word pair.*

36. Human : Oxygen *MP Police Constable 2022*
(a) Glucose : Power (b) Patient : Medicine
(c) Disease : Birth (d) Bed : Rest

37. Singer : Band *Haryana CET 2022*
(a) Painter : Painting (b) Dacoit : Robbery
(c) Flower : Bouquet (d) Musician : Song

38. Kingfisher : Bird *RRB NTPC 2021*
(a) Apple : Fruit (b) Cold : Hot
(c) Fat : Body (d) Fur : Cat

39. Tailor : Suit
(a) Scheme : Agent (b) Edit : Manuscript
(c) Revise : Writer (d) Mention : Opinion

40. Student : School : : ? *DSSSB 2019*
(a) Pencil : Write (b) Patient : Hospital
(c) Cup : Water (d) Milk : Protein

41. Golf : Course *SSC CGL (Tier-I) 2021*
(a) Ring : Boxing (b) Judo : Arena
(c) Cycling : Velodrome (d) Baseball : Rink

42. Love : Harmony *SSC CGL (Tier-I) 2024*
(a) Calm : Sad (b) Peace : Bliss
(c) Rage : Cool (d) Anger : Excitement

43. Wheel : Spoke *SSC CPO 2020*
(a) Table : Chair (b) House : Room
(c) Star : Galaxy (d) Chapter : Book

44. Dermatology : Skin *SSC CGL (Tier-I) 2020*
(a) Cardiology : Angiography
(b) Paediatrics : Lungs
(c) Orthopaedics : Bones
(d) Medicine : Treatment

45. Ohm : Electrical resistance : : ? *SSC (10+2) 2022*
(a) Power : Walt
(b) Volume : Litre
(c) Second : Time
(d) Pascal : Electric current

46. Select the words from among the given options that will replace the question marks in the given analogy, so that the relationship between the first term and the second term is the same as between the third term and the fourth term.
Cobbler : ? : : ? : Gold *RRB NTPC 2021*
(a) Leather; Jeweller (b) Shoe; Bride
(c) Goldsmith; Ornament (d) Merchant; Grain

Directions (Q. Nos. 47 and 48) *In the following questions, some words are given which are related in some way. The same relationship exists among the words in one of the four alternatives given under it. Find the correct alternatives.*

47. Road : Bus : Driver
(a) Track : Train : Passenger
(b) Watch : Ship : Driver
(c) Sky : Aeroplane : Pilot
(d) Paper : Letters : Reader

48. Iron : Silver : Gold
(a) Parents : Father : Mother
(b) Wheat : Barley : Cereal
(c) Tree : Brench : Fruit
(d) Deer : Lion : Wolf

Directions (Q. Nos. 49-52) *In each of the following questions, choose that word which has the same relationship among the given words.*

49. Stable, Burrow, Nest *RRB NTPC 2021*
(a) Den (b) Slum
(c) City (d) Herd

50. Cricket, Hockey, Baseball. *RRB NTPC 2021*
(a) Ground (b) Match (c) Play (d) Fight

51. Altimeter, Barometer, Dynamometer, Thermometer *RRB NTPC 2021*
(a) Heating equipment
(b) Navigation equipment
(c) Measuring instruments
(d) Weighing instruments

52. New Delhi, Beijing, Katmandu, Dhaka *RRB NTPC 2021*
(a) City (b) Capital
(c) Country (d) Japan

53. The names given below are related to a certain logic. From the options, select the name that can be made a part of this group of names.
Tarapur, Kundankulam, Kaiga, Kakrapar, Kalpakkam, Narora
(a) Koyna (b) Rawatbhata
(c) Ukai (d) Bhakranangal

Based on Letter Analogy

54. LPHK is related to NRJM in a certain way based on the English alphabetical order. In the same way, OSKN is related to QUMP. To which of the following is RVNQ related, following the same logic? *RPF SI 2024*
(a) XTPS (b) XTSP
(c) TXPS (d) TXSP

55. MNQP is related to STWV in a certain way based on the English alphabetical order. In the same way, ABED is related to GHKJ. To which of the following is IJML related, following the same logic? *SSC CHSL (Tier-II) 2024*
(a) OPRS (b) ROPS
(c) OPSR (d) PORS

56. UPTQ is related to OJNK in a certain way based on the English alphabetical order. In the same way, RMQN is related to LGKH. To which of the following options is NIMJ related, following the same logic? *Railway ALP 2024*
(a) HCGD (b) CHDG
(c) CHGD (d) HCDG

57. KBWJ is related to MZZG in a certain way based on the English alphabetical order. In the same way, OXCD is related to QVFA. To which of the following options is STIX related, following the same logic? *Railway ALP 2024*
(a) VRKU (b) URLU
(c) VSLT (d) TSLV

58. TPVS is related to LHNK in a certain way based on the English alphabetical order. In the same way, WSYV is related to OKQN. To which of the following options is RNTQ related, following the same logic? *RRB Technician Grade III 2024*
(a) JFLI (b) FJLI
(c) FJIL (d) JFIL

Directions (Q. Nos. 59-73) *In the following questions select the related letters from the given alternatives.*

59. E : H : : N : ? *UP Police Constable 2024*
(a) P (b) R (c) O (d) Q

60. P : Q : : T : ..... *UP Police Constable 2024*
(a) U (b) T (c) P (d) R

61. KR : NU : : TV : ? *DSSSB Primary Teacher 2019*
(a) XZ (b) VX (c) ZB (d) WY

62. AJN : DMQ : : PTW : ? *SSC (10+2) 2023*
(a) ITE (b) MZW
(c) SOH (d) SWZ

63. CKA : FND : : ? : GJP *UP Police ASI 2021*
(a) DGM (b) EHM
(c) DGN (d) EHN

64. DFH : HFD : : QSU : ? *SSC (10+2) 2022*
(a) UQS (b) USQ (c) UUS (d) SQO

65. Eea : aEE : : Ppb : ?
(a) PPP (b) BBP (c) bPP (d) EEA

66. NEAR : EARN : : GOAL : ? *CRPF Head Constable 2023*
(a) OALG (b) AOLG (c) OAGL (d) AOGL

67. BEST : WVHE : : CROP : ? *SSC CPO 2020*
(a) SRVC (b) SRUF
(c) RTUF (d) PRUM

68. SLOW : MPTX : : CAUGHT : ? *SSC CPO 2020*
(a) BDHIUV (b) BHIUVH
(c) WVHIUV (d) DBVHIU

69. BPMN : CQNO : : GTPL : ? *UP Police Constable 2024*
(a) EUQM (b) HURN
(c) DUQN (d) HUQM

70. LATYE : YTLEA : : NETAEO : ? *SSC Steno 2021*
(a) TONEEA (b) TONEAE
(c) TTNUAE (d) TQUNEA

71. LARTBZ : BLRTAZ : : PARENF : ? *SSC Steno 2021*
(a) RNPEAF (b) NPREAF
(c) NEARFP (d) NREAFP

72. ABRUPT : BZUQUN : : SUDDEN : ? *SSC MTS 2021*
(a) TSGZJH (b) URGFJP
(c) URFGJP (d) TSAHJH

73. BACTERIA : EXFWBUFX : : WOUNDS : ? *SSC CGL (Tier-I) 2022*
(a) ZLRQGV (b) YLRQFV
(c) ZLSQFW (d) ZRXQGV

Directions (Q. Nos. 74-78) *Select the option that is related to the fifth letter cluster in the same way as the fourth letter cluster is related to the third letter cluster and the second letter cluster is related to the first letter cluster.*

74. ACE : BDF : : EGI : FHJ : : HJL : ? *Delhi Police Constable 2022*
(a) NPR (b) LJH (c) LNP (d) IKM

75. JUG : LSI : : WIN : YGP : : APT : ? *RRB NTPC 2022*
(a) CRR (b) CNV (c) CNR (d) CRV

76. ACBO : PCDB : : JLKM : NLMK : : KJIH : ? *SSC GD 2023*
(a) JIKL (b) JILK
(c) IJKL (d) IJLK

77. QUEST : VUGWS : : REACH : JECGT : : SOLVE : ? *SSC GD 2023*
(a) GXNOV (b) GXNQU
(c) VONXG (d) UQNXG

Chapter Challenge Analogy

78. TEMPLE : SCJLGY : : CHURCH : BFRNXB : : MOSQUE : ? *SSC CPO 2023*
(a) LMPYPM (b) LMPYMP
(c) LPYMPM (d) LMPMPY

79. Select the pair which follows the same pattern as that followed by the two set of pairs given below. Both pairs follow the same pattern. *SSC (10 + 2) 2024*
CJM : FMP
AHL : DKO
(a) LTV : TVL (b) KOQ : PLJ
(c) NRS : QUV (d) GHA : AHG

80. Select the triad from the given options which follows the same pattern as followed by the two triads given below. Both the triads follow the same pattern. *RRB ALP (CBT-I) 2024*
JG-NK-RT, EB-IF-MO
(a) IF-MJ-QR (b) FC-JG-NO
(c) GD-KI-OQ (d) HE-LI-PR

81. Which of the following letter-clusters should replace # and % so that the pattern and relationship followed between the letter-cluster pair on the left side of :: is the same as that on the right side of ::?
: ORW : : RUZ : % *SSC CGL (Tier-II) 2025*
(a) # = VYD, % = KNK (b) # = VYD, % = LNS
(c) # = VYD, % = KNS (d) # = UYD, % = KNS

82. Which of the following letter-clusters should replace # and % so that the pattern and relationship followed between the letter-cluster pair on the left side of :: is the same as that on the right side of ::?
: VXB : : ACG : % *SSC CHSL (Tier-II) 2024*
(a) # = GIM, % = KMQ
(b) # = UVN, % = KMQ
(c) # = UWA, % = BDH
(d) # = HDN, % = BDH

Based on Number Analogy

83. 11 is related to 55 following a certain logic. Following the same logic, 12 is related to 60. To which of the following is 15 related following the same logic? *SSC (10+2)2024*
(a) 85 (b) 75
(c) 70 (d) 80

> **MRC*****
> ***(Most Repeating Concepts)***
> Question Nos. 83, 84, 85, 86, 87 and 88, the number analogy is presented in the form of sentences. This type of questions are important as far as SSC Exams are concerned especially SSC CGL, SSC MTS and SSC (10+2).

84. 13 is related to 21 following certain logic. Following the same logic, 35 is related to 43. To which of the following numbers is 66 related, following the same logic? *SSC CGL (Tier-I) 2024*
(a) 71 (b) 72 (c) 74 (d) 73

85. 17 is related to 159 following a certain logic. Following the same logic, 11 is related to 105. To which of the following is 13 related, following the same logic? *SSC CGL (Tier-II) 2025*
(a) 116 (b) 109
(c) 103 (d) 123

86. 17 is related to 102 following a certain logic. Following the same logic, 29 is related to 174. To which of the following is 39 related, following the same logic? *SSC CGL (Tier-I) 2024*
(a) 238 (b) 234 (c) 228 (d) 230

87. 89 is related to 78 following a certain logic. Following the same logic, 97 is related to 86. To which of the following is 72 related, following the same logic? *SSC CHSL (Tier-II) 2024*
(a) 68 (b) 59 (c) 61 (d) 66

88. 20 is related to 30 following a certain logic. Following the same logic, 30 is related to 45. Which of the following numbers is related to 120 using the same logic? *SSC CPO 2024*
(a) 80 (b) 75 (c) 70 (d) 60

Directions (Q. Nos. 89-94) *In each of the following questions, choose the number, which will replace the question mark.*

89. 16 : 48 : : 23 : ? *DSSSB Lab Asst. 2024*
(a) 66 (b) 58 (c) 69 (d) 54

90. 12 : 72 : : 6 : ? *HSSC CET 2022*
(a) 46 (b) 28 (c) 18 (d) 64

91. 5 : 42 : : 3 : ? *Rajasthan Police Constable 2022*
(a) 32 (b) 12 (c) 21 (d) 20

92. 27 : 14 : : 66 : ? *UP Police ASI 2021*
(a) 36 (b) 39 (c) 41 (d) 37

93. 4 : 28 : : 8 : ? *MP PSC 2021*
(a) 80 (b) 110 (c) 120 (d) 140

94. 7 : 57 : : 13 : ? *SSC Steno 2021*
(a) 163 (b) 153 (c) 183 (d) 143

Directions (Q. Nos. 95-98) *Select the option that is related to the fifth number in the same way as the second number is related to the first number and the fourth number is related to the third number.*

95. 7 : 21 : : 14 : 42 : : 18 : ? *SSC CGL (Tier-I) 2023*
(a) 57 (b) 54 (c) 63 (d) 72

96. 11 : 130 : : 7 : 58 : : 15 : ? *RRC Group D 2022*
(a) 234 (b) 248
(c) 216 (d) 224

97. 129 : 32 : : 109 : 27 : : 289 : ? *SSC (10+2) 2023*
(a) 54 (b) 96 (c) 72 (d) 28

98. 19 : 34 : : 5 : 6 : : 27 : ? *SSC CGL (Tier-I) 2023*
(a) 50 (b) 67 (c) 52 (d) 63

Directions (Q. Nos. 99-102) *Select the option that is related to the third term in the same way as the second term is related to the first term and the sixth term is related to the fifth term.*

99. 687 : 612 : : 713 : ? : : 621 : 546 **SSC CGL (Tier-I) 2022**
(a) 656 (b) 674
(c) 662 (d) 638

100. 38 : 78 : : 102 : ? : : 46 : 94 **SSC (10+2) 2022**
(a) 202 (b) 206
(c) 204 (d) 214

101. 144 : 36 : : 81 : ? : : 196 : 42 **SSC CGL (Tier-I) 2022**
(a) 30 (b) 23
(c) 27 (d) 29

102. 15 : 125 : : 27 : ? : : 36 : 1728 **SSC CGL (Tier-I) 2022**
(a) 689 (b) 749
(c) 790 (d) 729

MRC***
(Most Repeating Concepts)
Number analogy based on triple pairs of numbers (Q. Nos. 97, 98, 99, 100, 103, 104 and 105) are being repeatedly asked in SSC Exams (CGL, MTS, Steno etc).

Directions (Q. Nos. 103-105) *Select the option in which the number share the same relationship as that shared by the given number pair.*

103. 38 : 76 **SSC (10+2) 2023**
(a) 35 : 68 (b) 42 : 84
(c) 41 : 81 (d) 23 : 45

104. 12 : 65
13 : 70 **SSC (10+2) 2023**
(a) 14 : 65 (b) 15 : 80
(c) 16 : 75 (d) 18 : 85

105. 6 : 85 **SSC MTS 2023**
(a) 7 : 112 (b) 9 : 181
(c) 5 : 50 (d) 8 : 114

Directions (Q. Nos. 106-118) *Select the set in which the numbers are related in the same way as are the numbers of the given set.*

106. (71, 86, 101)
(94, 109, 124) **DP Head Constable 2022**
(a) (126, 141, 156) (b) (89, 103, 120)
(c) (107, 122, 142) (d) (112, 138, 150)

107. (7, 11, 33)
(14, 18, 54) **SSC CHSL (Tier-II) 2024**
(a) (5, 9, 36) (b) (16, 20, 40)
(c) (18, 21, 63) (d) (12, 16, 48)

108. (3, 5, 21) (4, 2, 14) **RRC Group D 2022**
(a) (6, 3, 12) (b) (8, 4, 28)
(c) (5, 2, 19) (d) (7, 1, 23)

109. (19, 9, 173)
(6, 17, 104) **SSC (10+2) 2024**
(a) (11, 4, 46) (b) (14, 4, 62)
(c) (8, 12, 94) (d) (7, 15, 105)

110. (13, 39, 6)
(9, 18, 4) **SSC CGL (Tier-I) 2022**
(a) (12, 48, 8) (b) (12, 50, 13)
(c) (15, 45, 3) (d) (20, 28, 8)

111. (215, 185, 135)
(276, 246, 196) **SSC CGL (Tier-II) 2025**
(a) (238, 208, 158) (b) (269, 229, 199)
(c) (294, 264, 224) (d) (255, 235, 205)

112. (8, 9, 431)
(11, 8, 1267) **SSC (10 + 2) 2023**
(a) (9, 12, 595) (b) (13, 14, 2011)
(c) (7, 5, 318) (d) (12, 10, 1528)

113. (16, 32, 54)
(29, 58, 80) **SSC CGL (Tier-I) 2023**
(a) (17, 35, 59) (b) (25, 50, 62)
(c) (24, 48, 70) (d) (23, 46, 62)

114. (46, 45, 93)
(56, 27, 141) **Delhi Police Constable 2022**
(a) (34, 22, 81) (b) (34, 21, 81)
(c) (39, 21, 81) (d) (34, 21, 82)

115. (30, 49, 19)
(37, 39, 2) **RPF SI 2024**
(a) (7, 29, 22) (b) (37, 58, 18)
(c) (17, 32, 12) (d) (18, 42, 21)

116. (36, 21, 35)
(43, 19, 53) **SSC CGL (Tier-I) 2023**
(a) (51, 34, 39) (b) (48, 37, 25)
(c) (44, 20, 54) (d) (35, 22, 34)

117. (3, 2, 162)
(6, 3, 3888) **SSC (10+2) 2023**
(a) (4, 3, 786) (b) (9, 3, 19783)
(c) (5, 2, 1350) (d) (7, 2, 4802)

118. (2, 5, 341)
(1, 7, 510) **SSC CPO 2023**
(a) (8, 2, 140) (b) (1, 2, 25)
(c) (2, 5, 56) (d) (3, 6, 64)

Directions (Q. Nos. 119 and 120) *In the following number-pairs, the second number is obtained by applying certain mathematical operations to the first number. Which numbers should replace X and Y so that the pattern followed by the two numbers on the left side of : : is same as that on the right side of : : ?*

119. X : 125 : :13 : Y **RRB ALP 2024**
(a) X = 12, Y = 173 (b) X = 11, Y = 173
(c) X = 11, Y = 169 (d) X = 12, Y = 169

120. X : 117 : : 15 : Y **RRB Tech. Grade III 2024**
(a) X = 7, Y = 193 (b) X = 9, Y = 195
(c) X = 9, Y = 193 (d) X = 7, Y = 195

121. Study the given pattern carefully and select the number that can replace the question mark (?) in it. *SSC CGL (Tier-I) 2023*

(4, 2, 6) (9, 3, 9) (24, 6, ?)

(a) 10 (b) 12 (c) 15 (d) 8

Based on Mixed Analogy

122. 'TABLE' is related to '726251522' and 'FORMS' is related to '21129148' in the same way as 'CHAIR' is related to .... *RRB NTPC 2022*

(a) 241926198 (b) 241296189
(c) 214926189 (d) 241926189

123. Select the term that is related to the third term in the same way as the second term is related to the first term.

BDF : 48 : : FHJ : ? *DSSSB 2019*

(a) 480 (b) 180 (c) 240 (d) 90

124. Select the option that is related to the third term in the same way as the second number is related to the first term. *RRB NTPC 2021*

XVI : 32 : : XXIV : ?

(a) 44 (b) 48
(c) 28 (d) 24

125. Choose the word/letter(s)/number which will replace the question mark.

WAITER : 242923 : : JUMPER : ? *RRB NTPC 2021*

(a) 312923 (b) 312623
(c) 302923 (d) 252923

126. GY16 is related to DV23 in a certain way. In the same way, OD11 is related to LA18. Following the same logic, LW13 is related to which of the following? *SSC MTS 2024*

(a) HS20 (b) IT20
(c) IS20 (d) HT19

Right Key

1. (c)	2. (d)	3. (b)	4. (c)	5. (b)	6. (c)	7. (d)	8. (a)	9. (d)	10. (b)
11. (c)	12. (b)	13. (d)	14. (c)	15. (b)	16. (b)	17. (b)	18. (d)	19. (b)	20. (b)
21. (d)	22. (b)	23. (b)	24. (c)	25. (b)	26. (b)	27. (c)	28. (a)	29. (a)	30. (c)
31. (d)	32. (c)	33. (c)	34. (d)	35. (c)	36. (b)	37. (c)	38. (a)	39. (b)	40. (b)
41. (c)	42. (b)	43. (b)	44. (c)	45. (c)	46. (a)	47. (c)	48. (d)	49. (a)	50. (c)
51. (c)	52. (b)	53. (b)	54. (c)	55. (c)	56. (a)	57. (b)	58. (a)	59. (d)	60. (a)
61. (d)	62. (d)	63. (a)	64. (b)	65. (c)	66. (a)	67. (b)	68. (a)	69. (d)	70. (a)
71. (b)	72. (a)	73. (a)	74. (d)	75. (b)	76. (c)	77. (b)	78. (d)	79. (c)	80. (d)
81. (c)	82. (c)	83. (b)	84. (c)	85. (d)	86. (b)	87. (c)	88. (a)	89. (c)	90. (c)
91. (d)	92. (a)	93. (c)	94. (c)	95. (b)	96. (a)	97. (c)	98. (a)	99. (d)	100. (b)
101. (c)	102. (d)	103. (b)	104. (b)	105. (b)	106. (a)	107. (d)	108. (b)	109. (a)	110. (a)
111. (a)	112. (c)	113. (c)	114. (b)	115. (a)	116. (a)	117. (d)	118. (b)	119. (b)	120. (b)
121. (b)	122. (d)	123. (a)	124. (b)	125. (a)	126. (b)				

Solutions

1. *(c)* As, 'Big' is antonym of 'Small'. Similarly, 'Thick' is antonym of Thin.

2. *(d)* As, 'Imphal' is the capital city of 'Manipur'. Similarly, 'Kohima' is the capital of 'Nagaland'.

3. *(b)* As, 'Taj Mahal' is a monument of 'India'. Similarly, 'Statue of Liberty' is a monument of 'USA'.

4. *(c)* As, the word 'Light' is the antonym of 'Darkness'. Similarly, 'Transparent' is the antonym of 'Opaque'.

5. *(b)* As, 'Precious' is a synonym of 'Valuable'. Similarly, 'Arid' is a synonym of 'Dry'.

6. *(c)* As, 'Pedal' is the part of 'Bicycle'. Similarly, 'Oar' is the part of 'Canoe'.

7. *(d)* 'Supply' is related to 'Demand' in the same way as 'Production' is related to 'Consumption'.

8. *(a)* As, 'Flourine' gas is a member of 'Halogen' family. Similarly, Helium gas is a member of 'Inert gas' family.

9. *(d)* As, 'Axe' used by 'Woodcutter' to Cut the wood. Similarly, 'Stethoscope' used by 'Doctor' to treat a patient.

10. *(b)* As, a 'Den' is the shelter of 'Lion'. Similarly, a 'Burrow' is the shelter of 'Rabbit'.

11. *(c)* In the given analogy, 'After' is the antonym of 'Before'. Following the same logic, the antonym of 'Enjoy' is 'Suffer'.

12. *(b)* As, 'Books' are kept in 'Library'. Similarly, 'Students' study in 'School'.

13. *(d)* As, 'Court' is the place where Lawyer works. Similarly, 'Parlour' is the place where 'Beautician' works.

14. *(c)* As, 'Moo' is the sound produced by 'Cow'. Similarly, 'Neigh' is the sound produced by 'Horse'.

15. *(b)* A 'Knife' is used to 'Cut'. Similarly, a 'Ladle' (a large long-handled spoon) is used to 'Serve'.

16. *(b)* As, 'Grip' and 'Hold' are synonyms of each other. Similarly, 'Synonym of 'Imbibe' is 'Absorb'.

17. *(b)* As, gravity was discovered. Similarly, the telephone was invented.

18. *(d)* As, 'Piglet' is the young one of Pig. Similarly, 'Cub' is the young one of 'Lion'.

19. *(b)* As, 'Telescope' is used to see 'Distant Objects'. Similarly, 'Microscope' is used to see the 'Tiny Objects'.

20. *(b)* As, a 'Frog', 'Jumps' to move forward. Similarly, a 'Snake', 'Drag' itself to move forward.

21. *(d)* As, 'Hongkong' is in 'China' in the same way 'Vatican' is situated in 'Rome'.

22. *(b)* As, 'Man' falls under the category of 'Mammal'. Similarly, 'Lizard' falls under the category of 'Reptile'.

23. *(b)* The young one of 'Ant' is called 'Antiling'. Similarly, the young one of 'Deer' is called 'Fawn'.

24. *(c)* As, 'Nairobi' is the capital of 'Kenya'. Similarly, 'Oslo' is the capital of 'Norway'.

> **TOP TIPS** To attempt this type of questions, candidates must have knowledge of country-capitals and state capitals.

25. *(b)* As, Amplify and Magnify are synonyms of each other. Similarly, synonym of Hinder is Obstruct.

26. *(b)* As, Insomnia is a disease in which there is a lack of sleep. Similarly, Alzheimer's is a disease in which there is a loss of memory.

27. *(c)* As, capital of 'Jordan' is 'Amman'. Similarly, capital of 'Qatar' is 'Doha'.

28. *(a)* As, 'Ballet' is directed by 'Choreographer'. Similarly, 'Clothes' are sewed by 'Tailor'.

29. *(a)* As, 'Radiology' measures 'Radiation'. Similarly, 'Seismology' measures 'Earthquake' intensity.

30. *(c)* In the given analogy, 'Pullet' refers to the young ones of 'Hens'. Following the same logic, the young one of a 'Kangaroo' is called 'Joey'.

31. *(d)* This analogy compares the chemical names of vitamins with their corresponding common names. 'Vitamin A' is also known as 'Retinol'. 'Vitamin C' is also known as 'Ascorbic acid'.

32. *(c)* The study of 'Heart' is called 'Cardiology'. Similarly, the study of 'Fungi' is called 'Mycology'.

33. *(c)* As, 'Pediatrics' is the branch of medical science that deals with the 'Children'. Similarly, 'Neurology' is branch of medical science that deals with the 'Brain'.

34. *(d)* As, person incharge of a 'Museum' is known as 'Curator'. Similarly, person incharge of a 'Prison' is called 'Jailor'.

35. *(c)* As, 'Green Pheasant' is the national bird of 'Japan'. Similarly, 'Peacock' is the national bird of 'India'.

36. *(b)* As, 'Oxygen' is necessary to 'Human' for living. Similarly, 'Medicine' is necessary to 'Patient' for living.

37. *(c)* As, 'Group' of Singers is called 'Band'. Similarly, 'Bunch' of 'Flowers' is called 'Bouquet'.

38. *(a)* As, 'Kingfisher' is a 'Bird'. Similarly, 'Apple' is a 'Fruit'.

39. *(b)* As, 'Suit' is stitched by 'Tailor'. Similarly, 'Manuscript' is 'Edited'.

40. *(b)* As, students go to school for study. Similarly, patients go to hospital for treatment.

41. (c) As, 'Course' is a ground for playing 'Golf'. Similarly, 'Velodrome' is an arena for track 'Cycling'.

42. *(b)* As, we know where there is love there is harmony too. Similarly, where there is peace there is bliss too.

43. *(b)* As, a Wheel has Spoke. Similarly, a House has Room.

44. *(c)* As, 'Dermatology' deals with problems related to 'Skin'. Similarly, 'Orthopaedics' deals with the problems related to 'Bones'.

45. *(c)* As, 'Ohm' is the unit of 'Electrical resistance'. Similarly, 'Second' is the unit of 'Time'.

46. *(a)* As, 'Cobbler' is makes the shoes from Leather. Similarly, Jeweller is makes the Jewellary from Gold.

47. *(c)* 'Bus' moves on 'Road' and is driven by 'Driver'. Likewise 'Aeroplane' flies in the 'Sky' and is driven by 'Pilot'.

48. (*d*) All the three belong to the same class. 'Iron', 'Silver' and 'Gold' are all metals and similarly, 'Deer', 'Lion' and 'Wolf' are all wild animals.

49. (*a*) Stable, Burrow and Nest all are related to animal places. Similarly, Den is related to wild mammal's place.

50. (*c*) All are types of play.

51. (*c*) All are the measuring instruments.

52. (*b*) All are the capital of different countries.

53. (*b*) As, Tarapur, Kundankulam, Kaiga, Kakrapar, Kalpakkam, Narora all are nuclear power plants and like these Rawatbhata is also a nuclear power plant.

54. (*c*) As, L P H K → +2 +2 +2 +2 → N R J M

and O S K N → +2 +2 +2 +2 → Q U M P

Similarly, R V N Q → +2 +2 +2 +2 → T X P S

TOP TIPS To attempt questions based on number analogy, the knowledge of positional values of letter in forward and reverse alphabet series is must. Generally analogies are drawn by applying some mathematical operations on these positional values.

55. (*c*) As, M N Q P → +6 +6 +6 +6 → S T W V

and A B E D → +6 +6 +6 +6 → G H K J

Similarly, I J M L → +6 +6 +6 +6 → O P S R

56. (*a*) As, U P T Q → −6 −6 −6 −6 → O J N K

and R M Q N → −6 −6 −6 −6 → L G K H

Similarly, N I M J → −6 −6 −6 −6 → H C G D

57. (*b*) As, K B W J → +2 −2 +3 −3 → M Z Z G

and O X C D → +2 −2 +3 −3 → Q V F A

Similarly, S T I X → +2 −2 +3 −3 → U R L U

58. (*a*) As, T P V S → −8 −8 −8 −8 → L H N K

and W S Y V → −8 −8 −8 −8 → O K Q N

Similarly, R N T Q → −8 −8 −8 −8 → J F L I

59. (*d*) As, 5 E : 8 H (+3)

Similarly, 14 N : 17 Q (+3)

60. (*a*) As, P —(+1)→ Q

Similarly, T —(+1)→ U

61. (*d*) As, K R → N U (+3, +3)

Similarly, T V → W Y (+3, +3)

62. (*d*) As, A J N → D M Q (+3, +3, +3)

Similarly, P T W → S W Z (+3, +3, +3)

63. (*a*) As, C K A → +3 +3 +3 → F N D

Similarly, D G M → +3 +3 +3 → G J P

64. (*b*) As, D F H → H F D

Similarly, Q S U → U S Q

65. (*c*) As, E e a → a E E (In capital letter)

Similarly, P p b → b P P (In capital letter)

66. (*a*) As, N E A R → E A R N

Similarly, G O A L → O A L G

67. (*b*) As, B E S T → (+3) → W V H E

Similarly, C R O P → (+3) → S R U F

68. (*a*) As, S L O W → +1 +1 +1 +1 → T M P X ⟶ MPTX (Alphabetical order)

Similarly, C A U G H T → +1 +1 +1 +1 +1 +1 → D B V H I U ⟶ BDHIUV (Alphabetical order)

69. *(d)* As,

B P M N
↓+1 ↓+1 ↓+1 ↓+1
C Q N O

Similarly,

G T P L
↓+1 ↓+1 ↓+1 ↓+1
[H U Q M]

70. *(a)* As,

L A T Y E ⇒ Y T L E A
(Arranged in alphabetical order from right to left)

Similarly,

N E T A E O ⇒ [T O N E E A]
(Arranged in alphabetical order from right to left)

71. *(b)* As,

L A R T B Z ⟶ B L R T A Z
1 2 3 4 5 6 ⟶ 5 1 3 4 2 6

Similarly,

P A R E N F ⟶ [N P R E A F]
1 2 3 4 5 6 ⟶ 5 1 3 4 2 6

> **TOP TIPS** Please note that in this type of questions, the arrangement is not only made on the basis of alphabetical order but it can also be made on the basis of some fixed pattern.

72. *(a)* As,

A B R U P T
↓+1 ↓−2 ↓+3 ↓−4 ↓+5 ↓−6
[B Z U Q U N]

Similarly,

S U D D E N
↓+1 ↓−2 ↓+3 ↓−4 ↓+5 ↓−6
[T S G Z J H]

73. *(a)* As,

B A C T E R I A
↓+3 ↓−3 ↓+3 ↓+3 ↓−3 ↓+3 ↓−3 ↓−3
E X F W B U F X

[Here, Vowel ⟶ − 3 and Consonant ⟶ + 3]

Similarly,

W O U N D S
↓+3 ↓−3 ↓−3 ↓+3 ↓+3 ↓+3
[Z L R Q G V]

74. *(d)* As,

A C E
↓+1 ↓+1 ↓+1
B D F

and

E G I
↓+1 ↓+1 ↓+1
F H J

Similarly,

H J L
↓+1 ↓+1 ↓+1
[I K M]

75. *(b)* As,

J U G
↓+2 ↓−2 ↓+2
L S I

and

W I N
↓+2 ↓−2 ↓+2
Y G P

Similarly,

A P T
↓+2 ↓−2 ↓+2
[C N V]

76. *(c)* As,

A C B O
(+1)
P C D B

and

J L K M
(+1)
N L M K

Similarly,

K J I H
(+1)
[I J K L]

77. *(b)* As,

Q U E S T
(+2)
V U G W S

and

R E A C H
(+2)
J E C G T

Similarly,

S O L V E
(+2)
[G X N Q U]

78. *(d)* As,

T E M P L E
↓−1 ↓−2 ↓−3 ↓−4 ↓−5 ↓−6
S C J L G Y

and

C H U R C H
↓−1 ↓−2 ↓−3 ↓−4 ↓−5 ↓−6
B F R N X B

Similarly,

M O S Q U E
↓−1 ↓−2 ↓−3 ↓−4 ↓−5 ↓−6
[L M P M P Y]

79. *(c)* As,

C J M
↓+3 ↓+3 ↓+3
F M P

and

A H L
↓+3 ↓+3 ↓+3
D K O

Similarly,

N R S
↓+3 ↓+3 ↓+3
[Q U V]

80. *(d)* As,

J $\xrightarrow{+4}$ N $\xrightarrow{+4}$ R
G $\xrightarrow{+4}$ K $\xrightarrow{+9}$ T

and

E $\xrightarrow{+4}$ I $\xrightarrow{+4}$ M
B $\xrightarrow{+4}$ F $\xrightarrow{+9}$ O

Similarly,

H $\xrightarrow{+4}$ L $\xrightarrow{+4}$ P
E $\xrightarrow{+4}$ I $\xrightarrow{+9}$ R

81. *(c)* Given,
: ORW : : RUZ : %
From option (c),
Taking, # = VYD and % = KNS
As,

[V Y D]
↓−7 ↓−7 ↓−7
O R W

Similarly,

R U Z
↓−7 ↓−7 ↓−7
[K N S]

82. *(c)* Given, # : VXB : : ACG : %
From option (c),
As,

[U W A]
↓+1 ↓+1 ↓+1
V X B

Similarly,

A C G
↓+1 ↓+1 ↓+1
[B D H]

⟶ UWA, % ⟶ BDH

83. *(b)* As, 11 is related to 55
⇒ $11 \times 5 = 55$
and 12 is related to 60
⇒ $12 \times 5 = 60$
Similarly, 15 is related to '?'
⇒ $15 \times 5 =$ [75]

84. (c) As, $13 \rightarrow 21 \Rightarrow 13 + 8 = 21$
and $35 \rightarrow 43 \Rightarrow 35 + 8 = 43$
Similarly, $66 \rightarrow 74 \Rightarrow 66 + 8 = \boxed{74}$

85. (d) As, $17 \times 9 = 153 + 6 = 159$
and $11 \times 9 = 99 + 6 = 105$
Similarly, $13 \times 9 = 117 + 6 = \boxed{123}$

86. (b) As, $17 \xrightarrow{\times 6} 102$
and $29 \xrightarrow{\times 6} 174$
Similarly, $39 \xrightarrow{\times 6} \boxed{234}$

87. (c) As, $(89, 78) \Rightarrow 89 - 11 = 78$
and $(97, 86) \Rightarrow 97 - 11 = 86$
Similarly, $(72, ?) \Rightarrow 72 - 11 = \boxed{61}$

88. (a) As, $20 : 30$, $20 \times \frac{3}{2} = 30$
and $30 : 45$, $30 \times \frac{3}{2} = 45$
Similarly, $\boxed{80} : 120$, $80 \times \frac{3}{2} = 120$

89. (c) As, $16 : 48$ ($\times 3$)
Similarly, $23 : \boxed{69}$ ($\times 3$)

90. (c) As, $12 : 72 \Rightarrow (12)^2 \div 2$
$\Rightarrow \quad 144 \div 2 = 72$
Similarly, $6 : ? \Rightarrow (6)^2 \div 2$
$\Rightarrow \quad 36 \div 2 = \boxed{18}$

91. (d) As, $5 : 42 \Rightarrow (5 + 1) \times (5 + 2) = 42$
Similarly, $3 : ? \Rightarrow (3 + 1) \times (3 + 2) = \boxed{20}$

92. (a) As, $27 : 14 \Rightarrow 2 \times 7 = 14$
Similarly, $66 : ? \Rightarrow 6 \times 6 = \boxed{36}$

93. (c) As, $(4^2 \times 2) - 4 = (32 - 4) = 28$
Similarly,
$(8^2 \times 2) - 8 = (128 - 8) = \boxed{120}$

> **TOP TIPS** Establishing analogies between numbers becomes easy and time saving, if candidate knows the square, cube, square root and cube roots of numbers in advance.

94. (c) As, $7 : 57 \Rightarrow 7^2 + (7 + 1)$
$= 49 + 8 = 57$
Similarly, $13 : ? \Rightarrow 13^2 + (13 + 1)$
$= 169 + 14 = \boxed{183}$

95. (b) As, $7 : 21 \Rightarrow 7 \times 3 = 21$
and $14 : 42 \Rightarrow 14 \times 3 = 42$
Similarly, $18 : ? \Rightarrow ? = 18 \times 3 = \boxed{54}$

96. (a) As, $11 : 130 \Rightarrow (11)^2 + 9 = 130$
and $7 : 58 \Rightarrow (7)^2 + 9 = 58$
Similarly, $15 : ? \Rightarrow (15)^2 + 9 = \boxed{234}$

97. (c) As, $129 : 32$
$(129 - 1) \div 4 = \frac{128}{4} = 32$
and $109 : 27$
$(109 - 1) \div 4 = \frac{108}{4} = 27$
Similarly, $289 : ?$
$(289 - 1) \div 4 = \frac{288}{4} = \boxed{72}$

98. (a) As, $19 : 34 \Rightarrow 19 - 2 = 17$
$\Rightarrow \quad 17 \times 2 = 34$
and $5 : 6 \Rightarrow 5 - 2 = 3 \Rightarrow 3 \times 2 = 6$
Similarly, $27 : ? \Rightarrow 27 - 2 = 25$
$\Rightarrow \quad 25 \times 2 = \boxed{50}$

99. (d) As, $687 : 612$
$\Rightarrow \quad 687 - 612 = 75$
and $621 : 546 \Rightarrow 621 - 546 = 75$
Similarly, $713 : ? \Rightarrow 713 - ? = 75$
$\therefore \quad ? = 713 - 75 = \boxed{638}$

100. (b) As, $38 : 78$ ($\times 2 + 2$)
and $46 : 94$ ($\times 2 + 2$)
Similarly, $102 : \boxed{206}$ ($\times 2 + 2$)

101. (c) As, $144 : 36 \Rightarrow \sqrt{144} = 12$
$\Rightarrow \quad 12 \times 3 = 36$
and $196 : 42 \Rightarrow \sqrt{196} = 14$
$\Rightarrow \quad 14 \times 3 = 42$
Similarly, $81 : ? \Rightarrow \sqrt{81} = 9$
$\Rightarrow \quad 9 \times 3 = \boxed{27}$

102. (d) As, $15 : 125 \Rightarrow (15 \div 3)^3$
$= 5^3 = 125$
and $36 : 1728 \Rightarrow (36 \div 3)^3$
$= 12^3 = 1728$
Similarly, $27 : ? \Rightarrow (27 \div 3)^3$
$= 9^3 = \boxed{729}$

103. (b) As,
$38 : 76$ ($\times 2$)
Similarly,
$\boxed{42 : 84}$ ($\times 2$)

104. (b) As, $12 : 65$
$\Rightarrow (12 \times 5) + 5 = 60 + 5 = 65$
and $13 : 70$
$\Rightarrow (13 \times 5) + 5 = 65 + 5 = 70$
Similarly, $15 : 80$
$\Rightarrow (15 \times 5) + 5 = 75 + 5 = \boxed{80}$

105. (b) As, $(6 : 85) \Rightarrow 6^2 + (6 + 1)^2$
$= 6^2 + 7^2 = 36 + 49 = 85$
Similarly, $9 : 181 \Rightarrow 9^2 + (9 + 1)^2$
$= 9^2 + (10)^2 = 81 + 100 = \boxed{181}$

106. (a) As, $(71, 86, 101)$ ($+15$, $+15$)
and $(94, 109, 124)$ ($+15$, $+15$)
Similarly, $(126, 141, 156)$ ($+15$, $+15$)

107. (d) As, $(7 \quad 11 \quad 33)$ ($+4$, $\times 3$)
and $(14 \quad 18 \quad 54)$ ($+4$, $\times 3$)
Similarly, $(12 \quad 16 \quad 48)$ ($+4$, $\times 3$)

108. (b) As, $(3, 5, 21)$
$\Rightarrow (3 + 5) \times 3 - 3 = 21$
and $(4, 2, 14) \Rightarrow (4 + 2) \times 3 - 4 = 14$
[Logic $(a, b, c) \Rightarrow (a + b) \times 3 - a = c$]
Similarly, $(8, 4, 28)$
$\Rightarrow \quad (8 + 4) \times 3 - 8 = 28$

109. (a) As, $(19, 9, 173)$
$\Rightarrow 19 \times 9 + 2 = 171 + 2 = 173$
and $(6, 17, 104)$
$\Rightarrow 6 \times 17 + 2 = 102 + 2 = 104$
Similarly, $(11, 4, 46)$
$\Rightarrow 11 \times 4 + 2 = 44 + 2 = 46$

110. (a) As, $(13, 39, 6)$
$\Rightarrow \quad 13 \times \frac{6}{2} = 13 \times 3 = 39$
and $(9, 18, 4) \Rightarrow 9 \times \frac{4}{2} = 9 \times 2 = 18$
Similarly, $(12, 48, 8)$
$\Rightarrow \quad 12 \times \frac{8}{2} = 12 \times 4 = 48$

111. (a) As, $(215, 185, 135)$
$\Rightarrow 215 - 30 = 185$
$\Rightarrow 185 - 50 = 135$

and (276, 246, 196)
$\Rightarrow 276 - 30 = 246$
$\Rightarrow 246 - 50 = 196$
Similarly, (238, 208, 158)
$\Rightarrow 238 - 30 = 208$
$\Rightarrow 208 - 50 = 158$

112. *(c)* As, (8, 9, 431)
$\Rightarrow 8^3 - 9^2 = 512 - 81 = 431$
and (11, 8, 1267)
$\Rightarrow 11^3 - 8^2 = 1331 - 64 = 1267$
Similarly, (7, 5, 318)
$\Rightarrow 7^3 - 5^2 = 343 - 25 = 318$

113. *(c)* As, (16, 32, 54)
$\Rightarrow 16 \times 2 = 32 \rightarrow 32 + 22 = 54$
and (29, 58, 80)
$\Rightarrow 29 \times 2 = 58 \rightarrow 58 + 22 = 80$
Similarly, (24, 48, 70)
$\Rightarrow 24 \times 2 = 48 \rightarrow 48 + 22 = 70$

114. *(b)* As, (46, 45, 93)
$\Rightarrow (46 + 45) + 2(46 - 45)$
$= 91 + 2 \times 1 = 93$
and (56, 27, 141)
$\Rightarrow (56 + 27) + 2(56 - 27)$
$= 83 + 2 \times 29$
$= 83 + 58 = 141$
Similarly, (34, 21, 81)
$\Rightarrow (34 + 21) + 2(34 - 21)$
$= 55 + 2 \times 13 = 55 + 26 = 81$

115. *(a)* As, (30, 49, 19) $\Rightarrow (49 - 30) = 19$
and (37, 39, 2) $\Rightarrow (39 - 37) = 2$
Similarly, (7, 29, 22) $\Rightarrow (29 - 7) = 22$

116. *(a)* As, (36, 21, 35)
$\Rightarrow 36 - 21 = 15 \Rightarrow 15 \times 2 + 5 = 35$
[Logic = (First number − Second number) × 2 + 5 = Third number]
and (43, 19, 53)
$\Rightarrow 43 - 19 = 24 \Rightarrow 24 \times 2 + 5 = 53$
Similarly, (51, 34, 39)
$\Rightarrow 51 - 34 = 17$
$\Rightarrow 17 \times 2 + 5 = 39$

117. *(d)* As, (3, 2, 162)
$\Rightarrow 3^4 \times 2 = 81 \times 2 = 162$
(6, 3, 3888) $\Rightarrow 6^4 \times 3$
$= 1296 \times 3 = 3888$
Similarly, (7, 2, 4802)
$\Rightarrow 7^4 \times 2 = 2401 \times 2 = 4802$

118. *(b)* As, (2, 5, 341) $\Rightarrow (2 + 5)^3 - 2$
$= 7^3 - 2 = 343 - 2 = 341$
and (1, 7, 510) $\Rightarrow (1 + 7)^3 - 2$
$= 8^3 - 2 = 512 - 2 = 510$
Similarly, (1, 2, 25) $\Rightarrow (1 + 2)^3 - 2$
$= 3^3 - 2 = 27 - 2 = 25$

119. *(b)* From option (b),
$(\boxed{11})^2 = 121 + 4 = 125$
$(13)^2 = 169 + 4 = \boxed{173}$
Hence, X = 11, Y = 173

120. *(b)* From option (b),
$X = \boxed{9} \times 13 = 117$
$Y = 15 \times 13 = \boxed{195}$
Hence, X = 9, Y = 195

121. *(b)* As, (4, 2, 6) $\Rightarrow \frac{4}{2} \times 3 = 6$
and (9, 3, 9) $\Rightarrow \frac{9}{3} \times 3 = 9$
Similarly, (24, 6, ?) $\Rightarrow \frac{24}{6} \times 3 = \boxed{12}$

122. *(d)* As,

T A B L E
↓ ↓ ↓ ↓ ↓ (Opposite letter positional value)
7 26 25 15 22

and

F O R M S
↓ ↓ ↓ ↓ ↓ (Opposite letter positional value)
21 12 9 14 8

Similarly,

C H A I R
↓ ↓ ↓ ↓ ↓ (Opposite letter positional value)
[24 19 26 18 9]

123. *(a)* As, B D F
↓ ↓ ↓ (Place value)
$2 \times 4 \times 6 = 48$

Similarly, F H J
↓ ↓ ↓ (Place value)
$6 \times 8 \times 10 = \boxed{480}$

124. *(b)* As, XVI : 32
$\Rightarrow$ XVI = 16 $\Rightarrow 16 \times 2 = 32$
and XXIV : ?
$\Rightarrow$ XXIV = 24 $\Rightarrow 24 \times 2 = \boxed{48}$

> **TOP TIPS** The candidate must have knowledge of roman number to attempt this type of questions.

125. *(a)* As,

W A I T E R
↓ ↓ ↓ ↓ ↓ ↓
(23+1) (9+20) (5+18)
↓ ↓ ↓
24 29 23

Similarly,

J U M P E R
↓ ↓ ↓ ↓ ↓ ↓
(10+21) (13+16) (5+18)
↓ ↓ ↓
[31 29 23]

126. *(b)* As,

G Y 16
↓ −3 ↓ −3 ↓ +7
D V 23

and

O D 11
↓ −3 ↓ −3 ↓ +7
L A 18

Similarly,

L W 13
↓ −3 ↓ −3 ↓ +7
[I T 20]

CHAPTER

02 Classification

Classification

The meaning of classification is choosing the odd one out. It is a process of classifying a word/letter/number or their groups on the basis of their shared characteristics and identifying the odd one out.
In this chapter, questions generally consist of four/five words/letters/numbers or their groups out of which three/four words/letters/numbers or their groups are similar to one another but one is different from them. Candidate has to find that odd word/ letter/number or group from the options.

Word Classification

In word classification, a group or pair of words are given, in which all except one are related to one another in a particular manner and thus, form a group. Candidate has to find that word / word-pair which is odd and does not belong to the group.
In this type of questions are generally based on the relationships like Country/Capital/ Currency, body parts and their study, etc.

e.g. Select the odd word from the given alternatives.

(a) Russia (b) Australia
(c) Cape town (d) China

Sol. (c) Except Cape town, all others are countries but Cape town is the capital of country South Africa.

Letter Classification

In letter classification, a group or pair of letters are given in which all except one are related to one another in a particular manner and thus form a group. Candidate has to find that odd letter/pair of letters from the options.
In this type questions are generally based on the relationship between positional values of letters in English alphabet, Vowels - Consonants, Number of letters, Mathematical operations between position of letters etc.

e.g. Select the odd pair of letters from the given group of letters.

(a) AE (b) PR
(c) TX (d) HL

Sol. (b) As, A → E (+4), P → R (+2)

T → X (+4), H → L (+4)

Except 'PR', there is a difference of 4 in the place values of each pair of letters.

Number Classification

In number classification, a number or pair of numbers are given in which all except one are related to one another in a particular manner and thus form a group. Candidate has to find that number/pair of numbers which doesn't belong to the group.
In this type of questions are generally based on Even-Odd numbers, Prime numbers, Multiplication and Divisibility of numbers, Squares, Square root, Cubes, Cube root etc.

e.g. Select the odd number from the given group.

(a) 15 (b) 27
(c) 33 (d) 26

Sol. (d) Except '26', all others are multiple of 3.

Mixed Classification

In mixed classification, a group of letters and numbers are given in which all except one, follow a certain patterns and related to one another. Candidate has to find that odd group of letters/numbers from the options.

e.g. Select the odd number from the given group.

(a) C-3 (b) E-5
(c) L-12 (d) S-20

Sol. (d) Except 'S-20', all others letters are given with their alphabetical positional values.

Score Booster

To solve questions based on classification, the candidate must have knowledge of numbers (their types and operations), vocabulary and some topics of general knowledge such as country-capital, currencies, state-capital, animals-places of dwelling, physical quantities-units etc.

Exam Approach Examples

Based on Word Classification

Directions (Ex. Nos. 1 and 2) *Find the odd word from the given options.*

Example 1 (a) Curd (b) Butter (c) Oil (d) Cheese

Sol. (*c*) Except 'oil' all others are obtained from milk.

Example 2 (a) Manama (b) Taka (c) Lusaka (d) Harare ***SSC CGL 2021***

Sol. (*b*) Except Taka (currency of Bangladesh), all others are capital of different countries.

Directions (Ex. Nos. 3 and 4) *Find the odd pair of words in the given questions.*

Example 3 (a) Petrol : Car (b) Ink : Pen (c) Garbage : Dustbin (d) Lead : Pencil

Sol. (*c*) Except 'Garbage : Dustbin', in all others first is required by the second for its functioning.

Example 4 (a) Shoes-Feet (b) Book-Pages (c) Spectacles-Lens (d) Flowers-Petals ***SSC CGL 2024***

Sol. (*a*) As, Book contains Pages, Spectacles have lens and flower contains petals but shoes does not contains feet actually it is worn on feet.

Example 5 In the given question, three out of four group of word are alike in a certain way and one is odd. Choose that odd group of words. ***SSC (10+2) 2023***

(a) Surgeon, Warrior, Cook (b) Labourers, Tailors, Sculptors
(c) Farmer, Mason, Doctor (d) Knife, Needle, Plumbline

Sol. (*d*) Except option (d) (Knife, Needle, Plumbline), all others are group of experts in different fields.

Based on Letter Classification

Directions (Ex. Nos. 6 and 7) *Find odd letter-pair among the given alternatives.* ***SSC CGL 2024***

Example 6 (a) YWA (b) LJO (c) JHL (d) OMQ

Sol. (*b*) As, ... and ... But,

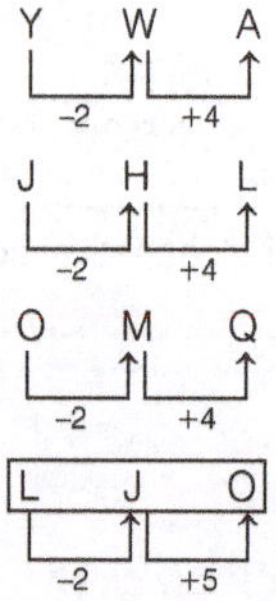

> ***Helping Tips***
> To solve such questions, it is very important to know positional values of letters in forward and reverse alphabetical series.

Example 7 (a) bac (b) aBc (c) Abc (d) ABc

Sol. (*a*) Except option (a) in all other options, only one letters is small alphabet, but in option (a) all the three letters are small alphabets.

Example 8 Find odd letter-cluster in the question given below.

(a) MNOL (b) AZCX (c) PKRI (d) PLRI

Sol. (*d*) As, ... and ... But,

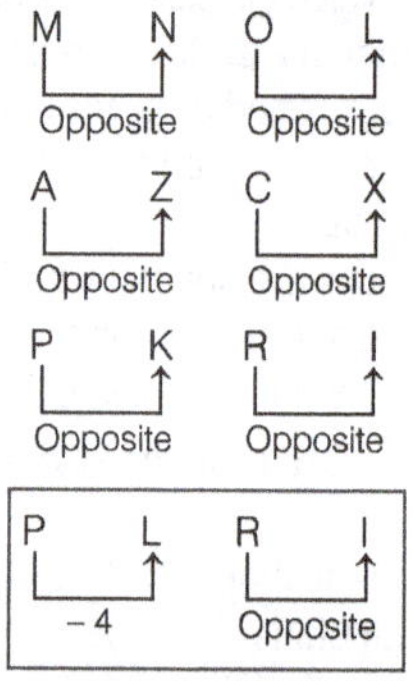

Example 9 Choose the odd letter-pair. ***DSSSB Lab Asst. 2024***

(a) RY : SZ (b) MP : NO (c) QW : RV (d) CE : DD

Sol. (*a*) As, ... and ... But,

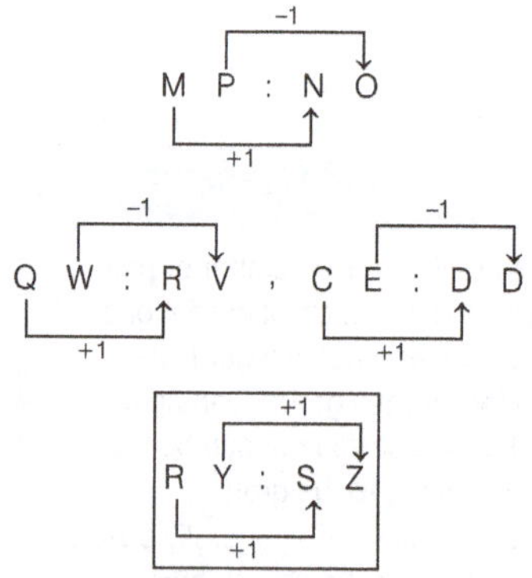

Example 10 Find the odd letter group.

(a) YWVT (b) NLKI (c) WVTS (d) SQPW

Sol. (*c*) As, ... and ... But,

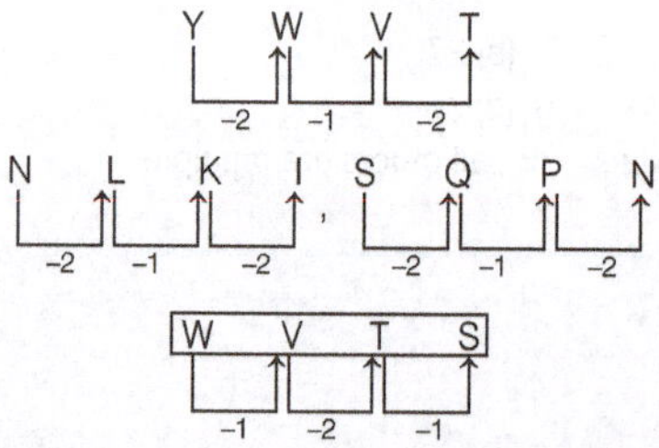

Based on Number Classification

Example 11 **Find the odd one out.**

(a) 19 (b) 17

(c) 13 (d) 12

Sol. (*d*) Expect 12, all others are prime numbers.

Directions (Ex. Nos. 12 and 13) *Find the odd number-pair among the given numbers.* ***SSC CGL 2024***

Example 12

(a) 24 : 4 (b) 36 : 24

(c) 12 : 8 (d) 72 : 48

Sol. (*a*) As, 36 : 24 (÷1.5), 12 : 8 (÷1.5)

and 72 : 48 (÷1.5) But, 24 : 4 (÷6)

Example 13 ***SSC (10+2) 2023***

(a) 13-163

(b) 9-77

(c) 18-320

(d) 24-572

Sol. (*a*) As,

$(9)^2 - 4 = 81 - 4 = 77$

$(18)^2 - 4 = 324 - 4 = 320$

$(24)^2 - 4 = 576 - 4 = 572$

But, $(13)^2 - 4 = 169 - 4 = \boxed{165 \neq 163}$

> **Helping Tips**
> To solve such questions, it is very important to have good knowledge of Squares, Cubes, Square roots and Cube roots of numbers.

Example 14 **Choose the odd number pair from the given alternatives.** ***SSC SGL (Tier I) 2024***

(a) 540-188-128 (b) 72-284-266

(c) 81-101-92 (d) 90-22-12

Sol. (*b*) As, 540-188-128

$\Rightarrow (188 - 128) \times 9 = 60 \times 9 = 540$

81-101-92 $\Rightarrow (101 - 92) \times 9 = 9 \times 9 = 81$

and 90-22-12

$\Rightarrow (22 - 12) \times 9 = 10 \times 9 = 90$

But, 72-284-266

$\Rightarrow (284 - 266) \times 9 = 18 \times 9 = 162 \neq 72$

> **Trending Concept**
> Questions based on number pairs are important, as they are being regularly asked in SSC, RRB-NTPC, UP-Police and MP-Police exams.

Based on Mixed Classification

Directions (Ex. Nos. 15-17) *Find the odd term from the given alternatives.*

Example 15 (a) 9IH (b) 11KP

(c) 13 MN (d) 3CX ***RRB NTPC 2021***

Sol. (*a*) As,

11KP ⇒ 11 → K (Place value), K → P (Opp. letter)

13MN ⇒ 13 → M (Place value), M → N (Opp. letter)

and

3CX ⇒ 3 → C (Place value), C → X (Opp. letter)

But,

9IH ⇒ 9 → I (Place value), I → H (−1)

Example 16 (a) L16 : U26 (b) H12 : X29

(c) C7 : I13 (d) T24 : S24

RRB NTPC 2022

Sol. (*c*) As,

L(12) 16 (+4) : U(21) 26 (+5)

H(8) 12 (+4) : X(24) 29 (+5)

and

T(20) 24 (+4) : S(19) 24 (+5)

But,

C(3) 7 (+4) : I(9) 13 (+4)

Example 17 ***SSC CGL 2024***

(a) Pentagon-5 (b) Triangle-3 sides

(c) Square-4 sides (d) Hexagon-8 sides

Sol. (*d*) Except "Hexagon-8 sides", the second word represent the number of sides of the first figure but Hexagon has 6 sides.

Chapter Challenge

Based on Word Classification

Directions (Q. Nos. 1-34) *In the following questions, choose the odd word/word-pair from the given options.*

1. (a) Cabbage (b) Mango (c) Apple (d) Banana
UPSSSC Forest Guard 2022

2. (a) India (b) China (c) Canada (d) Japan
MP Police Constable 2022

3. (a) Dictionary (b) Bibliography (c) Vocabulary (d) Synonyms books
Rajasthan Police Constable 2022

4. (a) Plotter (b) Keyboard (c) Webcam (d) Microphone
SSC CGL (Tier-I) 2021

5. (a) Roar (b) Shout (c) Scream (d) Mumble
SSC CGL (Tier-I) 2020

6. (a) Clove (b) Pepper (c) Onion (d) Cardamom
RRB NTPC 2021

7. (a) Pigeon (b) Crow (c) Sparrow (d) Ostrich
DSSSB Junior Assistant 2021

8. (a) Rickets (b) Hypertension (c) Gout (d) Arthritis
SSC CGL (Tier-I) 2021

9. (a) Drums (b) Tabla (c) Sitar (d) Mridangam
RRB NTPC 2021

10. (a) Empathy (b) Envy (c) Jealousy (d) Hatred
SSC CGL (Tier-I) 2021

11. (a) Shot Put (b) Discus Throw (c) Badminton (d) Hammer Throw
RRB NTPC 2024

12. (a) Padma Bhushan (b) Padma Vibhushan (c) Param Vir Chakra (d) Padma Shri
RRB NTPC 2021

13. (a) Square root (b) Square feet (c) Square metre (d) Square inch
DSSSB (Tier-I) Grade II 2024

14. (a) Lethargic (b) Passive (c) Vivacious (d) Sluggish
SSC CGL (Tier-I) 2021

15. (a) 1234 - Numbers (b) × + − ÷ - Text (c) ₹¥$£ - Currency (d) ABCD - Letters
SSC CGL (Tier-II) 2025

16. (a) Pyramid (b) Circle (c) Cuboid (d) Cylinder
UPSSSC 2024

17. (a) Lead (b) Tin (c) Copper (d) Steel
UP Police Constable 2024

18. (a) Circle (b) Square (c) Sphere (d) Triangle
UP Police Constable 2024

19. (a) Delhi (b) Puducherry (c) Chandigarh (d) Jammu and Kashmir
SSC (10+2) 2021

20. (a) Tea and Coffee (b) Pencil and Pen (c) Cycle and Scooter (d) Shirt and Tailor
UPSSSC Force Guard 2022

21. (a) Temple-Pray (b) Theater-Movies (c) Park-Swim (d) Restaurant-Dinner
SSC CGL (Tier-II) 2025

22. (a) Joy-Peace (b) Misery-Happiness (c) Problem-Concern (d) Worry-Fear
SSC CGL (Tier-I) 2024

23. (a) Television-Triangle (b) Birthday hat-Cone (c) Ball-Sphere (d) Ring-Circle
SSC (10+2) 2024

24. (a) Brick-Wall (b) Pulp-Paper (c) Wood-Fumiture (d) Metal-Ore
SSC (10+2) 2023

25. (a) Flag : Flagship (b) Court : Courtship (c) War : Worship (d) Friend : Friendship
UP Police SI 2021

26. (a) Refuse- Accept (b) Give- Take (c) Cold-Cool (d) Reward-Punishment
DSSSB 2024

27. (a) Melancholy : Gloomy (b) Negligent : Attentive (c) Dynamic : Robust (d) Lethargic : Laid back
SSC Steno 2020

28. (a) Bone-Orthopaedic (b) Uterus-Urologist (c) Stomach-Gastroenterologist (d) Eye-Ophthalmologist
SSC CGL (Tier-I) 2024

29. (a) Hospital-Doctors (b) School-Teachers (c) Theatre-Movies (d) Restaurant-Chefs
SSC CGL (Tier-II) 2023

30. (a) Libero : Volleyball (b) Bowling : Cricket (c) Point Gaurd : Hockey (d) Goalkeeper : Football
DSSSB DASS 2019

31. (a) Physiology- Body (b) Pedology-Fishes (c) Entomology-Insects (d) Selenography-Moon
SSC (10+2) 2023

32. (a) Scooter- Vehicle (b) Triangle-Figure
(c) Kidney-Organ (d) Fruit-Apple
SSC CHSL (Tier-I) 2023

33. (a) (Stock, Troupe, Robber)
(b) (Team, Council, Bouquet)
(c) (Crowd, Army, Herd)
(d) (Shoal, Flock, Chorus)

34. (a) (Igloo, Nun, Sty)
(b) (Web, Cottage, Palace)
(c) (Stable, Monastery, Hive)
(d) (Den, Byre, Barn) ***SSC (10+2) 2022***

Based on Letter Classification

Directions (Q. Nos. 35-65) *Find odd letter/ letter- cluster from the given alternatives.*

35. (a) P (b) I (c) B (d) N
SSC Steno 2019

36. (a) FG (b) AZ (c) QR (d) KL
UP Police Constable 2024

37. (a) QX (b) WC (c) PW (d) FM
SSC (10+2) 2023

38. (a) NJF (b) XSP (c) QMI (d) WSO
RRB NTPC (CBT-I) 2021

39. (a) YXW (b) UTR (c) DCA (d) TSQ

40. (a) ROL (b) RUO (c) VYS (d) PSM
SSC CPO 2022

41. (a) AGH (b) ZBD (c) QSU (d) MOQ
RRB Technician Grade IV 2024

42. (a) CHR (b) LRI (c) TZA (d) HNM
SSC Steno 2020

43. (a) CFD (b) GJH (c) KNM (d) JMK
DSSSB 2015

44. (a) NQT (b) VXB (c) ZBF (d) SUY
RPF SI 2024

45. (a) SWYX (b) LOQP (c) PTVU (d) RVXW
SSC CPO 2023

46. (a) JOTY (b) SXCH (c) GKPS (d) AFKP
SSC CGL (Tier-I) 2023

47. (a) LNSV (b) FHMP (c) BDIL (d) JLPT
SSC CPO 2022

48. (a) HEBY (b) SPLI (c) WTQN (d) OLIF
SSC CPO 2020

49. (a) WN-RU (b) NE-IK (c) TK-OR (d) QH-LO
RPF SI 2024

50. (a) GJJL (b) EHHK (c) ADDG (d) VYYB
SSC CGL (Tier I) 2023

51. (a) BFJN (b) DHLP (c) HJKP (d) JNRV

52. (a) QNOM (b) FRDP (c) MDKB (d) HLFJ
DP Head Constable 2022

53. (a) SXHP (b) UZFR (c) XCCU (d) VCDR
SSC CPO 2023

54. (a) LOKP (b) HMIL (c) KPLO (d) SXTW

55. (a) EVAF (b) CXBH (c) KPUZ (d) TGLQ
CUET VG 2022

56. (a) JRPV (b) GTMN (c) HSNM (d) EVKP
SSC Steno 2023

57. (a) WDLF
(b) YBXR
(c) PKSM
(d) IRMT
SSC CGL (Tier-I) 2022

> **MRC*****
> ***(Most Repeating Concepts)***
> The concept of opposite letters is used in (Q. Nos. 53, 55, 56, 57, 58) which is one of the most repeating concepts in exams such as SSC-CGL, SSC-Steno and Rajasthan Police Constable etc.

58. (a) BYAWD
(b) KPETG
(c) MNIQI
(d) CXOPB
Rajasthan Police Constable 2022

59. (a) KMQWF (b) DFJPX
(c) HJNTB (d) BDHNV ***CUET UG 2023***

60. (a) Bd Eg (b) Km Np
(c) Pr Su (d) Tw Xz ***DSSSB 2013***

61. (a) LH-PC (b) RX-VT
(c) NS-RO (d) RS-VO ***IB 2024***

62. (a) QL—OJ (b) WR—UP
(c) ID—GB (d) MS—LH ***RRB ALP 2024***

63. (a) DG-IL (b) CE-HK
(c) BE-GJ (d) AD-FI ***RPF SI 2024***

64. (a) QV-SX (b) KP-MR
(c) AD-CG (d) BG-DI ***RRB ALP 2024***

65. (a) DA-CF (b) JG-IM
(c) GD-FI (d) NK-MP
RRB Technician Grade III 2024

Based on Number Classification

Directions (Q. Nos. 66-95) *Select the odd number/number pair/number group from the options given below.*

66. (a) 2 (b) 3 (c) 7 (d) 4
RRB ALP (Tier-I) 2018

67. (a) $\sqrt{3}$ (b) $\sqrt{5}$ (c) $\sqrt{7}$ (d) $\sqrt{9}$
RRB NTPC 2021

68. (a) 863 (b) 345 (c) 463 (d) 601
UP Police ASI 2021

69. (a) 61 (b) 21 (c) 31 (d) 41
UP Police Head Operator 2024

70. (a) 256 (b) 36 (c) 1000 (d) 196
DSSSB 2022

71. (a) 289 (b) 353 (c) 467 (d) 281
UP Police ASI 2024

72. (a) 165 (b) 159 (c) 143 (d) 187
RRB NTPC (CBT-I) 2021

73. (a) 6341 (b) 6138 (c) 5423 (d) 1652
SSC CHSL (Tier-I) 2021

74. (a) 2105 (b) 6457 (c) 4328 (d) 3124
SSC CHSL (Tier-I) 2021

75. (a) 0 : 6 (b) 5 : 14 (c) 12 : 28 (d) 21 : 46
RRB NTPC 2021

76. (a) 14-41 (b) 9-28 (c) 12-37 (d) 17-52
DSSSB Warder (Male) 2019

77. (a) 14-126 (b) 31-280 (c) 25-225 (d) 12-108

78. (a) 12-96 (b) 15-120 (c) 13-104 (d) 16-118
RRB NTPC 2020

79. (a) 144 : 12 (b) 123 : 11
(c) 196 : 14 (d) 225 : 15
MP Police Constable 2022

80. (a) 1 : 2 (b) 4 : 17 (c) 3 : 12 (d) 2 : 5
UP Police Asst. Operator 2024

81. (a) 1-701 (b) 3-102 (c) 9-324 (d) 7-124
MP Police Constable 2022

82. (a) 3375-13500 (b) 2125-8600
(c) 2685-10740 (d) 1595-6380
SSC CHSL (Tier-I) 2023

83. (a) 19 : 25 (b) 3 : 5 (c) 23 : 29 (d) 13 : 17
RRB NTPC 2021

84. (a) 13-104 (b) 19-152 (c) 23-184 (d) 7-58
DSSSB Warder 2019

85. (a) 521-20 (b) 104-4 (c) 286-11 (d) 494-19
SSC CGL (Tier-II) 2025

86. (a) 18-198 (b) 13-144 (c) 31-341 (d) 22-242
SSC CGL (Tier-II) 2025

87. (a) 3333-6666 (b) 4444-8888
(c) 2222-4444 (d) 5555-7777
SSC CHSL (Tier-I) 2023

88. (a) 2-4-8 (b) 2-2-4 (c) 3-2-5 (d) 1-3-3
SSC CGL (Tier-I) 2024

89. (a) 112-103-94 (b) 76-67-54
(c) 94-85-76 (d) 87-78-69
SSC (10+2) 2024

90. (a) (17-51-147) (b) (10-30-90)
(c) (15-45-135) (d) (22-66-198)

91. (a) 81-118-91 (b) 52-68-51
(c) 99-104-71 (d) 21-38-31
SSC CGL (Tier-I) 2024

92. (a) 84 : 294 : 210 (b) 68 : 238 : 170
(c) 96 : 336 : 192 (d) 52 : 182 : 130
SSC CHSL (Tier-I) 2023

93. (a) 31-46-41 (b) 29-44-38
(c) 24-39-33 (d) 17-32-26
SSC (10+2) 2024

94. (a) 360-12-6 (b) 82-8-2 (c) 63-6-3 (d) 164-10-4
SSC CGL (Tier-I) 2024

95. (a) 11 : 21 : 121 (b) 7 : 15 : 49
(c) 2 : 3 : 4 (d) 9 : 17 : 81
SSC CGL (Tier-II) 2023

Based on Mixed Classification

Directions (Q. Nos. 96-101) *Select the odd letter-number pair from the options given below.*

96. (a) A12 (b) P16 (c) U21 (d) M13
RRB NTPC 2021

97. (a) & 300 # (b) & 200 # (c) & 400 # (d) & 10 #
UP Police Constable 2020

98. (a) BC6 (b) DE20 (c) CD12 (d) EF35
UP Police ASI 2021

99. (a) MN, 37 (b) RQ, 35 (c) HI, 17 (d) TS, 39
RRB NTPC 2022

100. (a) LR9 : PU55 (b) DL5 : HP25
(c) HP7 : LT35 (d) PJ3 : TN15
RRB NTPC 2022

101. (a) RED 7% (b) YELLOW 6 &
(c) PINK 4 # (d) GREEN 5*
UP Police Constable 2020

Right Key

1. (a)	2. (c)	3. (b)	4. (a)	5. (d)	6. (c)	7. (d)	8. (b)	9. (c)	10. (a)
11. (c)	12. (c)	13. (a)	14. (c)	15. (b)	16. (b)	17. (d)	18. (c)	19. (c)	20. (d)
21. (c)	22. (b)	23. (a)	24. (d)	25. (c)	26. (c)	27. (b)	28. (b)	29. (c)	30. (c)
31. (b)	32. (d)	33. (a)	34. (a)	35. (b)	36. (b)	37. (b)	38. (b)	39. (a)	40. (a)
41. (a)	42. (a)	43. (c)	44. (a)	45. (b)	46. (c)	47. (d)	48. (b)	49. (b)	50. (a)
51. (c)	52. (a)	53. (d)	54. (a)	55. (b)	56. (a)	57. (d)	58. (d)	59. (a)	60. (d)
61. (a)	62. (d)	63. (b)	64. (c)	65. (b)	66. (d)	67. (d)	68. (b)	69. (b)	70. (c)
71. (a)	72. (b)	73. (b)	74. (b)	75. (a)	76. (a)	77. (b)	78. (d)	79. (b)	80. (c)
81. (d)	82. (b)	83. (a)	84. (d)	85. (a)	86. (b)	87. (d)	88. (c)	89. (b)	90. (a)
91. (b)	92. (c)	93. (a)	94. (b)	95. (b)	96. (a)	97. (d)	98. (d)	99. (a)	100. (a)
101. (a)									

Chapter Challenge Classification

Solutions

1. (a) Except cabbage, all others are fruits while cabbage is a vegetable.
2. (c) Except Canada, all other countries are part of Asian Continent.
3. (b) Except Bibliography, all others contain list of words, whereas Bibliography is a list of books or sources used in the process of research or work.
4. (a) Except Plotter, all others are input devices.
5. (d) Except Mumble, all others are synonyms of each other.
6. (c) Except 'Onion' all others are spices.
7. (d) Except 'Ostrich' all other birds can fly but Ostrich is a flightless bird.
8. (b) Ricket, gout and Arthritis are related to bone disease. Whereas, Hypertension is related to high blood pressure.
9. (c) Except 'Sitar' all others i.e., Drums, Tabla and Mridangam are percussion instruments.
10. (a) Empathy is related to sympathy. Envy, Jealousy, Hatred have same relation.
11. (c) Except 'Badminton' all others are track and field events but Badminton is a racket sports.
12. (c) Except 'Param Vir Chakra' all others are Civilian award but Param Vir Chakra is a Military Gallantry award.
13. (a) Except 'Square root' all others are unit of area measurement but square root is a mathematical operation.
14. (c) In the given words Lethargic, Passive and Sluggish shown the quality of lazy person but vivacious is related to active so it's different from others.

> **TOP TIPS** To attempt this type of questions knowledge of english vocabulary and antonyms/synonyms is must.

15. (b) Except (b), in all other options, first one is denotation of second one.
16. (b) Except 'Circle' all others are 3-D shapes.
17. (d) Except Steel, all others are metals, whereas steel is an alloy.
18. (c) Except Sphere, all others are 2-D figure, whereas Sphere is a 3-D figure.
19. (c) Except Chandigarh, all are union territories with legislative assembly.
20. (d) Except 'Shirt and Tailor' in all other pairs both words are same type of things.
21. (c) Except (c), in all other options there is relation of place and action between the pair of word, while park does not use for the swim.
22. (b) Except 'Misery-Happiness', all other options are synonyms to each other.
23. (a) Except option (a), in all other options, things and their shapes are given, like (Ball-sphere) ball is having a spherical shape.
24. (d) Except option (d), in all other option, the second word represents the thing which is made up by the material given in first word. But in option (d), ore is not made by metal instead, metal is extracted from an ore.
25. (c) In all other pairs except (c), second is the abstract noun of first.
26. (c) Except 'cold-cool' the pairs of antonyms are given in the other options.
27. (b) Except option (b), all other word pairs are synonyms to each other. Here, Negligent and Attentive are antonym to each other.
28. (b) As, 'Orthopaedic' is a doctor treats issues related to 'bones'.
'Gastroenterologist' is a doctor treats issues related to 'Stomach'.
'Opthalmologist' is a doctor who treats issues related to 'eyes'.
But, 'Urologist' is a doctor who treats disease related to 'Urine' not 'Uterus'.
29. (c) Except option (c), in all others the first is a workplace where the second works.
30. (c) 'Libero' is a specific player position in Volleyball.
'Bowling' is a action in Cricket.
Goalkeeper is a specific player position in Football.
But, 'Point guard'is a specific player position in 'Basketball' not Hockey.
31. (b) Except 'Pedology-Fishes', first word is the study of second word, while Pedology is the study of soil.
32. (d) Except 'Fruit-Apple',first falls under category of second but in 'Fruit-Apple' second falls under category of first.
33. (a) Except, option (a), in all other options all the words refers to group of persons or things. But in option (a) 'Robber' is a person.
34. (a) Except, option (a), in all the other options, all three words are different places to live. Whereas in option (a), Nun is a woman who vows to dedicate her life to her religion.
35. (b) Except 'I' all others are consonants but 'I' is a vowel.
36. (b) As, F $\xrightarrow{+1}$ G, Q $\xrightarrow{+1}$ R, K $\xrightarrow{+1}$ L

But, A $\xrightarrow{\text{Opposite}}$ Z

∴ AZ is the odd one out.
37. (b) As, Q $\xrightarrow{+7}$ X, P $\xrightarrow{+7}$ W, F $\xrightarrow{+7}$ M

But, W $\xrightarrow{+6}$ C
38. (b) As, N $\xrightarrow{-4}$ J $\xrightarrow{-4}$ F ; Q $\xrightarrow{-4}$ M $\xrightarrow{-4}$ I

and W $\xrightarrow{-4}$ S $\xrightarrow{-4}$ O But, X $\xrightarrow{-4}$ S $\xrightarrow{-3}$ P
39. (a) As,

U $\xrightarrow{-1}$ T $\xrightarrow{-2}$ R ; D $\xrightarrow{-1}$ C $\xrightarrow{-2}$ A

and T $\xrightarrow{-1}$ S $\xrightarrow{-2}$ Q But, Y $\xrightarrow{-1}$ X $\xrightarrow{-1}$ W
40. (a) As, R $\xrightarrow{+3}$ U $\xrightarrow{-6}$ O

V $\xrightarrow{+3}$ Y $\xrightarrow{-6}$ S

P $\xrightarrow{+3}$ S $\xrightarrow{-6}$ M

But, R $\xrightarrow{-3}$ O $\xrightarrow{-3}$ L

41. (a) As, Z B D ; Q S U (+2, +2 ; +2, +2)

and M O Q (+2, +2)

But, A G H (+6, +1)

42. (a) As,

L —+6→ R I → (Opposite letter)

and

T —+6→ Z A → (Opposite letter)

H —+6→ N M → (Opposite letter)

But, C —+5→ H —+10→ R

43. (c) As, C F D , G J H (+3, −2 , +3, −2)

and

J M K (+3, −2) But, K N M (+3, −1)

44. (a) As, V X B ; Z B F (+2, +4 ; +2, +4)

and S U Y (+2, +4)

But, N Q T (+3, +3)

> **TOP TIPS** To solve such questions easily, it is very important to have knowledge of place value of letters in English alphabetical series.

45. (b) As, S —+4→ W —+2→ Y —−1→ X

P —+4→ T —+2→ V —−1→ U

R —+4→ V —+2→ X —−1→ W

But, L —+3→ O —+2→ Q —−1→ P

46. (c) As, A(1) F(6) K(11) P(16) (+5, +5, +5)

S(19) X(24) C(3) H(8) (+5, +5, +5)

and J(10) O(15) T(20) Y(25) (+5, +5, +5)

But, G(7) K(11) P(16) S(19) (+4, +5, +3)

47. (d) As, L —+2→ N —+5→ S —+3→ V

F —+2→ H —+5→ M —+3→ P

B —+2→ D —+5→ I —+3→ L

But, J —+2→ L —+4→ P —+4→ T

48. (b) As, H —−3→ E —−3→ B —−3→ Y

W —−3→ T —−3→ Q —−3→ N

O —−3→ L —−3→ I —−3→ F

But, S —−3→ P —−4→ L —−3→ I

49. (b) As, W N − R U (−9, +3)

T K − O R (−9, +3)

and Q H − L O (−9, +3)

But, N E − I K (−9, +2≠+3)

50. (a) As, E —+3→ H —+0→ H —+3→ K

A —+3→ D —+0→ D —+3→ G

V —+3→ Y —+0→ Y —+3→ B

But, G —+3→ J —+0→ J —+2→ L

51. (c) B —+4→ F —+4→ J —+4→ N

D —+4→ H —+4→ L —+4→ P

J —+4→ N —+4→ R —+4→ V

But, H —+2→ J —+1→ K —+5→ P

52. (a) As,

F R D P (−2, −2) , M D K B (−2, −2)

and

H L F J (−2, −2)

But,

Q N O M (−1, −2)

53. (d) As, S X H P (−8, Opposite letters) ; U Z F R (−8, Opposite letters)

and X C C U (−8, Opposite letters) ; But, V C D R (−11, +8)

54. (a) As, H M I L (+5, +3) ; K P L O (+5, +3)

S X T W (+5, +3); But, L O K P (+3, +5)

55. (b) As,

E V (Opposite) A F (+5) , T G (Opposite) L Q (+5)

and K P (Opposite) U Z (+5)

But, C X B H (Opposite, +6)

56. (a) As,

G T (Opposite letters) M N (Opposite letters) , H S (Opposite letters) N M (Opposite letters)

and E V (Opposite letters) K P (Opposite letters)

But, J R (Not opposite letters) P V (Not opposite letters)

57. (d) As, W D (Opposite) L F (−6)

Y B (Opposite) X R (−6)

and P K (Opposite) S M (−6)

But, I R (Opposite) M T (+7)

58. (d) As, B Y (Opposite letter) A W D (Opposite letter)

K P (Opposite letter) E T G (Opposite letter)

and M N (Opposite letter) I Q J (Opposite letter)

But, C X (Opposite letter) O P B (+12)

> **TOP TIPS** The sum of positional values of opposite letters in English alphabetical series is always 27
>
> e.g. A ⇌ Z (1) opposite (26)
>
> $1 + 26 = 27$

59. (a) As, D F J P X (+2, +4, +6, +8)

H J N T B (+2, +4, +6, +8)

B D H N V (+2, +4, +6, +8)

But, K M Q W F (+2, +4, +6, +9)

60. (d) As, B d E g (+2, +2)

K m N p (+2, +2)

P r S u (+2, +2)

But, T w X z (+3, +2)

61. (a) As,

R X - V T (+4, –4) N S - R O (+4, –4)

R S - V O (+4, –4) But, L H - P C (+4, –5)

62. (d) As, Q L - O J (+3; –5, –5)

W R - U P (+3; –5, –5)

I D - G B (+3; –5, –5)

But, M S - L H (–7; +6, –4)

63. (b) As, D G - I L (+2; +3, +3)

B E - G J (+2; +3, +3)

and A D - F I (+2; +3, +3)

But, C E - H K (+3; +2, +3)

64. (c) As, Q V - S X (+5, +5)

K P - M R (+5, +5)

and B G - D I (+5, +5)

But, A D - C G (+3≠+5, +4≠+5)

65. (b) As, D A - C F (–3, +3)

G D - F I (–3, +3)

and N K - M P (–3, +3)

But, J G - I M (–3, +4≠+3)

> **TOP TIPS** To solve these questions easily, the specific logic/rule must be applied within the letters of group in each option not within the letters of the two different groups.

66. (d) Except '4' all others are prime numbers.

67. (d) Except '$\sqrt{9}$' all others are irrational number, while '$\sqrt{9}$' is a rational number.

68. (b) As, $863 \Rightarrow 8+6+3=17$ (Prime number)

$463 \Rightarrow 4+6+3=13$ (Prime number)

$601 \Rightarrow 6+0+1=7$ (Prime number)

But, $345 \Rightarrow 3+4+5=12$ (Even number)

69. (b) Except '21' all others are prime numbers.

70. (c) Except '1000' all others are square of a number while '1000' is the cube of 10.

71. (a) Among the given numbers, except number 289, all other numbers are prime numbers, whereas 289 is a perfect square number.

72. (b) As, $165 \Rightarrow 1+5=6$ (middle digit)

$143 \Rightarrow 1+3=4$ (middle digit)

$187 \Rightarrow 1+7=8$ (middle digit)

But, $\boxed{159 \Rightarrow 9+1=10 \neq 5}$

73. (b) Except 6138, the sum of the digits of other numbers is 14.

As, $6+3+4+1=14$

$5+4+2+3=14$

$1+6+5+2=14$

But, $\boxed{6+1+3+8=18 \neq 14}$

74. (b) As, $2105 \Rightarrow 2\times5=10$

$4328 \Rightarrow 4\times8=32$; $3124 \Rightarrow 3\times4=12$

But, $\boxed{6457 \Rightarrow 6\times7=42 \neq 45}$

75. (a) As, $5:14 \Rightarrow 5\times2+4=14$

$12:28 \Rightarrow 12\times2+4=28$

$21:46 \Rightarrow 21\times2+4=46$

But, $\boxed{0:6 \Rightarrow 0\times2+4=4 \neq 6}$

76. (a) As, $9-28 \Rightarrow 9\times3+1=28$

$12-37 \Rightarrow 12\times3+1=37$

$17-52 \Rightarrow 17\times3+1=52$

But, $14-41 \Rightarrow \boxed{14\times3+1=43 \neq 41}$

77. (b) As, $14-126 \Rightarrow 126\div14=9$

$25-225 \Rightarrow 225\div25=9$

$12-108 \Rightarrow 108\div12=9$

But, $31-280 \Rightarrow \boxed{280\div31 \neq 9}$

78. (d) As, $12-96 = 12\times8=96$

$15-120 = 15\times8=120$

$13-104 = 13\times8=104$

But, $16-108 = \boxed{16\times8=128 \neq 108}$

79. (b) As, $144:12 \Rightarrow 12^2=144$

$196:14 \Rightarrow 14^2=196$

$255:15 \Rightarrow 15^2=225$

But $123:11 \Rightarrow \boxed{11^2=121 \neq 123}$

80. (*c*) As, $1:2 \Rightarrow (1)^2+1=2$

$4:17 \Rightarrow (4)^2+1=17$

$2:5 \Rightarrow (2)^2+1=5$

But, $3:12 \Rightarrow \boxed{(3)^2+1=10 \neq 12}$

81. (*d*) As, $1-701 \Rightarrow \frac{701}{1}=701$ (Divisible)

$3-102 \Rightarrow \frac{102}{3}=34$ (Divisible)

$9-324 \Rightarrow \frac{324}{9}=36$ (Divisible)

But, $7-124 \Rightarrow \frac{124}{7}=17\frac{5}{7}$ (Not divisible)

82. (*b*) As, 3375 — 13500 (×4)

and 2685 — 10740 (×4), 1595 — 6380 (×4)

But, $\boxed{2125 — 8500 \neq 8600}$ (×4)

83. (*a*) As, 3 : 5 → Pair of prime numbers

23 : 29 → Pair of prime numbers

13 : 17 → Pair of prime numbers

But, 19 : 25 → Not a pair of prime numbers.

84. (*d*) As, 13 — 104 (×8), 19 — 152 (×8)

and 23 — 184 (×8) But, $\boxed{7 — 58}$ (×8+2)

85. (*a*) As, (104-4) $\Rightarrow \frac{104}{26}=4$

(286-11) $\Rightarrow 286 \div 26 = 11$

and (494-19) $\Rightarrow 494 \div 26 = 19$

But, (521-20) $\Rightarrow \frac{521}{26}=20.03 \neq 20$

86. (*b*) As, (18-198) $\Rightarrow 18 \times 11 = 198$

(31-341) $\Rightarrow 31 \times 11 = 341$

and (22-242) $\Rightarrow 22 \times 11 = 242$

But (13, 144) $\Rightarrow 13 \times 11 = 143 \neq 144$

> **TOP TIPS** To solve these questions easily, it is important to have knowledge of squares, cubes of the numbers.

87. (*d*) As, 3333 — 6666 (×2)

and 2222 — 4444 (×2), 4444 — 8888 (×2)

But, $\boxed{5555 — 11110 \neq 7777}$ (×2)

88. (*c*) As, $2-4-8 \Rightarrow 4 \times 2 = 8$

$2-2-4 \Rightarrow 2 \times 2 = 4$

$1-3-3 \Rightarrow 1 \times 3 = 3$

But, $3-2-5 \Rightarrow \boxed{3 \times 2 = 6 \neq 5}$

89. (*b*) As, 112 − 103 − 94 ; 94 − 85 − 76 (−9, −9 ; −9, −9)

and 87 − 78 − 69 (−9, −9)

But, $\boxed{76 - 67 - 54 \neq 58}$ (−9, −9)

90. (*a*) As, $(10-30-90) \Rightarrow 10 \times 3 = 30$

$\Rightarrow 30 \times 3 = 90$

$(15-45-135) \Rightarrow 15 \times 3 = 45$

$\Rightarrow 45 \times 3 = 135$

$(22-66-198) \Rightarrow 22 \times 3 = 66$

$\Rightarrow 66 \times 3 = 198$

But, $\boxed{(17-51-147) \Rightarrow 17 \times 3 = 51 \Rightarrow 51 \times 3 = 153 \neq 147}$

91. (*b*) As, $81-118-91$

$\Rightarrow 81 \div 3 = 27 + 91 = 118$

and $99-104-71$

$\Rightarrow 99 \div 3 = 33 + 71 = 104$

$21-38-31 \Rightarrow 21 \div 3 = 7 + 31 = 38$

But, $52-65-51$

$\Rightarrow \boxed{52 \div 3 = 17.33 + 51 = 68.33 \neq 68}$

92. (*c*) As, 84 : 294 : 210 [∵ II-I=III]

$\Rightarrow 294 - 84 = 210$

$68 : 238 : 170 \Rightarrow 238 - 68 = 170$

$52 : 182 : 130 \Rightarrow 182 - 52 = 130$

But, 96 : 336 : 192

$\Rightarrow \boxed{336 - 96 = 240 \neq 192}$

93. (*a*) As, 29 − 44 − 38 ; 24 − 39 − 33 (+15, −6 ; +15, −6)

and 17 − 32 − 26 (+15, −6)

But, $\boxed{31 - 46 - 41}$ (+15, −5)

94. (*b*) As, $360-12-6=(6)^3+(12)^2$

$=216+144=360$

$63-6-3=(3)^3+(6)^2=27+36=63$

$164-10-4=(4)^3+(10)^2$

$=64+100=164$

But, $82-8-2=\boxed{(2)^3+(8)^2}$

$=8+64=72 \neq 82$

95. (*b*) As, 11 : 21 : 121

$=11 \times 2 = 22 - 1 = 21$

$=(11)^2=121$

and $2:3:4 = 2 \times 2 = 4 - 1 = 3$

$=(2)^2=4$

$9:17:81 = 9 \times 2 = 18 - 1 = 17$

$=(9)^2=81$

But, $7:15:49 = 7 \times 2 = 14 + 1 = 15$

$=(7)^2=49$

96. (*a*) Except A12, in all other terms letter are letter are written with their positional value.

97. (*d*) Except option (d), in all other options, there are two symbols and a 3-digit numbers.

98. (*d*) As,

B C ; D E

↓ ↓ ; ↓ ↓

$2 \times 3 = 6$; $4 \times 5 = 20$

and C D → $3 \times 4 = 12$

But, $\boxed{E\ F \rightarrow 5 \times 6 = 30 \neq 35}$

99. (*a*) As, (RQ, 35) ⇒ R Q

$18+17=35$

(HI, 17) ⇒ H I

$8+9=17$

(TS, 39) ⇒ T S

$20+19=39$

But, (MN, 37) ⇒ $\boxed{M\ N \quad 13+14=27 \neq 37}$

100. (*a*) As, D L 5 ; H P 25 (+4, +4, ×5)

and

H P 7 ; L T 35 (+4, +4, ×5) ; P J 3 ; T N 15 (+4, +4, ×5)

But, L R 9 ; P U 45 ≠ 55 (+4, +3, ×5)

101. (*a*) Except option (a), in all other options, given number represent the number of letters in each word.

CHAPTER

03 English Alphabet Test

English Alphabet Test

English alphabet test is based on finding the letter or its position in English alphabetical series (both forward and reverse) from left or right or on the basis of certain predefined conditions. English alphabetical series consists of 26 letters out of which 5 (A, E, I, O, U) are called vowel and rest are called constants.

Based on English Alphabet Position

In this type of questions, the position of a letter of the English alphabet is given and then the letter at a specific position to the right or to the left of that letter has to be found.

Sometimes in such questions, one has to find out how many letters are there or which letter is in the middle or between the positions (right or left) of any two letters.

e.g. Which of the following letters is 14th to the right of 6th letter from the left in the English alphabet?

(a) R (b) P (c) W (d) T

Sol. (d) According to the question,

A B C D E F G H I J K L M N O P Q R S [T] U V W X Y Z

6th from left → to the right → 14th

∴ Required letter = T

Based on Reverse Order

In this type of questions, letters of the English alphabet are written in reverse order from the beginning/half from the beginning and half from the end in several small blocks and then the letter at a specific place to the left or to the right of another letter has to be find out.

e.g. If English alphabet is written in reverse order, then what will be the 13th letter to the left of 3rd letter from right?

(a) P (b) N (c) R (d) Q

Sol. (a) English alphabet in reverse order

1 2 3 4 5 6 7 8 9 10 11 12 13 14 15 16 17 18 19 20 21 22 23 24 25 26

Z Y X W V U T S R Q (P) O N M L K J I H G F E D C B A

13th to the left ← 3rd from the right

∴ Required letter = P

Based on Rule/Condition

In this type of questions, one has to find the letter at a specific place to the left or to the right of a letter according to its position in the new series by eliminating some letters as per the given condition in the English alphabetical order.

e.g. If every third letter from the left of the English alphabet is removed, then the 9th letter from the left in the new series is

(a) N (b) O (c) M (d) K

Sol. (c) According to the question, new series

A B D E G H J K [M] N P Q S T V W Y Z

9th from left

∴ Required letter = M

Based on Letter-Word Problem

In this type of questions, a word is given and letters given in this word are to be arranged in alphabetical order or according to some other condition, and a new word is formed. Candidates are required to analyse this word and answer the given question.

e.g. The position of how many letters will remain unchanged, if each of the letter in the word 'FINGER' is arranged in alphabetical order?

(a) Two (b) One (c) Three (d) Four

Sol. (b) Given word → F I N G E [R]

Arrange alphabetical order → E F G I N [R]

So, position of 'R' remains unchanged. Hence, position of one letter remains unchanged.

Based on Letter-Pair

In such questions, candidate has to find out how many letter pairs are present in the given word, which have as many letters between them in the word as they have between them in the english alphabetical series, then the pair formed by these two letters is the required letter pair.

Note: Letter pairs should be formed in both forward and backward order.

e.g. How many pairs of letters are there in the word 'CONDITION', each of which has as many letters between them as they have between them in the English alphabetical order (both backwards and forward)?

(a) One (b) Two (c) Three (d) Four

Sol. (c) Given word,

3 15 14 4 9 20 9 15 14

C O N D I T I O N

Hence, there are three pairs in the given word CI, NO and NO.

Score Booster

Some important formulae to find the position of a letter in English alphabet are given below

- nth letter to the left of mth letter from right end $= (m + n)$th letter from the right end
- nth letter to the right of mth letter from left end $= (m + n)$th letter from the left end
- nth letter to the left of mth letter from left end $= (m - n)$th letter from the right end
- nth letter to the right of mth letter from right end $= (m - n)$th letter from the right end
- Total number of letters between mth letter from left and nth letter from right $= 26 -$ (Position of mth letter + Position of nth letter)

Exam Approach Examples

Based on English Alphabet Position

Example 1 Find the 11th letter to the left of 20th letter from the left in the English alphabet. *DP Head Constable 2022*

(a) D (b) J (c) K (d) I

Sol. (*d*) According to the question,

1 2 3 4 5 6 7 8 9 10 11 12 13 14 15 16 17 18 19 20 21 22 23 24 25 26
A B C D E F G H (I) J K L M N O P Q R S T U V W X Y Z

To the left
11th
From left
20th

Hence, 11th letter to the left of 20th letter from left is I.

Smart Approach

∴ In English alphabet, 11th letter to the left of 20th letter from left
= (20 − 11)th letter from left
= 9th letter from left = I

Helping Tips

While solving this type of question, it is important to remember the place value of letters in English alphabetical series.

Based on Reverse Order

Example 2 If letters of the English alphabets are written in reverse order, then which letter is 5th to the right of 12th letter from the right? *RRB NTPC 2022*

(a) L (b) G (c) O (d) J

Sol. (*b*) According to the question,

1 2 3 4 5 6 7 8 9 10 11 12 13 14 15 16 17 18 19 20 21 22 23 24 25 26
Z Y X W V U T S R Q P O N M (L) K J I H (G) F E D C B A

To the left
12th
5th to the right

Hence, 5th to the right of 12th letter from the right is G.

Smart Approach

In English alphabet, 5th to the right of 12th letter from right
= (12 − 5)th letter from the right end
= 7th letter from right
= G

Example 3 If the first half of the English alphabet series is reversed, which of the following will be the twelfth to the right of the seventh letter from the left end? *UP SI 2021*

(a) N (b) P (c) S (d) O

Sol. (*c*) According to the question,

First half reversed
MLKJIHGFEDCBANOPQRSTUVWXYZ

Twelfth letter to the right of the seventh letter from the left end
= (7 + 12)th letter
= 19th letter = S

Based on Rule/Condition

Example 4 If all the vowels are removed in the English alphabet series, which letter will be fifth to the right of the seventh letter from the left? *UP SI 2021*

(a) P (b) R (c) Q (d) N

Sol. (*a*) According to the question,
After removing vowel from the English alphabet series, we get

5th from right
(Left) B C D F G H [J] K L M N [P]
7th from left
Q R S T V W X Y Z (Right)

Hence, the letter 'P' is fifth to the right of the seventh letter from the left.

Trending Concept

Questions based on letter-word problems are being asked mostly in SSC CGL, CHSL, RRB NTPC, DP Head Constable UPSI, RRB ALP and RRC Group-D exams. They are important for upcoming exams.

Based on Letter-Word Problem

Example 5 The position of how many letters will remain unchanged, if each of the letters in the word 'SIGNATURE' is arranged in the English alphabetical order from left to right? *SSC CGL 2024*

(a) Three (b) One (c) Two (d) Four

Sol. (*b*)

Given word → S I [G] N A T U R E
Arranged in alphabetical order → A E [G] I N R S T U

Hence, position of one letter i.e. G, will remain unchanged.

Based on Letter-Pair

Example 6 How many such pairs of letters are there in the word CONVERTS (in both forward and backward directions) which have as many letters between them as they have in the English alphabetical order? *RRC Group D 2022*

(a) 2 (b) 4 (c) 5 (d) 3

Sol. (*b*) Given word,

3 15 14 22 5 18 20 19
C O N V E R T S

Hence, there are four pairs NO, ST, OT and NS.

Example 7 How many such pairs of letters are there in the word 'PRISTINE' (in both forward and backward directions) which have as many letters between them as they have in the English alphabetical order? *UP Police Head Operator 2024*

(a) 2 (b) 3 (c) 5 (d) 1

Sol. (*b*) Given word,
16 18 9 19 20 9 14 5
P R I S T I N E

Hence, there are three pairs, PS, PT and ST.

Chapter Challenge

Based on English Alphabet Position

1. Which of the following letter is fourth to the right of the twelfth letter from the right in the forward alphabetical series? ***SSC Steno 2023***
(a) P (b) H (c) S (d) K

2. Which of the following options is eight to the right of the 15th letter from the left in the English alphabet? ***RRB NTPC 2024***
(a) O (b) V (c) W (d) U

3. Which of the following words has its letter in alphabetical order? ***UP Police Constable 2019***
(a) Believe (b) Ceanse
(c) Beefy (d) Aerious

4. Which of the following words has its letter in alphabetical order? ***UP Police Constable 2024***
(a) Collops (b) Envelops
(c) Bloops (d) Adrops

5. In the following sequence the 6th letter to the right of the 18th letter from the left is ***RRB Group D 2018***
A B C D E F G H I J K L M N O P Q R S T U V W X Y Z
(a) Z (b) X (c) W (d) Y

6. Which of the following letter is 5th to the right of the 12th letter from the left of the English alphabet which written starting from left to right? ***RRB NTPC 2022***
(a) P (b) Q (c) E (d) H

7. Which of the following letter is sixth to the left of the nineteenth letter from the left in the forward alphabetical series? ***UP Police ASI 2021***
(a) M (b) B (c) Y (d) N

8. How many number of letters are there between 22nd letter from left and 8th letter from left in the English alphabet?
(a) 12 (b) 15 (c) 11 (d) 13

Based on Reverse Order

9. If the English alphabet is given in reverse order, then which is the 12th letter to the right of O? ***RRB NTPC 2021***
(a) C (b) A (c) B (d) E

10. If the first half of English alphabetical series is reversed, then which letter will be 12th to the right of 7th letter from the left end. ***UP Police SI 2021***
(a) N (b) P
(c) S (d) O

11. If the 1st half of the English alphabet is written in the backward order, then find the 15th letter to the left of 20th letter from left.
(a) H (b) I (c) Y (d) X

12. If letter of the English alphabet are written in reverse order then which letter is 2nd to the right of 9th letter from the left? ***RRB NTPC (CBT II) 2022***
(a) R (b) I (c) K (d) P

13. If the second half of the English alphabet is written in reverse order, which will be the 15th letter from the right? ***DP Constable 2020***
(a) M (b) L (c) K (d) J

14. If the letters of English alphabets are written in reverse order, which letter comes in the middle of the 13th letter and the 25th letter? ***RRB NTPC 2022***
(a) H (b) I (c) G (d) M

15. If all the English alphabets are arranged alphabetically in the reverse order. The difference of the positions of two vowels which appear in the beginning and in the end, is ***UP Police ASI 2021***
(a) 6 (b) 12 (c) 16 (d) 20

Based on Rule/Condition

16. If every 4th letter going from left to right of the English alphabet is deleted, then which of the following letter would be the 5th letter from the right in the new series obtained? ***RRB NTPC 2022***
(a) E (b) F (c) U (d) V

17. The following question is based on the series.
A B C D E F G H I J K L M N O P Q R S T U V W X Y Z
If the letters of the given series interchanged positions, so that A takes the place of Z and Z takes place of A and so on. What will be the 13th letter from the right? ***HSSC Police Constable 2021***
(a) L (b) O (c) M (d) N

18. If every 3rd letter from left to right of English alphabet is deleted, then what would be the 12th letter from right in the new series obtained? ***RRB NTPC 2021***
(a) J (b) T (c) K (d) S

19. In the English alphabet written in order from left to right, if the first and third letters are interchanged, second and fourth letters are interchanged and so on, which of the following will be the thirteenth letter from the left? ***RRB NTPC 2021***
(a) O (b) L (c) N (d) M

20. If all the English letter appearing at the even number position, except the multiples of 4, are removed, then which of the letter will come at the 13th place in the new alphabet series? ***UPSSSC VDO 2018***
(a) O (b) P (c) Q (d) R

Based on Letter Word Problem

21. The position(s) of how many letters will remain unchanged, if all the letters in the word 'ASTEROID' are arranged in English alphabetical order? *SSC CGL (Tier-I) 2024*

(a) Three (b) None (c) Two (d) One

22. The position of how many letters will remain unchanged, if each of the letters in the word BREAKDOWN is arranged in alphabetical order? *RRC Group D 2022*

(a) 1 (b) 4
(c) 2 (d) 3

> **MRC*****
> ***(Most Repeating Concepts)***
> Q. Nos. 22, 23, 27, 28, 29, 30 and 31 are very important from examination point of views. Questions on these concepts are being asked continuously in RRB NTPC, RRB Group-D, SSC CHSL, SSC CGL and CISF Head Constable exams.

23. If each letter of the word TYPING, is changed to the letter immediately preceding it in the English alphabetical order and the new group of letters thus formed is rearranged in English alphabetical order, then which letter is first to the right in the new rearranged group of letters? *RRB ALP 2024*

(a) O (b) X (c) M (d) S

24. If the letters in the word 'DISREPUTABLY' are rearranged as they appear in the English alphabet, then the position of how many letters will remain unchanged after the rearrangement? *CRPF Head Constable 2023*

(a) Three (b) Two (c) Zero (d) One

25. Each vowel in the word ICTERID is changed to the letter immediately following it in the English alphabetical order and each consonant is changed to the letter immediately preceding it in the English alphabetical order. How many letters will appear exactly twice in the group of letters thus formed? *RPF SI 2024*

(a) 2 (b) 1 (c) 3 (d) 0

26. The position of how many letters will remain unchanged if each of the letters in the word 'CONFIRM" is arranged in alphabetical order? *RRC Group D 2022*

(a) None (b) One (c) Two (d) Three

27. If the letters in the word BACKFIELDS are arranged as in the English alphabetical order, then which letter will be to the second right of the letter 'F', after the rearrangement? *CISF Head Constable 2023*

(a) E (b) K (c) L (d) C

28. Each of the letters in the word MUSICAL is arranged in alphabetical order. How many letters are there in the English alphabetical series between the letter which is fourth from the left and the one which is second from the right in the new letter cluster thus formed? *SSC CHSL (Tier-I) 2024*

(a) Seven (b) Six
(c) Eight (d) Five

29. Each of the letters in the word 'KEYBOARD' are arranged in the English alphabetical order. How many letters are in the English alphabetical order between the letter which is third from the right end and the second from the right end in the group of letters thus formed? *SSC CGL (Tier-I) 2024*

(a) Four (b) Three
(c) Two (d) One

30. Each vowel in the word CRICKET is changed to the letter following it in the English alphabetical order and each consonant is changed to the letter preceding it in the English alphabetical order. If each letter thus formed is arranged in alphabetical order, which letter will be fifth from the right? *RRC Group D 2022*

(a) J (b) F (c) B (d) Q

31. Each vowel in the word 'SIMILAR' is changed to the following letter in the English alphabetical order and each consonant is changed to the preceding letter in the English alphabetical order. How many letters are there in the English alphabetical order between the letter which is second from the left end and third from the left end in the group of letters thus formed? *SSC CGL 2024*

(a) Three (b) Two
(c) One (d) Four

32. If each vowel of the word 'CONSTRUCTION' is replaced by its next letter in the English alphabetical order and each consonant is replaced by its previous letter in the English alphabetical then, which letter will be 6th from the right in the letter group formed? *RRB ALP (CBT-I) 2024*

(a) V (b) Q (c) B (d) S

33. In the word MASTER, each consonant is changed to the letter immediately preceding it in the English alphabetical order and each vowel is changed to the letter immediately succeeding it in the English alphabetical order. How many consonants are present in the new group of letters thus formed? *RRB ALP 2024*

(a) Six (b) Four (c) Three (d) Five

Based on Letter Pair

34. How many such pairs of letters are there in the word DOLPHIN (in both the forward and backward directions) which have as many letters between them in the word as there are in the English alphabetical order? *RRB NTPC 2022*

(a) None (b) Four (c) Two (d) Three

35. How many such pairs of letters are there in the word DANCER (in both forward and backward directions) which have as many letters between them as there are in the English alphabetical order? *RRC Group D 2022*
(a) None (b) Three
(c) One (d) Two

36. How many such pairs of letters are there in the word LOVABLE (in both forward and backward directions) which have as many letters between them in the word as there are in the English alphabetical order? *RRC Group D 2022*
(a) 5 (b) 6
(c) 3 (d) 1

37. How many such pairs of letters are there in the word 'CLUSTERS' (in both forward and backward directions) which have as many letters between them in the word as there are in the English alphabetical order? *RRB NTPC 2022*
(a) 1 (b) 2
(c) 0 (d) 3

38. How many such pairs of letters are there in the word MASTER (in the forward direction) which have as many letters between them in the word as there are in the English alphabetical order? *RRC Group D 2022*
(a) 3 (b) 2 (c) 1 (d) 4

39. How many such pairs of letters are there in the word 'ABILITY' (in both forward and backward directions) each of which have as many letters between them in the word as there are in the English alphabetical order? *RRC Group D 2022*
(a) 1 (b) 2 (c) 3 (d) 4

40. How many such pairs of letters are there in the word REPUBLICAN (in both forward and backward directions) which have as many letters between them in the word as there are in the English alphabetical order? *RRC Group D 2022*
(a) 6 (b) 5 (c) 3 (d) 4

41. How many pairs of letters are there in the word TOMORROW (in both forward and backward directions) each of which has as many letters between them in the word as in the English alphabetical order? *RRC Group D 2022*
(a) 1 (b) 2 c) 3 (d) 4

Right Key

1. (c)	2. (c)	3. (c)	4. (c)	5. (b)	6. (b)	7. (a)	8. (d)	9. (a)	10. (c)
11. (b)	12. (d)	13. (b)	14. (a)	15. (d)	16. (c)	17. (c)	18. (a)	19. (a)	20. (c)
21. (d)	22. (c)	23. (b)	24. (d)	25. (b)	26. (b)	27. (b)	28. (b)	29. (c)	30. (a)
31. (c)	32. (a)	33. (a)	34. (b)	35. (c)	36. (d)	37. (d)	38. (b)	39. (a)	40. (c)
41. (a)									

Solutions

1. *(c)* According to the question,

A B C D E F G H I J K L M N O P Q R S T U V W X Y Z
4th right
12th from right end

Hence, required letter = S

2. *(c)* According to the question,

A B C D E F G H I J K L M N O P Q R S T U V W X Y Z
15th from left
8th from right

Hence, 'W' is eight to the right of the 15th letter from the left.

3. *(c)* Letter 'Beefy' word are arranged in the alphabetically order.
2 5 5 6 25
B E E F Y

4. *(c)* Letter 'Bloops' word are arranged in the alphabetically order.
2 12 15 15 16 19
B L O O P S

5. *(b)* According to the question,

1 2 3 4 5 6 7 8 9 10 11 12 13 14 15 16 17 18 19 20 21 22 23 24 25 26
A B C D E F G H I J K L M N O P Q R S T U V W X Y Z
18th from left
6th from right

Hence, the letter 'X' is 6th letter to the right of the 18th letter from the left.

Smart Approach

∴ Required letter = Letter from left side (18 + 6) = 24th letter from left = X

6. *(b)* According to the question,

1 2 3 4 5 6 7 8 9 10 11 12 13 14 15 16 17 18 19 20 21 22 23 24 25 26
A B C D E F G H I J K L M N O P Q R S T U V W X Y Z
12th from left
5th from right

Hence, 5th letter to the right of 12th letter from the left is Q.

7. (*a*) According to the question,

6th from left

A B C D E F G H I J K L [M] N O P Q R S T U V W X Y Z

19th from left

Hence, required letter = M

8. (*d*) According to the question,

1 2 3 4 5 6 7 8 9 10 11 12 13 14 15 16 17 18 19 20 21 22 23 24 25 26
A B C D E F G H I J K L M N O P Q R S T U V W X Y Z

From left — 13 letters

From left — 8th — 22nd

∴ Required number of letters = 13

Smart Approach

We have to find number of letters between 8th letter from left and 5th letter from right.

∴ Required number of letters = 26 − (8 + 5) = 26 − 13 = 13

9. (*a*) According to the question,

1 2 3 4 5 6 7 8 9 10 11 12 13 14 15 16 17 18 19 20 21 22 23 24 25 26
Z Y X W V U T S R Q P O N M L K J I H G F E D [C] B A

12th from right

Hence, the required letter is 'C'.

10. (*c*) On reversing the first half of alphabetical series,

M L K J I H [G] F E D C B A N O P Q R [S] T U V W X Y Z

7th from left — 12th from right

∴ Required letter = S

11. (*b*) According to the question,

13 12 11 10 9 8 7 6 5 4 3 2 1 14 15 16 17 18 19 20 21 22 23 24 25 26
M L K J (I) H G F E D C B A N O P Q R S T U V W X Y Z

To the left

15th — From left — 20th

∴ The required letter is 'I'.

12. (*d*) According to the question,

Z Y X W V U T S R Q [P] O N M L K J I H G F E D C B A

9th from left — 2nd to right

Hence, required letter = P

13. (*b*) According to the question,

A B C D E F G H I J K L M Z Y X W V U T S R Q P O N

15th from right

∴ Required letter = L

Smart Approach

15th letter from the right end comes in first part which remain unchanged.

∴ Letter from the right = (27 − 15) th letter from left

= 12th letter from the left = L

14. (*a*) According to the question,

1 2 3 4 5 6 7 8 9 10 11 12 13 14 15 16 17 18 19 20 21 22 23 24 25 26
Z Y X W V U T S R Q P O N M L K J I (H) G F E D C B A

Middle

Hence, 'H' comes in the middle of the 13th letter and the 25th letter.

TOP TIPS While solving this type of question, it is important to remember the opposite place value of the English alphabet in English alphabetical series.

15. (*d*) According to the question,

Reverse order of an English alphabet is as follows

Z Y X W V U T S R Q P O N M L K J I H G F E D C B A

6 12 18 22 26

Vowel that appear in beginning of new arrangement = U

U's position in the above arrangement = 6

and vowel that appear in the end in the new arrangement = A

A's position in the above arrangement = 26

∴ Required difference = 26 − 6 = 20

16. (*c*) According to the question,

1 2 3 4 5 6 7 8 9 10 11 12 13 14 15 16 17 18 19 20
A B C ~~D~~ E F G ~~H~~ I J K ~~L~~ M N O ~~P~~ Q R S ~~T~~ (U) V W ~~X~~ Y Z

5th from right

Hence, 'U' is the 5th letter from the right.

17. (*c*) According to the question, interchanging the position of letters, we get

Z Y X W V U T S R Q P O N [M] L K J I H G F E D C B A

13th from right

∴ Required letter = M

18. (*a*) According to the question,

When, every 3rd letter from left to right of English alphabet is deleted, new series obtained is

A B D E G H [J] K M N P Q S T V W Y Z

12th letter from right

Hence, the required letter is 'J'.

19. (*a*) According to the question,

First letter replaced with third, second with fourth.

Fifth with seventh and so on.

Thus, 13th letter will be replaced with 15th letter.

Hence, letter 'O' is the correct answer.

20. (*c*) According to the question,

D, H, L, P, T and X are not removed.

So, new series is

1 2 3 4 5 6 7 8 9 10 11 12 13 14 15 16 17 18 19
A C D E G H I K L M O P [Q] S T U W X Y

Hence, letter 'Q' is the 13th letter in the new series.

21. *(d)*

Given word → [A] S T E R O I D

Arranged in alphabetical order → [A] D E I O R S T

Hence, the position of one letter will remain unchanged.

22. *(c)*

Given word → B R E A [K] D [O] W N

Arranged in alphabetical order → A B D E [K] N [O] R W

Hence, position of two letter will remain unchanged.

23. *(b)*

Given word → T Y P I N G

After applying condition → S X O H M F

After arranging in alphabetical order → F H M O S [X] ← Right

Hence, letter X is first to the right in the new rearranged group of letters.

24. *(d)* According to the question,

Given word → D I S R E P U T A B L [Y]

After arranging in alphabetical order → A B D E I L P R S T U [Y]

Hence, the position of one letter, Y will remain unchanged.

25. *(b)*

Given word → I C T E R I D

+1 −1 −1 +1 −1 +1 −1

After applying condition → J B S F Q J C

Hence, letter J will appear exactly twice in the group of letters thus formed.

26. *(b)*

Given word → [C] O N F I R M

Arranged in alphabetical order → [C] F I M N O R

Hence, the letter 'C' will remain unchanged.

27. *(b)* According to the question,

Given word → B A C K F I E L D S

Arranged in alphabetical order → A B C D E F I [K] L S

2nd from right

Hence, letter 'K' is second right of the letter 'F'.

28. *(b)*

Given word → M U S I C A L

Arranged in alphabetical order → A C I L M S U

Letter fourth from the left → L

Letter second from the right → S

Hence, there are six letters between L and S i.e. M, N, O, P, Q and R.

29. *(c)*

Given word → K E Y B O A R D

Arranged in alphabetical order → A B D E K O R Y

Thus, there are two letter P and Q between R and O.

Hence, the correct answer is two.

30. *(a)*

Given word → C R I C K E T

−1 −1 +1 −1 −1 +1 −1

After applying condition → B Q [J] B J F S

5th from right

Hence, letter 'J' is fifth from the right.

31. *(c)*

Given word → S I M I L A R

−1 +1 −1 +1 −1 +1 −1

After applying condition → R J L J K B Q

Second letter from the left end = J

Third letter from the left end = L

Hence, there is only one letter between J and L i.e., K.

32. *(a)* According to the question,

Given word → C O N S T R U C T I O N

According to condition → B P M R S Q [V] B S J P M

6th from right

∴ Required answer is V.

33. *(a)*

Given word → M A S T E R

−1 +1 −1 −1 +1 −1

After applying condition → L B R S F Q

Hence, there are six consonants in the new group of letters thus formed.

34. *(b)*

Given word → D O L P H I N (4 15 12 16 8 9 14)

Hence, only four pairs are possible i.e., DH, DI HI and IL.

35. *(c)*

Given word → D A N C E R (4 1 14 3 5 18)

Hence, only one pair is possible i.e., AC.

36. *(d)*

Given word → L O V A B L E (12 15 22 1 2 12 5)

Hence, only one pair is possible i.e., AB.

37. *(d)*

Given word → C L U S T E R S (3 12 21 19 20 5 18 19)

Hence, three pair is possible i.e., ST, RT and SR.

38. *(b)*

Given word → M A S T E R (13 1 19 20 5 18)

Hence, there are two pairs of letter i.e., MR and ST.

39. *(a)*

Given word → A B I L I T Y (1 2 9 12 9 20 25)

Hence, only one pair of letter i.e., AB.

40. *(c)*

Given word → R E P U B L I C A N (18 5 16 21 2 12 9 3 1 14)

Hence, there are three pair of letter is possible i.e., PR, RU and BE.

41. *(a)*

Given word → T O M O R R O W (20 15 13 15 18 18 15 23)

Hence, only one pair of letter is possible i.e., RO.

CHAPTER

04 Word Formation

Word Formation

"Forming one or more meaningful words with the help of letters of a given word as per a particular rule/condition is called word formation".

Word formation or Not Formation Using Letters of the Given Word

In this type of questions, a word is given, followed by four other words. The candidate has to identify the word which can or cannot be formed by using the letters of the given word.

e.g. From the word COMPENSATION which word can be formed by using the letters of the given word, from the given four options.

(a) TINY (b) COPY

(c) MENTION (d) MOTIVE

Sol. (c) MENTION - All the letters of this word are present in the main word.

Hence, 'MENTION' can be formed from the letters of the given word 'COMPENSATION

Word Formation by Unscrambling Letters

In this type of questions, a set of English letters is given in a jumbled order. The candidate is required to arrange these letters to form a meaningful word.

e.g. Select the option from the following four possible arrangements of these numbers that forms a meaningful word.

L	P	C	E	I	N
1	2	3	4	5	6

(a) 6, 5, 3, 4, 1, 2 (b) 2, 4, 6, 3, 5, 1

(c) 3, 4, 1, 5, 2, 6 (d) 2, 4, 6, 3, 1, 5

Sol. (b) The meaningful word formed by given letters is

P	E	N	C	I	L
2	4	6	3	5	1

Forming a Meaningful Word with Selected Letters

In this type, information about an alphabet or a word along with some selected letters is given. It is necessary to make a meaningful word from the selected letters. Sometimes, it is also possible that more than one word can be made from these letters or no meaningful word can be made.

e.g. How many meaningful English words can be formed with the third, fifth, seventh and ninth letters of the word 'DOWNGRADED' using each letter once in each word?

(a) None (b) One (c) Two (d) Three

Sol. (b) Given word,

1	2	3	4	5	6	7	8	9	10
D	O	[W]	N	[G]	R	[A]	D	[E]	D

Only one meaningful English word. 'WAGE' can be formed by using the letters W, G, A and E.

Forming Meaningful Words using Given Letters

In this type, a word is given and the candidates are required to form as many meaningful English words as possible from the given word, using each letter only once in each word.

e.g. How many meaningful English words can be made with the letters IFEL, using each letter only once in each word?

(a) None (b) One

(c) Two (d) Three

Sol. (c) Only two meaningful words, 'FILE' and 'LIFE' can be formed from the letters 'IFEL' using each letter only once.

Formation of Meaningful Word by Adding Letters

In this type, some words are given and a new group of meaningful words has to be formed by adding letters before or after them.

It also includes questions based on forming two meaningful words by inserting a word in between the given word.

e.g. Which of the letter given in the options can be placed at the end of these letters to make them meaningful words?

LEN, SAN, WOR, SEE

(a) A (b) D (c) B (d) K

Sol. (b) By adding letter D after each word of the given group of words, new words will be formed LEND, SAND, WORD and SEED.

Choosing Different Words by Rearranging Jumbled Letters

In this type of questions, groups of jumbled letters are given as options. These jumbled letters have to be rearranged to form meaningful words and one word has to be selected which is different from other words.

e.g. Rearrange the jumbled letters to form meaningful words and choose the one which is different from the others.

(a) VEENS (b) ORFU (c) VIDEID (d) GHIET

Sol. (c) By arranging the given jumbled letters,

VEENS → SEVEN

ORFU → FOUR

VIDEID → DIVIDE

GHIET → EIGHT

Hence, except 'DIVIDE' all others are numbers whereas 'DIVIDE' is a mathematical operation.

Exam Approach Examples

Word Formation/Not Formation Using Letters of the Given Word

Example 1 From the given options, select the word which can be formed by using the letters of the given words.

IMMEDIATELY

(a) DIALECT (b) LIMITED
(c) DIAMETER (d) DICTATE

Sol. *(b)* LIMITED - All the letters of this word are present in the given word.

Hence, 'LIMITED' can be formed from the letters of the given word 'IMMEDIATELY.

> **Score Booster**
> To solve these questions, a good knowledge of English vocabulary and spellings is necessary.

Example 2 From the following options, choose the word which cannot be formed using the letters of the given words.

RRB NTPC 2021

CATASTROPHE

(a) STAR (b) CASTOR (c) TROPHY (d) TRAP

Sol. *(c)* The word 'TROPHY' cannot be formed using the letters of the given word 'CATASTROPHE' as the letter 'Y' is missing in the given word.

Word Formation by Unscrambling Letters

Example 3 A group of English letters is shown below in jumbled order. Select the combination of numbers such that the letters when arranged will form a meaningful word.

C P K T O E
1 2 3 4 5 6

HCET 2023

(a) 151426 (b) 215364 (c) 251364 (d) 415236

Sol. *(c)* Given word,

C P K T O E
1 2 3 4 5 6

The meaningful word formed by given letters is

P O C K E T
2 5 1 3 6 4

Hence, option (c) after arranging will form a meaningful word.

> **Helping Tips**
> To save time always try to place the letters according to the numbers provided in options rather than doing it on the basis of vocabulary knowledge.

Forming a Meaningful Word with Selected Letters

Example 4 In the alphabet series A B C D E F G H I J K L M N O P Q R S T U V W X Y Z, the letters in place of 20, 1, 7, 5 are used to form a meaningful word, find the second letter of that word.

RRB Group D 2018

(a) F (b) T (c) A (d) E

Sol. *(c)* According to the question,

In the given alphabetical series, the letter at 20th, 1st, 7th and 5th position = T, A, G, E

From letters T, A, G and E meaningful word formed is GATE.

Hence, the second letter of the meaningful word is A.

Example 5 If it is possible to make only one meaningful word from the fifth, sixth, seventh and eighth letters of the word 'DRINKING', then which will be the second letters from the left of that word? If more than one such word can be formed give 'X' as your answer. If no such word can be formed, give 'Z' as your answer.

(a) X (b) Z (c) I (d) N

Sol. *(c)* Given word, DRINKING

The fifth, sixth, seventh and eighth letters of the given word are K, I, N and G respectively,

Meaningful word = K [I] N G
2nd letter from left

Hence, the second letter from the left of new word will be I.

Choosing Different Words by Rearranging Jumbled Letters

Example 6 Rearrange the jumbled letters to make a meaningful word and then select the one which is different from the others.

(A) ARC (B) USB (C) LACES (D) LECCY

(a) A (b) C (c) B (d) D

Sol. *(b)* By arranging the given jumbled letters,

ARC ⇒ CAR
USB ⇒ BUS
LACES ⇒ SCALE
LECCY ⇒ CYCLE

Hence, 'SCALE' is different from all others as all others are modes of transport.

Formation of Meaningful Word by Adding Letters

Example 7 Which single letter can be placed before the following words to form new words?

EAT, OUR, IS, AS, AT

Delhi Police MTS 2019

(a) H (b) C (c) B (d) S

Sol. *(a)* By adding letter H before each word of the given group of words, new words will be formed = HEAT, HOUR, HIS, HAS, and HAT.

Forming Meaningful Words using Given Letters

Example 8 How many meaningful English words can be formed from R, O, W, D and C, using each letter mandatorily but only once in each word?

SSC CHSL (Tier-II) 2024

(a) More than two (b) None
(c) One (d) Two

Sol. *(c)* Given letters → R, O, W, D, C

The meaningful word formed by given letters is CROWD.

Hence, only one word can be formed by given letters.

Chapter Challenge

Word Formation/Not Formation using Letters of the given Word

Directions (Q. Nos. 1-8) *In each of the following questions, a word has been given, followed by four other words, one of which can be formed by using the letters of the given word. Find that word.*

1. MEASUREMENT *UP Police Constable 2024*
(a) MANTLE (b) RETUNES
(c) ASSURE (d) SUMMIT

2. INSTRUMENTALIST *UPSSSC 2018*
(a) INSTRUCT (b) TALISMAN
(c) ENTRUST (d) METRE

3. MONUMENT *SSC Steno 2016*
(a) TENENT (b) TENT
(c) MOUNT (d) MOVEMENT

4. REPUTATION
(a) TUTOR (b) PONDER
(c) REQUIRE (d) RETIRE

5. COMPANIONSHIP
(a) OPEN (b) OPIUM
(c) OPINION (d) NATION

6. DEDICATE
(a) DECIDE (b) DEMAND
(c) DERIDE (d) DEDUCE

7. MEASUREMENT
(a) ASSURE (b) MANTLE
(c) MASTER (d) SUMMIT

8. MUSPOPPAROTIH
(a) METAMORPHIC (b) PHILANTHROPIST
(c) HIPPOCAMPUS (d) HIPPOPOTAMUS

Directions (Q. Nos. 9-25) *From the given options, select the word which cannot be formed by using the letters of the given words.*

9. ADMINISTRATION *UP Police Constable 2024*
(a) MINISTER (b) RATION (c) MIND (d) STATION

10. SEPARATE *HCET 2022*
(a) PARADE (b) TREES (c) TEARS (d) ERASE

11. LAUGHTER *RRB NTPC 2020*
(a) GATE (b) GRUNT
(c) HATE (d) RATE

12. NATIONALISATION *UP (AO) 2024*
(a) SANITATION (b) INSTALLATION
(c) SALINATION (d) NOTATION

13. FRATERNAL *UPSSSC 2018*
(a) NARRATE (b) ERRATA
(c) FATHER (d) RENTAL

14. Russia is my country. *RRB NTPC 2021*
(a) Rain (b) Minor (c) Your (d) Cloud

15. ECCENTRICITY *SSC CGL 2017*
(a) NIECE (b) CREATE
(c) TRINITY (d) RETICENT

16. ADMINISTRATORS *SSC CPO 2016*
(a) STARDOM (b) TRAITOR
(c) DORMANT (d) MINISTER

17. PUNISHMENT *UP Police Constable 2024*
(a) PAIN (b) SENT (c) PENT (d) PUSH

18. APPLICATION *UP Police Constable 2024*
(a) POLONIA
(b) POINT
(c) OPTICAL
(d) ANTIC

> **MRC*****
> ***(Most Repeating Concepts)***
> In Q. Nos. 1, 9, 10, 14, 17, 18, 19 and 21 based on formation and not formation of words from the letters of the given word are important for UP Police Constable exams and Railway exams especially Railway NTPC

19. JURISPRUDENCE *SSC Steno 2016*
(a) PREJUDICE
(b) PRINCE
(c) PRUNE
(d) PRESIDENT

20. DAUGHTER *RRB NTPC 2020*
(a) DATE (b) TOUGH (c) GET (d) HURT

21. FLAMBOYANT *UP Police Constable 2018*
(a) LAMB (b) BOUT (c) MOAN (d) BOAT

22. TERRIFY *UPSSSC 2018*
(a) RIFT (b) FERRY (c) TIER (d) FEET

23. ENVIRONMENT *SSC CGL 2015*
(a) ENTRANCE (b) MOVE
(c) EMINENT (d) ENTER

24. TEMPERAMENT *DSSSB Grade-III 2017*
(a) TEMEPER (b) TESTER
(c) METER (d) PARENT

25. MERCHANDISE
(a) MESH (b) DICE
(c) CHARM (d) CHANCE

Word Formation by Unscrambling Letters

Directions (Q. Nos. 26-30) *In the given questions, a group of letters is given, which is numbered as 1, 2, 3, 4, 5, 6, 7 and 8. Four options are given below it.*

Find that option in which combining the letters according to the given number will form a meaningful word.

26. D U O P I M
1 2 3 4 5 6 *HCET 2022*
(a) 4, 3, 2, 5, 1, 6 (b) 6, 3, 1, 2, 5, 4
(c) 4, 3, 1, 5, 2, 6 (d) 4, 3, 2, 1, 6, 5

27. I G S N R A E O
1 2 3 4 5 6 7 8 *Rajasthan Police Constable 2022*
(a) 6, 3, 5, 2, 1, 4, 8, 7 (b) 8, 5, 2, 6, 4, 1, 3, 7
(c) 6, 3, 5, 2, 4, 1, 8, 7 (d) 3, 5, 2, 6, 3, 7, 8, 1

Chapter Challenge Word Formation

28. I A D O H E N S
1 2 3 4 5 6 7 8 *UPSSSC 2018*
(a) 3, 2, 5, 6, 8, 1, 4, 7 (b) 2, 3, 5, 6, 4, 8, 1, 7
(c) 2, 3, 5, 6, 8, 1, 4, 7 (d) 2, 3, 5, 6, 8, 4, 1, 7

29. G I C O D N
1 2 3 4 5 6
(a) 2, 1, 4, 3, 6, 5 (b) 4, 3, 2, 6, 5, 1
(c) 6, 5, 2, 3, 1, 4 (d) 3, 4, 5, 2, 6, 1

30. L N S A I G
1 2 3 4 5 6 *HCET 2023*
(a) 3, 5, 4, 2, 6, 1 (b) 2, 6, 3, 1, 4, 5
(c) 5, 4, 2, 1, 6, 3 (d) 3, 5, 6, 2, 4, 1

Forming a Meaningful Word with Selected Letters

31. In the alphabet ABCDEFGHIJKLMNOPQRSTUVWXYZ, a meaningful word is formed by taking letters from 15th, 18th, 16th, and 5th position.
The second letter of that meaningful word is *RRB Group D 2018*
(a) R (b) O
(c) M (d) P

32. If a meaningful English word is to be formed using the first, third, fifth and eighth letters of the word 'SOUVENIR' (each letter is to be used only once) then how many such words can be formed? *UP Police Constable 2024*
(a) More than 3 (b) 2
(c) 3 (d) 1

33. How many meaningful four-letter English words can be formed using the first, fourth, fifth and sixth letters (counted from left to right) of the word 'SAVOUR', using each letter only once in each word? *SSC (10+2) 2024*
(a) None (b) More than two
(c) Two (d) One

34. How many meaningful four-letter English words can be formed using the second, third, fifth and seventh letters (counted from left to right) of the word 'TOURIST' using each letter only once in each word? *SSC (10+2) 2024*
(a) None (b) Two
(c) More than two (d) One

35. If a meaningful word can be formed from the first, fourth, fifth, seventh, tenth, eleventh and twelfth letters of the word 'FELICITATIONS' then which letter will be the fifth letter of that word when counted from the right?
(a) I (b) N
(c) T (d) C

36. After interchanging the 3rd and 6th letters and the 4th and 9th letters as well as the 5th and 10th letters in the given words, which series will form a meaningful word after this rearrangement? *UP Police Constable 2024*
I. HRETIAGVSN
II. FLNESAGOMI
III. EXSONHTIAU
(a) Only I (b) Only II and III
(c) All I, II and III (d) Only III

Choosing Different words by Rearranging Jumbled Letters

Directions (Q. Nos. 37 and 38) *In each of the following questions, rearrange the jumbled letters to form meaningful words and choose the one which is different from the other.* *RRB NTPC 2016*

37. (a) LAFC (b) UKCGIDLN
(c) RILNIGHE (d) BCU

38. (a) ANDOMY (b) STEAUDY
(c) DIARFY (d) DHAIOLY

Formation of Meaningful Word by Adding Letters

39. In this question choose the correct letters that complete the first word and start the second word will go in brackets. The number of dots shown in brackets indicates the number of letters.
ST (...) PLE
(a) OPS (b) INK (c) RIP (d) ACK

40. Find the letter which can be placed before the following words to form entirely new words.
TILL, TABLE, PILE, TAB, PRING *SSC CGL 2015*
(a) P (b) N (c) S (d) B

41. Which single letter can be added after the following words to form new words? *SSC CGL 2015*
HAT, BAR, BAT, PIN, BATH
(a) A (b) E (c) B (d) D

Forming Meaningful Words Using Given Letters

42. How many independent words can be formed from the word 'BEHIND' in which the order of the letters remains unchanged and each letter is used once?
(a) One (b) Two *RRB NTPC 2016*
(c) Three (d) None of these

43. How many six-lettered meaningful words can be formed using all these letters but each letter only once in the word? *SSC CGL (Tier-II) 2025*
R F I G E D
(a) Three (b) Two (c) One (d) Four

Right Key

1. (b)	2. (c)	3. (c)	4. (a)	5. (c)	6. (a)	7. (c)	8. (d)	9. (a)	10. (a)
11. (b)	12. (b)	13. (c)	14. (d)	15. (b)	16. (d)	17. (a)	18. (a)	19. (d)	20. (b)
21. (b)	22. (d)	23. (a)	24. (b)	25. (d)	26. (c)	27. (b)	28. (c)	29. (d)	30. (d)
31. (b)	32. (a)	33. (c)	34. (a)	35. (d)	36. (b)	37. (c)	38. (d)	39. (c)	40. (c)
41. (b)	42. (b)	43. (c)							

Solutions

1. *(b)* The word 'RETUNES' can be formed from the given word as all the letters of 'RETUNES' are present in the given word 'MEASUREMENT'.

TOP TIPS While solving such questions, keep in mind that the letters in the formed word should be used as many times as they appear in the main word.

2. *(c)* The word ENTRUST can be formed using the letters of the given word 'INSTRUMENTALIST'. Because all its letters are present in the original word.

3. *(c)* The word MOUNT can be formed from the given word, as all the letters of this word are present in the original word MONUMENT.

4. *(a)* Only the word TUTOR can be formed from the letters of the given word REPUTATION, as all its letters are present in the original word.

5. *(c)* Only the word OPINION can be formed from the letters of the given word COMPANIONSHIP, as all its letters are present in the original word.

6. *(a)* The word DECIDE can be formed using the letters of the given word DEDICATE, as all its letters are present in the original word.

7. *(c)* The word MASTER can be formed using the letters of the given word MEASUREMENT, as all its letters are present in the original word.

8. *(d)* The word HIPPOPOTAMUS can be formed using the letters of the given word MUSPOPPAROTIH, as all its letters are present in the original word.

9. *(a)* The word MINISTER cannot be formed from the given word ADMINISTRATION, because the given word does not contain the letter 'E'.

10. *(a)* The word PARADE cannot be formed from the given word SEPARATE, because the given word does not contain the letter 'D'.

11. *(b)* The word GRUNT cannot be formed from the given word LAUGHTER, because the given word does not contain the letter 'N'.

12. *(b)* The word INSTALLATION cannot be formed from the given word NATIONALISATION, because the given word has only one 'L'.

13. *(c)* The word FATHER cannot be formed from the given word FRATERNAL, because the given word does not contain the letter 'H'.

14. *(d)* The word 'Cloud' can not be formed from the given sentence 'Russia is my country' because the given sentence does not have letters 'L' and 'D'.

15. *(b)* The word CREATE can not be formed from the given word ECCENTRICITY, because the given word does not contain the letter 'A'.

16. *(d)* The word MINISTER can not be formed from the given word ADMINISTRATORS, because the given word does not contain the letter 'E'.

17. *(a)* The word PAIN can not be formed from the given word PUNISHMENT, because the given word does not contain the letter 'A'.

18. *(a)* The word POLONIA cannot be formed using the letters of the given word APPLICATION, as the letter 'O' occurs once in the given word.

19. *(d)* The word PRESIDENT cannot be formed from the given word JURISPRUDENCE, because the given word does not contain the letter 'T'.

20. *(b)* The word TOUGH cannot be formed from the given word DAUGHTER, because the given word does not contain the letter 'O'.

21. *(b)* The word 'BOUT' cannot be formed from the given word FLAMBOYANT, because the given word does not contain the letter 'U'.

22. *(d)* The word FEET cannot be formed using the letters of the given word TERRIFY, as the letter 'E' occurs only once in the given word.

23. *(a)* The word ENTRANCE cannot be formed from the given word ENVIRONMENT, because the given word does not contain the letter 'C'.

24. *(b)* The word TESTER cannot be formed form the given word TEMPERAMENT, because the given word does not contain the letter 'S'.

25. *(d)* The word 'CHANCE' cannot be formed from the given word 'MERCHANDISE', because the given word does not contain the letter 'C'.

26. *(c)* The meaningful word formed by given letters is

P O D I U M
↓ ↓ ↓ ↓ ↓ ↓
4 3 1 5 2 6

Helping TIPS To solve such questions, it is very important for the student to have knowledge of English vocabulary.

27. *(b)* The meaningful word formed by given letters is

O R G A N I S E
↓ ↓ ↓ ↓ ↓ ↓ ↓ ↓
8 5 2 6 4 1 3 7

28. *(c)* The meaningful word formed by given letters is

A D H E S I O N
↓ ↓ ↓ ↓ ↓ ↓ ↓ ↓
2 3 5 6 8 1 4 7

29. *(d)* The meaningful word formed by given letters is

C O D I N G
↓ ↓ ↓ ↓ ↓ ↓
3 4 5 2 6 1

30. *(d)* The meaningful word formed by given letters is

S I G N A L
↓ ↓ ↓ ↓ ↓ ↓
3 5 6 2 4 1

31. *(b)* According to the question,

A B C D (E) F G H I J K L M N (O) (P) Q (R) S T U V W X Y Z

E → 5, O → 15, P → 16, R → 18

∴ Words formed from E, O, P and R = PORE and ROPE

Hence, required second letter = O

32. *(a)* The first, third, fifth and eighth letters of the given word SOUVENIR are S, U, E, R, respectively.

Meaningful words formed from letters S, U, E and R = SURE, RUSE, SUER, USER, RUES

Required total meaningful words = 5

Hence, more than 3 words are formed.

33. *(c)* The first, fourth, fifth and sixth letters of the given word SAVOUR are S, O, U, R respectively.

Meaningful words formed from letters S, O, U and R

= SOUR, OURS

Required total meaningful words = 2

Hence, two words are formed.

34. *(a)* The second, third, fifth and seventh letters of the given word 'TOURIST' are O, U, I, T respectively.

Hence, no meaningful word can be formed.

35. *(d)* Given word,

[F] E L [I] [C] I [T] A T [I] [O] [N] S

F (1st), I (4th), C (5th), T (7th), I (10th), O (11th), N (12th)

New word → F I [C] T I O N

C is 5th from the right

Hence, required letter = C

36. *(b)* Given word,

I. HRETIAGVSN

II. FLNESAGOMI

III. EXSONHTIAU

According to the question, after interchanging the 3rd and 6th letters and 4th and 9th letters, as well as 5th and 10th letters,

I. HRASNEGVTI

II. FLAMINGOES

III. EXHAUSTION

Therefore, only II and III will make a meaningful word after rearrangement.

37. *(c)* On arranging the given jumbled letters,

LAFC - CALF

UKCGIDLN - DUCKLING

RILNIGHE - HIRELING

BCU - CUB

So, all except 'HIRELING' are names of baby animals. While 'HIRELING' is a person employed on a fixed amount.

38. *(d)* On arranging the given jumbled letters,

ANDOMY - MONDAY

STEAUDY - TUESDAY

DIARFY - FRIDAY

DHAIOLY - HOLIDAY

Hence, HOLIDAY is different from others as all others are names of days of the week.

39. *(c)* The letters 'RIP' given in option (c) will complete the words given in the question as follows STRIP and RIPPLE.

40. *(c)* In the given words, if the first letter 'S' is introduced, then entirely new meaningful words will be formed- STILL, STABLE, SPILE, STAB, and SPRING.

41. *(b)* If the letter 'E' is added after the words HAT, BAR, BAT, PIN, BATH, then completely new meaningful words will be formed HATE, BARE, BATE, PINE, BATHE.

42. *(b)* As per the question, two independent words 'BE' and 'HIND' can be formed in which the order of the letters remains unchanged and each letter is used once.

43. *(c)* Only one meaningful word 'FRIDGE' can be formed using all the given letters when each letter is used once.

CHAPTER

05 Arrangement of Words

Arrangement of Words

The meaningful arrangement of words according to a certain logic or in the order in which they occur in English dictionary is called arrangement of words.

Questions asked in various examination consist of four, five or six words which are not arranged in any order. Candidates have to arrange these words in logical or dictionary order.

Based on Logical Order

In this type of questions, the words are arranged in a logical or meaningful order according to certain natural laws or universally accepted concepts. The given words may be such that they are related to a particular event or represent the various stages of a certain chained process from beginning to end.

e.g. Arrange the following words in a logical sequence.

1. Application **2. Selection**
3. Exam **4. Interview**
5. Advertisement

(a) 1, 2, 3, 4, 5 (b) 5, 1, 3, 4, 2
(c) 5, 3, 1, 4, 2 (d) 4, 5, 1, 2, 3

Sol. (b) The words are arranged according to the various stages in a job recruitment.

Advertisement → Application →
(5) (1)
Exam → Interview → Selection
(3) (4) (2)

⇒ 5, 1, 3, 4, 2

e.g. Arrange the following words in a logical or meaningful order.

1. Family **2. Community**
3. Member **4. Locality**
5. Country

(a) 3, 1, 2, 4, 5 (b) 3, 1, 2, 5, 4
(c) 3, 1, 4, 2, 5 (d) 3, 1, 4, 5, 2

Sol. (a) The logical or meaningful order of the words is as follows:

Member → Family → Community →
(3) (1) (2)
Locality → Country
(4) (5)

⇒ 3, 1, 2, 4, 5

Score Booster

To arrange the words in a meaningful order, it is very important for the candidates to have knowledge of the following relations.

(i) The process of occurence of any events/objects.
(ii) Decreasing and increasing order of the objects based on their sizes.
(iii) The sequence of life stages (life cycle) of different things or creatures.
(iv) Order of human body parts from top to bottom or bottom to top.
(v) Hierarchy of posts in government or private institutions.

Based on Dictionary Order

In this type of questions, the words are to be arranged in dictionary order. i.e in the order in which they occur in English dictionary.

e.g. Arrange the following words as per dictionary order.

1. Epitaxy **2. Episode**
3. Epigene **4. Epitome**
5. Epilogue

(a) 1, 2, 3, 4, 5 (b) 3, 2, 1, 5, 4
(c) 3, 5, 2, 1, 4 (d) 1, 3, 2, 5, 4

Sol. (c) The correct dictionary order of the words is as follows:

Epigene → Epilogue → Episode
(3) (5) (2)
→ Epitaxy → Epitome
(1) (4)

⇒ 3, 5, 2, 1, 4

e.g. Arrange the following words according to the dictionary.

1. Divide **2. Divisions**
3. Devine **4. Divest**
5. Direct

(a) 5, 4, 3, 1, 2 (b) 5, 4, 1, 3, 2
(c) 1, 2, 3, 4, 5 (d) 3, 5, 4, 1, 2

Sol. (d) The arrangement of words according to English dictionary is as follows:

Devine → Direct → Divest →
(3) (5) (4)
Divide → Divisions
(1) (2)

⇒ 3, 5, 4, 1, 2

Exam Approach Examples

Based on Logical Order

Example 1 From the given options, select the one in which the following are arranged is the most meaningful order:

1. Cosmos 2. Earth
3. Milky Way 4. Human *RRB NTPC 2021*

(a) 1, 2, 3, 4 (b) 1, 3, 4, 2
(c) 1, 3, 2, 4 (d) 1, 2, 4, 3

Sol. *(c)* The correct logical and meaningful order is

Cosmos → Milky way → Earth → Human
(1) (3) (2) (4)

Hence, the correct order is 1, 3, 2, 4

> **Helping Tips**
> To solve such questions, it is very important to have knowledge of scientific terminologies.

Example 2 Select the correct option that indicates the arrangement of the following words in a logical and meaningful order.

1. Senior secondary school 2. Primary school
3. Secondary school 4. Kindergarten
5. College *SSC Steno 2023*

(a) 4, 2, 3, 1, 5 (b) 4, 3, 2, 5, 1
(c) 2, 4, 3, 1, 5 (d) 4, 3, 2, 1, 5

Sol. *(a)* The correct logical and meaningful order is

Kindergarten → Primary School → Secondary School
(4) (2) (3)
→ Senior Secondary School → College
(1) (5)

⇒ 4, 2, 3, 1, 5

Direction (Ex. No. 3) *In the following example, arrange the given words in a logical and meaningful sequence and choose the correct sequence from the given alternatives.*

Example 3

1. Open email account 2. Compose email
3. Start computer 4. Enter email address
5. Write the content 6. Send the mail *SSC CGL (Tier I) 2022*

(a) 3, 1, 2, 6, 5, 4 (b) 2, 5, 1, 3, 4, 6
(c) 3, 1, 2, 4, 5, 6 (d) 3, 2, 6, 1, 5, 4

Sol. *(c)* The meaningful order represents the steps involved in sending an e-mail from computer

Start computer → Open email account → Compose mail
(3) (1) (2)
→ Enter email address → Write the content → Send the mail
(4) (5) (6)

So, the correct order is 3, 1, 2, 4, 5, 6.

Based on Dictionary Order

Example 4 Arrange the following words according to English dictionary. *CUET (UG) 2023*

1. Preach 2. Praise 3. Precinct 4. Precept

(a) 2, 1, 4, 3 (b) 2, 1, 3, 4 (c) 1, 2, 3, 4 (d) 4, 3, 2, 1

Sol. *(a)* On arranging the given words according to dictionary.

Praise → Preach → Precept → Precinct
(2) (1) (4) (3)

⇒ 2, 1, 4, 3.

Example 5 Select the option that indicates the correct arrangement of the given words in the order in which they appear in an English dictionary. *SSC CPO 2024*

1. Junction 2. Jupiter 3. Jungle 4. Jump 5. Juncture

(a) 1, 5, 4, 2, 3 (b) 4, 5, 1, 3, 2
(c) 1, 5, 3, 2, 4 (d) 4, 1, 5, 3, 2

Sol. *(d)* The correct dictionary order is

Jump → Junction → Juncture → Jungle → Jupiter
(4) (1) (5) (3) (2)

⇒ 4, 1, 5, 3, 2

> **Trending Concept**
> Questions based on dictionary arrangement are generally asked in various competitive exams (SSC, Bank, railway, DSSSB). They are very important as far as future exams are concerned.

Example 6 Select the option that represents the correct order of the given words as they would appear in an English dictionary. *SSC Steno 2023*

1. Logwood 2. Logarithm
3. Logically 4. Logophile
5. Logistic 6. Logotype

(a) 2, 3, 5, 1, 4, 6 (b) 2, 5, 3, 4, 6, 1
(c) 2, 3, 5, 4, 6, 1 (d) 2, 5, 3, 6, 1, 4

Sol. *(c)* The correct dictionary order is

Logarithm → Logically → Logistic → Logophile → Logotype → Logwood
(2) (3) (5) (4) (6) (1)

⇒ 2, 3, 5, 4, 6, 1

Example 7 After arranging the given words according to dictionary order, which word will come at 'Third' position?

1. Series 2. Serious
3. Serein 4. Serial 5. Serried *SSC CGL (Tier I) 2021*

(a) Series (b) Serein (c) Serial (d) Serious

Sol. *(a)* The correct dictionary order is

Serein → Serial → Series → Serious → Serried
(1) (2) (3) (4) (5)

It is clear from above that 'Series' will come at the third place.

Chapter Challenge

Based on Logical Order

Directions (Q. Nos. 1-14) *In each of the following questions, arrange the given words in a logical and meaningful sequence and choose the correct sequence from the given alternatives.*

1. 1. Delivery 2. Finished Paper 3. Dry 4. Pulp 5. Press **SSC CGL (Tier-II) 2025**
(a) 4, 5, 3, 2, 1 (b) 2, 5, 4, 3, 1
(c) 4, 1, 2, 5, 3 (d) 5, 4, 2, 3, 1

2. 1. Class 2. Admission 3. Result 4. Examination 5. Marking **SSC CGL (Tier-I) 2020**
(a) 5, 3, 4, 1, 2 (b) 2, 1, 4, 5, 3
(c) 3, 4, 2, 1, 5 (d) 2, 1, 5, 3, 4

3. 1. Paint 2. Plan 3. Furnish 4. Build 5. Live **RRB NTPC 2021**
(a) 2, 4, 1, 3, 5 (b) 2, 4, 5, 1, 3
(c) 2, 3, 5, 1, 4 (d) 2, 1, 4, 3, 5

4. 1. Design 2. Test 3. Conceptualize 4. Develop 5. Implement **SSC CGL (Tier-II) 2025**
(a) 1, 4, 5, 3, 2 (b) 3, 1, 4, 2, 5
(c) 3, 5, 2, 4, 1 (d) 3, 1, 5, 4, 2

5. 1. Earth 2. Venus 3. Mars 4. Saturn 5. Jupiter **SSC CPO 2023**
(a) 3, 1, 2, 4, 5 (b) 2, 3, 1, 4, 5
(c) 2, 1, 3, 5, 4 (d) 1, 2, 3, 5, 4

6. 1. Finger 2. Elbow 3. Wrist 4. Nail 5. Palm **Graduate Level 2023**
(a) 4, 5, 1, 3, 2 (b) 4, 1, 5, 3, 2
(c) 4, 1, 5, 2, 3 (d) 4, 1, 3, 5, 2

7. 1. Colonel 2. Field Marshal 3. Brigadier 4. Lieutenant 5. General **SSC CGL (Tier-I) 2020**
(a) 1, 2, 3, 5, 4 (b) 2, 5, 3, 1, 4
(c) 2, 5, 1, 4, 3 (d) 3, 5, 2, 4, 1

8. 1. Mansion 2. Cottage 3. Palace 4. Cabin 5. Villa **SSC CPO 2020**
(a) 2-4-1-5-3 (b) 2-1-3-4-5
(c) 4-2-5-1-3 (d) 3-1-2-4-5

9. 1. Car 2. Train 3. Cycle 4. Truck 5. Auto-rickshaw **SSC Steno 2022**
(a) 3, 1, 5, 4, 2 (b) 5, 1, 3, 2, 4
(c) 3, 4, 5, 2, 1 (d) 3, 5, 1, 4, 2

10. 1. Use the key 2. Open the door 3. Open the lock 4. Enter the room 5. Turn on lights **UP Police AO 2024**
(a) 1, 3, 5, 2, 4 (b) 1, 3, 2, 4, 5
(c) 1, 3, 4, 2, 5 (d) 5, 1, 3, 2, 4

11. 1. Kilogram 2. Gram 3. Quintal 4. Decigram 5. Milligram **SSC SPO 2020**
(a) 4, 5, 2, 3, 1 (b) 4, 5, 2, 1, 3
(c) 5, 4, 2, 1, 3 (d) 5, 2, 4, 1, 3

12. 1. South America 2. Africa 3. Europe 4. Australia 5. North America **UP Police (SI) 2021**
(a) 2, 1, 5, 3, 4
(b) 2, 5, 1, 3, 4
(c) 2, 5, 1, 4, 3
(d) 2, 1, 5, 4, 3

> **MRC*****
> ***(Most Repeating Concepts)***
> Q. Nos. 1, 4, 6, 12, 13, 17 these are very important from the examination point of view.
> Questions on these concepts are being asked recently in SSC and Railway exams.

13. 1. Set goals 2. Budget 3. Review 4. Invest 5. Assess **SSC CGL (Tier-II) 2025**
(a) 5, 1, 2, 3, 4 (b) 1, 5, 2, 4, 3
(c) 5, 2, 4, 3, 1 (d) 3, 5, 1, 2, 4

14. 1. Universe 2. Chennai 3. World 4. Asia 5. Tamil Nadu **SSC (10+2) 2021**
(a) 1, 4, 3, 5, 2 (b) 1, 3, 4, 2, 5
(c) 1, 3, 4, 5, 2 (d) 3, 1, 5, 4, 2

15. Arrange the following in a logical sequence from small to big.
1. Crocodile 2. Lizard 3. Whale 4. Housefly 5. Monkey **SSC CGL (Tier-I) 2020**
(a) 4, 2, 5, 1, 3 (b) 4, 5, 2, 1, 3
(c) 3, 5, 4, 1, 2 (d) 4, 3, 2, 1, 5

16. Select the correct option to arrange the following words in a logical and meaningful order on the basis of area (km^2). **SSC (10+2) 2023**
1. Atlantic ocean 2. Pacific ocean 3. Southern ocean 4. Arctic ocean 5. Indian ocean
(a) 4, 3, 1, 2, 5 (b) 4, 1, 3, 2, 5
(c) 4, 3, 5, 2, 1 (d) 4, 3, 5, 1, 2

Directions (Q. Nos. 17-20) *In each of the following questions, arrange the given words in a logical and meaningful sequence and choose the correct sequence from the given alternatives.*

17. 1. Plant 2. Pollination 3. Seed 4. Seedling 5. Fruit **SSC CGL (Tier-II) 2025**
(a) 4, 1, 2, 5, 3 (b) 3, 4, 1, 2, 5
(c) 3, 4, 1, 5, 2 (d) 4, 3, 1, 2, 5

18. 1. Kilobyte 2. Byte 3. Megabyte 4. Terabyte 5. Gigabyte 6. Bit **UGC NET 2018**
(a) 6, 2, 1, 3, 5, 4 (b) 6, 2, 1, 4, 3, 5
(c) 6, 2, 1, 3, 4, 5 (d) 6, 2, 1, 4, 5, 3

19. 1. Travel 2. Destination 3. Payment 4. Berth/Seat number 5. Reservation 6. Availability of berth/seat for reservation.
(a) 1, 2, 5, 4, 3, 6 (b) 2, 6, 3, 5, 4, 1
(c) 5, 3, 4, 1, 6, 2 (d) 6, 2, 5, 4, 3, 1

20. 1. Hexagon 2. Triangle 3. Pentagon 4. Square 5. Octagon **SSC (10+2) 2024**
(a) 3, 1, 5, 2, 4 (b) 1, 4, 3, 5, 2
(c) 2, 4, 3, 1, 5 (d) 2, 1, 3, 4, 5

Based on Dictionary Order

Directions (Q. Nos. 21-34) *In the following questions, which of the following options is in the order of the words given in the English dictionary.*

21. 1. Tune 2. Tone 3. Taste 4. Truth ***CRPF HC 2023***
(a) 3, 2, 1, 4 (b) 3, 2, 4, 1 (c) 3, 1, 4, 2 (d) 1, 2, 3, 4

22. 1. Orange 2. Orphan 3. Orbit
4. Orchard ***CISF ASI 2023***
(a) 1, 3, 4, 2 (b) 1, 3, 2, 4 (c) 1, 2, 4, 3 (d) 1, 2, 3, 4

23. 1. Pilot 2. Pigeon 3. Pipette 4. Pigment
(a) 2, 4, 1, 3 (b) 2, 1, 3, 4 (c) 4, 2, 3, 1 (d) 3, 2, 4, 1

24. 1. Deficient 2. Derived 3. Designed
4. Destined 5. Destination ***SSC CGL (Tier-I) 2023***
(a) 1, 2, 3, 5, 4 (b) 1, 2, 4, 3, 5
(c) 1, 2, 5, 3, 4 (d) 1, 3, 2, 5, 4

25. 1. HEIGHT 2. HINGE 3. HORSE
4. HATE 5. HUSTLE ***SSC GD Constable 2024***
(a) 4, 5, 3, 2, 1 (b) 4, 1, 2, 3, 5
(c) 4, 1, 2, 5, 3 (d) 4, 3, 2, 1, 5

26. 1. Head 2. Hold 3. Hammer
4. Hills 5. Hulk ***UPSSSC Forest Guard 2022***
(a) 31425 (b) 35412 (c) 45132 (d) 45312

27. 1. Boatyard 2. Boathouse 3. Boater
4. Boatman 5. Boating ***SSC CPO 2020***
(a) 2, 5, 3, 1, 4 (b) 3, 2, 5, 1, 4
(c) 3, 2, 5, 4, 1 (d) 2, 3, 5, 4, 1

28. 1. Knight 2. Kitchen
3. Kinship 4. Kinetic
5. Kind
SSC CHSL (Tier-I) 2022
(a) 5, 4, 3, 2, 1
(b) 5, 3, 4, 2, 1
(c) 5, 3, 2, 4, 1
(d) 5, 2, 3, 4, 1

> **MRC*****
> ***(Most Repeating Concepts)***
> Q. Nos. 24, 25, 27 and 28
> These are very important from the examination point of view. Question on these concepts are being asked continuously in SSC (CPO, CGL, CHSL) etc.

29. 1. Lollipop 2. Loincloth 3. Longways
4. Logician 5. Lonely ***CISF Head Constable 2023***
(a) 3, 2, 1, 5, 4 (b) 4, 2, 1, 5, 3
(c) 4, 3, 1, 5, 2 (d) 3, 4, 1, 5, 2

30. 1. Campus 2. Calendar 3. Capture 4. Capital
5. Calculate ***SSC CGL 2024***
(a) 3, 2, 1, 4, 5 (b) 3, 5, 4, 2, 1
(c) 5, 3, 2, 1, 4 (d) 5, 2, 1, 4, 3

31. 1. Serenity 2. Serpent 3. Serviceable
4. Sericulture 5. Serotonin ***CUET (UG) 2022***
(a) 1, 4, 5, 2, 3 (b) 1, 4, 2, 5, 3
(c) 3, 4, 5, 2, 1 (d) 2, 4, 5, 3, 1

32. 1. Profess 2. Product 3. Prosecute 4. Precaution
5. Proctor ***SSC Steno 2021***
(a) 2, 5, 4, 1, 3 (b) 3, 5, 2, 1, 4
(c) 4, 5, 2, 3, 1 (d) 4, 5, 2, 1, 3

33. 1. Campaigns 2. Catalytic 3. Candidature
4. Camphor 5. Cataracts ***SSC (10+2) 2022***
(a) 1, 3, 4, 2, 5 (b) 1, 2, 3, 4, 5
(c) 1, 4, 3, 2, 5 (d) 1, 5, 4, 3, 2

34. 1. Hooter 2. Hoodlum 3. Hoover 4. Hoodwink
5. Hoop ***CISF HC Min. 2022***
(a) 5, 2, 4, 1, 3 (b) 2, 4, 5, 1, 3
(c) 4, 2, 5, 3, 1 (d) 2, 5, 4, 3, 1

35. After arranging the given words according to dictionary order, which word will come at 'third' position?
1. Special 2. Speck 3. Species 4. Speckle
5. Spectacle ***SSC (10+2) 2023***
(a) Special (b) Speckle (c) Speck (d) Species

Directions (Q. Nos. 36-40) *In the following questions, which of the following options is in the order of the words given in the English dictionary.*

36. 1. Warriors 2. Warehouse
3. Warcraft 4. Warranty
5. Wardrobe 6. Wardenship ***SSC CGL (Tier-I) 2023***
(a) 3, 5, 6, 2, 1, 4 (b) 3, 5, 6, 2, 4, 1
(c) 3, 6, 5, 2, 1, 4 (d) 3, 6, 5, 2, 4, 1

37. 1. Enthusiasm 2. Enrollment 3. Enterprise
4. Ensure 5. Entangled 6. Entail ***SSC CGL 2023***
(a) 2, 4, 6, 5, 1, 3 (b) 2, 4, 6, 5, 3, 1
(c) 4, 2, 6, 5, 3, 1 (d) 2, 4, 5, 6, 3, 1

38. 1. Fontina 2. Fondue 3. Fondled 4. Fondant
5. Fontanel 6. Fonder ***SSC Steno 2023***
(a) 4, 6, 3, 2, 5, 1 (b) 6, 3, 4, 5, 1, 2
(c) 6, 4, 3, 2, 5, 1 (d) 4, 6, 3, 5, 1, 2

39. 1. Unfaithful 2. Unfamiliar 3. Uneasiness 4. Undone
5. Understand 6. Undetermined ***SSC CPO 2024***
(a) 5, 6, 4, 3, 2, 1 (b) 5, 6, 4, 3, 1, 2
(c) 5, 6, 4, 2, 1, 3 (d) 5, 6, 1, 2, 4, 3

40. 1. Humility 2. Humbug 3. Humanoid 4. Humidity
5. Humoresque 6. Humanity
7. Humectants ***SSC CGL (Tier-I) 2022***
(a) 6, 3, 2, 7, 4, 1, 5 (b) 6, 3, 2, 7, 1, 4, 5
(c) 6, 3, 7, 2, 1, 4, 5 (d) 6, 3, 7, 2, 4, 1, 5

41. If the given word are arranged in dictionary order, which word will come at the 'Fourth' Position?
SSC (10+2) 2023
1. Morning 2. More 3. Moral 4. Morbid 5. Morale
(a) Morning (b) More (c) Morale (d) Moral

42. Which one of the following word will come second place when it will arrange in the dictionary order. Exit, Exercise, Excuse, Exempt ***RRB NTPC (CBT-I) 2021***
(a) Exit (b) Excuse (c) Exempt (d) Exercise

43. Arrange the given word in dictionary order, and choose the word which come first. ***UP Police Constable 2019***
Refocus; Refinery; Reflexes; Reflector
(a) Refocus (b) Refinery (c) Reflector (d) Reflexes

Right Key

1. (a)	2. (b)	3. (a)	4. (b)	5. (c)	6. (b)	7. (b)	8. (c)	9. (d)	10. (b)
11. (c)	12. (b)	13. (b)	14. (c)	15. (a)	16. (d)	17. (b)	18. (a)	19. (b)	20. (c)
21. (b)	22. (a)	23. (a)	24. (a)	25. (b)	26. (a)	27. (c)	28. (a)	29. (b)	30. (d)
31. (a)	32. (d)	33. (c)	34. (b)	35. (c)	36. (d)	37. (b)	38. (a)	39. (b)	40. (a)
41. (b)	42. (c)	43. (b)							

Solutions

1. *(a)* The correct logical and meaningful order is,
Pulp (4) → Press (5) → Dry (3) → Finished paper (2) → Delivery (1)
⇒ 4, 5, 3, 2, 1

2. *(b)* The correct logical and meaningful order is
Admission (2) → Class (1) → Examination (4) → Marking (5) → Result (3)
⇒ 2, 1, 4, 5, 3

3. *(a)* The correct and meaningful order is
Plan (2) → Build (4) → Paint (1) → Furnish (3) → Live (5)
⇒ 2, 4, 1, 3, 5

4. *(b)* The correct logical and meaningful order is,
Conceptualize (3) → Design (1) → Develop (4) → Test (2) → Implement (5)
⇒ 3, 1, 4, 2, 5

5. *(c)* The logic used here is that the planets are arranged according to their distance from Sun in increasing order.
Venus (2) → Earth (1) → Mars (3) → Jupiter (5) → Saturn (4)
So, the correct order is 2, 1, 3, 5, 4.

6. *(b)* The correct logical and meaningful order is
Nail (4) → Finger (1) → Palm (5) → Wrist (3) → Elbow (2)
⇒ 4, 1, 5, 3, 2

7. *(b)* The correct logical and meaningful order is indicates the rank of Army personnel
Field Marshal (2) → General (5) → Brigadier (3) → Colonel (1) → Lieutenant (4)
⇒ 2, 5, 3, 1, 4

8. *(c)* The correct logical and meaningful order is
Cabin (4) → Cottage (2) → Villa (5) → Mansion (1) → Palace (3)
⇒ 4, 2, 5, 1, 3

9. *(d)* The correct logical and meaningful order is
Cycle (3) → Auto-rickshaw (5) → Car (1) → Truck (4) → Train (2)
⇒ 3, 5, 1, 4, 2

10. *(b)* The correct logical and meaningful order is
Use the key (1) → Open the lock (3) → Open the door (2) → Enter the room (4) → Turn on lights. (5)
⇒ 1, 3, 2, 4, 5

11. *(c)* The correct logical and meaningful order is
Milligram (5) → Decigram (4) → Gram (2) → Kilogram (1) → Quintal (3)
⇒ 5, 4, 2, 1, 3

12. *(b)* The logic used here is arrangement of continent according to area in decreasing order
Africa (2) → North America (5) → South America (1) → Europe (3) → Australia (4)
⇒ 2, 5, 1, 3, 4

> **TOP TIPS** To solve these type of question, arrange the group of words in a decreasing or increasing order. The criteria may be age, size, value, area, cost etc.

13. *(b)* The correct logical and meaningful order is,
Set goals (1) → Assess (5) → Budget (2) → Invest (4) → Review (3)
⇒ 1, 5, 2, 4, 3

14. *(c)* The correct logical and meaningful order is
Universe (1) → World (3) → Asia (4) Tamilnadu (5) Chennai (2)
⇒ 1, 3, 4, 5, 2

15. *(a)* The correct logical sequence from small to big
Housefly (4) → Lizard (2) → Monkey (5) → Crocodile (1) → Whale (3)
⇒ 4, 2, 5, 1, 3

16. *(d)* The correct logical and meaningful order on the basis of area is as shown below
Arctic ocean (4) → Southern ocean (3) → Indian ocean (5) → Atlantic ocean (1) → Pacific ocean (2)
⇒ 4, 3, 5, 1, 2

17. *(b)* The correct logical and meaningful order is,
Seed (3) → Seedling (4) → Plant (1) → Pollination (2) → Fruit (5)
⇒ 3, 4, 1, 2, 5

18. *(a)* The logical sequence of the given words is as below.
Bit (6) → Byte (2) → Kilobyte (1) → Megabyte (3) → Gigabyte (5) → Terabyte (4)
⇒ 6, 2, 1, 3, 5, 4

TOP TIPS If the arrangement is on the basis of size or magnitude, it can either in increasing order or in decreasing order.
In that case it will be ensured by analysing the order given in the options.

19. (b) The correct logical and meaningful order is
Destination
(2)
→Availability of berth/seat for reservation → Payment → Reservation
(6) (3) (5)
→ Berth/Seat number → Travel
(4) (1)
Hence, the correct order is 2, 6, 3, 5, 4, 1.

20. (c) The correct logical and meaningful order is,
Triangle → Square → Pentagon
(2) (4) (3)
→ Hexagon → Octagon
(1) (5)
⇒ 2, 4, 3, 1, 5

21. (b) The correct dictionary order is as given below.
Taste → Tone → Truth → Tune
(3) (2) (4) (1)
⇒ 3, 2, 4, 1

22. (a) The correct dictionary order is as given below.
Orange→ Orbit→ Orchard→ Orphan
(1) (3) (4) (2)
⇒ 1, 3, 4, 2

23. (a) The correct dictionary order is
Pigeon→ Pigment→Pilot→ Pipette
(2) (4) (1) (3)
⇒ 2, 4, 1, 3

24. (a) The correct dictionary order is
Deficient → Derived → Designed
(1) (2) (3)
→ Destination → Destined
(5) (4)
⇒ 1, 2, 3, 5, 4

25. (b) The correct dictionary order is
HATE → HEIGHT → HINGE
(4) (1) (2)
→ HORSE → HUSTLE
(3) (5)
⇒ 4, 1, 2, 3, 5

26. (a) The correct dictionary order is as shown below.
Hammer → Head → Hills → Hold
(3) (1) (4) (2)
→ Hulk
(5)
⇒ 3, 1, 4, 2, 5

TOP TIPS In this type of sequence, you need to arrange the words as per the order given in dictionary. In other words, you are required to arrange them alphabetically.

27. (c) The correct dictionary order is
Boater → Boathouse → Boating
(3) (2) (5)
→ Boatman → Boatyard
(4) (1)
⇒ 3, 2, 5, 4, 1

28. (a) The correct dictionary order is
Kind → Kinetic → Kinship
(5) (4) (3)
→ Kitchen → Knight
(2) (1)
⇒ 5, 4, 3, 2, 1

29. (b) The correct dictionary order of the words is as shown below.
Logician → Loincloth → Lollipop
(4) (2) (1)
→ Lonely → Longways
(5) (3)
⇒ 4, 2, 1, 5, 3

30. (d) The correct dictionary order is
Calculate → Calender → Campus
(5) (2) (1)
→ Capital → Capture
(4) (3)
⇒ 5, 2, 1, 4, 3

31. (a) Correct arrangement of the given words in the order in which they appear in an English dictionary, is
Serenity → Sericulture → Serotonin
(1) (4) (5)
Serpent → Serviceable
(2) (3)
⇒ 1, 4, 5, 2, 3

TOP TIPS For this arrangement, first we shall take the first letter of each word and then arrange the words in the order in which they appear in the english alphabet, then take the second letter and so on.

32. (d) The correct dictionary order is
Precaution → Proctor → Product
(4) (5) (2)
→ Profess → Prosecute
(1) (3)
⇒ 4, 5, 2, 1, 3

33. (c) The correct dictionary order is
Campaigns→ Camphor→ Candidature
(1) (4) (3)
→ Catalytic → Cataracts
(2) (5)
⇒ 1, 4, 3, 2, 5

34. (b) The correct dictionary order is
Hoodlum → Hoodwink → Hoop
(2) (4) (5)
→ Hooter → Hoover
(1) (3)
⇒ 2, 4, 5, 1, 3

35. (c) The correct dictionary order is
Special → Species → Speck
(1) (3) (2)
→ Speckle → Spectacle
(4) (5)
∴ 'Speck' will be at third position.

36. (d) The correct dictionary order is
Warcraft → Wardenship →
(3) (6)
Wardrobe → Warehouse →
(5) (2)
Warranty → Warriors
(4) (1)
⇒ 3, 6, 5, 2, 4, 1

37. (b) The correct dictionary order is
Enrollment → Ensure → Entail
(2) (4) (6)
→ Entangled→ Enterprise→Enthusiasm
(5) (3) (1)
⇒ 2, 4, 6, 5, 3, 1

38. (a) The correct dictionary order is
Fondant → Fonder → Fondled
(4) (6) (3)
→ Fondue → Fontanel → Fontina
(2) (5) (1)
⇒ 4, 6, 3, 2, 5, 1

39. (b) The correct dictionary order is
Understand→Undetermined→ Undone
(5) (6) (4)
→Uneasiness→Unfaithful → Unfamiliar
(3) (1) (2)
⇒ 5, 6, 4, 3, 1, 2

40. (a) The correct dictionary order is
Humanity → Humanoid
(6) (3)
→ Humbug → Humectants
(2) (7)
→ Humidity → Humility→ Humoresque
(4) (1) (5)
⇒ 6, 3, 2, 7, 4, 1, 5

41. (b) Dictionary order of the given word is shown below.
Moral → Morale → Morbid → More → Morning
Hence, fourth word is 'more'.

42. (c) Dictionary order of the given words is shown below.
Excuse→ Exempt→ Exercise → Exit
Hence, 'Exempt' come in the second place.

43. (b) After arranging the given word in dictionary order.
Refinery→Reflector→Reflexes→ Refocus
∴ Required word = Refinery.

CHAPTER

06 Coding-Decoding

Letter Coding

In letter coding, the letters of a word are replaced by certain other letters according to a specific pattern/rule to form a code. The candidates are required to detect the coding pattern/rule and answer the question(s) accordingly.

e.g. In a certain code language, 'DEER' is written as 'EGHV' then how will 'SOAP' be written in that language?

(a) TQCT (b) TCQT

(c) TQTC (d) TQDT

Sol. (d) As,

D E E R
+1 +2 +3 +4
E G H V

Similarly,

S O A P
+1 +2 +3 +4
T Q D T

Number Coding

In number coding, numerical code is assigned to the word/number/ letter and candidates are required to analyse the codes as per the correlation between these numbers and letters and answer the question. This correlation can be based on certain pattern according to the position of letters in English alphabet as per a given set of rules.

e.g. If 'RED' is coded as '6720', then how would 'GREEN' be coded?

(a) 1677199 (b) 1677209

(c) 14717209 (d) 9207716

Sol. (b) As, R E D ⟶ 6 7 20 (+2, +2, +2)

Similarly, G R E E N ⟶ 16 7 7 20 9 (+2, +2, +2, +2, +2)

Symbol Coding

In this type of questions, letters are coded as different symbols/numbers. Candidate has to analyse this code and then find the answer.

e.g. In a certain code language, 'GONE' is written as '5%2#' and 'MEDAL' is written as '4#3$@', then how will 'GOLD' be written in that code?

(a) 5@%3 (b) 5%@3 (c) 5#@3 (d) 5%#3

Sol. (b) As,

G O N E → 5 % 2 #

and

M E D A L → 4 # 3 $ @

Similarly, G O L D → 5 % @ 3

Coding-Decoding

Coding means to hide the meaning of any message and decoding means to understand the actual meaning of that message.

Fictitious Language Coding

In this type, some messages are provided in the code language and some codes are assigned to each word of the messages. The candidates are required to find the code of each word by finding the common code for two words and this process is followed to find the code for each word there after. Hence the entire message is decoded.

e.g. In a certain code language, 'BLUE' is coded as '1542' and 'ABLE' is coded as '1745'. What is the code for 'A' in the same code language?

(a) 7 (b) 1 (c) 4 (d) 5

Sol. (*a*) According to the question,

Ⓑ Ⓛ U Ⓔ ⟶ ① ⑤ ④ 2

A Ⓑ Ⓛ Ⓔ ⟶ ① 7 ④ ⑤

Hence, the code for A is 7.

Substitution Coding

In substitution coding, one word is coded as second word and the second word is coded as a third word. Similarly, the sequence continues further and the candidate has to find the code of the given word.

e.g. In a certain code language, if 'mustard' is called 'fruit', 'fruit' is called 'potato', 'potato' is called 'burger', 'burger' is called 'flower' and 'flower' is called rice, then what is rose?

(a) potato (b) rice (c) flower (d) fruit

Sol. (b) We know that, rose is a flower but here 'flower' is called 'rice'. So, rose is called as rice.

Conditional Coding

In conditional coding, letters/numbers/ symbols are given along with their codes. Candidates are required to find the codes for a particular letter/group/number/ symbols according to certain condition applied in different ways in the given questions and then find the correct answer according to given conditions.

e.g. Numbers and their letters-codes are given in the following table.

Number	3	7	2	8	6	5
Letter-code	K	E	F	Y	P	L

Find out which option has the correct coded form of the number group 8637.

(a) YKPE (b) YEPK (c) YLEP (d) YPKE

Sol. (d) According to the question,

8 → Y ; 6 → P ; 3 → K ; 7 → E

Hence, the code for 8637 is YPKE.

Exam Approach Examples

Based on Letter Coding

Example 1 If SCHEME is coded as TDIFNF, then what is the code for WONDER? *UPSSSC PET 2023*

(a) POXEFS (b) XPQFTF
(c) XOOESF (d) XPOEFS

Sol. (*d*) As,

S C H E M E
+1 +1 +1 +1 +1 +1
T D I F N F

Similarly,

W O N D E R
+1 +1 +1 +1 +1 +1
X P O E F S

Helping Tips

To solve such questions, it is very important to remember the positional value of letters in forward and reverse direction.

Example 2 If in a certain code language 'CAKE' written as 'ACIG' and 'GOLD' is written as 'EQJF', then how will 'WIRE' be written in the same language? *SSC MTS 2024*

(a) GUKP (b) UKPG
(c) GPUK (d) GUPK

Sol. (*b*) As, and

C A K E
−2 +2 −2 +2
A C I G

G O L D
−2 +2 −2 +2
E Q J F

Similarly,

W I R E
−2 +2 −2 +2
U K P G

Example 3 If BANKER is coded as CAMKFR, then how would INDIAN be coded? *SSC MTS 2011*

(a) JNEIBN (b) JNCIBN
(c) HMCIZN (d) JMCIZL

Sol. (*b*) As,

B A N K E R
+1 +0 −1 +0 +1 +0
C A M K F R

Similarly,

I N D I A N
+1 +0 −1 +0 +1 +0
J N C I B N

Trending Concept

Letter coding based questions are very important for the SSC CGL, MTS, CPO, DSSSB and Railway exams.

Example 4 If DRONE is coded as FUSSK, then what is the code for FLASH? *DSSSB 2021*

(a) HNCUJ (b) HODYM (c) HOEXN (d) HPDYO

Sol. (*c*) As,

D R O N E ⟶ F U S S K
(+2, +3, +4, +5, +6)

Similarly,

F L A S H ⟶ H O E X N
(+2, +3, +4, +5, +6)

Score Booster

1. By remembering the words 'EJOTY' and 'CFILORUX' we can easily find the position of letters of English alphabet.
   As:
   E J O T Y (It's a girl's name like jyoti)
   5 10 15 20 25 (They are in the form of multiplication of 5)
   C F I L O R U X (It's a name of a medicine like cifilox)
   3 6 9 12 15 18 21 24 (They are in the form of multiplication of 3)
2. If any two letters of the English alphabet, whose numerical value adds up to 27, then those two letters are opposite to each other.
   Such as: B (2) and (Y) 25 are opposite to each other.
3. The opposite value of the letters = 27 – Value of the corresponding letters.

Example 5 In a certain code language, if 'LIGHT' is coded as 'ORTSG', SWITCH is coded as HDRGXS, then how will WIRE be coded? *DSSSB 2024*

(a) DSIV (b) DRIV
(c) DRIW (d) DRJV

Sol. (*b*) As,

L I G H T
↕ Opposite letter
O R T S G

and

S W I T C H
↕ Opposite letter
H D R G X S

Similarly,

W I R E
↕ Opposite letter
D R I V

Based on Number Coding

Example 6 If 'BEAR' is coded as '25-22-26-9', then how will 'TIGER' be coded? *UP Police Constable 2024*

(a) 7-9-11-4-17
(b) 8-9-12-5-17
(c) 9-10-13-6-17
(d) 7-18-20-22-9

Sol. (*d*) As,

B E A R → 25 - 22 - 26 - 9 (Positional value of opposite letter)

Similarly,

T I G E R → 7 - 18 - 20 - 22 – 9 (Positional value of opposite letter)

Example 7 **In a certain code language, 'MAN' is coded as '15316' and 'SHE' is coded as '21107'. How will 'OUT' be coded in that language?** ***SSC CGL (Tier-I) 2024***

(a) 152120 (b) 172121 (c) 172322 (d) 152222

Sol. (*c*) As,

13 1 14
M A N
↓+2 ↓+2 ↓+2
15 3 16

and

19 8 5
S H E
↓+2 ↓+2 ↓+2
21 10 7

Similarly,

15 21 20
O U T
↓+2 ↓+2 ↓+2
17 23 22

Example 8 **In a certain code language, 'CRUST' is written as '201921183' and 'BLAME' is written as '5131122'. How will 'PLASTIC' be written in that language?** ***SSC CGL (Tier-I) 2022***

(a) 18204165138 (b) 73110209325
(c) 71642578102 (d) 39201911216

Sol. (*d*) As,

C R U S T → 20 19 21 18 3

and

B L A M E → 5 13 1 12 2

Similarly,

P L A S T I C → 3 9 20 19 1 12 16

Example 9 **In a certain code language, 'RAT' is coded as 39 and 'MICE' is coded as 30. How will 'ZEBRA' be coded in that language?** ***SSC CGL (Tier-I) 2023***

(a) 53 (b) 52 (c) 51 (d) 50

Sol. (*b*) As,

R A T → 18 + 1 + 20 = 39

and

M I C E → 13 + 9 + 3 + 5 = 30

Similarly,

Z E B R A → 26 + 5 + 2 + 18 + 1 = 52

Example 10 **In a certain code language, 'COIN' is written as '615928' and 'MINT' is written as '2692840'. How will 'HERO' be written in that language?** ***SSC (10+2) 2023***

(a) 81018 (b) 8101830
(c) 1653615 (d) 16536

Sol. (*c*) As,

3 15 9 14
C O I N
↓×2 ↓×1 ↓×1 ↓×2
6 15 9 28

[Consonant → ×2, Vowel → ×1]

and

13 9 14 20
M I N T
↓×2 ↓×1 ↓×2 ↓×2
26 9 28 40

Similarly,

8 5 18 15
H E R O
↓×2 ↓×1 ↓×2 ↓×1
16 5 36 15

Based on Symbol Coding

Example 11 **In a certain code language, 'BLAME' is written as '4%5@2' and "MEDIA" is written as @2Ω95. How will 'DELTA' be written in that language?** ***RRC Group D 2022***

(a) Ω2%35 (b) 2Ω%53 (c) 92%35 (d) 92$Ω5

Sol. (*a*) As,

B L A M E → 4 % 5 @ 2

and

M E D I A → @ 2 Ω 9 5

Similarly,

D E L T A → Ω 2 % 3 5

> ***Helping Tips***
> To find the code of the remaining letter, we can find directly with the help of the options.

Based on Fictitious Language Coding

Example 12 **In a certain code language, 'GAME' is coded as '8426' and 'MUST' is coded as '7853'. What is the code for 'M' in the same code language?** ***CISF Head Constable 2023***

(a) 7 (b) 3
(c) 2 (d) 8

Sol. (*d*) According to the question,

G A [M] E ⟶ [8] 4 2 6
[M] U S T ⟶ 7 [8] 5 3

∴ The code for M is 8.

Example 13 **In a certain code language, 'FEND' is coded as '9735' and 'FEUD' is coded as '3769'. What is the code for 'U' in the given code language?** ***RRB ALP 2024***

(a) 7 (b) 6 (c) 3 (d) 9

Sol. (*b*) According to the question,

(F)(E) N (D) ⟶ (9)(7)(3) 5
(F)(E) U (D) ⟶ (3)(7) 6 (9)

∴ Remaining letter U's code = 6

Example 14 In a certain code language, 'toys are gadgets' is coded as 'dj sq ty' and 'gadgets are machines' is coded as 'mp ty dj'. What is code for 'gadgets' in that language?

SSC CGL (Tier-I) 2024

(a) either 'ty' or 'mp' (b) either 'ty' or 'dj'
(c) dj (d) sq

Sol. (*b*) According to the question,

toys are gadgets ⟶ dj sq ty
gadgets are machines ⟶ mp ty dj

Hence, the code for gadgets is either 'ty' or 'dj'.

Based on Substitution Coding

Example 15 In a certain code language, if 'table' is called 'chair', 'chair' is called 'blackboard', 'blackboard' is called 'chalk', 'chalk' is called 'duster', 'duster' is called 'teacher', then where does the teacher write?

Rajasthan Police Constable 2022

(a) chair (b) duster
(c) blackboard (d) chalk

Sol. (*d*) We know that, the teacher writes on the 'blackboard' and in the question the 'blackboard' is called 'chalk'.

So, the teacher writes on the 'chalk'.

Example 16 In a certain code language, 'red' is called 'green', 'green' is called 'pink', pink is called 'brown' and 'brown' is called 'violet', then which coloured light is used to stop vehicles on traffic Signal? ***RRB NTPC 2022***

(a) Brown (b) Green (c) Red (d) Violet

Sol. (*b*) As we know that, we use 'red' coloured light to stop vehicles on traffic signal but here 'red' is called 'green'. So, 'green' light is used to stop vehicles.

Based on Conditional Coding

Example 17 In a certain code language, the letters are coded as per their alphabetical order (A as 1 and Z as 26). However, if a letter appears twice in a word at the second occurrence, it is coded with its reverse alphabetical position. Also, if a vowel appears between two consonants, its corresponding number gets doubled.

Which among the following is the correct code for GLASS?

RRB NTPC 2022

(a) 7121198 (b) 71221991 (c) 7122189 (d) 7122198

Sol. (*d*) According to the given conditions,

G	L	A	S	S
↓	↓	↓	↓	↓
7	12	2	19	8

Example 18 A group of numbers/symbols is coded using letters as per the table given below and the conditions which follow. The correct combination of codes following the conditions is your answer.

Code	Number/Symbol
B	I
F	&
I	2
K	9
A	*
V	7
S	3
U	$
E	8
Q	5
C	6
P	4
X	@
T	#

Conditions

(i) If the first element is a symbol and the second element is an even number, the first and the second elements are to be coded as €.

(ii) If both the first and the last elements are numbers, the codes for these two (the first and the last elements) are to be interchanged.

(iii) If last element is a symbol, the element is to be coded as β.

What will 5 @ & 2 7 be coded as? ***RRC Group D 2022***

(a) QXFIV (b) FXIQV (c) VXFIQ (d) VFXIV

Sol. (*c*) According to the question,

5	@	&	2	7
↓	↓	↓	↓	↓
V	X	F	I	Q

[Condition (ii) follows]

Chapter Challenge

Based on Letter Coding

1. If 'BEAT' is written as 'GIDV', then how will 'SOUP' be written? *UP AO 2024*
(a) ZSYS (b) XSXR
(c) XSYR (d) YSXR

2. If the code of CAT is DBU, then what is the code of DOG? *UP Police Constable 2024*
(a) EOF (b) DPF (c) EPH (d) EPF

3. If in a code language, 'PRIME' is written as 'KIRNV', then 'SPORT' would be written as in the same language. *RRB NTPC 2021*
(a) HKLIG (b) GJLHF
(c) GJKHF (d) HLLIG

> **MRC*****
> ***(Most Repeating Concepts)***
> Q. Nos. 3, 6, 16, 22, 28, 36, 48, 71, 76, and 89 are very important for SSC (CGL, MTS, CHSL, CPO), RRB (NTPC, Group D), State Police exam, etc.

4. In a certain code language, READING is coded as FJWILSN. How will FORMULA be coded in the same language? *RPF SI 2018*
(a) TKWFQZR (b) VSJQEPY
(c) VSQJPEY (d) WTKRFQZ

5. In a certain code, 'HUNTER' coded as 'UHNTRE'. How is 'MANAGE' coded in that code? *RRB JE 2019*
(a) MNAAEG (b) MAANGE
(c) AMNAEG (d) EGNAAM

6. In a certain code language, INCH is coded as CXID. What is the code for 'HUGE' in that code language? *SSC (10+2) 2023*
(a) ZCPC (b) ZBQC (c) ZBPC (d) ZBPD

7. In a certain code language JHMI is written as LPKM. How will YGAN be written in that code language? *Rajasthan Police Constable 2023*
(a) QDKA (b) PDJC
(c) QDJB (d) PEJB

8. In a certain code language, if WOMAN is coded as PXOOB, then how DREAM is coded in that code? *UP Police ASI 2021*
(a) ESGDP (b) ESGBN
(c) SEGNB (d) SEGPD

9. In a certain code language, it AMBER is coded as BNDHU, then how will LAUGH be coded in that code language? *UP Police ASI 2021*
(a) MBWHI (b) BMWKJ
(c) MBWJK (d) BMWIH

10. In a specific code language, 'TORQUE' is written as 'WSUUXI'. What is the code for 'GABENT' in the code language? *DSSSB 2019*
(a) JEEIQX (b) KFFJRX
(c) KEEJQX (d) JFEIQX

11. In a certain code language, ARITHEMATIC is written as MATICEHTIRA. How will ALGEBRA be written as in that language? *RRB NTPC 2021*
(a) BRAEGLA (b) ALGEARB
(c) ARBEGLA (d) GLAEBRA

12. In a certain code language INDIA is written as EJDME. Which of the following words would be coded as JAPEP? *DSSSB 2019*
(a) NEWPEL (b) BENGAL
(c) DELHI (d) NEPAL

13. If RAJESH is coded as SBKFTI, then how is URMILA coded? *DSSB 2018*
(a) TQLHKZ (b) VSNHMB
(c) BMJNSV (d) None of these

14. In a certain code language, if CHOICE is coded as EHIOCC, then how MARTIN is coded in that code? *UP Police ASI 2021*
(a) RAMNIT (b) AMTRNI
(c) NATRIM (d) NBSUJO

15. In a certain code, 'MOTHER' is written as 'JRQKBU', then how will 'PRINCIPAL' be written in that code? *HSSC Police Constable 2021*
(a) SULQFLSDO (b) MRFKZPMZI
(c) NRFKZLMXI (d) MUFQZLMDI

16. FUND is related to KSSB in a certain way based on the English alphabetical order. In the same way PQXZ is related to UOCX. To which of the given options is ZMHV related to, following same logic? *RPF SI 2024*
(a) GJMU (b) FLNT (c) EKMT (d) DKLS

17. In a certain code language, if CARPENTER is written as ACEENPRRT, then how will BLACKSMITH be written in the same code language? *SSC CPO 2020*
(a) LBCASKIMHT (b) ALBSKCIMHT
(c) ABCHIKLMST (d) CALBIMKSTH

18. In a certain code language, 'DEER' is written as 'EGHV' and 'ROOM' is written as 'SQRQ'. How will 'SOAP' be written in that language? *SSC (10+2) 2023*
(a) TQCT (b) TCQT (c) TQTC (d) TQDT

19. In a certain code language, 'CASE' is written as 'FTBD' and 'CAKE' is written as 'FLBD'. How will 'CALF' be written in that language? *SSC CGL (Tier-I) 2024*
(a) GMDB (b) GBMD
(c) GMBD (d) GBDM

20. In a certain code language, 'RUG' is coded as 'EPS' and 'SIT' is coded as 'RQG'. How will 'COP' be coded in the same language? *SSC CGL (Tier-I) 2024*
(a) MBO (b) NBM (c) NAM (d) MBM

21. If in a code language, 'TAP' is written as 'UUQ' and 'BEEP' is written as 'CAAQ', then how will 'LOW' be written in the same language? *SSC Steno 2021*
(a) MUX (b) MAE (c) MIX (d) MEA

22. In a certain code language, 'BOTH' is written as 'DQVJ' and 'DARE' is written as 'FCTG'. How will 'WILL' be written in that language? *SSC CGL (Tier-I) 2024*
(a) XJMM (b) YJMN (c) XKNM (d) YKNN

23. In a certain code language, 'LDWR' is coded as 'NGUQ' and 'BFKZ' is coded as 'DIIY'. What is the code for 'YTGX' in the given code language? *SSC (10+2) 2024*
(a) AWEW (b) ZVFV (c) YWFV (d) BWFV

24. In a certain code language, 'SITE' is written as 'WMXI' and 'MAKE' is written as 'QEOI'. How will 'TERM' be written in that language? *DP Constable 2023*
(a) WHVQ (b) WIUO (c) XIVQ (d) XHUP

25. In a certain code language, 'MENTOR' is coded as 'EMOUPS' and 'OCTAGON' is coded as 'COUBHPO'. What is the code for 'PENCIL' in the given code language? *SSC MTS 2023*
(a) EPLICN (b) LINCENP
(c) PLICNE (d) EPODJM

26. If in a certain code language, 'MUSSOORIE' is written as 'OTURQNTHG', then how will 'DELHI' be written in that code? *Haryana CET 2023*
(a) FCNFK (b) FCNGJ
(c) FDMGK (d) FDNGK

27. In a certain code language, if the word REGISTRATION is coded as TSIGERNOITAR, then how is the word CAMPFIRE coded in that language? *UPSSSC Forest Guard 2022*
(a) MACPRIFE (b) PMACERIF
(c) ERIFPMAC (d) FIRECAMP

28. In a certain code language, 'LIFETIME' is written as 'FGJMFNJU' and 'INTEGRAL' is written as 'FUOJMBSH'. How will 'INTEREST' be written in that language? *SSC CGL (Tier-I) 2023*
(a) FUOKUTGS (b) FUOJUTFS
(c) FUOJVUFS (d) ETNITSER

29. In a certain code language, 'GHOST' is written as 'ONGCB' and 'ABIDE' is written as 'UTMRQ'. How will 'RULES' be written in that language? *SSC CGL (Tier I) 2023*
(a) DAKQD (b) DAJQD
(c) DAJQC (d) WZQJX

30. In a certain code language, 'FLORA' is written as 'WQOLC' and 'MONEY' is written as 'PNPYE'. How will 'GOING' be written in the same code language? *CISF HC 2023*
(a) RHKSR (b) VBUDP (c) VNUPW (d) RMWEH

Based on Number Coding

31. In a certain code, 'MONEY' is written as '513141525'. How is 'BLACK' written in that code? *HSSC Police Constable 2021*
(a) 1321112 (b) 1321012 (c) 1213112 (d) 1231112

32. In a certain code language, 'THE' is coded as 33, then how will 'ANT' be coded in that code language? *UP Police SI 2021*
(a) 41 (b) 39 (c) 35 (d) 37

33. In a certain code language, 'YJM' is coded as '26-11-14' and 'SOP' is coded as '20-16-17'. What is the code for 'BTX' in the given code language ? *SSC MTS 2023*
(a) 3-21-25 (b) 5-22-24 (c) 5-23-25 (d) 4-22-24

34. If 95474 is written as KGFIF, then how will 82143 be written? *UP Police Constable 2024*
(a) JCDEF (b) JCDFE (c) JDCFE (d) JDCEF

35. If A is equal to 1. S is equal to 19 and G is equal to 7, how would you spell 'MASSAGE'? *RRB NTPC 2021*
(a) 1311919175 (b) 1311945375
(c) 1311919277 (d) 1311945355

36. In a certain code language, 'BLEACHERS' is coded as '63' and 'ABACAS' is coded as '42'. How will 'FIZZY' be coded in the same language? *SSC CGL (Tier-I) 2024*
(a) 44 (b) 45 (c) 35 (d) 52

37. In a certain code language, if storm = 15, apple = 6, virtue = 35, then cupboard = ? *SSC MTS 2021*
(a) 23 (b) 37 (c) 45 (d) 31

38. In a certain code language, 'PRO' is written as '48' and 'BAL' is written as '14'. What is the code for COH in that code language? *Rajasthan Police Constable 2022*
(a) 26 (b) 25 (c) 24 (d) 27

39. In a certain code language, 'DEAF' is written as '4516' and 'KILL' is written as '1191212'. How will 'LORD' be written in that language? *SSC CGL (Tier I) 2023*
(a) 1014145 (b) 1114166 (c) 1215184 (d) 1116641

40. In a certain code language, 'WJSL' is coded as '25–12–21–14' and 'DUOH' is coded as '6–23–17–10'. What is the code for 'PFKR' in the given language? *SSC CGL (Tier-I) 2024*
(a) 20–10–14–21 (b) 20–9–12–20
(c) 19–9–12–19 (d) 18–8–13–20

41. If in a code language HE is written as 26 and SHE is written as 64, then how will THEY be written in the same language? *Rajasthan Police Constable 2022*
(a) 163 (b) 116 (c) 113 (d) 136

42. If in a code language, 'ROHAN' is coded as '3136' and 'SHYAM' is coded as '4356', then how will you code 'RAM'? *SSC (10+2) 2021*
(a) 3412 (b) 2315 (c) 1234 (d) 1024

43. If in the code language, JOIN is written as 8574 and POKER is written as 95321, then how will JOKER be written? *UPSSSC 2018*
(a) 93596 (b) 83593 (c) 85321 (d) 93593

44. In a code language 'DICKINSON' is written as 357950210 and 'DIPP' is written as 3566, then how will 'PICNIC' be written in that code language? *BSSC (10+2) 2022*
(a) 650757 (b) 657057 (c) 657507 (d) 560757

45. In a certain language TRUE is coded as 1759, KICK is coded as 4384, CHAIN is coded as 82630. Now, what will be the 1st digit for KITCHEN in the same code? *UPSSSC Forest Guard 2022*
(a) 9 (b) 2 (c) 8 (d) 4

46. In a certain code language, 'PHONE' is coded as '78' as 'MOON' is coded as '52'. How will 'PLAN' be coded in that language? *CUET (UG) 2023*
(a) 43 (b) 98 (c) 65 (d) 66

47. In a certain code language, 'CYCLE' is coded as '242241522' and 'FINAL' is coded as '2118132615'. How will 'MUSIC' be coded in that language? *SSC CGL (Tier-I) 2024*
(a) 146192184 (b) 14681824
(c) 146191824 (d) 1421191824

48. In a certain code language, 'APPLE' is coded as 250 and 'BERRY' is coded as 340. How will 'LITCHI' be coded in the same language? *SSC CPO 2024*
(a) 330 (b) 306 (c) 305 (d) 350

49. If FRUIT is coded as 58281, then how is GRAPES coded? *DSSSB 2018*
(a) 718116519 (b) 791751
(c) 680649 (d) 680640

50. In a certain code language, 'MATHS' is written as '13320819' and 'HINDI' is written as '82714427'. How will 'PHYSICS' be written in that language? *SSC (10+2) 2022*
(a) 168251928319 (b) 168251923319
(c) 168251937319 (d) 168251927319

51. In a certain code language 'CLASS' is written as '81' and 'SECTION' is written as '104'. Then how will 'COLLEGE' be written in that code language? *Rajasthan Police Constable 2022*
(a) 130 (b) 123 (c) 143 (d) 134

52. If ACTOR is coded as 86739, then how would SPREAD be coded? *SSC MTS 2021*
(a) 829485 (b) 179514 (c) 718374 (d) 819263

53. In a certain code language, 'GCJL' is coded as '14-6-20-24' and 'WTRO' is coded as '46-40-36-30'. What is the code for 'BZKQ' in the given code language? *SSC (10+2) 2024*
(a) 4-52-22-34 (b) 2-52-22-34
(c) 4-52-21-32 (d) 3-51-20-33

54. In a certain code language, 'YEAH' is coded as '207'. 'BULK' is coded as '186'. What is the code for 'CORD' in that code language? *SSC (10+2) 2023*
(a) 204 (b) 236 (c) 208 (d) 242

55. In a certain code language, 'BELL' is written as '52225151' and 'CALL' is written as '42625151'. How will 'BEEP' be written in that language? *Delhi Police Head Constable 2022*
(a) 52221221 (b) 52222211
(c) 52222521 (d) 25222211

56. In a certain code language, 'BROTHER' is written as '30-14-17-12-24-27-14', then how will 'TADPOLE' be written in that code lanaguage? *Rajasthan Police Constable 2022*
(a) 12-31-26-16-17-19-27 (b) 12-32-28-16-17-20-27
(c) 12-31-28-16-17-20-27 (d) 12-32-28-16-17-19-27

57. In a certain language, 'MONEY' is coded as 68, 'RACE' is coded as 85, then 'FUNGI' will be coded as *HSSC Police Constable 2021*
(a) 79 (b) 83 (c) 78 (d) 85

58. If CABLES is coded as 720 and WEBINAR is coded as 819, then how will MANDOLIN be coded? *Delhi Police Constable 2020*
(a) 1027 (b) 1207 (c) 1702 (d) 1072

59. In a code language, 'ROSE' is coded as 228 and 'LOTUS' is coded as 435. How will 'ORCHID' be coded in the same language? *Delhi Police Head Constable 2022*
(a) 375 (b) 342 (c) 285 (d) 399

60. In a code language, 'DILIP' is coded as 46-36-30-36-22 and 'PRINCE' is coded as 22-18-36-26-48-44. How will 'FIROZ' be coded in the same language? *SSC CPO 2024*
(a) 42-36-18-24-2 (b) 2-36-18-42-52
(c) 56-36-18-32-52 (d) 48-36-18-38-6

Based on Symbol Coding

61. In a certain code language, "BOUTS" is written as "54%8#" and "ULTRA" is written as %38@9. How will 'BLARE' be written in that language? *RRC Group D 2022*
(a) 593#2 (b) 534#2
(c) 543@% (d) 539@2

Chapter Challenge Coding-Decoding

62. In a certain code language, 'WORSE' is written as 'K#2&6' and 'STEAK' is written as '&@689'. How will THORN be written in that language? *RRC Group D 2022*
(a) @5#27 (b) #5@86 (c) @5#86 (d) #5@27

63. If in a certain code language 'PRAISE' is written as '# @ $ 2 7 %' and 'RESPIRE' is written as '@ % 7 # 2 @ %', then how will 'REPAIR' be written in that code language? *MP Police Constable 2022*
(a) @%#2$@ (b) @%$#2@ (c) @%#$2@ (d) @%$2#@

Based on Fictitious Language Coding

64. In a certain code, 48 means 'which school' and 968 means 'college and school'. What is the code for school? *UP Police Constable 2024*
(a) 4 (b) 6 (c) 8 (d) 9

65. In a certain code language, 'bring the bags' is written as 'nd sm pf' and 'bags of gold' is written as 'rg tx sm'. How is 'bags' written in the given language? *SSC CPO 2024*
(a) rg (b) nd (c) sm (d) pf

66. In a certain code language, 'ATOM' is coded as '9613' and 'BOAT' is coded as '1938'. What is the code for 'B' in the given code language? *SSC MTS 2023*
(a) 9 (b) 8 (c) 3 (d) 1

67. In a certain code language, 'EARS' is coded as '4268' and 'NICE' is coded as '9723'. What is the code for 'E' in the given code language? *SSC CPO 2023*
(a) 3 (b) 2 (c) 9 (d) 4

68. In a certain code language, '4378' is coded as 'IDOL' and '7832' is coded as 'IDLE'. What is the code for '2' in that code language? *SSC (10+2) 2024*
(a) O (b) L (c) E (d) I

69. In a certain code language, 'revise the lesson' is written as 'rx cd st' and 'the lesson plan' is written as 'cd nq rx'. How is 'revise' written in the given language? *SSC CPO 2024*
(a) st (b) cd (c) rx (d) nq

70. In a certain code language, 'NATURE' is coded as '279346' and 'LEARNT' is coded as '794621'. What is the code for 'L' in the given code language? *SSC (10+2) 2023*
(a) 2 (b) 1 (c) 7 (d) 9

71. In a certain code language, 'DARK' is coded as '3284' and 'RAKE' is coded as '6438'. What is the code for 'E' in that language? *SSC (10+2) 2024*
(a) 6 (b) 3 (c) 4 (d) 8

72. In a certain code language, 'CURB' is coded as '3517' and 'BOAT' is coded as '4638'. What is the code for 'B' in the given code language? *SSC CGL (Tier-II) 2025*
(a) 4 (b) 7 (c) 3 (d) 8

73. In a certain code language, 'ARGOT' is coded as '12497' and 'GRAFT' is coded as '29743'. What is the code for 'F' in the given code language? *RRB ALP 2024*
(a) 7 (b) 3 (c) 2 (d) 4

74. In a certain code language,
'learn life lessons' is written as 'lo ma ku'
'lessons are good' is written as 'pi rh ma'
'lead good life' is written as 'lo ja pi'.
What is the code for 'learn' in the given code language? *UP Police SI 2021*
(a) ma (b) pi (c) ku (d) lo

75. In a certain code language 'TAPE' is coded as '4825', 'SHART' is coded as '93814' and 'TUBE' is coded as '4675'. What will be the code of letter 'E' in the same code language? *CUET UG 2023*
(a) 8 (b) 4 (c) 5 (d) 6

76. In a certain code language, 'he enjoys music' is coded as 'lo po jo' and 'music and dance' is coded as 'kb jo fk'. How is 'music' coded in the given language? *SSC CGL (Tier-II) 2025*
(a) jo (b) po (c) lo (d) fk

77. In a certain code
'123' means 'bright blue sky'
'145' means 'dark grey sky'
'378' means 'nice blue wall'
Which numerical is code for 'bright'?
(a) 1 (b) 2 (c) 3 (d) 4

78. In a code language,'he is waiting' is written as '269', 'she is ready' is written as '915', and 'he and she' is written as '271'. What will be the code for the word 'and' in this language? *SSC Steno 2021*
(a) 9 (b) 2 (c) 7 (d) 1

79. In a certain code language, 'live long' is coded as 'mu ae', 'road is long' is coded as 'ae si du' and 'game is live' is coded as 'si mu zt'. What is the code for the word game? *SSC CPO 2023*
(a) si (b) mu (c) zt (d) ae

80. In a code language, 'sweet fruits' is coded as 're de', 'mango is sweet' is coded as 'de me ke', 'orange is citrus' is coded as 'ke le pe', 'eat orange' is coded as 'pe ne'. What is the code for the word 'mango'? *SSC Constable (GD) 2023*
(a) pe (b) ke (c) de (d) me

81. In a code language, 'my mistake' is written as '62', 'nice shoes' is written as '45', 'people are nice' is written as '135' and 'big mistake' is written as '29'. How would 'my shoes' be written in that language? *SSC Steno 2021*
(a) 24 (b) 56
(c) 46 (d) 41

Based on Substitution Coding

82. If 'yellow' is called 'blue', 'blue' is called 'white', 'white' is called 'green', 'green' is called 'brown' and 'brown' is called 'red', what is the colour of 'milk'? ***RRB JE 2019***
(a) Blue (b) Green (c) White (d) Red

83. In a certain code language 'pink' is called 'wood', 'wood' is called 'pen', 'pen' is called 'colour' and 'colour' is called 'brown'. In this language, which of the following is used for writing? ***SSC CPO 2019***
(a) Pen (b) Pink (c) Brown (d) Colour

84. If in a certain code language, 'cricket' is called 'archery', 'archery' is called 'football' and 'football' is called 'volleyball', then which game is played with a bat?
(a) Volleyball (b) Archery (c) Cricket (d) Football

85. If 'orange' is called 'butter', 'butter' is called 'soap', 'soap' is called 'ink', 'ink' is called 'honey' and 'honey' is called 'orange', which of the following is used for washing clothes? ***RRB JE 2019***
(a) Ink (b) Honey (c) Soap (d) Orange

86. If 'book' is called 'pen' and 'pen' is called 'wheat' and 'wheat' is called 'chair' and 'chair' is called 'cup' and 'cup' is called 'book', then which of the following is edible? ***RRB NTPC 2021***
(a) Pen (b) Chair (c) Wheat (d) Book

87. If 'book' is called 'pen', 'pen' is called 'notebook', 'notebook' is called 'bag' and 'bag' is called 'school', then on what do we usually write? ***SSC Steno 2021***
(a) School (b) Book (c) Bag (d) Pen

88. If 'Autumn' is called 'Winter', 'Winter' is called 'Summer', 'Summer' is called 'Rainy', 'Rainy' is called 'cloudy', then in which season do we definitely wear woolen garments? ***RRB NTPC 2022***
(a) Cloudy (b) Rainy (c) Summer (d) Winter

Based on Conditional Coding

89. In this question, a set of numbers/symbols are coded using letters as per the table given below followed by the conditions. The correct combination of codes according to the conditions will be your answer.

Number/Symbol	=	$	6	8	<	?	/	2	5	!	@	7	3	^
Code	G	L	F	M	E	N	D	P	C	R	T	B	V	A

Conditions

(i) If the first element is a symbol and the last element is a number, then the first and last elements will be coded as © and ¥, respectively.
(ii) If the first element is an odd number and the last element is an even number, then the codes of these two should be interchanged.
(iii) If both the second and third elements are perfect squares, then the third element will be coded as the code for the second element.

What will '5 < = 2 @ 6' be coded as? ***RRC Group D 2022***
(a) FNGPTC (b) FEGPTC
(c) BELDTC (d) CEGPTF

90. In this question, a group of numbers/symbols is coded using letters as per the table given below and the conditions which follow. The correct combination of codes following the conditions is your answer.

Number/Symbol	7	5	E	%	&	4	8
Code	S	D	M	U	T	L	A

Conditions

(i) If the second element is an odd number and the last element is an even number, the codes for these two (the second and the last elements) are to be interchanged.
(ii) If the third element is an even number and the fifth element is a symbol, the codes for these two (the third and the fifth elements) are to be interchanged.
(iii) If the fifth element is a symbol and the sixth element is also a symbol, both these elements (the fifth and the sixth elements) are to be coded as R.

Question E 7 5 % & 4 % 8 ***RRC Group D 2022***
(a) MADURRUS (b) MATUDLUS
(c) MSDUTLUA (d) MADUTLUS

Right Key

1. (b)	2. (c)	3. (a)	4. (d)	5. (c)	6. (c)	7. (c)	8. (c)	9. (c)	10. (a)
11. (a)	12. (d)	13. (d)	14. (c)	15. (d)	16. (c)	17. (c)	18. (d)	19. (c)	20. (c)
21. (c)	22. (d)	23. (a)	24. (c)	25. (d)	26. (d)	27. (b)	28. (b)	29. (c)	30. (c)
31. (d)	32. (c)	33. (a)	34. (c)	35. (a)	36. (c)	37. (b)	38. (b)	39. (c)	40. (d)
41. (b)	42. (d)	43. (c)	44. (b)	45. (d)	46. (d)	47. (b)	48. (c)	49. (c)	50. (d)
51. (a)	52. (a)	53. (a)	54. (a)	55. (b)	56. (c)	57. (b)	58. (d)	59. (b)	60. (a)
61. (d)	62. (a)	63. (c)	64. (c)	65. (c)	66. (b)	67. (b)	68. (c)	69. (a)	70. (b)
71. (a)	72. (c)	73. (b)	74. (c)	75. (c)	76. (a)	77. (b)	78. (c)	79. (c)	80. (d)
81. (c)	82. (b)	83. (d)	84. (b)	85. (a)	86. (b)	87. (c)	88. (c)	89. (b)	90. (d)

Solutions

1. (b) As, B E A T
+5 +4 +3 +2
G I D V

Similarly, S O U P
+5 +4 +3 +2
X S X R

2. (c) As, C A T
+1 +1 +1
D B U

Similarly, D O G
+1 +1 +1
E P H

3. (a) As, P R I M E
Opposite letters
K I R N V

Similarly,
S P O R T
Opposite letters
H K L I G

4. (d) As, R E A D I N G
+5 +5 +5 +5 +5 +5 +5
F J W I L S N

Similarly,
F O R M U L A
+5 +5 +5 +5 +5 +5 +5
W T K R F Q Z

5. (c) As,
H U N T E R
U H N T R E

Similarly,
M A N A G E
A M N A E G

6. (c) As, I N C H
–5
C X I D

Similarly, H U G E
–5
Z B P C

7. (c) As, J H M I
+3 +3 +3 +3
L P K M

Similarly, Y G A N
+3 +3 +3 +3
Q D J B

8. (c) As, W O M A N
+1 +1 +2 +1 +1
P X O O B

Similarly, D R E A M
+1 +1 +2 +1 +1
S E G N B

9. (c) As, A M B E R
+1 +1 +2 +3 +3
B N D H U

Similarly, L A U G H
+1 +1 +2 +3 +3
M B W J K

10. (a) As, T O R Q U E
+3 +4 +3 +4 +3 +4
W S U U X I

Similarly, G A B E N T
+3 +4 +3 +4 +3 +4
J E E I Q X

11. (a) As, A R I T H E M A T I C
M A T I C E H T I R A

Similarly, A L G E B R A
B R A E G L A

12. (d) As,
I N D I A ⟶ E J D M E
–4 –4 0 +4 +4

Similarly,
N E P A L ⟶ J A P E P
–4 –4 0 +4 +4

13. (d) As,
R A J E S H ⟶ S B K F T I
+1 +1 +1 +1 +1 +1

Similarly,
U R M I L A ⟶ V S N J M B
+1 +1 +1 +1 +1 +1

14. (c) As,
C H O I C E
E H I O C C

Similarly,
M A R T I N
N A T R I M

15. (d) As, M O T H E R
–3 +3 –3 +3 –3 +3
J R Q K B U

Similarly,
P R I N C I P A L
–3 +3 –3 +3 –3 +3 –3 +3 –3
M U F Q Z L M D I

16. (c) As, F U N D
+5 –2 +5 –2
K S S B

and, P Q X Z
+5 –2 +5 –2
U O C X

Similarly, Z M H V
+5 −2 +5 −2
E K M T

17. (*c*) As,

C A R P E N T E R (Arranged according to alphabetical order)
A C E E N P R R T

Similarly,

B L A C K S M I T H
A B C H I K L M S T

18. (*d*) As, D E E R
+1 +2 +3 +4
E G H V

and R O O M
+1 +2 +3 +4
S Q R Q

Similarly, S O A P
+1 +2 +3 +4
T Q D T

19. (*c*) As, C A S E
+1 +1 +1 +1
F T B D

and C A K E
+1 +1 +1 +1
F L B D

Similarly, C A L F
+1 +1 +1 +1
G M B D

20. (*c*) As, R U G
−2 −2 −2
E P S

and S I T
−2 −2 −2
R Q G

Similarly, C O P
−2 −2 −2
N A M

21. (*c*) Here, the consonants are coded as + 1 alphabet and the vowels are coded as the previous vowel
(A → E → I → O → U)

As, T A P
+1 +1 [Here for A ⟶ U]
U U Q

and B E E P
+1 +1 [Here for E ⟶ A]
C A A Q

Similarly, L O W
+1 +1 [Here for O ⟶ I]
M I X

22. (*d*) As, B O T H
+2 +2 +2 +2
D Q V J

and D A R E
+2 +2 +2 +2
F C T G

Similarly, W I L L
+2 +2 +2 +2
Y K N N

23. (*a*) As, L D W R
+2 +3 −2 −1
N G U Q

and B F K Z
+2 +3 −2 −1
D I I Y

Similarly, Y T G X
+2 +3 −2 −1
A W E W

24. (*c*) As, S I T E
+4 +4 +4 +4
W M X I

and M A K E
+4 +4 +4 +4
Q E O I

Similarly, T E R M
+4 +4 +4 +4
X I V Q

25. (*d*) As, M E N T O R
+1 +1 +1 +1
E M O U P S

and O C T A G O N
+1 +1 +1 +1 +1
C O U B H P O

Similarly, P E N C I L
+1 +1 +1 +1
E P O D J M

26. (*d*) As,

M U S S O O R I E
+2 −1 +2 −1 +2 −1 +2 −1 +2
O T U R Q N T H G

Similarly, D E L H I
+2 −1 +2 −1 +2
F D N G K

27. (*b*) As, R E G I S T R A T I O N
T S I G E R N O I T A R

Similarly, C A M P F I R E
P M A C E R I F

28. (*b*) As,

L I F E T I M E
+1 +1
F G J M F N J U

and

I N T E G R A L
+1 +1
F U O J M B S H

Similarly,

I N T E R E S T
+1 +1
F U O J U T F S

29. (*c*) As,

G H O S T
T S L H G (Opposite letters)
−5 −5 −5 −5 −5
O N G C B

and A B I D E
Z Y R W V (Opposite letters)
−5 −5 −5 −5 −5
U T M R Q

Similarly, R U L E S ↕ I F O V H (Opposite letters) → −5 −5 −5 −5 −5 → D A J Q C

30. (c) As,

F L O R A ↕ U O L I Z (Opposite letters) → +2 +2 +3 +3 +3 → W Q O L C

and

M O N E Y ↕ N L M V B (Opposite letters) → +2 +2 +3 +3 +3 → P N P Y E

Similarly,

G O I N G ↕ T L R M T (Opposite letters) → +2 +2 +3 +3 +3 → V N U P W

31. (d) As,

13	15	14	5	25	Alphabetical order	5	13	14	15	25
M	O	N	E	Y	⟶	E	M	N	O	Y

Similarly,

2	12	1	3	11	Alphabetical order	1	2	3	11	12
B	L	A	C	K	⟶	A	B	C	K	L

32. (c) As, T H E → 20 + 8 + 5 = 33

Similarly, A N T → 1 + 14 + 20 = 35

33. (a) As, Y J M → +1 +1 +1 → 26 11 14

and S O P → +1 +1 +1 → 20 16 17

Similarly, B T X → +1 +1 +1 → 3 21 25

34. (c) As, 9 5 4 7 4 → +2 +2 +2 +2 +2 → K G F I F (11 7 6 9 6)

Similarly, 8 2 1 4 3 → +2 +2 +2 +2 +2 → J D C F E

35. (a) As, A $\xrightarrow{\text{Positional Value}}$ 1

S $\xrightarrow{\text{Positional Value}}$ 19

and G $\xrightarrow{\text{Positional Value}}$ 7

Similarly,

M A S S A G E → Positional value → 13 1 19 19 1 7 5

36. (c) As,

BLEACHERS $\xrightarrow{\text{Total number of letters} \times 7}$

$9 \times 7 = 63$

and ABACAS $\xrightarrow{\text{Total number of letters} \times 7}$

$6 \times 7 = 42$

Similarly, FIZZY $\xrightarrow{\text{Total number of letters} \times 7}$

$5 \times 7 = 35$

37. (b) Only vowel's place or sum of total vowels place is the code of the words.

∴ Storm = 15 (o's place),

Apple = 1 + 5 = 6, (Sum of a and e)

Virtue = 9 + 21 + 5 = 35 (Sum of i, u and e)

Similarly, Cupboard = 21 + 15 + 1 = 37 (Sum of u, o and a)

38. (b) As, P R O → 16+18+15 = 49−1 = 48

and B A L → 2+1+12 = 15−1 = 14

Similarly, C O H → 3+15+8 = 26−1 = 25

39. (c) As, D E A F → 4 5 1 6

and K I L L → 11 9 12 12

Similarly, L O R D → 12 15 18 4

40. (d) As, W J S L → +2 +2 +2 +2 → 25 − 12 − 21 − 14

and D U O H → +2 +2 +2 +2 → 6 − 23 − 17 − 10

Similarly, P F K R → +2 +2 +2 +2 → 18 − 8 − 13 − 20

41. (b) As, H E → 8 + 5 = 13 × 2 = 26

and S H E → 19 + 8 + 5 = 32 × 2 = 64

Similarly, T H E Y → 20 + 8 + 5 + 25 = 58×2 = 116

42. (d) As, ROHAN

$\Rightarrow (18+15+8+1+14)^2 = (56)^2 = 3136$

and SHYAM

$\Rightarrow (19+8+25+1+13)^2 = (66)^2 = 4356$

Similarly, RAM

$\Rightarrow (18+1+13)^2 = (32)^2 = 1024$

43. (c) As, J O I N → 8 5 7 4

and P O K E R → 9 5 3 2 1

Similarly, J O K E R → 8 5 3 2 1

44. (b) As, D I C K I N S O N → 3 5 7 9 5 0 2 1 0

and D I P P → 3 5 6 6

Similarly, P I C N I C
↓ ↓ ↓ ↓ ↓ ↓
6 5 7 0 5 7

45. (*d*) As, T R U E , K I C K
1 7 5 9 4 3 8 4

and C H A I N
8 2 6 3 0

Similarly, K I T C H E N
4 3 1 8 2 9 0

Ist digit = 4

46. (*d*) As,
P H O N E (Sum of opposite letter place value +1)
11 + 19 + 12 + 13 + 22 = 77+1=78

and
M O O N (Sum of opposite letter place value +1)
14 + 12 + 12 + 13 = 51+1=52

Similarly,
P L A N (Sum of opposite letter place value +1)
11 + 15 + 26 + 13 = 65+1= 66

47. (*b*) As, C Y C L E (Opposite letter positional value)
24 2 24 15 22

and F I N A L (Opposite letter positional value)
21 18 13 26 15

Similarly, M U S I C (Opposite letter positional value)
14 6 8 18 24

48. (*c*) [Logic-Sum of positional value of letters × 5]

APPLE ⇒

$1+16+16+12+5=50\times5=250$

and BERRY ⇒

$2+5+18+18+25=68\times5=340$

Similarly, LITCHI ⇒

$12+9+20+3+8+9=61\times5=$ 305

49. (*c*) As, $F \Rightarrow 6-1=5$

$R \Rightarrow 18 \Rightarrow 1+8-1=8$

$U \Rightarrow 21 \Rightarrow 2+1-1=2$

$I \Rightarrow 9 \Rightarrow 9-1=8$

$T \Rightarrow 20 \Rightarrow 2+0-1=1$

Similarly,

$G \Rightarrow 7 \Rightarrow 7-1=6$

$R \Rightarrow 18 \Rightarrow 1+8-1=8$

$A \Rightarrow 1 \Rightarrow 1-1=0$

$P \Rightarrow 16 \Rightarrow 1+6-1=6$

$E \Rightarrow 5 \Rightarrow 5-1=4$

$S \Rightarrow 19 \Rightarrow 1+9-1=9$

∴ GRAPES ⇒ 680649

50. (*d*) As, M A T H S
(A ×3)
13 3 20 8 19

[vowel → ×3]

and H I N D I
(I ×3, I ×3)
8 27 14 4 27

Similarly, P H Y S I C S
(I ×3)
16 8 25 19 27 3 19

51. (*a*) As,
C L A S S (Opposite letters value)
24 + 15 + 26 + 8 + 8=81

and
S E C T I O N (Opposite letters value)
8 + 22 + 24 + 7 + 18 + 12 + 13=104

Similarly,
C O L L E G E (Opposite letters value)
24 + 12 + 15 + 15 + 22 + 20 + 22= 130

52. (*a*) As,
26 24 7 12 9
A C T O R (Position in reverse alphabetical series)
(2+6) (2+4) 7 (1+2) 9
8 6 7 3 9

Similarly,
8 11 9 22 26 23
S P R E A D (Position in reverse alphabetical series)
8 (1+1) 9 (2+2) (2+6) (2+3)
8 2 9 4 8 5

53. (*a*) As,
7 3 10 12
G C J L
×2 ×2 ×2 ×2
14 6 20 24

and
23 20 18 15
W T R O
×2 ×2 ×2 ×2
46 40 36 30

Similarly,
2 26 11 17
B Z K Q
×2 ×2 ×2 ×2
4 52 22 34

54. (*a*) As, Y E A H (Opposite letters value)
2 + 22 + 26 +19 =69
⇒ 69 × 3 = 207

and B U L K (Opposite letters value)
25 + 6 + 15 +16 = 62
⇒ 62 × 3 = 186

Similarly, C O R D (Opposite letters value)
24 + 12 + 9 +23 = 68
⇒ 68 × 3 = 204

TOP TIPS Opposite letter position = 27 – Forward alphabetical position

55. (*b*) As,
B E L L
25 22 15 15 (Opposite letter place value)
52 22 51 51 (Reversing the number)

and
C A L L
24 26 15 15 (Opposite letter place value)
42 62 51 51 (Reversing the number)

Similarly, B E E P
25 22 22 11 (Opposite letter place value)
52 22 22 11 (Reversing the number)

56. (*c*) As, B R O T H E R
(Opposite position value) 25 9 12 7 19 22 9
+5 +5 +5 +5 +5 +5 +5
30 14 17 12 24 27 14

Similarly, T A D P O L E
(Opposite position value) 7 26 23 11 12 15 22
+5 +5 +5 +5 +5 +5 +5
12 31 28 16 17 20 27

57. (*b*) As, M O N E Y (Opposite positional value) → 14 + 12 + 13 + 22 + 2 = 63 + 5 = 68

and R A C E (Opposite positional value) → 9 + 26 + 24 + 22 = 81 + 4 = 85

[**Note** Sum of reverse alphabetical position of letters + Number of letters in the word]

Similarly,

F U N G I (opposite positional value) → 21 + 6 + 13 + 20 + 18 = 78 + 5 = 83

58. (*d*) As, CABLES

⇒ (24 + 26 + 25 + 15 + 22 + 8) × 6

= 120 × 6 = 720

[∵ Sum of opposite positional value × Total number of letters in word]

and WEBINAR

(4 + 22 + 25 + 18 + 13 + 26 + 9) × 7

= 117 × 7 = 819

Similarly, MANDOLIN

⇒ (14 + 26 + 13 + 23 + 12 + 15 + 18 + 13) × 8

= 134 × 8 = 1072

59. (*b*) As, R O S E → 18 + 15 + 19 + 5 = 57

⇒ 57 × 4 (Number of letters in word) = 228

and L O T U S → 12 + 15 + 20 + 21 + 19 = 87

⇒ 87 × 5 = 435

Similarly, O R C H I D → 15 + 18 + 3 + 8 + 9 + 4 = 57

⇒ 57 × 6 = 342

60. (*a*) As,

D I L I P (Place value of opposite letter): 23 18 15 18 11 → ×2 → 46 - 36 - 30 - 36 - 22

and P R I N C E: 11 9 18 13 24 22 → ×2 → 22 - 18 - 36 - 26 - 48 - 44

Similarly, F I R O Z: 21 18 9 12 1 → ×2 → 42 - 36 - 18 - 24 - 2

61. (*d*) As, B O U T S → 5 4 % 8 #

and U L T R A → % 3 8 @ 9

So, B L A R E → 5 3 9 @ 2

62. (*a*) As, W O R S E → K # 2 & 6

and S T E A K → & @ 6 8 9

So, T H O R N → @ 5 # 2 7

63. (*c*) As, P R A I S E → # @ $ 2 7 %

and R E S P I R E → @ % 7 # 2 @ %

Similarly, R E P A I R → @ % # $ 2 @

64. (*c*) According to the question,

4 ⑧ → which (school)

9 6 ⑧ → college and (school)

∴ The code for 'School' is '8'.

65. (*c*) According to the question,

bring the (bags) ⟶ nd (sm) pf

(bags) of gold ⟶ rg tx (sm)

∴ The code for bags is 'sm'.

66. (*b*) As,

Ⓐ Ⓣ Ⓞ M ⟶ ⑨ 6 ① ③

and B Ⓞ Ⓐ Ⓣ ⟶ ① ⑨ ③ 8

∴ The code for 'B' will be '8'.

67. (*b*) As, [E] A R S → 4 [2] 6 8

N I C [E] → 9 7 [2] 3

So, E is coded as 2.

68. (*c*) In the given code language,

4 ③⑦⑧ → ⓄⒹ O Ⓛ

⑦⑧③ 2 → ⓄⒹ Ⓛ E

Hence, the code of '2' is 'E'.

69. (*a*) According to the question,

[revise] (the) (lesson) = (rx) (cd) [st]

(the) (lesson) plan = (cd) nq (rx)

Hence, revise is coded as 'st'.

70. (*b*) According to the question,

[N][A][T]Ⓤ[R][E] → [2][7][9]③[4][6]

△L[E][A][R][N][T] → [7][9][4][6][2]△1

Hence, the code for 'L' is '1'.

71. (*a*) According to question,

D ⒶⓇⓀ ⟶ ③ 2 ⑧④

ⓇⒶⓀ E ⟶ 6 ④③⑧

Hence, code for 'E' = 6

72. (*c*) According to question,

C U R [B] ⟶ [3] 5 1 7

[B] O A T ⟶ 4 6 [3] 8

Hence, code for 'B' is '3'.

73. (*b*) According to the question,

ⒶⓇⒼ O Ⓣ ⟶ 1 ②④⑨⑦

ⒼⓇⒶ F Ⓣ ⟶ ②⑨⑦④ 3

Hence, code of 'F' is '3'.

74. (*c*) According to the question,

learn [life] (lessons) ⟶ [lo] (ma) ku

(lessons) are {good} ⟶ {pi} rh (ma)

lead {good} [life] ⟶ [lo] ja {pi}

Hence, the code for 'learn' is 'ku'.

> **TOP TIPS** To avoid confusion, mark the common words/letters with different shapes.

75. (*c*) According to the question,

[T] A P Ⓔ ⟶ [4] 8 2 ⑤

S H A R [T] → 9 3 8 1 [4]

[T] U B Ⓔ ⟶ [4] 6 7 ⑤

∴ The code for E is 5.

76. (*a*) According to the question,

he enjoys (music) → lo po (jo)

(music) and dance → kb (jo) fk

Hence, code of 'music' is 'jo'.

77. (*b*) According to the question,

(1) 2 [3] → bright [blue] (sky)

(1) 4 5 → dark grey (sky)

[3] 7 8 → nice [blue] wall

∴ The code for 'bright' is '2'.

78. (*c*) According to the question,

(she) [is] ready ⇒ [9] (1) 5

△he and (she) ⇒ △2 7 (1)

△he [is] Waiting ⇒ △2 6 [9]

Hence, code for 'and' is '7'.

79. (*c*) According to the question,

[Live] Long ⇒ [mu] ae

Road (is) Long ⇒ ae (si) du

{Game} (is) [Live] ⇒ (si) [mu] {zt}

∴ Game is coded as 'zt'.

80. (*d*) According to the given information,

[sweet] fruits → re [de]

mango (is) [sweet] → [de] me (ke)

orange (is) citrus → (ke) le pe

eat orange → pe ne

Clearly, 'mango' is coded as 'me'.

81. (*c*) According to the question,

my (mistake) ⇒ 6 (2)

[nice] shoes ⇒ 4 [5]

people are [nice] ⇒ 1 3 [5]

big (mistake) ⇒ (2) 9

Hence, the final code for 'my shoes' is 46.

82. (*b*) Colour of 'milk' is 'white' and here 'white' is 'green'. So, colour of milk is green.

83. (*d*) Pen is used for writing but here 'pen' is called 'colour'. So, colour is used for writing.

84. (*b*) As, we know that cricket is played with a bat and here 'cricket' is called as 'archery'.
So, archery is played with a bat.

85. (*a*) Soap is used for washing clothes and here 'soap' is called 'ink'. So, ink is used for washing clothes.

86. (*b*) Here, the only edible thing in question is wheat, which is called a chair in the question.
So, the edible thing is a chair.

87. (*c*) As, we know we usually write on notebook and here 'notebook' is called 'bag'. So, according to the given information we usually write on 'bag'.

88. (*c*) In winter season we definitely wear wollen garments and here winter is called summer.
Therefore, in summer season we definitely wear wollen garments.

89. (*b*) According to the question,

5	<	=	2	@	6
↓	↓	↓	↓	↓	↓
F E	G	P	T	C	

5 < = 2 @ 6 → F E G P T C

[condition (ii) follows]

90. (*d*) According to the question,

E 7 5 % & 4 % 8 → M A D U T L U S

[condition (i) follows]

CHAPTER

07 Series Test

Series Test

A sequence of numbers/letters /number and letters following a certain rule or pattern is called a series.

In this chapter, question consists of a series in which a term is missing or wrong. Candidate has to analyse the pattern and then find the missing or wrong term from the options.

Number Series

Number series refers to a sequence of numbers following a certain pattern based on various mathematical operations like addition, subtraction, multiplication, division, square, square root, cube, cube root etc., in which one term is missing. Candidate has to analyse that pattern and find that missing term.

e.g. The next term in 58, 60, 63, 68, 75, 86, ? will be

(a) 112 (b) 96 (c) 91 (d) 99

Sol. (d) The pattern of the series is,

58 → 60 → 63 → 68 → 75 → 86 → [99]

+2, +3, +5, +7, +11, +13

Hence, the series consists of a pattern of addition of consecutive prime number.

Alphabet Series

In this type of questions, a series of letter or group of letters of the English alphabet is given following a certain pattern, in which one or two letters or group of letters are missing. Candidate has to identify that pattern and then find the missing term.

e.g. What should come in the place of question mark (?).

UV, OY, IB, EE, ?

(a) ZK (b) AH (c) BI (d) BH

Sol. (b) The pattern of the series is,

U ⟶ O ⟶ I ⟶ E ⟶ [A]

V $\xrightarrow{+3}$ Y $\xrightarrow{+3}$ B $\xrightarrow{+3}$ E $\xrightarrow{+3}$ [H]

Note Vowels are in sequentially decreasing order.

Mixed (Alpha-Numeric) Series

In such questions, a series of numbers and letters of the English alphabet is given based on a certain rule/pattern in which one term is missing. Candidate has to identify that pattern and then, find the missing term.

e.g. Find the missing term in k11, m13, q17, s19, ?

(a) v24 (b) x25

(c) r20 (d) w23

Sol. (d) The pattern of the series is

k $\xrightarrow{+2}$ m $\xrightarrow{+4}$ q $\xrightarrow{+2}$ s $\xrightarrow{+4}$ [w]

11 $\xrightarrow{+2}$ 13 $\xrightarrow{+4}$ 17 $\xrightarrow{+2}$ 19 $\xrightarrow{+4}$ [23]

∴ The missing term = w23

Continuous Pattern Series

In this type, a continuous series of numbers or small/capital letters is given in which a group of letters or numbers is getting repeated following a particular pattern. Some blank spaces are given at the place of missing letters/numbers. Candidate has to find the letters/numbers which should come at the place of blank spaces and complete the given series.

e.g. Select the combination of letters that when sequentially placed in the blanks of the given series.

A B C _ A _ C C A B _ C _ B _ C

(a) ABBCC (b) CABBA

(c) CBCAC (d) ACCBA

Sol. (c) The pattern of the series is

A B C C / A B C C / A B C C / A B C C

∴ C B C A C will complete the series.

Finding the Wrong Term in the Series

In this type of questions, a series of number/letter/number-letter is given which follows a certain pattern and one of its term is incorrect and does not follow the pattern. Candidate is required to identify the pattern and then find out the wrong term.

e.g. Find the wrong term in the given series.

15, 31, 63, 127, 250

(a) 127 (b) 63 (c) 250 (d) 31

Sol. (c) The pattern of the series is,

15 → 31 → 63 → 127 → [250] (255)

×2+1, ×2+1, ×2+1, ×2+1

∵ $127 \times 2 + 1 = 255 \neq 250$

∴ 250 is the wrong term.

Exam Approach Examples

Based on Number Series

Example 1 What should come at the place of question mark (?).

710, 720, 730, 740, 750, ? *SSC MTS 2023*

(a) 770 (b) 780
(c) 790 (d) 760

Sol. (*d*) The pattern of the given series is,

710 → 720 → 730 → 740 → 750 → [760]
+10, +10, +10, +10, +10

Example 2 What should come at the place of '?' in the given series?

173, 151, 129, 107, ...?... *Delhi Police MTS 2019*

(a) 84 (b) 83
(c) 87 (d) 85

Sol. (*d*) The pattern of the given series is,

173 → 151 → 129 → 107 → [85]
−22, −22, −22, −22

Example 3 Which of the following numbers will replace the question mark (?) in the given series? *SSC CGL (Tier-I) 2024*

7, 13, ?, 145, 721, 4321

(a) 23 (b) 36
(c) 25 (d) 37

Sol. (*d*) The pattern of the given series is,

7 → 13 → [37] → 145 → 721 → 4321
(×2)−1, (×3)−2, (×4)−3, (×5)−4, (×6)−5

> **Helping Tips**
> If the terms of series is increasing quite rapidly. It means that the particular series is based on multiplication of numbers in its terms.

Example 4 Find the missing number in the following series.

1, 1, 2, 2, 6, 10, 42, ?, 1806 *CUET (UG) 2022*

(a) 1203 (b) 1389
(c) 1010 (d) 1302

Sol. (*c*) The pattern of the given series is,

1, 1, 2, 2, 6, 10, 42, [1010], 1806

Alternate terms (1, 2, 6, 42, 1806): 1^2+1, 2^2+2, 6^2+6, 42^2+42

Alternate terms (1, 2, 10, 1010): 1^3+1, 2^3+2, 10^3+10

Example 5 What should come at the place of question mark (?).

16, 22, 34, 58, 106, (?), 394 *UP Police Head Operator 2024*

(a) 288 (b) 202
(c) 178 (d) 175

Sol. (*b*) Pattern of the given series is,

16 → 22 → 34 → 58 → 106 → [202] → 394
+6, +12, +24, +48, +96, +192
×2, ×2, ×2, ×2, ×2

Based on Letter Series

Example 6 Select the letter from among the given options that can replace the question mark (?) in the following series.

P, N, J, H, ? *SSC CGL (Tier-I) 2021*

(a) D (b) B (c) E (d) C

Sol. (*a*) The pattern of the given series is,

P → N → J → H → [D]
−2, −4, −2, −4

Example 7 What should come at the place of question mark (?).

DE, FH, IL, MQ, ? *CISF ASI 2023*

(a) SV (b) RW (c) SW (d) RV

Sol. (*b*) The pattern of the given series is,

D →(+2) F →(+3) I →(+4) M →(+5) [R]
E →(+3) H →(+4) L →(+5) Q →(+6) [W]

Example 8 Select the letter-cluster that can replace the question mark (?) in the given letter-cluster series.

UKS, ZPX, EUC, JZH, ? *SSC CPO 2020*

(a) ODN (b) OEM (c) PEM (d) ODM

Sol. (*b*) The pattern of the given series is,

U →(+5) Z →(+5) E →(+5) J →(+5) [O]
K →(+5) P →(+5) U →(+5) Z →(+5) [E]
S →(+5) X →(+5) C →(+5) H →(+5) [M]

Example 9 Select the letter-cluster that can replace the question mark (?) in the given letter-cluster series.

BEV, FIR, JMN, NQJ, RUF, ? *RRB ALP (CBT-I) 2024*

(a) STU
(b) VYB
(c) TUS
(d) YVB

Sol. (*b*) The pattern of the given series is,

B →(+4) F →(+4) J →(+4) N →(+4) R →(+4) [V]
E →(+4) I →(+4) M →(+4) Q →(+4) U →(+4) [Y]
V →(−4) R →(−4) N →(−4) J →(−4) F →(−4) [B]

> **Helping Tips**
> To solve questions based on letter series, one should remember the place values and opposite place values of English alphabet.

Example 10 Select the letter-cluster that can replace the question mark (?) in the given letter-cluster series.

WKUL, SMQN, OOMP, KQIR, ? *MP Police Constable 2022*

(a) GIFT (b) KSIT (c) GSET (d) GIKT

Sol. (*c*) Pattern of the given series is as follow,

$W \xrightarrow{-4} S \xrightarrow{-4} O \xrightarrow{-4} K \xrightarrow{-4} \boxed{G}$

$K \xrightarrow{+2} M \xrightarrow{+2} O \xrightarrow{+2} Q \xrightarrow{+2} \boxed{S}$

$U \xrightarrow{-4} Q \xrightarrow{-4} M \xrightarrow{-4} I \xrightarrow{-4} \boxed{E}$

$L \xrightarrow{+2} N \xrightarrow{+2} P \xrightarrow{+2} R \xrightarrow{+2} \boxed{T}$

Based on Mixed (Alpha-Numeric) Series

Example 11 What should come at the place of question mark (?) in the following alpha-numeric series?

I2, J3, L7, O16, S32, ? *RRB Group-D 2022*

(a) X57 (b) Y60 (c) W55 (d) X60

Sol. (*a*) Pattern of the given series is as follow,

$I \xrightarrow{+1} J \xrightarrow{+2} L \xrightarrow{+3} O \xrightarrow{+4} S \xrightarrow{+5} \boxed{X}$

$2 \xrightarrow[+1^2]{} 3 \xrightarrow[+2^2]{} 7 \xrightarrow[+3^2]{} 16 \xrightarrow[+4^2]{} 32 \xrightarrow[+5^2]{} \boxed{57}$

Directions (Ex. Nos. 12 and 13) *What should come at the place of question mark (?) in the following alpha-numeric series?*

Example 12 AZ3B, CY6D, EX9F, ? *UP Police Constable 2024*

(a) IV15J (b) GW12H (c) NZ21O (d) KX18L

Sol. (*b*) Pattern of the given series is as follow,

$A \xrightarrow{+2} C \xrightarrow{+2} E \xrightarrow{+2} \boxed{G}$

$Z \xrightarrow{-1} Y \xrightarrow{-1} X \xrightarrow{-1} \boxed{W}$

$3 \xrightarrow{+3} 6 \xrightarrow{+3} 9 \xrightarrow{+3} \boxed{12}$

$B \xrightarrow{+2} D \xrightarrow{+2} F \xrightarrow{+2} \boxed{H}$

Example 13 HP16, ?, NV64, QY100, TB144 *SSC (10+2) 2023*

(a) JS36 (b) JR36
(c) KR49 (d) KS36

Sol. (*d*) Pattern of the given series is as follow,

$H \xrightarrow{+3} \boxed{K} \xrightarrow{+3} N \xrightarrow{+3} Q \xrightarrow{+3} T$

$P \xrightarrow{+3} \boxed{S} \xrightarrow{+3} V \xrightarrow{+3} Y \xrightarrow{+3} B$

$16 \quad \boxed{36} \quad 64 \quad 100 \quad 144$

$\uparrow \quad \uparrow \quad \uparrow \quad \uparrow \quad \uparrow$

$4^2 \xrightarrow{+2} 6^2 \xrightarrow{+2} 8^2 \xrightarrow{+2} 10^2 \xrightarrow{+2} 12^2$

Based on Continuous Pattern Series

Example 14 Find the correct alternative that when filled in the blanks in the same sequence will make the series logically complete.

_BX_ _X_B_X_X_ _X *SSC CHSL (Tier-I) 2023*

(a) XXBXXBXB (b) XBXBXBXX
(c) BBXXBXXX (d) BXXXBBBB

Sol. (*a*) The pattern of the given series is,

X B X / X B X / X B X / X B X / X B X

∴ XXBXXBXB will complete the series.

Example 15 Select the combination of letter that when placed from left to right in the same sequence in the blanks of the given series will complete the series.

_ _ LMT _ _ PLMT _ KPL _ _ _ KPLMT _ *RRC Group-D 2022*

(a) KPTKTMTTT (b) LPTKTMTTT
(c) KPTKTMTTM (d) KLTKTMTTT

Sol. (*a*) The pattern of the given series is,

K P L M T T /K P L M T T/ K P L M T T/ K P L M T T

∴ KPTKTMTTT will complete the series.

Trending Concept

Questions (Ex. 14, 15) based on continuous pattern series are being repeatedly asked in RRB Group D, SSC CHSL, MTS, CGL and CPO examination.

Finding the Wrong Term in the Series

Example 16 Find the wrong term in the given series.

109, 53, 24, 11, 4 *MP Police Constable 2022*

(a) 4 (b) 24
(c) 11 (d) 109

Sol. (*b*) Pattern of the given series is,

$109 \xrightarrow{-3 \div 2} 53 \xrightarrow{-3 \div 2} \boxed{24}\ (25) \xrightarrow{-3 \div 2} 11 \xrightarrow{-3 \div 2} 4$

Hence, wrong term = 24

Directions (Ex. Nos. 17 and 18) *Find the wrong term in the given series.*

Example 17 M, C, P, F, T, G, Y *RRB JE 2019*

(a) Y (b) C
(c) P (d) G

Sol. (*d*) Pattern of the given series is,

$C \xrightarrow{+3} F \xrightarrow{+4} \boxed{G}\ (J)$

$M \xrightarrow{+3} P \xrightarrow{+4} T \xrightarrow{+5} Y$

Hence, the wrong term is 'G'.

Example 18 3X5, 4U3, 2R4, 3O2, 1M3

UP Police Constable 2024

(a) 3O2 (b) 2R4
(c) 4U3 (d) 1M3

Sol. (*d*) Pattern of the given series is as follow,

$3 \xrightarrow{+1} 4 \xrightarrow{-2} 2 \xrightarrow{+1} 3 \xrightarrow{-2} \boxed{1}$

$X \xrightarrow{-3} U \xrightarrow{-3} R \xrightarrow{-3} O \xrightarrow{-3} \boxed{M}\ L$

$5 \xrightarrow{-2} 3 \xrightarrow{+1} 4 \xrightarrow{-2} 2 \xrightarrow{+1} \boxed{3}$

Hence, the wrong term is '1M3'.

Chapter Challenge

Based on Number Series

Directions (Q. Nos. 1-45) *In each of the following questions, find out the missing term of the series.*

1. 1, 1, 2, 3, 5, 8, 13, ? **SSC CPO 2024**
(a) 24 (b) 20 (c) 21 (d) 22

2. 4, 5, 7, 11, ?, 35 **Rajasthan Police Constable 2022**
(a) 17 (b) 18 (c) 21 (d) 19

3. 9, 13, 21, 33, ?, 69 **DSSSB Workshop 2024**
(a) 47 (b) 49 (c) 44 (d) 43

4. 7, 16, 41, 94, 249, ? **CUET (UG) 2022**
(a) 468 (b) 586 (c) 486 (d) 568

5. 5, 9, 18, 34, 59, ? **CRPF (HC) 2023**
(a) 94 (b) 93 (c) 95 (d) 90

6. 98, 50, 26, 14, ?, 5 **SSC CGL (Tier-II) 2025**
(a) 10 (b) 6 (c) 7 (d) 8

7. $\left[\frac{5}{9}\right], \left[\frac{14}{9}\right], \left[\frac{23}{9}\right], \left[\frac{32}{9}\right], \left[\frac{41}{9}\right]$, ? **SSC (10+2) 2024**
(a) $\left[\frac{50}{9}\right]$ (b) $\left[\frac{44}{9}\right]$ (c) $\left[\frac{51}{9}\right]$ (d) $\left[\frac{47}{9}\right]$

8. 1, 1, 9, 27, 25, 125, ?, 343 **UP Police Constable 2024**
(a) 34 (b) 22 (c) 37 (d) 49

9. 2, 9, 28, 65, 126, ? **UP Police (AO) 2024**
(a) 223 (b) 137 (c) 217 (d) 199

10. 9, 5, 6, 10.5, 23, ? **SSC CGL (Tier-II) 2025**
(a) 80 (b) 90 (c) 60 (d) 50

11. 129, 128, 124, 115, 99, ? **SSC (10+2) 2024**
(a) 71 (b) 74 (c) 72 (d) 73

12. 65, 88, 77, 98, 91, 108, ?, 118, 125 **SSC Steno 2020**
(a) 107 (b) 104 (c) 95 (d) 99

13. 11, 39, 75, 119, ...?... **UP Police Constable 2024**
(a) 171 (b) 161 (c) 191 (d) 181

14. 7, 16, 43, 124, 367, ? **SSC CPO 2024**
(a) 1066 (b) 1096 (c) 1076 (d) 1086

15. 286, 257, 230, 205, ?, 161 **DP Constable 2023**
(a) 178 (b) 192 (c) 188 (d) 182

16. 25, 40, 70, 115, 175, ? **SSC Constable (GD) 2022**
(a) 225 (b) 250 (c) 200 (d) 275

17. 433, 414, 376, 319, 243, ? **RRB Technician Grade III 2024**
(a) 148 (b) 162 (c) 124 (d) 136

18. 23, 27, 43, 79, 143, ? **SSC CGL (Tier-I) 2024**
(a) 240 (b) 243 (c) 200 (d) 250

19. 2, 3, 6, 18, ?, 1944 **SSC JE 2023**
(a) 118 (b) 126 (c) 108 (d) 112

20. 5, 19, 49, 101, ? **CISF HC (Min) 2022**
(a) 184 (b) 176 (c) 181 (d) 183

21. 1000, 759, 618, 545, 514, ? **UP Police Constable 2024**
(a) 504 (b) 502 (c) 507 (d) 505

22. $\frac{1}{121}, \frac{1}{11}$, 1, ?, 121 **SSC CPO 2023**
(a) 1 (b) 12 (c) 24 (d) 11

23. 8, 23, 38, 53, 68, ? **UP Police Constable 2024**
(a) 87 (b) 85 (c) 78 (d) 83

24. 15, 25, 45, 85, 165, ? **CRPF (HC) 2023**
(a) 315 (b) 325
(c) 363 (d) None of these

25. 39, 42, 48, 57, 69, ?, 102 **SSC CGL (Tier-I) 2023**
(a) 84 (b) 87 (c) 81 (d) 79

26. 125,25,5,?, $\frac{1}{5}, \frac{1}{25}, \frac{1}{125}$ **HCET 2023**
(a) 1 (b) –2 (c) 2 (d) –1
(e) None of these

27. 1, 6, 15, 28, ?, ?, 91 **SSC CPO 2024**
(a) 40, 60 (b) 45,66 (c) 44, 54 (d) 42, 54

28. 12, 37, 110, 331, 992, ? **CUET (UG) 2023**
(a) 2947 (b) 2867 (c) 2877 (d) 2977

29. 33, 80, 108, ?, 183, 230, 258 **SSC CGL (Tier-I) 2023**
(a) 155 (b) 143 (c) 138 (d) 160

30. 549, 525, 477, 405, 309, ? **RRB ALP (CBT-1) 2024**
(a) 189 (b) 139 (c) 145 (d) 167

31. $\frac{-1}{729}, \frac{-1}{81}, \frac{-1}{9}$, ? **CISF 2023**
(a) 1 (b) $\frac{-1}{3}$ (c) –1 (d) $\frac{1}{3}$

32. 6, 12, 5, 11, 4, 10, 3, ?, ? **CISF ASI 2023**
(a) 3, 9 (b) 9, 3 (c) 9, 2 (d) 2, 9

33. 19, 38, 35, ?, 135, 810 **SSC (10+2) 2022**
(a) 146 (b) 140 (c) 137 (d) 142

34. 213, 216, 221, 228, 237, ?, 261, ? **RPF SI 2024**
(a) 248, 276 (b) 259, 286 (c) 247, 275 (d) 246, 277

35. 3, 18, 90, 360, 1080, 2160, ?, 0 **UP Police Constable 2024**
(a) 1080 (b) 2160 (c) 0 (d) 360

36. 3, 20, 38, 52, 75, 82, 114,? **SSC CGL 2021**
(a) 118 (b) 101 (c) 110 (d) 104

37. 990, 962, 934,906, 878, ? **SSC (GD) 2024**
(a) 850 (b) 840 (c) 854 (d) 860

38. 146, 90, 56, 34, 22, ? **SSC MTS 2021**
(a) 12 (b) 14 (c) 16 (d) 10

39. 21, ?, 45, 180, 185 **SSC Steno 2020**
(a) 41 (b) 42 (c) 33 (d) 63

40. 25, 26, 53, 160, 641, ? *SSC (10+2) 2021*
(a) 3206
(b) 2908
(c) 3202
(d) 3403

> ***MRC******
> ***(Most Repeating Concepts)***
> Q. Nos. 17, 18, 25, 29, 33, 36, 37, 39 and 40 these type of questions frequently asked in SSC exam (CGL, (10+2) and MTS).

41. 361, 348, 335, 322, 309, ? *RRB ALP 2024*
(a) 290 (b) 300 (c) 296 (d) 294

42. 9, 72, 243, 576, ...?...... *UP Police Constable 2024*
(a) 1125 (b) 998 (c) 1250 (d) 876

43. 142, 150, 123, 187, 62, ? *SSC GD 2024*
(a) 285 (b) 281 (c) 300 (d) 278

44. 22, 4, 16, 24, 6, 36, 26, 8, 64, 28, 10, ? *SSC Steno 2019*
(a) 100 (b) 30 (c) 3 (d) 9

45. Find the missing numbers (A, B) in the series and find the value of B + A. *UP Police Constable 2024*
25, 36, 49, A, 81, B, 121
(a) 146 (b) 125 (c) 152 (d) 164

Based on Letter Series

Directions (Q. Nos. 46-86) *What should come in the place of question mark (?) in the following letter series?*

46. G, J, M, P, ? *SSC GD 2024*
(a) S (b) T (c) M (d) R

47. A, B, C, D, ?, F *MP Police Constable 2022*
(a) F (b) E (c) W (d) H

48. A, C, F, H, K, M, ?, ? *UP Police (AO) 2024*
(a) P, S (b) P, R (c) O, P (d) S, Q

49. N, O, Q,T, X, C, ? *CRPF (HC) 2023*
(a) I (b) H (c) J (d) L

50. J, K, M, ?, T, Y *Rajasthan Police Constable 2022*
(a) P (b) O (c) L (c) Q

51. A, D, H, M, S, ? *UP (AO) 2024*
(a) Y (b) U (c) Z (d) V

52. B, D, H, ?, V *DSSSB Workshop 2024*
(a) P (b) M (c) Q (d) N

53. BJ, CL, FO, KS, ? *UP Police Head Operator 2024*
(a) UX (b) EX (c) OT (d) RX

54. DA, HE, NK, RO, XU,? *UP Police Constable 2024*
(a) BY (b) AY (c) CY (d) XY

55. BEG, CFH, DGI, EHJ, ? *RRB ALP 2024*
(a) FGK (b) FIK (c) FKL (d) FGL

56. JLO, KMP, LNQ, MOR, ? *RRB Technician Grade III 2024*
(a) PNS (b) PSN (c) NSP (d) NPS

57. YUS, WSQ, UQO, SOM, ? *RRB ALP 2024*
(a) QMK (b) QOL
(c) RML (d) QKL

58. FNV, LUE, ?, XIW, DPF *SSC (10+2) 2024*
(a) UWZ (b) RBN (c) GQZ (d) HRY

59. DFH, KMO, RTV, YAC, ? *RRB ALP (CBT-I) 2024*
(a) FHJ (b) EGK (c) FIL (d) EGI

60. BDF, DHL, FLR, ? *CRPF (HC) 2023*
(a) HPX (b) HPY (c) HOX (b) IQY

61. DMQ, HUZ, LCI, PKR, ? *CUET (UG) 2023*
(a) TMO (b) TSB (c) TSA (d) TRA

62. VRS, TSO, PUK, NVG,? *Rajasthan Police Constable 2022*
(a) JWC (b) JXC (c) LWD (d) LXD

63. JMD, OHJ, ?, YXV, DSB *SSC (10+2) 2024*
(a) AOZ (b) TCP (c) RST (d) VCP

64. AYD, DVF, GRH, ?, MGL *UP Police Head Operator 2024*
(a) JMJ (b) GLJ (c) HLK (d) FMI

65. OLR, REZ, UXH, XQP, ? *SSC (10+2) 2023*
(a) ALX (b) AJX (c) AQX (d) BJY

66. CHO, DIP, EJQ, ? *SSC CPO 2024*
(a) FKR (b) HMR (c) EJL (d) DIL

67. KJI, HGF, EDC, BAZ, YXW, ? *CISF ASI 2023*
(a) UTS (b) STU (c) VUT (d) WUT

68. ABC, EFG, IJK, MNO, QRS, ? *CRPF (HC) 2023*
(a) VWX (b) UVW (c) STU (d) TUV

69. LAP, KEQ, JIR, ?, HUT, GAU, FEV *UPSSSC 2018*
(a) IIS (b) IOT (c) IOS (d) IIT

70. HLA, BFU, VZO, PTI, ? *RRB ALP (CBT-I) 2024*
(a) JMC (b) JNB (c) JMB (d) JNC

71. SQO, LJH, ECA, ? *SSC CPO 2020*
(a) XVT (b) YWV (c) XUS (d) YWU

72. WVE, UTG, SRI, QPK, ? *SSC (10+2) 2022*
(a) NMO (b) MNO (c) MON (d) ONM

73. RSX, NQW, JOV, FMU, ? *SSC CGL 2022*
(a) CJS (b) BKT (c) BLT (d) DKS

74. YEF, VFI, SGL, PHO, ? *RRB Technician Grade III 2024*
(a) NMR (b) MIR (c) NMQ (d) IMR

75. HIF, KLI, NOL, QRO, ? *RPF SI 2024*
(a) TUR (b) TUS (c) SVR (d) TVS

76. CALI, ZEGO, WIBU, TMWA,? *CUET (UG) 2022*
(a) QQRG (b) QSPF (c) QPSF (d) QRQE

77. FDKI, GCMG, ?, IAQC *SSC CPO 2024*
(a) HBNF (b) HBLE (c) HBPF (d) HBOE

78. JOQW, LQSY, ?, PUWC *SSC (10+2) 2023*
(a) MRTZ (b) KPRX (c) NSUA (d) AUSN

79. YZUW, ?, QTQU, MQOT, INMS *SSC CGL (Tier-I) 2024*
(a) UWVS (b) USWV (c) WUSV (d) UWSV

80. HEWC, KIRI, ?, QQHU, TUCA *SSC CPO 2024*
(a) PRZO (b) NMMO
(c) NBTO (d) JLSO

81. BWUT,?, ZUSR, EZXW, XSQP *SSC Steno 2021*
(a) CTXV (b) CXVU
(c) CYTW (d) CZAB

82. BOMP, DPOQ, ?, HRSS *SSC JE 2023*
(a) FQQR (b) FQRR
(c) FPQR (d) FQQS

83. ELSV, FJVR, GHYN, ?, IDEF *CISF 2023*
(a) GHFJ (b) HFBJ
(c) HFJB (d) HBJF

84. AEJOT, XBGLQ, UYDIN, ? *RRB NTPC (CBT-II) 2022*
(a) RUBDG (b) RVAFK
(c) RVBGJ (d) RVBFJ

85. ZVRN, VSPM, RPNL, ?, JJJJ *SSC CGL (Tier-I) 2024*
(a) RNLK
(b) RMLN
(c) RNLL
(d) NMLK

86. PJVG, VBZB, BTDW, HLHR, ? *SSC CPO 2023*
(a) NDLM
(b) MDLM
(c) NDLN
(d) MDLN

Trending Concept

Questions based on number or letter series are generally in trend as far as SSC (CGL, MTS, JE) exams, railway exams and UP Police constable exams are concerned. These type of questions are also being asked multiple times in each set.

Based on Mixed (Alpha-Numeric) Series

Directions (Q. Nos. 87-96) *What should come at the place of question mark (?) in the following alpha-numeric series?*

87. C-3, E-5, G-7, I-9, ?, ?
(a) M-18, K-14 (b) K-11, M-13
(c) X-24, M-21 (d) O-15, X-24

88. C, 81, E, 64, ?, 49, I, ?, K *UPPSC 2016*
(a) G, 36 (b) F, 36 (c) G, 32 (d) H, 24

89. B9U, E16R, H25O, ? *RRB NTPC 2021*
(a) K36L (b) J34L
(c) M38N (d) L36M

90. UE 88, VG 84, WI 80, XK 76, ? *SSC CGL (Tier-I) 2024*
(a) YN73 (b) YM72
(c) ZM72 (d) ZN71

91. EZ 10, ?, ID 36, KF 49, MH 62 *SSC (10+2) 2023*
(a) FC 21 (b) GB 23
(c) HC 21 (d) FB 22

92. JZI3, LVL9, ?, PNR81, RJU243 *RPF SI 2024*
(a) NGR 17 (b) MPO 15 (c) BYR 21 (d) NRO 27

93. A1Z1, X3C3, E3V4, T9G7, ? *UP Police Constable 2019*
(a) H20R11 (b) I27R11
(c) I27S12 (d) H20S12

94. XD 45, YE 53, ?, AG 58, BH 55 *SSC (10+2) 2023*
(a) ZF 54 (b) ZF 50
(c) ZG 52 (d) AF 51

95. TJM10, ULP12, VNS14, WPV16, XRY18, ? *SSC GD 2024*
(a) YSZ20 (b) YTB20
(c) YTB21 (d) YSZ21

96. FM61, EK58, DI55, CG52, ? *SSC CGL (Tier-I) 2024*
(a) BF48 (b) BE49
(c) CE46 (d) CD44

Based on Continuous Pattern Series

Directions (Q. Nos. 97-113) *What should come at the place of question mark (?) in the following series?*

97. DE_G YUA_TK_G OAQ_ *SSC (10+2) 2023*
(a) FGVG (b) FGVA
(c) BCHL (d) VGFA

98. CB_W V_SP_NLI HG_BA_XU *SSC (10+2) 2024*
(a) XUOEZ (b) ZUOEZ
(c) XUOFY (d) XUOEY

99. A_A_CAB_B_A_ _BCABA_C *SSC (10+2) 2024*
(a) BBACABB (b) BBACBAB
(c) BABACBA (d) BBABBCB

100. _c_dd_ca_cbddb_a *SSC MTS 2021*
(a) caddb (b) cdaba
(c) abbac (d) abcac

101. REMRRE_R_EEMRRE_M_ *SSC CHSL (Tier-II) 2024*
(a) MRME (b) EMER
(c) MREM (d) REME

102. _BCD_ _ABC_ _E_BC_ _ _ABC_DE *RRB NTPC (CBT-II) 2022*
(a) ADEADDEDDD (b) ADDADDEDDE
(c) AADEDDDDED (d) ADEDDADDED

103. LMBA_HOLMBAC_OLM_ACHOL _BACHOL_ *SSC CGL (Tier-I) 2024*
(a) CMHBM (b) CHMBM
(c) CHBMM (d) CHMMB

104. _ml_nl_mlm_l_mlmn_ *SSC CPO 2017*
(a) nnmmll (b) nmlnml
(c) mnlnlm (d) nmnnnl

105. YR_TYRG_YRGR_RG_ *CISF HC (Min) 2022*
(a) GSYQ (b) SYPG
(c) SYTR (d) STRP

106. _JHH_HH_HHJ_ *SSC JE 2023*
(a) HJHJ (b) HJHH
(c) HJJH (d) HHJJ

107. A_DF GI_L MOP_ _UVX YA_D *SSC CGL (Tier-II) 2023*
(a) BJQRB (b) CJRSB
(c) CJQRB (d) BJRSB

108. nm_ _mpn_ _ nmpnm_ _ _pnm_ _mp *Rajasthan Constable 2022*
(a) mnmmmnmmn (b) mnmpmnmmn
(c) mnpmmpmmn (d) mnmnmnmmn

109. CL_VEC_ _WECLO_ _C_O_E *SSC CGL (Tier-I) 2023*
(a) OLPXELY (b) OLOXELY
(c) OLOXFMY (d) OLOYELZ

110. _ba_ _abac_ _ba_aa_ _ca *Rajasthan Police Constable 2022*
(a) acbaacba (b) abaaacba
(c) acaaacba (d) acabaaac

111. C_EF HNE_ _NEP RN_U WNE_ *SSC (10+2) 2024*
(a) FHOSM (b) CAHKL
(c) PAWER (d) NKMEZ

112. _VJRWB_ _RWBVL_ _BV_ _W *SSC CGL (Tier-I) 2023*
(a) BVKRWMR (b) AVKRWMR
(c) AWKRXNR (d) BWKRWMR

113. GA_BM_PB SA_B YAB_ _AHB *SSC (10+2) 2024*
(a) CHFJK (b) JAVBE
(c) AWBUY (d) MFGTY

Finding the Wrong Term in the Series

Directions (Q. Nos. 114-125) *Which one of the following does not come in the sequence? (wrong term in the series)*

114. 1, 3, 12, 60, 340 *UP Police Constable 2024*
(a) 340 (b) 3
(c) 12 (d) 60

115. 2, 6, 18, 54, 161, 486 *RRB NTPC 2021*
(a) 18 (b) 2 (c) 486 (d) 161

116. 4, 7, 13, 21, 34 *UP Police Constable 2024*
(a) 21 (b) 7 (c) 34 (d) 13

117. 324, 109, 36, 12, 4 *RRB NTPC 2021*
(a) 12 (b) 4
(c) 324 (d) 109

118. 4, 11, 6, 12, 10, 15, 16, 20, 22, 27 *MP Police Constable 2022*
(a) 16 (b) 6 (c) 10 (d) 22

119. 9, 15, 24, 34, 51, 69 *RRB JE 2019*
(a) 34 (b) 51
(c) 15 (d) 24

120. 486, 482, 478, 474, 472, 466, 462 *UP Police Constable 2024*
(a) 466 (b) 478
(c) 472 (d) 474

121. 104, 108, 54, 58, 29, 31 *SSC CPO 2022*
(a) 54 (b) 58
(c) 108 (d) 31

122. 33792, 8448, 2148, 528, 132, 33, 8.25 *SSC Steno 2020*
(a) 2148 (b) 528
(c) 8448 (d) 132

123. AZ, EV, IR, NO, QJ *RRB JE 2019*
(a) QJ (b) EV
(c) NO (d) IR

124. AA, BD, CJ, DJ, EM *RRB JE 2019*
(a) AA (b) DJ
(c) CJ (d) BD

125. A1, C9, E25, G49, I89 *UP Police Constable 2024*
(a) C9 (b) E25
(c) I89 (d) G49

Right Key

1. (c)	2. (d)	3. (b)	4. (d)	5. (c)	6. (d)	7. (a)	8. (d)	9. (c)	10. (c)
11. (b)	12. (a)	13. (a)	14. (b)	15. (d)	16. (b)	17. (a)	18. (b)	19. (c)	20. (c)
21. (d)	22. (d)	23. (d)	24. (b)	25. (a)	26. (a)	27. (b)	28. (d)	29. (a)	30. (a)
31. (c)	32. (c)	33. (b)	34. (a)	35. (b)	36. (c)	37. (a)	38. (a)	39. (b)	40. (a)
41. (c)	42. (a)	43. (d)	44. (a)	45. (d)	46. (a)	47. (b)	48. (b)	49. (a)	50. (a)
51. (c)	52. (d)	53. (d)	54. (a)	55. (b)	56. (d)	57. (a)	58. (b)	59. (a)	60. (a)
61. (c)	62. (b)	63. (b)	64. (a)	65. (b)	66. (a)	67. (c)	68. (b)	69. (c)	70. (d)
71. (a)	72. (d)	73. (b)	74. (b)	75. (a)	76. (a)	77. (d)	78. (c)	79. (d)	80. (b)
81. (b)	82. (a)	83. (b)	84. (b)	85. (d)	86. (a)	87. (b)	88. (a)	89. (a)	90. (b)
91. (b)	92. (d)	93. (b)	94. (b)	95. (b)	96. (b)	97. (a)	98. (b)	99. (b)	100. (c)
101. (c)	102. (d)	103. (c)	104. (d)	105. (a)	106. (c)	107. (b)	108. (a)	109. (b)	110. (c)
111. (d)	112. (a)	113. (b)	114. (a)	115. (d)	116. (a)	117. (d)	118. (d)	119. (a)	120. (c)
121. (d)	122. (a)	123. (c)	124. (c)	125. (c)					

Solutions

1. (*c*) Pattern of the given series is,
$1+1=2, 1+2=3, 2+3=5,$
$3+5=8, 5+8=13, 8+13=\boxed{21}$

2. (*d*) Pattern of the given series is,

4 5 7 11 [19] 35
+1 +2 +4 +8 +16
×2 ×2 ×2 ×2

3. (*b*) Pattern of the given series is,

9 13 21 33 [49] 69
+4 +8 +12 +16 +20
+4 +4 +4 +4

4. (*d*) Pattern of the given series is,

×6–1 ×6+3
7 16 41 94 249 [568]
×6–2 ×6+4

5. (*c*) Pattern of the given series is,

5 9 18 34 59 [95]
$+2^2$ $+3^2$ $+4^2$ $+5^2$ $+6^2$

6. (*d*) Pattern of the given series is,

98 50 26 14 [8] 5
÷2+1 ÷2+1 ÷2+1 ÷2+1 ÷2+1

7. (*a*) Pattern of the given series is,

+9 +9 +9 +9 +9
$\frac{5}{9}$ $\frac{14}{9}$ $\frac{23}{9}$ $\frac{32}{9}$ $\frac{41}{9}$ $\boxed{\frac{50}{9}}$

8. (*d*) Pattern of the given series is,

1, 1, 9, 27, 25, 125, [49,] 343,
1^2 1^3 3^2 3^3 5^2 5^3 7^2 7^3

9. (*c*) Pattern of the given series is,

2 9 28 65 126 [217]
1^3+1 2^3+1 3^3+1 4^3+1 5^3+1 6^3+1

10. (*c*) Pattern of the given series is,

9 5 6 10.5 23 [60]
×.5+.5 ×1+1 ×1.5+1.5 ×2+2 ×2.5+2.5

11. (*b*) Pattern of the given series is,

129, 128, 124, 115, 99, [74]
–1 –4 –9 –16 –25
1^2 2^2 3^2 4^2 5^2

12. (*a*) Pattern of the given series is,

+10 +10 +10
65 88 77 98 91 108 [107] 118 125
+12 +14 +16 +18

13. (*a*) Pattern of the given series is,

11, 39, 75, 119, [171]
+28 +36 +44 +52
+8 +8 +8

14. (*b*) Pattern of the given series is,

7, 16, 43, 124, 367, [1096]
+9 +27 +81 +243 +729
3^2 3^3 3^4 3^5 3^6

15. (*d*) Pattern of the given series is,

286 257 230 205 [182] 161
–29 –27 –25 –23 –21
+2 +2 +2 +2

16. (*b*) Pattern of the given series is,

25, 40, 70, 115, 175, [250]
+15 +30 +45 +60 +75
+15 +15 +15 +15

17. (*a*) Pattern of the given series is,

433 414 376 319 243 [148]
–19 –38 –57 –76 –95
–19 –19 –19 –19

18. (*b*) Pattern of the given series is,

23 27 43 79 143 [243]
+4 +16 +36 +64 +100
$(2)^2$ $(4)^2$ $(6)^2$ $(8)^2$ $(10)^2$

TOP TIPS To solve such questions, it is very important for candidate to remember the square of numbers at least from 1 to 30.

19. (*c*) Pattern of the given series is,
2, 3, 6, 18, ?, 1944
$2\times3=6$
$3\times6=18$
$6\times18=\boxed{108}$
$18\times108=1944$

20. (*c*) Pattern of the given series is,

5 19 49 101 [181]
+14 +30 +52 +80
+16 +22 +28
+6 +6

21. (*d*) Pattern of the given series is,

1000 759 618 545 514 [505]
–241 –141 –73 –31 –9
+100 +68 +42 +22
–32 –26 –20
+6 +6

22. (*d*) Pattern of the given series is,

$\frac{1}{121}$ $\frac{1}{11}$ 1 [11] 121
×11 ×11 ×11 ×11

23. (*d*) Pattern of the given series is,

8 23 38 53 68 [83]
+15 +15 +15 +15 +15

24. (*b*) Pattern of the given series is,

15 25 45 85 165 [325]
+10 +20 +40 +80 +160
×2 ×2 ×2 ×2

25. (*a*) Pattern of the given series is,

39 42 48 57 69 [84] 102
+3 +6 +9 +12 +15 +18
+3 +3 +3 +3 +3

26. (*a*) Pattern of the given series is,

125 25 5 [1] $\frac{1}{5}$ $\frac{1}{25}$ $\frac{1}{125}$

÷5 ÷5 ÷5 ÷5 ÷5 ÷5

27. (*b*) Pattern of the given series is,

1, 6, 15, 28, [45], [66], 91

+5 +9 +13 +17 +21 +25

+4 +4 +4 +4 +4

Hence, required numbers are 45 and 66.

> **TOP TIPS** If the difference between every two terms of the series is fixed or minimum, then the operations of addition or subtraction can be used.

28. (*d*) Pattern of the given series is,

12 37 110 331 992 [2977]

×3+1 ×3–1 ×3+1 ×3–1 ×3+1

29. (*a*) Pattern of the given series is,

33 $\xrightarrow{+47}$ 80 $\xrightarrow{+28}$ 108 $\xrightarrow{+47}$ [155] $\xrightarrow{+28}$ 183 $\xrightarrow{+47}$ 230 $\xrightarrow{+28}$ 258

30. (*a*) Pattern of the given series is,

549, 525, 477, 405, 309, [189]

–24 –48 –72 –96 –120

–24 –24 –24 –24

31. (*c*) Pattern of the given series is,

$\frac{-1}{729}$ $\frac{-1}{81}$ $\frac{-1}{9}$ [–1]

×9 ×9 ×9

32. (*c*) Pattern of the given series is,

6 12 5 11 4 10 3 [9] [2]

+6 –7 +6 –7 +6 –7 +6 –7

33. (*b*) Pattern of the given series is,

19 38 35 [140] 135 810

×2 –3 ×4 –5 ×6

34. (*a*) Pattern of the given series is,

213 216 221 228 237 [248] 261 [276]

+3 +5 +7 +9 +11 +13 +15

35. (*b*) Pattern of the given series is,

3 18 90 360 1080 2160 [2160] 0

×6 ×5 ×4 ×3 ×2 ×1 ×0

36. (*c*) Pattern of the given series is,

3 20 38 52 75 82 114 [110]

+17 +18 +14 +23 +7 +32 –4

+1 –4 +9 –16 +25 –36

1^2 $-(2)^2$ 3^2 $-(4)^2$ 5^2 $-(6)^2$

37. (*a*) Pattern of the given series is,

990 962 934 906 878 [850]

–28 –28 –28 –28 –28

38. (*a*) Pattern of the given series is,

146 – 90 = 56

90 – 56 = 34

56 – 34 = 22

34 – 22 = [12]

39. (*b*) Pattern of the given series is,

21 [42] 45 180 185

×2 +3 ×4 +5

40. (*a*) Pattern of the given series is,

25 26 53 160 641 [3206]

×1+1 ×2+1 ×3+1 ×4+1 ×5+1

41. (*c*) Pattern of the given series is,

361 348 335 322 309 [296]

–13 –13 –13 –13 –13

42. (*a*) Pattern of the given series is,

9 72 243 576 [1125]

9×1^3 9×2^3 9×3^3 9×4^3 9×5^3

43. (*d*) Pattern of the given series is,

142 150 123 187 62 [278]

$+2^3$ -3^3 $+4^3$ -5^3 $+6^3$

44. (*a*) Pattern of the given series is,

22 4 16 24 6 36 26 8 64 28 10 [100]

+2 +2 +2

4^2 6^2 8^2 10^2

45. (*d*) Pattern of the given series is,

25, 36, 49, [64], 81, [100], 121

5^2 6^2 7^2 8^2 9^2 10^2 11^2

A = 64 and

B = 100

∴ B + A = 100 + 64 = [164]

46. (*a*) Pattern of the given series is,

G J M P [S]

+3 +3 +3 +3

47. (*b*) Pattern of the given series is,

A B C D [E] F

+1 +1 +1 +1 +1

48. (*b*) Pattern of the given series is,

A $\xrightarrow{+2}$ C $\xrightarrow{+3}$ F $\xrightarrow{+2}$ H $\xrightarrow{+3}$ K $\xrightarrow{+2}$ M $\xrightarrow{+3}$ [P] $\xrightarrow{+2}$ [R]

49. (*a*) Pattern of the given series is,

N $\xrightarrow{+1}$ O $\xrightarrow{+2}$ Q $\xrightarrow{+3}$ T $\xrightarrow{+4}$ X $\xrightarrow{+5}$ C $\xrightarrow{+6}$ [I]

50. (*a*) Pattern of the given series is,

J $\xrightarrow{+1}$ K $\xrightarrow{+2}$ M $\xrightarrow{+3}$ [P] $\xrightarrow{+4}$ T $\xrightarrow{+5}$ Y

51. (*c*) Pattern of the given series is,

A $\xrightarrow{+3}$ D $\xrightarrow{+4}$ H $\xrightarrow{+5}$ M $\xrightarrow{+6}$ S $\xrightarrow{+7}$ [Z]

52. (*d*) Pattern of the given series is,

B $\xrightarrow{+2}$ D $\xrightarrow{+4}$ H $\xrightarrow{+6}$ [N] $\xrightarrow{+8}$ V

53. (*d*) Pattern of the given series is,

B $\xrightarrow{+1}$ C $\xrightarrow{+3}$ F $\xrightarrow{+5}$ K $\xrightarrow{+7}$ [R]

J $\xrightarrow{+2}$ L $\xrightarrow{+3}$ O $\xrightarrow{+4}$ S $\xrightarrow{+5}$ [X]

54. (*a*) Pattern of the given series is,

D $\xrightarrow{+4}$ H $\xrightarrow{+6}$ N $\xrightarrow{+4}$ R $\xrightarrow{+6}$ X $\xrightarrow{+4}$ [B]

A $\xrightarrow{+4}$ E $\xrightarrow{+6}$ K $\xrightarrow{+4}$ O $\xrightarrow{+6}$ U $\xrightarrow{+4}$ [Y]

55. (*b*) Pattern of the given series is,

B $\xrightarrow{+1}$ C $\xrightarrow{+1}$ D $\xrightarrow{+1}$ E $\xrightarrow{+1}$ [F]

E $\xrightarrow{+1}$ F $\xrightarrow{+1}$ G $\xrightarrow{+1}$ H $\xrightarrow{+1}$ [I]

G $\xrightarrow{+1}$ H $\xrightarrow{+1}$ I $\xrightarrow{+1}$ J $\xrightarrow{+1}$ [K]

56. (*d*) Pattern of the given series is,

J $\xrightarrow{+1}$ K $\xrightarrow{+1}$ L $\xrightarrow{+1}$ M $\xrightarrow{+1}$ [N]

L $\xrightarrow{+1}$ M $\xrightarrow{+1}$ N $\xrightarrow{+1}$ O $\xrightarrow{+1}$ [P]

O $\xrightarrow{+1}$ P $\xrightarrow{+1}$ Q $\xrightarrow{+1}$ R $\xrightarrow{+1}$ [S]

57. (*a*) Pattern of the given series is,

Y $\xrightarrow{-2}$ W $\xrightarrow{-2}$ U $\xrightarrow{-2}$ S $\xrightarrow{-2}$ [Q]

U $\xrightarrow{-2}$ S $\xrightarrow{-2}$ Q $\xrightarrow{-2}$ O $\xrightarrow{-2}$ [M]

S $\xrightarrow{-2}$ Q $\xrightarrow{-2}$ O $\xrightarrow{-2}$ M $\xrightarrow{-2}$ [K]

58. (*b*) Pattern of the given series is,

$$F \xrightarrow{+6} L \xrightarrow{+6} \boxed{R} \xrightarrow{+6} X \xrightarrow{+6} D$$
$$N \xrightarrow{+7} U \xrightarrow{+7} \boxed{B} \xrightarrow{+7} I \xrightarrow{+7} P$$
$$V \xrightarrow{+9} E \xrightarrow{+9} \boxed{N} \xrightarrow{+9} W \xrightarrow{+9} F$$

59. (*a*) Pattern of the given series is,

$$D \xrightarrow{+7} K \xrightarrow{+7} R \xrightarrow{+7} Y \xrightarrow{+7} \boxed{F}$$
$$F \xrightarrow{+7} M \xrightarrow{+7} T \xrightarrow{+7} A \xrightarrow{+7} \boxed{H}$$
$$H \xrightarrow{+7} O \xrightarrow{+7} V \xrightarrow{+7} C \xrightarrow{+7} \boxed{J}$$

60. (*a*) Pattern of the given series is,

$$B \xrightarrow{+2} D \xrightarrow{+2} F \xrightarrow{+2} \boxed{H}$$
$$D \xrightarrow{+4} H \xrightarrow{+4} L \xrightarrow{+4} \boxed{P}$$
$$F \xrightarrow{+6} L \xrightarrow{+6} R \xrightarrow{+6} \boxed{X}$$

61. (*c*) Pattern of the given series is,

$$D \xrightarrow{+4} H \xrightarrow{+4} L \xrightarrow{+4} P \xrightarrow{+4} \boxed{T}$$
$$M \xrightarrow{+8} U \xrightarrow{+8} C \xrightarrow{+8} K \xrightarrow{+8} \boxed{S}$$
$$Q \xrightarrow{+9} Z \xrightarrow{+9} I \xrightarrow{+9} R \xrightarrow{+9} \boxed{A}$$

62. (*b*) Pattern of the given series is,

$$V \xrightarrow{-2} T \xrightarrow{-4} P \xrightarrow{-2} N \xrightarrow{-4} \boxed{J}$$
$$R \xrightarrow{+1} S \xrightarrow{+2} U \xrightarrow{+1} V \xrightarrow{+2} \boxed{X}$$
$$S \xrightarrow{-4} O \xrightarrow{-4} K \xrightarrow{-4} G \xrightarrow{-4} \boxed{C}$$

63. (*b*) Pattern of the given series is,

$$J \xrightarrow{+5} O \xrightarrow{+5} \boxed{T} \xrightarrow{+5} Y \xrightarrow{+5} D$$
$$M \xrightarrow{-5} H \xrightarrow{-5} \boxed{C} \xrightarrow{-5} X \xrightarrow{-5} S$$
$$D \xrightarrow{+6} J \xrightarrow{+6} \boxed{P} \xrightarrow{+6} V \xrightarrow{+6} B$$

64. (*a*) Pattern of the given series is,

$$A \xrightarrow{+3} D \xrightarrow{+3} G \xrightarrow{+3} \boxed{J} \xrightarrow{+3} M$$
$$Y \xrightarrow{-3} V \xrightarrow{-4} R \xrightarrow{-5} \boxed{M} \xrightarrow{-6} G$$
$$D \xrightarrow{+2} F \xrightarrow{+2} H \xrightarrow{+2} \boxed{J} \xrightarrow{+2} L$$

65. (*b*) Pattern of the given series is,

$$O \xrightarrow{+3} R \xrightarrow{+3} U \xrightarrow{+3} X \xrightarrow{+3} \boxed{A}$$
$$L \xrightarrow{-7} E \xrightarrow{-7} X \xrightarrow{-7} Q \xrightarrow{-7} \boxed{J}$$
$$R \xrightarrow{+8} Z \xrightarrow{+8} H \xrightarrow{+8} P \xrightarrow{+8} \boxed{X}$$

66. (*a*) Pattern of the given series is,

$$C \xrightarrow{+1} D \xrightarrow{+1} E \xrightarrow{+1} \boxed{F}$$
$$H \xrightarrow{+1} I \xrightarrow{+1} J \xrightarrow{+1} \boxed{K}$$
$$O \xrightarrow{+1} P \xrightarrow{+1} Q \xrightarrow{+1} \boxed{R}$$

67. (*c*) Pattern of the given series is,

$$K \xrightarrow{-3} H \xrightarrow{-3} E \xrightarrow{-3} B \xrightarrow{-3} Y \xrightarrow{-3} \boxed{V}$$
$$J \xrightarrow{-3} G \xrightarrow{-3} D \xrightarrow{-3} A \xrightarrow{-3} X \xrightarrow{-3} \boxed{U}$$
$$I \xrightarrow{-3} F \xrightarrow{-3} C \xrightarrow{-3} Z \xrightarrow{-3} W \xrightarrow{-3} \boxed{T}$$

68. (*b*) Pattern of the given series is,

$$A \xrightarrow{+4} E \xrightarrow{+4} I \xrightarrow{+4} M \xrightarrow{+4} Q \xrightarrow{+4} \boxed{U}$$
$$B \xrightarrow{+4} F \xrightarrow{+4} J \xrightarrow{+4} N \xrightarrow{+4} R \xrightarrow{+4} \boxed{V}$$
$$C \xrightarrow{+4} G \xrightarrow{+4} K \xrightarrow{+4} O \xrightarrow{+4} S \xrightarrow{+4} \boxed{W}$$

69. (*c*) Pattern of the given series is,

$$L \xrightarrow{-1} K \xrightarrow{-1} J \xrightarrow{-1} \boxed{I} \xrightarrow{-1} H \xrightarrow{-1} G \xrightarrow{-1} F$$
$$A \xrightarrow{+1\text{vowel}} E \xrightarrow{+1\text{vowel}} I \xrightarrow{+1\text{vowel}} \boxed{O} \xrightarrow{+1\text{vowel}} U \xrightarrow{+1\text{vowel}} A \xrightarrow{+1\text{vowel}} E$$
$$P \xrightarrow{+1} Q \xrightarrow{+1} R \xrightarrow{+1} \boxed{S} \xrightarrow{+1} T \xrightarrow{+1} U \xrightarrow{+1} V$$

> **TOP TIPS**
> In English alphabetical series, there are 5 vowels (a, e, i, o, u) and 21 consonants. Sometimes separate operations are being performed on vowels in a series.

70. (*d*) Pattern of the given series is,

$$H \xrightarrow{-6} B \xrightarrow{-6} V \xrightarrow{-6} P \xrightarrow{-6} \boxed{J}$$
$$L \xrightarrow{-6} F \xrightarrow{-6} Z \xrightarrow{-6} T \xrightarrow{-6} \boxed{N}$$
$$A \xrightarrow{-6} U \xrightarrow{-6} O \xrightarrow{-6} I \xrightarrow{-6} \boxed{C}$$

71. (*a*) Pattern of the given series is,

$$S \xrightarrow{-7} L \xrightarrow{-7} E \xrightarrow{-7} \boxed{X}$$
$$Q \xrightarrow{-7} J \xrightarrow{-7} C \xrightarrow{-7} \boxed{V}$$
$$O \xrightarrow{-7} H \xrightarrow{-7} A \xrightarrow{-7} \boxed{T}$$

72. (*d*) Pattern of the given series is,

$$W \xrightarrow{-2} U \xrightarrow{-2} S \xrightarrow{-2} Q \xrightarrow{-2} \boxed{O}$$
$$V \xrightarrow{-2} T \xrightarrow{-2} R \xrightarrow{-2} P \xrightarrow{-2} \boxed{N}$$
$$E \xrightarrow{+2} G \xrightarrow{+2} I \xrightarrow{+2} K \xrightarrow{+2} \boxed{M}$$

73. (*b*) Pattern of the given series is,

$$R \xrightarrow{-4} N \xrightarrow{-4} J \xrightarrow{-4} F \xrightarrow{-4} \boxed{B}$$
$$S \xrightarrow{-2} Q \xrightarrow{-2} O \xrightarrow{-2} M \xrightarrow{-2} \boxed{K}$$
$$X \xrightarrow{-1} W \xrightarrow{-1} V \xrightarrow{-1} U \xrightarrow{-1} \boxed{T}$$

74. (*b*) Pattern of the given series is,

$$Y \xrightarrow{-3} V \xrightarrow{-3} S \xrightarrow{-3} P \xrightarrow{-3} \boxed{M}$$
$$E \xrightarrow{+1} F \xrightarrow{+1} G \xrightarrow{+1} H \xrightarrow{+1} \boxed{I}$$
$$F \xrightarrow{+3} I \xrightarrow{+3} L \xrightarrow{+3} O \xrightarrow{+3} \boxed{R}$$

75. (*a*) Pattern of the given series is,

$$H \xrightarrow{+3} K \xrightarrow{+3} N \xrightarrow{+3} Q \xrightarrow{+3} \boxed{T}$$
$$I \xrightarrow{+3} L \xrightarrow{+3} O \xrightarrow{+3} R \xrightarrow{+3} \boxed{U}$$
$$F \xrightarrow{+3} I \xrightarrow{+3} L \xrightarrow{+3} O \xrightarrow{+3} \boxed{R}$$

76. (*a*) Pattern of the given series is,

$$C \xrightarrow{-3} Z \xrightarrow{-3} W \xrightarrow{-3} T \xrightarrow{-3} \boxed{Q}$$
$$A \xrightarrow{+4} E \xrightarrow{+4} I \xrightarrow{+4} M \xrightarrow{+4} \boxed{Q}$$
$$L \xrightarrow{-5} G \xrightarrow{-5} B \xrightarrow{-5} W \xrightarrow{-5} \boxed{R}$$
$$I \xrightarrow{+6} O \xrightarrow{+6} U \xrightarrow{+6} A \xrightarrow{+6} \boxed{G}$$

77. (*d*) Pattern of the given series is,

$$F \xrightarrow{+1} G \xrightarrow{+1} \boxed{H} \xrightarrow{+1} I$$
$$D \xrightarrow{-1} C \xrightarrow{-1} \boxed{B} \xrightarrow{-1} A$$
$$K \xrightarrow{+2} M \xrightarrow{+2} \boxed{O} \xrightarrow{+2} Q$$
$$I \xrightarrow{-2} G \xrightarrow{-2} \boxed{E} \xrightarrow{-2} C$$

78. (*c*) Pattern of the given series is,

$$J \xrightarrow{+2} L \xrightarrow{+2} \boxed{N} \xrightarrow{+2} P$$
$$O \xrightarrow{+2} Q \xrightarrow{+2} \boxed{S} \xrightarrow{+2} U$$
$$Q \xrightarrow{+2} S \xrightarrow{+2} \boxed{U} \xrightarrow{+2} W$$
$$W \xrightarrow{+2} Y \xrightarrow{+2} \boxed{A} \xrightarrow{+2} C$$

79. (*d*) Pattern of the given series is,

$$Y \xrightarrow{-4} \boxed{U} \xrightarrow{-4} Q \xrightarrow{-4} M \xrightarrow{-4} I$$
$$Z \xrightarrow{-3} \boxed{W} \xrightarrow{-3} T \xrightarrow{-3} Q \xrightarrow{-3} N$$
$$U \xrightarrow{-2} \boxed{S} \xrightarrow{-2} Q \xrightarrow{-2} O \xrightarrow{-2} M$$
$$W \xrightarrow{-1} \boxed{V} \xrightarrow{-1} U \xrightarrow{-1} T \xrightarrow{-1} S$$

80. (*b*) Pattern of the given series is,

$$H \xrightarrow{+3} K \xrightarrow{+3} \boxed{N} \xrightarrow{+3} Q \xrightarrow{+3} T$$
$$E \xrightarrow{+4} I \xrightarrow{+4} \boxed{M} \xrightarrow{+4} Q \xrightarrow{+4} U$$
$$W \xrightarrow{-5} R \xrightarrow{-5} \boxed{M} \xrightarrow{-5} H \xrightarrow{-5} C$$
$$C \xrightarrow{+6} I \xrightarrow{+6} \boxed{O} \xrightarrow{+6} U \xrightarrow{+6} A$$

81. (*b*) Pattern of the given series is,

$$B \xrightarrow{+1} \boxed{C} \xrightarrow{-3} Z \xrightarrow{+5} E \xrightarrow{-7} X$$
$$W \xrightarrow{+1} \boxed{X} \xrightarrow{-3} U \xrightarrow{+5} Z \xrightarrow{-7} S$$
$$U \xrightarrow{+1} \boxed{V} \xrightarrow{-3} S \xrightarrow{+5} X \xrightarrow{-7} Q$$
$$T \xrightarrow{+1} \boxed{U} \xrightarrow{-3} R \xrightarrow{+5} W \xrightarrow{-7} P$$

82. (*a*) Pattern of the given series is,

$$B \xrightarrow{+2} D \xrightarrow{+2} \boxed{F} \xrightarrow{+2} H$$
$$O \xrightarrow{+1} P \xrightarrow{+1} \boxed{Q} \xrightarrow{+1} R$$
$$M \xrightarrow{+2} O \xrightarrow{+2} \boxed{Q} \xrightarrow{+2} S$$
$$P \xrightarrow{+1} Q \xrightarrow{+1} \boxed{R} \xrightarrow{+1} S$$

83. (*b*) Pattern of the given series is,

$$E \xrightarrow{+1} F \xrightarrow{+1} G \xrightarrow{+1} \boxed{H} \xrightarrow{+1} I$$
$$L \xrightarrow{-2} J \xrightarrow{-2} H \xrightarrow{-2} \boxed{F} \xrightarrow{-2} D$$
$$S \xrightarrow{+3} V \xrightarrow{+3} Y \xrightarrow{+3} \boxed{B} \xrightarrow{+3} E$$
$$V \xrightarrow{-4} R \xrightarrow{-4} N \xrightarrow{-4} \boxed{J} \xrightarrow{-4} F$$

84. (*b*) Pattern of the given series is,

$A \xrightarrow{-3} X \xrightarrow{-3} U \xrightarrow{-3} \boxed{R}$
$E \xrightarrow{-3} B \xrightarrow{-3} Y \xrightarrow{-3} \boxed{V}$
$J \xrightarrow{-3} G \xrightarrow{-3} D \xrightarrow{-3} \boxed{A}$
$O \xrightarrow{-3} L \xrightarrow{-3} I \xrightarrow{-3} \boxed{F}$
$T \xrightarrow{-3} Q \xrightarrow{-3} N \xrightarrow{-3} \boxed{K}$

85. (*d*) Pattern of the given series is,

$Z \xrightarrow{-4} V \xrightarrow{-4} R \xrightarrow{-4} \boxed{N} \xrightarrow{-4} J$
$V \xrightarrow{-3} S \xrightarrow{-3} P \xrightarrow{-3} \boxed{M} \xrightarrow{-3} J$
$R \xrightarrow{-2} P \xrightarrow{-2} N \xrightarrow{-2} \boxed{L} \xrightarrow{-2} J$
$N \xrightarrow{-1} M \xrightarrow{-1} L \xrightarrow{-1} \boxed{K} \xrightarrow{-1} J$

> **TOP TIPS** To solve this type of questions candidate must remember the forward and reverse alphabetical positions of letters.

86. (*a*) Pattern of the given series is,

$P \xrightarrow{+6} V \xrightarrow{+6} B \xrightarrow{+6} H \xrightarrow{+6} \boxed{N}$
$J \xrightarrow{-8} B \xrightarrow{-8} T \xrightarrow{-8} L \xrightarrow{-8} \boxed{D}$
$V \xrightarrow{+4} Z \xrightarrow{+4} D \xrightarrow{+4} H \xrightarrow{+4} \boxed{L}$
$G \xrightarrow{-5} B \xrightarrow{-5} W \xrightarrow{-5} R \xrightarrow{-5} \boxed{M}$

87. (*b*) Pattern of the given series is,

C-3 E-5 G-7 I-9 $\boxed{K\text{-}11}$ $\boxed{M\text{-}13}$
(letters: +2 +2 +2 +2 +2; numbers: +2 +2 +2 +2 +2)

88. (*a*) Pattern of the given series is,

C 81 E 64 $\boxed{G}$ 49 I $\boxed{36}$ K
(letters: +2 +2 +2 +2; numbers: 9^2, 8^2, 7^2, 6^2)

89. (*a*) Pattern of the given series is,

B 9 U E 16 R H 25 O $\boxed{K\ 36\ L}$
(first letters: +3 +3 +3; numbers: 3^2, 4^2, 5^2, 6^2; last letters: –3 –3 –3)

90. (*b*) Pattern of the given series is,

$U \xrightarrow{+1} V \xrightarrow{+1} W \xrightarrow{+1} X \xrightarrow{+1} \boxed{Y}$
$E \xrightarrow{+2} G \xrightarrow{+2} I \xrightarrow{+2} K \xrightarrow{+2} \boxed{M}$
$88 \xrightarrow{-4} 84 \xrightarrow{-4} 80 \xrightarrow{-4} 76 \xrightarrow{-4} \boxed{72}$

91. (*b*) Pattern of the given series is,

$E \xrightarrow{+2} \boxed{G} \xrightarrow{+2} I \xrightarrow{+2} K \xrightarrow{+2} M$
$Z \xrightarrow{+2} \boxed{B} \xrightarrow{+2} D \xrightarrow{+2} F \xrightarrow{+2} H$
$10 \xrightarrow{+13} \boxed{23} \xrightarrow{+13} 36 \xrightarrow{+13} 49 \xrightarrow{+13} 62$

92. (*d*) Pattern of the given series is,

$J \xrightarrow{+2} L \xrightarrow{+2} \boxed{N} \xrightarrow{+2} P \xrightarrow{+2} R$
$Z \xrightarrow{-4} V \xrightarrow{-4} \boxed{R} \xrightarrow{-4} N \xrightarrow{-4} J$
$I \xrightarrow{+3} L \xrightarrow{+3} \boxed{O} \xrightarrow{+3} R \xrightarrow{+3} U$
$3 \xrightarrow{\times 3} 9 \xrightarrow{\times 3} \boxed{27} \xrightarrow{\times 3} 81 \xrightarrow{\times 3} 243$

93. (*b*) Pattern of the given series is,

A (+2) → C, Z (–2) → X, X (–2) → V, C (+2) → E, E (+2) → G, V (–2) → T, T (–2) → $\boxed{R}$, G (+2) → $\boxed{I}$

Number series 1, 3, 3, 9, ?
$\Rightarrow 1 \times 3 = 3$
$\Rightarrow 3 \times 3 = 9$
$\Rightarrow 3 \times 9 = \boxed{27}$
and 1, 3, 4, 7, ?
$\Rightarrow 1 + 3 = 4$
$\Rightarrow 3 + 4 = 7$
$\Rightarrow 4 + 7 = \boxed{11}$
Hence, next term willl be I27R11.

94. (*b*) Pattern of the given series is,

$X \xrightarrow{+1} Y \xrightarrow{+1} \boxed{Z} \xrightarrow{+1} A \xrightarrow{+1} B$
$D \xrightarrow{+1} E \xrightarrow{+1} \boxed{F} \xrightarrow{+1} G \xrightarrow{+1} H$
$45 \xrightarrow{+8} 53 \xrightarrow{-3} \boxed{50} \xrightarrow{+8} 58 \xrightarrow{-3} 55$

95. (*b*) Pattern of the given series is,

$T \xrightarrow{+1} U \xrightarrow{+1} V \xrightarrow{+1} W \xrightarrow{+1} X \xrightarrow{+1} \boxed{Y}$
$J \xrightarrow{+2} L \xrightarrow{+2} N \xrightarrow{+2} P \xrightarrow{+2} R \xrightarrow{+2} \boxed{T}$
$M \xrightarrow{+3} P \xrightarrow{+3} S \xrightarrow{+3} V \xrightarrow{+3} Y \xrightarrow{+3} \boxed{B}$
$10 \xrightarrow{+2} 12 \xrightarrow{+2} 14 \xrightarrow{+2} 16 \xrightarrow{+2} 18 \xrightarrow{+2} \boxed{20}$

96. (*b*) Pattern of the given series is,

$F \xrightarrow{-1} E \xrightarrow{-1} D \xrightarrow{-1} C \xrightarrow{-1} \boxed{B}$
$M \xrightarrow{-2} K \xrightarrow{-2} I \xrightarrow{-2} G \xrightarrow{-2} \boxed{E}$
$61 \xrightarrow{-3} 58 \xrightarrow{-3} 55 \xrightarrow{-3} 52 \xrightarrow{-3} \boxed{49}$

97. (*a*) Pattern of the given series is,

$D \xrightarrow{-5} Y \xrightarrow{-5} T \xrightarrow{-5} O$
$E \xrightarrow{-10} U \xrightarrow{-10} K \xrightarrow{-10} A$
$\boxed{F} \xrightarrow{-5} A \xrightarrow{-5} \boxed{V} \xrightarrow{-5} Q$
$G \xrightarrow{+0} \boxed{G} \xrightarrow{+0} G \xrightarrow{+0} \boxed{G}$

∴ Required term = FGVG

98. (*b*) Pattern of the given series is,

$C \xrightarrow{-7} V \xrightarrow{-7} \boxed{O} \xrightarrow{-7} H \xrightarrow{-7} A$
$B \xrightarrow{-7} \boxed{U} \xrightarrow{-7} N \xrightarrow{-7} G \xrightarrow{-7} \boxed{Z}$
$\boxed{Z} \xrightarrow{-7} S \xrightarrow{-7} L \xrightarrow{-7} \boxed{E} \xrightarrow{-7} X$
$W \xrightarrow{-7} P \xrightarrow{-7} I \xrightarrow{-7} B \xrightarrow{-7} U$

∴ Required term = ZUOEZ

99. (*b*) Pattern of the given series is,
A <u>B</u> A <u>B</u> C / A B <u>A</u> B <u>C</u> / A <u>B</u> <u>A</u> B C / A B A <u>B</u> C
Required combination = BBACBAB

100. (*c*) Pattern of the given series is,
<u>a</u> c <u>b</u> d / d <u>b</u> c a / <u>a</u> c b d / d b <u>c</u> a
⇒ a b b a c

101. (*c*) Pattern of the given series is,
R E M / R R E <u>M</u> / R <u>R</u> E E M / R R E <u>E</u> M <u>M</u>
∴ Required combination = M R E M

102. (*d*) Pattern of the given series is,
<u>A</u> B C D <u>D</u> <u>E</u> / A B C <u>D</u> <u>D</u> E / <u>A</u> B C <u>D</u> <u>D</u> <u>E</u> / A B C <u>D</u> D E
⇒ ADEDDADDED

103. (*c*) Pattern of the given series is,
L M B A <u>C</u> H O / L M B A C <u>H</u> O / L M <u>B</u> A C H O / L <u>M</u> B A C H O / L <u>M</u> ⇒ C H B M M

104. (*d*) Pattern of the given series is,
<u>n</u> ml <u>m</u> nl / <u>n</u> ml m <u>n</u> l / <u>n</u> ml mn <u>l</u>
⇒ nmnnnl

105. (*a*) Pattern of the given series is,
Y R G <u>T</u> / Y R G <u>S</u> / Y R G <u>R</u> / <u>Y</u> R G <u>Q</u>
(–1 –1 –1)
⇒ GSYQ

106. (*c*) Pattern of the given series is,
<u>H</u> J H / <u>H</u> J H / H <u>J</u> H / H J <u>H</u>
⇒ HJJH

107. (*b*) Pattern of the given series is,

$A \xrightarrow{+6} G \xrightarrow{+6} M \xrightarrow{+6} \boxed{S} \xrightarrow{+6} Y$
$\boxed{C} \xrightarrow{+6} I \xrightarrow{+6} O \xrightarrow{+6} U \xrightarrow{+6} A$
$D \xrightarrow{+6} \boxed{J} \xrightarrow{+6} P \xrightarrow{+6} V \xrightarrow{+6} \boxed{B}$
$F \xrightarrow{+6} L \xrightarrow{+6} \boxed{R} \xrightarrow{+6} X \xrightarrow{+6} D$

⇒ CJRSB

108. (*a*) Pattern of the given series is,
From option (a)
nm <u>m</u> <u>n</u> mp / n <u>m</u> <u>m</u> nmp / nm <u>m</u> <u>n</u> <u>m</u> <u>p</u> / nm <u>m</u> <u>n</u> mp
⇒ m n m m m n m m n

109. (*b*) In the given series start with word 'CLOVE' and fourth letter is increases by 1.
C L O V E / C L O W E / C L O X E / C L O Y E
(+1 +1 +1)
Hence, the correct answer is 'OLOXELY'.

110. (*c*) Pattern of the given series is,

a ba c a / abac a / a ba c a / a b a c a

⇒ acaaacba

> **TOP TIPS** In this type of questions the repeating pattern can be easily find out by placing the letters given in the option in the blank spaces one by one separately.

111. (*d*) Pattern of the given series is,

+5 +5 +5 +5

C N E F / H N E K / M N E P / R N E U / W N E Z

+5 +5 +5 +5

⇒ NKMEZ

112. (*a*) Pattern of the given series is,

BVJRW / BVKRW / BVLRW / BVMRW

+1 +1 +1

⇒ BVKRWMR

113. (*b*) Pattern of the given series is,

+6 +6 +6 +6

G A J B / M A P B / S A V B / Y A B B / E A H B

+6 +6 +6 +6

⇒ JAVBE

114. (*a*) Pattern of the given series is,

1 3 12 60 [340] (360)

×3 ×4 ×5 ×6

Hence, '340' is wrong term.

115. (*d*) Pattern of the given series is,

2 6 18 54 [161] (162) 486

×3 ×3 ×3 ×3 ×3

Hence, '161' is wrong term.

116. (*a*) Pattern of the given series is,

4 7 13 [21] (22) 34

+3 +6 +9 +12

+3 +3 +3

Hence, '21' is the wrong term.

117. (*d*) Pattern of the given series is,

324 [109] (108) 36 12 4

÷3 ÷3 ÷3 ÷3

Hence, '109' is the wrong term.

118. (*d*) Pattern of the given series is,

+1 +3 +5 +7

4 11 6 12 10 15 16 20 [22] (24) 27

+2 +4 +6 +8

Hence, '22' is the wrong term.

119. (*a*) Pattern of the given series is,

9 15 24 [34] (36) 51 69

+6 +9 +12 +15 +18

+3 +3 +3 +3

Hence, '34' is the wrong term.

120. (*c*) Pattern of the given series is,

486 482 478 474 [472] (470) 466 462

−4 −4 −4 −4 −4 −4

Hence, '472' is the wrong term.

121. (*d*) Pattern of the given series is,

104 108 54 58 29 [31] (33)

+4 ÷2 +4 ÷2 +4

Hence, '31' is the wrong term.

122. (*a*) Pattern of the given series is,

33792 8448 [2148] (2112) 528 132 33 8.25

÷4 ÷4 ÷4 ÷4 ÷4 ÷4

Hence, '2148' is the wrong term.

123. (*c*) Pattern of the given series is,

A →(+4) E →(+4) I →(+4) [N] (M) →(+4) Q

Z →(−4) V →(−4) R →(−4) [O] (N) →(−4) J

Hence, 'NO' is the wrong term.

124. (*c*) Pattern of the given series is,

A →(+1) B →(+1) [C] →(+1) D →(+1) E

A →(+3) D →(+3) [J] (G) →(+3) J →(+3) M

Hence, 'CJ' is the wrong term.

125. (*c*) Pattern of the given series is,

$(1)^2$ $(3)^2$ $(5)^2$ $(7)^2$ $(9)^2$

A1 C9 E25 G49 [I 89] (I 81)

+2 +2 +2 +2

Hence, I89 is the wrong term.

CHAPTER 08

Conditional Number/ Letter/Symbol

Conditional Number / Letter / Symbol

In this chapter some numbers /letters/symbols in a series or in a group are given which are to be arranged according to a certain rule/condition. Based on that rule/conditions candidate has to find certain number/letter/symbol or total number of elements in the group/series.

Based on Number Series

In this type, a number series is given along with some condition and based on this condition, the candidate needs to find the desired number or it's total numbers as asked in the question.

e.g. In series 1891358913915791 how many times the digit 9 is immediately preceded by 8 and followed by 1?

(a) 0 (b) 1 (c) 2 (d) 3

Sol. (c) According to the series,

1891358913915791

∴ Required 9's are 2.

Based on Letter Series

In this type, a series of letters is given along with some condition, and based on this condition, candidate needs to find the desired letters and total number of letters as asked in the question.

e.g. In series BCNKLJOKIUKJLOKJLN, How many L are there which is immediately preceded by J.

(a) 0 (b) 1 (c) 3 (d) 2

Sol. (d) According to the given series,

B C N K L J O K I U K J L O K J L N

∴ Required L's are 2.

Based on Numbers, Letters and Symbols Series

In this type, a series of letters, numbers and symbols are given along with some condition. The candidate needs to find the desired number, letter or symbol as asked in the question.

e.g. In series K $ 9 # 23 V 1 * 4 @ 3 & A 12 How many numbers are there which are immediately preceded and followed by a symbol?

(a) 0 (b) 1 (c) 2 (d) 3

Sol. (d) According to the series,

K $ 9 # 23 V 1 * 4 @ 3 & A 12

∴ The required numbers are 3.

Based on Conditional Rearrangement

In this type, a number or group of letters or numbers is given along with some conditions. The candidate needs to rearrange the given group of numbers or letters and find out the desired number or letter asked in the question.

e.g. In the digits of the numbers 597841 are arranged in descending order, then the positions of how many digits will remain unchanged?

(a) Zero (b) One
(c) Two (d) Three

Sol. (d) Given numbers → 5 9 7 8 4 1

After rearranging the numbers → 9 8 7 5 4 1

∴ Only three digits will remain unchanged.

Score Booster

While solving such type of questions, candidates must read the conditions carefully given in the question and must know the right and left direction of series or, preceding and following terms of a given term in a series.

Exam Approach Examples

Based on Number Series

Example 1 How many such 5's are there in the following series which are not immediately preceded and followed by 1?

2 6 2 5 3 5 7 3 5 1 3 5 4 3 5 9 1 2 3 5 1 4 6 3 5 1 8 2 3

UP Police Head Operator 2024

(a) 5 (b) 3 (c) 4 (d) 8

Sol. (*b*) Given series,

2 6 2 5 3 5 7 3 5 1 3 5 4 3 5 9 1 2 3 5 1 4 6 3 5 1 8 2 3

Hence, according to the given condition, required 5 are 3.

Example 2 Which number has come maximum time in the following number series?

5 4 3 3 5 4 8 8 3 2 5 3 6 5 5

(a) 5 (b) 4 (c) 3 (d) 2

Sol. (*a*) Given series, 5 4 3 3 5 4 8 8 3 2 5 3 6 5 5

8 = 2 times, 6 = 1 times, 5 = 5 times, 4 = 2 times

3 = 4 times, 2 = 1 time

Clearly, 5 has come maximum times.

Based on Letter Series

Example 3 If all the vowels are deleted in the given series, then what will be the position of 'Q' from the left end?

DSSSB Workshop Assistant 2024

H J L D S R I Q H B E F P L X A Z J K L

(a) 5th

(b) 6th

(c) 8th

(d) 7th

Sol. (*d*) On deleting the vowels in the given series

H J L D S R Q H B F P L X Z J K L

7th from the left

Hence, the position of Q will be 7th from the left end.

> **Helping Tips**
>
> English alphabet series consists of 26 alphabets out of which 5 (A, E, I, O, U) are called vowels and rest of the alphabets are called consonants.

Example 4 In the following letter series, how many 'JKL' are there which are immediately followed by N?

BCNKLJKLMJKLQJKLMNJKLABJKL

JKLMNJKLSKTKJLLKJNJKLJLTKLT *RRB NTPC CBT-1 2021*

(a) 1 (b) 0

(c) 2 (d) 3

Sol. (*b*) Given series is,

BCNKL JKL M JKL Q JKL MN JKL AB JKL

JKL MN JKL SKTKJLLKJN JKL JLTKLT

Hence, the 'JKL' which are immediately followed by N is '0'.

Based on Number, Letter and Symbol Series

Example 5 If the first half of the given series is written in reverse order, which letter/number will come at the fourteenth place to the left of the sixth place from the right?

U345TETCE463DR45S3403T *Rajasthan Police Constable 2022*

(a) C (b) 4 (c) E (d) 3

Sol. (*c*) Given series,

U 3 4 5 T E T C E 4 6 3 D R 4 5 S 3 4 0 3 T

First half

After writing the first half in reverse order,

6 4 E C T E T 5 4 3 U 3 D R 4 5 S 3 4 0 3 T

Fourteenth to the left Sixth from right

∴ Required letter is E.

Example 6 T%N9*M$3U=L8Y@G&3E>W&4RF!K.

Find out the total number of symbols that are immediately preceded by a number and immediately followed by a letter.

RRC Group D 2022

(a) 1 (b) 2 (c) 4 (d) 3

Sol. (*a*) Given series is,

T% N 9 * M $ 3 U = L 8 Y @ G & 3 E > W & 4 R F ! K.

∴ Required symbol is 1.

Based on Conditional Rearrangement

Example 7 If each digit of the number 7148356 is arranged in ascending order from left to right, then with respect to the original number, the positions of how many digits will remain unchanged?

(a) Three (b) One (c) None (d) Two

Sol. (*b*)

Given numbers ⟶ 7 1 4 8 3 5 6

After arranging in ascending order ⟶ 1 3 4 5 6 7 8

Hence, the number of unchanged digit is one.

Example 8 If the first and the third digit in each numbers are interchanged, then how many odd numbers are formed in the new arrangement.

DSSSB Workshop Assistant 2024

> **Trending Concept**
>
> This type of questions (based on number series) are important for DSSSB and Railway exams. (NTPC and Group D)

964 348 667 679 678

(a) 3 (b) 2 (c) 4 (d) 1

Sol. (*b*) Given numbers ⟶ 964 348 667 679 678

After interchanging the first and third digit of each number,

469 843 766 976 876

Hence, only 2 odd numbers i.e. 469 and 843 are formed.

Chapter Challenge

Based on Number Series

1. Refer to the following number series and answer the question.
(Left) 7 5 3 3 9 1 4 6 2 7 8 3 7 5 6 8 9 1 3 9 5 3 (Right)
Find the sum of all the odd numbers in the above number series. *RRC Group D 2022*
(a) 90 (b) 80 (c) 70 (d) 100

2. Refer to the given series and answer the question that follows (all numbers are single-digit numbers only).
(Left) 5 7 0 5 5 0 9 5 5 9 8 2 9 1 2 8 6 6 9 8 6 9 4 7 2 1 0 1 2 5 (Right)
What is the sum of the 10th digit from the left and the 4th digit from the right? *RRB Technician Grade III 2024*
(a) 10 (b) 9 (c) 8 (d) 11

3. Refer to the given series and answer the question that follows (all numbers are single-digit numbers only).
(Left) 2 7 5 3 1 5 8 7 7 4 0 6 3 1 2 1 9 2 2 6 5 0 8 6 2 7 5 3 9 3 (Right)
What is the sum of the Ist digit from the left and the 15th digit from the right? *RRB Technician Grade III 2024*
(a) 10 (b) 9 (c) 3 (d) 5

4. Which number comes least in the given series?
8 4 6 7 3 4 3 7 8 3 4 4 5 6 3 4 6 4 3 4 8
(a) 8 (b) 7 (c) 5 (d) 4

5. How many 4's are there in the series which comes between two 5s?
3 4 4 5 4 5 4 2 1 4 5 4 5 7 4 5 4 5
(a) 4 (b) 5 (c) 6 (d) 3

6. How many 7's immediately preceded by 6 but not immediately followed by 4 are there in the following series?
7 4 2 7 6 4 3 6 7 5 3 5 7 8 4 3 7 6 7 2 4 0 6 7 4 3
(a) One (b) Two (c) Four (d) Six

7. How many 7's are there in the given series which are immediately preceded by 6 but not immediately followed by 8?
3 4 8 7 6 1 5 6 7 8 4 9 6 7 5
(a) 1 (b) 2
(c) 3 (d) 4

8. (Left) 1 4 6 7 4 3 2 5 6 7 3 4 6 5 1 3 4 5 2 4 5 1 5 7 (Right)
In above series, if every second number is removed from the left then which number will be at the eight from the left? *RRC Group D 2022*
(a) 5 (b) 7 (c) 1 (d) 3

9. Refer to the given series and answer the question that follows (all numbers are single-digit numbers only, and all counting is to be done from left to right).
(Left) 1 2 8 2 4 1 7 6 1 7 3 2 9 7 5 1 7 8 6 8 2 4 3 9 4 6 6 2 (Right)
How many such odd digits are there, each of which is immediately preceded by a perfect square and immediately followed by an even digit? (**Note** I will be considered as a perfect square.) *RRB Technician Grade III 2024*
(a) 4 (b) 1 (c) 2 (d) 3

10. 2 5 6 9 8 0 3 8 6 7 2 5 2 2 6 8 3 6 5 3
How many such numbers are there in the series each of which is immediately preceded by an even number and immediately followed by an odd number? *RRC Group D 2022*
(a) 3 (b) 4 (c) 5 (d) 2

11. 6 3 5 3 5 6 3 2 2 2 5 1 9 5 4 8 9 5 2 7
How many such numbers are there in the series each of which is immediate preceded by an odd number and immediately followed by an even number? *RRC Group D 2022*
(a) 5 (b) 3 (c) 4 (d) 2

12. In the following series, how many times number 8 is not followed by number 4 but is preceded by number 5? *RRB NTPC 2021*
6 58 23 58 12 58 34 35 65 45 86 58 458
(a) 2 (b) 3 (c) 4 (d) 5

13. 56 32 4888 92 66 588 343 In the above series, how many 8's are there which are not divisible by the number on their left but are exactly divisible by the number on their right? *RRB ALP 2018*
(a) 3 (b) 1 (c) 2 (d) 4

14. If in the number sequence 8 7 2 1 4 5 6 3 2 8 4 5, all the odd numbers are increased by one and all the even numbers are increased by one then the new number sequence are arranged in ascending order, which will be the fifth digit from the right? *UP SI 2021*
(a) 7 (b) 4 (c) 8 (d) 6

Based on Letter Series

15. How many letters are immediately followed by L in the given letter series? *UP B.Ed 2011*
C P M L M M R L T L D E S L
(a) 4 (b) 5 (c) 3 (d) 6

16. In the given series, how many 'S' are there which are immediately preceded and immediately followed by 'K'. *UP Police Constable 2022*

S S K S K S R K S P O K S K S K S
(a) 3 (b) 2 (c) 4 (d) 5

17. (Left) G H U B Q R P M E N S T A V L M A (Right)
How many such vowels are there which are immediately preceded and followed by a consonant?
RRC Group D 2022
(a) 4 (b) 6 (c) 3 (d) 1

18. How many D's are there in the following series which are immediately followed by W but not immediately preceded by K?
K D C W K D W N K G D W W D H K V D W Z D W *RRB NTPC 2021*
(a) 1 (b) 3 (c) 2 (d) 4

19. K I O X J E T R U L E B A C K J M N
How many such vowels are there in the series, each of which immediately followed by two consonants together? *RRC Group D 2022*
(a) 2 (b) 3 (c) 4 (d) 1

20. Y A B U Y H I R J S B R X M P Q S D I R A Y E F G
How many such consonants are there, which are immediately preceded and immediately followed by a vowel? *RRC Group D 2022*
(a) 4 (b) 2 (c) 1 (d) 3

21. In the below series, how many L's are there which are not immediately preceded by R and not immediately followed by T?
Z Q S T L R M N Q N R T U V X R L A S L T Q R S L T
(a) 2 (b) 1 (c) 3 (d) 5

22. K D N C I C L O A S C S O P M C O D K C V N D C M M
How many consonants are there in the given series between the letter that is fifth from the right end and the letter that is sixth from the left end of the given series? *RRC Group D 2022*
(a) Eleven (b) Eight (c) Three (d) Thirteen

23. (Left) B Z C T B Z T E S B C Z T W A Z T F Z T U K R B Z T V (Right)
How many Z are there in the series which are immediately followed by T but not immediately preceded by B? *RRC Group D 2022*
(a) Five (b) Two (c) Four (d) Three

24. How many T's are both immediately preceded and followed by 'E' in the following series?
UP Police Constable 2018
E T E T T M E E E T E T E T E T T E E T T T E E E T E T E T E T T E E T E
(a) 7 (b) 6 (c) 5 (d) 8

25. How many M's occur in the following series such that it is preceded by W and followed by V?
X U V M R S T M W N V M W O P M W U V M W A C W M V H P N V W M W T U N
(a) 3 (b) 2 (c) 1 (d) 5

26. In the following series, how many K's are there which are immediately preceded by N and immediately followed by U?
A B C D K N L J M N K S T R Z N K U A N K U B W X N K L S
(a) 6 (b) 2 (c) 3 (d) 4

27. In the following letter series, how many 'BCN' are present such that letter C is in the middle and letters B and N are on either side of it?
B C M X N C X N B X N C B N C B Y B C X N B C N A B O N M Z C B
(a) 4 (b) 2 (c) 5 (d) 3

Based on Number, Letter and Symbol Series

> **MRC*****
> ***(Most Repeating Concepts)***
> (Q. Nos. 28-40) Which are based on mixed series (Letter, numbers and symbols) are being repeatedly asked in Railway NTPC and Group D examination. They are very important for future railway examinations.

28. If all the numbers are dropped from the given arrangement, which of the following will be the ninth to the left of S?
2 R Q 4 A 5 $ I ^ 9 R # E % 8 S * P
RRB NTPC 2021
(a) A (b) $
(c) Q (d) I

29. The number of symbols that are preceded by a number in the given expression is ....
R+JM2$#QR?*O@7F3 *RRB ALP 2018*
(a) 4 (b) 1 (c) 3 (d) 2

30. Refer to the following letter, number and symbol series and answer the question that follows. Counting to be done from left to right only.
(Left) D R & F 1 7 Q * 9 E D 4 W W % I6 L 3 * € $ (Right)
If all the numbers are dropped from the series, which of the following will be fourth from the left?
RPF SI 2024
(a) * (b) F (c) Q (d) E

31. Refer to the given number and symbol series and answer the question that follows. Counting to be done from left to right only.
(Left) 7 3 @ 1 7 3 ^ 4 & 3 Ω 9 # * £ 5 (Right)
How many such symbols are there, each of which is immediately preceded by a number and also immediately followed by a number? *RRB ALP 2024*
(a) Four (b) Three
(c) Five (d) More than five

32. # 9 1 @ 4 * 7 ^ 5 3 # 9 1 < 5 4 @ 3 $ # 2 * 6 ! 4 2 & 9 < 3 6
How many such numbers are there which are immediately preceded by a symbol and immediately followed by an even number? ***RRC Group D 2022***
(a) 4 (b) 3 (c) 6 (d) 5

33. Study the given arrangement and answer the following question. ***UPSSSC 2018***
A S A T @ # ₹ P Q 1 2 4 S U T
If all the numbers and symbols are removed then which vowel will occur most frequent times?
(a) U (b) T (c) S (d) A

34. How many such consonants are there in the following arrangement, each of which is immediately followed by a vowel but not preceded by a number?
TRB50%U7C4#KFS2UE*18I3V@9IX@LAB
RRB NTPC 2021
(a) Two (b) More than three (c) Three (d) One

35. L @ S * J ^ B U # W R < E @ N S # B * H ! A & L < W Q ***RRC Group D 2022***
How many symbols are immediately followed by a consonant and immediately preceded by a vowel?
(a) 4 (b) 2 (c) 3 (d) 1

36. How many such digits are there in the following sequence, each of which is immediately preceded by as well as immediately followed by a letter?
A B 7 C D 9 Z Y * P 2 M © K S 3 ↑ 5 N T
RRB NTPC 2021
(a) One (b) Two (c) Four (d) Three

37. 7 T % N 9 * M S 3 U = L 8 Y @ G & 3 E > 5 & R 3 ! K # 7 % H = Y 6.
Find out the total number of letters that are immediately followed by a number and immediately preceded by a symbol. ***RRC Group D 2022***
(a) 1 (b) 2 (c) 4 (d) 3

38. (Left) 3 ^ % 7 2 4 £ 3 ¥ 4 δ @ 8 8 & 6 @ 1 (Right)
How many such numbers are there in the above sequence each of which is immediately followed by a symbol and also immediately preceded by a symbol?
RRC Group D 2022
(a) 3 (b) 2 (c) 4 (d) 1

39. B 5 R 1 @ E K 4 F 7 © D A M 2 P 3 % 9 H I W 8 * 6 U I $ V Q #
Which of the following is the 7th to the left of the 17th from the left end of the above arrangement?
(a) 7 (b) W (c) * (d) 4

40. Rafer to the following letter, number and symbol series and answer the question that follows. Counting to be done from left to right only.
(Left) G E * S D Y # 3 R 6 K & 5 4 @ C & T % 7 2 (Right)
How many such letters are there which are immediately preceded by a number and also immediately followed by a symbol? ***RPF SI 2024***
(a) 3 (b) 0 (c) 2 (d) 1

41. Study the given arrangement and answer the following question. ***UPSSSC 2018***
S D B M 1 4 8 6 3 % T @ © U K 5 V 1 W $ Y 2 B E 6 # 9 D H 8 G & Z N
How many symbols are there each of which immediately followed by letter but not immediately preceded by number?
(a) Four (b) Two (c) Three (d) One

Based on Conditional Rearrangement

42. If the digits of the number 2079816 are arranged in descending order from left to right, then which digit will come exactly in the middle? ***RRC Group D 2022***
(a) 8 (b) 2 (c) 6 (d) 7

43. If 1 is added to each odd digit and 2 is subtracted from each even digit in the number 7123546, what will be sum of the highest and lowest digits in the new number thus formed? ***RPF SI 2024***
(a) 6 (b) 7 (c) 8 (d) 9

44. If all the digits of the number is written in descending order within the number, then how many digits will not change their positions?
8 3 2 4 5 7 1 ***CRPF HC 2023***
(a) None (b) One (c) Two (d) Three

45. If 2 is added to each odd digit and 1 is subtracted from each even digit in the number 23584617, how many digits will appear more than once in the new number thus formed? ***SSC (10+2) 2024***
(a) Three (b) None (c) One (d) Two

46. From the given numbers 452, 243, 361, 579 and 674, if in each number, the first and the second digits of each number are interchanged, then which of the following will be the highest number?
(**Example** 697-First digit = 6, second digit = 9 and third digit = 7) ***RRC Group D 2022***
(a) 361 (b) 579 (c) 452 (d) 674

47. This question is based on the five, three-digit numbers given below.
(Left) 589 365 451 749 159 (Right)
(Example: 697 – First digit = 6, second digit = 9 and third digit = 7) (**Note** All operations to be done from left to right.)
If all the numbers are arranged in ascending order, the position of how many numbers will remain unchanged? ***RPF SI 2024***
(a) One (b) Four
(c) Three (d) Two

48. Each of the digits in the number 5238641 is arranged in ascending order from left to right. The position(s) of how many digits will remain unchanged as compared to that/those in the original number? *SSC CGL (Tier-II) 2025*
(a) None (b) One (c) Two (d) Three

49. The following question is based on the five three-digit numbers given below.
(Left) 815 458 512 630 235 (Right)
If the third digit of second largest number is added in the second digit of the lowest number, what will be the result? *RRC Group D 2022*
(a) 5 (b) 6 (c) 3 (d) 2

50. If 2 is added to each odd digit and 1 is subtracted from each even digit in the number 2586473, which of the following digits will be third from the left in the new number thus formed? *RPF SI 2024*
(a) 7 (b) 5 (c) 9 (d) 1

51. Each of the digits in the number 3571869 is arranged in ascending order from left to right. The position(s) of how many digits will remain unchanged as compared to that/those in the original number? *SSC CGL (Tier-II) 2025*
(a) None (b) One (c) Two (d) Three

52. (Left) BOW SAD LOW RAY (Right)
How many letters are there in the English alphabetical order between the second letter of the first word from the right and the second letter of the first word from the left? *RRC Group D 2022*
(a) Thirteen (b) Eight (c) Fifteen (d) Twelve

53. GYM HIP JAM LAC PIC
If the first letter of all the words is changed to the following letter of the English alphabetical series, how many words will have more than one vowel? (same or different vowel) *RRC Group D 2022*
(a) Two (b) One (c) Three (d) Zero

54. If the numbers given below are arranged in descending order, then what will be the difference between the fifth number from the right and the fourth number from the left? *RRC Group D 2022*
(Left) 202, 323, 266, 182, 315, 285, 193, 217, 231, 186 (Right)
(a) 27 (b) 49 (c) 37 (d) 29

55. If in each number, one is added to each even digit and two is subtracted from each odd digit, then what will be the difference between the middle digit of the second number from the right end and the last digit of the second number from the left end? *DSSSB Workshop Assistant 2024*
748 623 543 422 298
(a) 5 (b) 3 (c) 4 (d) 2

56. The following question is based on the given information.
PLAN FORE RAMP RANG SAND
If in each word, the fourth letter is changed to the next letter in the English alphabetical order, how many letter clusters thus formed will have two vowels? *RRB NTPC 2022*
(a) Two (b) Three (c) None (d) One

57. This question is based on the five three-digit numbers given below.
465 638 359 987 563
If the positions of the first two digits in each number are reversed, then the difference between the first digit of the greatest number and the first digit of the lowest number is equal to
(Example. 697-First digit = 6, second digit = 9 and third digit = 7) *RRC Group D 2022*
(a) 7 (b) 6 (c) 4 (d) 5

Directions (Q. Nos. 58-60) *The questions given below are based on the following series.*
A B @ ☆ $ d 1 2 f G h 9 Z u V n M N Q O ? E & 8
DSSSB Grade II 2015

58. Three of the following four options are alike based on their position so form a group. Find one which does not belong to that group?
(a) ☆1G (b) d@f (c) 2$B (d) VN?

59. In the following series, what should come in place of question mark (?).
1nE, 2NO, fOM, ?, h82
(a) G&Z (b) GE9
(c) 3&Z (d) None of these

60. If first half of the series is written in the reverse order, then which element will be 11th to the left of 21st from the left end?
(a) G (b) h (c) ☆ (d) @

Right Key

1. (b)	2. (b)	3. (c)	4. (c)	5. (d)	6. (b)	7. (a)	8. (c)	9. (c)	10. (b)
11. (c)	12. (d)	13. (b)	14. (d)	15. (a)	16. (a)	17. (c)	18. (b)	19. (b)	20. (d)
21. (b)	22. (a)	23. (d)	24. (d)	25. (c)	26. (b)	27. (d)	28. (c)	29. (b)	30. (b)
31. (a)	32. (b)	33. (d)	34. (d)	35. (c)	36. (d)	37. (c)	38. (a)	39. (a)	40. (d)
41. (c)	42. (c)	43. (c)	44. (d)	45. (a)	46. (d)	47. (d)	48. (c)	49. (c)	50. (a)
51. (b)	52. (a)	53. (b)	54. (b)	55. (d)	56. (a)	57. (d)	58. (b)	59. (d)	60. (d)

Solutions

1. *(b)* The odd numbers in given series are

7, 5, 3, 3, 9, 1, 7, 3, 7, 5, 9, 1, 3, 9, 5, 3

$\therefore$ Required sum $= 7 + 5 + 3 + 3 + 9 + 1 + 7 + 3 + 7 + 5 + 9 + 1 + 3 + 9 + 5 + 3 = 80$

2. *(b)* In the given series,

10th digit from left = 9

4th digit from right = 0

$\therefore$ Sum of these digits = 9 + 0 = 9

3. *(c)* In the given series,

1th digit from the left = 2

15th digit from the right = 1

$\therefore$ Sum of these digits = 2 + 1 = 3

4. *(c)* Given series,

8 4 6 7 3 4 3 7 8 3 4 4 5 6 3 4 6 4 3 4 8

8 = 3 times, 7 = 2 times, 6 = 3 times,

5 = 1 times, 4 = 7 times, 3 = 5 times

Clearly, 5 comes least in the series.

5. *(d)* Given series,

3 (4) (4) 5 (4) 5 (4) 2 1 (4) 5 (4) 5 7 (4) 5 (4) 5

✓ = Condition fulfilled × = Condition not fulfilled

$\therefore$ Required 4 = 3 times

6. *(b)* Given series,

(7) 4 2 (7) 6 4 3 6 (7) 5 3 5 (7) 8 4 3 7 6 (7) 2 4 0 6 (7) 4 3

✓ = Condition fulfilled × = Condition not fulfilled

Clearly, there are two such 7's.

7. *(a)* Given series,

3 4 8 (7) 6 1 5 6 (7) 8 4 9 6 (7) 5

✓ = Condition fulfilled × = Condition not fulfilled

$\therefore$ Required 7 = 1 time

8. *(c)* Given number series is,

(Left) 1 4 6 7 4 3 2 5 6 7 3 4 6 5 1 3 4 5 2 4 5 1 5 7 (Right)

After removing every second number from the left

1 6 4 2 6 3 6 [1] 4 2 5 5

Eight from left

Hence, the required number is 1.

> **Smart Approach**
>
> Here, after removing digits (elements), candidates are not required to make new arrangement.
>
> While, use $2n - 1$ (where, n = asked term)
>
> $= 2 \times 8 - 1 = 16 - 1 = 15$th term $= 1$

9. *(c)* Given series is,

1 2 8 2 4 <u>1 7 6</u> 1 7 3 2 9 7 5 <u>1 7 8</u> 6 8 2 4 3 9 4 6 6 2

Hence, according to the given condition required odd digits are 2.

10. *(b)* Given number series is,

2 5 6 9 <u>8 0 3</u> <u>8 6 7</u> 2 5 2 2 <u>6 8 3</u> <u>6 5 3</u>

Hence, required numbers are 4.

11. *(c)* Given series is,

6 3 5 [3 5 6] [3 2 2] 2 5 1 9 [5 4 8] [9 5 2] 7

Hence, the required numbers are 4.

12. *(d)* Given series is,

6 <u>58</u> 23 <u>58</u> 12 <u>58</u> 34 35 65 4<u>58</u> 6 58 4<u>58</u>

$\therefore$ Required numbers of 8's are 5.

13. *(b)* Given number series is,

56 32 4888 92 66 5<u>8</u>8 343

Thus, here is only '8' which is not divisibly by number on their left but are exactly divisible by the number on their right.

14. *(d)* According to the question,

8 7 2 1 4 5 6 3 2 8 4 5 [odd → +1, even → +1]

↓ ↓ ↓ ↓ ↓ ↓ ↓ ↓ ↓ ↓ ↓ ↓

9 8 3 2 5 6 7 4 3 9 5 6

$\Rightarrow$ 2 3 3 4 5 5 6 6 7 8 9 9 (Right)

5th

Hence, required number = 6

15. *(a)* Given series is,

C P <u>M L</u> M M <u>R L</u> <u>T L</u> D E <u>S L</u>

Thus, there are only 4 letters which are followed by L in the given series.

16. *(a)* Given series is,

S S [K S K] S R K S P O [K S] [K] S K S

Hence, the required 'S' are 3.

17. *(c)* Given series is,

G <u>H U B</u> Q R P <u>M E N</u> S <u>T A V</u> L M A

$\therefore$ The required vowels are '3'.

18. *(b)* Given series is,

K D C W K D W N K <u>G D W</u> W D H K <u>V D W</u> <u>Z D W</u>

Thus, there are only 3 D's which are immediately followed by W but not immediately preceded by K.

19. *(b)* The given series is, K I O X J E T R U L E B A C K J M N

Hence, there are 3 vowels, which are immediately followed by two consonant together.

20. *(d)* Given series is, Y A B U Y H I R J S B R X M P Q S D I R A Y E F G

∴ The required consonants are 3.

21. *(b)* Given series is,

Z Q S T L R M N Q N R T U V X R L A S L T Q R S L T

Thus, there is only 1 L which is not immediately preceded by R and not immediately followed by T.

22. *(a)* Given series is,

K D N C I C L O A S C S O P M C O D K C V N D C M M

6th from left   5th from right

The required consonants are L, S, C, S, P, M, C, D, K, C, V = 11

23. *(d)* Given series is,

(Left) B Z C T B Z T E S B C Z T W A Z T F Z T U K R B Z T V (Right)

Hence, the required Z are 'three'.

24. *(d)* There are '8' T's here which are immediately preceded and followed by E the given series.

E T E T T M E E E T E T E T E T T E E T

T T E E E T E T E T E T T

E E T E

25. *(c)* X U V M R S T M W N V M W O P M W U V M W A C W M V H P N V W M W T U N

Clearly, there is one M which is preceded by W and followed by V.

26. *(b)* Given series,

A B C D K N L J M N K S T R Z N K U A N K U B W X N K L S

✓ = Condition fulfilled   × = Condition not fulfilled

∴ Required number of K = 2 times

27. *(d)* Given series,

B C M X N C X N B X N C B N C B Y B C X N B C N A B O N M Z C B

Hence, the required 'BCN' are 3.

28. *(c)* Given arrangement is,

2 R Q 4 A 5 $ I ^ 9 R # E % 8 S * P

After dropping all the numbers,

R Q A $ I ^ R # E % S * P

9th to the left

Thus, the letter which is 9th to the left of S is 'Q'.

29. *(b)* The given arrangement is,

R + J M 2 $ # Q R ? * O @ 7 F 3

Hence, the number of symbols which are preceded by a number is '1'.

30. *(b)* Given series, D R & F 1 7 Q * 9 E D 4 W W % I 6 L 3 * € $

On dropping all the numbers

D R & F Q * E D W W % I L * € $

4th from left

∴ Required letter is F.

31. *(a)* Given series is, 7 3 @ 1 7 3 ^ 4 & 3 π 9 # * £ 5

Hence, according to the given condition required symbols are 4.

32. *(b)* Given arrangement is, # 9 1 @ 4 * 7 ^ 5 3 # 9 1 < 5 4 @ 3 $ # 2 * 6 ! 4 2 & 9 < 3 6

Hence, the numbers which are immediately preceded by a symbol and immediately followed by an even number is '3'.

33. *(d)* Given arrangement is, A S A T @ # ₹ P Q 1 2 4 S U T

After removing all numbers and symbols.

A S A T P Q S U T

Hence, vowel 'A' occurs most frequent i.e. 2 times.

34. *(d)* Given arrangement is,

T R B 5 0 % U 7 C 4 # K F S 2 U E * I 8 I 3 V @ 9 I X @ L A B

Hence, the required consonants are only 'one'.

35. *(c)* Given arrangement is,

L @ S * J ^ B U # W R < E @ N S # B * H ! A & L < W Q

Hence, the required symbols are '3'.

36. *(d)* Given sequence is, A B 7 C D 9 Z Y * P 2 M © K S 3 ↑ 5 N T

Hence, the required digits are 'three'.

37. *(c)* Given arrangement is, 7 T % N 9 * M S 3 U = L 8 Y @ G & 3 E > 5 & R 3 ! K # 7 % H = Y 6

Hence, required letters are 4.

38. *(a)* Given sequence is,

(Left) 3 ^ % 7 2 4 £ 3 ¥ 4 δ @ 8 8 & 6 @ 1 (Right)

Hence, the required numbers are '3'.

39. *(a)* Given series,

1	2	3	4	5	6	7	8	9	10	11	12	13	14	15	16	17
B	5	R	1	@	E	K	4	F	7	©	D	A	M	2	P	3

To the left

From left

7th   17th

18	19	20	21	22	23	24	25	26	27	28	29	30	31
%	9	H	I	W	8	*	6	U	I	$	V	Q	#

Smart Approach

7th to the left of 17th from the left end = (17 − 7) = 10 th from left end = 7

40. *(d)* Given series,

G E * S D Y # 3 R 6 K & 5 4 @ C & T % 7 2

Hence, according to the given condition, required letter is 1.

41. *(c)* In the given arrangement,

S D B M 1 4 8 6 3 % T @ © U K 5 V 1 W $ Y 2 B E 6 # 9 D H 8 G & Z N

Hence, there are 'three' such symbols which are immediately followed by letter but not immediately preceded by number.

42. (*c*) Given numbers is → 2079816

After arranging the number in descending order → 987[6]210

Hence, the digit '6' will come exactly in the middle.

43. (*c*) Given number is, 7123546

According to the question,

7	1	2	3	5	4	6
+1 ↓	+1 ↓	−2 ↓	+1 ↓	+1 ↓	−2 ↓	−2 ↓
8	2	0	4	6	2	4

Highest digit = 8

Lowest digit = 0

∴ Sum of these two digits = 8 + 0 = 8

44. (*d*) Given numbers → [8] 3 2 [4] 5 7 [1]

After rearranging the number → [8] 7 5 [4] 3 2 [1]

Hence, only three digits will remain unchanged.

45. (*a*) Given number is,

23584617

According to the question,

2	3	5	8	4	6	1	7
−1 ↓	+2 ↓	+2 ↓	−1 ↓	−1 ↓	−1 ↓	+2 ↓	+2 ↓
1	(5)	△7	△7	[3]	(5)	[3]	9

∴ 3 digits i.e. 5, 7, 3 will appear more than once in the new number.

46. (*d*) Given numbers are,

452, 243, 361, 579, 674

After interchanging first and second digit of each number, we have

542, 423, 631, 759, [764]

The highest number will be 764 i.e. 674.

47. (*d*) Given, three digit numbers,

589, 365, 451, 749, 159

On arranging in ascending order.

159, 365, 451, 589, 749

∴ Position of 3 numbers i.e. 365 & 451 will remain unchanged.

48. (*c*) Given number → 5 [2] [3] 8 6 4 1

After arranging the digits in ascending order → 1 [2] [3] 4 5 6 8

Hence, two digits will remain unchanged.

49. (*c*) Given series is,

(Left) 815 458 512 630 235 (Right)

The second largest number = 630

∴ Third digit of this number = 0

The smallest number = 235

∴ Second digit of this number = 3

Hence, required sum = 0 + 3 = 3

50. (*a*) Given number is,

2586473

According to the question,

2	5	8	6	4	7	3
−1 ↓	+2 ↓	−1 ↓	−1 ↓	−1 ↓	+2 ↓	+2 ↓
1	7	7	5	3	9	5

3rd from the left

∴ Digit 7 is the third from the left in the new number.

51. (*b*) Given number → 3 5 7 1 8 6 [9]

After arranging the digits in ascending order → 1 3 5 6 7 8 [9]

Hence, 1 digit will remain unchanged.

52. (*a*) Given series is,

(Left) BOW SAD LOW RAY (Right)

First word from the right = RAY

∴ Second letter of the word = A

First word from the left = BOW

Second letter of the word = O

∴ Required letters are

= O (15) − A (1) − 1

= 14 − 1 = 13

53. (*b*) Given series is,

GYM	HIP	JAM	LAC	PIC
+1 ↓	+1 ↓	+1 ↓	+1 ↓	+1 ↓
HYM	[IIP]	KAM	MAC	QIC

Hence, only one word will have more than one vowel.

54. (*b*) Given series is,

(Left) 202, 323, 266, 182, 315, 285, 193, 217, 231, 186 (Right)

After arranging into descending order,

323, 315, 285, 266, 231, 217, 202, 193, 186, 182

Number fifth from the right = 217

Number fourth from the left = 266

∴ Required difference = 266 − 217 = 49

55. (*d*) Second number from the right end is → 4 2 2

On changing the digits

4	2	2
+1 ↓	+1 ↓	+1 ↓
5	(3)	3

(3) ← Middle digit

Second number from the left end

On changing the digits

6	2	3
+1 ↓	+1 ↓	−2 ↓
7	3	(1)

(1) ← Last digit

∴ Required difference = 3 − 1 = 2

56. (*a*) The given series is,

PLAN FORE RAMP RANG SAND

Changing the fourth letter in each word to the next letter in English alphabetical order,

P L A N → P L A O (N +1 → O), F O R E → F O R F (E +1 → F)

R A M P → R A M Q (P +1 → Q), R A N G → R A N H (G +1 → H)

S A N D → S A N E (D +1 → E)

Hence, two words i.e. PLAO and SANE have two vowels letters.

57. (*d*) The given series is

⇒ 465 638 359 987 563

After reversing the position of first two digit

⇒ 645 368 539 897 653

The greatest number = 897

∴ First digit = 8

The lowest number = 368

∴ First digit = 3

∴ Required difference = 8 − 3 = 5

58. (*b*) From options,

☆ $\xrightarrow{+3}$ 1 $\xrightarrow{+3}$ G, 2 $\xrightarrow{-3}$ \$ $\xrightarrow{-3}$ B

V $\xrightarrow{+3}$ N $\xrightarrow{+3}$? but d $\xrightarrow{-3}$ @ $\xrightarrow{+6}$ f

59. (*d*) In the given series,

1 $\xrightarrow{+1}$ 2 $\xrightarrow{+1}$ f $\xrightarrow{+1}$ [G] $\xrightarrow{+1}$ h

n $\xrightarrow{+2}$ N $\xrightarrow{+2}$ O $\xrightarrow{+2}$ [E] $\xrightarrow{+2}$ 8

E $\xrightarrow{-2}$ O $\xrightarrow{-3}$ M $\xrightarrow{-4}$ [Z] $\xrightarrow{-5}$ 2

∴ ? = G E Z

60. (*d*) The given series have 24 elements,

11th to the left of 21st from the left means 10th from the left.

But the first half (12 elements) are written in reverse order.

Hence, the required element will be third from the left end i.e. @.

CHAPTER

09 Direction and Distance

Based on Direction

In this type of questions, initial direction of a person's movement along with the various turns in various directions taken during course of journey is given.

The candidates need to determine the final direction in which the person is moving or final direction with respect to the initial point.

e.g. Joulie starts walking towards West after walking 2 km she turns right and walks 3 km, then she turns to her left and walks 4 km. In which direction is she walking now?

(a) West (b) East (c) North (d) South

Sol. (a) According to the question,

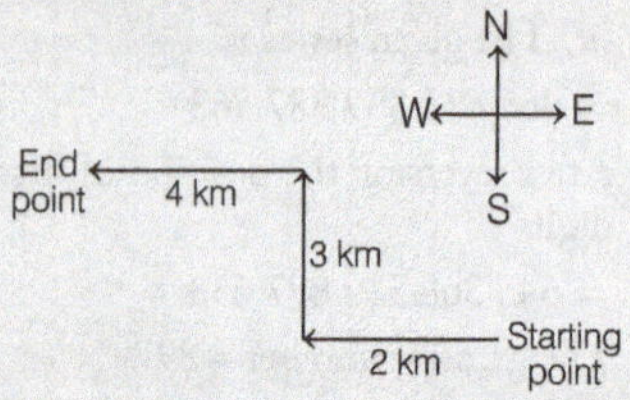

Hence, Joulie is walking towards West.

Based on Distance

In this type of questions, path covered by a person/thing along with distance covered is given.

The candidates are required to find out the shortest distance or total distance between initial position and final position of the given person/thing.

e.g. A person travels 4 km towards North, then he moves 6 km towards East and then he moves 4 km towards North. Find total distance covered by him.

(a) 6 km (b) 14 km

(c) 8 km (d) 10 km

Sol. (b) According to the question,

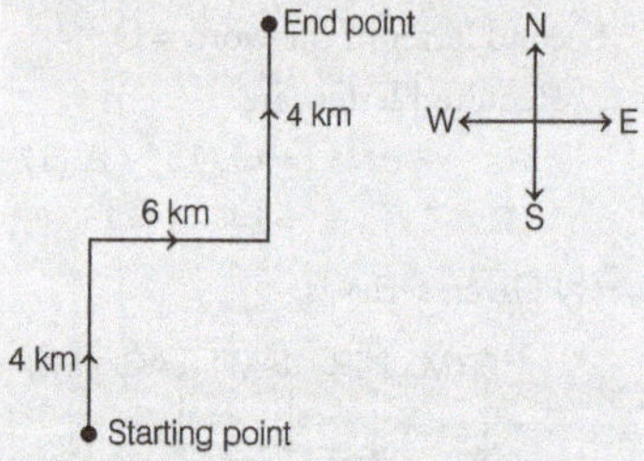

$\therefore$ Total distance = 4 + 6 + 4 = 14 km

Based on Both Distance and Direction

In this type of questions, some information related to a person/thing moving in different directions along with distances covered by him, is given.

The candidates are required to find out both distance and direction asked in the question.

e.g. Gaurav exits from the backdoor of his North-facing house and walks 25 m straight, then he takes a left turn and walks 36 m, then he turns left and walks 47 m. He turns left again and walks 36 m. How far and in which direction is he from his house now?

(a) 22 m, North (b) 11 m, North

(c) 22 m, South (d) 11 m, South

Sol. (a) According to the question,

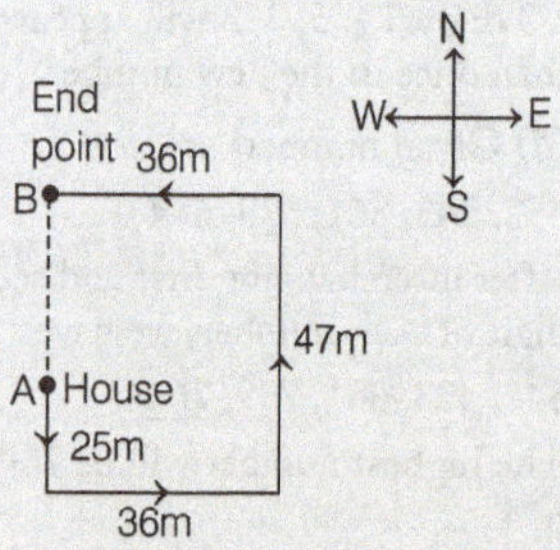

Now, he is in North direction from his house and the distance of Gaurav from his house = (47 – 25) = 22 m

Pythagoras Theorem

We can find the minimum distance between two points by using Pythagoras theorem.

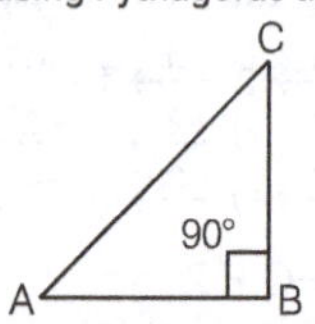

e.g. In ΔABC, AB = Base, BC = Perpendicular and AC = Hypotenuse

Then, by Pythagoras theorem,

Minimum distance = $AC = \sqrt{(AB)^2 + (BC)^2}$

Direction and Distance

When we move in different paths from a fixed point (initial point) then these paths are called directions and the total length of path covered by moving from intial point to the final (stoppage) point is called distance.

The main objective of this chapter is to test the knowledge of candidates regarding various directions and covered distance.

Score Booster

To solve the questions easily, visualisation of directions, rotation of directions and knowledge of Pythagoras theorem is very important.

Main Directions

There are four main directions *viz*. East, West, North and South as shown in the figure given below.

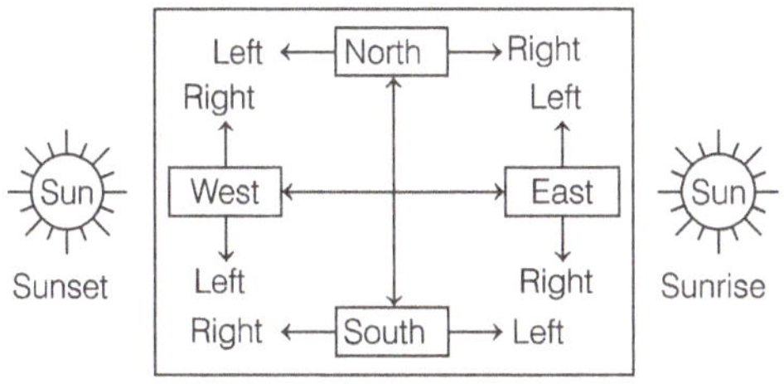

Cardinal Directions (Sub-directions)

The direction between two main directions is called cardinal direction or sub-directions.

i.e. N-E (North-East), N-W (North-West), S-E (South-East) and S-W (South-West).

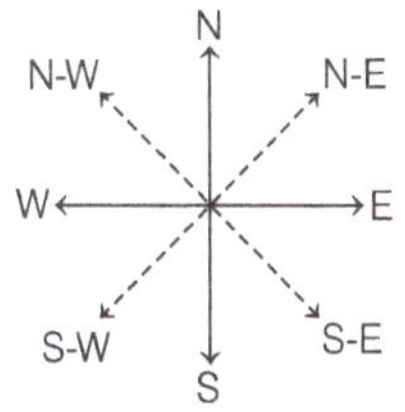

Angle of Movement

For solving questions based on angle of movement, it is necessary to know the rotations which are given below

(i) Movement towards the right is called clockwise (CW) movement.

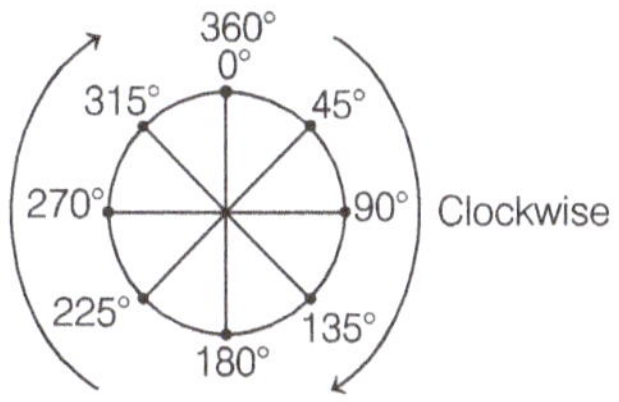

(ii) Movement towards the left is called anti-clockwise (ACW) movement.

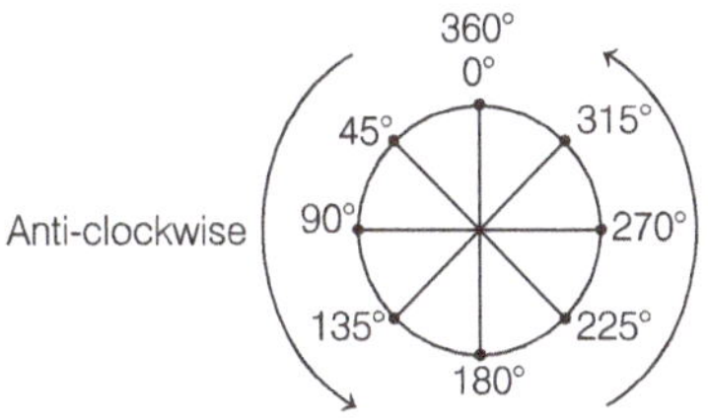

Concept of Shadow

In the morning, when the Sun rises in the East, the shadow of any person or object is in the West direction.

Similarly, in the evening, when the Sun sets in the West, the shadow of a person or an object is towards the East.

Shadow at the Time of Sunrise

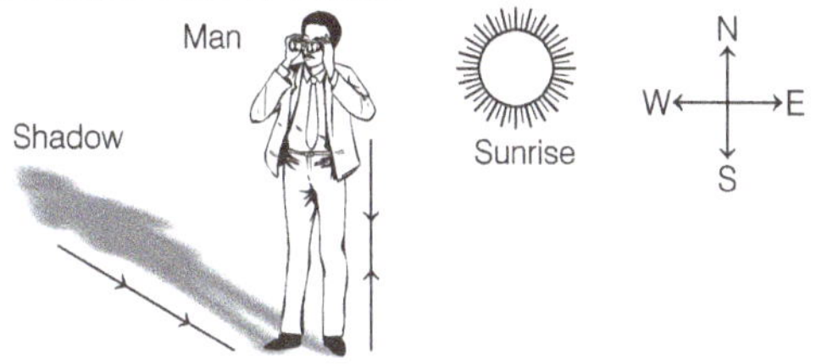

Shadow at the Time of Sunset

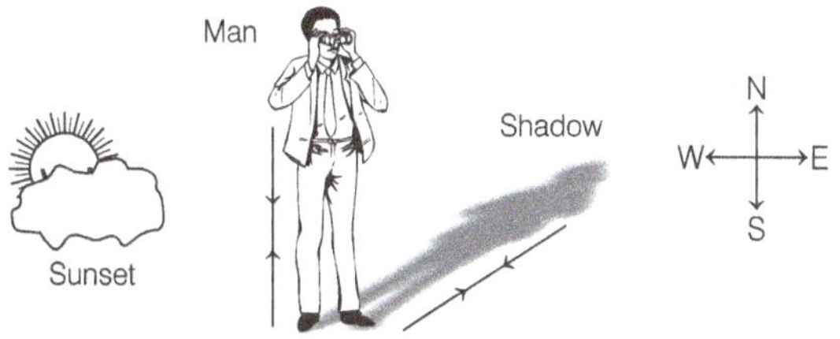

At 12 : 00 noon, there will be no shadow as the rays of the Sun are vertically downwards at that time.

Use the following table to find the shadow formed by a person or object.

Direction	At Sunrise	At Sunset
East	Back	Front
West	Front	Back
North	Left	Right
South	Right	Left

Concept Booster Points

- If we turn to the right from a point, then we should turn to our right or in clockwise direction making an angle of 90°. Similarly, if we turn to the left from a point, then we should turn to our left or in anti-clockwise making an angle of 90°.
- The minimum distance between two specific points is found by using Pythagoras theorem.
- If the starting direction of on object or person is not given in the question. In this situation, the directions are determined according to the question by moving the object or person in any direction at start.

Exam Approach Examples

Based on Direction

Example 1 **Vani starts from Point A and drives 6 km towards West. She then takes a left turn, drives 8 km. She then turns left and drives 6 km to reach Point B. In which direction is Point B with respect to Point A?** ***SSC CPO 2024***

(a) North (b) South (c) South-West (d) South-East

Sol. (*b*) According to the question,

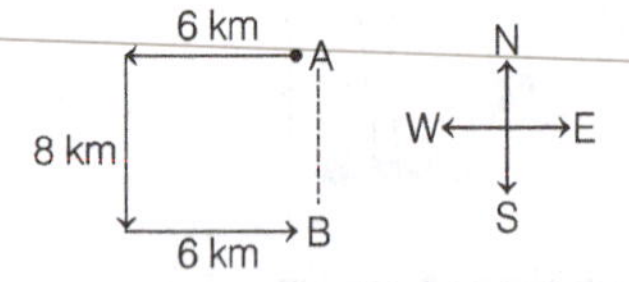

∴ Point B is in South direction with respect to Point A.

Example 2 **Umesh is standing facing the South-West direction. He then takes a 90° clockwise turn. After that, he takes a 135° clockwise turn. He finally takes a 90° anti-clockwise turn. In which direction is he facing now?** ***RRC Group-D 2022***

(a) West (b) North (c) North-East (d) North-West

Sol. (*b*) According to the question,

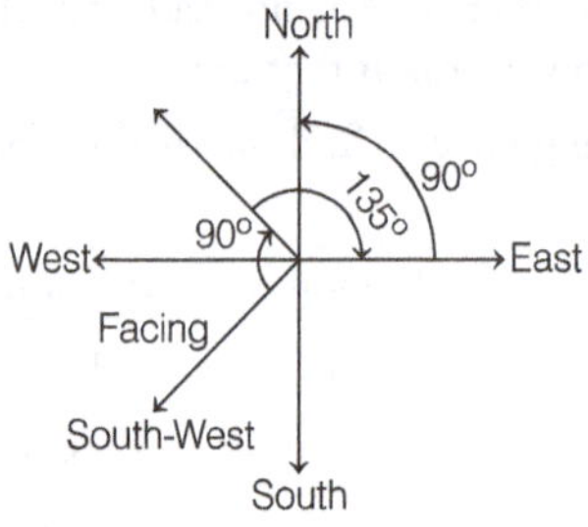

Hence, Umesh is facing 'North' direction.

Based on Distance

Example 3 **A person moves in North direction by 9 km, then turns left and moves by 4 km, again turns left and moves by 10 km, again turns left and moves by 4 km. How far the person is from initial position?** ***UP Police Constable 2024***

(a) 14 km (b) 9 km (c) 1 km (d) 4 km

Sol. (*c*) According to the question,

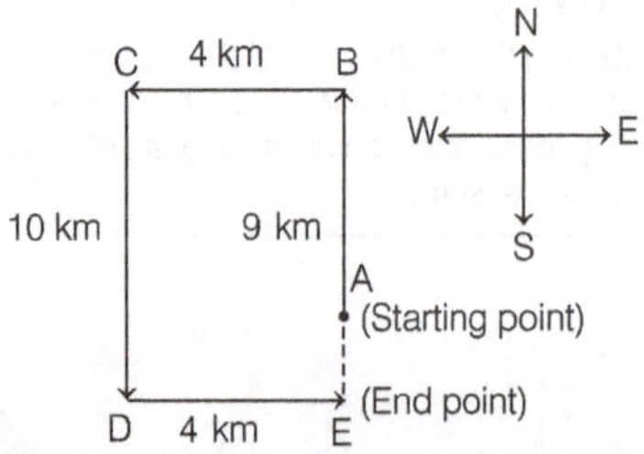

Hence, the distance

$$AE = DC - AB = 10 - 9 = 1 \text{ km}$$

Based on Direction and Distance

Example 4 **Ahmet's house faces North. He came out of his house and walked straight for 40 m, turned left and walked for 30 m. He, then turned right and walked for 35 m. Finally, he took another two successive right turns and covered 30 m and 25 m respectively, to reach his final destination. How far and in which direction is he from his house now?** ***SSC CPO 2022***

(a) 25 m due East (b) 15 m due North
(c) 25 m due South (d) 50 m due North

Sol. (*d*) According to the question,

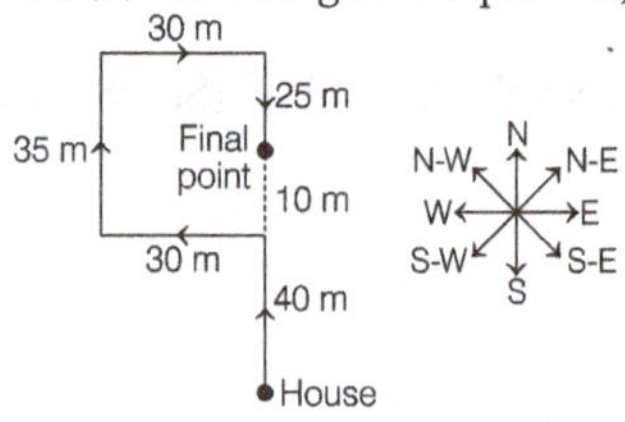

Trending Concept

This type of questions based on distance and directions are being repeatedly asked in SSC (CGL, CPO, MTS) examination and Rajasthan Police Constable examinations.

Distance between house and end point

$$= 40 + (35 - 25) = 50 \text{ m}$$

Hence, Ahmet is in 50 m North from his house.

Example 5 **Ashwini starts from his office and drives 90 km towards East. Then, he turns right and drives 20 km. Again he turns right and drives 30 km. Then, again he turns right and drives 100 km and reaches his final destination. In which direction his office is situated with respect to the final destination and what is the shortest distance between his office and the final destination?** ***Rajasthan Police Constable 2022***

(a) 100 km, South-West
(b) 10 km, West
(c) 100 km, North-East
(d) 10 km, East

Sol. (*a*) From the given information,

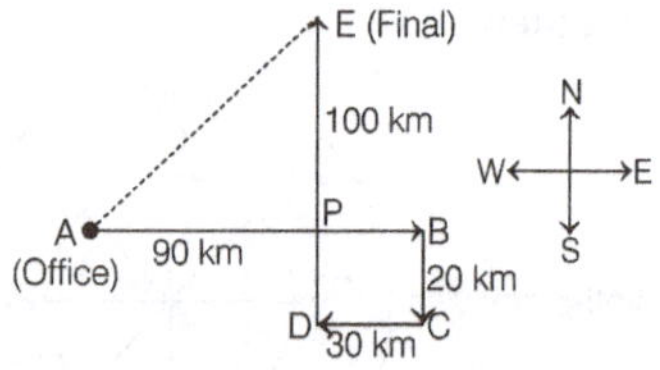

The shortest distance between office and final destination = AE

$$= \sqrt{AP^2 + PE^2}$$
$$= \sqrt{(AB - CD)^2 + (DE - DP)^2}$$
$$= \sqrt{(90 - 30)^2 + (100 - 20)^2}$$
$$= \sqrt{3600 + 6400} \text{ km}$$
$$= 100 \text{ km}$$

Direction of Ashwini's office with respect to final destination is South-West.

Chapter Challenge

Based on Direction

1. In the morning, Dev was standing facing North. He turned right and walked 15 m. Then, he turned left and walked 20 m. In which direction was he standing now? ***DSSSB 2019***
(a) South (b) East (c) West (d) North

2. Mr. Z walks 5 km towards the South, then turns right. After walking 3 km, he turns to the left and walks 6 km. What direction is he facing right now? ***CRPF Head Constable 2023***
(a) North-East (b) South
(c) South-West (d) West

3. Anita is standing facing the North direction. Then, she turns 135° anti-clockwise. After that, she turns 90° clockwise, in which direction is she facing now? ***RRC Group D 2022***
(a) North-East (b) South-West
(c) North-West (d) South-East

4. After walking 8 km, a boy turned right and walked 5 km. He then took a left turn and walked 9 km. If he stood facing West direction finally, towards which direction did he walk the first 8 km? ***UP SI 2021***
(a) East (b) North (c) South (d) West

5. In a playground, Raman is standing to the South of Sheetal. Reshma is standing to the East of Sheetal. In which direction is Raman standing from Reshma? ***Rajasthan Police Constable 2022***
(a) North-East (b) North
(c) South-West (d) South

6. Shyam travels 7 km North, then he turns to his right and walks 3 km. He again turns to his right and moves 7 km forward. Now, in which direction is he from his starting point? ***UP Police Constable 2024***
(a) West (b) South
(c) North (d) East

7. Facing West, Suresh turns 45 degrees in the clockwise direction and then another 180 degrees in the same direction and then 270 degrees in the anti-clockwise direction. Which direction is he facing now? ***DSSSB 2019***
(a) South-East (b) North-West
(c) North-East (d) South-West

8. A man walks 5 km toward South and then turns to the right. After walking 3 km he turns to the left and walks 5 km. Now in which direction is he from the starting place? ***Delhi Police MTS 2018***
(a) West (c) South
(b) North-East (d) South-West

9. A man is facing North direction. He turns 135° in anti-clockwise direction and then 90° in the clockwise direction. Which direction is he facing now? ***Haryana CET 2023***
(a) North (b) North-West (c) West
(d) North-East (e) Not attempted

10. Gopal goes towards East from Point X, and turns anti-clockwise at 4 right angles and moves straight after each turn, in which direction he is facing now? ***UPSSSC 2022***
(a) East (b) West
(c) North (d) None of these

11. A boy is standing in a lawn facing North direction. If the boy turns 65 degrees in clockwise direction and 155 degrees in anti-clockwise direction, which direction will he face now? ***UP SI 2021***
(a) East (b) South (c) North (d) West

12. Two trucks, A and B, start from the same warehouse. Truck A goes 12 km North, then turns to its left and goes 5 km. Meanwhile truck B goes 10 km East, then turns left and moves 12 km, then turns to its left and goes 5 km. Now, in which direction is truck A with respect to B? ***UPSSSC 2022***
(a) East (b) North-West
(c) West (d) None of these

13. Shanmukh comes out of a bank and walks 90m towards South. Then, he takes a right turn and walks 110m. Then, he takes a right turn and walks 90m. Finally, he again takes a right turn and walks 220m. In which direction is he now with respect to the bank? (All turns are 90 degree turns only) ***RRC Group D 2022***
(a) South (b) North (c) West (d) East

14. Ashok went 8 km South and turned West and walked 3 km. Again he turned North and walked 5 km. He took a final turn to East and walked 3 km. In which direction was Ashok from the starting point? ***RRB JE 2019***
(a) East (b) North (c) West (d) South

15. Sunil starts walking from Point R. He walks 28 m towards the West, turns right and walks for 20 m to reach Point M. He, then takes a left turn walks for 30 m, takes a left turn and walks for 28 m to reach Point S. He finally takes a left turn and walks for 48 m to reach Point Z. In which direction is Point Z with respect to Point R?
(All turns are 90° turns only) ***RRB NTPC 2022***
(a) South-West (b) North-West
(c) South (d) North

16. When I was going to office from my house, early morning, my shadow was formed on my left hand side. In which direction is my house from the office? ***SSC MTS 2021***
(a) North-West (b) North
(c) South (d) East

17. One morning, Chitrashi and Ayaan sit facing each other. If the shadow of Ayaan falls to the left of Chitrashi, then in which direction is Ayaan facing? *SSC CGL (Tier I) 2022*

(a) South (b) North (c) East (d) West

18. If the minute hand of a clock points towards the South at 12:00 am, then in which direction will the minute hand point at 3:00 am in the same clock? *SSC CPO 2020*

(a) South (b) West (c) North (d) East

19. Reshma walked towards the South. After 500 m, she reached her friend Rehana's house. After meeting her friend, Reshma walked towards the East for 500 m and then turned right and walked for another 500 m. From there, she turned right and walked for 1 km. Finally, she turned to her right and walked for 1 km to reach her college. In which direction is her college from Rehana's house? *SSC Steno 2021*

(a) North (b) South-East
(c) North-West (d) South

Based on Distance

20. A boy rode his bicycle Northwards, then turned left and moved 1 km and again turned left and rode 2 km. He found himself exactly 1 km West of his starting point. How far did he ride Northwards initially? *HSSC Police Constable 2021*

(a) 1 km (b) 3 km (c) 2 km (d) 5 km

21. A person moves from home 7 km towards North, then turns right and moves 8 km, again turns right and moves 7 km, again turns right and moves 3 km. How far a person from his home (in km)? *UPSSSC 2022*

(a) 15 (b) 5
(c) 11 (d) None of these

22. Hari walked 17 km towards East, after that he turned left and walked 15 km. Now, he turned left again and walked 17 km. How far is he from the starting point? *DSSSB 2019*

(a) 15 km (b) 17 km
(c) 21 km (d) 19 km

23. Ram leaves his home at 5:00 a.m and starts running towards North and runs 50 km, then he turns right and runs 30 km. Finally, he turns right and runs for 50 km. How far is he from his home? *SSC JE 2023*

(a) 40 km (b) 20 km (c) 50 km (d) 30 km

24. Two persons A and B, stand at the same point. A walks 6 km East, takes a right turn and walks 4 km and turns left and walks 2 km. B walks 3 km towards West; turns right and walks 2 km; turns right again and walks 11 km. How far is A from B? *UP SI 2021*

(a) 10 km (b) 6 km (c) 12 km (d) 8 km

25. Anita starts from her house and cycles 6 km towards the South and then turns left and cycles 8 km. She again turns left and cycles for X km to reach her school. Point A is to the West of her school and also 3 km to the North of her house. What is the value of X? *SSC CPO 2022*

(a) 3 km (b) 9 km (c) 11 km (d) 7 km

26. Vijendra walks a certain distance, X m, from his home towards the West. Then, he turns left and walks 23 m. After that, he turns left and walks 36 m. Then, he turns left again to walk 23 m. He finally turns left and walks 18 m to reach his home. Find the value of X. *SSC CGL (Tier I) 2022*

(a) 41 (b) 18 (c) 20 (d) 22

27. Point A is 18 m to the East of Point B. Point B is 22 m to the North of Point C. Point D is 11 m to the West of Point C. Point E is 11 m to the South of Point D. Point X is 29 m to the East of Point E.
What is the shortest distance between Point A and Point X? *RRB NTPC 2022*

(a) 11 m (b) 33 m (c) 21 m (d) 10 m

28. A woman walked 9 km towards East, took a right turn and walked 9 km, took another right turn and walked 4 km. She then walked 14 km towards North and turned right and walked 11 km. She then finally took a right turn and walked 5 km. How far is she from the starting point? *UP SI 2021*

(a) 13 km (b) 20 km (c) 18 km (d) 16 km

29. B was taking a morning walk. She started from a point and walked 50 m towards East. She then takes a right turn, walks 30 m, turns right again, and walks 50 m. She takes a final left turn, walks 10 m and stops. How far is she from the starting point? (All turns are 90 degree turns only) *RRC Group D 2022*

(a) 20 m (b) 50 m (c) 40 m (d) 30 m

30. Kripal starts driving from his home and drives 37 km towards South. From there he turns left and drive 31 km. Then, he turns right and drives 27 km. Then, he turns left and drives a certain distance of Y km. After that, he turns left and drives 57 km. Now, he finally, turns left and drives 58 km to reach a bank, which is exactly 7 km South of his home. Find the value of Y in km. *SSC Steno 2020*

(a) 22 (b) 27 (c) 36 (d) 55

31. Two buses start from opposite points towards each other on a main road, 185 km apart. The first bus runs for 35 km and takes a right turn and runs for 17 km. It then turns left and runs for another 42 km and takes the left turn to reach the main road, in the meantime, due to a minor breakdown, the other bus has run only 36 km along the main road. What would the distance between the two buses be at this point? *RRB NTPC 2020*

(a) 72 km (b) 75 km (c) 80 km (d) 85 km

32. Ganesh is standing at a point. He walks 20 m East, then 10 m South, then 35 m West and at last 5 m towards East. What is the distance between his initial point and final point? ***MP Police Constable 2022***
(a) 20 m (b) $10\sqrt{2}$ m (c) 35 m (d) 5 m

33. Shyam lal goes 8 km in West from a certain point. Then, he moves to his right and goes 8 km. In the end he goes 25 km in South-East direction. How far is he from starting point? ***HP Police Constable 2022***
(a) 10 km (b) 20 km (c) 15 km (d) None of these

34. Pratiksha leaves from her home for her college. She walks 48 m towards West. After that, she turns towards North and walk 32 m. Then, she turns right and walks 54 m. Then, she goes 40 m toward the South and reaches her college. What is the shortest distance between her home and the college? ***DSSSB 2019***
(a) 15 m (b) 20 m (c) 9 m (d) 10 m

Based on Direction and Distance

35. Manick walked 40 m towards North, took a left turn and walked 20 m. He again took a left turn and walked 40 m. How far and in which direction is he from the starting point? ***CUET UG 2023***
(a) 20 m, East (b) 20 m, North
(c) 20 m, West (d) 100 m, South

36. Sarita walks 24 m towards West, then turns to her right and walks 24 m and then turns to her left and walks 16 m. Again she turns to her left and walks 24 m. How far and in which direction is Sarita from her starting point? ***Haryana CET 2023***
(a) 40 m, North (b) 40 m, West
(c) 32 m, North (d) 448 m, West
(e) Not attempted

37. Shahid starts from Point A and drives 20 km towards West. He then takes a left turn, drives 20 km, turns left and drives 15 km. He then takes a left turn and drives 12 km. He takes a final right turn, drives 5 km and stops at Point P. How far (shortest distance) and towards which direction should he drive in order to reach Point A again? (All turns are 90 degree turns only unless otherwise specified.) ***RRB Technician Grade III 2024***
(a) 10 km towards South (b) 5 km towards North
(c) 8 km towards East (d) 8 km towards North

38. Ramdin started from his office and walked 15 km in the South direction and reached the bus stop, and then turned to his left and walked 8 km straight on the road. From there, he turned to his left, walked 15 km and reached the Central Library. After this, he turned to his left again and walked 4 km to reach his hostel. How far and in which direction is the hostel with respect to his office? ***RRB NTPC 2022***
(a) 12 km towards North (b) 7 km towards South
(c) 4 km towards West (d) 4 km towards East

39. Namit starts from a Point 'Z' and travels 4 km towards West to reach 'Y'. Then, he takes a left turn and covers 2.5 times the distance covered between 'Y' and 'Z' and reaches at Point 'X'. From there he takes a left turn and travels 4 km to reach destination 'B'. Then, he takes a left turn and covers some distance and walks 2 km ahead of Z to reach Point 'A'. What is the shortest distance between 'A' and 'B' and the direction of B with respect to A? ***Rajasthan Police Constable 2022***
(a) 12 km, North (b) 12 km, South
(c) 8 km, North (d) 8 km, South

40. Joya comes out of a bank and walks 14 m towards North. Then, she turns left and walks 20 m. Then, she turns left again and walks 36 m. Now, she turns left and walks 65 m. In which direction should she turn now and what distance should she walk in order to reach a hospital that is 45 m East of the bank? ***SSC Steno 2020***
(a) Right, 29 m (b) Left, 29 m
(c) Right, 22 m (d) Left, 22 m

41. Prince drives 8 km towards East from Point A. He takes a right turn and drives 3 km. Again, he takes a right turn and drives 5km. He takes a right turn and drives 8 km. Finally, he takes a left turn and drives 3 km to reach Point B. How far and towards which direction should he drive now in order to reach Point A again? ***SSC Steno 2022***
(a) 3 km towards West (b) 5 km towards South
(c) 2 km towards East (d) 4 km towards North

42. Rayan starts from Point A and drives 13 km towards East. He then takes a left turn, drives 5 km, turns left and drives 15 km. He then takes a left turn and drives 11 km. He takes a final left turn, drives 2 km and stops at Point P. How far (shortest distance) and towards which direction should he drive in order to reach Point A again? (All turns are 90 degree turns only unless specified.) ***RPF SI 2024***
(a) 6 km to the South (b) 5 km to the South
(c) 6 km to the North (d) 5 km to the North

> **MRC*****
> ***(Most Repeating Concepts)***
> Q. Nos. 25, 30, 31, 32, 33, 34, 35, 36 and 42 which are based on finding distances are very important from examination point of view. These types of questions are being repeatedly asked in SSC (CGL, Steno), State Police Constable (HP and MP) and Railway exams (NTPC).

43. Karan drives 6 km towards North from Point A. He takes a left turn and drives 3 km. Again he takes a left turn and drives 3 km. He takes a left turn and drives 6 km. He takes a right turn and drives 3 km to reach Point B. How far and towards which direction should he drive in order to reach Point A again? ***SSC CPO 2023***
(a) 4 km towards North (b) 2 km towards South
(c) 3 km towards West (d) 5 km towards East

44. Rajesh is walking towards North. After walking 10 m he turns to the right and walks 40 m to the shop L. Now, he turns to the left and walk 24 m. He again turns to the left and walk 12 m to arrive at hospital P. Now, finally he walks 22 m in his opposite direction. How far and in which direction is shop L from its end point? ***DSSSB 2019***

(a) 26 m, North-East (b) 28 m, South-West
(c) 26 m, South-West (d) 28 m, North-East

45. Rupali goes to office from her house via a specific route. Initially, she travels 17 km towards the North, then turns right towards the East and travels 15 km. From there, she again takes a right turn and travels 17 km. Now, she turns left and travels 7 km and finally reaches her office. In which direction and how many kilometers away (considering the shortest distance) is she from her house? (All turns are 90° turns only) ***RRB NTPC 2022***

(a) West, 22 km (b) West, 29 km
(c) East, 24 km (d) East, 22 km

46. A boy leaves his house. He travels 6 km towards South, then travels 8 km towards West and further travels 9 km towards South. How far and in which direction is he from his house now? ***NTA CUET UG 2024***

(a) 13 km, South-West (b) 17 km, South-West
(c) 17 km, North-West (d) 13 km, West

47. Nalin starts from Point Y and drives 8 km towards North. He then takes a right turn, drives 23 km, turns right and drives 29 km. He then takes a left turn and drives 14 km. He takes a left turn, drives 21 km and stops at Point Z. How far (shortest distance) and towards which direction should he drive in order to reach Point Y again? (All turns are 90 degrees turns only unless specified) ***RRB ALP 2024***

(a) 29 km towards the South
(b) 37 km towards the West
(c) 26 km towards the North
(d) 21 km towards the East

48. Ratan walks 15 m towards the North and then turns right and walks 23 m. Then, he turns left and walks 16m. After that, he turns left and walks 11 m. Then, he turns right and walks 17 m. Then, he turns left and walks 12 m. He finally turns right and walks 19 m. In which direction and how far is he now with reference to the starting point? ***SSC CPO 2022***

(a) South, 51 m (b) North, 52 m
(c) North, 48 m (d) North, 67 m

49. Neetu steps out from her classroom and walks 25 m towards the East. She takes a right turn and walks 20 m. She takes a right turn again and walks 62 m. Again, she takes a right turn and walks 91 m. She takes a right turn again and walks 62 m. Again, she takes a right turn and walks 35 m. She takes a right turn again and walks 25 m. She takes a final right turn and walks 15 m to reach Point X. How far and in which direction is Point X from Neetu's classroom?
(All turns are 90 degree turns only) ***RRC Group D 2022***

(a) 51 m, North (b) 55 m, North
(c) 51 m, South (d) 55 m, South

Right Key

1. (d)	2. (b)	3. (c)	4. (d)	5. (c)	6. (d)	7. (d)	8. (d)	9. (d)	10. (a)
11. (d)	12. (c)	13. (d)	14. (d)	15. (a)	16. (c)	17. (a)	18. (a)	19. (c)	20. (c)
21. (b)	22. (a)	23. (d)	24. (b)	25. (b)	26. (b)	27. (b)	28. (d)	29. (c)	30. (b)
31. (a)	32. (b)	33. (d)	34. (d)	35. (c)	36. (b)	37. (d)	38. (d)	39. (b)	40. (d)
41. (b)	42. (c)	43. (c)	44. (c)	45. (d)	46. (b)	47. (b)	48. (d)	49. (a)	

Solutions

1. (*d*) According to the question,

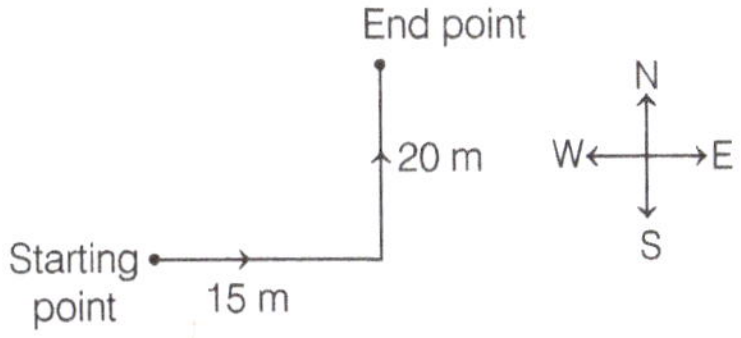

Hence, Dev was standing in "North" direction.

2. (*b*) According to the question,

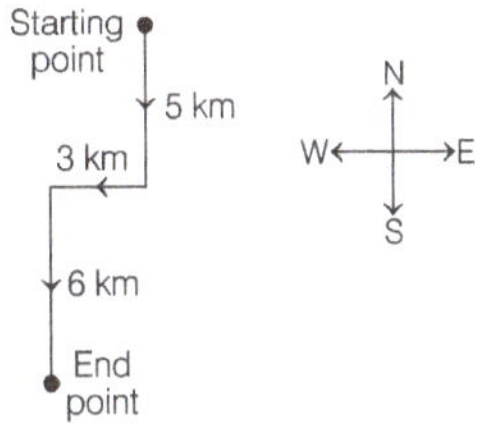

Hence, Mr. Z facing South direction right now.

TOP TIPS To solve this type of questions knowledge of left and right turn along with different directions is important.

3. (*c*) According to the question,

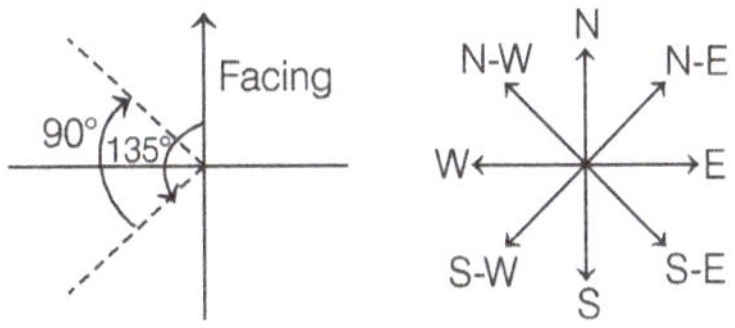

Hence, Anita is now facing North-West direction.

4. (*d*) According to the question,

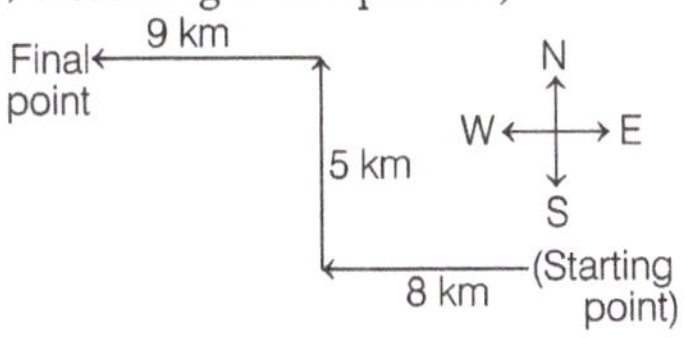

Hence, it is clear from the above that boy walk 8 km in West direction.

5. (*c*) According to the question,

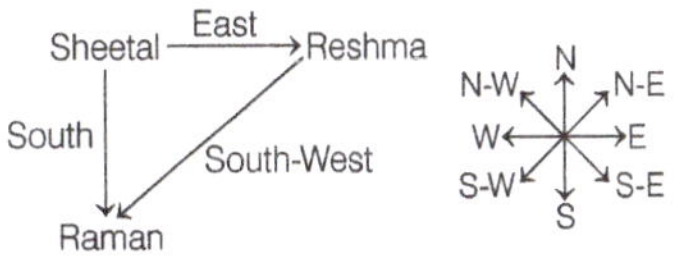

∴ Raman is to the South-West of Reshma.

6. (*d*) According to the question,

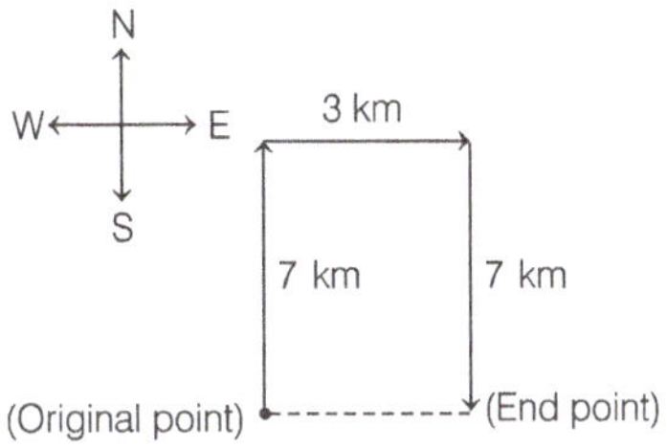

Hence, he is in East direction from his starting point.

7. (*d*) According to the question,

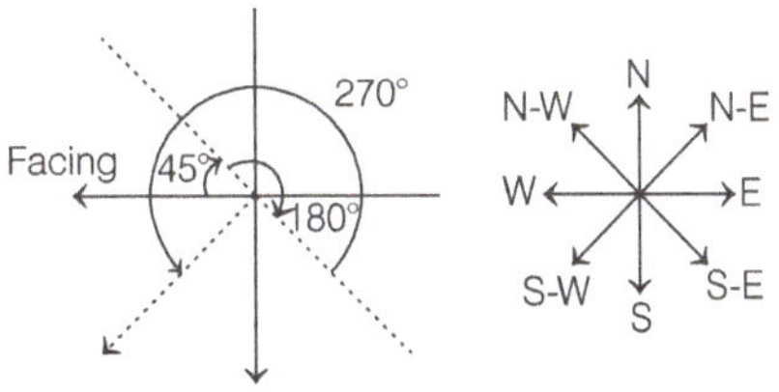

Hence, Suresh is facing 'South-West' direction.

8. (*d*) According to the question,

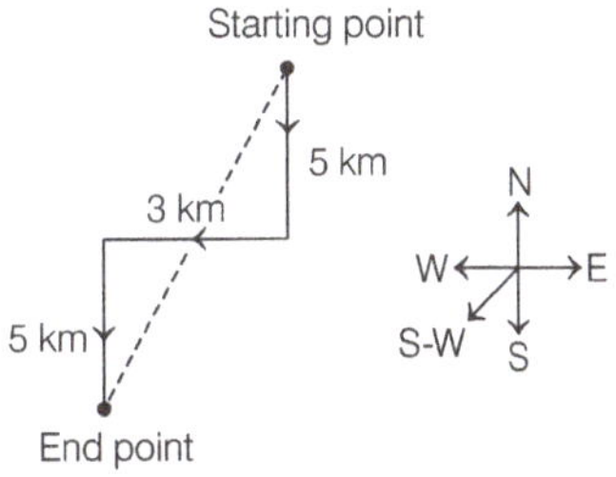

Hence, the man is in "South-West" from the starting point.

9. (*d*) The direction diagram is as shown below,

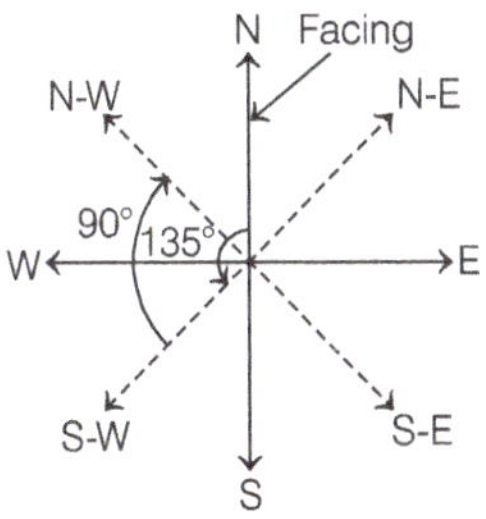

Hence, he is facing North-East direction.

10. (*a*) Gopal's movements are shown below,

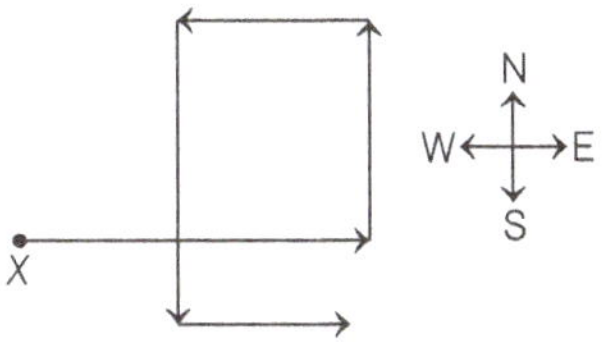

Hence, Gopal is facing in East direction now.

11. (*d*) According to the question,

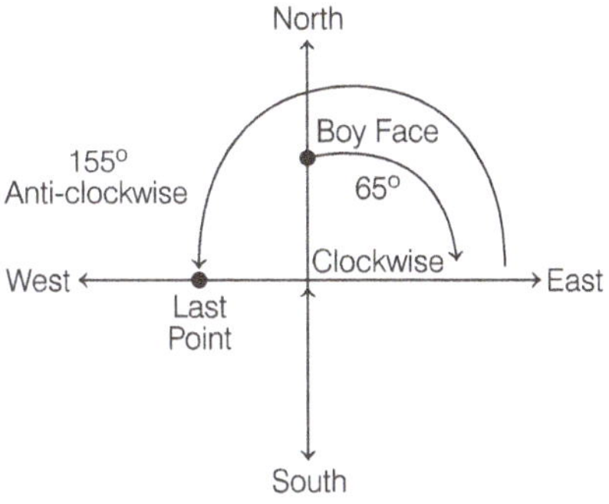

Clearly, at last he was facing towards 'West' direction.

TOP TIPS To solve this type of questions a candidate must have knowledge of clockwise and anti-clockwise rotation and concepts of angles.

12. (*c*) The movements of both the trucks are shown below,

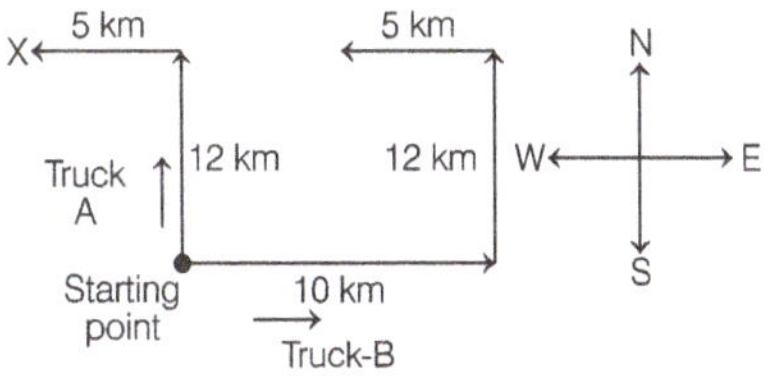

Hence, Truck A is in West direction with respect to Truck B.

13. (*d*) According to the question,

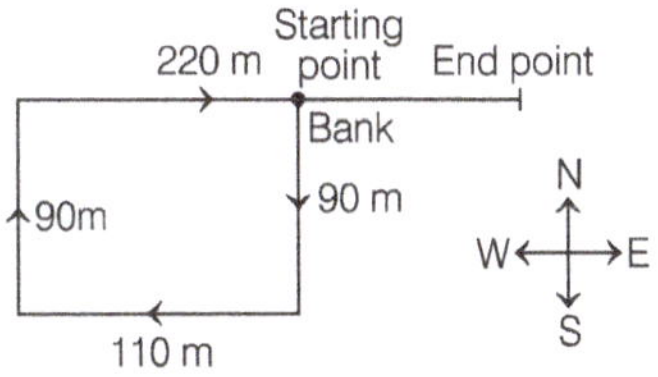

Hence, Shanmukh is in 'East' direction with respect to the Bank.

14. *(d)* According to the question,

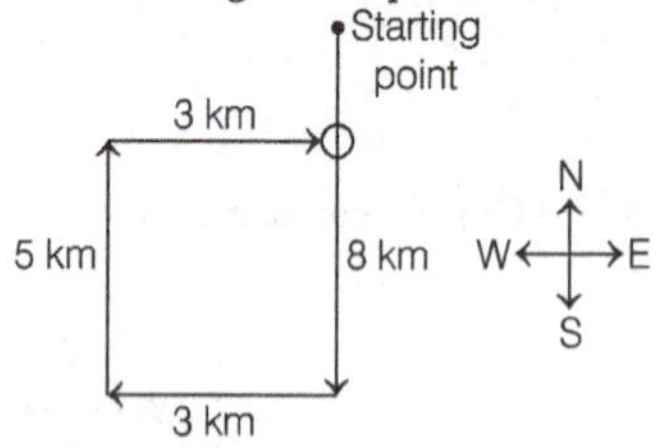

∴ Ashok was in South direction from starting point.

15. *(a)* According to the question,

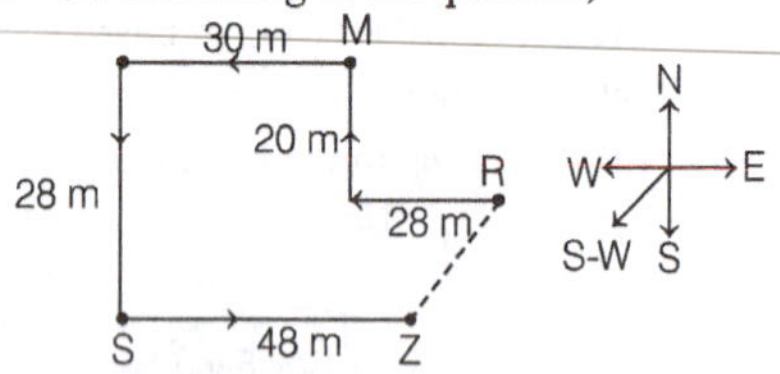

Hence, Point Z is in South-West direction with respect to Point R.

16. *(c)* According to the question,

Hence, the home is in South direction with respect to the office.

17. *(a)* According to the question,

Since, Sun rises in East direction. Hence, Ayaan is facing in South direction.

18. *(a)* According to the question,

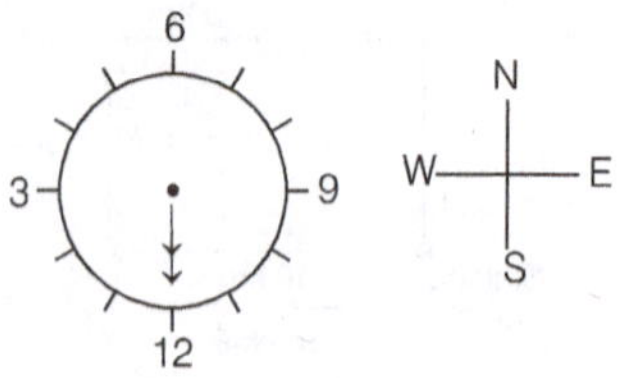

∴ When it is 3 : 00 am in this clock, minute hand comes at 12, so it points South again.

19. *(c)* According to the question,

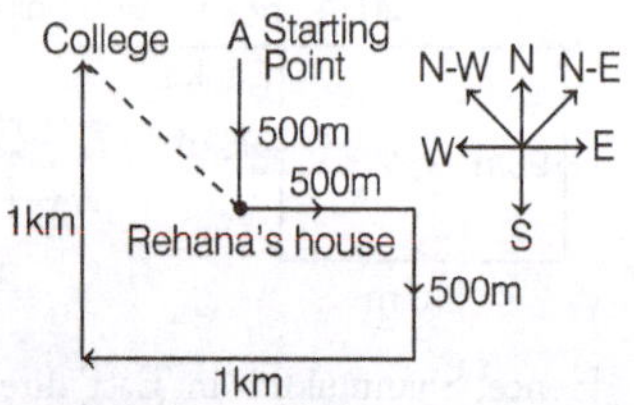

Hence, her college is in North-West direction from Rehana's house.

20. *(c)* According to the question,

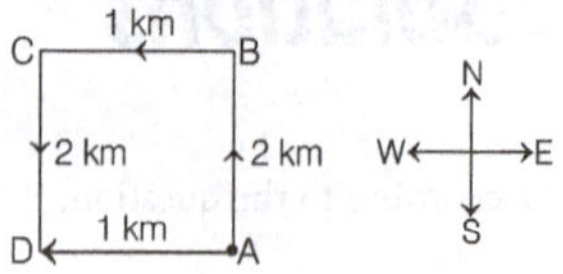

A = Initial point
D = End point
AB = CD = 2 km
∴ He rides 2 km towards North.

21. *(b)* The movements of person is as shown below,

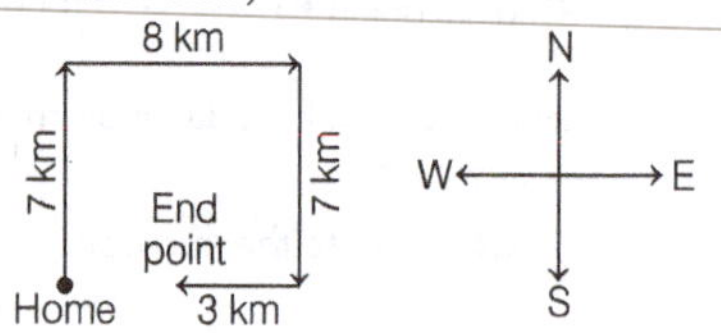

∴ Required distance
= 8 − 3 = 5 km

22. *(a)* According to the question,

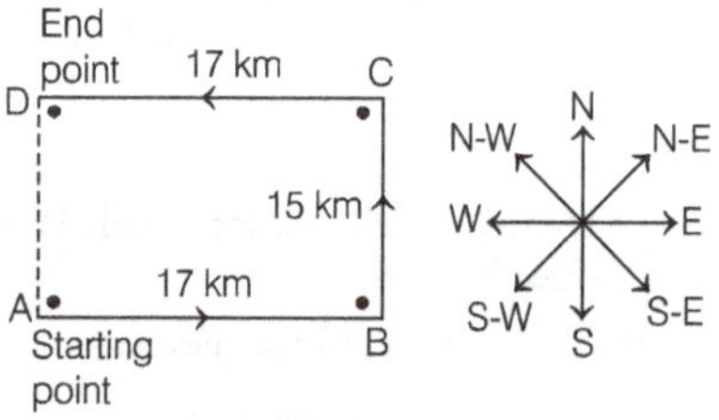

AD = BC = 15 km
Hence, Hari is 15 km far from the starting point.

23. *(d)* According to the question,

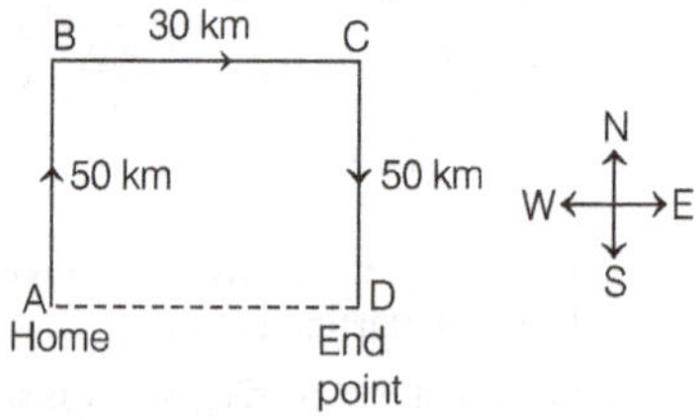

Here, AD = BC = 30 km
Hence, Ram is 30 km far from his home.

24. *(b)* According to the question,

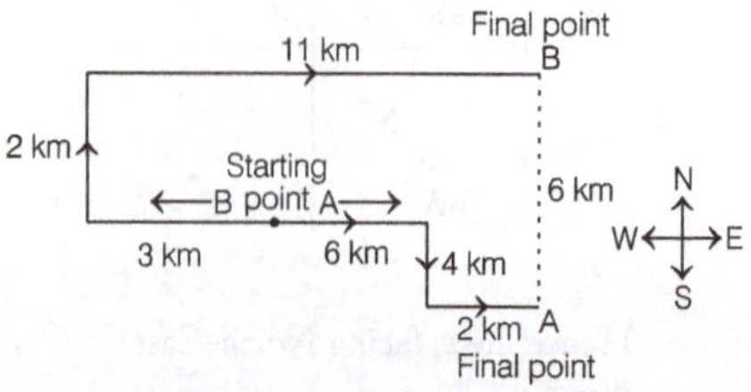

Clearly, A is '6 km' far from B.

25. *(b)* According to the question,

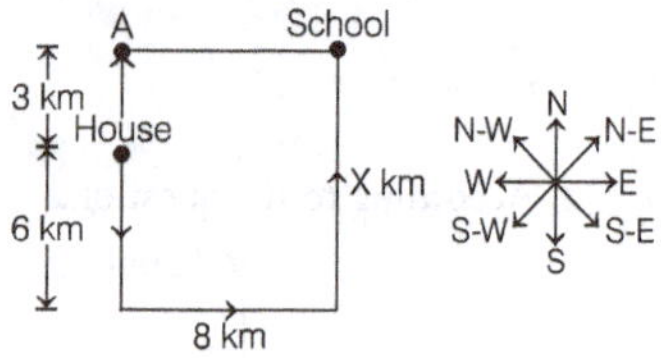

∴ X = 3 km + 6 km = 9 km
Hence, value of X is 9 km.

26. *(b)* According to the question,

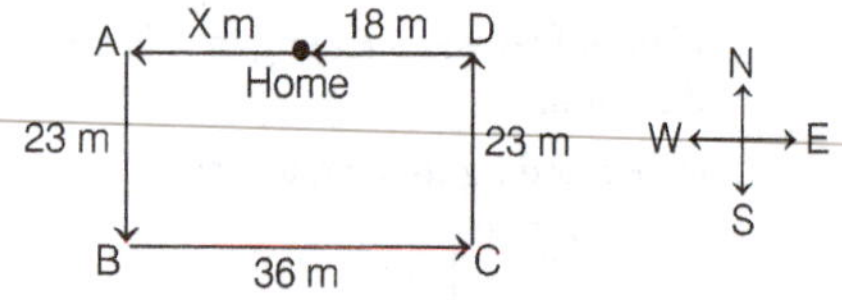

∵ AD = BC ⇒ X + 18 = 36
∴ X = 36 − 18 = 18 m

27. *(b)* According to the question,

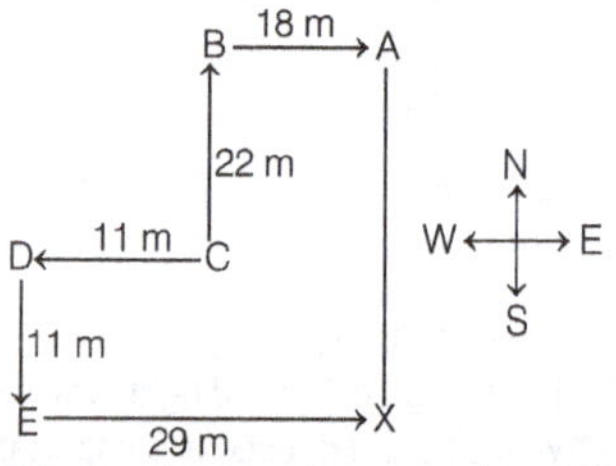

Hence, distance between A and X
= 22 + 11 = 33 m

28. *(d)* According to the question,

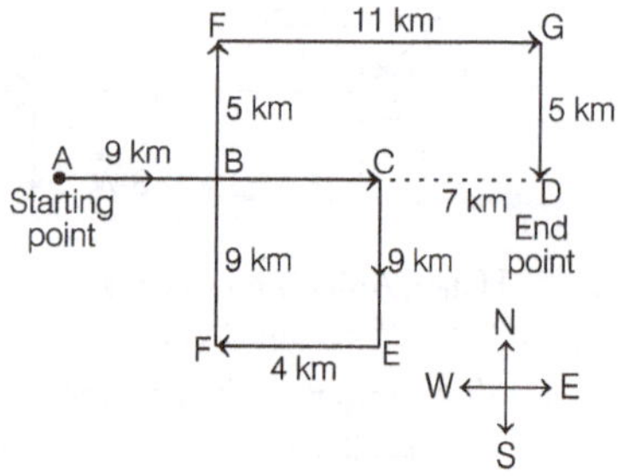

BC = FE = 4 km, AB = 9 − 4 = 5 km
CD = FG − BC = 11 − 4 = 7 km
Hence, required distance
= 4 + 5 + 7 = 16 km

29. *(c)* According to the question,

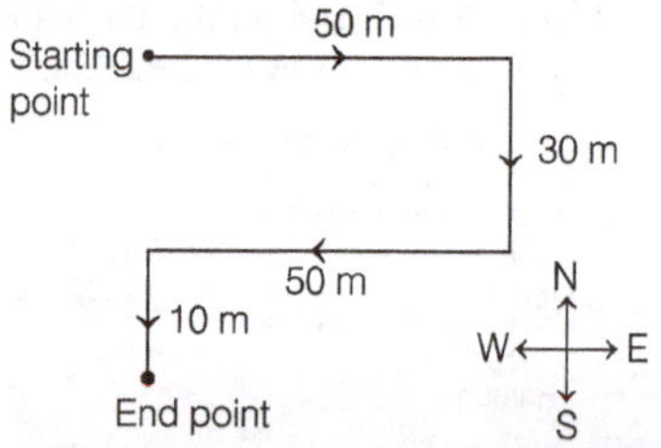

Hence, distance between starting point and end point
= 30 + 10 = 40 m

30. *(b)* According to the question,

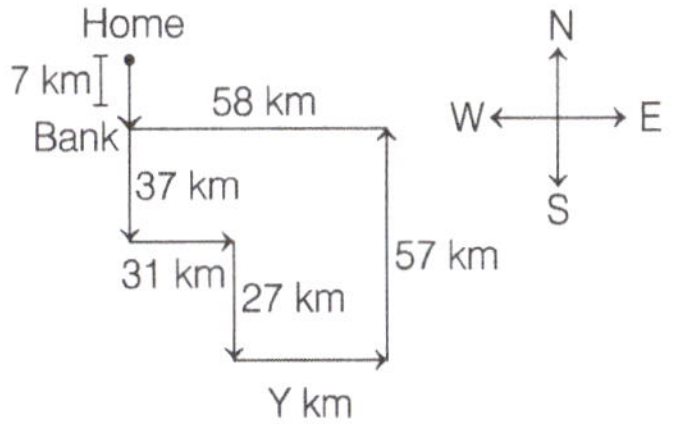

$\therefore$ Value of Y = 58 – 31

= 27 km

31. *(a)* According to the question,

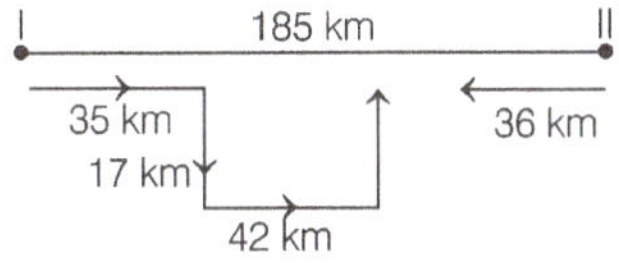

Distance between both buses

= 185 – (35 + 42 + 36)

= 185 – 113 = 72 km

32. *(b)* According to the question,

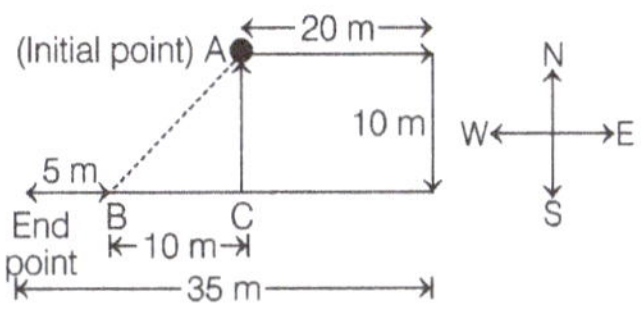

$\therefore$ Distance between initial point and final point,

$$AB = \sqrt{AC^2 + BC^2}$$

$$= \sqrt{(10)^2 + (10)^2}$$

$$= \sqrt{200}$$

$$= 10\sqrt{2} \text{ m}$$

33. *(d)* According to the question,

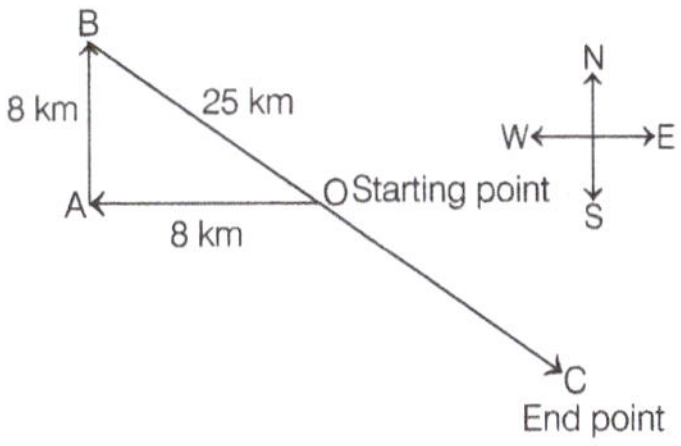

In ΔOAB,

$$OB^2 = OA^2 + AB^2$$

(Pythagoras theorem)

$$\Rightarrow \quad OB^2 = 8^2 + 8^2$$

$$\Rightarrow \quad OB = 8\sqrt{2}$$

$$\therefore \quad OC = BC - OB$$

$$= (25 - 8\sqrt{2}) \text{ m}$$

34. *(d)* According to the question,

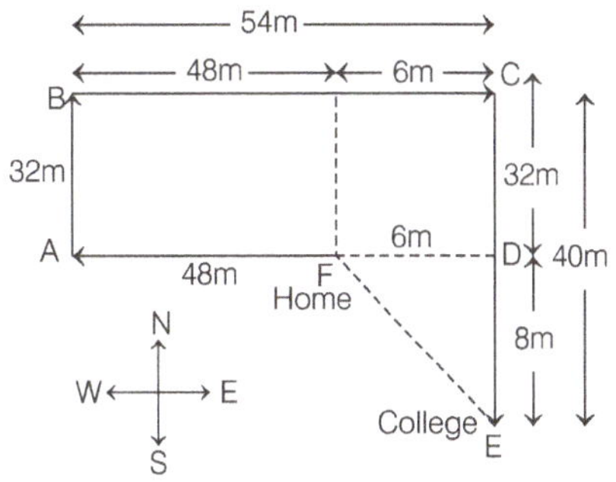

$\therefore$ Shortest distance

$$= EF = \sqrt{(ED)^2 + (DF)^2}$$

$$= \sqrt{(8)^2 + (6)^2} = \sqrt{100}$$

$$= 10 \text{ m}$$

35. *(c)* According to the question,

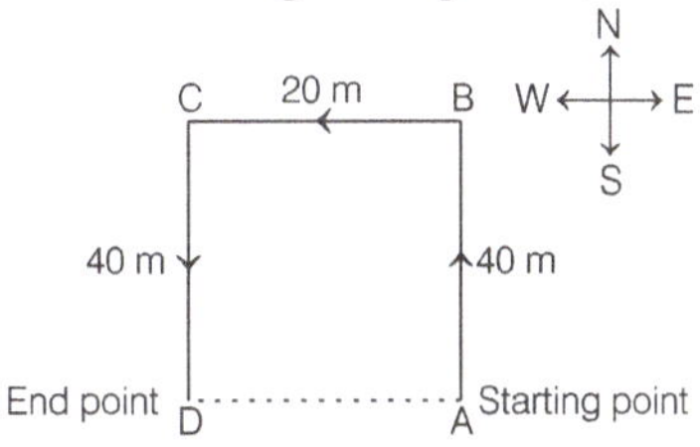

AD = BC = 20 m

Thus, D is 20 m to the West of A.

36. *(b)* According to the question,

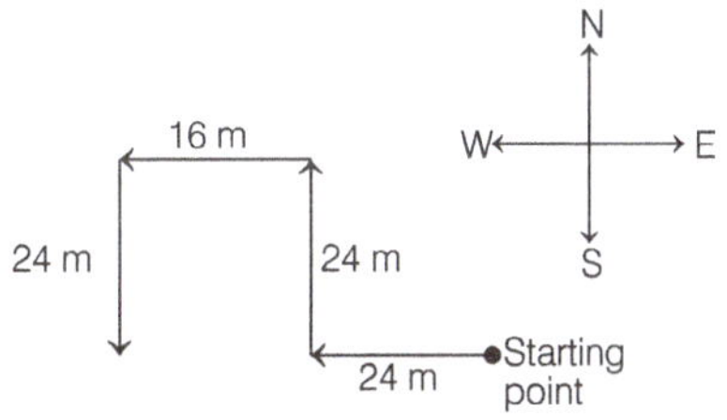

$\therefore$ Required distance

= 24 + 16 = 40 m

Hence, Sarita is in 40 m, West from her starting point.

37. *(d)* According to the question,

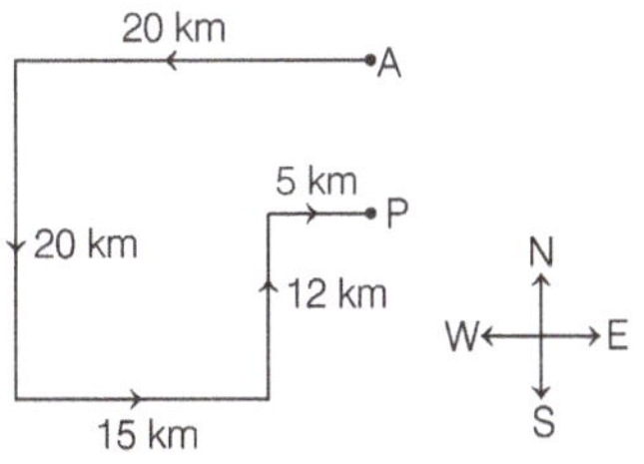

Required distance = AP

= 20 – 12 = 8 km

Hence, Shahid drives 8 km towards North to reach point A.

38. *(d)* According to the question,

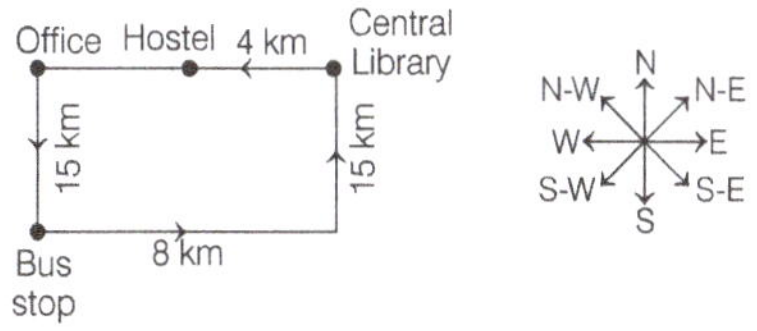

Distance between Ramdin's office and hostel = 8 – 4 = 4 km

Hence, Ramdin's hostel is in 4 km, East with respect to his office.

39. *(b)* According to the question,

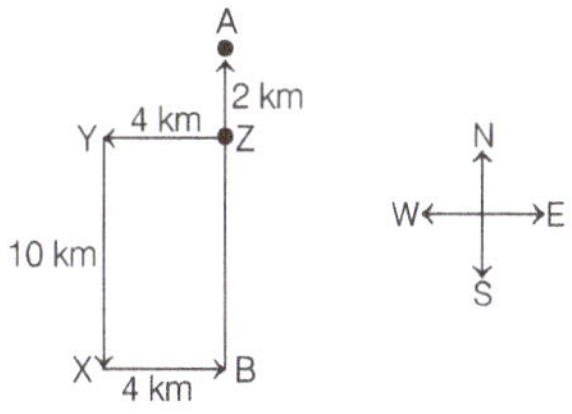

Distance between 'A' and 'B'

= BZ + ZA

= 10 + 2

= 12 km

B is in 'South' direction with respect to 'A'.

40. *(d)* According to the question,

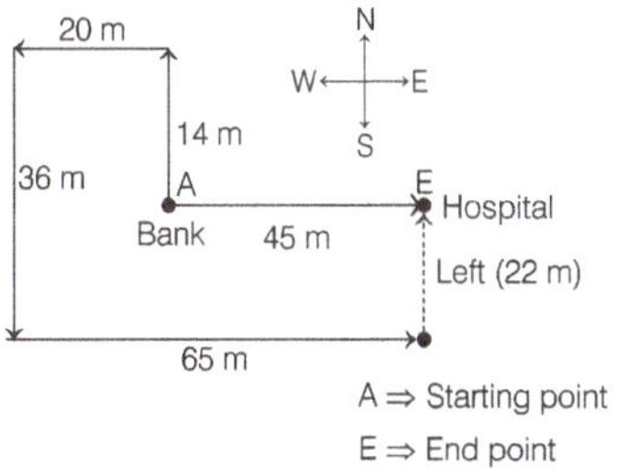

Now, she should move North (left) (36 – 14 = 22 m) to reach point E, which is hospital.

41. *(b)* According to the question,

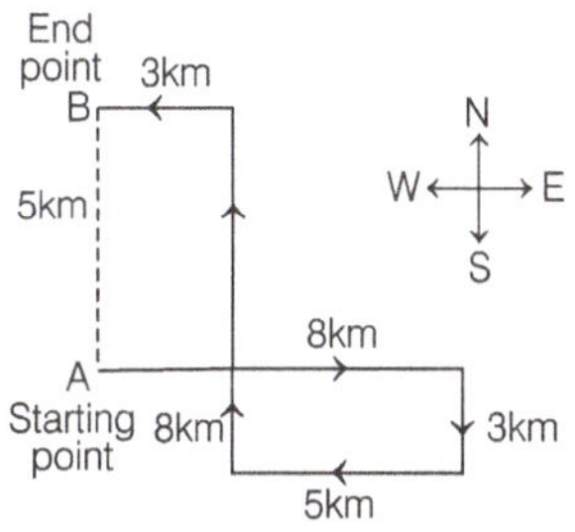

Hence, Prince should drive 5 km South to reach Point A.

42. *(c)* According to the question,

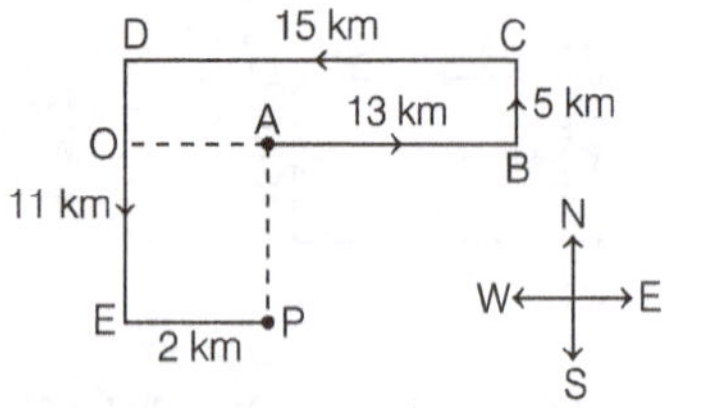

OD = BC = 5 km

∴ AP = DE − OD (∵ OE = AP)

= 11 − 5 = 6 km

Hence, Rayan drive 6 km to the North to reach point A.

43. *(c)* According to the question,

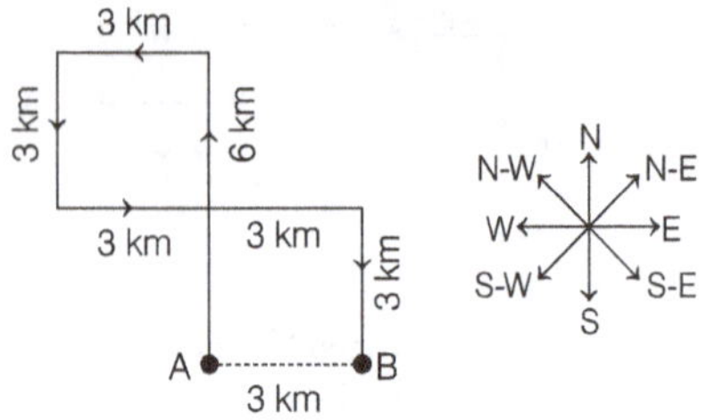

Distance between points A and B = 3 km

Hence, Karan should drive 3 km West from Point B in order to reach Point A again.

44. *(c)* According to the question,

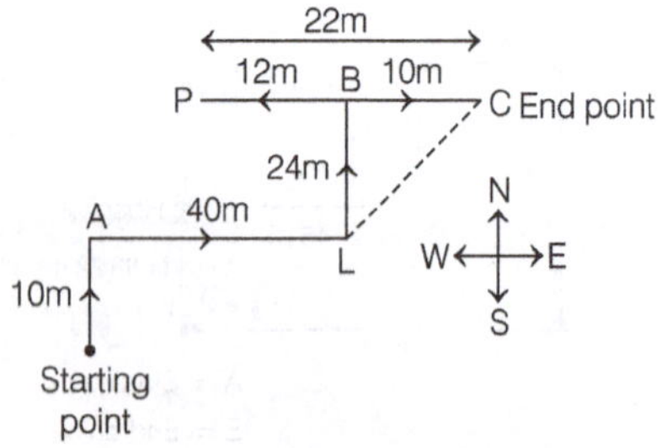

By Pythagoras theorem,

$LC = \sqrt{LB^2 + BC^2} = \sqrt{(24)^2 + (10)^2}$

$= \sqrt{576 + 100} = \sqrt{676} = 26$ m

Hence, shop L is in 26 m South-West from the end point.

45. *(d)* According to the question,

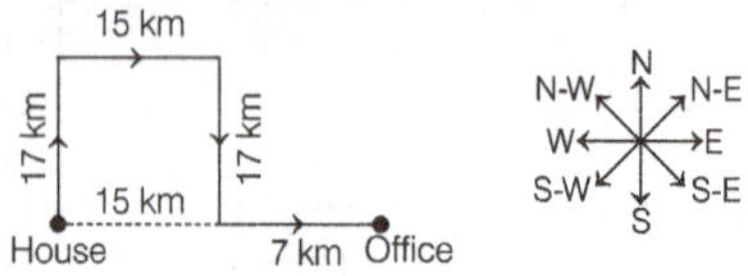

∴ Shortest distance between Rupali's house and office = 15 + 7 = 22 km

Hence, Rupali's office is in 22 km East from her house.

46. *(b)* 17 km from his starting point and is in South-West direction from his house.

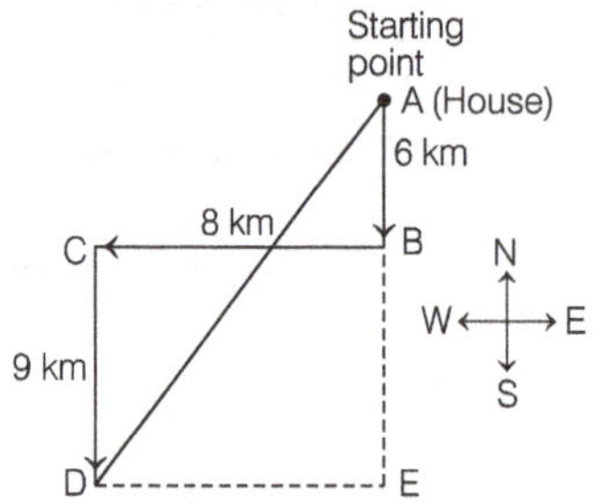

AE = 6 + 9 = 15 km

DE = BC = 8 km

∴ $AD = \sqrt{(15)^2 + (8)^2}$

$= \sqrt{225 + 64} = \sqrt{289} = 17$ km

He is 17 km from his starting point and is in South-West direction from his house.

47. *(b)* According to the question,

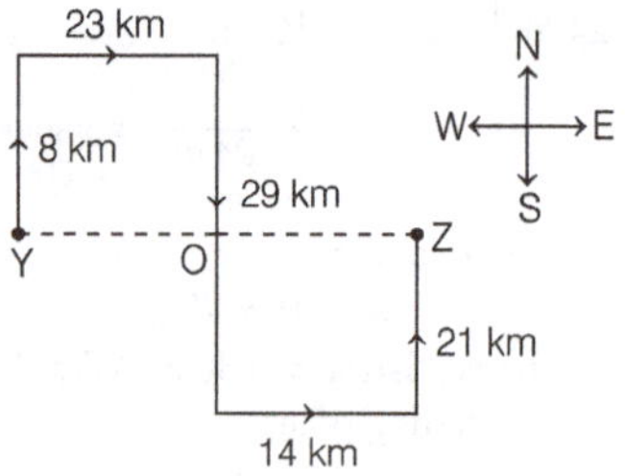

⇒ YZ = YO + OZ

= 23 + 14

= 37 km

Hence, Nalin drive 37 km towards the West to reach point Y.

48. *(d)* According to the question,

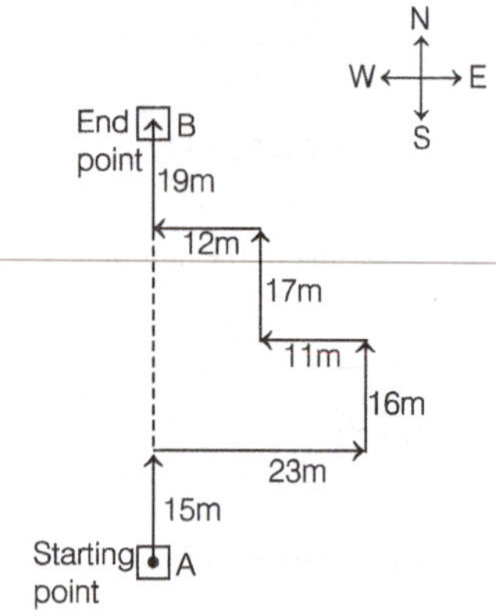

Distance between Point A and B

= 15 + 16 + 17 + 19 m

= 67 m

Hence, Point B is in the North of Point A.

49. *(a)* According to the question,

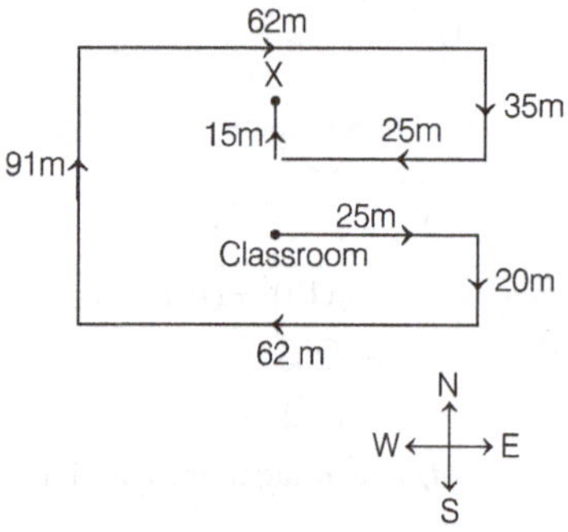

Distance between starting point and

X = 91 − 35 − 20 + 15 = 36 + 15

= 51 m in North

CHAPTER

10 Blood Relation

Blood Relation

Blood relation between two individuals is defined as a relation between them by the virtue of their birth or by their marriage. Blood relation based questions show the relationship among members of the family. The chain of relationship is given in the form of information and on the basis of this information. Candidate has to find relationship between any two members.

Based on Fact

In these type of questions, some information based on the relationship between one or two generations is usually given, which directly or indirectly presents the relationships between the generations. Based on the information, it is required to deduce the relation between the two individual which is asked by drawing a family chart.

e.g. Rani has a son named Anup. Ram is Rani's brother. Neeta has a daughter named Reena. Neeta is Ram's sister. How is Anup related to Reena?

(a) Brother (b) Nephew
(c) Cousin (d) Father

Sol. (c) According to the question,

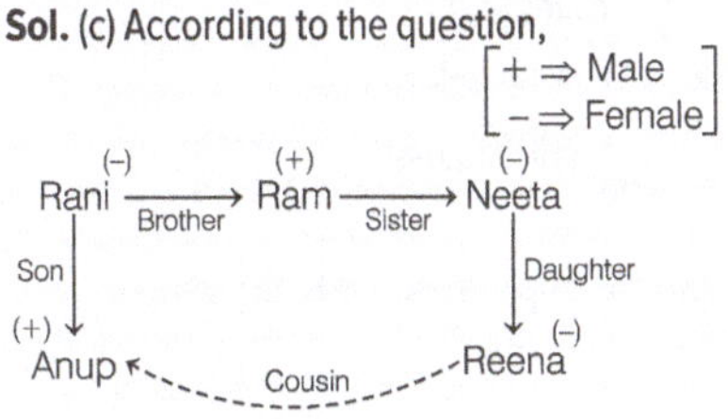

Hence, Anup is 'cousin' of Reena.

Based on Codes and Mathematical Symbol

In this type of questions, the relations are represented by particular codes or by mathematical symbol such as +, $, *, s, #, @, ! etc. By decoding these symbols or codes, candidates need to find the correct relationship.

e.g. In a certain code language,
A+B means 'A is the mother of B'.
A–B means 'A is the brother of B'.
A×B means 'A is the wife of B'.
A÷B means 'A is the father of B'.
Based on the above, how is M related to P, if 'M+N÷O×P–Q'?

(a) Wife's father's mother
(b) Mother's husband
(c) Brother' wife
(d) Daughter

Sol. (a) According to the given information,

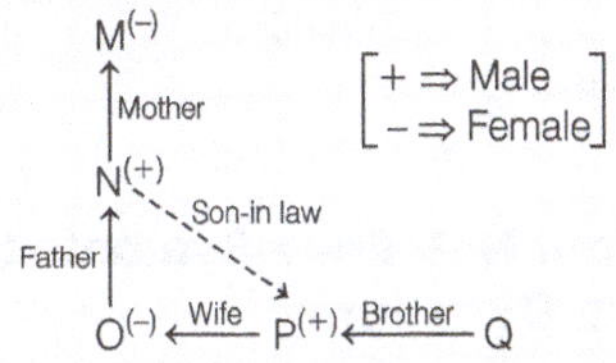

Hence, M is 'wife's father's mother of P.

Based on Photograph/ Conversation

In these type of questions, a person gives information to another person either about a particular person in a photograph or a person present in front of him.

Using the information, candidate is required to establish a relationship between a given person and the person in the photograph/the person about whom the information is provided.

e.g. Anita points to a man saying that he is the son of the brother of her mother. How is the man related to Anita?

(a) Cousin (b) Father's brother
(c) Father's father (d) Father

Sol. (a) According to the question,

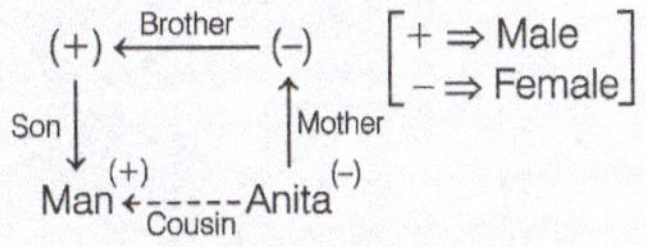

Hence , man is the 'cousin' of Anita.

Relation from One Generation to Next Generation

Generation	Male	Female
Three generation above	Paternal great grand father/Maternal great grand father	Paternal great grand mother/Maternal great grand mother
	Paternal great grand father-in-law	Paternal great grand mother-in-law
	Maternal great grand father-in-law	Maternal great grand mother-in-law
Two generation above	Paternal grand father	Paternal grand mother
	Maternal grand father	Maternal grand mother
One generation above	Father, Father-in-law, Paternal uncle, Maternal uncle	Mother, Mother-in-law, Paternal aunt, Maternal aunt
Self generation	Self, Brother, Brother-in-law, Cousin, Husband	Self, Sister, Sister-in-law, Cousin, Wife
One generation below	Son, Son-in-law, Nephew	Daughter, Daughter-in-law, Niece
Two generation below	Grandson	Grand daughter
Three generation below	Great grandson	Great grand daughter

Important Notations/Symbols to Solve Blood Relation Questions

Given below are some standard symbols and notations, they will help you to solve the questions by expressing the given information in the form of a relation tree.

- ⊕⟶ Male
- ⊖⟶ Female
- ⊕⟷⊖ Husband-Wife
- ⊕——⊕ Brother-Brother
- ⊖——⊖ Sister-Sister
- ⊕——⊖ Brother-Sister
- ⊕ | ⊕ Father-Son
- ⊕ ↓ ⊖ Father-Daughter
- ⊖ ↓ ⊕ Mother-Son
- ⊖ ↓ ⊖ Mother-Daughter

Important Relation for Expressing Relationships

1. Father can be expressed as follows

Father →
- Mother's husband
- Paternal grand parent's son
- Paternal uncle's/paternal aunt's brother
- Maternal grand father's/maternal grand mother's son-in-law
- Maternal uncle's/aunt's brother-in-law

2. Mother can be expressed as follows

Mother →
- Father's wife
- Grand parent's daughter-in-law
- Maternal uncle's/aunt's sister
- Maternal grand father's/maternal grand mother's daughter
- Paternal uncle's/aunt's sister-in-law
- Maternal aunt's sister-in-law

3. Paternal aunt can be expressed as follows

Paternal aunt →
- Father's/paternal uncle's sister
- Mother's sister-in-law
- Paternal grand parent's daughter

4. Maternal uncle can be expressed as follows

Maternal uncle →
- Mother's brother
- Father's brother-in-law
- Maternal grand father's/maternal grand mother's son

5. Paternal grandfather can be expressed as follows

Paternal grand father →
- Father's/paternal uncle's father
- Mother's father-in-law
- Paternal grand mother's husband

6. Maternal grandfather can be expressed as follows

Maternal grand father →
- Mother/maternal uncle's father
- Father's father-in-law
- Maternal grand mother's husband

Exam Approach Examples

Based on Facts

Example 1 **W is the brother of X. V is the father of W. X is the husband of Z. Z is the sister of A. Who is the father-in-law of Z?** ***CUET (UG) 2023***

(a) X (b) V (c) A (d) W

Sol. (*b*) According to the given information,

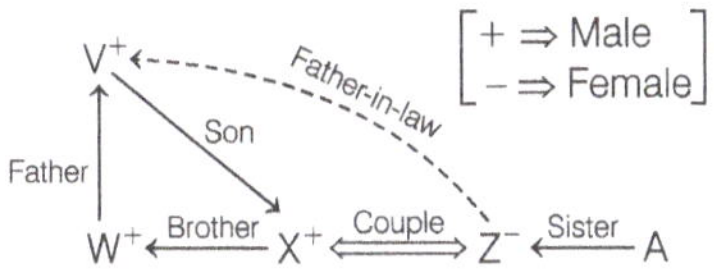

Hence, V is the father-in-law of Z.

Example 2 **A and B are brothers and their materal uncles are C and D. E is the wife of D and sister-in-law of F and F is the only daughter of G. G is the materal grandmother of B. How is F related to A?** ***RRB NTPC 2021***

(a) Maternal grandmother (b) Sister
(c) Mother (d) Maternal aunt

Sol. (*c*) According to the given information,

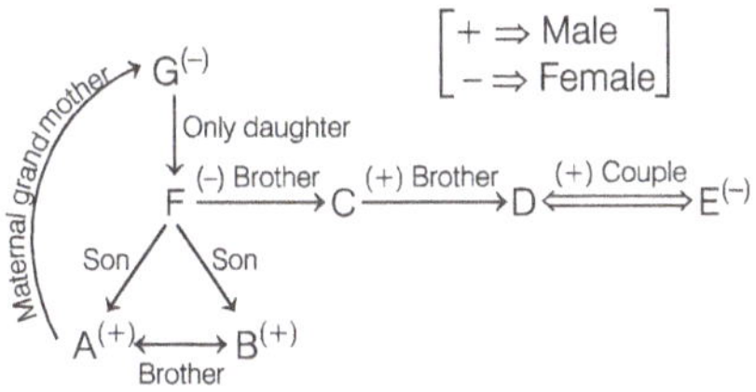

Hence, F is the mother of A.

Example 3 **A is the sister of B. C is the mother of B. D is the father of C. E is the mother of D, so how is A related to D?** ***UP Police Constable 2024***

(a) Grand daughter (b) Daughter
(c) Grand mother (d) Grand father

Sol. (*a*) According to the given information,

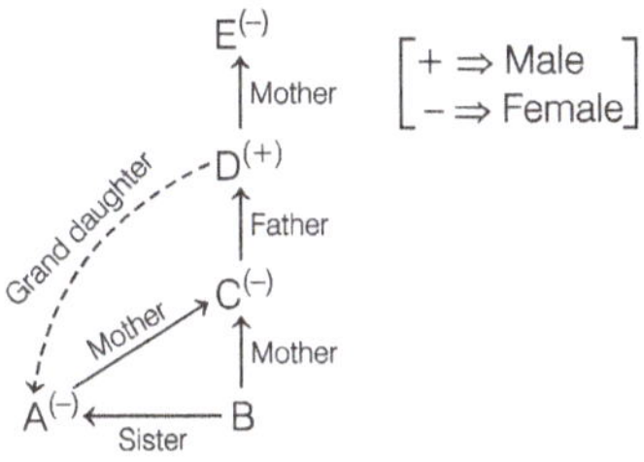

Hence, A is the grand daughter of D.

> **Helping Tips**
> Such questions should always be solved with the help of diagram because every relationship will become very clear to you in a step by step manner.

Example 4 **H is the brother of I. G is the brother of H. I is the son of J. J is the sister of K. How is J related to G?** ***SSC (10+2) 2023***

(a) Daughter (b) Mother-in-law
(c) Aunt (d) Mother

Sol. (*d*) According to the given information,

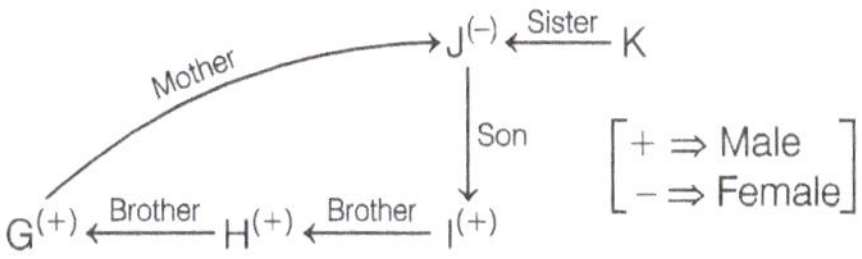

Hence, J is the mother of G.

Based on Conversation/Photograph

Example 5 **At a wedding reception, a man pointed to the groom and said that the groom was the brother of the son of his grand father's son. What is the relation of groom with the man?** ***SSC CPO 2024***

(a) Father (b) Uncle
(c) Brother-in-law (d) Brother

Sol. (*d*) According to the given information,

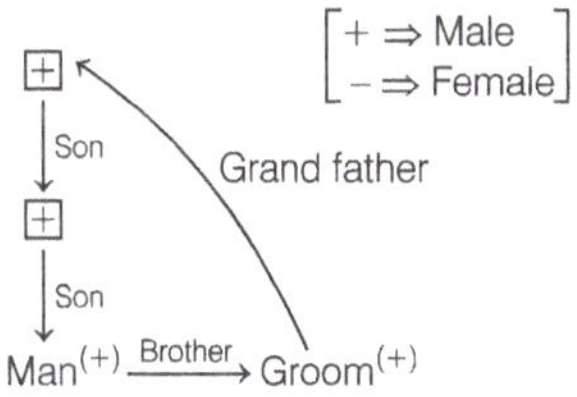

Hence, groom is the brother of man.

Example 6 **Pointing to the photograph of a man, Neha said, "His sister's brother is the only son of my father-in-law." How is that person related to Neha?** ***Rajasthan Police Constable 2022***

(a) Brother (b) Father
(c) Grandfather (d) Husband

Sol. (*d*) According to the given information,

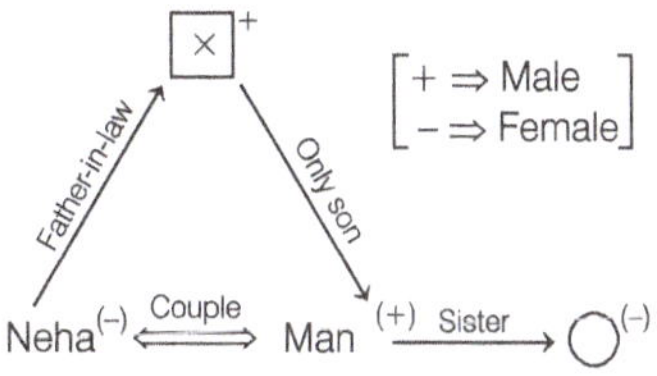

Hence, the man is Neha's husband.

> **Helping Tips**
> By expressing the relationship is the form of your family relationship, it will become easier to solve the questions.

Based on Codes and Mathematical Symbols

Example 7 In a certain code language,

A # B means 'A is the sister of B'.

A @ B means, 'A is the son of B'.

A & B means, 'A is the wife of B'.

A % B means, 'A is the father of B'.

If P & Q % L # R & K, then how is Q related to R?

SSC CGL (Tier-I) 2024

(a) Mother (b) Father (c) Sister (d) Wife

Sol. (*b*) According to the given information,

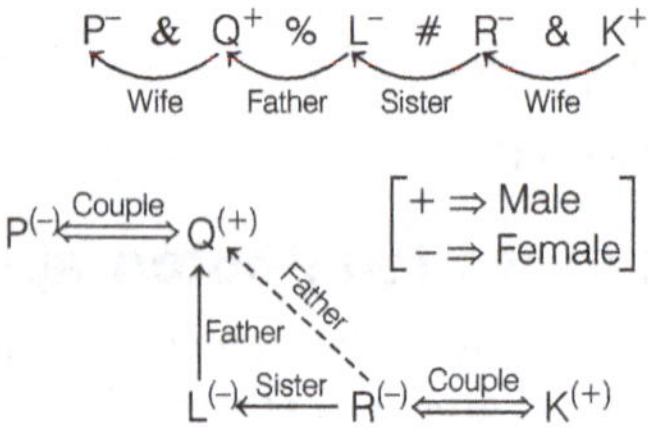

Trending Concept

All three types of questions on blood relation are very important for the current exams (SSC, Railway, State exams).

Hence, Q is the father of R.

Example 8 'A + B' means, 'A is the brother's wife of B'.

'A − B' means, 'A is the sister of B'.

'A × B' means, 'A is the wife of B'.

'A ÷ B' means, 'A is the daughter of B'.

If 'G + K − L ÷ M × Q', then how is G related to Q.

SSC CPO 2024

(a) Sister (b) Sister-in-law

(c) Son's wife (d) Daughter

Sol. (*c*) According to the given information,

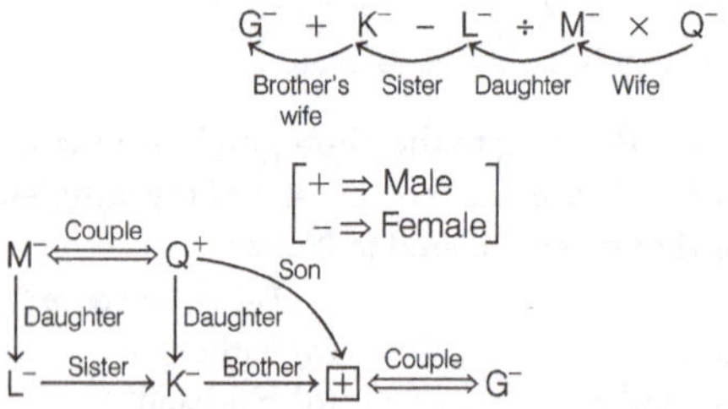

Hence, G is the son's wife of Q.

Example 9 'A + B' means, 'A is the father of B'.

'A − B' means, 'A is the mother of B'.

'A × B' means, 'A is the husband of B'.

'A ÷ B' means, 'A is the sister of B'.

If C ÷ M − S − K + T × Q, then which of the following statement is not correct?

CISF HC Min 2022

(a) K is the father-in-law of Q

(b) S is the father's father of T

(c) S is the sister's daughter of C

(d) M is the mother's mother of K

Sol. (*b*) According to the given information,

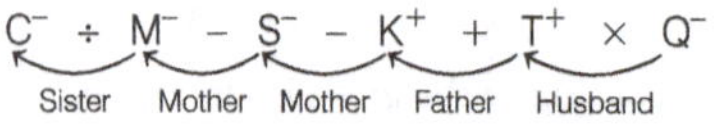

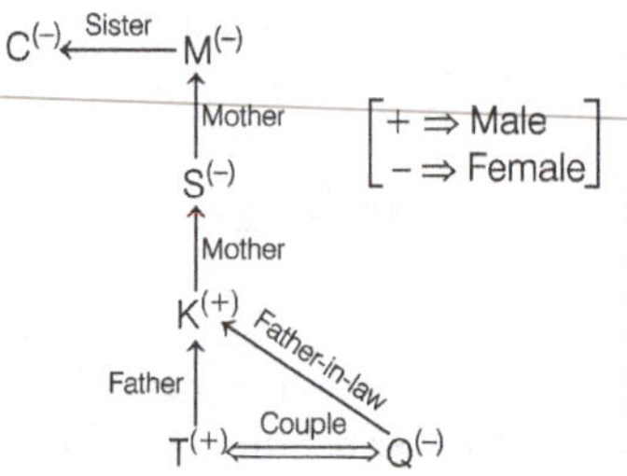

Helping Tips

To solve the questions based on blood relations, the older generation is shown at the top and the younger generation is shown at the bottom in the relation diagram.

Hence, the statement S is the father of T's father is wrong because S is the mother of T's father.

Example 10 'R + Q' means, 'R is the father of Q', 'R × Q' means, 'R is the brother of Q' and 'R − Q' means, 'R is the sister of Q', then which of the following means N is the aunt of P?

UP Police Head Operator 2024

(a) N − M + P (b) N − M × P

(c) N × M − P (d) N × P + M

Sol. (*a*) From option (a),

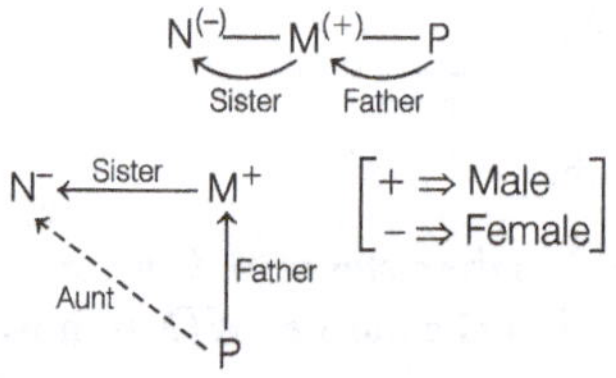

Hence, N is the aunt of P.

TOP TIPS

- First of all, it should be divided between which two person the relationship is to be found.
- The intermediate relationships given in the question should be ensured.
- Determine the gender of a person based on the information gives in the question and do not guess the gender of the person based on the name given in the question.

Chapter Challenge

Based on Facts

> **MRC*****
> **(Most Repeating Concepts)**
> Question Nos. 1, 4, 11, 14, 17, 19 and 20 are very important from the examination point of view. Question on these concepts are being asked continously in UP Police examination.

1. A is the brother of B. C is the father of D. E is the mother of B. A and D are brothers. How is E related to C? *UP Police Constable 2024*
(a) Wife
(b) Sister-in-law
(c) Niece
(d) Sister

2. If Suman is the wife of the son of Rajesh's wife, then how is Suman related to Rajesh? *SSC (10+2) 2023*
(a) Daughter-in-law (b) Wife
(c) Sister (d) Sister-in-law

3. If X is the husband of Aamir's mother's sister, then how is X related to Aamir? *RRB Group-D 2018*
(a) Father (b) Brother (c) Uncle (d) Nephew

4. Y is the sister of P. K is the father of Y and T is the wife of K. How is P related to T? *UP Police Asst. Operator 2024*
(a) Either maternal grand father or maternal grand mother
(b) Either son or daughter
(c) Either father or mother
(d) Either elder brother or elder sister

5. How is the mother of Abhishek's father's wife related to Abhishek? *CISF ASI 2023*
(a) Paternal grand mother (b) Aunt
(c) Mother (d) Maternal grand mother

6. If Q is the brother of the son of R's son, then how is Q related to R? *HCET 2023*
(a) Son (b) Uncle (c) Grandson (d) Cousin

7. Q is the mother of R. P is the husband of Q. S is the brother of R. How is P related to S? *SSC CGL (Tier II) 2023*
(a) Brother-in-law (b) Brother
(c) Father (d) Son

8. L is the wife of Q. P is the mother of M. J is the father of L. M is the sister of H. J is the husband of H. How is P related to L? *CISF Head Constable 2023*
(a) Nephew (b) Brother-in-law
(c) Maternal grand mother (d) Aunt

9. Suppose A is the daughter of B, B is the daughter of C, C is the brother of D and D is the mother of E. If E is female, then how is A related to E? *UPSSSC 2018*
(a) Nephew (b) Niece
(c) Brother (d) Sister

10. U is the father of N. N is the sister of T. T is the wife of I. I is son of L. How is U related to L. *SSC CGL Tier-II 2025*
(a) Son's wife's sister (b) Son's wife's father
(c) Son's wife (d) Son's wife's mother

11. Eena is the mother of Jatin. Pratap is the father of Bani. Sukrit is the son of Garv. Suyog's only sister is married to Garv. Suyog is the son of Anshum. Eena's husband is the only son of Pratap. Bani is the mother of Sukrit. How is Pratap related to Jatin? *SSC Steno 2021*
(a) Maternal grandfather (b) Paternal grandfather
(c) Uncle (d) Father

12. S is the brother of D. D is the father of F. F is the mother of G. G is the wife of H. How is S related to H? *RPF SI 2024*
(a) Wife's mother's mother's father
(b) Wife's mother's father's brother
(c) Wife's mother's father's father
(d) Wife's mother's mother's brother

13. P is the daughter of Q. Q is the mother of R. S is the brother of R, then how is S related to P? *HSSC Police Constable 2021*
(a) Grandfather (b) Brother
(c) Father (d) Son

14. K is the wife of L and M is the sister of L. N is the daughter of K, while O is the mother of M. How is O related to K? *UP Police Constable 2024*
(a) Father-in-law (b) Mother-in-law
(c) Mother (d) Father

15. Komal is Daman's wife. Radhika is Arpan's mother. Sayantani is Malay's daughter and Malay is Karthik's brother. Sayantani's mother Radhika is Daman's daughter-in-law. How is Komal related to Karthik? *SSC Steno 2020*
(a) Maternal grand mother (b) Mother
(c) Paternal grand mother (d) Sister

16. Ganesh was walking with the grand daughter of the father of his mother's brother. Who was he walking with? *SSC CGL (Tier-I) 2023*
(a) Mother (b) Grand daughter
(c) Daughter (d) Cousin

17. Suresh's sister is Ram's wife. Ram is Rani's brother. Ram's father is Madhur. Sheetal is Ram's grandmother. Reema is Sheetal's daughter-in-law. Rohit is Rani's brother's son. How is Rohit related to Suresh? *UP Police Constable 2024*
(a) Nephew (b) Brother
(c) Brother-in-law (d) Son

18. If 'Ravi' is the brother of 'Priya', 'Priya' is the daughter of 'Savita' and 'Vaibhav' is the father of 'Nonu', who is the only son of Savita's father-in-law. How is 'Ravi' related to 'Vaibhav'? *Rajasthan Police Constable 2022*

(a) Father (b) Grand father
(c) Grandson (d) Grand daughter

19. There are seven member in a family from four generations. There are only two married couples. W is the mother of Q. G is the husband of W. H is the daughter-in-law of W. G has only one son. F is the grand daughter of G. E is the brother of F. B is the materal grandson of H. E is unmarried. How is E related to G? ***UP Police Head Operator 2024***
(a) Grandson (b) Father
(c) Maternal grand father (d) Maternal uncle

20. Among her children, Ganga's favourites are Ram and Rekha. Rekha is Sharad's mother, whom his maternal uncle Mithun loves the most. The head of the family is Ramlal, who is succeeded by his son Gopal and Mohan. Gopal and Ganga have been married for 35 yr and have 3 children. What is the relationship between Mithun and Mohan? ***UP Police Constable 2024***
(a) Nephew (b) Son
(c) Brother (d) Uncle

Based on Conversation/Photograph

21. K said to L, "You are the daughter of the son-in-law of my husband." How is L related to K? ***UP Police Constable 2019***
(a) L is the grand daughter of K
(b) L is the daughter of K
(c) L is the son-in-law of K
(d) L is the father of K

22. Pointing to a girl, Rohan said, "She is the elder of the two sisters of the son of my father's wife". Then, how is the girl related to Rohan? ***DP Head Constable 2022***
(a) Father's sister (b) Grandmother
(c) Mother (d) Sister

23. A man said to a woman, "Your mother's husband's sister is my aunt". How is the woman related to the man? ***CRPF (HC) 2023***
(a) Sister (b) Mother
(c) Cousin (d) Either (a) or (c)

24. Pointing to a man in a photograph, Ram said, "He is the only son of my grandfather and husband of my mother". How is that man related to Ram? ***MP Police Constable 2022***
(a) Uncle (b) Ram's grandfather's brother
(c) Brother (d) Father

25. Introducing a girl, Anthony said, "She is the daughter of the daughter of my maternal aunt's mother". How is the girl related to Anthony? ***UP Police Constable Re-Exam 30 Aug 2024***
(a) Niece (b) Nephew
(c) Brother (d) Sister

26. Pointing to Rita, Nikhil said, "I am the only son of her mother's son". How is Rita related to Nikhil? ***UPSSSC PET 2021***
(a) Aunt (b) Niece (c) Mother (d) Cousin

27. Pointing to a girl, Ankit said, "This girl is the wife of my mother's grandson". How is Ankit related to that girl? ***HCET 2022***
(a) Father (b) Uncle
(c) Son (d) Father-in-law

28. Pointing to Falguni, Hardik said, "The son of her only brother is the brother of my wife". How is Falguni related to Hardik? ***UPSSSC PET 2022***
(a) Father-in-law's sister (b) Niece
(c) Maternal Aunt (d) Grandmother

29. Pointing to the photograph of a man, Rajni said, "He is the brother of the daughter of the wife of my husband". How is that man related to Rajni? ***CISF HC (Min) 2022***
(a) Father (b) Brother (c) Grandfather (d) Son

30. Introducing Kajal, Varsha said, "she is the sister of the son of the wife of my husband". How is Varsha related to Kajal? ***DSSSB Workshop 2024***
(a) Daughter (b) Sister (c) Mother (d) Son

31. Pointing to a girl, Priyanka said that the girl is the daughter of the only son-in-law of my mother's husband. How is Priyanka related to that girl? ***CISF ASI 2023***
(a) Aunt (b) Maternal grandmother
(c) Daughter (d) Mother

32. Pointing to a woman, a man said, "Her father is the only son of my father." How is the man related to the woman? ***UGC NET 2018***
(a) Father of woman (b) Brother of woman
(c) Brother-in-law of woman (d) Father-in-law of woman

33. Looking at a family photograph, F pointed to A and said, "She is the wife of B who is the father of E, who is the sister of D, who is the father of my sister G." How is B related to F? ***SSC Steno 2022***
(a) Father's brother (b) Son
(c) Father's father (d) Father

34. Rahul said to a man, "Yesterday I defeated the only brother of my grandmother's daughter". Whom did Rahul defeat? ***HSSC Police Constable 2021***
(a) Son (b) Father (c) Brother (d) Cousin

Based on Codes and Mathematical Symbols

35. In a certain code language,
$A + B$ means 'A is the mother of B',
$A - B$ means 'A is the brother of B',
$A \times B$ means 'A is the wife of B' and
$A \div B$ means 'A is the father of B'.
Based on the above, how is U related to Z if '$U + V \div W - Y \times Z$'? ***SSC CGL Tier-II 2025***

Chapter Challenge Blood Relation

(a) Wife's Father's Sister (b) Wife's Mother's Mother
(c) Wife's Mother's Sister (d) Wife's Father's Mother

36. In a certain code language,
'A % B' means 'A is the father of B'.
'A @ B' means 'A is the brother of B'.
'A & B' means 'A is the daughter of B'.
'A # B' means 'A is the mother of B'.
If E @ M # N % Q @ R & P, then how is N related to P? ***Delhi Police 2022***
(a) Son-in-law (b) Wife
(c) Son (d) Husband

37. 'I × J' means 'I is the mother of J'.
'I + J' means 'I is the husband of J'.
'I ÷ J' means 'I is the sister of J'.
'I – J' means 'I is the brother of J'.
In the expression 'Q ÷ X + Y × Z', how is 'Q' related to 'Z'. ***SSC Constable (GD) 2024***
(a) Wife (b) Daughter
(c) Father's sister (d) Mother's sister

38. 'A + B' means 'A is the brother of B'.
'A – B' means 'A is the wife of B'.
'A × B' means 'A is the father of B'.
'A ÷ B' means 'A is the sister of B'.
Using the same meaning of mathematical operators given above, find out how T is related to Z in 'T × X ÷ Y + Z'? ***SSC (10+2) 2024***
(a) Father (b) Father-in-law
(c) Sister-in-law (d) Brother

39. In a certain code language,
A + B means 'A is the mother of B'.
A – B means 'A is the brother of B',
A × B means 'A is the wife of B',
A ÷ B means 'A is the father of B'.
and A # B means 'A is the daughter of B'.
How is R related to T
if 'Q # R × P ÷ K × T'? ***RRB ALP 2024***
(a) Daughter's daughter (b) Wife's mother
(c) Son's wife (d) Son's daughter

40. In a certain code language,
A % B means 'A is the mother of B'.
A # B means 'A is the brother of B'.
A @ B means 'A is the wife of B'.
A & B means 'A is the father of B'.
If P & Q % R # S @ T, then how is P related to T?
(a) Wife's brother ***SSC (10+2) 2024***
(b) Father of wife's mother
(c) Brother of wife's mother
(d) Wife's father

41. In a certain code language,
'A + B' means 'A is the father of B'.
'A – B' means 'A is the mother of B'.
'A ÷ B' means 'A is the daughter of B'.
If M ÷ J + O – Q, then how is M related to Q?
Rajasthan Police Constable 2022
(a) Niece (b) Sister
(c) Daughter (d) Maternal aunt

42. 'A = B' means 'A is the father of B'.
'A $ B' means 'A is the sister of B'.
'A * B' means 'A is the mother of B'.
'A ? B' means 'A is the son of B'.
If M ? C $ J * Z, then how is J related to M?
CISF 2023
(a) Maternal aunt (b) Sister
(c) Brother (d) Maternal grand mother

43. In a certain code language,
'A + B' means 'A is the brother of B'.
'A – B' means 'A is the son of B'.
'A × B' means 'A is the wife of B'.
and 'A ÷ B' means 'A is the father of B'.
If 'P – Q ÷ R × S + T', then how is Q related to S?
RRB ALP 2024
(a) Father (b) Wife's brother
(c) Husband's brother (d) Wife's father

44. 'P × Q' means 'P is the father of Q'.
'P * Q' means 'P is the sister of Q'.
'P + Q' means 'P is the brother of Q'.
'P – Q' means 'P is the mother of Q'.
'P ÷ Q' means 'P is the son of Q'.
'P = Q' means 'P is the daughter of Q'.
If 'V × W + X * Y = Z', then how is V related Z?
MP Police Constable 2022
(a) Wife (b) Brother
(c) Sister (d) Husband

45. In a certain code language,
'A + B' means 'A is the sister of B'.
'A – B' means 'A is the mother of B'.
'A × B' means 'A is the husband of B'.
and 'A ÷ B' means 'A is the father of B'.
If 'M + U – H ÷ S × N', then how is S related to U?
SSC (10+2) 2023
(a) Father's son (b) Wife's father
(c) Sister's son (d) Son's son

46. 'A + B' means 'A is the father of B'.
'A – B' means 'A is the mother of B'.
'A * B' means 'A is the brother of B'.
and 'A ÷ B' means 'A is the daughter of B'.
If S ÷ T * U + Z, then which of the following is correct? ***UP (AO) 2024***
(a) S is the daughter of Z
(b) Z is the aunt of S
(c) S is the mother of Z
(d) S is the cousin of Z

47. 'A # B' means 'A is the sister of B'.
'A $ B' means 'A is the father of B'.
'A @ B' means 'A is the wife of B'.
'A % B' means 'A is the brother of B'.
Which of the following options means J is the father of R? *CUET (UG) 2022*
(a) J @ C $ K % M # R (b) C @ J $ K % M # R
(c) C @ J % K $ M # R (d) C @ R $ K % M # J

48. In a certain code language,
A + B means 'A is the mother of B',
A – B means 'A is the brother of B',
A × B means 'A is the wife of B' and
A ÷ B means 'A is the father of B'. *SSC CGL Tier-II 2025*
Based on the above, how is U related to Z if 'U – V × W ÷ Y + Z'?
(a) Mother's mother's father
(b) Mother's father's brother
(c) Mother's mother's brother
(d) Mother's father's father

49. In a certain code language,
P + Q means 'P is the mother of Q',
P – Q means 'P is the brother of Q',
P × Q means 'P is the wife of Q' and
P ÷ Q means 'P is the father of Q'. *SSC CGL Tier-II 2025*
Based on the above, how is U related to Z if 'U– V + W ÷ Y × Z'?
(a) Wife's father's mother's brother
(b) Wife's father's mother's father
(c) Wife's mother's mother's father
(d) Wife's mother's mother's brother

50. If 'A & B' means 'A is the father of B' and 'A @ B' means 'A is the sister of B', then which of the following expression means 'H is the father of M'? *SSC (10+2) 2021*
(a) H @ K @ P & M (b) K & H @ P @ M
(c) M & K @ P @ H (d) H & K @ P @ M

51. In a certain code language,
'P + Q' means 'P is the daughter of Q'.
'P × Q' means 'P is the son of Q'.
'P – Q' means 'P is the wife of Q'.
Then which option in the following expression 'A + B – C × D' is true? *RRB NTPC 2022*
(a) B is the son of D (b) A is the son's daughter of D
(c) A is the son of D (d) C is the wife of D

52. In a certain code language,
A + B means 'A is the brother of B',
A – B means 'A is the wife of B',
A × B means 'A is the father of B',
and A ÷ B means 'A is the sister of B'.
How is P related to T if 'P × Q ÷ R – S × T' ? *RRB Technician Grade III 2024*
(a) Father's father (b) Mother's brother
(c) Mother's father (d) Father's brother

53. If 'A $ B' means 'A is the father of B', 'A # B' means 'A is the mother of B', 'A × B' means 'A is the sister of B', then how is W related to U in W # X × Y $ U? *UP Police Constable 2024*
(a) Grand mother (b) Mother
(c) Grand father (d) Mother-in-law

54. If C % D means 'C is the wife of D', C & D means 'C is the father of D' and C $ D means 'C is the daughter of D', then what will 'X $ Y % W & Z' mean, if W has only one daughter?
(a) X is the son of Z
(b) Z is the mother's sister of X
(c) X is the sister of Z
(d) Z is the sister of X

> **Trending Concept**
> Question based on coded blood relation being asked in the examination like SSC CGL, MTS and RRB NTPC.

55. In a certain code language,
'A + B' means 'A is the mother of B'.
'A – B' means 'A is the father of B'.
'A $ B' means 'A is the son of B'.
'A % B' means 'A is the sister of B'.
'A / B' means 'A is the wife of B'.
and 'A = B' means 'A is the brother of B'.
Which of the following means A is the daughter of K? *SSC CGL (Tier-I) 2024*
I. A + K / J – P = D
II. J % P = K + A = D
III. K + A / P – D % J
IV. D + K = A / P – J
(a) IV (b) I (c) III (d) II

Right Key

1. (a)	2. (a)	3. (c)	4. (b)	5. (d)	6. (c)	7. (c)	8. (c)	9. (b)	10. (b)
11. (b)	12. (b)	13. (b)	14. (b)	15. (b)	16. (d)	17. (a)	18. (c)	19. (a)	20. (a)
21. (a)	22. (d)	23. (a)	24. (d)	25. (d)	26. (a)	27. (d)	28. (a)	29. (d)	30. (c)
31. (d)	32. (a)	33. (c)	34. (b)	35. (d)	36. (d)	37. (c)	38. (a)	39. (b)	40. (b)
41. (d)	42. (a)	43. (d)	44. (d)	45. (d)	46. (d)	47. (b)	48. (c)	49. (a)	50. (d)
51. (b)	52. (c)	53. (a)	54. (c)	55. (c)					

Solutions

1. *(a)* According to the given information,

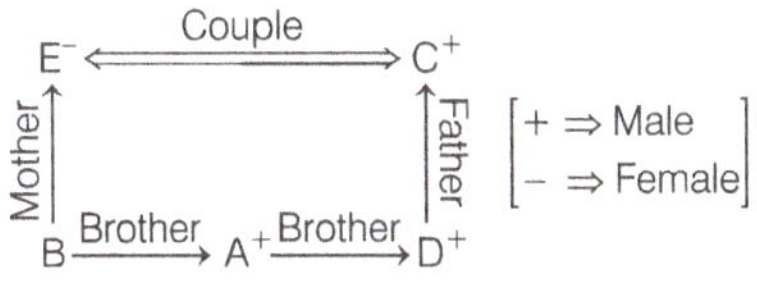

Hence, E is the wife of C.

2. *(a)* According to the given information,

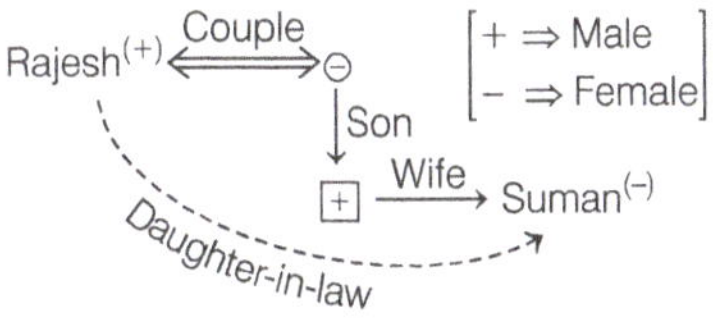

Hence, Suman is the daughter-in-law of Rajesh.

3. *(c)* According to the given information,

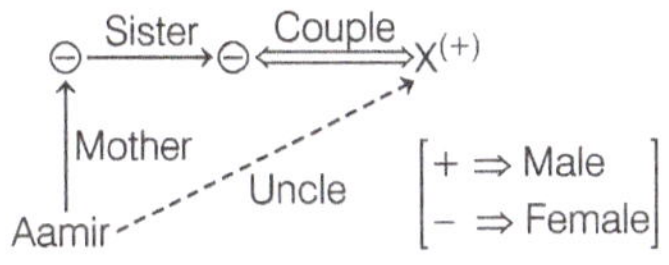

Hence, X is the uncle of Aamir.

4. *(b)* According to the given information,

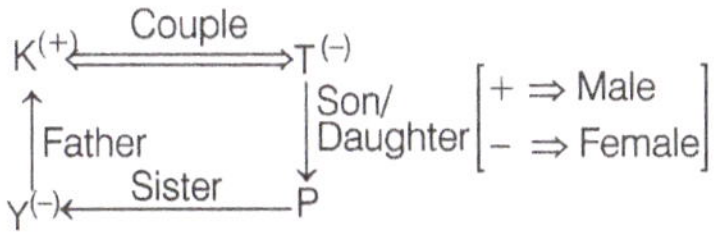

The gender of P is not known from the question.

Hence, P is either the son or daughter of T.

5. *(d)* According to the given information,

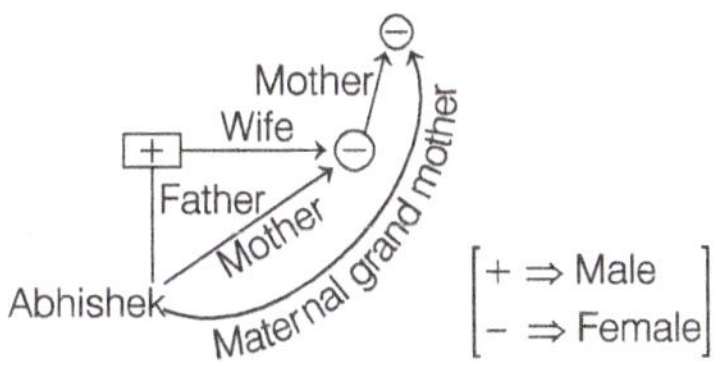

Hence, the mother of Abhishek's father's wife will be Abhishek's maternal grand mother.

6. *(c)* According to the given information,

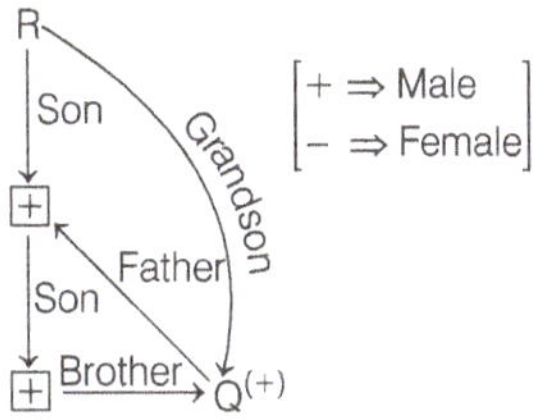

Hence, Q is the grandson of R.

7. *(c)* According to the given information,

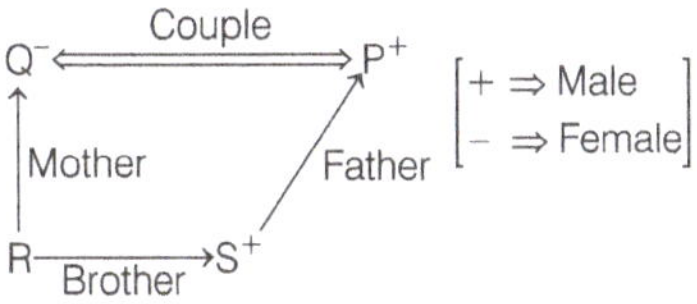

Hence, P is the father of S.

8. *(c)* According to the given information,

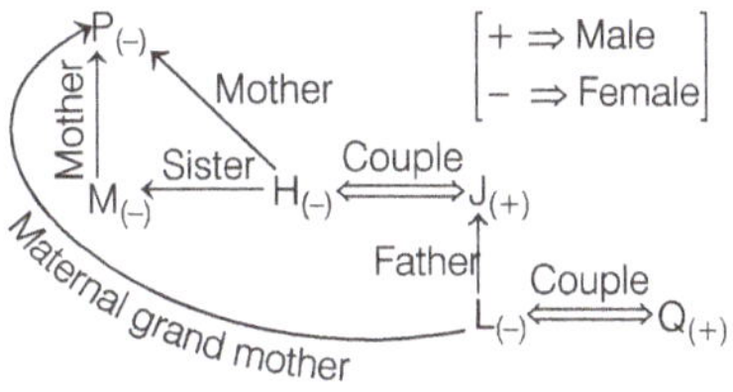

Hence, P is the maternal grand mother of L.

9. *(b)* According to the given information,

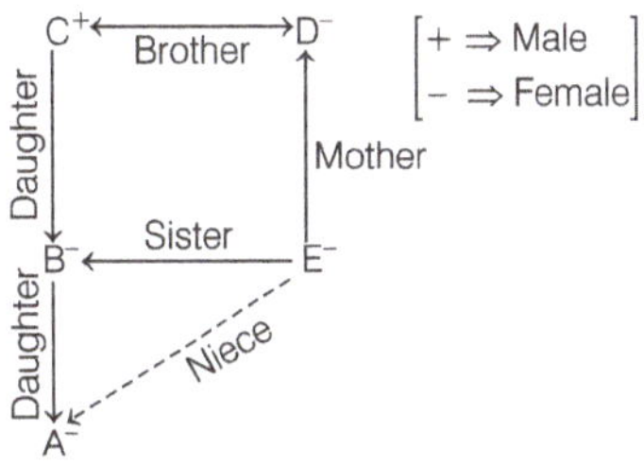

Hence, A is the niece of E.

10. *(b)* According to the question,

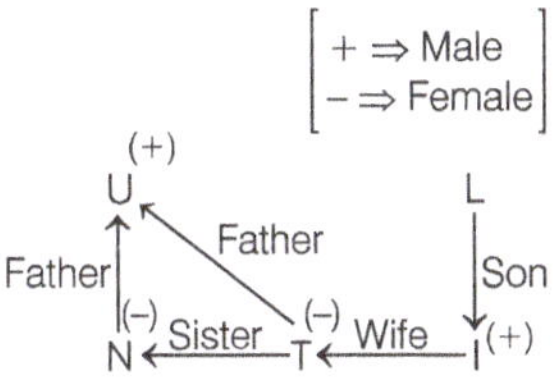

It is clear from the above diagram that U is L's son's wife's father.

11. *(b)* According to the given information,

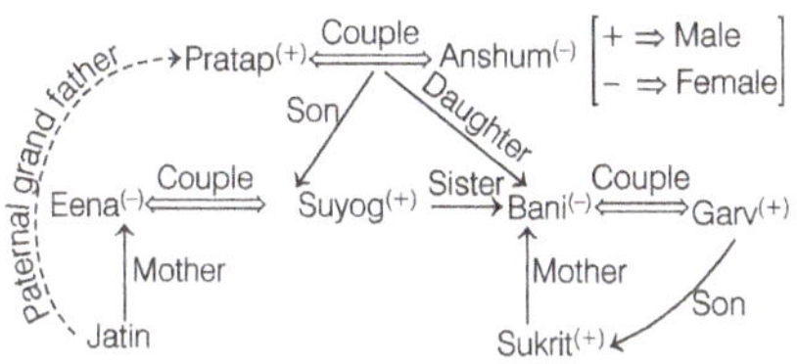

Hence, Pratap is the paternal grand father of Jatin.

12. *(b)* According to the question,

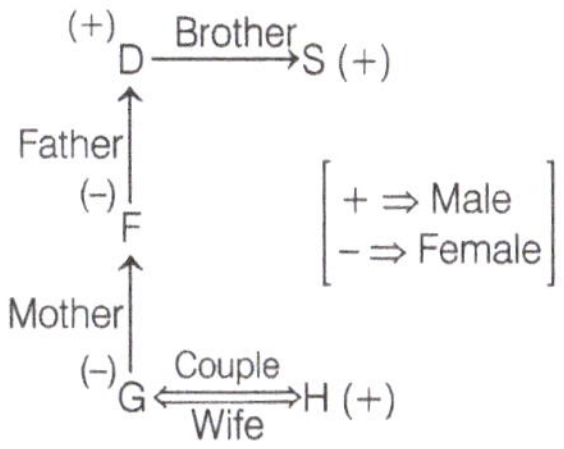

From the above diagram it is clear that S is H's wife's mother's father's brother.

13. *(b)* According to the given information,

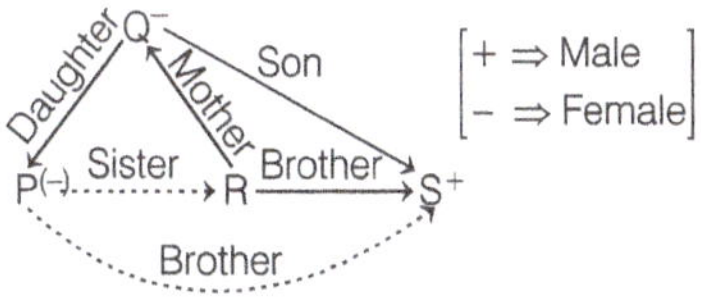

Hence, S is the brother of P.

14. *(b)* According to the given information,

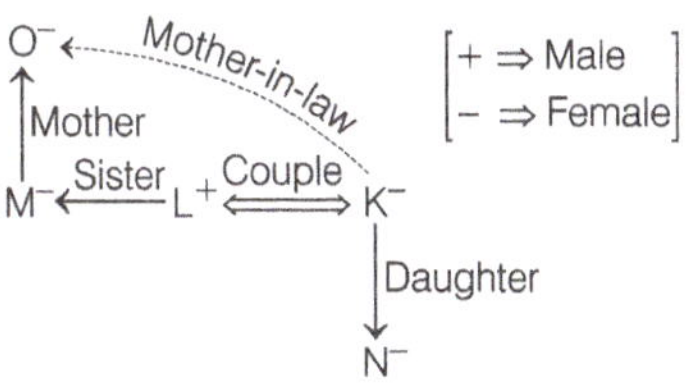

Hence, O is the mother-in-law of K.

15. *(b)* According to the given information,

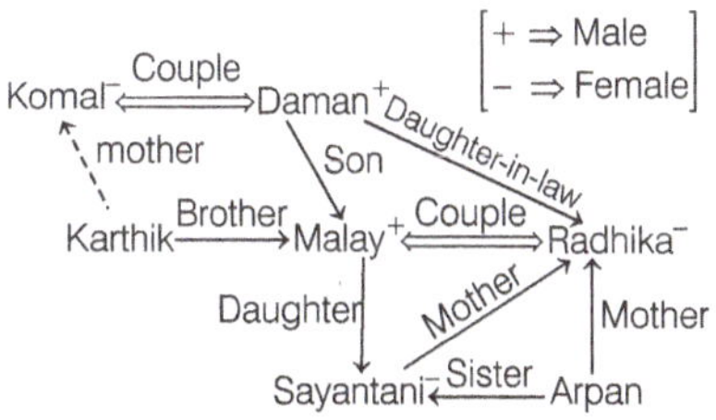

Hence, Komal is the mother of Kartik.

16. (*d*) According to the given information,

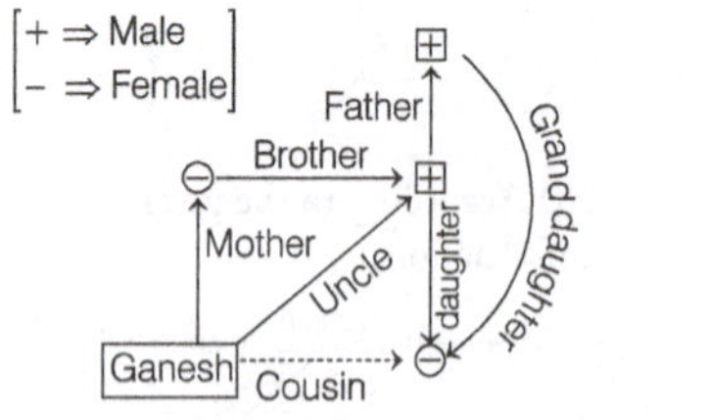

Hence, Ganesh was walking with his 'cousin'.

17. (*a*) According to the given information,

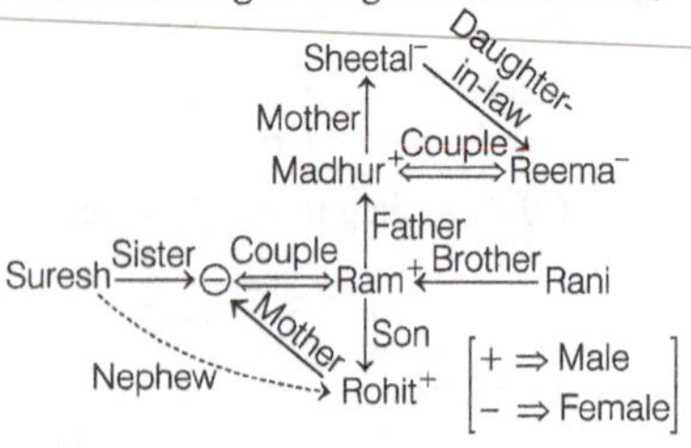

Hence, Rohit is the nephew of Suresh.

18. (*c*) According to the given information,

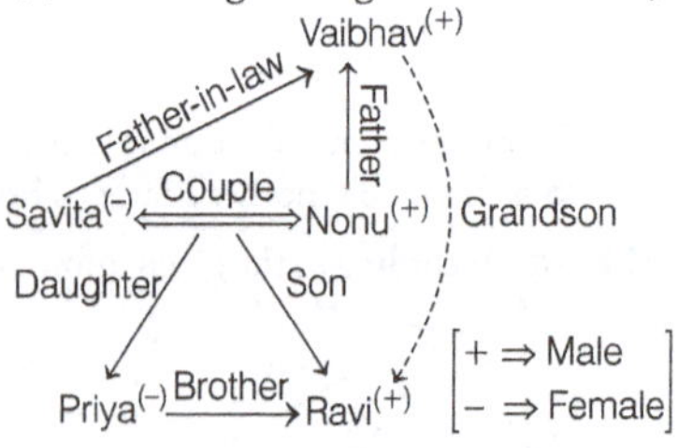

Hence, Ravi is the grandson of Vaibhav.

19. (*a*) According to the given information,

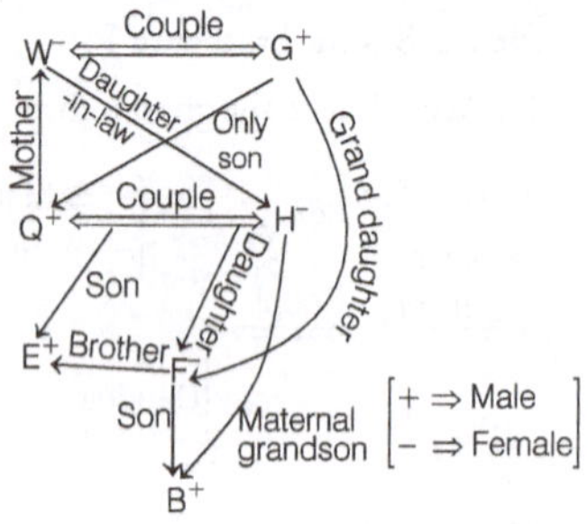

Hence, E is the grandson of G.

20. (*a*) According to the given information,

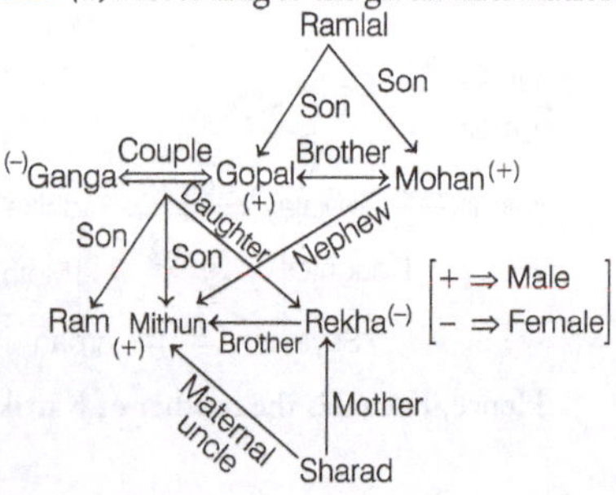

Hence, Mithun is the nephew of Mohan.

21. (*a*) According to the given information,

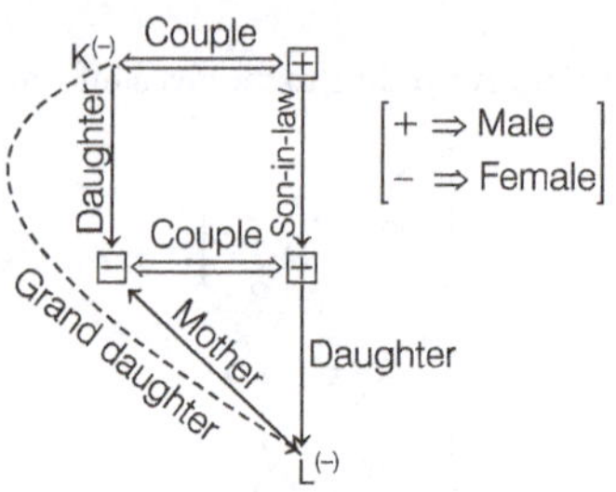

Hence, L is the grand daughter of K.

22. (*d*) According to the given information,

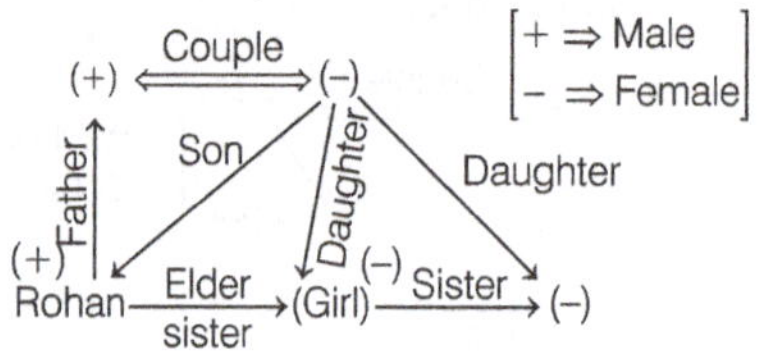

Hence, girl is the sister of Rohan.

23. (*a*) According to the given information,

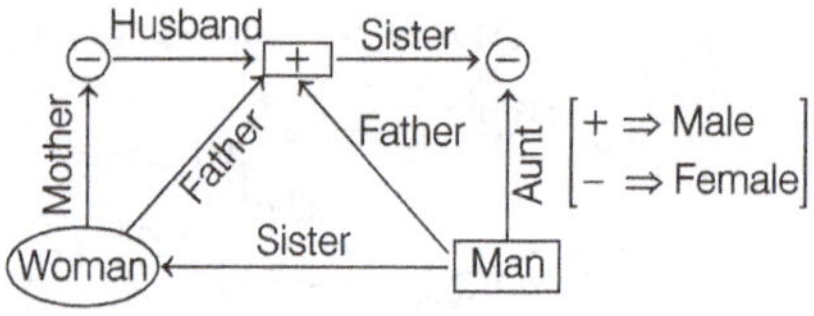

Hence, woman is the sister of man.

24. (*d*) According to the given information,

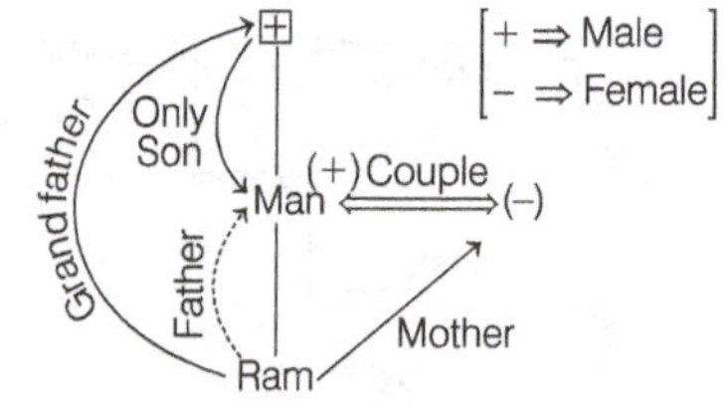

Hence, man is the father of Ram.

25. (*d*) According to the given information,

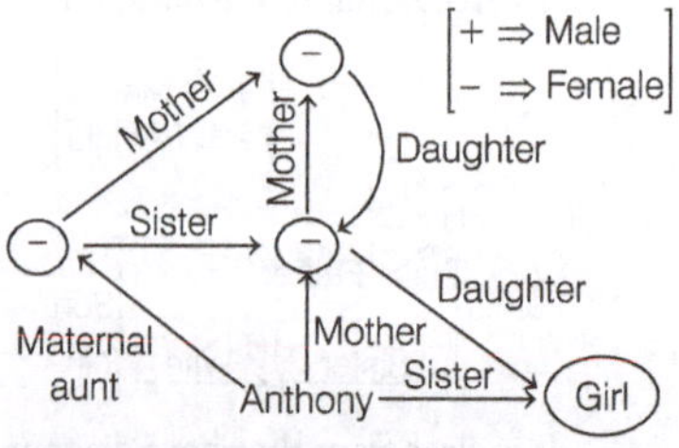

Hence, girl is the sister of Anthony.

26. (*a*) According to the given information,

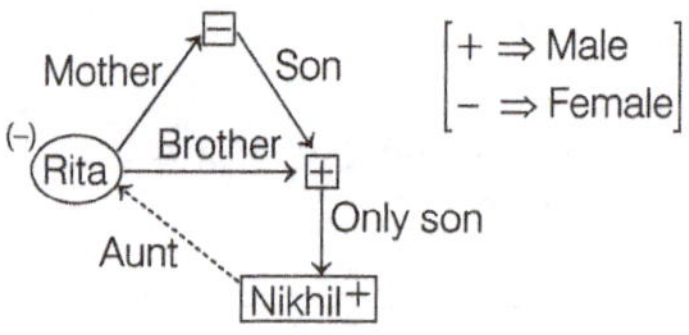

Hence, Rita is the aunt of Nikhil.

TOP TIPS Never assume "only son" means the only child.

27. (*d*) According to the given information,

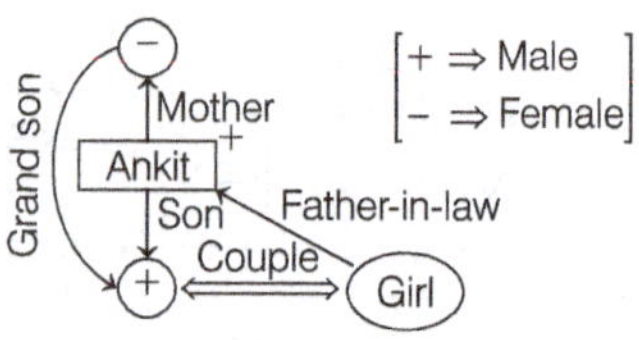

Hence, Ankit is the father-in-law of that girl.

28. (*a*) According to the given information,

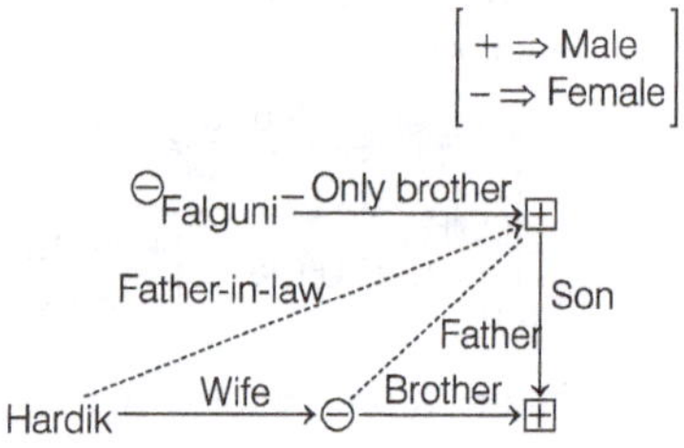

Hence, Falguni is the sister of Hardik's father-in-law.

29. (*d*) According to the given information,

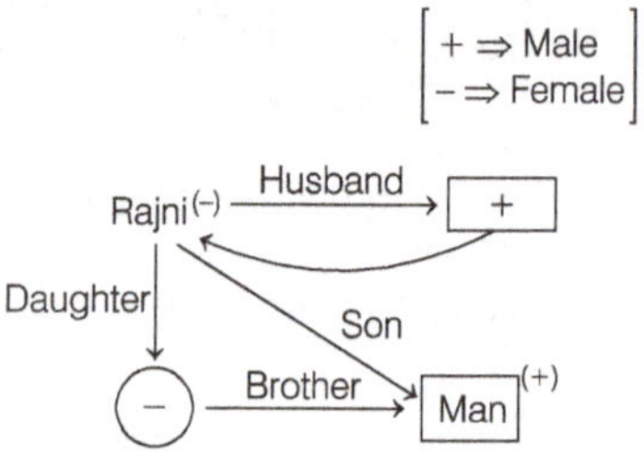

Hence, man is the son of Rajni.

30. (*c*) According to the given information,

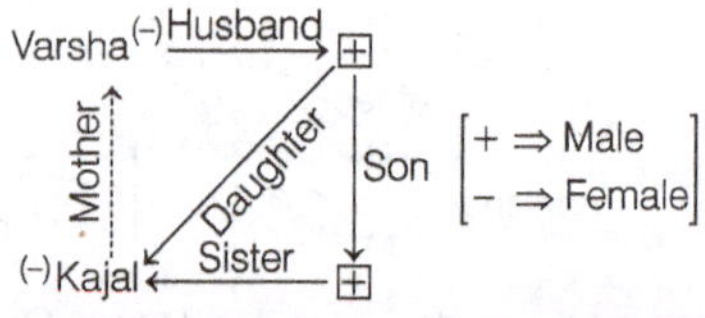

Hence, Varsha is the mother of Kajal.

31. (*d*) According to the given information,

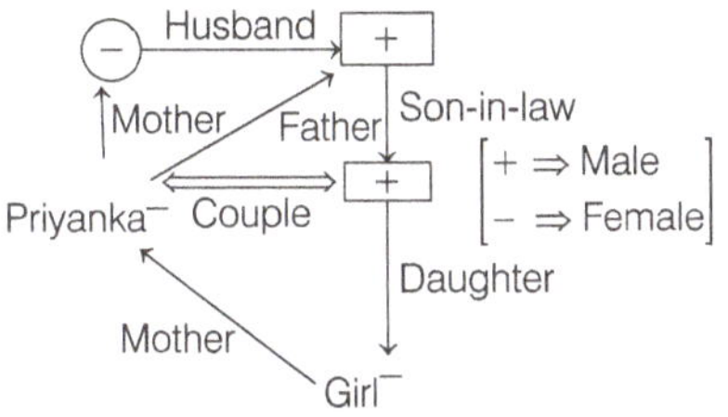

Hence, Priyanka is the mother of that girl.

32. (*a*) According to the given information,

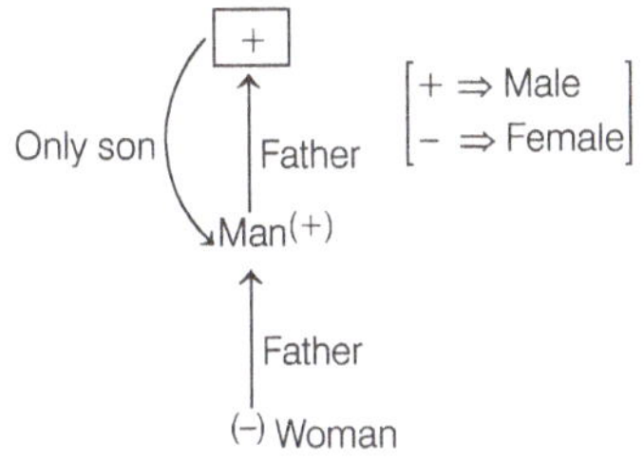

So, the man is the father of the woman.

33. (*c*) According to the given information,

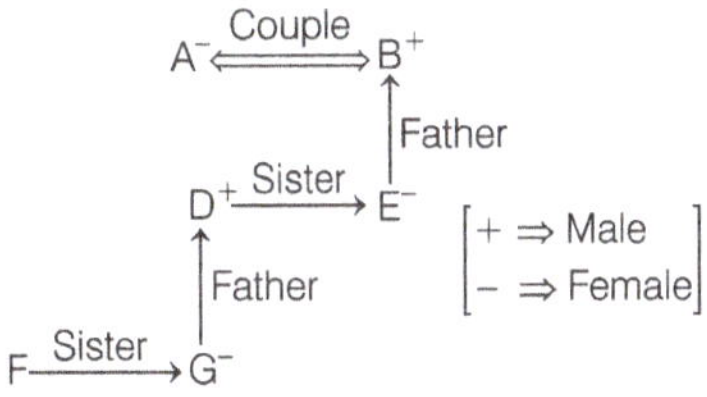

Hence, B is the father's father of F.

34. (*b*) According to the given information,

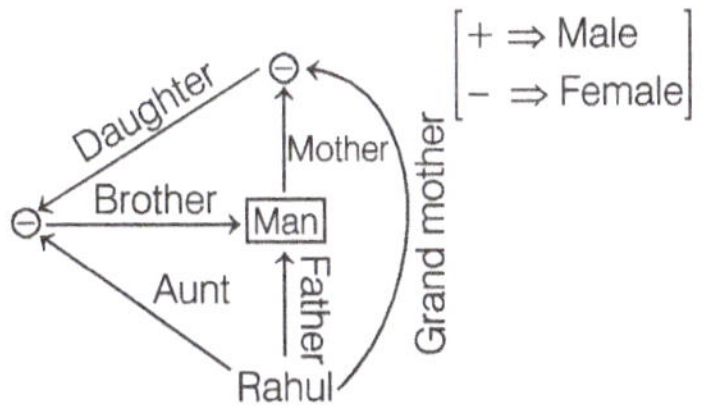

Hence, Rahul defeated his father.

35. (*d*) According to the given information,

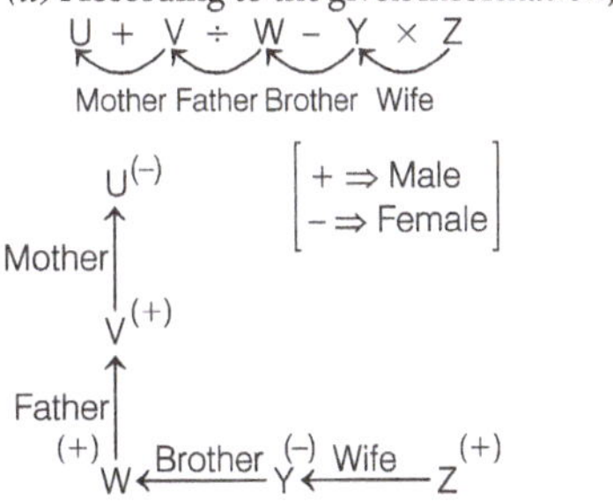

From the above diagram it is clear that U is Z's wife's father's mother.

36. (*d*) According to the given information,

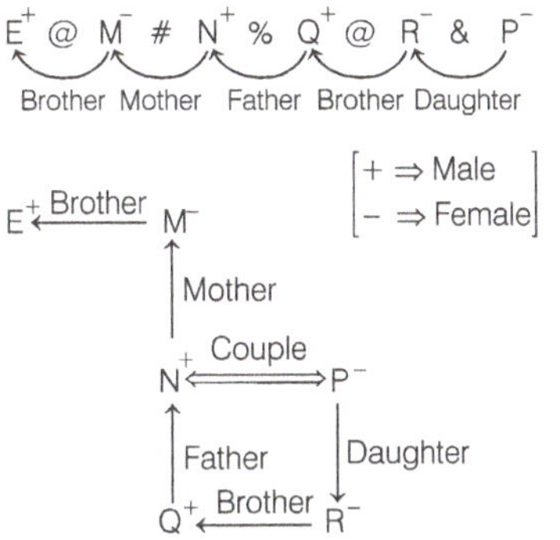

Hence, N is the husband of P.

37. (*c*) According to the given information,

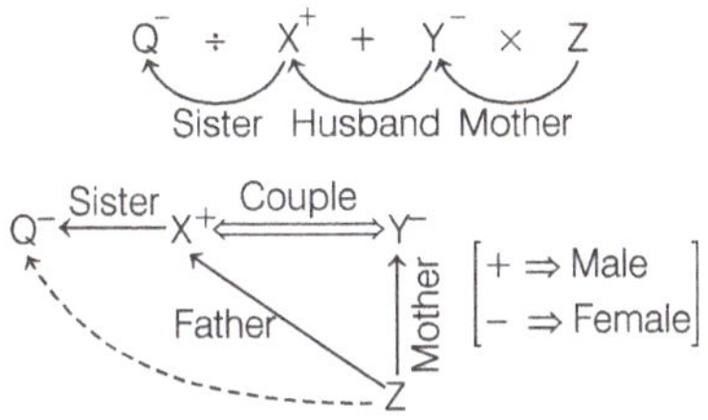

Hence, Q is the father's sister of Z.

38. (*a*) According to the given information,

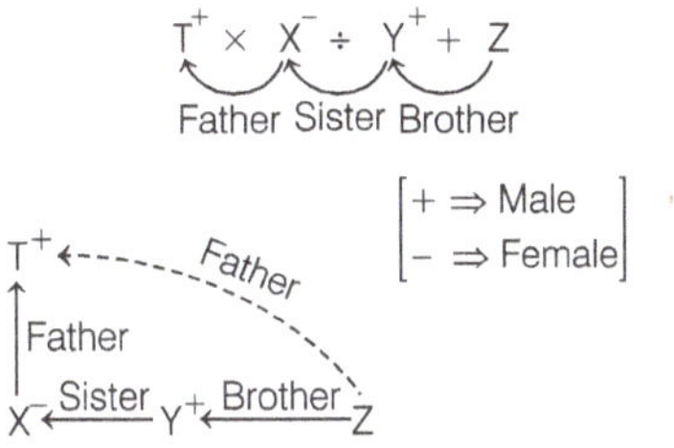

Hence, T is the father of Z.

39. (*b*) According to the given information,

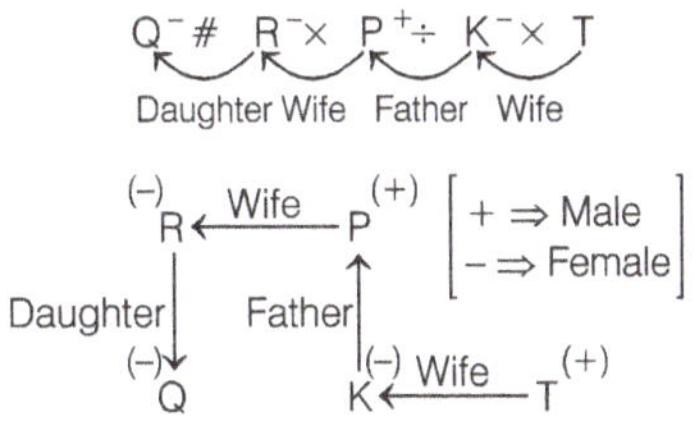

From the above diagram it is clear that R is T's wife's mother.

40. (*b*) According to the given information,

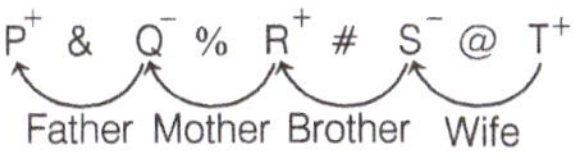

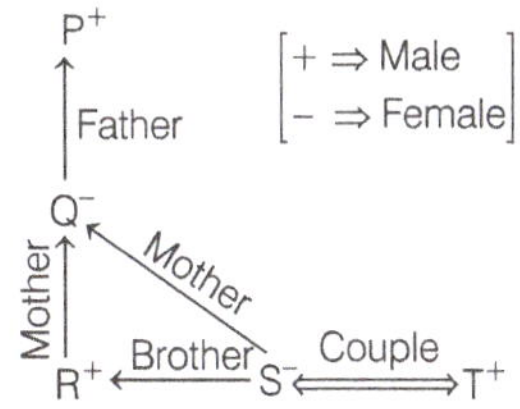

Hence, P is the father of T's wife's mother.

41. (*d*) According to the given information,

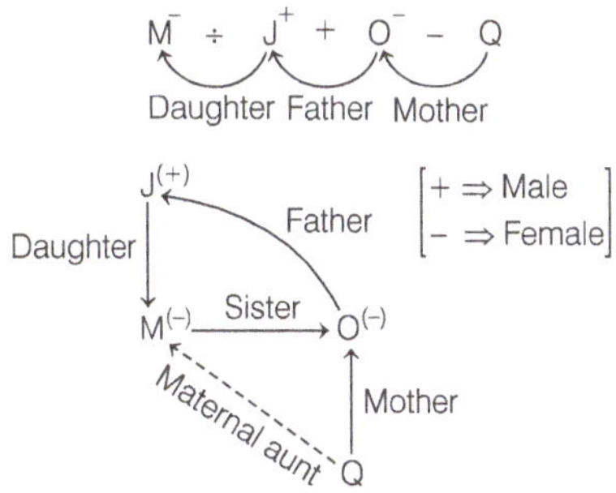

Hence, M is the maternal aunt of Q.

42. (*a*) According to the given information,

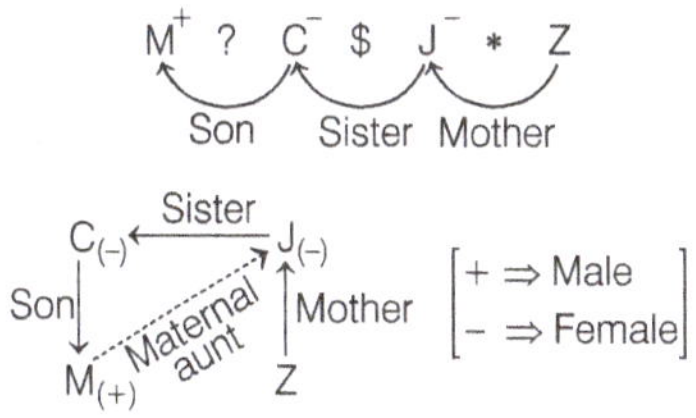

Hence, J is the maternal aunt of M.

43. (*d*) According to the given information,

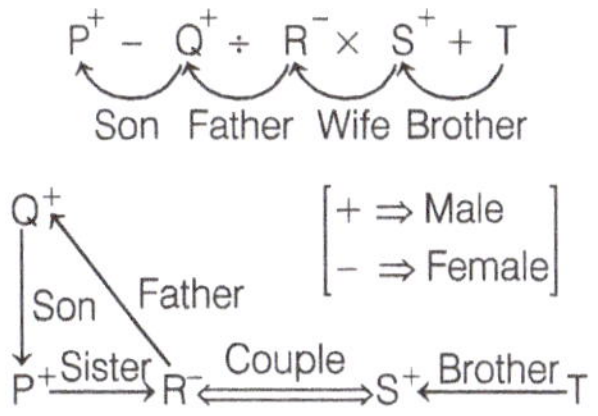

Hence, Q is the wife's father of S.

44. (*d*) According to the given information,

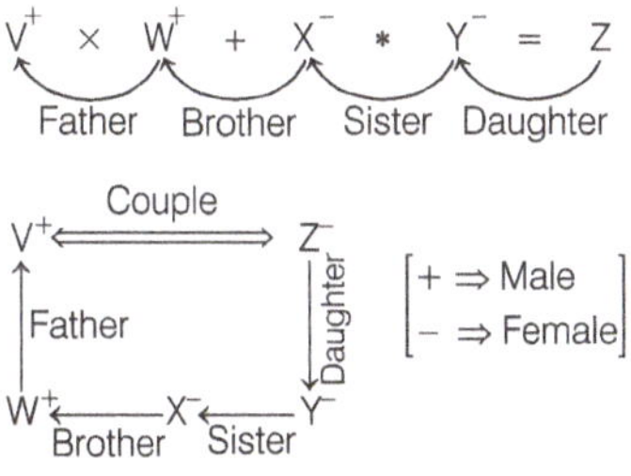

Hence, V is the husband of Z.

45. (*d*) According to the given information,

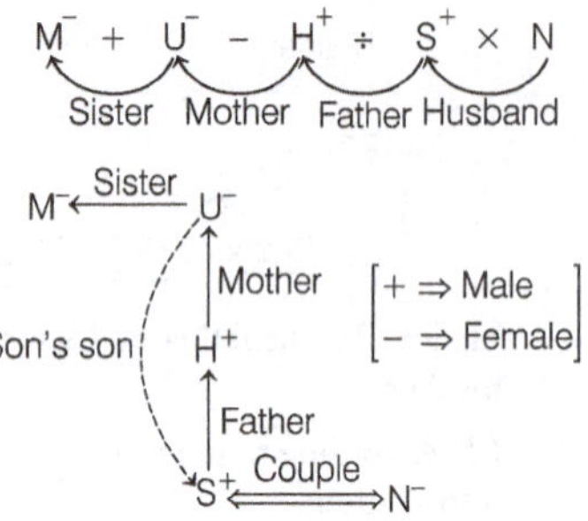

Hence, S is the son's son of U.

46. (*d*) According to the given information,

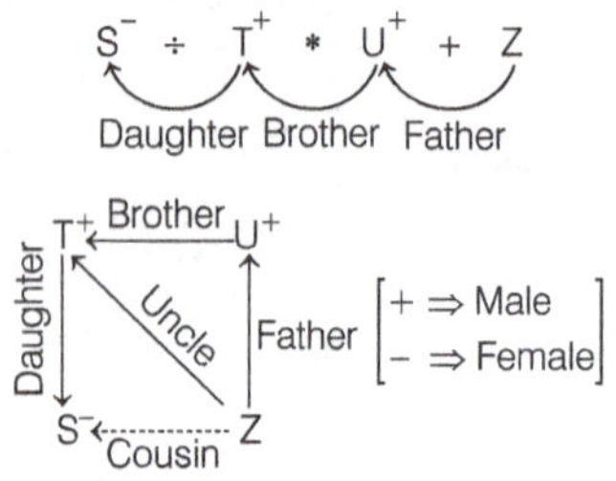

Hence, S is the cousin of Z.

47. (*b*) According to the given information,

From option (b),

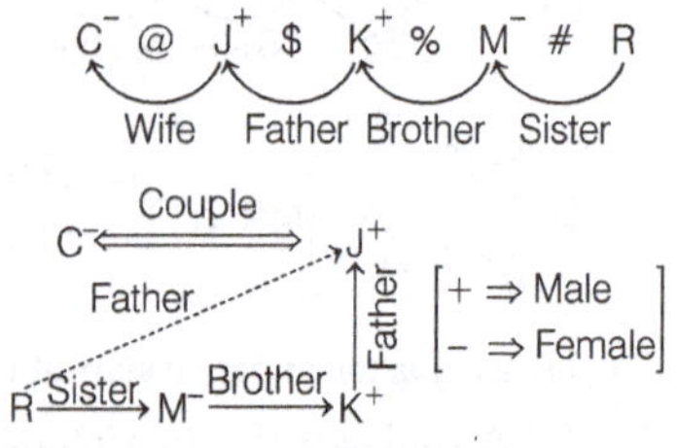

Hence, J is the father of R.

48. (*c*) According to the given information,

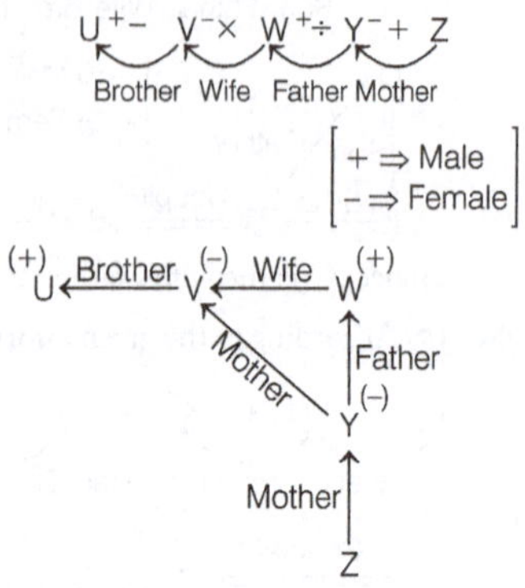

From the above diagram, it is clear that U is mother's mother's brother of Z.

49. (*a*) According to the given information,

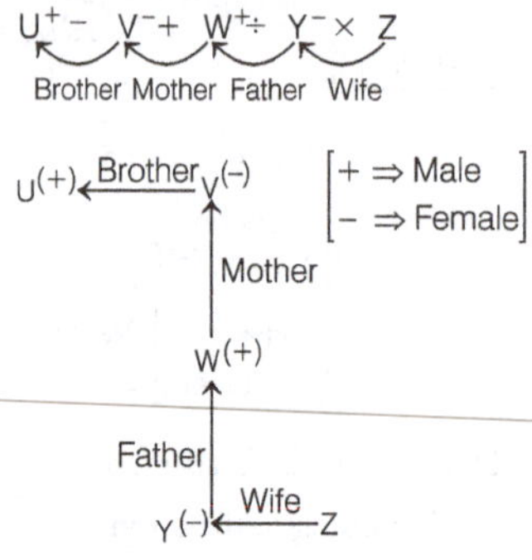

From the above relation diagram it is clear that U is Z's wife's father's mother's brother.

50. (*d*) From option (d),

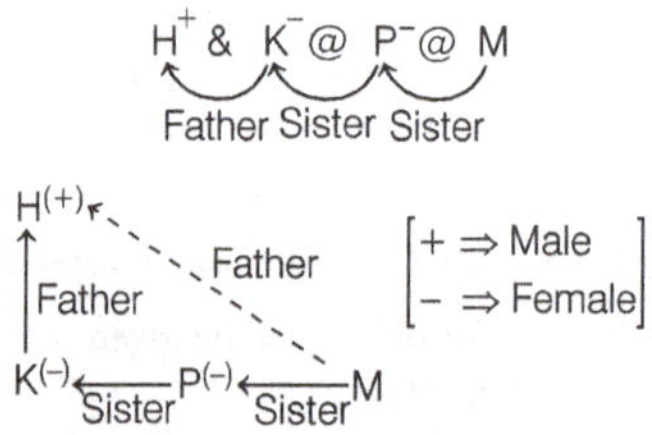

Hence, H is the father of M.

51. (*b*) According to the given information,

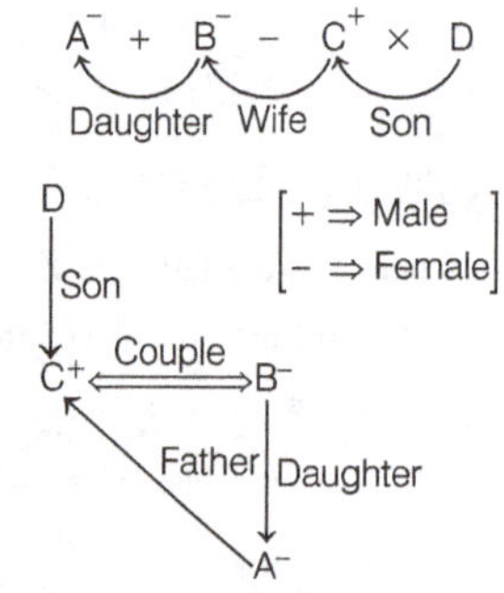

Hence, A is the son's daughter of D.

52. (*c*) According to the given information,

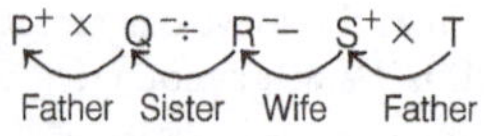

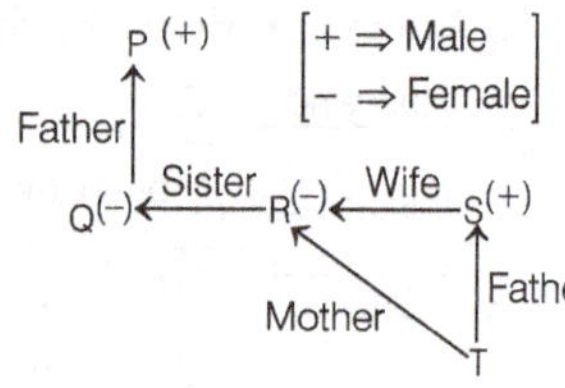

From the above relation diagram it is clear that P is mother's father of T.

53. (*a*) According to the given information,

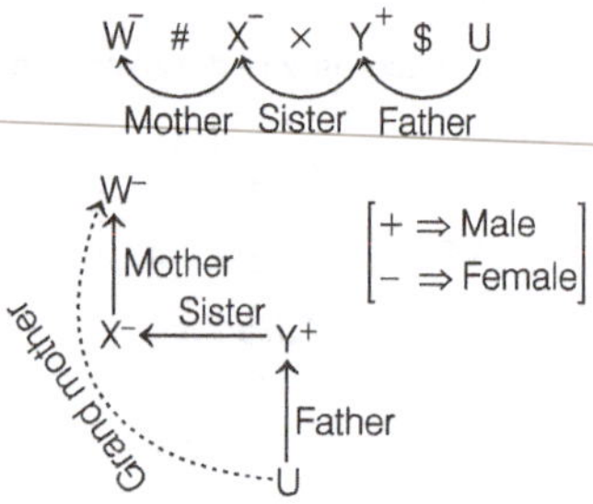

Hence, W is the grand mother of U.

54. (*c*) According to the given information,

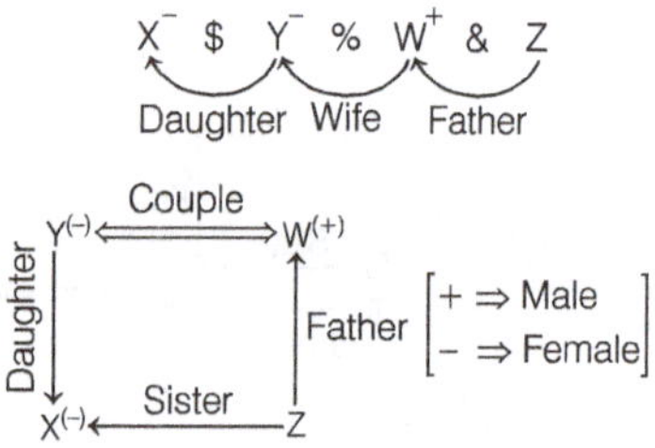

Hence, X is the sister of Z.

55. (*c*) From option (c),

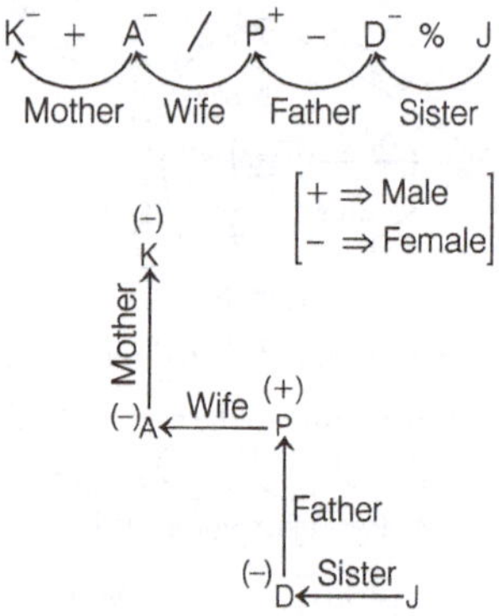

Hence, A is the daughter of K.

CHAPTER

11 Ranking Arrangement Test

Ranking Arrangement Test

The process of arranging two or more persons, objects or places in a sequence by making relative comparisons with other persons, objects or places on the basis of their quality, quantity, size, position/situation etc. is called ranking arrangement.

This type of questions are based on comparison of objects or persons and their position in the row and finding the total number of persons/objects in a row.

Ranking Test

This type of questions are generally based on finding the position of a person or object from right/left and from top/bottom in a row/class and the total number of objects or persons in a row/class.

e.g. If Rohit is ranked 19th from the top among 45 boys, then what will be his position from the bottom?

(a) 29 (b) 27

(c) 26 (d) 30

Sol. (b) According to the question,

Rohit's rank from the top = 19

Total number of boys = 45

∴ Rohit's rank from the bottom

= (Total number of boys + 1) – Rohit's rank from the top

= (45 + 1) – 19

= 46 – 19

= 27

Arrangement Test

This types of questions are generally based on the comparison of two or more persons or objects on the basis of their characterstics such as age, weight, quality, size, ability and intelligency etc. Under this position of objects and persons is know by arranging them in a required order.

e.g. Four friends A, B, C and D divide some amount among themselves in such a way that A gets one less than B, C gets 5 more than D and D gets 3 more than B. Who gets the least amount?

(a) A (b) C

(c) D (d) B

Sol. (a) According to the question,

$B > A$ ...(i)

$C > D$ ...(ii)

$D > B$ ...(iii)

On arranging the equations

$C > D > B > A$

Hence, A gets the least amount.

Score Booster

The position or rank can be calculated with the help of following formulae

1. Total number of persons in a row = (Rank of a person from upper or left end + Rank of that person from lower or right end) – 1
2. Rank of a person from upper or left end = (Total number of persons in row – Rank of that person from lower or right end) + 1
3. Rank of a person from lower or right end = (Total number of persons in row – Rank of that person from upper or left end) + 1
4. In case of interchanging of positions
   (a) Total number of persons = (Initial position of 1st person + Interchanged position of 2nd person) – 1
   (b) New position of 2nd person = (Difference in the two positions of 1st person) + Initial position of 2nd person
5. Formula for finding the number of persons between two given persons
   (a) For non-overlapping condition, number of persons between two people
   = The total number of persons – Sum of position of two different persons from opposite sides.
   (b) For overlapping condition, number of persons between two persons
   = (Sum of position of two different persons from opposite end – Total number of persons) – 2

Exam Approach Examples

Based on Ranking Test

Example 1 **There are 46 students in the class. If Aruna's rank is 12th from the top, then what is her rank from the bottom?**

(a) 36 (b) 37 (c) 35 (d) 34

Sol. (*c*) According to the question,

Aruna's rank from bottom

= (Total students – Aruna's rank from top) + 1

= (46 – 12) + 1 = 35th

Example 2 **A group of 10 students are sitting in a row according to their age. Rohan is sixth from the beginning and his friend Shomya is ninth from the end of the row. How many students are sitting between them?** *CUET (UG) Section III 2023*

(a) 3 (b) 4 (c) 2 (d) 5

Sol. (*a*) According to the question,

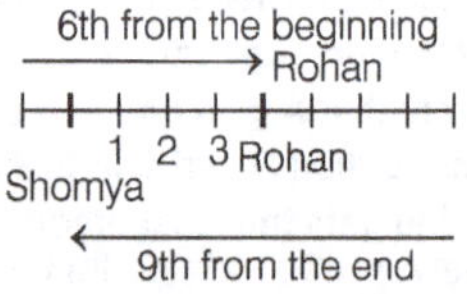

So, there are three students sitting between them.

Example 3 **In a class of 40 students, a boy is ranked 12th from the top. When 10 boys joined, his rank was dropped by one. What is his new rank from the last?** *UP Police SI 2021*

(a) 38 (b) 32
(c) 24 (d) 30

Sol. (*a*) Total number of students in class = 40

Rank of boy from top = 12th

According to the question,

New numbers of students in class = 40 + 10 = 50

and new rank of boy from top = 12 + 1 = 13 th

Hence, new rank from last = (50 – 13) + 1 = 37 + 1 = 38

Example 4 **All persons in a row are facing North. A is 9th to the left of B who is at the extreme right. A has 3 persons on the left. What is the total number of persons in the row?** *UP Police SI 2021*

(a) 13 (b) 15
(c) 14 (d)12

Sol. (*a*) According to the question, the arrangement is as follows,

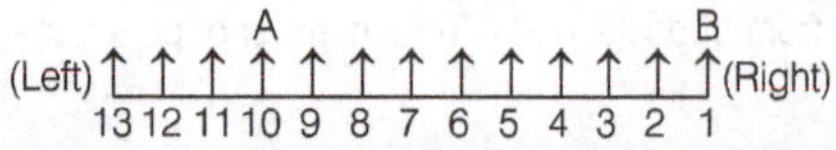

If B is at extreme right end, then A will be at 10th position. So, 3 persons on the left of A means there are 13 persons in the row.

There are total 13 persons in the row.

Example 5 **All 32 students in a class are standing in a row facing North. Akash is 12th from the right end while Priya is 18th from the left end. How many people are standing between Akash and Priya?** *SSC CGL (Tier-II) 2023*

(a) Two (b) Four (c) Three (d) Five

Sol. (*a*) Total students in a class = 32

Akash is 12th from right end and Priya is 18th from left end.

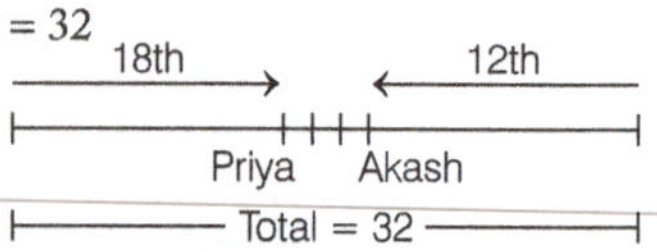

Students standing between Akash and Priya

= 32 – (18 + 12) = 32 – 30 = 2

Hence, two people are standing between Akash and Priya.

Based on Arrangement Test

Example 6 **Five friends took a test. Payal scored more than Komal. Reena scored less than Payal. Simi scored more than Tanu but less than Komal. Who among them scored the highest?** *CUET (UG) Section III 2023*

(a) Reena (b) Komal (c) Payal (d) Tanu

Sol. (*c*) According to the question, the arrangement is as follow,

Payal > Komal, Reena > Simi > Tanu

Hence, Payal scored the highest marks.

Example 7 **Speed of six bikes T1, T2, T3, T4, T5 and T6 are compared. Speed of T6 is more than only three bikes. No two bikes have same speed. Speed of T4 is more than T2 but less than T6. Speed of T3 is not less than T5. Speed of T2 and T5 is not least. How many bikes have less speed than T3?** *SSC MTS 2023*

(a) 0 (b) 1 (c) 3 (d) 5

Sol. (*d*) According to the question,

T3 > T5 > T6 > T4 > T2 > TI

Hence, total 5 bikes have less speed than T3.

> **Helping Tips**
> The words 'old' and 'young' are used for age whereas words 'tall' and 'short' are used for height.

Example 8 **The weights of seven women W_1, W_2, W_3, W_4, W_5, W_6 and W_7 are compared. W_4 weighs more than W_7. W_5 weighs more than only three women and W_2 weighs less than only W_1 and W_3. If W_7 weighs the least, then what is the minimum number of women who are heavier than W_6?** *CUET (UG) 2023*

(a) 2 (b) 3 (c) 1 (d) 4

Sol. (*d*) According to the question,

$W_4 > W_7$

(W_5 > Three women)

W_1 and $W_3 > W_2$

(W_7 → (least)

∴ W_1 and $W_3 > W_2 > W_5 > W_6 > W_4 > W_7$

Hence, the minimum number of women who are heavier than W_6 is 4.

Chapter Challenge

Based of Ranking Test

1. Disha ranks 23rd from the top in a class of 28 students. What is her rank from the bottom? ***DSSSB Lab Asst. 2024***
(a) 4th (b) 6th (c) 7th (d) 5th

2. The total number of students in a class is 25. From the bottom, Mamta's rank is 8. What is her rank from the top? ***CISF ASI 2023***
(a) 18th (b) 35th (c) 32nd (d) 30th

3. There are 42 students in a class. If Kritika is 18th from the top, what is her position from the bottom? ***RRB NTPC 2022***
(a) 25th (b) 24th (c) 26th (d) 23rd

4. Ram's position is thirteen from upwards in a class of 53 students. What will be his position from downwards? ***HP Police Constable 2022***
(a) 42 (b) 43
(c) 41 (d) 40

> ***MRC******
> ***(Most Repeating Concepts)***
> Question Nos. 2, 3, 4, 9, 10, 11 and 12 based on ranking test are being repeatedly asked in examinations such as HP Police Constable, RRB NTPC and SSC CHSL examination. They are important for upcoming examination.

5. In a class, Shambhu is 10th from the top and 36th from the bottom. How many students are there in the class? ***UP Police Constable 2024***
(a) 47 (b) 45 (c) 44 (d) 43

6. Paras ranked 5th from the top and 24th from the bottom in his class. How many students are there in his class? ***SSC CGL (Tier-II) 2025***
(a) 29 (b) 26 (d) 27 (d) 28

7. Nik ranked 89th from the bottom and 19th from the top in his class. How many students are there in his class? ***RPF SI 2024***
(a) 107 (b) 121 (c) 111 (d) 99

8. In a row of people all facing North, Shreya is 11th from the left end. Ravi is 12th from the left end. Ravi is exactly between Shreya and Rahul. If Rahul is 15th from the right end of the line, how many people are there in the row? ***RRB Technician Grade III 2024***
(a) 29 (b) 45 (c) 28 (d) 27

9. Sunita is ranked 10th from the top and 18th from the bottom in her class. How many students are there in the class? ***SSC CHSL (Tier-II) 2023***
(a) 27 (b) 28 (c) 30 (d) 29

10. Rahul ranked 16th from the top and 21st from the bottom in his class in an examination. If only 21 students failed the exam, then how many students in his class passed? ***RRB NTPC 2022***
(a) 19 (b) 17 (c) 15 (d) 21

11. In a row of 17 boys, A is at 16th position from right end and B is at 9th position from left end. Then, how many boys are there between A and B? ***MP Police Constable 2022***
(a) 6 (b) 4 (c) 5 (d) 7

12. Prasad ranked eleventh from the top and twenty fourth from the bottom among those who had passed in the mid-term examination in a class. If four students had failed in the mid-term examination, what was the total number of students in that class? ***RRB NTPC 2021***
(a) 37 (b) 36 (c) 35 (d) 38

13. In a row of boys, Akash is fifth from the left and Nikhil is eleventh from the right. If Akash is twenteeth from the right, how many boys are sitting, between Akash and Nikhil? ***HSSC Police Constable 2021***
(a) 13 (b) 15 (c) 14 (d) 12

14. In a row of children, Hari is eleventh from left and Manjula is seventeenth from the right. If they interchange their places Hari will be seventeenth from the left. Which of the following will be in the new position of Manjula from right? ***Haryana Police Constable 2021***
(a) Eleventh (b) Twenty ninth
(c) Twenty third (d) Nineteenth

15. There are 33 people in a row. Anushya is sixth from the left corner and Divyasha is eighth from the right corner. Shyamala is exactly in the middle of Anushya and Divyasha, so find the rank of Shyamala from the right corner. ***UP Police Head Operator 2024***
(a) 22nd (b) 20th (c) 19th (d) 18th

16. In a row of 23 persons facing North, person A is 15th from the right. After shifting him two place to the right from his present position, what is his position now from the left? ***UP Police ASI 2021***
(a) 13th (b) 10th (c) 11th (d) 12th

17. Paresh is 14th from the left and Dileep is 16th from the right in a line of students. When both Paresh and Dileep interchange their positions, the position of Dileep becomes 21st from the right. How many students are there in the line? ***SSC Steno 2020***
(a) 35 (b) 34 (c) 33 (d) 36

18. In a row of 33 trees, if a monkey is shifted 7 trees to the right end, then it will be sitting on 20th tree from the left end. What was its initial position from the right end of the row? ***MP Police Constable 2022***
(a) 24th (b) 14th (c) 18th (d) 21st

19. In the morning prayer of a school, Chanchal was 8th from the front, while Prince was 11th from the back

in the same row. If they swap their positions, Chanchal becomes 22nd from the front. What is the number of students in the row? **SSC MTS 2021**

(a) 32 (b) 30
(c) 31 (d) 33

> **MRC*****
> ***(Most Repeating Concepts)***
> Q. Nos. 4, 7, 9, 10, 16, 19, 21, 25, 26 and 27 are very important from the examination point of view. The concept based on the rank of a person from top or bottom, from left or right end, interchanging of positions are mainly being asked in RRB NTPC, SSC Steno, SSC CGL, State police, RRC Groud D examination.

20. A stands in the 13th position from the front of the queue and there are 2 persons between A and B. B stands after A. If the first 8 persons are removed from the queue, then what is the position of B from the front of the queue ? **UP Police SI 2021**

(a) 5 (b) 6 (c) 8 (d) 7

21. Avinash is ranked 11th from the top in the class and Ira is ranked 7th from the bottom. If their positions get interchanged, Avinash will rank 15th from the top and Ira is ranked 11th from the bottom. How many total students appeared for the exams? **RRB NTPC 2022**

(a) 23 (b) 20 (c) 21 (d) 22

22. All 20 students of a class are sitting in a straight row facing East. Ram is 8th from the right end and Sita is 16th from the left end. How many students are sitting between Ram and Sita? **RRC Group D 2022**

(a) 3 (b) 2 (c) 4 (d) 8

23. X is 7th from the top while Y is 16th from the bottom in the class ranking. If they interchange their positions, then X becomes 21st from the top. What will be the position of Y from the bottom? **SSC CPO 2020**

(a) 16th (b) 29th (c) 21st (d) 30th

24. 83 people are sitting in a row. Aaru is sitting at 27th from the left end of the row and Pihu is sitting at 41st from the right end of the row. Ana is sitting exactly between Aaru and Pihu. What is the position of Ana from the left end? **RRC Group D 2022**

(a) 35th (b) 33rd (c) 37th (d) 34th

25. In a row of 28 students, Jamuna was 12th from the extreme left end and Ganga was 19th from the extreme right end. If Saraswati was seated exactly between them, then what was Saraswati's position from the right end? Assume that the students were seated facing North. **RRB NTPC 2022**

(a) 17th (b) 16th (c) 20th (d) 18th

Based on Arrangement Test

26. Ram is taller than Shyam but not as much as Rajan. Arjun is taller than Sohan and shorter than Shyam. Who is the shortest? **HP Police Constable 2022**

(a) Rajan (b) Ram (c) Arjun (d) Sohan

27. Radha is younger than Sunita but elder to Reeta. Reeta is elder to Geeta. Shyam is elder to Reeta but younger than Radha. Who is the youngest? **MP Police Constable 2022**

(a) Shyam (b) Reeta (c) Radha (d) Geeta

28. In a group of five children (K, L, O, M, N) with different heights. K is the tallest while L is the shortest. O is the second shortest person in that group. M is taller than N. Who among them is the third tallest? **RRB NTPC 2022**

(a) M (b) L (c) O (d) N

29. Ram is taller than Mohan and Sohan, while Sohan is taller than Shyam. Also, Mohan is taller than Sohan. Who among the following is the Shortest? **CRPF (HC) 2023**

(a) Shyam (b) Mohan (c) Ram (d) Sohan

30. A is taller than B. C and D are of equal height. E is shorter than B but taller than D. F is shorter than C, who is shorter than B. Who is the shorter among all? **SSC Steno 2021**

(a) F (b) E (c) D (d) C

31. Umesh is older than Satish. Suresh is younger than Neeraj but older than Umesh, Tarun is older than Ritesh but younger than Satish, Manish is the youngest. Who is the oldest among them? **SSC MTS 2023**

(a) Ritesh (b) Neeraj (c) Satish (d) Suresh

32. Speed of five cars C_1, C_2, C_3, C_4 and C_5 are compared. Speed of C_1 is more than only one car. Speed of C_5 is more than four cars. Speed of C_4 is more than C_1 but less than C_3 and C_5. Speed of how many cars is less than the speed of C_3? **SSC MTS 2023**

(a) 0 (b) 1 (c) 3 (d) 2

33. Price of five cars A, L, J, M and T are compared. Price of A is the least. No two cars have the same price. Price of J is less than T, L and M. Price of neither T nor L is the highest. Price of T is less than L. Price of how many cars is more than the price of T? **SSC MTS 2023**

(a) 1 (b) 3 (c) 2 (d) 0

34. I, J, K, L, M, N and O are seven friends having different ages. I is elder than K but younger than J. K is elder than N but younger than I. J is elder than I but younger than 2 persons. L is elder than J. M is not the eldest and O is the youngest. The age of how many people is between I and N? **SSC CPO 2022**

(a) 0 (b) 2 (c) 3 (d) 1

35. Seven people A, B, C, D, E, F and G, scored different marks (out of 100) in an exam. G scored the lowest marks. B scored second highest marks, which were 80. A scored 72. E scored more than F but less than C. Marks scored by C were a multiple of 11 and less than 70. The sum of marks scored by C and F was 120. What is the score of F? **SSC CGL (Tier-II) 2025**

(a) 56 (b) 54
(c) 50 (d) 55

36. Six persons A, B, C, D, E and F were engaged in a group discussion. A spoke immediately before D but immediately after B. B spoke immediately after F. If C spoke immediately after D but before E, then who among the following started the discussion?

RRB NTPC 2022

(a) F (b) D (c) E (d) B

> ***MRC******
> ***(Most Repeating Concepts)***
> Q. Nos. 33, 34, 38, 41, 42, 44, are very important. The question based on comparison of age, height, weight, score, speed of car, etc. are being asked in SSC Steno, MTS, RRB NTPC and RRB Group D examination.

37. A, B, C, D, E, F and G are of different heights. A is taller than only two people. D is shorter than only G. F is taller than A but shorter than B. C is shorter than E. How many people are shorter than E?

SSC Steno 2023

(a) Four (b) One (c) None (d) Three

38. Six girls named Natasha, Yuvika, Aditi, Tanya, Shehnaaz and Daljit are of different heights. Tanya is the shortest. Aditi's height is greater than Natasha and one other girl. Shehnaaz's height is less than Daljit, who is shorter than Yuvika. Who is the third tallest among these six girls?

RRC Group D 2022

(a) Yuvika (b) Aditi (c) Shehnaaz (d) Daljit

39. In a group of seven friends Mysha, Myra, Heer, Tia, Yash, Sia and Aarav each has a different height. Sia is third tallest among her friends. Mysha is third shortest among the friends. Aarav is taller than Yash and Sia. Heer and Tia are shorter than Myra. Aarav is not the tallest in the group. Who is the tallest of them all?

SSC Steno 2023

(a) Heer (b) Yash (c) Myra (d) Tia

40. Amongst six friends A, D, F, G, L and S, each has a different age. S is older than only four other friends. D is older than only one friend. G is older than L but younger than A. A is not the oldest. Who is the youngest among all the friends?

RRB Group-D 2022

(a) F (b) S
(c) L (d) G

41. Number of wickets taken by six bowlers Anil, Kamal, Laxman, Mohan, Bittu and Rahul are compared. Number of wickets taken by Kamal are more than only the number of wickets taken by Anil. Number of wickets taken by Bittu are less than only two bowlers. Number of wickets taken by Mohan are not more than Bittu. Who among the following has taken more wickets than Bittu?

SSC MTS 2023

(a) Rahul (b) Kamal
(c) Anil (d) Mohan

42. A person has put some sweets in boxes B_1, B_2, B_3, B_4 and B_5 respectively. The number of sweets in B_2 is less than the number of sweets in B_3 and B_1. The number of sweets in B_1 is less than the number of sweets in B_4 and more than the number of sweets in B_5. The number of sweets in B_3 is less than the number of sweets in B_5.
Which of the following options is correct according to above information?

MP Police Constable 2022

(a) The number of sweets in B_3 is more than the number of sweets in B_1.
(b) The total number of sweets in B_1 and B_5 is less than the total number of sweets in B_3 and B_2.
(c) The number of sweets in B_1 is more than the number of sweets in B_4.
(d) The number of sweets in B_2 is the least.

43. Amongst six friends Uday, Vikrant, William, Xena, Yasir and Ziya, each has a different height. Vikrant is taller than only three other friends. Ziya is only taller than Xena and William is only shorter than Uday. Given that no two friends have the same height, find who is the third shortest among all the friends?

SSC CHSL (Tier-I) 2023

(a) Yasir (b) Uday (c) Ziya (d) Willian

44. Seven friends-M, N, O, P, Q, R and S, each has a different height. Only two people are taller than Q. P is taller than Q but shorter than O. M is taller than R but shorter than S. Only three people are taller than S. N is the shortest among all. The height of how many persons is between the heights of Q and R?

SSC CHSL (Tier-I) 2022

(a) 2 (b) 4 (c) 1 (d) 3

45. The marks of seven students A, B, C, D, E, F and G in a test were given as follows. A's score was exactly between E's and F's scores. B's score was more than only G's score. C's score was immediately more than B's score. F's score was more than E's score and F did not score the highest. Who scored the highest marks in the test?

SSC MTS 2022

(a) A (b) G (c) E (d) D

46. There are five girls in a group. K is the second tallest. P is taller than M. R is taller than M. N is taller than P. Which of the following sequences about their height is not possible?

RRB NTPC 2021

(a) N > K > R > P > M (b) R > K > N > P > M
(c) N > K > P > R > M (d) R > K > P > N > M

47. Six classmates appeared in an exam. Yatharth scored more marks than Karan. Parth's marks were less than Amrita. Vineeta scored more marks than Parth. Parth scored exactly the same marks as Yatharth. Girish did not score more marks than Karan. Vineeta scored less marks than Amrita. Which of the

following options is not correct according to above information? ***RRB NTPC 2022***
(a) Karan scored less marks than Vineeta
(b) Girish scored less marks than Parth
(c) Amrita scored more marks than Karan
(d) Yatharth scored more marks than Amrita

48. Five people C, D, X, Y and Z each scored different marks in the same test. All scores are in whole numbers only. D scored the second lowest and D's score was 40. X scored more than D but less than the one who scored 45. 45 was not the highest score. C's score is an even number. C did not score the least. Y scored 6 marks less than Z. Which of the following can be a possible score of C? ***RRB NTPC 2022***
(a) 38 (b) 44 (c) 46 (d) 42

49. Mona, Rahul, Vikas, Kavita, Poonam and Khushi, each has a different height. They are standing in a line according to their heights in an increasing order. Vikas is taller than only one person. Only Rahul is standing between Khushi and Vikas. Mona is shorter than only one person. Exactly two people are standing between Poonam and Rahul. Who is the shortest person in this group? ***RRC Group D 2022***
(a) Kavita (b) Vikas (c) Rahul (d) Poonam

50. Seven students of a coaching centre, Param, Qazi, Ravi, Suresh, Tanvir, Uday and Varsha, have obtained different percentages. Param scored the second-highest percentage in the centre. The percentage scored by Varsha was more than only one person. Suresh's percentage was more than Tanvir's but less than Param's. Three people got more percentage than Tanvir and three got lesser than Tanvir. Neither Ravi nor Qazi received the lowest percentage. Whose percentage was the lowest? ***SSC MTS 2023***
(a) Tanvir (b) Param (c) Uday (d) Qazi

Right Key

1. (b)	2. (a)	3. (a)	4. (c)	5. (b)	6. (d)	7. (a)	8. (d)	9. (a)	10. (c)
11. (a)	12. (d)	13. (a)	14. (c)	15. (d)	16. (c)	17. (b)	18. (d)	19. (a)	20. (c)
21. (c)	22. (b)	23. (d)	24. (a)	25. (d)	26. (d)	27. (d)	28. (d)	29. (a)	30. (a)
31. (b)	32. (c)	33. (c)	34. (d)	35. (b)	36. (a)	37. (b)	38. (c)	39. (c)	40. (c)
41. (a)	42. (d)	43. (a)	44. (a)	45. (d)	46. (d)	47. (d)	48. (c)	49. (a)	50. (c)

Solutions

1. *(b)* Rank of Disha from bottom
= 28 − (Rank of Disha from top) + 1
= 28 − 23 + 1 = 6th

2. *(a)* Total number of students in a class
= 25
Mamta's rank from bottom = 8
∴ Rank of Mamta from the top in a class = (25 − 8) + 1 = 17 + 1 = 18th

3. *(a)* According to the question,
Kritika's rank from bottom
= (42 − 18) + 1 = 25th

4. *(c)* Total number of students = 53
Position of Ram from upwards = 13th
∴ Position of Ram from downwards
= (53 − 13) + 1 = 41th

5. *(b)* According to the question,

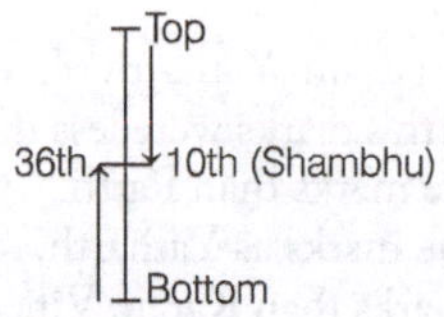

Given, Shambhu is 10th from top and 36th from bottom.
∴ Total number of students in the class
= (10 + 36) − 1 = 46 − 1 = 45

6. *(d)* According to the question,

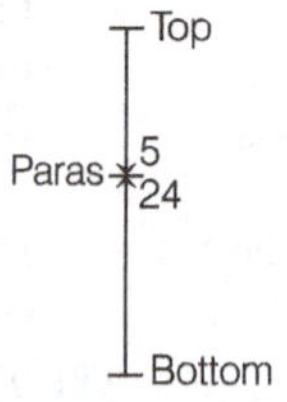

∴ Total number of students in the class
= (5 + 24) − 1 = 29 − 1 = 28

7. *(a)* According to the question,

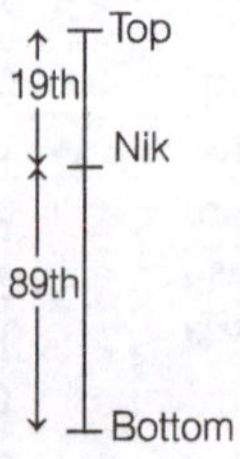

Given, Nik is 19th from the top and 89th from bottom.
∴ Total number of students in the class
= (19 + 89) − 1 = 108 − 1 = 107

8. *(d)* According to the question,

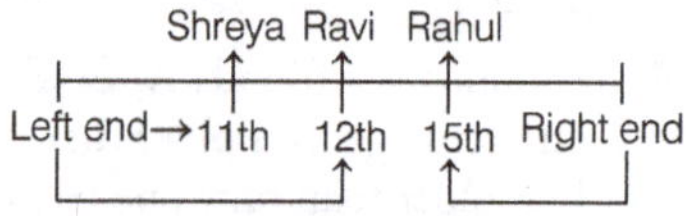

∴ Total number of people in the row
= (12 + 15) = 27

9. *(a)* Sunita ranked from the top = 10th
Sunita ranked from the bottom = 18th
So, students are there in the class
= (10 + 18) − 1 = 27

TOP TIPS In order to find the total number of persons in a row/class etc., don't forget to add (−1) in the sum of positions.

10. *(c)* According to the question,
Rahul ranked from the top = 16th
Rahul ranked from the bottom = 21st

We know that,

Total students = (Top + Bottom) – 1

= (16 + 21) – 1 = 37 – 1 = 36

Number of failed students = 21

∴ Number of passed students

= 36 – 21 = 15

11. (*a*) According to the question,

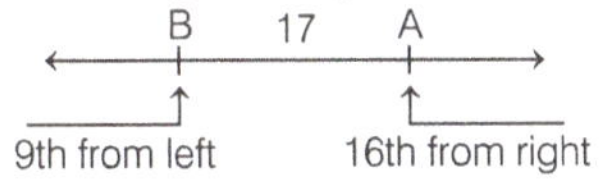

Position of A from left

= (17 – 16) + 1 = 2

Number of boys between A and B

= (9 – 2) – 1 = 6

12. (*d*) According to the question,

Total students passed

= (11 + 24) – 1 = 34

∵ Four students failed in the exam.

So, total students = 34 + 4 = 38

Hence, there is total 38 students in the class.

13. (*a*) According to the question,

Position of Nikhil from right = 11th

Position of Akash from right = 25th

∴ Number of boys between Akash and Nikhil = 25 – 11 – 1 = 13

14. (*c*) According to the question,

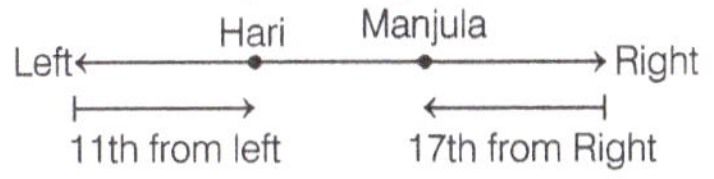

After exchange the places

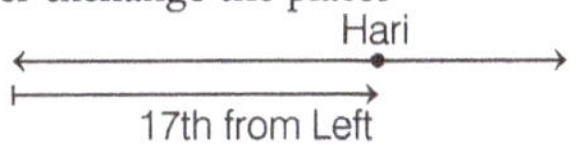

∴ Total number of children in row

=(17 + 17) – 1 = 33

∴ New position of Manjula from right

=(33 – 11) + 1 = 23rd

15. (*d*) Given, total number of persons in the row = 33

Position of Anushya from left in the row = 6th

Position of Divyasha from right in the row = 8th

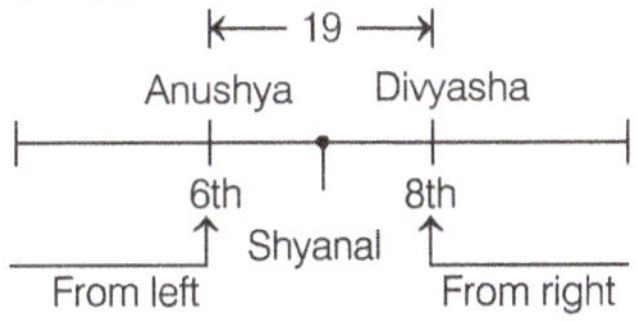

Number of persons between Anushya and Divyasha = 33 – (6 + 8) = 19

So, the rank of Shyamala from the right corner is

⇒(8 + 9) + 1 ⇒ 18th

16. (*c*) According to the question,

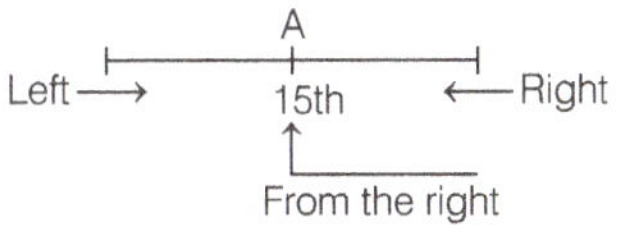

Now, changing position

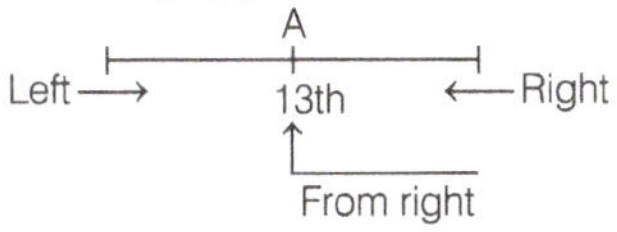

Now, position of A from left is

= (23 – 13) + 1 = 10 + 1 = 11th

> **TOP TIPS** While solving such questions, keep in mind the change of place. That is, carefully observe the new and previous positions of the persons.

17. (*b*) According to the question,

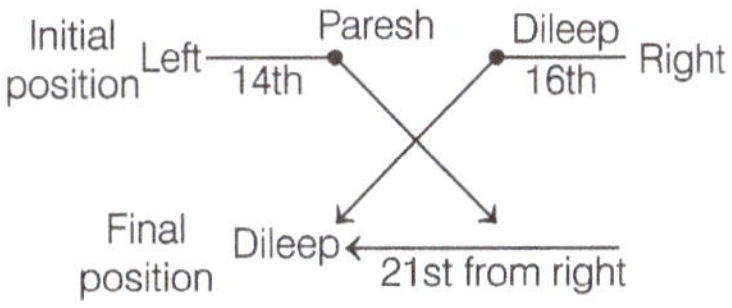

∴ Total students in the line

= (14 + 21) – 1 = 35 – 1 = 34

18. (*d*) According to the question,

Total number of trees in the row = 33

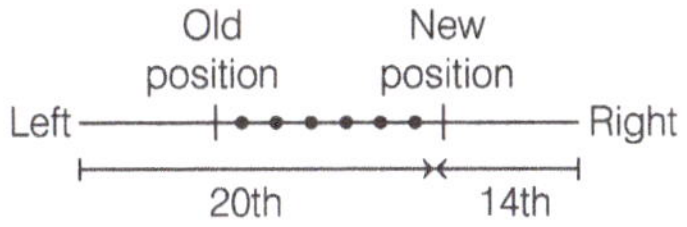

∴ Its new position from right end

= 33 – 20 + 1 = 14th

Its initial position from right end

= 14 + 7 = 21st

19. (*a*) From front

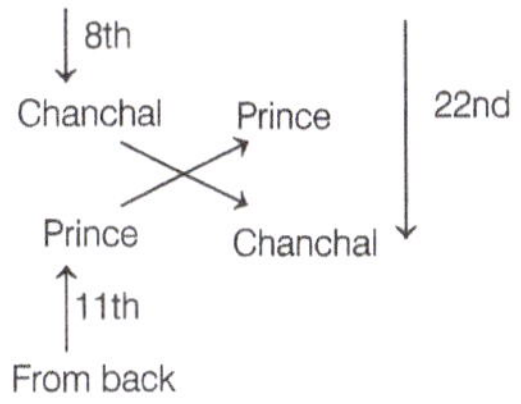

∴ Total number of students

= 22 + 11 – 1 = 32

20. (*c*) According to the question,

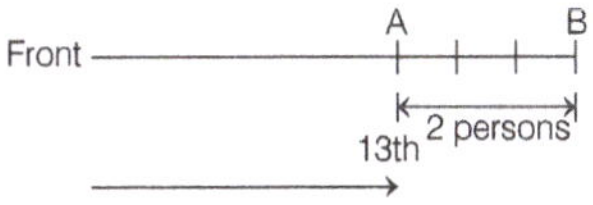

∵ Position of B from the front of the queue = (13 + 2 + 1) = 16th

Now, position of B after removing 8 persons = (16 – 8) = 8th

21. (*c*) According to the question,

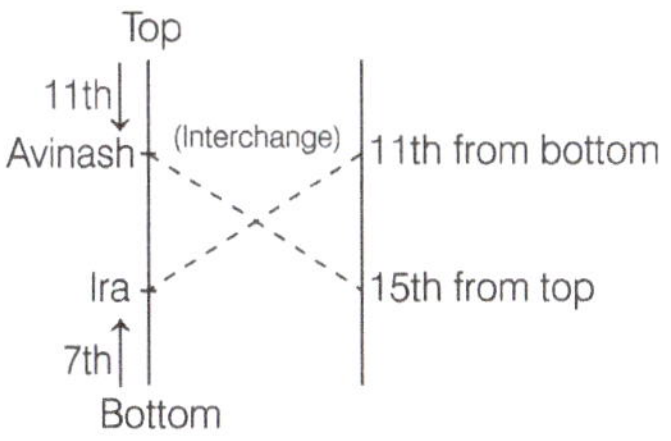

Total student = (15 + 7) – 1 = 21

22. (*b*) According to the question,

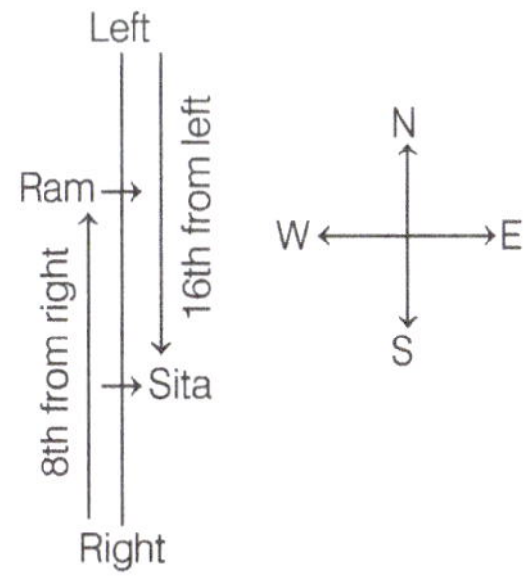

Position of Ram from left

= (20 – 8) + 1 = 13th

∴ Number of students between Ram and Sita = (16 – 13 – 1) = 2

> **Smart Approach**
>
> ∴ Number of students between Ram and Sita = (8 + 16 – 20) – 2 = 4 – 2 = 2

23. (*d*) According to the question,

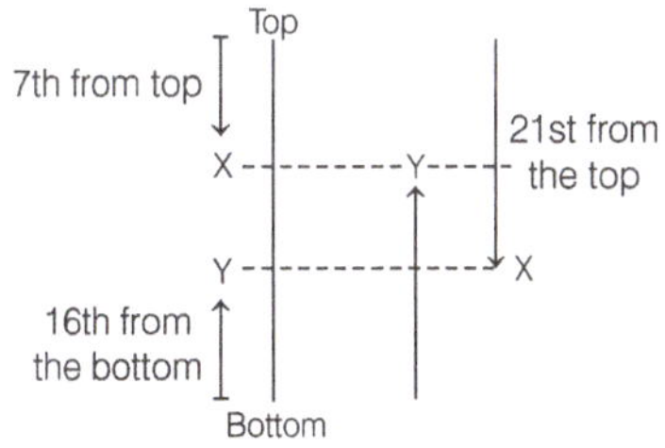

We know that,

Total students = 16 + 21 – 1 = 36

∴ Position of Y from bottom

= 36 – 7 + 1 = 30th

> **Smart Approach**
>
> Position of Y from bottom = (21 – 7 + 16)
>
> = (14 + 16) = 30th

24. (*a*) According to the question,

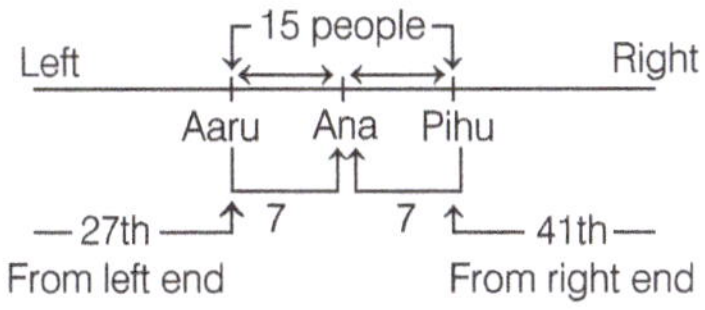

Number of people in between Aaru and Pihu = 83 – (27 + 41)
= 83 – 68 = 15

Ana is sitting exactly between Aaru and Pihu.

∴ Number of people in between Aaru and Ana = (15 – 1) ÷ 2 = 7

∴ The position of Ana from left end
= 27 + 7 + 1 = 35th

25. (*d*) According to the question,

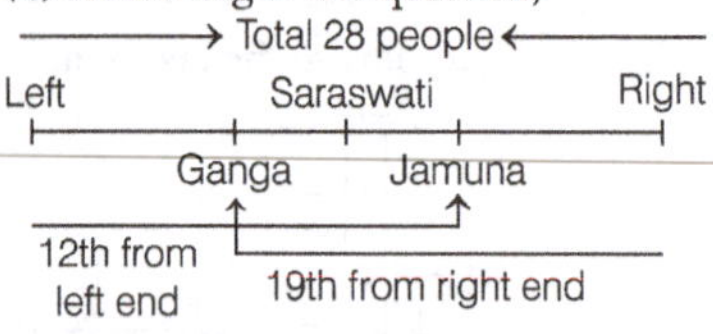

Position of Jamuna from right
= 28 – 12 + 1 = 17th

Saraswati is seated exactly between Jamuna and Ganga.

So, position of Saraswati from right is 18th.

26. (*d*) According to the question,
Rajan > Ram > Shyam > Arjun > Sohan
∴ Sohan is the shortest.

27. (*d*) According to question,
Sunita > Radha > Shyam > Reeta > Geeta
∴ Geeta is the youngest.

28. (*d*) According to the question,
K > M > (N) > O > L
Hence, 'N' is the third tallest children.

29. (*a*) According to the question,
Ram > Mohan/Sohan ...(i)
Sohan > Shyam ...(ii)
Mohan > Sohan ...(iii)
By combining Eqs. (i), (ii) and (iii), we get
Ram > Mohan > Sohan > Shyam
Hence, Shyam is the shortest among them.

TOP TIPS Generally sign '>' is used for Taller and sign '<' is used for shorter.

30. (*a*) According to the question,
A > B ...(i)
C = D ...(ii)
D < E < B ...(iii)
F < C < B ...(iv)
On combining all, we get
A > B > E > D = C > F
Hence, F is shortest among all.

31. (*b*) According to the question,
Neeraj > Suresh > Umesh > Satish > Tarun > Ritesh > Manish
Hence, 'Neeraj' is the oldest among all.

32. (*c*) According to the question,
$C_5 > C_3 > C_4 > C_1 > C_2$
Hence, speed of 3 cars are less than the speed of C_3.

33. (*c*) According to the question,
M > L > T > J > A
Hence, price of 2 cars is more than price of T.

34. (*d*) According to the question,
L > M > J > I > K > N > O
Hence, the age of one person is between I and N.

35. (*b*) According to the question,
D > B > A > C > E > F > G
(80) (72) (66) (54)
C + F = 120
66 + F = 120
F = 120 – 66
= 54
Hence, the score of F is 54.

36. (*a*) According to the question,

1	F
2	B
3	A
4	D
5	C
6	E

Hence, F started the discussion.

37. (*b*) According to the question,
G > D > B > F > A > E > C
Hence, only 'one' people is shorter than 'E'.

38. (*c*) According to the question,
Yuvika > Daljit > Shehnaaz > Aditi > Natasha > Tanya
Hence, 'Shehnaaz' is the third tallest girl.

39. (*c*) According to the question,
Myra > Aarav > Sia > Yash > Mysha > Heer/Tia > Heer/Tia.
Hence, 'Myra' is the tallest among all.

40. (*c*) According to the question,
S > _ > _ > _ > _ ...(i)
D > _ ...(ii)
A > G > L ...(iii)
A is not the oldest ...(iv)
On combining Eqs. (i), (ii), (iii) and (iv), we get
F > S > A > G > D > L
Hence, L is the youngest among all the friends.

41. (*a*) According to the question,
Laxman/Rahul > Rahul/Laxman > Bittu > Mohan > Kamal > Anil
Here Rahul and Laxman both has taken more wickets than Bittu.
But, According to the options, Rahul has taken more wickets than Bittu.

42. (*d*) According to question,
arrangement of boxes in the increasing order is
$B_4 > B_1 > B_5 > B_3 > B_2$
∴ The number of sweets is least in B_2.

43. (*a*) According to the information, final arrangement is as follows,
Uday > William > Vikrant > Yasir > Ziya > Xena
Hence, 'Yasir' is third shortest among all.

44. (*a*) According to the question,
O > P > Q > S > M > R > N
Hence, the height of two persons is between the heights of Q and R.

45. (*d*) The arrangement of students according to the marks is as follows,
D > F > A > E > C > B > G
Hence, D score the highest marks.

46. (*d*) According to the given information,
N > P > M ...(i)
R > M ...(ii)
K is second tallest.
Hence, R > K > P > N > M is not possible sequence of their heights because N is taller than P.

47. (*d*) According to the question,
Amrita > Vineeta > Yatharth = Parth > Karan > Girish
Hence, option (d) i.e. Yatharth scored more marks than Amrita is incorrect.

48. (*c*) According to the question,
C (Even number) > Z (45) > X > D (40) > Y (39)
It can be clearly seen that, C scores more than 45 and is an even number.
From all four options available, possible value of C's score is 46.

49. (*a*) According to the question,
Poonam > Mona > Khushi > Rahul > Vikas > Kavita
Hence, Kavita is the shortest person in this group.

50. (*c*) According to the question,
Qazi/Ravi > Param > Suresh > Tanvir > Qazi/Ravi > Varsha > Uday
∴ Percentage of 'Uday' was the lowest.

CHAPTER

12 Sitting Arrangement

Sitting Arrangement

Sitting arrangement is a process of arranging people or objects in a specific order based on given conditions or information.

Linear Arrangement

In this type, some information regarding people/objects are given in the jumbled manner.

Based on this information all the people/objects have to be arranged in a linear order in one row or two rows facing the same or different direction.

It can be divided into following types:-

I. Arrangement in a single row

(i) Facing towards North

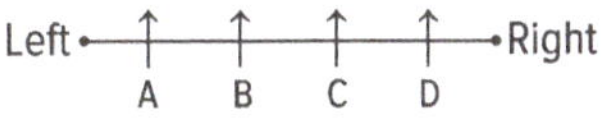

(ii) Facing towards South

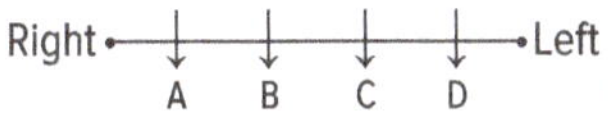

(iii) Facing towards East

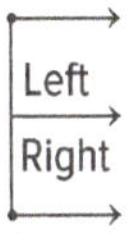

(iv) Facing towards West

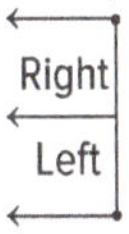

II. Arrangement in two rows

There can be two situation in this

(i) When face is in the opposite directions

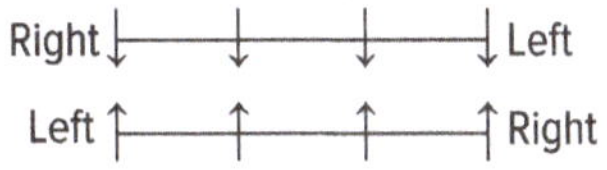

(ii) When face is in the same direction

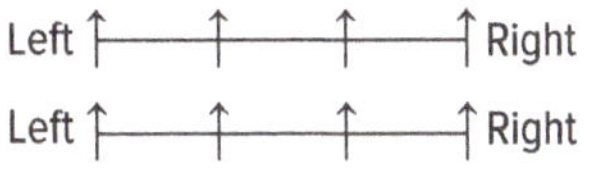

Circular Arrangement

In this type, some information regarding some people/objects are given in a jumbled format.

Based on this jumbled information, all the given people or objects are to be arranged around a circle in which their faces can be towards center or outside the center or both situation can be possible simultaneously.

I. Facing towards the centre

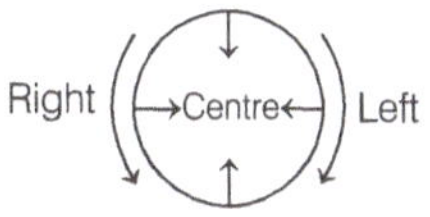

II. Facing outside the centre

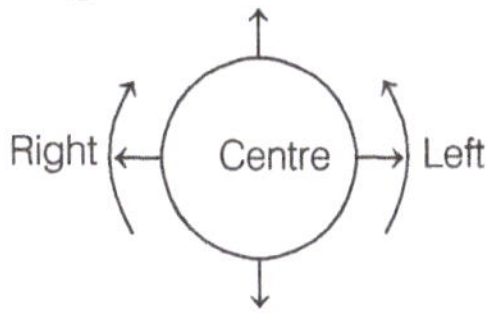

Square, Rectangular or Polygonal Arrangement

In this type, some random information regarding some people/objects are given to arrange them in square, rectangular or polygonal order.

Based on this information, all the given people/objects are to be arranged at the corners or middle of the sides of the square or rectangle. Their faces can be towards or outside the centre or both the situations can be possible simultaneously.

Note In the square, rectangular or polygonal arrangement the left side or right side of a person/object is just like circular order arrangement.

Square arrangement

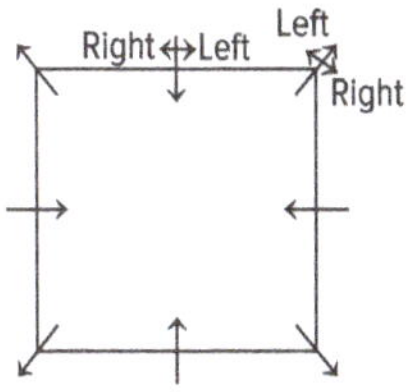

Hexagonal Arrangement

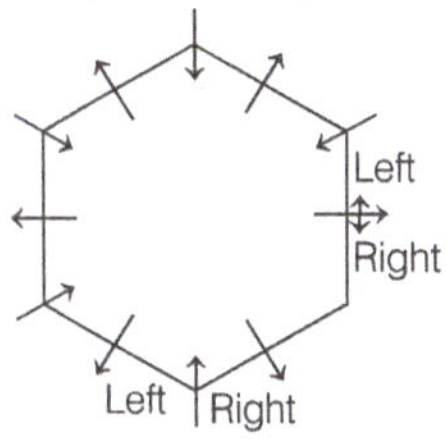

Score Booster

To solve the questions of sitting arrangement. Carefully counting the number of people, drawing a diagram to visualize the arrangement, breaking down information sentence by sentence, noting relative positions (left/right) and considering clockwise/anticlockwise directions if applicable, all while merging observations to build a complete picture of the seating layout.

Exam Approach Examples

Based on Linear Arrangement

Example 1 Six friends, K, L, M, N, O and P are sitting in a straight line. All are facing North. K is between M and N. O is third to the right of M. P is third to the left of K. M is to the immediate right of L. Which two persons are sitting at the corners? ***SSC Steno 2021***

(a) P and O (b) O and N (c) P and N (d) N and L

Sol. (*a*) According to the given information,

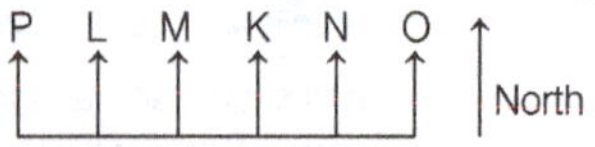

So, P and O are sitting at the corners.

Example 2 Five girls K, L, N, P and V are sitting in a row facing South (not necessarily in this order). L sits second to the right of P. V sits immediate right of K. Two girls are sitting between V and N. How many girls are sitting to the right of K? ***DSSSB Lab Asst. 2024***

(a) 3 (b) 2
(c) 1 (d) 4

Sol. (*c*) According to the given information,

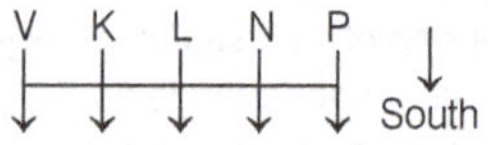

∴ Only one girl (V) is sitting to the right of 'K'.

> **Helping Tips**
> While solving such questions, a candidate should know about
> (i) The arrangement given or asked in the questions.
> (ii) The directions in which the person/ things are facing.

Example 3 Six persons A, B, C, D, E and F are sitting in two rows with three persons in each row. If E is not the end of any row. D is second to the left of F. C, the neighbour of E, is sitting diagonally opposite to D. B and F sit adjacent to each other. Who is sitting in front of B ? ***BSSC (10+2) 2022***

(a) A (b) E (c) C (d) D

Sol. (*b*) According to the given information,

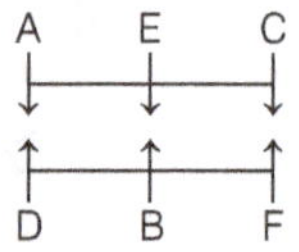

Hence, E is sitting in front of B.

Example 4 A certain number of people are sitting in a row facing the North direction. 'T' is sitting to the immediate right of 'U'. 'Y' is sitting 5th to the left of 'U'. 'Z' is an immediate neighbour of both 'T' and 'P'. 'V' is sitting 5th to the left of 'T'. 'O' is sitting at one extreme end and there is only one person sitting between 'O' and 'Y'.

If no other person is sitting in the row, what is the total number of people seated? ***SSC (10+2) 2024***

(a) 11 (b) 12
(c) 13 (d) 14

Sol. (*a*) According to the given information,

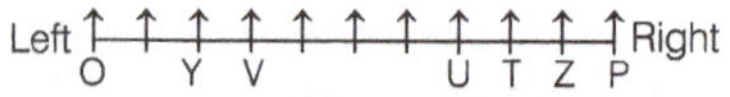

Hence, the total number of persons seated in the row is 11.

Example 5 Ten people are sitting in two parallel rows 1 and 2. A, B, C, D and E are sitting in row 1 facing North and V, W, X, Y and Z are sitting in row 2 facing South in such a way that each member in row 1 faces a member of row 2. A sits second from the right end of the row. W faces an immediate neighbour of A. X sits third to the right of W. The one who faces X, sits to the immediate right of B. Only one person sits between B and C. V sits to the immediate right of Y. D does not sit at any of the extreme ends of the row. Who faces Z? ***RRB NTPC 2022***

(a) E (b) C
(c) D (d) B

Sol. (*d*) According to the given information,

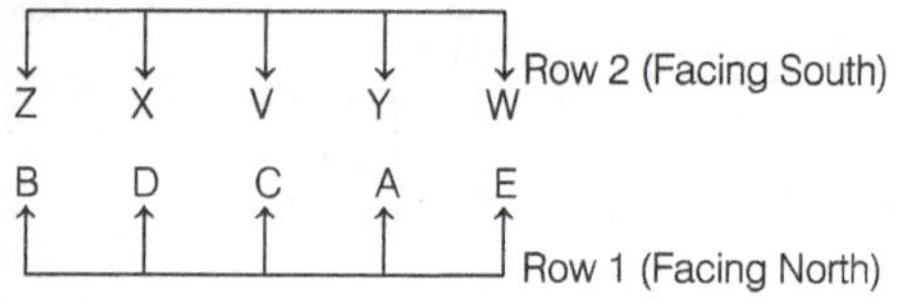

Hence, 'B' faces 'Z'.

Based on Circular Arrangement

Example 6 Six persons, A, B, C, D, E and F are sitting around a circular table. All are facing the center of the table. Only two persons are sitting between D and A. F is to the immediate right of C. E is second to the right of F. E is second to the left of A. Who is sitting to the immediate right of F ? ***RRC Group D 2022***

(a) E (b) C
(c) A (d) D

Sol. (*d*) According to the given information,

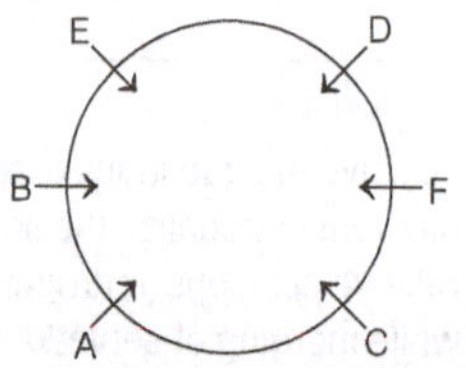

Hence, D is sitting immediate right of F.

> **Helping Tips**
> If information about the direction of person/things is not given in the question, then candidates can arrange the given/things as per their convenience and taking left/right in relation to it.

Example 7 K, L, M, N, O and P are six friends sitting around a circular table facing opposite to the centre. M is sitting to the immediate left of O and immediate right of K. K is sitting to the immediate right of N. L is sitting to the immediate left of N. P is sitting between L and O. Who is sitting to the immediate right of P? ***SSC GD Constable 2023***

(a) L (b) O
(c) P (d) M

Sol. (*a*) According to the given information,

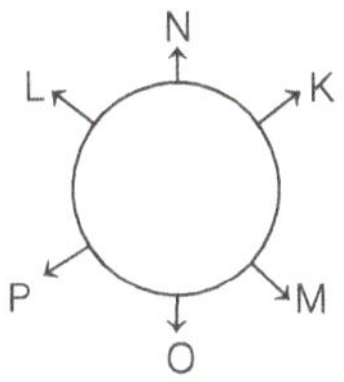

Trending Concept
This type of question based on linear and circular arrangement are repeatedly asked in SSC and railway exams.

Clearly, 'L' is sitting immediate right of P.

Example 8 M, N, O, X, Y and Z are sitting around a circular table facing the centre (but not necessarily in the same order). O is an immediate neighbour of Y. Z sits second to the right of O. X is the immediate neighbour of both M and N. M is not an immediate neighbour of O. Who sits to the immediate left of Y? ***SSC CGL (Tier-II) 2025***

(a) N (b) O
(c) X (d) M

Sol. (*b*) According to the given information,

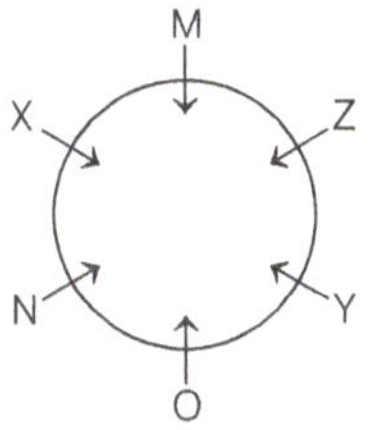

Hence, O sits to the immediate left of Y.

Example 9 L, P, R, V, X, Y and Z are sitting around a circular table facing the centre. Only one person sits between V and L, when counted from the right of V. Only one person sits between L and X. Only one person sits between V and Z. Only two people sit between R and X. Only one person sits between P and Z. Who sits to the immediate right and left of Y, respectively? ***RRB ALP 2024***

(a) Z and V (b) V and X
(c) V and Z (d) X and Z

Sol. (*c*) According to the question,

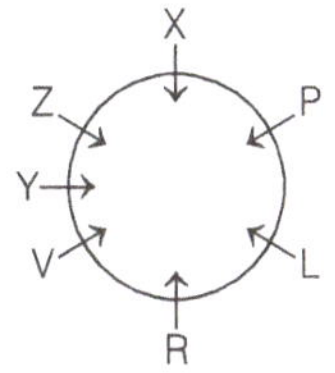

Hence, V and Z sits to the immediate right and left of Y, respectively.

Based on Square, Rectangular or Polygonal Arrangement

Example 10 D, E, F, G, H, I, J and K are sitting around a square table facing the center of the table. Some of them are sitting at the corners, while some are sitting at the exact center of the sides. K sits third to the right of I. K sits at one of the corners, E sits second to the left of G.G sits at any of the corners. E is an immediate neighbour of I and D. F sits third to the right of J. H is the immediate neighbour of F and K. How many people sit between I and F, when counted from the left to I? ***SSC MTS 2023***

(a) Two (b) Four (c) One (d) Three

Sol. (*a*) According to the given information,

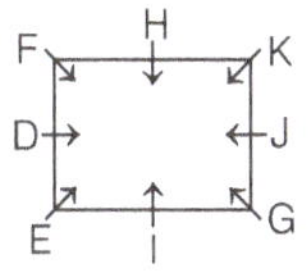

Hence, two people sit between I and F, when counted from left of I.

Example 11 Six persons P, Q, R, S, T and U were sitting around a hexagon table facing the centre. U was sitting opposite to P, who was to the immediate left of R. S was sitting to the immediate right of U and T was exactly between P and S. What was the sitting location of Q? ***SSC CPO 2020***

(a) Immediate left of P (b) Opposite to T
(c) Opposite to S (d) Opposite to R

Sol. (*b*) According to the given information,

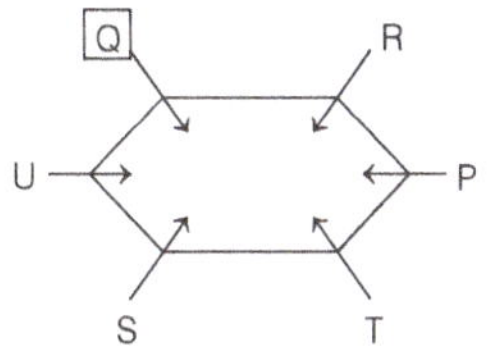

Hence, Q is sitting exactly opposite of T.

Chapter Challenge

Based on Linear Arrangement

1. Seven people, A, B, C, D, E, F and G, are sitting in a row, facing north. Only five people sit between C and D. B sits third from the right end. G sits to the immediate right of C. E sits third to the right of A. How many people sit between G and F? **RRB ALP 2024**
(a) Four (b) Three (c) One (d) Two

2. P, Q, R, S, T and U are sitting on a wall and all of them are facing North.
R is to the immediate left of U.
Q is at an extreme end and has U as his neighbour.
Only T is between R and P. Who is sitting to the left of P? **DSSSB PGT 2023**
(a) R (b) T (c) U (d) S

3. Five girls Babita, Lita, Mita, Rita and Tina are playing a game. They are sitting in a row facing towards the North. Mita is sitting at the West end and Tina is sitting at the East end. Lita and Rita are sitting together next to each other. Babita is sitting to the immediate left of Lita and to the right of Mita. Who is sitting second from the East end? **SSC MTS 2023**
(a) Rita (b) Lita (c) Babita (d) Tina

4. Six friends P, Q, R, S, T and U are standing in a row facing North but not necessarily in the same order. 'P' is to the left of 'T' and to the right of 'R'. 'Q' is on the right of 'T' but to the left of 'S'. Who are the neighbours of 'Q'? **Haryana CET 2023**
(a) T and S (c) P and R
(b) T and U (d) P and T
(e) Not attempted

5. Rahul, Mehul, Priya, Payal, Dhyani and Dharmi are sitting in a row facing North. Dhyani and Dharmi are in the centre. Rahul and Mehul are at the ends. Priya is sitting to the immediate left of Rahul. How many persons are there to the right of Payal? **UPSSSC 2022**
(a) 1 (b) 4 (c) 3 (d) 2

6. Six friends M, N, O, P, Q and R are sitting in a row facing South. N is exactly in between P and Q. O is to the immediate left of R.
M is to the immediate right of P. If Q is at the extreme left of the row, then who is sitting to the immediate left of O? **SSC GD Constable 2023**
(a) Q (b) M (c) N (d) P

7. Seven people A, B, C, D, E, F and G are sitting in a straight row, facing North. Only two people sit to the right of D. G is an immediate neighbour of D. Only three people sit between A and G. Only two people sit between B and C. E is not an immediate neighbour of C. F sits to the immediate right of G. Who sits to the immediate left of A? **SSC CPO 2023**
(a) E (b) C (c) D (d) B

> **MRC*****
> ***(Most Repeating Concepts)***
> Question Nos. 7, 10, 14 and 18 are very important from examination point of view. Question based on these concepts are being asked in SSC (MTS, CGL, CPO) and RRB NTPC examination.

8. Six people, Deepak, Gauri, Babita, Ira, Farheen and Hema are sitting in a straight line, facing North. Deepak sits 2nd from the left end. Gauri sits 2nd to the right of Deepak. Ira sits 2nd to the right of Gauri. Farheen sits 3rd to the left of Ira. Babita sits 2nd to the left of Farheen. Who sits 3rd to the right of Deepak? **SSC MTS 2023**
(a) Farheen (b) Hema (c) Babita (d) Ira

9. Seven people, A, B, C, D, E, F and G are sitting in a straight line, facing North. Only three people sit in the left of D. Only two people sit between D and A. B sits fifth to the right of C. G sits to the immediate right of E but somewhere to the left of A. Who sits to the extreme right? **SSC CGL (Tier-II) 2023**
(a) B (b) A (c) E (d) G

10. Seven people U, M, K, G, B, R and D are sitting in a straight line, facing South. Only two people sit in the left of B. M sits third to the right of G. U is the immediate neighbour of M and B. D sits to the immediate left of K. How many people sit between D and G ? **SSC MTS 2023**
(a) Two (b) Three (c) One (d) Four

11. Seven people S, T, U, V, W, X and Y are sitting in a straight line, facing North. Only two people sit to the right of W. Only three people sit between S and W. U is the immediate neighbour of T and X. X is not the immediate neighbour of W. V sits third to the right of T. Who is sitting between W and V? **SSC MTS 2023**
(a) T (b) Y (c) U (d) X

12. Eight people are sitting in two parallel rows with 4 people each, in such a way that there is equal distance between adjacent persons. In Row I - L, O, V and E are seated and all of them are facing South. In Row II - P, I , C and T are seated and all of them are facing North. C sits next to the person at the extreme left end of their row and is exactly opposite O. V sits at the extreme left end of their row and is exactly opposite T. E is the immediate neighbour of V and is exactly opposite P. Who sits at the extreme left end of the row of people facing North? **SSC CPO 2022**
(a) P (b) T (c) C (d) I

Chapter Challenge Sitting Arrangement

13. Seven people. A, B, D, L, X, Y and Z are sitting in a row, facing north. Only Z sits to the right of D. Only three people sit to the left of A. Only three people sit between D and L. Y sits at some place to the left of X but at some place to the right of B. How many people sit between B and X?
RRB Technician Grade III 2024
(a) One (b) Two (c) Three (d) Four

14. Two teams consisting of 3 players in each team, are participating in a debate competition. Three players in one team are sitting facing the three players of the other team. K and L are sitting facing each other. N and O are in different teams. M is sitting facing N. P is at one of the corners. N is sitting to the immediate right of L.
Which of the following are members of the same team? *SSC CPO 2020*
(a) N, L and M (b) O, K and N
(c) K, M and P (d) L, N and P

15. Eight friends A, B, C, D, E, F, G and H are sitting in two lines of four persons each. Both the lines are facing each other. A is facing D. E is to the immediate left of G. H is to the immediate right of B. C is facing G. F is facing H. B is to the immediate right of the person who is facing G. D is to the immediate left of F. Which four persons are sitting in the same line? *CUET UG 2022*
(a) A, B, C, H (b) B, C, D, H
(c) A, C, F, G (d) C, D, E, F

16. Eight people are sitting in two parallel rows containing four people each in such a way that there is equal distance between adjacent persons.
In the first row, J, K, L and M are seated and all of them are facing the South.
In the second row, S, T, U and V are seated and all of them are facing the North.
Thus, each person faces another person from the other row.
The person facing L is sitting second to the left of V. J is sitting third to the right of M. S is sitting second to the left of U.
Who amongst the following faces S?
DP Head Constable 2022
(a) L (b) K (c) J (d) M

17. Ten people are sitting in two parallel rows 1 and 2. A, B, C, D and E are sitting in row 1 facing the North and V, W, X, Y and Z are sitting in row 2 facing the South, in such a way that each member in row 1 faces a member of row 2. A sits second from the left end of the row. V faces an immediate neighbour of A. W sits second to the left of V. The one who faces W, sits to the immediate left of B. E sits at one of the positions to the right of B. Z faces an immediate neighbour of E. Neither X nor D sit at any of the extreme ends of the row. Who faces D ?
RRB NTPC 2022
(a) X (b) Z (c) W (d) V

18. 8 students Ani, Bini, Cina, Dia, Eva, Fin, Gim and Haz are sitting in a row facing towards North (not necessarily in the same order). Only four students are sitting between Cina and Bini and one among Cina and Bini is sitting at the end of row. Only three students are sitting between Bini and Ani. Only two students are sitting between Gim and Haz.
Dia is sitting to the immediate right of Ani and Ani is fifth to the left of Haz. Who among the given options could be seated to the immediate left of Bini?
RRB NTPC 2021
(a) Haz (b) Eva (c) Gim (d) Ani

19. Seven people Tanu, Rano, Beena, Shirin, Kanak, Aditya and Anshul are sitting in a straight row, facing North. Only two people sit to the left of Tanu. Only three people sit between Tanu and Rano. Beena sits second to the right of Shirin. Beena is an immediate neighbour of Rano. Kanak sits to the immediate right of Aditya.
Who sits at the extreme right end of the row?
SSC Steno 2023
(a) Aditya (b) Kanak (c) Anshul (d) Rano

20. Eight friends Kajal, Sneha, Pooja, Anjum, Ram, Priya, Pranjali and Jivan are seated in a straight line, facing North, but not necessarily in the same order. Jivan sits at the extreme right end of the line. Only four people sit between Jivan and Sneha. Both Kajal and Pooja are immediate neighbours of Sneha. Only two people sit between Pooja and Pranjali. Pranjali is not an immediate neighbour of Jivan. Anjum sits second to left of Priya.
Who amongst the following sit exactly between Pooja and Pranjali? *DSSSB 2019*
(a) Anjum, Kajal (b) Kajal, Sneha
(c) Priya, Jivan (d) Anjum, Ram

21. X is sitting to the immediate right of Y. X moves 5 places to the right and Y moves 5 places to the left and both reach the extremes. What is the total number of persons in the row? *UP Police SI 2021*
(a) 12 (b) 8 (c) 10 (d) 9

22. There are seven persons Anmol, Fuzail, Raju, Enamul, Dinesh, Badal and Chaman each of different professions Lawyer, Judge, Police, Professor, Architect, Engineer and Doctor but not necessarily in same order, sitting in a row facing towards North direction as per the given information.
- There is no person is sitting to the left of Judge.

- Dinesh is sitting exactly in the middle of row.
- Raju is sitting third to the left of Chaman.
- Lawyer is sitting between Police and Anmol.
- Fuzail is a Professor sitting to the one end of row.
- Badal is an Engineer and Raju is a Lawyer.
- Dinesh is neither Police nor Lawyer.

Which of the following statement is/are true based on the given arrangement? **IB 2024**

I. Anmol is sitting to the left end of the row.
II. Enamul is sitting third to the left of Badal.
III. Doctor is sitting to the right of Chaman.

(a) Only Arrangement II is true
(b) Arrangements I and II are true
(c) All Arrangements I, II and III are true
(d) Only Arrangement I is true

Based on Circular Arrangement

23. G, H, I, J, K, L and O are sitting around a circular table facing to the centre of the table. L sits third to the left of G. H sits second to the left of O. Only G sits between J and H. K is not an immediate neighbour of L. How many people sit between I and K, when counted from the right of I ? **RPF SI 2024**

(a) Two (b) One (c) Three (d) Four

24. E, F , G, H, I and J are sitting around a circular table facing the center. J sits immediate left of I. G sits second to the right of I. E sits second to the right of G. H sits second to the left of F.
Who sits third to the right of E? **SSC MTS 2023**

(a) F (b) H (c) I (d) J

25. Manoj, Pranay, Esha, Wasim, Tina and Diksha are sitting in a circle facing the centre. Manoj sits opposite to Esha who is to the right of Diksha and who is not adjacent to Pranay or Wasim. Esha sits between Pranay and Diksha. Who sits to the left of Wasim? **DSSSB 2019**

(a) Pranay (b) Manoj
(c) Tina (d) Esha

26. O, P, Q, R, S and T are sitting around a circular table facing the centre (but not necessarily in the same order). P sits second to the left of T. S sits third to the right of Q. Q is not an immediate neighbour of P. O sits second to the right of S. Which of the following represents the position of O with respect of R? **SSC CGL (Tier-II) 2025**

(a) Third to the left (b) Second to the left
(c) Immediate right (d) Third to the right

27. Six persons are sitting in a circle and are facing the centre. Ananya is facing Bhuv. Bhuv is to the immediate right of Ranbir and the immediate left of Yash. Yash is to the immediate left of Johar. Taara is to the immediate right of Ananya.
Who is sitting to the immediate right of Taara ? **CRPF Head Constable 2023**

(a) Yash (b) Bhuv (c) Johar (d) Ranbir

28. Six people E, H, K, M, S and U are seated in a circle facing the centre. U and H are immediate neighbours of M. E is the only person sitting between K and S. H is to the immediate right of S. Who is the immediate right of U? **NTA CUET (UG) 2024**

(a) M (b) E (c) K (d) S

29. Shagun, Pragya, Yati, Lovey, Savi and Frooti are sitting around a circular table facing the centre. Shagun sits 2nd to the left of Pragya. Yati sits 2nd to the left of Shagun. Lovey sits 3rd to the left of Yati. Savi sits 2nd to the left of Lovey. Who sits 3rd to the left of Shagun? **SSC MTS 2023**

(a) Pragya (b) Lovey (c) Savi (d) Frooti

30. A, B, C, D, E and F are sitting in a circle facing center. D is sitting immediate right of B. B and F are not immediate neighbours. 'C' is sitting exactly between 'A' and 'D'. Who are the neighbours of F? **HSSC CET 2022**

(a) A and B (b) C and D (c) B and D (d) A and E

31. Six friends are sitting in a circle facing the centre of the circle. Veena and Sadvi are the immediate neighbours of Pooja. Anil and Guna are the immediate neighbours of Giri. Anil is to the immediate left of Veena. Who is to the immediate right of Veena? **RRB NTPC 2022**

(a) Guna (b) Anil (c) Pooja (d) Sadvi

32. Six people were seated around a circular table facing the centre. B is sitting to the immediate right of E. Only A is between F and D. Only C is between D and B. Who is sitting just left of E ? **CRPF Head Constable 2023**

(a) C (b) D (c) A (d) F

33. Six students Aarav, Bhavya, Chetan, Diya, Esha and Farhan are sitting in a circle facing the center. Bhavya sits to the immediate right of Aarav. Diya is not sitting next to Aarav or Farhan. Esha, who is sitting to the immediate left of Farhan, is also sitting to the immediate right of Chetan. Who is the immediate neighbour of both Diya and Esha? **SSC GD Constable 2024**

(a) Aarav (b) Chetan
(c) Bhavya (d) Farhan

Directions (Q. Nos. 34 and 35) *Study the following information carefully and answer the questions given below.*

Six friends are sitting in a circle. All of them are facing the centre. Kanak sits third to the right of Sona. Kapil is an immediate neighbour of Mani. Goldy sits second to the right of Mani. Sona is an immediate neighbour of Kapil and Suresh. **SSC CPO 2023**

34. Who sits second to the left of Kanak ?
(a) Suresh (b) Kapil (c) Goldy (d) Mani

35. Who sits to the immediate right of Goldy ?
(a) Sona (b) Kapil (c) Kanak (d) Suresh

36. Seven boys B_1, B_2, B_3, B_4, B_5, B_6 and B_7 are sitting around a circular table facing towards the centre (not necessarily in the same order). B_1 is third to the left of B_7. B_4 is to immediate left of B_1. B_2 is second to the left of B_6. B_6 is not an immediate neighbour of B_5.
Who are the immediate neighbours of B_3? *SSC MTS 2022*
(a) B_5 and B_4 (b) B_6 and B_7
(c) B_1 and B_2 (d) B_4 and B_6

37. Seven friends, Subhi, Prince, Ketan, Vishal, Mahima, Krish and Naitik are sitting around a circular table with their backs towards the centre. Subhi is sitting to the immediate right of Prince. Naitik and Krish are not sitting to the immediate left or right of Vishal. Vishal is sitting third to the left of Prince. Mahima is sitting to the immediate right to Vishal.Who is sitting third to the right of Prince ? *SSC CGL (Tier I) 2022*
(a) Naitik (b) Ketan (c) Mahima (d) Krish

> **MRC*****
> ***(Most Repeating Concepts)***
> Question Nos. 24, 27, 31, 32, 37, 40 and 45 are very important from examination point of view. Question based on these concept are being asked in SSC (MTS), RRB NTPC, CRPF Head Constable and DP Head Constable examination.

38. Seven girls, Mansi, Shweta, Monika, Payal, Aarti, Kajal and Laxmi are sitting around a circular table facing opposite to the centre (not necessarily in the same order). Aarti is second to the left of Kajal. Monika is third to the right of Kajal. Mansi is not the immediate neighbour of Kajal. Laxmi is second to the left of Mansi. Payal is not the immediate neighbour of Laxmi. Who is second to the left of Laxmi ? *SSC MTS 2023*
(a) Mansi (b) Aarti (c) Kajal (d) Payal

39. A, B, E, G, P, L and M are sitting around a circular table facing the centre. Only two people sit between A and M when counted from the right of A. Only three people sit between P and L when counted from the right of L. M sits to the immediate right of L. E sits to the immediate right of G. Who sits fourth to the right of B? *RRB Technician Grade III 2024*
(a) P (b) G (c) M (d) E

40. Eight friends, P, Q, R, S, T, U, V and W are sitting around a circular table, facing towards the centre of the table.
P is an immediate neighbour of U and S. R is second to the left of S and V is fourth to the right of P. Two people are sitting between U and V. T is not an immediate neighbour of either U or V. If T is third to the left of U and W is an immediate neighbour of V. Where is Q sitting? *DP Head Constable 2022*
(a) Immediate left of U (b) Immediate left of S
(c) Third to the right of T (d) Third to the left of R

41. Eight persons are sitting around a circular table facing the centre. Z is an immediate neighbour of both U and V. Z is second to the left of X. S is an immediate neighbour of both U and T. U sits third to the left of X. W is an immediate neighbour of T. Y sits second to the right of V. Who sits third to the left of T? *RRC Group D 2022*
(a) X (b) Z (c) W (d) Y

42. Seven persons, Mayank, Manjeet, Naresh, Jitender, Suman, Jitu and Jeevan are sitting around a circular table, some are facing inwards and some are facing outwards. Suman is facing inside and sitting 4th to the right of Mayank. Mayank is sitting 2nd to the left of Jitu. Jitu is facing outwards and is sitting next to the left of Jeevan. Jeevan is sitting 3rd to the right of Suman. Manjeet is not the immediate neighbour of Mayank and Jitu. Manjeet is sitting 2nd to the left of Mayank. Naresh is not sitting 3rd to the right of Jitu. Who among the following is an immediate neighbour of Mayank? *RRB NTPC 2021*
(a) Jeevan (b) Jitu (c) Manjeet (d) Suman

43. Palak, Quincy, Ramesh, Shyam, Timir, Umang, Vandan and Willa are sitting around a circular table facing the centre of the table. Palak sits third to the right of Willa and third to the left of Quincy. Shyam sits second to the right to Timir. Vandan sits second to the left of Ramesh. Timir is not neighbour of Quincy while Umang is neither a neighbour of Timir nor of Willa. Who is sitting to the immediate right of Quincy? *UPSSSC Forest & Wild Life Guard 2022*
(a) Vandan (b) Umang (c) Willa (d) None of these

44. Eight friends are sitting around a circular table at equal distances with their back towards the centre of the table. Ishin is sitting to the immediate right of Anshu. Amina is not an immediate neighbour of Dhruv. Only three people sit between Harmeet and Fiza. Dhruv is to the immediate left of Varun. There are only two people between Mohit and Harmeet. Fiza is sitting to the immediate left of Anshu. Only three people sit between Ishin and Varun. Who is sitting to the immediate left of Harmeet ? *RRB NTPC 2022*
(a) Dhruv (b) Varun (c) Amina (d) Ishin

45. Five friends Amit, Bablu, Chirag, Deepak and Eklavya each having different occupations Advocate, Boxer, Coach, Doctor and Engineer are sitting around a circular table facing the centre.

1. Bablu is a Boxer and Deepak is a Doctor.
2. Amit sits second to the right of Chirag, who is a Coach.
3. The Boxer will never sit immediately next to the Coach.
4. The Doctor and Boxer are immediate neighbours of each other.

Who sits to the immediate right of Chirag? **RRB NTPC 2022**

(a) Deepak (b) Bablu (c) Amit (d) Eklavya

Based on Square, Rectangular and Polygonal Arrangement

46. Eight professors of a college namely X, Y, Z, A, B, C, D and E are sitting around a square table in such a way that four of them sit at the four corners of the table while other four sit on each side of the table are sitting in the middle facing each other. C sits immediate right of A, who faces Z. E sits opposite to X, who sits immediate right of Y. B sits immediate left of Y and faces C. Who among the following faces Y? **SSC MTS 2023**

(a) Z (b) D (c) A (d) C

47. A, B, C, D, E, F, G and H are sitting around a square table facing the centre of the table. Some of them are sitting at the corners, while some are sitting at the exact centre of the sides. Only three people sit between C and D. Both C and D sit at the centres of the sides of the table. A sits third to the left of D. B is neither an immediate neighbour of C nor D. F sits third to the right of B. E sits to the immediate right of H.

Who sits third to the right of G? **DP Constable 2022**

(a) D (b) H (c) B (d) C

48. A, B, C, D, J, K, L and M are sitting around a square table facing the centre of the table. Four of them are sitting at either of the corners while the other four are sitting at the exact centre of either of the sides. D sits at one of the corners of the table. Only two people sit between D and C, when counted from the left of D. Only three people sit between C and B. M sits third to the left of B. K sits to the immediate right of M. A is neither an immediate neighbour of B nor C. J sits to the immediate left of A. Who sits second to the right of L? **RRB NTPC 2022**

(a) C (b) K (c) J (d) M

49. A, B, C, D, E, F, G and H are sitting around a square table facing outwards. Some of them are sitting at the corners while some are sitting at the exact centre of the sides. A is sitting to the immediate left of B and right of H. H is sitting between A and G. F is sitting to the immediate left of G and right of E. D is sitting between E and C. C is sitting to the immediate right of B. Who is sitting between C and E? **SSC Steno 2022**

(a) D (b) B (c) G (d) A

50. Eight friends A, B, C, D, E, F, G and H are sitting around a square table facing the centre.

I. B is facing D and is sitting to the right of E.
II. F, who is a neighbour of D, is facing G.
III. There are two persons between C and H. H is not facing E.

Who might be sitting between C and E, if there is only person between them? **SSC MTS 2021**

(a) D (b) A (c) G (d) B

51. Amir, Bunty, Leslie, Pradeep, Eshan, Faiz, Gaurav and Harish are sitting around a square table facing the centre of the table. Some of them are sitting at the corners, while some are sitting at the exact centre of the sides. Pradeep sits third to the right of Gaurav. Pradeep sits at one of the corners. Bunty sits second to the right of Faiz. Faiz does not sit at any of the corners. Bunty is not an immediate neighbour of Pradeep. Harish is an immediate neighbour of Amir. Harish does not sit at any of the middle of the sides. Only one person sits between Harish and Leslie. Who sits third to the right of Amir? **SSC GD Constable 2023**

(a) Eshan (b) Leslie (c) Bunty (d) Gaurav

52. Eight relatives P, Q, R, S, T, V, W and Y are sitting around a square table in such a way that four of them sit at four corners of the square while four sit in the middle of each of four sides, all of them facing the centre of the square. P sits third to the left of V. R is not an immediate neighbour of V. Only one person sits between V and W. S sits second to the right of Q. R is not an immediate neighbour of P. T sits second to the left of P. Who sits fourth to the right of P? **SSC CPO 2022**

(a) V (b) T (c) S (d) R

53. Eight friends, Janak, Kuldeep, Punit, Kavita, Naveen, Azad, Vikas and Anil are sitting around a square table, four of them are sitting at the four corners and the rest four are sitting at the middle of each of four sides of the table. The ones who sit at the corners face the centre, while those who are sitting in the middle of the sides face away opposite to the centre of the table.

Janak faces the centre and is third to the right of Azad. Naveen faces the centre, but is not an immediate neighbour of Azad. Only one person is sitting between Azad and Vikas. Kavita is sitting second to the right of Kuldeep. Kuldeep faces the centre. Punit is not an immediate neighbour of Janak.

Which of the following statements is true regarding Punit? *RRB NTPC 2022*

(a) Punit is an immediate neighbour of Azad
(b) Punit faces away from the centre of the table
(c) Kuldeep sits third to the left of Punit
(d) Punit is an immediate neighbour of both Azad and Janak

54. On all the five corners of pentagon, five people Ram, Rohan, Sunita, Seema and Chandan sit in a specific order facing towards the centre. Ram is to the immediate left of Rohan. Sunita is not an immediate neighbour of Ram. Chandan is an immediate neighbour of both Sunita and Seema. *RRB NTPC 2022*

What will be the position of Sunita with respect to Ram?

(a) Sunita occupies third place from Ram in the anti-clockwise direction
(b) Sunita occupies third place from Ram in the clockwise direction
(c) Sunita occupies second place from Ram in the clockwise direction
(d) Sunita occupies first place from Ram in the anti-clockwise direction

Right Key

1. (c)	2. (d)	3. (a)	4. (a)	5. (b)	6. (b)	7. (b)	8. (b)	9. (b)	10. (b)
11. (b)	12. (d)	13. (c)	14. (d)	15. (a)	16. (c)	17. (c)	18. (b)	19. (d)	20. (b)
21. (a)	22. (b)	23. (c)	24. (b)	25. (a)	26. (b)	27. (d)	28. (c)	29. (d)	30. (d)
31. (c)	32. (d)	33. (b)	34. (b)	35. (d)	36. (d)	37. (b)	38. (c)	39. (d)	40. (d)
41. (a)	42. (a)	43. (a)	44. (c)	45. (d)	46. (b)	47. (b)	48. (d)	49. (a)	50. (d)
51. (a)	52. (c)	53. (b)	54. (b)						

Solutions

1. *(c)* According to the given information,

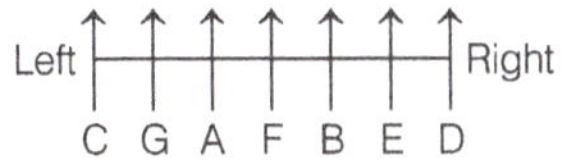

Hence, there is only one person sits between G and F.

2. *(d)* According to the given information,

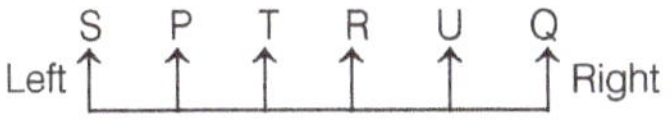

∴ S is sitting to the left of P.

3. *(a)* According to the question, the sitting arrangement is as given below,

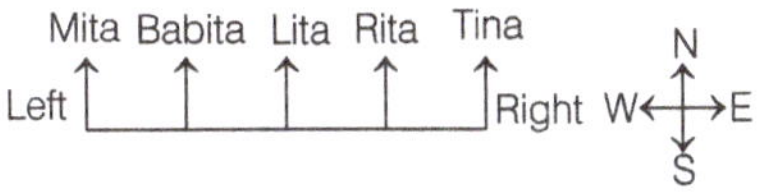

Clearly, from above diagram, Rita is sitting second from the East end.

4. *(a)* According to the given information,

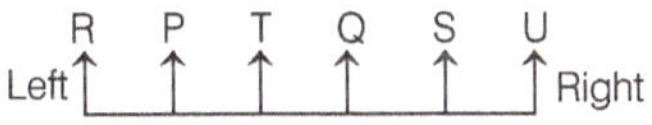

Hence, T and S are the neighbours of Q.

5. *(b)* According to the given information,

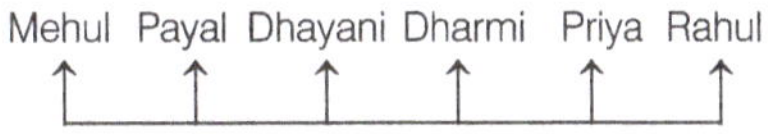

Hence, there are four persons to the right of Payal.

TOP TIPS First arrange the definite statements in a row and then arrange the Probable/ uncertain and statements with less condition in a row.

6. *(b)* According to the given information,

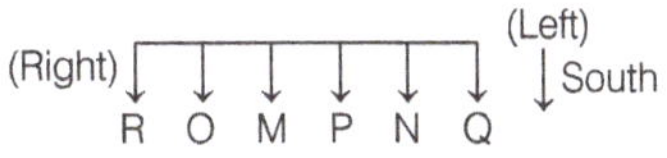

Clearly, 'M' is sitting immediate left of 'O'.

7. *(b)* According to the given information,

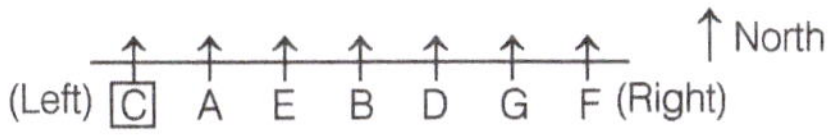

Hence, C sits to the immediate left of A.

8. *(b)* According to the given information,

∴ Hema sits 3rd to right of Deepak.

9. *(b)* According to the given information,

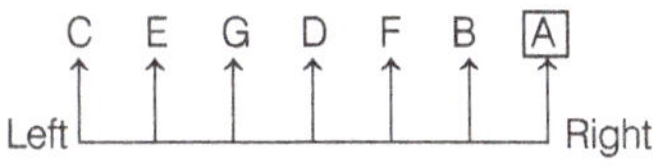

Hence, A sits to the extreme right.

10. *(b)* According to the given information,

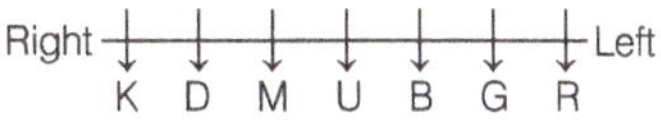

Hence, there are three people sit between D and G.

11. *(b)* According to the given information,

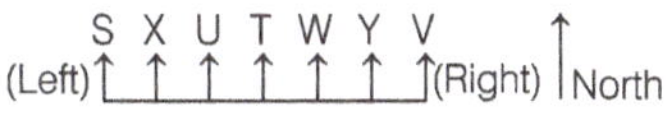

Clearly, 'Y' is sitting between W and V.

12. *(d)* According to the given information,

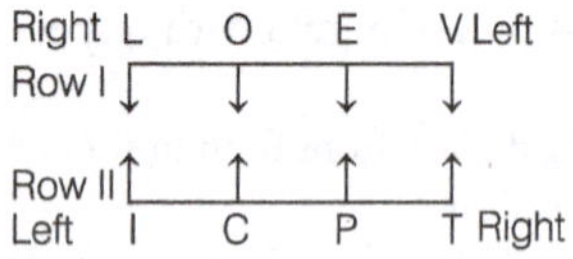

Hence, I sits at the extreme left end of the row of people facing North.

13. *(c)* According to the given information,

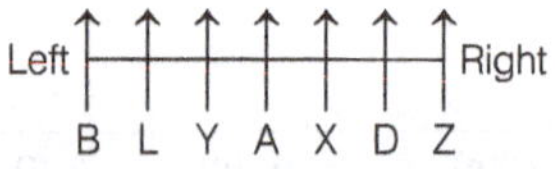

Hence, three people sit between B and X.

14. *(d)* According to the given information,

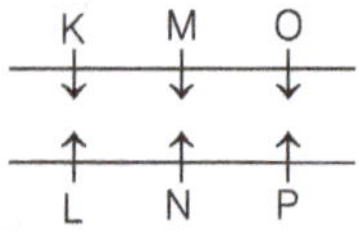

Hence, L, N and P are in same team.

15. *(a)* According to the given information,

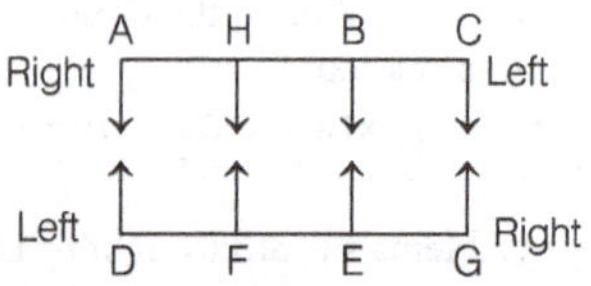

∴ A, B, C and H are sitting in the same line.

16. *(c)* According to the given information,

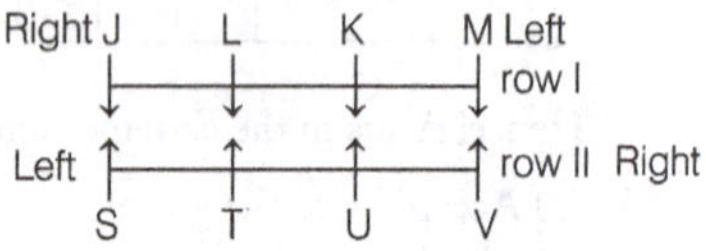

Hence, the person facing S is J.

17. *(c)* According to the given information,

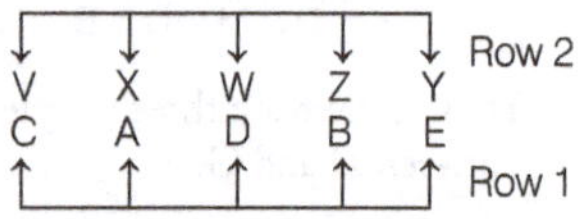

Hence, W faces D.

18. *(b)* According to the given information,

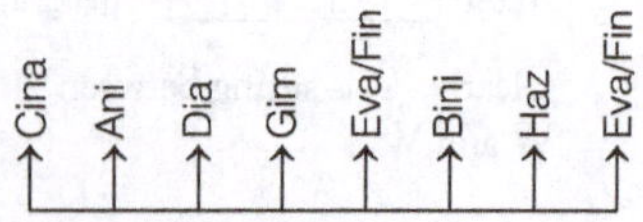

One who can be seated to the immediate left of Bini is either Eva or Fin.

But according to the option 'Eva' can be seated to the immediate left of Bini.

19. *(d)* According to the given information,

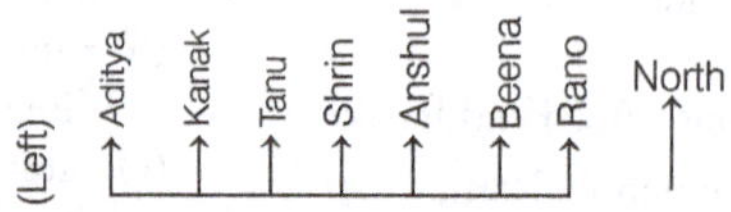

Hence, 'Rano' is sitting extreme right of the row.

20. *(b)* According to the information,

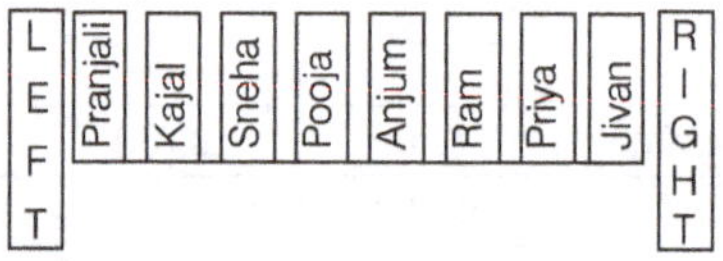

Hence, Kajal and Sneha sit exactly between Pooja and Pranjali.

21. *(a)* When X is sitting to the immediate right of Y.

Then,

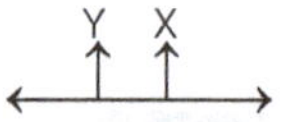

and when X moves 5 places to right and Y moves 5 places to the left and both reach extremes.

Then,

Hence, total number of persons

$= 5 + 5 + 2 = 12$

22. *(b)* According to the given information,

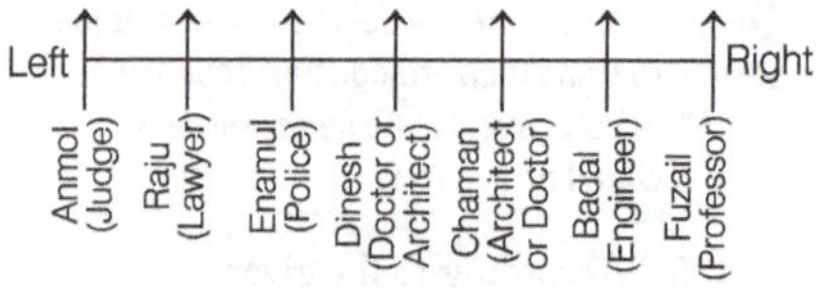

Statements I. (✓) II. (✓) III. (✗)

Hence, Arrangements I and II are true.

23. *(c)* According to the given information,

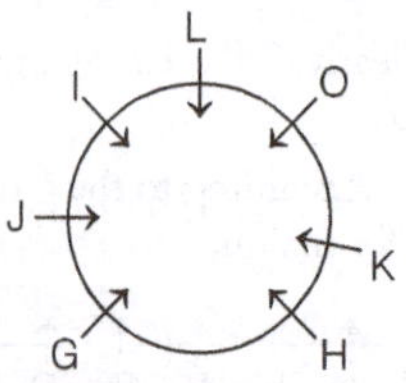

Hence, there are three persons sit between I and K, when counted from the right of I.

24. *(b)* According to the given information,

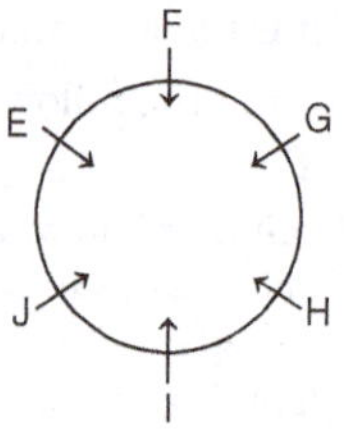

Hence, H sits third to the right of E.

25. *(a)* According to the information,

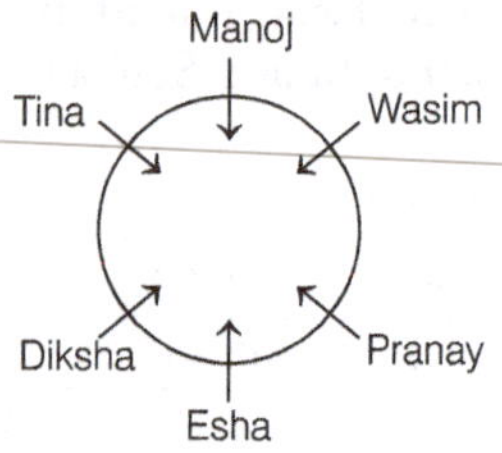

Hence, Pranay sits to the left of Wasim.

TOP TIPS While solving such questions arrange the person first about whom exact information is given.

26. *(b)* According to the given information,

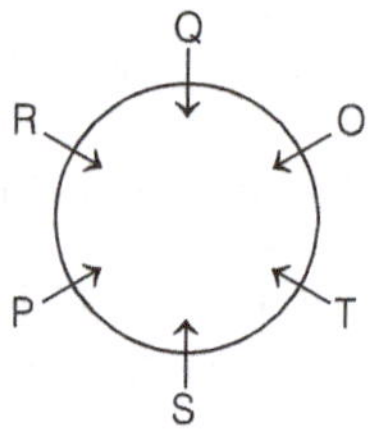

Hence, O is second to the left of R.

27. *(d)* According to the given information,

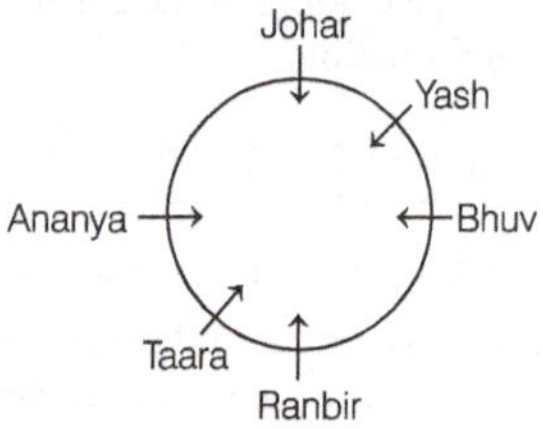

Hence, Ranbir is sitting to the immediate right of Taara.

28. *(c)* According to the question,

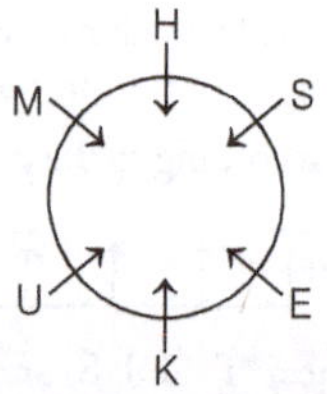

Hence, K is the immediate right of U.

29. *(d)* According to the given information,

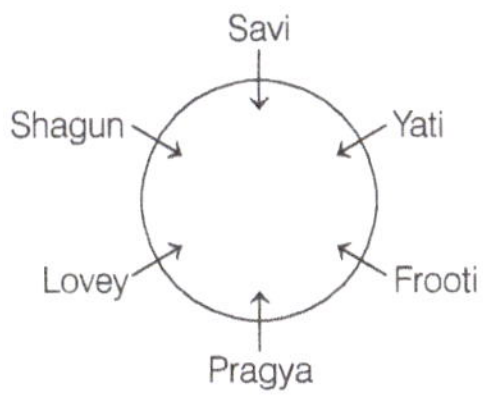

∴ Frooti sits 3rd to the left of Shagun.

30. *(d)* According to the given information,

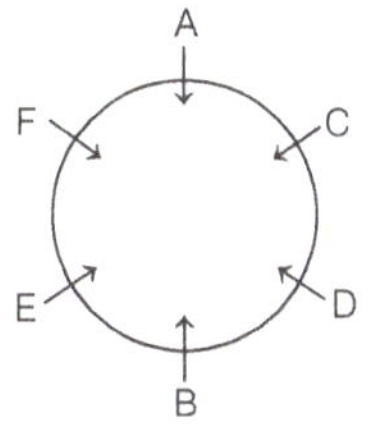

Hence, A and E are neighbour of F.

31. *(c)* According to the given information,

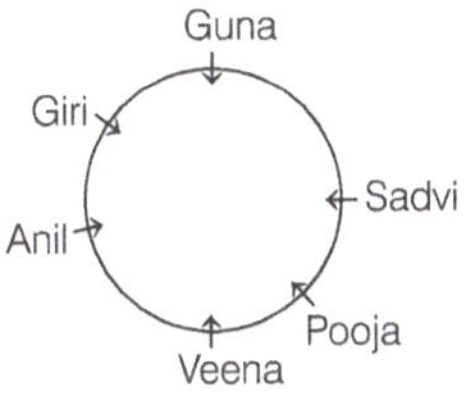

Hence, 'Pooja' sits immediate right of Veena.

32. *(d)* According to the given information,

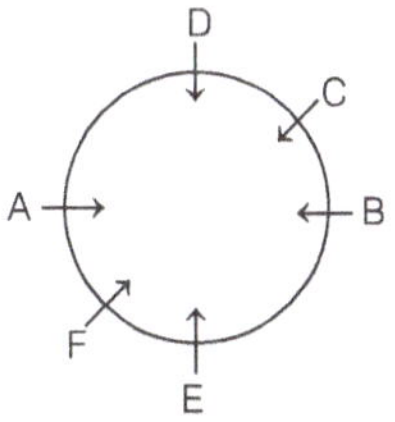

Hence, F is sitting just left of E.

33. *(b)* According to the given information,

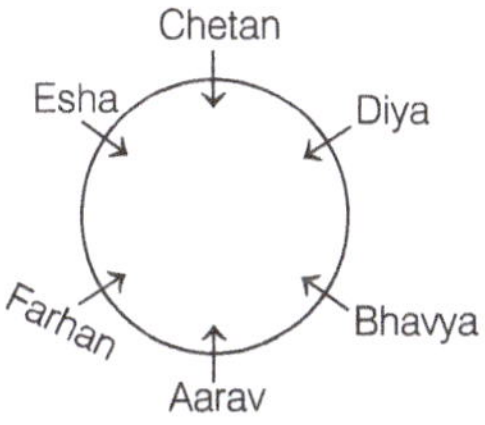

∴ Chetan is the immediate neighbour of both Diya and Esha.

Sol. (Q. Nos. 34 and 35) According to the given information,

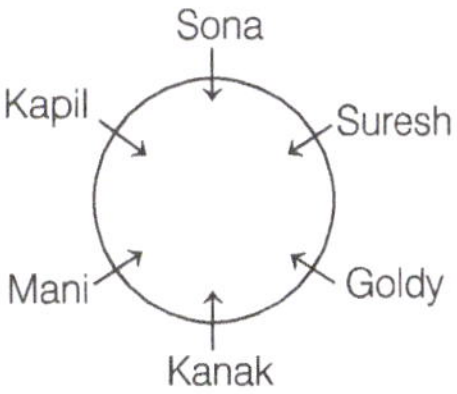

34. *(b)* Kapil sits second to the left of Kanak .

35. *(d)* Suresh sits to the immediate right of Goldy.

36. *(d)* According to the given information,

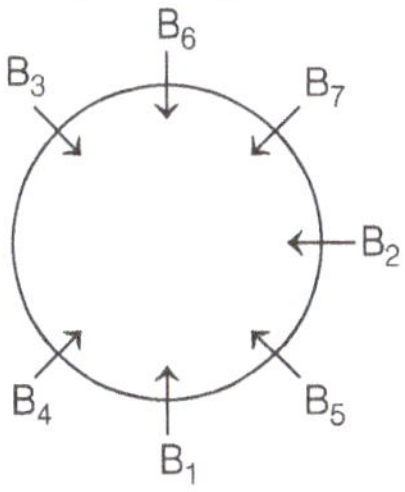

So, B_4 and B_6 are the immediate neighbours of B_3.

37. *(b)* According to the given information,

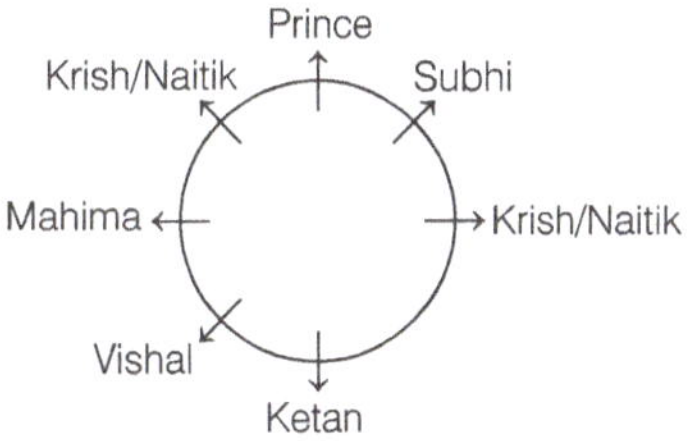

Hence, Ketan sits third to the right of Prince.

38. *(c)* According to the given information,

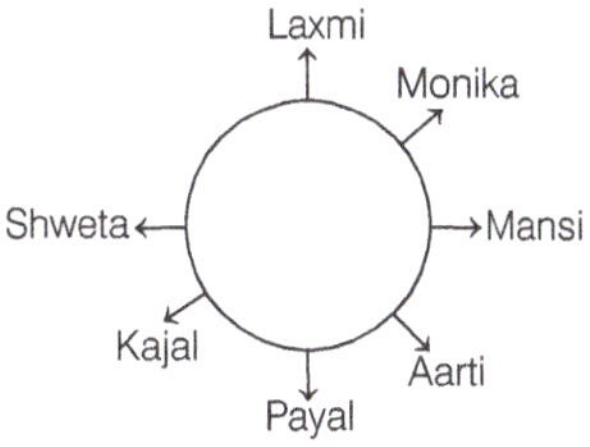

Hence, Kajal sits second to the left of Laxmi.

39. *(d)* According to the given information,

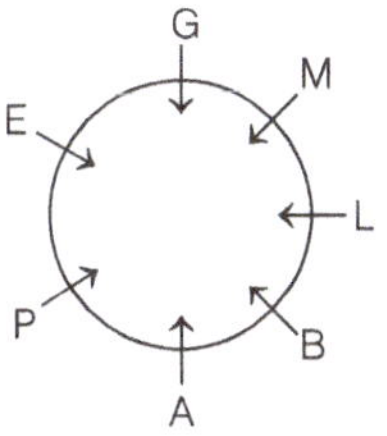

Hence, E sits fourth to the right of B.

40. *(d)* According to the given information,

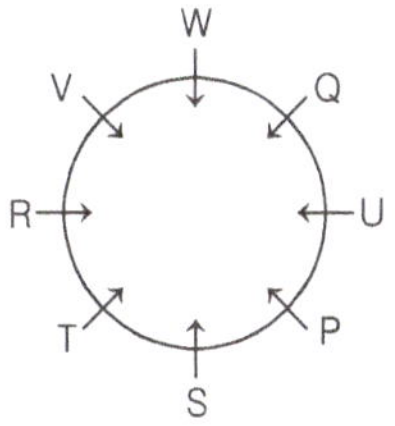

Hence, Q is sitting third to the left of R.

41. *(a)* According to the given information,

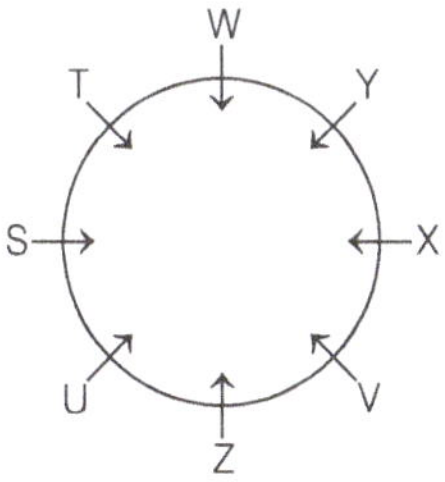

Hence, X sits third to the left of T.

42. *(a)* According to the given information,

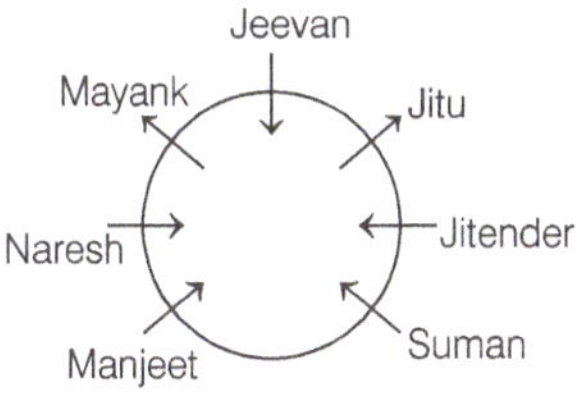

Jeevan and Naresh immediate neighbour of Mayank.

43. *(a)* According to the question,

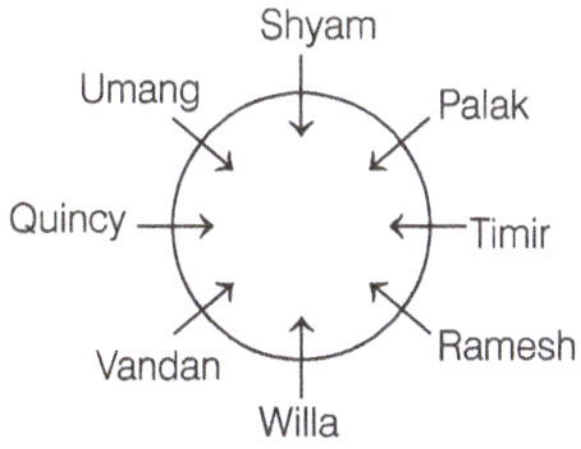

Hence, Vandan is sitting to the immediate right of Quincy.

44. *(c)* According to the given information,

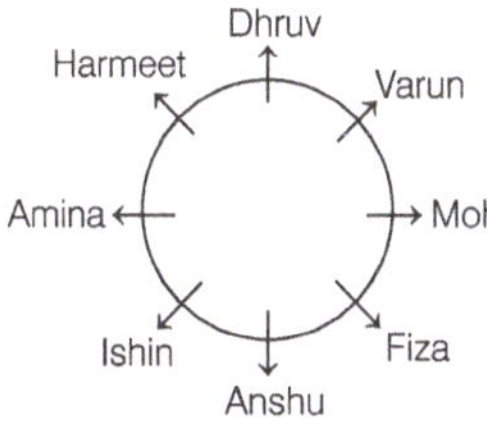

Hence, Amina is sitting to the immediate left of Harmeet.

45. *(d)* According to the given information,

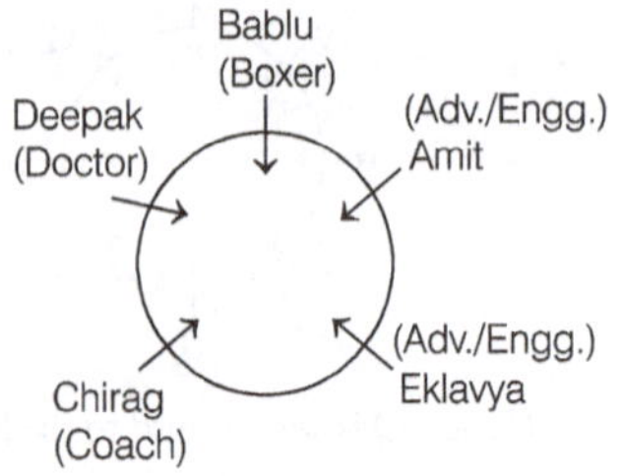

Hence, Eklavya sits to the immediate right of Chirag.

46. *(b)* According to the given information,

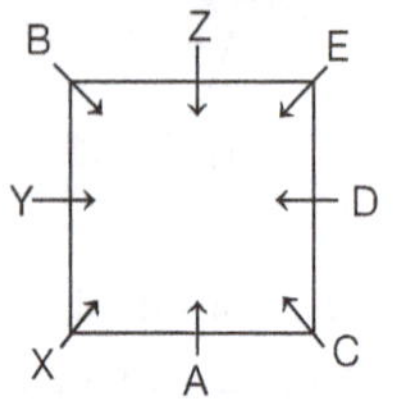

Hence, D faces Y.

47. *(b)* According to the given information,

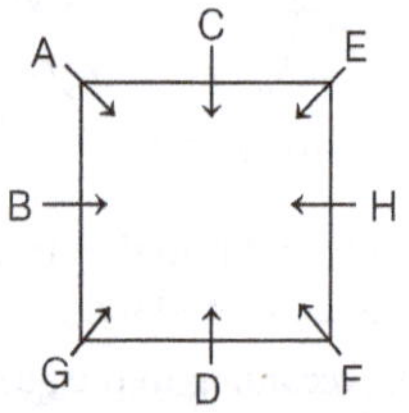

Hence, H sits third to the right of G.

48. *(d)* According to the given information,

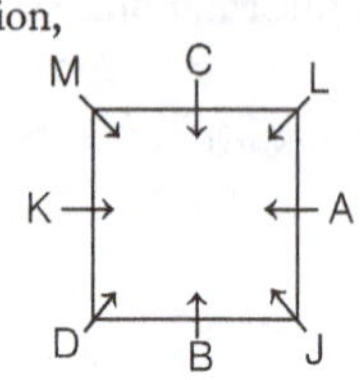

Hence, M sits second to the right of L.

49. *(a)* According to the given information,

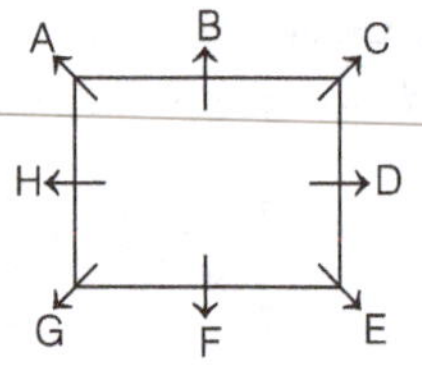

Hence, D is sitting between C and E.

50. *(d)* According to the given information,

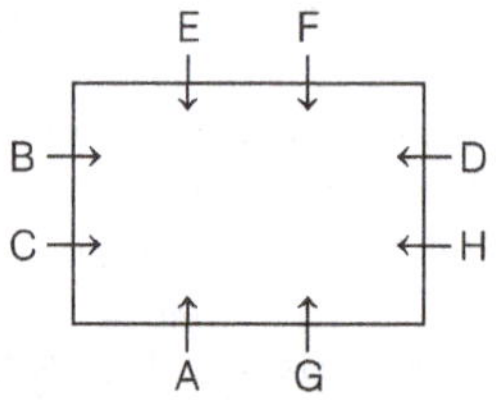

Hence, B is siting between C and E.

51. *(a)* According to the given information,

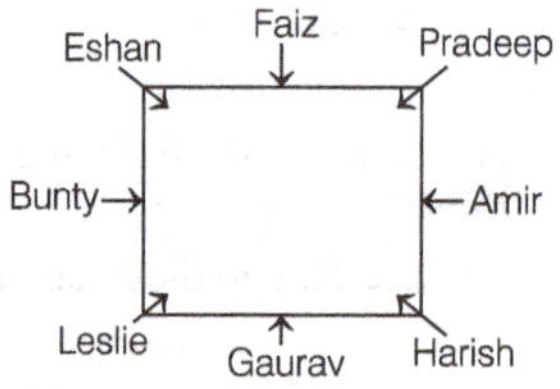

Clearly, Eshan is sitting third to the right of Amir.

52. *(c)* According to the given information,

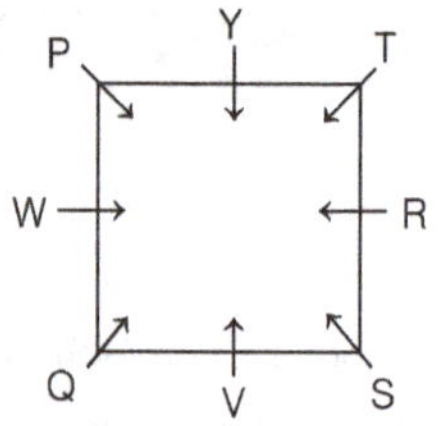

Hence, S sits fourth to the right of P.

53. *(b)* According to the given information,

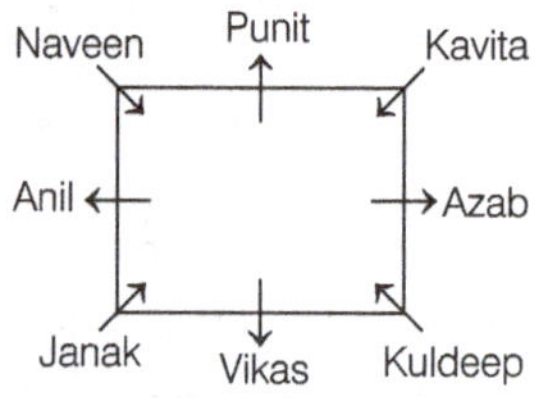

Hence, 'Punit' faces away from the centre of the table.

54. *(b)* According to the given information,

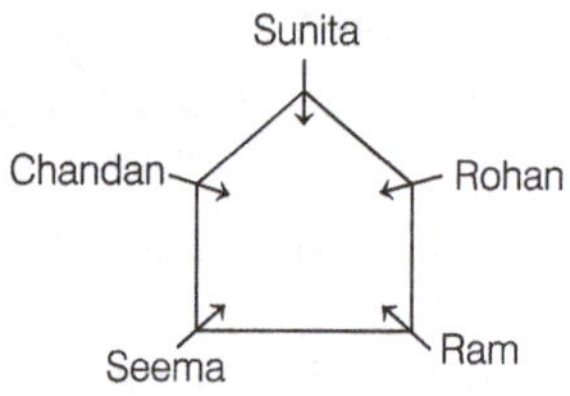

Hence, Sunita occupies third place from Ram in the clockwise direction.

CHAPTER

13 Puzzle Test

Based on Classification

In this type of question, certain items belonging to different groups or possessing different qualities are given along with some clues, with the help of which it is required to group the items having common properties and analyse the given items to answer the questions accordingly.

e.g. Raj, Vikram, Amit, Amar and Shivani are five friends. Raj, Vikram and Amit are intelligent. Raj, Amar and Shivani are hard working. Amar, Amit and Shivani are teachers. Raj, Vikram and Shivani are scholar. Who among the given friends is neither hardworking nor a scholar?

(a) Amit (b) Vikram (c) Shivani (d) Raj

Sol. (a) According to the question,

Friend	Qualities Achievements			
	Intelligent	Hard Woking	Teacher	Scholar
Raj	✓	✓	×	✓
Vikram	✓	×	×	✓
Amit	✓	×	✓	×
Amar	×	✓	✓	×
Shivani	×	✓	✓	✓

Hence, Amit is neither hard working nor a scholar.

Based on Box and Floor

In this type, some information is given regarding the box or floors. Candidate has to arrange that data in an appropriate structure and answer the question.

e.g. There are five boxes K, L, M, N and O arranged one above the other. Box M is placed above box N. Box O is placed below Box K. Box N is placed above K. Box L is placed below O. Which among the following is the bottom most box?

(a) O (b) L
(c) K (d) M

Sol. (b) According to the question,

M
N
K
O
L

Hence, 'L' is the bottom most box.

Based on Conditions, Grouping and Team formation/Designation

In this type, conditions regarding the selection or non-selection of persons or objects with respect to one another and depending on their designations are given on the basis of which a team is to be formed and questions are to be answered accordingly.

e.g. A student has exactly four books A, B, C and D. Out of which he has to choose exactly three books to put in a bag. Any combination is acceptable, provided it satisfies the following conditions.

If A is selected, then C cannot be selected. If B is selected, then D is also selected.

Choose the combination of books from the options given below which satisfies the given three conditions.

(a) ABC (b) ACD
(c) CBD (d) None of these

Sol. (c) CBD satisfies both the conditions. So, it will be acceptable.

Puzzle Test

A group of statements which despite being completely true, reveal vague meanings but when these statements are arranged or tabulated, reveal completely clear meanings. Such statement are called puzzles. The process of finding out the clear meaning of these statements is called puzzle test.

Based on Day/Data/Month

In this type, some clues are given regarding the order of occurrence of certain events. The candidate is required to analyse the given information, frame the right sequence and then answer the questions accordingly.

e.g. A tourist group plans to visit six places A, B, C, D, E and F or different days of the same week (starting on Monday and ending on Saturday). During their tour, they visited place D on Monday. They visited only one place between visiting place B and place D. They visited place F the immediate next day of visiting place C. They neither visited place C nor place A on Thursday. On which day did they visit place E?

(a) Friday (b) Saturday (c) Thursday (d) Tuesday

Sol. (c) According to the question,

Day	Monday	Tuesday	Wednesday	Thursday	Friday	Satur.
Place	D	A	B	E	C	F

Hence, they visited place E on Thursday.

Based on Family Blood Relation

In this type, some clues are provided regarding relationship amongst different members of a family, together with their professions, qualities, colours, dresses etc. Candidates have to analyse the whole information and then answer the given questions accordingly.

e.g. A family consists of 7 people with three couples. The artist is married to the politician and they have three children. The teacher is the sister-in-law of the accountant, who is the wife of the engineer. The doctor and businessman are brothers. Who among the following could be the husband of the teacher?

(a) Politician (b) Engineer (c) Accountant (d) Doctor

Sol. (d) According to the given information,

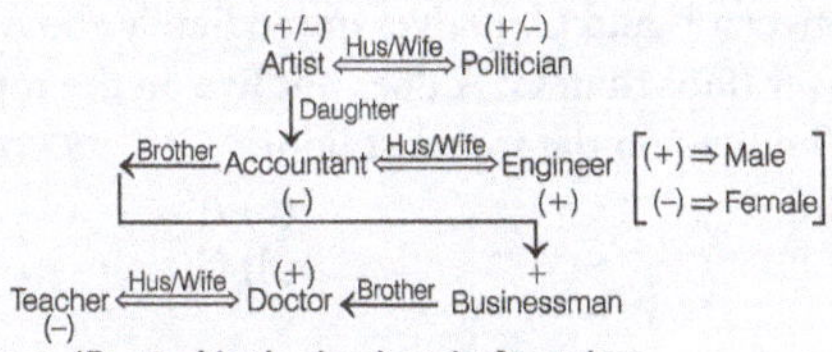

Hence, 'Doctor' is the husband of teacher.

Exam Approach Examples

Based on Classification

Examles 1 **Four students P, Q, R and S learn one language each from among English, French, Spanish and German. P and R do not learn Spanish, S learns French. If P does not learn German, then who learns English?** *SSC Steno 2020*

(a) Q (b) R
(c) S (d) P

Sol. (*d*) According to the question,

Language	Students
English	P
French	S
Spanish	Q
German	R

From the above table, it is clear that P learn English.

Based on Box and Floor

Example 2 **Six bags, A, B, C, D, E and F are kept one above another (not necessarily in the same order). Only three bags are kept between B and D. Bag A is kept above E but below C. There are only two bags between A and F. B is kept above D. D is not kept below F. If we re-arrange these bags in alphabetical order from top to bottom, then the position of how many bags will remain the same?** *RRB NTPC 2021*

(a) One (b) Two
(c) Zero (d) Three

Sol. (*a*) According to the given information,

B
C
A
E
D
F

Trending Concept

Puzzles based on box and floor are being asked in the current exams (RRB NTPC and SSC CHSL). It is very important for upcoming examination.

After arranging them in alphabetic order from top to the bottom (A, B, C, D, E, F). Hence, only 'F' will remain the same.

Example 3 **A, B, C, D, E and F live on six different floors of the same building. The lowermost floor in the building is numbered 1, the floor above it, number 2, and so on, till the topmost floor is numbered 6. E lives on an odd-numbered floor, but not on floor number 5. Only one person lives between E and C. D lives immediately above F. B lives on a lower floor than C. A does not live on the topmost floor. Who lives on the topmost floor?** *SSC CHSL (Tier-II) 2024*

(a) B (b) A
(c) D (d) C

Sol. (*c*) According to the question,

Floor	Person
6	D
5	F
4	A
3	C
2	B
1	E

$\therefore$ D lives on topmost floor.

Helping Tips

While attempting question based on puzzle, recheck the solution by matching the given information again, to ensure that no contradictory statement is present.

Based on Conditions, Grouping and Team Formation/Designation

Example 4 **A team of 5 members is to be selected from 6 men A, B, C, D, E and F and 6 women P, Q, R, S, T and U have to be selected together. If B is selected then neither U nor Q can be selected. Among A, B, S and T exactly two persons are to be selected. If E is selected, then neither S nor B can be selected. If A is selected, then B will be selected. Which of the following is the correct selection of the team ?** *RRB NTPC 2021*

(a) C, U, B, P, R (b) P, R, S, T, D
(c) P, R, A, B, S (d) C, Q, A, B, S

Sol. (*b*) From the given options,

Option (a), C and U have to be selected together. So, this cannot be the team.

Option (c), As among A, B, S and T exactly two person to be selected. So, this can not be the team.

Option (d), As B is selected. So, Q can not be the part of team.

Hence, option (b) is correct.

Based on Day/Date/Month

Example 5 **In a year end examination, 6 Papers - Maths, Physics, Geography, Economics, Chemistry, History are scheduled on 6 consecutive days of a week (Monday - Saturday)**

1. **Maths Paper is after the Chemistry paper, with a 1-day gap between them.**
2. **Physics paper is on Monday.**
3. **Geography paper is not on the last day.**
4. **History paper, which is scheduled on the previous day of the Maths paper, has a two-day gap with the Physics paper.**

Which paper is scheduled on Saturday? *SSC MTS 2021*

(a) Chemistry (b) Economics
(c) History (d) Maths

Sol. (*b*) According to the given information,

Day	Subject
Monday	Physics
Tuesday	Geography
Wednesday	Chemistry
Thursday	History
Friday	Math
Saturday	Economics

Hence, Economics paper is scheduled on Saturday.

Example 6 **Vishakha joined five different hobby classes viz. Painting, Dancing, Modelling, Singing and Cooking. She attends each class on different day of the same week from Monday to Friday but not necessarily in the same order. She attends Modelling class on Wednesday. She attends neither paniting nor Dancing class on Thursday and Friday. She attends Cooking class on Friday.**

On which day does she attend Singing class ? ***[RRB NTPC 2022]***

(a) Tuesday (b) Monday

(c) Thursday (d) Data is inadequate

Sol. (*c*) According to the question,

Day	Hobby classes
Monday	Painting/Dancing
Tuesday	Dancing/Painting
Wednesday	Modelling
Thursday	Singing
Friday	Cooking

Hence, Vishakha attend singing class on Thursday.

Based on Family Blood Relation

Example 7 **P, Q, R, S, T and U are 6 members of family in which there are two married couples. T, a teacher, is married to a doctor who is mother of R and U. Q, the lawyer, is married to P. P has one son and one grandson. Of the two married ladies one is a housewife. There is also one student and one male engineer in the family.**

Which of the following is true about the granddaughter of the family? ***SSC CGL 2018***

(a) She is a lawyer

(b) She is an engineer

(c) She is a student

(d) She is a doctor

Sol. (*c*) According to the given information, arrangement is as follows,

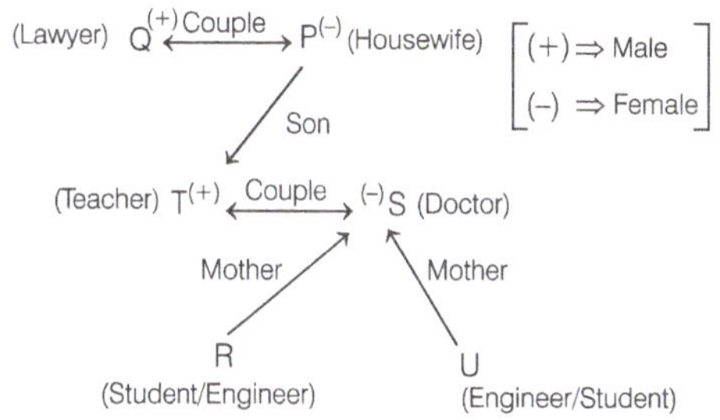

So, the granddaughter of the family is a student and either R or U is a student.

Example 8 **A family consists of 7 people with three couples. The artist is married to the politician and they have three children. The teacher is the sister-in-law of the accountant, who is the wife of the engineer. The doctor and businessman are brothers. Who among the following could be the husband of the teacher ?** ***[RRB NTPC 2021]***

(a) Politician (b) Engineer

(c) Accountant (d) Doctor

Sol. (*d*) According to the given information, arrangement is as follows.

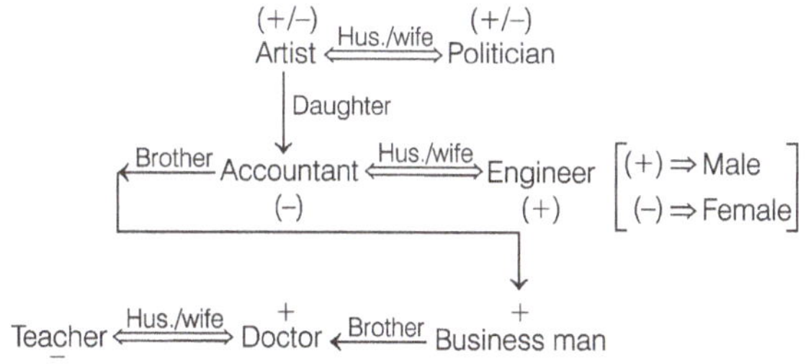

Hence, 'Doctor' is the husband of teacher.

Chapter Challenge

Based on Classification

1. Five students A, B, C, D and E study in different schools K, L, M, N and O, but not necessarily in the same order. Each one likes only one subject, viz Hindi, Mathematics, Science, Social Science and English. C studies in M. B does not like Social Science. D likes English and studies in N. The students of L likes Mathematics. E likes Hindi but is neither from O nor L. B studies in O. Which one of the following students studies in school L and likes Mathematics? *RRB NTPC 2022*
(a) B (b) A (c) D (d) C

> **MRC*****
> ***(Most Repeating Concepts)***
> Q. Nos. 1, 3, 6 and 10 are very important from the examination point of view. Question on this concept are continuously being asked in RRB (NTPC) examination.

2. Among A, B, C, D, E and F, only one person likes the colour black, among them, only two study in class 12th, while the rest study in class 10th, only C is in the same class as F. D likes the colour pink. None of those studying in 12th like the colour black. One person likes one colour. Neither A nor E likes the colour black. Who among them likes the colour black? *RRB NTPC 2022*
(a) B (b) F (c) C (d) A

3. Five friends, Purva, Roshan, Vibhor, Luna and Anuj are wearing five different coloured T-shirts, red, black, purple, yellow and blue. Each of the friends is allergic to one of the following : nuts, dairy, cats, fish and dust, such that no two has the same allergy. Luna is allergic to cats but is not wearing a purple T-shirt. The one wearing a yellow T-shirt has dust allergy. Purva is wearing a black T - shirt but is not allergic to dairy or fish. Vibhor is wearing a purple T - shirt but does not have fish allergy. Luna is wearing a blue T - shirt. Roshan is wearing a red T - shirt. Who is allergic to dust ? *RRB NTPC 2022*
(a) Vibhor (b) Purva (c) Roshan (d) Anuj

4. Five friends, Puneet, Jatin, Gautam, Arshil and Tina, like five different subjects namely Maths, English, Science, Computer and Hindi, but not necessarily in the same order. Each of the friends also like one sport, namely Cricket, Hockey, Badminton, Football and Basketball, such that no two has the same favourite sport.
Tina like Science but does not like Hockey. The one who likes Hindi also likes Basketball. Arshil like Badminton but does not like Computer or English. Gautam likes Hockey but does not like English or Maths. Arshil does not like Football Puneet likes Cricket. Who likes Hindi? *RRB NTPC 2022*
(a) Jatin (b) Arshil (c) Puneet (d) Gautam

Based on Box and Floor

5. Seven boxes A, B, C, D, E, F and G are kept one over the other but not necessarily in the same order. F is kept third from the top. Only two boxes are kept between B and G. D is kept immediately above G. Only three boxes are kept between E and A. D is kept at one of the positions below F. E is not kept at the top-most position. Which box is kept fourth from the top? *RRB ALP 2024*
(a) E (b) B (c) C (d) A

6. F, G, H, I, J and Q live on six different floors of the same building. The lowermost floor in the building is numbered 1, the floor above it, number 2 and so on, till the topmost floor is numbered 6. No one lives below J. Only two people lives between J and G. Only I lives above Q. H lives on an even numbered floor. How many people live between F and Q? *RPF SI 2024*
(a) Two (b) Three
(c) One (d) Four

7. Y, Z, A, B, C and D live on six different floors of the same building. The lowermost floor in the building is numbered 1, the floor above it number 2, and so on till the topmost floor is numbered 6.Only Y lives on the floor between the floors occupied by D and C. B lives on an even numbered floor, but not on floor 6. Z lives on the lowermost floor. D is immediately above B. Who is on the topmost floor? *RRC Group D 2022*
(a) C (b) Y (c) D (d) A

8. Five friends P, Q, R, S and T live in a five-storeyed building numbered from 1 (lowest floor) to 5 (top most floor). Each of them lives on different floors of the building. R lives on the floor below Q's floor. T does not live on the top floor. There are equal number of people living above and below the floor on which S lives. Two people live between the floors where T and R live. Q does not live just above or below the floor where S lives. Who lives on second floor? *RRC Group D 2022*
(a) P (b) S (c) T (d) R

9. Q, W, E, R, T and Y live on seven different floors of the same building with one floor being vacant. The lowermost floor in the building is numbered 1, the floor above it, number 2 and so on till the topmost floor is numbered 7. T lives on the 7th floor and W lives on the 1st floor. Only Y lives between R and W

and there is no vacant floor between R and W. The 5th floor is occupied by E. Only Q lives between T and E. Which floor is vacant. ***RRC Group D 2022***

(a) 6 (b) 4
(c) 2 (d) 3

10. Rohan lives in a seven-storeyed building. The top floor of the building is numbered as seven and the lowermost floor is numbered as one. Diya who is Rohan's friend lives somewhere above the floor where Rohan lives. Every Sunday Rohan goes two floors below to his colleague Atul's flat to eat and drink together. If there are three floors between Rohan's and Diya's floor, on which floor does Rohan live? ***RRC Group D 2022***

(a) Third floor (b) First floor
(c) Second floor (d) Fourth floor

11. G, H, I, J, K and L live on six different floors of the same building. The lowermost floor in the building is numbered 6, the floor above it is numbered 5 and so on till the topmost floor is numbered 1. J lives on an even numbered floor. G and K each live on an odd numbered floor. I lives on floor number 2. H lives on an odd numbered floor, immediately above L and immediately below I. G does not live on the topmost floor. Who lives on the lowermost floor? ***RRC Group D 2022***

(a) J (b) K (c) L (d) G

12. Six boxes, red, green, yellow, pink, blue and orange are kept vertically, one above the other (but not necessarily in the same order). The red box is placed at an odd number position when counted from the bottom but it is not in the fifth position. The red box is placed immediately above the yellow box. Only two boxes are placed between the yellow box and the orange box. Only two boxes are placed between the blue box and the pink box and only one box is placed between the blue box and the green box. Which box is placed third from the top? ***RRC Group D 2022***

(a) Blue (b) Green
(c) Pink (d) Red

13. Five boxes containing different fruits, namely strawberry, apple, litchi, cherry and pear, are kept one above the other, but not necessarily in the same order. The strawberry box is in the exact middle of the stack. The pear box is immediately below the litchi box. Only the apple box is in between the cherry and strawberry boxes. The box at the bottom most position contains pears. Which box is second from the top? ***RRC Group D 2022***

(a) Pear (b) Litchi
(c) Cherry (d) Apple

14. P, Q, R, S, T and U live on six different floors of the same building. The lowermost floor in the building is numbered 1, the floor above it is numbered 2, and so on till the topmost floor is numbered 6. Exactly three persons live between the floors of R and Q. T lives on the floor immediately above P's floor. U lives on the floor immediately above Q's floor. R lives on the floor immediately below S's floor. T lives on floor number 4. Q does not live on floor number 5. Who lives on floor number 6? ***RRC Group D 2022***

(a) U (b) R
(c) S (d) P

15. The houses of seven friends Rekha, Bharti, Shilpi, Jai, Tarun, Ravi and Nausheen are on seven different floors of the same building. The ground floor of the building is numbered 1, the floor above it is numbered 2 and so on till the topmost floor is numbered 7. Five persons live between the floors on which Jai and Rekha live. There are two floors between the houses of Tarun and Ravi. Tarun lives at one of the floors below Ravi's floor. Ravi's house is not on the topmost floor. Nausheen's house is immediately above Tarun's house. Only two persons live between the houses of Nausheen and Jai. Only two persons live above Bharti's house. Who among the following lives on floor number 4? ***RRC Group D 2022***

(a) Tarun (b) Bharti
(c) Nausheen (d) Jai

16. Six companies P, Q, R, S, T and U, are situated on different floors of a 6-floored building, but not necessarily in the same order. The lowermost floor of the building is numbered 1, the floor above it is numbered as 2, and so on, up to the topmost floor, which is numbered as 6. Company Q is not situated at floor number 1, Company P has five companies situated below it's floor. There are only two companies situated between the floors of companies T and P also between the companies Q and U. Company S is situated on an odd number floor, but not on the lowest floor. Which company is situated on floor number 1. ***RRB NTPC 2022***

(a) P (b) U (c) R (d) T

Based on Conditions, Grouping and Team Formation/Designation

17. A student has exactly eight books A, B, C, D, E , F, G and H, from which he must choose exactly five to be put in a bag. Any combination is acceptable, provided it meets the following conditions.

If A is chosen, F cannot be chosen.

If B is chosen, E must also be chosen.

If D is chosen, G must also be chosen.
Choose from the given options below, the combination of books which satisfies given three conditions. **RRB NTPC 2022**

(a) B, D, E, F, G (b) B, C, D, F, G
(c) A, B, D, E, F (d) A, B, C, D, G

18. A team is to be selected from 9 players A, B, C, D, E, F, G, H and M. There will be six players in the team. A cannot be selected with B. G cannot be selected with H. H and A should be in the same team. E cannot be selected with F. C cannot be selected with H but always must be selected with D. Which of the following is a correct selection of the team? **RRB NTPC 2021**

(a) A, D, G, E, C and H (b) B, C, D, E, H and M
(c) A, C, D, E, G and M (d) B, C, D, E, G and M

19. Six persons A, B, C, D, E and F are going to any one place among six different places Delhi, Mumbai, Punjab, Odisha, Goa and UP (not necessarily in the same order). No two persons are going to the same place. B is not going to Delhi. E is going to Odisha. F is not going to Delhi and Goa. D is going to Mumbai. A and C are not going to UP. A is not going to Delhi. Who is going to Delhi? **RRB NTPC 2021**

(a) E (b) B (c) C (d) A

20. There are six persons, A, B, C, D, E and F. A, B, C and F are male and other two are female. The height of A is 5.2 feet, B is 5.7 feet, C is 5.9 feet, D is 5.4 feet, E is 6.0 feet and F is 6.1 feet. Out of these all, A, B, C and E like sugar and D and F like salt. Persons who have a height of more than 5.5 feet wear black and others wear white.
Who among these is the sugar-loving male who does not wear black? **RRB NTPC 2022**

(a) C (b) A
(c) D (d) B

21. There are six girls Mayuri, Kavyanjali, Divya, Poonam, Neha and Vidya. Each girl likes a different colour - red, blue, purple, yellow, green and pink. Divya likes red colour. Poonam does not like green and yellow colour. Neha likes purple colour. Vidya does not like pink and green colour. Mayuri likes blue colour. Which of the following girl and colour combinations is correct? **RRB NTPC 2022**

(a) Kavyanjali - Pink (b) Neha - Blue
(c) Vidya - Yellow (d) Poonam - Green

22. Five students Radha, Sujit, Mihir, Anshul and Vikas have a total of five books on the subjects of Accountancy, Business Studies, Mathematics, Economics and English, written by authors Jain, Kohli, Das, Sharma and Edwin. Each student has only one book on one of the five subjects.

- Jain is the author of the Accountancy book, which is not owned by Vikas or Radha.
- Anshul owns the book written by Edwin.
- Mihir owns the Mathematics book.
- Vikas has the English book, which is not written by Kohli.
- The Economics books is written by Sharma.

Identify the author of the Business Studies book. **RRB NTPC 2021**

(a) Sharma (b) Jain (c) Edwin (d) Das

23. Five clothes, sweater, jacket, coat, gloves and trousers, are made of different fabrics, wool, fur, velvet, flannel and taffeta, but not necessarily in the same order. Also, each has a different colour, red, orange, black, white and yellow, but not necessarily in the same order.
The jacket and trousers are not made of velvet. The sweater is orange in colour. The coat is made of fur but it is not black or red in colour. The gloves are yellow in colour but are not made of flannel or taffeta. The orange coloured item is made of wool. The jacket is made of flannel and is neither black nor white in colour. The trouser is not white in colour. Which item is made of velvet? **RRB NTPC 2022**

(a) Trousers (b) Sweater
(c) Gloves (d) Coat

Based on Day/Date/Month

24. Each of P, Q, R, S, T, U and V has an exam on a different day of a week, starting from Monday and ending on Sunday of the same week. Q has the exam on Saturday. Only two people have exams between S and Q. R has the exam before S, but after P. U has the exam immediately after T. On which of the following days does V have the exam?

(a) Saturday (b) Sunday
(c) Friday (d) Thursday

25. A company sold six different cars Swift, Santro, Creta, Audi, I10 and Magna during a period of Monday to Saturday. Only one car was sold on a particular day. No car was sold twice. Atleast four cars were sold after the car Santro. The car Magna was sold on Tuesday.
The car Audi was sold immediately after the car Creta and car Creta was sold atleast before three cars. Both the cars Santro and I10 were sold atleast before one car. On which day was Swift car sold? **RRB NTPC 2021**

(a) Thursday (b) Friday
(c) Monday (d) Saturday

26. J, K, L, M, N and O are six teachers. Each one teaches a different subject out of Hindi, English, Math, Science, Social Science and Arts, not necessarily in the same order. Each of them teaches on only one day, from Monday to Saturday, not necessarily in the same order. J teaches Arts on Saturday. L teaches neither English nor Social Science, but he teaches on Thursday. Wednesday is reserved for Maths taught by K. O teaches Science a day before N. Social Science is taught a day before Arts. Which subject is taught by L? *SSC GD 2022*
(a) Hindi (b) Maths (c) Science (d) Arts

27. Six people, A, B, C, D, E and F, travelled in different years 2010, 2012, 2014, 2016, 2018 and 2020 (but not necessarily in the same order). C travelled in 2018. Only three people travelled between D and A. A travelled after D. Only one person travelled between F and E. F travelled before E. Who travelled in 2014? *RRC Group D 2022*
(a) D (b) B (c) F (d) E

28. Six persons, P, Q, R, S, T and U travelled in different months of the same year viz. January, February, March, July, September and December. R travelled in September. Only one person travelled between R and T. No one travelled between U and P. P travelled in a month after U. More than two people travelled between P and S. Who among them travelled in July? *RRC Group D 2022*
(a) T (b) Q (c) P (d) S

29. Each of A, B, C, D and E has an exam on a different day of a week starting from Monday and ending on Friday of the same week. C has an exam on Friday. Only one person has exam between C and E. A do not have exam on the first day of their schedule. B has an exam immediate day before C. How many people have exam after A?
(a) None (b) One (c) Three (d) Two

30. Six persons, A, B, C, D, E and F, travelled in different months of the same year, viz. January, March, May, July, September and November. None of them travelled after B and he travels just after C. Only three people travelled before E. A travelled just after F. D did not travel in the month of May. Who among the following travelled in May? *RRC Group D 2022*
(a) F (b) A
(c) C (d) E

Based on Family Blood Relation

31. Six family members, A, B, C, D, E, F are working as a team on a family project of renovating a house. Each person has been given a single task. A is B's son and is in charge of flooring. B is C's sister and is in charge of water issues. C is D's wife and is in charge of electric works. D is in charge of foundation related work and his son E is in charge of interior decoration. F, who is D's brother, is in charge of roof. What work is assigned to A's cousin? *RRB NTPC 2021*
(a) Interior decoration
(b) Roof
(c) Electrical work
(d) Foundation related work

32. A family includes six members A, B, C, X, Y and Z. There are two married couples, B is an engineer and the father of Y, Z is the grandfather of C and is a scientist. X is the grandmother of Y and is a painter, Y and C are sisters and are cricketers. A is the mother of C and an actor. There is one engineer, one scientist, one actor, one painter and two cricketers in the group. Which of the following options is a group of male members only? *RRB NTPC 2021*
(a) BZA (b) BZ
(c) ZY (d) BZY

Right Key

1. (b)	2. (a)	3. (d)	4. (a)	5. (b)	6. (c)	7. (d)	8. (a)	9. (b)	10. (a)
11. (a)	12. (a)	13. (d)	14. (c)	15. (c)	16. (b)	17. (a)	18. (d)	19. (c)	20. (b)
21. (c)	22. (c)	23. (c)	24. (b)	25. (d)	26. (a)	27. (d)	28. (b)	29. (c)	30. (b)
31. (a)	32. (b)								

Solutions

1. (*b*) According to the question, arrangement of students, subjects and schools is as follows

Student	School Name	Subject
A	L	Mathematics
B	O	Science
C	M	Social Science
D	N	English
E	K	Hindi

Hence, Student A studies in School L and likes Mathematics.

2. (*a*) According to the question, arrangement of class and person is as follows

Person	Class	Black	Pink
A	10th	×	
B	10th	✓	
C	12th	×	
D	10th	×	✓
E	10th	×	
F	12th	×	

Hence, B likes the colour black.

3. (*d*) According to the question, arrangement of friends colour of T-shirts and allergic is as follows,

Friend	Colour of T-shirt	Allergic to
Purva	Black	Nuts
Roshan	Red	Fish
Vibhor	Purple	Dairy
Luna	Blue	Cats
Anuj	Yellow	Dust

Hence, Anuj is allegric to dust.

4. (*a*) According to the question, arrangement of friends, subjects and sports is as follows

Friend	Subject	Sport
Puneet	English	Cricket
Jatin	Hindi	Basketball
Gautam	Computer	Hockey
Arshil	Maths	Badminton
Tina	Science	Football

Hence, Jatin likes Hindi.

5. (*b*) According to the given information,

A
C
F
B
E
D
G

Hence, box 'B' is kept fourth from the top.

6. (*c*) According to the given information,

Floor	Name
6	I
5	Q
4	G
3	F
2	H
1	J

Hence, one person lives between F and Q.

7. (*d*) According to the question,

Floors	Members
6	A
5	C
4	Y
3	D
2	B
1	Z

Hence, 'A' lives on the topmost floor.

8. (*a*) According to the question,

Floor	Name
5	Q
4	R
3	S
2	P
1	T

Hence, 'P' lives on the second floor.

9. (*b*) According to the question,

Floor	Name
7	T
6	Q
5	E
4	Vacant
3	R
2	Y
1	W

∴ Hence, 4th floor is vacant.

TOP TIPS While solving this question, systematically eliminate option that no longer fit or make sense based on the given information.

10. (*a*) According to the question,

7th floor	Diya
6th floor	
5th floor	
4th floor	
3rd floor	Rohan
2nd floor	
1st floor	Atul

Hence, Rohan lives on the third floor.

11. (*a*) According to the question,

Floor	Persons
1	K
2	I
3	H
4	L
5	G
6	J

Hence, 'J' lives on the lowermost floor.

12. (*a*) According to the question,

6	Green
5	Orange
4	Blue
3	Red
2	Yellow
1	Pink

Hence, box 'blue' is placed third from the top.

13. (*d*) According to the question,

Cherry
Apple
Strawberry
Litchi
Pears

Hence, box 'Apple' is second from the top.

14. *(c)* According to the question,

Floor	Name
6	S
5	R
4	T
3	P
2	U
1	Q

Hence, 'S' lives on the floor number 6.

15. *(c)* According to the question,

Floors	Friends
7	Jai/Rekha
6	Ravi
5	Bharti
4	Nausheen
3	Tarun
2	Shilpi
1	Jai/Rekha

Hence, 'Nausheen' lives on the floor number '4'.

TOP TIPS While solving the puzzle carefully review your solution to ensure it does not contradict any information provided.

16. *(b)* According to the question,

Floors	Companies
6	P
5	S
4	Q
3	T
2	R
1	U

Hence, Company 'U' situated on floor number 1.

17. *(a)* According to the question, option (b), (c) and (d) does not satisfy the given condition, as, E is not choosen with B in option (b) and (d) and F is chosen with A in option (c). Only option (a) follows the given condition. Hence, option (a) is the correct combination of books.

18. *(d)* If we take A and H in the team, we cannot take B and G in the team. Also, C and D being together cannot be selected with H. In this way we are left with only 5 players. So, we have to take B and G in the team, excluding A and H. We take either E or F.

But according to the options, we take E. Hence, B, C, D, E, G and M is the correct option.

19. *(c)* According to the question,

Person	Place
A	Goa/Punjab
B	UP/Goa/Punjab
C	Delhi
D	Mumbai
E	Odisha
F	UP/Punjab

Hence, 'C' is going to Delhi.

20. *(b)* According to the question,

Persons	Male/ Female	Height in feet	Sugar/ Salt	Colour
A	Male	5.2	Sugar	White
B	Male	5.7	Sugar	Black
C	Male	5.9	Sugar	Black
D	Female	5.4	Salt	White
E	Female	6.0	Sugar	Black
F	Male	6.1	Salt	Black

Hence, A is the sugar-loving male who does not wear black colour.

Helping TIPS While solving this question use the information which is clearly provided and avoid making assumptions that may lead to wrong solution.

21. *(c)* According to the question,

Girls	Colour
Divya	Red
Poonam	Pink
Neha	Purple
Vidya	Yellow
Mayuri	Blue
Kavyanjali	Green

Hence, 'Vidya-Yellow' is the correct answer.

22. *(c)* According to the question,

Students	Books	Authors
Sujit	Accountancy	Jain
Radha	Economics	Sharma
Mihir	Mathematics	Kohli
Anshul	Business Studies	Edwin
Vikas	English	Das

So, Edwin is the author of the Business Studies book.

23. *(c)* According to the question,

Jacket	Flannel	Red
Sweater	Wool	Orange
Coat	Fur	White
Gloves	Velvet	Yellow
Trousers	Taffeta	Black

Hence, gloves are made up of velvet.

24. *(b)* According to the given information,

Day	Person
Monday	P
Tuesday	R
Wednesday	S
Thursday	T
Friday	U
Saturday	Q
Sunday	V

Hence, V have the exam on 'Sunday'.

25. *(d)* According to the question,

Days	Cars
Monday	Santro
Tuesday	Magna
Wednesday	Creata
Thursday	Audi
Friday	I10
Saturday	Swift

Hence, swift car was sold on 'Saturday'.

26. *(a)* According to the question,

Day	Teacher	Subject
Monday	O	Science
Tuesday	N	English
Wednesday	K	Maths
Thursday	L	Hindi
Friday	M	Social Science
Saturday	J	Arts

Hence, 'Hindi' is taught by L.

27. *(d)* According to the question,

Peoples	Years
F	2010
D	2012
E	2014
B	2016

Peoples	Years
C	2018
A	2020

Hence, E travelled in 2014.

28. *(b)* According to the question,

Persons	Months
U	January
P	February
T	March
Q	July
R	September
S	December

Hence, 'Q' among them travelled in July.

29. *(c)* According to the question,

Days	Persons
Monday	D
Tuesday	A
Wednesday	E
Thursday	B
Friday	C

From the above table, it is clear that three persons (E, B and C) have their exams after A.

30. *(b)* According to the question,

Months	Peoples
January	D
March	F
May	A
July	E
September	C
November	B

Hence, A travelled in month of May.

31. *(a)* According to the question,

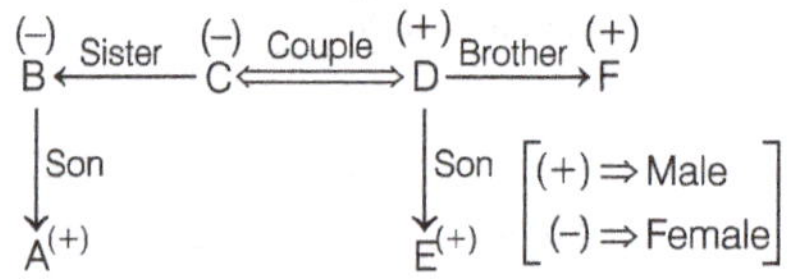

A	Flooring
B	Water issue
C	Electric work
D	Foundation
E	Interior Decoration
F	Roof

Hence, A's cousin is E and 'interior decoration' work assigned to E.

32. *(b)* According to the given information, arrangement is as follows,

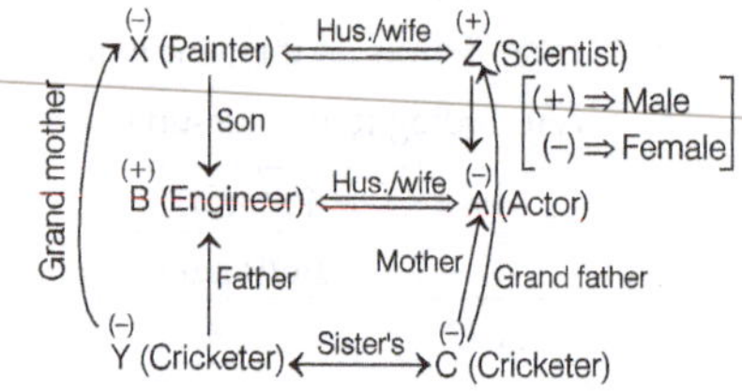

Clearly, B and Z are male members.

Hence, the correct answer is BZ.

CHAPTER

14 Clock and Calendar

Clock

A clock is a device that expresses the time interval in hours, minutes and seconds. Generally, a clock has following four components

1. Dial, 2. Hour hand 3. Minute hand, 4. Second hand.

Clocks are divided into 12 hour and 60 minute slots.

The basic structure of a clock is as follows

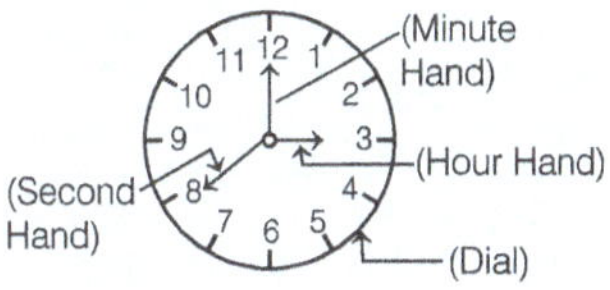

Based on the Image of the Clock

When an imaginary image of a clock is formed by a mirror, it is called the image of the clock. In this type of questions, candidates need to determine the original position of the hour and minute hands of the clock based on the position of the hour and minute hands as seen in the mirror/water image or *vice-versa*.

e.g. If it is 2 O'clock in a clock, then what time will be seen in the mirror image?

(a) 8:00 (b) 9:30 (c) 10:00 (d) 10:30

Sol. (c) According to the question,

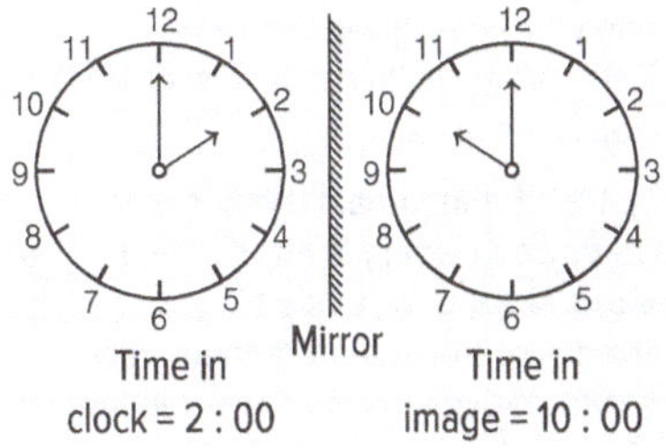

Based on Angle

In this type, questions are based on the angular distance covered by the hands. In this type, candidates are asked to find the angle between the hour hand and the minute hand of the clock.

e.g. What will be the angle between the two hands of clock at 4:40?

(a) 120° (b) 100°

(c) 90° (d) 130°

Sol. (b) Angle made by the hour hand at 4:40

$\therefore$ We know, $\theta = \left|\frac{11}{2}M - 30\,H\right|$

$\Rightarrow \quad \theta = \left|\frac{11}{2} \times 40 - 30 \times 4\right|$

[M = Minute, H = Hour]

$\Rightarrow \quad \theta = |220° - 120°|$

$\Rightarrow \quad \theta = 100°$

$\therefore$ Required angle = 100°

Based on the Positions of Clock Hands Fast Clock/Slow Clock

In this type, questions are based on the positions of the hands of the clock/fast clock and slow clock. Candidates are asked questions about the positions of the hands such as when they meet, are opposite to each other are at right angles to each other or at any other angle or whether to clock is fast or slow.

e.g. How many times in a day do the hour and minute hands of a clock are opposite to each other?

(a) 21 (b) 22

(c) 20 (d) 24

Sol. (b) Both the hands of a clock are opposite to each other 11 times in every 12 hours.

$\therefore$ The hour and minute hands of a clock are opposite to each other 22 times in a day.

Based on Specific Time

In the questions asked in this, candidates have to determine the exact time using information like the time of meeting/interview/ missing bus or train/getting information etc. based on a given particular situation.

e.g. Mohit reach the meeting place 20 min before 8:50 O'clock. On reaching Mohit found that he had arrived 30 min before the person who was 40 min late. What was the scheduled time of the meeting?

(a) 8:20 (b) 8:10 (c) 8:00 (d) 8:05

Sol. (a) Mohit's arrival time

= 8:50 – 20 min = 8:30 O'clock

Time of the person who was 40 min late

8 : 30 + 30 min = 9 O'clock

Hence, the actual time of the meeting

= 9:00 – 40 min = 8:20 O'clock

Score Booster

To solve questions based on clock it is very important to have knowledge about the distance travelled by the hands, of clock angles covered and its images.

Calendar

Calendar is a source which shows the mutual relations between day, week, month and year through a table. The smallest unit of a calendar is a day and 7 days together make a week. There are 12 months or 365/366 days in a year.

Based on Finding the Day

1. When the Reference Day is Given

In this type, questions are based on finding the day of a particular date. The questions asked from the candidate related to the day of a particular date or the day of another date according to a reference date.

e.g. If March 17, 2006 was Tuesday, then what day of the week will March 17, 2008 be?

(a) Wednesday (b) Friday

(c) Tuesday (d) Saturday

Sol. (b) Given,

17th March, 2006 is Tuesday.

Number of odd days from 17th March 2006 to 17th March 2008

(1 ordinary and 1 leap year)

Odd days $= 2 \times 1 + 1 \times 1 = 2 + 1 = 3$

Hence, 17th March, 2008 is Tuesday + 3 days = Friday

2. When the Reference Day is Not Given

To find the day of a particular date when the specific day is not given, follow the following steps

I. 1st January 1 A.D. was Monday and hence the questions are solved on this basis.

II. Find the number of odd days till the date for which the date is asked. Then divide that number by 7 and subtract the number of extra days obtaind from it. The day of that date can be find out.

e.g. What day was October 2, 1809?

(a) Sunday (b) Monday

(c) Tuesday (d) Wednesday

Sol. (b) Number of odd days till 2nd October, 1809 odd days = Odd days in 1800 years + Odd days in 8 years + Odd days till 2nd October in 1809

$= 0 + 3 + (2 \times 2 + 6 \times 1) + 3 + 0 + 3 + 2 + 3 + 2 + 3 + 3 + 2 + 2 = 36 = \frac{36}{7} = 1$ Odd day

Hence, day on 2nd October, 1809 was Monday.

Finding Day Based on Week Day

In this type of questions, a particular day of the week or month is taken as the base and then another day of the week or month is found.

e.g. If the 11th of a month is falls three days after Monday, then what day will be on the 27th of the same month.

(a) Saturday (b) Tuesday

(c) Monday (d) Wednesday

Sol. (a) Three days after Monday

= Monday + 3 = Thursday

i.e. 11th is Thursday, so 11 + 14 = 25th will also be Thursday.

Hence, the day of 27th = Thursday + 2

= Saturday

Based on Memory

In this type of questions, dates are given by two or more persons. The common date among the dates given by them is considered as the particular day which is asked in the question.

e.g. Mohit remembers that his elder sister's anniversary is after 11 January and before 16 January, while his younger sister correctly remembers that their elder sister's anniversary is after 9 January but before 13 January. On which date of January was their sister's anniversary.

(a) 12 (b) 11

(c) 13 (d) 15

Sol. (a) Anniversary according to Mohit

→ ⑫, 13, 14, 15

According to Mohit's sister

→ 10, 11, ⑫

Hence, anniversary of Mohit's elder sister is on 12 January.

Score Booster

To solve the questions to based on calender (it is very important) have knowledge about the odd days and having knowledge of ordinary and leap years.

Mirror Image of a Clock

In mirror image, the position of the mirror is perpendicular and the image of the object placed in front of the perpendicular mirror appears, laterally inverted i.e. the left side of the clock appears on the right side and the right side on the left.

Time in Clock	1	2	3	4	5	6	7	8	9	10	11	12
Time in Mirror	11	10	9	8	7	6	5	4	3	2	1	12

If the time is between 1 and 11 O'clock,

Actual time = 11:60 – Time in the mirror

If the time is between 11 and 1 O'clock,

Actual time = 23 : 60 – Time in the mirror

Important Facts/Points Related to the Clock

- The measurement of the entire circumference of the clock dial is equal to 360°.
- The minute hand makes an angle of 6° in 1 min.
- The hour hand makes an angle of 30° in 1 hour and $\frac{1^\circ}{2}$ in 1 min.
- Angle between the hands of clock, $\theta = \left|\frac{11}{2}M - 30H\right|$

  where, M = Minute and H = Hour

  Value of θ is always positive.
- In every 12 hours the hour and minute hands meet 11 times.
- In every 12 hours the hour and minute hands are opposite to each other 11 times.
- In every 12 hours the hour and minute hands are at right angles 22 times.

Calendar

In this topic, questions are asked related to ordinary years, leap years, odd days, the day of a particular/specific date of the calendar, the repetition of the calendar, etc.

Ordinary Year

Years which are not exactly divisible by 4 are ordinary or normal years. An ordinary year has 365 days. i.e., 52 week and 1 days

e.g. 1927,1831, 2007, 2013, 2033 etc. are ordinary years.

Leap Year

Years which are exactly divisible by 4 are leap years. It has 366 days i.e. 52 weeks and 2 days.

Among the century years, the leap year will be the one which is divisible by 400. Apart from this, all other century years are ordinary years.

e.g. 2000, 2400, 1932, 1948, 2800 etc. are leap years.

Concept of Odd Days

In a given period, the number of days more than the complete weeks are called odd days.

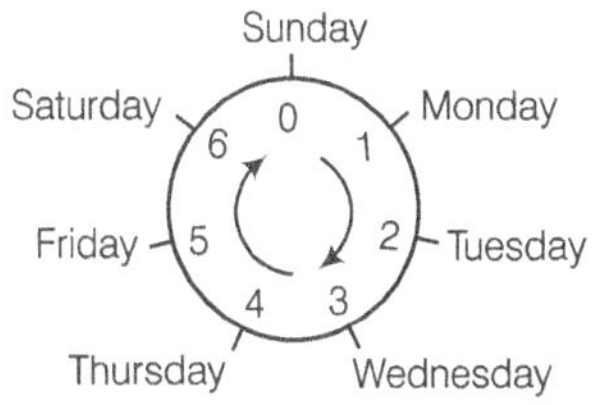

To find the odd days, divide the number of days by 7. The quotient obtained in this process of division indicates the complete cycle of days i.e. week and the remainder indicates the odd days. If we start from Monday, then in a time period of 8 days, we will get 1 full week and 1 extra day or 1 odd day. In a complete cycle of days, all the days of a week come one after the other. After this, the days start recurring again.

e.g. (i) Number of odd days in 30 days = $\frac{30}{7}$

= 4 full weeks + 2 remaining days

Number of odd days = 2

Note Number of odd days cannot be more than 6.

On the basis of the above rule, we can find out the number of odd days in the months of the year as given in the table below,

Month	January	February (Ordinary year)	February (Leap year)	March	April	May	June	July	August	September	October	November	December
No. of odd days	3	0	1	3	2	3	2	3	3	2	3	2	3

Odd days in Century Years

- Number of odd days in 100 years = 5
- Number of odd days in 200 years = 3
- Number of odd days in 300 years = 1
- Number of odd days in 400 years = 0

Important Facts Related to the Calendar

- In an ordinary year, the first days of the given months are the same.

  January ↔ October ; February ↔ March ↔ November,
  April ↔ July ; September ↔ December
- In a leap year, the first days of the given months are the same.

  January ↔ April ↔ July ; February ↔ August
  March ↔ November ; September ↔ December
- The first and last day of an ordinary year are the same.
- The first and last day of a leap year are unequal i.e. the last day is one day ahead of the first day.
- The first day of a century can be Monday, Tuesday, Thursday, Friday or Saturday.
- The last day of a century can be Wednesday, Friday or Sunday. But can not be Tuesday, Thursday or Saturday.

Exam Approach Examples

Based on the Image of the Clock

Example 1 **Select the time which represents the exact mirror image of 9:30 on a clock.** *RRB ALP 2018*

(a) 2:30 (b) 6:30 (c) 7:30 (d) 4:30

Sol. (*a*) Correct time = 12:00 − 9:30 = 2:30

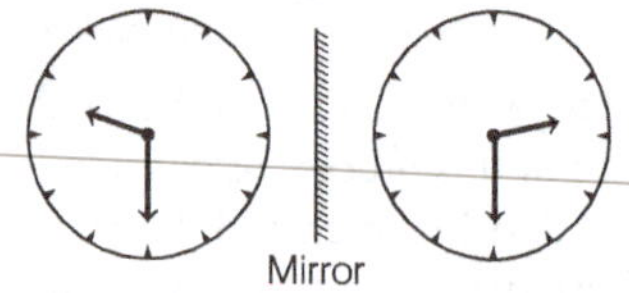

Example 2 **If the time shown in the mirror image of a 12 hour clock is 3:25, what is the actual time?** *RRC Group-D 2022*

(a) 9:35 (b) 8:35 (c) 8:45 (d) 7:45

Sol. (*b*) Time of the clock in the mirror image = 3:25

Actual time on clock = (12:00 − 3:25) = 8:35 O'clock.

Based on Angle

Example 3 **What is the angular distance covered by the second hand of an accurate clock in 12 min?** *RRC Group-D 2022*

(a) 4762° (b) 5120° (c) 4320° (d) 5611°

Sol. (*c*) Angular distance covered by second hand in 1 min = 360°

Angular distance covered by the second hand in 12 min

$= 12 \times 360° = 4320°$

Example 4 **Find the angle between the hour hand and the minute hand of a clock at 6:10.** *UPSSSC PET 2022*

(a) 138° (b) 125° (c) 115° (d) 180°

Sol. (*b*) Time = 6:10

Here, Hour (H) = 6, Minute (M) = 10

$\therefore$ Required angle, $\theta = \left|\frac{11}{2}M - 30H\right| = \left|\frac{11}{2} \times 10 - 30 \times 6\right|$

$= |55 - 180| = 125°$

Example 5 **If the minute hand of a clock is at 12 and the hour hand is making an angle of 120° with it in the direction of its motion, then the time will be in the clock.** *Rajasthan Patwari 2016*

(a) 4:00 O'clock (b) 5:00 O'clock
(c) 3:50 O'clock (d) 4:30 O'clock

Sol. (*a*) We know that, the hour hand makes an angle of 30° in 1 hour.

$= \frac{120}{30} = 4$ hours

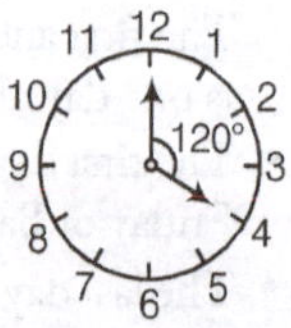

120° angle will be formed in 4 hours.

Now, since the minute hand is at 12.

Hence, required time = 4:00 O'clock

Based on the Positions of Clock Hands/Fast Clock/Slow Clock

Example 6 **How many times in a day do the hands of a clock meet each other?**

(a) 21 (b) 22
(c) 24 (d) 20

Sol. (*b*) The two hands of a clock meet 11 times in every 12 hours.

Therefore, the two hands of a clock move together in a day (24 hours) = 11 × 2 = 22 times.

Example 7 **A clock which is 10 min behind in 24 hours was corrected at 8 am on Monday. Now the clock is showing 1 pm on Tuesday, what will be the correct time?** *DSSSB Grade IV 2019*

(a) 12 : 36 pm (b) 1 pm
(c) 12 : 56 pm (d) 12 : 48 pm

Sol. (*d*) Time difference from Monday 8 am to Tuesday 1 pm

= 29 hours

Now, 24 hours 10 min $= 24 + \frac{10}{60} = \frac{144+1}{6} = \frac{145}{6}$ hours

$\because \frac{145}{6}$ hours of given clock = 24 hours of actual clock

$\therefore$ 29 hours of given clock $= 24 \times \frac{6}{145} \times 29 = \frac{144}{5} = 28\frac{4}{5}$ hours

= 28 hours 48 min (actual clock's)

$\therefore$ Actual time = 1:00 − (29:00 − 28:48)

= 1:00 − 0:12 = 12:48 pm

Example 8 **At 8 am on Sunday, a clock is found to be 5 min behind. Then, it starts gaining and at 8 pm on Monday, it is found to be 5 min ahead. At what time was it perfectly accurate?** *RRB JE 2019*

(a) 2 am, Monday (b) 8 pm, Monday
(c) 8 am, Monday (d) 6 am, Monday

Sol. (*a*) Given,

On Sunday at 8 am, the clock is found to be 5 min behind.

And on Monday at 8 pm, it is found to be 5 min fast.

$\therefore$ Total time from 8 am on Sunday to 8 pm on Monday is

= 36 hours

$\because$ The clock got (5 + 5) = 10 min fast in 36 hours

To show correct time, the clock should be only 5 min fast.

$\because$ 10 min fast in 36 hours.

$\therefore$ It will be 5 min fast $= \frac{36}{10} \times 5 = 18$ hours

$\therefore$ Time when the clock will show correct time

= 8 : 00 am + 18 : 00 hours

= 2 : 00 am, Monday

Based on Specific Time

Example 9 **The bus for Delhi leaves after every 35 min. The enquiry officer told a passenger that the bus for Delhi has left just 10 min ago and the next bus will leave at 9:35. Tell at what time the enquiry officer gave the information to the passenger?** *UPSSSC 2016*

(a) 9 : 10 (b) 8 : 55
(c) 9 : 08 (d) 15 minutes past 9

Sol. (*a*) Time at which the enquiry officer informed the passenger about the departure of the next bus = 9 : 35

Leaving time of the previous bus = 9 : 35 − 35 min = 9 : 00 O'clock

∴ Time at which the enquiry officer informed the passenger

= 9 : 00 + 10 min = 9 : 10 O'clock

Based on Finding the Day of the Date

Example 10 **If December 19, 1992 is Saturday, what day of the week will December 22, 2009 be?** *SSC (10+2) 2023*

(a) Tuesday (b) Sunday
(c) Saturday (d) Thursday

Sol. (*a*) Given, 19 December, 1992 is Saturday.

Number of odd days from 19 December, 1992 to19 December, 2009 $= 13 \times 1 + 4 \times 2$ [∵ leap year = 4]

$= 13 + 8$

$= \frac{21}{7} = 0$ (odd day)

Number of odd days from 19 December to 22 December in year 2009 odd days = 3

Total number of odd days = 0 + 3 = 3

So, 22 December, 2009 = Saturday + 3 days = Tuesday

Example 11 **What was the day of the week on 26 January, 1989?** *RRB ALP 2018*

(a) Tuesday (b) Thursday
(c) Sunday (d) Monday

Sol. (*b*) Number of odd days till 26th January, 1989

= Odd days in 1600 years

+ Odd days in 300 years

+ Odd days in 88 years

+ Odd days in 26 days

$= 0 + 1 + (22 \times 2 + 66) + 5$

$= 0 + 1 + 110 + 5 = 116$ days

= 16 weeks 4 odd days

Hence, the day on 26th January, 1989 was Thursday.

> **Trending Concept**
> Questions based on finding the day of a date are currently being asked in all exams (SSC, Railway and UP Police). It is very important for the upcoming exams.

Finding Day Based on Week Day

Example 12 **Meena returned to her home 3 days before her scheduled time. Meena's sister Reena arrived five days late from the day on which Meena was supposed to return. If Meena returned on Thursday, on which day did Reena return?** *UP AO 2024*

(a) Friday (b) Sunday
(c) Saturday (d) Wednesday

Sol. (*a*) The day on which Meena returns home = Thursday

According to the question,

The scheduled day of Meena's return home is Thursday + 3

= Sunday

The day on which Reena returns home is Sunday + 5 = Friday

Example 13 **Priyanka's birthday is on the third Friday of a month. The fourth day of the same month is the first Monday of the month. What is the date of Priyanka's birthday?** *HCET 2023*

(a) 22 (b) 15
(c) 23 (d) 21

Sol. (*b*) Fourth day of the month = Monday

First day of the month = Monday −3 = Friday

So, other dates on Friday = 8, 15, 22, 29

Hence, Priyanka's birthday is 15.

Based on Memory

Example 14 **Mita correctly remembers that her father's birthday falls after July 8 but before July 12. Mita's brother correctly remembers that her father's birthday falls after July 10 but before July 15. Find on which day Mita's father was born?**

(a) 10 July
(b) 11 July
(c) 10 or 11 July
(d) Cannot be known

Sol. (*b*) Birthday of Mita's father

According to Mita → 9, 10, (11) July

According to Mita's brother

→ (11), 12, 13, 14 July

∴ Required day = Common date 11 July

> **Helping Tips**
> **Repetition of Calendar**
> The calendar will be repeated in 6 years or 11 years.
> (i) If the year immediately preceding the given year is a leap year. Then, it will be repeated in 6 years.
> (ii) If the year immediately preceding the given year is an ordinary year, then it will repeated in 11 years.
> - The leap year calendar is repeated after 28 years.

Chapter Challenge

Based on the Image of the Clock

1. Looking in a mirror shows that the time on an analog clock (with hands) is 1:30, so tell what is the correct time? *UPSSSC VDO 2016*
(a)10 : 30 (b) 6 : 30
(c) 10 min past 6 (d) 4 : 30

2. The image of the clock in the mirror shows 3:15. What will be the correct time? *SSC CPO 2016*
(a) 8 : 45 (b) 10 : 45 (c) 7 : 45 (d) 9 : 45

3. A clock marked only with 3, 6, 9 and 12 O'clock is placed in front of a mirror. A person sees the time stopped at 9:50 in the mirror image. What is the real time?
(a) 3 : 00 (b) 2 : 40 (c) 2 : 10 (d) 3 : 15

4. The image of a clock was visible in the mirror. The time on the clock was 5:25. If the image of the clock formed in the mirror is reflected again in another mirror, then what time will be displayed in the image of the clock formed in this second mirror?
(a) 5:25 (b) 6:35
(c) 20 min past 5 (d) 6:30

> **MRC*****
> ***(Most Repeating Concepts)***
> Q. Nos. 2, 4, 5, 10, 12 are very important from the examination point of view. Questions on these concepts are continuously being asked in SSC, Railway, UPSSSC Competitive examinations.

Based on Angle

5. A clock is started at noon. At 4:10, the hour hand has turned. *UP Police Constable 2024*
(a) 135° (b) 130° (c) 120° (d) 125°

6. If the hour hand of a clock moves forward by 18°, then by how many degrees will the minute hand move in the same time? *RRB ALP 2018*
(a) 168° (b) 276° (c) 196° (d) 216°

7. How much angular distance does the minute hand of a clock telling correct time cover in a period of 3 hours 10 min? *RRC Group-D 2022*
(a) 1000° (b) 1202° (c) 978° (d) 1140°

8. A clock is started at noon. At 5:20, the hour hand has turned. *UP Police Constable 2024*
(a) 160° (b) 150° (c) 155° (d) 145

9. Find the angle between the hour hand and minute hand of a clock at 8:20. *UPSSSC PET 2022*
(a) 130° (b) 122°
(c) 149° (d) 190°

10. What is the acute angle between the minute hand and the hour hand at 4:37 pm? *RRB ALP 2018*
(a) 83.5° (b) 18° (c) 18.5° (d) 6.5°

11. Find the angle between the hands of the clock at 3:30 O'clock. *RRB JE 2019*
(a) 120° (b) 90° (c) 105° (d) 75°

12. What will be the angle between the minute and hour hands of a clock at 5:35? *CGPSC 2016*
(a) $40\frac{1°}{2}$ (b) $46\frac{1°}{2}$ (c) $42\frac{1°}{2}$ (d) 43°
(e) None of these

13. When a wall clock shows 3:25, O'clock what will be the acute angle between the hour hand and the minute hand? *UPPSC 2016*
(a) 60° (b) 52.5° (c) 47.5° (d) 42°

14. At what time between 2:30 pm and 3:30 pm will the clock hands be together (one above the other)? *RRC Group D 2022*
(a) $3:11\frac{4}{16}$ (b) $3:16\frac{4}{11}$
(c) $3:14\frac{11}{16}$ (d) $3:14\frac{6}{11}$

15. What is the time when the clock hands between 2 and 3 make a 90° angle with each other?
(a) $2:27\frac{3}{11}$ (b) 2 : 30
(c) $2:28\frac{3}{11}$ (d) 2 : 25

16. Tell the time when the angle between the 4 and 5 O'clock hands will be 30°.
(a) $4:20\frac{4}{11}$ (b) $4:16\frac{4}{11}$
(c) 4 : 30 (d) 5 : 00

17. When will the clock hands meet between 1 and 2?
(a) 1 : 30 (b) $1:5\frac{5}{11}$
(c) 1 : 10 (d) None of these

Based on the Positions of Clock Hands/Fast Clock/Slow Clock

18. How many times in a week, the hour hand and minute hand of a clock are at right angles to each other? *RRB ALP 2018*
(a) 44 (b) 24 (c) 54 (d) 308

19. If the minute hand of a clock moves at the rate of 9° per minute, then how many minutes will the clock be ahead in half an hour? *DSSSB 2018*
(a) 20 min (b) 12 min
(c) 15 min (d) None of these

20. A clock gains 5 min every hour. How much angle will the second hand cover in one minute?
(a) 360° (b) 360.5° (c) 390° (d) 380°

21. My watch is 3 min behind on Monday at 2 pm and 5 min ahead on Wednesday at 2 pm. When will it have shown the correct time?
(a) Tuesday at 6 am (b) Tuesday at 8 am
(c) Wednesday at 4 am (d) Wednesday at 8 am

22. A clock gains 60 min every 24 hours. It was set at 10 am. What will be the correct time the next day when the clock shows 4 pm?
(a) 2 : 48 pm (b) 2 : 30 pm
(c) 10 min past 3 (d) 5 min past 4

23. On Sunday at 12 noon my watch was 5 min ahead and Hamid's watch was 6 min slow. On Wednesday at 8 pm I found out that my watch was 1 min slow and Hamid's watch was 3 min fast. Tell me when my and Hamid's watches would have shown the same time? (Time has to be calculated relative to the correct time)
(a) Tuesday at 10 : 40 am (b) Tuesday at 10 : 40 pm
(c) Monday at 10 O'clock (d) Tuesday at 10 O'clock

Based on Specific Time

24. The worker switched on a bulb at 2:39:40 and switched it off at 12:30:34 on the same day. For how long did the bulb burn? *RRB ALP 2018*
(a) 09 h 50 min 54 sec (b) 10 h 09 min 06 sec
(c) 06 h 09 min 09 sec (d) 12 h 40 min 06 sec

25. Ajay leaves for the bus stop to go to office 15 min earlier than usual. It takes 10 min to reach the bus stop from home. He reaches the bus stop at 8:40 am. Tell me at what time he reaches home on normal days?
(a) 8 : 30 am (b) 8 : 45 am
(c) 8 : 55 am (d) None of these

26. A train leaves for Ghaziabad from Delhi Railway Station every 55 min. Ashok came to know from the enquiry window that the train had left 20 min ago and the next train will leave at 10:35. Ashok could find out from the enquiry window at what time the train would leave. *UP B.Ed 2010*
(a) 10 O'clock (b) 9 : 40 O'clock
(c) 10 : 15 O'clock (d) 11 : 50 O'clock

27. A bus goes to Ludhiana every four hours. The bus is announced 20 minutes after it leaves for Ludhiana. The next bus will leave at 4:30 pm, so at what time will it be announced? *Uttarakhand VDO 2016*
(a) 12:40 pm (b) 12:50 pm
(c) 12:30 pm (d) 1:00 pm

28. The letters of the English alphabet are arranged in the dial of a wall clock in anti-clockwise direction in such a way that instead of 12, there is A. If this sequence continues, then at 3:30 pm. What will be the position of the hour hand?
(a) Between I and J (b) Between H and J
(c) Between C and D (d) Between J and K

29. In a school, the class starts at 1 pm and lasts till 3:52 pm. If there are 4 periods in this time and 4 min are left before each period to go from one room to another, then tell how many minutes does one period last? *UPSSSC 2018*
(a) 39 min (b) 40 min (c) 41 min (d) 42 min

30. A bus leaves for Chennai every 40 min from a stand. An enquiry clerk tells a man that the bus left 10 min ago and the next bus will leave at 10:45 am. At what time was this information given to the man? *FCI Assistant 2015*
(a) 10:25 am (b) 09:55 am
(c) 10:15 am (d) 10:35 am

Based on Finding the Day of the Date

31. Which of the following is a leap year? *SSC CGL (Tier I) 2023*
(a) 1998 (b) 1354 (c) 1675 (d) 1076

32. Which of the following is not a leap year? *UP Police Constable 2024*
(a) 2004 (b) 2024 (c) 2020 (d) 2014

33. If 18 February 2005 is Friday, then what day will be 18 February 2007? *UPSSSC PET 2021*
(a) Sunday (b) Monday
(c) Tuesday (d) Wednesday

34. 11 January, 2018 was Thursday, so what day will be 11 June, 2019? *RRB ALP 2018*
(a) Sunday (b) Wednesday
(c) Tuesday (d) Monday

35. If 25th August, 2006 was Friday, then what day of the week was it on 25th August, 2018? *SSC (10+2) 2024*
(a) Wednesday
(b) Sunday
(c) Saturday
(d) Thursday

MRC***
(Most Repeating Concepts)
Q. Nos. 32, 35, 38, 46 and 57 are very important from the examination point of view. Questions on these concepts are continuously being asked in UP Police, SSC, Railway examinations.

36. If May 28, 2015 was Thursday, what day of the week will it be on April 24, 2023? *SSC (10+2) 2023*
(a) Wednesday (b) Sunday (c) Friday (d) Monday

37. Shamita's birth anniversary was on Sunday, March 15, 2020. So, what day was her husband's birth anniversary, which was on May 31, 2020? *RRB NTPC (CBT-II) 2022*
(a) Friday (b) Sunday (c) Tuesday (d) Wednesday

38. If March 20, 2001 is Tuesday, then what day will April 23, 2021? *SSC (10+2)2023*
(a) Tuesday (b) Wednesday
(c) Friday (d) Monday

39. If December 31, 2003 was Wednesday, then what day was on March 7, 2005? *SSC CPO 2022*
(a) Tuesday (b) Sunday (c) Saturday (d) Monday

40. If 31st January, 2009 was Saturday, then what day of the week was 30th January, 2013? *SSC CGL 2023*
(a) Tuesday (b) Wednesday
(c) Monday (d) Friday

41. If January 15, 1996 is Monday, then what day of the week will be March 30, 1997? *SSC (10+2) 2023*
(a) Monday (b) Tuesday (c) Sunday (d) Wednesday

42. If January 1, 2013 was Wednesday, then what day of the week was January 2, 2014? *STET 2020*
(a) Wednesday (b) Thursday
(c) Tuesday (d) Friday

43. Which day of the week was July 20, 2009? *SSC Steno 2020*
(a) Saturday (b) Tuesday (c) Monday (d) Sunday

44. What day of the week on January 10, 2006? *RRC Group-D 2022*
(a) Wednesday (b) Monday
(c) Tuesday (d) Thursday

45. Which day of the week will be on 1 January, 2022? *RRB JE 2019*
(a) Sunday (b) Monday (c) Thursday (d) Saturday

Finding Day Based on Week Day

46. If the fourth day of a month is Sunday, then which of the following days will be the sixth day before the thirteenth day of the same month? *UP Police Constable 2018*
(a) Sunday (b) Tuesday (c) Saturday (d) Friday

47. If the fourth day of a month is Saturday, then which day will be 5 days before the 26th day of that month? *UPPSC 2018*
(a) Monday (b) Tuesday (c) Friday (d) Sunday

48. All Saturdays and Sundays in a month are holidays. If the month is January, then how many holidays will there be in that month? *CGPSC 2019*
(a) 8 (b) 9 (c) 10
(d) The information is incomplete
(e) None of these

49. If the fourth day of a month is Friday, then which of the following will be the third day after the twenty-fifth day of the same month? *UP Police Constable 2019*
(a) Wednesday (b) Tuesday
(c) Sunday (d) Monday

50. If the fifth day of the month is 4 days before Friday, then what day will be on the 22nd of that month? *DSSSB Warder 2019*
(a) Wednesday (b) Tuesday
(c) Thursday (d) Friday

51. If two days before yesterday was Friday, then what day is the day after tomorrow will be? *Bihar TET 2020*
(a) Monday (b) Sunday
(c) Saturday (d) Wednesday

52. If today is Friday, then what day will it be after 72 days? *SSC CGL 2023*
(a) Thursday (b) Sunday
(c) Friday (d) Tuesday

53. If today is Thursday, then what day will it be after 91 days? *RRB NTPC 2021*
(a) Thursday (b) Wednesday
(c) Friday (d) Monday

54. If tomorrow is Sunday, then which day of the week will be 121 days from today? *RRC Group-D 2022*
(a) Sunday (b) Wednesday
(c) Tuesday (d) Monday

55. If Republic Day in India in 1980 was on Saturday and X was born on 3rd March, 1980 and Y is four days older than X, then Y was born on
(a) Thursday (b) Friday
(c) Wednesday (d) None of these

56. If 1st January is Friday, then what day will be the 1st of March in a leap year?
(a) Tuesday (b) Wednesday
(c) Thursday (d) Friday

Based on Memory

57. Rama remembers that she met her brother on Saturday, which was the day after the 20th day of a month. If the first day of that month was Tuesday, on which date did Rama meet her brother? *RRB NTPC (CBT-I) 2022*
(a) 23 (b) 24 (c) 25 (d) 26

58. An application comes to an office in the afternoon, which is given to the concerned branch the next day. The next day the application is presented to the concerned officer from the concerned branch who disposes of it on the same day i.e. Friday. On which day was the application received?
(a) Monday (b) Wednesday
(c) Tuesday (d) Saturday last week

59. Mohini went to the movies nine days ago. She goes to the movies only on Thursdays. What day of the week is today?
(a) Saturday (b) Thursday
(c) Sunday (d) Tuesday

60. Sanjeev remembers that his brother Manvendra's date of birth is after 20th but before 28th August. Reeta remembers that Manvendra's date of birth is before 22nd but after 12th August. Tell me what is Manvendra's date of birth?
(a) 22 August (b) 20 August
(c) 21 August (d) 26 August

Right Key

1. (a)	2. (a)	3. (c)	4. (a)	5. (d)	6. (d)	7. (d)	8. (a)	9. (a)	10. (a)
11. (d)	12. (c)	13. (c)	14. (b)	15. (a)	16. (b)	17. (b)	18. (d)	19. (c)	20. (c)
21. (b)	22. (a)	23. (b)	24. (a)	25. (b)	26. (a)	27. (b)	28. (a)	29. (b)	30. (c)
31. (d)	32. (d)	33. (a)	34. (c)	35. (c)	36. (d)	37. (b)	38. (c)	39. (d)	40. (b)
41. (c)	42. (d)	43. (c)	44. (c)	45. (d)	46. (c)	47. (b)	48. (d)	49. (d)	50. (c)
51. (d)	52. (b)	53. (a)	54. (d)	55. (a)	56. (a)	57. (d)	58. (b)	59. (a)	60. (c)

Solutions

1. *(a)* According to the question,

Time in the mirror = 1:30   Actual time = 10:30

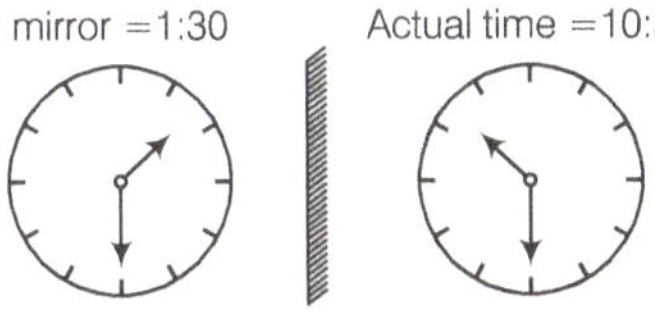

So, it will be 10:30 in the mirror.

Smart Approach

Correct time = 11:60 − 1:30 = 10:30

2. *(a)* According to the question, if we consider the image of the clock as the correct time and find its reflection, then we will know the actual time.

Time in the mirror = 3:15   Actual time = 8:45

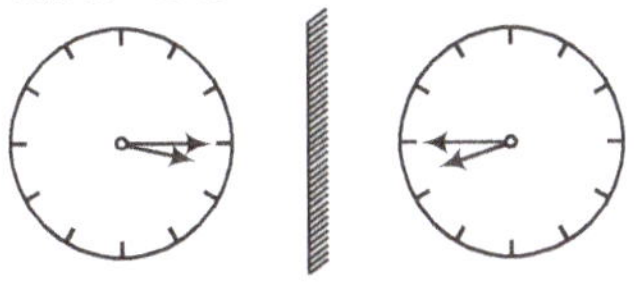

Therefore, the correct time on the clock will be 8:45.

3. *(c)* As per the question,

Time in the mirror = 9:50   Actual time = 2:10

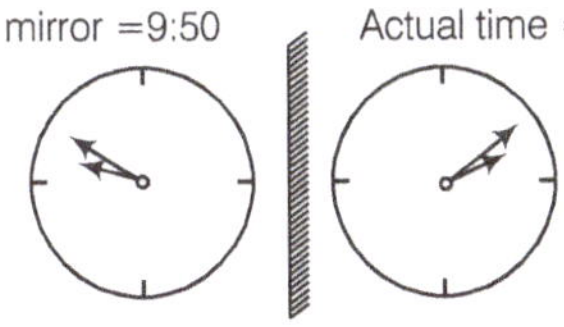

So, the actual time is 2:10.

4. *(a)* According to the question,

Actual time = 5:25   Time in first image = 6:35

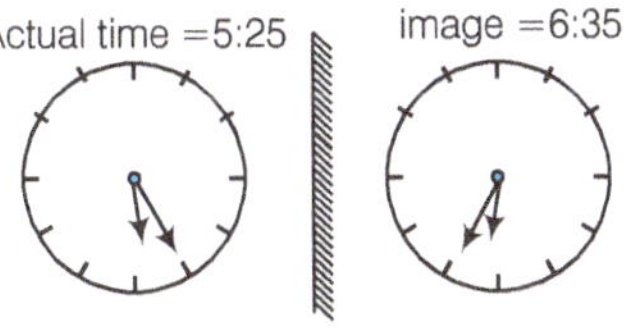

Time in second image = 5:25

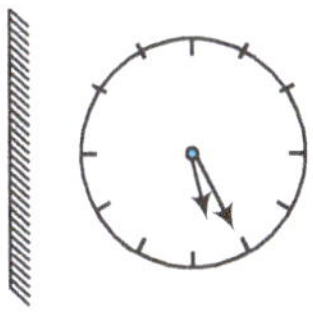

5. *(d)* Angle made by the hour hand in 4 hours = $30^\circ \times 4 = 120^\circ$

Angle made by hour hand in 10 min

$$= \frac{30^\circ}{60} \times 10 = 5^\circ$$

Hence, angle made by the hour hand at 4 : 10 = $120^\circ + 5^\circ = 125^\circ$

6. *(d)* The hour hand takes 1 min to rotate $\frac{1^\circ}{2}$.

It takes $\frac{1}{1/2} = 2$ min to rotate 1°.

∴ It will take $18 \times 2 = 36$ min to rotate 18°.

Now, the minute hand moves 6 in 1 min.

∴ In 36 min, it will move

$36 \times 6^\circ = 216^\circ$.

7. *(d)* 3 hour 10 min

$= 3 \times 60 + 10 = 190$ min

Minute hand covers an angular distance in 1 min = 6°

∴ Angle covered by …minute hand in 190 min = $6 \times 190^\circ = 1140^\circ$

TOP TIPS To solve such questions, it is very important to have knowledge of angular distance travelled by the hands.

8. *(a)* Given, time = 5:20 = $\left[5 + \frac{20}{60}\right]$

$$= 5 + \frac{1}{3} = \frac{16}{3} \text{ hours}$$

The hour hand rotates in 12 hours

$= 360^\circ$

∴ In $\frac{16}{3}$ hours the hour hand will rotate

$$= \frac{360}{12} \times \frac{16}{3} = 160^\circ$$

9. *(a)* Given, time = 8:20

Here, H = 8 and M = 20

∴ Required angle, $\theta = \left|30H - \frac{11}{2}M\right|$

$$= \left|30 \times 8 - \frac{11}{2} \times 20\right|$$

$$= 240^\circ - 110^\circ = 130^\circ$$

10. *(a)* Here, H = 4 and M = 37

∴ Required angle = $\left|30H - \frac{11}{2}M\right|$

$$= \left|30 \times 4 - \frac{11}{2} \times 37\right|$$

$$= \left|120^\circ - 203.5^\circ\right|$$

$$= 83.5^\circ$$

11. *(d)* Given, H = 3 and M = 30

∴ Required angle = $\left|\frac{11}{2}M - 30H\right|$

$$= \left|\frac{11}{2} \times 30 - 30 \times 3\right|$$

$$= 165^\circ - 90^\circ = 75^\circ$$

12. *(c)* In 5 hours 35 min or $\frac{67}{12}$ hours,

angle made by hour hand

$$= \left(\frac{360^\circ}{12} \times \frac{67}{12}\right) = 167.5^\circ$$

In 35 min, angle made by minute hand

$$= \frac{360 \times 35}{60} = 210^\circ$$

∴ Required angle

$$= 210^\circ - 167.5^\circ = 42.5^\circ$$

13. (*c*) Given, H = 3 and M = 25

$\therefore$ Required angle $= \left|\frac{11}{2}M - 30H\right|$

$= \left|\frac{11}{2} \times 25 - 30 \times 3\right|$

$= 137.5° - 90°$

$= 47.5°$

14. (*b*) Angle between the hands

$= \left|\frac{11}{2}M - 30H\right|$

M = minute hand, H = hour hand

The hands of a clock cannot be together between 2:30 - 3:00

H = 3, angle = 0

$\left|\frac{11}{2}M - 90\right| = 0 \Rightarrow M = \frac{180}{11} = 16\frac{4}{11}$

$\therefore$ Required time $= 16\frac{4}{11}$ min past 3

Smart Approach

$M = \frac{60}{11} \times T_1 = \frac{60}{11} \times 2 = \frac{120}{11} = 10\frac{10}{11}$

$M = \frac{60}{11} \times T_2 = \frac{60}{11} \times 3 = \frac{180}{11} = 16\frac{4}{11}$

15. (*a*) Let the angle of 90° formed at 2 : M.

$\theta = \left|\frac{11}{2}M - 30H\right|$

[$\theta = 90°$, H = 2, M = ?]

$\Rightarrow \quad 90° = \frac{11}{2}M - 30 \times 2$

$\Rightarrow \frac{11}{2}M = 90° + 60°$

$\Rightarrow \frac{11M}{2} = 150°$

$\Rightarrow \quad M = \frac{300}{11} = 27\frac{3}{11}$

Hence, the required time $= 27\frac{3}{11}$ min past 2.

16. (*b*) Here, $\theta = 30°$, H = 4, M = ?

$\theta = \left|30H - \frac{11}{2}M\right|$

$\Rightarrow 30° = 30 \times 4 - \frac{11}{2}M$

$\Rightarrow \frac{11}{2}M = 120 - 30$

$= \frac{90 \times 2}{11} = \frac{180}{11} = 16\frac{4}{11}$

Therefore, an angle of 30° will be hands at $4:16\frac{4}{11}$.

17. (*b*) At 1 O'clock the distance between the two hands is 5 min. So, when the minute hand covers a distance of 5 min more than the hour hand, then both the hands will meet each other.

Time taken by the two hands to meet

$= 5 \times \frac{12}{11} = \frac{60}{11}$ min $= 5\frac{5}{11}$ min

Hence, the hands will meet at $01{:}5\frac{5}{11}$.

18. (*d*) Because the hour hand and the minute hand of a clock are at right angles twice in 1 hour.

But in 24 hours, the hour hand and minute hand of the clock will be at right angles 22 × 2 = 44 times.

Therefore, both the hands of the clock will be at right angles to each other in a week = 44 × 7 = 308 times

19. (*c*) Angular distance covered by the minute hand in 1 min $= \frac{360°}{60} = 6°$

But according to the question, the minute hand moves at the rate of 9° in 1 min.

Difference in angular distance covered

$= (9° - 6°) = 3°$

$\therefore$ Distance covered in 1 min = 6°

$\therefore$ Time taken to cover 3° distance

$= \frac{1}{6} \times 3 = \frac{1}{2}$ min

The clock fasts $\frac{1}{2}$ min in 1 min.

The clock will be fast in 30 min

$= 30 \times \frac{1}{2} = 15$ min fast.

20. (*c*) The clock gains 5 min in every hour the clock gains in one min $= \frac{5}{60}$

$\therefore$ Angular distance covered in 5 min

$= \frac{5}{60°} \times 360° = 30°$

Therefore, the second hand will rotate through 360° + 30° = 390° in one minute.

21. (*b*) The clock moved forward in 48 hours = 8 min

In 6 hours it moved forward = 1 min

Hence, it will take 18 hours from 2:00 pm on Monday to move ahead by 3 min

i.e. 2:00 pm + 18 hours = 20 O'clock

i.e. on Tuesday morning at 8 O'clock the clock showed the correct time.

22. (*a*) There will be 30 hours from 10 am on the first day to 4 pm on the second day i.e. when the fast clock shows 4 pm on the second day, then it will have moved 30 hours according to itself but when the fast clock will show 25 hours, then the actual time will be 24 hours. Hence, when the fast clock will move 30 hours.

Then, the actual time will be

$= \frac{24}{25} \times 30\text{ h} = 28\frac{4}{5}\text{ h}$

= 28 hours 48 min

$\therefore$ Actual time = 28 h 48 min from 10 am on the first day = 2 : 48 pm

23. (*b*) Sunday 12 noon to Wednesday evening 8 O'clock.

Total time period = 80 h

In 80 h,

First clock losses = 6 min

and second clock gains = 9 min

Time difference gained in 80 h

= 15 min

$1\text{ min} = \frac{80}{15}$

$\therefore$ In 11 min gained

$= \frac{80}{15} \times 11 = 58\frac{2}{3}$ h

= 2 days 10 h 40 min

So, both the clocks will show the same time at = Sunday (12 noon) + 2 days 10 h 40 min

= Tuesday at 10 : 40 pm

24. (*a*) Required time period

= 12:30:34 − 02:39:40 = 09:50:54

i.e. the bulb remained lit for 9 h 50 min 54 sec.

25. (*b*) The time of departure of Ajay from the house is given as

= 8:40 − 0:10 = 8:30 am

Ajay leaves 15 min earlier than usual days. So, on usual days he leaves the house at 8 : 30 + 00 : 15

i.e. 8:45 am

26. (*a*) According to the question, the departure time of the next train

= 10:35 am

Departure time of the previous train

= 10:35 − 55 min = 9:40 O'clock

Time of inquiry

= 9:40 O'clock + 20 min

= 10:00 O'clock

27. (*b*) According to the announcement, the next bus departure time is 4:30 O'clock.

Since, the bus leaves every 4 hours.

Time of the previous bus

$= 4{:}30 - 4{:}00 = 12{:}30$ pm

Now, since the announcement was made 20 min after the first bus left.

Correct time of announcement

$= 12{:}30 + 20$ min $= 12{:}50$ pm

28. (*a*) The position of the dial of the clock will be as follows,

Hence, the hour hand will be between I and J at $3\frac{1}{2}$ O'clock.

29. (*b*) Let the time of one period be t min.

As per the question,

$4 \times t + 4 \times (4-1) = 03{:}52 - 01{:}00$

$\Rightarrow 4 \times t + 4 \times 3 = 02{:}52$ (2 hours 52 min)

$\Rightarrow 4 \times t + 12 = (2 \times 60 + 52)$

$\Rightarrow 4t = 172 - 12 \Rightarrow 4t = 160$ min

$\therefore t = 40$ min

30. (*c*) Since, the bus leaves every 40 min and as per the information given by the clerk, the bus left 10 min ago, the person got the information $(40-10) = 30$ min before the next bus leaves.

If the next bus leaves at 10:45 am, then the time when the person got the information will be 30 min before 10:45 am i.e. 10:15 am.

(10:45 – 30 min = 10:15)

31. (*d*) Leap year is exactly divisible by '4'.

So, from option (d), $\frac{1076}{4} = 269$

$\therefore$ 1076 is a leap year.

32. (*d*) The year 2014 is not a leap year. All other years are exactly divisible by 4.

33. (*a*) Given, 18th February, 2005 is Friday,

Then 18th February, 2006 will be (Friday + 1) Saturday.

Hence, 18th February, 2007 will be (Saturday + 1) Sunday.

34. (*c*) Total number of days from 11th January, 2018 to 11th June, 2019 = 516

Number of odd days

$= 516 \div 7 = 5$ days

$\therefore$ Required day = Thursday + 5 days

= Tuesday

35. (*c*) 25th August, 2006 = Friday

Day of 25 August, 2018 is Friday + 9 (ordinary year) + 3 (leap year)

$=$ Friday $+ 9 + (2 \times 3)$

$=$ Friday $+ 15 =$ Saturday

36. (*d*) Given,

Day of 28th May, 2015 = Thursday

Odd days in remaining days in year 2015

$= 3 + 2 + 3 + 3 + 2 + 3 + 2 + 3$

$= 21 \div 7 = 0$ (odd days)

Odd days from year 2016 to 2022

$= 2 + 1 + 1 + 1 + 2 + 1 + 1$

$= \frac{9}{7} = 2$ (odd days)

Odd days from 1 January 2023 to 24 April 2023 $= 3 + 0 + 3 + 24$

$= \frac{30}{7} = 2$ (odd days)

Total odd days $= 0 + 2 + 2 = 4$

So, day on 24 April 2023

= Thursday + 4 = Monday

37. (*b*) According to the question,

Day on 15th March, 2020 = Sunday

Total days from 15th March to 31st May $= 16 + 30 + 31 = 77$

Odd days from 15th March to 31st May = 0

(Remainder in $77 \div 7 = 0$)

Hence, 31st May, 2020 was Sunday.

38. (*c*) Day of 20th March, 2001

= Tuesday,

Odd days from 20th March, 2001 to 23rd April, 2021

= Odd days from 20th March, 2001 to 20th March, 2021 + Odd days from 21st March, 2021 to 23rd April, 2021

$= (5 \times 2 + 15) + (11 + 23)$

(2004, 2008, 2012, 2016, 2020 are leap years)

$= 25 + 34 = 59$

$= 7 \times 8 + 3 = 3$ (odd day)

So, day on 23rd April, 2021

= Tuesday + 3 = Friday

39. (*d*) Number of odd days from 31 December 2003 to 31 December 2004 = 2 (2004 is a leap year)

1st January 2005 to 7th March 2005

Number of odd days

$= 3 + 0 + 7 = 10$

$\therefore$ Total number of odd days

$(10 + 2) \div 7 = 5$ (odd days).

$\therefore$ Day on 7th March, 2005

= Wednesday + 5 = Monday

40. (*b*) Number of odd days from 31st January, 2009 to 31st January 2013

$= 1 + 1 + 2 + 1 = 5$ (odd days)

$\therefore$ Day of 31st January, 2013

= Saturday + 5 = Thursday

$\therefore$ Day of 30th January, 2013

= Thursday – 1 = Wednesday

41. (*c*) Given,

15th January 1996 is Monday.

Since, 1996 is a leap year.

Hence, 15th January 1997 will be Wednesday.

Number of days between 15th January 1997 and 30th March 1997

$= 16 + 28 + 30 = 74$

$= 7 \times 10 + 4 = 4$ (odd days)

Hence, the day on 30th March 1997

= Wednesday + 4 days

= Sunday

42. (*d*) Total odd days from 1st January 2013 to 2nd January 2014

$= 1 + 1 = 2$ (odd days)

$\because$ Day of 1st January, 2013

= Wednesday

$\therefore$ Day of 2nd January 2014

= Wednesday + 2

= Friday

43. (*c*) Odd days till the year 2000 = 0

Odd days from 2001 to 2008

$= 2 \times 2 + 6 \times 1$

$= 4 + 6 = 10 = 10 \div 7 = 3$

(Years 2004 and 2008 are leap years)

Odd days in the year 2009

$= 3 + 0 + 3 + 2 + 3 + 2 + 6 = 19$

Total odd days $= 19 \div 7 = 5$

Total number of odd days till 20th July, 2009

$= 0 + 3 + 5 = 8 \div 7 = 1$ (odd day)

$\therefore$ Required day = Monday

TOP TIPS To solve this type of questions Candidate must have good knowledge about odd days.

44. *(c)* Number of odd days till 10th January, 2006 = Odd days in 2000 years + Odd days in 5 years + Odd days in 10 days

$= 0 + 2 \times 1 + 4 \times 1 + 3$

$= 2 + 4 + 3 = 9$

$= 7 \times 1 + 2 = 2$ (odd days)

Hence, the day on 10th January 2006 is Tuesday.

45. *(d)* Total number of odd days till January 1, 2022 = Odd days in 2000 years + Odd days in 21 years + 1 odd day

$= 0 + 5 \times 2 + 16 \times 1 + 1 = 27$

Total odd days = $27 \div 7 = 6$

Total odd days = 6 odd days

1 January, 2022 will be a Saturday.

46. *(c)* Day of the 4th of the month

= Sunday

∴ Sixth day before the 30th day of the month i.e. $30 - 6 = 24$th day

$= \text{Sunday} + \dfrac{(24-4)}{7}$ odd days

= Sunday + 6 (odd days) = Saturday

47. *(b)* ∵ The fourth day of the month is Saturday.

∴ 11th, 18th, 25th day of the month is also Saturday.

Now, the day 5 days before the 26th day is the 21st day.

∴ 21st day = 18th day + 3 days

Hence, 21st day will be the day 3 days after Saturday i.e. Tuesday.

48. *(d)* January month has 31 days i.e. 4 weeks and 3 days. Since, the first day of the month is not known, the number of Saturdays and Sundays in January cannot be found.

49. *(d)* 4th of the month is Friday.

11th of the month is Friday.

18th of the month is Friday.

25th of the month is Friday.

∴ 3rd day after 25th of the month

= Friday + 3 = Monday

50. *(c)* 5th day of the month

= Friday − 4 = Monday

Other Mondays in the month

= 12th, 19th, 26th

∴ Day of 22nd = 19th + 3

= Monday + 3 = Thursday

51. *(d)* Two days before yesterday

= Friday

∴ Yesterday's day = Friday + 2

= Sunday

Today's day = Monday

Tomorrow's day = Tuesday

∴ Day after tomorrow = Wednesday

52. *(b)* Number of odd days in 72 days

= Remainder of $72 \div 7 = 2$(odd days)

∴ Day after 72 days = Friday + 2

= Sunday

53. *(a)* Number of odd days in 91 days

= Remainder of $91 \div 7 = 0$ (odd days)

∴ Day after 91 days = Thursday + 0

= Thursday

54. *(d)* Tomorrow = Sunday

∴ Today = Saturday

Total number of odd days in 121 days

Remainder of $121 \div 7 = 2$ (odd days)

∴ Day of the week after 121 days

= Saturday + 2 = Monday

55. *(a)* Day of Republic Day in 1980

i.e. 26 January 1980 = Saturday

Odd days till 3 March 1980

$= 5 + 29 + 3 = 37$

= 5 weeks and 2 days (odd days)

∴ Day of 3 March 1980

= Saturday + 2 = Monday

Since, Y is four days older than X, so his birthday will be four days before X's birthday.

∴ Y was born on = Monday − 4

= Thursday

56. *(a)* Given, 1st January = Friday

∴ 8, 15, 22, 29 January = Friday

And 30th January = Saturday

31st January = Sunday

1st February = Monday

∴ 8, 15, 22, 29 February = Monday

Hence, 1st March = Tuesday

57. *(d)* According to the question,

The first day of the month = Tuesday

∴ 8th, 15th, 22nd, 29th day of the month will also be Tuesday.

Rama met her brother after the 20th day.

∵ Tuesday + 4 days = Saturday

∴ 26th will be Saturday after the 20th day.

58. *(b)* Day of receipt of the application

= Day of disposal − 2 = Friday − 2

= Wednesday

Hence, the application was received on Wednesday.

59. *(a)* Since, every week has seven days and the same day comes again on the seventh day. So, the day falling two days ago = Thursday

So, the day falling today

= Thursday + 2 = Saturday

60. *(c)* According to Sanjeev,

Manvendra's date of birth = (21) − 27

According to Rita,

Manvendra's date of birth = 13 − (21)

So, Manvendra's date of birth

= 21 August (common date)

CHAPTER

15 Mathematical Operations

Mathematical Operations

The process of solving a given mathematical expression or equation by changing the actual signs/letters/ symbols as per the instruction given in the question is called mathematical operations.

Substitution of Symbols

In this type of questions, some instructions about mathematical symbols along with the equation in which symbols are present, is given.

The candidate need to find the value of the equation or expression by substituting the symbols given in the equation.

e.g. In the following equation if '+' and '–' are interchanged, '×' and '÷' are interchanged, then what will come at the place of question mark (?).

$4515 \times 5 - 431 \div 3 + 821 = ?$

(a) 1575 (b) 1335 (c) 1375 (d) 1775

Sol. (c) Given expression,

$4515 \times 5 - 431 \div 3 + 821$

According to the question, after substituting the signs,

$$4515 \div 5 + 431 \times 3 - 821$$
$$= 903 + 1293 - 821$$
$$= 2196 - 821 = 1375$$

Interchanging the Signs and Numbers

In this type of questions, some instructions are given along with an equation. According to the instruction certain signs or numbers are to be interchanged with each other to balance the given equation.

The candidates are required to choose that pair of signs or numbers from the options and solve the equation.

e.g. Which of the two numbers should be interchange to make the given equation correct?

$144 + 108 \div 12 - 16 \times 6 = 24$

(a) 12, 6 (b) 108, 6 (c) 108, 144 (d) 12, 16

Sol. (c) Given equation,

$144 + 108 \div 12 - 16 \times 6 = 24$

From option (c), by interchanging 108 and 144,

$$108 + 144 \div 12 - 16 \times 6 = 24$$
$$\Rightarrow \quad 108 + 12 - 96 = 24$$
$$\Rightarrow \quad 120 - 96 = 24 \Rightarrow 24 = 24$$

Based on Special Case

In this type of questions, an unsolved equation is given along with some solved equations which follow some special pattern or rule.

On the basis of that particular rule, candidates have to solve the unsolved equation and find the correct answer accordingly.

e.g. If $4 \times 6 = 1812$, $5 \times 8 = 2415$, $6 \times 9 = 2718$, then 7×6 is equal to

(a) 1821 (b) 2428 (c) 3035 (d) 3642

Sol. (a) As, $4 \times 6 \Rightarrow (6 \times 3)\ (4 \times 3) \Rightarrow 1812$

and, $5 \times 8 \Rightarrow (8 \times 3)\ (5 \times 3) \Rightarrow 2415$

$6 \times 9 \Rightarrow (9 \times 3)\ (6 \times 3) \Rightarrow 2718$

Similarly, $7 \times 6 \Rightarrow (6 \times 3)\ (7 \times 3) \Rightarrow 1821$

Balancing the Equation

In this type of questions, an equation is given with some blank spaces or with some '*' symbols in place of its actual signs. The candidate needs to fill those blank spaces or replace '*' symbols with actual signs given in the options which balances the given equation.

e.g. Choose the correct combination of arithmetical signs to replace the * symbols and balance the given equation.

7 * 5 * 8 * 4 * 2 * 4 * 35

(a) × + ÷ + – = (b) + ÷ × + – =

(c) – × + = × ÷ (d) ÷ × + × ÷ =

Sol. (a) From option (a),

$$7 \times 5 + 8 \div 4 + 2 - 4 = 35$$
$$\Rightarrow \quad 7 \times 5 + 2 + 2 - 4 = 35$$
$$\Rightarrow \quad 35 + 4 - 4 = 35$$
$$\Rightarrow \quad 35 = 35$$

Identifying Balanced Equation After Interchanging the Signs/Numbers

In this type of questions, some equations are given as options in which instead of mathematical signs, some blank spaces or other symbols/letters are given.

The candidate is required to replace these blank spaces or other symbols/letters according to the question and find a balanced equation by solving.

e.g. If '→' means '+', '←' means '–', ↑ means '÷' and '↓' means '×' and '↗' means '=', then which of the following option is correct?

(a) $2 \downarrow 5 \leftarrow 6 \rightarrow 2 \nearrow 6$

(b) $5 \rightarrow 7 \leftarrow 3 \uparrow 2 \nearrow 4$

(c) $3 \downarrow 6 \uparrow 2 \rightarrow 3 \leftarrow 6 \nearrow 5$

(d) $7 \leftarrow 43 \uparrow 6 \downarrow 1 \nearrow 4$

Sol. (a) From option (a),

Given equation, $2 \downarrow 5 \leftarrow 6 \rightarrow 2 \nearrow 6$

By interchanging the signs,

$$2 \times 5 - 6 + 2 = 6 \Rightarrow 10 - 6 + 2 = 6$$
$$\Rightarrow \quad 12 - 6 = 6 \Rightarrow 6 = 6$$

Exam Approach Examples

Based on Substitution of Symbols

Example 1 If '+' means 'subtraction', '–' means 'multiplication', '÷' means 'addition' and '×' means 'division', then what is the value of the following expression?

$14 - 19 + 240 \times 16 \div 61$ *SSC CGL (Tier-I) 2023*

(a) 284 (b) 312 (c) 247 (d) 329

Sol. (*b*) Given expression, $14 - 19 + 240 \times 16 \div 61$

After interchanging signs, we get

$= 14 \times 19 - 240 \div 16 + 61$ [By using BODMAS rule]

$= 266 - 15 + 61 = 327 - 15 = \boxed{312}$

Example 2 If $p + q$ means $p - q$, $p - q$ means $p \times q$, $p \times q$ means $p \div q$ and $p \div q$ means $p + q$, then find the value of

$25 + 48 \times 6 \div 12 - 2$ *RRB NTPC 2020*

(a) 39 (b) 52 (c) 41 (d) 17

Sol. (*c*) Given expression, $25 + 48 \times 6 \div 12 - 2$

According to the question, substituting the signs,

$+ \rightarrow -$	$- \rightarrow \times$
$\times \rightarrow \div$	$\div \rightarrow +$

$25 - 48 \div 6 + 12 \times 2 = 25 - 8 + 24 = 49 - 8 = \boxed{41}$

Based on Balancing the Equation

Example 3 Select the combination of signs that when sequentially placed in the given blanks will make the equation correct.

7_3_4_12_6 = 19 *UPSSSC 2022*

(a) +, ÷, ×, – (b) ×, –, +, ÷ (c) –, ×, +, ÷ (d) ÷, ×, +, –

Sol. (*b*) Given expression, 7_3_4_12_6 = 19

By option (b), $7 \times 3 - 4 + 12 \div 6 = 19$ (Using BODMAS rule)

$\Rightarrow 7 \times 3 - 4 + 2 = 19 \Rightarrow 21 - 4 + 2 = 19$

$\Rightarrow 23 - 4 = 19 \Rightarrow 19 = 19$

Example 4 Select the correct combination of mathematical signs to sequentially replace the * signs and balance the given equation.

11 * 7 * 345 * 5 * 31 = 115 *SSC CGL (Tier-II) 2023*

(a) +, ×, ÷, – (b) ×, +, ÷, – (c) ÷, ×, +, – (d) ÷, –, +, ×

Sol. (*b*) Given equation, 11 * 7 * 345 * 5 * 31 = 115

From option (b),

$11 \times 7 + 345 \div 5 - 31 = 115 \Rightarrow 77 + 69 - 31 = 115 \Rightarrow 115 = 115$

Based on Interchanging the Signs and Numbers

Example 5 Which of the two numbers should be interchanged to balance the given equation?

$2 + 10 \times 12 - 4 \div 24 = 8$ *SSC CPO 2024*

(a) – and + (b) ÷ and + (c) ÷ and – (d) × and ÷

Sol. (*c*) Given equation is, $2 + 10 \times 12 - 4 \div 24 = 8$

From option (c), by interchanging '÷' and '–' signs, we get

$\Rightarrow 2 + 10 \times 12 \div 4 - 24 = 8 \Rightarrow 2 + 10 \times 3 - 24 = 8$

$\Rightarrow 2 + 30 - 24 = 8 \Rightarrow 8 = 8$

Example 6 Which two numbers should be interchanged to make the given equation correct?

$72 - 56 + (13 + 19) \times 2 - 95 \div 5 + 17 = 76$

(Note: Interchange should be done of the entire number and not individual pairs of a given number.) *RRB ALP 2024*

(a) 19 and 5 (b) 19 and 17
(c) 17 and 56 (d) 13 and 17

Sol. (*b*) Given equation,

$72 - 56 + (13 + 19) \times 2 - 95 \div 5 + 17 = 76$

From option (b), on interchanging 19 and 17

$72 - 56 + (13 + 17) \times 2 - 95 \div 5 + 19 = 76$

$\Rightarrow 72 - 56 + 30 \times 2 - 19 + 19 = 76$

$\Rightarrow 72 - 56 + 60 = 76$

$\Rightarrow 132 - 56 = 76$

$\Rightarrow 76 = 76$

Based on Identifying Balanced Equation After Interchanging the Signs/Numbers

Example 7 In the following statement A, B, C, D and E denotes +, –, ×, ÷ and =, respectively. Which of the following statement is correct? *SSC JE 2023*

(a) 8A6C5D15B14E4 (b) 8A6C3D15E14B4
(c) 8A6C5D15E24B4 (d) 8A6C5D15E14B4

Sol. (*d*) From option (d) expression as,

8A6C5D15E14B4

On substituting signs we have,

$8 + 6 \times 5 \div 15 = 14 - 4$

$\Rightarrow 8 + 6 \times \frac{5}{15} = 14 - 4$

$\Rightarrow 8 + 2 = 14 - 4$

$\Rightarrow 10 = 10$

Helping Tips

To solve questions of this chapter we need to solve the equation using BODMAS rule.

Based on Special Case

Example 8 If 8A7 = 56 and 9A11 = 99, then 16A15 = ? *SSC (10+2) 2023*

(a) 260 (b) 220
(c) 240 (d) 280

Sol. (*c*) As, $8A7 = 8 \times 7 = 56$

and, $9A11 = 9 \times 11 = 99$

Similarly, $16A15 = 16 \times 15 = \boxed{240}$

Chapter Challenge

Based on Substitution of Symbols

1. If '+' means '÷', '–' means '+', '×' means '–' and '÷' means '×', then what will be the value of $[\{(14\times6)-(4\div3)\}+(6-4)]\div3$? *CISF 2023*
(a) 1 (b) 9 (c) 3 (d) 6

> ***MRC******
> ***(Most Repeating Concepts)***
> Question Nos. 2, 4, 8, 15, 20, 22, 28, 36, 45, 61, 65 and 74 are very important for SSC (CGL, CPO, CHSL), DSSSB, UP Police Constable and Railway NTPC exams.

2. What will come in the place of the question mark (?) in the following equation if '+' and '×' are interchanged and '–' and '÷' are interchanged?
$95-19\times4+6\div16=?$ *SSC CGL (Tier-I) 2024*
(a) 13 (b) 12 (c) 14 (d) 11

3. What will come in the place of '?' in the following equation, if '÷' and '–' are interchanged and '×' and '+' are interchanged?
$7+4\div18-3\times2=?$ *SSC CGL (Tier-I) 2024*
(a) 16 (b) 20 (c) 18 (d) 24

4. If 'I' stands for '×', 'J' stands for '+', 'K' stands for '÷' and 'L' stands for '–', what will come in place of the question mark (?) in the following equation?
(40 J 32 K 4) I 5 L 155 J 7 I 9 = ? *SSC CPO 2024*
(a) 126 (b) 156 (c) 134 (d) 148

5. If '×' means '–', '÷' means '+', '+' means '×', then, $18\times5\div5+6$ is equal to *CRPF HC 2023*
(a) 58 (b) 49 (c) 43 (d) 37

6. If 'A' stands for '÷', 'B' stands for '×', 'C' stands for '+' and 'D' stands for '–', what will come in place of the question mark (?) in the following equation?
96 A 4 D 5 B 7 C 20 = ? *SSC CPO 2024*
(a) 9 (b) 2 (c) 4 (d) 7

7. If '+' means '–', '–' means '×', '× means '÷', '÷' means '+', what will come in place of the question mark (?) in the given equation?
$99\times33-70\div90+100=?$ *SSC CPO 2024*
(a) 100 (b) 201 (c) 300 (d) 200

8. In a certain code language, '+' represents '×', '–' represents '+', '×' represents '÷' and '÷' represents '–'. Find the answer of the following question.
$16\div8\times4-2+1=?$ *UP Police Constable 2018*
(a) 22 (b) 27 (c) 16 (d) 13

9. What will come in the place of '?' in the following equation, if '+' and '–' are interchanged and '×' and '÷' are interchanged?
$4-5\div9+6\times2=?$ *SSC CGL (Tier-I) 2024*
(a) 42 (b) 46 (c) 36 (d) 38

10. If 'A' stands for '÷', 'B' stands for '×', 'C' stands for '+' and 'D' stands for '–', what will come in place of the question mark (?) in the following equation?
228 B 5 C 89 D 328 A 4 = ? *SSC CPO 2024*
(a) 1774 (b) 1174
(c) 1147 (d) 1474

11. If '<' means '–', '!' means '×', '>' means '+' and '$' means '÷', then what is the value of the following expression?
205 > 210 $ 15 ! 2 < 19 *SSC CGL (Tier-I) 2023*
(a) 242 (b) 238
(c) 214 (d) 226

12. If '+' means '–', '–' means '÷', '×' means '+' and '÷' means '×', what will be the value of the following expression?
$16\times9+5\div4-2=?$ *SSC CPO 2024*
(a) 20 (b) 15
(c) 40 (d) 35

13. What will come in the place of (?) in the following equation, if '+' and '–' are interchanged and also '×' and '÷' are interchanged?
$11\div12-78\times6+54=?$ *SSC CPO 2024*
(a) 104 (b) 91
(c) 86 (d) 99

14. If A represents '+', B represents '×' C represents '–' and D represents '÷', then what will be the value of the following equation?
(45D9) B5A8B (7A3C6) C (28D(4D4))
CUET UG 2022
(a) 38 (b) 82 (c) 35 (d) 29

15. If M represents 'Addition', N represents 'Multiplication', O represents 'Subtraction' and P represents 'Divide', then what will be the value of the following equation?
16M3O5N4P2 = ? *DSSSB 2024*
(a) 11 (b) 13 (c) 7 (d) 9

16. If 'A' stands for '+', B' stands for '–', 'C' stands for '×' and 'D' stands for '÷', what will come in place of the question mark (?) in the following equation?
69 D 3 A 4 C 7 B 10 = ? *SSC CPO 2024*
(a) 39 (b) 41 (c) 37 (d) 35

17. If 'A' stands for '+', 'B' stands for '–', 'C' stands for '×' and 'D' stands for '÷', what will come in place of the question mark (?) in the following equation?
6 C 7 C 8 B 71 A 11 B 32 C 2 = ? *SSC CPO 2024*
(a) 198 (b) 228
(c) 212 (d) 192

18. If 'I' stands for '×', 'J' stands for '+', 'K' stands for '÷' and 'L' stands for '–', what will come in place of the question mark (?) in the following equation?
17 I (11 L 8 J 4) L 148 K 4 J 22 = ? *SSC CPO 2024*
(a) 114 (b) 128
(c) 104 (d) 98

19. If '÷' means '+', '−' means '÷', '×' means '−' and '+' means '×', then what will be the value of $\frac{24-8\div6+4\times7}{8+3\times19}=?$ *SSC Steno 2019*

(a) 7 (b) 4 (c) 1 (d) 5

20. If 'I' represents '+', 'J' represents '×', 'K' represents '÷' and 'L' represents '−', then what will come in place of the question mark (?) is the following equation?

38 I (3 J 4) L (16 K 2) I 11 = ? *RRB ALP (CBT-I) 2024*

(a) 61 (b) 34 (c) 53 (d) 47

21. If 'W' stands '+', 'X' stands '−' 'Y' stands '×' and 'Z' stands '÷', then 12Y4W18X40Z4 = ? *CISF ASI 2023*

(a) 54 (b) 52 (c) 56 (d) 50

22. If '−' stands divide, '+' stands multiplication, '÷' stands subtraction and '×' stands addition, then

$18\times36-6\div2+3=?$ *UP Police Constable 2024*

(a) 20 (b) 18 (c) 22 (d) 24

23. If A represents '+', B represents '×', C represents '−' and D represents '÷' then what will be the value of 96D3B8C25A14 = ? *CISF 2023*

(a) 217 (b) 245 (c) 234 (d) 254

24. If '+' means '−', '−' means '×', '×' means '÷' and '÷' means '+', then what will come in place of the question mark (?) in the following equation?

$114\div85\times5-4+33=?$ *SSC JE 2023*

(a) 149 (b) 161 (c) 158 (d) 136

25. What will come in the place of the question mark (?) in the following equation, if '+' and '−' are interchanged and '×' and '÷' are interchanged?

$87\div3+35-88\times11=?$ *SSC (10+2) 2024*

(a) 231 (b) 233 (c) 234 (d) 232

26. What will come in the place of the question mark (?) in the following equation if '+' and '−' are interchanged and '×' and '÷' are interchanged?

$161\div4+75\times5-4=?$ *SSC CGL (Tier-II) 2023*

(a) 533 (b) 633 (c) 643 (d) 543

27. What will come in the place of the question mark (?) in the following equation, if '+' and '−' are interchanged and '×' and '÷' are interchanged?

$125\div5+19-190\times19=?$ *SSC (10+2) 2024*

(a) 606 (b) 636 (c) 616 (d) 626

28. If 'A' stands for '÷', 'B' stands for '×', 'C' stands for '+' and 'D' stands for '−', what will be come in place of the question mark (?) in the following equation?

55 B 5 D 13 B 2 C 14 A 7 D 15 B 5 C 102 A 2 C 15 = ? *SSC CGL (Tier-II) 2025*

(a) 291 (b) 203
(c) 177 (d) 242

29. What will come in the place of the question mark (?) in the following equation, if '+' and '÷' are interchanged and '−' and '×' are interchanged?

$28\div90+6-5\times17=?$ *SSC (10+2) 2024*

(a) 84 (b) 82 (c) 80 (d) 86

30. What will come in the place of the question mark (?) in the following equation, if '+' and '−' are interchanged and '×' and '÷' are interchanged?

$24\div10+68\times2-16=?$ *SSC (10+2) 2024*

(a) 242 (b) 222 (c) 252 (d) 232

31. If '+' means '−', '−' means '×', '×' means '÷' and '÷' means '+', what will come in place of '?' in the following equation?

$62\div12\times3-8+5=?$ *SSC Steno 2023*

(a) 89 (b) 94 (c) 87 (d) 99

32. If 'A' stands for '+', 'B' stands for '−', 'C' stands for '÷' and 'D' stands for '×', what will come in place of the question mark '?' in the following equation?

18C6D18A6B18 = ? *RRB Technician Grade III 2024*

(a) 62 (b) 7 (c) 42 (d) 67

33. What will come in the place of the question mark (?) in the following equation, if '+' and '−' are interchanged and '×' and '÷' are interchanged?

$98\div7+288\times2-144\times3-152\div2+120=?$ *SSC CGL (Tier-II) 2025*

(a) 774 (b) 671 (c) 632 (d) 743

34. If '+' means '−', '−' means '×', '×' means '÷', '÷' means '+', then what will come in place of the question mark (?) in the following equation?

$62-2\div7+14\times7=?$ *RRB ALP 2024*

(a) 129 (b) 133 (c) 143 (d) 131

35. If '<' means '−', '!' means '×', '>' means '+' and '$' means '÷', then what is the value of the following expression?

183 > 39 $ 13 ! 6 < 26 *SSC CGL (Tier-I) 2023*

(a) 175 (b) 160 (c) 193 (d) 181

36. If P = 3, Q = 6, R = 77, S = 11 and T = 8, then which of the following numbers will replace the question mark (?).

$P\times R\div S+T-Q=?$ *UP Police Head Operator 2024*

(a) 41 (b) 23 (c) 35 (d) 53

Based on Balancing the Equation

Directions (Q. Nos. 37-47) *Select the correct combination of mathematical signs that can sequentially replace the * signs and balance the equation.*

37. 10*2*1*8*11*8 *SSC CPO 2024*

(a) ÷, −, ×, +, = (b) +, −, −, +, =
(c) +, −, ×, ÷, = (d) ÷, −, ×, −, =

38. 150*3*10*2*7 = 46 *SSC CGL (Tier-I) 2023*

(a) +, −, ÷, ×, = (b) ÷, +, −, ×, =
(c) ×, +, ÷, −, = (d) −, ×, +, ÷, =

39. 6 * 2 * 0 * 8 = 20 *SSC CPO 2024*

(a) −, ×, + (b) +, ×, +
(c) +, +, × (d) ×, +, +

40. (37 * 13) * 6 * 3 * 7 *Rajasthan Police Constable 2022*
(a) ÷ + × = (b) − ÷ + =
(c) + ÷ × = (d) × + ÷ =

41. 24 * 4 * 16 * 4 * 15 = 85 *SSC CPO 2020*
(a) ÷, +, ×, − (b) ÷, −, +, ×
(c) ×, +, ÷, − (d) −, ÷, +, ×

42. (18 * 3) * 7 * 15 * 5 = 0 *UP AO 2024*
(a) +, −, ×, − (b) +, +, ×, ÷
(c) +, ×, −, ÷ (d) +, ÷, −, ÷

43. 40 * 15 * 3 * 72 * 9 * 77 *SSC (10+2) 2021*
(a) +, ÷, −, ×, = (b) ×, ÷, +, −, =
(c) +, ×, −, ÷, = (d) +, ×, ÷, −, =

44. 242 * 11 * 76 * 34 * 2 * 32 *DP Constable 2023*
(a) ÷, −, +, ×, = (b) ÷, +, −, =, ×
(c) ÷, +, −, ×, = (d) +, ÷, −, =, ×

45. 256 * 4 * 9 * 3 * 14 = 51 *SSC CGL (Tier-I) 2023*
(a) ×, +, −, ÷ (b) ×, ÷, +, −
(c) ÷, ×, −, + (d) ÷, −, ×, +

46. 12 * 6 * 3 * 2 * 8 * 4 *DP Constable 2023*
(a) +, ×, −, ÷, = (b) +, −, ×, +, =
(c) +, −, ×, ÷, = (d) +, ×, −, =, ÷

47. ((100 * 2) * 2) * 10 = 59 *RRB Group D 2018*
(a) −, ÷, + (b) −, ×, ÷ (c) +, ×, × (d) +, ÷, ÷

Based on Interchanging the Signs and Numbers

Directions (Q. Nos. 48-59) *Which two signs/numbers should be interchanged to make the equation given below correct?*

48. $588 \div 28 \times 32 + 72 - 160 = 760$ *SSC CGL (Tier-I) 2023*
(a) + and × (b) ÷ and − (c) − and + (d) ÷ and +

49. $10 \div 63 \times 7 + 90 - 80 = 100$ *SSC CPO 2024*
(a) × and ÷ (b) − and ÷
(c) × and − (d) + and −

50. $8 - 2 \times 49 \div 7 + 2 = 11$ *DP Constable 2023*
(a) + and × (b) − and + (c) − and × (d) ÷ and −

51. $15 \times 3 \div 15 - (45 \times 3) - 10 + (13 \div 2) = 76$ *SSC CPO 2023*
(a) ÷ and + (b) ÷ and × (c) × and ÷ (d) × and −

52. $20 \div 6 + 10 - 5 \times 2 = 2$ *CUET UG 2023*
(a) 10 and 20 (b) 5 and 6
(c) 5 and 10 (d) 6 and 10

53. $22 - 16 \div (3 \times 4) + 6 = 8$ *SSC Steno 2021*
(a) − and + (b) − and × (c) ÷ and × (d) ÷ and +

54. $4 \div 8 + 5 - 6 \times 2 = 34$ *RRB NTPC (CBT-II) 2022*
(a) + and − (b) × and +
(c) ÷ and × (d) ÷ and +

55. $294 + 14 \times 4 \div 16 - 67 = 33$ *SSC CGL (Tier-I) 2023*
(a) + and ÷ (b) + and −
(c) × and ÷ (d) − and ÷

56. $15 \div 3 + 2 \times 10 - 6 = 14$ *RRB ALP 2018*
(a) + and × (b) + and −
(c) ÷ and − (d) ÷ and +

57. $24 - 8 \div 4 + 5 \times 3 = 14$ *Rajasthan Police Constable 2022*
(a) ÷ and × (b) × and −
(c) + and ÷ (d) ÷ and −

58. $16 - 18 \times 216 \div 432 + 40 = 20$ *CUET UG 2022*
(a) × and + (b) ÷ and −
(c) × and ÷ (d) + and −

59. $28 + 12 - 21 \div 7 \times 4 = 60$ *SSC GD 2024*
(a) × and − (b) × and ÷
(c) + and ÷ (d) × and +

60. Which two signs should be interchanged to make the given equation correct?
$3 \times 12 - 6 \div 2 + 12 = 16$ *SSC CGL (Tier-I) 2023*
(a) ÷ and + (b) × and ÷
(c) − and ÷ (d) − and +

61. Which two numbers should be interchanged to make the given equation correct?
$15 \times 5 - 75 + (300 \div 6) + 3 \times 19 = 115$
(**Note** Numbers must be interchanged and not the constituent digits e.g., if 2 and 3 are to be interchanged in the equation $43 \times 3 + 4 \div 2$, then interchanged equation is $(43 \times 2 + 4 \div 3)$)
SSC (10+2) 2024
(a) 15 and 6 (b) 15 and 19
(c) 6 and 5 (d) 6 and 3

62. What will be the value of equations (I) and (II) respectively after interchanging the given two signs?
× and −
I. $7 \times 8 - 6 + 15 \div 3$
II. $8 - 9 \times 2 + 45 \div 5$ *SSC (GD) Constable 2024*
(a) −36 and 79 (b) −8 and 10
(c) 56 and 18 (d) 84 and 42

63. By interchanging the given two signs which of the following equation will be correct?
× and − *SSC (10+2) 2023*
I. $11 + 6 \times 8 - 8 \div 2 = 15$
II. $15 - 4 \times 3 + 6 \div 1 = 63$
(a) Only II (b) Both I and II
(c) Only I (d) Neither I nor II

64. Which two signs and numbers need to be interchanged to make the following equation correct?
$24 - (9 \div 12) + (84 \times 4) + 28 = 23$ *SSC CGL (Tier-I) 2023*
(a) 24 and 28, − and ÷ (b) 24 and 28, × and ÷
(c) 9 and 4, ÷ and × (d) 12 and 4, ÷ and ×

Based on Identifying Balanced Equation After Interchanging the Signs/Numbers

65. If 'A' stands for '÷', 'B' stands for '×', 'C' stands for '+' and 'D' stands for '−', then the resultant of which of the following will be 218? *SSC (10+2) 2024*
(a) 32 A 8 D 160 B 2 C 42
(b) 32 B 8 D 160 C 2 A 42
(c) 32 B 8 D 160 A 2 C 42
(d) 32 C 8 D 160 A 2 B 42

66. By interchanging the given two numbers which of the following equation will be correct?
4 and 3 **SSC (10+2) 2023**
(a) $3 \times 4 \div 2 + 7 = 17$ (b) $7 \times 4 + 3 \div 1 = 30$
(c) $4 + 3 \times 7 - 2 = 29$ (d) $4 \times 3 + 7 - 5 = 16$

67. By interchanging the given two numbers which of the following equation will be correct?
2 and 8 **SSC CGL (Tier-I) 2022**
(a) $8 \div 1 + 4 \times 2 - 3 = 18$
(b) $7 \times 2 + 6 \div 3 - 8 = 60$
(c) $2 \times 4 - 8 + 6 \div 3 = 33$
(d) $8 \times 4 + 6 - 2 \div 1 = 6$

68. On interchanging the given two signs + and – and two numbers 17 and 216 (not digits), which of the following equations will be correct?
I. $10 \times 216 + 17 \div 6 - 13 = 146$
II. $7 \times 216 + 41 - 17 \div 36 = 81$ **SSC MTS 2022**
(a) Only I (b) Only II
(c) Neither I nor II (d) Both I and II

69. By interchanging the given two numbers which of the following equation will be not correct?
9 and 6 **SSC CGL (Tier-I) 2022**
(a) $7 + 6 \times 4 \div 9 - 8 = 5$
(b) $6 \times 8 - 9 \div 3 + 5 = 75$
(c) $9 \times 7 + 4 \div 1 - 6 = 38$
(d) $7 \times 6 \div 3 + 9 - 8 = 19$

70. If '+' means '÷', '×' means '+', '–' means '×' and '÷' means '–', then which of the following equations will be correct? **SSC Steno 2016**
(a) $33 - 4 \div 5 \times 6 + 2 = 130$
(b) $33 \times 4 - 5 + 6 \div 2 = 26$
(c) $33 \div 4 \times 5 + 6 - 2 = 30$
(d) $33 - 4 + 5 \div 6 \times 2 = 24$

71. If '×' sign is replaced to '÷' sign and number '3' is replaced to '2', then which of the equation given below will be correct? **SSC CPO 2018**
(a) $3 \div 2 \times 2 + 2 - 3 = 1$ (b) $3 \times 2 \div 2 + 2 - 3 = 2$
(c) $2 \times 3 - 2 + 2 \div 3 = 0$ (d) $2 \times 3 \div 2 + 2 - 3 = 0$

72. If '–' and '÷' interchanged and '+' and '×' interchanged, then which of the equation given below will be correct?
(a) $32 \times 21 + 9 \div 184 - 8 = 198$
(b) $32 + 21 - 9 \times 184 \div 8 = 198$
(c) $32 \div 21 + 9 - 184 \times 8 = 198$
(d) $32 + 21 \times 9 - 184 \div 8 = 198$

Based on Special Case

73. If 8#2@5 = 21 and 4#6@2 = 26, then what will be 3#7@9 ? **RRB JE 2019**
(a) 40 (b) 30 (c) 47 (d) 52

74. If 9$12#4 = 27 and 7$18#9 = 14, then 6$15#3 = ? **UP Police Head Operator 2024**
(a) 45 (b) 25 (c) 30 (d) 60

75. If $a \sim b = a^2 + b$, $a \wedge b = b^2 + a$, then the value of (3 ~ 6)^2. **UP Police Constable 2024**
(a) 23 (b) 18 (c) 21 (d) 19

76. If 4@9#3= 1 and 4@8#4=2, then 5@6#2 = ? **UP AO 2024**
(a) 5 (b) 2 (c) 6 (d) 9

77. Which of the following options will best complete the relationship given below?
19(413)22 11(431)32 42(???)12 **RRB JE 2019**
(a) 154 (b) 514 (c) 145 (d) 541

78. Some equations given below are solved on the basis of a certain system. On the same basis find out the correct answer from among the four options for the unsolved equation.
45 – 25 = 2, 78 – 45 = 3, 61 – 40 = ? **UPSSSC 2018**
(a) 1 (b) 5 (c) 2 (d) 6

79. If 4*2@3=6, 18*6@4=12, then what will be the value of 24*3@8=? **SSC (10+2) 2023**
(a) 21 (b) 27 (c) 72 (d) 56

80. According to the code, the digits 0, 1, 2, 3, 4 are represented by A, B, C, D, E, respectively. Find the value of [(B + E) – (D + A)] **UP Police Constable 2024**
(a) –2 (b) 1 (c) 3 (d) 2

Right Key

1. (d)	2. (a)	3. (d)	4. (d)	5. (c)	6. (a)	7. (d)	8. (c)	9. (b)	10. (c)
11. (c)	12. (b)	13. (b)	14. (d)	15. (d)	16. (b)	17. (c)	18. (c)	19. (b)	20. (c)
21. (c)	22. (b)	23. (b)	24. (a)	25. (c)	26. (b)	27. (c)	28. (d)	29. (d)	30. (b)
31. (a)	32. (c)	33. (a)	34. (a)	35. (a)	36. (b)	37. (a)	38. (b)	39. (d)	40. (b)
41. (c)	42. (d)	43. (c)	44. (b)	45. (d)	46. (b)	47. (a)	48. (c)	49. (a)	50. (c)
51. (b)	52. (b)	53. (d)	54. (c)	55. (a)	56. (a)	57. (d)	58. (c)	59. (a)	60. (c)
61. (b)	62. (a)	63. (a)	64. (d)	65. (c)	66. (c)	67. (d)	68. (c)	69. (c)	70. (a)
71. (b)	72. (a)	73. (b)	74. (c)	75. (d)	76. (b)	77. (d)	78. (c)	79. (d)	80. (d)

Solutions

1. *(d)* Given equation,

$[\{(14 \times 6) - (4 \div 3)\} + (6 - 4)] \div 3$

After substituting the signs, we get

$[\{(14 - 6) + (4 \times 3)\} \div (6 + 4)] \times 3$

$= [\{8 + 12\} \div 10] \times 3$

$= [20 \div 10] \times 3$

$= 2 \times 3 = 6$

2. *(a)* Given expression,

$95 - 19 \times 4 + 6 \div 16$

After interchanging the signs, we get

$95 \div 19 + 4 \times 6 - 16$

$= 5 + 24 - 16$

$= 29 - 16 = 13$

3. *(d)* Given expression,

$7 + 4 \div 18 - 3 \times 2 = ?$

After interchanging the signs, we get

$7 \times 4 - 18 \div 3 + 2$

$= 28 - 6 + 2$

$= 30 - 6 = 24$

4. *(d)* Given expression,

(40 J 32 K 4) I 5 L 155 J 7 I 9

After interchanging the signs,

$(40 + 32 \div 4) \times 5 - 155 + 7 \times 9$

$= 48 \times 5 - 155 + 63$

$= 240 - 155 + 63$

$= 148$

5. *(c)* Given equation,

$18 \times 5 \div 5 + 6$

After substituting the signs, we get

$18 - 5 + 5 \times 6$

$= 18 - 5 + 30$

$= 48 - 5 = 43$

6. *(a)* Given expression,

96 A 4 D 5 B 7 C 20

After substituting the signs,

$96 \div 4 - 5 \times 7 + 20$

$= 24 - 35 + 20$

$= 44 - 35 = 9$

7. *(d)* Given expression,

$99 \times 33 - 70 \div 90 + 100$

After interchanging the signs,

$99 \div 33 \times 70 + 90 - 100$

$= 210 + 90 - 100$

$= 200$

8. *(c)* Given expression,

$16 \div 8 \times 4 - 2 + 1$

After substituting the signs, we get

$16 - 8 \div 4 + 2 \times 1$

$= 16 - 2 + 2 = 16$

9. *(b)* Given expression,

$4 - 5 \div 9 + 6 \times 2$

After interchanging '+' and '–', '×' and '÷', we get

$4 + 5 \times 9 - 6 \div 2$

$= 4 + 45 - 3 = 49 - 3 = 46$

10. *(c)* Given expression,

228 B 5 C 89 D 328 A 4

After interchanging the signs,

$228 \times 5 + 89 - 328 \div 4$

$= 1140 + 89 - 82$

$= 1229 - 82 = 1147$

11. *(c)* Given expression,

205 > 210 \$ 15 ! 2 < 19

On substituting the signs, we get

$205 + 210 \div 15 \times 2 - 19$

[By using BODMAS rule]

$= 205 + 28 - 19 = 214$

12. *(b)* Given expression,

$16 \times 9 + 5 \div 4 - 2$

After interchanging the signs,

$16 + 9 - 5 \times 4 \div 2$

$= 16 + 9 - 10 = 15$

13. *(b)* Given expression,

$11 \div 12 - 78 \times 6 + 54$

After interchanging the signs,

$11 \times 12 + 78 \div 6 - 54$

$= 132 + 13 - 54$

$= 145 - 54 = 91$

14. *(d)* Given expression, (45 D 9) B 5 A 8 B (7 A 3 C 6) C (28 D (4 D 4))

On substituting the signs, we get

$= (45 \div 9) \times 5 + 8 \times (7 + 3 - 6) - (28 \div (4 \div 4))$

$= 5 \times 5 + 8 \times 4 - (28 \div 1)$

$= 25 + 32 - 28$

$= 57 - 28 = 29$

15. *(d)* Given equation,

16 M 3 O 5 N 4 P 2 = ?

On replacing letter with signs, we get

$16 + 3 - 5 \times 4 \div 2 = ?$

$\Rightarrow \quad 19 - 5 \times 2 = ?$

$\Rightarrow \quad ? = 19 - 10 = 9$

16. *(b)* Given expression,

69 D 3 A 4 C 7 B 10

After interchanging the signs,

$69 \div 3 + 4 \times 7 - 10$

$= 23 + 28 - 10$

$= 51 - 10 = 41$

17. *(c)* Given expression,

6 C 7 C 8 B 71 A 1 1 B 32 C 2

After interchanging the signs,

$6 \times 7 \times 8 - 71 + 11 - 32 \times 2$

$= 336 - 71 + 11 - 64$

$= 347 - 135 = 212$

18. *(c)* Given expression,

17 I (11 L 8 J 4) L 14 8 K 4 J 22 = ?

After interchanging the signs,

$17 \times (11 - 8 + 4) - 148 \div 4 + 22$

$= 17 \times 7 - 37 + 22$

$= 119 - 37 + 22 = 104$

19. *(b)* Given expression,

$\dfrac{24 - 8 \div 6 + 4 \times 7}{8 + 3 \times 19}$

After substituting the sign,

$\dfrac{24 \div 8 + 6 \times 4 - 7}{8 \times 3 - 19}$

$= \dfrac{3 + 24 - 7}{24 - 19} = \dfrac{20}{5} = 4$

20. *(c)* Given expression,

38 I (3 J 4) L (16 K 2) I 11 = ?

On replacing letter with signs, we get

$38 + (3 \times 4) - (16 \div 2) + 11$

$= 38 + 12 - 8 + 11$

$= 61 - 8 = 53$

21. *(c)* Given equation,

12 Y 4 W 18 X 40 Z 4 = ?

On replacing letter with signs, we get

$12 \times 4 + 18 - 40 \div 4$

$= 12 \times 4 + 18 - 10$

$= 48 + 18 - 10$

$= 66 - 10 = 56$

22. *(b)* Given equation,

$18 \times 36 - 6 \div 2 + 3 = ?$

After changing the signs,

$18 + 36 \div 6 - 2 \times 3$

$= 18 + 6 - 2 \times 3$

$= 18 + 6 - 6 = 18$

23. *(b)* Given equation,

96 D 3 B 8 C 25 A 14 = ?

On replacing letter with signs, we get

$96 \div 3 \times 8 - 25 + 14$

$= 32 \times 8 - 25 + 14$

$= 256 - 25 + 14$

$= 270 - 25 = 245$

24. *(a)* Given equation,

$114 \div 85 \times 5 - 4 + 33 = ?$

After changing the signs,

$114 + 85 \div 5 \times 4 - 33$
$= 114 + 17 \times 4 - 33$
$= 114 + 68 - 33$
$= 182 - 33 = 149$

25. *(c)* Given equation,
$87 \div 3 + 35 - 88 \times 11 = ?$
After interchanging signs, we get
$? = 87 \times 3 - 35 + 88 \div 11$
$= 261 - 35 + 8$
$= 269 - 35 = 234$

26. *(b)* Given equation,
$161 \div 4 + 75 \times 5 - 4 = ?$
After interchanging the signs, we get
$? = 161 \times 4 - 75 \div 5 + 4$
$= 161 \times 4 - 15 + 4$
$= 644 - 15 + 4$
$= 648 - 15 = 633$

27. *(c)* Given equation,
$125 \div 5 + 19 - 190 \times 19 = ?$
After interchanging signs, we get
$125 \times 5 - 19 + 190 \div 19$
$= 625 - 19 + 10$
$= 635 - 19 = 616$

28. *(d)* Given expression
55 B 5 D 13 B 2 C 14 A 7 D 15 B 5 C 102 A 2 C 15 = ?
After changing letters with signs,
$55 \times 5 - 13 \times 2 + 14 \div 7 - 15 \times 5 + 102 \div 2 + 15$
$= 275 - 26 + 2 - 75 + 51 + 15$
$= 343 - 101 = \boxed{242}$

29. *(d)* Given equation,
$28 \div 90 + 6 - 5 \times 17 = ?$
After interchanging signs, we get
$28 + 90 \div 6 \times 5 - 17 = ?$
$\Rightarrow 28 + 15 \times 5 - 17 = ?$
$\Rightarrow 28 + 75 - 17 = ?$
$\Rightarrow 103 - 17 = ?$
$\therefore ? = 86$

30. *(b)* Given equation,
$24 \div 10 + 68 \times 2 - 16 = ?$
After interchanging signs, we get
$24 \times 10 - 68 \div 2 + 16 = ?$
$\Rightarrow 240 - 34 + 16 = ?$
$\Rightarrow 256 - 34 = ?$
$\therefore ? = 222$

31. *(a)* Given equation,
$62 \div 12 \times 3 - 8 + 5 = ?$
After interchanging the signs, we get
$62 + 12 \div 3 \times 8 - 5 = ?$
$= 62 + 4 \times 8 - 5$
$= 62 + 32 - 5$
$\therefore ? = 94 - 5 = 89$

32 *(c)* Given expression,
18 C 6 D 18 A 6 B 18
On interchanging the letters with signs,
$18 \div 6 \times 18 + 6 - 18$
$= 3 \times 18 + 6 - 18$
$= 54 + 6 - 18$
$= 60 - 18 = \boxed{42}$

33. *(a)* Given expression,
$98 \div 7 + 288 \times 2 - 144 \times 3 - 152 \div 2 + 120 = ?$
On interchanging the signs, we get
$98 \times 7 - 288 \div 2 + 144 \div 3 + 152 \times 2 - 120$
$= 686 - 144 + 48 + 304 - 120$
$= 1038 - 264 = \boxed{774}$

34. *(a)* Given expression,
$62 - 2 \div 7 + 14 \times 7 = ?$
On interchanging the signs, we get
$62 \times 2 + 7 - 14 \div 7$
$= 62 \times 2 + 7 - 2$
$= 124 + 7 - 2$
$= 131 - 2 = \boxed{129}$

35. *(a)* Given expression,
183 > 39 $ 13 ! 6 < 26
After substituting the signs, we get
$183 + 39 \div 13 \times 6 - 26$
$= 183 + 3 \times 6 - 26$
$= 183 + 18 - 26$
$= 201 - 26 = 175$

36. *(b)* Given,
$P = 3, Q = 6, R = 77, S = 11, T = 8$
Given equation, $P \times R \div S + T - Q = ?$
On changing the letters,
$3 \times 77 \div 11 + 8 - 6$
$= 3 \times 7 + 8 - 6$
$= 21 + 8 - 6$
$= 29 - 6 = 23$

37. *(a)* Given expression, 10 * 2 * 1 * 8 * 11 * 8
From option (a), on placing the signs, we get
$10 \div 2 - 1 \times 8 + 11 = 8$
$\Rightarrow 5 - 1 \times 8 + 11 = 8$
$\Rightarrow 5 + 11 - 8 = 8$
$\Rightarrow 16 - 8 = 8$
$8 = 8$

38. *(b)* Given equation,
150 * 3 * 10 * 2 * 7 = 46
From option (b), on placing the signs, we get
$150 \div 3 + 10 - 2 \times 7 = 46$
$\Rightarrow 50 + 10 - 2 \times 7 = 46$
$\Rightarrow 50 + 10 - 14 = 46$
$\Rightarrow 60 - 14 = 46$
$\Rightarrow 46 = 46$

TOP TIPS To save time, candidates should try to, do small calculations in mind.

39. *(d)* Given equation,
6 * 2 * 0 * 8 = 20
From option (d), on placing the signs, we get
$6 \times 2 + 0 + 8 = 20$
$\Rightarrow 12 + 8 = 20$
$\Rightarrow 20 = 20$

40. *(b)* Given expression,
(37 * 13) * 6 * 3 * 7
From option (b), on placing signs, we get
$(37 - 13) \div 6 + 3 = 7$
$\Rightarrow 24 \div 6 + 3 = 7$
$\Rightarrow 4 + 3 = 7$
$\Rightarrow 7 = 7$

41. *(c)* Given equation,
24 * 4 * 16 * 4 * 15 = 85
From option (c), on placing signs, we get
$24 \times 4 + 16 \div 4 - 15 = 85$
$\Rightarrow 24 \times 4 + 4 - 15 = 85$
$\Rightarrow 96 + 4 - 15 = 85$
$\Rightarrow 100 - 15 = 85$
$\Rightarrow 85 = 85$

42. *(d)* Given equation,
(18 * 3) * 7 * 15 * 5 = 0
From option (d), on placing signs, we get
$(18 + 3) \div 7 - 15 \div 5 = 0$
$\Rightarrow 21 \div 7 - 15 \div 5 = 0$
$\Rightarrow 3 - 3 = 0$
$\Rightarrow 0 = 0$

43. *(c)* Given expression,
40 * 15 * 3 * 72 * 9 * 77
From option (c), on placing signs, we get
$40 + 15 \times 3 - 72 \div 9 = 77$
$\Rightarrow 40 + 45 - 8 = 77$
$\Rightarrow 85 - 8 = 77$
$\Rightarrow 77 = 77$

44. *(b)* Given expression,
242 * 11 * 76 * 34 * 2 * 32
From option (b), on placing signs, we get
$242 \div 11 + 76 - 34 = 2 \times 32$
$\Rightarrow 22 + 76 - 34 = 64$
$\Rightarrow 98 - 34 = 64$
$\Rightarrow 64 = 64$

45. *(d)* Given expression,
$256 * 4 * 9 * 3 * 14 = 51$
From option (d), on placing signs, we get
$256 \div 4 - 9 \times 3 + 14 = 51$
$\Rightarrow 64 - 27 + 14 = 51$
$\Rightarrow 78 - 27 = 51$
$\Rightarrow 51 = 51$

46. *(b)* Given expression,
$12 * 6 * 3 * 2 * 8 * 4$
From option (b), on placing signs, we get
$12 \div 6 - 3 \times 2 + 8 = 4$
$\Rightarrow 2 - 3 \times 2 + 8 = 4$
$\Rightarrow 2 - 6 + 8 = 4$
$\Rightarrow 10 - 6 = 4$
$\Rightarrow 4 = 4$

47. *(a)* Given equation,
$((100 * 2) * 2) * 10 = 59$
From option (a), on placing signs, we get
$((100 - 2) \div 2) + 10 = 59$
$\Rightarrow (98 \div 2) + 10 = 59$
$\Rightarrow 49 + 10 = 59$
$\Rightarrow 59 = 59$

48. *(c)* Given equation,
$588 \div 28 \times 32 + 72 - 160 = 760$
From option (c), interchanging – and +,
$588 \div 28 \times 32 - 72 + 160 = 760$
$\Rightarrow \left(\frac{588}{28} \times 32\right) - 72 + 160 = 760$
$\Rightarrow 672 - 72 + 160 = 760$
$\Rightarrow 832 - 72 = 760$
$\Rightarrow 760 = 760$

49. *(a)* Given equation,
$10 \div 63 \times 7 + 90 - 80 = 100$
From option (a), interchanging × and ÷,
$10 \times 63 \div 7 + 90 - 80$
$= 10 \times 9 + 90 - 80$
$= 90 + 90 - 80$
$= 180 - 80 = 100$

50. *(c)* Given equation,
$8 - 2 \times 49 \div 7 + 2 = 11$
From option (c), interchanging – and ×,
$8 \times 2 - 49 \div 7 + 2 = 11$
$\Rightarrow 8 \times 2 - 7 + 2 = 11$
$\Rightarrow 16 - 7 + 2 = 11$
$\Rightarrow 18 - 7 = 11$
$\Rightarrow 11 = 11$

51. *(b)* Given equation,
$15 \times 3 \div 15 - (45 \times 3) - 10 + (13 \div 2) = 76$
From option (b), interchanging the signs ÷ and ×, we get
$15 \div 3 \times 15 - (45 \div 3) - 10 + (13 \times 2) = 76$
$\Rightarrow 75 - 15 - 10 + 26 = 76$
$\Rightarrow 101 - 25 = 76$
$\Rightarrow 76 = 76$

52. *(b)* Given equation,
$20 \div 6 + 10 - 5 \times 2 = 2$
From option (b), interchanging 5 and 6, we get
$20 \div 5 + 10 - 6 \times 2 = 2$
$\Rightarrow 4 + 10 - 6 \times 2 = 2$
$\Rightarrow 4 + 10 - 12 = 2$
$\Rightarrow 14 - 12 = 2$
$\Rightarrow 2 = 2$

53. *(d)* Given equation,
$22 - 16 \div (3 \times 4) + 6 = 8$
From option (d), interchanging the signs ÷ and +, we get
$22 - 16 + (3 \times 4) \div 6 = 8$
$\Rightarrow 22 - 16 + 12 \div 6 = 8$
$\Rightarrow 22 - 16 + 2 = 8$
$\therefore 8 = 8$

54. *(c)* Given equation,
$4 \div 8 + 5 - 6 \times 2 = 34$
From option (c), interchanging the signs ÷ and ×, we get
$4 \times 8 + 5 - 6 \div 2 = 34$
$\Rightarrow 32 + 5 - 3 = 34$
$\Rightarrow 37 - 3 = 34$
$\therefore 34 = 34$

55. *(a)* Given expression,
$294 + 14 \times 4 \div 16 - 67 = 33$
From option (a), interchanging the signs + and ÷, we get
$294 \div 14 \times 4 + 16 - 67 = 33$
$\Rightarrow 21 \times 4 + 16 - 67 = 33$
$\Rightarrow 84 + 16 - 67 = 33$
$\Rightarrow 100 - 67 = 33$
$\therefore 33 = 33$

56. *(a)* Given expression,
$15 \div 3 + 2 \times 10 - 6 = 14$
From option (a), interchanging the signs + and ×, we get
$15 \div 3 \times 2 + 10 - 6 = 14$
$\Rightarrow 5 \times 2 + 10 - 6 = 14$
$\Rightarrow 10 + 10 - 6 = 14$
$\Rightarrow 20 - 6 = 14$
$\Rightarrow 14 = 14$

57. *(d)* Given equation,
$24 - 8 \div 4 + 5 \times 3 = 14$
From option (d), interchanging the signs ÷ and –, we get
$24 \div 8 - 4 + 5 \times 3 = 14$
$\Rightarrow 3 - 4 + 15 = 14$
$\Rightarrow 18 - 4 = 14$
$\therefore 14 = 14$

58. *(c)* Given equation,
$16 - 18 \times 216 \div 432 + 40 = 20$
From option (c), interchanging the signs × and ÷, we get
$16 - 18 \div 216 \times 432 + 40 = 20$
$\Rightarrow 16 - 18 \times \frac{1}{216} \times 432 + 40 = 20$
$\Rightarrow 16 - 36 + 40 = 20$
$\Rightarrow 56 - 36 = 20$
$\Rightarrow 20 = 20$

59. *(a)* Given equation,
$28 + 12 - 21 \div 7 \times 4 = 60$
From, option (a), interchanging the signs × and –, we get
$28 + 12 \times 21 \div 7 - 4 = 60$
$\Rightarrow 28 + 12 \times 3 - 4 = 60$
$\Rightarrow 28 + 36 - 4 = 60$
$\Rightarrow 60 = 60$

60. *(c)* Given expression,
$3 \times 12 - 6 \div 2 + 12 = 16$
From option (c), after interchanging the signs '–' and '÷', we get
$3 \times 12 \div 6 - 2 + 12 = 16$
$\Rightarrow 6 - 2 + 12 = 16$
$\Rightarrow 16 = 16$

61. *(b)* Given expression,
$15 \times 5 - 75 + (300 \div 6) + 3 \times 19 = 115$
From option (b), after interchanging numbers 15 and 19, we get
$19 \times 5 - 75 + (300 \div 6) + 3 \times 15$
$= 95 - 75 + 50 + 45$
$= 190 - 75 = 115$

62. *(a)* From equation I,
$7 \times 8 - 6 + 15 \div 3$
After interchanging the signs,
$7 - 8 \times 6 + 15 \div 3$
$= 7 - 8 \times 6 + 5$
$= 7 - 48 + 5$
$= 12 - 48 = \boxed{-36}$
From equation II,
$8 - 9 \times 2 + 45 \div 5$
After interchanging the signs,
$8 \times 9 - 2 + 45 \div 5$
$= 8 \times 9 - 2 + 9$
$= 72 - 2 + 9$
$= 81 - 2 = \boxed{79}$

63. *(a)* Given equation,
I. $11 + 6 \times 8 - 8 \div 2 = 15$

After interchanging the signs × and –, we get

$11+6-8\times8\div2=15$

$\Rightarrow\quad 11+6-8\times\frac{8}{2}=15$

$\Rightarrow\quad 11+6-8\times4=15$

$\Rightarrow\quad 11+6-32=15$

$\Rightarrow\quad 17-32=15$

$\Rightarrow\quad -15\neq15$ (incorrect)

II. $15-4\times3+6\div1=63$

After interchanging the signs × and –, we get

$15\times4-3+6\div1=63$

$\Rightarrow\quad 15\times4-3+6=63$

$\Rightarrow\quad 60-3+6=63$

$\Rightarrow\quad 66-3=63$

$\Rightarrow\quad 63=63$ (correct)

Hence, only equation II is correct.

64. (*d*) Given expression,

$24-(9\div12)+(84\times4)+28=23$

From option (d), after replacing signs and numbers, we get

$24-(9\times4)+(84\div12)+28=23$

$\Rightarrow\quad 24-36+7+28=23$

$\Rightarrow\quad 59-36=23$

$\Rightarrow\quad 23=23$

65. (*c*) After interchanging letters with signs, we get

From option (c),

32 B 8 D 160 A 2 C 42

$=32\times8-160\div2+42$

$=256-80+42$

$=298-80=218$

66. (*c*) From option (c),

$4+3\times7-2=29$

After interchanging the numbers, we get

$3+4\times7-2=29$

$\Rightarrow\quad 3+28-2=29$

$\Rightarrow\quad 31-2=29$

$\Rightarrow\quad 29=29$

67. (*d*) By interchanging 2 and 8, in option (d),

$8\times4+6-2\div1=6$

After interchanging 2 and 8,

$2\times4+6-8\div1=6$

$\Rightarrow\quad 8+6-8=6$

$\Rightarrow\quad 6=6$

68. (*c*) I. $10\times216+17\div6-13=146$

After interchanging the numbers 17 and 216 and signs + and –, we get

$10\times17-216\div6+13=146$

$=10\times17-216\div6+13$

$=10\times17-36+13$

$=170-36+13$

$=183-36$

$=147\neq$ RHS

II. $7\times216+41-17\div36=81$

After interchanging the numbers 17 and 216 and signs + and –, we get

$7\times17-41+216\div36=81$

$=7\times17-41+216\div36$

$=7\times17-41+6$

$=119-41+6=125-41$

$=84\neq$ RHS

Hence, neither I nor II is correct.

69. (*c*) By interchanging 9 and 6, from option (c),

$9\times7+4\div1-6=38$

After interchanging

$6\times7+4\div1-9=38$

$\Rightarrow\quad 42+4-9=38$

$\Rightarrow\quad 46-9=38$

$\Rightarrow\quad 37\neq38$

70. (*a*) From option (a),

$33-4\div5\times6+2=130$

After interchanging the signs,

$33\times4-5+6\div2=130$

$\Rightarrow\quad 132-5+3=130$

$\Rightarrow\quad 135-5=130$

$\Rightarrow\quad 130=130$

71. (*b*) From option (b),

$3\times2\div2+2-3=2$

After interchanging the signs and numbers,

$2\div3\times3+3-2=3$

$\Rightarrow\quad \frac{2}{3}\times3+3-2=3$

$\Rightarrow\quad 2+3-2=3$

$\Rightarrow\quad 3=3$

72. (*a*) From option (a),

$32\times21+9\div184-8=198$

After interchanging the signs,

$32+21\times9-184\div8=198$

$\Rightarrow\quad 32+189-23=198$

$\Rightarrow\quad 221-23=198$

$\Rightarrow\quad 198=198$

73. (*b*) Here, # ⇒ × and @ ⇒ +

As, 8 # 2 @ 5 $=8\times2+5$

$=16+5=21$

and 4 # 6 @ 2 $=4\times6+2$

$=24+2=26$

Similarly, 3 # 7 @ 9 $=3\times7+9$

$=21+9=\boxed{30}$

74. (*c*) Here, \$ ⇒ × and # ⇒ ÷

As, 9 \$ 12 # 4 = 27

$\Rightarrow\ 9\times12\div4$

$\Rightarrow\quad 9\times3=27$

and 7 \$ 18 # 9 = 14

$\Rightarrow\ 7\times18\div9=7\times2=14$

Similarly, 6 \$ 15 # 3 = ?

$\Rightarrow\ 6\times15\div3=6\times5=\boxed{30}$

75. (*d*) Given,

$a\sim b=a^2+b,\ a\hat{\ }b=b^2+a$

$(3\sim6)\hat{\ }2$

According to the question,

$(3^2+6)\hat{\ }2=15\hat{\ }2$

$=2^2+15=\boxed{19}$

76. (*b*) Here, @ ⇒ – and # ⇒ ÷

As, 4 @ 9 # 3 = 1

$\Rightarrow\ 4-9\div3=4-3=1$

and 4 @ 8 # 4 = 2

$\Rightarrow\ 4-8\div4=4-2=2$

Similarly, 5 @ 6 # 2 = ?

$\Rightarrow\ 5-6\div2=5-3=\boxed{2}$

77. (*d*) As, 19(413)22 $\Rightarrow 19+22=41$

and $4-1=3\Rightarrow413$

and 11(431)32 $\Rightarrow11+32=43$

and $4-3=1\Rightarrow431$

Similarly, 42(???)12

$\Rightarrow\ 42+12=54$

and $5-4=1\Rightarrow541$

So, ??? = $\boxed{541}$

78. (*c*) As, $4\underline{5}-2\underline{5}\Rightarrow4-2=2$

(diff. of unit digits)

and $\underline{7}8-\underline{4}5\Rightarrow7-4=3$

Similarly, $\underline{6}1-\underline{4}0\Rightarrow6-4=\boxed{2}$

79. (*d*) Here, * ⇒ ÷ and @ ⇒ ×

As, $4\div2\times3=6$ and $18\div6\times4=12$

Similarly, $24\div3\times7=\boxed{56}$

80. (*d*) Given, A = 0, B = 1,

C = 2, D = 3, E = 4

$\therefore\ [(B+E)-(D+A)]$

$=(1+4)-(3+0)$

$=5-3=\boxed{2}$

CHAPTER

16 Mathematical Reasoning

Mathematical Reasoning

Questions based on mathematical reasoning are based on general mathematical rules and ages. Their aim is to develop general intellectual and logical ability. To solve these questions, mathematical ability as well as logical ability and intellectual and practical knowledge are required.

Based on Arithmetic

This type of questions are based on arithmetical concepts such as ratio-proportion, percentage, profit-loss and pipes and tanks etc.

e.g. The ratio of the sum and difference of two numbers is 7:6. Find the ratio of these two numbers.

(a) 12:1 (b) 11:2
(c) 3:4 (d) 13:1

Sol. (d) Let the numbers be x and y.
According to the question,

$$\frac{x+y}{x-y}=\frac{7}{6}$$

$\Rightarrow$ $6x + 6y = 7x - 7y$

$\Rightarrow$ $x = 13y \Rightarrow \frac{x}{y}=\frac{13}{1}=13:1$

Based on Linear Equations

In this type of questions, the given information is solved by representing it in a linear equation.

e.g. In a group of 1600 persons, there are some captains and soldiers. They are all travelling by bus. There is one captain for 15 soldiers. How many captains are there in the group?

(a) 95 (b) 75 (c) 100 (d) 150

Sol. (c) Let the number of captains = x
Then, number of soldiers = $15x$
According to the question, $x + 15x = 1600$

$\Rightarrow$ $16x = 1600 \Rightarrow x=\frac{1600}{16}=100$

$\therefore$ Number of captains = 100

Based on Venn Diagram

While solving such questions, first make a Venn diagram of the statements and then solve the questions with the help of Venn diagram.

e.g. In a class of 100 students, 36 have taken music, 52 have taken arts and 4 have taken both arts and music. How many students in the class have taken neither music nor arts?

(a) 12 (b) 16
(c) 32 (d) 48

Sol. (b) Total number of students = 100

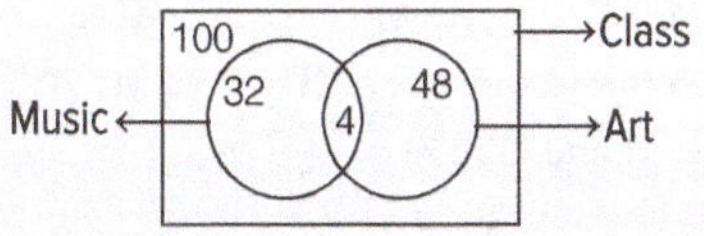

Number of students taking neither music nor art in the class

$= 100 - (32 + 48 + 4) = 100 - 84 = 16$

Based on Age

In this type of questions, the candidate is asked to find out the current age of a particular person or his age some years ago or after some years with the help of given information.

Note If the age of a person at present is x yr, then his age after n yr will be $(x + n)$ yr and his age n yr ago will be $(x-n)$ yr.

e.g. The sum of the ages of four people is 80 yr. What was their average age 5 yr ago?

(a) 10 yr (b) 25 yr
(c) 15 yr (d) 20 yr

Sol. (c) $\because$ Sum of ages of four persons = 80 yr
Sum of ages 5 yr ago $= 80 - 5 \times 4$
$= 80 - 20 = 60$

$\therefore$ Their average age 5 yr ago

$$=\frac{60}{4}=15 \text{ yr}$$

Score Booster

A candidate should familiarize with common formulas (e.g. sum of n terms in an arithmetic progression, simple interest, profit and loss, algebric equation etc.) Learn shortcuts like vedic math tricks, approximation and mental math.

Exam Approach Examples

Based on Arithmetic

Example 1 **The ratio of the sum and difference of two numbers is 6: 5. Find the ratio of these two numbers.** ***CUET (UG) 2022***

(a) 7 : 5 (b) 2 : 3 (c) 11 : 1 (d) 3 : 2

Sol. (*c*) Let the numbers be x and y.

According to the question, $\frac{x+y}{x-y} = \frac{6}{5}$

$\Rightarrow 5x + 5y = 6x - 6y \Rightarrow x = 11y \Rightarrow \frac{x}{y} = \frac{11}{1} = 11:1$

Example 2 **The average salary of the entire teaching staff in a college is ₹ 2000 per day. The average salary of male teachers is ₹ 2500 and the average salary of female teachers is ₹ 1200. If the number of male teachers is 16, find the number of female teachers in the college.** ***SSC CGL 2022***

(a) 18 (b) 12 (c) 14 (d) 10

Sol. (*d*) Let the number of female teachers in the college = x

Number of male teachers = 16

According to the question,

$16 \times 2500 + x \times 1200 = (16 + x) \times 2000$

$\Rightarrow 40000 + 1200x = 32000 + 2000x$

$\Rightarrow 800x = 8000$

$\Rightarrow x = 10$

Hence, the number of female teachers in the college = 10

Helping Tips

To solve the problems on mathematical reasoning, a candidate should have a knowledge of concepts of arithmetic or basic mathematics.

Based on Linear Equation

Example 3 **Arjun is reading a book. On Monday he reads 1/3 of the book. On Tuesday he reads 3/10 of the remaining pages. He has 28 pages left to read. How many pages are there in the book?** ***UP Police Head Operator 2024***

(a) 55 pages (b) 48 pages
(c) 72 pages (d) 60 pages

Sol. (*d*) Let the total number of pages in the book = x

Total pages read by Arjun on Monday = $x \times \frac{1}{3} = \frac{x}{3}$ pages

Remaining pages = $x - \frac{x}{3} = \frac{3x - x}{3} = \frac{2x}{3}$ pages

Again, total pages read by Arjun on Tuesday $= \frac{2x}{3} \times \frac{3}{10} = \frac{x}{5}$

According to the question, $\frac{2x}{3} - \frac{x}{5} = 28$

$\Rightarrow \frac{10x - 3x}{15} = 28 \Rightarrow 7x = 28 \times 15$

$\Rightarrow x = \frac{28 \times 15}{7} = 60$ pages

Example 4 **Rajan and Manu go to the market. Rajan buys 3 erasers and 5 pens for ₹ 105, while Manu buys 4 erasers and 6 pens for ₹ 130. What is the price of an eraser?** ***MP Police Constable 2022***

(a) ₹ 25 (b) ₹ 30 (c) ₹ 20 (d) ₹ 10

Sol. (*d*) Let the price of an eraser and a pen be ₹ x and ₹ y, respectively.

According to the question,

$3x + 5y = 105$ ...(i)

$4x + 6y = 130$ ...(ii)

Eq. (i) × 4 – Eq. (ii) × 3,

$12x + 20y - 12x - 18y = 420 - 390$

$\Rightarrow 2y = 30$

$\therefore y = \frac{30}{2} = 15$

Putting the value of y in Eq. (i),

$3x + 75 = 105 \Rightarrow 3x = 30$

$\Rightarrow x = \frac{30}{3} = 10$

Hence, the cost of one eraser is ₹ 10.

Trending Concept

The question based on arithmetic reasoning are asked in current examination of UP Police constable, SSC CPO, Steno, CUET (UG), UP Police (Head operator) SSC CGL, RRB Group D. These questions are important for the upcoming examination.

Based on Venn Diagram

Example 5 **In a class of 40 students, 15 students play cricket and 15 students play tennis and 5 students play both the games, then the number of students who do not play any of the games is?** ***UP Police Constable 2024***

(a) 10 (b) 15 (c) 35 (d) 25

Sol. (*b*) According to the question,

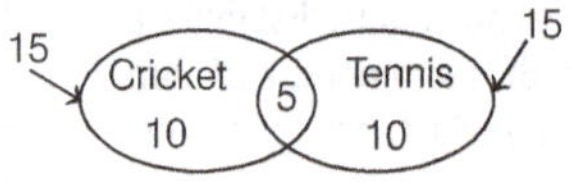

Hence, the number of students who do not play any sport is

$= 40 - (10 + 5 + 10) = 15$

Based on Age

Example 6 **A and B are friends and A is 2 yr older than B. A's father D is twice as old as A and B is twice as old as his sister C. The difference between the ages of D and C is 40 yr. Find the age of A.** ***RRB Group D 2018***

(a) 25 yr (b) 26 yr (c) 15 yr (d) 40 yr

Sol. (*b*) Let the age of A = x yr and age of B = $x - 2$ yr

Age of A's father D = $2x$ yr and C's age = $\frac{x-2}{2}$ yr

According to the question, $2x - \left(\frac{x-2}{2}\right) = 40$

$\Rightarrow 4x - x + 2 = 80 \Rightarrow 3x = 78 \Rightarrow x = 26$

Hence, the age of A = 26 yr.

Chapter Challenge

Based on Arithmetic

1. A basket of mangoes contains one bad mango for every 30 mangoes. If 3 out of every 4 bad mangoes are considered unsaleable and 12 mangoes in the basket are unsaleable, how many mangoes are there in the basket? ***UP Police Constable 2024***
(a) 480 (b) 320 (c) 420 (d) 240

2. A farmer has 17 sheeps out of which all except 9 die, then how many sheep are left? ***UP Police Head Operator 2024***
(a) 17 (b) 10 (c) 9 (d) 8

3. Richa, Rohini, Roli, Roshan and Rita are five friends. Each of them has eight balls. Rohini gives three balls to Roshan, who gives five balls to Richa. Richa gives four balls to Roli, who in turn gives three balls to Rita. Rita gives-two balls each to Roshan and Rohini. After the final distribution, how many balls do all the five friends have in total. ***RRB NTPC (CBT-I) 2021***
(a) 48 (b) 36 (c) 35 (d) 40

4. In a hospital, some patients are waiting to consult the doctor about their illness. 40 patients have diabetes and 30 patients have high blood pressure. 22 patients have both diabetes and high blood pressure while 17 patients have neither diabetes nor high blood pressure. What is the total number of patients waiting in the hospital? ***UPSSSC 2018***
(a) 56 (b) 65 (c) 87 (d) 109

5. The number of apples in a basket doubles every minute. If the basket is filled with apples in one hour, then when was the basket half full? ***UP Police Constable 2024***
(a) 59 min
(b) 55 min
(c) 38 min
(d) 47 min

> *MRC****
> ***(Most Repeating Concepts)***
> Q. Nos. 1, 2, 5, 8, 9, 10, 13, 17, 18, 21, 23, 26, 27, 32, 33, 35, 36, 38, 44 and 52 are important from the examination point of view. The questions based on mathematical reasoning are asked in current examination of UP Police Head Constable, UP Police Head Operator, UPSSSC, RRB NTPC, SSC CHSL, Steno, CGL, RRB JE, RRB ALP.

6. John was buying petrol at the rate of ₹ 80 per liter till last month. Now, he buys it at the rate of ₹ 85 per liter. By what per cent did the price of petrol increase compared to last month? ***SSC (10+2) 2020***
(a) 6.25% (b) 8.35% (c) 10% (d) 5.5%

7. Out of a group of 25 tourists, 10 can speak Gujarati, 12 can speak Marathi, 5 can speak Gujarati as well as Marathi. Find the number of people who can speak neither Gujarati nor Marathi. ***UPSSSC 2018***
(a) 6 (b) 7 (c) 8 (d) 9

8. Sonu and his friend Rahul went for shopping. Sonu had ₹ 500, while Rahul had ₹ 240. Sonu spent twice as much on shopping as Rahul. Now, Sonu has three times more money left than Rahul. How much money did Sonu spend? ***SSC Steno 2016***
(b) ₹ 220 (a) ₹ 60 (c) ₹ 440 (d) ₹ 120

9. Four boxes weight 30, 40, 50 and 100 kg, respectively. Which of the following cannot be the total weight, in kg, of any combination of these boxes and a box in a combination can be used only once? ***SSC CGL 2017***
(a) 190 (b) 180 (c) 160 (d) 140

10. A father invited some boys and girls on his son's birthday. The number of boys was 2 less than the girls. The father gave ₹ 10 to all the boys and ₹ 20 to all the girls as gifts. If the total amount spent was ₹ 280, then find the number of boys. ***UPSSSC 2016***
(a) 8 (b) 10 (c) 12 (d) 14

11. Five students A, B, C, D and E appeared in an examination. If C got 5 marks less than B, D got 10 marks more than B and 20 marks less than A, E got 22 marks more than B and B got a total of 40 marks, then how many marks did A get? ***UPSSSC 2016***
(a) 52 (b) 60 (c) 64 (d) 70

12. A monkey is climbing a tree. He usually climbs at 10 steps per hour. When the clock reaches an odd hour he halves his speed. If he started climbing at 12.00 noon, how far did he climb by 11.00 am the next day? ***DSSSB Head Clerk 2018***
(a) 175 (b) 285 (c) 295 (d) 185

13. A school canteen charges ₹ 20 for lunch and ₹ 4 for milk per day. How much money will Ramesh have to spend on these items for 5 days? ***BSSC (10+2) 2020***
(a) ₹ 240 (b) ₹ 24 (c) ₹ 120 (d) ₹ 100

14. A farmer has 45 buffaloes. All died except 13. How many buffaloes are left? ***DSSSB Grade-II 2019***
(a) 45 (b) 32 (c) 0 (d) 13

15. Flights to Ahmedabad depart every 5 h. The last flight left 25 min ago. If the time now is 10:45 am, what is the time of the next flight? ***DSSSB Grade-IV 2017***
(a) 2:20 am (b) 3:20 pm (c) 3:35 am (d) 3:55 pm

16. In a particular conference of 100 people, there are 29 Indian women and 23 Indian men. Out of these Indians, 4 are doctors and 24 are either ordinary men or doctors. There are no foreign doctors. Find the number of women doctors attending the conference. ***Delhi Police MTS 2019***
(a) 3 (b) 2 (c) 1 (d) 4

17. A tap can fill a 1250 L tank in 4 h, while another tap can fill the same tank in 8 h. An emptying tap can empty the tank in 6 h. If all the three taps are opened simultaneously, how much time will it take to fill the tank completely? **SSC CPO 2020**

(a) 4.5 h (b) 5 h (c) 4.8 h (d) 4.2 h

18. Disha's salary is ₹ 3000 more than Pratima's salary. The ratio of Disha and Pratima's salary is 17:15 respectively. What is Pratima's salary? **SSC (10+2) 2020**

(a) ₹ 26750 (b) ₹ 22500 (c) ₹ 25500 (d) ₹ 27250

19. A person has money in the form of coins of denominations of ₹ 5, ₹ 2 and ₹ 1. The total number of coins is 150. What is the total amount that the person has? Which additional information given below will be required to answer the above question? **UPSSSC 2018**

(a) The number of ₹ 5 denomination coins was 25
(b) The number of ₹ 1, ₹ 2 and ₹ 5 coins were in the ratio 3 : 2 : 1
(c) The number of ₹ 1 coins was thrice the number of ₹ 5 coins
(d) The number of ₹ 2 coins was twice the number of ₹ 5 coins

20. In a retail shop, there were 54 almirah. Each almirah had 28 rack. Each rack contained 10 boxes. Each box contained 4 shirts. One day 500 boxes were sold and 250 were purchased. How many shirts were there on that day?

(a) 60380 (b) 59360 (c) 59580 (d) 59480

21. A monkey climbs a smooth pole 12 m high. He climbs 2 m in the first minute and slides down, 1 m in the next minute. If this sequence continues, then in how many minutes will he reach the top of the pole? **MP Police Constable 2022**

(a) 21 (b) 15 (c) 10 (d) 20

22. ₹ 1875 is divided among A, B and C in such a way that A's share is half of the combined share of B and C and B's share is one fourth of the combined share of A and C. C's share is how much more than A's share? **SSC CGL 2020**

(a) ₹ 200 (b) ₹ 225 (c) ₹ 250 (d) ₹ 500

23. A basket contains twelve dozen apples. Two dozen are added later. Ten apples are rotten and are removed. The remaining are transferred equally into two baskets. How many apples are in each? **UP Police Constable 2024**

(a) 168 (b) 89
(c) 158 (d) 79

24. A machine that cuts a ribbon into pieces of 10 m takes 6 sec to cut once. How long will it take to completely cut a 3 km long ribbon into pieces?

(a) 174 sec (b) 180 sec
(c) 1794 sec (d) 1800 sec

25. At a fancy dress party with 200 people, 30% of the guests are dressed as animals. 40% of the remaining guests are dressed as birds. 50% of the remaining guests are dressed as clowns. The remaining guests are dressed as plants. How many guests are dressed as plants? **SSC Steno 2021**

(a) 62 (b) 56 (c) 70 (d) 42

26. In a survey, 60% of people preferred option A and 40% preferred option B. If there were a total of 500 respondents, how many people preferred option A? **UP Police Constable 2024**

(a) 200 (b) 400 (c) 100 (d) 300

Based on Linear Equation

27. In a college, the total number of students who opted for either Biology or Chemistry is 150. Later, 12 students who opted for Biology changed their choice and opted for Chemistry. Now, the number of students in Biology is half the number of students in Chemistry. Now, how many students are there in Chemistry? **SSC Steno 2020**

(a) 104 (b) 100 (c) 88 (d) 94

28. The sum of the ages of X, Y and Z is 27. X is 2 yr older than Y and the age of Y is twice of Z. Find the age of Y. **RRB JE 2019**

(a) 12 (b) 5 (c) 8 (d) 10

29. There are as many chickens as there are sheep in a farm. There are twice as many men as there are goats and twice as many goats as there are sheep. If the total number of legs is 44, how many men are there in the farm? **UPSSSC 2018**

(a) 14 (b) 12 (c) 6 (d) 8

30. Daisy has one-third as much as David. David has one-third as much as Francis. All together there are 111. How much does Francis have? **BSSC (10+2) 2017**

(a) 27 (b) 36 (c) 48 (d) 68

31. A herd consists of some cows, bulls and 45 hens. One cowherd looks after every 15 animals. The number of bulls is twice that of cows. If the total number of heads is 186 less than the number of legs (including cowherds), then how many cowherds are there? **UPSSSC 2016**

(a) 6 (b) 8 (c) 10 (d) 12

Based on Venn Diagram

32. In a class of 40 students, 20 chosen only Biology and 15 chosen Mathematics but not Biology. It is given that each student chosen either Mathematics, or Biology or both. Find the number of students who chosen both Mathematics and Biology. **UP Police Constable 2024**

(a) 15 (b) 5 (c) 20 (d) 40

33. In a survey of 140 students, it was found that 60 students like to play video games, 70 students like to play indoor games and 75 students like to play outdoor games. In addition, 30 students like both indoor and outdoor games, 18 like both video games and outdoor games, 42 like both video games and indoor games and 8 like all types of games. Using a Venn diagram, find the number of students who play only outdoor games. ***UP Police Constable 2024***
(a) 64 (b) 35 (c) 32 (d) 57

34. In a music class, 12 students can play flute, 11 can play guitar and 10 can play violin. 6 students can play flute as well as guitar and 3 of them can play violin as well. 3 students can play only guitar and 4 students can play only violin. How many students can play only flute? ***UPSSSC 2018***
(a) 4 (b) 5 (c) 6 (d) 7

35. 40% people read newspaper X and 50% people read newspaper Y. 10% people read both the newspapers, How many people do not read either of the newspapers? ***UPSSSC PET 2022***
(a) 15% (b) 25% (c) 20% (d) 30%

Based on Age

36. The ratio of the ages of A and B after 5 yr will be 7:5 and the difference between their ages will be 4 yr. What are the present ages (in years) of A and B respectively? ***CRPF (HC) 2023***
(a) 5, 9 (b) 6, 5 (c) 9, 5 (d) 9, 6

37. Six people named W, X, Y, Z, T and U, each are of different ages.The age of Y is 30. The age of T is five times the age of Z. The age of W is half the age of X. The age of Z is one-fourth the age of W. The age of Y is two times the age of T. If the age of X is half the age of U, what is the age of U? ***RPF SI 2024***
(a) 35 (b) 45 (c) 38 (d) 48

38. The sum of the ages of Reena and her father is 60 yr and the difference between their ages is 36 yr. Find the age of Reena's father. ***SSC Steno 2021***
(a) 48 yr (b) 52 yr
(c) 58 yr (d) 60 yr

39. The sum of the present ages of father and son is 45 yr. 5 yr ago, the ratio of their ages was 6:1. Find the present age of the father. ***RRB ALP 2018***
(a) 25 yr. (b) 40 yr (c) 35 yr (d) 30 yr

40. Ram's age is one-sixth of his father's age. After 10 yr, Ram's father's age will be twice as Vimal's age. If Vimal's 8th birthday was 2 yr ago, then how old is Ram? ***Rajasthan Patwari 2016***
(a) 24 (b) 30
(c) $6\frac{2}{3}$ (d) None of these

41. Nisha and Deepak are a married couple and they have a daughter named Tanya. At present, Deepak is 5 yr older than Nisha and Nisha is three times older than Tanya. If Tanya is 10 yr old, what was the age of her father when his daughter was born? ***SSC CGL 2019***
(a) 20 yr (b) 35 yr (c) 25 yr (d) 30 yr

42. Last year my age was a perfect square number. Next year it will be a cube number. Tell me my present age (in years).
(a) 26 (b) 24 (c) 25 (d) 27

43. The average of the present ages of Amit and Anil is 32 yr. If Amit is 6 yr older than Anil, what is Anil's present age? ***SSC Steno 2016***
(a) 29 yr (b) 38 yr (c) 26 yr (d) 19 yr

44. My age is 2 yr less than twice the age of my brother. If I am 18 yr old, then how old is my brother? ***Bihar Forest Guard 2020***
(a) 8 yr (b) 12 yr (c) 9 yr (d) 10 yr

45. Umesh, Vikram, Veena, Suman and Yash are five cousins. Suman is half the age of Vikram. Vikram is half the age of Umesh. Yash is half the age of Suman. If Yash is 4 yr old, then how old is Umesh? ***DSSSB warder 2019***
(a) 48 (b) 16 (c) 8 (d) 32

46. Sachin is 7 yr younger than Rahul. If the ratio of their ages is 7:9 respectively, then what is Sachin's age?
(a) 16 yr (b) 18 yr (c) 28 yr (d) 24.5 yr

47. Akshar and Manvita have just celebrated their silver wedding anniversary and also the birthday of their eldest son 'Sanju'. If Sanju's age is 18 yr after his parents' marriage and his ratio of age and golden anniversary of marriage of his parents is 5: 21, then after how many years of marriage was Sanju born? ***SSC CGL 2021***
(a) 8 yr (a) 12 yr
(c) 15 yr (d) 10 yr

48. Read the question given below
What is the average age of Aman, Boman and Chaman? Read the statement given below:
The ratio of the ages of Aman, Boman and Chaman is 6:5:3 respectively. Which additional information given below will be required to answer the above question?. ***UPSSSC 2018***
(a) Boman is older than the average age of the three people.
(b) The difference between the ages of Boman and Chaman is twice the difference between the ages of Aman and Boman.
(c) Aman is twice as old as Chaman.
(d) Aman was 9 yr older than Boman on Chaman's first birthday.

49. Sami, 12 yr old, is three times older than his brother Vinay. How old will Sami be when he becomes twice as old as Vinay? ***SSC CPO 2016***
(a) 14 yr (b) 16 yr (c) 20 yr (d) 18 yr

50. 10 yr ago, the age of a father was $3\frac{1}{2}$ times more than the age of his son and after 10 yr from now, the age of the father will be $2\frac{1}{4}$ times more than the age of his son. What is the sum of the ages of the father and son at present? ***SSC CGL 2018***
(a) 120 yr (b) 115 yr (c) 110 yr (d) 100 yr

51. Harshad's age is four times the age of his son Vijay. Four years ago, Sudha's age was six times the age of her son Vijay. What is Sudha's present age? Which additional information given below will be required to answer the above question? ***UPSSSC 2018***
(a) After four years, the difference between the ages of Harshad and Sudha will be four years.
(b) Four years later, the sum of the ages of Harshad and Sudha will be 8 more than the sum of their present ages.
(c) Four years ago, the sum of the ages of Harshad, Vijay and Sudha was 12 less than the sum of their present ages.
(d) The average age of Harshad, Vijay and Sudha is an even number.

52. The captain of a cricket team of 11 members is 29 yr old and the wicketkeeper is four years older than the captain. If the age of the captain and the wicketkeeper is excluded, then age of the rest of the players is two years less than the average age of whole team. What is the average age of the team? ***UP Police Constable 2024***
(a) 23 yr (b) 21 yr
(c) 22 yr (d) 24 yr

Right Key

1. (a)	2. (c)	3. (d)	4. (b)	5. (a)	6. (a)	7. (c)	8. (c)	9. (c)	10. (a)
11. (d)	12. (a)	13. (c)	14. (d)	15. (b)	16. (c)	17. (c)	18. (b)	19. (b)	20. (d)
21. (a)	22. (c)	23. (d)	24. (c)	25. (d)	26. (d)	27. (b)	28. (d)	29. (d)	30. (a)
31. (a)	32. (b)	33. (b)	34. (b)	35. (c)	36. (c)	37. (d)	38. (a)	39. (c)	40. (d)
41. (c)	42. (a)	43. (a)	44. (d)	45. (d)	46. (d)	47. (a)	48. (d)	49. (b)	50. (c)
51. (a)	52. (c)								

Solutions

1. *(a)* According to the question,
Mangoes which are not saleable = 12
Total bad mangoes $= \frac{12}{3} \times 4 = 16$
There are 30 mangoes in the basket with 1 bad mango
Total mangoes in the basket with 16 bad mangoes
$= 30 \times 16 = 480$ mangoes

2. *(c)* Total number of sheep the farmer has = 17
According to the question,
All the sheep die except 9.
∴ Total number of sheeps left with the farmer = 9

3. *(d)* According to the question,
The total number of balls remains the same before and after distribution.
∴ Total number of balls the five friends have $= 5 \times 8 = 40$

4. *(b)* According to the question,
Diabetes patients = 40
High blood pressure patients = 30
Patients with both diabetes and high blood pressure = 22
Patients with neither of the illness = 17
∴ Total number of patients waiting
$= (40 + 30 - 22) + 17 = 48 + 17 = 65$

5. *(a)* The basket is completely filled with apples in 60 min.
As, the number of apples in the basket doubles every minute, it becomes half filled in 59 min.
∴ Hence, half the basket is filled in 59 min.

6. *(a)* Price of petrol till last month
= ₹ 80 per liter
Current price of petrol = ₹ 85 per liter
∴ Required percentage increase
$= \frac{85-80}{80} \times 100 = \frac{5}{8} \times 10 = \frac{25}{4} = 6.25\%$

7. *(c)* Total number of people who speak either Gujarati or Marathi
$= 10 + 12 - 5 = 17$
∴ Number of people who speak neither Gujarati nor Marathi
$= 25 - 17 = 8$

8. *(c)* Let Rahul's expenditure $= x$
Then, Sonu's expenditure $= 2x$
According to the question,
$500 - 2x = 3(240 - x)$
$\Rightarrow 500 - 2x = 720 - 3x \Rightarrow x =$ ₹ 220
∴ Expenditure of some
$= 2x = 2 \times 220 =$ ₹ 440

9. *(c)* $190 = 40 + 50 + 100$
$180 = 30 + 50 + 100$
$160 \neq 50 + 100$
$140 = 40 + 100$
Clear from the above that the combination 160 kg is not correct.

10. *(a)* Let the number of boys $= x$
Then, number of girls $= x + 2$
According to the question,
∴ $x \times 10 + (x + 2) \times 20 = 280$
$\Rightarrow 10x + 20x + 40 = 280$

$\Rightarrow \quad 30x = 240 \Rightarrow x = 8$

So, number of boys = 8

11. *(d)* According to the question,

$B = 40, E = 40 + 22 = 62$

$D = 40 + 10 = 50$

$A = 50 + 20 = 70$

$C = 40 - 5 = 35$

So, the marks of A = 70

12. *(a)* Total time from 12:00 noon to 11 : 00 am next day = 23 h.

In 23 h there will be 12 even hours and 11 odd hours.

$\therefore$ Total number of steps

$= 12 \times 10 + 11 \times \frac{10}{2}$

$= 120 + 55 = 175$ steps

13. *(c)* Total expenditure of Ramesh for 5 days = $20 \times 5 + 4 \times 5$

$= 100 + 20 =$ ₹ 120

14. *(d)* Total buffaloes farmer has = 45

According to the question, except 13 all died, which means that out of all, 13 buffaloes are alive.

So, the number of buffaloes left with the farmer = 13

15. *(b)* Given, flight to Ahmedabad departs at every 5 h.

According to the question,

Last flight time

10 : 45 – 0 : 25 = 10 : 20 am

$\therefore$ Next flight time

= (10 : 20 + 5 : 00) = 3 : 20 pm

16. *(c)* Number of Indian men = $m = 23$

Number of Indian women = $w = 29$

Number of Indian doctors = $d = 4$

According to the question,

There are 24 Indian people who are either ordinary men or doctors.

Now, since the number of men is 23.

Number of women doctors attending the conference = (24 – 23) = 1

$\therefore$ 1 female doctor is present in the conferenec.

17. *(c)* Part filled by first tap in 1 h = $\frac{1}{4}$

Part filled by second tap in 1 h = $\frac{1}{8}$

Part emptied by emptying tap in 1 h = $\frac{1}{6}$

According to the question,

When all the three taps are opened together part filled in 1 h

$= \frac{1}{4} + \frac{1}{8} - \frac{1}{6} = \frac{5}{24}$

$\therefore$ Time taken to fill tank when all three taps are opened together = $\frac{24}{5}$ h = 4.8 h

18. *(b)* Let Pratima's salary = ₹ x

$\therefore$ Disha's salary = ₹ $(x + 3000)$

According to the question,

The ratio of Disha's and Pratima's salary = $\frac{17}{15} \Rightarrow \frac{x + 3000}{x} = \frac{17}{15}$

$\Rightarrow 15x + 45000 = 17x$

$\Rightarrow \quad 17x - 15x = 45000$

$\Rightarrow \quad 2x = 45000$

$\therefore \quad x = 22500$

$\therefore$ Pratima's salary = ₹ 22500

19. *(b)* Total number of coins = 150

From option (b),

The number of ₹ 1, ₹ 2 and ₹ 5 coins are $3x$, $2x$ and x, respectively.

$3x + 2x + x = 150$

$\Rightarrow \quad 6x = 150 \Rightarrow x = 25$

Now, value of all types of coins can be found. So, option (b) is required to answer the question.

20. *(d)* Total number of shirts

$= 54 \times 28 \times 10 \times 4 = 60480$

Boxes sold = 500

Boxes purchased = 250

Number of boxes left

= (500 – 250) = 250

$\therefore$ Number of shirts in 250 boxes

$= 250 \times 4 = 1000$

So, total number of shirts there on that day = 60480 – 1000 = 59480

21. *(a)* Height of the pole is 12 m.

The monkey climbs up 2 m in the first minute and slides down 1 m in the next minute i.e. in 2 min it can climb only 2 – 1 = 1 m.

Since, the monkey climbs up 1 m in 2 min.

$\therefore$ Monkey will climb up (12 – 2)m = 10 m in $10 \times 2 = 20$ min and the remaining 2 m will be climbed in the next minute.

Hence, the required time

= 20 + 1 = 21 min

22. *(c)* According to the question,

$A + B + C =$ ₹ 1875 ...(i)

$A = \frac{B + C}{2}$

$2A = B + C$ ...(ii)

and $B = \frac{A + C}{4}$

$4B = A + C$ ...(iii)

From Eqs. (i) and (ii), we get

$3A = 1875 \Rightarrow A =$ ₹ 625

From Eqs. (i) and (iii), we get

$5B = 1875 \Rightarrow B =$ ₹ 375

$\Rightarrow$ On putting value of A and B in Eq. (i), we get

$C = 1875 - 625 - 375 = 875$

Therefore, the difference between C's share and A's share is

$= C - A = 875 - 625 =$ ₹ 250

23. *(d)* Initially, apples in the basket = 12 dozen

Total apples after adding 2 dozen

$= (12 + 2) \times 12 = 14 \times 12 = 168$

After removing 10 rotten apples, the remaining apples are = 168 – 10 = 158

Again, as per the question,

Remaining apples are transferred equally into two baskets, then the total number of apples in each basket is

$= \frac{158}{2} = 79$

24. *(c)* We know that, 1 km = 1000 m

Time taken by machine to cut 10 m of tape = 6 sec

$\therefore$ Time taken to cut 3000 m or 3 km of tape $= \frac{3000}{10} \times 6 = 1800$ sec

Since, when 20 m tape is left at the end, the machine will have to be used only once. So, required time

= 1800 – 6 = 1794 sec

25. *(d)* Total number of people = 200

Number of people dressed as animals

$= \frac{30}{100} \times 200 = 60$

Number of people remaining

$= 200 - 60 = 140$

Number of people dressed as birds

$= \frac{40}{100} \times 140 = 56$

Number of people remaining

$= 140 - 56 = 84$

Number of dressed as clowns

$= \frac{50}{100} \times 84 = 42$

Number of people dressed as plants

$= 84 - 42 = 42$

Number of guests dressed as plants is 42.

26. *(d)* Given, total respondents = 500

$\therefore$ People preferred option A

$= 500 \times \frac{60}{100} = 300$

27. *(b)* Let the number of students who opted for Biology = x

Then, number of students who opted for Chemistry = $150 - x$

After 12 students changed their choices, then

Number of students who opted for Biology = $x - 12$

Number of students who opted for Chemistry $= 150 - x + 12 = 162 - x$

According to the question,

$$x - 12 = \frac{162 - x}{2}$$

$$\Rightarrow \quad 2x - 24 = 162 - x$$

$$\Rightarrow \quad 3x = 186 \Rightarrow x = 62$$

$\therefore$ Number of students in Chemistry $= 162 - 62 = 100$

28. *(d)* Given, $X + Y + Z = 27 \quad \ldots(i)$

and $X = Y + 2 \quad \ldots(ii)$

$Y = 2Z \quad \ldots(iii)$

From Eqs. (ii) and (iii), we get

$X = 2Z + 2 \quad \ldots(iv)$

On putting the value of X and Y from Eqs. (iii) and (iv) in Eq. (i), we get

$$2Z + 2 + 2Z + Z = 27$$

$$\Rightarrow \quad 5Z = 27 - 2 \Rightarrow 5Z = 25$$

$$\Rightarrow \quad Z = \frac{25}{5} \Rightarrow Z = 5$$

$\therefore$ The age of $Y = 2Z = 2 \times 5 = 10$ yr

29. *(d)* Let the number of sheep be x.

Then, the number of goats $= 2x$

Number of men is $4x$

Number of chickens is x.

According to the question,

$$x \times 4 + 2x \times 4 + 4x \times 2 + 2x = 44$$

$$\Rightarrow \quad 4x + 8x + 10x = 44$$

$$\Rightarrow \quad 22x = 44 \Rightarrow x = 2$$

$\therefore$ Number of men $= 4x = 4 \times 2 = 8$

30. *(a)* Let Francis have x.

$\therefore$ David has $= x + \frac{x}{3} = \frac{3x + x}{3} = \frac{4x}{3}$

and Daisy has $= \frac{4x}{3} + \frac{4x}{3} \times \frac{1}{3}$

$$= \frac{4x}{3} + \frac{4x}{9} = \frac{12x + 4x}{9} = \frac{16x}{9}$$

According to the question,

$$x + \frac{4x}{3} + \frac{16x}{9} = 111$$

$$\Rightarrow \quad \frac{9x + 12x + 16x}{9} = 111$$

$$\Rightarrow \quad 37x = 111 \times 9$$

$$\Rightarrow \quad x = \frac{111 \times 9}{37} = 27$$

So, Francis have = 27.

31. *(a)* Let the number of cows $= x$

$\therefore$ Number of bulls $= 2x$

and number of hens = 45

So, cowherds $= \frac{x + 2x + 45}{15}$

According to the question,

$$45 \times 2 + 4x + 8x + 2 \times \frac{2x + x + 45}{15} - 45 - x - 2x - \frac{3x + 45}{15} = 186$$

$$\Rightarrow 90 + 12x + \frac{6x + 90}{15} - 45 - 3x - \frac{3x + 45}{15} = 186$$

$$\Rightarrow 1350 + 180x + 6x + 90 - 675 - 45x - 3x - 45 = 2790$$

$$\Rightarrow 720 + 138x = 2790$$

$$\Rightarrow \quad 138x = 2070 \Rightarrow x = 15$$

$\therefore$ Number of cowherds

$$= \frac{30 + 15 + 45}{15} = \frac{90}{15} = 6$$

32. *(b)* According to the question,

Total number of students in a class = 40

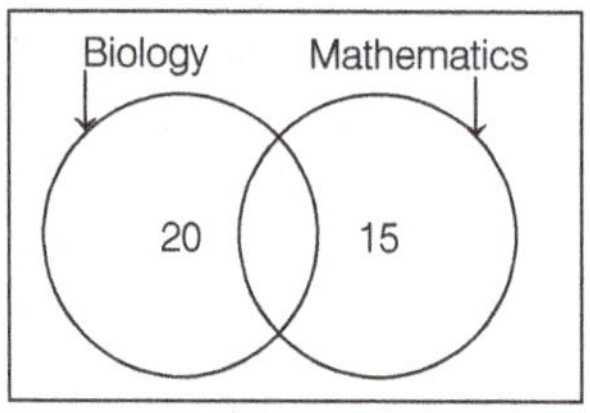

It is given that each student chosen either Mathematics or Biology or both.

$\therefore$ Number of students who chosen both Mathematics and Biology

$$= 40 - (20 + 15) = 5$$

33. *(b)* According to the question,

Total number of students = 140

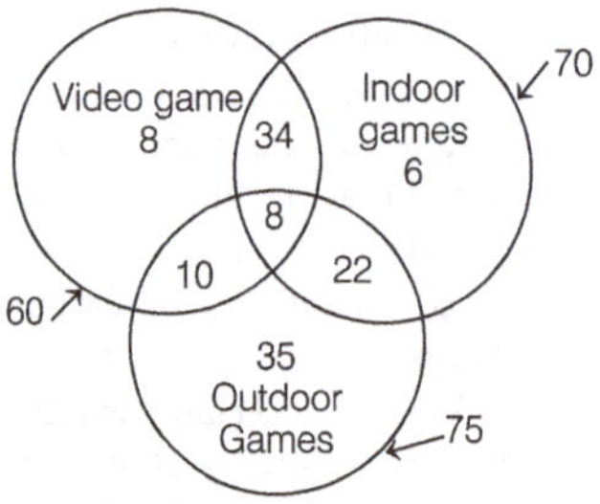

Hence, 35 students play only outdoor games.

TOP TIPS While representing data, keep in mind the difference between 'two' and 'only two'.

34. *(b)* According to the question,

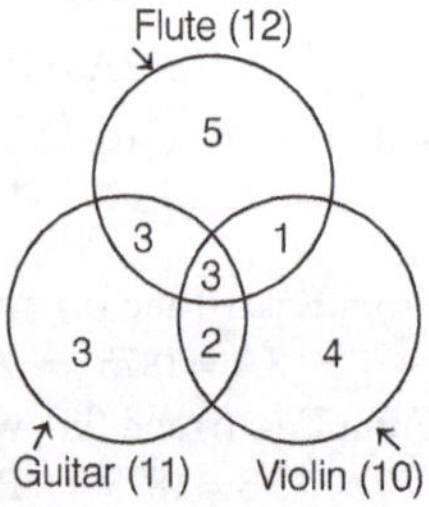

Only Guitar and violin players

$$11 - (3 + 3 + 3) = 2$$

Only Flute and violin players

$$= 10 - (4 + 3 + 2) = 1$$

$\therefore$ Only flute players

$$= 12 - (3 + 3 + 1) = 5$$

35. *(c)* According to the question,

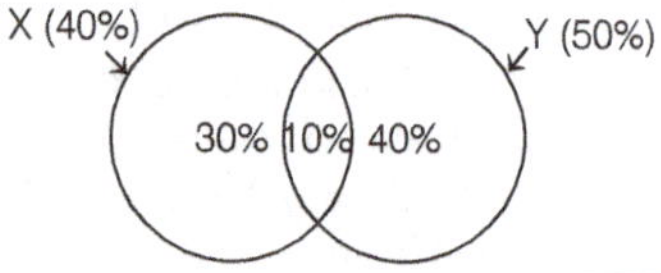

Number of people who read neither of the newspapers.

$$= [100 - (30 + 10 + 40)]\%$$

$$= (100 - 80)\% = 20\%$$

36. *(c)* Let the ages of A and B after 5 yr be $7x$ and $5x$, respectively.

As per the question, $(7x - 5x) = 4$

$$\Rightarrow \quad 2x = 4 \therefore x = 2$$

Present age of A

$$= 7x - 5 = 7 \times 2 - 5 = 9 \text{ yr}$$

and present age of B $= 5x - 5$

$$= 5 \times 2 - 5 = 5 \text{ yr}$$

Hence, the present age of A and B is 9 yr and 5 yr, respectively.

37. *(d)* Given, age of Y = 30

Age of $T = \frac{30}{2} = 15$

($\because$ Y' age is two times the age of T)

Age of $Z = \frac{15}{5} = 3$

($\because$ T age is five times the age of Z)

Let suppose age of $U = x$

$\therefore$ Age of $X = \frac{x}{2}$

($\because$ X age is half the age of U)

Now, age of $W = \frac{x}{4}$

($\because$ W age is half the age of X)

So, age of $Z = \frac{1}{4}$ (age of W)

Age of $Z = \frac{1}{4} \times \frac{x}{4} = \frac{x}{16}$

According to the question,

$$\Rightarrow \quad \frac{x}{16} = 3 \Rightarrow x = 48$$

Hence, age of $U = x = 48$

38. *(a)* Let the age of Reena's father be x yr.

Then, Reena's age $= (x - 36)$ yr

According to the question,

$$x + x - 36 = 60 \Rightarrow 2x = 96 \Rightarrow x = 48$$

Hence, Reena's father is 48 yr old.

39. *(c)* Let the present age of father $= x$ yr

$\therefore$ Present age of son $= 45 - x$ yr

According to the question,

$$\frac{x-5}{45-x-5}=\frac{6}{1}$$

$\Rightarrow\quad x-5=240-6x$

$\Rightarrow\quad 7x=245 \Rightarrow x=\frac{245}{7}$

$\Rightarrow\quad x=35$ yr

So, the present age of father = 35 yr

TOP TIPS The difference between ages of two persons always remains constant.

40. *(d)* Given, Vimal's present age = 10 yr

Age of Ram's father after 10 yr

$=(10+10)\times 2=40$ yr

Present age of Ram's father

$=40-10=30$ yr

Ram's age $=\frac{30}{6}=5$ yr

41. *(c)* Present age of Tanya = 10 yr

$\therefore$ Present age of Nisha = $10\times 3=30$ yr

Present age of Deepak = $30+5=35$ yr

$\because$ Age of Deepak at the time of birth of his daughter $=35-10=25$ yr

42. *(a)* Form option *(a)*, according to the given question,

Let my present age be 26 yr.

Then, last year age $=26-1=25$ yr

$=(5)^2$ yr

Next year age $=26+1=27$ yr

$=(3)^3$ yr

43. *(a)* Let the present age of Anil = x yr.

Then, present age of Amit = $(x+6)$ yr.

According to the question,

$x+x+6=2\times 32$

$\Rightarrow\quad 2x+6=64 \Rightarrow 2x=64-6$

$\Rightarrow\quad 2x=58 \Rightarrow x=29$

So, present age of Anil = 29 yr.

44. *(d)* Let my brother's age = x yr.

$\therefore$ My age $=(2x-2)$ yr

According to the question,

$2x-2=18 \Rightarrow x=10$ yr

So, my brother's age = 10 yr

45. *(d)* Yash's age = 4 yr

Suman's age $=4\times 2=8$ yr

Vikram's age $=8\times 2=16$ yr

$\therefore$ Umesh's age $=16\times 2=32$ yr

46. *(d)* Let Sachin's age = $7x$ yr and Rahul's age = $9x$ yr.

According to the question,

$9x-7x=7 \Rightarrow 2x=7 \Rightarrow x=\frac{7}{2}$

$\therefore$ Sachin's age $=7\times\frac{7}{2}=\frac{49}{2}=24.5$ yr

47. *(a)* Let Sanju's present age = x yr

Sanju's age on the silver anniversary of his parents' marriage

$=x-(25-18)=(x-7)$ yr

Sanju's age on the golden anniversary of his parents marriage $=(x+25)$ yr

According to the question,

$$\frac{x-7}{x+25}=\frac{5}{21}$$

$\Rightarrow\quad 21x-147=5x+125$

$\Rightarrow\quad 16x=272 \Rightarrow x=17$ yr

$\therefore$ Sanju was born after $25-17=8$ yr of his parents' marriage.

48. *(d)* According to the statement, the ages of Aman, Boman and Chaman are $6x$, $5x$ and $3x$, respectively.

According to the option *(d)*, on Chaman's first birthday, Aman was 9 yr older than Boman and the difference between the ages of Aman and Boman will always be 9 yr that is

$6x-5x=9 \Rightarrow x=9$

Hence, option *(d)* is required to find the average age of the three.

49. *(b)* If Sami's age is 12 yr, then his brother's age will be 4 yr. Let's say after x yr Sami's age will be twice the age of Vinay.

Then, according to the question,

$12+x=2(4+x)$

$\Rightarrow\quad 12+x=8+2x \Rightarrow x=4$

Since, after 4 yr Sami will be twice as old as his brother. So, after 4 yr Sami's age $=12+4=16$ yr

Smart Approach

Sami's age = 12 yr

Vinay's age $=\frac{12}{3}=4$ yr

After 4 yr

Sami's age $=12+4=16$ yr

Vinay's age $=4+4=8$ yr

50. *(c)* Let the present ages of the father and the son be x yr and y yr, respectively.

Then, according to the question,

10 yr ago, $x-10=3\frac{1}{2}(y-10)$

$\Rightarrow\quad x-10=\frac{7}{2}(y-10)$

$\Rightarrow\quad 2x-20=7y-70$

$\Rightarrow\quad 2x-7y=-50 \quad ...(i)$

Again, as per the question

After 10 yr, $x+10=2\frac{1}{4}(y+10)$

$\Rightarrow\quad x+10=\frac{9}{4}(y+10)$

$\Rightarrow\quad 4x+40=9y+90$

$\Rightarrow\quad 4x-9y=50 \quad ...(ii)$

On solving Eqs. (i) and (ii), we get value of $y=30$

On putting the value of y in Eq. (i), we get

$2x-210=-50 \Rightarrow x=80$ yr

$\therefore$ At present, the sum of the ages of father and son

$=x+y=80+30=110$ yr

51. *(a)* Let Vijay's age = x yr

According to the question,

Harshad's age = $4x$ yr

Four year ago, Sudha's age $=6(x-4)$

$\therefore$ Sudha's present age

$=6(x-4)+4=6x-20$

From option *(a)*, after four years, the difference between the ages of Harshad and Sudha is four year.

$\therefore (4x+4)-(6x-20+4)=4$

$\Rightarrow\quad 4x+4-6x+16=4$

$2x=20-4=16$

$x=8$

$\therefore$ Present age of Sudha $=6\times 8-20$

$=48-20=28$ yr

Hence, option (a) is required to find the answer of the question.

52. *(c)* Given, age of captain = 29 yr

Age of wicket-keeper $=29+4=33$ yr

Let the average age of remaining 9 players = x yr

According to the question,

$$x+2=\frac{9x+29+33}{11}$$

$\Rightarrow\quad 11x+22=9x+29+33$

$\Rightarrow\quad 2x=40 \Rightarrow x=20$

So, average age of the team $=x+2$

$=20+2=22$ yr

CHAPTER 17 Inserting the Missing Characters

Inserting the Missing Characters

In 'inserting the missing character', some letters/numbers/combination of letters and numbers are arranged in a table or in a geometrical figure on the basis of a certain logical and mathematical calculation and one number/letter/combination of letter and number is left missing in the figure. Candidate has to analyse that pattern and find that missing character.

Based on Numbers

In this type of questions, some numbers are arranged in diagrams or geometrical shapes on the basis of some logical and mathematical operations (such as addition, subtraction, multiplication, division, square, square root, cube and cube root etc). In which one term is missing. Candidate has to analyse the pattern and find that missing term.

e.g. What will come at the place of question mark (?) in the given question?

5	7	8
4	6	6
2	3	?
10	14	12

(a) 2 (b) 4 (c) 6 (d) 3

Sol. (b) As in the first column,

$$(5 \times 4) \div 2 = 10$$

and in second column,

$$(7 \times 6) \div 3 = 14$$

Similarly in third column,

$$(8 \times 6) \div ? = 12$$

$$? = \frac{48}{12} = \boxed{4}$$

Based on English Letters

In this type of questions, letters are arranged in a table or geometrical figure according to a certain rule/pattern (by mathematical operations on their positional values) and one term is missing. Candidate has to analyse that rule or pattern and on basis of that find that missing term.

e.g. In the given figure, what will come at the place of '?'.

B	D	G
E	G	J
G	I	?

(a) L (b) K (c) E (d) Z

Sol. (a) As, in first row, $B \xrightarrow{+2} D \xrightarrow{+3} G$

In second row, $E \xrightarrow{+2} G \xrightarrow{+3} J$

Similarly in third row, $G \xrightarrow{+2} I \xrightarrow{+3} \boxed{L}$

Based on Letters and Numbers

In this type of questions, combination of letters and numbers are arranged in a geometrical figure following a certain rule/pattern on the basis of certain mathematical operations and one term is missing. Candidate has to analyse that pattern/rule and find the missing term.

e.g. Find the missing term in the given figure.

A_2	C_4	E_6
G_3	I_5	?
M_5	O_9	Q_{14}

(a) L_{10} (b) K_{15} (c) K_8 (d) I_{15}

Sol. (c) As, in first row, $A \xrightarrow{+2} C \xrightarrow{+2} E$ and $2 + 4 = 6$

and in third row, $M \xrightarrow{+2} O \xrightarrow{+2} Q$ and $5 + 9 = 14$

Similarly, in second row, $G \xrightarrow{+2} I \xrightarrow{+2} \boxed{K}$ and $3 + 5 = \boxed{8}$

$\therefore$ $? = \boxed{K_8}$

Score Booster

To attempt this type of question, analysing and finding pattern is the first and foremost step. Please remember that patterns can be established vertically as well as horizontally (in case of table) or even diagonally (in case of geometrical figures).
In case of letters, patterns are generally based on operations of positional values of letters in English alphabetical series.

Exam Approach Examples

Based on Numbers

Directions (Ex. Nos. 1-4) *Study the given pattern carefully and select the number that can replace the question mark* (?).

Example 1

82	91	100
63	72	81
24	33	?

SSC MTS 2023

(a) 56 (b) 34
(c) 48 (d) 42

Trending Concept

Questions related on numbers frequently asked in different exams (MTS, RRB, CGL). Questions based on these concepts are very important for upcoming exams.

Sol. (*d*) As, in first row, 82 + 9 = 91 and 91 + 9 = 100

In second row, 63 + 9 = 72 and 72 + 9 = 81

Similarly, in third row, 24 + 9 = 33 and 33 + 9 = 42

Example 2

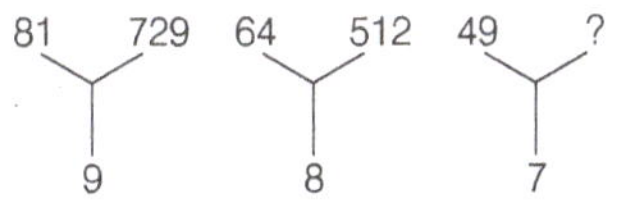

BSSC (10+2) 2023

(a) 444 (b) 515 (c) 343 (d) 314

Sol. (*c*) As, in figure I,

$9^1 = 9, 9^2 = 81$ and $9^3 = 729$

and in figure II,

$8^1 = 8, 8^2 = 64$ and $8^3 = 512$

Similarly, in figure III,

$7^1 = 7, 7^2 = 49$ and $7^3 = \boxed{343}$

Helping Tips

To solve such questions, it is very important to have knowledge of square, cubes, square roots and cube roots of numbers.

Example 3

2	3	4	25
5	7	2	71
1	5	6	?

(a) 31 (b) 33 (c) 37 (d) 43

Sol. (*a*) As, in Ist row, $2 \times 3 \times 4 = 24 \Rightarrow 24 + 1 = 25$

and in IInd row, $5 \times 7 \times 2 = 70 \Rightarrow 70 + 1 = 71$

Similarly, in IIIrd row, $1 \times 5 \times 6 = 30 \Rightarrow 30 + 1 = \boxed{31}$

Example 4

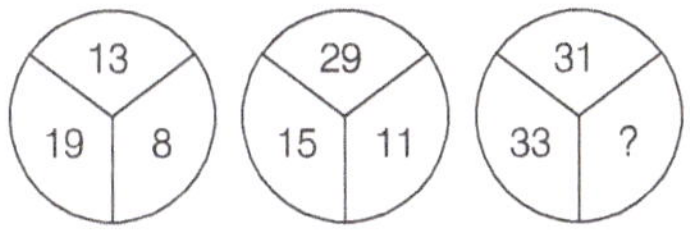

Bihar Forest Guard 2020

(a) 14 (b) 16 (c) 18 (d) 12

Sol. (*b*) As, in figure Ist, $13 + 19 = 8 \times 4 = 32$

and in figure IInd, $29 + 15 = 11 \times 4 = 44$

Similarly, in figure IIIrd,

$31 + 33 = ? \times 4 \Rightarrow ? = \frac{64}{4} = \boxed{16}$

Based on English Letters

Directions (Ex. Nos. 5 and 6) *Study the given pattern carefully and select the letter that can replace the question mark* (?).

Example 5

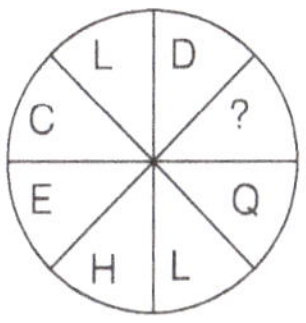

RRB NTPC 2021

(a) W (b) U (c) A (d) X

Sol. (*a*) According to the question,

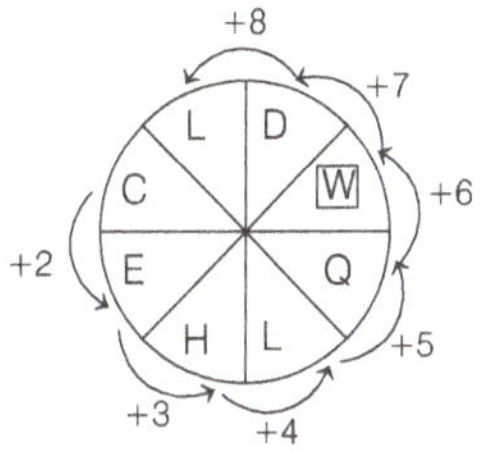

∴ ? = W

Example 6

R	X	?
D	V	L
N	B	F

Bihar STET 2020

(a) Q (b) S (c) R (d) T

Sol. (*c*) As, in column Ist, N(14) + D(4) = R(18)

and in column IInd, B(2) + V(22) = X(24)

Similarly, in column IIIrd, $\boxed{\text{F(6)}}$ + L(12) = R(18)

Based on Letters and Numbers

Example 7 **Find the missing term in the given question.**

RRB NTPC 2021

B_3	E_4	H_7
K_8	N_9	?
T_{11}	W_{13}	Z_{24}

(a) Q_{21} (b) R_{12} (c) Q_{17} (d) P_{12}

Sol. (*c*) As, in row Ist,

$B \xrightarrow{+3} E \xrightarrow{+3} H; 3 + 4 = 7$

and in row IIIrd,

$T \xrightarrow{+3} W \xrightarrow{+3} Z; 11 + 13 = 24$

Similarly, in row IInd,

$K \xrightarrow{+3} N \xrightarrow{+3} \boxed{Q}; 8 + 9 = \boxed{17}$

∴ $? = Q_{17}$

Chapter Challenge

Based on Numbers

Directions (Q. Nos. 1-41) *Find the missing numbers in the questions given below.*

1.

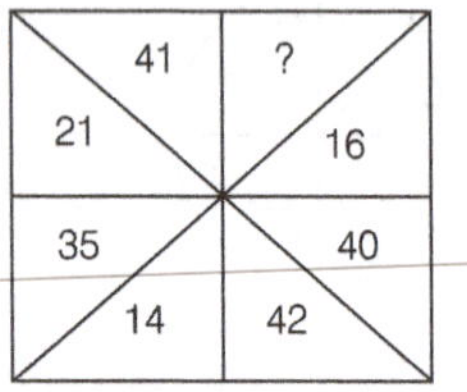

MPPSC 2018

(a) 12 (b) 13
(c) 14 (d) 15

2.

963	2	844
464	?	903

Haryana Police Constable 2021

(a) 2 (b) 25
(c) 1 (d) 66

3.

RRB NTPC 2021

(a) 4 (b) 6 (c) 2 (d) 5

4.

8	10	15	13
6	5	7	4
4	6	8	8
6	11	16	?

MPPSC 2021

(a) 17 (b) 19 (c) 21 (d) 23

5.

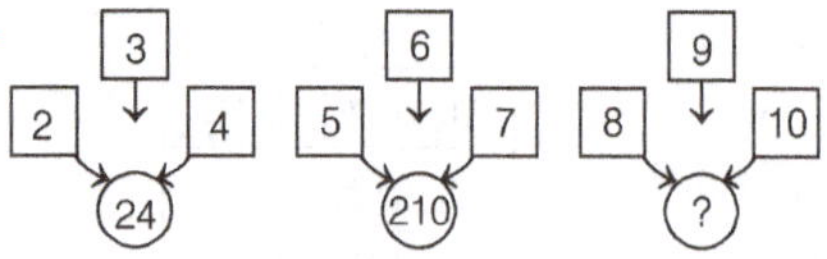

RRB NTPC 2022

(a) 9 (b) 27 (c) 270 (d) 720

6.

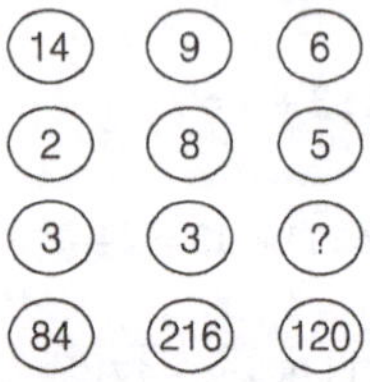

RRB JE 2019

(a) 8 (b) 6
(c) 7 (d) 4

7.

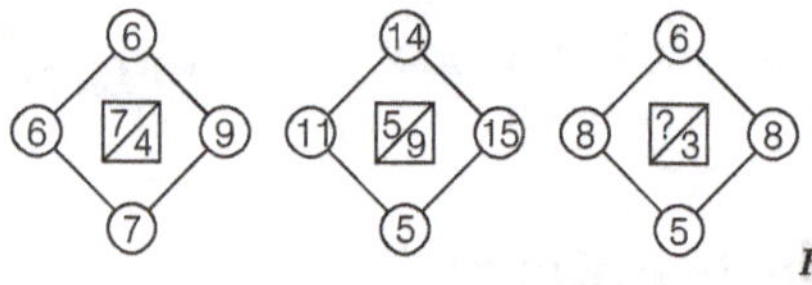

RRB NTPC 2021

(a) 3 (b) 2
(c) 9 (d) 7

8.

19	6	37
21	8	45
72	14	?

CISF Head Constable 2023

(a) 114 (b) 144
(c) 124 (d) 134

9.

4	2	6
9	3	9
24	6	?

SSC CGL (Tier-I) 2023

(a) 10 (b) 12
(c) 15 (d) 8

10.

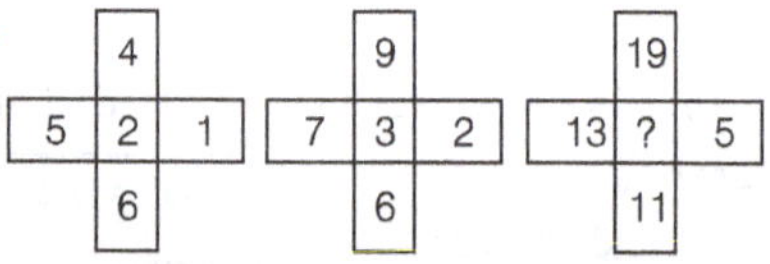

MPPSC 2018

(a) 4 (b) 6 (c) 8 (d) 10

11.

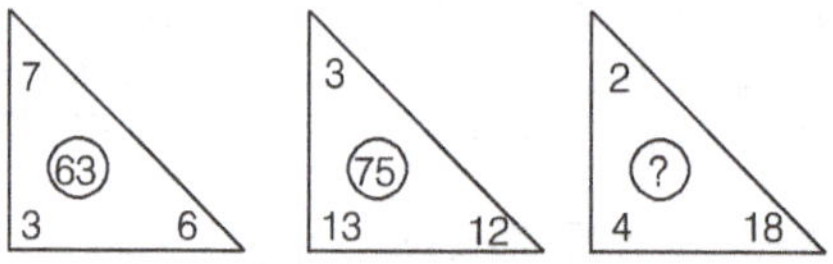

RRB NTPC 2021

(a) 87 (b) 144 (c) 22 (d) 44

12.

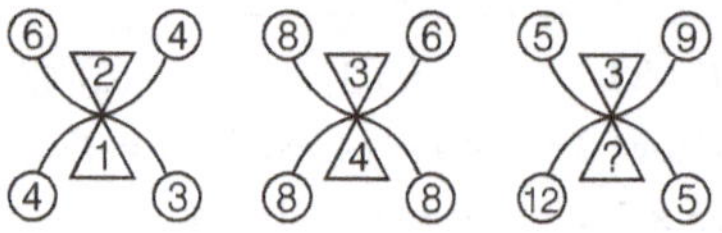

RRB NTPC 2021

(a) 3 (b) 2 (c) 4 (d) 1

13.

5	8	32
9	6	48
7	9	?

Bihar TET 2020

(a) 54 (b) 45 (c) 49 (d) 53

14.

13	16	52
15	24	90
23	36	?

CUET UG 2022

(a) 81 (b) 108 (c) 207 (d) 117

15.

86	82	56
74	67	47
54	48	?

SSC (10+2) 2022

(a) 34 (b) 38 (c) 32 (d) 37

16.

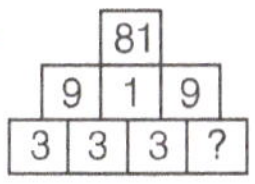

RRB JE 2019

(a) 4 (b) 2 (c) 3 (d) 1

17.

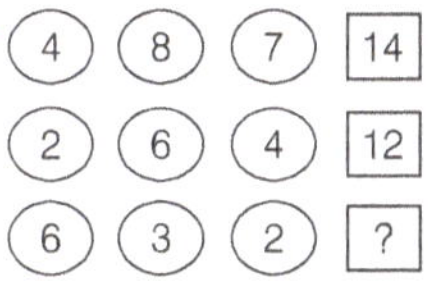

RRB NTPC 2022

(a) 10 (b) 6 (c) 8 (d) 1

18.

6	8	34
3	2	10
11	18	?

SSC (10+2) 2022

(a) 47 (b) 84 (c) 74 (d) 48

19.

25	24	122
31	27	143
35	29	?

SSC MTS 2021

(a) 197 (b) 157 (c) 114 (d) 222

20.

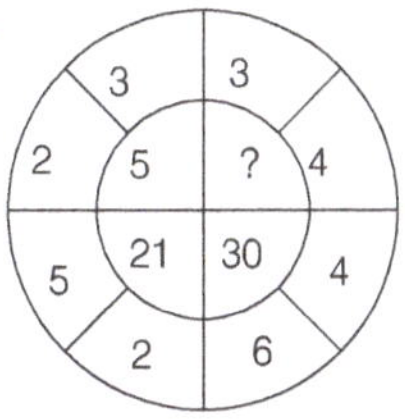

BSSSC CGL 2016

(a) 10 (b) 9 (c) 8 (d) 7

21.

11	29	22
17	23	?
112	208	156

SSC Steno 2020

(a) 17 (b) 20
(c) 26 (d) 16

> **MRC*****
> ***(Most Repeating Concepts)***
> Questions based on arrangement of numbers in a table or matrix (Q. Nos. 17, 21, 22, 23) are repeatedly asked in (SSC exams (10+2), Steno, MTS and RRB NTPC). They are very important for upcoming exams.

22.

5	14	3
3	24	7
9	30	?

SSC CGL (Tier-I) 2023

(a) 7 (b) 5 (c) 13 (d) 9

23.

6	12	78
6	15	99
3	13	?

SSC MTS 2021

(a) 49 (b) 45 (c) 54 (d) 50

24.

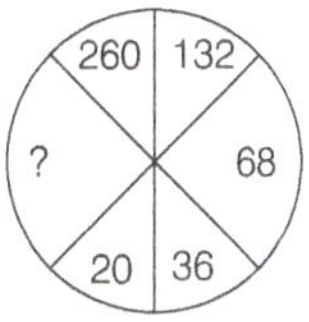

CRPF HC 2023

(a) 12 (b) 10 (c) 9 (d) 8

25.

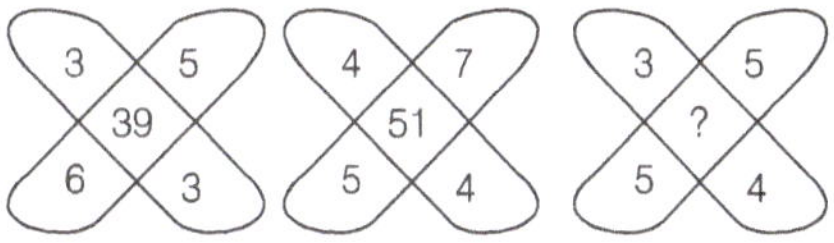

RRB ALP 2018

(a) 35 (b) 47 (c) 45 (d) 37

26.

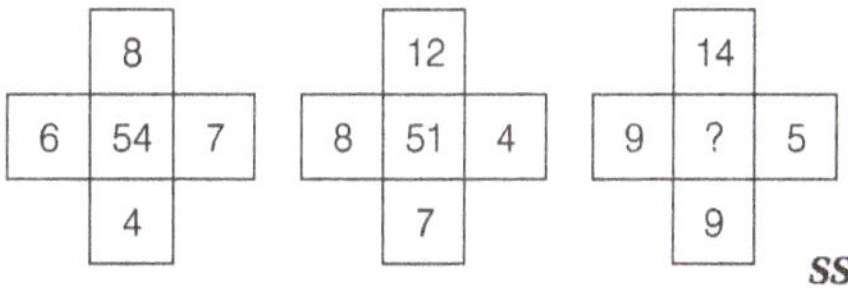

SSC CPO 2018

(a) 53 (b) 76 (c) 71 (d) 68

27.

5	12	65
7	14	105
9	13	?

Delhi Police Constable 2020

(a) 102 (b) 126 (c) 120 (d) 135

28.

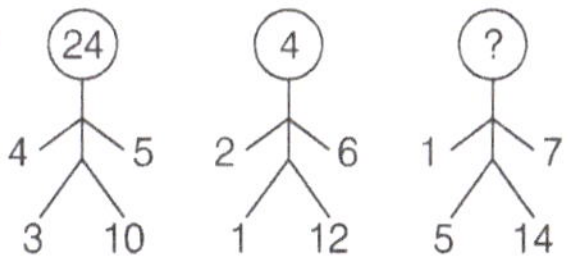

BSSSC (10+2) 2020

(a) 25 (b) 20 (c) 10 (d) 15

29.

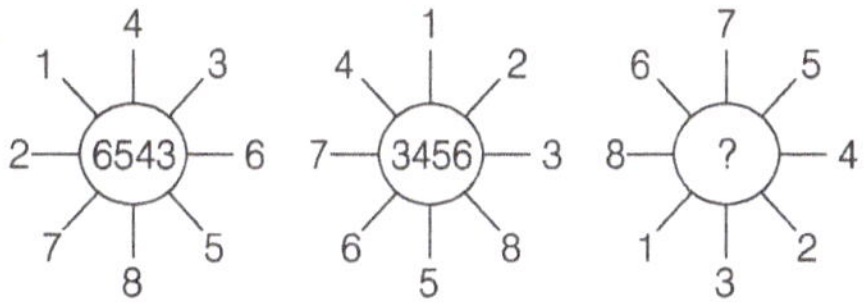

SSC CGL (Tier-I) 2020

(a) 3564 (b) 5364 (c) 6543 (d) 5634

30.

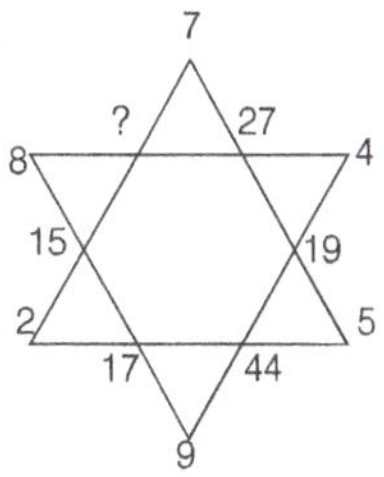

RRB JE 2019

(a) 55 (b) 58 (c) 52 (d) 59

31.

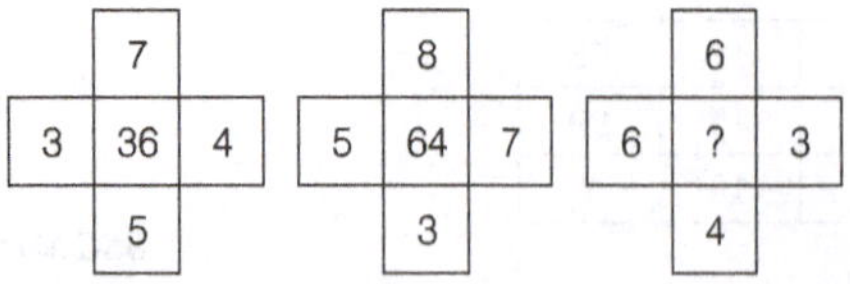

BSSSC (10+2) 2018

(a) 25 (b) 27 (c) 49 (d) 28

32.

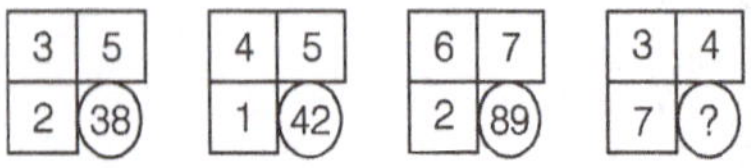

RRB NTPC 2022

(a) 84 (b) 31 (c) 74 (d) 14

33.

36	49	43
42	64	?
24	36	30

SSC CPO 2020

(a) 38 (b) 32 (c) 34 (d) 36

34.

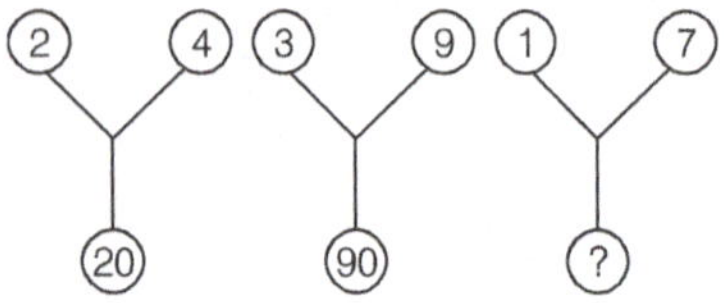

WB PSC 2018

(a) 160 (b) 100 (c) 50 (d) 75

35.

9	34	72
7	26	56
23	90	?

SSC (10+2) 2022

(a) 184 (b) 148 (c) 146 (d) 164

36.

3	9	2
8	6	8
5	3	?

SSC CGL (Tier-I) 2023

(a) 22 (b) 13 (c) 10 (d) 5

37.

4	3	6
3	5	3
337	706	?

SSC Steno 2020

(a) 1377 (b) 895
(c) 1456 (d) 1123

38.

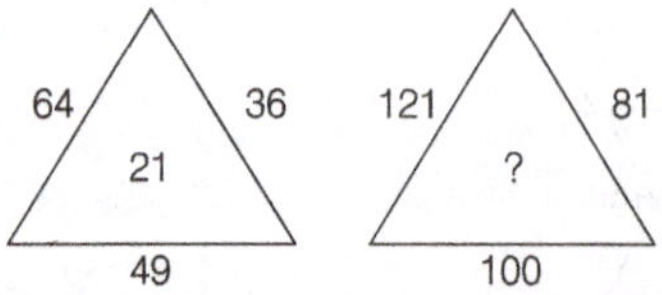

(a) 40 (b) 30
(c) 20 (d) 10

39.

125	25	10
216	49	13
27	121	?

CUET UG 2023

(a) 16 (b) 8
(c) 12 (d) 14

40.

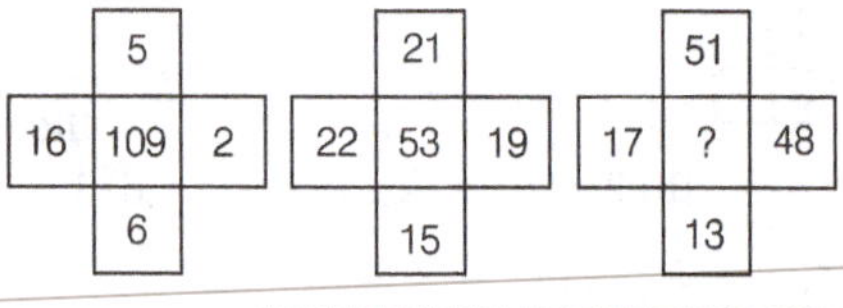

UPSSSC Forest Guard and Wildlife Guard 2022

(a) 7 (b) 25 (c) 49 (d) 129

41.

2	5	8	51
4	7	9	65
3	3	8	47
1	8	4	?

CG Revenue Inspector 2017

(a) 48 (b) 44
(c) 42 (d) None of these

Based on Letters

Directions (Q. Nos. 42-49) *Find the missing letters in the given questions.*

42.

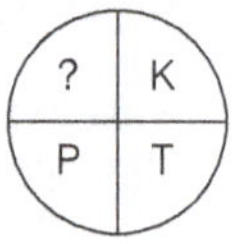

BSSSC (10+2) 2018

(a) M (b) H (c) G (d) U

43.

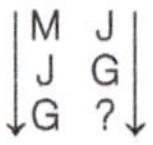

DSSSB 2015

(a) D (b) E (c) C (d) J

44.

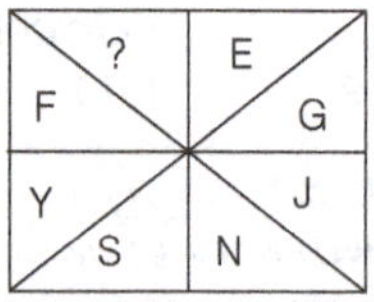

RRB NTPC 2021

(a) N (b) W
(c) X (d) P

45.

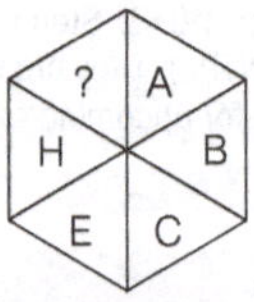

BSSSC (10+2) 2020

(a) M (b) J
(c) K (d) L

46.

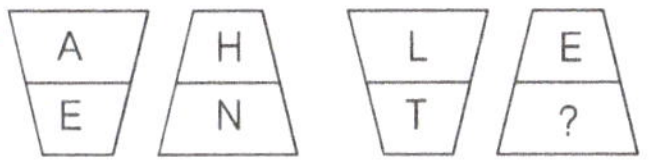

DSSSB TGT/PGT 2017

(a) W (b) O (c) V (d) U

47.

P	J	O
A	D	I
O	F	?

(a) F
(b) G
(c) H
(d) K

> ***MRC******
> ***(Most Repeating Concepts)***
> Questions based on finding missing letters are being repeatedly asked in RRB NTPC, DSSSB and BSSS examinations. They are very important for upcoming examination.

48.

N	R	V
Q	M	?
P	T	X
O	K	G

RRB NTPC 2021

(a) I (b) W (c) H (d) Z

49.

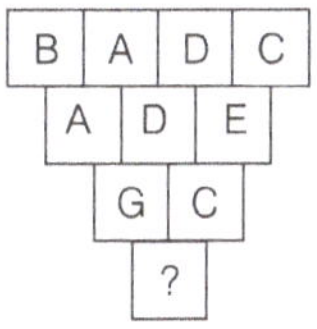

RRB NTPC 2021

(a) J (b) H (c) I (d) F

Based on Letters and Numbers

Directions (Q. Nos. 50-57) *Find the missing elements in the questions given below.*

50.

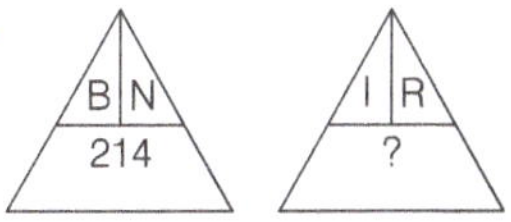

DSSSB 2019

(a) 1024 (b) 1121 (c) 918 (d) 821

51.

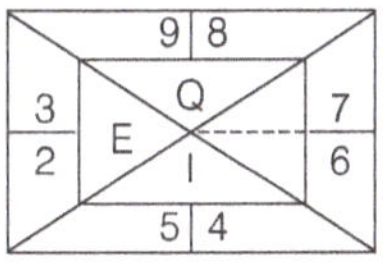

UP (Lower Subordinate) 2018

(a) R (b) N (c) M (d) L

52.

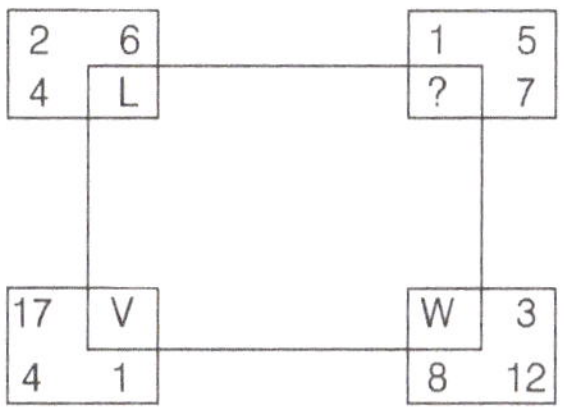

RRB NTPC 2021

(a) N (b) H (c) K (d) M

53.

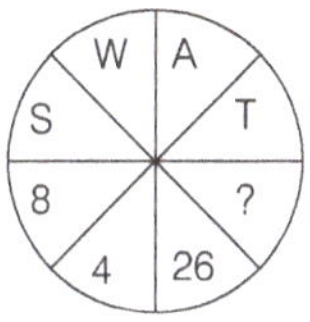

RRB NTPC 2021

(a) 20 (b) 6 (c) 14 (d) 7

54.

JL4	KM5	LN20
MO7	NP3	OQ21
PR6	QS8	?

UPSSSC Conductor Exam 2015

(a) RT14 (b) TR48 (c) RT48 (d) SR48

55.

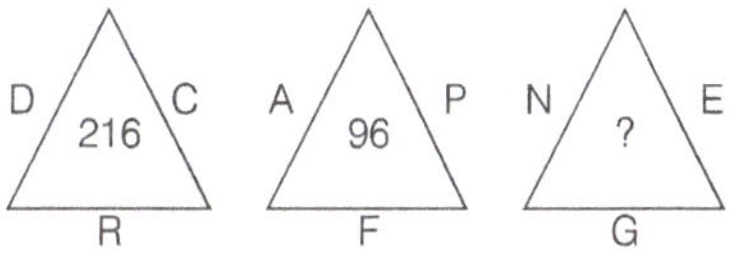

(a) 835 (b) 88 (c) 490 (d) 75

56.

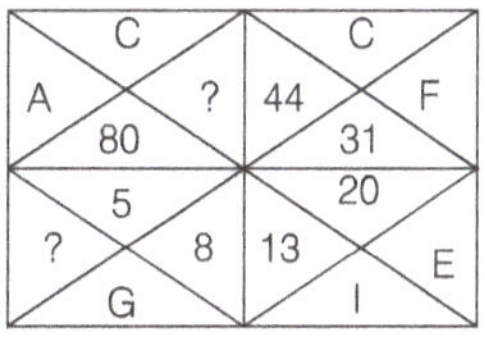

NTA CUET UG 2024

(a) 59 and K (b) 61 and L
(c) 61 and K (d) 59 and L

57.

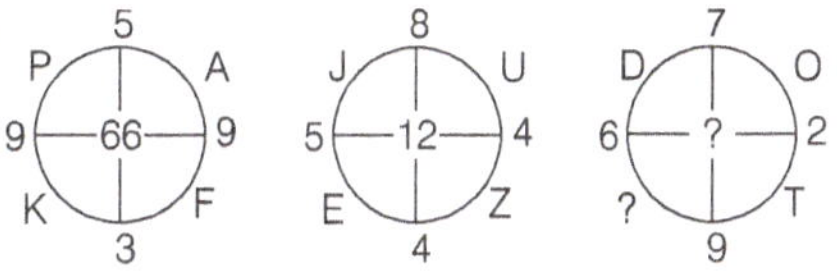

(a) 53 and Z (b) 51 and Y
(c) 50 and Y (d) 52 and U

Right Key

1. (d)	2. (a)	3. (a)	4. (a)	5. (d)	6. (d)	7. (c)	8. (a)	9. (b)	10. (b)
11. (d)	12. (c)	13. (a)	14. (c)	15. (a)	16. (c)	17. (d)	18. (c)	19. (b)	20. (d)
21. (a)	22. (a)	23. (a)	24. (a)	25. (d)	26. (d)	27. (b)	28. (c)	29. (b)	30. (a)
31. (d)	32. (c)	33. (c)	34. (c)	35. (a)	36. (c)	37. (a)	38. (b)	39. (d)	40. (b)
41. (c)	42. (c)	43. (a)	44. (a)	45. (a)	46. (b)	47. (a)	48. (a)	49. (a)	50. (c)
51. (c)	52. (d)	53. (d)	54. (c)	55. (c)	56. (b)	57. (b)			

Solutions

1. *(d)* As, $21 + 35 = 56$

and $14 + 42 = 56$ and $16 + 40 = 56$

Similarly, $41 + ? = 56$

$\Rightarrow ? = 56 - 41 \Rightarrow ? = \boxed{15}$

2. *(a)* As, in the first row,

$963 \Rightarrow 9 + 6 + 3 = 18$

and $844 \Rightarrow 8 + 4 + 4 = 16$

$\Rightarrow 18 - 16 = 2$

Similarly, in second row,

$464 \Rightarrow 4 + 6 + 4 = 14$

and $903 \Rightarrow 9 + 0 + 3 = 12$

$\Rightarrow 14 - 12 = \boxed{2}$

3. *(a)* As, in first figure, $9 \times 4 = 36$

and in second figure, $8 \times 7 = 56$

Similarly, in third figure,

$6 \times 8 = \boxed{4}8 \Rightarrow ? = \boxed{4}$

4. *(a)* As, in first column,

$8 - 6 = 2 \Rightarrow 6 - 4 = 2$

and in second column,

$11 - 10 = 1 \Rightarrow 6 - 5 = 1$

and in third column,

$16 - 15 = 1 \Rightarrow 8 - 7 = 1$

Similarly, in fourth column,

$8 - 4 = 4 \Rightarrow ? - 13 = 4$

$\therefore ? = 4 + 13 = \boxed{17}$

5. *(d)* As, in first figure, $2 \times 3 \times 4 = 24$

and in second figure, $5 \times 6 \times 7 = 210$

Similarly, in third figure

$8 \times 9 \times 10 = \boxed{720}$

6. *(d)* As, in first column, $14 \times 2 \times 3 = 84$

and in second column, $9 \times 8 \times 3 = 216$

Similarly, in third column,

$6 \times 5 \times ? = 120$

$\Rightarrow 30 \times ? = 120$

$\Rightarrow ? = \frac{120}{30} \Rightarrow ? = \boxed{4}$

7. *(c)* As, in first figure,

$6 + 9 + 7 + 6 = 7 \times 4 = 28$

and in second figure,

$14 + 15 + 5 + 11 = 5 \times 9 = 45$

Similarly, in third figure,

$6 + 8 + 5 + 8 = ? \times 3$

$\Rightarrow 27 = ? \times 3 \Rightarrow ? = \boxed{9}$

8. *(a)* As, in row I,

$19 + (3 \times 6) = 19 + 18 = 37$

and in row II,

$21 + (3 \times 8) = 21 + 24 = 45$

Similarly, in row III,

$72 + (3 \times 14) = 72 + 42 = \boxed{114}$

9. *(b)* As, in first row,

$(4, 2, 6) \Rightarrow \frac{4}{2} \times 3 = 6$ (Third number)

and in second row,

$(9, 3, 9) \Rightarrow \frac{9}{3} \times 3 = 9$ (Third number)

Similarly, in third row

$(24, 6, ?) \Rightarrow \frac{24}{6} \times 3 = \boxed{12}$

10. *(b)* As, in first figure,

$\frac{(4 + 6) - (5 + 1)}{2} = \frac{10 - 6}{2} = 2$

and in second figure,

$\frac{(9 + 6) - (7 + 2)}{2} = \frac{15 - 9}{2} = 3$

Similarly, in third figure

$\frac{(19 + 11) - (13 + 5)}{2} = \frac{30 - 18}{2} = \boxed{6}$

11. *(d)* As, in first figure,

$(3 + 6) \times 7 = 63$

and in second figure,

$(13 + 12) \times 3 = 75$

Similarly, in third figure

$(4 + 18) \times 2 = ?$

$\therefore ? = 22 \times 2 = \boxed{44}$

12. *(c)* As, in first figure,

$(6 \times 4) \times 1 = 24, (4 \times 3) \times 2 = 24$

and in second figure,

$(8 \times 6) \times 4 = 192, (8 \times 8) \times 3 = 192$

Similarly, in third figure

$(12 \times 5) \times 3 = 180$ and $(5 \times 9) \times ? = 180$

$\Rightarrow 45 \times ? = 180$

$? = \frac{180}{45} = \boxed{4}$

13. *(a)* As, in first row,

$5 \times 8 - 8 = 40 - 8 = 32$

and in second row,

$9 \times 6 - 6 = 54 - 6 = 48$

Similarly, in third row,

$7 \times 9 - 9 = 63 - 9 = \boxed{54}$

> **TOP TIPS** To solve these type of pattern we should apply BODMAS rule during numerical operations.

14. *(c)* From Ist row, $13 \times \frac{16}{4} = 52$

and from IInd row, $15 \times \frac{24}{4} = 90$

Similarly,

from IIIrd row, $23 \times \frac{36}{4} = \boxed{207}$

15. *(a)* As, in Ist row,

$(86 + 82) \div 3 = 168 \div 3 = 56$

and in IInd row,

$(74 + 67) \div 3 = 141 \div 3 = 47$

Similarly, in IIIrd row,

$(54 + 48) \div 3 = 102 \div 3 = \boxed{34}$

16. *(c)* As, pattern followed in the figure is,

81 $\Rightarrow 81$

9 | 1 | 9 $\Rightarrow 9 \times 1 \times 9 = 81$

3 | 3 | 3 | ? $\Rightarrow 3 \times 3 \times 3 \times ? = 81$

$\Rightarrow 27 \times ? = 81 \Rightarrow ? = \frac{81}{27} = \boxed{3}$

17. *(d)* As, in first row,

$(8 \times 7) \div 4 = 56 \div 4 = 14$

and in second row,

$(6 \times 4) \div 2 = 24 \div 2 = 12$

Similarly, in third row,

$(3 \times 2) \div 6 = 6 \div 6 = \boxed{1}$

18. *(c)* As, in first row,

$(6 \times 2) + (8 \times 3) - 2$

$= 12 + 24 - 2 = 34$

and in second row

$(3 \times 2) + (2 \times 3) - 2 = 6 + 6 - 2 = 10$

Similarly, in third row,

$(11 \times 2) + (18 \times 3) - 2$

$= 22 + 54 - 2 = \boxed{74}$

19. *(b)* As, in first row,

$(25 \times 2) + (24 \times 3) = 50 + 72 = 122$

and in second row,

$(31 \times 2) + (27 \times 3) = 62 + 81 = 143$

Similarly, in third row

$(35 \times 2) + (29 \times 3) = 70 + 87 = \boxed{157}$

20. *(d)* In lower half of the circle,

$(5 + 2) \times 3 = 7 \times 3 = 21$

$\Rightarrow (6 + 4) \times 3 = 10 \times 3 = 30$

In upper half of the circle,

$2 + 3 = 5, 3 + 4 = \boxed{7}$

21. *(a)* As, in Ist column

$(11 + 17) \times 4 = 112$

and in IInd column

$(29 + 23) \times 4 = 208$

Similarly, in IIIrd column

$(22 + x) \times 4 = 156 \Rightarrow 88 + 4x = 156$

$\Rightarrow \quad 4x = 156 - 88 \Rightarrow 4x = 68$

$\Rightarrow \quad x = \boxed{17}$

22. (a) As, in first row,

$5 + (3 \times 3) = 5 + 9 = 14$

and in second row,

$3 + (7 \times 3) = 3 + 21 = 24$

Similarly in third row,

$9 + (? \times 3) = 30$

$\Rightarrow (? \times 3) = 30 - 9$

$\Rightarrow ? = \frac{21}{3} = 7$

$\therefore \quad ? = \boxed{7}$

23. (a) As, in first row,

$(6 \times 12) + (12 - 6) = 72 + 6 = 78$

and in second row,

$(6 \times 15) + (15 - 6) = 90 + 9 = 99$

Similarly, in third row

$(3 \times 13) + (13 - 3) = 39 + 10 = \boxed{49}$

24. (a)

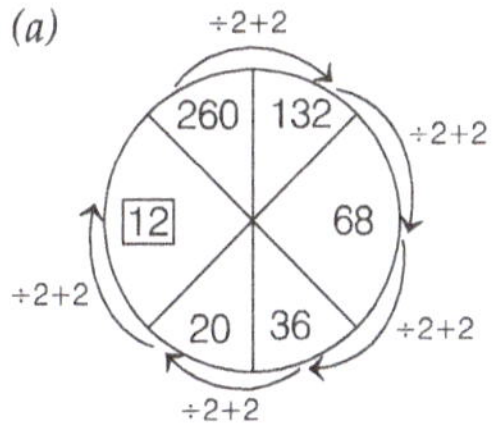

25. (d) As, in figure I,

$(6 \times 5) + (3 \times 3) = 30 + 9 = 39$

and in figure II,

$(4 \times 4) + (5 \times 7) = 16 + 35 = 51$

Similarly, in figure III,

$(3 \times 4) + (5 \times 5) = 12 + 25 = \boxed{37}$

26. (d) As, in first figure,

$6 \times 7 + (8 + 4) = 42 + 12 = 54$

and in second figure,

$8 \times 4 + (12 + 7) = 32 + 19 = 51$

Similarly, in third figure,

$9 \times 5 + (14 + 9) = 45 + 23 = \boxed{68}$

27. (b) As, in first row,

$5 \times 12 + 5 = 60 + 5 = 65$

and in second row,

$7 \times 14 + 7 = 98 + 7 = 105$

Similarly, in third row

$9 \times 13 + 9 = 117 + 9 = \boxed{126}$

28. (c) As, in first figure,

$(4 \times 3) \times (10 \div 5) = 12 \times 2 = 24$

In second figure,

$(2 \times 1) \times (12 \div 6) = 2 \times 2 = 4$

Similarly, in third figure,

$(5 \times 1) \times (14 \div 7) = 5 \times 2 = \boxed{10}$

29. (b) As, in first figure,

$4 + 8 = 12$ and $\frac{12}{2} = 6$

$3 + 7 = 10$ and $\frac{10}{2} = 5$

$6 + 2 = 8$ and $\frac{8}{2} = 4$

$5 + 1 = 6$ and $\frac{6}{2} = 3$

$\therefore$ Middle number $= 6543$

and the number in second figure will be obtained using same way.

Similarly, in third figure

$7 + 3 = 10$ and $\frac{10}{2} = 5,$

$5 + 1 = 6$ and $\frac{6}{2} = 3,$

$4 + 8 = 12$ and $\frac{12}{2} = 6$

$6 + 2 = 8,$ and $\frac{8}{2} = 4$

$\therefore$ Middle number $= \boxed{5364}$

30. (a) As, in the given figure is solve in clockwise direction starting from 7.

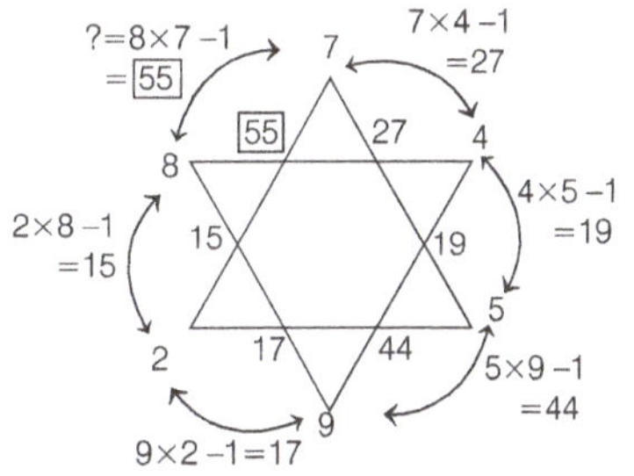

31. (d) As, in first figure,

$(7 \times 4) + 5 + 3 = 28 + 5 + 3 = 36$

and in second figure,

$(8 \times 7) + 3 + 5 = 56 + 3 + 5 = 64$

Similarly in third figure,

$(6 \times 3) + 4 + 6 = 18 + 4 + 6 = \boxed{28}$

32. (c) As, in first figure, $5^2 + 3^2 + 2^2 = 38$

In second figure, $5^2 + 4^2 + 1^2 = 42$

In third figure, $7^2 + 6^2 + 2^2 = 89$

Similarly, in fourth figure,

$4^2 + 3^2 + 7^2 = \boxed{74}$

33. (c) As, in Ist row,

$36, 49, 43 \Rightarrow 49 = (36 - 43)^2$

$\Rightarrow \quad 49 = 49$

and in IIIrd row,

$24, 36, 30 \Rightarrow 36 = (30 - 24)^2$

$\Rightarrow \quad 36 = 36$

Similarly, in IInd row,

$42, 64, ? \Rightarrow 64 = (42 - ?)^2$

$\Rightarrow \quad \sqrt{64} = 42 - ?$

$\therefore \quad ? = 42 - 8 = \boxed{34}$

34. (c) As, in first figure,

$2^2 + 4^2 = 4 + 16 = 20$

and in second figure,

$3^2 + 9^2 = 9 + 81 = 90$

Similarly in third figure

$1^2 + 7^2 = 1 + 49 = \boxed{50}$

TOP TIPS To attempt this of questions candidate must have knowledge of squares and cubes of numbers.

35. (a) As, in first row,

$9 \times 4 - 2 = 36 - 2 = 34$

$\Rightarrow (34 + 2) \times 2 = 36 \times 2 = 72$

In second row,

$7 \times 4 - 2 = 28 - 2 = 26$

$\Rightarrow (26 + 2) \times 2 = 28 \times 2 = 56$

Similarly, in third row,

$23 \times 4 - 2 = 92 - 2 = 90$

$\Rightarrow (90 + 2) \times 2 = 92 \times 2 = \boxed{184}$

36. (c) As in first row,

$(3, 9, 2) = 9 \times \frac{2}{3} = \frac{18}{3} = 6$

and in second row,

$(8, 6, 8) = 6 \times \frac{8}{8} = \frac{48}{8} = 6$

Similarly, in third row,

$(5, 3, ?) = \frac{3 \times ?}{5} = 6$

$\Rightarrow \quad ? = 5 \times \frac{6}{3} = \frac{30}{3} = \boxed{10}$

37. (a) As, in Ist column

$4^4 + 3^4 = 256 + 81 = 337$

and in IInd column

$3^4 + 5^4 = 81 + 625 = 706$

Similarly, in IIIrd column

$6^4 + 3^4 = 1296 + 81 = \boxed{1377}$

38. (b) As, in figure Ist,

$\sqrt{64} + \sqrt{36} + \sqrt{49} = 8 + 6 + 7 = 21$

Similarly, in figure IInd,

$\sqrt{121} + \sqrt{81} + \sqrt{100}$

$= 11 + 9 + 10 = \boxed{30}$

39. (d) As, in Ist row,

$\sqrt[3]{125} + \sqrt{25} = 5 + 5 = 10$

In 2nd row,

$\sqrt[3]{216} + \sqrt{49} = 6 + 7 = 13$

Similarly in IIIrd row,

$\sqrt[3]{27} + \sqrt{121} = 3 + 11 = \boxed{14}$

40. *(b)* As, in 1st figure,
$(16-6)^2+(5-2)^2=10^2+3^2$
$=100+9=109$
In 2nd figure,
$(22-15)^2+(21-19)^2=7^2+2^2$
$=49+4=53$
Similarly, in 3rd figure,
$(17-13)^2+(51-48)^2=4^2+3^2$
$=16+9=\boxed{25}$
$\therefore$? = 25

41. *(c)* As, $2\times2+5\times3+8\times4=51$
$4\times2+7\times3+9\times4=65$
and $3\times2+3\times3+8\times4=47$
Similarly, $1\times2+8\times3+4\times4=42$
$?=\boxed{42}$

42. *(c)* As, P(16) + K(11) = 27
Similarly, T(20) + $\boxed{\text{G(7)}}$ = 27

43. *(a)* As,
M $\xrightarrow{-3}$ J $\xrightarrow{-3}$ G
Similarly,
J $\xrightarrow{-3}$ G $\xrightarrow{-3}$ $\boxed{D}$

44. *(a)* According to the question,
E $\xrightarrow{+2}$ G $\xrightarrow{+3}$ J $\xrightarrow{+4}$ N $\xrightarrow{+5}$
S $\xrightarrow{+6}$ Y $\xrightarrow{+7}$ F $\xrightarrow{+8}$ $\boxed{N}$

45. *(a)* As, 1 + 2 → 3
(A) + (B) (C)
2 + 3 → 5
(B) + (C) (E)
3 + 5 → 8
(C) + (E) (H)
Similarly, 5 + 8 → 13
(E) + (H) $\boxed{\text{(M)}}$
$\therefore$? = M

46. *(b)* According to the question,
A $\xrightarrow{+4}$ E, H $\xrightarrow{+6}$ N, L $\xrightarrow{+8}$ T, E $\xrightarrow{+10}$ $\boxed{O}$

> **TOP TIPS** To solve these kind of questions easily, candidate must know the alphabetical place values of letters.

47. *(a)* As, in column Ist,
P(16) – A(1) = O(15)
and in column IInd,
J(10) – D(4) = F(6)
Similarly, in column IIIrd,
O(15) – I(9) = $\boxed{\text{F(6)}}$

48. *(a)* As, in 1st and IIIrd row,
N $\xrightarrow{+4}$ R $\xrightarrow{+4}$ V
P $\xrightarrow{+4}$ T $\xrightarrow{+4}$ X
and in IInd and IVth row,
Q $\xrightarrow{-4}$ M $\xrightarrow{-4}$ $\boxed{I}$
O $\xrightarrow{-4}$ K $\xrightarrow{-4}$ G

49. *(a)* As, in Ist row,
⇒ B(2) + A(1) + D(4) + C(3)
= 2 + 1 + 4 + 3 = 10
and in IInd row,
A(1) + D(4) + E(5) = 1 + 4 + 5 = 10
and in IIIrd row,
G(7) + C(3) = 7 + 3 = 10
Similarly, in IVth row, $\boxed{\text{J(10)}}$ = 10

50. *(c)* As, in first figure,
B → 2, N → 14
Similarly, in second figure,
I → $\boxed{9}$, R → $\boxed{18}$

51. *(c)* As, 3 + 2 = 5 → E
And, 9 + 8 = 17 → Q
And, 5 + 4 = 9 → I
Similarly, 7 + 6 = 13 → $\boxed{M}$

52. *(d)* As, in upper square,
6 + 2 + 4 = 12 → L
and, in lower square,
17 + 4 + 1 = 22 → V
and, in second lower square
8 + 12 + 3 = 23 → W
Similarly in second upper square,
1 + 5 + 7 = 13 → $\boxed{M}$

53. *(d)* According to the question,
S(19) + 8 = 27; W(23) + 4 = 27
A(1) + 26 = 27; T(20) + ? = 27
? = 27 – 20 = $\boxed{7}$

54. *(c)* As, in first row,

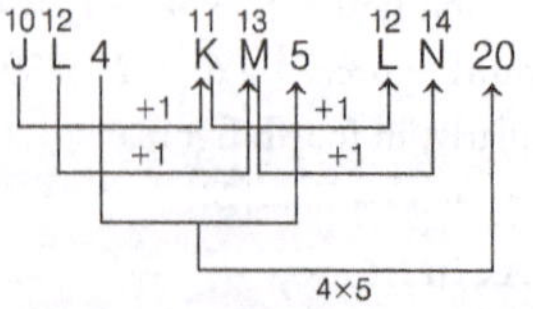

and in second row,

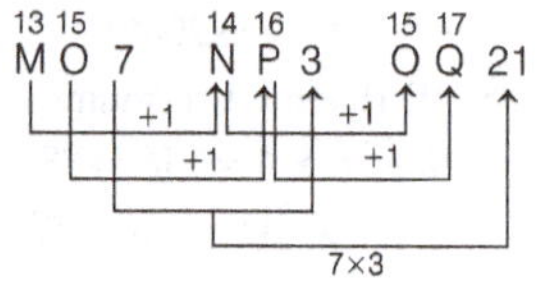

Similarly, in third row,

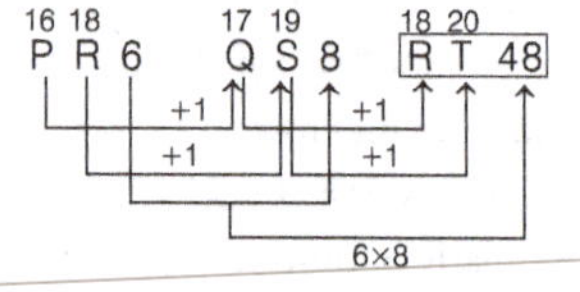

55. *(c)* As, D × C × R
↓ ↓ ↓
4 × 3 × 18 = 216
and A × P × F
↓ ↓ ↓
1 × 16 × 6 = 96
Similarly, N × E × G
↓ ↓ ↓
14 × 5 × 7 = $\boxed{490}$

56. *(b)* The pattern of the series is as follows,
5 $\xrightarrow{+3}$ 8 $\xrightarrow{+5}$ 13 $\xrightarrow{+7}$ 20 $\xrightarrow{+11}$ 31 $\xrightarrow{+13}$ 44 $\xrightarrow{+17}$ $\boxed{61}$ $\xrightarrow{+19}$ 80
Adding continuous prime numbers.
And in alphabets,
A $\xrightarrow{+2}$ C, C $\xrightarrow{+3}$ F, E $\xrightarrow{+4}$ I, G $\xrightarrow{+5}$ $\boxed{L}$
Required term (?) = 61, L

57. *(b)* As, in figure I, $9\times9-5\times3=66$
and in figure II, $8\times4-5\times4=12$
Similarly, in figure III
$9\times7-6\times2=\boxed{51}$
Again,
As, in figure I
A $\xrightarrow{+5}$ F $\xrightarrow{+5}$ K $\xrightarrow{+5}$ P
and, in figure II
U $\xrightarrow{+5}$ Z $\xrightarrow{+5}$ E $\xrightarrow{+5}$ J
Similarly, in figure III
O $\xrightarrow{+5}$ T $\xrightarrow{+5}$ $\boxed{Y}$ $\xrightarrow{+5}$ D
Required term = 51 and Y.

CHAPTER 18

Mathematical Statements and Conclusions (Inequality)

Statements and Conclusions

In this chapter, some mathematical statements are usually given consisting of letters and mathematical symbols or other signs and below these two or more conclusions based on the statements are given. The candidate is required to read the given statements and then choose which of the conclusion(s) is/are definitely true.

In these questions, both the statements and conclusions are formed using mathematical symbols ($>, \geq, <, \leq, =$). We can divide these symbols into two groups.

(i) Greater family; Group ($>, \geq, =$)

(ii) Lesser family; Group ($<, \leq, =$)

Simple Inequalities

In this type of questions, certain relations between different sets of elements in terms of real symbols such as 'less than' (<), 'greater than' (>), 'equal to' (=) etc, are given followed by some conclusions. The candidate is required to analyse the given statements and then decide which of the conclusion/conclusion(s) is/are definitely true.

e.g. Read the given statement and conclusions carefully. Decide which of the given conclusion(s) is/are definitely true from the statement?

Statement $A > B > C \leq D < E \leq F$

Conclusions I. $C < F$ **II.** $C = F$

(a) Only Conclusion I is true

(b) Only Conclusion II is true

(c) Neither Conclusion I nor II is true

(d) Both Conclusions I and II are true

Sol. (a) According to the question,

$A > B > C \leq D < E \leq F$

Conclusions I. $C < F$ (✓)

II. $C = F$ (✗)

Hence, only Conclusion I is true.

Coded Inequalities

In coded inequalities all the signs ($>, <, =, \geq, \leq$) are written in coded form. i.e. substituted symbols are used in place of real symbols e.g. the sign of greater than (>) can be coded as ϕ/@/*/$ etc.

The candidates are required to replace the codes with real signs and then choose which of the given conclusion/conclusions is/are definitely true.

e.g. 'P#Q' means, P is greater than Q.
'P$Q' means, P is neither greater than nor smaller than Q.

Read the following statement and decide which of these conclusion(s) is/are correct?

Statement A # B $ C $ D # E

Conclusions I. A#D II. B$E

(a) Only Conclusion II is true

(b) Only Conclusion I is true

(c) Both Conclusions I and II are true

(d) Neither Conclusion I nor II is true

Sol. (b) According to the question,

$A > B = C = D > E$

# → >	$ → =

Conclusions I. $A > D$ (✓) II. $B = E$ (✗)

Hence, only Conclusion I is true.

Table of Important Signs with their Meaning

Signs	Meaning	Example	Explanation
=	Equal to	A = B	(i) A is equal to B. (ii) A is neither greater nor smaller than B.
>	Greater than	A > B	(i) A is greater than B. (ii) A is neither smaller than nor equal to B
<	Less than	A < B	(i) A is less than B. (ii) A is neither greater than nor equal to B.
≥	Greater than or equal to	A ≥ B	(i) A is greater than or equal to B. (ii) A is not less than B.
≤	Less than or equal to	A ≤ B	(i) A is less than or equal to B. (ii) A is not greater than B.
≠	Not equal to	A ≠ B	(i) A is not equal to B. (ii) A is either greater than or less than B.

Condition for "Either-or" Case

An 'either' situation will arise between any two conclusions if the following conditions are fulfilled.

(i) Both the conclusions are false.

(ii) Both the variables of both the conclusions must be same.

(iii) Check the symbols.

Such as (i) < and = or > and = are together.

(ii) < and ≥ or > and ≤ are together.

Score Booster

While verifying the truth of the conclusion between any two elements, if the symbols of both the groups i.e. big family and small family group come in between, then in this situation no relation can be formed between those two elements.

Exam Approach Examples

Based on Simple Inequality

Directions (Ex. Nos. 1 and 2) *Read the given statements and conclusions carefully. Decide which of the given conclusion(s) is/are definitely true from the statement?*

Example 1 Statement $F > B < E \le C = D \ge A > G$

Conclusions I. $G < F$ II. $C > G$ ***SSC (10+2) 2023***

(a) Only Conclusion II is true
(b) Both Conclusions I and II are true
(c) Only Conclusion I is true
(d) Neither Conclusion I nor II is true

Sol. (*a*) According to the statement,

$$F > B < E \le C = D \ge A > G$$

Conclusions I. $G < F$ (✗) II. $C > G$ (✓)

Hence, only Conclusion II is true.

> **Trending Concept**
> These questions based on simple inequalities and coded inequalities are asked in current examination of SSC CHSL, CGL, RRB NTPC, RRB Group-D, RPF Constable.

Example 2 Statement $S = A < P > R \le T < U$

Conclusions I. $U > A$ II. $S \le T$ ***DSSSB (Grade-IV) 2019***

(a) Only Conclusion II follows
(b) Only Conclusion I follows
(c) Either Conclusion I or II follows
(d) Neither Conclusion I nor II follows

Sol. (*d*) According to the statement,

$$S = A < P > R \le T < U$$

Conclusions I. $U > A$ (✗) II. $S \le T$ (✗)

Hence, neither Conclusion I nor II follows.

Example 3 Read the given statement and conclusion carefully. Decide which of the given conclusion(s) is/are true based on the given statement?

Statement $K \ge L > M < N \le X$

Conclusions I. $X > M$ II. $X > L$
III. $M < K$ IV. $L > K$ ***RRB NTPC 2022***

(a) Only Conclusion I is true
(b) Both Conclusions I and III are true
(c) Both Conclusions I and IV are true
(d) Only Conclusion II is true

Sol. (*b*) **Statement** $K \ge L > M < N \le X$

Conclusions I. $X > M$ (✓) II. $X > L$ (✗)
III. $M < K$ (✓) IV. $L > K$ (✗)

Hence, both Conclusions I and III are true.

Based on Coded Inequality

Example 4 'A&B' means 'A is smaller than B'.
'A@B' means 'A is equal to B'.
If 'P & Q @ Y & Z & T', then who is the greatest?

RRB NTPC (CBT-II) 2022

(a) Y (b) T
(c) P (d) Z

Sol. (*b*) According to the question,

$$A \& B \Rightarrow A < B$$
$$A @ B \Rightarrow A = B$$
$$P \& Q @ Y \& Z \& T$$
$$\Rightarrow P < Q = Y < Z < T$$

Hence, 'T' is the greatest.

> **Helping Tips**
> In order to solve coded inequalities questions, first decode symbols one by one then add decoded operator in the given statements and conclusions.

Example 5 Four statements are given followed by three conclusions. The meaning of the symbols used is as follows.
P & Q means P is neither greater nor smaller than Q.
P # Q means P is neither greater than nor equal to Q.
P @ Q means P is neither smaller than nor equal to Q.
P % Q means P is not greater than Q.
P $ Q means P is not smaller than Q.
Read the following statements and decide which of the following conclusion(s) is/are correct?

Statement C & D, A # M
C @ T, T @ A

Conclusions I. C @ A
II. D @ A
III. M & T ***DSSSB (Grade-II) 2019***

(a) Only Conclusions II and III are true
(b) All Conclusions I, II and III are true
(c) Only Conclusions I and III are true
(d) Only Conclusions I and II are true

Sol. (*d*) According to the question,

& ⇒ = ; # ⇒ < ; @ ⇒ > ; % ⇒ ≤ ; $ ⇒ ≥

$C = D, A < M, C > T, T > A$

$$\Rightarrow D = C > T > A < M$$

Conclusions
I. $C @ A \Rightarrow C > A$ (✓)
II. $D @ A \Rightarrow D > A$ (✓)
III. $M \& T \Rightarrow M = T$ (✗)

Hence, only Conclusions I and II are true.

Chapter Challenge

Based on Simple Inequality

Directions (Q. Nos. 1-6) *Read the given statement and conclusions carefully. Decide which of the given conclusion(s) is/are definitely true from the statement?*

1. **Statement** $A = F \geq S > H < Z > R = G$
Conclusions I. $S < G$
II. $S \geq A$ *RRC Group-D 2022*
(a) Only Conclusion I is true
(b) Only Conclusion II is true
(c) Both Conclusions I and II are true
(d) Neither Conclusion I nor II is true

2. **Statement** $S < G < X = T > W > Q < R$.
Conclusions I. $W < X$
II. $Q = S$ *RRB NTPC 2021*
(a) Both Conclusions I and II follow
(b) Either Conclusion I or II follows
(c) Only Conclusion II follows
(d) Only Conclusion I follows

3. **Statement** $A > B > C \leq D = E \leq F$
Conclusions I. $C < F$ II. $C = F$
(a) Neither Conclusion I nor II is true
(b) Either Conclusion I or II is true
(c) Only Conclusion II is true
(d) Only Conclusion I is true

4. **Statement** $W = H \leq G < C \geq T = L > M$
Conclusions I. $W < T$
II. $C > M$ *RRB NTPC 2022*
(a) Neither Conclusion I nor II is true
(b) Both Conclusions I and II are true
(c) Only Conclusion II is true
(d) Only Conclusion I is true

5. **Statement** $Z = E \geq R > G < Y > Q = F$
Conclusions I. $R < F$
II. $R \geq Z$ *SSC CGL (Tier-II) 2023*
(a) Both Conclusions I and II are true
(b) Only Conclusion II is true
(c) Only Conclusion I is true
(d) Neither Conclusion I nor II is true

6. **Statement** $A = B \geq C \leq D > G < E < F$
Conclusions I. $B > F$
II. $C < A$ *SSC CGL (Tier-II) 2023*
(a) Only Conclusion I is true
(b) Only Conclusion II is true
(c) Neither Conclusion I nor II is true
(d) Both Conclusions I and II are true

Directions (Q. Nos. 7-10) *In these questions, a relationship between different elements is shown in the statements. The statements are followed by conclusions. Study the conclusions based on the given statements and select the appropriate answer.*
(a) Only Conclusion I is true
(b) Only Conclusion II is true
(c) Neither Conclusion I nor II is true
(d) Both Conclusions I and II are true

7. **Statement** $P \leq L \geq M \geq N = U < V < G$
Conclusions I. $P > V$
II. $G \leq L$ *SSC (10+2) 2024*

8. **Statement** $Z > F \geq A = B = G > S < E$
Conclusions I. $Z < A$
II. $G < F$ *SSC CGL (Tier-I) 2023*

9. **Statement** $T \geq M < W = P \geq Q > R \leq S$
Conclusions I. $P \leq M$
II. $Q > T$ *SSC (10+2) 2024*

10. **Statement** $M < K \leq N > P = J > O \geq L$
Conclusions I. $N > L$
II. $O = M$ *SSC (10+2) 2023*

11. In this question, a statements is followed by two conclusions numbered I and II. Decide which of the two conclusion(s) is/are true based on the given statement?

> ***MRC******
> ***(Most Repeating Concepts)***
> Q. Nos. 1, 2, 4, 6, 7, 8, 10 and 12 are very important from the examination point of view. The concept of simple inequality is being repeatedly asked in SSC CGL, CHSL, Steno, RRB NTPC and UP Police SI examination.

Statement $M < N \leq O = S > T \geq W > Z$
Conclusions I. $M \leq T$
II. $N < Z$ *SSC CHSL (Tier-II) 2024*
(a) Only Conclusion II is true
(b) Only Conclusion I is true
(c) Both Conclusions I and II are true
(d) Neither Conclusion I nor II is true

12. In this question, relationship between different elements is shown in the statements. This statement is followed by two conclusions.
Statements $K > I > T = C, N \geq E > H \leq C$
Conclusions I. $I \geq C$
II. $K > C$
Choose the appropriate one from the following options. *UP Police SI*
(a) Only Conclusion I follows
(b) Only Conclusion II follows
(c) Neither I nor II follows
(d) Both Conclusions I and II follow

13. Read the given statements and conclusions carefully. Decide which of the given conclusion(s) is/are definitely true from the statement?

Statements

$C > U \leq S < T = O > D \geq Y, Z = O \leq P$

Conclusions I. $Z > Y$

II. $C < O$ ***RRB JE 2019***

(a) Only Conclusion I follows
(b) Both Conclusions I and II follow
(c) Only Conclusion II follows
(d) Either Conclusion I or II follows

Directions (Q. Nos. 14-16) *In the following questions, relationship between different elements is shown in the statements. These statements are followed by two conclusions. Read them carefully and mark the appropriate answer.*

(a) Both Conclusions I and II follow
(b) Only Conclusion I follows
(c) Neither Conclusion I nor II follows
(d) Only Conclusion II follows

14. **Statements** $X < Y, X = J, Y \leq M, Z \leq J$

Conclusions I. $Y = J$

II. $M > Z$ ***RRB NTPC 2022***

15. **Statements** $M \leq N < O, A \geq B < C = O$

Conclusions I. $N > B$

II. $C > M$ ***RRB NTPC 2022***

16. **Statements** $A > B \leq C, P < Q \geq A$

Conclusions I. $B \leq P$

II. $C \leq Q$ ***RRB NTPC 2022***

Directions (Q. Nos. 17-19) *In the questions below are given a statement followed by Conclusions* I, II *and* III. *On the basis of the given statements, find out which of the following conclusion(s) is/are true ?*

17. **Statements** $B < R \leq E = V; V < I = T > Y$

Conclusions I. $B > V$ II. $R < T$

III. $V > Y$ ***RPF Constable 2019***

(a) Only I and III (b) Only II and III
(c) Only II (d) All are true

18. **Statements**

$B = S \geq T < H = A; C > Q = U < T < D;$
$F > E > D = K$

Conclusions I. $K > Q$ II. $B > C$

III. $C > K$ ***RPF SI 2018***

(a) Only II and III (b) Only I
(c) Only III (d) Only I and II

19. **Statement** $F \leq H < J \geq V > E$

Conclusions I. $H < V$ II. $J > E$

III. $F < E$ ***RRB JE 2019***

(a) Only Conclusion II is true
(b) Only Conclusions I and III are true
(c) Only Conclusion III is true
(d) Only Conclusion I is true

20. A statement is followed by four conclusions. Which of the conclusion(s) is/are true based on the given statement? ***SSC CGL (Tier-I) 2023***

Statement $I < M < F \leq D \leq S = J$

Conclusions I. $S < M$

II. $F = S$

III. $I > J$

IV. $M < D$

(a) Only Conclusion IV is true
(b) Both Conclusions I and III are true
(c) Only Conclusion II is true
(d) Conclusions IV and II are true

21. If $G = E < D < R$ and $E = Y > K > Q$, then which of the following option is not correct? ***SSC Steno 2021***

(a) $G < Q$ (b) $R > Q$
(c) $G < R$ (d) $Y < R$

22. If $U = M > J = R$ and $J = S < T$, then which of the following option is not correct? ***SSC Steno 2020***

(a) $J < T$ (b) $M > T$
(c) $J < U$ (d) $R = S$

23. If $N > H > Q = X$ and $H = F = C < T$, then which of the following option is not correct? ***SSC Steno 2020***

(a) $N > X$ (b) $H < T$
(c) $Q < C$ (d) $C < X$

24. If $F = C < B = E$ and $D < C = A < E$, then which of the following option is not correct? ***SSC Steno 2023***

(a) $A < B$ (b) $E > D$
(c) $A = F$ (d) $A > E$

25. If $D = B > C = F$ and $F < B = E < A$, then which of the following option is not correct? ***SSC Steno 2023***

(a) $A > C$ (b) $A < F$
(c) $E = D$ (d) $F < E$

Directions (Q. Nos. 26-28) *Each statement given below is followed by four options. Based on the given statement, find out which option is true ?*

26. **Statement** $L \leq H = P > O > D \geq S = U$ ***RRC Group-D 2022***

(a) $L \leq P$ (b) $U \geq D$ (c) $L > D$ (d) $L > O$

27. **Statement** $R > T \geq N > U = S \leq Z < V$ ***RRB NTPC 2022***

(a) $R > U$ (b) $N < Z$
(c) $V < T$ (d) $T = S$

28. In this question, two statements are followed by four conclusions given as options. Decide which conclusion is definitely true, based on the given statements?

Statements $A < B \geq C > D$

$C > E \geq F = G$ ***SSC CGL (Tier-II) 2025***

(a) $G > C$ (b) $D < F$
(c) $A < E$ (d) $B > G$

Based on Coded Inequality

29. Study the given statement and conclusions carefully and decide which of the given conclusions logically follows from the statement?

P # Q means P is greater than Q.

P $ Q means P is either greater than or equal to Q.

P = Q means P is smaller than Q.

Statement

C $ E, F # C, D = E

Conclusions I. C # D II. E # D ***DSSSB TGT 2023***

(a) Only Conclusion II follows
(b) Both Conclusions I and II follow
(c) Only Conclusion I follows
(d) Either Conclusion I or II follows

> **Trending Concept**
> Q. Nos. 29 and 30 based on coded inequalities are being repeatedly asked in DSSSB TGT, Grade II examination, it is very important for upcoming examinations.

30. Four statements are given followed by three conclusions.

The meaning of the symbols used in them is as follows.

P @ Q means P is neither smaller nor greater than Q.

P # Q means P is neither greater than nor equal to Q.

P & Q means P is neither smaller than nor equal to Q.

P % Q means P is not greater than Q.

P $ Q means P is not smaller than Q.

Now read the following statements and decide which of the conclusion(s) is/are correct?

Statements

S @ Z; J # Q; S & P; P & J

Conclusions I. S & J II. Z & J

III. Q @ P ***DSSSB (Grade II) 2019***

(a) Conclusions I and II are true
(b) All Conclusions I, II and III are true
(c) Conclusions I and III are true
(d) Only Conclusions II and III are true

Directions (Q. Nos. 31-33) *In the following questions, the symbols @, ©, $, % and # are used with the meaning as illustrated below.*

'A $ B' means 'A is not smaller than B'.

'A © B' means 'A is neither smaller than nor greater than B'.

'A @ B' means 'A is neither smaller than nor equal to B'.

'A # B' means 'A is not greater than B'.

'A % B' means 'A is neither greater than nor equal to B'.

In each of the following questions, assuming the given statements to be true, find which of the three Conclusion(s) I, II and III given below is/are definitely true?

31. **Statements** K © P, P @ Q, Q $ R

Conclusions I. K @ R II. R % P

III. Q % R

(a) I and II are true (b) II and III are true
(c) Only III is true (d) All are true

32. **Statements** D © K, K # F, F @ P

Conclusions I. P @ D II. K # P

III. F $ D

(a) Only I is true (b) Only II is true
(c) Only III is true (d) II and III are true

33. **Statements** M @ D, D © V, V $ W

Conclusions I. W @ M II. M % V

III. D $ W

(a) Both II and III are true (b) Only II is true
(c) Only III is true (d) Only I is true

Right Key

1. (d)	2. (d)	3. (b)	4. (c)	5. (d)	6. (c)	7. (c)	8. (c)	9. (c)	10. (a)
11. (d)	12. (b)	13. (a)	14. (d)	15. (d)	16. (c)	17. (c)	18. (b)	19. (a)	20. (a)
21. (a)	22. (b)	23. (d)	24. (d)	25. (b)	26. (a)	27. (a)	28. (d)	29. (b)	30. (a)
31. (d)	32. (c)	33. (c)							

Solutions

1. *(d)* Given statement,

$A = F \geq S > H < Z > R = G$

Conclusions I. $S < G =$ (✗)

II. $S \geq A$ (✗)

Hence, neither Conclusion I nor II is true.

2. *(d)* Given statement,

$S < G < X = T > W > Q < R$

Conclusions I. $W < X$ (✓)

II. $Q = S$ (✗)

Hence, only Conclusion I follows.

3. *(b)* Given statement,

$A > B > C \leq D = E \leq F$

Conclusions I. $C < F$ (✗)

II. $C = F$ (✗)

Here, Conclusions I and II makes a complementary pair.

Hence, either Conclusion I or II is true.

4. *(c)* Given statement,

$W = H \leq G < C \geq T = L > M$

Conclusions I. $W < T$ (✗)

II. $C > M$ (✓)

Hence, only Conclusion II is true.

5. *(d)* Given statement,

$Z = E \geq R > G < Y > Q = F$

Conclusions

I. $R < F$ (✗)

II. $R \geq Z$ (✗)

Hence, neither Conclusion I nor II is true.

6. *(c)* Given statement,

$(A = B \geq C \leq D > G < E < F)$

Conclusions I. $B > F$ (✗)

II. $C < A$ (✗)

Hence, neither Conclusion I nor II is true.

7. *(c)* Given statement,

$P \leq L \geq M \geq N = U < V < G$

Conclusions I. $P > V$ (✗)

II. $G \leq L$ (✗)

Hence, neither Conclusion I nor II is true.

8. *(c)* Given statement,

$Z > F \geq A = B = G > S < E$

Conclusions I. $Z < A$ (✗)

II. $G < F$ (✗)

Hence, neither Conclusion I nor II is true.

9. *(c)* Given statement,

$T \geq M < W = P \geq Q > R \leq S$

Conclusions I. $P \leq M$ (✗)

II. $Q > T$ (✗)

Hence, neither Conclusion I nor II is true.

10. *(a)* Given statement,

$M < K \leq N > P = J > O \geq L$

Conclusions I. $N > L$ (✓)

II. $O = M$ (✗)

Hence, only Conclusion I is true.

11. *(d)* Given statement,

$M < N \leq O = S > T \geq W \geq Z$

Conclusions I. $M \leq T$ (✗)

II. $N < Z$ (✗)

Hence, neither Conclusion I nor Conclusion II is true.

12. *(b)* Given statement,

$K > I > T = C \quad N \geq E > H \leq C$

On combining

$K > I > T = C \geq H < E \leq N$

Conclusions I. $I \geq C$ (✗)

II. $K > C$ (✓)

Hence, only Conclusion II follows.

13. *(a)* Given statement,

$C > U \leq S < T = O > D \geq Y$ ...(i)

$Z = O \leq P$ ...(ii)

Conclusions I. $Z > Y$ (✓)

II. $C < O$ (✗)

Hence, only Conclusion I follows.

TOP TIPS While combining the statements, arrange maximum parts given in question in one line.

14. *(d)* According to the statements,

$Z \leq J = X < Y \leq M$

Conclusions I. $Y = J$ (✗)

II. $M > Z$ (✓)

Hence, only Conclusion II follows.

15. *(d)* According to the statement,

$M \leq N < O = C > B \leq A$

Conclusions I. $N > B$ (✗)

II. $C > M$ (✓)

Hence, only Conclusion II follows.

16. *(c)* According to the statement,

$P < Q \geq A > B \leq C$

Conclusions I. $B \leq P$ (✗)

II. $C \leq Q$ (✗)

Hence, neither Conclusion I nor II follows.

17. *(c)* According to the statement,

$B < R \leq E = V < I = T > Y$

Conclusions I. $B > V$ (✗)

II. $R < T$ (✓)

III. $V > Y$ (✗)

Hence, only Conclusion II is true.

18. *(b)* According to the statement,

$B = S \geq T < H = A$ ...(i)

$C > Q = U < T < D$ ...(ii)

$F > E > D = K$ ...(iii)

From Eqs. (ii) and (iii),

$C > Q = U < T < D = K < E < F$

From Eqs. (i) and (ii),

$B = S \geq T > U = Q < C$

Conclusions

I. $K > Q$ (✓) II. $B > C$ (✗)

III. $C > K$ (✗)

Hence, only Conclusion I is true.

19. *(a)* Given statement,

$F \leq H < J \geq V > E$

Conclusions

I. $H < V$ (✗) II. $J > E$ (✓)

III. $F < E$ (✗)

Hence, only Conclusion II is true.

20. *(a)* Given statement,

$I < M < F \leq D \leq S = J$

Conclusions

I. $S < M$ (✗) II. $F = S$ (✗)

III. $I > J$ (✗) IV. $M < D$ (✓)

Hence, only Conclusion IV is true.

21. *(a)* Given statement,

$G = E < D < R$ and $E = Y > K > Q$

$\Rightarrow G = E = Y > K > Q$

$\Rightarrow R > D > E > Y > K > Q$

From options,

(a) $G < Q$ (✗)

(b) $R > Q$ (✓)

(c) $G < R$ (✓)

(d) $Y < R$ (✓)

Hence, $G < Q$ is not correct.

22. *(b)* Given statement,

$U = M > J = R$ and $J = S < T$

$\Rightarrow U = M > J = S < T$

$\Rightarrow R = J = S$

From options,

(a) $J < T$ (✓)

(b) $M > T$ (✗)

(c) $J < U$ (✓)

(d) $R = S$ (✓)

Hence, $M > T$ is not correct.

23. *(d)* Given statements,

$N > H > Q = X$ and $H = F = C < T$

$\Rightarrow X = Q < H = F = C$

From options,

(a) $N > X$ (✓)

(b) $H < T$ (✓)

(c) $Q < C$ (✓)

(d) $C < X$ (✗)

Hence, $C < X$ is incorrect.

24. *(d)* Given statement,

$F = C < B = E$ and $D < C = A < E$

$\Rightarrow F = A = C < B$

From options,

(a) $A < B$ (✓)

(b) $E > D$ (✓)

(c) $A = F$ (✓)

(d) $A > E$ (✗)

Hence, $A > E$ is not correct.

25. *(b)* Given statements,

$D = B > C = F$ and $F < B = E < A$

$\Rightarrow D = B > C = F < B = E < A$

From options,

(a) $A > C$ (✓) (b) $A < F$ (✗)

(c) $E = D$ (✓) (d) $F < E$ (✓)

Hence, '$A < F$' is not correct.

26. *(a)* Given statement,

$L \leq H = P > O > D \geq S = U$

From options,

(a) $L \leq P$ (✓) (b) $U \geq D$ (✗)

(c) $L > D$ (✗) (d) $L > O$ (✗)

Hence, option (a) is true.

27. *(a)* Given statement,

$R > T \geq N > U = S \leq Z < V$

From options,

(a) $R > U$ (✓) (b) $N < Z$ (✗)

(c) $V < T$ (✗) (d) $T = S$ (✗)

Hence, option (a) is true.

28. *(d)* According to the statements,

$A < B \geq C > D, C > E \geq F = G$

$\Rightarrow D < C > E \geq F$

$\Rightarrow A < B \geq C > E \geq F = G$

From options,

(a) $G > C$ (✗) (b) $D < F$ (✗)

(c) $A < E$ (✗) (d) $B > G$ (✓)

Hence, option (d) is true.

> **TOP TIPS** If $a \geq b > c$, then $a > c$ is always true.

29. *(b)* According to the question,

$P \# Q \Rightarrow P > Q$

$P \$ Q \Rightarrow P \geq Q$

$P = Q \Rightarrow P < Q$

Statement $C \geq E$; $F > C$; $D < E$

$\Rightarrow F > C \geq E > D$

Conclusions

I. $C > D$ (✓) II. $E > D$ (✓)

Hence, both Conclusions I and II follow.

30. *(a)* According to the question,

$P @ Q \rightarrow P = Q$

$P \# Q \rightarrow P < Q$

$P \& Q \rightarrow P > Q$

$P \% Q \rightarrow P \leq Q$

$P \$ Q \rightarrow P \geq Q$

Statement $S = Z, J < Q, S > P, P > J$

$\Rightarrow Z = S > P > J < Q$

Conclusions

I. $S \& J \Rightarrow S > J$ (✓)

II. $Z \& J \Rightarrow Z > J$ (✓)

III. $Q @ P \Rightarrow Q = P$ (✗)

Hence, Conclusions I and II are true.

Sol. (Q. Nos. 31-33) According to the given information,

$A \$ B \rightarrow A \geq B$

$A © B \rightarrow A = B$

$A @ B \rightarrow A > B$

$A \# B \rightarrow A \leq B$

$A \% B \rightarrow A < B$

31. *(d)* Given statements,

$K © P, P @ Q, Q \$ R$

$\Rightarrow K = P, P > Q, Q \geq R$

$\Rightarrow K = P > Q \geq R$

Conclusions

I. $K @ R \rightarrow K > R$ (✓)

II. $R \% P \rightarrow R < P$ (✓)

III. $Q \% K \rightarrow Q < K$ (✓)

Hence, all conclusions are true.

32. *(c)* Given statements,

$D © K, K \# F, F @ P$

$\Rightarrow D = K, K \leq F, F > P$

$\Rightarrow D = K \leq F > P$

Conclusions

I. $P @ D \rightarrow P > D$ (✗)

II. $K \# P \rightarrow K \leq P$ (✗)

III. $F \$ D \rightarrow F \geq D$ (✓)

Hence, only Conclusion III is true.

33. *(c)* Given statements,

$M @ D, D © V, V \$ W$

$\Rightarrow M > D, D = V, V \geq W$

$\Rightarrow M > D = V \geq W$

Conclusions

I. $W @ M \rightarrow W > M$ (✗)

II. $M \% V \rightarrow M < V$ (✗)

III. $D \$ W \rightarrow D \geq W$ (✓)

Hence, only Conclusion III is true.

CHAPTER

19 Decision Making

Decision Making

Decision making is a process in which a final decision is taken by analysing the pros and cons of the given information. In decision making questions, some conditions are given. Candidates need to analyse the given conditions and then decide the suitable decision from the given options.

There are two types of questions which are generally asked

(i) Situational Response Question

(ii) Data Decision/Eligibility Test.

Based on Situational Response

The immediate reaction of a person to an event occurring in a particular situation is called 'situational reaction'.

In these questions, information is given about an incident that happened in a particular situation and four/five immediate reactions regarding the incident are given as options. Candidates, need to find out which answer is appropriate for the given question.

e.g. Today is your sister's birthday. And you have been instructed to work overtime in your firm due to some emergency. What will you do in such a situation?

(a) Will ignore it

(b) Be responsible and do your duty

(c) Request your management to give you some time off so, that you can celebrate with your sister

(d) Do not want to answer

Sol. (c) In this situation sister's birthday and company's urgent work both are important. The persons should not ignore any of them completely. So, the best possible decision is that the person must request management to give him sometime off so, that he can celebrate sister's birthday and then complete the work.

Data Decision/Eligibility Test

In data decision making, some information or instructions are given. Just below them, some special conditions or conditions along with sub-conditions are given. On the basis of these instructions, it has to be decided which decision is completely appropriate and correct for a person.

e.g. Study the following information carefully and answer the question given below.

The following are the criteria for selection of the principal of a college by a number of people. He

I. Must have completed PhD in any subject.

II. Have 10 years of experience in this field.

If a candidate fulfills all the above criteria. Except

A. I above but has a PhD is incomplete, the case will be referred to the Dean of the institution.

B. If there is no experience as per clause II above, the case will be referred to the Chairman.

Nasiman completed his PhD. He is 46 years old and has 10 years of experience as Principal.

(a) The matter shall be referred to the Chairman.

(b) The matter will be referred to the Dean.

(c) The data is inadequate.

(d) Selection has to be made.

Sol. (d) Since, Nasiman follows all the required criteria, therefore he is to be selected.

Score Booster

While selecting the options in questions based on decision making ability, one should use his practical knowledge and experience so that appropriate decision can be taken.

Exam Approach Examples

Based on Situational Response

Example 1 **You are a Finance Minister of any country. There is recession in the economy of that country. What best action would you take?** ***HSSC CET 2022***

(a) Try to get money from international agencies.
(b) Implement good financial policies to enhance the economy of the country.
(c) Divert the mind of the public to other issues.
(d) Try to borrow money from other countries.
(e) None of the above

Sol. (*b*) According to the statement as a Finance Minister we have to implement good financial policies to enhance the country's economy forward.

Example 2 **You are the executive officer of a polling station. During polling, a Maoist group comes and intimidates the voters and fires bullets in the air. What will you do in such a situation?**

(a) The voting will be stopped immediately.
(b) Inform the police force deployed there and ask them to secure all important documents.
(c) Ask the police to oppose the Maoists with force.
(d) We will save lives by giving the Maoists whatever they want.

Sol. (*b*) In such a situation, the police force deployed there should be informed and all the important documents should be secured, which is the most appropriate option among all.

Option (a) A decision to stop voting immediately would be a boost to the Maoist efforts.

Option (c) Asking the police to resist forcefully would not be an appropriate because this task comes under the police's specialised area. Option (d) The decision to save life by surrendering to the Maoists would be cowardly. Such a decision can be taken only in a situation of no choice.

Based on Data Decision/Eligibility Test

Example 3 **A multinational company ABC has the following criteria for selecting executive trainees.**

Candidates must fulfill the following requirements. ***Rajasthan Police Constable 2022***

a. Diploma or Degree in Business Administration with above 60% marks.
b. Be below 27 yr of age as on September 30, 2022.
c. Have at least 2 yr of experience in project management. However, the candidate must satisfy all of the above criteria except the following.
d. (a) but scores 75% marks in the interview, his/her case is to be referred to the Director, Human Resources.
e. At (b), if the candidate fulfills (a) and (c) but his age is six months more or less than the prescribed age, his case is to be sent to the Recruitment Incharge G for backup.

Shyam Sundar is a B.B.A and secured 70% marks. He has three years of experience in management. He was born on May 16, 1994. What will be the decision in his case?

(a) He will be selected
(b) He will not be selected
(c) His/her case is to be referred to the Director, Human Resources
(d) Their case is to be referred to the recruitment incharge

Sol. (*b*) Age of Shyam Sundar (from 16th May, 1994 to 30th September, 2022) = 28 yr 4 months 14 days. Shyam Sundar fulfills requirement (a) and requirement (c). But his age is more than 27 yr. Hence, he will not be selected.

Example 4 **Read the following information carefully and answer the question given below.**

> **Helping Tips**
> If any important eligibility is not given in the information, then always think that the candidate is not to be selected.

Sudeep is applying for residential accommodation in IOCL Panipat company. To get residential accommodation from IOCL company, the employee must fulfill the following criteria. ***RRB Group-D 2018***

(i) He must have worked in the company for at least 10 yr and in department ABC for at least 4 yr.
(ii) His family should consist of a maximum of five members.
(iii) Have at least 5 yr of service remaining before attaining the retirement age of 58 yr.
(iv) He/she should not be the owner or co-owner of a house (if one of the spouses is the owner.) For cases where an employee.

A. fulfills all the conditions except (i) above and has joined the company as a manager, shall be referred to as a Director.
B. fulfills all the conditions except (iii) above and is working as a senior manager in the company, he shall be referred to as the Managing Director.

If transferred from any other city, condition (i) may be deleted.

Based on the above conditions, decide whether to provide accommodation to Sudeep. Whether the matter will be referred to higher authority. All the matters are presented on July 31, 2016. Sudeep has been transferred from another office and his age as on February 6, 2016 was 53 yr.

He has been working in the company for the last 20 yr out of which he has worked in ABC department for 6 yrs. There are 4 members in his family and neither he nor his wife owns any house.

(a) His case will be referred to the Director.
(b) Sudeep will be provided company accommodation.
(c) His case will be referred to the Managing Director.
(d) Sudeep will not be provided company accommodation.

Sol. (*d*) Since, Sudeep does not have at least 5 yr of service left before his retirement age of 58 yr, Sudeep will not be provided company accommodation.

Example 5 Study the following information carefully and answer the question given below.

Following are the conditions for selection of Assistant General Manager HR in an organisation. The candidate must have

(i) Be a graduate with at least first class.
(ii) Should not be more than 25 yr of age as on August 15, 2018.
(iii) Have secured minimum 50% marks in the entrance examination.
(iv) Should be fluent in English.

If a candidate fulfills all the criteria except (i) but is a post graduate with minimum 55% marks, his/her case should be referred to the Chairman. If a candidate fulfills all the criteria except (iii) but has secured minimum 45% marks in the entrance examination, he/she will be waitlisted.

Ravi is fluent in English. He is a graduate with first division and scored 58% marks in the entrance exam. He was born on June 1, 1991. ***UP Police (AO) 2023***

(a) The candidate should not be admitted.
(b) The candidate should be waitlisted.
(c) The candidate should be sent to the Speaker.
(d) The candidate must be admitted.

Sol. (*a*) Ravi does not fulfill all the criteria as his age is more than 25 yr as on August 15, 2018, so he should not be admitted in the organisation.

Example 6 Consider the following conditions for the selection of faculty members in a Computer Education Centre. ***UP Police Constable 2024***

1. Age between 23 to 28 yr.
2. Work experience or programming experience.
3. Post Graduate Degree in Computer Applications with minimum 60% marks.
4. Minimum 25 marks out of 50 in interview.
5. If the candidate does not have PG, the matter should be referred to senior faculty member.
6. If the candidate does not have work experience, the matter is to be referred to the Principal of the Institute.
7. If the candidate fulfills all the qualifications except age limit, the case is to be referred to the Director of the Centre.

Trending Concept

The questions based on decision making are asked in current examination of UP Police AO, RRB Group D, Rajasthan Police Constable, UP Police Constable. These questions are important for the upcoming examination.

Based on the following information what action should be taken for Babli Sarkar?

Babli Sarkar: MCA with 68% marks. Age 30 years. 2.5 years experience as a programmer. Scored 40 marks in interview.

(a) The candidate is to be selected as Junior Faculty Member
(b) Data is insufficient
(c) The matter is to be referred to the Director of the Centre
(d) The candidate is not to be selected

Sol. (*c*) The candidate fulfills all the eligibility criteria except age limit.

∴ The matter should be referred to the Director of the Centre.

Chapter Challenge

Based on Situational Response

1. You were about to enter a mall when you heard the sound of a gunshot and at the same time you saw three people coming out of the mall. They fled in a white car. You note down the number of that car. After entering the mall, you came to know that a person has been shot and robbed. The person is injured, but his condition is not serious. In such a situation, you
   (a) continue doing your work as usual because other people are helping the victim and the incident is recorded on CCTV
   (b) offer assistance and take the victim to hospital
   (c) call the police, give them the car number and also call an ambulance
   (d) inform the mall management/security personnel and demand immediate action from them

2. You are given the responsibility of hiring boats at short notice in a flood-affected area. On checking the prices quoted by the boat owners, you find that the lowest price is almost three times more than the government approved rate. What will you do in such a situation?
   (a) Cancel their offer and ask for new prices.
   (b) Will accept the lowest price.
   (c) Refer the matter to the government.
   (d) Threaten boat owners that their licences may be cancelled.

3. You have been invited by the Public Service Commission of your state to appear for an interview for the post of Food Distribution Officer. You reach the railway station but see a long queue at the ticket window. The train is about to leave. You board the train without buying a ticket. On seeing a ticket checker enter your compartment, you decide
   (a) hiding in the toilet
   (b) requesting the ticket checker to permit him to travel without ticket on the ground of need to attend an interview
   (c) to submit oneself to legal proceedings
   (d) to start a quarrel with the ticket checker

4. You are incharge of implementing a family planning programme in an area where there is strong opposition to the current policy. You want to convince residents of the need to have small families. What would be the best way to communicate this message?
   (a) To rationally explain to the residents the need for family planning for improving health and quality of life.
   (b) Encouraging late marriage and proper spacing between children.
   (c) Providing incentives for adopting family planning devices.
   (d) Urging residents to talk directly to people who have been sterilised or are using contraception.

5. When you are passing by the conference room of your office and you see that all the fans are running and the lights are on, while there is no one in the conference room. What will you do?
   (a) Report to the officer-in-charge.
   (b) Ask the peon to switch off the fans and lights.
   (c) You will switch off the fans and lights yourself.
   (d) You will do nothing and walk away thinking it is none of your business.

6. As a citizen you have some work with a government department. The concerned officer calls you repeatedly and gestures you to give bribe without saying anything directly. You want to get your work done. What will you do?
   (a) Will give bribe
   (b) Act as if you do not understand her hints and stick to your application
   (c) Approach higher authority for assistance with verbal complaint regarding bribery gestures
   (d) Send a formal complaint

7. You are the chairman of a State Sports Committee. You have received a complaint and later it is found that the age of a medal winning athlete in the junior age group is five days more than the prescribed criteria. What will you do?
   (a) Ask the inquiry committee to give clarification.
   (b) Ask the athlete to return the medal.
   (c) Ask the athlete to produce an affidavit from the court declaring his age.
   (d) Ask the members of the Sports Committee for their opinion.

8. You need money to pay your examination fees urgently. While walking on the road, you find a wallet full of money.
   What will you do?
   (a) You will keep the money with yourself and deposit your examination fee.
   (b) You will try to find the owner of the wallet.
   (c) You will hand over the wallet to the police.
   (d) You will distribute wealth among the poor.

9. A woman wants to buy the following items in the given range.
   1. Tomatoes are between ₹ 40 and ₹ 45 per kg.
   2. Grapes are in the price range of ₹ 80 and ₹ 90 per kg.
   3. Milk packets are available at ₹ 23 per litre.

   From which of the following shops he will definitely get all his items? *RRB NTPC 2016*

A. Shop S sells tomatoes at ₹ 22.5 per half kg, grapes at ₹ 24 per kg and milk at ₹ 32 per litre.
B. Shop H sells grapes at ₹ 21 per quarter kilo, milk at ₹ 12.5 per half litre and tomatoes at ₹ 22 per half kilo.
C. Shop Q sells milk at ₹ 11.5 per half litre, tomatoes at ₹ 21 per half kg and grapes at ₹ 43 per half kg.
D. Shop P sells tomatoes at ₹ 23 per half kg, grapes at ₹ 23.5 per kg and milk at ₹ 85 per litre.

(a) B (b) D (c) C (d) A

Based on Data Decision/Eligibility Test

10. Read the given statement and decisions carefully and decide which of the two decisions logically follow(s) from the statement.

Statement

Students are confused regarding the choice of appropriate course/stream for higher education.

Decisions

I. Consider their interests, aptitudes and competencies while deciding on their choice.
II. Seek guidance from an education and career counsellor. *RRB NTPC 2021*

(a) Only Decision I follows
(b) None of the given decisions follow
(c) Both Decisions I and II follow
(d) Only Decision II follows

11. Study the given information carefully and answer the question that follows.

The administration has set the following criteria for the selection of a teacher in school. The candidate must.

A. Be a graduate with at least 50% marks.
B. Have a qualified bachelor's degree in education.
C. Not be less than 21 yr and not more than 32 yr as on July 1, 2021.
D. For a candidate with Master in Education, the school board may relax the upper age limit.

Rahul Verma is teaching in a reputed school. He is a 1st class graduate. He was 23 yr old when he joined the previous school as a teacher. He has also completed B.ed. *RRB NTPC 2022*

(a) The case is to be referred to the school board
(b) The data given are not sufficient to take a decision
(c) The candidate is not to be appointed
(d) The candidate is to be appointed

12. XYZ a shipping corporation company, decides to recruit management trainees for one of its plants. The company laid down the following criteria for selecting candidates

A. Should be a marine engineering graduate with a minimum of 65% marks
B. Should have done an internship of at least 1 yr with some shipping company
C. Should not be less than 21 yr of age and more than 29 yr of age as on July 1, 2020
D. Should have secured a minimum of 75% marks in the common entrance test

Anirudh who was born on March 12, 1993 is a Marine Engineer with 61% marks and has done an internship for a period of 14 months with a renowned shipping company. He has been working as a supervisor in a company for the past 2 yr. He has secured 80% marks in the common entrance test.

Based on the above date(you cannot assume anything else), decide whether Anirudh is eligible for the above post. *RRB NTPC 2022*

(a) He should be selected
(b) Data is insufficient to take a decision
(c) He should be recruited but at a lower post
(d) He should be rejected

13. A college has set of following criteria for admission to the MBA programme.

I. Candidate must have secured at least 75% in graduation.
II. Candidate must have secured at least 50% marks in the entrance examination.
III. Candidate age should be minimum of 21 yr as of June 1, 2021.
IV. Candidate must be a citizen of India.

However, a candidate who fulfills all the above conditions except

A. Subject to condition (IV), but he has been residing in India for the last five years and may be admitted temporarily.
B. The case of condition (I), but who has participated in national level games may be considered by the admission committee.

Consider and decide the case of the following candidate. Rohan is a 25 year old male, who has graduated in science with 80% marks and passed the entrance exam with 75% marks. *Rajasthan Police Constable 2022*

(a) He will be selected
(b) He will not be selected
(c) His case will be referred to the admission committee
(d) Information is not enough to make a decision

14. Following are the criteria for selection of Accounts Manager in XYZ Agro limited.

A. Candidate must be a postgraduate in commerce.
B. Candidate's age should be between 21 to 40 yr as on January 1, 2021.
C. If a candidate doesn't fulfill criteria A but has MBA with a specialisation in Accounts and Finance; his/her case will be referred to the Board of Trustees, which may grant provisional permission to the candidate to appear in an interview.
D. Candidates fulfilling criteria A and B will be called for an interview.

E. A candidate who has secured 50% stipulated marks from the interviewers in the interview will be short listed for probation.

F. Such a candidate/candidates who has been awarded Grade B or above by his/her Manager will be finally selected.

Based on the above criteria decide which of the following should be taken in the case of following candidate?

Post graduation in Commerce. Sameer secured 70% contract marks in the interview. His age was 35 yr as on July 31, 2000. ***Rajasthan Police Constable 2022***

(a) He will be put on probation
(b) Eventually he will be selected
(c) He will be rejected
(d) His case will be referred to the Board of Trustees

15. Given below is a decision followed by two Statements I and II. Read the information carefully and select the correct option.

Decision

Many private schools in country F have decided to discontinue assessments for students until grade 7. All students will be promoted to the next grade irrespective of how they have performed.

Statements

I. A survey in country F showed that students who were assessed regularly had much better grasp on concepts than those who did not have assessments on a regular basis.

II. As per the current curriculum of grades 4 to 7 in country F, 70-80% of all subject matter consists of basics which are very important for higher education. ***RRC Group-D 2022***

(a) Statement I weakens the decision but Statement II is neutral.
(b) Both Statements I and II strengthens the decision.
(c) Statements I is neutral but Statement II strengthens the decision.
(d) Both Statements I and II weakens the decision.

16. A decision followed by two Statements I and II are given. Study the given information carefully and choose the correct option.

Decision The management of Telecom Company D has decided to postpone their hiring process for next 2 months.

Statements

I. Company D has just signed on for the country's biggest project, which is expected to start in a few weeks and they'll need a huge workforce to get it done on time.

II. Due to change in management, the attrition rate in Company D has increased by 12%. ***RRC Group D 2022***

(a) Statement I does not support the decision and Statement II is a neutral statement.
(b) Both the Statements I and II do not support the decision.
(c) Both the Statements I and II support the decision.
(d) Statement I is a neutral statement and Statement II supports the decision.

> ***MRC******
> ***(Most Repeating Concepts)***
> Question Nos. 9, 10, 11, 12, 13, 14, 16, 17, 18, 21 and 22 are important from the examination point of view. These type of questions are asked in examination-RRB NTPC, UP Police Constable, Rajasthan Police Constable, RRC Group-D, UP Police Head Operator.

Directions (Q. Nos. 17-19) *Following are the criteria for selection of computer professionals in an organisation.*

Candidate ***UP Police Constable 2024***

1. Be a Computer Engineer or MCA with first class having minimum 65% marks.
2. Have secured at least 50% marks in the selection Test.
3. Have secured at least 40% marks in the interview.
4. Not be less than 21 yr and not more than 30 yr of age as on October 1, 2005.

In case of candidate who satisfies all other criteria, except

A. At (1) above, but is an Electronics Engineer with 70% marks, the case may be referred to the GM, Recruitment.

B. At (2) above, but is having at least 2 yr experience of working as a Systems Analyst, the case may be referred to the Chairman, Recruitment Committee.

In each of the following question, information about one candidate is given. You have to analyse it with reference to the above criteria and condition and then decide the appropriate course of action. You are not to assume anything other than the given information. All these cases are given to you as on October 1, 2005.

17. Sanjay is a Civil Engineer with 75% marks. He was born on July 6, 1976. He scored 70% marks in the selection test and 42% marks in the interview.

(a) If the case is to be referred to the GM, Recruitment.
(b) If the case is to be referred to the Chairman, Recruitment Committee
(c) If the candidate is to be selected
(d) If the candidate is not to be selected

18. Modi Jay did MCA in year 1998 with 70% marks at the age of 22 yr. He scored 55% marks in interview and 55% marks in the selection test. He joined an IIT company in year 1999 as programmer and got promoted as systems analyst in December, 2002.

(a) If the case is to be referred to the GM, Recruitment
(b) If the case is to be referred to the Chairman, Recruitment Committee
(c) If the candidate is to be selected
(d) If the candidate is not to be selected

19. Divya is a Computer Engineer with 80% marks. She scored more than 55% marks in interview and in the selection test. She has worked in XYZ company as a systems analyst for more than 5 yr.

(a) Data inadequate
(b) If the case is to be referred to the Chairman, Recruitment Committee
(c) If the candidate is to be selected
(d) If the candidate is not to be selected

20. Study the following information carefully and answer the question given below. Following are the conditions for selection of System Manager in an organisation. The candidate must have

(i) Should be a Graduate Engineer in IT, Computer Science or Electronics with at least 60% marks.
(ii) Should be at least 30 years and not more than 40 years of age as on September 1, 2009.
(iii) Should have secured at least 40% marks in the written examination.
(iv) Should have secured at least 50% marks in the selection interview.
(v) Should have at least 10 years post qualification work experience in the systems department of an organisation.

If a candidate fulfills all the criteria except (i) but has secured less than 60% marks in ME-IT or Computer Science, the case will be referred to DGM-Systems. If a candidate fulfills all the criteria except (v) but has at least five years of post qualification work experience as Deputy System Manager, the case will be referred to GM-Systems.

Prakash has secured 62% marks in BE Computer Science. He has been working in the systems department of an organisation since July 1999 after completion of BE. He was born on April 4, 1974. He secured 55% marks in the selection interview and 45% marks in the written examination.

UP Police Head Operator 2024

(a) The candidate cannot be selected
(b) The candidate should be referred to GM-Systems
(c) The candidate should be selected
(d) The candidate should be referred to DGM-Systems

21. The owner of a small shop maintains inventory based on the following parameters.

1. Shampoo sachets which cost between ₹ 4 to ₹10 per sachet.
2. The price of chocolate per piece ranges between ₹ 1 to ₹ 60.
3. Dry fruits cost more than ₹ 125 per 100 grams.
4. The price of milk packets per litre ranges between ₹ 21 to ₹ 29.

Which of the following lists will definitely not be found in his shop?

A. Shampoo A, ₹ 4 per sachet; chocolate B, ₹ 1.5 per piece and dry fruits C, ₹ 250 per 125 grams
B. Shampoo P, ₹ 5 per sachet; milk packets, Q ₹ 23 per litre and dry fruits R, ₹ 150 per 100 grams
C. Shampoo X, ₹ 5 per sachet, chocolate Y, ₹ 1 per piece and dry fruits Z, ₹ 100 per 100 g
D. Shampoo L, ₹ 4 per sachet; Milk packets M, ₹ 24.5 per packet and chocolate N, ₹ 35 per piece and dry fruits O, ₹ 350 per 200 grams

(a) C (c) D (b) A (d) B

22. A company wants to hire some candidates for computer related work. They must meet the following criteria.

1. Candidate must have secured minimum 65% marks in class 10th or equivalent examination.
2. Candidate must have knowledge of MS Word and Excel.
3. Candidate must have knowledge of either C or C + +.

Who among the following is the company definitely going to hire?

A. M scored 70% marks in class 10th and knows only C and MS Word.
B. S has learned C and has created a program, he also knows MS Word and Excel and he has scored 63% marks in class 10th exam.
C. H has 68% marks in the 10th class examination. He also knows MS Word and Excel but does not have any other computer knowledge.
D. U has knowledge of C + +, MS Word and Excel and has scored 65% marks in class 10th exam

(a) B (b) D (c) C (d) A

Right Key

1. (c)	2. (b)	3. (c)	4. (d)	5. (c)	6. (b)	7. (b)	8. (c)	9. (c)	10. (c)
11. (b)	12. (d)	13. (d)	14. (a)	15. (d)	16. (b)	17. (d)	18. (c)	19. (a)	20. (c)
21. (a)	22. (b)								

Solutions

1. *(c)* In this situation, we will inform the police about the incident and give them the number of the car and also call an ambulance for the injured person.

2. *(b)* Accepting the lowest price is the appropriate solution to the situation. Options (a) or (c) would take time to acquire the boats, whereas you have to deal with the situation quickly, as you have to hire the boats on short notice. Option (d) would be inappropriate.

   Thus, option (b) is the balanced approach.

3. *(c)* According to options (a) and (d), hiding in the toilet or quarreling with the ticket checker is wrong. According to option (b), requesting the ticket checker to travel without a ticket on the grounds of needing to attend an interview is wrong.

   Hence, the best option is (c) to present yourself before the ticket checker for legal action.

4. *(d)* This type of problem requires human skills, as people will share experiences through direct interactions with those who have undergone sterilisation and those who are using contraceptives.

   So, option (d) would be the right solution because the logic will not be understood by those who are orthodox and uneducated. There can be an option of encouragement but it is a long term process.

5. *(c)* When you are passing by the conference room of your office and you see that all the fans are running and lights are on even though there is no one in the conference room, it is your moral responsibility to switch off the fans and lights yourself.

6. *(b)* In this situation the problem is based on the question, since the officer is not clearly asking for bribe but is only hinting, in such a situation the solution would be to stick to your application without paying attention to his hints.

7. *(b)* In this type of problem, the decision can be taken by directive style of decision making. Here, the authorised person will take the decision according to the existing rules and his position. Here, it has been proved that the athlete has crossed the age limit.

   Hence, options (a) and (d) are not possible. Affidavit of declaration of age cannot deny the true fact. Hence, option (c) is also not correct. Its only solution can be option (b).

TOP TIPS To solve such questions, first read all the options carefully. Eliminate the options that can be eliminated and choose the most appropriate option.

8. *(c)* Option (c) is the correct answer. You will hand over the wallet to the police, which is practical and legal.

   Option (a) is not correct because it is unethical and illegal to keep the wallet and deposit your examination fee.

   Option (b) is not practically correct but is morally correct.

   Option (d) is not correct because that money doesn't belong to him, so distributing that money will be an immoral act.

9. *(c)* The woman will definitely get all her items from the shop Q. Because the price of milk there is ₹ 23 per liter, the price of tomatoes is ₹ 42 per kg and the price of grapes is ₹ 86 per kg.

10. *(c)* Students are confused so they consider their interests, aptitudes and competencies for deciding on choice and seek guidance from career and education counsellor.

    Hence, both Decisions I and II follow.

11. *(b)* Rahul Verma was 23 yr old when he joined the previous school as teacher. His present age cannot be determined from this. Hence, the data is insufficient.

12. *(d)* As, Anirudh fulfill the condition B, C and D, but not A because he has scored 61% marks in marine engineering graduate where as the requirement was 65%, so he should be rejected by the company XYZ.

13. *(d)* Information is not enough to make a decision, because it is not clear, whether Rohan is an Indian citizen or not.

14. *(a)* Sameer satisfies the conditions A, B and E. Therefore, he will be put on probation.

15. *(d)* Both the statements focus on the importance of assessment for student. But, decision talks about discontinuing the assessment.

    Hence, both Statements I and II weakens the decision.

16. *(b)* In both the statements, company is sharing the need to hire the employees. But, decision talks about postponing the hiring process.

    Hence, both the statements do not support the decision.

Sol. (Q. Nos. 17-19)

Q. Nos.	Candidate	1	2	3	A	B
17	Sanjay	×	✓	✓	–	–
18	Modi Jay	✓	✓	✓		3
19	Divya	✓	✓	✓	–	✓

17. *(d)* According to the information, Sanjay is not to be selected because condition (1) is not fulfilled by Sanjay.

18. *(c)* According to the given information, Modi Jay is selected because all conditions are fulfilled by Modi Jay.

19. *(a)* According to the information, Divya's age is not given in the question.

    Hence, data is inadequate.

20. *(c)* Prakash satisfies all the selection conditions given in the question, hence he should be selected.

21. *(a)* The price of dry fruits in the shop is more than ₹ 125 per 100 grams but the dry fruit Z in list C is priced at ₹ 100 per 100 grams. Hence, the items in list C will not be available in his shop.

22. *(b)* M violates condition (2) S violates condition (1) and H does not follow condition (3). Therefore, they will not be appointed. Only U follows all the conditions. Therefore, U will be appointed.

CHAPTER

20 Cube, Cuboid and Dice

Cube and Cuboid

Cube and cuboid are three-dimensional shapes that consist of 6 faces, 8 vertices and 12 edges. The primary difference between them is a cube has all its sides equal whereas the length, width and height of a cuboid are different. For example Ludo's dice is a cube and match box is a cuboid.

Cutting/Colouring of Cube or Cuboid

The questions asked under these are based on cutting a cube or cuboid into smaller cubes like top cube, middle cube etc. or cutting after colouring (in one or more colours) and getting coloured smaller cubes.

e.g. A cube of side 18 cm is painted yellow on all the faces and then cut into smaller cubes of sides 3 cm each. Find the number of smaller cubes that have only two faces painted.

(a) 36 (b) 48
(c) 20 (d) 64

Sol. (b) Here, $n = \dfrac{\text{Side of bigger cube}}{\text{Side of smaller cube}} = \dfrac{18}{3} = 6$

Number of smaller cubes that have only two faces painted $= 12(n-2) = 12 \times (6-2) = 12 \times 4 = 48$

Based on Counting of Blocks

In this type of questions, a mixed figure is given which is made up of various parts/blocks like cube and cuboid etc. candidates have to find the number of these small parts/blocks.

e.g. How many cubes are there in the following figure?

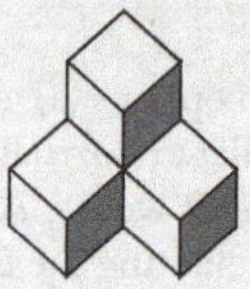

(a) 3 (b) 4 (c) 5 (d) 6

Sol. (b) Number of cubes in the column containing 2 cubes $= 2 \times 1 = 2$

Number of cubes in the column containing 1 cube $= 1 \times 2 = 2$

$\therefore$ Total number of cubes $= 2 + 2 = 4$

Dice

Dice is a three-dimensional structure having six faces like a cube and cuboid but all the faces have equal length in dice. It is having different numbers 1 to 6, dots or some letters on all its faces.

Based on Close Dice

In this type of questions, one or more than one position of the closed dice is given. Under closed dice, questions related to only one position, two positions and more than two positions are asked and according to some specific rules, numbers/points/letters/colours etc., are found on the opposite surfaces of a certain surface.

e.g. Two different positions of the same dice are given below. Find the alphabet opposite of C.

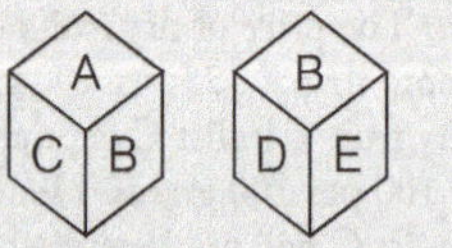

(a) E (b) A (c) B (d) D

Sol. (a) Here, B is common in both the positions.
So, starting from B in clockwise direction.

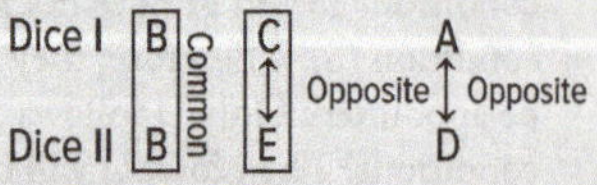

So, the alphabet E is opposite to C.

Based on Open Dice

The questions asked under these are based on spread dice/open dice. Just as the spread surface are shown from a closed dice, similarly the spread surfaces are used to form a dice. The questions in these are mainly based on making a cube/dice by folding the surfaces of the open dice and finding the opposite digit/letter/symbol.

e.g. Select the dice which cannot be formed on folding the given sheet?

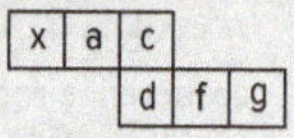

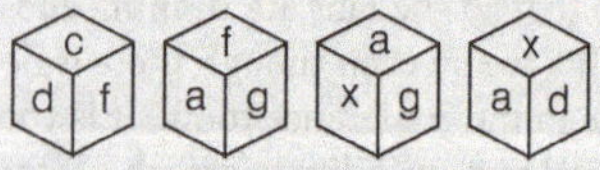

(a) (b) (c) (d)

Sol. (b) According to the question,
Forming dice by folding a given sheet along a line.

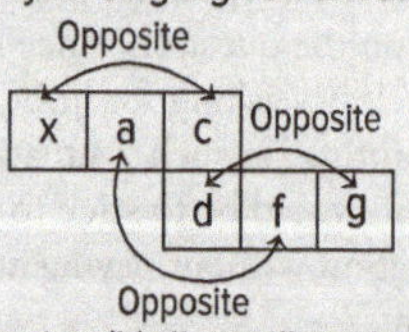

From given option (b) dice will not be formed as 'a' and 'f' are opposite to each other.

Score Booster

To boost your score in cube, cuboid and dice memorize the formula of cube and cuboid. Practice questions involving opposite faces, rotations and finding possible outcomes. Learn shortcut for identifying correct pattern in unfolded dice.

Surface

Any cube or cuboid or dice has six surfaces (faces), out of which three surfaces are visible and three surfaces are not visible, i.e., are hidden.

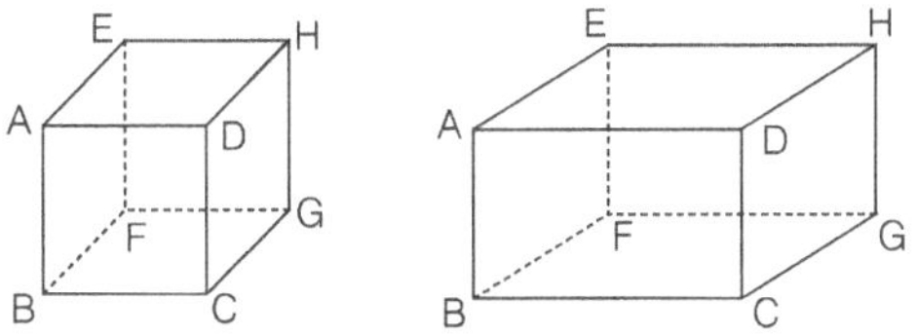

In the above figure, ABCD, ADHE, CDHG, EFGH, BCGF and ABFE are six surfaces (faces), of these, ABCD, ADHE and CDHG are visible surfaces, while EFGH, BCGF and ABFE are invisible surfaces.

In the above figure, the opposite surfaces are as follows

ABCD-front surface ⎤ Opposite
EFGH-rear surface ⎦

ADHE top surface ⎤ Opposite
BCGF bottom surface ⎦

ABFE left surface ⎤ Opposite
DCGH right surface ⎦

Top/Corner/Vertices

Any cube or cuboid or dice has eight corners (vertices), out of which seven are visible and one corner is not visible, i.e., hidden.

In the given figure, A, B, C, D, E, F, G and H are eight corners (vertices) where F is not visible.

Edge

Any cube or cuboid or dice has twelve edges, out of which nine are visible and three edges are not visible, i.e. hidden. In the given figure, AB, BC, CD, AD, AE, EH, HD, HG, CG, BF, FG and EF are the twelve edges.

Cutting of Cube

After cutting a cube into smaller equal cubes, the cubes located on its different parts are identified as follows.

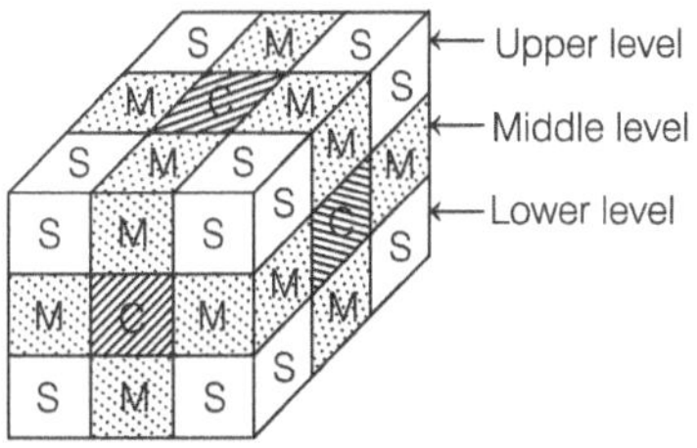

where, S = Vertex cube, M-Middle cube, C = Central cube and N = Inner central cube

(i) **Vertex Cubes** Such cubes are located at every vertex, i.e. corner. Their number is always eight for each cube, because any cube has eight corners or vertices.

(ii) **Middle Cubes** Such cubes lie exactly in the middle of each edge.

(iii) **Central Cubes** Such cubes are located exactly at the centre of each surface (face).

(iv) **Internal Central Cube** Such cubes are located in the middle of each surface (face) inside the central cube. They are not visible from outside. It is also called nucleus cube.

Important Formulae Related to Cube

- The total number of times a big cube can be divided into smaller cubes will be $(N) = (n)^3$. Where, n = total number of small cubes obtained after dividing a big cube into smaller cubes. One side of the big cube is one side of the small cube.
- Total number of top cubes = 8
- Total number of middle cubes = $12(n-2)$
- Total number of central cubes = $6(n-2)^2$
- Total number of inner central cubes = $(n-2)^3$
- Number of cuts = $3(n-1)$

Cutting a Cuboid

If a cuboid is cut into small identical cubes, then the total number of small cubes

$$= \frac{\text{Volume of the bigger cuboid}}{\text{Volume of the smaller cuboid}}$$

$$= \frac{\text{Length of cube} \times \text{Breadth} \times \text{Height}}{(\text{Side of smaller cube})^3}$$

For example If a cuboid whose length is 5 cm, width is 3 cm and height is 4 cm, then the total number of small cubes with side 1 cm is

$$= \frac{\text{Volume of bigger cuboid}}{\text{Volume of smaller cuboid}}$$

$$= \frac{5 \times 3 \times 4}{1} = 60$$

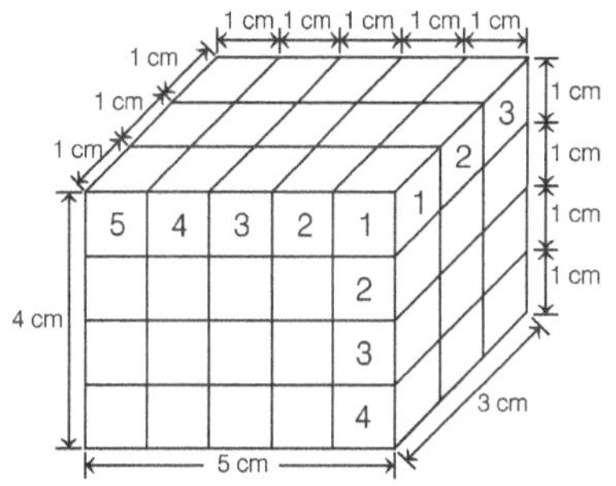

If the segments cut along the length of the cuboid are represented by Nl, segments cut along the width by Nb and segments cut along the height by Nh, then the total number of small cubes = $Nl \times Nb \times Nh$

Colouring and Cutting a Cube

If a large cube is painted with one or more colours and then it is divided into smaller and equal cubes, then the cubes located on different parts are identified in the following manner.

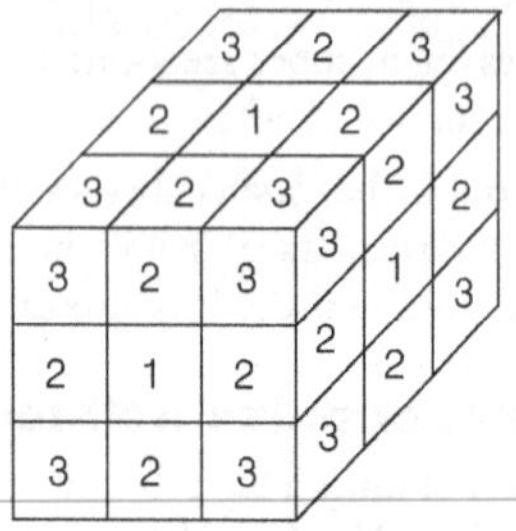

Number of Cubes When a Large Cube is Painted and Cut

- Number of smaller cubes = n^3
- Number of smaller cubes painted on three surfaces = 8
- Number of smaller cubes painted on two surfaces = $(n-2)\times 12$
- Number of smaller cubes painted on a surface = $(n-2)^2 \times 6$
- Number of smaller cubes painted on no surface = $(n-2)^3$

Colouring and Cutting a Cuboid

Under this, a cuboid is painted with one or more colours like a cube and then cut into smaller cubes.

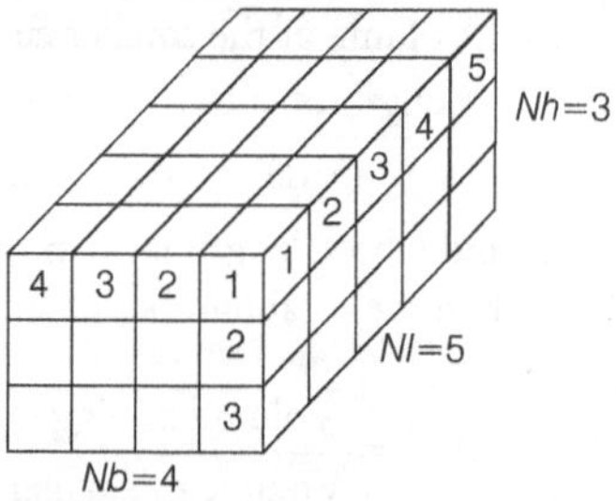

If all the sides of the painted cuboid are represented by segments and the segments cut along the length of the cuboid are represented by Nl, segments cut along the width are represented by Nb and segments cut along the height are represented by Nh, then

(i) Total number of small cubes whose four or more surfaces are colored = 0

(ii) Total number of such small cubes whose three surfaces are painted = 8

(iii) Total number of small cubes whose two surfaces are painted $= 4(Nl-2)+4(Nb-2)+4(Nh-2)$
$= 4[(Nl-2)+(Nb-2)+(Nh-2)]$

(iv) Total number of small cubes whose one surface is painted
$= 2(Nl-2)(Nb-2)+2(Nl-2)(Nh-2) + 2(Nb-2)+(Nh-2)$
$= 2[(Nl-2)(Nb-2) + (Nl-2)(Nh-2)+(Nb-2)(Nh-2)]$

(v) Total number of such small cubes whose none of the surfaces is painted $= (Nl-2)(Nb-2)(Nh-2)$

Types of Dice

If numbers or points from 1 to 6 are shown on the surfaces of a dice, then we can divide such a dice into two parts in the following manner.

1. **Normal Dice** In this type of dice the sum of the numbers on opposite surfaces is not 7, but the sum of the numbers on any two adjacent surfaces can be 7.

   As,

   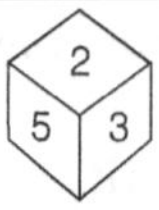

   $2+5=7$

   Hence the given dice is a normal dice.

   If the number opposite to 2 is asked, it can be any one of 1, 4 and 6.

2. **Standard Dice** The sum of the numbers on opposite sides of this type of dice is always 7. And if the sum of two adjacent sides is not 7, then it can be a standard dice.

   e.g.,

   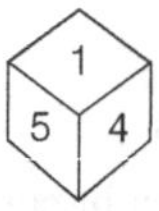

   1+4=5
   4+5=9
   1+5=6

   Hence, the given dice is a standard dice.

   In this type of dice, if the opposite number of any number is asked, then that number will be subtracted from 7

   i.e. 1 opposite $\rightarrow 7-1=6$

   2 opposite $\rightarrow 7-2=5$

Different Positions of the Dice

I. When a Single Position of the Dice is Given

If only one position of the dice is given in the question asked, then first of all it should be found out whether the given dice is a standard dice or an ordinary dice. The solution of the question should be found on this basis only.

e.g., In the dice given below, which number will be on the opposite side of number 3?

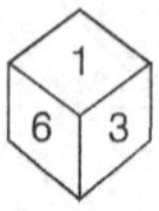

(a) 3 (b) 5
(c) 2/5 (d) 2/4/5

Sol. (*d*) In the given dice, $6+1=7$

So, this is a normal dice.

Hence, the number opposite to 3 is 2/4/5 (can be any one.)

II. When Two Positions of the Dice are Given

Two positions X and Y of the dice are shown below.

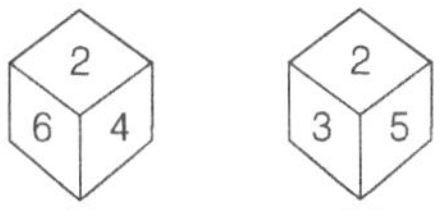

X Y

Case I When only one digit is common in two positions of the dice then starting from the common digit, write it in different series in clockwise order.

e.g. For dice X	2	Common	4	Opposite	6	Opposite
For dice Y	2		5		3	

Hence, 4 is opposite to 5,

6 is opposite to 3 and 2 is opposite to 1.

Case II When two numbers are common in both the positions of the dice.

e.g. 2 and 3 numbers are common in both the positions,

X Y

So, the remaining two digits will be opposite to each other. Hence, there will be 5 opposite to 4.

III. When Three or Four Positions of the Dice are Given,

We will first consider the pattern of that dice in which the number appears for which the question is asked and by keeping any one of the dice patterns together, we will find the answer with the help of the rules given for two dice patterns.

e.g. As shown below are the four patterns of a dice, which number will be on the face opposite to the number '1'?

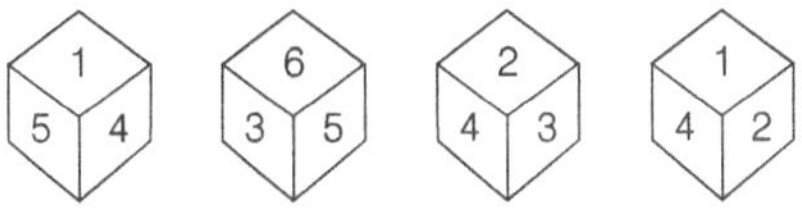

(a) 6 (b) 4 (c) 2 (d) 3

Sol. (*d*) 5 is common from positions (i) and (ii), writing clockwise from 5, from position (i) to position (ii).

From Dice I → 5 [1] 4

From Dice II → 5 [3] 6

Hence, '1' is the face opposite to '3'.

Open Dice

When a dice or a cube is formed by folding a sheet of paper, then some of the forms or patterns are as follows,

1 lies opposite to 6
2 lies opposite to 4
3 lies opposite to 5

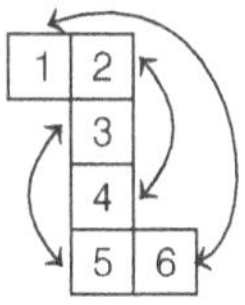

1 lies opposite to 5
2 lies opposite to 4
3 lies opposite to 6

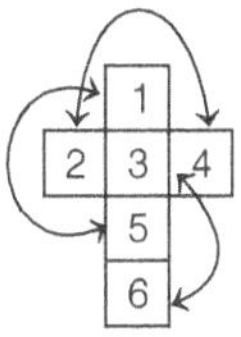

1 lies opposite to 4
2 lies opposite to 6
3 lies opposite to 5

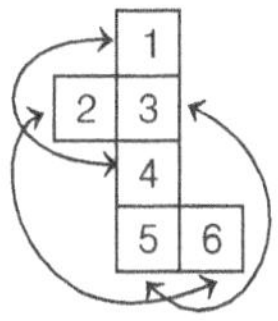

1 lies opposite to 3
2 lies opposite to 5
4 lies opposite to 6

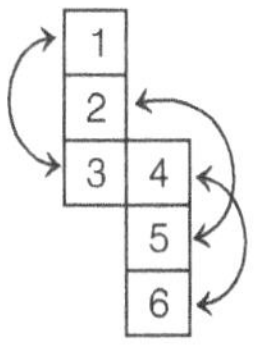

1 lies opposite to 4
2 lies opposite to 5
3 lies opposite to 6

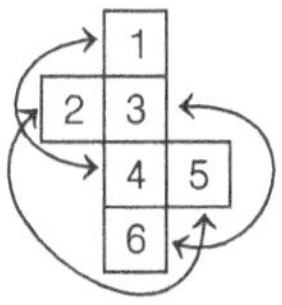

Exam Approach Examples

Based on Cutting/Colouring of Cube/Cuboid

Example 1 **A cube has each side 6 cm. In how many smaller cubes of side 1 cm each can it be divided?**

(a) 36 (b) 12
(c) 18 (d) 216

Sol. (*d*) Each side of bigger cube will be divided into 6 parts.

It means, $n = \frac{\text{Side of bigger cube}}{\text{Side of smaller cube}} = \frac{6}{1} = 6$

$\therefore$ Required number of smaller cubes $= (n)^3 = (6)^3 = 216$

Example 2 **How many smaller cubes of 1 cm side can be formed with a solid cube of 3 cm side?**

(a) 3 (b) 6 (c) 9 (d) 27

Sol. (*d*) Required number of smaller cubes

$$= \frac{\text{Volume of bigger cube}}{\text{Volume of smaller cube}}$$

$$= \frac{(3)^3}{1^3} = (3)^3 = 27$$

Example 3 **How many times will a solid cube of 4 cm side be cut to obtain smaller cubes of 2 cm side?**

(a) 2 (b) 3 (c) 5 (d) 7

Sol. (*b*) Required number of cuts $= \left(\frac{\text{Side of bigger cube}}{\text{Side of smaller cube}} - 1\right) \times 3$

$$= \left(\frac{4}{2} - 1\right) \times 3 = (2-1) \times 3 = 3$$

Example 4 **A cube having 24 cm side is divided into 64 smaller cubes of equal volume. Find the side of smaller cubes?**

(a) 5 cm (b) 6 cm
(c) 3 cm (d) 4 cm

Sol. (*b*) Here, number of smaller cubes

$= (n)^3 = 64$

$\Rightarrow n = \sqrt[3]{64} = 4$

$\therefore n = \frac{\text{Side of bigger cube}}{\text{Side of smaller cube}}$

$\Rightarrow 4 = \frac{24}{\text{Side of smaller cube}}$

$\therefore$ Side of smaller cube $= \frac{24}{4} = 6$ cm

Helping Tips

If we want to cut a piece of wood or a rod into two equal parts, we cut it once. Similarly, if we want to cut a piece of wood or a rod into three equal parts, we cut it twice; if we want to cut into four equal parts, we cut it three times; if we want to cut it into further more then same process is so on. We can say that if we want to cut a piece of wood or a rod into n equal parts, we cut in $(n-1)$ times.

Example 5 **A cube has to be painted in such a way that there is no similar colour on adjacent faces. How many colours are needed for this?**

(a) 3 (b) 4 (c) 6 (d) 2

Sol. (*a*) Clearly, when opposite faces are painted with different colours, then colours on adjacent faces will be different.

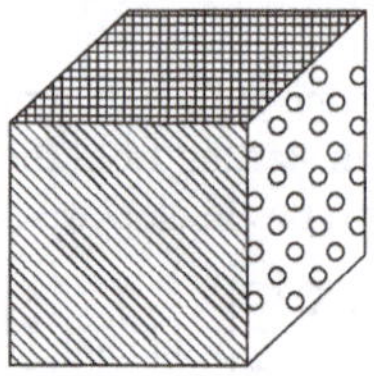

As we know that,

Number of pairs of opposite faces = 3

$\therefore$ Required number of colours = 3

Example 6 **A cube of side 18 cm is painted all its surfaces yellow and then cut into smaller cubes of side 3 cm. Find the number of such smaller cubes which have only two surfaces painted.** *SSC CGL 2022*

(a) 36 (b) 48 (c) 20 (d) 64

Sol. (*b*) Here, $n = \frac{\text{Side of larger cube}}{\text{Side of smaller cube}} = \frac{18}{3} = 6$

Total number of small cubes whose only two faces are painted

$$= 12\,(n-2)$$
$$= 12\,(6-2)$$
$$= 12 \times 4 = 48$$

Based on Counting of Blocks

Example 7 **How many cubes are invisible in the given picture?** *CRPF HC 2023*

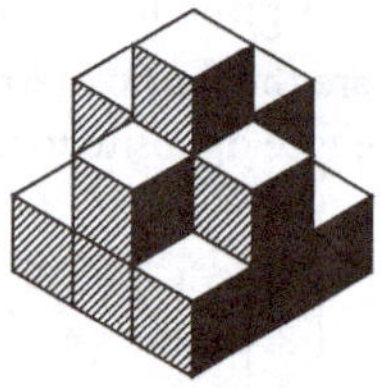

(a) 5 (b) 6 (c) 10 (d) 15

Sol. (*a*) According to the question,

Total number of cubes in the first row from the top = 1

Total number of cubes in the second row from the top = 5

Total number of cubes in the third row from the top = 9

Total number of visible cubes in the first row from the top = 1

Total number of visible cubes in the second row from the top = 4

Total number of visible cubes in the third row from the top = 5

$\therefore$ Total number of required invisible cubes

$$= (1+5+9) - (1+4+5)$$
$$= 15 - 10 = 5$$

Based on Close Dice

Example 8 **Which number will appear on the face opposite to number 1 in the dice given below?**

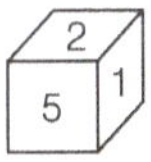

(a) 2 (b) 6
(c) 4 (d) None of these

Sol. (*d*) In the given dice = 5 + 2 = 7 (so, it is a normal dice)

In this, the number on the surface opposite to 1 can be any one of 3, 6 and 4.

Example 9 **Two positions of a dice are given below. What will come on the face opposite to the face containing 'F' on it?** ***IB 2024***

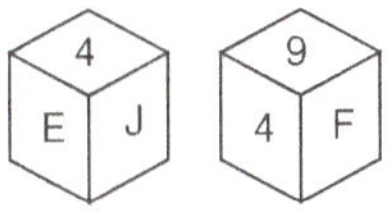

(a) J (b) 9 (c) 4 (d) E

Sol. (*d*) From the both positions of dice, number '4' is common. So, starting from '4' write all numbers/letters in clockwise direction.

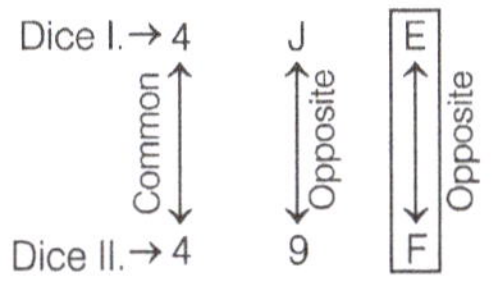

Hence, letter 'E' will come on the face opposite to the face containing 'F'.

> ***Helping Tips***
> To solve such questions, it is very important to know the opposite sides of the dice. Two opposite faces of dice never seen together in any dice.

Example 10 **Three different positions of the same dice are shown. Select the symbol that will be on the face opposite to the one showing '+'.**

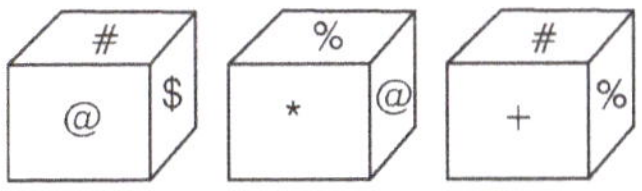

SSC CGL (Tier I) 2020

(a) # (b) $ (c) * (d) @

Sol. (*d*) From dice I and dice III, '#' is common in both the dices.

So, on writing clockwise from #.

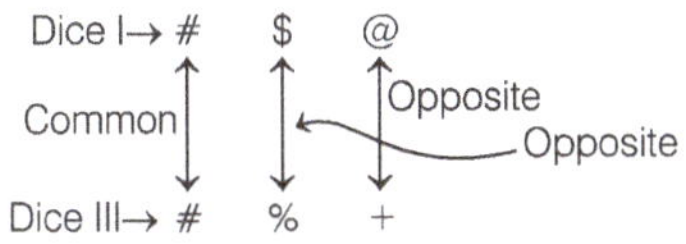

Hence, '@' is opposite to '+'.

Based on Open Dice

Example 11 **A cube is made by folding the given sheet. In the cube so formed what would be the symbol on the opposite side of the '#' symbol?**

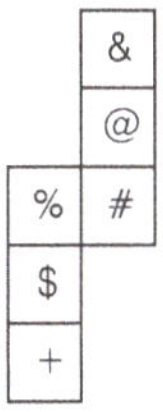

SSC CGL (Tier I) 2021

(a) $ (b) +
(c) & (d) %

Sol. (*c*) According to the question,

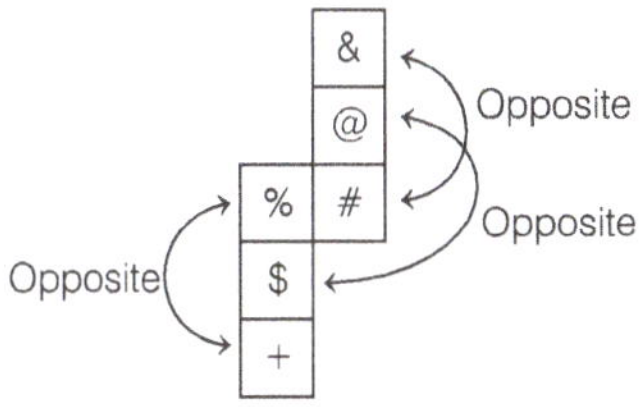

Here, '&' is opposite to '#', '%' is opposite to '+' and '@' is opposite to '$'.

So, it is clear that '#' is opposite to '&'.

Example 12 **Select the box that cannot be formed by folding the given unfolded box.** ***SSC CGL (Tier I) 2020***

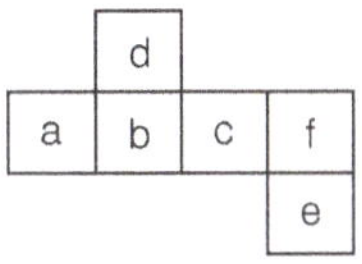

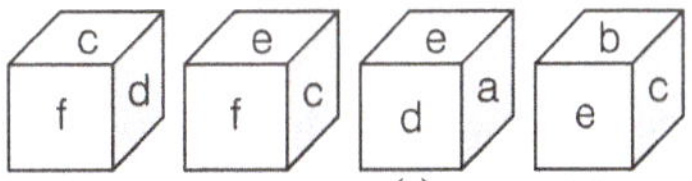

(a) (b) (c) (d)

> ***Trending Concept***
> Question based on open dice are being asked in the current exams like SSC CGL, SSC CHSL and RRB NTPC. It is very important for these examination.

Sol. (*c*) According to the question, from option (c) will not be formed as 'd' and 'e' are opposite to each other.

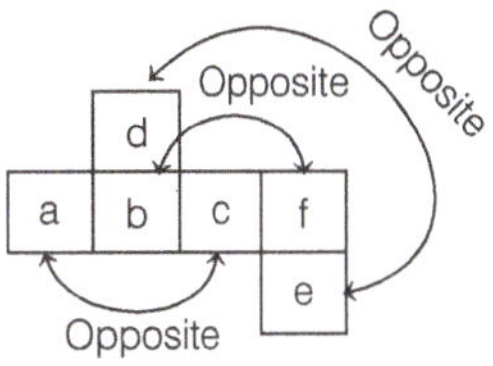

Chapter Challenge

Based on Cutting/Colouring of Cube/Cuboid

1. If small cubes of side 3 cm are made from a solid cube of size 18 cm, then how many cubes will be formed in total? **UPSSSC 2016**
(a) 216 (b) 24 (c) 124 (d) 6

2. A cube is divided into 125 parts. The side of the smaller cubes obtained from this division is 3 cm, then what would be the side of the larger cube?
(a) 5 cm (d) 12 cm (a) 10 cm (d) 15 cm

3. If a coloured cube of side 25 cm is divided into smaller cubes of side 5 cm, then how many such small cubes will be obtained, whose atleast two surfaces will be coloured?
(a) 50 (b) 44 (c) 36 (d) 8

4. A big cube is made by arranging 64 cubes of side 1 cm. Then, how many such cubes will be there in this arrangement, whose none of the surfaces will be visible from outside?
(a) 27 (b) 1 (c) 9 (d) 8

5. There is a cuboid of dimensions $4 \times 3 \times 3$ cm. The opposite faces of dimension 4×3 are painted yellow. The opposite faces of other dimensions 4×3 are painted red. The opposite faces of dimension 3×3 are painted green. Now the cuboid is cut into small cubes of side 1 cm. How many such small cubes are there which have three faces coloured? **UP Police Constable 2024**
(a) 20 (b) 16 (c) 8 (d) 12

6. A cubic wooden block has dimensions of length 6 cm, breadth 4 cm and height 1 cm. Two faces measuring 4 cm × 1 cm are painted black. Two faces measuring 6 cm × 1 cm are painted red. Two faces measuring 6 cm × 4 cm are painted green. The block is divided into 6 equal cubes of side 1 cm (with 6 cm side), 4 equal cubes of side 1 cm (with 4 cm side). If the black and green cubes are removed, how many cubes will remain? **UP Police Constable 2024**
(a) 16 (b) 8 (c) 12 (d) 4

7. A cube is painted green on all sides. It is then cut into 64 smaller cubes of equal size. How many of these smaller cubes are painted on only one side?
(a) 16 (b) 24 (c) 4 (d) 6

8. Three colours have been used to paint a cube. The colour arrangement is such that no colour is used on two adjacent surfaces. After this it is cut into 64 smaller cubes, then the maximum number of such cubes painted with any one colour will be
(a) 6 (b) 7 (c) 8 (d) 9

Directions (Q. Nos. 9-11) *Study the following information carefully and answer the given questions.* **CGPSC 2019**

(i) A wooden cuboid has length 4 cm, breadth 3 cm and height 5 cm.
(ii) Opposite sides of 5 cm × 4 cm are painted red.
(iii) The opposite side of 4 cm × 3 cm is painted blue.
(iv) The remaining two sides are painted green.
(v) Now the cuboid is cut into cubes of 1 cm × 1 cm × 1 cm.

9. How many cubes will have only one colour?
(a) 12 (b) 16 (c) 22 (d) 28

10. How many cubes will have all three colours?
(4) 14 (b) 12 (c) 10 (d) 8

11. How many cubes will not have any colour?
(a) 0 (b) 6 (c) 4 (d) 2

Directions (Q. Nos. 12-15) *Study the information given below carefully and answer the questions based on it.*

(i) There is a rectangular wooden block whose length is 6 cm, width 4 cm and height 2 cm.
(ii) The two sides having dimensions 4 cm × 2 cm are painted blue.
(iii) Both the sides having dimensions 6 cm × 2 cm are painted black.
(iv) Both the sides having dimensions 6 cm × 4 cm are painted red.
(v) This block is cut in such a way that it is converted into small cubes of equal side 1 cm each.

12. How many such cubes will there be, whose three surfaces are painted and three surfaces are unpainted?
(a) 4 (b) 24 (c) 8 (d) 16

13. What is the total number of cubes?
(a) 24 (b) 48 (c) 96 (d) 12

14. How many such cubes are there which have only two surfaces painted?
(a) 8 (b) 16 (c) 24 (d) 32

15. How many cubes are there whose none of the sides are coloured?
(a) 4 (b) 0 (c) 16 (d) 32

Based on the Counting of Blocks

16. Find the total number of cubes in the given figure. **SSC (10+2) 2023**

(a) 10 (b) 8 (c) 11 (d) 9

> **MRC*****
> ***(Most Repeating Concepts)***
> Q. Nos. 2, 5, 16 and 18 are very important from the examination point of view. Questions on these concept are continuously being asked in UP Police, SSC (CPO, 10+2) examination.

17. Find the total number of cubes in the given figure.

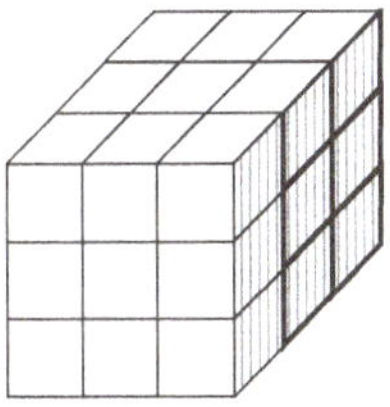

(a) 3 (b) 9 (c) 27 (d) 81

18. Find the number of cubes arranged in the given figure. *UP Police Constable 2024*

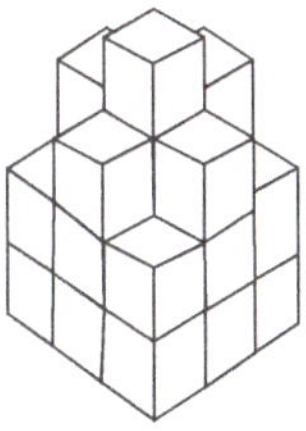

(a) 20 (b) 24 (c) 16 (d) 21

Based on Close Dice

19. The position of a dice is shown below. Which number is on the face opposite to 4 in this dice?

(a) 1 (b) 3 (c) 5 (d) None of these

20. Two different positions of the same dice are given below. Which is the number on the face opposite the face containing 5? *SSC CGL (Tier I) 2024*

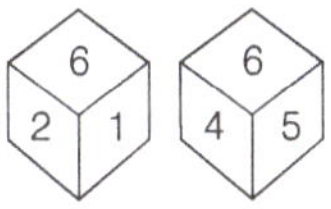

(a) 1 (b) 6 (c) 2 (d) 3

21. A dice has its faces marked by symbols θ and %. Two positions of the same dice are given below. Which face is opposite to face %? *SSC CPO 2024*

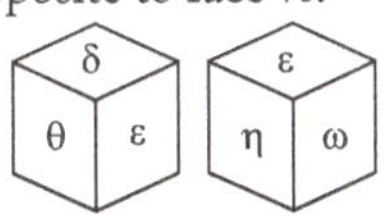

(a) η (b) θ (c) ω (d) ε

22. Two different positions of the same dice are shown, having letters H, I, J, K, L and M written on its faces are shown. *SSC CGL 2024*

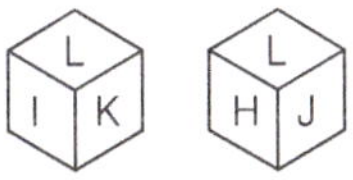

Which letter is on the face opposite to the face having H on it?

(a) K (b) I (c) J (d) M

23. Two different positions of the same dice, with the symbols $, @, !, *, ∞ and ÷ are shown. Find the symbol on the face opposite the face showing '÷'. *SSC GD Constable 2023*

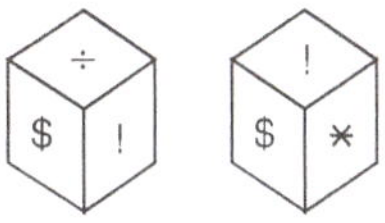

(a) @ (b) ! (c) * (d) ∞

MRC***
(Most Repeating Concepts)
Q. Nos. 20, 22, 26, 29, 34, 42, 45 and 46 are very important from the examination point of view. Questions on these concept are continuously being asked in SSC CGL, CHSL, Railway UP Constable examination.

24. Six letters P, Q, S, T, U and V are written on different faces of a dice. Two positions of this dice are shown in the figure. Find the letter on the face opposite to T. *SSC CGL (Tier-II) 2025*

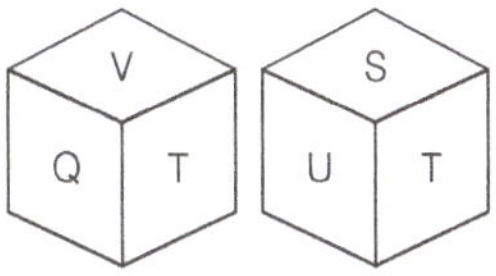

(a) V (b) P (c) S (d) U

25. Two different positions of the same dice are shown, each with six faces numbered 1 to 6.
Select the number that will appear on the face opposite to the face showing 1. *CISF Head Constable 2023*

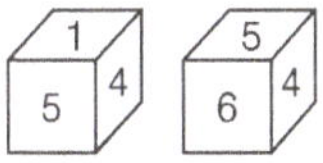

(a) 4 (b) 6 (c) 3 (d) 5

26. Two dimensions of the same dice are given. Which letter will be on the face opposite to the face having the letter D? *SSC (10+2) 2024*

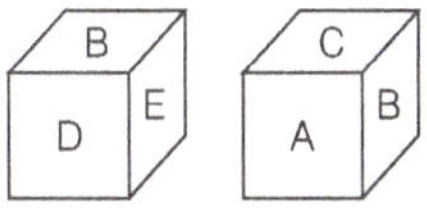

(a) B (b) F (c) E (d) C

27. Two different positions of the same dice are shown, the six faces of which are coloured Red, Green, Blue, Yellow, Black and White. Select the colour that will be on the face opposite to the one coloured Yellow. *SSC (10+2) 2022*

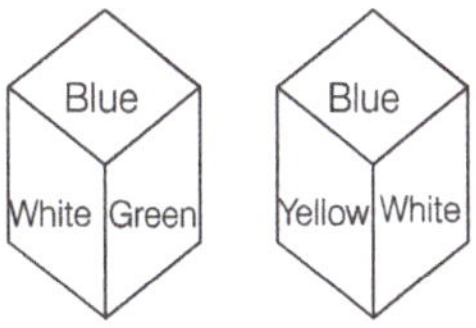

(a) Green (b) Black
(c) Red (d) White

28. Three different positions of the same dice are shown. Study the same and identify which of the following statements is correct? **CUET 2022**

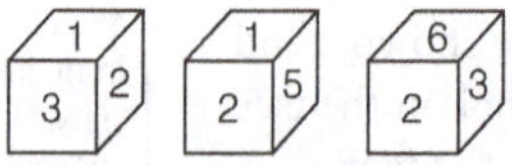

(a) 1 is opposite to 4 (b) 3 is opposite to 6
(c) 6 is opposite to 1 (d) 5 is opposite to 2

29. Three different positions of the same dice are given. Find the number on the face opposite to the face showing '4'. **SSC CPO 2024**

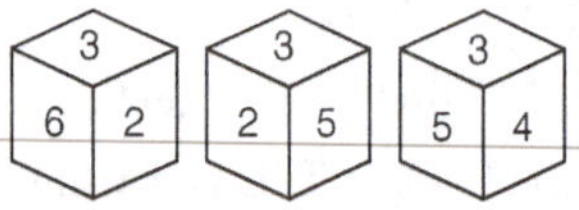

(a) 5 (b) 2 (c) 1 (d) 6

30. Three different positions of the same dice are shown. Find the number on the face opposite the face showing 3? **SSC GD Constable 2023**

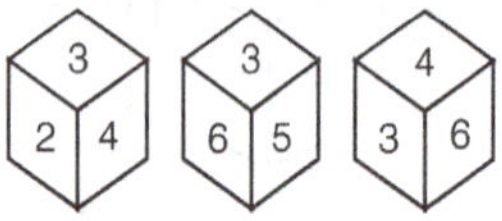

(a) 2 (b) 4 (c) 1 (d) 6

31. Three different positions of the same dice are shown. Find the number on the face opposite to the face showing '6'. **DP Constable 2023**

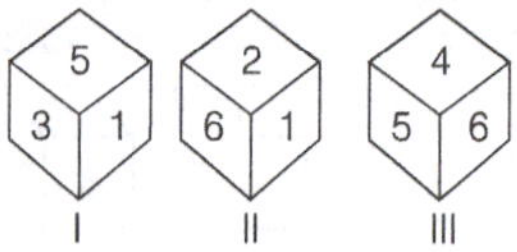

(a) 3 (b) 1 (c) 5 (d) 4

32. Three different positions of the same dice are shown. Find the number on the face opposite the face showing '6'. **SSC GD Constable 2023**

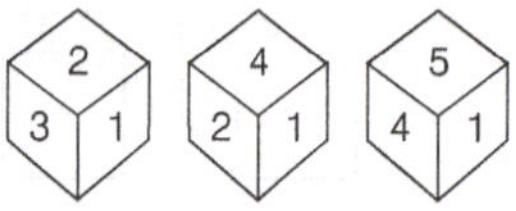

(a) 3 (b) 5 (c) 1 (d) 2

33. Three different positions of the same dice are shown. Find the number on the face opposite the face showing '1'. **SSC CGL (Tier I) 2023**

(a) 5 (b) 6 (c) 2 (d) 3

34. Three different positions of the same dice are shown below. Find the number of dots on the face opposite to the face on which two dots are given. **UP Police Head Operator 2024**

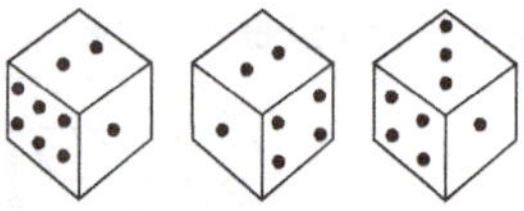

(a) 3 (b) 5 (c) 4 (d) 6

35. Six numbers 1, 2, 3, 4, 5 and 6 are written on different faces of a dice. Three positions of this dice are shown in the given figure. Find the number on the face opposite to the number 3. **SSC CGL 2024**

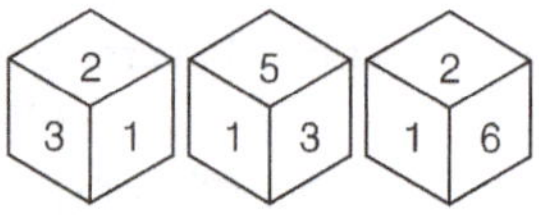

(a) 2 (b) 1 (c) 4 (d) 6

36. 1, 2, 3, 4, 5 and 6 are written on different faces of a dice. Three different positions of the same dice are shown below. Find the number on the face opposite to the one showing '2'. **SSC Steno 2023**

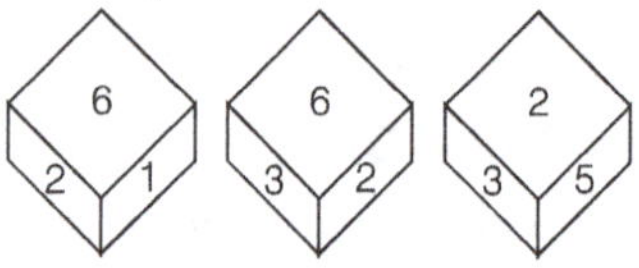

(a) 3 (b) 1 (c) 4 (d) 5

37. Three different positions of the same dice are shown. Which number will be on the face opposite to the face showing '4'? **CISF 2023**

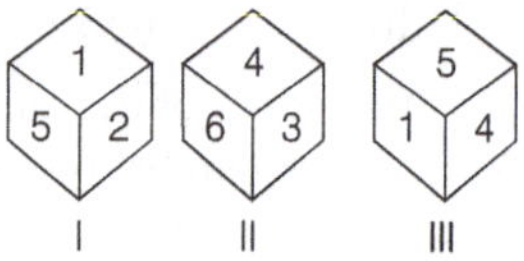

(a) 3 (b) 6 (c) 1 (d) 2

38. Six numbers 21, 22, 23, 24, 25 and 26 are written on different faces of a dice. Three positions of this dice are shown in the figure. Find the number on the face opposite to 24. **SSC CGL (Tier-I) 2024**

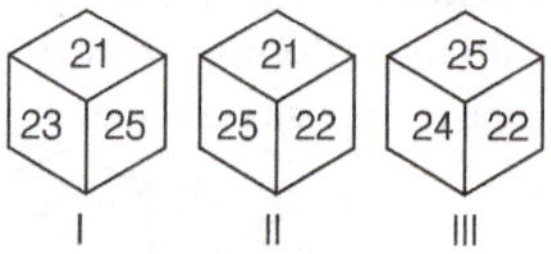

(a) 22 (b) 21
(c) 26 (d) 25

39. Four different positions of the same dice are given below. Find the number opposite of 23. **SSC GD Constable 2024**

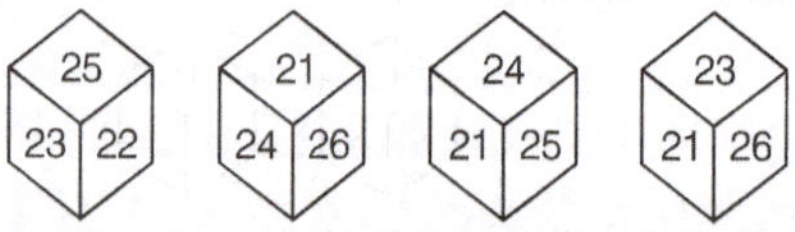

(a) 24 (b) 25
(c) 26 (d) 21

40. Four different positions of a cube are shown in the figure. Which of the following colours is on the face opposite to the face that has black written on it?

RRB NTPC CBT-I 2020

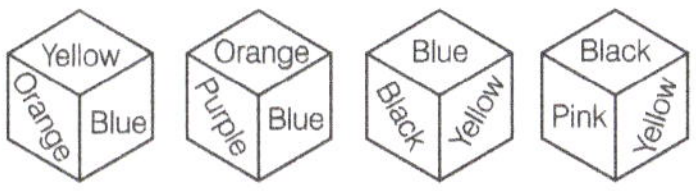

(a) Purple (b) Orange (c) Blue (d) Pink

41. Four positions of the same dice are shown. Select the number that will be on the face opposite to the one showing '3'. *SSC CGL (Tier I) 2020*

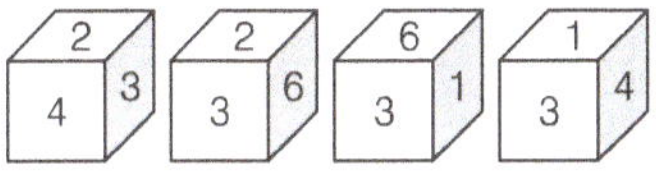

(a) 6 (b) 2 (c) 4 (d) 5

Based on Open Dice

42. A cube is constructed by folding the given sheet along the lines shown. In the cube so formed, what would be the word on the opposite side of 'Ball'?

SSC CGL (Tier-I) 2024

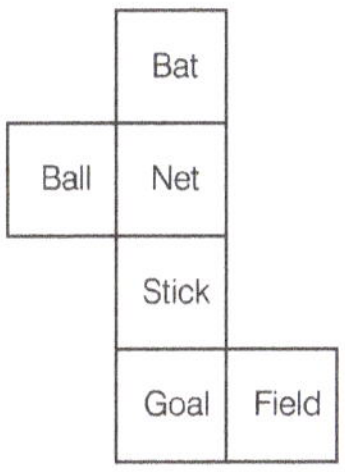

(a) Field (b) Goal (c) Stick (d) Bat

43. If the given figure is folded to form a cube, which alphabet will come on the face opposite to 'a'?

Rajasthan Police Constable 2022

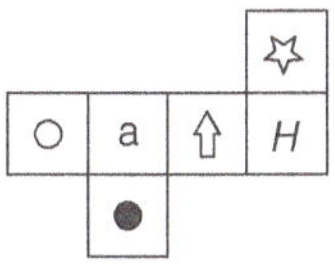

(a) ● (b) ☆ (c) ○ (d) *H*

44. On folding the given dice, which letter will be opposite to the letter '*n*'? *SSC GD Constable 2024*

(a) j (b) h (c) r (d) p

45. What would be the Roman numeral on the opposite side of 'VI', if the given sheet is folded to form a cube? *SSC (10+2) 2024*

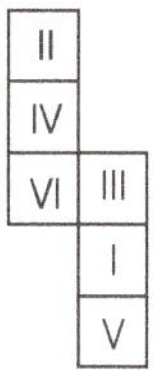

(a) V (b) III (c) I (d) II

46. When the given figure is folded to form a cube which face is opposite to face A? *UP (AO) 2024*

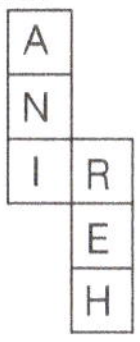

(a) E (b) I (c) H (d) R

47. When the following figure is folded to form a cube, which letter-number will be on the face opposite to the face showing the letter-number 'A1'? (The elements are shown to indicate the sides only.)

SSC CPO 2023

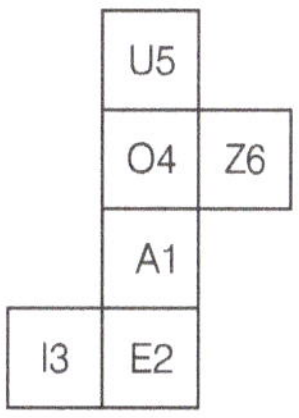

(a) U5 (b) O4 (c) I3 (d) E2

48. Two orientations of a dice are shown. This dice can be obtained by folding which of the option figure along the lines? *CUET 2022*

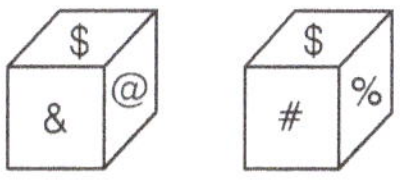

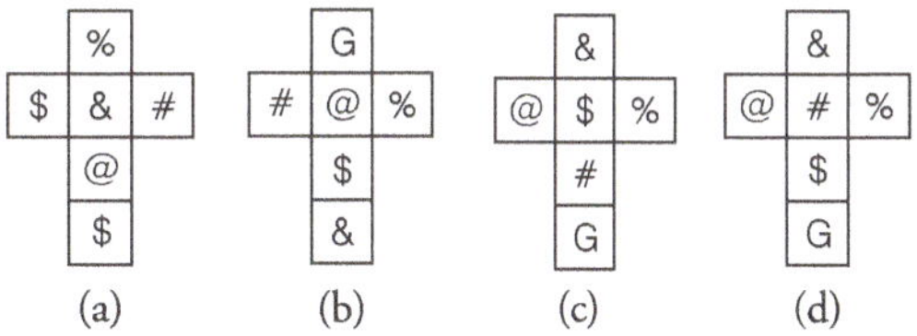

49. Select the cube that can be formed by folding the given sheet along the lines. *SSC CGL (Tier I) 2022*

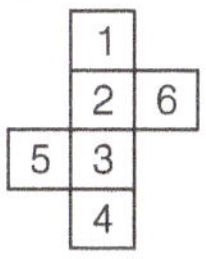

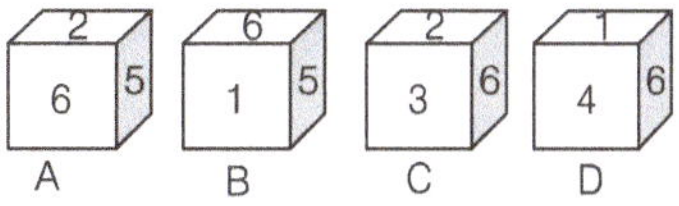

(a) Only D (b) Only A and C
(c) Only C and D (d) Only B

50. Select the box that can be formed by folding the given sheet along the lines. *RRB NTPC 2021*

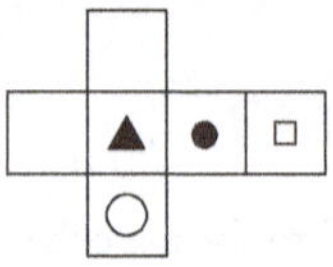

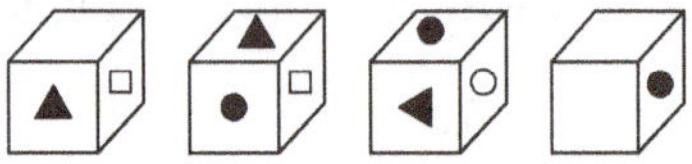

(a) (b) (c) (d)

51. Which of the following cubes is not based on the unfolded cube?

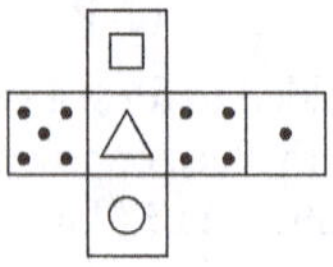

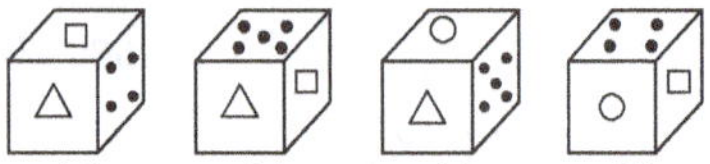

(a) (b) (c) (d)

52. Which cube in the answer figure cannot be made based on the expanded cube in the question figure? *UP Police Constable 2019*

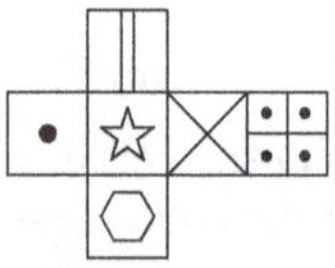

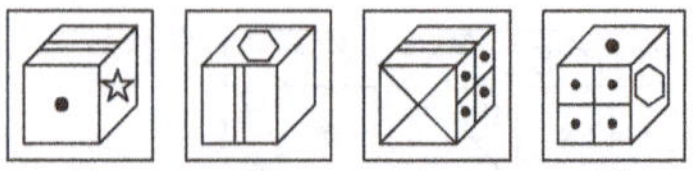

(a) (b) (c) (d)

53. Select the cube that can be formed by folding the given sheet along the lines. *SSC CGL (Tier-I) 2022*

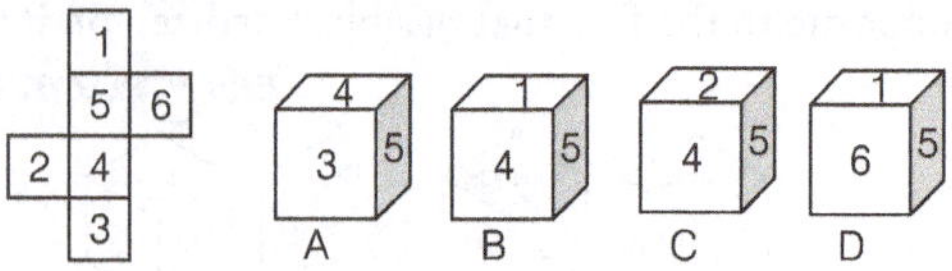

(a) Only C and D (b) Only A and B
(c) Only A and C (d) Only A, B and C

54. If the given sheet is folded to form a cube, which of the given figures is/are possible? (The elements are shown to indicate the sides only). *SSC CPO 2023*

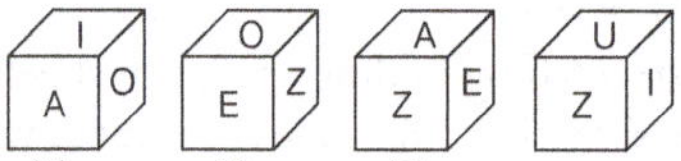

(1) (2) (3) (4)

(a) 1 and 2 (b) 1, 2 and 4
(c) 2 and 3 (d) Only 3

55. If the given sheet is folded to form a cube, which of the following figures is possible? *SSC CPO 2023*

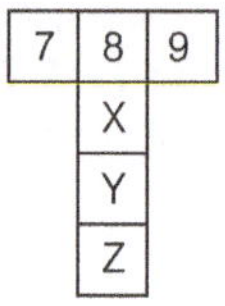

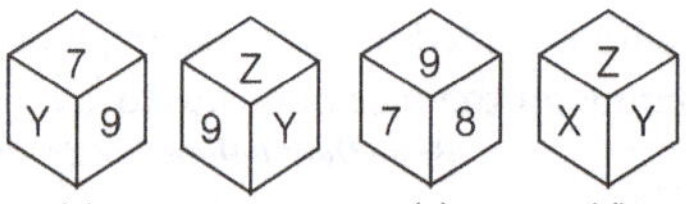

(a) (b) (c) (d)

Right Key

1. (a)	2. (d)	3. (b)	4. (d)	5. (c)	6. (a)	7. (b)	8. (c)	9. (c)	10. (d)
11. (b)	12. (c)	13. (b)	14. (c)	15. (b)	16. (a)	17. (c)	18. (b)	19. (b)	20. (a)
21. (d)	22. (b)	23. (c)	24. (b)	25. (b)	26. (d)	27. (a)	28. (c)	29. (b)	30. (c)
31. (a)	32. (c)	33. (d)	34. (a)	35. (d)	36. (c)	37. (d)	38. (b)	39. (a)	40. (b)
41. (d)	42. (a)	43. (d)	44. (a)	45. (d)	46. (b)	47. (a)	48. (c)	49. (c)	50. (c)
51. (d)	52. (b)	53. (a)	54. (d)	55. (b)					

Solutions

1. *(a)* Here, $n = \frac{18}{3} = 6$

Total number of small cubes

$= (6)^3 = 216$

2. *(d)* Here, $n = \sqrt[3]{125} = 5$

Side of bigger cube

$= n \times$ Side of smaller cube

$= 5 \times 3 = 15$ cm

3. *(b)* Because the number of cubes with atleast two coloured surfaces will also include cubes with three coloured surfaces.

Number of cubes with atleast two surfaces coloured = Number of cubes with two surfaces coloured + Number of cubes with three surfaces coloured

$= (5-2) \times 12 + 8 \quad \left[\because n = \frac{25}{5} = 5\right]$

$= 44$

4. *(d)* Here, $n = \sqrt[3]{64} = 4$

$\therefore$ Number of cubes whose no surface is visible from outside $= (n-2)^3$

$= (4-2)^3 = 8$

5. *(c)* We know that the number of a cube with three coloured surfaces is always '8'.

6. *(a)*

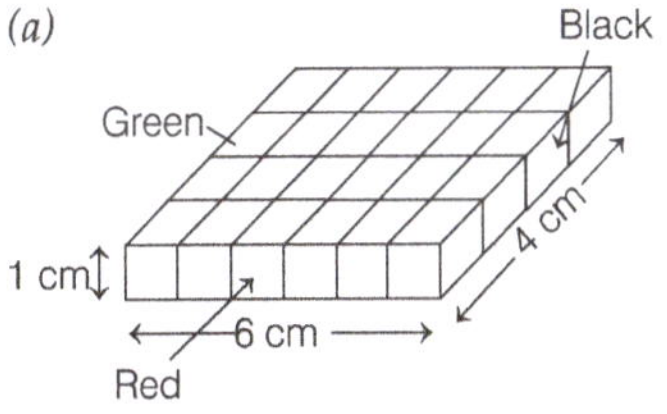

If both black and green coloured cubes are removed from the above block, then the number of remaining cubes will be $= 6 \times 4 - 4 \times 2 = 24 - 8 = 16$

7. *(b)* Let the side of the cube be cut into x equal parts. Then, number of cubes, $x^3 = 64 \Rightarrow x = 4$

Number of cubes painted on one side

$= 6(x-2)^2 = 6(4-2)^2$

$= 6 \times 4 = 24$

Hence, number of cubes painted on one side = 24

> **TOP TIPS** Number of central cube $= 6(n-2)^2$ where 6 represents to the number of surfaces of cube.

8. *(c)* According to the question, each colour is used on two surfaces and cut into 64 small cubes, $n = \sqrt[3]{64} = 4$ Hence, number of cubes coloured on one surface $= (n-2)^2 \times 2$

$= (4-2)^2 \times 2 = 8$

Sol. (Q. Nos. 9-11) According to the given information,

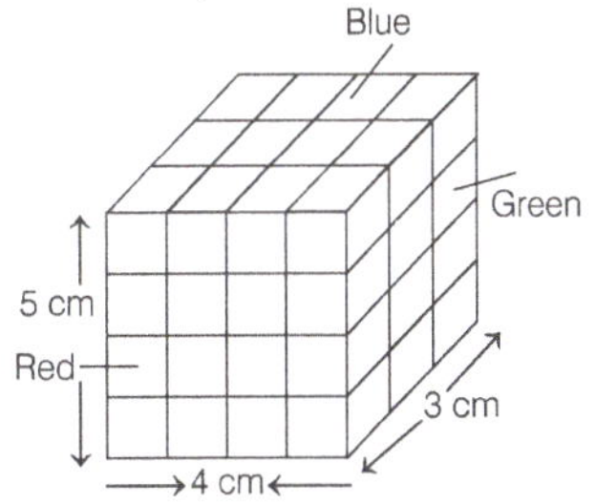

9. *(c)* There are cubes of 5 cm $\times$ 4 cm on both the surfaces of which both are of only one colour

$= 2(5-2) \times (4-2) = 2 \times 3 \times 2 = 12$

Similarly, cubes of 4 cm $\times$ 3 cm with both surfaces having only one colour

$= 2(4-2) \times (3-2) = 2 \times 2 \times 1 = 4$

and cubes of 5cm $\times$ 3 cm with only one colour on both surfaces

$= 2(5-2)(3-2) = 2 \times 3 \times 1 = 6$

Total cubes of only one colour

$= 12 + 4 + 6 = 22$

10. *(d)* Number of cubes having three colours = 8

11. *(b)* Number of cubes with no colour

$= (5-2) \times (4-2) \times (3-2)$

$= 3 \times 2 \times 1 = 6$

Sol. (Q. Nos. 12-15) It is clear from the diagram given below that there are 24 cubes in each surface.

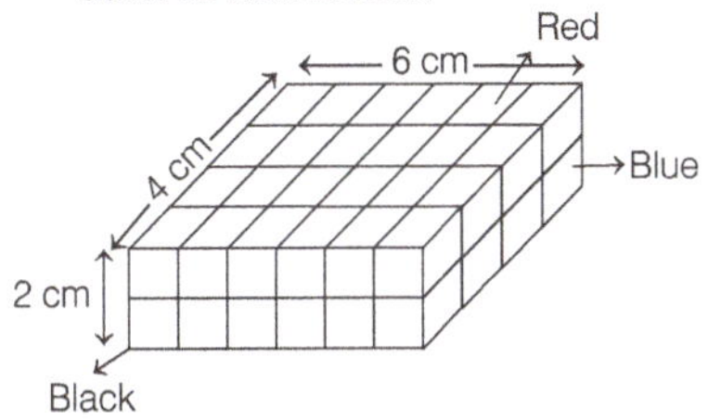

12. *(c)* We know that only edge cube has three painted surfaces and three unpainted surfaces, also the number of edge cubes is always 8.

So, the number of required cubes = 8

13. *(b)* According to the question, it is clear from the above diagram that there are 24 cubes in each layer of the rectangular block.

So, the number of required cubes

$24 \times 2 = 48$

14. *(c)* We know that only two surfaces are painted of the middle cubes. So, by finding the central cube and the edge cube and subtracting them from the total number of cubes, we will find the middle cubes, which will be cubes painted on only two surfaces.

So, the number of required cubes

$= 48 - (8 \times 2 + 8) = 48 - 24 = 24$

15. *(b)* There is no such cube.

16. *(a)* Total number of cubes in columns containing 1 cube $= 1 \times 3 = 3$

Number of cubes in a column of 2 cubes $= 2 \times 2 = 4$

Number of cubes in a column of 3 cubes $= 3 \times 1 = 3$

Total number of cubes $= 3 + 4 + 3 = 10$

17. *(c)* It is clear from the given figure that there are 3 cubes in each of the 9 columns.

$\therefore$ Total number of cubes

$= 9 \times 3 = 27$ cubes

18. *(b)* Number of cubes in Ist row

$= 3 \times 3 = 9$

Number of cubes in IInd row $= 3 \times 3 = 9$

Number of cubes in IIIrd row

$= 4 + 1 = 5$

Number of cubes in on the top = 1

$\therefore$ Total number of cubes

$= 9 + 9 + 5 + 1 = 24$

19. *(b)* In the given dice, the sum of any two adjacent face is not equal to 7. So, it is a standard dice and in this dice sum of values of opposite faces is equal to 7.

Hence, 4 is the face opposite to 3.

20. *(a)* 6 is common in both position of dice.

On writing clockwise from 6.

Dice I → 6 | 1 | 2

Dice II → 6 | 5 | 4

(1 ↕ 5, 2 ↕ 4 Opposite)

So, '1' is opposite to the face containing 5.

21. *(d)* In both the dices, ε is common. So, moving in a clockwise direction from common.

Dice I ε θ δ
Common | Opposite | Opposite
Dice II ε ω η

∴ ε is opposite to remaining symbol %.

22. *(b)* From both positions of dice, letter 'L' is common. Therefore, on writing clockwise from 'L'

Dice I L | K | I
Dice II L | J | H
Opposite

Hence, letter I is opposite to H.

> **TOP TIPS** If the same letter appears on any corresponding surface, then the letter on other corresponding surfaces are opposite to each other.

23. *(c)* In both figures the position of '$' and '!' is common. So, remaining surfaces are opposite to each other.

Hence, '*' is opposite to '÷'.

24. *(b)* Here, letter T is common in both the positions of dice.

So, on writing clockwise from 'T'.

Position I→ T Q V
Common | Opposite | Opposite
Position II→ T U S

Hence, remaining face 'P' is opposite to 'T'.

> **Smart Approach**
>
> Here, S, U, V and Q are on the adjacent faces of T.
>
> Hence, remaining letter 'P' will be on the opposite face of T.

25. *(b)* In the given dice number 5 and 4 are common in both the position. Hence, number '6' is opposite to number 1.

26. *(d)* Here letter B is common in both positions. So, on writing clockwise from letter 'B'.

Dice I → B → E → D
Dice II → B → A → C
Opposite

Hence, letter C will be opposite to letter D.

27. *(a)* Blue and White colours are common in both the positions of dice, then the remaining two colours will be opposite to each other. So, Green will be opposite to Yellow.

28. *(c)* In position II and III, 2 is common. So, on writing clockwise from '2'.

Position II → 2 1 5
Opposite | Opposite
Position III → 2 6 3

Hence, option (c) is correct 6 is opposite to 1.

29. *(b)* Here, in dice I and III number 3 is common. So, moving in a clockwise direction from common number.

Dice I 3 2 6
Common | Opposite | Opposite
Dice II 3 4 5

Hence, 2 is opposite to 4.

30. *(c)* From I and II dice we can write as

Dice I ⇒ 3 4 2
Dice II ⇒ 3 5 6
Opposite

Hence, '1' is opposite to '3'.

31. *(a)* In dice I and II, 1 is common.

On writing clockwise from common number.

Dice I ⟶ 1 3 5
Common | Opposite | Opposite
Dice II ⟶ 1 6 2

Hence, '6' is opposite to '3'.

32. *(c)* From all the positional of dice, it is clear that, 2, 3, 4 and 5 are on the faces adjacent to 1.

Hence, '6' will be opposite to '1'.

33. *(d)* From the position of dice II and III. Faces '6' and '2' are common.

Hence, '1' is opposite to '3'.

34. *(a)* In the given dice II and III dot 4 and 1 is common in both the position. Hence, dot '3' is opposite to the dot '2'.

> **TOP TIPS** 3 will be opposite to 2 only if, in the both the positions of a dice. The direction of rotation of both the common digits is opposite to each other.

35. *(d)* From dice I and III, two faces i.e., 2 and 1 are common.

So, the remaining faces i.e., 3 and 6 will be opposite to each other.

Hence, number 6 will be opposite to the number 3.

36. *(c)* From dice I and III 2 is common. So, moving in clockwise direction from common.

Dice I→ 2 6 1
Common | Opposite | Opposite
Dice III→ 2 5 3

So, the remaining number 4 is opposite face to 2.

37. *(d)* From the given dice I and III number 5 and 1 are common in both the position.

Hence, '2' is opposite to '4'.

38. *(b)* From dice I and III number '25' is common in both the position on rotating clockwise from the common face.

Dice I ⟶ 25 23 21
Opposite
Dice III ⟶ 25 22 24

Hence, number 21 is the opposite to number 24.

39. *(a)* From the dice II and IV,

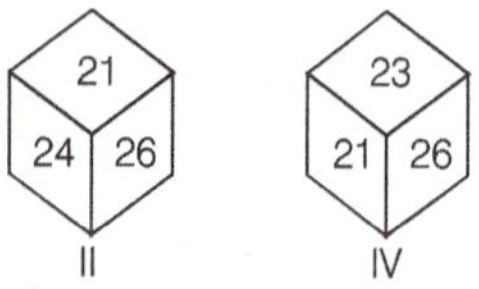

Here, we can see that 21 and 26 are common in both dices.

So, the opposite face of 23 is 24.

40. *(b)* From Ist and IIIrd position of dice, we can see that colour yellow and blue are common in both.

Hence, colour orange will be on the opposite face that has black.

41. *(d)* From I and III position of dice, 3 is common in both positions of dice. Now, start with 3, writing all the remaining numbers in clockwise direction.

Dice I→ 3 4 2
Common | Opposite | Opposite
Dice II→ 3 6 1

Here, number 3 is opposite to the remaining number 5.

42. *(a)* According to the question,

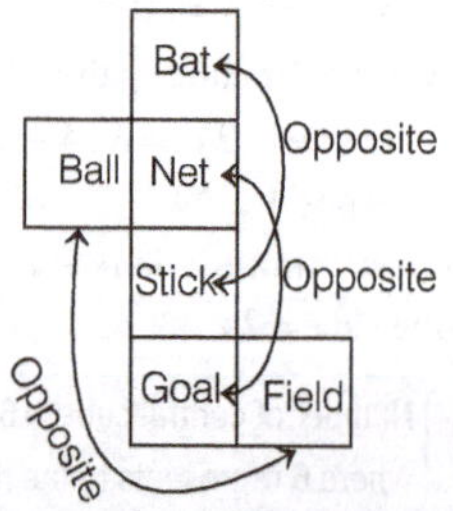

Hence, Field is opposite to Ball.

> **TOP TIPS** Any surface has four adjacent surfaces and one opposite surface. Two opposite surfaces are not connected together by any edge or vertex.

43. *(d)* According to the question,

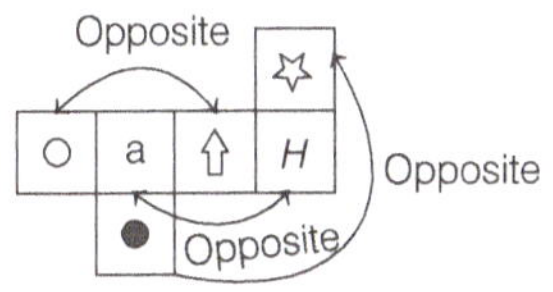

Hence H is opposite to 'a'.

44. *(a)* On folding the given dice

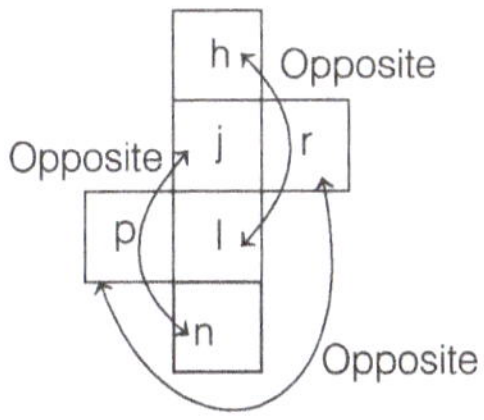

∴ 'n' is opposite to the 'j'.

45. *(d)* According to the question,

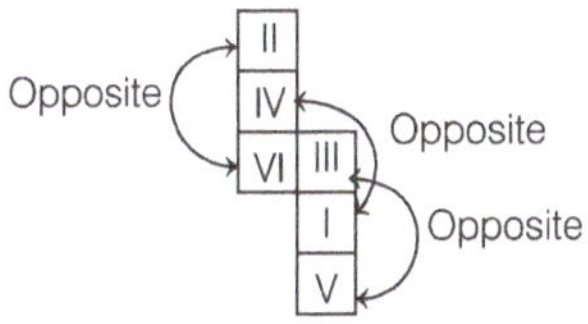

Hence, II is opposite side of VI.

46. *(b)* According to the given open dice,

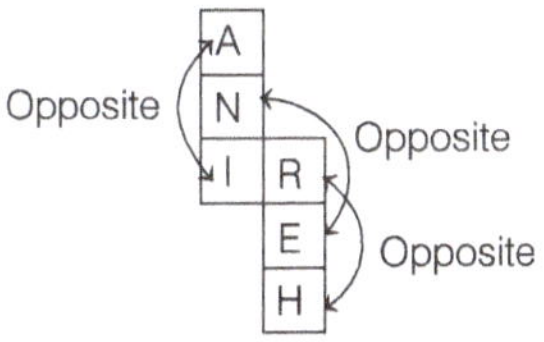

Hence, A is opposite to I.

47. *(a)* According to the question,

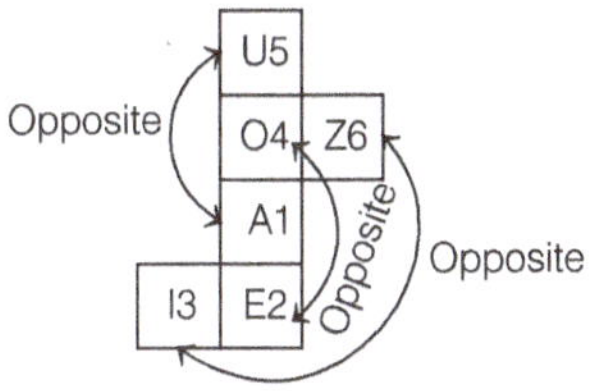

Hence, U5 is opposite to A1.

48. *(c)* According to the given positions of a dice, it is clear that @ is opposite to % and & is opposite to #.

Therefore, the dice would like below figure when unfolded.

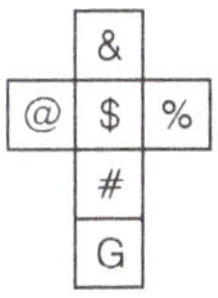

49. *(c)* Here, 1, 2 and 5 are opposite faces of 3, 4 and 6, respectively.

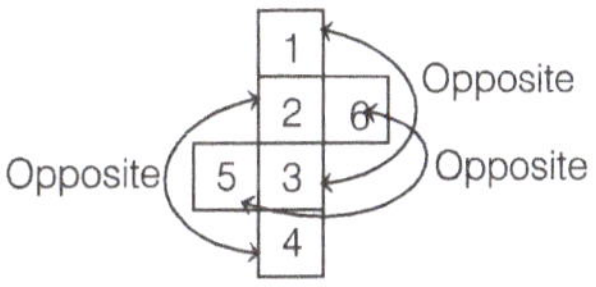

By folding the given sheet, cube (C) and cube. (D) can be formed.

> **TOP TIPS** The vertices of two opposite faces never connect to each other, meaning vertices remain separate.

50. *(c)* According to the given open dice.

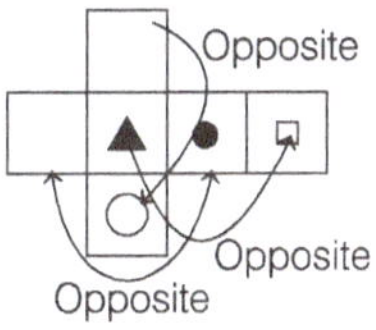

Hence, the option (c) has the same pair of opposite faces.

51. *(d)* According to the question,

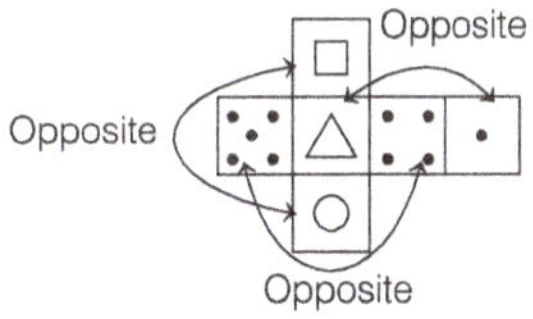

So, △ is infront and □ is to be right side. There should be five dots on the top.

Hence, the correct answer is figure option (d).

52. *(b)* According to the given open dice.

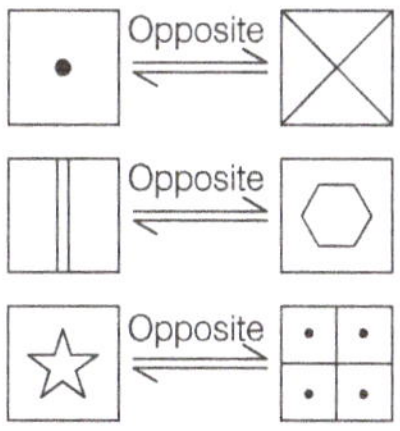

Hence, option (b) cannot be made from the given open dice.

53. *(a)* From the given open dice,

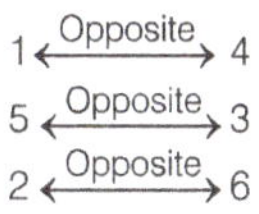

In figure A, 3 is opposite to 5.

And in figure B, 1 is opposite to 4.

So, these are not folded dice by using given open dice.

Hence, only C and D are possible folds for given open dice.

54. *(d)* According to the question,

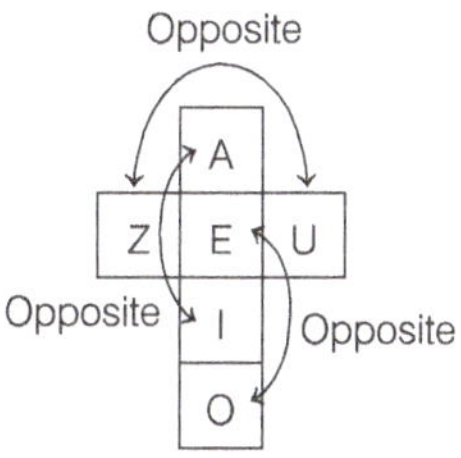

Hence, only figure 3 is possible.

55. *(b)* As per the question,

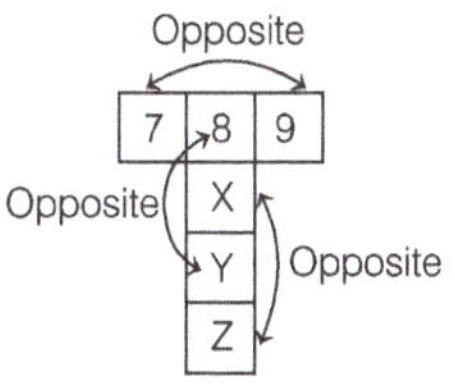

Hence, option (b) is the possible figure.

CHAPTER

21 Venn Diagram

Venn Diagram

Venn diagrams are used to show a logical relationship between given groups of elements. Questions asked in this chapter, are based upon two or more persons, objects or groups based on which appropriate relationship has to be found. Various geometric shapes like, circle, triangle, square, rectangle etc. are used to represent these diagrams.

Based on Relationship Identity

In this type of questions, two or more objects are given followed by some diagrams as options. The candidates have to identify the relationship among these objects and select the diagram which correctly represents that relationship.

e.g. Choose the venn diagram that best represent the relationship between the given group of classes.

(i) Wives, Sisters and Women

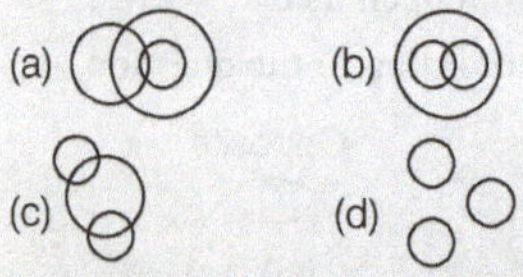

Sol. (b) According to the question,

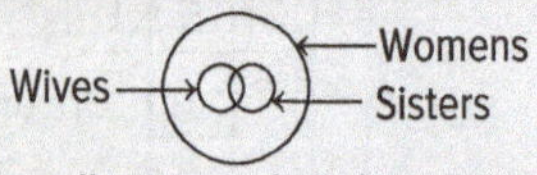

Hence, all wives and mothers are women and some wives may be mothers.

(ii) Kanpur, Varanasi and Meerut

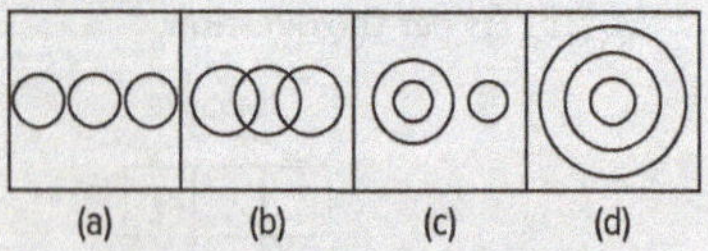

Sol. (a) Kanpur, Varanasi and Meerut all are cities of Uttar Pradesh but they are entirely different from one another. This can be expressed by option (a).

Based on Analytical Venn Diagram

In this type of questions, a venn diagram comprising of different geometrical figure is given. Each figure in diagram represents a certain class. The candidate is required to study and analyse the figure carefully, then answer the question based on it.

e.g. In the given figure, if triangle represents healthy people, rectangle represents old people and circle represents men, then

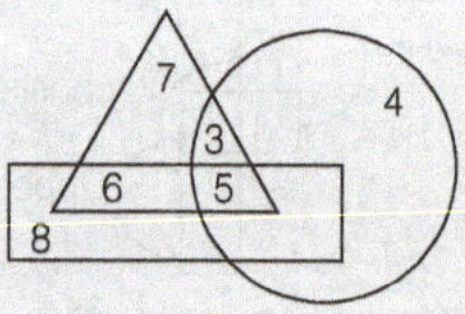

(i) Find the total number of men.

(a) 12 (b) 8
(c) 10 (d) 5

Sol. (a) According to the given diagram,

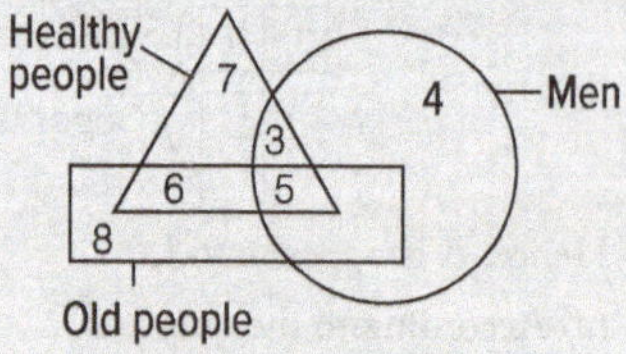

Total number of men = 4 + 3 + 5 = 12

(ii) Find the number of healthy people who are neither men nor old.

(a) 7 (b) 14
(c) 8 (d) 4

Sol. (a) According to the given diagram,
The number of healthy people who are neither men nor old is = 7
Hence, the correct answer is 7.

Score Booster

Venn diagram is a part of linguistic general intelligence test. In which it is necessary to have practical knowledge or logical understandings to solve the questions.

Exam Approach Examples

Based on Relationship Identity

Directions (Ex. Nos. 1-6) *Select the venn diagram that best represents the relationship between the following classes.*

Example 1 Mango, Fruit, Banana *SSC (10+2) 2023*

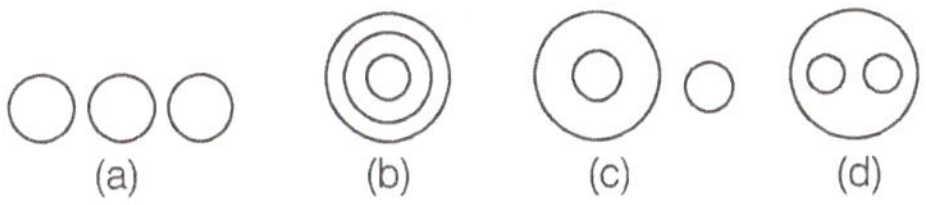

Sol. (*d*) The venn diagram of the given words is

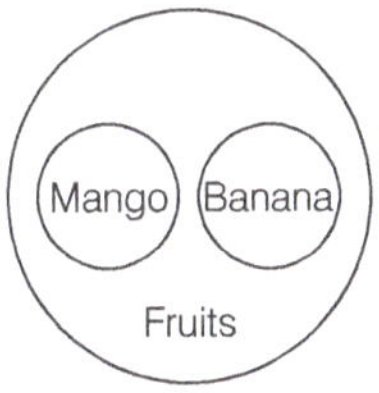

Both Mango and Banana are different type of fruits.

Example 2 Pencil, Eraser, Sharpener *SSC CPO 2023*

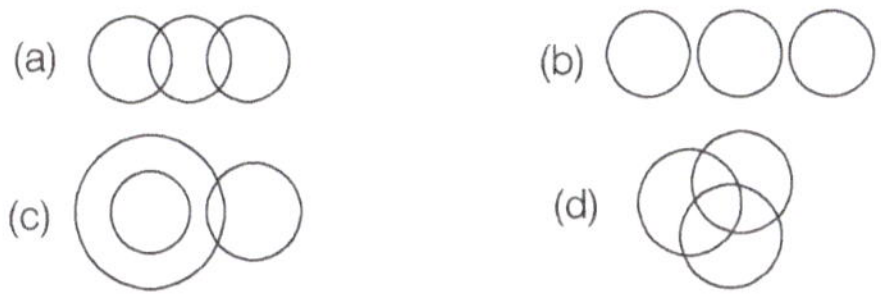

Sol. (*b*) The venn diagram of the given words is

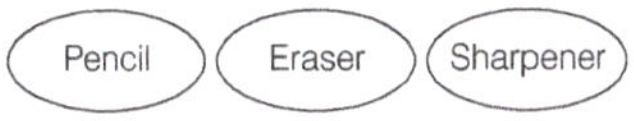

As, pencil, eraser and sharpener all are different from one another.

Example 3 Lawyers, Human beings, Married People *RRB NTPC 2022*

Sol. (*b*) The venn diagram of the given words is

Some lawyers are married people and some married people are lawyers but all lawyers and married people are human beings.

Example 4 Mobile, Book, Digital Device *SSC CGL 2023*

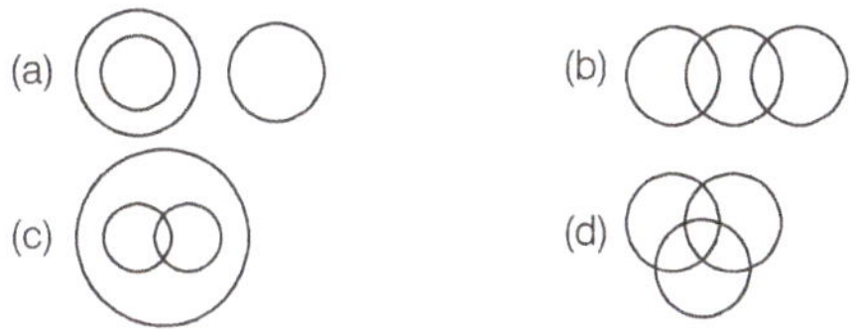

Sol. (*a*) The venn diagram of the given words is

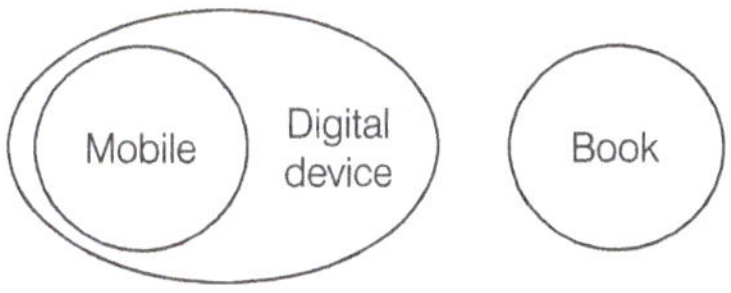

As, all mobiles are digital devices but book is different.

Example 5 Doctors, Artists, Men *DSSSB 2017*

Sol. (*a*) The venn diagram of the given words is

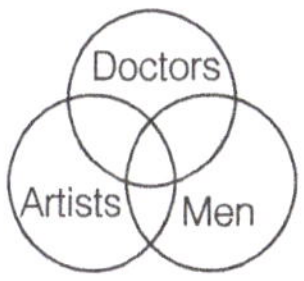

Some men can be both Doctors and Artists and some men also can be both Doctors and Artists.

Example 6 Solids, Liquids, Gasses *RRB NTPC 2021*

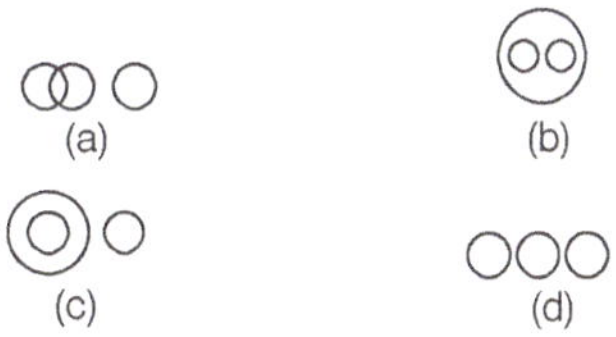

Sol. (*d*) The venn diagram of the given words is

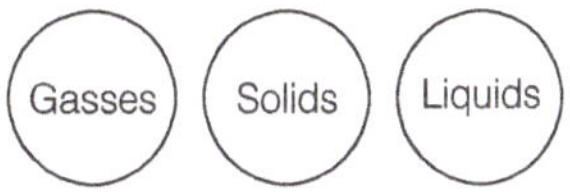

All are states of matter but they are different to each other.

> **Helping Tips**
> To solve these type of questions, candidates must have knowledge about topics of general science and general knowledge.

Based on Analytical Venn Diagram

Directions (Ex. Nos. 7-11) *Study the given diagram carefully and answer the questions.*

Example 7 **Which of the following number in the venn diagram represents Businessmen and Architect but not Police?** ***UP Police SI 2021***

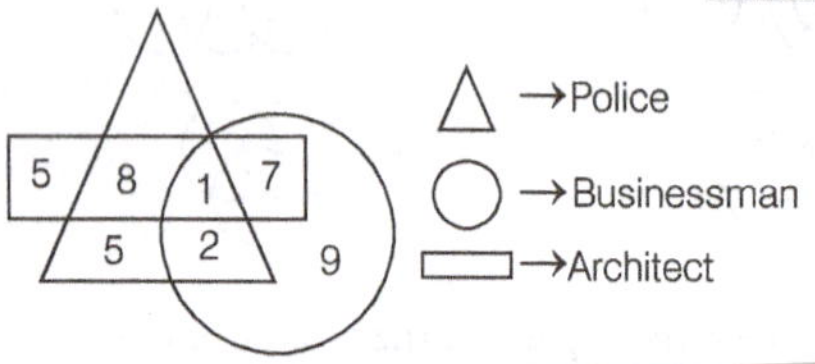

(a) 1 (b) 7 (c) 2 (d) 8

Sol. (*b*) As per given venn diagram,

Number 7 represents businessman and architect but not police.

Example 8 **The numbers in different sections indicate the number of persons.**

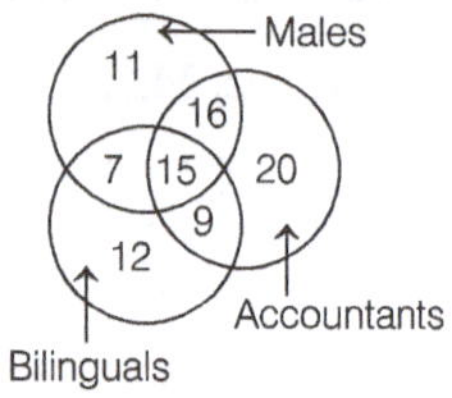

How many such accountants are there who are also bilinguals? ***RRC Group D 2022***

(a) 15 (b) 24 (c) 9 (d) 22

Sol. (*b*) As per given venn diagram,

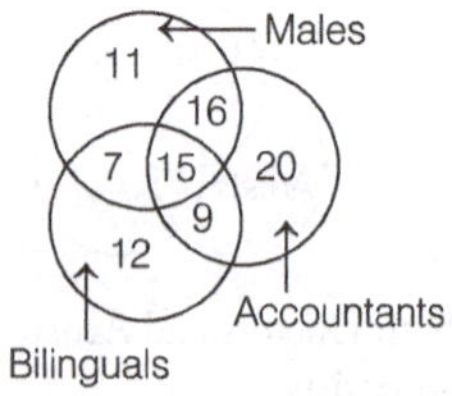

Number of persons who are accountants as well as bilinguals

$= 15 + 9 = 24$

Example 9 **How many doctors are both players and artists?**

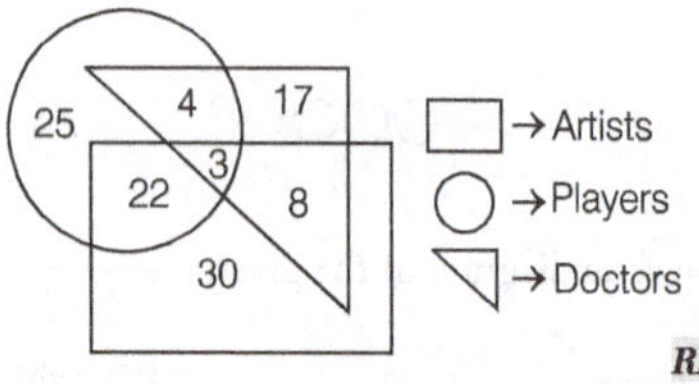

RRB NTPC 2021

(a) 3 (b) 13 (c) 6 (d) 8

Sol. (*a*) The number of doctors who are both players and artists = 3

Example 10 **In the following diagram, the circle represents 'rural folk' the triangle represents 'businessmen' and the rectangle represents 'graduates'.** ***SSC CGL 2021***

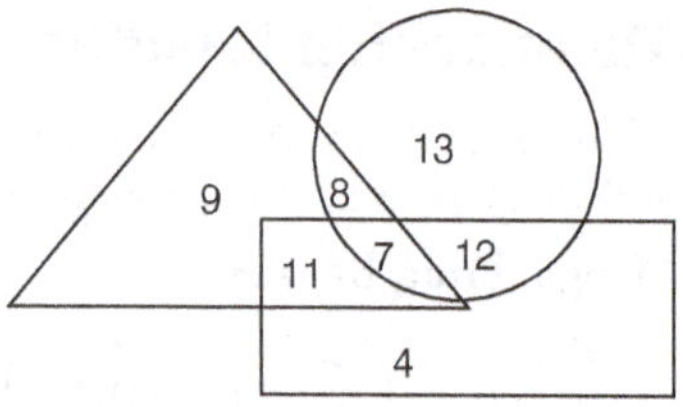

What is the number of rural businessmen, who are not graduates?

(a) 7

(b) 8

(c) 15

(d) 11

Sol. (*b*) As per given venn diagram,

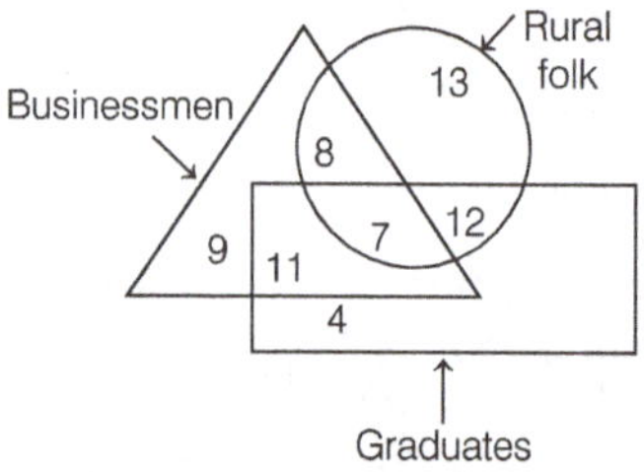

> ***Trending Concept***
>
> The question based on these concepts are being asked in (RRB NTPC, SSC, CPO, 10+2, CGL, DSSSB, UP Police SI and RRC Group D).

∴ The number of rural businessmen who are not graduate = 8

Example 11 **In the venn diagram given below, the square represents 'boys', the circle represents 'tall persons', the pentagon represents 'North Indians' and the rectangle represents 'food lovers'. The numbers given in the diagram represents the number of persons of that particular category.**

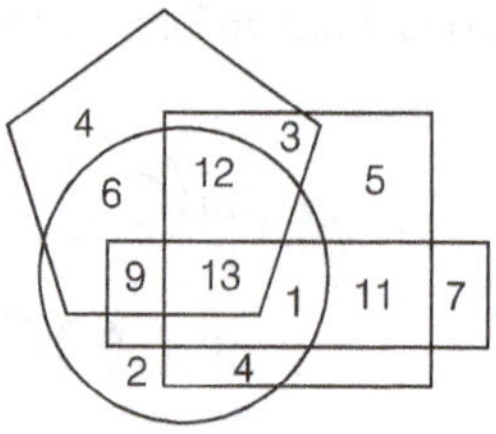

How many North Indian boys are tall persons but are not food lovers? ***DSSSB 2019***

(a) 12 (b) 25

(c) 13 (d) 16

Sol. (*a*) North Indian boys who are tall persons but not food lovers can be represented by the number present in the square, the pentagon and the circle but not in the rectangle. i.e. 12.

Chapter Challenge

Based on Relationship Identity

Directions (Q. Nos. 1-30) *Select the venn diagram that best illustrates the relationship between the given classes.*

1. Day, Hour, Month ***MP Police Constable 2022***

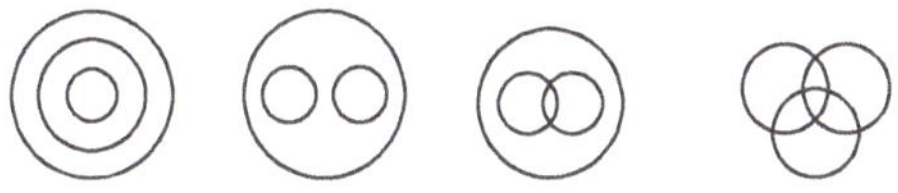

(a) (b) (c) (d)

2. Banana, Cabbage, Fruits ***Rajasthan Police Constable 2022***

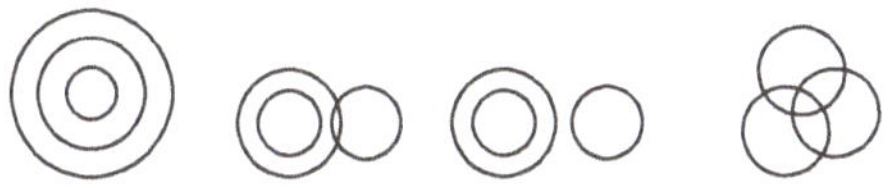

(a) (b) (c) (d)

3. Plum, Litchi, Fruits ***CUET UG 2023***

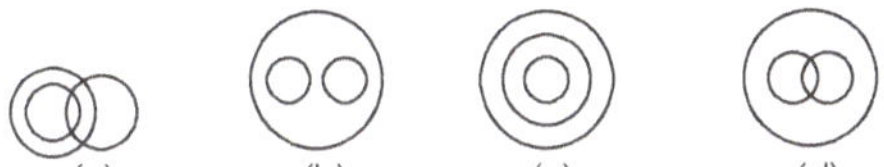

(a) (b) (c) (d)

4. Husband, Family, Wife ***UP Police Constable 2024***

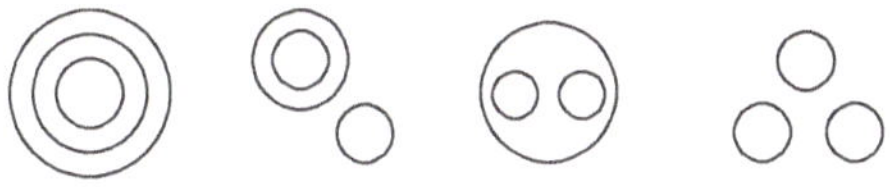

(a) (b) (c) (d)

5. Lotus, Lily, Mango ***SSC (10+2) 2023***

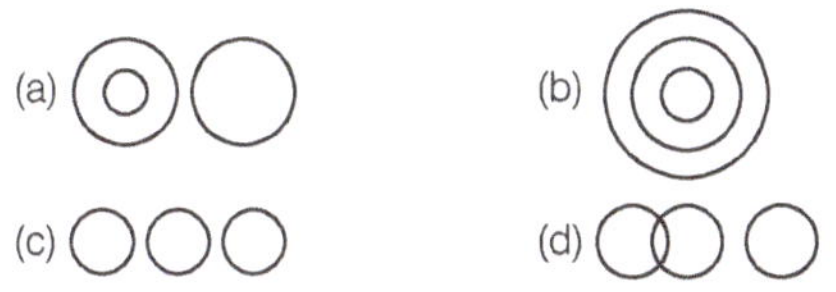

> *MRC****
> ***(Most Repeating Concepts)***
> Question Nos. 5, 8, 10, 15, 22, 31 and 32 are very important from examination point of view. Questions based on these concepts are being repeatedly asked in UP Police Constable, RRB (NTPC, ALP), SSC (CGL, CHSL, Steno, CPO), Delhi Police (DP) Head Constable, State Police Exams.

6. Gold, Silver, Jewellery ***SSC CPO 2022***

7. Crockery, Cups, Plates ***DSSSB 2019***

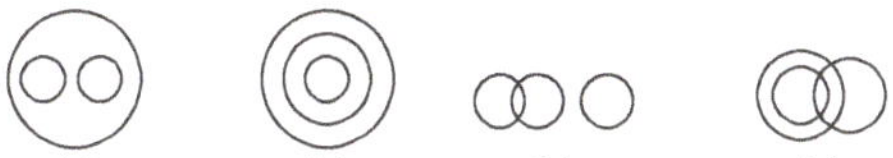

(a) (b) (c) (d)

8. India, Gujarat, Surat ***UP Police Constable 2024***

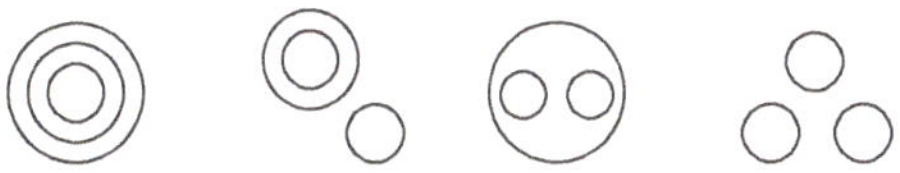

(a) (b) (c) (d)

9. King, Father, Queen ***SSC (10+2) 2022***

(a) (b) (c) (d)

10. Humans, Birds, Mammals ***RRB NTPC 2021***

(a) (b) (c) (d)

11. Human beings, Society, Family ***SSC Steno 2022***

(a) (b) (c) (d)

12. Lion, Tiger, Animals ***RRB ALP 2018***

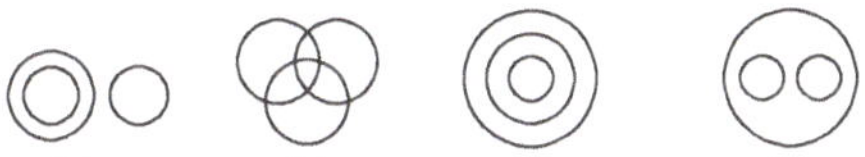

(a) (b) (c) (d)

13. Karnataka, India, Asia ***RRB ALP 2018***

(a) (b) (c) (d)

14. Herbivorous, Tiger, Animals ***BSSC (10+2) 2022***

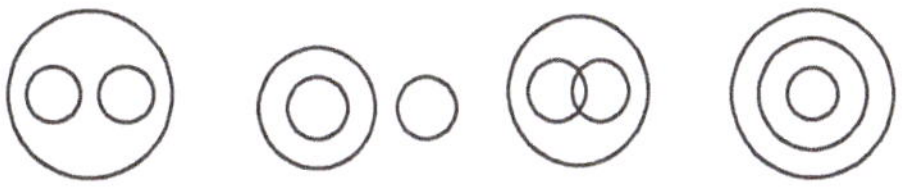

(a) (b) (c) (d)

15. Ticket, Aeroplane, Rail ***SSC CGL (Tier I) 2023***

(a) (b) (c) (d)

16. Rats, Cats, Mammals ***DSSSB 2019***

(a) (b) (c) (d)

17. Animals, Lions, Jackals *SSC CPO 2024*

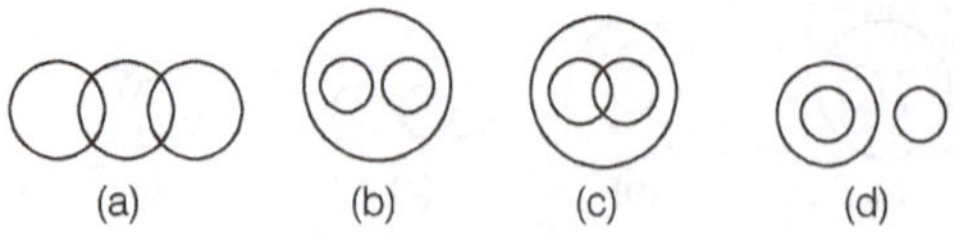

18. Profit, Dividend, Bonus *Delhi Police Constable 2022*

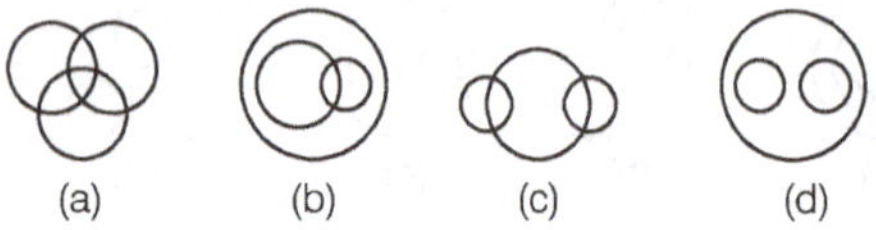

19. Singers, Athletes, Girls *UP Police SI 2021*

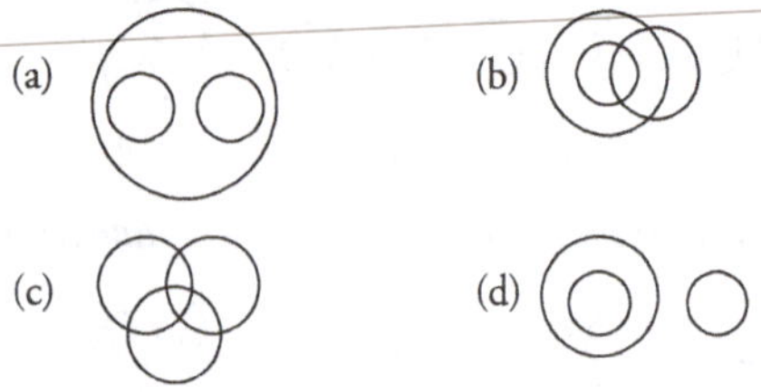

20. Sports, Cricket, Cockroach *RRB NTPC 2020*

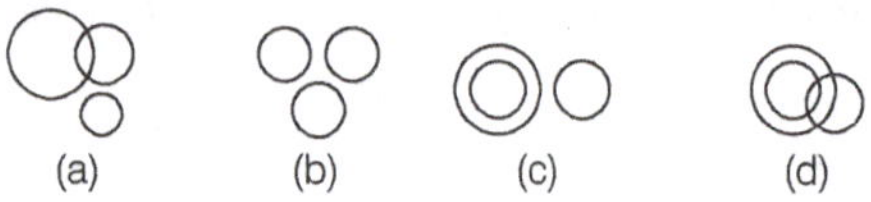

21. Surgery, Calligraphy, Art *RRB NTPC 2021*

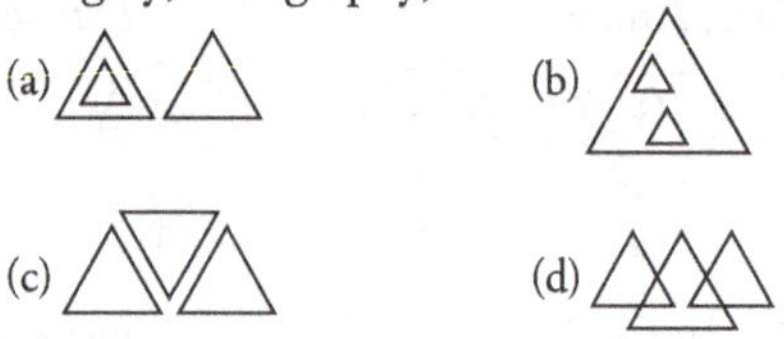

22. Brothers, Fathers, Mothers *SSC (10+2) 2022*

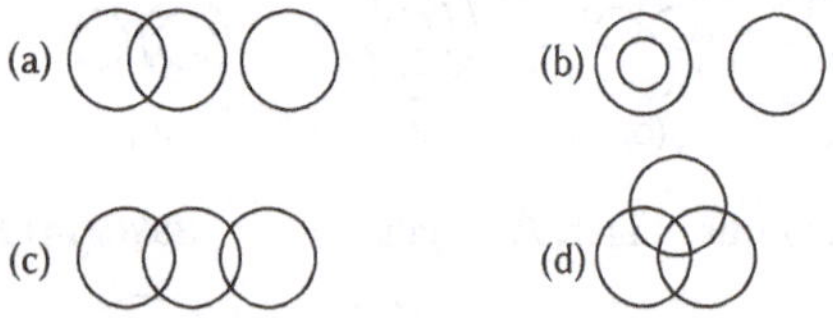

23. Actors, Comedians, Politicians *SSC CGL (Tier-I) 2023*

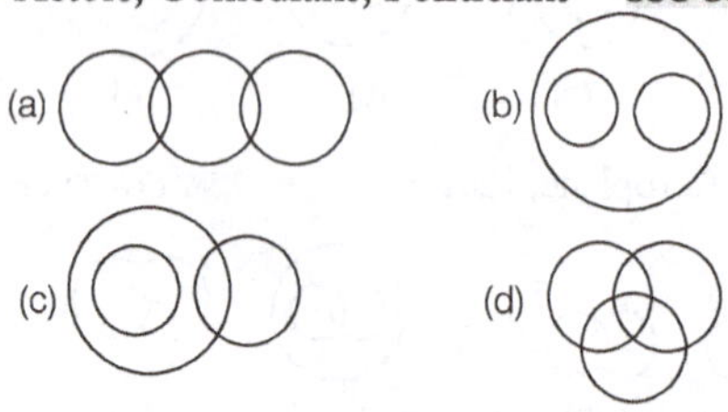

24. Employee, Manager, Woman *Rajasthan Police Constable 2022*

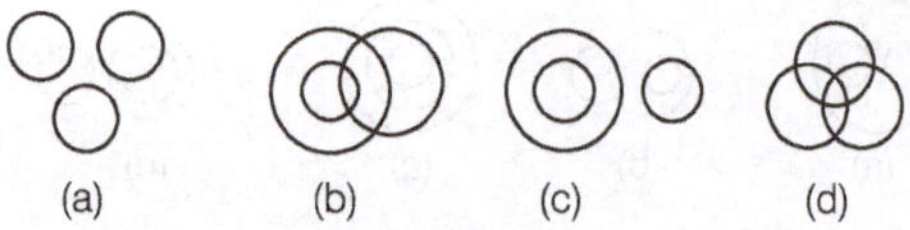

25. Charcoal, Black Colour, Classroom Board *SSC MTS 2021*

26. Mouse, Rodent, Snake *DSSSB 2019*

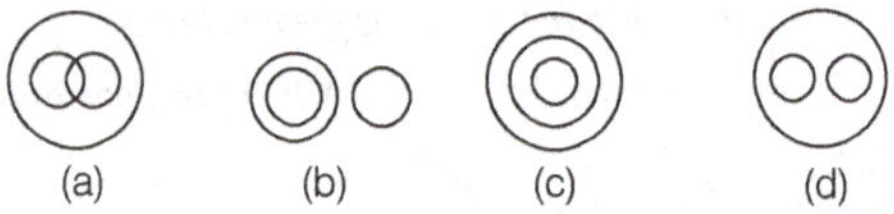

27. Communication, Telephone, Letter *RRB NTPC 2020*

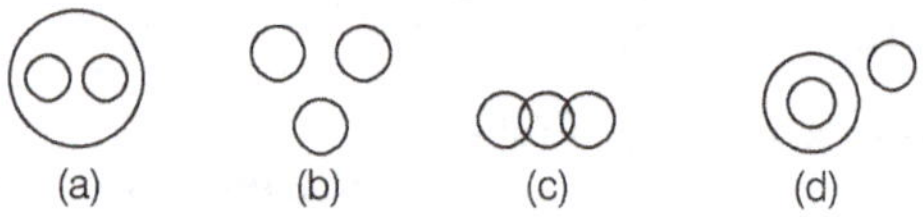

28. Men, Gynaecologist, Doctor *DSSSB 2019*

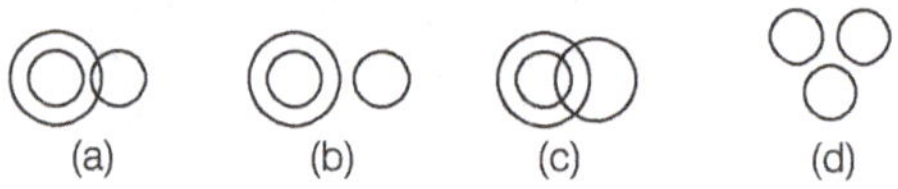

29. Vegetable, Woman, Lion, Parrot *RRB JE 2018*

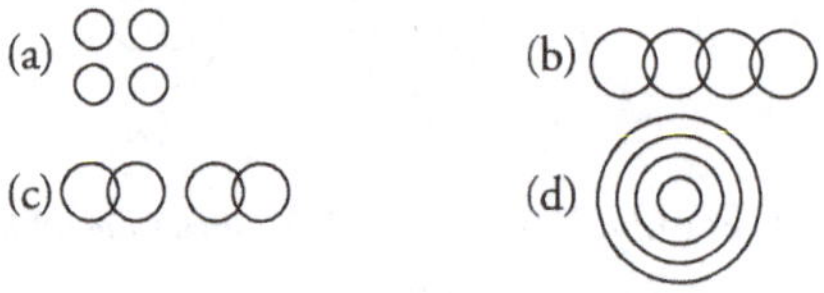

30. India, Delhi, Assam, Guwahati. *CUET UG 2022*

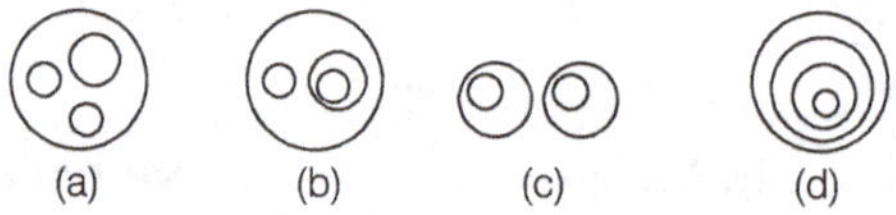

Directions (Q. Nos. 31-34) *Select the set of classes the relationship among which is best illustrated by the venn diagram given below.*

31. *DP Head Constable 2022*

(a) Beverage, Tea, Coffee
(b) Elephant, Deer, Tiger
(c) Doctor, MBA, Engineer
(d) Clock, Fan, Refrigerator

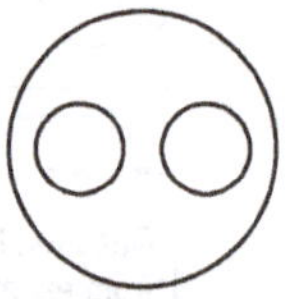

32. *SSC CGL (Tier I) 2022*

(a) Fathers, Brothers, Males
(b) Grandfathers, Fathers, Males
(c) Literates, Engineers, Farmers
(d) Mothers, Aunts, Doctors

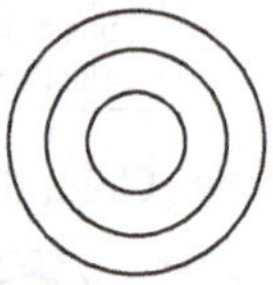

33.

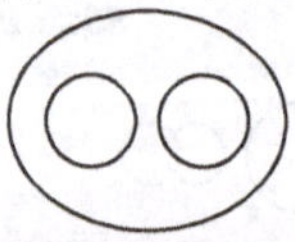

MP Police Constable 2022

(a) Flower, Yellow, Rose
(b) Boy, Player, Student
(c) Living Being, Women, Birds
(d) Male, Father, Police officer

34. 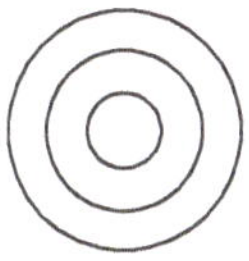

SSC CPO 2021

(a) Males, Fathers, Sons
(b) Sisters, Females, Mothers
(c) Fathers, Males, Doctors
(d) Engineers, Brothers, Males

Based on Analytical Venn Diagram

35. In the given figure, if triangle represents healthy people, rectangle represents old persons and circle represents men, then what is the number of those men who are healthy but not old? *UP Police Constable 2024*

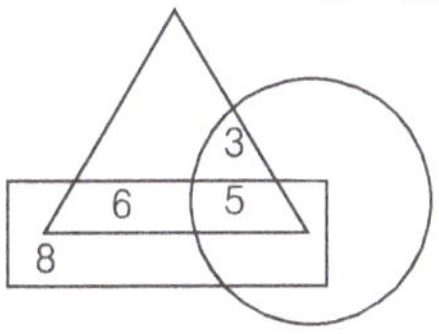

(a) 8 (b) 6 (c) 3 (d) 5

36. In the following figure the numbers represent Indians, leaders and singers. Which of the number represents a person who is an Indian leader but not a singer. *BSSC (10+2) 2022*

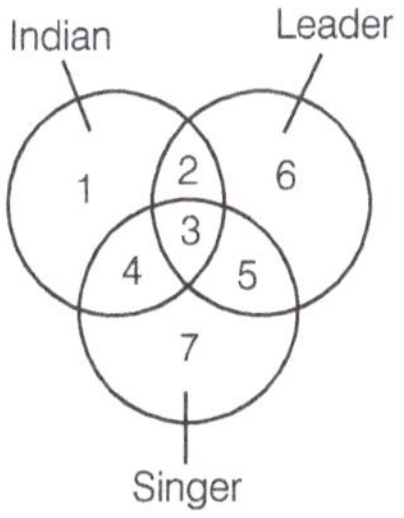

(a) 2 (b) 3
(c) 4 (d) 5

37. The numbers in different sections indicate the number of persons. The circle represents sports persons, the square represents 'coaches' and the triangle represents administrators.
How many sports persons are there who are also coaches but not administrators? *RRC Group D 2022*

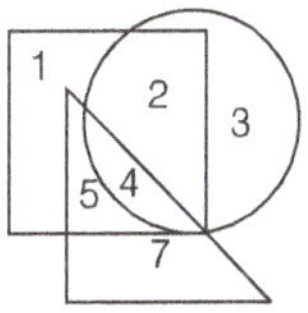

(a) 2
(b) 1
(c) 4
(d) 3

> ***MRC******
> ***(Most Repeating Concepts)***
> Q. Nos. 37, 38, 40, 41, 42, 46, 48 and 49 are very important from examination point of view. Question based on these concept are continuously being asked in RRC Group D, DSSSB Ass, State Police, SC CHSL Teacher and UP SI exams.

38. Which of the following numbers in venn diagram represents only brave police ? *UP Polcie ASI 2021*

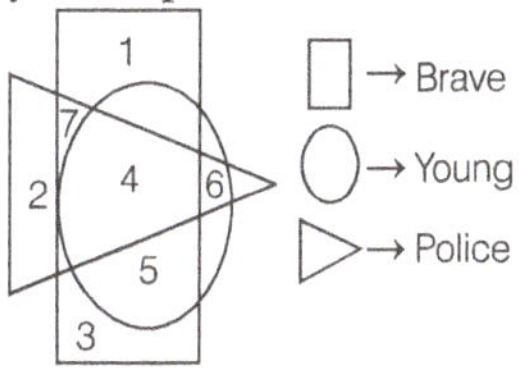

(a) 4 (b) 5
(c) 6 (d) 7

39. How many balls are neither bat nor tyre? *SSC (10+2) 2023*

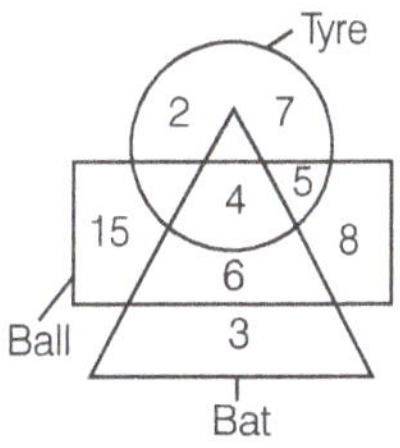

(a) 15 (b) 21 (c) 23 (d) 8

40. The numbers in different sections indicate the number of persons who visited different countries. How many people visited either Australia or Switzerland but not India ? *Delhi Police Head Constable 2022*

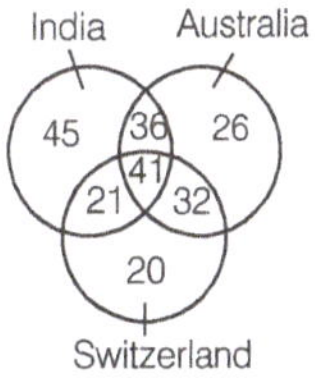

(a) 58 (b) 52 (c) 46 (d) 78

41. How many blue are red?

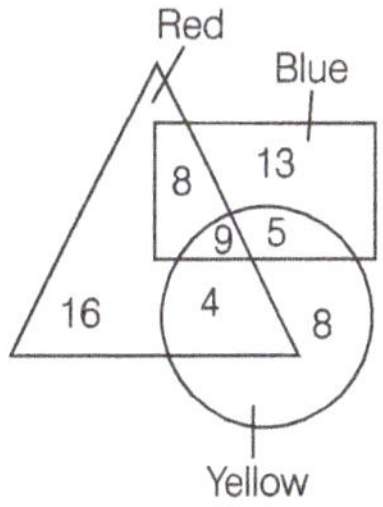

DSSSB 2019

(a) 9 (b) 17 (c) 13 (d) 8

42. Study the following figure and answer the question given below. *UP Police Constable 2024*

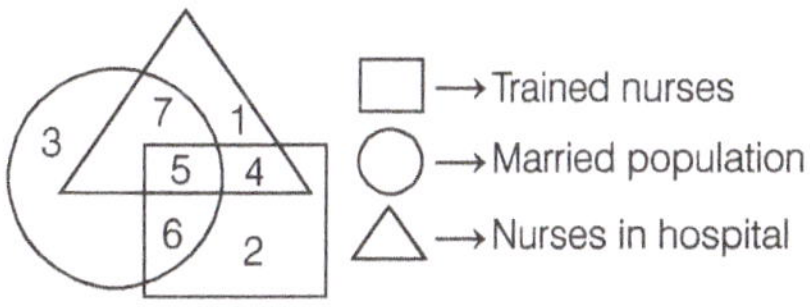

What is represented by the number 7 ?

(a) Married trained nurses
(b) Married nurses in the hospital
(c) Trained nurses
(d) Unmarried trained nurses

43. How many paper are not bottles? ***SSC (10+2) 2022***

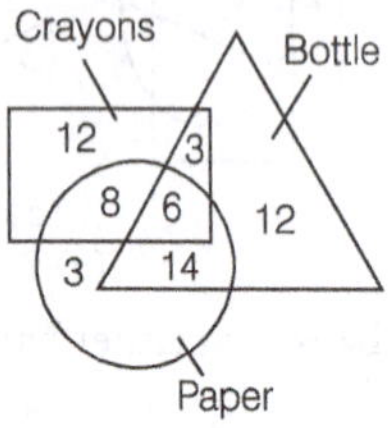

(a) 17 (b) 14 (c) 11 (d) 8

44. Study the venn diagram given below and answer the question that follows.

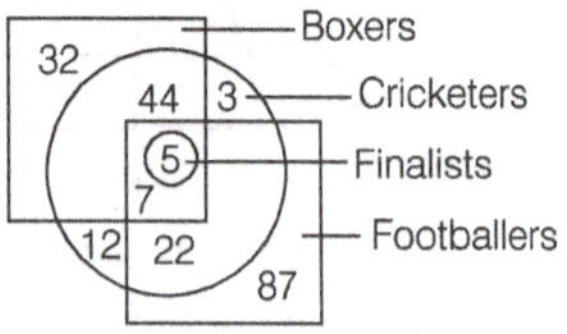

How many cricketers are neither boxers nor footballers? ***RRC Group D 2022***
(a) 12 (b) 3 (c) 15 (d) 20

45. How many talented students can sing as well as dance?

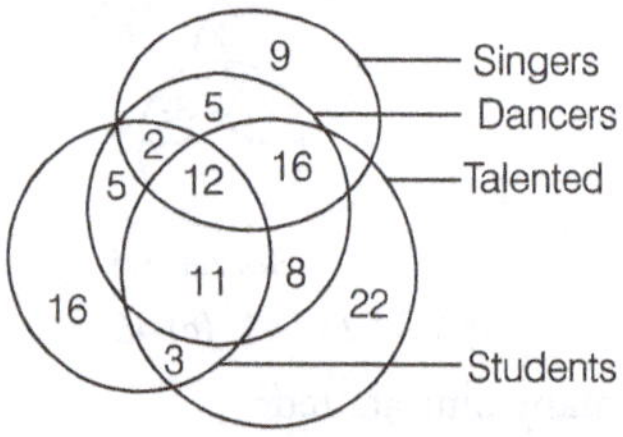

Rajasthan Police Constable 2022
(a) 14 (b) 12 (c) 33 (d) 30

46. Which of the following numbers in the venn diagram represents only mojitos and chocolates, where the biggest triangle represents juices, the second bigger triangle represents mojitos, circle represents chocolates and square represents ice-cream? ***UP Police SI 2021***

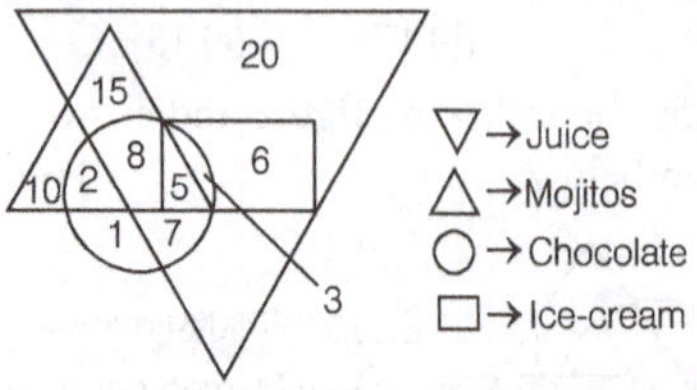

(a) 5 (b) 8 (c) 2 (d) 1

47. In the venn diagram given below, 'circle' represents 'women'; 'triangle' represents 'married', 'rectangle' represents 'under 30 yr and 'square' represents 'employed people'. The numbers given in the diagram indicate the number of persons in that particular category. How many unmarried men under the age of 30 are unemployed? ***Rajasthan Police Constable 2022***

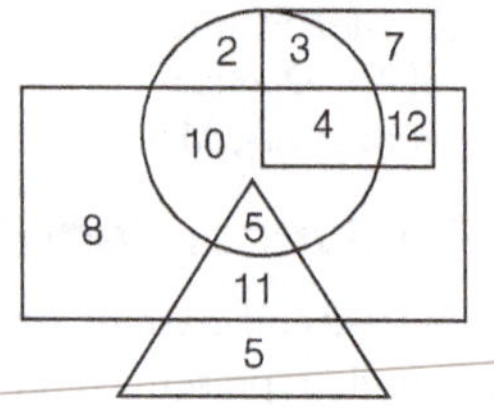

(a) 2 (b) 8 (c) 10 (d) 4

48. Study the venn diagram given below and answer the question that follows.

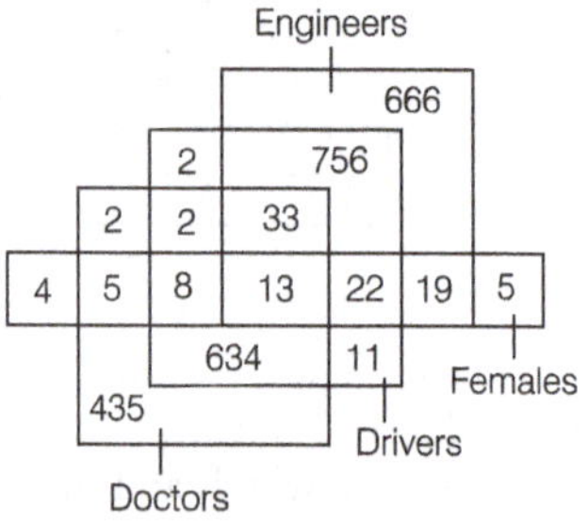

How many female engineers are drivers but not doctors? ***RRC Group D 2022***
(a) 22 (b) 8 (c) 13 (d) 19

49. The hexagon represents women, the circle represents writers and the quadrilateral represent Bengali. ***RRB NTPC 2021***

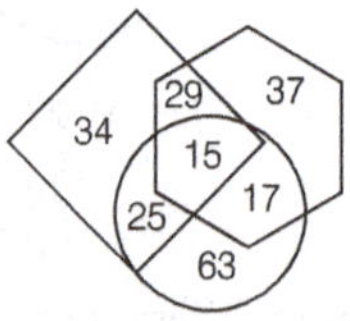

How many women writers are Bengali?
(a) 57 (b) 32 (c) 15 (d) 40

50. Study the venn diagram given below and answer the question that follows.

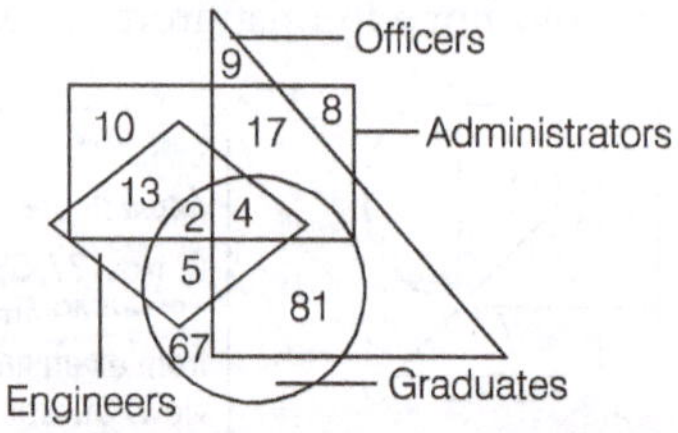

How many non-graduate officers neither adminitrators nor engineers? ***RRB Group D 2022***
(a) 9 (b) 76
(c) 67 (d) 8

Right Key

1. (a)	2. (c)	3. (b)	4. (c)	5. (c)	6. (d)	7. (a)	8. (a)	9. (b)	10. (c)
11. (c)	12. (d)	13. (c)	14. (a)	15. (a)	16. (a)	17. (b)	18. (d)	19. (c)	20. (c)
21. (a)	22. (a)	23. (d)	24. (b)	25. (d)	26. (b)	27. (a)	28. (c)	29. (a)	30. (b)
31. (a)	32. (b)	33. (c)	34. (a)	35. (c)	36. (a)	37. (a)	38. (d)	39. (c)	40. (d)
41. (b)	42. (b)	43. (c)	44. (c)	45. (b)	46. (c)	47. (b)	48. (a)	49. (c)	50. (a)

Solutions

1. *(a)* The venn diagram of the given words is

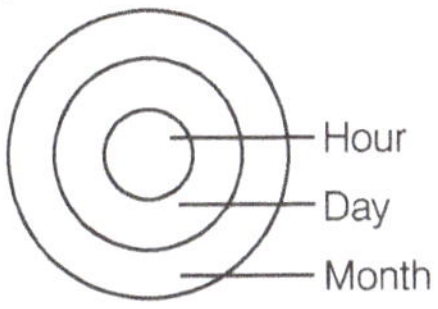

2. *(c)* The venn diagram of the given words is

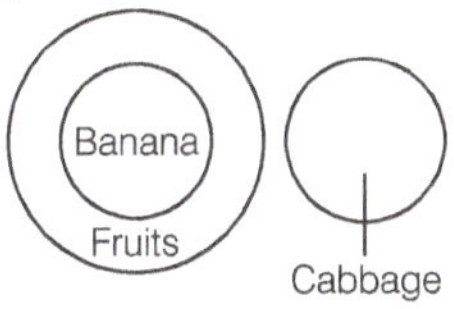

Banana is a fruit, whereas cabbage is different. Cabbage is a vegetable.

3. *(b)* The venn diagram of the given words is

As, both litchi and plum are the fruits.

4. *(c)* The venn diagram of the given words is

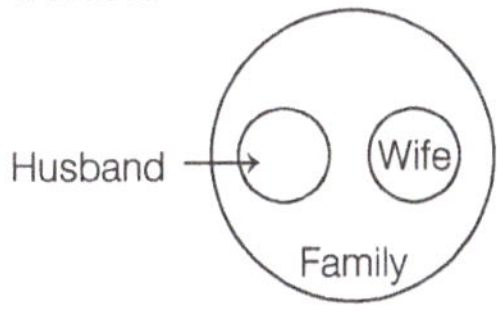

Husband and wife are different, but they come under the family.

5. *(c)* The venn diagram of the given words is

Here, Lotus, Lily and Mango are different from each other.

6. *(d)* The venn diagram of the given words is

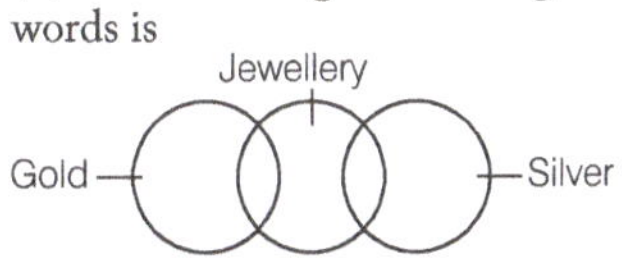

Some jewellery is made of silver and some jewellery is made of gold.

7. *(a)* The venn diagram of the given words is

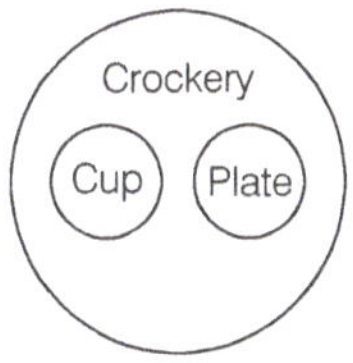

Cup and plate are different kind of crockery.

8. *(a)* The venn diagram of the given words is

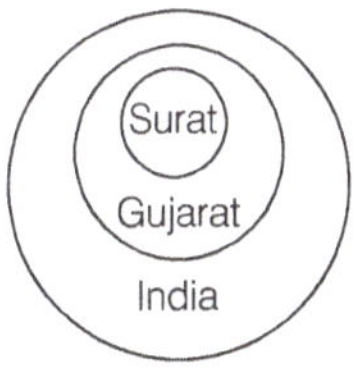

Surat is a city of Gujarat and Gujarat is a state of India.

9. *(b)* The venn diagram of the given words is

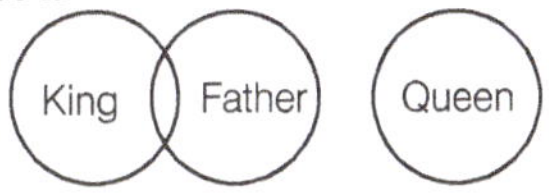

Some kings are father but queen is a female and different from the other two.

10. *(c)* According to the venn diagram,

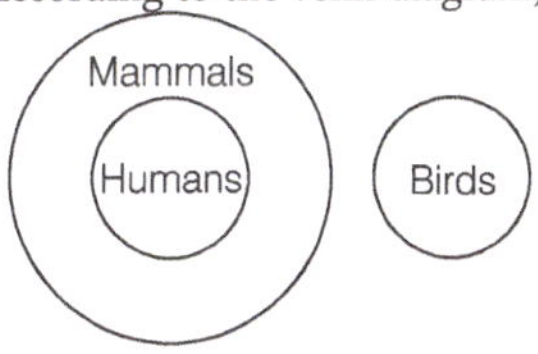

Humans are mammals but bird are aves.

11. *(c)* The venn diagram of the given words is

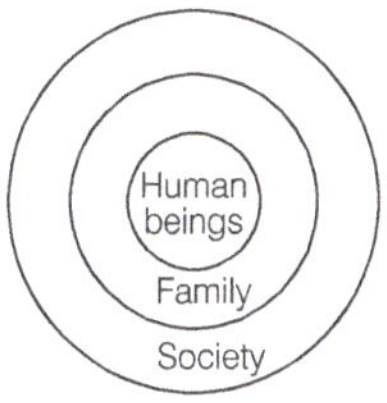

As, human being is the part of the family and family is the part of the society.

12. *(d)* The venn diagram of the given words is

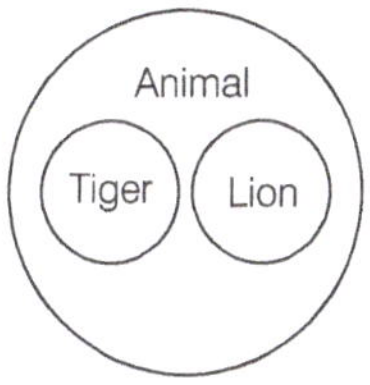

As, lion and tiger are different from each other but both are animals.

13. *(c)* The venn diagram of the given words is

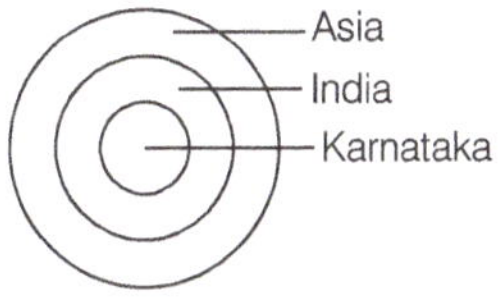

As, karnatakes is a state in India and India is in Asia.

14. *(a)* The venn diagram of the given words is

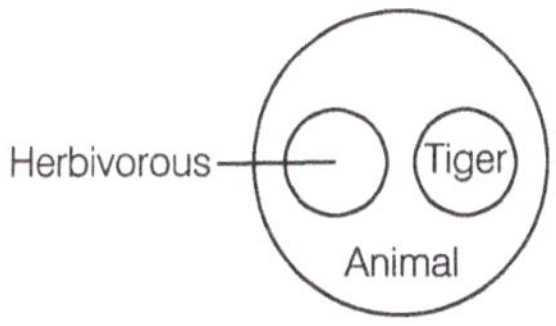

Since, herbivorous and tiger both are animals but tiger is not a herbivorous animal.

15. *(a)* The venn diagram of the given words is

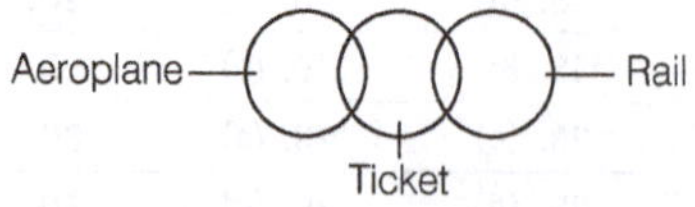

We need tickets in aeroplane and rail both.

16. *(a)* The venn diagram of the given words is

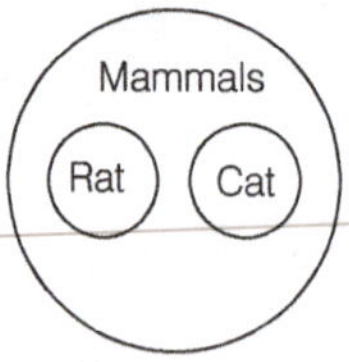

Rat is different from cat but both are mammals.

17. *(b)* The venn diagram of the given words is

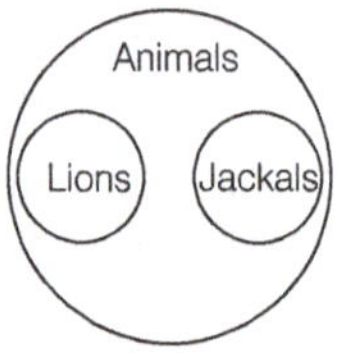

As, both lion and Jackal are animals, but both are different from each other.

18. *(d)* The venn diagram of the given words is

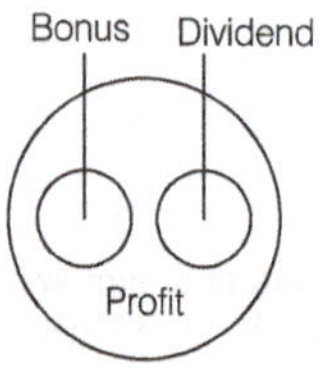

Bonus and dividend are different from each other but both are the part of profit.

19. *(c)* The venn diagram of the given words is

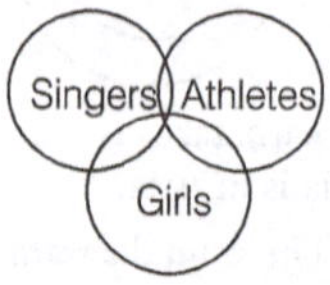

Some girls are singers and athletes and *vice-versa.*

20. *(c)* The venn diagram of the given words is

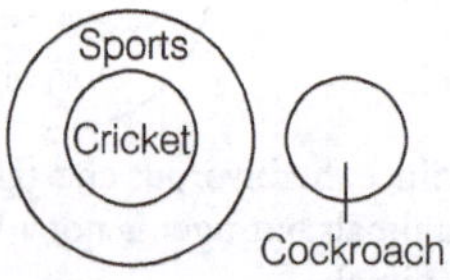

As, cricket is a sport and cockroach is different from them.

21. *(a)* The venn diagram of the given words is

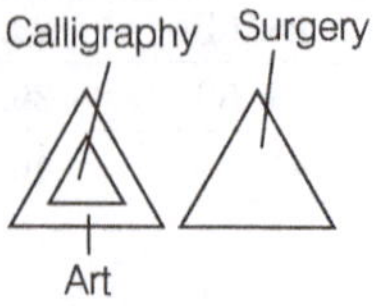

Calligraphy is an art but surgery is different from them.

22. *(a)* The venn diagram of the given words is

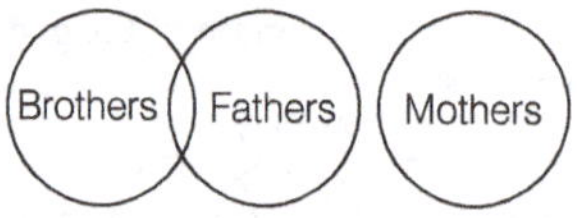

As, some brothers are fathers but mothers are different from them.

23. *(d)* The venn diagram of the given words is

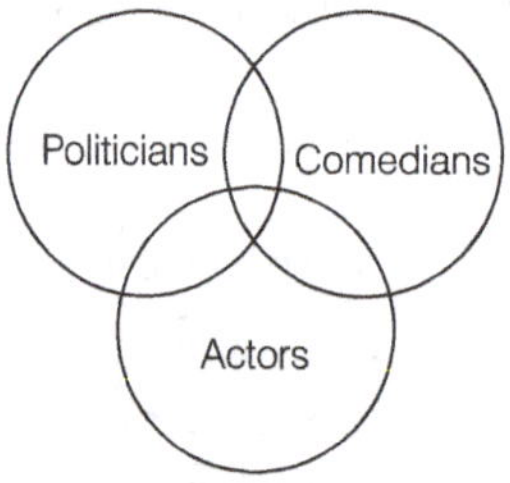

Some actors may be comedians and politicians and some comedians may be politicians.

24. *(b)* The venn diagram of the given words is

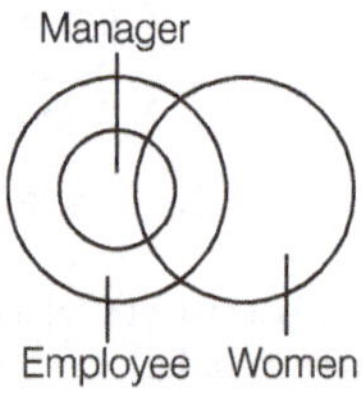

All manager are employees and some women can be manager and employee.

25. *(d)* The venn diagram of the given words is

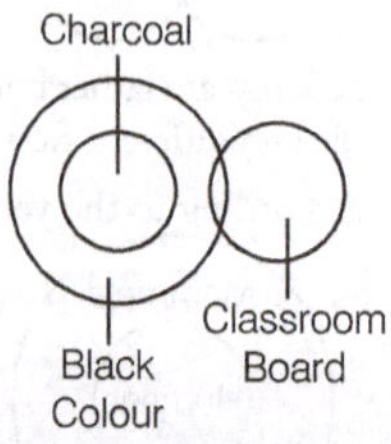

Charcoal is black in colour and some classroom boards are black in colour.

26. *(b)* The venn diagram of the given words is

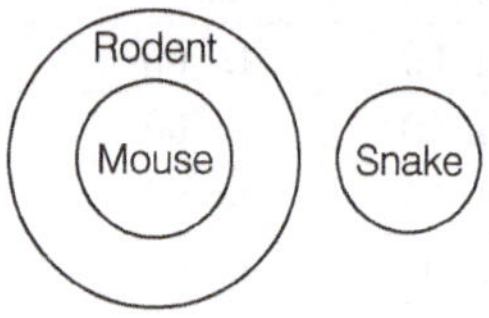

Mouse is small rodent, while snake are reptiles and they are carnivores with long narrow body and no legs.

27. *(a)* The venn diagram of the given words is

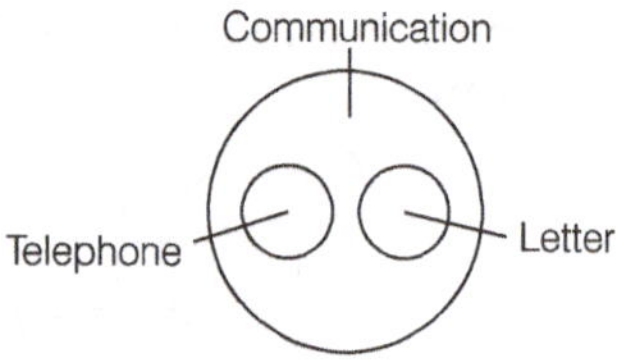

Both telephone and letter are forms of communication.

28. *(c)* The venn diagram of the given words is

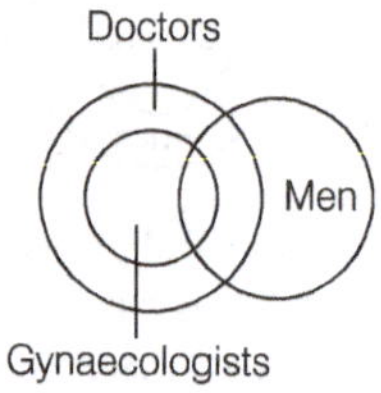

Some men may be Gynaecologists and *vice-versa.*

All gynaecologists are doctors.

Some men may be doctors and *vice-versa.*

29. *(a)* The venn diagram of the given words is

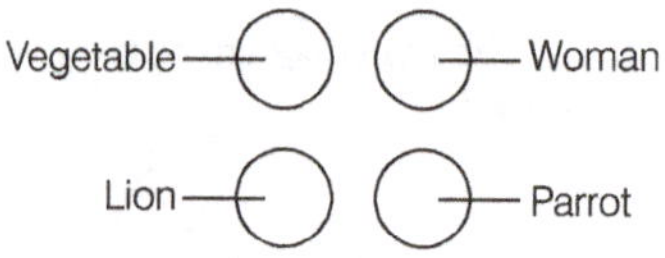

All are different from one another.

30. *(b)* The venn diagram of the given words is

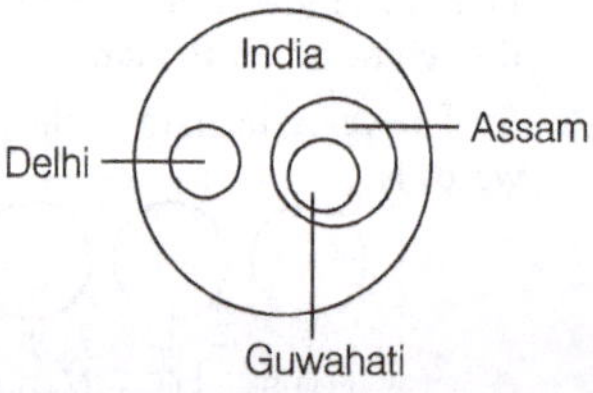

As, Guwahati is in Assam and both Assam and Delhi is in India.

31. *(a)* The venn diagram of the given words is

Both tea and coffee are beverages.

32. *(b)* The venn diagram of the given words is

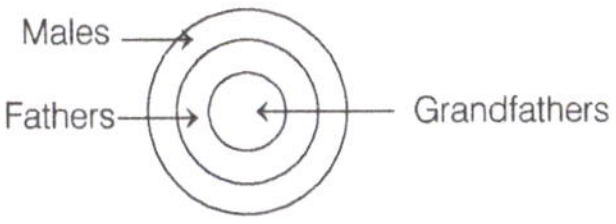

All grandfathers are fathers and both are males.

33. *(c)* The venn diagram of the given words is

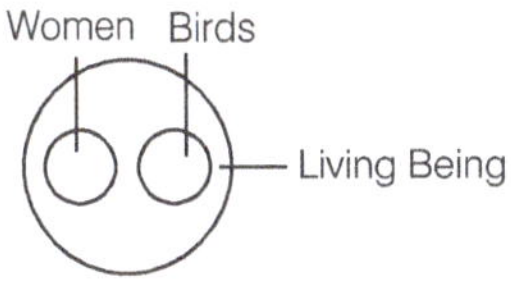

Both, women and birds are living beings.

34. *(a)* The venn diagram of the given words is

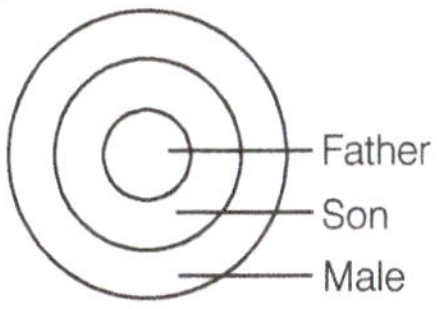

As, all fathers are son and all sons are males.

35. *(c)* According to the venn diagram,

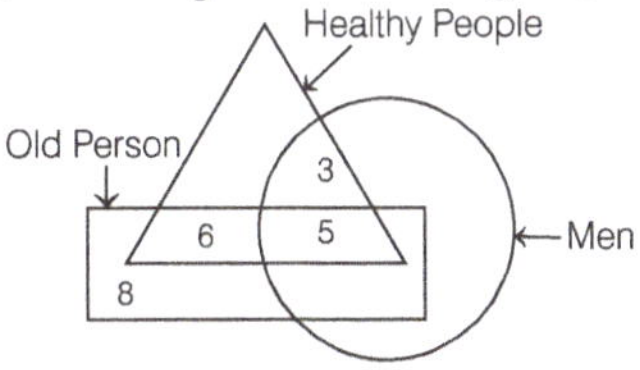

Hence, the number of those men who are healthy but not old = 3

36. *(a)* Hence, the number '2' represents Indian who are leaders but not singers.

37. *(a)* According to the venn diagram,

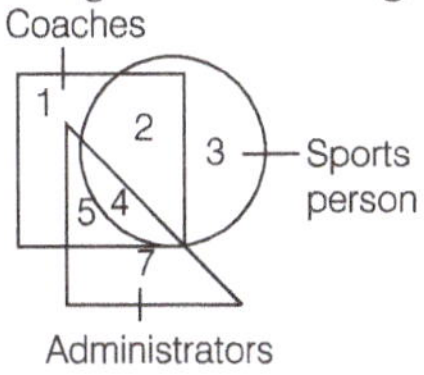

Number of sports person who are also coaches, but not administrators = 2

TOP TIPS To attempt this type to questions, the candidate must know how the identify different shapes such as circle, square and rectangles etc.

38. *(d)* According to the given venn diagram, The number representing only brave police = 7

39. *(c)* According to the venn diagram,

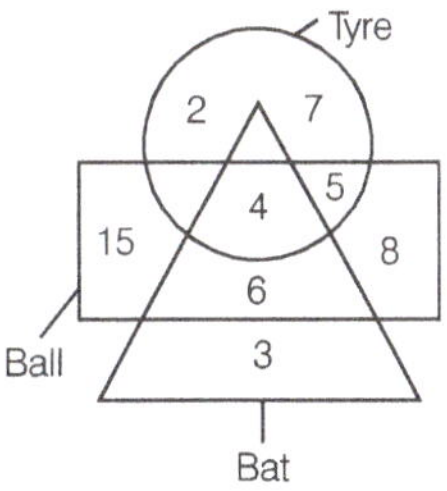

∴ Numbers of balls which are neither bat nor tyre = 15 + 8 = 23

40. *(d)* According to the venn diagram, The total number of people visited either Australia or Switzerland but not India = 26 + 32 + 20 = 78

41. *(b)* According to the venn diagram, Common numbers under both rectangular and triangular part

8 + 9 = 17

Therefore, a total of 17 blue are red.

42. *(b)* According to the venn diagram, number 7 is represented married nurses in the hospital.

43. *(c)* Number of papers which are not bottles = 8 + 3 = 11

44. *(c)* According to the venn diagram,

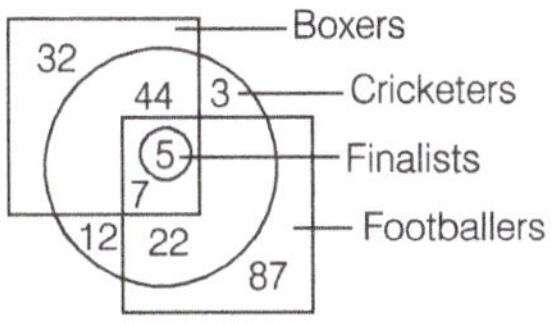

The number of cricketers who are neither boxers nor footballers

= 12 + 3 = 15

45. *(b)* According to the venn diagram, 12 talented students can sing as well as dance.

46. *(c)* According to the venn diagram, Number which represents only mojitos and chocolates = 2

47. *(b)* According to the venn diagram,

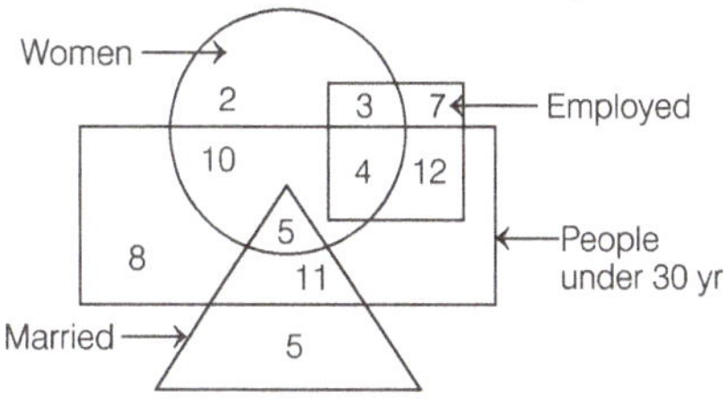

So, the number which represent unmarried men under the age of 30 are unemployed should be enclosed by only rectangle i.e. 8.

48. *(a)* According to the venn diagram,

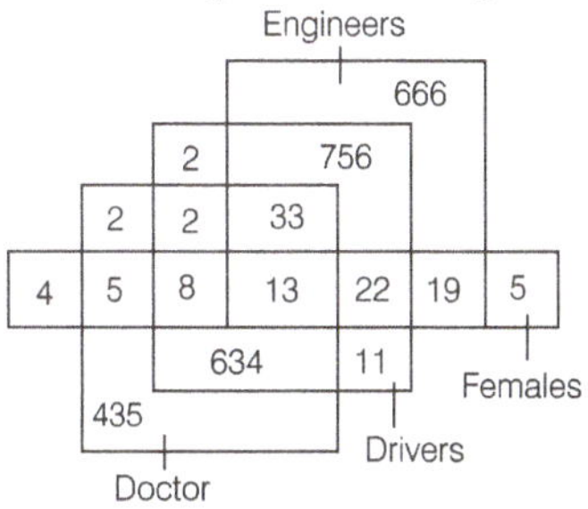

Clearly, only 22 female engineers are drivers but not doctors.

49. *(c)* According to the venn diagram,

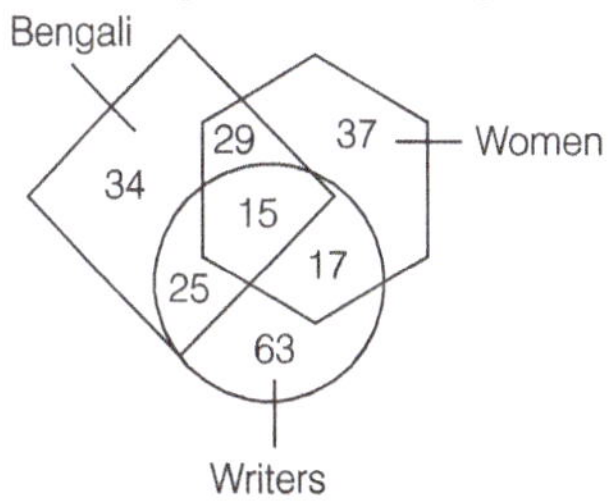

The women writers who are Bengali is 15.

50. *(a)* According to the venn diagram,

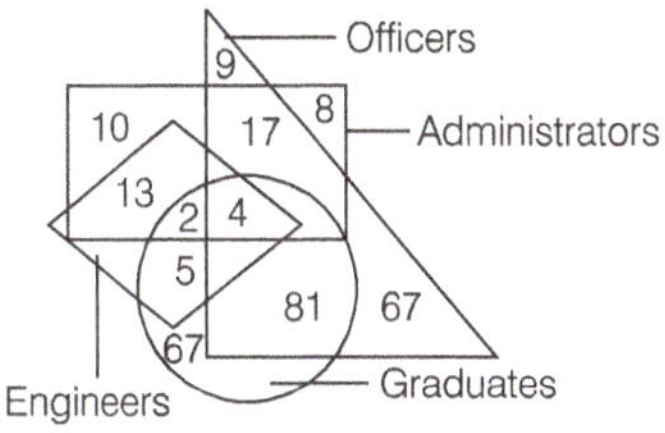

Hence, non graduates officers who are neither administrators nor engineers are = 9

CHAPTER 22 Syllogism

Syllogism

The word syllogism is derived from the greek word "syllogismos" which means "conclusion, inference or deduction". Thus, syllogism is the process by which two or more ideas/propositions/ statements are taken together and a logical conclusion is drawn from them. Even if the given proposition/statement is different from reality, we always consider them to be true and arrive at a conclusion.

Based on Two Statements

In these types of questions, two statements are given followed by two or more conclusions. Taking these statements to be true even if they seem to be at variance with commonly known facts or we have to decide which of the conclusions logically follows from the given statements.

e.g. Which of the given conclusions logically follows from the given statements?

Statements

Some octopus are fish.

Some fish are frogs.

Conclusions

I. Some frogs are fish.

II. Some fish are octopus.

(a) Only Conclusion I follows

(b) Either Conclusion I or I follows

(c) Only Conclusion II follows

(d) Both the conclusions follow

Sol. (d) According to the statements,

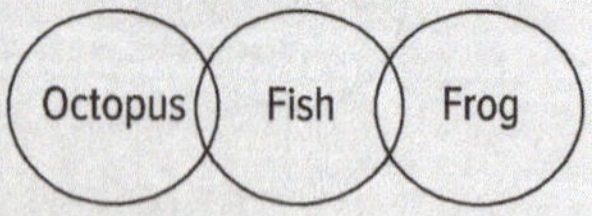

Conclusions I. (✓) II. (✓)

Hence, both the conclusions follow.

Based on Three or More Statements

In these types of questions, three or more statements are given followed by two or more conclusions. Taking these statements to be true, even if they seem to be at variance with commonly known facts, it is to be ascertained which of the given conclusions logically follows from the given statements.

e.g. Which of the given conclusions logically follows from the given statements?

Statements

All cities are towns.

Some towns are states.

No states are continents.

Conclusions

I. Some cities are states.

II. No city is a continent.

(a) Only Conclusion II follows

(b) Neither Conclusion I nor II follows

(c) Only Conclusion I follows

(d) Both Conclusions I and II follow

Sol. (b) According to the statements,

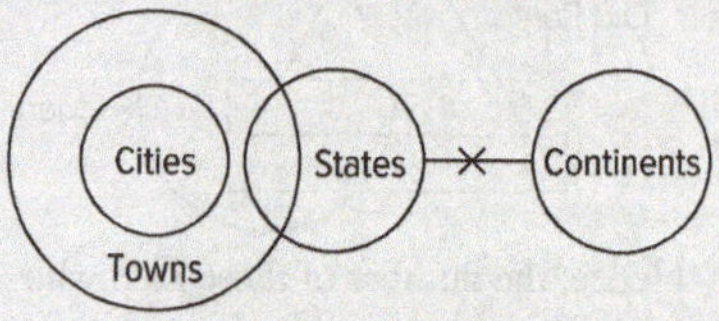

Conclusions I. (✗) II. (✗)

Hence, neither Conclusion I nor II follows.

Score Booster

- Draw conclusions solely based on given information. This will help you avoid mistakes and improve your accuracy.
- Pay attention to keywords like "All', 'No', "Some". and "Some not" as they define relationships. This will help you identify the type of statement and draw accurate conclusions.
- Sometimes contradictory conclusions can help to eliminate incorrect options. This will save your time and reduce the risk of

To solve the questions based on syllogism, it is necessary to have knowledge of the following terms

Statement

A statement is a type of proposition that expresses a relationship between terms.

The statement has four parts, which are as follows

(i) **Quantifier** → A word which expresses quantity is called a quantifier. Some words; like 'all', 'some' and 'none' are called quantifiers.

(ii) **Subject** → A word about which something is said, is called the subject word.

(iii) **Predicate** → Something said about someone which expresses its characteristic is called predicate.

(iv) **Copula** → It is that part or word of the statement which establishes relationship between the subject and the predicate.

e.g. All the boys are smart.

All	the boys	are	smart.
↑	↑	↑	↑
Quantifier	Subject	Copula	Predicate

Here information is given about boys. So 'boys' is the subject and the word 'all' expresses their quantity. So 'all' is a quantifier word while 'smart' is the quality which shows the characteristic of the subject. So 'smart' is the predicate word and the word 'are' establishes the relation between the predicate and the subject. So, the word 'are' is the conjunction.

Term

Such words or groups of words, which are used as subject and predicate in a sentence, are called terms.

e.g. Radhika is an honest girl.

In this sentence Radhika, honest and girl are three different words.

Syllogism is based on the following three principles.

(i) **Minor Term** This is the subject of the conclusion.

(ii) **Middle Term** A term which is common in two or more given statements and establishes a relationship between the two statements is called the middle term.

(iii) **Major Term** It is the predicate of the conclusion.

As,

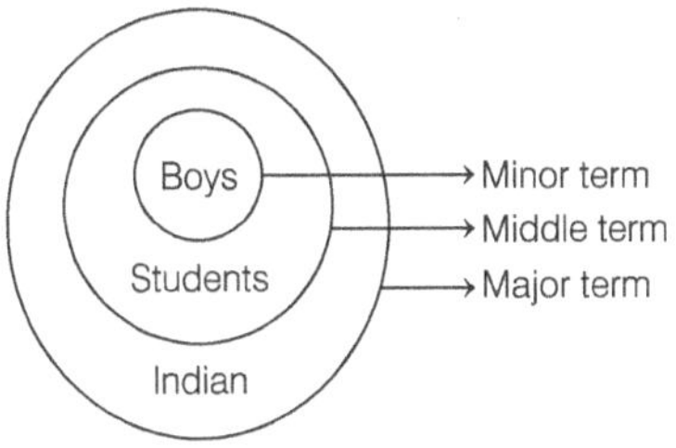

e.g.

Minor term		Middle term
↑		↑
All boys	are	**Students**
All **Students**	are	Indian
↑		↑
Middle term		Major term

Classification of Logical Sentences

Classification of logical sentences is done on the basis of quality and quantity in the following manner.

1. Universal Statement or Sentence

A statement or sentence in which the whole thing is said about a single objective is called an universal sentence'. For example, universal statements are of the following two types

e.g. All human beings are mortal.

(i) **Universal Affirmative Statement or Sentence** A statement which gives a positive information and fully include the subject is called a 'universal affirmative statement' and is denoted by 'A'.

e.g. All cows are animals.

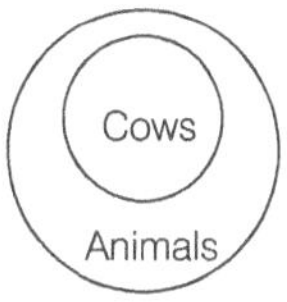

(ii) **Universal Negative Statement or Sentence** A statement which gives a negative information and fully exclude the subject is called a 'universal negative statement' and is denoted by 'E'.

e.g. No cow is an animal.

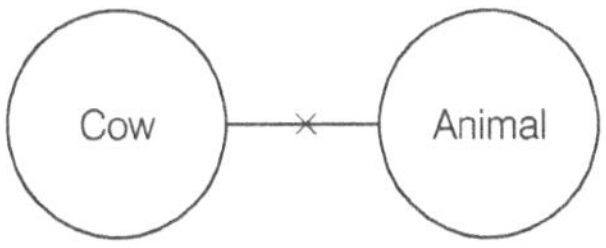

2. Particular Statement or Sentence

A statement or sentence in which some parts of the subject are mentioned is called a 'Particular statement. For example, some people are rich. Particular statements are of the following two types

(i) **Particular Affirmative Statement or Sentence**
A statement which gives a positive information and only partly include the subject is called a 'particular affirmative statement' and is denoted by 'I'.

e.g. Some cows are animals.

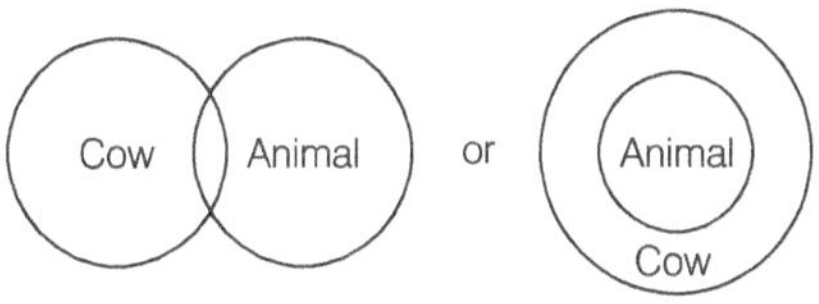

(ii) **Particular Negative Statement or Sentence**
A statement which gives a negative information and only partly exclude the subject is called a 'particular negative statement' and is denoted by 'O'.

e.g. Some people are not rich.

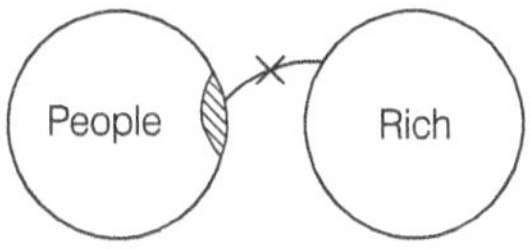

Method of Solving Syllogism

The simplest method of solving questions related to syllogism is the venn diagram method, which is as follows.

Venn Diagram Method In this method we draw separate diagrams for all the given statements and connect the diagrams together as much as possible and draw conclusions based on the connected diagrams.

Basic Venn Diagram Representation

Types of Propositions	Venn Diagram
All S are P	Always 
No S are P	Always 
Some S are P	Either  Some S are P [Some S are not P]
	or  Some S are P [All P are S]
	or  Some S are P [All S are P]
Some S are not P	Either  Some S are not P [Some S are P]
	or  Some S are not P [All P are S]
	or  Some S are not P [No S are P]

Some Basic Statements and Conclusions

1. All A are B.
All C are A.
Conclusions
All C are B.
Some B are C.

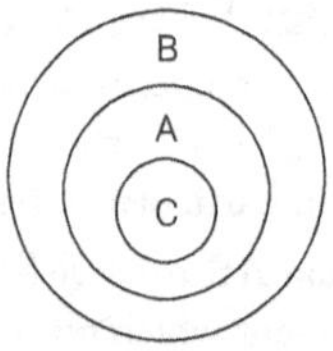

2. All A are B.
All A are C.
Conclusion
Some C are B.

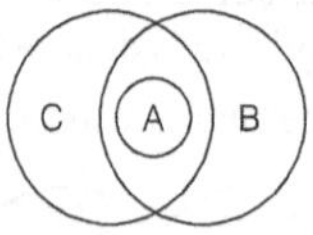

3. All A are B.
Some A are C.
Conclusion
Some C are B.

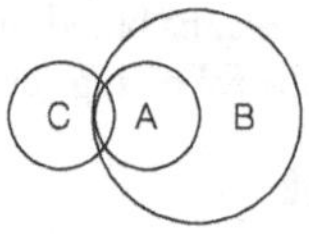

4. No A is B.
All C are A.
Conclusion
No C is B.

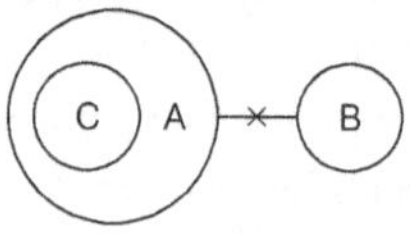

5. No A is B.
All A are C.
Conclusion
Some C are not B.

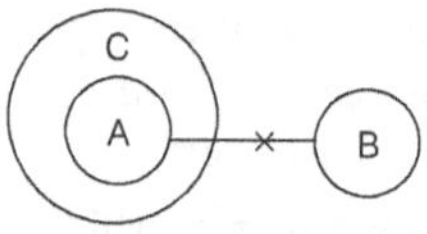

6. No A is B.
Some C are A.
Conclusion
Some C are not B.

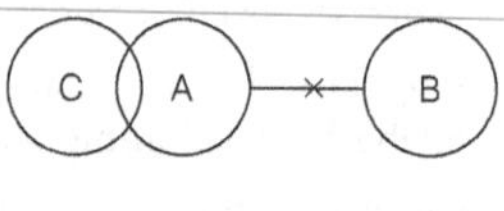

7. All B are A.
Some C are not A.
Conclusion
Some C are not B.

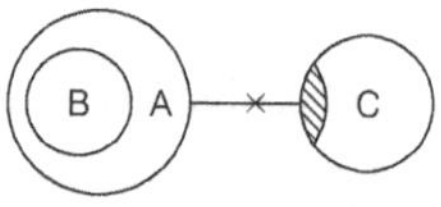

8. Some A are not B.
All A are C.
Conclusion
Some C are not B.

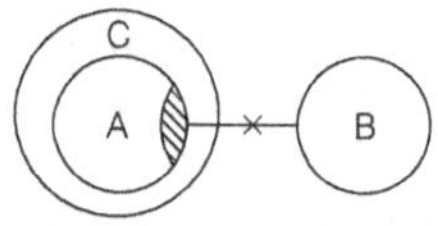

Note Probable conclusions are those conclusions (which are neither completely true nor completely false, there is only a possibility of them being true.

"Either/or" Situation

An "either-or" situation will arise if the following four conditions apply

(i) Both the conclusions must be logically false.
(ii) The subject and predicate should be the same in both the conclusions.
(iii) One of the two conclusions must be positive and the other negative.
(iv) Both the conclusions should be complementary pairs of each other.

Note 'All' and "None" will not be complementary pairs. So there will be no "either or" situation between them.

Exam Approach Examples

Based on Two Statements

Directions (Ex. Nos. 1-4) *In the questions below are given two statements followed by some conclusions. You have to take the given statements to be true even if they seem to be at variance with commonly known facts. Read all the conclusions and then decide which of the given conclusions logically follows from the given statements without disregarding commonly known facts?*

Example 1 Statements

Some Bed are table.

No table is chair. ***RRB ALP (CBT-I) 2024***

Conclusions

I. All tables are beds.

II. Some chairs are beds.

(a) Only Conclusion II follows from the statements
(b) Only Conclusion I follows from the statements
(c) Conclusions I and II follow from both the statements
(d) Neither Conclusion I nor II follows from the statements

Sol. (*d*) According to statements,

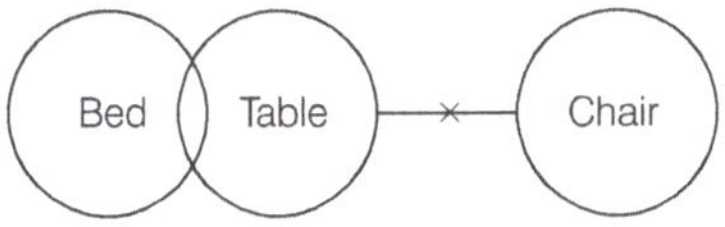

Conclusions I. (✗) II. (✗)

Hence, neither Conclusion I nor II follows.

Example 2 Statements

Some movies are dramas.

Some dramas are fiction. ***SSC CPO 2023***

Conclusions

I. Some movies are fiction.

II. All fiction are movies.

(a) Only Conclusion I follows
(b) Only Conclusion II follows
(c) Neither Conclusion I nor II follows
(d) Both Conclusions I and II follow

> **Helping Tips**
> If all the statements are positive in nature, then all the negative conclusions will be false.

Sol. (*c*) According to statements,

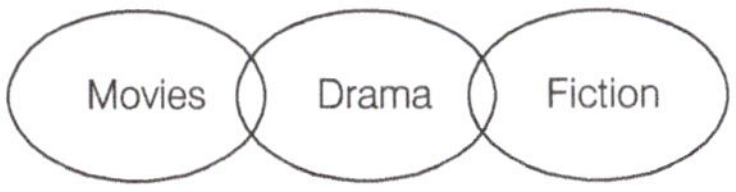

Conclusions I. (✗) II. (✗)

So, neither Conclusion I nor II follows.

Example 3 Statements

Some athletes are businessmen.

All businessmen are rich. ***RRB NTPC (CBT II) 2022***

Conclusions

I. Some athletes are rich.

II. No athlete is rich.

(a) Only Conclusion I follows
(b) Both Conclusions I and II follow
(c) Only Conclusion II follows
(d) Neither Conclusion I nor II follows

Sol. (*a*) According to the statements,

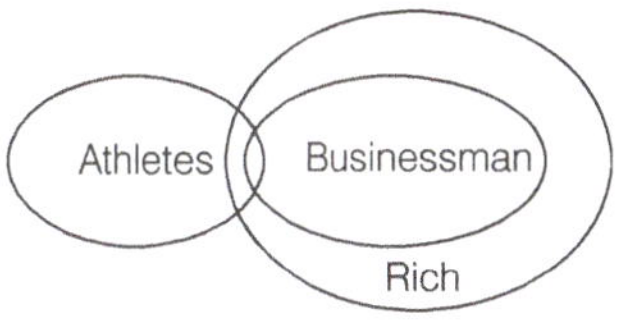

Conclusions I. (✓) II. (✗)

Hence, only Conclusion I follows.

Example 4 Statements

No park is a house.

All field is a park. ***SSC (10+2)2021***

Conclusions

I. No house is a field.

II. Some parks are fields.

III. Some houses are fields.

(a) All the conclusions follow
(b) Both Conclusions I and II follow
(c) Both Conclusions II and III follow
(d) Only Conclusion II follows

Sol. (*b*) According to the statements,

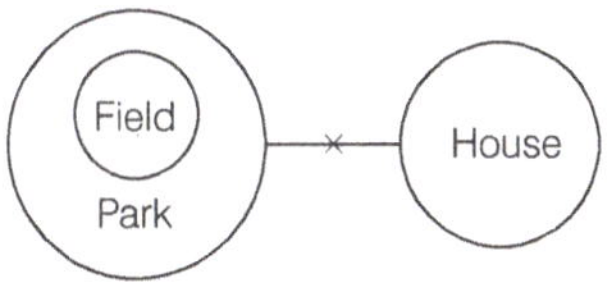

Conclusions I. (✓) II. (✓) III. (✗)

Hence, both Conclusions I and II follow.

Based on More than Two Statements

Directions (Ex. Nos. 5-8) *In the questions below are given three or more statements followed by some conclusions. Assuming the statements to be true, even if they seem to be at variance with commonly known facts, decide which of the conclusions logically follow(s) from the statements. Do they?*

Example 5 Statements

No rose is an orchid.

All roses are lilies.

All lilies are lotus. ***SSC (10+2) 2024***

Conclusions

I. Some lilles are orchids.

II. Some lotus are orchids.

III. All lilies are orchids.
(a) Both Conclusions I and III follow
(b) Both Conclusions II and III follow
(c) Neither Conclusion I, II nor III follows
(d) Both Conclusions I and II follow

Sol. (*c*) According to statements,

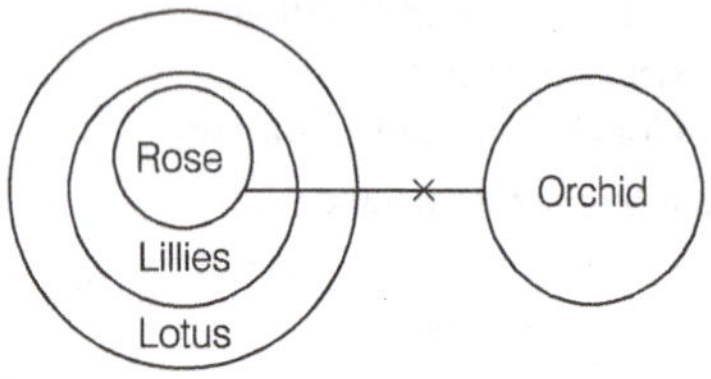

Conclusions I. (✗) II. (✗) III. (✗)

Hence, neither Conclusion I, II nor III follows.

Example 6 Statements

Some tears are drops.
Some drops are streams.
All streams are rivers.

SSC CGL (Tier I) 2024

> **Helping Tips**
> Never assume anything while solving the questions of this chapter. Follow only the data mentioned in the question and do not make any additional assumptions.

Conclusions
I. All tears can never be rivers.
II. Some drops are rivers.
III. All tears being streams is a possibility.
(a) Both Conclusions I and II follow
(b) Only Conclusion I follows
(c) Both Conclusions II and III follow
(d) Only Conclusion III follows

Sol. (*c*) According to statements,

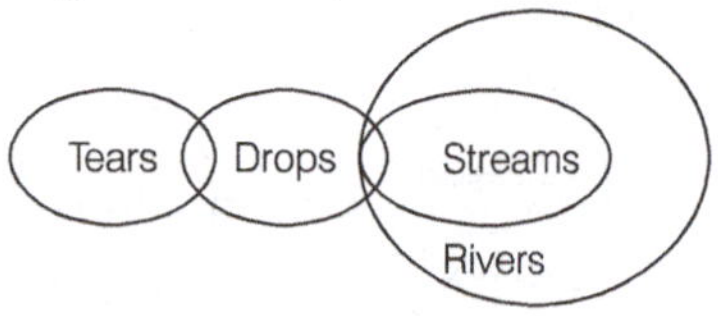

Conclusions I. (✗) II. (✓) III. (✓)

Hence, both Conclusions II and III follow.

Example 7 Statements

All plastics are fruits.
All fruits are books.
No books are trousers.

RRB NTPC 2021

Conclusions
I. Some books are plastic.
II. No trousers are plastic.
III. Some fruits are plastic.
IV. Some trousers are fruits.
(a) Conclusions I, II and III follow
(b) Conclusions I and II follow
(c) Conclusions II, III and IV follow
(d) Conclusion I and III follow

Sol. (*a*) According to the statements,

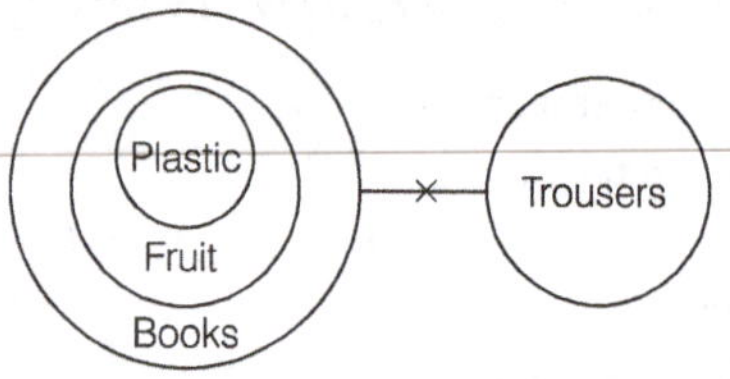

Conclusions I. (✓) II. (✓)
III. (✓) IV. (✗)

Therefore, Conclusions I, II and III follow.

Example 8 Statements

All sheeps are cows.
Some cows are horses.
All horses are jackals.

SSC CGL (Tier-II) 2025

Conclusions
I. Some jackals are cows.
II. Some horses are sheeps.
(a) Both Conclusions I and II follow
(b) Only Conclusion II follows
(c) Only Conclusion I follows
(d) Neither Conclusion I nor II follows

Sol. (*c*) According to the statements,

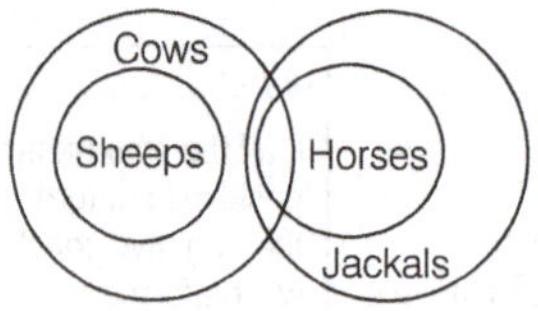

Conclusions I. (✓)
II. (✗)

Hence, only Conclusion I follows.

> **Trending Concept**
> Questions based on three statements are being asked in current examination (RRB Group D, NTPC, ALP), SSC (CPO, CGL). These questions are important for the upcoming examination.

Chapter Challenge

Based on Two Statements

Directions (Q. Nos. 1-32) *Read the given statements and conclusions carefully. Assuming the information given in the statements to be true, even if it seems to be at variance with commonly known facts, decide which of the given conclusions logically follows from the given statements.*

1. Statements All lemons are potatoes.
Some lemons are papayas. ***RRB ALP 2024***

Conclusions
I. Some potatoes are papayas.
II. All papayas are potatoes.
(a) Only Conclusion I follows
(b) Only Conclusion II follows
(c) Both Conclusions I and II follow
(d) Neither Conclusion I nor II follows

> ***MRC******
> ***(Most Repeating Concepts)***
> Question Nos. 1, 3, 11, 12, 14, 17 and 18 are very important from the examination point of view. Questions on these concepts are being asked regularly in Railway (ALP, Technician), SSC (CPO, 10+2) and DSSSB examinations.

2. Statements All fishes are birds.
All birds are animals. ***RRB ALP (CBT-I) 2024***

Conclusions
I. All animals are fishes.
II. Some birds are fishes.
(a) Conclusion follows from both Statements I and II
(b) Only Conclusion II follows from the statements
(c) Neither Conclusion I nor II follows from the statements
(d) Only Conclusion I follows from the statements

3. Statements Some giraffes are rhinos.
All rhinos are tigers. ***RRB ALP 2024***

Conclusions
I. Some tigers are giraffes.
II. All tigers are rhinos.
(a) Only Conclusion II follows
(b) Neither Conclusion I nor II follows
(c) Only Conclusion I follows
(d) Both Conclusions I and II follow

4. Statements Some cushions are bells.
All cushions are machines.

Conclusions ***RRB Technician Grade III 2024***
I. All machines are cushions.
II. Some bells are machines.
(a) Only Conclusion II follows
(b) Both Conclusions I and II follow
(c) Only Conclusion I follows
(d) Neither Conclusion I nor II follows

5. Statements All flowers are trees.
All leaves are flowers.
CISF Head Constable 2023

Conclusions
I. All trees are flowers.
II. All leaves are trees.
(a) Only Conclusion II follows
(b) Conclusions I and II follow
(c) Only Conclusion I follows
(d) Neither Conclusion I nor II follows

6. Statements Some dogs are fishes.
Some fishes are birds. ***HCET 2023***

Conclusions
I. Some dogs are birds.
II. Some birds are dogs.
(a) Both Conclusions I and II follow
(b) Neither Conclusion I nor II follows
(c) Only Conclusion I follows
(d) Only Conclusion II follows
(e) Do not wish to answer

7. Statements All animals are dogs.
Some dogs are dangerous. ***HCET 2023***

Conclusions
I. All animals are dangerous.
II. Some dogs are animals.
(a) Only Conclusion I follows
(b) Only Conclusion II follows
(c) Both Conclusions I and II follow
(d) Neither Conclusion I nor II follows
(e) Do not wish to answer

8. Statements All peelers are funnels.
Some peelers are spatulas.

Conclusions ***CUET (UG) 2022***
I. Some peelers are not funnels.
II. Some spatulas are peelers.
(a) Neither I nor II follows
(b) Both Conclusions I and II follow
(c) Only Conclusion I follows
(d) Only Conclusion II follows

9. Statements All computers are calculators.
All calculators are boxes.

Conclusions ***SSC (10+2) 2021***
I. All computers are boxes.
II. Some boxes are computers.
(a) Both Conclusions I and II follow
(b) Neither Conclusion I nor II follows
(c) Only Conclusion II follows
(d) Only Conclusion I follows

10. Statements Some appliances are electronics.
Some electronics are tubelights.

Conclusions ***SSC CPO 2019***
I. Some appliances are tube lights.
II. No tubelight is an appliance.

(a) Only Conclusion II follows
(b) Only Conclusion I follows
(c) Either Conclusion I or II follows
(d) Neither Conclusion I nor II follows

11. **Statements** Some roads are vehicles.
Some vehicles are trees.

Conclusions
I. Some trees are roads.
II. All vehicles are trees.
(a) Both Conclusions I and II follow
(b) Only Conclusion I follows
(c) Neither Conclusion I nor II follows
(d) Only Conclusion II follows

12. **Statements** Some apples are oranges.
All oranges are fruits. ***SSC CPO 2023***

Conclusions
I. All apples are fruits.
II. Some fruits are oranges.
(a) Only Conclusion II follows
(b) Neither Conclusion I nor II follows
(c) Both Conclusions I and II follow
(d) Only Conclusion I follows

13. **Statements** All teas are juices.
All juices are cocktails. ***SSC CPO 2023***

Conclusions
I. All teas are cocktails.
II. All cocktails are definitely juices.
(a) Only Conclusion II follows
(b) Only Conclusion I follows
(c) Both Conclusions I and II follow
(d) Neither Conclusion I nor II follows

14. **Statements** All Hulk are Thor.
All Thor are Flash. ***SSC (10+2) 2023***

Conclusions
I. All Hulk are Flash.
II. No Thor is Hulk.
(a) Both Conclusions I and II follow from the statements
(b) Neither Conclusion I nor II follows from the statements
(c) Only Conclusion I follows from the statements
(d) Only Conclusion II follows from the statements

15. **Statements** All birds are cows.
Some cows are dogs. ***SSC JE 2023***

Conclusions
I. Some dogs are birds.
II. Some cows are birds.
(a) Both Conclusions I and II follow
(b) Only Conclusion II follows
(c) Neither Conclusion I nor II follows
(d) Only Conclusion I follows

16. **Statements** Some roses are lilies.
Some lilies are jasmines. ***DP Constable 2023***

Conclusions
I. Some jasmine are rose.
II. All jasmine are rose.
(a) Only Conclusion II follows
(b) Both Conclusions I and II follow
(c) Neither of Conclusions I nor II follows
(d) Only Conclusion I follows

17. **Statements** No toffee is chocolate.
No chocolate is candy.
DSSSB Workshop 2024

Conclusions
I. No toffee is candy.
II. Some candy are chocolates.
(a) Only Conclusion II follows
(b) Only Conclusion I follows
(c) Neither Conclusion I nor II follows
(d) Both Conclusions I and II follow

18. **Statements** Some rivers are lakes.
No lake is stream. ***DSSSB Workshop 2024***

Conclusions
I. No stream is a lake.
II. Some streams are rivers.
(a) Only Conclusion I follows
(b) Neither Conclusion I nor II follows
(c) Both Conclusions I and II follow
(d) Only Conclusion I follows

19. **Statements** All crows are brains.
No-brain are falcons.

Conclusions ***Rajasthan Police Constable 2022***
I. All crows are falcons.
II. Some falcons are brain.
(a) Only Conclusion I follows
(b) Only Conclusion II follows
(c) Both Conclusions I and II follow
(d) Neither Conclusion I nor II follows

20. **Statements** All balloons are cakes.
No cake is toffee. ***CISF ASI 2023***

Conclusions
I. No balloon is a toffee.
II. All cakes are balloons.
(a) Neither Conclusion I nor II follows
(b) Only Conclusion I follows
(c) Only Conclusion II follows
(d) Both Conclusions I and II follow

21. **Statements** Some drivers are racers.
Some racers are pilots. ***SSC MTS 2019***

Conclusions
I. Some pilots are drivers.
II. No pilot is a driver.
(a) Either Conclusion I or II follows
(b) Only Conclusion I follows
(c) Neither Conclusion I nor II follows
(d) Only Conclusion II follows

22. **Statements** All flowers are trees.
All trees are fruits. ***SSC MTS 2019***

Conclusions
I. Some fruits are flowers.
II. All flowers are fruits.
(a) Both Conclusions I and II follow
(b) Only Conclusion I follows
(c) Either Conclusion I or II follows
(d) Only Conclusion II follows

23. Statements Some bulbs are LEDs.
Some LEDs are tubelights. *SSC CPO 2018*
Conclusions
I. Some tubelights are bulbs.
II. No tubelight is a bulb.
(a) Only Conclusion I follows
(b) Only Conclusion II follows
(c) Either Conclusion I or II follows
(d) Neither Conclusion I nor II follows

24. Statements All hurricanes are cyclones.
All cyclones are tornadoes. *RRB ALP 2018*
Conclusions
I. Some tornadoes are hurricanes.
II. Some cyclones are hurricanes.
(a) Only Conclusion I follows
(b) Both Conclusions I and II follow
(c) Neither Conclusion I nor II follows
(d) Only Conclusion II follows

25. Statements Some pencils are sticks.
All sticks are trees. *UPSSSC 2018*
Conclusions
I. All sticks are pencils.
II. All pencils are trees.
(a) Only Conclusion I follows
(b) Only Conclusion II follows
(c) Either Conclusion I or II follows
(d) Neither Conclusion I nor II follows

26. Statements Some trees are flowers.
No flower is red. *SSC Constable (GD) 2024*
Conclusions
I. All trees are red.
II. All red are flowers.
III. Some trees are not red.
(a) Only Conclusion II follows from the statements
(b) Conclusions II and III follow from both the statements
(c) Only Conclusion III follows from the statements
(d) All the conclusions follow from the statements

27. Statements No fish is a pen.
All keys are pens. *SSC MTS 2021*
Conclusions
I. No key is a pen.
II. No pen is a key.
III. Some pens are keys.
IV. Some keys are fishes.
(a) Only Conclusion III follows
(b) Only Conclusion I follows
(c) Conclusions I and II follow
(d) Conclusion I and IV follow

28. Statements All bats are birds.
Some rats are bats. *SSC CGL 2022*
Conclusions
I. Some rats are birds.
II. Some birds are bats.
III. All rats are bats.
(a) Conclusions I and III follow
(b) Conclusions I and II follow
(c) Only Conclusion II follows
(d) Only Conclusion I follows

29. Statements Some blankets are scarves.
All rooms are blankets. *RRB NTPC 2021*
Conclusions
I. Some scarves are blankets.
II. Some rooms are scarves.
(a) Both Conclusions I and II follow
(b) Only Conclusion I follows
(c) Only Conclusion II follows
(d) Neither Conclusion I nor II follows

30. Statements Some mobiles are tablets.
All tablets are laptops. *SSC CPO 2022*
Conclusions
I. Some laptops are mobiles.
II. Some mobiles are laptops.
III. All mobiles are laptops.
(a) All the conclusions follows
(b) Conclusion I follows
(c) Conclusions II and III follow
(d) Conclusions I and II follow

31. Statements No yellow is green.
Some pink are yellow. *CUET (UG) 2023*
Conclusions
I. No green is yellow.
II. Some yellow are pink.
III. All green are pink.
(a) Conclusions I and II follow
(b) Conclusions I, II and III follow
(c) Conclusions II and III follow
(d) Only Conclusion III follows

32. Statements Some rivers are oceans.
All oceans are beaches. *SSC CPO 2023*
Conclusions
I. Some rivers are beaches.
II. All oceans are rivers.
(a) Both Conclusions I and II follow
(b) Only Conclusion I follows
(c) Neither Conclusion I nor II follows
(d) Only Conclusion II follows

Based on More than Two Statements

Directions (Q. Nos. 33-58) *Read the following statements and conclusions carefully. Consider the information given in the statements as true, even if it seems to be at variance with commonly known facts, and decide which of the given conclusions logically follow(s) from the statements?*

33. Statements All apples are plums.
Some plums are berries.
Some berries are coconuts. ***SSC (10+2) 2024***

Conclusions
I. Some berries are plums.
II. All plums are apples.
III. Some coconuts are berries.
(a) Only Conclusion III follows from the statements
(b) Conclusions I and III follow from both the statements
(c) Only Conclusion II follows from the statements
(d) Only Conclusion I follows from the statements

> ***MRC******
> ***(Most Repeating Concepts)***
> Question Nos. 33, 35, 37, 40, 44, 48, 51 and 56 are very important from the examination point of view. Question on these concept are being asked regularly in SSC CGL, SSC MTS and RRB NTPC.

34. Statements All camels are donkeys.
Some cats are camels.
All dolphins are cats. ***RRB NTPC 2022***

Conclusions
I. All dolphins are donkeys.
II. Some dolphins are donkeys.
III. Some donkeys are cats.
IV. All cats are donkeys.
(a) Conclusions II and III follow
(b) Only Conclusion III follows
(c) Conclusions I and III follow
(d) Only Conclusion IV follows

35. Statements All oranges are apples.
All apples are kiwis.
Some apples are grapes. ***RPF SI 2024***

Conclusions
I. Some kiwis are grapes.
II. Some oranges are grapes.
(a) Only Conclusion II follows
(b) Neither Conclusion I nor II follows
(c) Both Conclusions I and II follow
(d) Only Conclusion I follows

36. Statements Some rice is white.
Some rice is brown.
No white is wheat. ***SSC (10+2) 2024***

Conclusions
I. Some wheat is brown.
II. Some rice is not wheat.
III. Some brown is not white.
(a) Both Conclusions I and III follow
(b) Only Conclusion II follows
(c) Both Conclusions II and III follow
(d) Only Conclusion III follows

37. Statements Some crayon is colour.
No colour is water.
Some water is liquid.
SSC CHSL (Tier-II) 2024

Conclusions
I. Some crayon is liquid.
II. Some crayon is not water.
III. Some liquid is not colour.
(a) Only Conclusion III follows
(b) Both Conclusions I and III follow
(c) Only Conclusion II follows
(d) Both Conclusions II and III follow

38. Statements All shirts are pants.
All pants are ties.
No ties are jeans.

Conclusions ***RRB Technician Grade III 2024***
I. No jeans are pants.
II. All pants are shirts.
(a) Only Conclusion II follows
(b) Both Conclusions I and II follow
(c) Neither Conclusion I nor II follows
(d) Only Conclusion I follows

39. Statements All cranes are mixers.
Some mixers are trucks.
All trucks are vanes. ***SSC (10+2) 2023***

Conclusions
I. No crane is a vane.
II. Some vanes are mixers.
(a) Conclusions I and II follow from statements
(b) Only Conclusion I follows from the statements
(c) Only Conclusion II follows from the statements
(d) Neither Conclusion I nor II follows from the statements

40. Statements Some desks are trays.
Some trays are plates.
Some plates are desks. ***SSC CGL 2023***

Conclusions
I. All desks are plates.
II. All plates are desks.
III. Some plates are trays.
IV. All trays are desks.
(a) Only Conclusion IV follows
(b) Only Conclusion III follows
(c) Only Conclusion II follows
(d) Only Conclusion I follows

41. Statements Some butter are honey.
Some honey is bread.
All bread is jam. ***SSC (10+2) 2022***

Conclusions
I. Some jam are honey.
II. All honey are butter.
III. Some jam are butter.
(a) Conclusions I and II follow
(b) Conclusions I and III follow
(c) Only Conclusion II follows
(d) Only Conclusion I follows

42. Select the option which cannot be concluded from the given statements.

Statements Some keys are boats.
Some boats are pipes.
All pipes are fish. ***SSC (10+2) 2024***

Conclusions
(a) Some boats are keys (b) Some fish are keys
(c) Some pipes are boats (d) Some fish are boats

43. **Statements** Some keys are chains.
All chains are locks.
No lock is a rock. ***SSC (10+2) 2024***

Conclusions
I. No rock is a key.
II. At least some keys are locks.
(a) Only Conclusion II follows
(b) None of the conclusions follows
(c) Both Conclusions I and II follow
(d) Only Conclusion I follows

44. **Statements** Some bells are pumps.
All pumps are skates.
All bells are kites. ***SSC (10+2) 2024***

Conclusions
I. Some kites are skates.
II. Some skates are bells.
III. Some skates are pumps.
(a) Conclusions I and II follow from statements
(b) Conclusions I, II and III follow from all the statements.
(c) Conclusions II and III follow from both the statements
(d) Conclusions I and III follow from both the statements

45. **Statements** Some boxes are cartons.
All cartons are papers.
Some cartons are utensils. ***SSC CGL 2024***

Conclusions
I. No boxes are utensils.
II. Some papers are utensils.
(a) Only Conclusion I follows
(b) Only Conclusion II follows
(c) Neither Conclusion I nor II follows
(d) Both Conclusions I and II follow

46. **Statements** All bats are balls.
All balls are badminton.
All badminton are wickets.

Conclusions ***SSC GD Constable 2024***
I. All bats are wickets.
II. Some badminton are bats.
(a) Neither Conclusion I nor II follows
(b) Only Conclusion II follows
(c) Only Conclusion I follows
(d) Both Conclusions I and II follow

47. **Statements** Some pens are books.
Some books are cars.
Some cars are spoons. ***SSC CGL (Tier II) 2023***

Conclusions
I. Some spoons are pens.
II. Some books are pens.
(a) Both Conclusions I and II follow
(b) Only Conclusion I follows
(c) Neither Conclusion I nor II follows
(d) Only Conclusion II follows

48. **Statements**
No cards are parcels.
All cards are envelopes.
Some envelopes are bags.
SSC CGL 2024

Conclusions
I. All envelopes can never be parcels.
II. No card is a bag.
III At least some bags are postcards.
(a) Only Conclusions II and III follow
(b) Only Conclusions I and II follow
(c) Only Conclusion II follows
(d) Only Conclusion I follows

49. **Statements** Some fries are cakes.
All burgers are cakes.
All cakes are chips. ***RRB NPTC 2022***

Conclusions
I. All fries are chips.
II. Some chips are fries.
III. All burgers are chips.
(a) All the conclusions follow
(b) Only Conclusions II and III follow
(c) Only Conclusions I and II follow
(d) Only Conclusions I and III follow

50. **Statements** All rice are pulses.
All pulses are cereals.
All cereals are food items. ***SSC CGL 2023***

Conclusions
I. All rice are food items.
II. All pulses are food items.
III. Some foods are cereals.
(a) Conclusions I and III follow
(b) Conclusions II and III follow
(c) Only Conclusions I and II follow
(d) All the conclusions follow

51. **Statements** Some cars are bikes.
All bikes are trucks.
Some trucks are buses. ***SSC MTS 2024***

Conclusions I. Some trucks are cars.
II. All buses are cars.
III. Some cars are buses.
IV. All bikes are buses.
(a) Conclusions I and IV follow
(b) Conclusions II and III follow
(c) Only Conclusion I follows
(d) Conclusions I, II and IV follow

52. **Statements** All cats are dogs.
Some dogs are birds.
All bears are birds. ***RRC Group-D 2022***

Conclusions I. Some bears are cats.
II. All birds being dogs is a possibility.
III. Some birds are cats.
(a) Conclusion III is true
(b) Conclusion I is true
(c) Conclusions I and II are true
(d) Conclusion II is true

53. **Statements** Some flowers are petals.
Some birds are petals.
No birds are flowers. *RRC Group D 2022*

Conclusions
I. Some petals are birds.
II. Some flowers are birds.
III. Some petals are flowers.
(a) Only Conclusions I and III follow
(b) Only Conclusion III follows
(c) None of the Conclusion follows
(d) Only Conclusion II follows

54. **Statements** No pumpkin is guava.
No guava is peas.
Some peas are potatoes. *SSC JE 2023*

Conclusions
I. Some pumpkins are potatoes.
II. Some peas are pumpkins.
III. Some pumpkins are not potatoes.
(a) Only Conclusion I follows
(b) Either Conclusion I or III follows
(c) Only Conclusion II follows
(d) None of the conclusion follows

55. **Statements** All iron are zinc.
Some copper are gold.
No gold is zinc. *CISF HC (Min) 2022*

Conclusions
I. Some iron can be gold.
II. No iron is gold.
III. Some copper are zinc.
(a) Only Conclusion II follows
(b) Only Conclusions I and III follow
(c) Either Conclusion I or II follows
(d) Only Conclusion I follows

56. **Statements** All bags are pants.
All pants are eggs.
All eggs are flowers. *DP Constable 2023*

Conclusions
I. All pants are flowers.
II. All pants are bags.
III. All flowers are bags.
IV. All flowers are pants.
(a) Only Conclusion IV follows
(b) Only Conclusion I follows
(c) Only Conclusion III follows
(d) Only Conclusion II follows

57. **Statements** All mice are cats.
All lions are cats.
All deer are lions. *HCET 2022*

Conclusions
I. All deer are cats.
II. Some deer are mice.
III. Some cats are deer.
(a) Conclusions II and III follow
(b) Conclusions I and III follow
(c) Only Conclusion II follows
(d) Conclusions I and II follow
(e) Do not wish to answer

58. **Statements** All dolls are robots.
Some robots are toys.
Some toys are cycles. *SSC CGL Tier-II 2025*

Conclusions
I. Some toys are dolls.
II. No cycle is a robot.
(a) Only Conclusion I is true
(b) Only Conclusion II is true
(c) Neither Conclusion I nor II is true
(d) Both Conclusions I and II are true

59. You are given three groups of arguments, each containing three sentences. Select those groups in which the third statement is the logical conclusion of the first two statements. *RRB NTPC 2020*

(A) I. All shops are showrooms.
II. No showroom is a mall.
III. All shops are not malls.

(B) I. No Japanese can dance.
II. All Americans people are books.
III. Americans and Japanese can dance.

(C) I. No P is Q. II. No Q is R.
III. No P is R.

(a) Only B
(b) Only C
(c) Only A
(d) Only B and C

Trending Concept
Question No. 59 is the question based on new concept which has been asked in the RRB NTPC exam.

Right Key

1. (a)	2. (b)	3. (c)	4. (a)	5. (a)	6. (b)	7. (b)	8. (d)	9. (a)	10. (c)
11. (c)	12. (a)	13. (b)	14. (c)	15. (b)	16. (c)	17. (c)	18. (a)	19. (d)	20. (b)
21. (a)	22. (a)	23. (c)	24. (b)	25. (d)	26. (c)	27. (a)	28. (b)	29. (b)	30. (d)
31. (a)	32. (b)	33. (b)	34. (b)	35. (d)	36. (b)	37. (d)	38. (d)	39. (c)	40. (b)
41. (d)	42. (b)	43. (a)	44. (b)	45. (b)	46. (d)	47. (d)	48. (d)	49. (b)	50. (d)
51. (c)	52. (d)	53. (a)	54. (b)	55. (a)	56. (b)	57. (b)	58. (c)	59. (c)	

Solutions

1. *(a)* According to the statements,

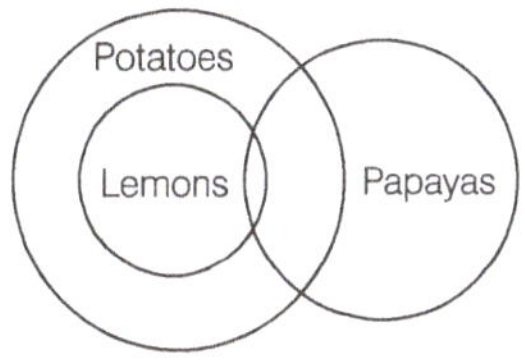

Conclusions I. (✓) II. (✗)

Hence, only Conclusion I follows.

2. *(b)* According to the statements,

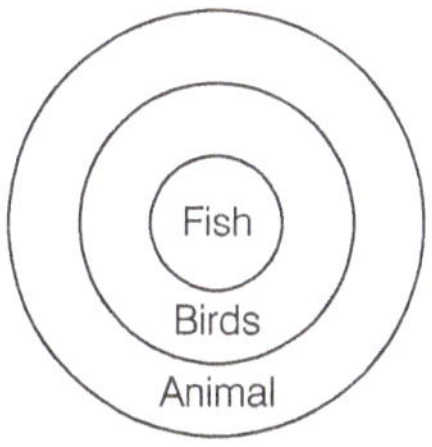

Conclusions I. (✗) II. (✓)

Hence, only Conclusion II follows.

3. *(c)* According to the statements,

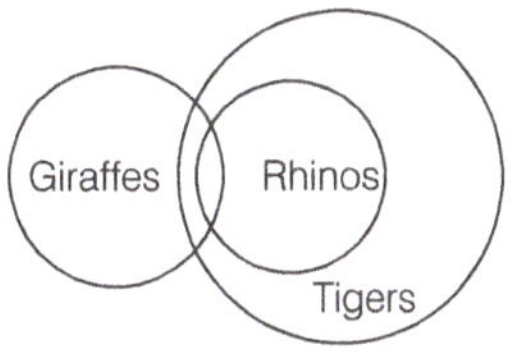

Conclusions I. (✓) II. (✗)

Hence, only Conclusion I follows.

4. *(a)* According to the statements,

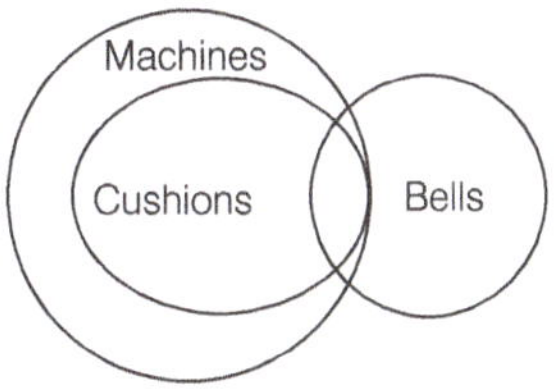

Conclusions I. (✗) II. (✓)

Hence, only Conclusion II follows.

5. *(a)* According to the statements,

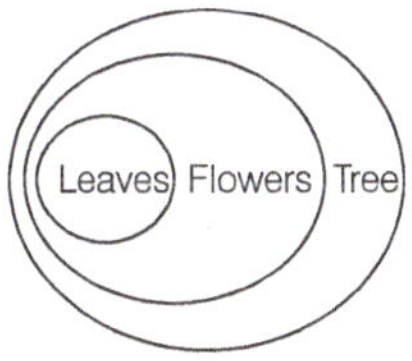

Conclusions I. (✗) II. (✓)

Hence, only Conclusion II follows.

6. *(b)* According to the statements,

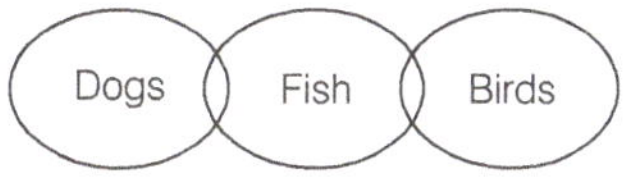

Conclusions I. (✗) II. (✗)

Hence, neither Conclusions I nor II follows.

7. *(b)* According to the statements,

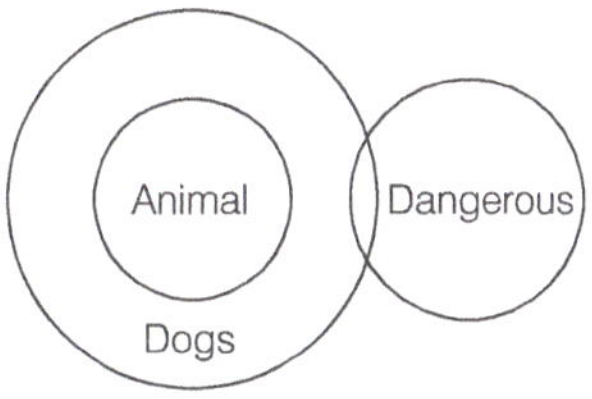

Conclusions I. (✗) II. (✓)

Hence, only Conclusion II follows.

8. *(d)* According to the statements,

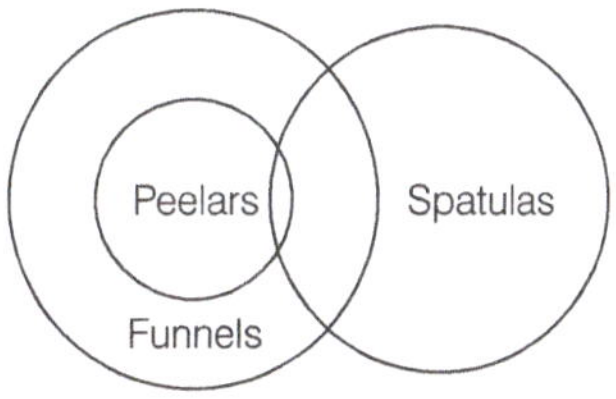

Conclusions I. (✗) II. (✓)

Hence, Conclusion II follows.

9. *(a)* According to the statements,

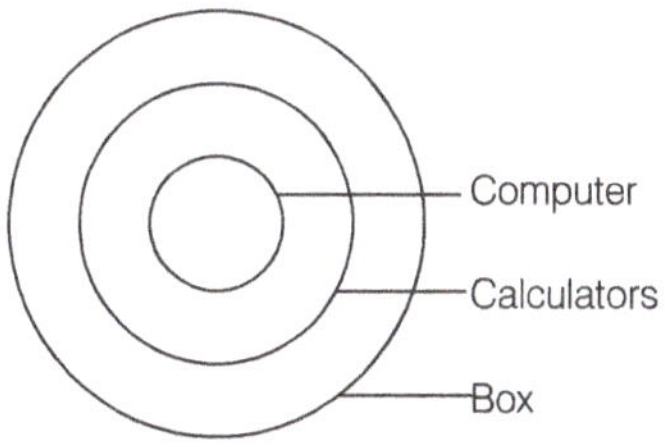

Conclusions I. (✓) II. (✓)

Both Conclusions I and II follow.

10. *(c)* According to the statements,

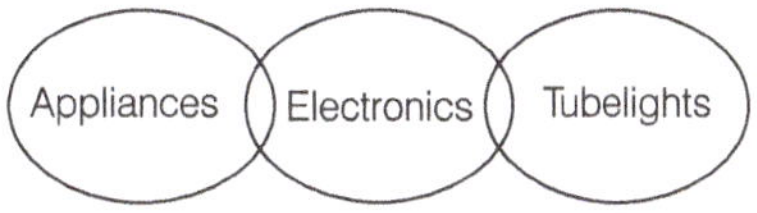

Conclusions I. (✗) II. (✗)

or

Hence, either Conclusion I or II follows.

> **TOP TIPS** There are mainly three different type of complementry pairs:
> - Some + No
> - Some + Some not
> - All + Some not

11. *(c)* According to the statements,

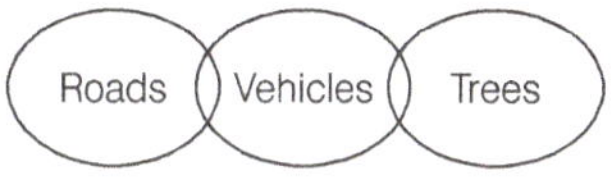

Conclusions I. (✗) II. (✗)

Hence, neither Conclusion I nor II follows.

12. *(a)* According to the statements,

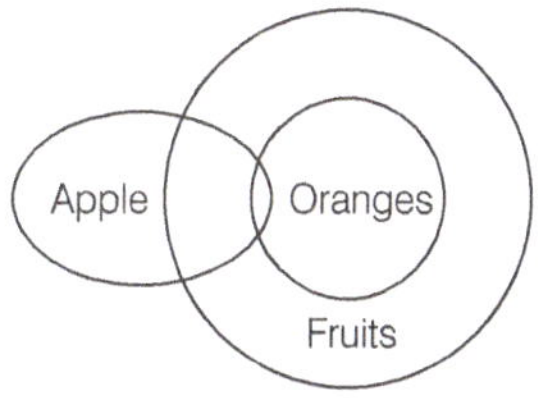

Conclusions I. (✗) II. (✓)

Hence, only Conclusion II follows.

13. *(b)* According to the statements,

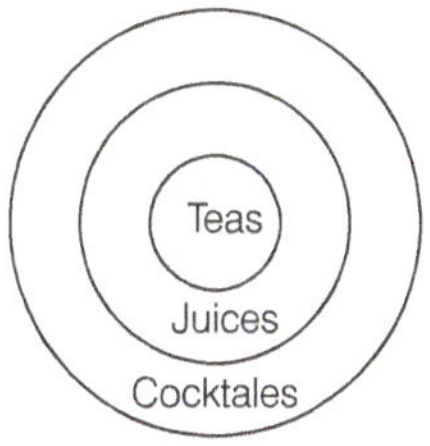

Conclusions I. (✓) II. (✗)

Hence, only Conclusion I follows.

14. *(c)* According to the statements,

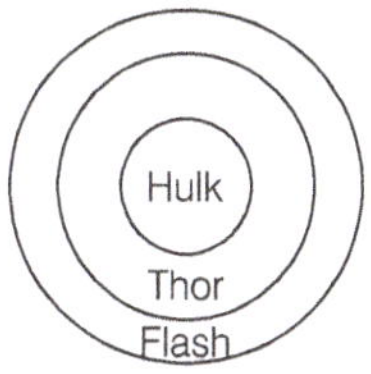

Conclusions I. (✓) II. (✗)

Hence, only Conclusion I follows.

> **TOP TIPS** A positive statement leads to a positive conclusion and a negative statement leads to a negative conclusion.

15. *(b)* According to the statements,

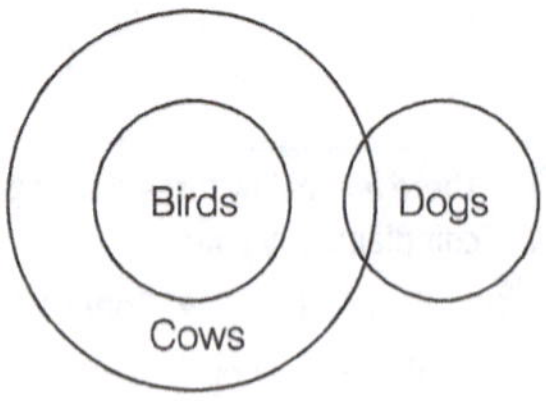

Conclusions I. (✗) II. (✓)

Hence, only Conclusion II follows.

16. *(c)* According to the statements,

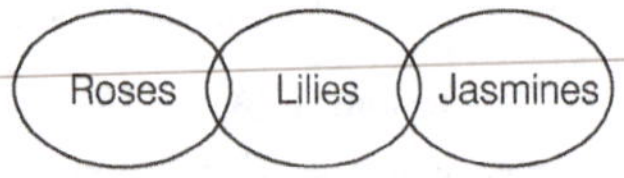

Conclusions I. (✗) II. (✗)

Hence, neither Conclusion I nor II follows.

17. *(c)* According to the statements,

Conclusions I. (✗) II. (✗)

Hence, neither Conclusion I nor II follows.

18. *(a)* According to the statements,

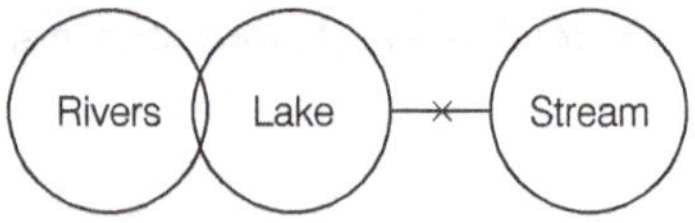

Conclusions I. (✓) II. (✗)

Hence, only Conclusion I follows.

19. *(d)* According to the statements,

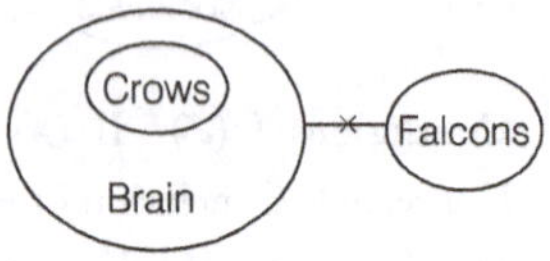

Conclusions I. (✗) II. (✗)

Hence, neither Conclusion I nor II follows.

20. *(b)* According to the statements,

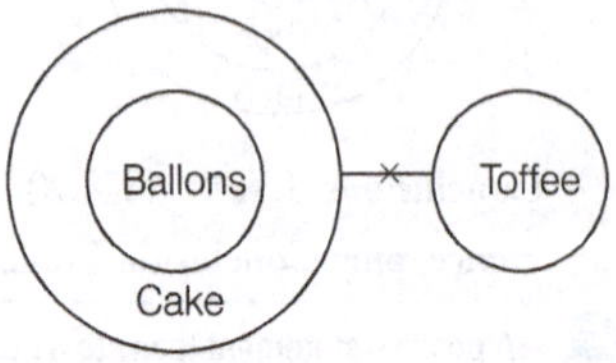

Conclusions I. (✓) II. (✗)

Hence, only Conclusion I follows.

21. *(a)* According to the statements,

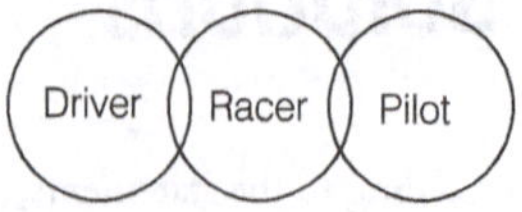

Conclusions I. (✗) II. (✗)

or

Hence, either Conclusion I or II follows.

22. *(a)* According to the statements,

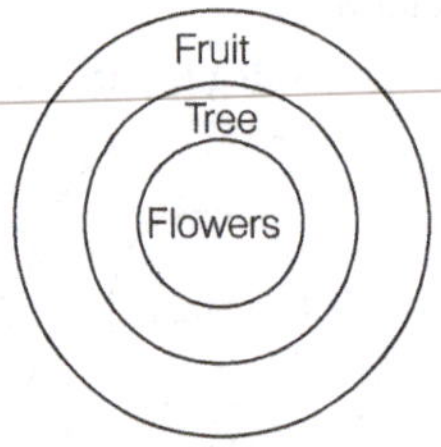

Conclusions I. (✓) II. (✓)

Hence, both Conclusions I and II follow.

23. *(c)* According to the statements,

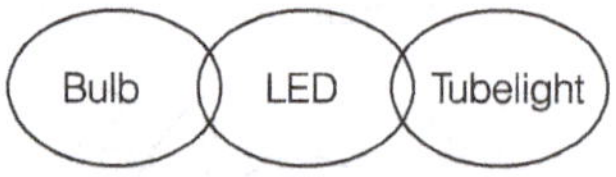

Conclusions I. (✗) II. (✗)

or

Hence, either Conclusion I or II follows.

TOP TIPS When both the conclusion are false then we should check the 'either' or condition once.

24. *(b)* According to the statements,

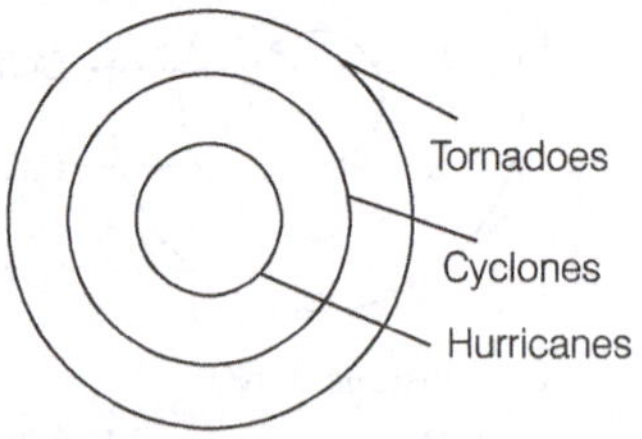

Conclusions I. (✓) II. (✓)

Hence, both Conclusions I and II follow.

25. *(d)* According to the statements,

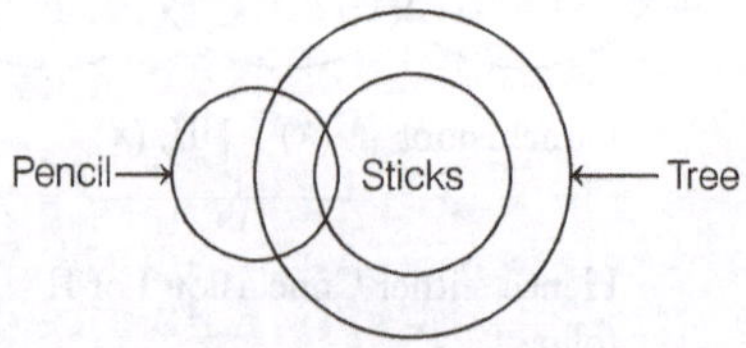

Conclusions I. (✗) II. (✗)

Hence, neither Conclusion I nor II follows.

26. *(c)* According to the statements,

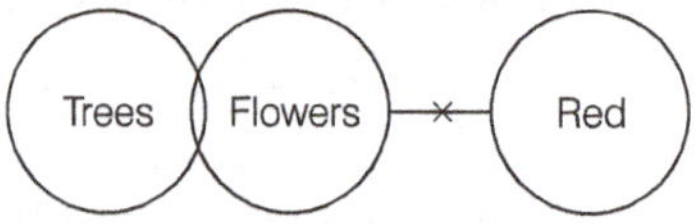

Conclusions I. (✗) II. (✗) III. (✓)

Hence, only Conclusion III follows.

27. *(a)* According to the statements,

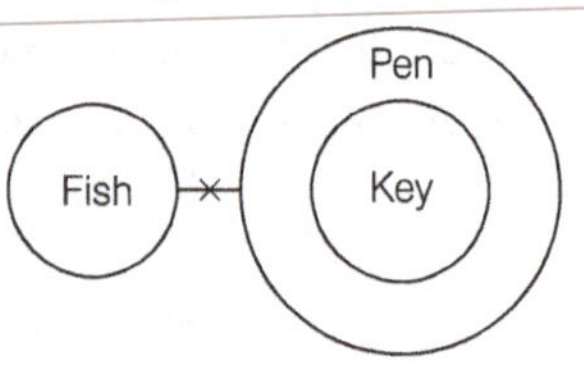

Conclusions I. (✗) II. (✗) III. (✓) IV. (✗)

Hence, only Conclusion III follows.

28. *(b)* According to the statements,

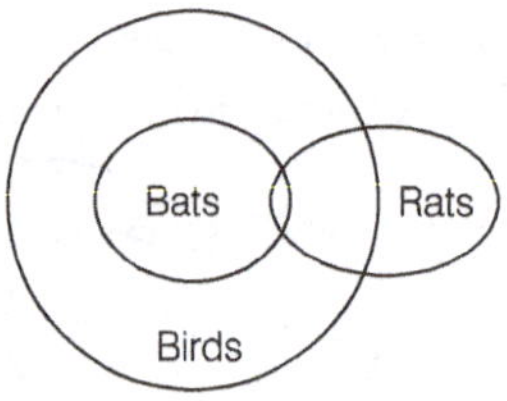

Conclusions I. (✓) II. (✓) III. (✗)

Hence, only Conclusions I and II follow.

29. *(b)* According to the statements,

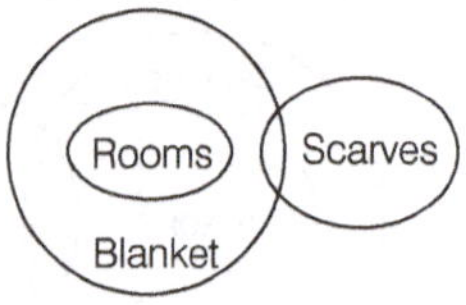

Conclusions I. (✓) II. (✗)

Hence, only Conclusion I follows.

30. *(d)* According to the statements,

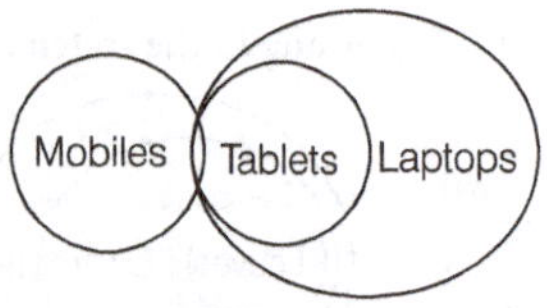

Conclusions I. (✓) II. (✓) III. (✗)

Hence, Conclusions I and II follow.

31. *(a)* According to the statements,

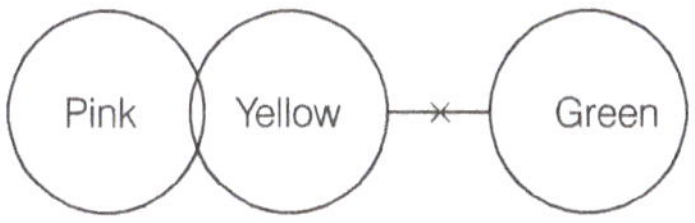

Conclusions I. (✓) II. (✓) III. (✗)

Hence, only Conclusions I and II follow.

32. *(b)* According to the statements,

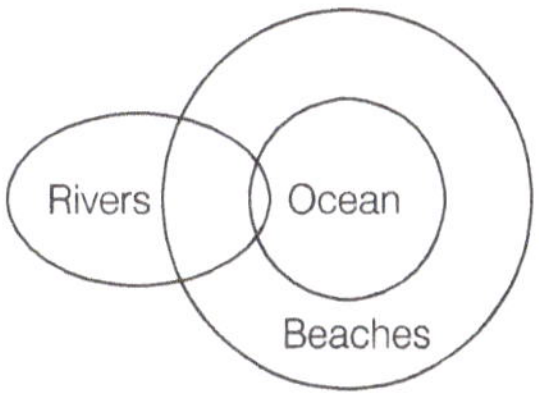

Conclusions I. (✓) II. (✗)

Hence, only Conclusion I follows.

33. *(b)* According to the statements,

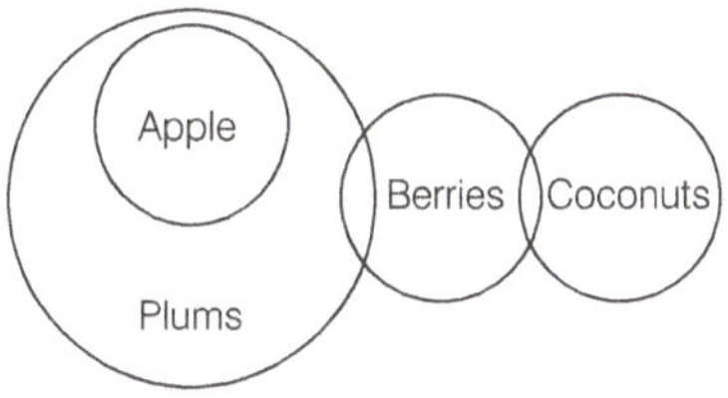

Conclusions I. (✓) II. (✗) III. (✓)

Hence, only Conclusions I and III follow.

34. *(b)* According to the statements,

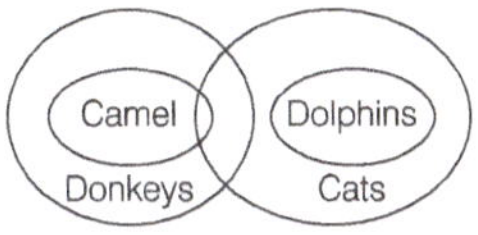

Conclusions I. (✗) II. (✗) III. (✓) IV. (✗)

Hence, only Conclusion III follows.

35. *(d)* According to the statements,

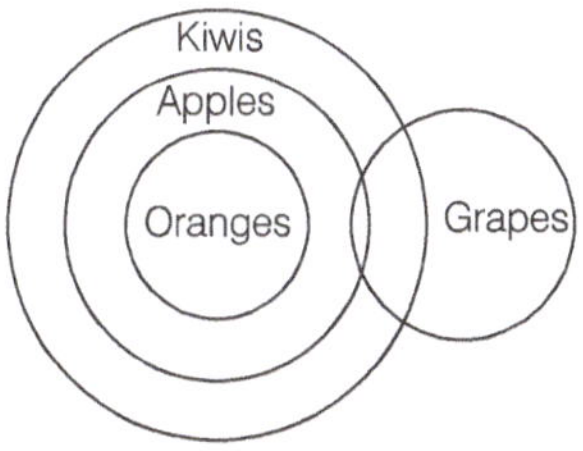

Conclusions I. (✓) II. (✗)

Hence, only Conclusion I follows.

36. *(b)* According to the statements,

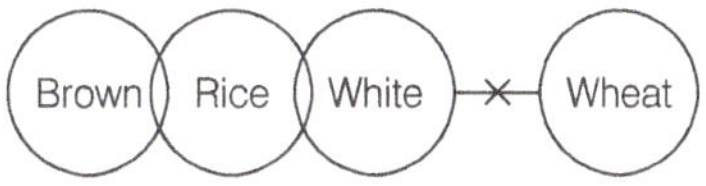

Conclusions I. (✗) II. (✓) III. (✗)

Hence, only Conclusion II follows.

37. *(d)* According to the statements,

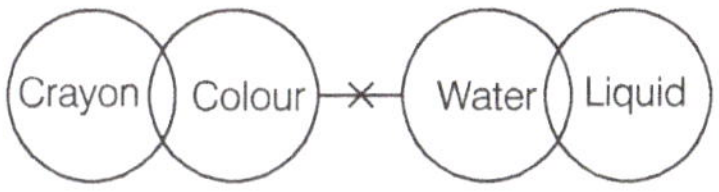

Conclusions I. (✗) II. (✓) III. (✓)

Hence, both Conclusions II and III follow.

38. *(d)* According to the statements,

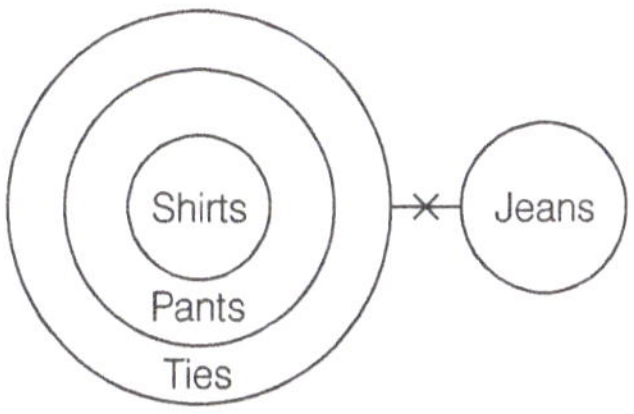

Conclusions I. (✓) II. (✗)

Hence, only Conclusion I follows.

39. *(c)* According to the statements,

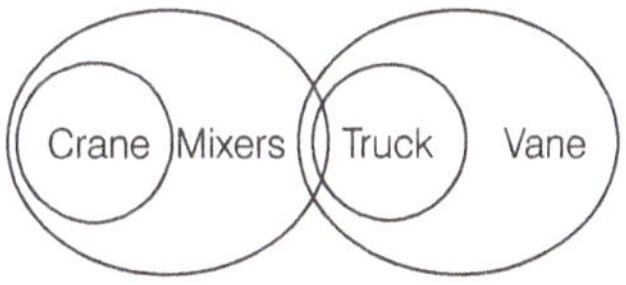

Conclusions I. (✗) II. (✓)

Hence, only Conclusion II follows.

40. *(b)* According to the statements,

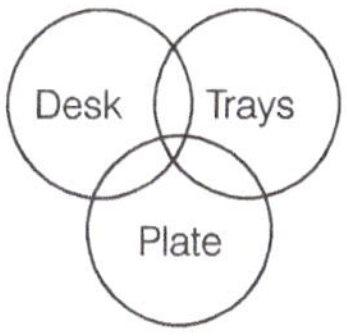

Conclusions I. (✗) II. (✗) III. (✓) IV. (✗)

Hence, only Conclusion III follows.

41. *(d)* According to the statements,

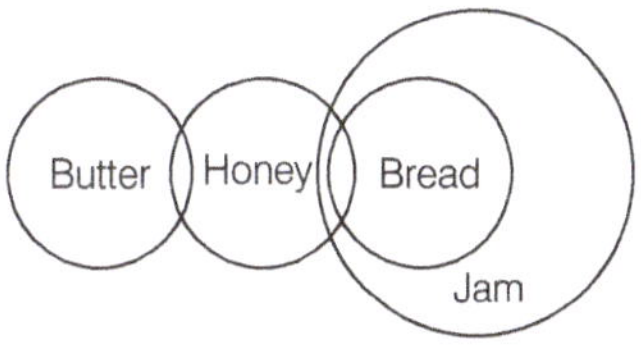

Conclusions I. (✓) II. (✗) III. (✗)

Hence, only Conclusion I follows.

42. *(b)* According to the statements,

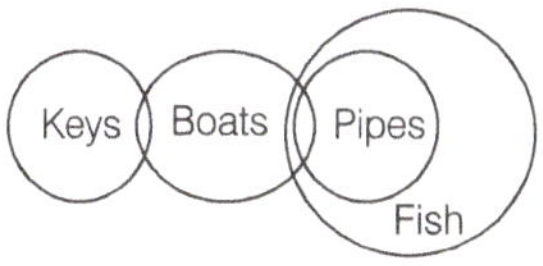

Conclusions (a) (✓) (b) (✗) (c) (✓) (d) (✓)

Hence, conclusion (b) cannot be concluded.

43. *(a)* According to the statements

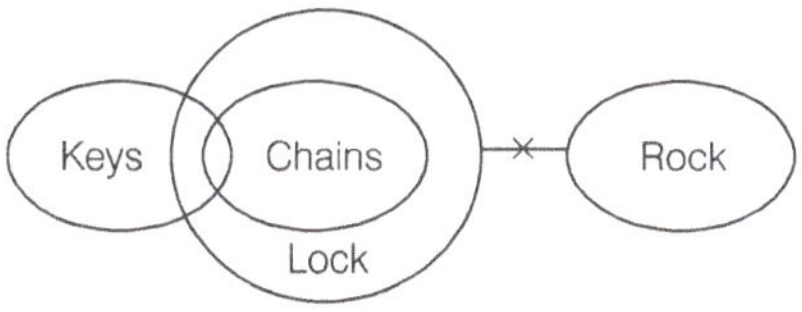

Conclusions I. (✗) II. (✓)

Hence, only Conclusion II follows.

44. *(b)* According to the statements,

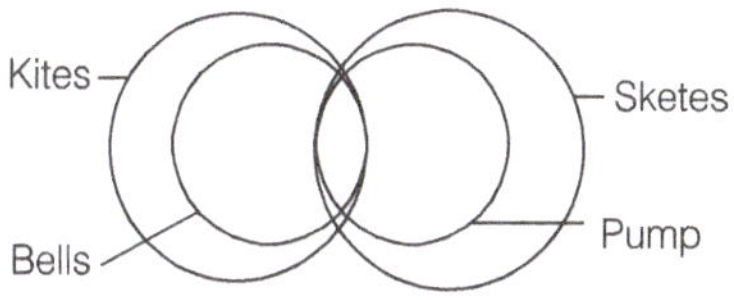

Conclusions I. (✓) II. (✓) III. (✓)

Hence, Conclusions I, II and III follow.

45. *(b)* According to the statements,

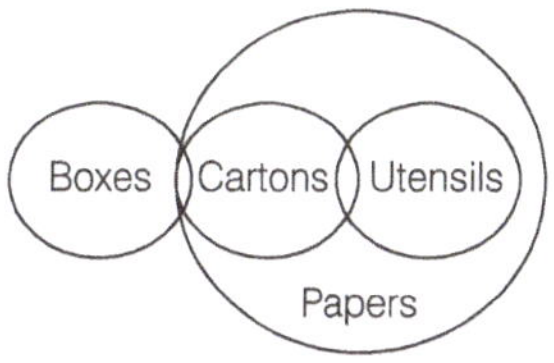

Conclusions I. (✗) II. (✓)

Hence, only Conclusion II follows.

46. *(d)* According to the statements,

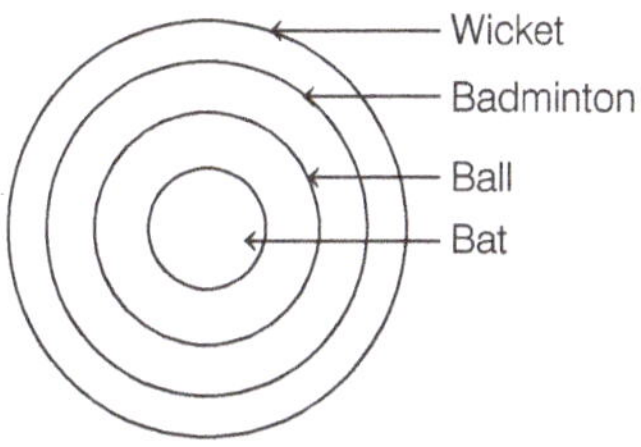

Conclusions I. (✓) II. (✓)

Hence, both Conclusions I and II follow.

47. *(d)* According to the statements,

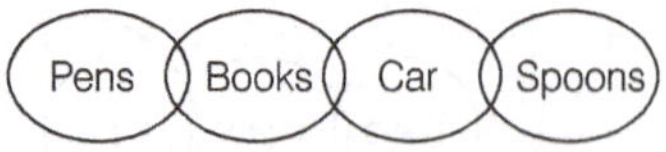

Conclusions I. (✗) II. (✓)

Hence, only Conclusion II follows.

48. *(d)* According to the statements,

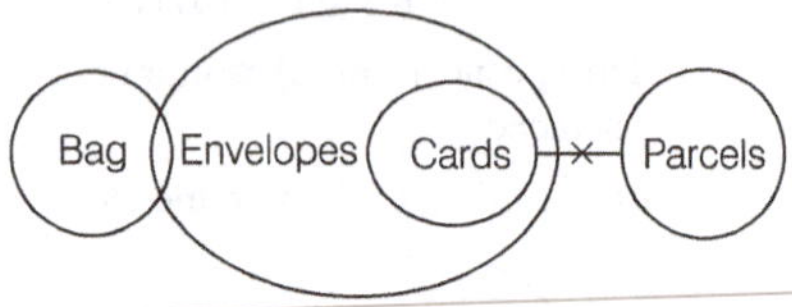

Conclusions I. (✓) II. (✗) III. (✗)

Hence, only Conclusion I follows.

49. *(b)* According to the statements,

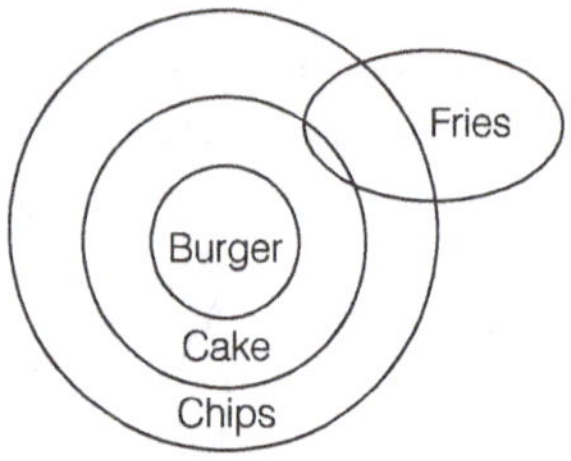

Conclusions I. (✗) II. (✓) III. (✓)

Hence, only Conclusions II and III follow.

50. *(d)* According to the statements,

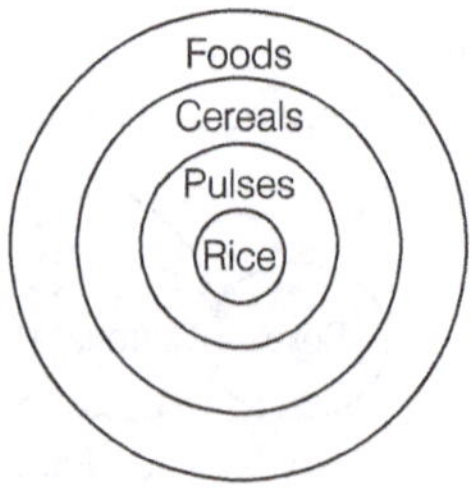

Conclusions I. (✓) II. (✓) III. (✓)

Hence, all the conclusions follow.

51. *(c)* According to the statements,

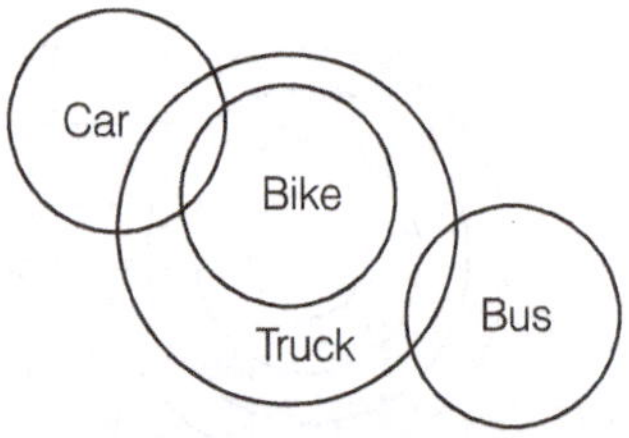

Conclusions I. (✓) II. (✗) III. (✗) IV. (✗)

Hence, only Conclusion I follows.

52. *(d)* According to the statements,

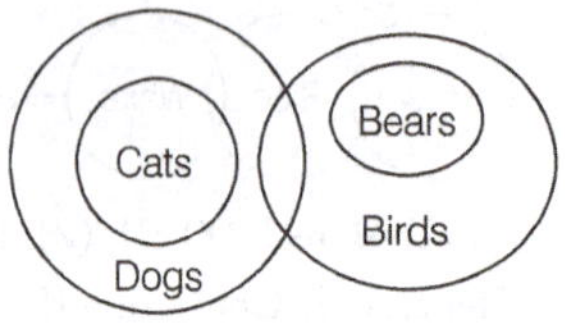

Conclusions I. (✗) II. (✓) III. (✗)

Hence, only Conclusion II follows.

TOP TIPS If the possible conclusions in any one of the possible (probable) diagrams are true, then the possibility in conclusion is considered to be true.

53. *(a)* According to the statements,

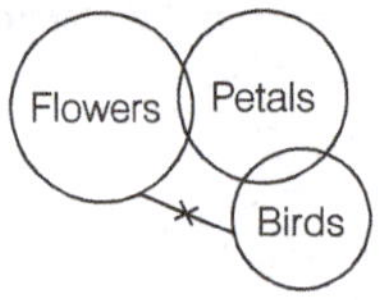

Conclusions I. (✓) II. (✗) III. (✓)

Hence, only Conclusion I and III follow.

54. *(b)* According to the statements,

Conclusions I. (✗) II. (✗) III. (✗)

(I or III)

Hence, either Conclusion I or III follows.

55. *(a)* According to the statements,

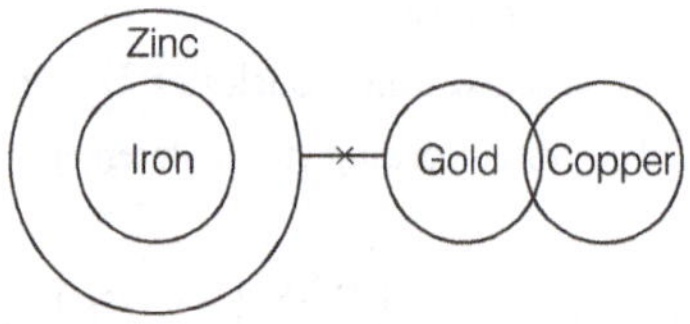

Conclusions I. (✗) II. (✓) III. (✗)

Hence, only Conclusion II follows.

56. *(b)* According to the statements,

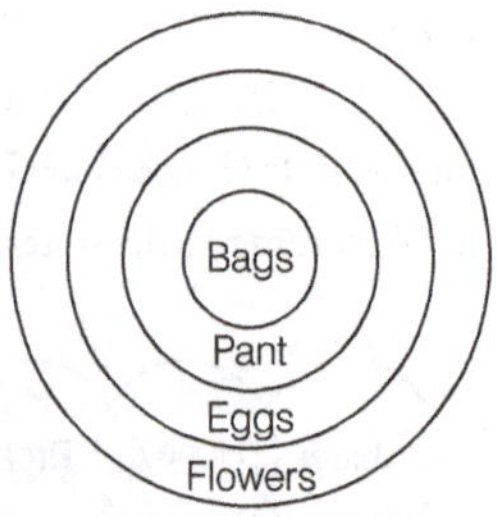

Conclusions I. (✓) II. (✗) III. (✗) IV. (✗)

Hence, only Conclusion I follows.

57. *(b)* According to the statements,

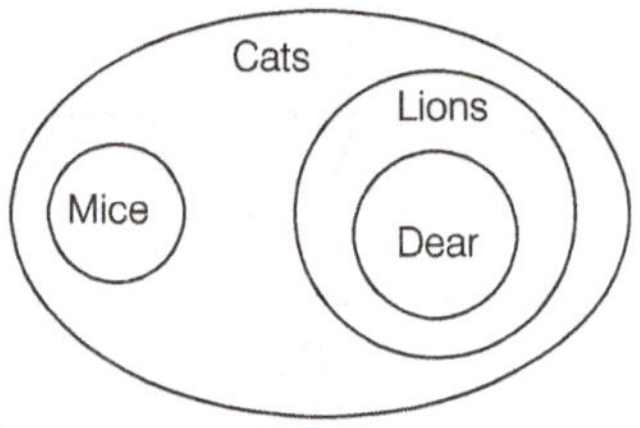

Conclusions I. (✓)
II. (✗)
III. (✓)

Hence, only Conclusions I and III follow.

58. *(c)* According to the statements,

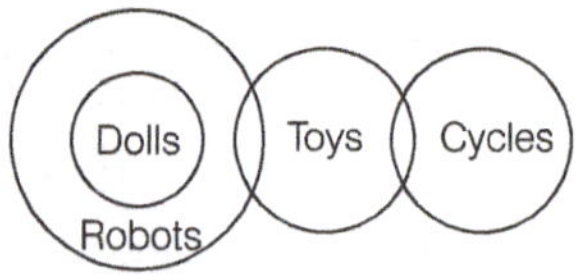

Conclusions I. (✗) II. (✗)

Hence, neither Conclusion I nor II is true.

59. *(c)* According to the statements,

From group A

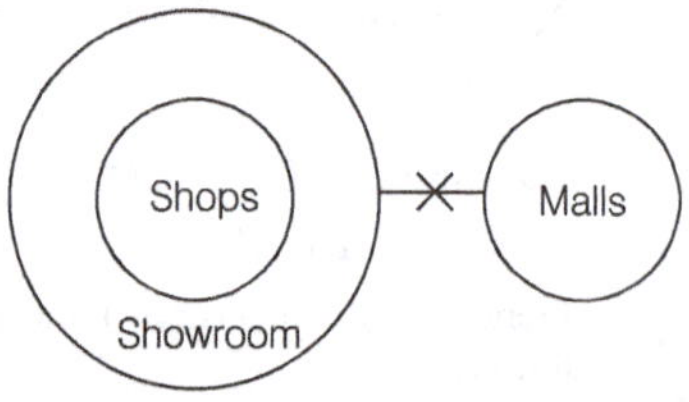

From group B

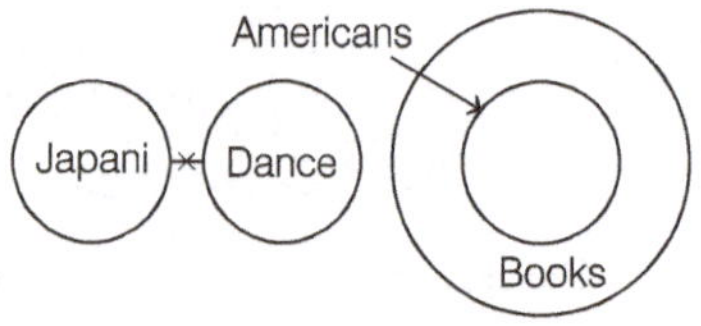

From group C

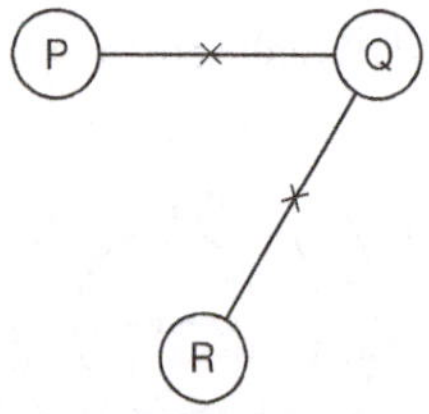

Hence, only in group A the third statement is the conclusion of the first two statements.

CHAPTER

23 Statement and Conclusions

Statement and Conclusions

A statement is an expression or information given in relation to any subject 'conclusion' means a fact that can truly be inferred from the contents of a given statement or passage. Assuming the facts of these statement to be true, one has to find out which of the given conclusions is true.

Based on Two Conclusions

In this type of questions one statement with two conclusions is given and candidate has to analyse which of the given conclusions logically follows from the statement.

e.g. Consider the given statement to be true and decide which of the conclusion(s) logically follow(s) from the statement?

Statement

The best way to escape from a problem is to solve it.

Conclusions

I. Your life will be dull if you don't face a problem.

II. To escape from problems, you should always have some solutions with you.

(a) Only Conclusion I follows

(b) Only Conclusion II follows

(c) Either I or II follows

(d) Neither I nor II follows

Sol. (d) Statement doesn't suggests that problems make any one's life dull or not. So, Conclusion I does not follows. The statement emphasizes on need to solve a problem except ascape it. However, it does not suggest that the person facing problem always has some solution. Hence, neither Conclusion I nor II follow.

Score Booster

- If certain words such as all, always, at least, only, each and so on are used in the conclusion, such words make the conclusion invalid or unclear. Always read the statement very carefully and try to find keywords from them. These keywords play an important role in analysing valid or invalid conclusion.
- Matters related to past and future are considered false in the conclusion.

Based on Three/Four Conclusions

In this type of questions, one or more than one statements and three/four conclusions are given candidate has to analyse which of the given conclusion/conclusions definitely (follows/follow) from the statement.

e.g. Read the given statements and conclusions carefully and decide which of the conclusions logically follow(s) from the statements?

Statements

All girls in my class are good dancers.

All good dancers are acrobats.

Some boys in my class are acrobats.

Conclusions

I. Some boys in my class are good dancers.

II. All acrobats in my class are good dancers.

III. All girls in my class are acrobats.

(a) Only Conclusion III follows

(b) Both Conclusions II and III follow

(c) Both Conclusions I and II follow

(d) Only Conclusion I follows

Sol. (a) All girls in my class are good dancer and good dancer are acrobats. So, all girls in my class are acrobats is correct.

Hence, only Conclusion III follows.

Exam Approach Examples

Based on Two Conclusions

Example 1 In the following question, a statement is followed by two Conclusions I and II. Consider the statement and the following conclusions and decide which of the conclusion/conclusions logically follows from the statement.

Statement The new government's policy aims to reduce carbon emissions by 50% within the next decade.

Conclusions

I. The government will immediately ban all vehicles running on fossil fuels.

II. The government will shut down all coal-fired power plants. *SSC (10+2) 2023*

(a) Only Conclusion I follows
(b) Only Conclusion II follows
(c) Neither Conclusion I nor II follows
(d) Both Conclusions I and II follow

***Sol.** (c)* Conclusion I is specifically about fossil fuels and Conclusions II is specifically about power plants, while statement is to reduce carbon emissions.

Hence, neither Conclusion I nor II follows.

Helping Tips

If the government order or rule and constitutional amendment has been discussed in the statement, then conclusion which is related to the statement, will be true.

Example 2 A statement is followed by two Conclusions I and II. You have to consider the statement to be true, even if it seems to be at variance from commonly known facts. You are to decide which of the given conclusions can definitely be drawn from the given statements and indicate your answer accordingly.

Statement

India is a country of multiple languages.

Conclusions

I. All Indians should learn multiple languages.

II. Every country has multiple languages. *DSSSB 2021*

(a) Only Conclusion II follows
(b) Neither Conclusion I nor II follows
(c) Only Conclusion I follows
(d) Both the Conclusions follow

***Sol.** (b)* India is a country of multiple languages. This statement does not implies that Indians should learn multiple languages. Statement does not provide any information regarding Conclusion II. Hence, neither Conclusion I nor II follows.

Based on Three/Four Conclusions

Example 3 In the question below two statements followed by three conclusions numbered I, II and III are given. You have to assume everything in the statements to be true, then consider the three conclusions together and decide which of them logically follows beyond a reasonable doubt from the information given in the statements.

Statements Water has no shape, has volume.
The knowledge is like water, flowed from one side to other.

Conclusions

I. The knowledge is interdisciplinary.

II. The knowledge is bound within a specific area.

III. The knowledge influences the core of mental activity directly. *UP Police Constable 2024*

(a) Both Conclusions I and III follow
(b) Both Conclusions I and II follow
(c) Only Conclusion I follows
(d) Only Conclusion II follows

***Sol.** (a)* According to the statements, Conclusions I and III follow. Knowledge how from one side to other so, it is interdisciplinary. It is also true that knowledge influences the thoughts minds and actions of persons.

Example 4 Choose the Conclusion(s) which logically follow(s) from the given statements.

Statements MS Dhoni is a popular cricketer.
All cricketers are fit and healthy.
MS Dhoni earns a handsome amount every year through advertisements of various products.

Conclusions

I. All popular cricketers earn a handsome amount through advertisement.

II. MS Dhoni is fit and healthy.

III. MS Dhoni, being famous, advertises only famous product. *RRB NTPC 2021*

(a) Both Conclusions I and III follow
(b) Only Conclusion II follows
(c) Only Conclusion III follows
(d) Both Conclusions I and II follow

***Sol.** (b)* From the given statements, it can be concluded that MS Dhoni is fit and healthy. But, Dhoni earns handsome amount, it does not mean all cricketers earn handsome amount. Dhoni, being famous, not necessarily means that he advertises famous products only.

Hence, only Conclusion II follows.

Trending Concept

Recently such questions which are based on logical reasoning on cause and effect, public welfare schemes which where launched by government and other topics are currently being asked in Railway, UP Police, SSC Freauently.

Chapter Challenge

Based on Two Conclusions

Directions (Q. Nos. 1-8) *In each of the following questions, a statement is followed by two conclusions I and II. Consider the statement and the following conclusions and decide which of the conclusion/conclusions logically follows from the statement.*

Give answer
(a) If only Conclusion I follows
(b) If only Conclusion II follows
(c) If neither Conclusion I nor II follows
(d) If both Conclusions I and II follow

1. **Statement** India's largest lender bank has announced that it will be allowing customers to exchange ₹ 2000 notes without a requisition slip for amounts up to ₹ 20000.

Conclusions
I. No one will be allowed to withdraw an amount of more than ₹ 20000.
II. No requisition slip is required for exchange of up to ₹ 20000. ***SSC (10+2) 2023***

2. **Statement** Death will not see time.

Conclusions ***MP Police Constable 2022***
I. Man has to die one day.
II. Death can come at any time in life.

3. **Statement** The increase in the population of a country is a major challenge for the policy makers there.

Conclusions
I. After a certain time population of that country will decreases.
II. The increasing population will have an impact on the availability of resources in the country. ***Rajasthan Police Constable 2022***

4. **Statement** A friend in need is a friend indeed.

Conclusions
I. A person who helps you in difficults situations is your friend.
II. Your enemies can also sometimes have a change of heartand help you in times of need. ***RRB NTPC 2021***

5. **Statement** Road offers the fastest connectivity between Agra and Delhi. ***SSC MTS 2019***

Conclusions
I. There is no rail connectivity between Agra and Delhi.
II. There is no air connectivity between Agra and Delhi.

6. **Statement** Before leaving for college, Sita is learning to cook basic meals from her mother.

Conclusions
I. Sita didn't know how to cook.
II. Sita wants to throw a party for her friends before leaving for college. ***RRC Group-D 2022***

7. **Statement** Every Australian speaks 6 languages and Antony speaks 6 languages.

Conclusions
I. Antony is an Australian.
II. People from other countries do not speak 6 languages. ***UP Police SI 2021***

8. **Statement** The residents of Jane's place should save water every summer.

Conclusions
I. The residents of Jane's place may face water shortage during the summer season.
II. The residents of Jane's palce will have enough water during winter. ***UP Police ASI 2021***

> ***MRC******
> ***(Most Repeating Concepts)***
> Questions based on one statement and two conclusions (Q. Nos. 2, 7, 8) are being repeately asked in different exams (MP Police, UPASI, DSSSB) and are very important for upcoming exams.

9. In this question one statement is given, followed by two Conclusions I and II. You have to consider the statements to be true even if it seems to be at variance from commonly known facts. You have to decide which of the given Conclusions, if any follows from the given statement.

Statement
Aman is shortlisted for the interview process based on his application for the post of investment analyst at BCD firm.

Conclusions
I. Aman will be selected as the investment analyst at BCD firm.
II. Aman will not be selected as the investment analyst at BCD firm. ***DSSSB 2021***

(a) Only Conclusion II follows
(b) Either Conclusion I or II follows
(c) Only Conclusion I follows
(d) Neither Conclusion I nor II follows

10. Consider the given statement to be true and decide which of the given conclusions can definitely be drawn from the given statements.

Statement
People think that paying tax to the government is a burden and waste Hence, they avoid paying tax or don't pa tax promptly.

Conclusions
I. Government should create awarenes among the people that paying tax helps to build nation.
II. Tax should be increased so that more money is collected. ***RRB ALP 2018***

(a) Both Conclusions I and II follow
(b) Only Conclusion I follows
(c) Neither Conclusion I nor II follows
(d) Only Conclusion II follows

11. Read the following statements and identify the logically correct conclusion from the given information.

Statements Milk will become poison, if kept in a copper utensil.

Poison is good for consumption and health.

Conclusions

I. People should consume milk which is kept in a copper pot.

II. Consumption of poison should be avoided.

RRB NTPC 2022

(a) Only Conclusion I follows
(b) Only Conclusion II follows
(c) Neither Conclusion I nor II follows
(d) Both Conclusions I and II follow

12. Consider the given statements to be true and decide which of the conclusions logically follow(s) from the statements.

Statements

Sachin is a good batsman.

Batsmen are intelligent.

Conclusions

I. All intelligent people are batsman.

II. Sachin is intelligent. ***RRB ALP 2018***

(a) Both Conclusions I and II follow
(b) Neither Conclusion I nor II follows
(c) Only Conclusion I follows
(d) Only Conclusion II follows

13. Read the given statements and conclusions carefully and decide which of the given conclusions logically follow (s) from the statements.

Statement Every child in the village goes to school. Kabir goes to school regularly.

Conclusions

I. Kabir is an obedient students.

II. Kabir comes from village. ***UP Police ASI 2021***

(a) Only Conclusion I follows
(b) Only Conclusion II follows
(c) Neither Conclusion I nor II follows
(d) Both Conclusions I and II follow

14. A statement is given followed by two conclusions numbered I and II. You have to assume everything in the statement to be true and decide which of the conclusions logically follow(s) beyond a reasonable doubt from the information given in the statement.

Statement

It is reported that heavy and erratic rainfall has destroyed many agricultural crops and farmers are in debt.

Conclusions

I. Farmers need not repay the debt.

II. Prices of groceries and other essential food items such as lentils and grains will surge. ***RRB Group D 2022***

(a) Neither Conclusion I nor II follows
(b) Both Conclusions I and II follow
(c) Only Conclusion I follows
(d) Only Conclusion II follows

15. A statement is given followed by two conclusions numbered I and II. You have to assume everything in the statement to be true and decide which of the conclusions logically follow(s) beyond a reasonable doubt from the information given in the statement.

Statement

Sale up to 70% on all clothing item in the store and online.

Conclusions

I. All clothing items are 70% off during the sale period.

II. There are some clothing items that are not on sale.

RRB Group D 2022

(a) Neither Conclusion I nor II follows
(b) Only Conclusion II follows
(c) Only Conclusion I follows
(d) Both Conclusions I and II follow

16. A statement is followed by two conclusions. Choose the correct options considering the statement to be true irrespective of the commonly known facts.

Statement

Don't throw garbage here. If you violate this non littering sign, a fine of ₹ 5000 will be imposed.

Conclusions

I. The same fine is charged for litterin! offence everywhere.

II. This warning is written at every public place of non-littering zone. ***RRB NTPC 2021***

(a) Neither Conclusion I nor II follows
(b) Only Conclusion I follows
(c) Only Conclusion II follows
(d) Both Conclusions I and II follow

Directions (Q. Nos. 17-22) *In each of the following questions, a statements is followed by two conclusion I and II. Consider the statements and the following conclusions and decide which of the conclusion/conclusions logically follows from the statement.*

Give answer

(a) If only Conclusion I follows
(b) If only Conclusion II follows
(c) If neither Conclusion I nor II follows
(d) If both Conclusions I and II follow

17. **Statement** In a T-20 cricket match, total wickets taken by a team were 9. Out of these, 6 wickets were taken by spinners.

Conclusions

I. 80% of the bowlers in the team were spinners.

II. The opening bowlers of the team were spinners.

RRB NTPC 2020

18. **Statement** United Nation has adopted 21st June as World Yoga day. This has promoted India's glorious tradition all over the world.

Conclusions

I. Yoga is practiced only on 21st June.

II. More people are coming to India to practice Yoga.

SSC CPO 2019

19. **Statement** Ram and Shyam always get first and second ranks in class.

Conclusions

I. Ram always gets the first rank while Shyam gets the second rank.

II. The competition between Ram and Shyam is as tough as nails. ***UPSSSC VDO 2018***

20. **Statement** The Prime Minister has made clear that his government will make concerted effort for the upliftment of poor farmers and announced an annual pension for them.

Conclusions

I. Government understands that the condition of poor farmers needs immediate attention.

II. No benefits are announced for other sections of society. ***SSC CPO 2019***

21. **Statement** Population increase coupled with depleting resources in going to be the scenario of many developing countries in the days to come.

Conclusions

I. The population of developing countries will not continue to increase in the future.

II. It will be very difficult for the government of developing countries to provide their people a decent quality of life. ***RRB Group D 2022***

22. **Statement** The government has been supplying free medicines, since 2014 and so far 75 thousand disease affected people have been benefited although size of the affected population is 100 times of this number.

Conclusions

I. Every affected person is benefiting from the supply of free medicines by the government.

II. Providing free medicines to the affected people is a good scheme implemented by the Indian government. ***UP Police ASI 2021***

23. Read the given statement and conclusions carefully and decide which of the conclusions logically follow(s) from the statement.

Statement

Increasing use of non-biodegradable plastic will pose a grave threat to plant and animal life in the long run.

Conclusions

I. If non-biodegradable plastic is banned, humanity will not face extinction.

II. Humanity will not be impacted by extensive use of plastic. ***RRB NTPC 2021***

(a) II follows but I does not follow
(b) I and II follow
(c) Neither I nor II follows
(d) I follows but II does not follow

Directions (Q. Nos. 24-26) *Each of these questions has a statement followed by two conclusions I and II. Consider the statement and the following conclusions. Decide which of the conclusion follows from the statement.*

Give answer

(a) If Conclusion I follows
(b) If Conclusion II follows
(c) If both Conclusions I and II follow
(d) If neither Conclusion I nor II follows

24. **Statement** 'On October 2, let us pledge to make the country free of single-use plastic.' - Prime Minister of India ***SSC CPO 2019***

Conclusions

I. All Indians should reduce and then completely eliminate the consumption of single-use plastic like packaged drinking water.

II. India is going to be completely plastic free on October 2.

25. **Statement** The National Skill Development committee conducted an assessment among their trainers and found the performance below mandatory level. ***UPSSSC Junior Assistant 2020***

Conclusions

I. The committee should immediately organise remedial courses and training to improve standards.

II. The committee should terminate poor performers and hire new trainers.

26. **Statement** Fruits and vegetables grown at home are far more healthy as compared to those fetched from markets, as those are kept under artificial refrigeration and preservation to make them look fresh. ***RRB Group D 2018***

> ***MRC******
> ***(Most Repeating Concepts)***
> Questions based on conclusions (Q. Nos. 26, 27, 30, 37) are repeatdly asked in different exams (NTPC, RRB-JE, ALP) They are very important for upcoming railway exams.

Conclusions

I. Fruits and vegetables in the market are kept under artificial refrigeration and preservation.

II. Fruits and vegetables grown at home are more healthy.

27. In this question, a statement is given followed by two conclusions. Choose the conclusion(s) which best fit(s) logically. ***RRB JE 2019***

Statement We do not educate children for the purpose of educating them. We want to prepare them for life.

Conclusions

I. Our system of education is defective.

II. Vocational education is the real education.

(a) Neither Conclusion I nor II follows
(b) Only Conclusion II follows
(c) Only Conclusion I follows
(d) Both Conclusions I and II follow

28. Consider the given statements to be true and decide which of the conclusions logically follow(s) from the statements.

Statements There is an increase in the price of essential commodities due to a strike by the transporters.

Conclusions

I. Government should buy their own vehicles to transport the essential goods.

II. Government should negotiate with transporters to withdraw the strike. ***RRB ALP 2018***

(a) Only Conclusion I follows
(b) Only Conclusion II follows
(c) Neither Conclusion I nor II follows
(d) Both Conclusions I and II follow

29. In this question, a statement is given followed by two conclusions. Choose the conclusion(s) which best fit(s) logically.

Statement Candidates should be young, energetic and dynamic in the age group of 27 to 32 years.

Conclusions

I. Persons below 27 years are not energetic.

II. Persons above 32 years are not young. ***RRB JE 2019***

(a) Only Conclusion II follows
(b) Both Conclusions I and II follow
(c) Neither Conclusion I nor II follows
(d) Only Conclusion I follows

30. Consider the given statement true and decide which of the conclusions logically follow(s) from the information given in the statement.

Statement

The population in metro cities is increasing tremendously which leads to the shortage of living space and a drop in living conditions of the people.

Conclusions

I. Government should re-plan city development.

II. Government should demolish illegal buildings and build cottages for people. ***RRB ALP 2018***

(a) Only Conclusion II follows
(b) Only Conclusion I follows
(c) Neither Conclusion I nor II follows
(d) Both Conclusions I and II follow

31. Consider the given statement is true and decide which of the conclusions logically follow(s) from the information given in the statement.

Statements India is one of the world's largest suppliers of generic medicines to the developing world.

Conclusions

I. India is a developing country.

II. India is not the only country which supplies generic medicines to the world. ***UPASI 2021***

(a) Only Conclusion I follows
(b) Only Conclusion II follows
(c) Both Conclusions I and II follows
(d) Neither I nor II follows

32. In this question, a statement is given followed by two conclusions numbered I and II. You have to assume everything in the statement to be true, then consider the two conclusions together and decide which of them logically follows beyond a reasonable doubt from the information given in the statement. ***RPF SI 2019***

Statement "The MT pen costs ₹ 25 per piece", read a board in a stationery shop.

Conclusions

I. The cost of 5 MT pen is ₹ 125.

II. The cost of the pen is very high.

Choose the appropriate one from the following options

(a) Only Conclusion I follows (b) Only Conclusion II follows
(c) Either I or II follows (d) Neither I nor II follows

33. Read the given statement and conclusions carefully and decide which of the conclusions logically follow(s) from the statement.

Statement Of all the mobile phones manufacturers in Korea, the 'Maxto' brand has the highest sale.

Conclusions

I. The quality of no other mobile phones in Korea is as high as that of 'Maxto'.

II. The number of sales of all the brands of mobile phones manufactured in Korea is known. ***RRB NTPC 2021***

(a) Only Conclusion I follows
(b) Either Conclusion I or II follows
(c) Only Conclusion II follows
(d) Neither Conclusion I nor II follows

Based on Three/Four Conclusions

34. Assuming that the given statement is true: find out which of the four alternative (s) is definitely true.

Statement No newspaper is read by an illiterate.

A. All newspapers that are read, are read by post graduates.

B. Some newspapers that are read, are read by post graduates.

C. Some newspapers are not read by illiterates.

D. No illiterate ever reads a newspaper. ***RRB NTPC 2021***

(a) Only A & B (b) Only C & D
(c) Only A (d) Only B

35. Read the given statement and conclusions carefully and decide which of the conclusions logically follow(s) from the statement.

Statement "My husband will drive me to the Hudson shopping Mall because my hand is not in a healthy condition to drive our car", X told Y.

Conclusions

I. X will not go to Hudson Shopping Mall walking.
II. X is married.
III. Y is married.
IV. X knows how to drive a car. ***RRB NTPC 2021***

(a) Only Conclusions I, II and IV follow
(b) Only Conclusions I and II follow
(c) Only Conclusions II and IV follow
(d) Only Conclusions II, III and IV follow

36. Read the given statements and conclusions carefully and decide which of the conclusions logically follow(s) from the statements.

Statements

Some of the dance forms taught in all the dance classes of Delhi are Hip-Hop, Contemporary and Kathakali.

None of the dance classes of Delhi teach Kuchipudi.

Some of the dance classes of Delhi teach Salsa and Odissi.

Conclusions

I. Salsa is taught in every dance class in Delhi.
II. Some of the dance classes of Delhi do not teach Kathakali.
III. There isn't a single dance class in Delhi that doesn't teach Hip-Hop. ***RRB NTPC 2021***

(a) Both Conclusions I and III follow
(b) Only Conclusion III follows
(c) Only Conclusion I follows
(d) Both Conclusions I and II follow

37. Read the given statements and conclusions carefully and decide which of the conclusions logically follows from the statements.

Statements

Some of the beverages sold at this cafeteria are coffee.

None of the beverages sold are tea.

All the beverages sold at this cafeteria are very aromatic and tasty.

MRC***
(Most Repeating Concepts)
Question Nos. 34, 35 and 36 based on three or more conclusions are very important from the examination point of view. Question on these concept are continuously being asked in RRB (NTPC) exams.

Conclusions

I. Every coffee sold at this cafeteria is very aromatic.
II. Some espressos sold at this cafeteria are cappuccinos.
III. Some of the tea sold at this cafeteria is not aromatic.

RRB NTPC 2021

(a) Only Conclusions I and II follow
(b) Only Conclusions I and III follow
(c) Only Conclusion III follows
(d) Only Conclusion I follows

38. Read the given statements and conclusions carefully and decide which of the conclusions logically follows from the statements.

Statements All the clothes sold in my boutique are of high standard.

None of the brands except Cara and Cucci are sold at my boutique.

Some Cucci accessories like bags and makeup are also sold.

Conclusions

I. My boutique sells clothes and accessories.
II. Cara and Cucci brands have clothes of high standard.
III. Some of the accessories sold at my boutique are of Cucci. ***RRB NTPC 2021***

(a) Only Conclusion I follows
(b) Only Conclusion I and II follow
(c) All the Conclusions I, II and III follow
(d) Only Conclusion III follows

39. Read the given statement and conclusions carefully and decide which of the given conclusions logically follow(s) from the statements.

Statement Hard work is poor man's wealth.

Conclusions

I. A poor man is always a hard worker.
II. A poor man earns wealth through his hard work.
III. A wealthy man is always a hard worker.

(a) Only Conclusion I and III follow
(b) Only Conclusion II follows
(c) Both Conclusions I and II follow
(d) Neither Conclusions I nor II follows

Direction (Q. No. 40) *In the following questions, two statements are given followed by four conclusions (a), (b), (c) and (d). You have to consider the statements to be true even if they seem to be at variance from commonly known facts. You have to decide which of the given conclusions, if any, follow from the given statements.*

40. During the last summer vacation, Ankit went to a summer camp where he took part in hiking, swimming and boating. This summer, he is looking forward to a music camp where he hopes to sing, dance and learn to play the guitar.

Based on the above information, four conclusions, as given below, have been made.

Which one of these logically follows from the information given above?

(a) Ankit's parents want him to play the guitar
(b) Ankit prefers music to outdoor activities
(c) Ankit goes to some type of camp every summer
(d) Ankit likes to sing and dance

Right Key

1. (b)	2. (d)	3. (b)	4. (a)	5. (c)	6. (a)	7. (c)	8. (a)	9. (b)	10. (b)
11. (a)	12. (d)	13. (c)	14. (d)	15. (a)	16. (a)	17. (c)	18. (c)	19. (b)	20. (a)
21. (b)	22. (c)	23. (c)	24. (a)	25. (c)	26. (c)	27. (a)	28. (b)	29. (c)	30. (b)
31. (b)	32. (a)	33. (a)	34. (b)	35. (a)	36. (b)	37. (d)	38. (c)	39. (b)	40. (c)

Solutions

1. *(b)* According to the statement, requisition slip is not required for amount up to ₹ 20000, it does not mean that customers cannot withdraw amount of more than ₹ 20000.
Hence, only Conclusion II follows.

2. *(d)* Both Conclusions I and II follow as death is inevitable and it can come anytime in life.

3. *(b)* Conclusion I doesn't follow from the statement. As, this is a hypothetical situation.
Conclusion II follows from the statement. The increasing population will have an impact on the availability of resources in the country.

4. *(a)* According to the statement, a friend who help when help is needed is a true friend but it doesn't say anything about enemies.
Hence, only Conclusion I follows.

5. *(c)* Statement mentions about road connectively between Delhi and Agra, but it doesn't say anything about rail and air connectivity.
Hence, neither Conclusion I nor II follows.

6. *(a)* From the given statement, it can be concluded that Sita didn't know how to cook. But, there is no mention of a party. Hence, only Conclusion I follows.

7. *(c)* Antony speaks 6 languages, but that does not mean he is an Australian. Many people in the world can speak 6 or more languages. Hence, Conclusion I does not follow. Every Australian can speak 6 languages. This does not mean that people from other countries cannot speak 6 languages. Hence, Conclusion II also does not follow.
Hence, neither Conclusion I nor II follows.

8. *(a)* According to the given statement, the residents of Jane's place should save water, so that they do not face water shortage during summer season.
Hence, only Conclusion I follows.

9. *(b)* Aman was shortlisted for the interview. Therefore he may be selected finally or rejected. Hence, either Conclusion I or II follows.

10. *(b)* If government create awarness among people that the tax paying is helpful in building a nation then people definitely understand that paying tax is not a burden or waste of money.
Hence, only Conclusion I follows.

11. *(a)* According to the statement, milk in copper utensil becomes poison, which is good for health and shouldn't be avoided.
Hence, only Conclusion I follows.

12. *(d)* As given, Sachin is a good batsman that means Sachin is a batsman. All batsman are intelligent, that means Sachin is intelligent but we are not sure all intelligent are batsman. Hence, only Conclusion II follows.

13. *(c)* Both the conclusions do not follow. Because, it is not clear in the statement whether only village child or city child comes to the school. It is also not clear whether Kabir is an obedient student.
Hence, neither Conclusion I nor II follows.

14. *(d)* If agricultural crops are destroyed prices of groceries and other essential food will surge. Hence, only Conclusion II follows.

15. *(a)* There is a sale UP to 70%. This means that on all the clothes there is a maximum 70% off but it is not a fixed value. For instant discounts may be 30%, 40% and so on. And it is written that the sale is on all the cloths. So neither Conclusion I nor II follows.

> **TOP TIPS** If advice, result, diagonsis, publicity or advertisement is given in the statement and the conclusion is directly related to the statement, then that conclusion will be true.

16. *(a)* It is clear that the charge is only for throwing garbage not for every littering offence and also it is not written at every public place of non litering zone. Hence, neither Conclusion I nor II follows.

17. *(c)* From the given statements, Conclusion I is false as number of spinners and number of bowlers are not given.
Conclusion II is false, as there is no support to this conclusion in the given statement.
Hence, neither Conclusion I nor II follows.

18. *(c)* Statement doesn't mention anything about the number of people coming to India and moreover yoga is not practiced only on yoga day.
Hence, neither Conclusion I nor II follows.

19. *(b)* From the given statement, only Conclusion II follows because in statement, it is not mentioned that who comes first or who comes second but it is quite evident that there is a tough competition between both.

20. *(a)* The action taken by the government indicates that the government understands the condition of poor farmers and they need immediate attention. Conclusion II is not related to the given statement.
Hence, only Conclusion I follows.

21. *(b)* According to the statement, Conclusion I doesn't follow from the statement, because it is opposite in meanings to the statement, but Conclusion II follows from the statement the government of developing countries will not be able to provide their people a decent quality of life.

Hence, only Conclusion II follows.

22. *(c)* According to the given statement, the government is supplying free medicines to the disease affected people. But it can't be said that every diseased person is benefiting from them. Moreover nothing can be said about the impact of this scheme. Hence, neither Conclusion I nor II follows.

23. *(c)* According to the given statement, it is clear that neither I nor II follows.

24. *(a)* The statement given by PM indicates that all Indians eliminate should reduce and then completely the consumption of single use plastic. But we cannot say that India is going to be completely plastic free on October 2. Hence, only Conclusion I follows.

25. *(c)* From the given statement it is clear that the committee should immediately organise remedial courses and training to improve standards.

26. *(c)* Both conclusions follow as both are clearly stated in the statement.

27. *(a)* According to the question, we do not educate children for the purpose of educating them. We want to prepare them for life but both the conclusions do not satisfy the statement.

Hence neither Conclusion I nor II follows.

TOP TIPS If the statement is positive in nature then its conclusion will also be positive.

28. *(b)* According to the given statement only Conclusion II follows as government should negotiate with transporters to withdraw the strike.

29. *(c)* Statement says candidate should be energetic in the age group of 27 to 32. But in conclusion I, it says that person below 27 year are not energetic. So, it does not follow and in conclusion II it says that persons above 32 years are not young so it also does not follow the statements.

Hence, neither Conclusion I nor II follows.

30. *(b)* In the statement (is not mentioned) the existence of illegal buildings. So, Conclusion II is does not follow.

Since in the statement it is given the issue of living space in the city, it can be concluded that Government should re-plan city development.

Hence, only Conclusion I follows.

31. *(b)* From the given statement, we can't conclude whether India is a developing country or not, so Conclusion I does not follows. Since India is world's largest suppliers of generic medicines, so its conclude that India is not only suppliers.

Hence, only Conclusion II follows.

32. *(a)* As MT pen costs ₹ 25 per piece. So, the cost of 5 MT pen is ₹ 125 is correct.

But the second conclusion is not true.

Hence, only Conclusion I follows.

33. *(a)* The brand maxto has the highest sale, so the of sales of each brand is known. There is nothing mention of the quality of mobile phones in the statement.

Hence, only Conclusion I follows.

34. *(b)* From the given statements, it can be concluded that an illiterate can not read newspapers.

Hence, only Conclusion C and D follows.

35. *(a)* According to the statement, it is clear that X's husband will drive so she will not go to Hudson mall walking. X has a husband. So, X is married.

But marital status of Y is not known.

Hence, only Conclusions I, II and IV follow.

36. *(b)* According to the question, there isn't a single dance class in Delhi and doesn't teach Hip-Hop.

Hence, only Conclusion III follows.

37. *(d)* From the question it is clear that every coffee sold at this cafeteria is very aromatic.

Hence, only Conclusion I follows.

38. *(c)* From the statement we can say that all the conclusions follow.

39. *(b)* A poorman is not necessarily always hard working.

Although, he can earn with hard work, but hard work is not the only way to earn.

Hence, only Conclusion II follows.

40. *(c)* No reasons are specified in the question for going to different camps. As, Ankit has been going to different camps since the past two year, so it can be said that he goes to some type of camp every summer.

CHAPTER

24 Statement and Arguments

Statement and Arguments

The information given related to any topic is called a statement.

An argument is a fact that is given by someone to support or oppose a statement.

In this chapter, a statement concerned with an issue is given, followed by certain arguments in favour or against that statement. Considering the statement and arguments given in the question, it has to be decided that which of the arguments is given in favour or against the given statement is strong and which argument is weak.

Based on Two Arguments

In this type of questions, a statement is followed by two arguments. On the basis of the given statement, candidate has to find out the strong and weak argument and select the answer with the help of options.

e.g. A statement is given followed by two arguments. Decide which of the argument(s) is/are strong with respect to the statement?

Statement

Should government increase the budget allocation for participation in international sporting events.

Arguments

I. Yes, because India also has many talented youth in sports, but our country is unable to perform well due to lack of resources.

II. No, India is a poor country and this money should be used for welfare activities.

(a) If only Argument II is strong

(b) If only Argument I is strong

(c) If both Arguments I and II are strong

(d) If both Arguments I and II are not strong

Sol. (b) Investing in sports also have economic benefits. Moreover, winning players and athletes bring praise and glory to the nation. Hence, only Argument I is strong.

Based on Three or More Arguments

In this type of questions, a statement is given followed by three or more arguments. Based on this statement, the weak and strong arguments have to be identified and the argument has to be chosen which is completely based on the statement.

e.g. The given statement is followed by three or four arguments. Decide which of the option is correct about the given arguments?

Statement Should there be only few banks in place of numerous smaller banks in India?

Arguments

I. Yes, this will help secures the investor's money as these big banks will be able to withstand intermittent market related shocks.

II. No, large number of people will lose their job as after the merger many employees will be redundant.

III. Yes, this will help consolidate the entire banking industry and will lead to healthy competition.

(a) None is strong argument

(b) I and III are strong arguments

(c) II and III are strong arguments

(d) I and II are strong arguments

(e) All are strong arguments

Sol. (e) Argument I is strong because larger banks are better equipped to handle economic downturns; which can protect investors money.

Argument II is also strong because when banks merge, there's often a need to streamline operations, which can lead to job cuts.

Argument III is strong as well, fewer larger banks can lead to a more concentrated and efficient banking sector.

So, all are strong arguments.

Score Booster

- If the argument is suggestive, comparative, deceptive, inconsistent, or unclear, then the argument is weak.
- Arguments based on assumptions about a person, an idea, a newspaper, a leader, etc, are weak.
- If the argument contains words like "only", "only this", "only one", etc., then the argument is weak.
- If any argument compares a country with its policies, then that argument is weak.
- Arguments based on words like "magic", "mystery", "miracle" and such emotions are weak.
- Arguments that contradict the prevailing Indian constitutional and legal foundations are weak.

Exam Approach Examples

Based on Two Arguments

Directions (Ex. Nos. 1-3) *A statement is given followed by two arguments. Decide which of the argument(s) is/are strong with respect to the statement?*

Give answer
(a) If only Argument I is strong
(b) If only Argument II is strong
(c) If both Arguments I and II are strong
(d) If neither Argument I nor II is strong

Example 1 **Statement** Should parents invest as much in educating their daughters as much as they spend on educating their sons? ***UP Police Constable 2018***

Arguments

I. No, almost all data points to the fact that boys are way more intelligent than girls.

II. No, though girls may be intelligent, parents have to keep money aside for their marriages.

Sol. (*d*) Argument I is weak, as it is totally gender based and absurd.

Argument II is also weak, as it is a socially regressive mindset. Educating girls will make them more stronger both socially and financially.

Hence, neither Argument I nor II is strong.

Example 2 **Statement** Should small countries like Nepal not have defence forces? ***RRB Group-D 2018***

Arguments

I. No, other countries do not rely on violence.

II. Yes, many people in Nepal are peace loving and preachers of non-violence.

> **Helping Tips**
> To solve such questions, a candidate should have knowledge of topics general awareness and general science.

Sol. (*d*) According to the statement, the question has been raised whether a small country like Nepal should have an army or not. None of the given arguments is able to answer this question properly. Hence, neither Argument I nor Argument II is strong.

Example 3 **Statement** Education for all children up to the age of 14 yr. Should it be made mandatory? ***UP Police Asst. Operator 2024***

Arguments

I. Yes, this will help in ending the system of forced employment of children. Will get help.

II. Yes, this will increase the standard of living.

> **Trending Concept**
> This type of questions are mainly asked in current examination such as RRB NTPC, Group-D, UP Police ASI, UP Police Constable, UPSSSC etc.
> Statement and Argument based questions are important for the upcoming examination.

Sol. (*a*) Making education compulsory for all children up to the age of 14 yr will help in eliminating the system of forced employment of children. Hence, only Argument I is supported.

Based on Three or More Arguments

Directions (Ex. Nos. 4 and 5) *In the following questions, a statement is given, followed by three/four arguments. Study the statement carefully and mark the appropriate alternatives.*

Example 4 **Statement** Should the government impose restrictions on access to sensitive information to the journalists to avoid the media hype?

Arguments

I. Yes, the media creates hype and publishes distorted information at times.

II. No, journalists should have an access to all the information as media is the best source to expose the malfunctions in the society.

III. Yes, at times it leads to harassment of those who are affected and alleged to be involved in the crisis.

(a) All I, II and III are strong
(b) Arguments I and II are strong
(c) Arguments II and III are strong
(d) Only Argument II is strong

Sol. (*a*) All the arguments strongly support the given statement. Hence, all the three arguments are strong.

Example 5 **Statement** Should the consumption of aerated drinks be banned in India?

Arguments

I. Yes, this is the only way to reduce the risk of exposing people to some disease.

II. No, each individual should have right to choose what he wants.

III. No, there is no confirmed evidence that such products have adverse effects on human body.

IV. Yes, it is banned in many countries also.

(a) Only I is strong
(b) I and II are strong
(c) Only III is strong
(d) I and IV are strong

> **Helping Tips**
> It is not appropriate to completely ban any item. Arguments in favour of a ban are mostly weak.

Sol. (*c*) Argument I is a weak argument, because of the word 'only'.

Argument II is also a weak argument, because it is the duty of the government to save its citizens from harmful products.

Argument III is strong as a product must not be banned unless its harmful effects have been proved. Argument IV is weak, because we cannot blindly follow other countries.

Chapter Challenge

Based on Two Arguments

Directions (Q. Nos. 1-23) *A statement is given followed by two arguments. Decide which of the argument(s) is/are strong with respect to the statement?*

Give answer

(a) If only Argument I is strong
(b) If only Argument II is strong
(c) If both Arguments I and II are strong
(d) If neither Argument I nor II is strong

1. **Statement** Citing rising costs, private schools have increased their fees by 20 per cent for this academic year. ***RRC Group-D 2022***

Arguments

I. This year the government has reduced the taxes levied on private schools by 8 per cent.
II. The teachers union is protesting against the decision to cut the salaries of private schools by 15 per cent.

2. **Statement** Oils should be totally removed from our diet. ***RRB NTPC 2021***

Arguments

I. Yes, removing oils from our diet will keep the budget in check.
II. No, some types of oils are essential for us as our body cannot produce them on its own.

> ***MRC******
> ***(Most Repeating Concepts)***
> Q. Nos. 3, 4, 5, 8, 10, 15, 21, 25 and 35 are very important from the examination point of view. These types of questions are being asked regularly in UP Police related examinations.

3. **Statement** Should people who throw household garbage on the road be punished ? ***UP Police ASI 2021***

Arguments

I. Yes, throwing garbage on the road is a bad habit, because it hinders the objective of keeping the environment clean.
II. No, it will not have a serious impact on wildlife and habitat.

4. **Statement** In a newspaper publishing confirmed news, a man read that "People are dying from a disease caused by a deadly virus". Should this be taken seriously? ***UP Police ASI 2021***

Arguments

I. Yes, the newspaper publishes only verified news.
II. No, if it is declared fake news, then there is no need to take it seriously.

5. **Statement** Should adult education programs be given priority over compulsory education programmes?

Arguments ***UP Police Head Operator 2024***

I. No, it will also help in the success of compulsory education programmes.
II. Yes, this will help eliminate adult illiteracy.

6. **Statement** Should there be a complete ban on mining coal in India?

Arguments

I. Yes, the present stock coal will not last long, if we continue mining at the present rate.
II. No, we do not have alternate energy source of sufficient quantity.

7. **Statement** Should there be a ban on smoking in public places? ***UP Police SI 2021***

Arguments

I. Yes, this will decrease the possibility of fire disasters.
II. No, they are not effective.

8. **Statement** Should speed breakers on roads be outlawed? ***UPSSSC Mandi Parishad 2018***

Arguments

I. No, speed breakers are a simple way to reduce vehicle speed.
II. Yes, some people fail to see the speed breakers at night.

9. **Statement** Should you work hard till you make your signature into an autograph? ***RRB ALP 2018***

Arguments

I. Work until you no longer have to introduce yourself.
II. Work hard to become financially secure.

10. **Statement** Should government ban the use of plastic bags? ***UP Police SI 2021***

Arguments

I. Yes, plastic bags take lot of time to decompose.
II. No, other countries have not banned the use of plastic bags.

11. **Statement** Are the best things in life free?

Arguments ***RRB ALP 2018***

I. Life gives us so many opportunities for free and yet most of us waste it.
II. Smile, friends, family, good talk, good sleep and happy memories are all free.

12. **Statement** Should students cheating in exams be punished? ***RRB NTPC 2021***

Arguments

I. No, cheating is common among successful people.
II. Yes, as the exams are conducted to assess the potentiality of an individual, so they should give exams honestly.

13. Statement Should the mid-day meal given in government schools be stopped?

UP Police Constable 2019

Arguments

I. No, it provides at least one meal to underprivileged children.

II. Yes, it provides the wrong incentives to go to school.

> **MRC*****
> ***(Most Repeating Concepts)***
> Question Nos. 13, 16, 20, 24, 28 and 31 are very important from the examination point of view. These types of questions are being currently asked in Railway (Group-D, NTPC, ALP) related examinations.

14. Statement What is the solution to avoid the occurrence of mosquitoes? *RRB Group D 2018*

Arguments

I. We should remove dirty and stagnant water. We should use mosquito repellent and other gadgets to avoid mosquito bites.

II. There is no way to eliminate mosquitoes. They are produced in a particular season. We should only make arrangements for prevention.

15. Statement Should Ganesh buy a new motorcycle?

UPSSSC 2018

Arguments

I. Yes, Ganesh's old motorcycle, which he has been using to go to his office for the last 15 years, he is often facing problems in commuting on that motorcycle.

II. No, the new motorcycles will increase the existing problem of pollution.

16. Statement Should complete education be made free for women and girls of all ages in India? *CGPSC 2019*

Arguments

I. No, it will weaken our present social structure.

II. Yes, this is the only way to bring back the pride of Indian women.

17. Statement Should Indian scientists working abroad be called back to India? *UPSSSC 2018*

Arguments

I. Yes, they should serve the motherland first and forget about discoveries, honours, facilities etc.

II. No, we have enough talent, let them be where they want.

18. Statement Farmers in Village X should switch to crops that require comparatively less water for irrigation as compared to sugarcane.

Arguments *RRC Group D 2022*

I. Availability of water for irrigation has been on a constant decline in Village X for the last few years.

II. Main source of income of farmers in Village X is through sale of sugarcane crop to the nearby sugar factories.

19. Statements Should a child from a not-so-affluent family in India be allowed to follow his/her passion?

UP Police Constable 2018

Arguments

I. Yes, these days if a child is allowed to pursue her/his interests, she/he can excel in it, even financially.

II. No, even today our country does not have a strong social security system and establishing oneself in unconventional fields is time-consuming and can be financially taxing.

20. Statement

Hydroelectricity is a cleaner and greener energy than other forms of power generation. *SSC CGL (Tier-II) 2025*

Arguments

I. Hydroelectric plants almost have nil CO_2 emissions.

II. Hydroelectric power projects submerge huge amounts under water thereby affecting local flora and fauna.

21. Statements Should a cricket team have more than one captain during a match? *UP Police Constable 2018*

Arguments

I. No, one needs to make decisions on the sports and there won't be time to resolve conflicting ideas between the captains on the field if such a scenario emerges.

II. Yes, it is always better to have more brains coming to an understanding before taking a decision.

22. Statement Fake news has become a problem of the 21st century all over the globe. *RRC Group D 2022*

Arguments

I. A global level mechanism is needed to combat this worldwide problem.

II. Problems related to fake news are only present in India.

23. Statement Should all the drugs patented and manufactured in western countries be first tried out on sample basis before giving license for sale to general public in India?

Arguments

I. Yes, many such drugs require different doses and duration for Indian population and hence it is necessary.

II. No, this is just not feasible and hence cannot be implemented.

24. A statement is given followed by two arguments I and II. Read the statement and the arguments carefully and select the appropriate answer from the given options.

Statement

Floods caused widespread damage to crops in Odisha this year.

Arguments

I. There has been a bumper production of food grains in Odisha this year.

II. The number of crop insurance claims has seen a significant increase in Odisha this year. *RRC Group D 2022*

(a) Argument I weakens, while Argument II strengthens the statement
(b) Both Arguments I and II weaken the statement
(c) Argument II weakens, while Argument I strengthens the statement
(d) Both Arguments I and II strengthen the statement

25. Study the statements and arguments carefully, and choose the appropriate answer from the given alternatives.

Statement

Children should be allowed to use mobile phones from an early age.

Arguments

I. Continuous use of mobile phone, causes distraction for children.

II. Lots of educational apps encourage enjoyable competition among kids, while also enhancing the way they learn new things. *RRC Group-D 2022*

(a) Both I and II do not support the statement
(b) Both I and II support the statement
(c) I does not support the statement while II supports the statement
(d) II does not support the statement while I supports the statement

26. A question is given followed by two arguments. Decide which of the argument(s) is/are strong with respect to the question?

Question Should all criminals be given severe punishments?

Arguments

I. Yes, it will induce fear in criminals and crime would reduce greatly.

II. No, Human life is precious, and criminals should also be given a chance to improve. *RRB NTPC 2021*

(a) Both Arguments I and II are strong
(b) Only Argument II is strong
(c) Only Argument I is strong
(d) Neither Argument I nor II is strong

27. A statement is given followed by two arguments. Decide which of the argument(s) is/are strong with respect to the statement?

Statement Healthcare services should be nationalised.

Arguments

I. Healthcare services are provided nationally in many countries.

II. Nationalisation of healthcare services will reduce the career prospects of doctors. *RRB NTPC 2021*

(a) Argument I is strong
(b) Argument II is strong
(c) Either Arguments I and II is strong
(d) Neither Argument I nor argument II is strong

28. A statement is given followed by two arguments I and II. Read the statement and the arguments carefully and select the appropriate answer from the given options.

Statement

In spite of all apartments having the same square foot area, rents of the apartments above the 6th floor are higher in most high-rise apartment buildings.

Arguments

I. It is riskier to live on higher floors, since the dependence on lifts is much more critical than the lower floors which can be accessed by stairs.

II. Air pollution is several times lower on higher floors than on the lower floors. *RRC Group D 2022*

(a) Argument I weakens, while Argument II strengthens the statement
(b) Both Arguments I and II weaken the statement
(c) Both Arguments I and II strengthen the statement
(d) Argument II weakens, while Argument I strengthens the statement

29. Read the given statement and the arguments carefully and select the appropriate answer from the given options.

Statement

The monsoon season influences the lives of Mumbai people in many ways.

Arguments

I. Water logging is a common issue in Mumbai during the monsoon.

II. Generally people enjoy the monsoon season in Mumbai. *RRC Group D 2022*

(a) Both I and II weaken the statement
(b) II weakens while I strengthens the statement
(c) I weakens while II strengthens the statement
(d) Both I and II strengthen the statement

Based on Three or More Arguments

Directions (Q. Nos. 30-32) *In the following questions, a statement is given followed by theee/four arguments. Study the statement carefully and mark the appropriate alternative.*

30. Statement Should the income generated out of agricultural activities be taxed?

Arguments

I. No, farmers are otherwise suffering from natural calamities and low yield coupled with low procurement price and their income should not be taxed.

II. Yes, majority of the population is dependent on agriculture and hence their income should be taxed to argument the Government resources.

III. Yes, many big farmers earn much more than majority of the service earners and they should be taxed to remove the disparity.

(a) All are strong (b) II and III are strong
(c) Only I is strong (d) I and II are strong

31. **Statement** Should there be complete ban on Indian professionals seeking jobs elsewhere after getting their education in India?

Arguments

I. Yes, this is the only way to sustain present rate of technological development in India.

II. No, the Indians settled abroad send huge amount of foreign exchange and this constitute a significant part of foreign exchange reserve.

III. No, the practical knowledge gained by Indians by working in other countries help India develop its economy.

(a) None is strong
(b) I and II are strong
(c) Only III is strong
(d) II and III are strong

32. **Statement** Should India go in for computerisation in all possible sectors? ***UP Police Constable 2024***

Arguments

I. Yes, it will bring efficiency and accuracy in the work.

II. No, it will be an injustice to the monumental human resources which are at present underutilised.

III. No, computerisation demands a lot of money. We should not waste money on it.

IV. Yes, when advanced countries are introducing computers in every field, how can India afford to lag behind.

(a) II and III are strong
(b) I and III are strong
(c) Only I is strong
(d) I and II are strong

Right Key

1. (d)	2. (b)	3. (a)	4. (b)	5. (b)	6. (b)	7. (a)	8. (a)	9. (a)	10. (a)
11. (c)	12. (b)	13. (a)	14. (a)	15. (a)	16. (d)	17. (d)	18. (c)	19. (a)	20. (a)
21. (a)	22. (a)	23. (a)	24. (a)	25. (c)	26. (a)	27. (d)	28. (a)	29. (d)	30. (b)
31. (a)	32. (c)								

Solutions

1. *(d)* Both the arguments are not directly associated with given statements. So, neither Arguments I nor II is strong.

> **TOP TIPS** To solve such type of questions, candidate must be aware of the current existing laws, financial and educational situations in a country/state.

2. *(b)* As, some types of oils are essential for us as our body cannot produce them on its own. So, only Argument II is strong.

3. *(a)* Only Argument I is strong, because throwing garbage on the road is a bad habit and it hinders the objective of keeping the environment clean.

4. *(b)* Only Argument II is strong, because if the news is declared as fake news, then there is no need to take it seriously.

5. *(b)* Giving priority to adult education programmes over compulsory education programmes will help in eliminating adult illiteracy.

Hence, only Argument II is supported.

6. *(b)* Argument I is a weak argument as it is not relevant to 'complete ban'. Argument II is strong as banning in such a scenario will lead us into great trouble.

Note : Arguments in favour of a ban are mostly weak but not always.

7. *(a)* Only Argument I is strong because cigarette smoking related fires are among the top causes of fire related fatalities. So, banning smoking in public places can substantially reduce fire disasters.

8. *(a)* Argument I is strong as speed breakers reduces speed.

Argument II is weak as people fails to see speed breakers because of the absence of proper lighting. Road lighting should be improved instead of eliminating speed breakers.

9. *(a)* If a person works hard that he no longer needs to introduce himself, he would be a celebrity and people will ask for his autograph. And, if someone work hard only for becoming financialy secure, it doesn't make them famous or a celebrity.

Hence, only Argument I is strong.

10. *(a)* Plastic takes long time to decompose. So, Argument I is strong.

Argument II is weak because it is not necessary that, our country should follow the same thing which other countries are doing.

11. *(c)* Both the Arguments I and II are strong because life gives us many opportunities for free moreover smile, friends, family, good talk, good sleep and happy memories are all free.

12. *(b)* Argument I is not strong, even if cheating is common it can not be considered right and children must be taught not to cheat. Argument II is strong because exams are to assess the potential of a student and should be given with honesty.

Hence, only Argument II is strong.

13. *(a)* According to the statement, only Argument I is strong because stopping mid-day meal in government schools will have a direct impact on the nutritional status of underprivileged children whereas Argument II is illogical. So, only Argument I is strong.

14. *(a)* Argument I is strong with respect to Argument II. To avoid the breeding of mosquitoes, we should remove dirty and stagnant water. We should use mosquito repellent and other similar resources to avoid mosquito bites.

15. *(a)* According to the question, only Argument I is strong. Since, Ganesh is having problems with transportation, mainly because of his old motorcycle. Therefore, he should buy a new motorcycle.

16. *(d)* Free education is essential for those women or girls who belong to economically backward families. Therefore, free education should be on economic basis. Free education alone will not bring back the dignity of women. Hence, both the Arguments are not strong.

17. *(d)* Argument I does not present any valid reason why Indian scientists working abroad should be called back to India and Argument II is also not strong.

Hence, both the Arguments are not strong.

18. *(c)* Both the Arguments are strong because, if water supply for irrigation is declining, then switching to less water consuming crops will save the water. Moreover, farmers would be able to increase sugarcane production because of availability of extra water.

19. *(a)* Argument I is strong. If children are allowed to pursue their passion, they can become successful and financially stable even, if they are not from, so affluent families. Argument II is weak because if a child is hardworking and talented, then he can be successful and can make a mark in unconventional fields also.

Hence, only Argument I is strong.

20. *(a)* Argument I supports the statement. The lack of CO_2 emissions is a significant environmental advantage of hydroelectricity, as it reduces greenhouse gas emissions associated with fossil fuel-based power generation.

While Argument II challenges the statement hydroelectricity may have low CO_2 emissions, it can have adverse environmental impact, such as habitat destruction and disruption of ecosystems.

Hence, only Argument I is strong.

21. *(a)* Having two captains can sometimes lead to conflict in opinions which would take time to reach a decision. But in sports sometimes quick decision is needed. So, only Argument I is strong.

22. *(a)* Argument I is strong, as given in the statement that fake news has become a problem of the 21st century all over the globe and need some mechanism to eliminate it.

But, fake news are only present in India not in whole world is not true.

Hence, Argument II weakens while Argument I strengthens the statement.

23. *(a)* Clearly, health of the citizens is an issue of major concern for the government. So, a product like drugs must be first studied and tested before giving license for its sale.

24. *(a)* Argument I weakens the statement as nothing has been mentioned about the production of food grains in Odisha.

Argument II is strong, as due to floods in Odisha, there has been a lot of damage to the crop, then there will be a decrease in the production of the crop there, so number of crop insurance claims has seen a significant increase in Odisha this year.

25. *(c)* Argument II is strong, as because it states that lots of educational apps encourage enjoyable competition among kids, while also enhancing the way they learn new things.

Hence, only Argument I is strong.

26. *(a)* Both the arguments are strong as all the criminals should be given severe punishment as it will create fear among the criminals and there will be a lot of reduction in crime.

All criminals should not be punished severely, human life is precious and criminals should also be given a chance to reform.

> **TOP TIPS** To solve such questions easily, you should consider the statement, extract the effective meaning and reach the conclusion.

27. *(d)* Neither Argument I nor Argument II is strong, as both the arguments are different from the statements.

28. *(a)* Argument I weakens, while Argument II strengthens the statement.

29. *(d)* As from the given statement, both the arguments strengthen the statement.

30. *(b)* Argument I is not strong as it is not always true.

Argument II is strong as in order to increase revenue the government should bring more persons under the cap of taxation.

Argument III is also strong as it is true that many big farmers earn much and hence should be taxed.

31. *(a)* Argument I is weak because of the word only.

Argument II is not strong as it is true that Indians earning abroad increases foreign exchange reserve but it will create a situation of brain-drain in the country.

Argument III is weak as the Indians can also gain practical knowledge by working in their own country.

So, none of the arguments is strong.

32. (c) Yes, India go in for computerisation in all possible sectors because it will bring efficiency and accuracy in the work.

Hence, option (c) is the correct answer.

CHAPTER

25 Statement and Assumptions

Statement and Assumptions

The information given related to any subject is called a statement. Assumption is a thought that is assumed or presumed or indirectly imagined. It represents the reality contained in a statement. It means, things that are not said explicitly but are inferred from the statement or reveal the thinking which is hidden in the statements are called assumptions.

Based on Two Assumptions

In this type of questions, a statement is given followed by two assumptions related to it. Candidates have to consider the statement true and find out which of the given assumptions is implicit in the statement.

e.g. In the question given below, a statement is given followed by two Assumptions I and II. Consider the statement and decide which of the given assumptions is implicit?

Statement

Anil advised Sanjay to go to Goa *via* Mumbai by train.

Assumptions

I. Sanjay wants to go to Goa.

II. Anil gives advice to everyone.

(a) If neither I nor II is implicit

(b) If both I and II are implicit

(c) If only Assumption II is implicit

(d) If only Assumption I is implicit

Sol. (d) Anil advises Sanjay to go to Goa. Based on this, the assumption is that Sanjay wants to go to Goa. It is not clear that Anil advises everyone.

Hence, only Assumption I is correct.

Based on Three or more Assumptions

In this type of questions, a statement and three or more assumptions are given. The candidates have to consider the statement true and find out which assumption is implicit in the statement.

e.g. Read the given statement and the following assumptions and decide which of the assumptions is implicit in the statement? Select the correct options.

Statement

'Work hard to succeed in the examination. A' advises B.

Assumptions

I. B listens to A's advice.

II. Passing the examination is desirable.

III. Hard practice leads to success.

(a) None of these

(b) All I, II and III are implicit

(c) Only I and III are implicit

(d) Only I and II are implicit

Sol. (b) A gives advice to B. Based on this, the assumption that follows is that B listens to A's advice. Passing the examination is desirable and hard work leads to success.

Hence, all the assumptions are implicit.

Score Booster

- While solving the questions of this chapter, one should properly understand the exact meaning of the statement and imagine the assumption.
- If any assumption shows improvement, advice, suggestion, beneficial effect and result, then such assumption will be valid.
- A sentence with presupposition should not contain words like each, all, what, why, and, so, etc.
- If certain words, such as probably, can, usually, etc., are attached to a preconceived sentence, it is usually valid.
- If an assumption talks about the past or the future, it is generally not valid.
- Government instructions are generally expected to be followed by the general public, so it is valid as an assumption.
- No assumption should be broader than the statement.
- There should not be repetition of statement in the assumption.
- If some words like only, solid/strong, best etc, are present in the assumption, then such assumption is invalid.

Exam Approach Examples

Based on Two Assumptions

Directions (Ex. No. 1 and 2) *Each question below consists of a statement followed by two assumptions, numbered I and II. An assumption is something that is either assumed or taken for granted. You have to consider the statement and the assumptions given below it and decide which of the assumptions is implicit in the statement.*

Give answer

(a) Only Assumption I is implicit
(b) Only Assumption II is implicit
(c) Neither Assumption I nor II is implicit
(d) Both Assumptions I and II are implicit

Example 1 **Statement**

Nowadays many entrance exams are gradually shifting from 'offline' to 'online' exams.

Assumptions

I. The online system is more efficient.

II. Online system creates more employment opportunities.

UPPSC 2018

Sol. (*a*) There are more transparency in the online system and it is also easier to evaluate the exams, but the assumption that the online system creates more employment opportunities is not implicit in the statement.

Example 2 **Statement**

It is important to open some more hospitals in village X.

Assumptions

I. The number of hospitals existing in village X is not sufficient to meet the needs of its residents.

II. Having more hospitals will help meet the growing needs of healthcare institutions in village X.

RRB NTPC 2021

> ***Helping Tips***
> While solving such questions, candidates should have an understanding of the beneficial effects and results. Also, the assumption should be simple and general.

Sol. (*a*) The number of hospitals existing in village X is not sufficient to meet the needs of its residents. Hence, it is important to open some more hospitals in village X. Hence, only Assumption I is implicit.

Based on Three or more Assumptions

Example 3 **In this question, a statement is given, followed by three Assumptions I, II and III. You have to take the statement to be true even if it seems to be at variance with commonly known facts. You have to decide which of the given assumptions, If any, logically supports the given statement.**

UP Police Head Operator 2024

Statement

An advertisement by a computer company for computer literate housewives. "A rare opportunity to become a professional while you are at home."

Assumptions

I. Some housewives aspire to become professionals simultaneously.

II. The computer industry is growing at a rapid pace.

III. It is possible to be a professional as well as a housewife.

(a) All the assumptions are implicit
(b) Assumptions I and III are implicit
(c) Assumptions I and II are implicit
(d) Assumptions II and III are implicit

Sol. (*b*) This advertisement is for housewives who wish to become professionals and it is possible to be a housewife as well as a professional.

Hence, Assumptions I and III are implicit.

Example 4 **A retailer aims to generate higher sales by attracting more customers to the store. They have increased their marketing budget on activities and promotions.**

Identify which of the following assumptions is implicit in the above statement?

UPSSSC 2018

(a) Higher marketing expenditure will lead to employee motivation and efficiency.
(b) Activities and promotions will increase footfall in the store and more customers mean more purchases and more business.
(c) Higher marketing expenditure will improve negotiating power with vendors and increase margins.
(d) Increase in marketing expenditure will improve product availability and reduce opportunity loss due to out-of-stock.

Sol. (*b*) If the store increases its budget on activities and promotions, the number of customers visiting the store will increase and the increased number of customers will lead to more purchases and more business, allowing the store to achieve its higher sales target.

Hence, Assumption (b) is implicit in the given statement.

> ***Trending Concept***
> Question based on statement and assumption are asked in examination such as UP Police Head Operator, UPSSSC, RRB NTPC, RRB Group-D.
> It is very important for the upcoming examination.

Chapter Challenge

Based on Two Assumptions

Directions (Q. Nos. 1-10) *In each of the questions below, a statement is given followed by two assumptions, numbered I and II. Consider the statement and the given assumptions and decide which of the two assumptions is implicit in the statement.*

(a) Only Assumption I is implicit
(b) Only Assumption II is implicit
(c) Neither Assumption I nor II is implicit
(d) Both Assumptions I and II are implicit

1. **Statement** "When our son starts going to college, you will have to give him pocket money of ₹ 100 daily." Mother instructing her husband. ***RRB ALP 2019***
   Assumptions
   I. College going students have some daily expenses.
   II. Boys need not be given any pocket money until they start going to college.

2. **Statement** To reach Bangalore quickly from Mumbai, take a flight. ***RRB NTPC 2021***
   Assumptions
   I. Bangalore and Mumbai are connected by air service.
   II. There is no other means of transport to go from Bangalore to Mumbai.

3. **Statement** Eating food heated in plastic utensils causes cancer, so it should be avoided. ***RRC Group D 2022***
   Assumptions
   I. Simply storing food in plastic containers is not harmful to health.
   II. There are non-plastic utensils available that can be used to heat food.

4. **Statement** All mammals are warm-blooded animals.
   Assumptions ***SSC (10+2) 2024***
   I. Dogs are warm-blooded animals.
   II. All warm-blooded animals are mammals.

5. **Statement** The demand for smartphones and laptops has increased significantly since online classes started in schools. ***RRC Group D 2022***
   Assumptions
   I. People are buying smartphones and laptops to enable their children to attend online classes.
   II. Desktop computers cannot be used to attend online classes.

6. **Statement** One should wake up early in the morning and do exercise. ***SSC (10+2) 2022***
   Assumptions
   I. It is not possible to exercise at any other time of the day.
   II. People who exercise early in the morning are more fit than those who do not exercise.

7. **Statement** The fuel prices in India are increasing day by day and there is no upper limit to the increase in its price. ***SSC CGL (Tier-II) 2023***
   Assumptions
   I. The central and state governments have not cut their special taxes on fuel.
   II. The effect of inflation in the international market is responsible for the rising prices of fuel.

8. **Statement** A software engineer changes his jobs more frequently than other professionals. ***Rajasthan Police Constable 2022***
   Assumptions
   I. Software engineers are more greedy.
   II. The job requirements of a software engineer are more challenging.

9. **Statement** The customer can avail banking services at his home. ***RRB NTPC 2022***
   Assumptions
   I. This will create problems for the bank.
   II. Customers will be very happy with this service.

10. **Statement** 27 years of imprisonment made Mihir Kalal the President. ***UP Police Constable 2024***
    Assumptions
    I. Whoever remains in prison for 27 years will become the President.
    II. Imprisonment is a qualification to become President.

11. **Statement** 'State B government has now decided to create a department for information technology to help coordinate and adopt information technology' is a news item.
    If the above statement is true, which of the following assumptions must have been made while making the statement?
    (a) State B is considered lax in taking any step in public interest.
    (b) State B has achieved greater success in information and technology as compared to other state governments.
    (c) Each state needs to coordinate and regulate information and technology work.
    (d) State B has the necessary funds to spend on such activities.

12. **Statement** 'Swachh Bharat', keep your city clean, campaign launched by the apartment association did not get much response from its residents.
    Considering the above statement and the given assumptions, decide which assumption is implicit in the statement. ***RRB ALP 2018***
    Assumptions
    I. Local residents do not want to keep their apartments clean.
    II. The Association failed in the campaign.

(a) Only Assumption I is implicit
(b) Only Assumption II is implicit
(c) Neither Assumption I nor II is implicit
(d) Both Assumptions I and II are implicit

Directions (Q. Nos. 13-27) *A statement is given followed by two assumptions I and II. You have to decide which of the given assumptions is/are implicit in the statement, assuming all the information given in the statement to be true.*

(a) Only Assumption II is implicit
(b) Both Assumptions I and II are implicit
(c) Only Assumption I is implicit
(d) Neither Assumption I nor II is implicit

13. Statement "To keep the employees engaged with the company, we should reward them with monthly benefits," the president of the company told the manager. ***RRC Group D 2022***

Assumptions

I. Employees will be happy with monthly benefits.
II. Employees will be punctual.

14. Statement Rekha's investment in the stock market at this time is just a gamble. ***Rajasthan Police Constable 2022***

Assumptions

I. She may suffer loss in the stock market.
II. She may get good returns in the stock market.

15. Statement To expand its business, a new company now needs more employees. ***RRB NTPC 2021***

Assumptions

I. The current staff is inefficient.
II. Business can always be expanded by hiring new employees.

16. Statement The Union Ministry of Road Transport and Highways is preparing to build a super expressway to connect Delhi and Mumbai, which will allow travellers to complete the 1400 km long journey within 12 hours. ***RRC Group D 2022***

Assumptions

I. The condition of the road between the two cities is very bad.
II. At present there is no road connecting these two cities in India.

> **MRC*****
> ***(Most Repeating Concepts)***
> Questions Nos. 1, 4, 7, 10, 16, 28 and 34 are important from the examination point of view. Questions based on these concepts are important for examination such as SSC CGL, UP Police Constable, Group D NTPC ALP, MPPSC etc.

17. Statement Can India become a terrorism free country in future? ***RRB NTPC 2021***

Assumptions

I. India has declared a zero tolerance policy.
II. India's security establishment is working hard on all fronts.

18. Statement Children share their feelings more with their friends than with their parents. ***RRB NTPC 2021***

Assumptions

I. Children feel that their friends will understand their feelings better than their parents.
II. Children nowadays are not friendly with their parents.

19. Statement Warning "Consumption of alcohol is injurious to health". ***RRB ALP 2018***

Assumptions

I. No warning is required.
II. People who do not consume alcohol remain healthy.

20. Statement 'Oh what if' is better than 'what if'.

Assumptions ***UPSSSC 2018***

I. You should try before giving up because of the problems.
II. Even if you fail, you will learn how to deal with the problem.

21. Statement Only dead fish go with the flow.

Assumptions ***UPSSSC 2018***

I. Fish cannot swim with the flow.
II. Every person must have the ability to think and take decisions.

22. Statement Crying children are able to attract more attention of the parents. ***RRB Group D 2018***

Assumptions

I. They are unable to communicate properly.
II. Parents are caught up in their work and leave the children to play by themselves.

23. Statement Even after providing improved variety of cotton seeds, the cotton crop continues to be poor.

Assumptions

I. Cotton yield was expected to increase after introduction of improved variety seeds.
II. Before the introduction of improved variety seeds the cotton yield was sufficient.

24. Statement There should be uniformity in charging various fees in government aided schools.

Assumptions

I. Government subsidies come from collecting money from people through taxes.
II. While giving subsidy the government may have imposed some conditions regarding maintaining uniformity in fees.

25. Statement Retired IAS officer Shri Rai has taken over as the Director of All India Nuclear Research Institute. It is hoped that now the administration of the institute will improve.

Assumptions

I. There was no Director in the institute before Mr. Rai.
II. The Director is expected to look after the administration of the Institute.

Chapter Challenge Statement and Assumptions

26. **Statement** The government has started a scheme to provide coaching to students from weaker sections so that they can improve their educational level.

Assumptions

I. Coaching classes will help the students from weaker sections of the society to do well academically.

II. Students from weaker sections of the society are educationally backward.

27. **Statement** 'Army should be immediately deployed in this area to restore peace and normalcy' - A news item.

Assumptions

I. Army's help can also be taken for such purposes.

II. Only the Army can restore peace.

Directions (Q. Nos. 28-32) *Each of the following questions consists of a statement followed by two assumptions I and II given below it. You have to consider the given assumptions and decide which of the assumptions is/are strong in the statement. Choose the correct answer from the given options.* ***MPPSC 2018***

(a) Assumption I is strong
(b) Assumption II is strong
(c) Both assumptions I and II are strong
(d) Neither assumption I nor II is strong

28. **Statement** Conservation of rivers is very important nowadays.

Assumptions

I. It will reduce the water crisis.

II. It will protect our ecological life system.

29. **Statement** Many government services have now been brought under the Right to Information (RTI) Act.

Assumptions

I. It will bring more transparency.

II. This will bring more accountability.

30. **Statement** All citizens have the right to challenge the decisions of lower courts in the High Court.

Assumptions

I. Lower courts are not efficient while High Courts are better.

II. There may be a possibility of error in decision.

31. **Statement** Parliamentary democracy operates in many countries.

Assumptions

I. It represents the aggregate opinion of the public.

II. It always fulfills the aspirations of the people.

32. **Statement** Almost all appointments have a probation period of one or two years and confirmation of the job takes place after the probation period.

Assumptions

I. The employer does not know much about the employee.

II. The employer wants more work done during the probation period.

Based on Three or more Assumptions

Directions (Q. Nos. 33-36) *In each of the questions below is given a statement followed by three assumptions, numbered I, II and III respectively. Considering the statement and the given assumptions, find out which of the three assumptions is implicit in the statement.*

33. **Statement** The manager of a garment company announced, "We are going to expand our company, so we need to hire more tailors."

Assumptions

I. The existing tailors are not able to make modern designs.

II. There will be more sales after expansion.

III. There is a need to produce more before expanding. ***RRB Group D 2018***

(a) Only Assumption I is implicit
(b) Only Assumption II is implicit
(c) Both Assumptions I and III are implicit
(d) Both Assumptions II and III are implicit

34. **Statement** Read the instructions before you start playing the game.

Assumptions

I. The game is being held.

II. No blind person is playing.

III. The players are literate. ***RRB Group D 2018***

(a) Only Assumption I is implicit
(b) All Assumptions are implicit
(c) No Assumption is implicit
(d) Assumptions I and III are implicit

35. **Statement** Think in high groups without paying huge price -Book a luxurious flat with us, this is an advertisement of a building construction company for its prestigious project.

Assumptions

I. It is possible to join the select group of rich people through hard work.

II. Living in style without paying heavy price is the criterion of high people in the society.

III. Booking a luxurious flat has now become very easy.

(a) Only Assumption II is implicit
(b) Only Assumption III is implicit
(c) Both Assumptions II and III are implicit
(d) None of the above

36. **Statement** There is no proper staff in certain labour and industrial courts of this state. The posts of judges and stenographers are lying vacant. Statement of a retired judge of 'X' state.

Assumptions

I. Adequate number of employees and judges helps in smooth functioning of the Industrial and Labour Court.

II. The State is not concerned about the condition of the Labour and Industrial Court.

III. The physical facilities of an office help in increasing the efficiency of its employees.

(a) Only Assumption I is implicit
(b) Only Assumption II is implicit
(c) Assumptions I and III are implicit
(d) All Assumptions are implicit

37. I like to shop at those stores which have more offers and discounts, so, I choose to shop more at GMart and less at Bills Bazaar.

Identify which of the following assumptions is implicit in the above statement? ***UPSSSC 2018***

(a) Both GMart and Bills Bazaar offer more offers and discounts.
(b) There are no offers and discounts in the Bills Bazaar.
(c) GMart has more offers and discounts than Bills Bazaar.
(d) Bills Bazaar has more offers and discounts than GMart.

Right Key

1. (a)	2. (a)	3. (b)	4. (a)	5. (a)	6. (c)	7. (c)	8. (c)	9. (b)	10. (c)
11. (c)	12. (b)	13. (c)	14. (b)	15. (d)	16. (d)	17. (b)	18. (c)	19. (d)	20. (d)
21. (a)	22. (b)	23. (c)	24. (d)	25. (a)	26. (b)	27. (c)	28. (c)	29. (c)	30. (b)
31. (a)	32. (a)	33. (d)	34. (b)	35. (c)	36. (d)	37. (c)			

Solutions

1. *(a)* College going students have some daily expenses. Hence, only Assumption I is implicit.

2. *(a)* It is clear from the given statement that Bangalore and Mumbai are connected by air service. Hence, only Assumption I is implicit. It is not stated in the statement that there is no other means of going from Bangalore to Mumbai. Hence, Assumption II is not implicit.

3. *(b)* Assumption I says that storing food only in plastic containers is not harmful, hence contradicts the statement.

Assumption II says that we can use other utensils for heating the food as the statement says that plastic utensils should be avoided for heating the food.

Therefore, only Assumption II is implicit.

4. *(a)* All mammals are warm blooded and dog is a mammal. So, we can say that dog is also warm-blooded animal. we can't say that all warm-blooded animals are mammals.

Hence, only Assumption I is implicit.

TOP TIPS How immediate conclusions are drawn from the law of change can be seen in the chapter called Syllogism.

5. *(a)* People are buying smartphones and laptops to enable their children to attend online classes, which has led to a significant increase in the demand for smartphones and laptops.

Hence, only Assumption I is implicit.

6. *(c)* Exercise can be done at any time. Hence, neither Assumption I nor II is implicit.

7. *(c)* Reduction in fuel taxes will reduce the price of fuel. There are many reasons for the increase in fuel prices.

Therefore, neither Assumption I nor II is implicit.

8. *(c)* Neither Assumption I nor II is implicit. Software engineers change their jobs frequently to improve their career, search for new opportunities and increment in salary.

9. *(b)* 'The consumer can avail banking services at his home'.

From the above statement we can say that if banking services become easy for the consumer, then the consumer will be very happy with this service. Also the bank will get more profit from this service because the number of their customers will increase. Hence, only Assumption II is implicit.

10. *(c)* The statement does not show that being in Jail for 27 years made Mihir Kalal the President. There may be other reasons or events for this and the statement does not say that imprisonment is a qualification for becoming the President. Hence, neither Assumption I nor II is implicit.

11. *(c)* It is clear from the given statement that every state needs to coordinate and regulate information and technology work because one of the things mentioned in the statement is to create a department.

Hence, Assumption (c) is implicit in the given statement.

12. *(b)* It can be clearly said from the given statement that the association has failed in the campaign, but we cannot say that the local residents do not want to keep their apartments clean.

Hence, only Assumption II is implicit.

13. *(c)* According to the statement, the president of the company told the manager that we should reward the employee with monthly benefits. With such rewards, the employees will be happy and will also work well. But nothing has been said about punctuality in the statement. So, only Assumption I is implicit.

14. *(b)* It is given in the statement that investment by Rekha in the stock market is a gamble, from this it is clear that either Rekha should buy shares or the market may incur losses or it may also give good returns. Hence, both Assumptions I and II are implicit.

15. *(d)* It is clear from the given statement that neither Assumption I nor II is implicit as it is not true that a business can always expand by hiring new employees and the statement does not say that the present staff is inefficient.

16. *(d)* The statement neither says that the condition of the road is bad nor that there is no road connecting these two cities in India. Hence, neither Assumption I nor II is implicit.

17. *(b)* Both the Assumptions are important and interlinked to become a terror free country in the future.

18. *(c)* Because children feel that their friends will understand their feelings better than their parents, children share their feelings more with their friends than with their parents. Therefore, only Assumption I is implicit.

19. *(d)* The statement warns that alcohol consumption is harmful for health. It does not follow from this that warning is not needed nor does it follow from this that people who do not consume alcohol remain healthy.
Hence, neither Assumption I nor II is implicit.

TOP TIPS Such warnings are often issued by governments and social organisations "in the public Interest", and there is a specific reason for issuing them.

20. *(d)* Both the Assumptions emphasise on not giving up and continuously trying.
Hence, neither Assumption I nor II is implicit.

21. *(a)* Only Assumption II is implicit, because here the synonym of fish is a common human. The human goes with the crowd, who does not have the power to think and understand.
Therefore, a person should take a decision after thinking carefully.

22. *(b)* Crying babies attract more attention from parents, from this it can be inferred that children are unable to communicate well. It can also be assumed that parents get busy with their work and leave the children to play on their own. It is clear that both the Assumptions are implicit in the statement.

23. *(c)* Before giving improved seeds, the cotton yield was not sufficient, so improved variety seeds were given. Hence, Assumption II is totally irrelevant, but it is quite clear that after giving improved variety seeds, the cotton yield was likely to increase. Hence, only Assumption I is implicit in the statement.

24. *(d)* Since, none of the Assumptions is related to the statement, neither any tax nor any conditions are discussed in the statement. Hence, neither Assumption I nor II is implicit in the statement.

25. *(a)* Mr. Rai has been appointed as the Director to look after the administration of the institute. Hence, Assumption II is implicit in the statement, while Assumption I is irrelevant, because it is not stated in the statement that the institute was running without a Director before Mr. Rai.

26. *(b)* Students from weaker sections of society have been deprived of coaching due to lack of money, as a result of which they are educationally backward, but if the government provides them coaching facilities, then definitely coaching classes will help them and they will be able to improve their educational level.
Hence, both Assumptions I and II are implicit in the statement.

27. *(c)* Army should be immediately deployed in the area to restore peace and normalcy. Only Assumption I is consistent with the statement because army is used by the government to establish peace.
Assumption II is irrelevant because the Army alone cannot restore peace in any area. The government has other resources as well.

28. *(c)* Both Assumptions I and II are strong, because conservation of rivers will naturally reduce water crisis and conservation of water will also protect the life system.

29. *(c)* Both Assumptions I and II are strong because the Right to Information (RTI) Act brings transparency as well as ensures accountability of government departments.

30. *(b)* Having a High Court in the country does not mean that the lower courts are not efficient, but it is definitely possible that there may be an error in the decision, if a citizen is not satisfied with the justice of the lower court, then he can go to the High Court. Therefore, only Assumption II is strong.

31. *(a)* Assumption I is strong because in Parliamentary democracy there is direct rule or representation of the people and the elected representatives inform the Parliament about the problems of the people. Assumption II is irrelevant because Parliamentary democracy cannot always fulfill the aspirations of everyone.

32. *(a)* The purpose of probation period is not to get more work done but to let the employer know whether the employee is capable of doing the work. How much understanding does he have and how is his behaviour at the workplace. The probation period is also a way to provide training to the employer.
Therefore, only Assumption I is strong.

33. *(d)* According to the statement, the manager of the company has announced that they are going to expand their company, so, they need to hire more tailors. So, Assumptions II and III are implicit in the statement, while Assumption I is not implicit in the statement.

34. *(b)* It is clear from the given statement that the game is being organised and the instructions are being asked to be read i.e. the players are literate and no player is blind. Hence, all the Assumptions are implicit.

35. *(c)* It is clear from the given statement that living in luxury without paying a heavy price is the criterion of the upper class people in the society and now it has become very easy to book a luxurious flat. The advertiser knows the preferences of the people and taking advantage of this, he tempts people, which also benefits the people. Hence, both Assumptions II and III are implicit.

36. *(d)* All the three Assumptions are implicit because there is no proper place in the statement and all the terms are lying vacant.

37. *(c)* Since, a person prefers to shop at those stores which have more offers and discounts, a person shops more at GMart and less at Bills Bazaar. This means Gmart has more offers and discounts than Bills Bazaar.

CHAPTER

26 Statement and Courses of Action

Statement and Courses of Action

Course of Action is the feasible step to be taken after an event has happened or is about to happen.

In this chapter, a situation is presented and some courses of action are suggested in the context of that situation.

Candidates have to identify the correct course of action, which either reduces the problem or improves the situation. Course of action should be feasible and should relate with the practical aspect of life.

Based on Two Courses of Action

In this type of questions, a statement is given followed by two courses of action numbered I and II.

The candidate is required to understand the statement, analyse the problem or issue mentioned by it and then decide which of the courses of action logically follows.

e.g. A statement followed by two courses of action numbered I and II are given below. You have to assume everything in the statement to be true and on the basis of the information given in the statement, decide which of the suggested courses of action logically follows for pursuing.

Statement Trade Unions slow down the industrial production.

Courses of Action

I. Trade Unions should be banned.

II. Industry should employ persons on temporary basis.

(a) If only I follows

(b) If only II follows

(c) If both I and II follow

(d) If either I or II follows

Sol. (b) If the industry employs persons on temporary basis then it can improve its productions. So, only course of action II follows.

Score Booster

In simple problems, the course of action should be simple. Make a plan for action, prioritize the tasks and complete them in a systematic manner. Also keep time management and problem solving in mind during taking the action.

Based on Three Courses of Action

In this type of questions, a statement is given followed by three courses of action numbered I, II and III. The candidate is required to assess the given situation and take the administrative decision with regard to the given problem and provide requisite courses of action to be take to lesson the extremities of the problem.

e.g. Statement

The weather bureau has recently forecasted next week's weather of Kashmir in which it said that there is going to be a heavy snowfall for the whole week.

Courses of Action

I. The weather bureau should propagate the information throughout Kashmir through various platforms.

II. The civic bodies must make arrangements to remove snow from roads.

III. The news must be stopped from spreading outside the state.

(a) Only II follows

(b) Only III follows

(c) Both I and II follow

(d) All I, II and III follow

Sol. (c) The weather bureau should propagate the information throughout Kashmir through various platforms and also the civic bodies must make arrangements to remove snow from roads. So, both I and II follow.

Questions asked under this chapter consists of a statement or a problem given in the form of a statement. After that, the required action is given to deal with these problems/situations. Candidates have to analyze the action closely and decide which action/actions would be appropriate in the given circumstances.

The aim of this chapter is to test the candidate's ability to take administrative decisions and the logical ability to take appropriate action.

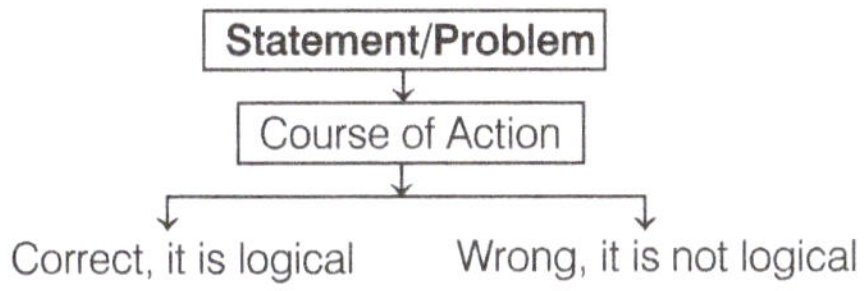

Problems can be divided into the following two types

1. **Ordinary Problem** A problem that requires improvement rather than immediate action. This includes exploitation, juvenile delinquency, unemployment, malnutrition, etc.
2. **Complex Problem** A problem which requires quick and concrete action in a planned manner. It includes communal riots, extremism, epidemic, war, dispute, earthquake etc.

Concept Booster Points

- The action should be directly related to the problem.
- The method of solution should be positive i.e. do not adopt negative action.
- The solution should be practical and should not create any other problems.
- The actions should be sequential according to the nature of the problem.
- All decisions taken on the basis of proceedings should be inspired by the spirit of public welfare based on established law and order, constitutional rules.
- In terms of trend, if the problem given in the statement is complex then the action should be quick.
- There should be uniformity in the decision taken as a proceeding; no action should be narrow or biased.
- The action should not be induced by any outside pressure or pressure group.
- Such action should be chosen which is universally acceptable and acceptable to all.
- If any action is only with words, it weakens the action and the problem should be solved on the basis of experience.
- The proceedings should not be based on personal opinion.

In this chapter two types of questions asked which is given below.

Based on Two Courses of Action

Example 1 **Statement** **There is a large increase in migration of villagers to urban areas as repeated crop failure has put them into finanical problems.**

Course of Action *SSC CGL (Tier-II) 2023*

I. The villagers should be provided with an alternate source of income in their villages which will make them stay there only.

II. To ensure their survivial, the migrated villagers should be given access to all housing options in urban areas.

(a) If only I follows
(b) If only II follows
(c) If both I and II follow
(d) If either I or II follows

Sol. *(a)* Clearly, increased migration would add burden on city's infrastructure. So, attempts should be made to make the villagers comfortable in their villages itself. So, only Course of Action I follows.

Helping Tips

To solve this type of questions the candidates must have the ability to take administrative decisions, a sense of public welfare based on constitutional rules.

Based on Three Courses of Action

Example 2 **Statement Over 27000 bonded labourers identified and freed are still awaiting rehabilitation.**

Courses of Action

I. More cases of bonded labourers should be identified.

II. Till the proper rehabilitation facilities are available, the bonded labourers should not be freed.

III. The impediments in the way of speedy and proper rehabilitation of bonded labourers should be removed.

(a) If Actions I and II follow
(b) If Actions I and III follow
(c) If Action III follows
(d) Both Actions II and III follow

Sol. *(c)* Only Course of Action III provides a feasible and effective solution to combat the problem, that impediments in the way of speedy and proper rehabilitation should be removed while Courses of Action I and II are not effective.

Trending Concept

Questions based on individual action, official action etc., are being asked in the different examination (CGL, ALP, CHSL) these are very important for upcoming exams.

Chapter Challenge

Based on Two Courses of Action

Directions (Q. Nos. 1-8) *Each question given below has a statement followed by two courses of action numbered* I *and* II. *A course of action is a step or administrative decision to be taken for improvement follow up or further action in regard to the problem, policy, etc., on the basis of the information given in the statement. You have to assume everything in the statement to be true, then decide which of the two suggested courses of action logically follows for pursuing.*

Give answer

(a) If only I follows
(b) If only II follows
(c) If either I or II follows
(d) If neither I nor II follows

1. **Statement** Voltage fluctuation in A's home has damaged many of his new electrical appliances.

Courses of Action ***SSC (10+2) 2024***

I. A should consult an electrician and install a device to safeguard appliances against fluctuations in voltage.

II. A must replace all the appliances.

2. **Statement** There is a huge increase in the migration of citizens of Country X to foreign countries as the unemployment rate has been increasing in Country X. ***RRB NTPC 2022***

> ***MRC******
> ***(Most Repeating Concepts)***
> Question Nos. 1, 2, 7, 11, 14 and 18 are very important for exam point of view. Question on these concepts important for RRB NTPC, CHSL, ALP Exam.

Courses of Action

I. The citizens of Country X should be provided with alternate sources of income.

II. Substantial fees should be imposed on all foreign travels by the citizens of Country.

3. **Statement** Many private schools in Bangalore charge more fees than the government- prescribed limits. ***RRB ALP 2018***

Courses of Action

I. Strict action should be taken against such schools.

II. Such schools should be shut down.

4. **Statement** A man wants to get admission in a certain unique elite club. ***UPSSSC Mandi Parishad 2018***

Courses of Action

I. Find and complete the procedure to get entry into the club.

II. Get admission into another club.

5. **Statement** Many villages face flood fury every year in the monsoon. ***CGPSC 2018***

Courses of Action

I. Timely evacuation of the people is necessary.

II. The government should take measures to control floods by building dams etc.

6. **Statement** School uniform is a burden on the poor parents. ***CGPSC 2018***

Courses of Action

I. Poor parents should stop buying school uniform.

II. Schools can provide subsidy on school uniforms.

7. **Statements** Due to heavy rain in Bangalore, the normal lives of the citizens are paralysed. ***RRB ALP 2018***

Courses of Action

I. Government should take measures to help people and avoid life and property destruction.

II. Government should provide free treatment in all the hospitals of Bangalore.

8. **Statement** Teachers in India still teach using traditional methods and are not aware of modern methods of teaching. ***RRB ALP 2018***

Courses of Action

I. Orientation should be done for teachers to change their method of teaching.

II. There should be a pay hike for teachers who teach in modern methods.

9. In this question, a statement is followed by two courses of actions, numbered I and II. You must assume everything in the statement to be true and on the basis of the information given in the statement, decide which of the courses of actions logically follow(s) for pursuing.

Statement

In spite of the principal's repeated warnings, a child was caught with a hidden mobile phone in the school.

Courses of Action ***SSC CHSL (Tier-II) 2024***

I. The mobile phone should be taken away from the child and the parents should be called to the school.

II. The child should be punished for committing this mistake.

(a) Only I follows (b) Both I and II follow
(c) Neither I nor II follows (d) Only II follows

10. Read the given statement and courses of action carefully. Assuming that the information given in the statement is true, even if it appears to be at variance with commonly known fact, decide which of the given courses of action logically follow(s) from the statement. *RRB NTPC 2021*

Statement

Road accidents are going to increase day by day.

Courses of Action

I. Government should start awareness programmes that promote following traffic rules strictly.

II. Government should put a limit on registration of new vehicles.

(a) Neither I nor II follows
(b) Only I follows
(c) Either I or II follows
(d) Only II follows

11. In this question, a statement is follwed by two courses of action, numbered I and II. You must assume everything in the statement to be true and on the basis of the information given in the statement, decide which of the course of action/s logically follows for pursuing.

Statement

Many people have complained to the Finance Ministry regarding a delay in receiving refunds of their Income Tax returns. *SSC CGL (Tier-II) 2025*

Courses of Action

I. The Finance Ministry must institute an enquiry into the complaints received regarding delay in income tax refunds.

II. The Finance Ministry must compensate the income tax payees by paying interest on their refunds for the duration of the delay.

(a) Both I and II follow (b) Only I follows
(c) Neither I nor II follows(d) Only II follows

Directions (Q. Nos. 12 and 13) *In each of the question below is given a statement followed by two courses of action. Course of action is a step for administrative decision to be taken for improvement, follow-up or further action in regard to the problem, policy etc. On the basis of the information given in the statement, you have to assume everything in the statement to be true, then decide which of the given suggested courses of action is/are logically worth pursuing.*

Give answer

(a) If only I follows
(b) If only II follows
(c) If either I or II follows
(d) If both I and II follow

12. Statement The police department has come under a cloud with recent revelations that atleast two senior police officers are suspected to have been involved in the illegal sale of a large quantity of weapons from the state police armoury.

Courses of Action

I. A thorough investigation should be ordered by the State Government to find out all those who are involved into the illegal sale of arms.

II. State police armoury should be kept under Central Government control.

13. Statement The State Government has decided to declare 'Kala Azar' as a notifiable disease under the Epidemic Act. Under the Epidemic Act, 1897, family members or neighbours of the patient are liable to be punished in case they did not inform the State Authorities.

Courses of Action

I. Efforts should be made to efficiently implement the Act.

II. The cases of punishment should be propagated through mass media, so that more people become aware of the stern action.

Based on Three Courses of Action

Directions (Q. Nos. 14-16) *In each question given below has a statement followed by three courses of action numbered* I, II *and* III. *Assuming the statements to be true, decide which of the three courses of action most logically follows.*

Give answer

(a) Only II follows
(b) Only III follows
(c) Both I and II follow
(d) All I, II and III follow

14. Statement If Ritu studies effectively for 6 h daily from today, she will be able to pass the exam which is due after 10 days. *RRB NTPC 2022*

Courses of Action

I. Ritu must effectively study Science for 6 h daily for 10 days to be able to prepare enough to pass her exam.

II. Ritu must plan her time ahead of preparation and give sufficient time to every subject.

III. Ritu must not play during these days which are crucial for her for preparation for exams.

15. Statement The vehicular traffic in New Delhi area has increased considerably these days making it difficult for people to reach on time to Railway Station as vehicles frequently face traffic jams at various places.

Courses of Action

I. The vehicles which are not bound to Railway Station should not be allowed to play on the road connecting the New Delhi area to the Railway Station.

II. The load of vehicular traffic should be diverted through several link roads during the peak hours.

III. The time table of trains should be prepared so as to avoid the congestion during the peak hours.

16. Statement Every year during monsoon, the condition of most of the roads in the city deteriorates causing immense problem to the commuters.

Courses of Action

I. The civic body should include a heavy penalty clause while awarding future contracts for road repairs.

II. The civic officials incharge of maintenance of city roads should be asked to explain why the condition of the roads worsens every year.

III. General public should avoid taking their vehicles out during monsoon.

17. Read the given statement and courses of action carefully and decide which of the courses of action logically follows from the statement.

Statement

The weather bureau has recently forecast next week's weather of Kashmir in which it said that there is going to be a heavy snowfall for the whole week. ***RRB NTPC 2021***

Courses of Action

I. The weather bureau should propagate the information throughout Kashmir through various platforms.

II. The civic bodies must make arrangements to remove snow from roads.

III. The news must be stopped from spreading outside the state.

(a) All the Actions I, II and III follow
(b) Only Action III follows
(c) Only Action II and III follow
(d) Only Action I and II follow

18. Read the given statement and courses of action carefully and decide which of the courses of action logically follows from the statement.

Statement

An epidemic disease has spread in an XYZ area due to contaminated water in a nearby pond. ***RRB NTPC 2021***

Courses of Action

I. Awareness of preventive measures regarding the spread of that disease must be communicated in that area and in the areas nearby.

II. The people of XYZ area must be shifted to other areas populated with healthy people.

III. The contaminated water body must be treated.

(a) Only Actions I and II follow
(b) Only Actions I and III follow
(c) Only Action III follows
(d) Action I, II and III follow

Right Key

1. (a)	2. (a)	3. (a)	4. (a)	5. (b)	6. (b)	7. (a)	8. (a)	9. (b)	10. (b)
11. (a)	12. (a)	13. (d)	14. (a)	15. (a)	16. (c)	17. (d)	18. (b)		

Solutions

1. *(a)* According to the statement as of voltage fluctuation A's home has damaged many of new electrical appliances for the future safety. A should consult an electrician and install a device to safeguard appliances against fluctuation in voltage, but replacement of all the appliances is not the good idea. Hence, only Course of Action I follows.

2. *(a)* An, alternate source of income should be provided to the citizens to reduce unemployment and migration of citizen to foreign countries, while imposing fees on foreign travel won't help to stop migration. Hence, only I follows.

3. *(a)* As, many private schools in Bangalore charge more fees than the government-prescribed limits. So, strict action should be taken against such schools. Hence, only Course of Action I follows.

4. *(a)* Only I follows, if man wants to take admission in a certain unique elite club, then he must find and complete the procedure to get entry into the club.

5. *(b)* The government should build dams and also take other measures to control floods, so that the villages will not have to face flood fury every year in the monsoon. Hence, only II follows.

6. *(b)* The correct course of action for the given statement is schools should provide subsidy on school uniforms.

   Hence, only II follows.

7. *(a)* Yes, government should take measures to help people and avoid life and property destruction. So, only I follows.

TOP TIPS While solving such questions, it is very important to have knowledge of social benefits, social Justice and health services.

8. *(a)* As, per given statement orientation should be done for teachers to change their method of teaching. Hence, only Course of Action I follows.

9. *(b)* Since the act has been repeated despite various warnings. So, the parents of the child should be called for a meeting and also give punishment to set example for him and others is inevitable. Thus, course I and II shall follow.

10. *(b)* According to the question, it is clear that if we have to control or reduce the road accidents, the Government should start awareness programmes that promote following trafic rules strictly.

    Hence, only I follows.

TOP TIPS To solve simple problems, quick and unreasonable action or steps should be avoided, rather the action should be taken in a systematic manner.

11. *(a)* According to the given statement regarding delay in refund of people's Income Tax returns, Finance Ministry must institute an inquiry and also Finance Ministry must compensate the tax payers by paying interest on their refunds.

    Hence, both Courses of Action I and II follow.

12. *(a)* Keeping the State police armoury under the supervision of Central Government control is not the right course of action to bring the guilty to the book. However, an investigation may help to reveal those involved into the illegal acts.

    Hence, only action I is the right course of action.

13. *(d)* It is given in the statement that 'Kala Azar' has been declared as notifiable disease. Since, it is a good effort by the Government, hence effort should be made to implement the Act. Moreover, a deterrent in the form of punishment will ensure effective implementation of the Act.

    Hence, both I and II follow.

14. *(a)* From the given statement it is clear that Ritu must plan her time ahead of preparation and give sufficient time to every subject. Hence, only II follows.

15. *(a)* During the peak hours, the load of vehicular traffic should be diverted through several link roads.

    Hence, Course of Action II follows.

16. *(c)* Action I follows because such a clause would act as a deterrent to inferior standard construction.

    Action II is also a good step as it will make officials responsible.

    Hence, both I and II follow.

17. *(d)* As, recently forecast next week's weather of Kashmir in which it said that there is going to be a heavy snowfall for the whole week.

    So, Courses of Action I and II follow.

18. *(b)* According to the given statement it clear that awareness must be communicated in that area and areas nearby also the contaminated water body must be treated.

    Hence only I and III follow.

CHAPTER

27 Assertion and Reason

Assertion is a strong statement and **Reason** is an explanation about that particular statement.

This type of questions consist of two statements, an assertion and a reason. The candidate must first determine whether each statement is true. If both are true, then it is required to analyse whether the reason is the correct explanation of the assertion.

Sometimes both assertion and reason are correctly stated facts but the reason does not correctly explain the assertion. So, different possibilities can exist between these two statements and accordingly the correct answer is marked from the given alternatives.

Example 1 Read the given statements (Assertion and Reason) carefully and select the most appropriate option with respect to them. ***RRB NTPC 2021***

Assertion (A) Greenland is entirely green.

Reason (R) Polar regions have snow round the year.

(a) Both A and R are true, but R is not the correct explanation of A
(b) Both A and R are false
(c) Both A and R are true and R is the correct explanation of A
(d) A is false but R is true

Sol. (*d*) As, greenland falls in polar region so, there is snow not greenery. Hence, A is false but R is true.

Trending Concept

Questions based on assertion and reason is important for SSC CGL and Railway (NTPC, ALP) exam.

Direction (Ex. No. 2) *Choose the correct alternative from the following options for the Assertion (A) and Reason (R) given below.*

Give answer

(a) If both 'A' and 'R' are true and 'R' is the correct explanation of 'A'
(b) If both 'A' and 'R' are true but 'R' is not the correct explanation of 'A'
(c) If 'A' is true but 'R' is false
(d) If 'A' is false but 'R' is true

Example 2 Assertion (A) We prefer to wear white clothes in winter.

Reason (R) White clothes are good reflectors of heat.

Sol. (*d*) We prefer to wear dark clothes in winter as, they absorb the heat and keep the body warm. However, white clothes are good reflectors of heat that's why we do not prefer to wear white clothes in winter. Hence, A is false but 'R' is true.

Directions (Ex. Nos. 3 and 4) *In each of the following questions, there are two statements labelled as Assertion (A) and Reason (R).*

Give answer

(a) If both 'A' and 'R' are true and 'R' is the correct explanation of 'A'
(b) If both 'A' and 'R' are true but 'R' is not the correct explanation of 'A'
(c) If 'A' is true but 'R' is false
(d) If both 'A' and 'R' are false

Example 3 Assertion (A) Ventilators are provided near the roof.

Reason (R) Conduction takes place better near the roof.

Sol. (*c*) Air, upon heating, rises and so can be thrown out of a room through high ventilators. This is the reason why ventilators are provided near the roof.

Helping Tips

To solve questions based on assertion and reason, one should have a proper knowledge of general knowledge and general science.

Example 4 Assertion (A) Uttar Pradesh is called the 'Sugar Bowl' of India.

Reason (R) Uttar Pradesh is the leading sugarcane producer.

Sol. (*a*) Uttar Pradesh is the leading sugarcane producer of India and this is the reason why this state is called 'Sugar Bowl' of India.

Example 5 Given below is an Assertion followed by two possible reasons numberd I and II. Read the statement carefully and decide which of the two explain(s) the event/observation/information given in the statement.

Assertion Even though Company X is the biggest exporter of wheat in the country, it is not among one of the biggest profit earning companies in the country. ***RRB Technician Grade III 2024***

Reasons

I. Trading in other materials other than wheat, like iron, is much more profitable.

II. Company X has heavy miscellaneous expenditure.

(a) Only I is a possible reason
(b) Neither I nor II is a possible reason
(c) Both I and II are possible reasons
(d) Only II is a possible reason.

Sol. (*c*) According to the given statement, Both reason I and II provide possible explanations for why company X might not be among the top profit-earning companies despite being the biggest wheat exporter. The higher profitability of other materials and the presence of heavy miscellaneous expenses could both contribute to lower profit margins.

Hence, both I and II are the possible reasons.

Score Booster

Sometimes both Assertion (A) and Reason (R) can be true, but they might not be connected to each other. Don't assume one statement explains the other unless it is clearly stated.

Chapter Challenge

1. An Assertion (A) and Reason (R) are given below. Choose the correct alternatives.

   Assertion (A) Leakages in household gas cylinders can be detected.

   Reason (R) LPG has a strong smell.

   (a) Both A and R are true and R is the correct explanation of A
   (b) Both A and R are true and R is not the correct explanation of A
   (c) Both A and R are false
   (d) A is true but R is false

Directions (Q. Nos. 2-4) *In each of the following question, there are two statements labelled as Assertion* (A) *and Reason* (R).

Give answer

(a) If both 'A' and 'R' are true and 'R' is the correct explanation of 'A'
(b) If both 'A' and 'R' are true but 'R' is not the correct explanation of 'A'
(c) If 'A' is true but 'R' is false
(d) If both 'A' and 'R' are false

2. **Assertion** (A) Shimla is colder than Delhi.

   Reason (R) Shimla is at higher altitude as compared to Delhi.

3. **Assertion** (A) Silver is not used to make wires.

   Reason (R) Silver is a bad conductor.

4. **Assertion** (A) In India, females have higher life expectancy than the males.

   Reason (R) Females receive a better diet.

Directions (Q. Nos. 5-7) *Read the given Assertion (A) and a Reason (R) carefully and choose the option that accurately describes the relationship between them.*

(a) Both 'A' and 'R' are true but 'R' is not the correct explanation of 'A'
(b) 'A' is false but 'R' is true
(c) 'A' is true but 'R' is false
(d) Both 'A' and 'R' are true and 'R' is the correct explanation of 'A'

5. **Assertion (A)** Most cars in India are Right hand drive cars i.e. the driver is seated on the right side of the car.

   Reason (R) Indian car companies do not have the knowledge or capacity to make left hand drive cars.

   RRB NTPC 2021

6. **Assertion (A)** Trees grow against gravity.

   Reason (R) Nature defies gravitational law.

   RRB NTPC 2021

7. **Assertion (A)** All prime numbers are odd numbers.

   Reason (R) Prime numbers can only be divided by itself or 1. ***RRB NTPC 2021***

Directions (Q. Nos. 8 and 9) *Select an option which is true regarding the following two statements labelled Assertion* (A) *and Reason* (R).

Give answer

(a) 'A' is true but 'R' is false
(b) Both 'A' and 'R' are true and 'R' is the correct explanation of 'A'
(c) Both 'A' and 'R' are true but 'R' is not the correct explanation of 'A'
(d) Both 'A' and 'R' are false

8. **Assertion (A)** A satellite is not a planet.

   Reason (R) Planets do not revolve around other planets.

   RRB NTPC 2022

9. **Assertion (A)** Some people have darker skin colour.

   Reason (R) Some people have blood of darker colour.

   RRB NTPC 2022

> ***MRC******
> ***(Most Repeating Concepts)***
> Questions Nos. 5, 8, 9, 16, 17 and 20 are very important for the examination point of view. These type of questions are being. asked in examination like RRB NTPC, ALP, MP Police Constable and SSC CGL.

Directions (Q. Nos. 10 and 11) *Choose the correct alternative from the following options for the Assertion* (A) *and Reason* (R) *given below.*

Give answer

(a) if both 'A' and 'R' are true and 'R' is the correct explanation of 'A'
(b) if both 'A' and 'R' are true but 'R' is not the correct explanation of 'A'
(c) if 'A' is true but 'R' is false
(d) if 'A' is false but 'R' is true

10. **Assertion** (A) Methane gas released by some industries leads to global warming.

    Reason (R) Methane is a heavy gas and it settles in the lower regions of the atmosphere.

    UPSSSC Mandi Parishad 2018

11. **Assertion** (A) Railway tracks are longer during the day than at night.

    Reason (R) Days are hotter and metal expands due to heat. ***UPSSSC Mandi Parishad 2018***

Directions (Q. Nos. 12-15) *Each of these questions has an Assertion* (A) *and a Reason* (R).

Give answer

(a) If both 'A' and 'R' are true and 'R' is the correct explanation of 'A'

(b) If both 'A' and 'R' are true but 'R' is not the correct explanation of 'A'

(c) If 'A' is true but 'R' is false

(d) If both 'A' and 'R' are false

12. **Assertion (A)** Inside the Earth, metals are present in molten state.

Reason (R) Earth absorbs the Sun's rays.

13. **Assertion (A)** In India, the judiciary is independent of the executive.

Reason (R) Judiciary favours the government and helps in the implementation of its plans.

14. **Assertion (A)** Red-green colour blindness occurs with more frequency in males than in females.

Reason (R) Females have two chromosomes and males have one.

15. **Assertion (A)** Salt is added to cook food at higher altitudes.

Reason (R) Temperature is lower at higher altitudes.

16. A statement is given below followed by two possible reasons numbered I and II. Read the statement carefully and decide which of the two reasons best explains the event/observation/information given in the statement.

Do you think so?

Assertion (A) On June 14, 2023, long queues were seen outside electricity bill payment counters in city X.

Reason (R) *RRB ALP (CBT-I) 2024*

I. The last date for payment of electricity bills in city X is 15th of every month.

II. In June 2023, many people were not able to pay electricity bills online due to server failure.

(a) Only I is a possible cause

(b) Both I and II are possible reasons

(c) Only II is a possible reason

(d) Neither I nor II is the possible cause

17. Given below is statement followed by two possible reasons numbered I and II. Read the statement carefully and decide which of the two explain(s) the event observation/information given in the statement.

Statement The railway authorities have decided to run two holiday special trains on Tuesday and Friday from City A to City B from 19th October 2023 to 5th January 2024. *RRB ALP 2024*

Reasons

I. Flights from City A to City C are booked to capacity, and airlines are planning to increase the number of flights operating between City A and City C form August 2023.

II. Many migrants from City B who work in city A travel back to City B on trains from October to January for the festivals. The existing trains cannot accommodate this increase in passenger demand.

(a) Neither I nor II is a possible reason

(b) Only I is a possible reason

(c) Only II is a possible reason

(d) Both I and II are possible reasons

18. The following question consists of two statements, one labelled as 'Assertion' and the other as 'Reason'. You have to examine these two statements carefully and choose the correct answer to the question from the given options.

Assertion (A) Benefits of sprinkler system.

Reason (R) Sprinkler system is very expensive and difficult to install. *MP Police Constable 2022*

(a) Both A and R are true

(b) A is false but R is true

(c) A is true but R is false

(d) Both A and R are false

19. The following question consists of two statements one labelled as 'Assertion' and the other as 'Reason'. You have to examine these two statements carefully and choose the correct answer to the question from the given options.

Assertion (A) Energy obtained from fossil fuels is not green energy.

Reason (R) Burning fossil fuels like petrol, diesel or natural gas releases toxic gases and soot particles.

MP Police Constable 2023

(a) A is true, but R is false

(b) Both A and R are false

(c) A is false but R is true

(d) Both A and R are true

20. Given below is a statement followed by two possible reasons numbered I and II. Read the statement carefully and decide which of the two explain(s) the event/observation/information given in the statement?

Assertion

In India, large cities have attracted migrant population from across rural parts of the country. According to 2011 census, in India's six largest metros (Delhi, Mumbai, Chennai, Bengaluru, Kolkata and Hyderabad), approximately 48% of the residents were migrants. *SSC CGL (Tier-II) 2023*

Reasons

I. Migration happens due to availability of better career and economic prospects in cities.

II. Migration happens because people like travelling and exploring new cities.

(a) Only I is a possible reason
(b) Neither I nor II is a possible reason
(c) Both I and II are possible reasons
(d) Only II is a possible reason

Directions (Q. Nos. 21-26) *Choose the correct alternative from the following options for the Assertion* (A) *and Reason* (R) *given below.*

Give answer

(a) if both 'A' and 'R' are true and 'R' is the correct explanation of 'A'
(b) if both 'A' and 'R' are true but 'R' is not the correct explanation of 'A'
(c) if 'A' is true but 'R' is false
(d) if 'A' is false but 'R' is true

21. **Assertion** (A) India is a democratic country.
Reason (R) People elect their own representatives who form the government. ***MAT 2018***

22. **Assertion** (A) In India, 2nd October, is observed as 'Martyr's Day'.
Reason (R) Pt. Nehru was the first Prime Minister of India. ***MAT 2018***

23. **Assertion** (A) Copper is used to make electrical wires.
Reason (R) Copper is a good conductor of electricity. ***MAT 2018***

24. **Assertion (A)** Methane gas released by some industries leads to global warming.
Reason (R) Methane is a heavy gas and it settles in the lower regions of the atmosphere. ***UPSSSC Mandi Parishad 2018***

25. **Assertion (A)** Railway tracks are longer during the day than at night.
Reason (R) Days are hotter and metal expands due to heat. ***UPSSSC Mandi Parishad 2018***

26. **Assertion (A)** India celebrates its Independence Day on 15th August.
Reason (R) India became independent on 15th August 1947. ***MAT 2018***

Right Key

1. (a)	2. (a)	3. (c)	4. (d)	5. (c)	6. (c)	7. (b)	8. (c)	9. (c)	10. (a)
11. (a)	12. (c)	13. (c)	14. (a)	15. (b)	16. (b)	17. (c)	18. (d)	19. (d)	20. (a)
21. (a)	22. (d)	23. (a)	24. (a)	25. (a)	26. (a)				

Solutions

1. *(a)* LPG contains ethyl mercaptan which has strong smell. Because of this, smell leakages in household gas cylinders can be detected.

2. *(a)* Both 'A' and 'R' are true and 'R' is the correct explanation of 'A'. As compared to Delhi, Shimla is situated at a higher altitude and temperature decreases by 1°C for every 165 m of ascent.

3. *(c)* Silver is not used to makes wires, hence 'A' is true but silver is not a bad conductor, it is a good conductor. Hence, 'R' is false.

4. *(d)* 'A' is false because of high birth rate and negligence, females have lower life expectancy than males in India. Although a better diet is a requirement for females but they do not receive that. Thus, both 'A' and 'R' are false.

5. *(c)* 'A' is true but 'R' is false. Cars in India are right hand drive cars but it does not mean that Indian companies do not have knowledge to make left hand drive cars.

6. *(c)* 'A' is true but 'R' is false. Gravitational force of earth attracts everything to its core and trees grow against gravity. But, the nature follows the gravitational laws, it doesn't defies the gravitational law.

7. *(b)* 'A' is false but 'R' is true. Prime numbers are the numbers that can be divided by itself and 1 only. But, it is not necessary that all prime numbers are odd numbers only. As, 2 is even prime number.

TOP TIPS To solve such questions, read both statements carefully and then analyze the assertion and reason are true, after whether that check whether the Reason (R) correctly explains the Assertions (A).

8. *(c)* Satellite is not a planet and planets do not revolve around other planets. Hence, Both 'A' and 'R' are true but 'R' is not the correct explanation of 'A'.

9. *(c)* Some people have darker skin colour and some people have darker blood colour.
Both 'A' and 'R' are true but 'R' is not the correct explanation of 'A'.

10. *(a)* 'A' is true, because methane gas causes global warming. 'R' is true and properly explains 'A' that methane gets settled in troposphere and stratosphere. Methane molecule breaks down into carbondioxide and water and carbondioxide causes green house effect which is the major cause of global warming.

11. *(a)* Assertion bears the fact of thermal expansions in metal. There is a small increment in the dimensions of metalic substances when slowly treated with heat. Hence, both 'A' and 'R' are true and 'R' is the correct explanation of 'A'.

12. *(c)* Inside the Earth, due to high temperature and pressure keep the metals in molten state. The Earth does not absorb the Sun's rays but reflects them.

Hence, 'A' is true but 'R' is false.

13. *(c)* 'A' is true but 'R' is false. As in India, the judiciary is completely independent of the executive and it has no interference in the government affairs.

14. *(a)* Men are much more likely to be colourblind than women because the genes responsible for the most common, inherited colour blindness are on the X chromosome.

Male have only one X chromosome, while females have two X and Y chromosome.

So, 'R' is correct explanation of 'A'.

15. *(b)* As pressure decreases at higher altitudes, water boils much below 100°C, so that the food does not get sufficient heat for being cooked. Salt increases the boiling point of water. 'A' is true as Temperature is lower at higher altitudes.

So, 'R' is also true but not the correct explanation of 'A'.

16. *(b)* According to the statement, both the reasons can be inferred from the long queue for payment of electricity bills. Hence, both I and II are possible reasons.

17. *(c)* According to the given statement, Reason I talks about flights between City A and City C. It is irrelevant to the decision of running special trains between City A and City B.

Reason II directly relates to the increased passenger demand during the festival season (October to January) from City A to City B. The existing trains cannot handle this demand, which justifies the need for additional special trains.

Therefore, only Reason II is a possible reason for the railway authorities decision.

18. *(d)* Through sprinkler system, water is sprayed in the air. It falls on the land surface in the form of artificial rain. This method saves 50% of irrigation water, due to which 2 to 2.5 times more area can be irrigated simultaneously. Installing a Sprinkler Irrigation. System it is expensive.

Hence both Statement (A) and Reason (R) are false.

19. *(d)* Both Assertion (A) and (R) is true, and (R) is the correct explanation of (A). The process of formation of fossil fuels is called fossilization. Burning of fossil fuels like petrol, diesel or natural gas releases toxic gases and soot particles, which pollute the atmosphere. Hence, it is not green energy.

20. *(a)* People migrate to town and cities mainly in search of a job. They go in search of jobs due to lack of employment opportunities available to them in the villages.

Hence, only I is a possible reason.

21. *(a)* Both the 'A' and 'R' are true and the 'R' is correct explanation of 'A'. India, being a democracy, it is a government run by the representatives elected by its people.

22. *(d)* 'A' is false as 2nd October is observed as International Day of non-violence. But 'R' is true.

23. *(a)* Both the 'A' and 'R' are true and the R is correct explanation of A. As, we use copper to make electrical wires because it is a good conductor of electricity.

24. *(a)* 'A' is true, because methane gas causes global warming. 'R' is true and properly explains 'A' that methane gets settled in troposphere and stratosphere. Methane molecule breaks down into carbondioxide and water and carbondioxide causes green house effect which is the major cause of global warming.

25. *(a)* Assertion bears the fact of thermal expansions in metal. There is a small increment in the dimensions of metalic substances when slowly treated with heat.

Hence, both 'A' and 'R' are true and 'R' is the correct explanation of 'A'.

26. *(a)* Both the 'A' and 'R' are true and the 'R' is the correct explanation of 'A'.

As, India became independent on 15th August, 1947, so its Independence Day is celebrated every year on 15th August.

CHAPTER

28 Cause and Effect

Cause and Effect

In cause and effect, two or more statements or one event are given. The given statements can either be independent causes or effects of independent causes or common causes. It is also possible that one of these statements is the effect of the other statement. In this, the statements are classified as either 'cause' or 'effect'. According to the statements, the relationship existing between them has to be understood well and has to be found correctly.

Based on Two Statements

In this type of questions, there are two statements, which are either cause or an effect. (or they can be effects of independent causes). Out of these two statements, the cause and effect have to be found out.

e.g. In the following question, two statements I and II are given. There may be a relation between statement and cause or they may be independent cause or they may be effects of independent causes.

Statements

I. Most of the students of the school passed in mathematics in the annual examination.

II. Most of the students of the school failed in english in the annual examination.

Given answer

(a) Statement I is the cause and statement II is the effect.

(b) Statement II is the cause and statement I is the effect.

(c) Statements I and II are both effects of a common cause

(d) Statements I and II are both effects of independent causes.

Sol. (c) Most of the students of the school passed in mathematics in the annual examination and most of the students failed in english in the annual examination, both these statements are different. There is no relation between these two statements. Therefore, it can be said that both the statements are effects of a common cause.

Based on more than Two Statements/Effect

In this type of questions, more than two statements are given which can either be a cause or an effect of a particular situation given in the question. Candidate has to analyse the statements and choose the correct options.

e.g. The government has decided to build an eight-lane superhighway in the state so that vehicles can travel at high speed. Which one of the following could be the effect that is implicit in the above statements?

(a) The government has sufficient resources to construct the proposed superhighway.

(b) The people of the state can oppose this decision of the government because the government will take away their agricultural land to build the highway.

(c) It may be difficult for the government to nominate a suitable contractor to construct the highway.

(d) There are no other highways in the state which can be used for transportation of goods.

Sol. (a) The government has decided to build an eight-lane superhighway across the state so that vehicles can travel at high speed. From the given statement, it can be inferred that the government has sufficient resources to build the proposed superhighway.

Score Booster

In questions based on cause and effect, decisions should be taken according to the statements after carefully understanding the relationship existing between them.

Exam Approach Examples

Based on Two Statements

Directions (Ex. Nos. 1 and 2) *In each question below are given two statements I and II. These statements may be either independent causes or effects of independent causes or common causes. One of these statements may be the effect of the other statement. Read both the statements and decide which of the following answer options correctly depicts the relationship between these two statements?*

Example 1 **Statements** *RRB NTPC 2021*

I. Police has increased vigilance till late night.

II. Incidents of petty crimes have decreased late at night.

(a) Both Statements I and II are effects of the same cause
(b) Both Statements I and II are independent causes
(c) Statement I is the possible cause and Statement II is its possible effect
(d) Statement II is the possible cause and Statement I is its possible effect

Sol. (*c*) Police has increased vigilance during late nights is the possible cause and decrease in the incidents of petty crimes during late night hours is its possible effect.

Trending Concept

Questions based on two statements are being repeatedly asked in Railway-(Group D, NTPC) and UPSSSC examination.

Example 2 **Statements**

I. Several incidents of theft have been recorded in jewellery shops in the remote suburbs of the city.

II. Shopkeepers of the city and suburbs have demanded the police authority to improve the security situation.

(a) Statement I is the cause and Statement II is the effect
(b) Statement II is the cause and Statement I is the effect
(c) Both Statements I and II are independent causes
(d) Both Statements I and II are effects of independent causes

Sol. (*a*) Many incidents of theft have been recorded in the jewellery shops in the outlying suburbs of the city due to which the shopkeepers of the city and suburbs have demanded the police authority to improve the security situation. Hence, Statement I is the cause and Statement II is its effect.

Example 3 **In the given question two Statements I and II are given. These statements may be either independent causes or effects of independent causes or common causes. One of these statements may be the effect of the other statement. Read both the statements and decide which of the following answer choices correctly describes the relationship between these two statements?**

Statements

I. Many plant and animal species are becoming extinct with the passage of time and the ecological balance is getting disturbed.

II. Large scale deforestation is taking place for the development of infrastructure and expansion of towns and cities.

(a) Both Statements I and II are independent causes
(b) Statement II is the cause and Statement I is the effect
(c) Statement I is the cause and Statement II is the effect
(d) Both Statements I and II are effects of some common cause

Sol. (*a*) On the basis of the given two statements, it can be said that the extinction of plant and animal species over time and the large-scale deforestation for the expansion of towns and cities are two different things. Hence, it can be said that both Statements I and II are independent causes.

Based on more than Two Statements/Effects

Example 4 **Statement Cement manufacturing companies have increased the prices of cement by about 15% with immediate effect.**

Which of the following is/are the possible effects of the above statement?

I. The government will instruct cement manufacturing companies to reduce the price increase to 5%.

II. The prices of residential flats and commercial companies will see an upward trend.

III. Construction companies may stop all ongoing construction projects with immediate effect.

(a) Only Statement II
(b) Only Statement I
(c) Only Statement III
(d) Both Statements II and III

Sol. (*d*) Only II and III effects can occur in the given statement, because cement manufacturing companies have increased the prices of cement by about 15% with immediate effect. The possible effect of this reason will be that the prices of residential flats and commercial companies will show an upward trend, and it is also possible that construction companies may stop construction projects with immediate effect.

Helping Tips

In the given questions, the cause always occurs before the effect. Therefore, we should first find out what the effect is?

Example 5 **Statement In the first two months of monsoon, the condition of the city roads has deteriorated a lot and there are big potholes on the roads. Which of the following can be the possible effect of the above statement?**

(a) The Municipal Corporation had repaired the city roads with good quality material before the onset of monsoon
(b) A large number of people suffer spinal cord injuries after regularly travelling long distances on intra-city roads
(c) In past, the Municipal Corporation has been careful in selecting contractors for repairing roads
(d) People always complain about potholes on the roads during the monsoon months

Sol. (*b*) A large number of people have suffered spinal injuries due to long distance travelling regularly due to huge potholes on the roads.

Therefore, the effect of the given statement is in option (b).

Chapter Challenge

Based on Two Statements

1. Without assuming anything beyond the given information, choose the correct nature of relationship between Event A and Event B.

Event A Ronit went to the dentist.

Event B Ronit had a toothache. ***RRB NTPC 2021***

(a) Event B is the effect and Event A is its immediate and major cause
(b) Event A is the effect but Event B is not its immediate and major cause
(c) Event B is the effect but Event A is not its immediate and major cause
(d) Event A is the effect and Event B is its immediate and major cause

> ***MRC******
> ***(Most Repeating Concepts)***
> Questions Nos. 1, 2, 3, 7, 8, 9, 13, 15, 16 are important from the examination point of view. The questions based on cause and effect are repeatedly asked in RRB NTPC and UPSSSC examination.

2. Two Statements, I and II have been given. These statements may be independent causes or effects of independent causes or a common cause. One of the statements may be the effect of the other statement. Read both the statements and select the correct option. ***SSC (10+2) 2024***

I. Refreshing and delicious salads are full of antioxidants, Vitamin A, Vitamin C, folate, calcium, fibre and phytonutrients, which are good for health.
II. It is a perfect way to begin our day with salads in order to lead a healthy life.

(a) Both I and II are independent causes
(b) II is the cause and I is its possible effect
(c) I is the cause and II is its possible effect
(d) Both I and II are effects of independent causes

3. Two Statements I and II have been given. These statements may be independent causes or effects of independent causes or a common cause. One of the statements may be the effect of the other statement. Read both the statements and select the correct option. ***SSC (10+2) 2024***

I. All undergraduate exams scheduled for tomorrow in Balasore have been cancelled by the university. New dates will be announced early next week.
II. High winds and very heavy rains are expected in Balasore tomorrow as the cyclone makes a landfall by 3 pm.

(a) II is the cause and I is its possible effect
(b) Both I and II are effects of independent causes
(c) Both I and II are independent causes
(d) I is the cause and II is its possible effect

Directions (Q. Nos. 4-6) *In the questions given below, two statements* I *and* II *are given in each question. These statements may be causes of independent events, their effects, independent events or independent causes. One of these statements may be the effect of the other. Read both the statements and decide which of the following answer options correctly represents the relationship between these two statements?*

Give answer

(a) If Statement I is the cause and Statement II is the effect
(b) If Statement II is the cause and Statement I is the effect
(c) If both Statements I and II are independent causes
(d) If both Statements I and II are effects of independent causes
(e) If both the statements are effects of a common cause

4. **Statements**

I. It is the moral duty of every person in the society to make better efforts to reduce air pollution to protect the health of all the citizens of his country.
II. Due to the tremendously increasing amount of air pollution in our country, many people are getting affected by asthma.

5. **Statements**

I. Groundwater level at every location in Delhi has increased due to last year's monsoon rains.
II. Last year many trains had to be cancelled due to waterlogging on the railway tracks.

6. **Statements**

I. The government has recently fixed the fees for professional courses in unauthorized institutes.
II. Last year, parents of students studying in unauthorized institutes protested against charging of fees higher than the standard prescribed fees.

Directions (Q. Nos. 7-11) *In each question below are given two Statements* I *and* II. *These statements may be either independent causes or effects of independent causes. One of these statements may be the effect of the other statement. Read both the statements and decide which of the following answer options correctly represents the relationship between these two statements?*

Give answer

(a) Statement I is the cause and Statement II is its effect
(b) Statement II is the cause and Statement I is its effect
(c) Both Statements I and II are independent causes
(d) Both Statements I and II are effects of independent causes
(e) If both the statements are effects of a common cause

7. **Statements**

I. There is a possibility of heavy rainfall in the urban areas in the next 48 h.
II. The inter-club cricket tournament scheduled for the week has been cancelled.

8. **Statements**

I. Although there are a large number of mobile phone users in rural India, computers and Internet are still a distant dream.

II. Recently there has been a large scale migration of people from rural areas to urban areas.

9. **Statements**

I. The municipal authority asked all schools in the city to remain closed for the next two days.

II. A big storm is likely to hit the city in the next two days.

10. **Statements**

I. The majority shareholders of the company decided to purchase the shares of the minority shareholders.

II. The company has been incurring losses for the last three quarters.

11. **Statements**

I. In the evening, the roads are jam packed with vehicles, due to which the speed of vehicles reduces considerably.

II. The level of air pollution has increased a lot in the recent past.

Based on more than Two Statements/Effects

12. Sales of four-wheelers in the last six months have declined significantly compared to the number of four-wheelers sold in the same period last year.

Which of the following could be the possible cause of the above phenomenon?

Statements

I. The government has imposed higher excise duty on four-wheelers earlier this year.

II. Petrol prices have increased a lot in the last eight months.

III. Interest rates on housing and car loans have been increasing for the last seven months.

(a) Statements I, II and III (b) Statements I and III
(c) Statements II and III (d) Only Statement II
(e) Only Statement I

13. Given below is a statement (Cause) followed by possible effects numbered I, II and III. Read the 'Cause' carefully and decide which of the three can be the possible effect/s? ***SSC CGL (Tier-II) 2025***

Cause Heavy rains yesterday in City X have caused flooding in many areas including the railway station and airport.

Effects

I. Railways has announced a delay in the departure of three trains scheduled to start from City X this morning.

II. A number of flights were unable to land in the airport of City X last evening.

III. Finance ministry has extended the date for filing tax returns by a month.

(a) Only I is a possible effect
(b) Both I and II are possible effects
(c) Both II and III are possible effects
(d) Only II is a possible effect

14. Given below is a statement (Cause) followed by possible effects numbered I, II and III. Read the 'Cause' carefully and decide which of the three can be possible effect/s? ***SSC CGL (Tier-II) 2025***

Cause Many people in City X have reported receiving two electricity bills this month, instead of one.

Effects

I. The Electricity Board has published the details of areas where power shutdowns are expected tomorrow in City X.

II. The municipal commissioner of City X has clarified that the technical glitch which led to multiple electricity bills being generated would be resolved within 48 h.

III. Long queues were seen outside the electricity board offices in many localities.

(a) Only II is a possible effect
(b) Both I and II are possible effects
(c) Only I is a possible effect
(d) Both II and III are possible effects

15. **Statement** Last week the authorities raided three different business houses.

Which of the following can be a possible outcome of the above statement?

(a) Three business houses are regular defaulters in paying their income tax
(b) The Income Tax Department had received secret information regarding illegal activities in three business houses
(c) The Government has decided to look into the matter and has appointed an enquiry committee
(d) Other business houses took immediate action to pay all their income tax dues to avoid raids on their establishments
(e) The authorities intend to raid many more business houses in the area

16. It has been reported in several leading newspapers that the current year's monsoon may be below expected levels, as many parts of the country are still not receiving adequate rainfall.

Which of the following can be the possible outcome of the above situation?

(a) People from areas affected by low rainfall may migrate to urban areas
(b) The government may announce ex-gratia compensation for all the affected farmers in these areas
(c) The government can declare these areas as drought affected areas
(d) People may blame the government and protest if they do not get enough water for farming
(e) None of the above

17. After the government announced a policy of compensation for farmers in exchange for the acquisition of their land, farmers demanded written proof of this policy. Which of the following could possibly be the reason for demanding written proof ?

(a) In earlier such policies farmers could not protest against inadequate compensation for their land

(b) The compensation assured in the policy was very low

(c) The farmers did not want to surrender their land to the government

(d) Farmers are demanding a certain percentage of the income from their land from the government

(e) The only option to pressurize the government to formulate a compensation policy for farmers is to demand proof

18. **Effect** Due to the decrease in the number of devotees, the temple in the religious place has become desolate.

Which of the following could be the possible reason for the above effect?

(a) A structural engineer had visited the temple a month ago and declared the structure unsafe

(b) The funds accumulated by devotees over many years are rapidly depleting

(c) The local corporation has announced a large sum of money for the renovation of the temple

(d) In the village where there are religious places, there are qualified priests to perform religious rituals

(e) Recently a famous actor visited the temple and had darshan of the deity.

Right Key

1. (d)	2. (c)	3. (a)	4. (b)	5. (a)	6. (b)	7. (a)	8. (d)	9. (b)	10. (c)
11. (d)	12. (a)	13. (b)	14. (d)	15. (d)	16. (c)	17. (a)	18. (a)		

Solutions

1. *(d)* Ronit went to the dentist because he had a toothache. So, Event A is the effect and Event B is its immediate and prime cause.

2. *(c)* The correct answer is that Statement I is the cause and Statement II is its possible effect. To maintain a healthy life, we should began our day with salads because salads are full of antioxidants, vitamins, fibre and phytonutrients which are good for health.

3. *(a)* When heavy rains are expected in Balasore tomorrow due to the cyclone. So, all exams scheduled for tommorow in Balasore have been suspended by the university. So, Statement II is the cause of the bad wheather and Statement I is the possible effect of it.

4. *(b)* Air pollution causes many fatal diseases like asthma, cancer, allergy, cough etc. Therefore, it is the moral duty of every person in the society to protect the environment around him from air pollution. Hence, Statement II is the cause and Statement I is its effect.

5. *(a)* It is clear from Statement I that Delhi received heavy rainfall last year, as a result of which the groundwater level has increased. Hence, Statement I is the cause and Statement II is its effect.

> **TOP TIPS** Sometimes the word 'result' is used in place of 'effect' in questions. Don't get confused by this, follow the same procedure to solve the question.

6. *(b)* It is clear from Statement II that the fees have been fixed by the government only after the protest by the parents. Hence, Statement II is the cause and Statement I is its effect.

7. *(a)* There is a possibility of heavy rain in the urban area in the next 48 h due to which the inter-club cricket tournament scheduled for the week has been cancelled. Hence, Statement I is the cause and Statement II is its effect.

8. *(d)* Although there are a large number of mobile phone users in rural India, computers and the Internet are still a distant dream. Recently, people have migrated from rural areas to urban areas on a large scale.

   Hence, both Statements I and II are effects of independent causes.

9. *(b)* A big storm is expected to hit the city in the next two days, so the municipal authority has asked to close all the schools in the city for the next two days. Hence, Statement II is the cause and Statement I is its effect.

10. *(c)* The company has been incurring losses for the last three quarters. Despite this, the majority shareholders of the company have decided to buy the shares of the minority shareholders. Hence, both Statements I and II are independent causes.

11. *(d)* It is true that the level of air pollution has increased a lot in the recent past and it is also true that in the evening the roads are jam packed with vehicles, due to which the speed of vehicles reduces considerably, but both the Statements are different.

    Hence, both Statements I and II are effects of independent causes.

12. *(a)* At the beginning of this year the government, has imposed higher excise duty on four-wheelers. Petrol prices have increased a lot in the last eight months and interest rates on housing and car loans have been increasing for the last seven months, due to which the sale of four-wheelers in the last six months has decreased a lot compared to the number of four-wheelers sold in the same period last year. Hence, the possible reason for the given event can be all the three Statements I, II and III.

13. *(b)* According to the question, Effect I and II are a direct and logical consequence of the heavy rains and flooding at the airport. Effect III is not a direct consequence of the heavy rains and flooding. There is no logical connection between the weather event and tax filling deadline extension. Therefore, both I and II are possible effects.

14. *(d)* According to the question, Effect I is not a direct consequence of receiving two electricity bills. Effect II is a probable effect as it's reasonable to assume that the authorities would address the issue and provide a resolution, especially if it affects many people. Effect III is also a possible effect as if people receive duplicate bills, they might visit the electricity board offices for clarification or to resolve the issue, leading to longer queues.

15. *(d)* Last week, the officials raided three different business houses, as a result of which other business houses took immediate action to pay all their income tax dues to avoid raids on their establishments. Hence, option (d) is the correct answer.

16. *(c)* It is clear from the newspaper reports that the current year's monsoon may be less than the expected level as many parts of the country are still not receiving adequate rainfall, due to which the government may declare these areas as drought-hit areas.

17. *(a)* The reason why the government demands written proof of compensation from farmers in exchange for acquiring their land is that under earlier such policies farmers could not protest against inadequate compensation for their land.

18. *(a)* A structural engineer visited the temple a month ago and declared the structure unsafe, due to which the number of devotees visiting the temple decreased and the temple became deserted. Hence, option (a) is the correct answer.

CHAPTER

01 Figure Analogy

Analogy

Analogy means similarity. Two figures which are similar in some way or look alike or have similar properties are called analogies and their property is called similarity. In such questions, the relation between both the figures of the first part is established on the basis of which the missing figure of the second part has to find out.

Based on Real Objects

In this type of questions, the relationships between the figures are based on objects visible in daily life.

e.g. In the question given below, the first group is of question figures and the second group is of answer figures. Two pairs of figures are given in the question figure. Just as the figures of the first pair are related to each other, find the second figure of the second pair on the basis of the same relationship.

Question Figures

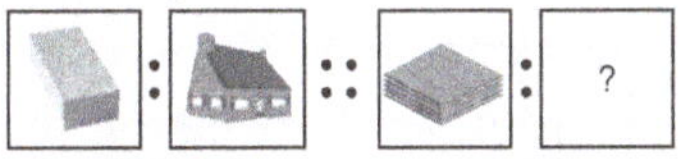

Answer Figures

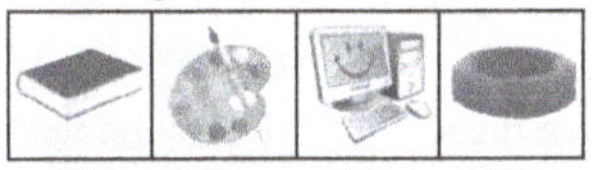

(a) (b) (c) (d)

Sol. (a) As, a house is made from bricks, in the same way a book is made from pages of paper.

Based on Rotation

In this type of questions, the change from one figure to another figure depends on the rotation of the figure. Under this, the second figure rotates at a certain angle in clockwise or anti-clockwise direction with respect to the first figure.

e.g. Find the figure that comes in place of the question mark.

Question Figures

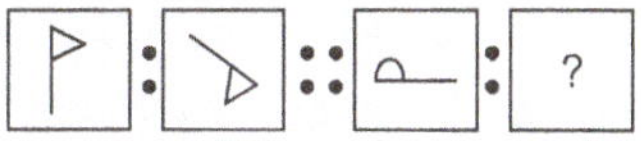

Answer Figures

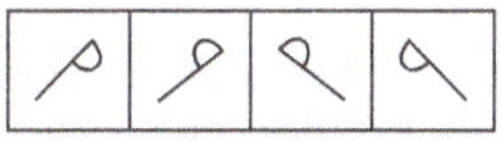

(a) (b) (c) (d)

Sol. (a) After observing the question figures, it is found that the first figure of the first pair of question figures rotates 135° clockwise to form the second figure. Similarly, the first figure of the second pair of question figures rotates 135° clockwise to form the second figure, which will look similar to answer figure (a).

Based on Water/Mirror Image

In this type of questions, the change between the figures is also based on the properties of water/mirror image, under this the second figure is the water or mirror image of the first figure.

e.g. Find the figure that comes in place of the question mark.

Question Figures

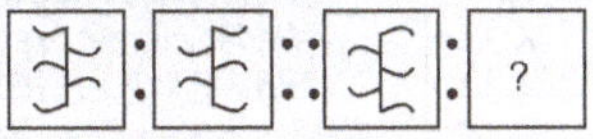

Answer Figures

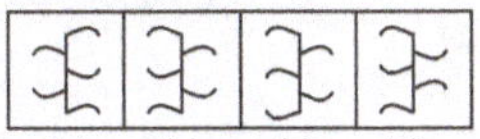

(a) (b) (c) (d)

Sol. (b) After observing the question figures, it is found that the mirror image of the first figure of the first pair of question figures is the second figure. Similarly, the mirror image of the first figure of the second pair of question figures will be the required answer figure, which will look similar to answer figure (b).

Score Booster

Candidates need to understand tricks to understand the figure analogy-check the figure rotation, figure interchange or figure dislocation patterns. Also, regular practice is highly important to develop a better understanding of identifying the relationship.

Based on Splitting/Joining /Transforming Figures Design

In this type of questions, the transformation between figures is based on the division, combining and mutual transformation of the figures design.

e.g. Find the figure that comes in place of the question mark.

Question Figures

Answer Figures

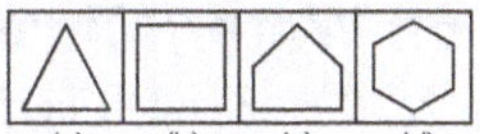

(a) (b) (c) (d)

Sol. (c) After observing the question figures, it is found that the first figure of the first pair of question figures has three sides, which changes to one more sided figure (quadrilateral) in the second figure. Similarly, the first figure of the second pair has four sides, which will change to a five sided figure in the second figure and it will look similar to answer figure (c).

Exam Approach Examples

Based on Real Objects

Example 1 **In the following question, question figures and answer figures are given. A special relationship is established between the first figure and the second figure of the first pair of question figures. The same relationship is established between the first figure of the second pair and one of the alternative figures. Choose this alternative figure.**

Question Figures

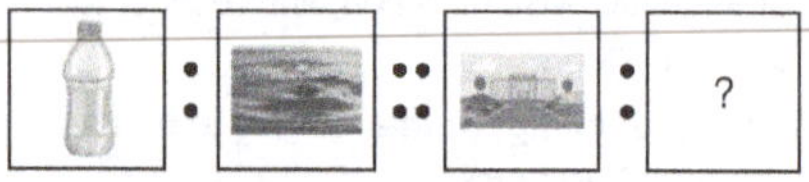

Answer Figures

(a) (b) (c) (d)

Sol. (*a*) As, water is filled in a bottle, in the same way vehicles (cars) are parked in a parking space.

Based on Rotation

Example 2 **In the following question, select the figure which is related to the third figure in the same way as the first figure is related to the second figure.**

Question Figures

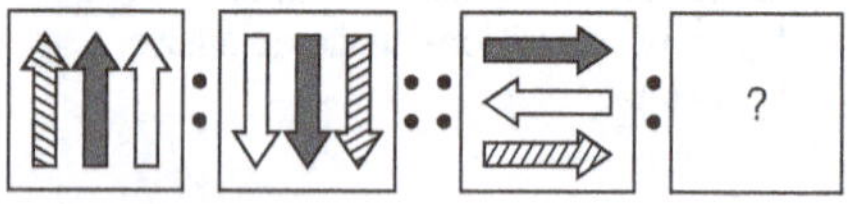

RRB Group-D 2018

Answer Figures

(a) (b) (c) (d)

> **Helping Tips**
> While solving such questions, candidates have to imagine where each part of the object will appear in its image and should mentally turn the object to confirm their answer.

Sol. (*a*) In the first pair, the second figure is obtained by rotating the first figure by 180°.

Similarly, in the second pair, by rotating the first figure 180°, answer figure (a) will be obtained.

Based on Water/Mirror Image

Directions (Ex. Nos. 3 and 4) *In the following questions, select the figure which is related to the third figure in the same way as the first figure is related to the second figure.*

Example 3 Question Figures

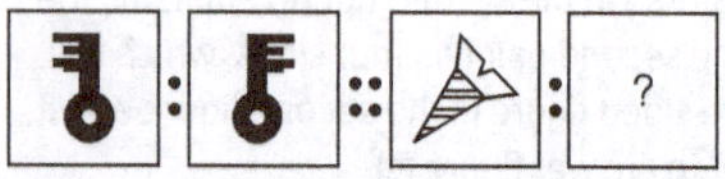

Answer Figures

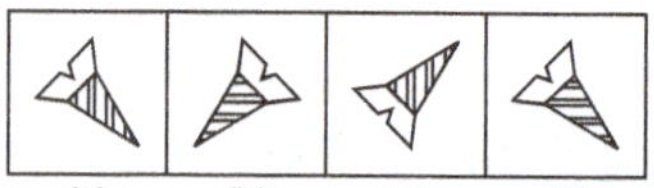

(a) (b) (c) (d)

Sol. (*d*) On observing the question figure, it is clear that the second figure of the first pair is the mirror image of the first figure.

Similarly, the mirror image of the first figure of the second pair will be the figure in option (d).

Example 4 Question Figures

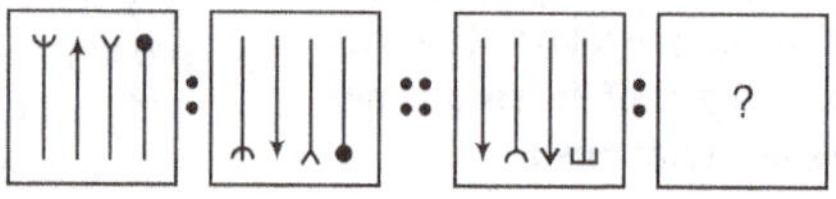

Answer Figures

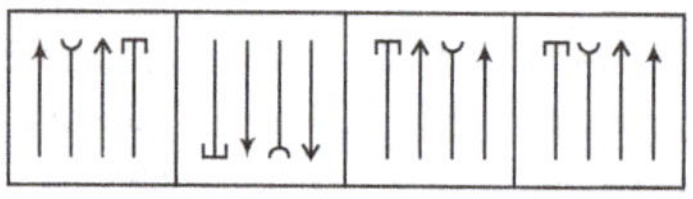

(a) (b) (c) (d)

Sol. (*a*) When the first figure of the first pair of question figures is seen in water, the second figure is obtained as water image.

Similarly, the water image of the first figure of the second pair will be look like the figure in option (a).

Based on Splitting/Joining/Transforming Figures Design

Example 5 **In the following question, select the figure which is related to the third figure in the same way as the first figure is related to the second figure.**

Question Figures ***UP Police Head Operator 2024***

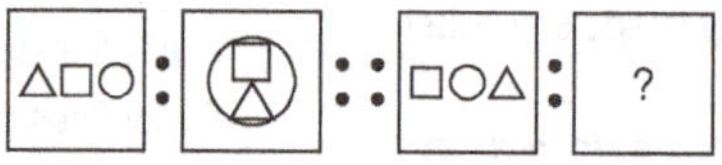

Answer Figures

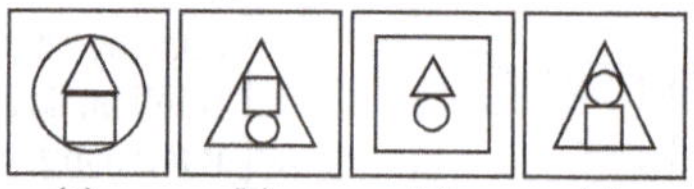

(a) (b) (c) (d)

> **Trending Concept**
> Questions based on analogy (division/ joining/ transformation) are being asked in current exams (RRB, UP Police, UPSSSC). They are very important for upcoming exams.

Sol. (*d*) In the first pair the following changes occur.

As,

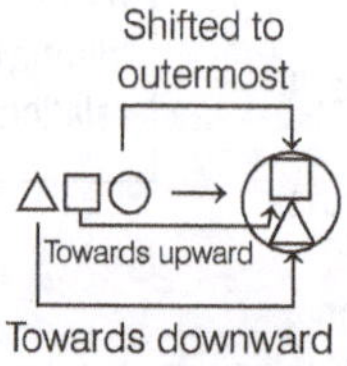

Similarly,

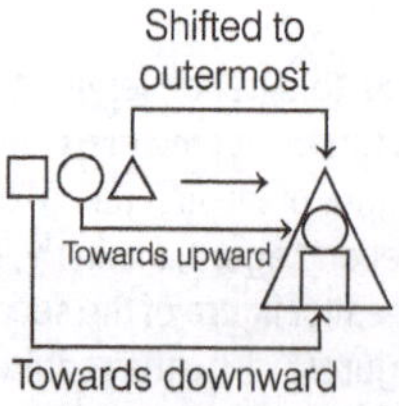

Chapter Challenge

Based on Real Objects

Directions (Q. Nos. 1 and 2) *In the questions given below, the first group is of question figures and the second group is of answer figures. Two pairs of figures are given in the question figure. Find the second figure of the second pair on the basis of the relationship in which the figures of the first pair are related to each other.*

1. Question Figures

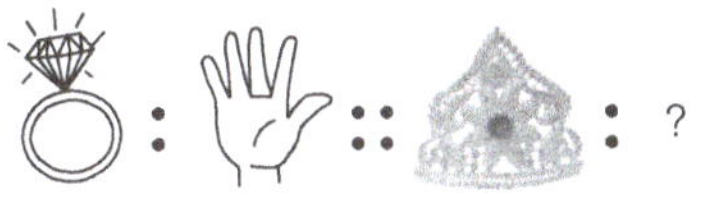

RRB ALP 2018

Answer Figures

(a) (b) (c) (d)

2. Question Figures

RRB ALP 2018

Answer Figures

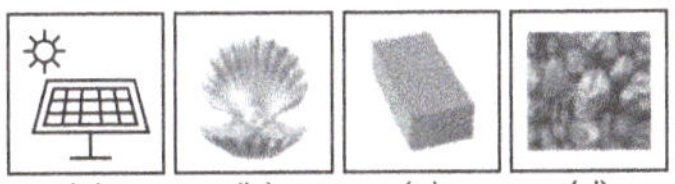

(a) (b) (c) (d)

Based on Rotation

Directions (Q. Nos. 3-13) *In the following questions, choose the figure related to the third figure in the same way as the first figure is related to the second figure.*

3. Question Figures

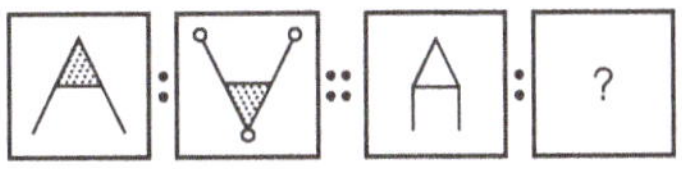

Answer Figures

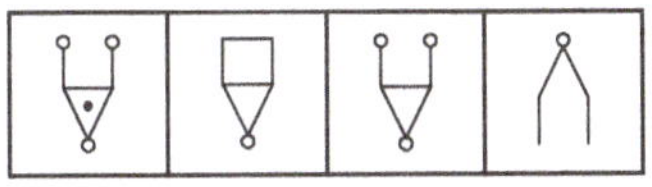

(a) (b) (c) (d)

4. Question Figures

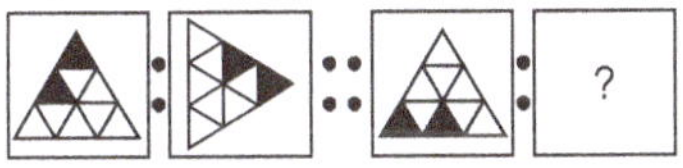

RRB Group D 2018

Answer Figures

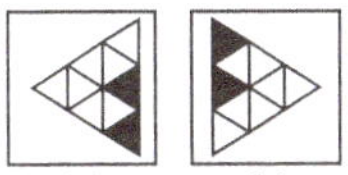

(a) (b)

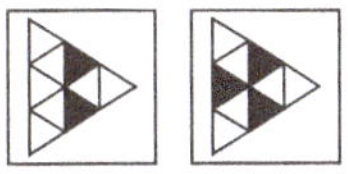

(c) (d)

> ***MRC******
> ***(Most Repeating Concepts)***
> Q. Nos. 1, 2, 4, 6, 8, 9, 11, 12, 16 and 17 are important from the examination point of views. Questions on these concepts are continuously being asked in RRB ALP, UPSSSC, UP (AO), CRPF HC exams.

5. Question Figures

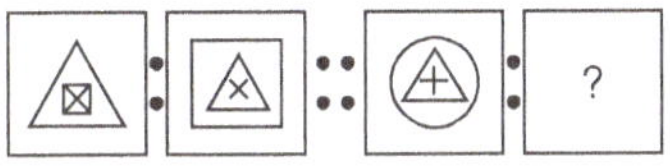

UPSSSC 2018

Answer Figures

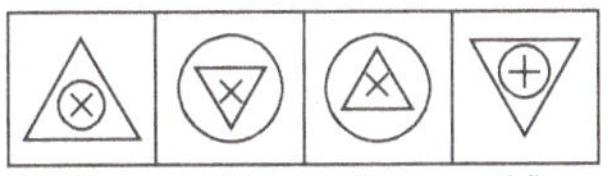

(a) (b) (c) (d)

6. Question Figures

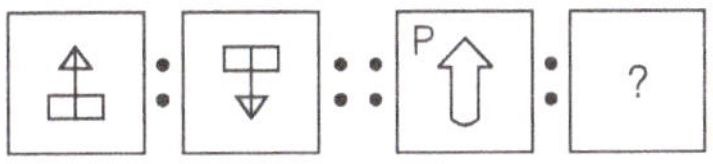

SSC CGL (Tier II) 2023

Answer Figures

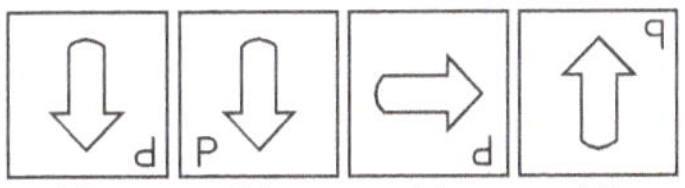

(a) (b) (c) (d)

7. Question Figures

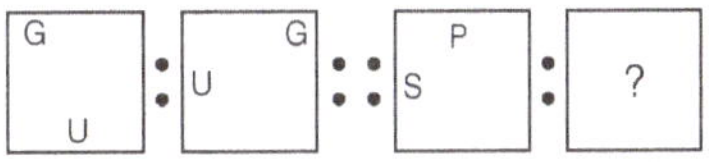

Rajasthan Police Constable 2022

Answer Figures

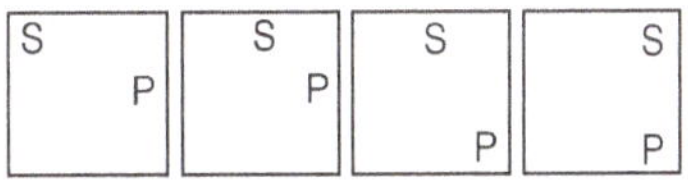

(a) (b) (c) (d)

8. Question Figures

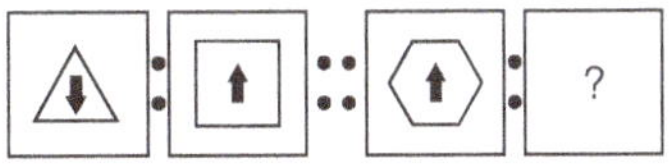

UPSSSC 2018

Answer Figures

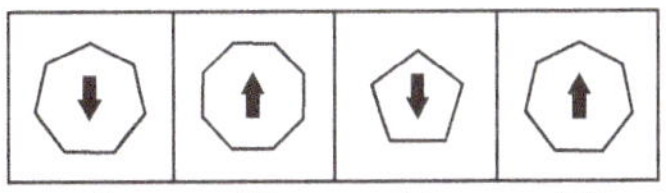

(a) (b) (c) (d)

9. Question Figures

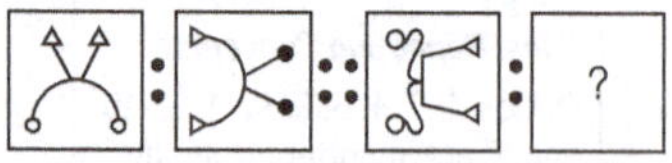

UPSSSC 2018

Answer Figures

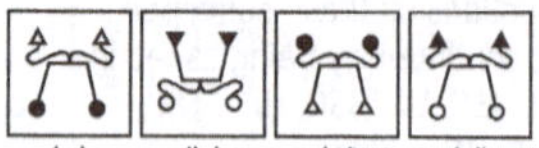

(a) (b) (c) (d)

10. Question Figures

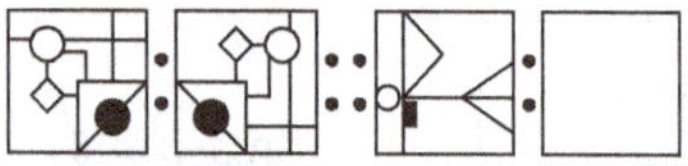

Answer Figures

(a) (b) (c) (d)

11. Question Figures

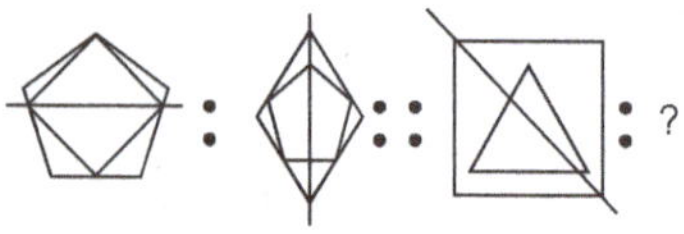

Rajasthan Police Constable 2022

Answer Figures

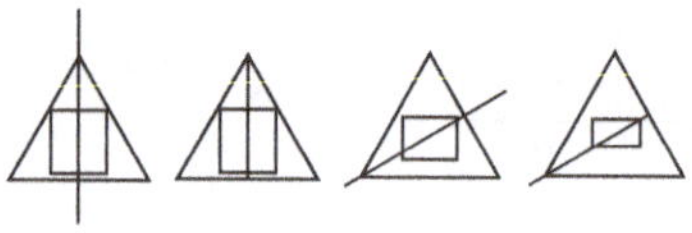

(a) (b) (c) (d)

12. Question Figures

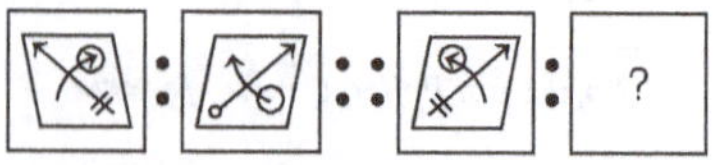

UP (AO) 2024

Answer Figures

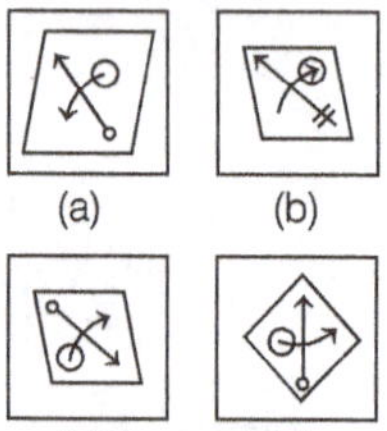

(a) (b) (c) (d)

> **MRC*****
> ***(Most Repeating Concepts)***
> Q. Nos. 6, 9, 12, 17, 18, 19, 24 and 25 important from the examination point of view. Such type of question continuously being asked in SSC-CGL, UPSSSC, RRB Group D, Constable, CHSL exams.

13. Question Figures

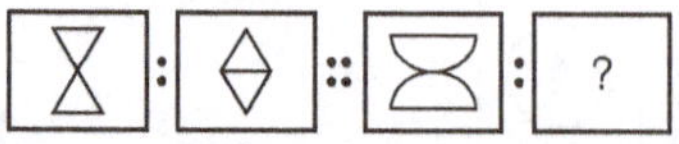

Answer Figures

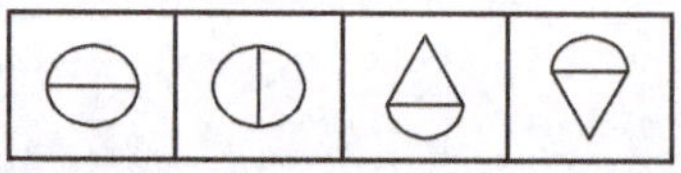

(a) (b) (c) (d)

Based on Water/Mirror Image

Directions (Q. Nos. 14-16) *In the following questions, choose the figure related to the third figure in the same way as the first figure is related to the second figure.*

14. Question Figures

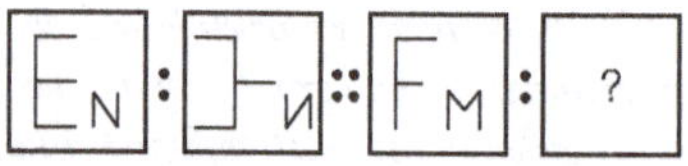

Answer Figures

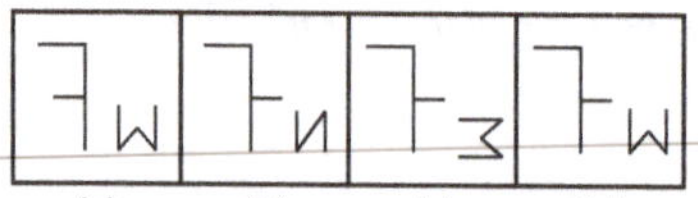

(a) (b) (c) (d)

15. Question Figures

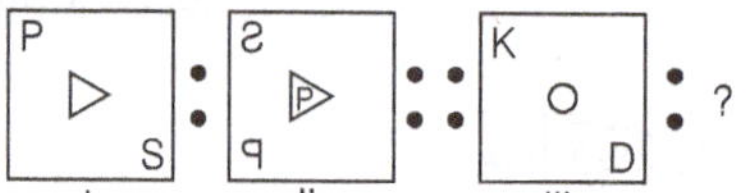

I II III

Answer Figures

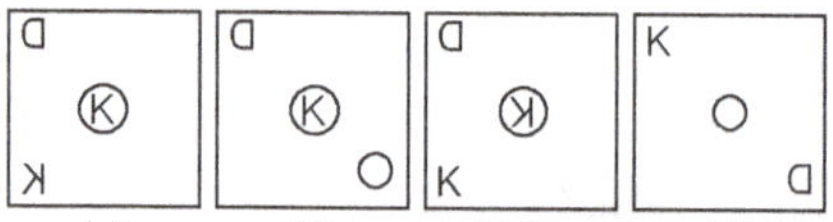

(a) (b) (c) (d)

16. Question Figures

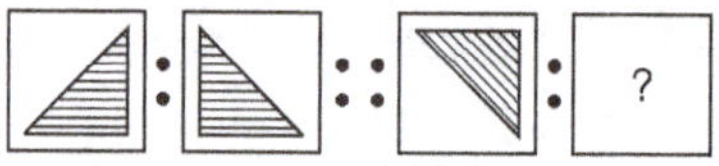

CRPF HC 2023

Answer Figures

(a) (b) (c) (d)

Based on Splitting/Joining/ Transforming Figures Design

Directions (Q. Nos. 17-25) *In the following questions, choose the figure related to the third figure in the same way as the first figure is related to the second figure.*

17. Question Figures

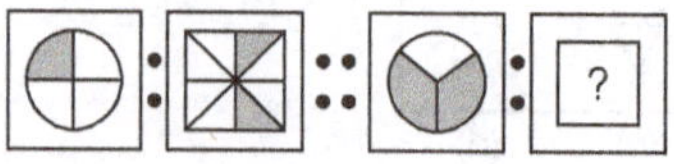

UP Police Constable 2019

Answer Figures

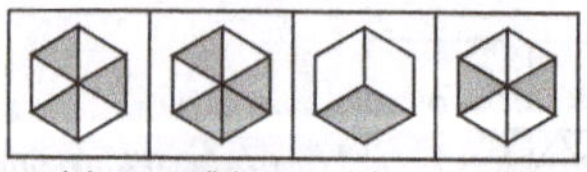

(a) (b) (c) (d)

18. Question Figures

RRB Group D 2018

Answer Figures

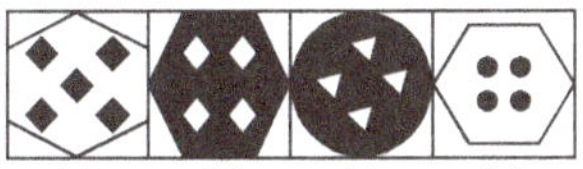

(a) (b) (c) (d)

19. **Question Figures**

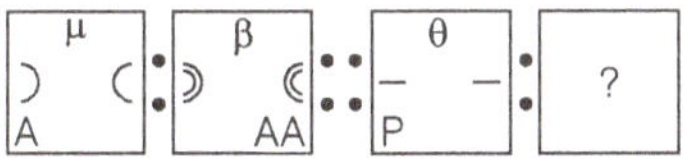

Answer Figures

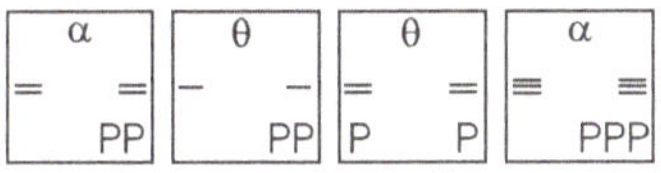

(a) (b) (c) (d)

20. **Question Figures**

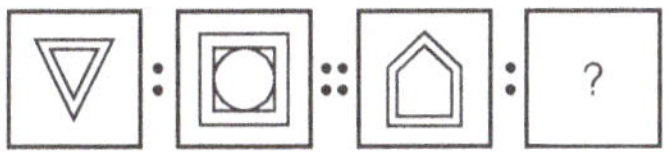

Answer Figures

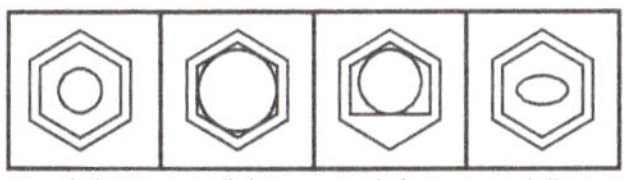

(a) (b) (c) (d)

21. **Question Figures**

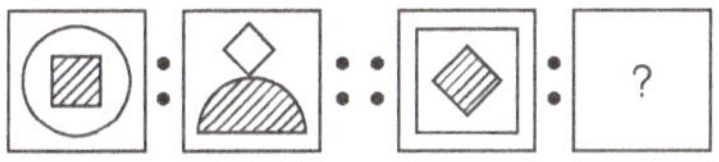

Answer Figures *MP Police Constable 2022*

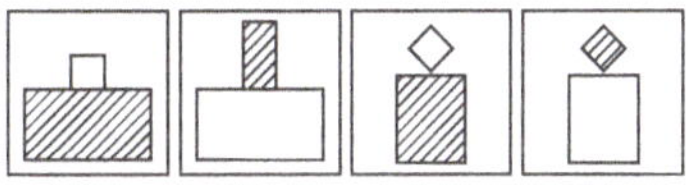

(a) (b) (c) (d)

22. **Question Figures**

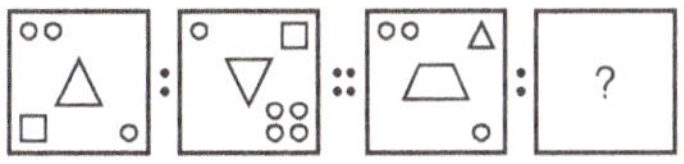

Answer Figures

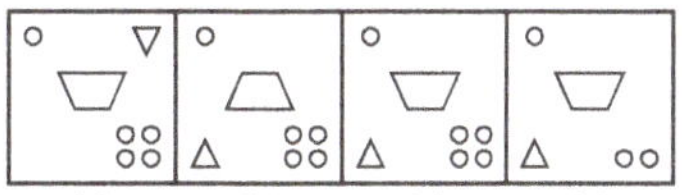

(a) (b) (c) (d)

23. **Question Figures**

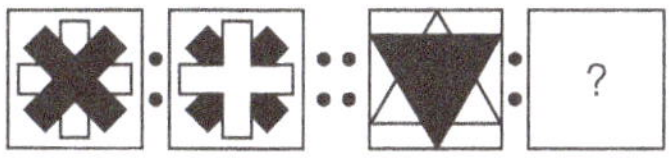

RRB Group D 2018

Answer Figures

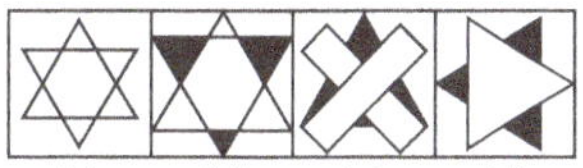

(a) (b) (c) (d)

24. **Question Figures**

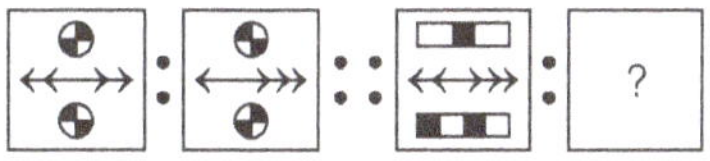

MP Police Constable 2022

Answer Figures

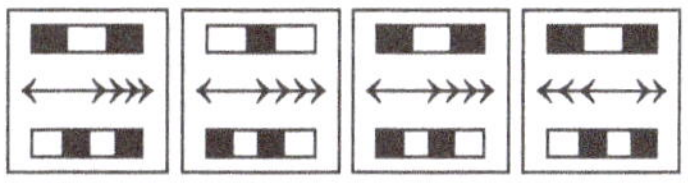

(a) (b) (c) (d)

25. **Question Figures**

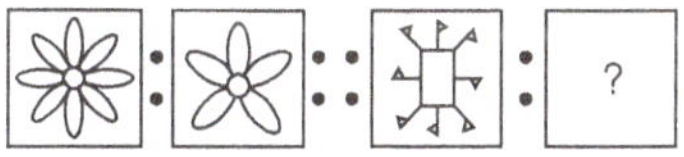

SSC (10+2) 2024

Answer Figures

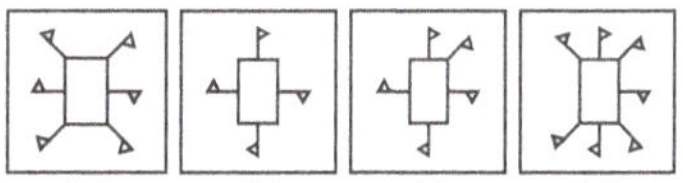

(a) (b) (c) (d)

Right Key

1. (a)	2. (d)	3. (c)	4. (b)	5. (d)	6. (a)	7. (b)	8. (a)	9. (a)	10. (b)
11. (c)	12. (a)	13. (a)	14. (d)	15. (a)	16. (d)	17. (b)	18. (b)	19. (a)	20. (b)
21. (a)	22. (c)	23. (b)	24. (a)	25. (c)					

Solutions

1. *(a)* As, a ring is worn on the finger, in the same way a crown is worn on the head.
2. *(d)* As, water is taken out from a well, in the same way coal is taken out from a coal mine.
3. *(c)* The second figure of the first pair has been formed by inverting the first figure and adding a small circle on all three vertices. Hence, option figure (c) will replace the question mark.

4. *(b)* In the first pair, the second figure is obtained by rotating the first figure 90° clockwise. Similarly, in the second pair, the answer figure (b) will be obtained by rotating the first figure 90° clockwise.
5. *(d)* From the first figure of the question figure to the second figure, the middle figure rotates 180° and becomes the outer figure and the outer figure becomes the middle figure. By following the same pattern, the figure of option (d) will be obtained from the third figure.
6. *(a)* In the first pair, the second figure is obtained by rotating the first figure 180° in the anticlockwise direction. Similarly, in the second pair, the first figure is rotated 180° in the anticlockwise direction to get option figure (a).
7. *(b)* Both the letters of the first figure are moved 1 step clockwise. Similarly, by changing the third figure, option figure (b) will be obtained.
8. *(a)* In the given pair, the three-sided figure becomes a four-sided figure and the arrow rotates 180°. Similarly, in the next pair, the six-sided figure becomes a seven-sided figure and the arrow rotates 180°. Hence, the figure in option (a) will be the correct answer.
9. *(a)* The whole figure rotates 90° clockwise and the designs of circle and triangle interchanges their position, also the circles turn black. Thus, option figure (a) will be obtained as the correct option.
10. *(b)* As, after rotating the first figure 90° in clockwise direction we get the second figure. Similarly, when we rotate 90° clockwise of third figure we will get the option figure (b) as the fourth figure.
11. *(c)* To get the second figure in the given pair, the outer part of the first figure comes inside and the inner part comes out and the line rotates 90° clockwise. Similarly, the figure in option (c) will come in place of (?).

TOP TIPS Trace the figure on a piece of paper, then pivot the paper around the centre of rotation.

12. *(a)* In the first figure, the straight arrow (↑) turns 90° clockwise in the second figure and a small circle (O) is added in place of (=) below the arrow. The curved arrow (↩) turns 90° anticlockwise and the big circle (O) is added to the back part of this arrow. On applying the same sequence in the third figure, the option figure (a) will be obtained.

TOP TIPS To solve such questions, it is very important to have knowledge about anticlockwise and clockwise direction of rotation and angles.

13. *(a)* As, in the first figure of the question figure, both the triangles are inverted and joined to their bases. Similarly, if the semicircles are inverted and joined to their bases, then answer figure (a) will be obtained.
14. *(d)* Since (E) is inverted to form ∃ and the middle line is moved backwards ⅂ and 'N' is inverted to form as water image 'И'. On doing same changes answer figure (d) will replace the question mark.
15. *(a)* Following the same pattern answer figure (a) will replace the question mark.

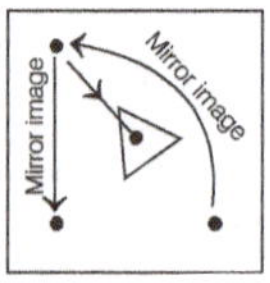

16. *(d)* As, the second figure is the mirror image of the first figure. Similarly, option figure (d) in the second pair is the mirror image of the first figure.
17. *(b)* As, in the first figure of the first pair, 4 parts are divided into 8 parts and the number of shaded parts is doubled. Similarly, by changing the first figure of the second pair, answer figure (b) will be obtained.
18. *(b)* As, the shaded part in the first figure changes to unshaded and unshaded part changes to shaded in the second figure. Similarly, by changing the third figure, answer figure (b) will be obtained.
19. *(a)* As, in the given analogy from first to second figure of first pair, symbol changes to new symbol, curve increases by one on both part as well as letter shifted to bottom right corner and increases by one. Similarly, on following same pattern in second pair we will get the option figure (a).
20. *(b)* From first figure to second figure of the first pair, one side is increase in both the designs and a circle is formed in the middle by touching all the sides of the inner design. Similarly, by making changes in the second pair, the figure option (b) will be obtained.
21. *(a)* As, the circle changes to a semicircle and the square to a small rhombus in the next figure. Similarly, the big square in the second pair changes to a rectangle and the rhombus in the square changes to a small square and the shaded figure inside each pair becomes unshaded and *vice-versa*. Hence, next figure will be option figure (a).
22. *(c)* As, in first to the second figure, the inner design rotates 180° and the small designs follows the pattern as,

Hence, option figure (c) will replace the question mark.

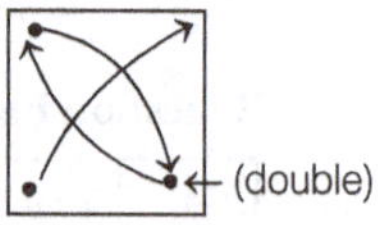

23. *(b)* In the first to second figure, the unshaded part comes up and the shaded part goes down. Similarly, in the second pair, the answer figure (b) will come in place of the question mark (?).
24. *(a)* As, the shaded and unshaded parts in the first figure of the first pair are interchanged and an arrow symbol on the left is replaced on the right in the second figure. Similarly, if the same change is made in the first figure of the second pair, then the answer figure (a) will be obtained.
25. *(c)* As, by removing three leaves in the first figure, we will get the second figure.

Similarly, by removing three flags from the first figure of second pair, we will get answer figure (c).

CHAPTER

02 Figure Classification

Figure Classification

Figure classification means to classify the given shapes/objects on the basis of some similar properties. In the questions based on this chapter, four or five options are given out of which all except one have the same quality, characteristic or a certain pattern, candidates have to understand that pattern and identify the odd one i.e. different figure.

Based on the Shape and Subshapes (Elements) of the Figures

This type of questions are usually based on the number of shapes, relationship between internal-external elements/shapes, changed shapes and position of shapes and subshapes etc.

e.g. Choose the odd figure from the given figures.

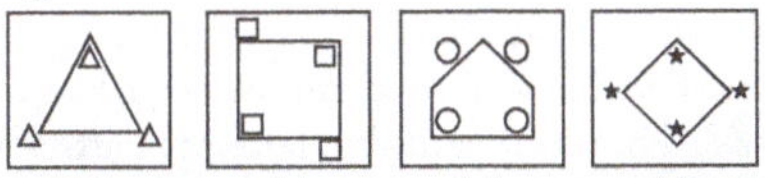

(a) (b) (c) (d)

Sol. (a) After carefully observing the above figures, it is found that except figure (a), in all other figures the number of designs inside and outside the main design is the same, while in figure (a) there is one design inside the main design and two designs outside it.

Based on the Sides and Nature of Line of Figures

This type of questions are usually based on the number of sides, nature of lines, construction, format and special properties of the complete figure etc.

e.g. Choose the odd figure from the given figures.

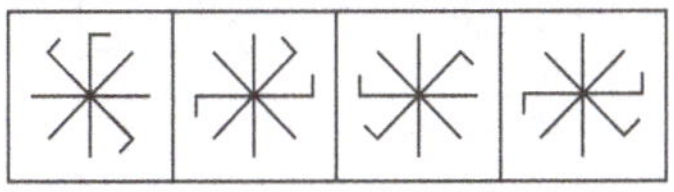

(a) (b) (c) (d)

Sol. (d) Let us consider the two adjacent bent lines as a pair. Then, in each figure except (d), there are two straight lines between the bent pair and the remaining bent line when the direction of bent is considered.

Based on Similarity, Rotation and Division of Figures

This type of questions are usually based on the properties of the shapes such as similarity, rotation of shapes/figure, division of shapes, shaded and unshaded shapes, etc.

e.g. Choose the odd figure from the given figures.

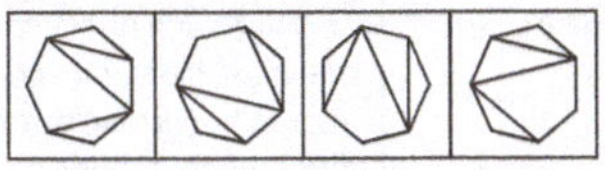

(a) (b) (c) (d)

Sol. (a) All figures except (a) are similar and can be obtained from one another by rotation in clockwise or anti-clockwise direction.

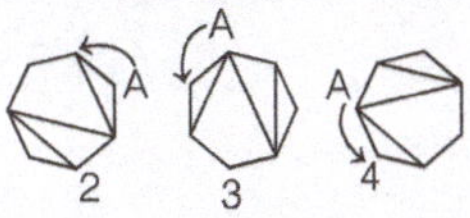

Based on Letter Figures and Real Objects

This type of questions are usually related to classification between letter-shapes and real objects. Apart from this, questions are also based on mirror and water images of letters.

e.g. Choose the odd figure from the given figures.

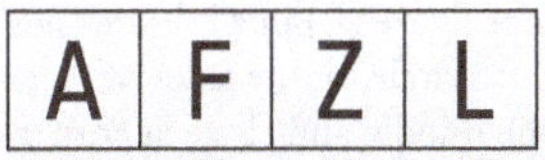

(a) (b) (c) (d)

Sol. (d) In all figures except figure (d), alphabets are made up of three straight lines, while L is made of using two straight lines.

> ***Score Booster***
>
> While solving the questions of this chapter, carefully observe the similarities and dissimilarities of the shapes (based on properties and size) and the patterns of the shapes.

Exam Approach Examples

Based on the Shape and Subshapes (Elements) of the Figures

Example 1 Choose the odd figure from the given figures.

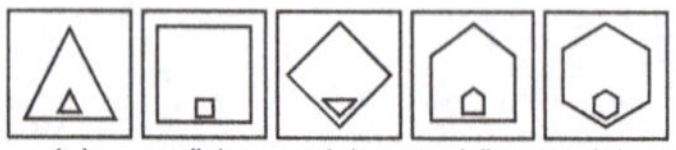

(a) (b) (c) (d) (e)

Sol. (*c*) After carefully observing the above figures, it is found that except figure (c), in all other figures the inside and outside designs are the same, whereas in figure (c) the inside and outside designs are different.

Based on Sides and Nature of Line of Figures

Example 2 Choose the odd figure from the given figures.

(a) (b) (c) (d) (e)

Sol. (*e*) After observing the given figures, it is found that except figure (e), all other figures are formed by three sides, while figure (e) is formed by four sides.

Example 3 Choose the odd figure from the given figures.

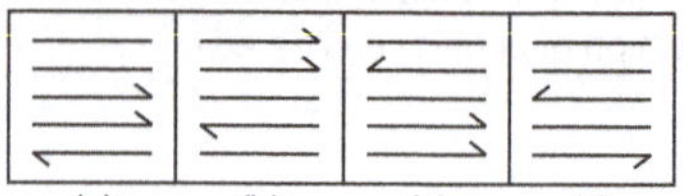

(a) (b) (c) (d)

Sol. (*d*) Except figure option (d) all the figures have three bend lines while in figure (d) only two bend lines. Hence, figure option (d) is odd among all.

Based on Similarity, Rotation and Division of Figures

Example 4 Four of the following five figures are alike in a certain way and thus form a group. Which figure does not belong to that group? ***RPF SI 2024***

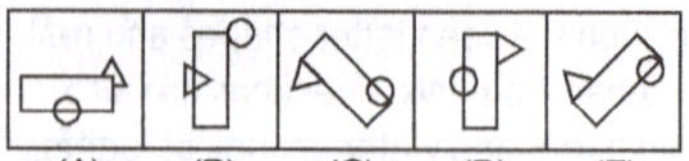

(A) (B) (C) (D) (E)

(a) D (b) B (c) A (d) C

Sol. (*b*) Except figure (B) in all figures position of triangle at corner of rectangle and circle on the sides of rectangle while in figure (B) triangle on the middle and circle at corner of the rectangle. Hence, figure (B) does not belong to that group.

Example 5 Choose the odd figure from the given figures.

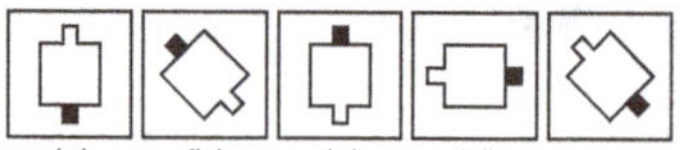

(a) (b) (c) (d) (e)

Sol. (*d*) After observing the above figures, it is found that in all the figures except figure (d), the outer white part and the middle part of the square is open, whereas in figure (d) the outer white part is closed by the side.

Trending Concept

Questions based on rotation and division of figures are asked in current examination of RRB Group-D, RRB NTPC, ALP, UP Police Constable frequently.

Example 6 Choose the odd figure from the given figures.

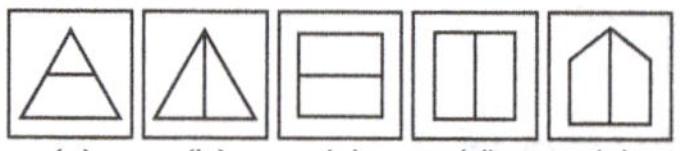

(a) (b) (c) (d) (e)

Sol. (*a*) After carefully observing the above figures, it is found that except figure (a), all other figures are divided into two equal parts, whereas figure (a) is divided into two parts, but both the parts are not equal.

Based on Letter Figures and Real Objects

Example 7 Choose the odd figures from the given figures.

(a) (b) (c) (d)

Sol. (*d*) Except the letter 'O', all other letters of the English alphabet are consonants while the letter 'O' is a vowel.

Helping Tips

To solve such questions one must have knowledge about vowel and consonant of english alphabet.

Example 8 Choose the odd figure from the given figures.

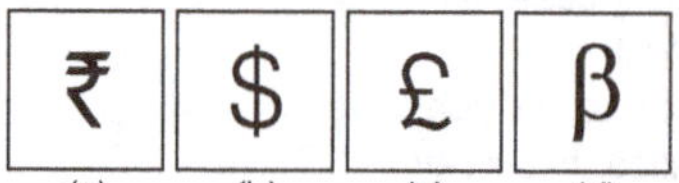

(a) (b) (c) (d)

Sol. (*d*) Except 'β', all the other symbols represent currencies of different nations.

₹ → Rupes (India)

$ → Dollar (USA)

£ → Pound (England)

Helping Tips

To solve such questions one must have knowledge about the currencies of different countries and their symbols.

Chapter Challenge

Based on the Shape and Subshapes (Elements) of the Figures

Directions (Q. Nos. 1-40) *Choose the odd figure from the given figures.*

1.
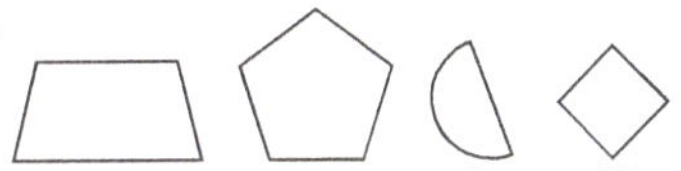
(A) (B) (C) (D)

UPSSSC 2018

(a) A (b) B
(c) C (d) D

2.
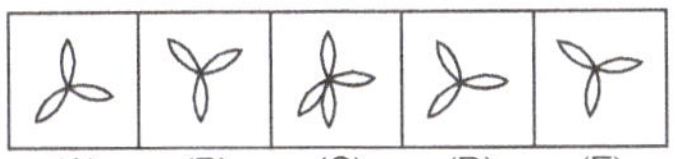
(A) (B) (C) (D) (E)

RRB Group-D 2018

(a) A (b) E
(c) C (d) D

3.
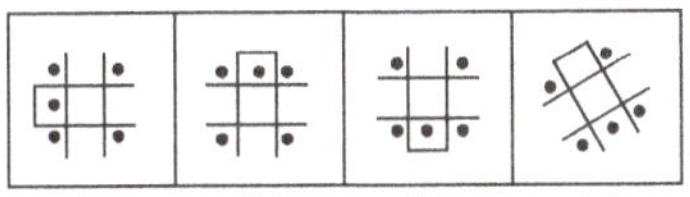
(a) (b) (c) (d)

UP Police AO 2024

4.
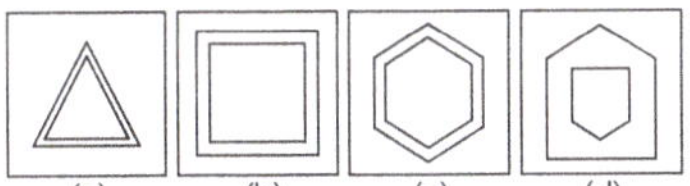
(a) (b) (c) (d)

UP Police Head Operator 2024

5.
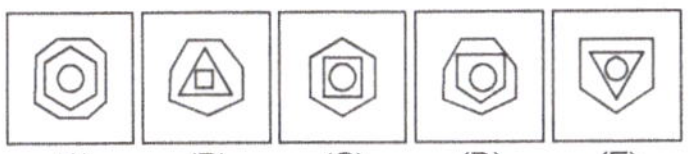
(A) (B) (C) (D) (E)

SSC CGL (Tier-II) 2023

(a) D (b) A
(c) C (d) B

6.
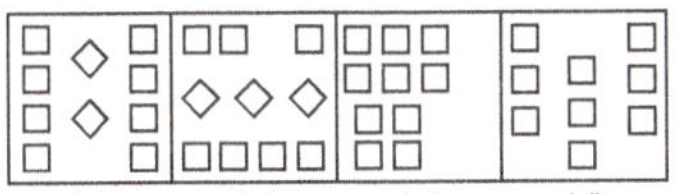
(a) (b) (c) (d)

RRB ALP 2018

7.
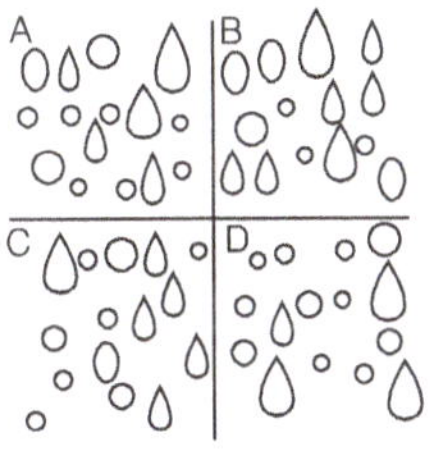

RRB Group-D 2018

(a) D (b) A
(c) C (d) B

8.
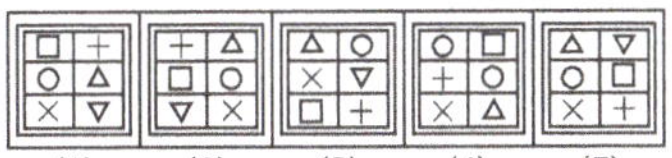
(1) (2) (3) (4) (5)

Delhi Police MTS 2018

(a) 1 (b) 2 (c) 3 (d) 4

9.
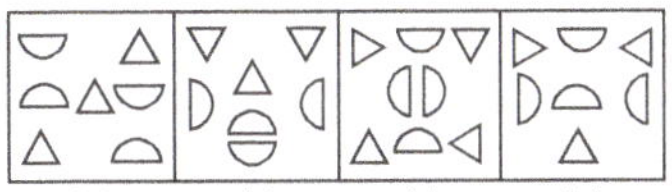
(a) (b) (c) (d)

RRB ALP 2018

10.
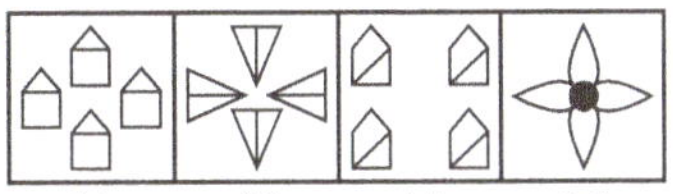
(a) (b) (c) (d)

11.
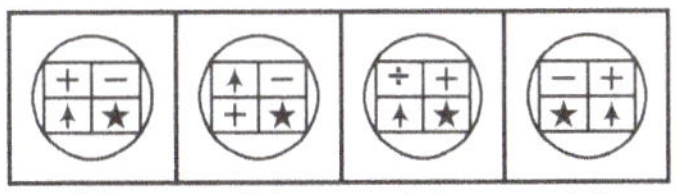
(a) (b) (c) (d)

Based on Sides and Nature of Line of Figures

12.
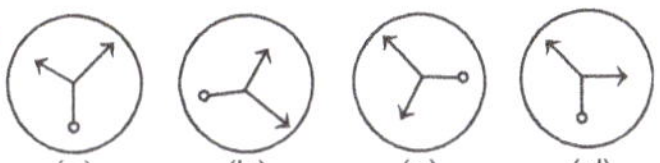
(a) (b) (c) (d)

UP Police Constable 2018

13.
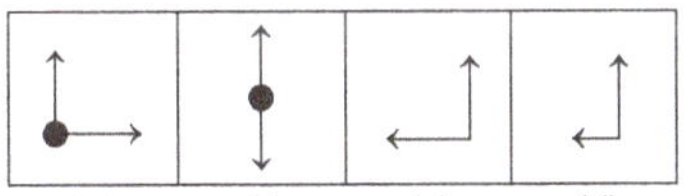
(a) (b) (c) (d)

RRB ALP 2018

14.
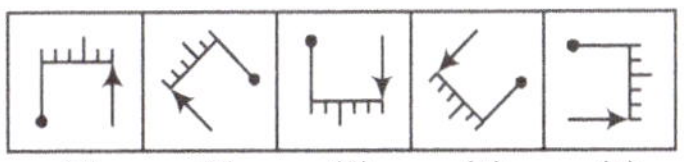
(1) (2) (3) (4) (5)

CISF ASI 2023

(a) 2 (b) 4
(c) 3 (d) 1

15.
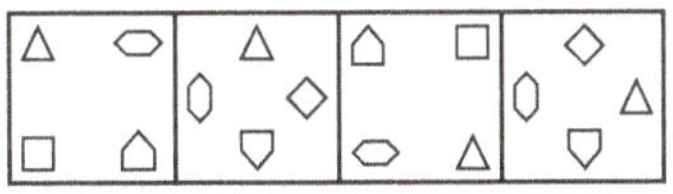
(a) (b) (c) (d)

16.
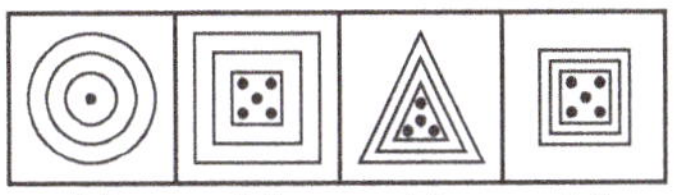
(a) (b) (c) (d)

17.
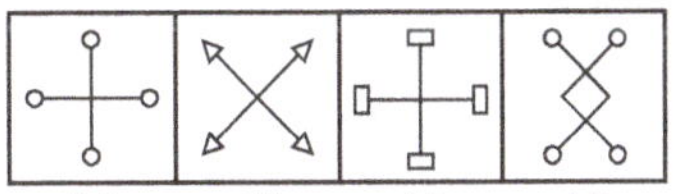
(a) (b) (c) (d)

Based on Similarity, Rotation and Division of Figures

18.

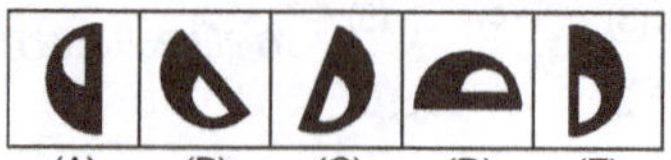

(A) (B) (C) (D) (E)

UPSSSC 2018

(a) C (b) B (c) A (d) E

19.

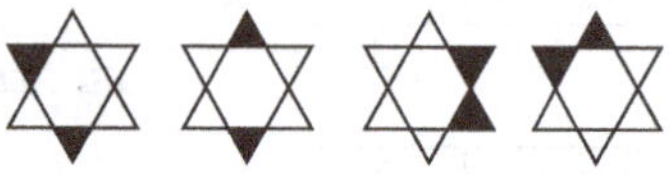

(a) (b) (c) (d)

RRB ALP 2018

20.

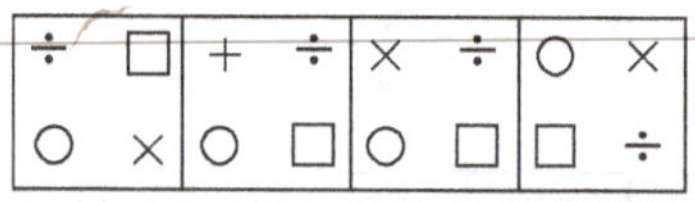

(a) (b) (c) (d)

RRB NTPC 2021

21.

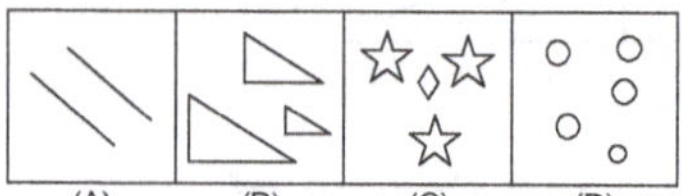

(A) (B) (C) (D)

RRB ALP 2018

(a) C (b) A (c) B (d) D

22.

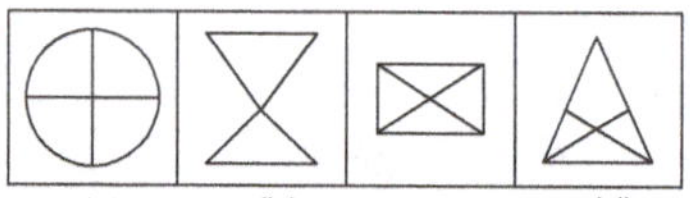

(a) (b) (c) (d)

CRPF HC 2023

23.

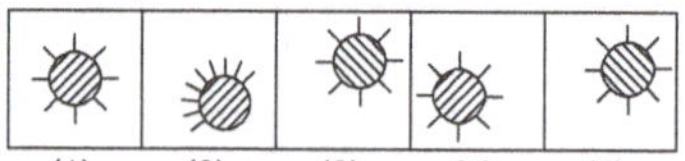

(1) (2) (3) (4) (5)

CISF ASI 2023

(a) 3 (b) 2 (c) 4 (d) 1

24.

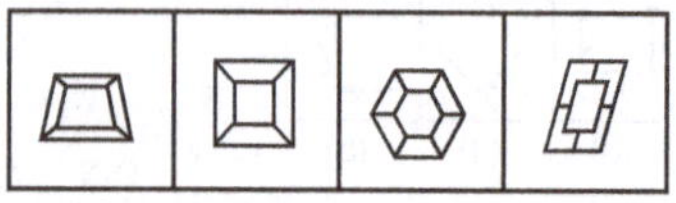

(a) (b) (c) (d)

25.

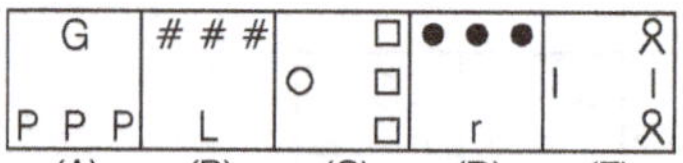

(A) (B) (C) (D) (E)

SSC CGL (Tier-II) 2025

(a) A (b) E (c) B (d) D

26.

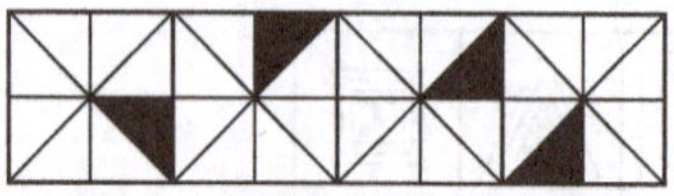

(a) (b) (c) (d)

27.

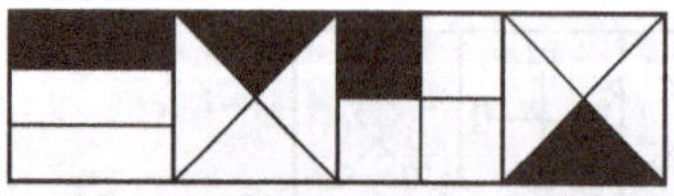

(a) (b) (c) (d)

28.

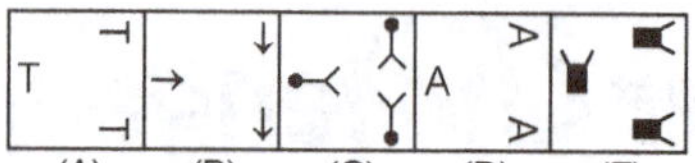

(A) (B) (C) (D) (E)

(a) A (b) B (c) C (d) D

29.

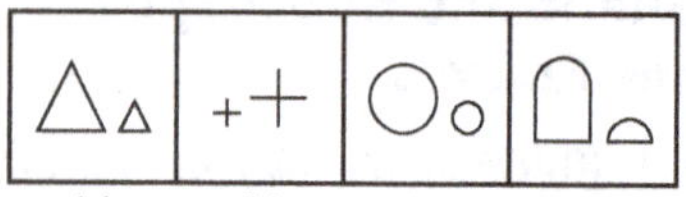

(a) (b) (c) (d)

30.

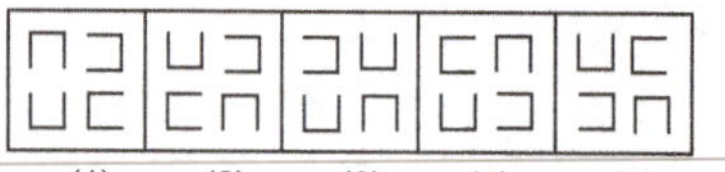

(1) (2) (3) (4) (5)

UP Police Constable 2024

(a) 4 (b) 3 (c) 1 (d) 2

31.

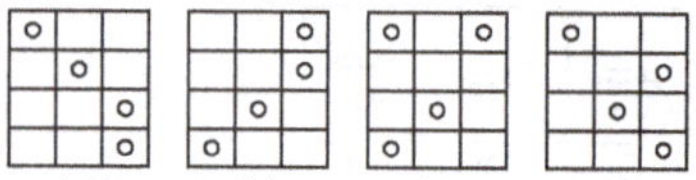

(a) (b) (c) (d)

DSSSB Workshop 2024

32.

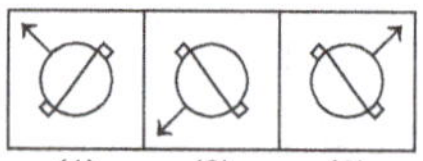

(1) (2) (3)

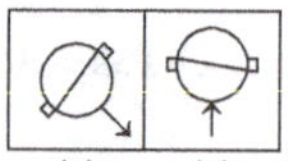

(4) (5)

UP Police Constable 2024

(a) 4 (b) 2
(c) 3 (d) 5

> **MRC*****
> ***(Most Repeating Concept)***
> Q. Nos. 1, 3, 20, 28 and 32 are very important from the examination point of view. Questions based on Rotation, Division, Letters, Shape Elements etc., are being asked in UPSSSC, UP Police, RRB, ALP, RRB NTPC, SSC CGL etc. exams.

33.

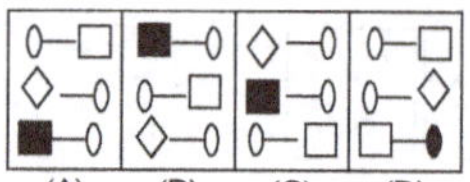

(A) (B) (C) (D)

RRB NTPC 2021

(a) A (b) C (c) B (d) D

34.

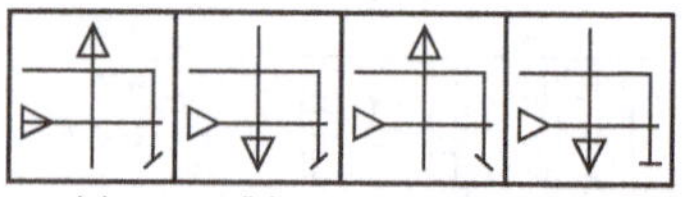

(a) (b) (c) (d)

RRB ALP 2023

35.

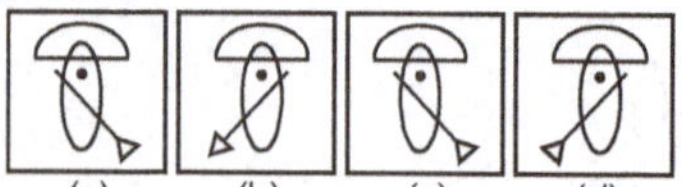

(a) (b) (c) (d)

Based on Letter Figures and Real Objects

36.

(a) (b) (c) (d)

RRB ALP 2018

37.

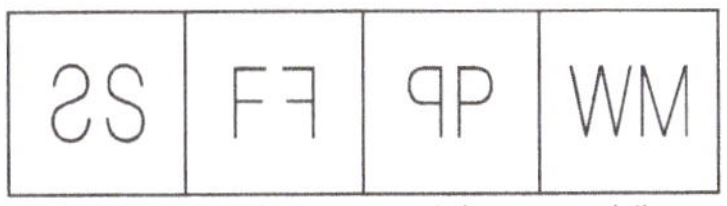

(a) (b) (c) (d)

38.

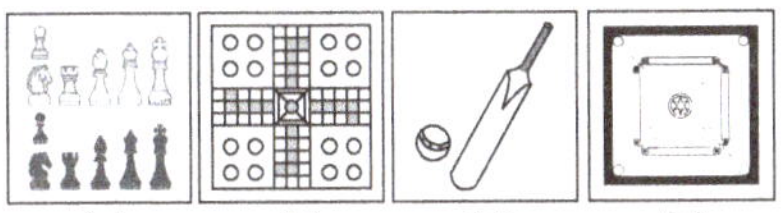

(a) (b) (c) (d)

39.

H X P	Q M R	P O R	K W Q
O R K	X H O	M W K	R O P
W Q M	K W P	H X Q	I M X
(a)	(b)	(c)	(d)

RRB ALP 2019

40.

H Q Y	X Q Y	X T Z	Q S X
N I X	Z S H	N Q S	Y Q N
O S Z	N O I	H Y O	I H Z
(a)	(b)	(c)	(d)

UP Police Constable 2018

Right Key

1. (c)	2. (c)	3. (d)	4. (d)	5. (d)	6. (d)	7. (d)	8. (d)	9. (c)	10. (d)
11. (c)	12. (d)	13. (b)	14. (d)	15. (d)	16. (a)	17. (d)	18. (b)	19. (a)	20. (a)
21. (a)	22. (b)	23. (b)	24. (d)	25. (b)	26. (c)	27. (a)	28. (c)	29. (d)	30. (b)
31. (c)	32. (d)	33. (d)	34. (a)	35. (b)	36. (d)	37. (d)	38. (c)	39. (d)	40. (c)

Solutions

1. *(c)* Except figure (C), all other figures are made of straight lines.

2. *(c)* Except figure (C), all other figures have only three leaves.

3. *(d)* In all the figures except option figure (d), the point is inside the closed rectangle but in figure (d) the point is inside the open rectangle.

4. *(d)* In all the three figures except option figure (d), the outer and inner figure are same. In figure (d), the inner figure is the water image of the outer figure.

5. *(d)* All the figures except figure (B) have a circle in the middle, but figure (B) has a square in the middle. So, figure (B) does not belong to the group.

6. *(d)* All the figures except figure (d) have 10 quadrilaterals but figure (d) has 9 quadrilaterals.

   Hence, figure (d) is different from the others.

7. *(d)* All except figure (B) have 15 designs, while figure (B) has 14 designs.

8. *(d)* All figures except figure (4) have 2 triangles. While figure 4 has only one triangle.

9. *(c)* All figures except figure (c) have 4 semicircles and 3 triangles. While in figure (c) the number of semicircles and triangles is '4'.

10. *(d)* Four figures are given in options (a), (b) and (c) but in option (d) all the four figures are combined to form a single figure, i.e. the figure in option (d) is different from the other figures.

11. *(c)* The elements of the shapes in options (a), (b) and (d) include '+', '–', '↑' and '★' while the elements of the shape in option (c) do not include '–' but instead include the element '÷'.

    Hence, the shape in option (c) is different from the other three.

12. *(d)* All except figure (d) have a big arrow (↑) to the right of the small arrow (↑), while figure (d) has a big arrow to the left of the small arrow.

    Hence, figure (d) is different from the other three.

13. *(b)* In all the figures except option figure (b), an angle of 90° is formed between the two lines.

    In option figure (b) an angle of 180° is formed between them.

14. *(d)* In figure (1) there is a small line between '↑' and the big middle line. In all the other figures there are two small lines between '↑' and the big middle line.

15. *(d)* The figures given in options (a), (b) and (c) are in ascending or descending order based on the number of their sides but the figures given in option (d) are not arranged in this order.

    Hence, the figure in option (d) is different from the other figures.

16. *(a)* All the shapes except option (a) have sides but option (a) has the shape of a circle, which has no sides.

    Hence, it is different from the other three shapes.

17. *(d)* In option (d) a small quadrilateral is formed from the line segments, whereas this is not the case in other figures.

Hence, the figure in option (d) is different from all the others.

18. *(b)* All the figures except figure (B) are similar when rotated.

Hence, figure (B) is different from all others.

19. *(a)* In all the figures except figure (a), the shaded portion is a part of both the triangles, while in figure (a) the shaded portion is in only one triangle.

20. *(a)* In all the figures except option figure (a), the arithmetic symbol and geometric figure are paired together. But in option (a) they are at diagonal.

21. *(a)* All the figures except figure (C) have the same geometrical figure/symbol, but not in figure (C).

22. *(b)* In all the figures except option figure (b), two lines inside the geometrical figure divide the figure into four parts.

Hence, option (b) is different from the others.

23. *(b)* In all the figures except figure (2) the lines outside the circle are equally spaced and these lines spread across the entire circle.

Hence, figure (2) is different from the others.

24. *(d)* In all other figures, the outer and inner figures are joined vertex to vertex by line segments, while in the figure of option (d), the sides are joined side to side. Hence, it is different from other figures.

25. *(b)* Except figure (E) all the figures have three consecutive and same symbol/letter while in figure (E) three consecutive symbols are not same. Hence, figure (E) is not belong to that group.

26. *(c)* By rotating any one of the figures given in options (a), (b) and (d), the other two figures will be obtained, but by rotating any of them, the figure in option (c) will not be obtained.

Hence, the figure in option (c) is different from the other figures.

> **TOP TIPS** To solve such questions it is very important to have knowledge about rotation of shapes.

27. *(a)* In the other three figures, three parts are white and one part is black, but in the figure of option (a) only two parts are white and one part is black. Hence, it is different from the other three figures.

28. *(c)* Except figure (c) on rotating middle left letter/symbol 90° clockwise, we get two letter/symbol at top right and bottom right corner while in figure (c) bottom right shape doesn't follow the same pattern. Hence, figure (c) does not belong to that group.

29. *(d)* In the figures of options (a), (b) and (c), both the figures are the same, only one is bigger, the other is smaller; while in option (d) both the figures are different.

Hence, the figure of option (d) is different from the other three.

30. *(b)* Except the subfigures given in figure (3), in all other figures the faces of the subfigures are open in all four directions. Hence, option (b) is the correct answer.

31. *(c)* Except option figure (c), all other figures have a circle in only one box of each row, but in figure (c) there are circles in two boxes of the first row. Hence, figure (c) is different.

32. *(d)* In all the figures except figure (5) the arrows are opposite to the circumference of the circle but in figure (5) they are towards the circumference of the circle. These can be obtained by rotating them from each other.

33. *(d)* In all the figures except figure (D), the square is shaded, but in figure (D), the circle is shaded.

34. *(a)* In all the three figures (b), (c) and (d), one of the triangles is empty and the other has a line, while in option (a) both the triangles have a line.

Hence, the figure in option (a) is different from the other three figures.

35. *(b)* Except figure (b), in all other figures one vertex of the triangle is connected to the line, whereas in figure (b) one side is connected to the line.

36. *(d)* All are media of transmitting information while headphones are media of receiving information.

Hence, option (d) will be the required answer.

37. *(d)* In all the figures except figure (d), the two designs are mirror images of each other while in figure (d) the two designs are water images of each other.

> **TOP TIPS** To solve this type of questions, one must have knowledge of english alphabets (vowels or consonants) and their shapes. Knowledge of real objects that we regularly and daily see in are surrounding is also desirable.

38. *(c)* Option figure (c) i.e. except the game of cricket, all others are indoor games while cricket is an outdoor game.

39. *(d)* Option figure (d) has a letter I. All other figures have letter H. So, option figure (d) is different from the rest.

40. *(c)* The figure given in option (c) contains the letter T which is not in any other figure.

Hence, the figure given in option (c) is different from the other three.

CHAPTER

03 Figure Series

Figure Series

The literal meaning of series is to arrange the figure in a sequential manner.

The questions asked from this chapter have two parts in which the first part is called question figures and the second part is called answer figures. Three, four or five figures are given in the question figures. In every next figure of the question figure, there is a change according to a certain rule or in a sequential manner and the candidates have to understand this change and find out the answer figure which will complete the series.

Based on Number of Lines or Sides of Figures

In this type of questions, a series is formed by changing (increasing or decreasing) the number of lines or sides of the given figures.

e.g. Select the next figure in the following figure series.

Question Figures

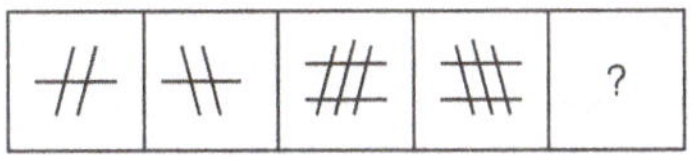

Answer Figures

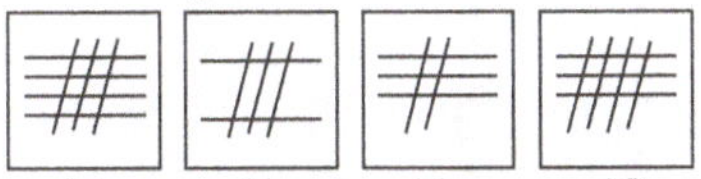

(a) (b) (c) (d)

Sol. (d) In the each next term of the given figure series is inverted as compared to the first figure and one horizontal line and one vertical line is increased alternately. In this way, in place of question mark in the series, the answer figure (d) will come.

Based on Rotation of Figures

In this type of questions, the next figure is formed when each figure (elements) is rotated in a certain order. Candidates have to identify the order of this change and select the answer figure that comes in place of the question mark from the given answer figures.

e.g. Select the figure that comes next in the following figure series.

Question Figures

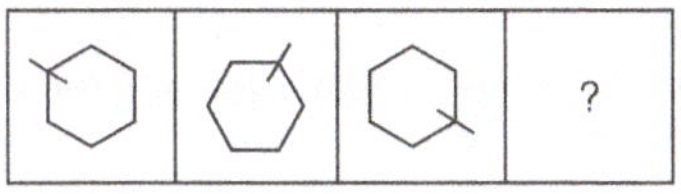

Answer Figures

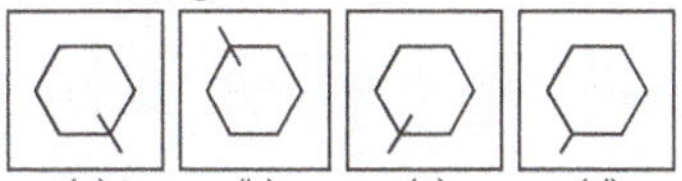

(a) (b) (c) (d)

Sol. (c) In each next term of the given figure series, the entire figure rotates 90° clockwise. Thus, in place of the question mark, the answer figure (c) will come.

Based on the Changes of Position of the Figure

In such questions, the positions of the elements of the given figure series keep changing in a certain order. By identifying the order of this change, the answer figure that comes in place of the question mark has to be selected from the given answer figures.

e.g. Select a figure from the given options which can come at the place of question mark (?) in the following series.

Question Figures

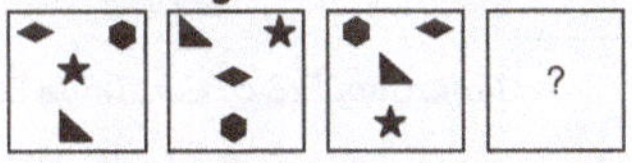

Answer Figures

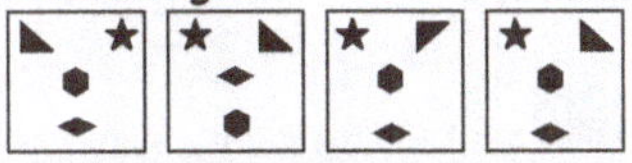

(a) (b) (c) (d)

Sol. (d) In the given figure series, the small figures are changing their position in each next term according to the following pattern.

So, answer figure (d) will come in place of question mark (?).

Score Booster

In this type of questions sometimes two series are given in alternate order whose pattern are different, so we should analyse the question figure very carefully to solve the problem.

Based on Change in Shape and Size

In this type of questions, the figure change in a certain order based on their shape and size. The answer figure that comes in place of the question mark has to be identified from the given answer figures by identifying the changes in the shapes.

e.g. Which figure will continue the sequence the series given below?

Question Figures

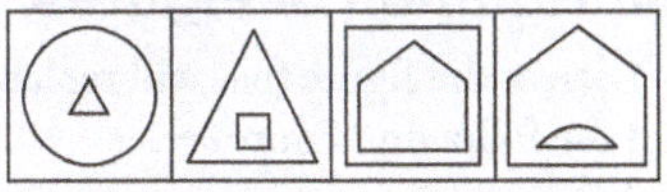

Answer Figures

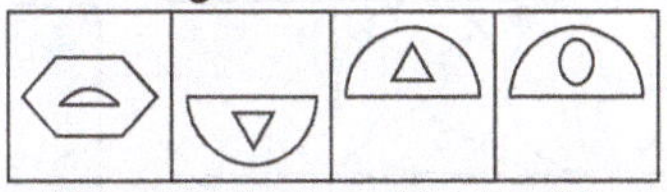

(a) (b) (c) (d)

Sol. (d) In every next figure of the question figure, the inner design becomes the outer design and a new design formed inside it. If this sequence continues further, then the answer figure (d) will be obtained.

Exam Approach Examples

Based on Number of Lines or Sides of Figures

Example 1 **Identify the figure given in the options which when put in place of the question mark (?) will logically complete the series.** ***RPF SI 2024***

Question Figures

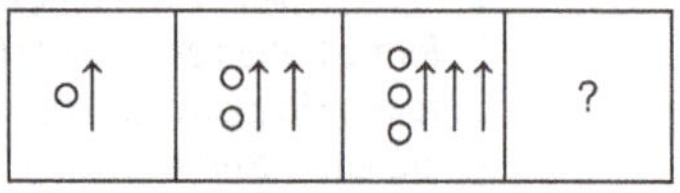

Answer Figures

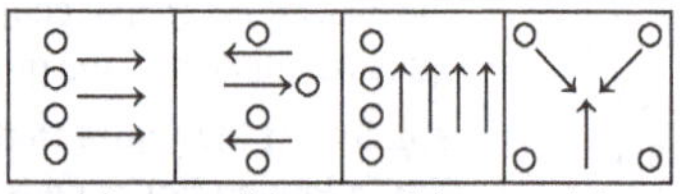

(a) (b) (c) (d)

Sol. (*c*) In the given series in each next consecutive figure number of circle and arrow increases by one at same orientation. Hence, the next figure will be figure option (c).

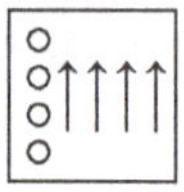

Example 2 **Select the figure from the options that can replace the question mark (?) and complete the given series.**

Question Figures ***SSC CHSL (Tier-II) 2024***

Answer Figures

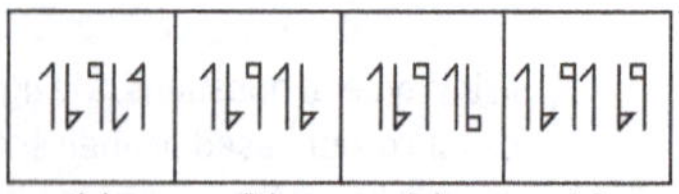

(a) (b) (c) (d)

Sol. (*b*) In the given figure series, three designs 1, ʟ and ˥ are adding to the consecutive steps in cyclic manner. So, the option (b) will complete the given series.

Based on Rotation of Figures

Example 3 **Select the figure that will replace the question mark (?) in the following figure series.** ***SSC CPO 2020***

Question Figures

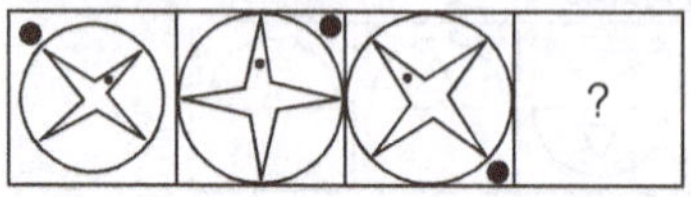

Answer Figures

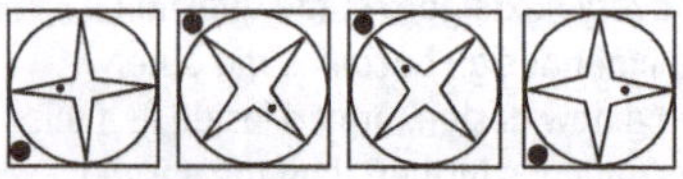

(a) (b) (c) (d)

> **Helping Tips**
>
> To solve such questions, it is very important to have knowledge related to rotation of shapes at different angles and also there should be knowledge about clockwise and anticlockwise direction of rotation.

Sol. (*a*) In the given figure series, in every next term the design inside the circle is rotating 45° anticlockwise and the small shaded circle moves to the next corner in clockwise direction. In this way, answer figure (a) will come in place of question mark (?) in the series.

Based on Change in Position of Figures

Example 4 **Identify the figure given in the options which when placed in place of the question mark (?) will logically complete the series.** ***SSC (10+2) 2024***

Question Figures

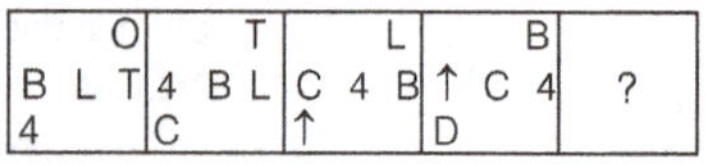

Answer Figures

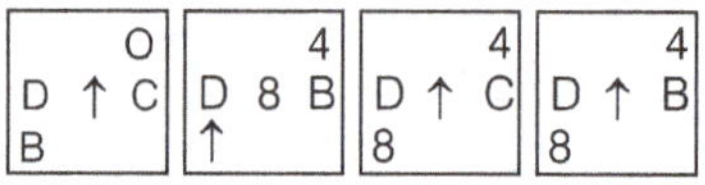

(a) (b) (c) (d)

Sol. (*c*) Every next figure in the given figure series follows the following pattern,

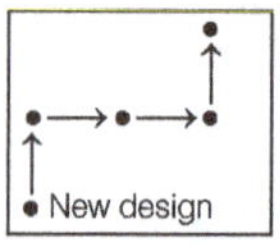

Hence, the figure in option (c) will be the next figure in the series.

> **Trending Concept**
>
> This type of questions are asked in current examination of CGL, CHSL, CPO etc. These are important for the upcoming examination.

Based on Change in Shape and Size

Example 5 **Which figure will continue the series given below?**

Question Figures

Rajasthan Police Constable 2018

Answer Figures

(a) (b) (c) (d)

Sol. (*a*) In the given figure series in every next step the two designs interchange their position and the colour of the smaller and bigger figure changes alternatively.

Thus, the next figure in the sequence will be answer figure (a).

Chapter Challenge

Based on Number of Lines or Sides of Figures

Directions (Q. Nos. 1-5) *In each of the following questions given below which one from the four answer figures should come at the place of '?' to complete the series logically.*

1. Question Figures

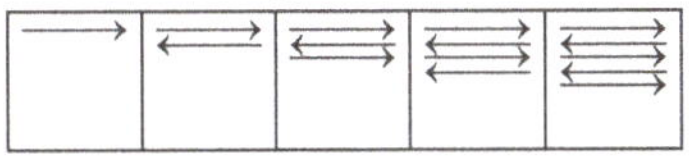

MP Police Constable 2022

Answer Figures

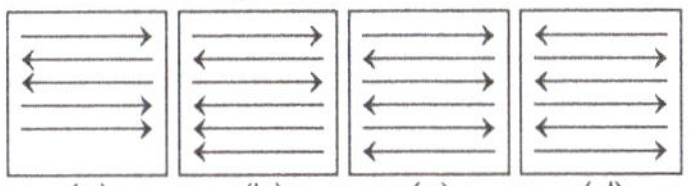

(a) (b) (c) (d)

2. Question Figures

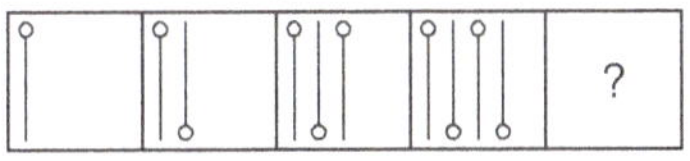

CUET UG 2023

Answer Figures

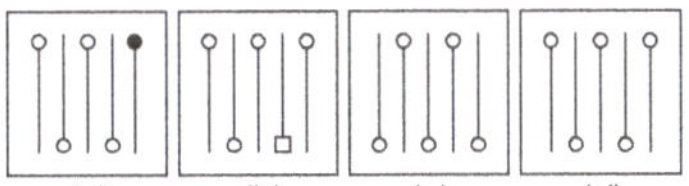

(a) (b) (c) (d)

3. Question Figures

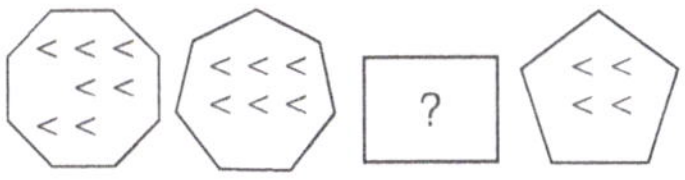

RRB NTPC 2020

Answer Figures

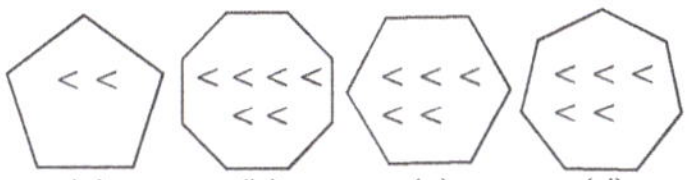

(a) (b) (c) (d)

4. Question Figures

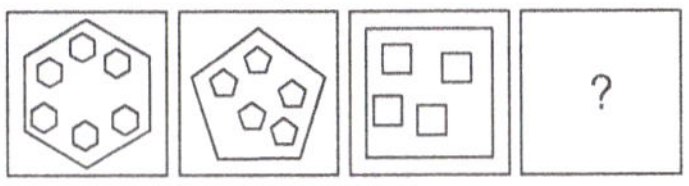

DP Constable 2023

Answer Figures

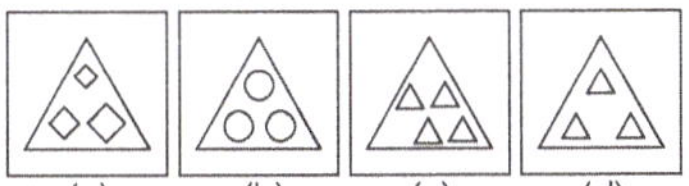

(a) (b) (c) (d)

5. Question Figures

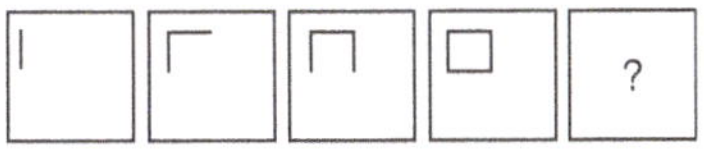

SSC GD Constable 2024

Answer Figures

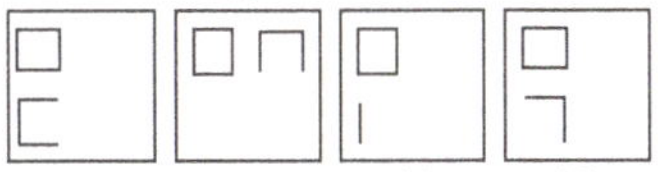

(a) (b) (c) (d)

Based on Rotation of Figures

Directions (Q. Nos. 6-10) *Find the figure which will come next in the given figure series.*

6. Question Figures

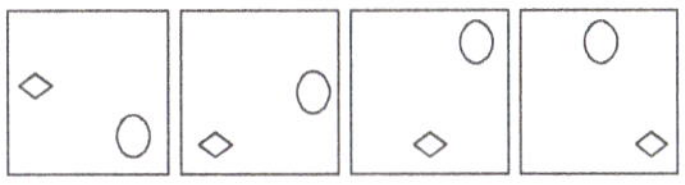

RRB ALP 2018

Answer Figures

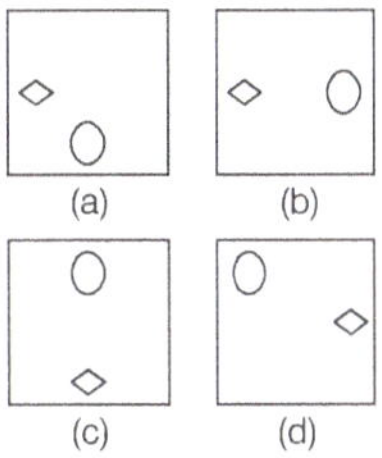

> ***MRC******
> ***(Most Repeating Concepts)***
> Question Nos. 2, 3, 5, 11, 13, 16, 21 and 28 are important from the examination point of view. Questions based on figure series are asked in examination SSC CGL, CHSL, CPO, CUET (UG), RRB NTPC, ALP, DSSSB, SSC GD etc.

7. Question Figures

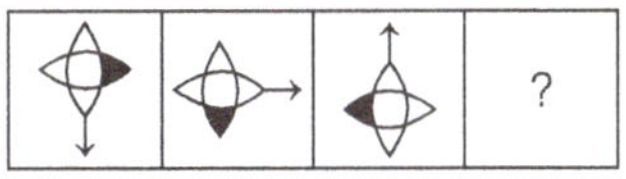

SSC GD Constable 2024

Answer Figures

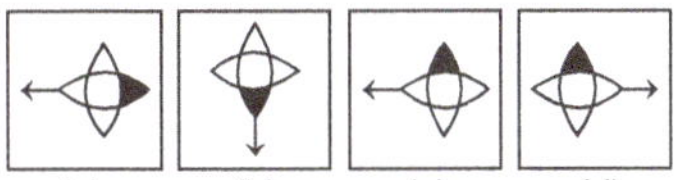

(a) (b) (c) (d)

8. Question Figures

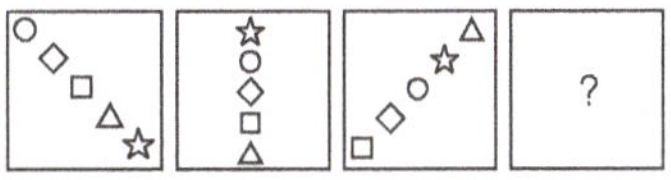

CUET (UG) 2022

Answer Figures

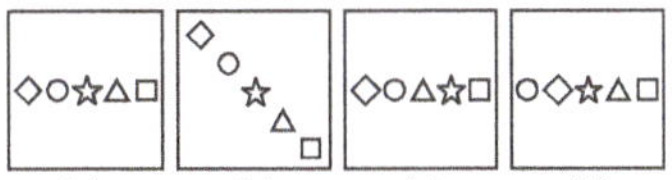

(a) (b) (c) (d)

9. Question Figures

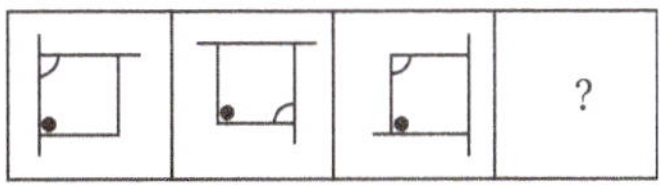

SSC CPO 2018

Answer Figures

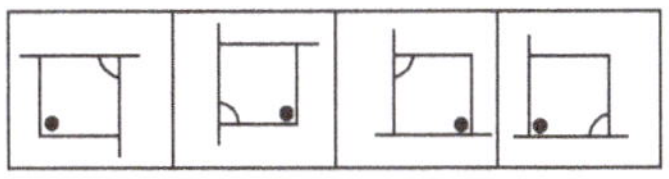

(a) (b) (c) (d)

10. Question Figures

DP Constable 2023

Answer Figures

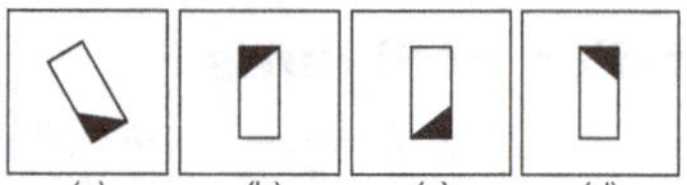

(a) (b) (c) (d)

Based on Change in Position of Figures

Directions (Q. Nos. 11-22) *Find the figure that will come next in the given figure series.*

11. Question Figures

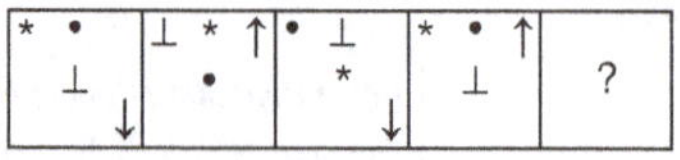

SSC CGL (Tier-II) 2025

Answer Figures

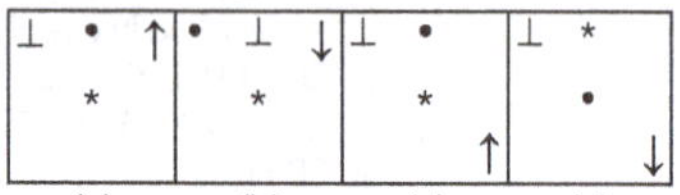

(a) (b) (c) (d)

12. Question Figures

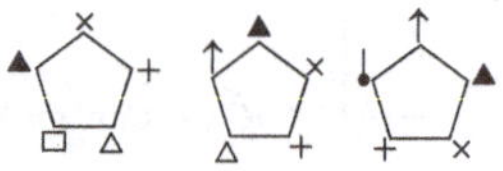

SSC MTS 2021

Answer Figures

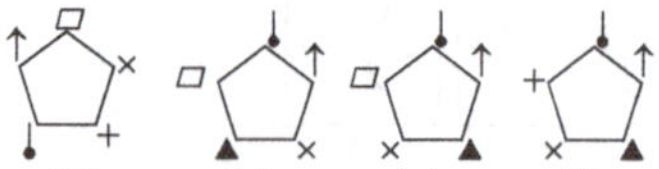

(a) (b) (c) (d)

13. Question Figures

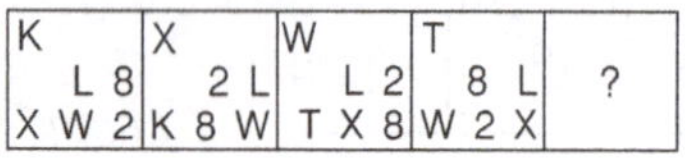

SSC CGL Tier-I 2024

Answer Figures

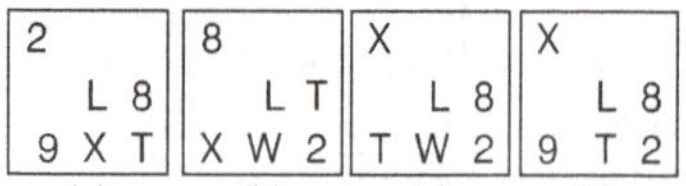

(a) (b) (c) (d)

14. Question Figures

BLAST	LBPTS	SLBPT	LSCTP	?

SSC CGL (Tier-I) 2023

Answer Figures

(a)	(b)	(c)	(d)
SLDPT	SCTPL	PLTSC	PLSCT

15. Question Figures

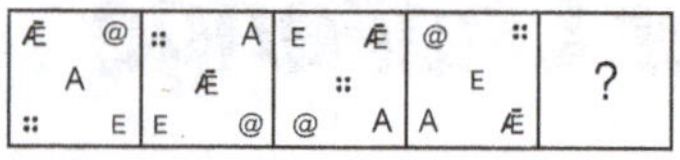

SSC CPO 2024

Answer Figures

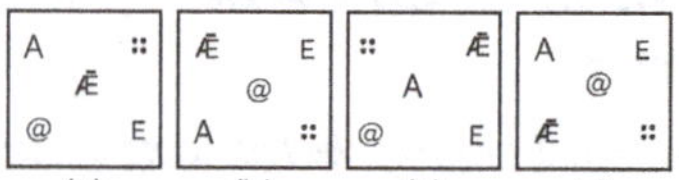

(a) (b) (c) (d)

16. Question Figures

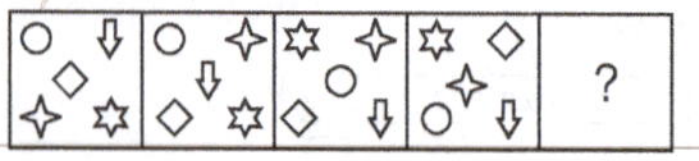

SSC CPO 2024

Answer Figures

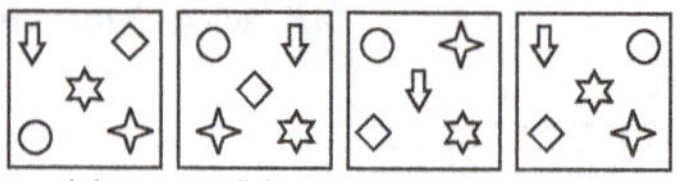

(a) (b) (c) (d)

17. Question Figures

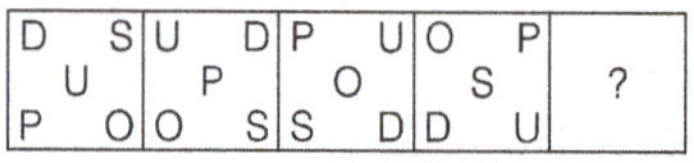

SSC CGL (Tier-I) 2024

Answer Figures

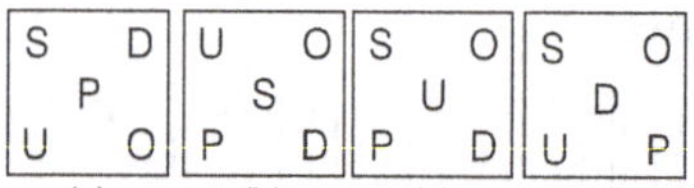

(a) (b) (c) (d)

18. Question Figures

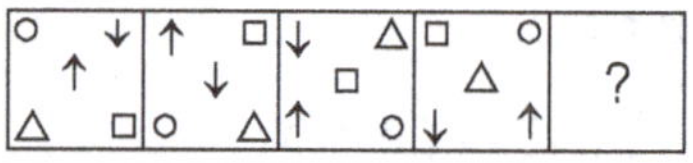

SSC CGL Tier-I 2024

Answer Figures

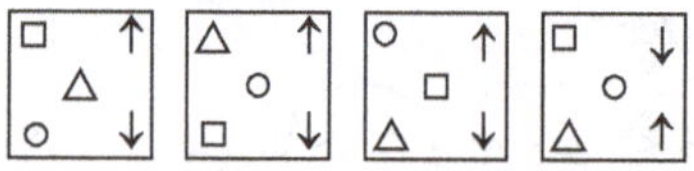

(a) (b) (c) (d)

19. Question Figures

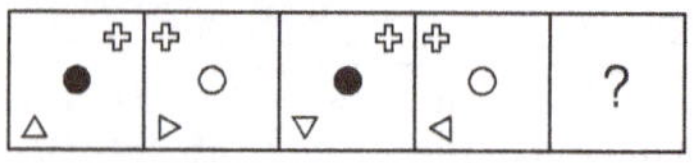

CISF HC Min. 2022

Answer Figures

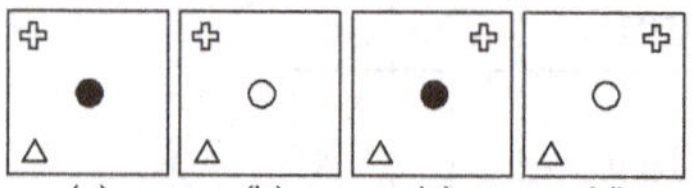

(a) (b) (c) (d)

20. Question Figures

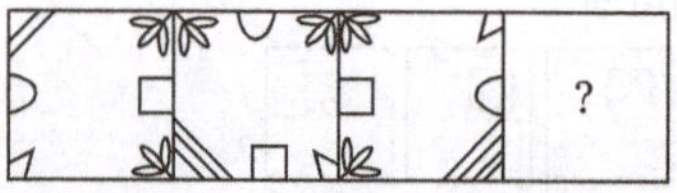

CG Patwari 2019

Chapter Challenge Figure Series

Answer Figures

(a) (b) (c) (d)

21. Question Figures

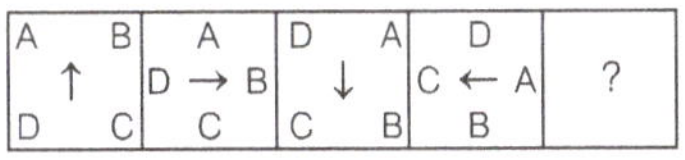

SSC CGL (Tier-II) 2025

Answer Figures

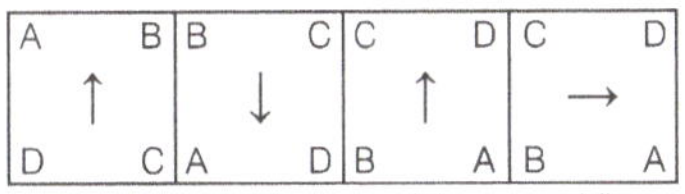

(a) (b) (c) (d)

22. Question Figures

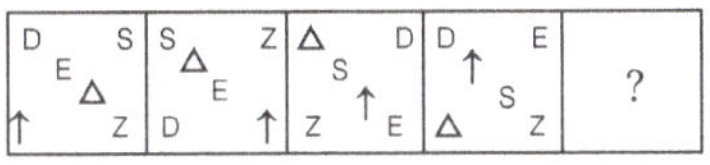

SSC CGL (Tier-I) 2023

Answer Figures

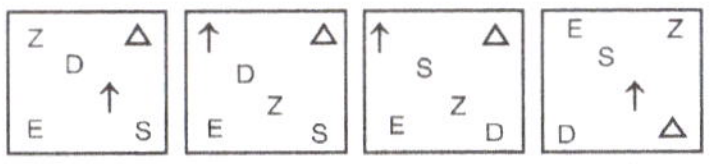

(a) (b) (c) (d)

Based on Change in Shape and Size

Directions (Q. Nos. 23-31) *Find the figure that will come next in the given figure series.*

23. Question Figures

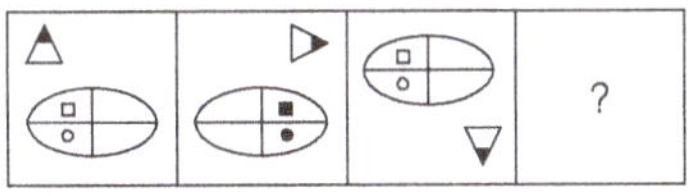

SSC Steno 2020

Answer Figures

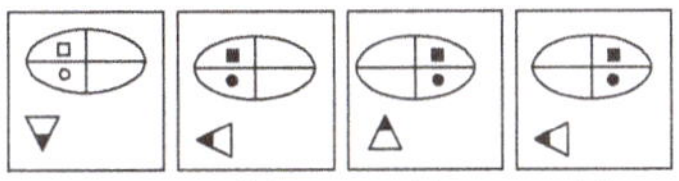

(a) (b) (c) (d)

24. Question Figures

SSC CPO 2024

Answer Figures

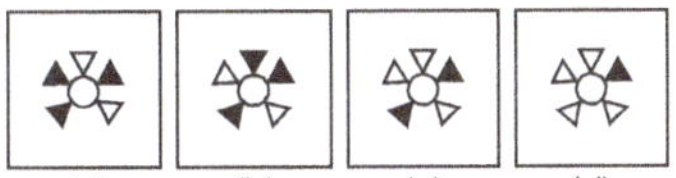

(a) (b) (c) (d)

25. Question Figures

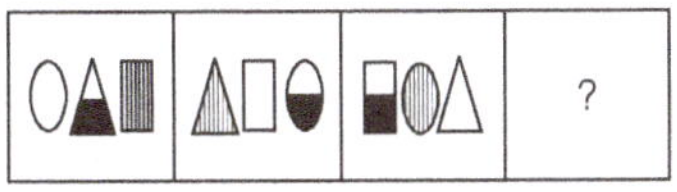

SSC (10+2) 2021

Answer Figures

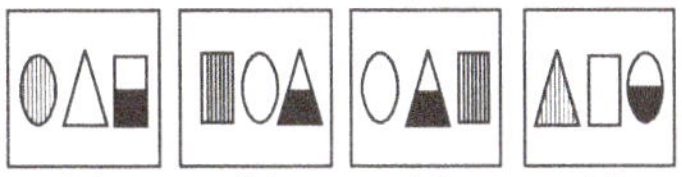

(a) (b) (c) (d)

26. Question Figures

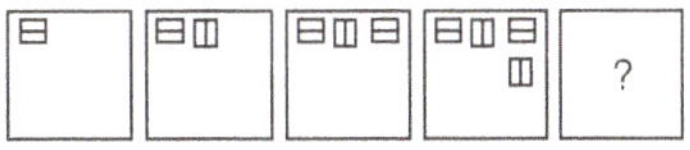

SSC GD Constable 2024

Answer Figures

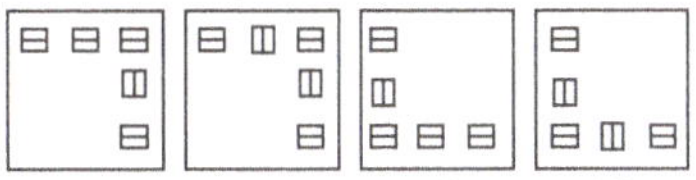

(a) (b) (c) (d)

27. Question Figures

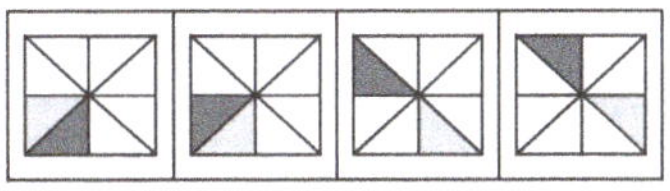

Rajasthan Police Constable 2018

Answer Figures

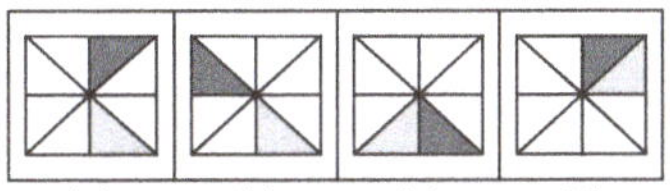

(a) (b) (c) (d)

28. Question Figures

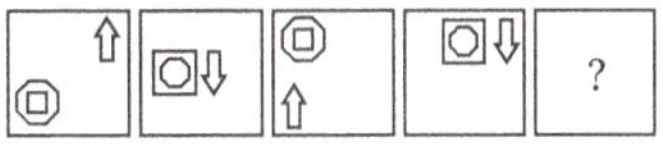

SSC (10+2) 2024

Answer Figures

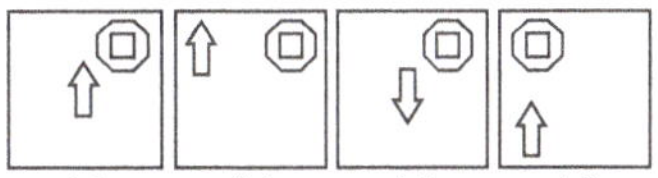

(a) (b) (c) (d)

29. Question Figures

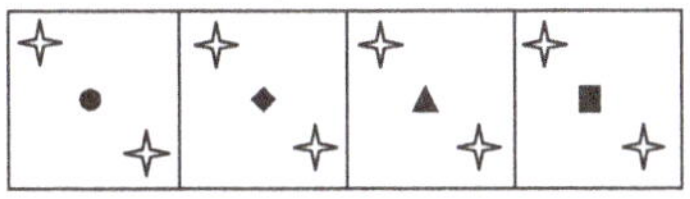

UP Police Constable 2019

Answer Figures

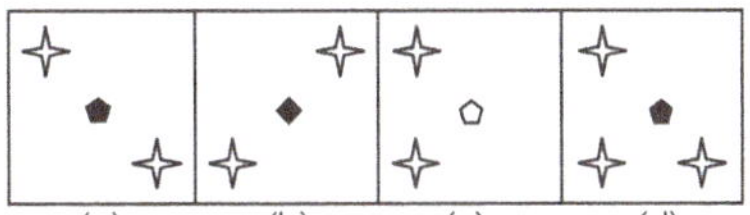

(a) (b) (c) (d)

MRC***

(Most Repeating Concepts)

Question Nos. 2, 3, 5, 11, 13, 16, 21 and 28 are important from the examination point of view. Questions based on figure series are asked in examination SSC CGL, CHSL, CPO, CUET (UG), RRB NTPC, ALP, DSSSB, SSC GD etc.

30. Question Figures

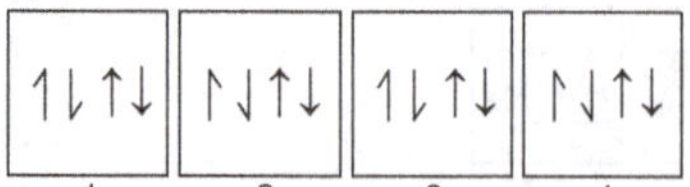

1 2 3 4

SSC CPO 2023

Answer Figures

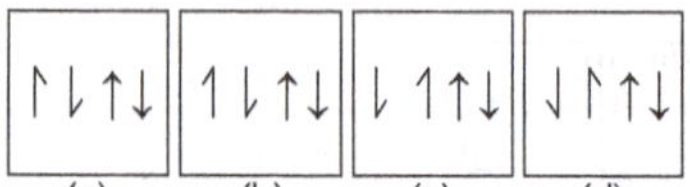

(a) (b) (c) (d)

31. Question Figures

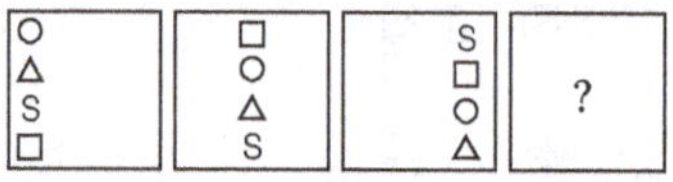

DSSSB 2024

Answer Figures

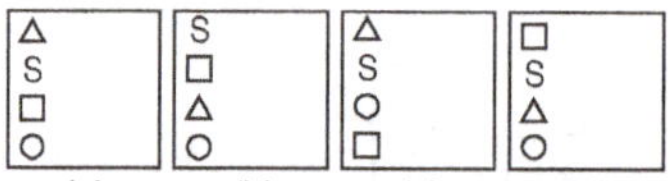

(a) (b) (c) (d)

Right Key

1. (c)	2. (d)	3. (c)	4. (d)	5. (c)	6. (d)	7. (c)	8. (a)	9. (d)	10. (d)
11. (d)	12. (c)	13. (d)	14. (d)	15. (d)	16. (a)	17. (d)	18. (b)	19. (c)	20. (d)
21. (c)	22. (b)	23. (d)	24. (c)	25. (c)	26. (b)	27. (d)	28. (a)	29. (a)	30. (b)
31. (a)									

Solutions

1. *(c)* After observing the question figures, it is found that in every next figure, one arrow is added in the opposite direction of previous arrow. Hence, answer figure (c) will come in the given figure series.

2. *(d)* In the given figure series, a pin is adding to the right in each next term. The top of the pin is opposite to the previous pin each time.

Thus, in place of question mark answer figure (d) will come.

3. *(c)* In every next figure, one '<' sign and one side is decreasing. The figure that comes in place of question mark will have 5 number of '<' and 6 sides.

Hence, option figure (c) is the next figure in the series.

4. *(d)* The number of sides of every next outer figure is decreasing by one.

The shape of the smaller figure inside is same as the outer figure and their number of sides is same as the number of sides of the outer figure.

Hence, answer figure (d) will come at the place of question mark (?).

5. *(c)* In the given figure series, one line is being added continuously in the clockwise direction.

Hence, answer figure (c) will come at the place of question mark (?).

6. *(d)* In each next figure, both designs are moving half step in anticlockwise direction.

So, answer figure (d) will be the next figure in the series.

7. *(c)* In the given figure series, in each next figure the shaded portion is moving 90° clockwise and the arrow (↓) is moving 90° anticlockwise.

So, the option figure (c) will come in place of '?' in the given series.

8. *(a)* In the given figure series, group of small figures is rotating in 45° clockwise direction and following the pattern given below.

Hence, answer figure (a) will comes at the place of question mark.

9. *(d)* In each step, the main figure is rotating 90° clockwise and design look like arc (◡) change their position diagonally and small dark circle remain at their position.

Hence, the next figure will be the figure in option (d).

10. *(d)* Figure series is divided into two alternate parts.

First series (1st, 3rd, 5th figure)

Second series (2nd, 4th, 6th in figure)

11. *(d)* In the given series arrow is shifting one step in anticlockwise direction and in next figure arrow move back to their previous position and rotate 180° its direction in each step. Position of other symbols are as follows.

Hence, the next figure will be option figure (d).

12. *(c)* In the given series, the small figures at the top in each next term are moving in clockwise direction as per the following pattern and the figure at the left side of the base is changing in every term.

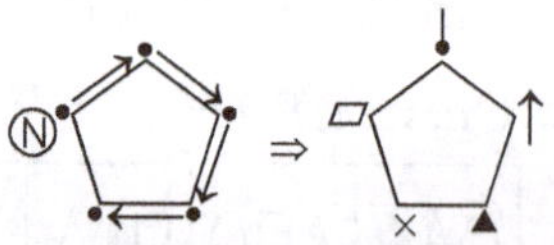

The figure given in option (c) will come next in the figure series.

13. *(d)* The given series follows the following alternate pattern,

From fig. 1 to 2 From fig. 2 to 3
From fig. 3 to 4 From fig. 4 to 5

Hence, the correct figure is option (d).

14. *(d)* There are two alternate series in the given question, which are as follow,

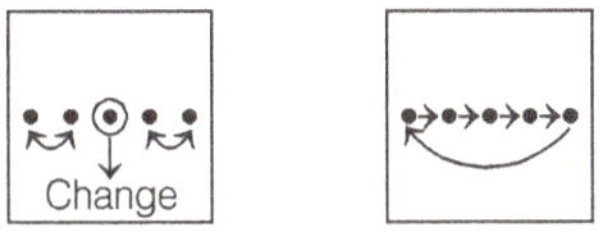

From figure 1 to 2 and 3 to 4 From figure 2 to 3 and 4 to 5

Hence, figure given in option (d) will replace the question mark.

15. *(d)* The series follows the pattern, which is as follows,

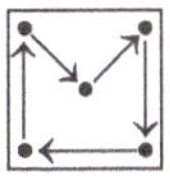

So, 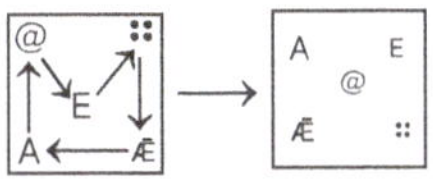

Hence, the next figure in the series will be option figure (d).

16. *(a)* The pattern of the series is as follows,

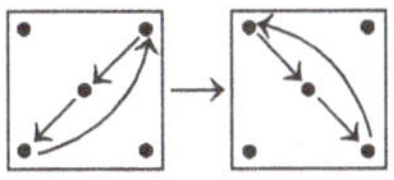

I to II II to III

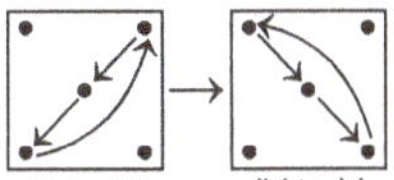

III to IV IV to V

Hence, the next figure will be option figure (a).

> **TOP TIPS** While solving such questions, observe the series of figures carefully and solve the question keeping in mind the change and replacement pattern of the elements contained in the figures.

17. *(d)* The pattern of the series is as follows,

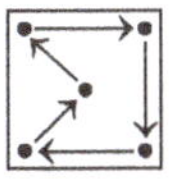

Hence, option figure (d) will replace the question mark.

18. *(b)* The pattern of the series is as follows,

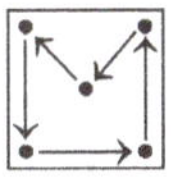

So, following the same sequence, figure (b) will complete the series.

19. *(c)* Symbol (✣) moves one step clockwise and anticlockwise, alternative in each figure. The circle is being shaded in alternate order and is fixed at its place. The triangle is rotating at its place in 90° clockwise direction.

Hence, option figure (c) will be the next figure of the series.

20. *(d)* Here in the question figures, the corner designs shift one place in the anticlockwise direction and the designs in the middle of the sides shift one place in the clockwise direction and one line is added in every next position. In this way, answer figure (d) will come in place of the question mark.

21. *(c)* In the given series letters are moving half step in clockwise direction in each consecutive figure and symbol arrow (↑) is rotating 90° in clockwise direction.

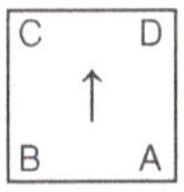

Thus, the next figure will be option figure (c).

22. *(b)* The alternate sequence of the pattern of the given figure series will be as follow.

(i-ii) (ii-iii) (iii-iv)

(iv-v) (v)

23. *(d)* In each next term of the given series, the shapes inside the circle move to the front part and become shaded or unshaded, alternatively. Apart from this, the triangular shape moves one step in clockwise direction and rotates 90° in clockwise direction.

24. *(c)* In the given figure series, in each next figure, one shaded and one unshaded on triangle are being added in alternate order in clockwise direction. Thus, following the sequence, the next figure will be answer figure (c).

25. *(c)* In each next term of the given figure series, the figures shift from right to left and the design inside them changes from left to right. In this way, the answer figure (c) will come in place of the question mark (?) in the series.

26. *(b)* In each step of the given figure series, the number of sub-figures is increasing by 1 in clockwise direction both horizontally and vertically in alternate order. Hence, option figure (b) will replace the question mark.

27. *(d)* In the given sequence of figures, the light black shaded part and the black shaded part move forward one place each in anticlockwise and clockwise direction, respectively. Thus, the next figure in the series will be figure (d).

28. *(a)* In each next figure, the regular octagon and square figure moves half step clockwise direction and interchange their positions. In addition, the arrow-shaped figure moves down diagonally and rotates 180°. This sequence continues. Thus, in place of the question mark, there will be option figure (a).

29. *(a)* In the given series, position and number of stars remain same and shaded shape in middle is getting replaced by a new shape and no shape is repeating itself. From the given options, only figure given in option (a) is the possible next figure.

Hence, figure given in option (a) will replace the question mark.

30. *(b)* In the given figure series, the first and third figures are similar and the second and fourth figures are similar. Therefore, the next figure in the series will be similar to the third figure.

31. *(a)* The order of the figure given in the question is as follows,

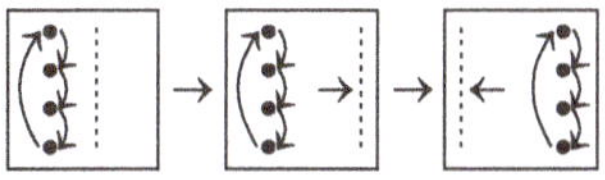

From figure 1 to 2 From figure 2 to 3 From figure 3 to 4

Hence, the figure in option (a) will come in place of the question mark (?).

CHAPTER

04 Figure Completion

Figure completion is a process of finding out the missing part of an incomplete figure to complete it. In this chapter, candidates deal with the questions in which a part, generally 1/4th part of the figure is missing and they asked to find the missing part. Candidates are required to understand the general structure of the figure, then choose the correct alternative.

e.g. Identify the missing part of the question figure and select it from given answer figures.

Question Figure

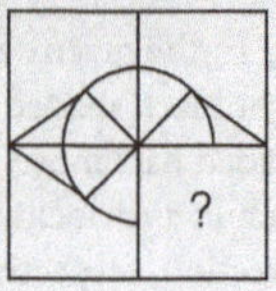

Answer Figures

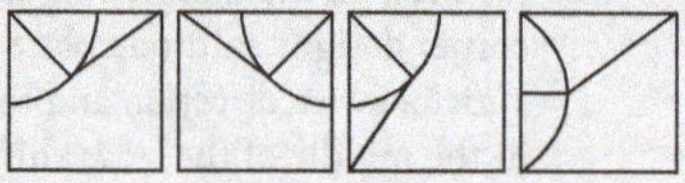

(a) (b) (c) (d)

Sol. (*a*) Answer figure (a) will complete the pattern in the question figure.

> **Score Booster**
>
> If the answer figure appears same, but has been rotated, then the figure whose orientation is least changed is the correct option figure. The figure to be placed at '?' can be given in any rotated form of figure. Candidates can rotate the figure to select the correct answer figure.

Directions (Ex. Nos. 1-3) *Identify the missing part of the question figure and select it from given answer figures.*

Example 1 Question Figure *CUET (UG) 2023*

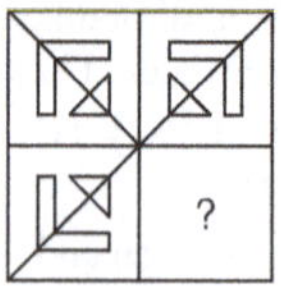

Answer Figures

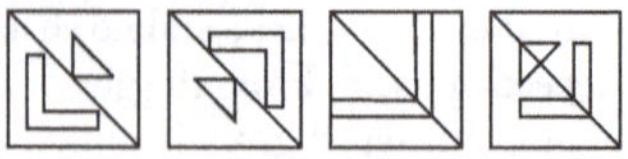

(a) (b) (c) (d)

Sol. (*d*) Answer figure (d) will complete the pattern in the question figure.

Example 2 Question Figure *SSC MTS 2022*

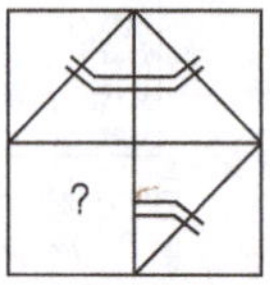

Answer Figures

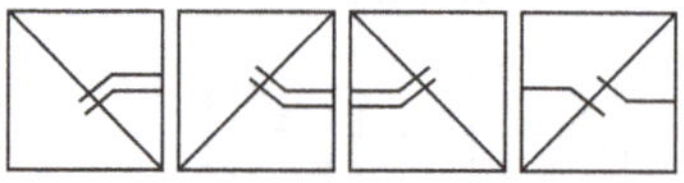

(a) (b) (c) (d)

Sol. (*a*) Answer figure (a) will complete the pattern in the question figure.

Example 3 Question Figure

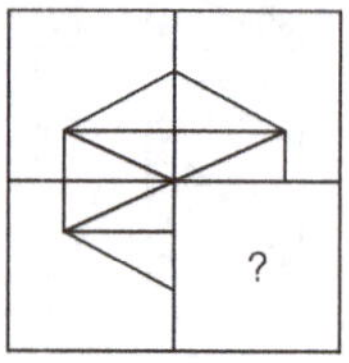

RPF SI 2019

Answer Figures

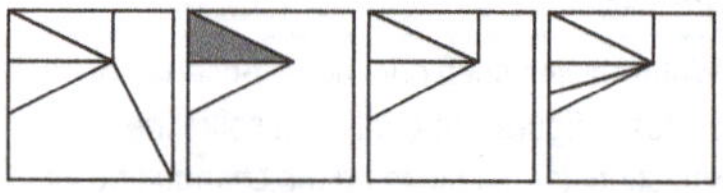

(a) (b) (c) (d)

Sol. (*c*) Answer figure (c) will complete the pattern in the question figure.

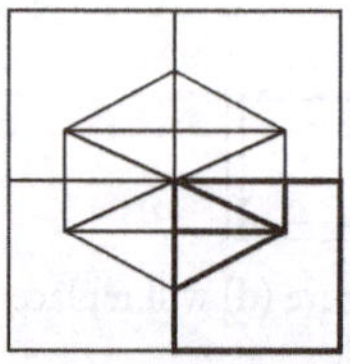

Chapter Challenge

Directions (Q. Nos. 1-35) *In each of the following questions, select a figure from the given four alternatives, which when placed in the blank space of question figure would complete the pattern.*

1. Question Figure

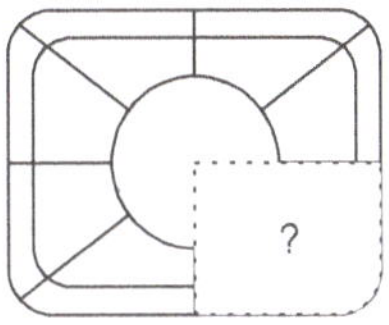

DSSSB 2019

Answer Figures

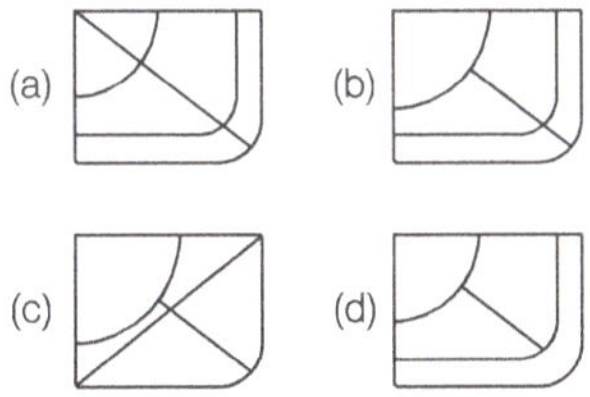

2. Question Figure

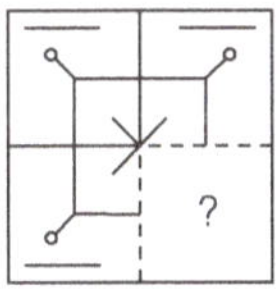

SSC CGL (Tier-I) 2024

Answer Figures

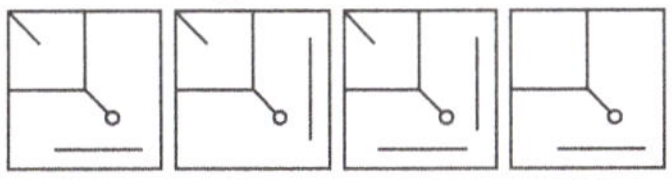

(a) (b) (c) (d)

3. Question Figure

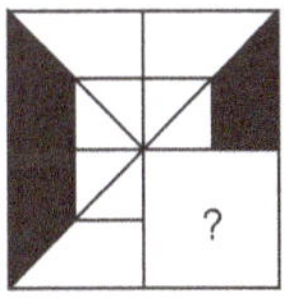

UP Police (SI) 2021

Answer Figures

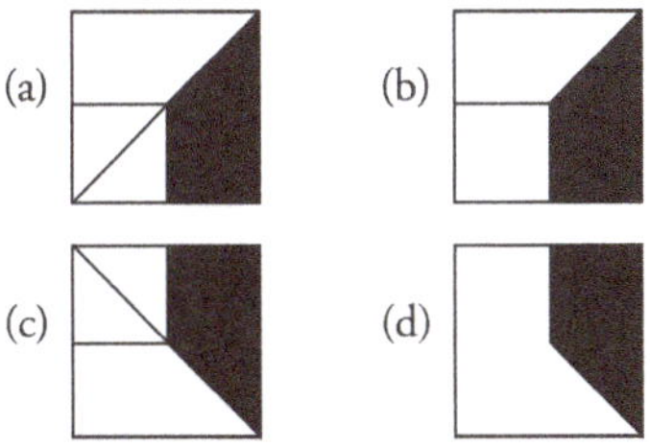

4. Question Figure

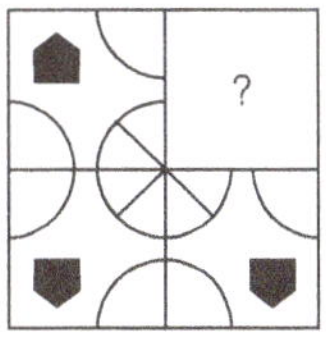

SSC GD Constable 2024

Answer Figures

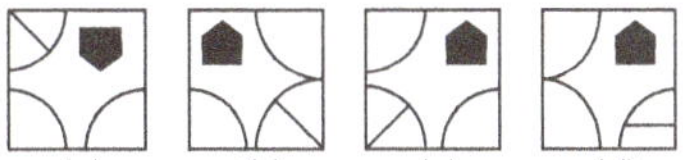

(a) (b) (c) (d)

5. Question Figure

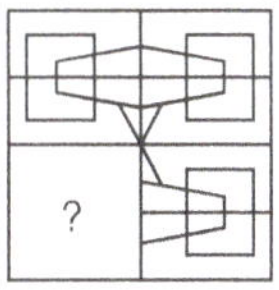

DSSSB 2019

Answer Figures

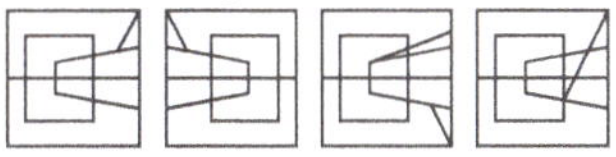

(a) (b) (c) (d)

6. Question Figure

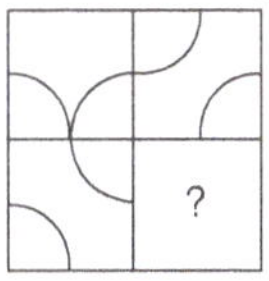

RRB ALP 2018

Answer Figures

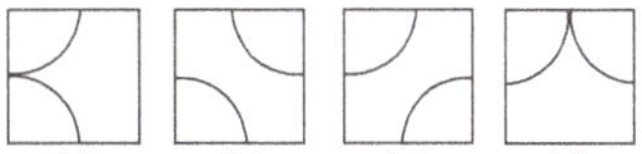

(a) (b) (c) (d)

7. Question Figure

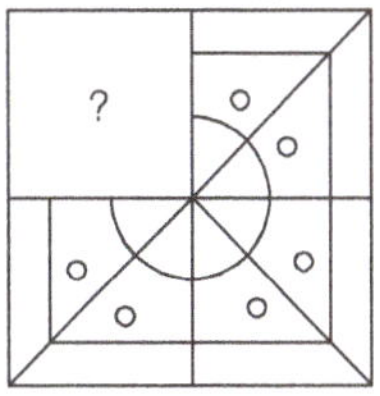

UP Police (SI) 2021

Answer Figures

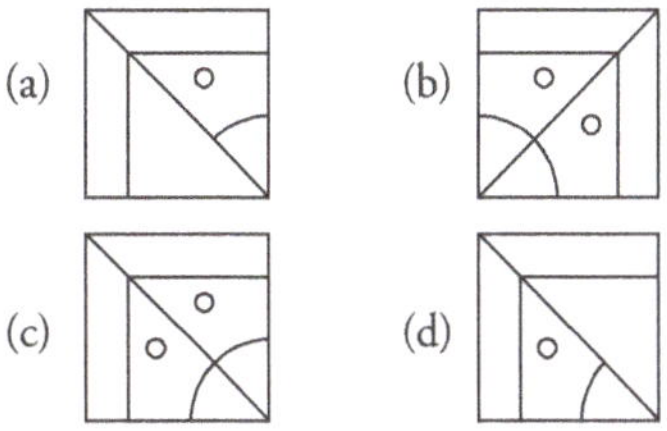

8. Question Figure

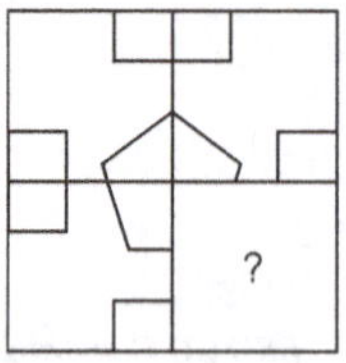

SSC MTS 2023

Answer Figures

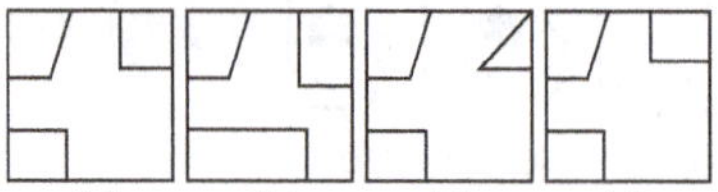

(a) (b) (c) (d)

9. Question Figure

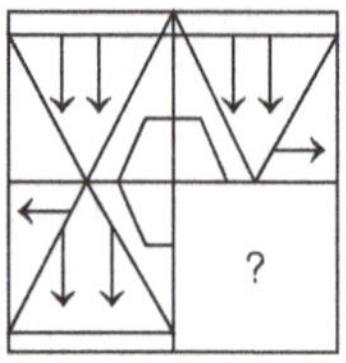

SSC Steno 2022

Answer Figures

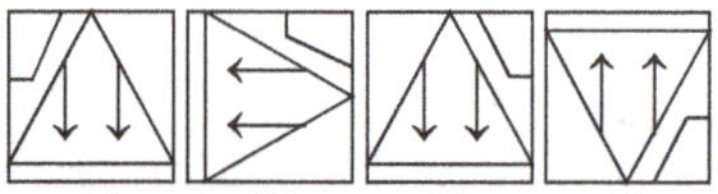

(a) (b) (c) (d)

10. Question Figure

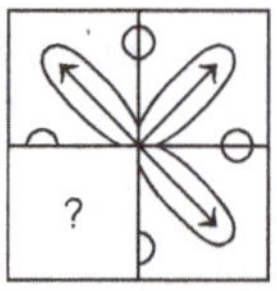

DSSSB 2019

Answer Figures

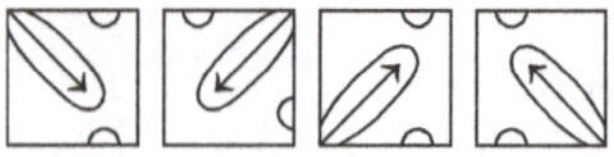

(a) (b) (c) (d)

11. Question Figure

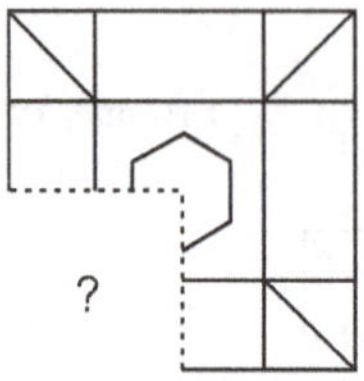

SSC CGL (Tier-II) 2025

Answer Figures

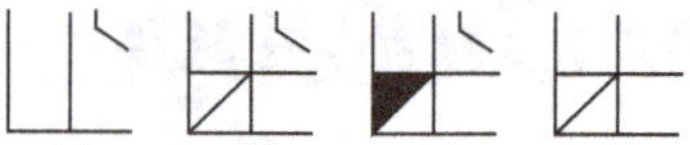

(a) (b) (c) (d)

12. Question Figure

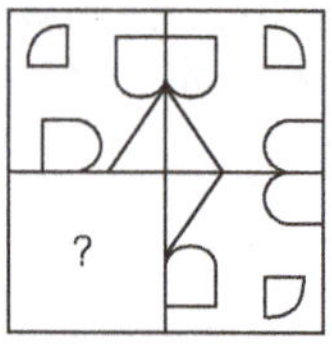

SSC MTS 2023

Answer Figures

(a) (b) (c) (d)

13. Question Figure

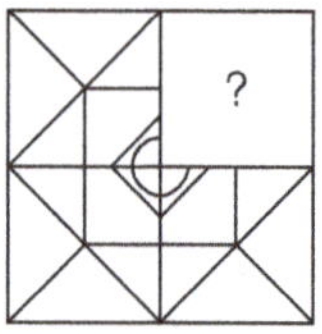

AFCAT 2018

Answer Figures

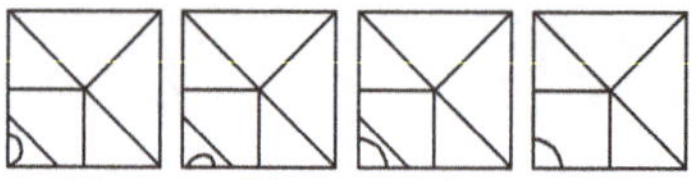

(a) (b) (c) (d)

14. Question Figure

Chhattisgarh Patwari 2019

Answer Figures

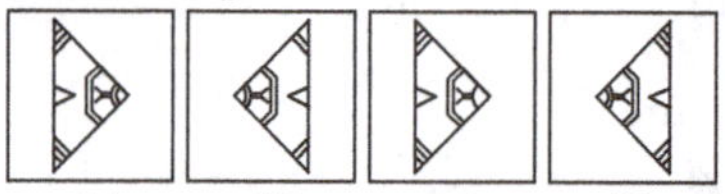

(a) (b) (c) (d)

15. Question Figure

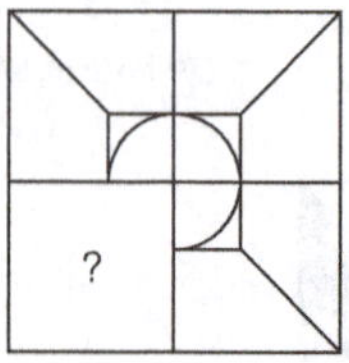

RPF Constable 2019

Answer Figures

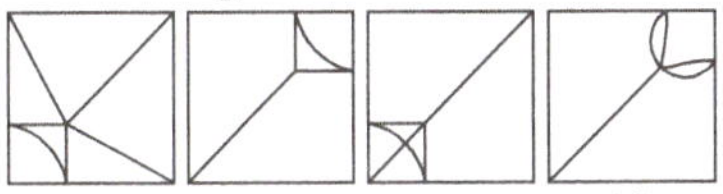

(a) (b) (c) (d)

16. Question Figure

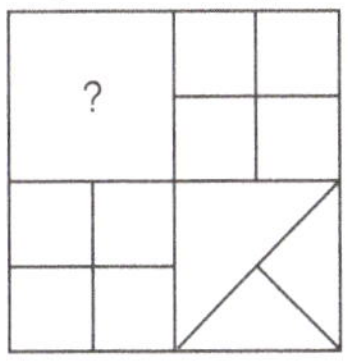

RRB JE 2019

Answer Figures

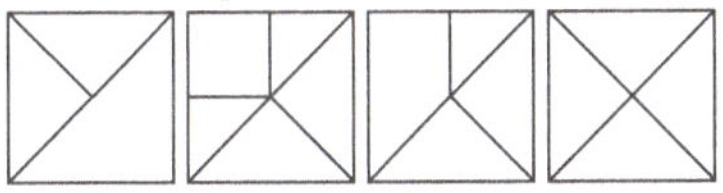

(a) (b) (c) (d)

17. Question Figure

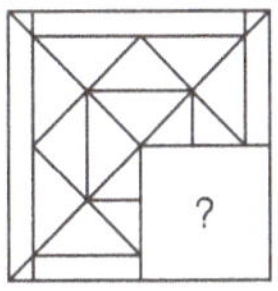

DSSSB 2019

Answer Figures

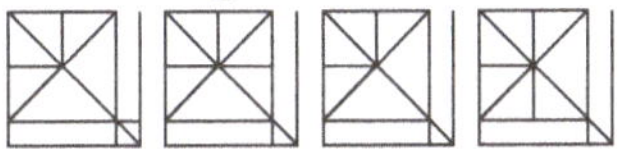

(a) (b) (c) (d)

18. Question Figure

Delhi Police Constable 2020

Answer Figures

(a) (b) (c) (d)

19. Question Figure

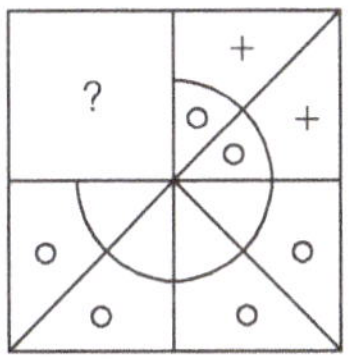

RRB JE 2019

Answer Figures

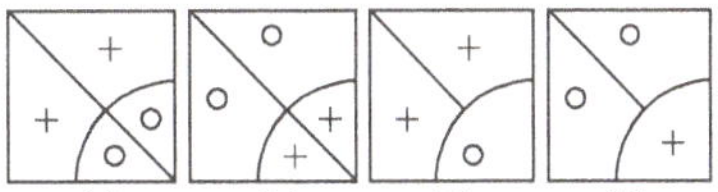

(a) (b) (c) (d)

20. Question Figure

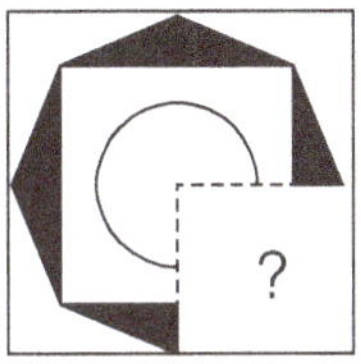

SSC CGL (Tier-II) 2025

Answer Figures

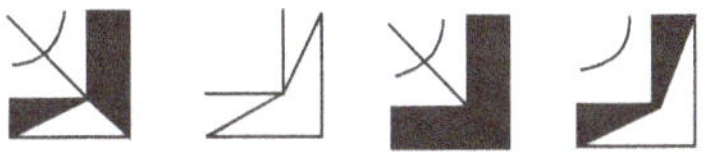

(a) (b) (c) (d)

21. Question Figure

SSC MTS 2021

> ***MRC******
> ***(Most Repeating Concepts)***
> Q. Nos. 2, 4, 8, 9, 12, 21 and 25 is frequently being asked the examination like SSC CGL, MTS, CPO and GD Constable.

Answer Figures

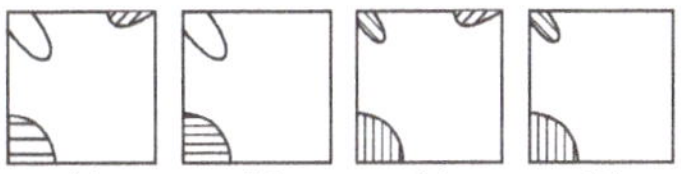

(a) (b) (c) (d)

22. Question Figure

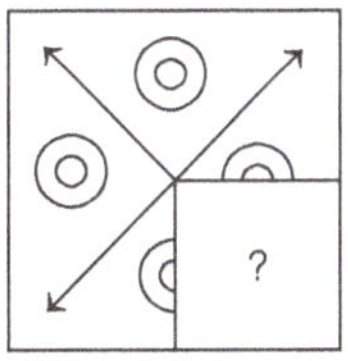

RRB JE 2019

Answer Figures

(a) (b) (c) (d)

23. Question Figure

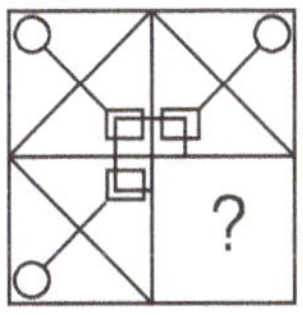

Delhi Police Constable 2020

Answer Figures

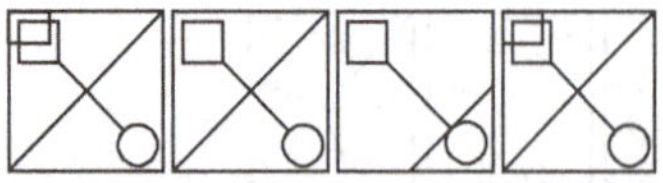

(a) (b) (c) (d)

24. Question Figure

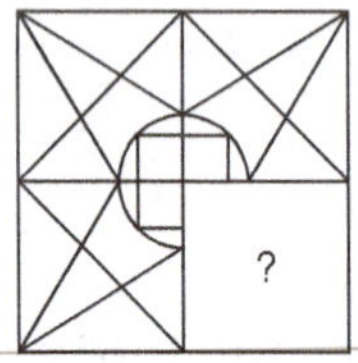

RRB SI 2019

Answer Figures

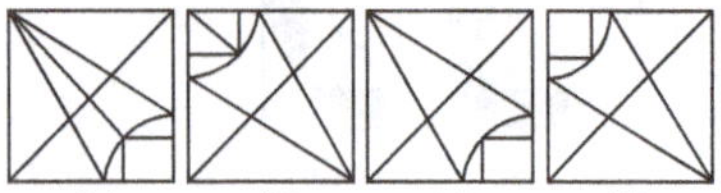

(a) (b) (c) (d)

25. Question Figure

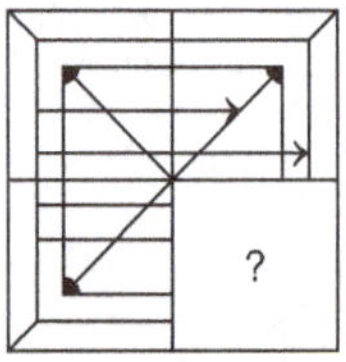

SSC Steno 2022

Answer Figures

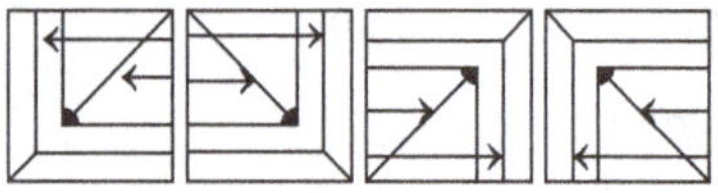

(a) (b) (c) (d)

26. Question Figure

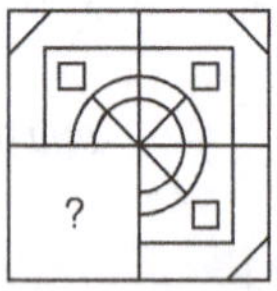

DSSSB 2019

Answer Figures

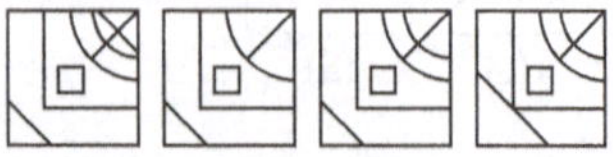

(a) (b) (c) (d)

27. Question Figure

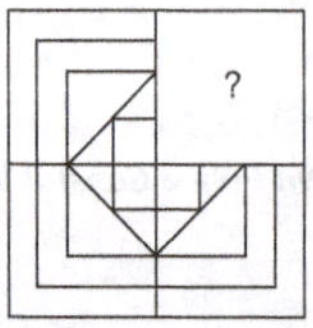

MP Police Constable 2022

Answer Figures

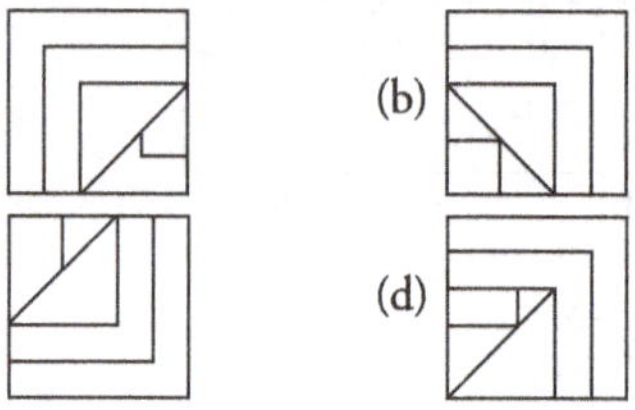

(a) (b) (c) (d)

28. Question Figure

RRB Group D 2018

Answer Figures

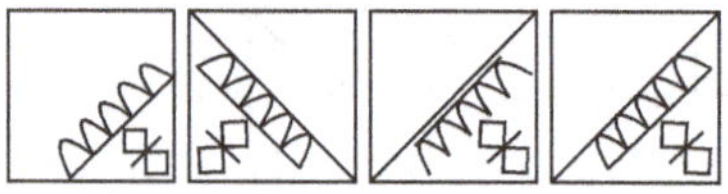

(a) (b) (c) (d)

29. Question Figure

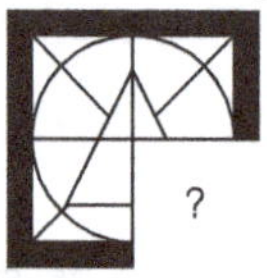

UP Police (ASI) 2021

Answer Figures

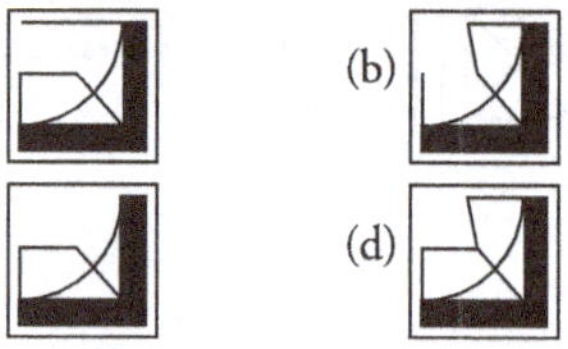

(a) (b) (c) (d)

30. Question Figure

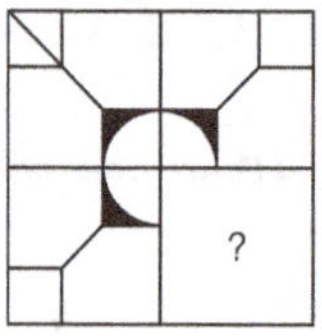

RPF Constable 2019

Answer Figures

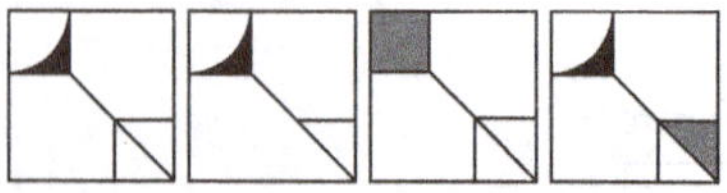

(a) (b) (c) (d)

31. Question Figure

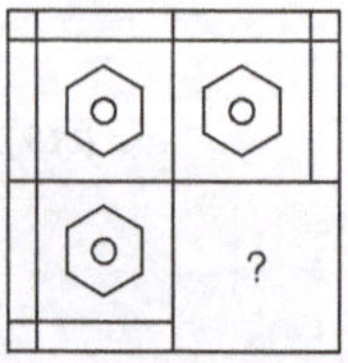

RPF Constable 2019

Chapter Challenge Figure Completion

Answer Figures

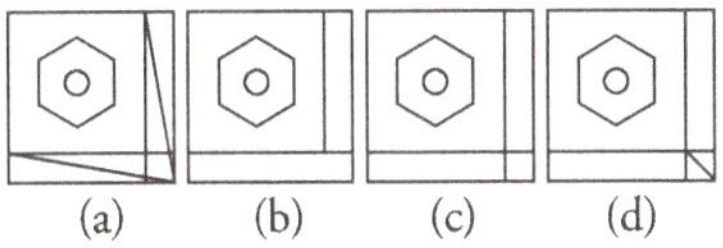

32. Question Figure

RRB ALP 2018

Answer Figures

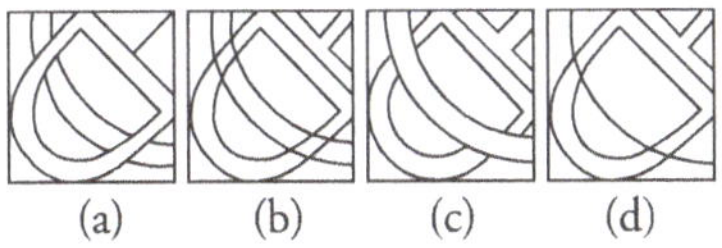

33. Question Figure Answer Figures

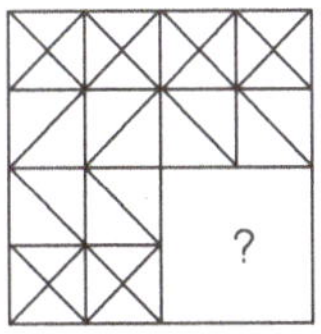

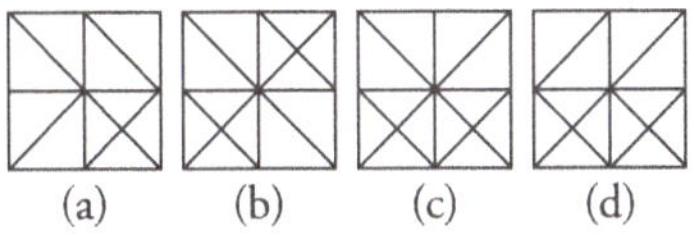

AFCAT 2018

34. Question Figure

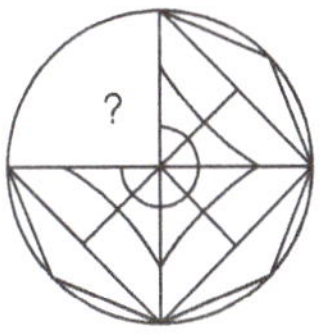

RRB ALP 2018

Answer Figures

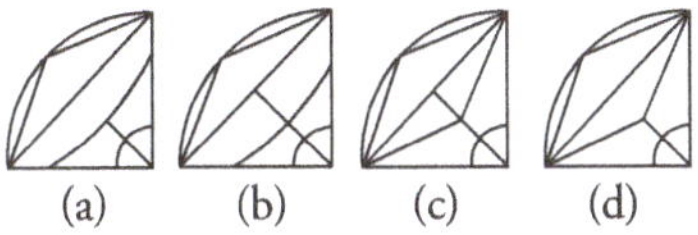

35. Question Figure

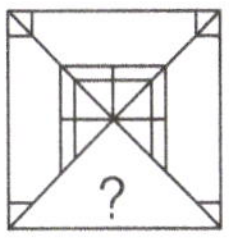

Delhi Police Constable 2020

Answer Figures

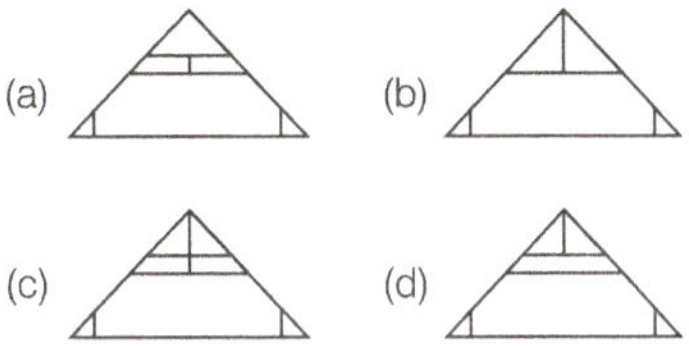

36. Question Figure

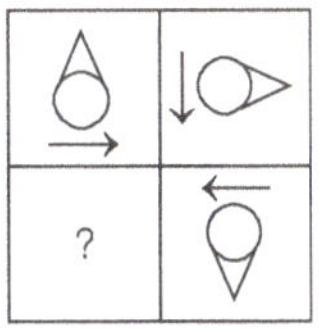

SSC MTS 2023

Answer Figures

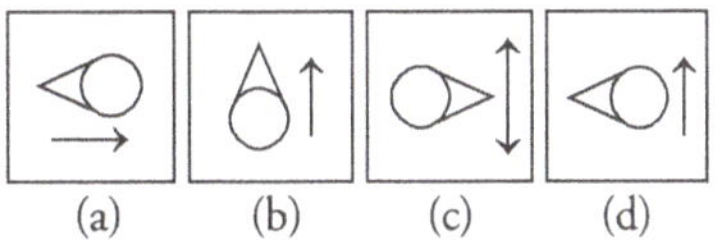

37. Question Figure

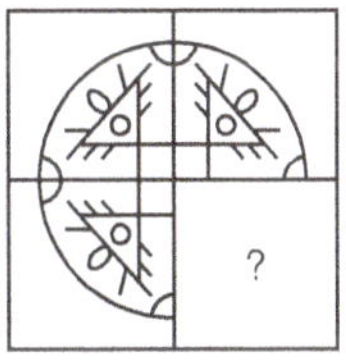

BSSC (10+2) 2022

Answer Figures

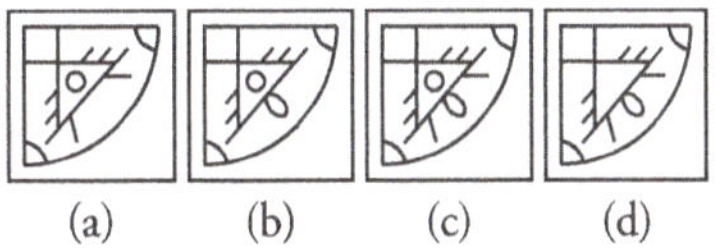

Right Key

1. (b)	2. (a)	3. (c)	4. (c)	5. (a)	6. (c)	7. (c)	8. (d)	9. (a)	10. (b)
11. (b)	12. (a)	13. (c)	14. (d)	15. (b)	16. (a)	17. (c)	18. (b)	19. (a)	20. (d)
21. (a)	22. (d)	23. (d)	24. (d)	25. (b)	26. (c)	27. (b)	28. (a)	29. (d)	30. (a)
31. (c)	32. (c)	33. (d)	34. (b)	35. (c)	36. (d)	37. (c)			

CHAPTER

05 Figure Formation

Figure Formation

Formation of figures refers to the use of pieces of different designs to construct a desired figure.
It requires a high visualisation skill, as different fragmented parts of a figure are combined to form the desired figure.
In this chapter, two sets of figures are given namely problem figure and answer figures. A candidate is asked to arrange the different components/pieces of the problem figure, so as to form one of the answer figures.

Based on Arrangement of the Figures

In this type of questions, a candidate is required to select a figure from the answer figures, that can be formed by arranging the pieces given in the question figure.

e.g. In the following question, find a figure from the answer figures that can be formed by joining the pieces given in the question figure.

Question Figure

Answer Figures

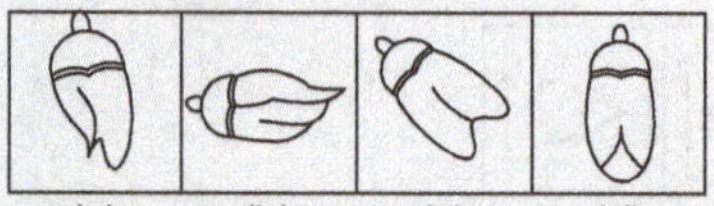

(a) (b) (c) (d)

Sol. (b) Figure given in option (b) can be formed by joining the pieces given in the question figure.

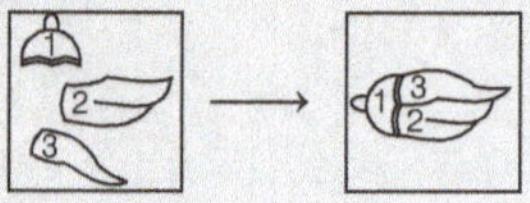

Fragmentation of a Figure into Simple Parts

In this type of questions, question figures are to be formed using the pieces given in one of the answer figures and the candidate is required to find out the correct answer figure. Sometimes, pieces of boundary lines of the question figure are also given in the answer figure, then in this case, these pieces are also counted for the formation of question figure.

e.g. In the following question, find the figure from the given answer figures, that can form the question figure.

Question Figure

Answer Figures

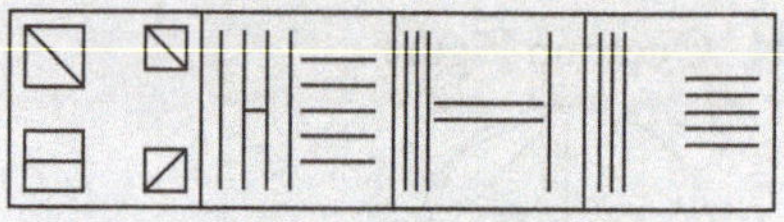

(a) (b) (c) (d)

Sol. (c) The question figure can be formed by joining the pieces given in option (c) as shown below.

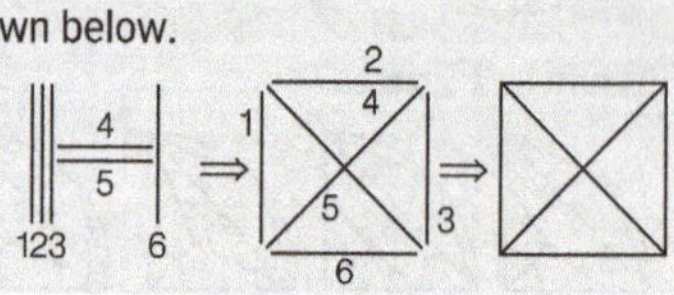

Based on Formation of Triangle/Square

In this type of questions, a triangle (equilateral, isosceles etc.) or a square is to be formed by joining three or four figures out of a group of five or six figures of different designs.
A candidate is required to find out the correct combination of figure from the given alternative which can be joined to form the required figure.

e.g. In the following question, five figure are given. Out of them, find the three figures that can be joined to form an equilateral triangle.

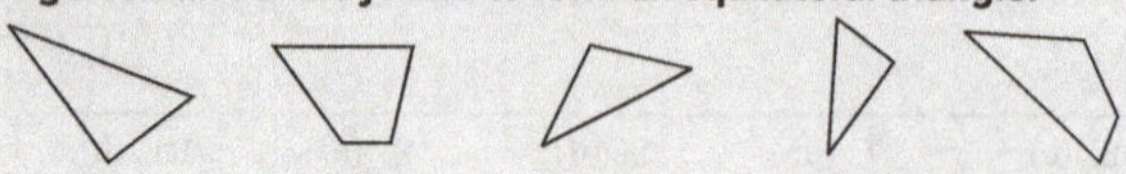

(A) (B) (C) (D) (E)

(a) ABC (b) BCD (c) CDE (d) BDE

Sol. (c) Figures C, D and E can be joined together to form an equilateral triangle.

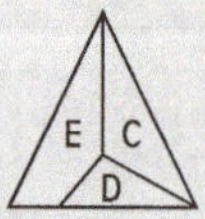

Score Booster

- If the question has complex shapes/figures, then do not select the answer option just by looking at it. Try drawing the shapes yourself on paper once, this will reduce the chances of error.
- Read the instructions carefully because sometimes you are asked to construct not only the question figure but also other geometrical figures like square, triangle etc.

Exam Approach Examples

Based on Arrangement of the Figures

Example 1 In the following question, find a figure from the answer figure that can be formed by joining the pieces given in the question figure.

Question Figure

Answer Figures

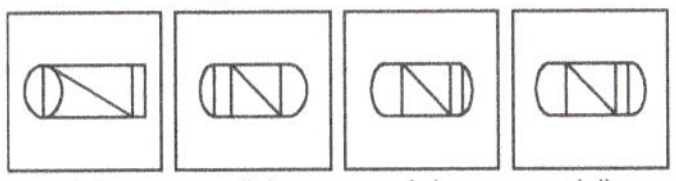

(a) (b) (c) (d)

Sol. *(d)* Figure given in option (d) can be formed by joining the pieces given in the question figure.

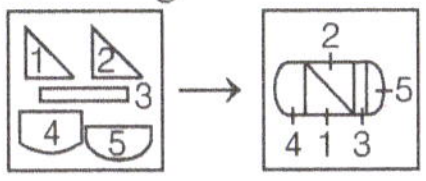

Fragmentation of a Figure into Simple Parts

Example 2 In the following question, find the figure from the given answer figures, that can form the question figure.

Question Figure

Helping Tips

Select the answer figure only when all the pieces of the question figure are present in it.

Answer Figures

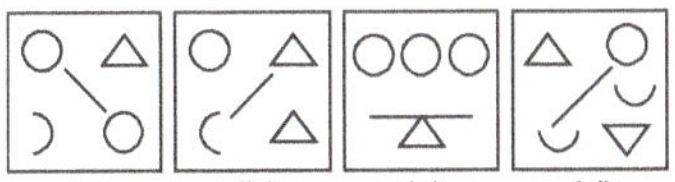

(a) (b) (c) (d)

Sol. (a) The question figure can be formed by joining the pieces given in option (a).

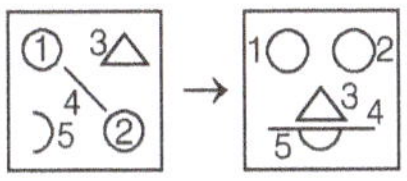

Example 3 Which of the following answer figure patterns can be combined to form the question figure?

UP Police Constable 2018

Trending Concept

These type of questions are very important for UP Police Constable and UPSSSC examination.

Question Figure

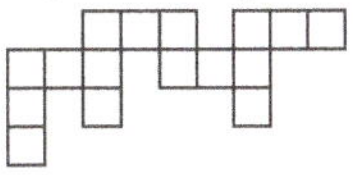

Answer Figures

Sol. *(d)* The question figure can be formed by joining the pieces given in option (d).

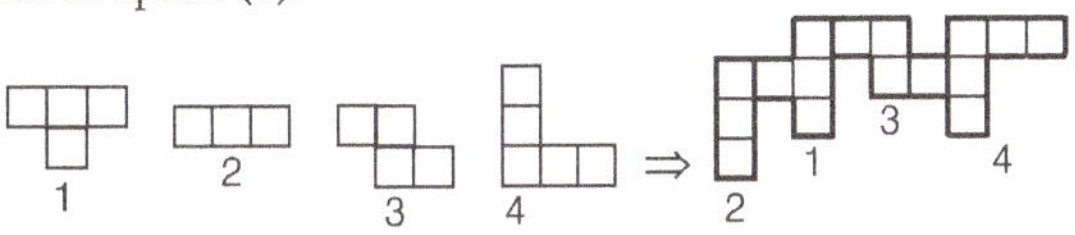

Based on Formation of Triangle/Square

Example 4 From the given figures, find those 3 figures which when fitted together form a square.

UP Police Constable 2024

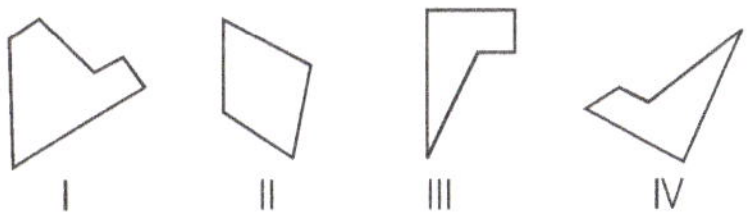

(a) I, II, IV
(b) II, III, IV
(c) I, III, IV
(d) I, II, III

Sol. *(b)* The square can be formed by joining the pieces in option (b).

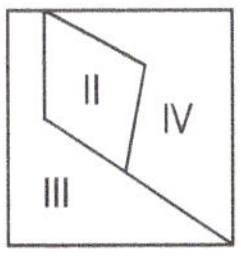

Chapter Challenge

Based on Arrangement of the Figures

Directions (Q. Nos. 1-11) *In the questions given below, find out which of the figures can be formed using the pieces given in the question figure?*

1. Question Figure Answer Figures

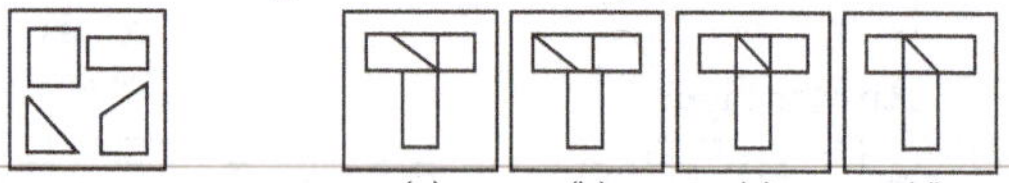

(a) (b) (c) (d)

SSC CPO 2019

> *MRC****
> ***(Most Repeating Concepts)***
> Questions Nos. 1, 2, 3, 4, 6, 9 and 10 are very important from the examination point of view. These types of questions are being repeatedly asked in SSC CGL, MTS, CPO, UP Police Constable, UPSSSC examination.

2.

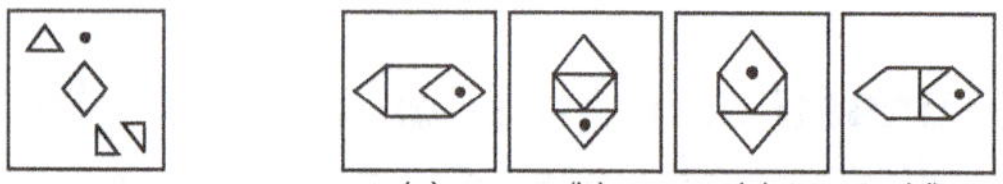

(a) (b) (c) (d)

SSC MTS 2019

3.

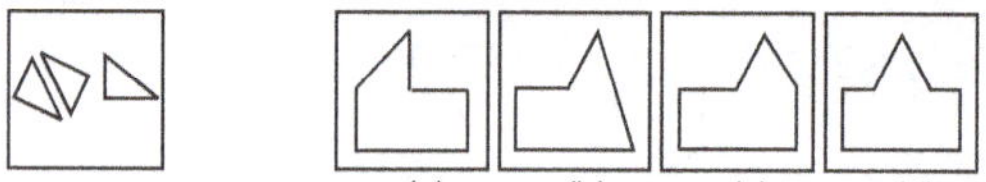

(a) (b) (c) (d)

UP Police Constable 2024

4.

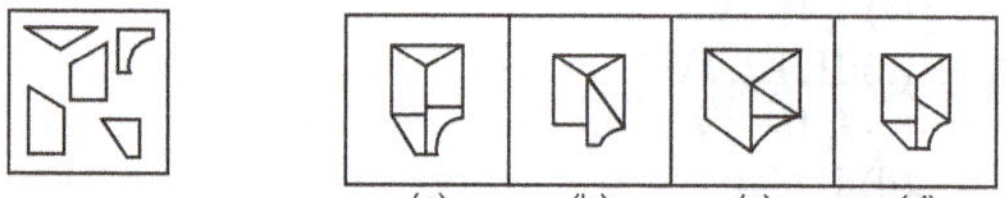

(a) (b) (c) (d)

SSC CGL (Tier-I) 2020

5.

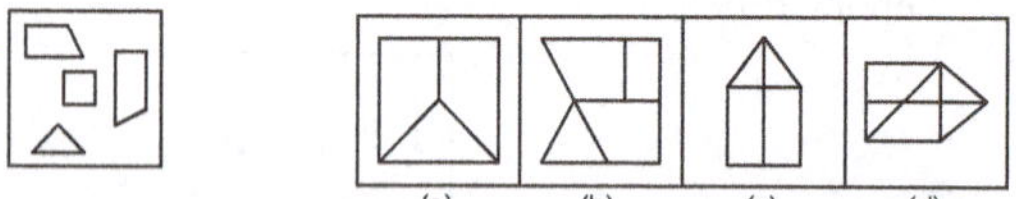

(a) (b) (c) (d)

SSC CGL (Tier-I) 2020

6.

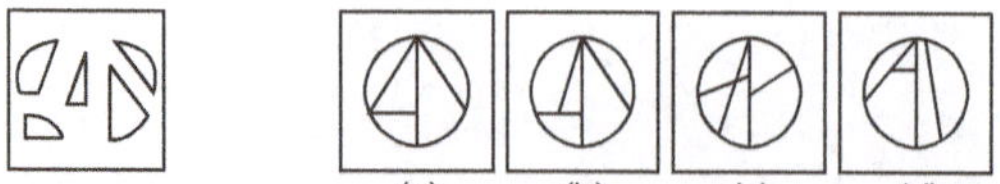

(a) (b) (c) (d)

UPSSSC Combined Exercise Trainer 2018

7.

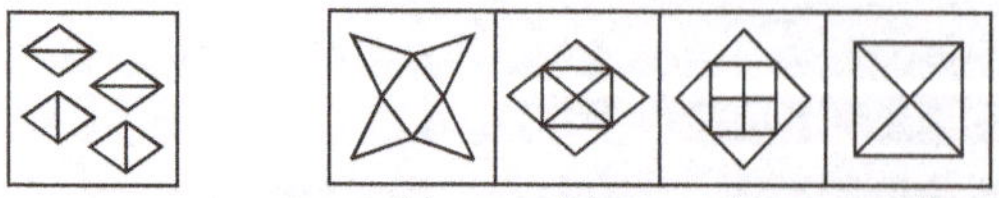

(a) (b) (c) (d)

UPSSSC 2018

8. Question Figure Answer Figures

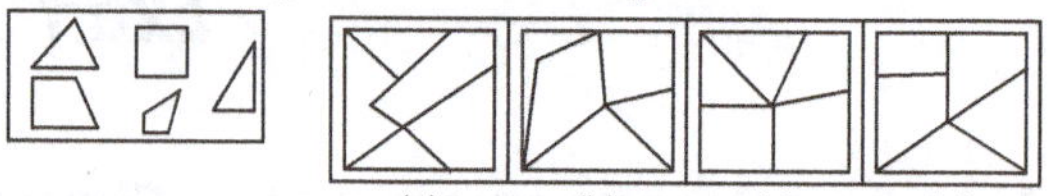

(a) (b) (c) (d)

9.

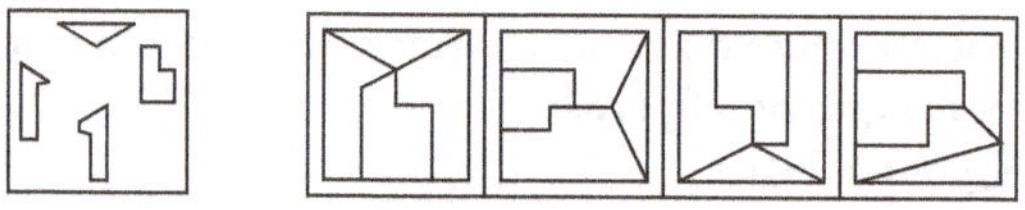

(a) (b) (c) (d)

RRC Group D 2018

10.

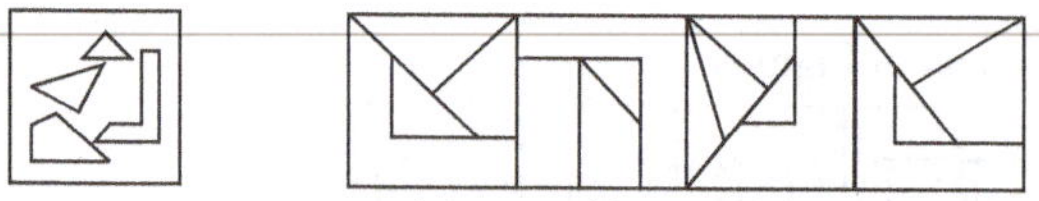

(a) (b) (c) (d)

SSC CGL (Tier-I) 2020

11.

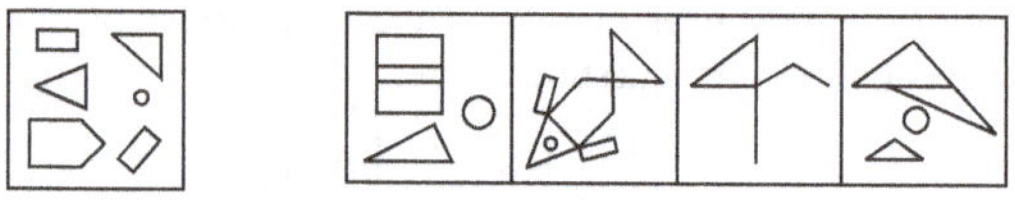

(a) (b) (c) (d)

Fragmentation of a Figure into Simple Parts

Directions (Q. Nos. 12-17) *In each of the following questions, find the figure from the given answer figures, that can form the question figure.*

12. Question Figure Answer Figures

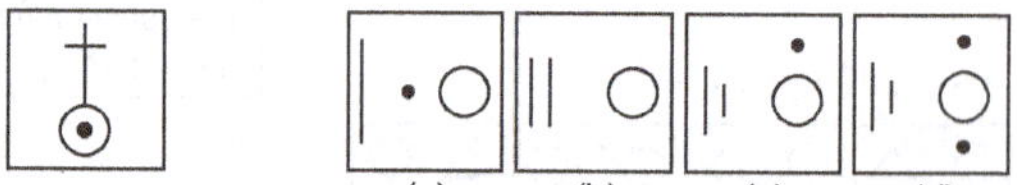

(a) (b) (c) (d)

13.

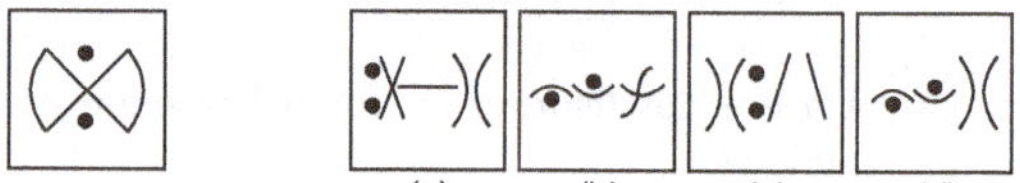

(a) (b) (c) (d)

14.

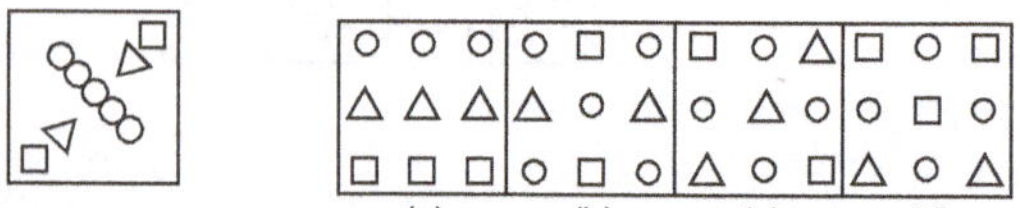

(a) (b) (c) (d)

UPSSSC 2020

15.

(a) (b) (c) (d)

16. Question Figure Answer Figures

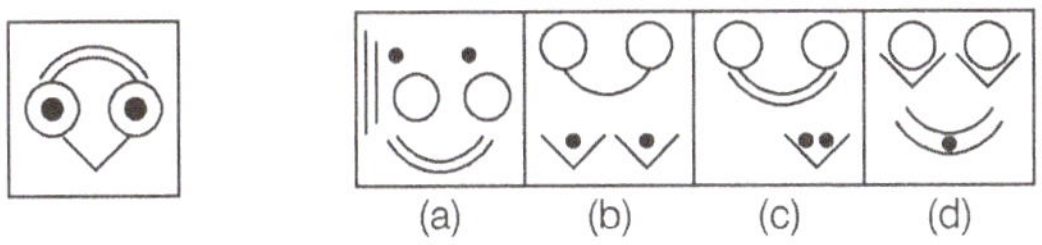

(a) (b) (c) (d)

17. Question Figure

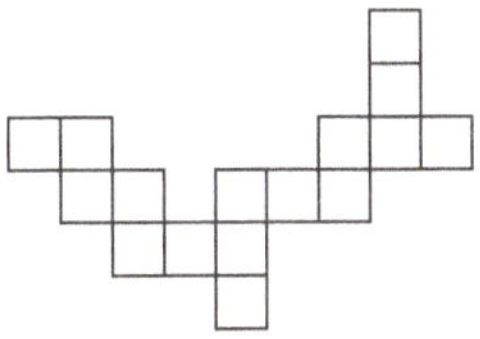

UPSSSC 2018

Answer Figures

(a) 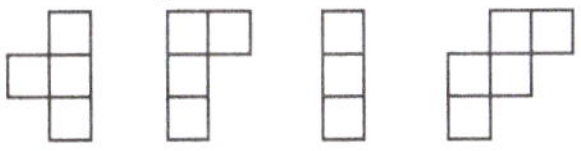

(b) 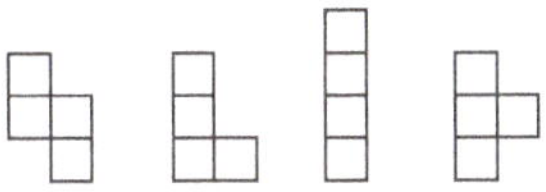

(c) 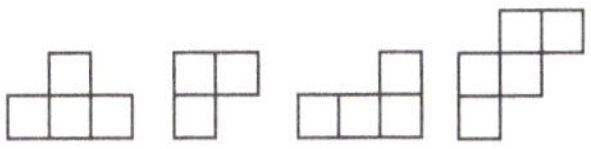

(d) 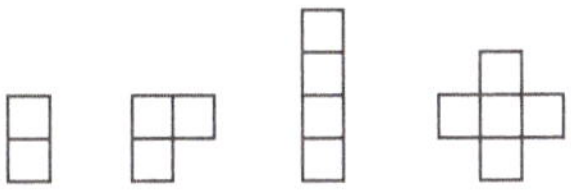

Based on Formation of Triangle/Square

Directions (Q. Nos. 18-21) *In each of the following questions five figures are given. Out of them, find the three figures that can be joined to form an equilateral triangle.*

18. 

(A) (B) (C) (D) (E)

(a) BCD (b) ABC
(c) CDE (d) BCE

19. 

(A) (B) (C) (D) (E)

(a) BCD (b) ACD
(c) CDE (d) BDE

20. 

(A) (B) (C) (D) (E)

(a) ABC (b) BCD
(c) CDE (d) BDE

21. 

(A) (B) (C) (D) (E)

(a) ABE (b) BCE
(c) ADE (d) BDE

Directions (Q. Nos. 22-25) *In each of the following questions, five figures are given. Out of them, find the three figures that can be joined to form a square.*

22. 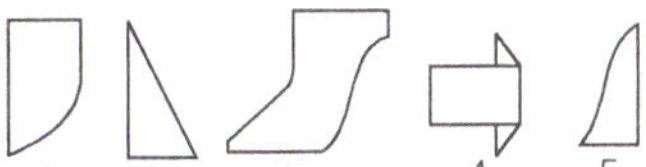

1 2 3 4 5

RPF Constable 2019

(a) 1, 3, 4 (b) 1, 4, 5
(c) 1, 3, 5 (d) 2, 3, 4

> ***MRC******
> *(Most Repeating Concepts)*
> Question Nos. 22, 23, 24 and 25 are important from examination point of view. These type of questions are generally asked in RPF SI and Constable examination.

23. 

1 2 3 4 5

RPF SI 2019

(a) 1, 3, 4 (b) 2, 4, 5
(c) 1, 3, 5 (d) 2, 3, 4

24. 

1 2 3 4 5

RPF SI 2019

(a) 1, 3, 4 (b) 1, 4, 5
(c) 2, 3, 4 (d) 1, 2, 3

25. 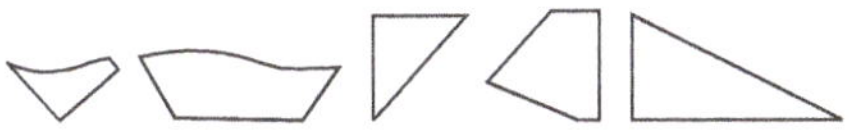

1 2 3 4 5

RPF SI 2019

(a) 1, 3, 5 (b) 2, 4, 5
(c) 3, 4, 5 (d) 2, 3, 4

Right Key

1. (d)	2. (c)	3. (a)	4. (a)	5. (b)	6. (b)	7. (b)	8. (c)	9. (c)	10. (a)
11. (b)	12. (c)	13. (c)	14. (b)	15. (b)	16. (c)	17. (c)	18. (b)	19. (c)	20. (c)
21. (c)	22. (c)	23. (a)	24. (a)	25. (c)					

CHAPTER

06 Embedded Figures

Embedded Figures

When a simple figure is hidden or embedded in a complex figure, then such a figure is called embedded figure. In this type of questions usually one question figure with four answer figures are given. Out of these answer figures, that figure has to be chosen in which the question figure is embedded or which is itself is embedded in the question figure.

When Question Figure is Embedded in Answer Figure

In this type of questions, a question figure along with four answer figures is given. Candidate has to find that answer figure out of the given options in which the question figure is embedded.

e.g. Find the answer figure in which the question figure (X) is embedded. (Rotation is not allowed)

Question Figure

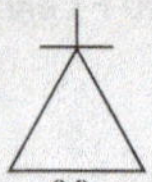

(X)

Answer Figures

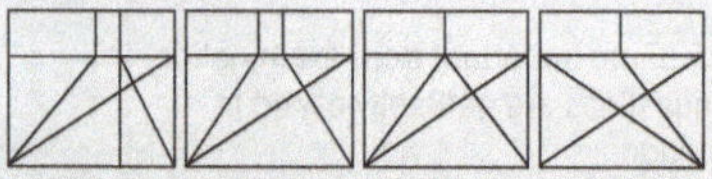

(a) (b) (c) (d)

Sol. (c) The question figure (X) is embedded in answer figure (c).

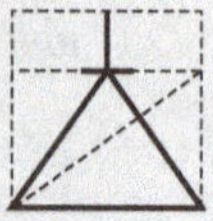

When Answer Figure is Embedded in Question Figure

In this type of questions, a question figure along with four answer figures is given. The candidate has to find out that answer figure from the given options which is embedded in the question figure as its part.

e.g. Select the answer figure which is embedded in the question figure.

Question Figure

Answer Figures

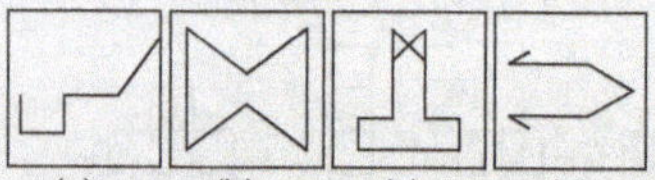

(a) (b) (c) (d)

Sol. (a) Answer figure (a) is embedded in the question figure.

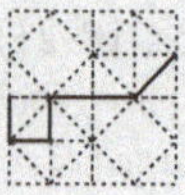

Score Booster

To solve questions involving complex figures or shapes, try drawing the shape on paper, which reduces the chance of error.

There are two types of questions asked from this chapter in the exam.

When Question Figure is Embedded in Answer Figure

Example 1 Choose the answer figure out of the given option in which the question figure (X) is embedded.

Question Figure — Answer Figures — *SSC (10+2) Tier-I 2019*

(X)

(a) (b) (c) (d)

Sol. (*b*) The question figure (X) is embedded in answer figure (b).

Helping Tips

This type of questions can be easily solved by analysing the options. Some options (answer) figures can be easily eliminated by just looking at them.

When Answer Figure is Embedded in Question Figure

Example 2 Find the answer figure out of the given options which is embedded in the question figure.

Question Figure — Answer Figures — *CISF Head Operator 2023*

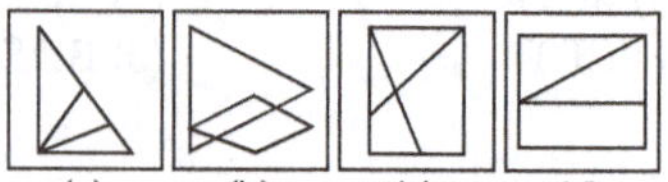

(a) (b) (c) (d)

Sol. (*a*) Answer figure (a) is embedded in the given question figure.

Trending Concept

Questions based on embedded figures are currently asked in SSC CGL, CHSL, CPO, RRB ALP, CISF and UP Police. They are very important for upcoming examinations.

Chapter Challenge

When Question Figure is Embedded in Answer Figure

Directions (Q. Nos. 1-33) *Choose the correct option among the answer figures in which the question figure is embedded.*

1. Question Figure Answer Figures *CISF ASI 2023*

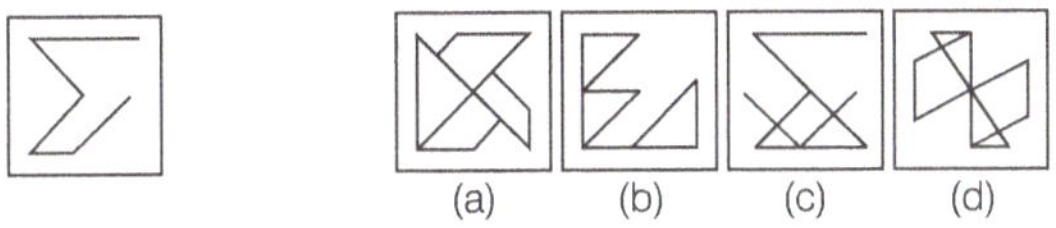

2. Question Figure Answer Figures

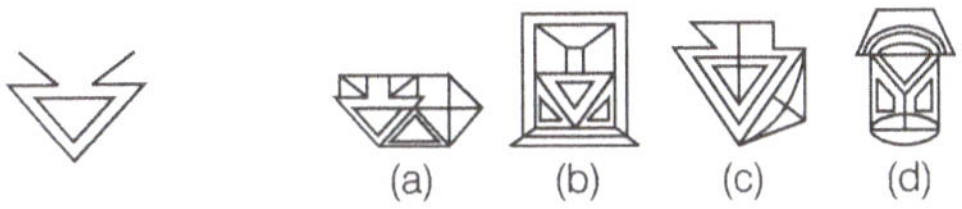

DP Constable 2023

3. Question Figure Answer Figures

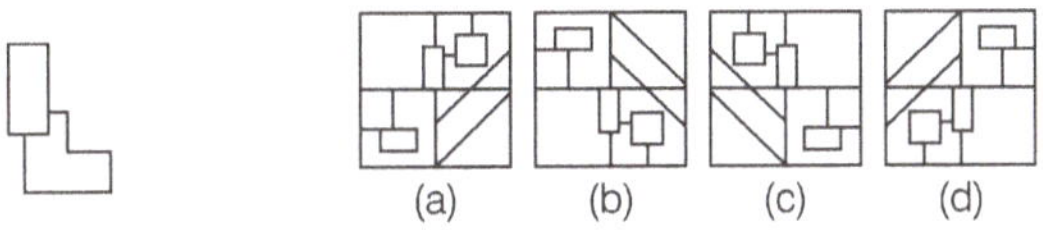

SSC CPO 2024

4. Question Figure Answer Figures

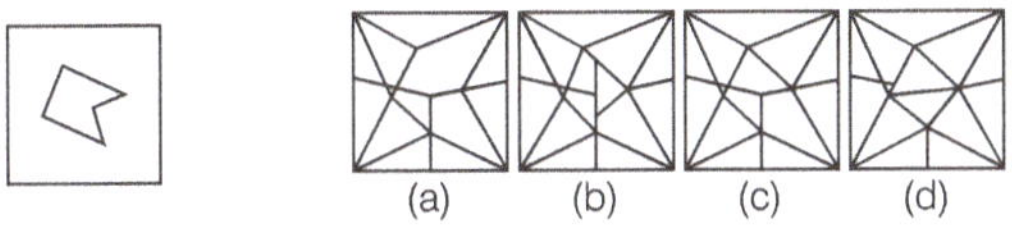

SSC CGL (Tier I) 2023

5. Question Figure Answer Figures

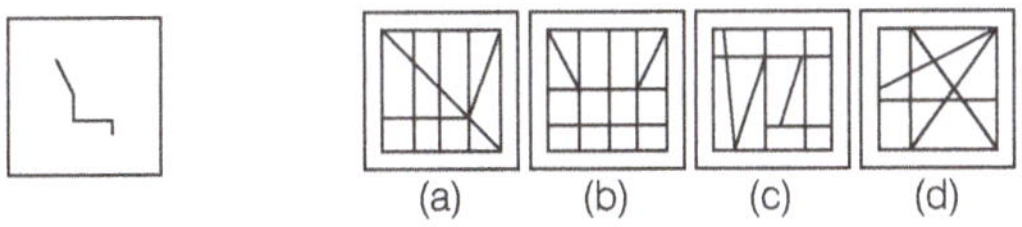

SSC (10+2) 2023

6. Question Figure Answer Figures

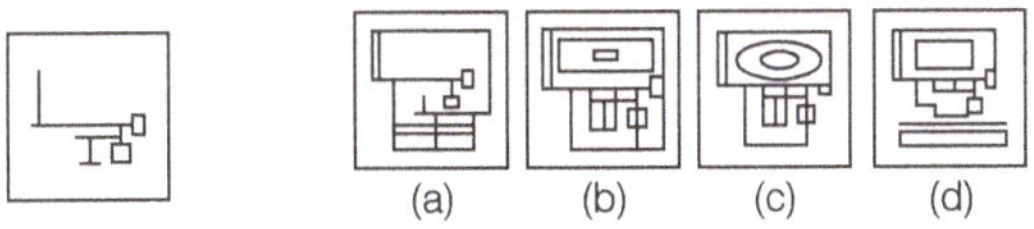

SSC (10+2) 2020

7. Question Figure

SSC CPO 2024

> **MRC*****
> ***(Most Repeating Concepts)***
> In Q. Nos. 3, 4, 5, 6, 7, 13, 14 are very important from examination point of view. These type to questions are being repeatedly asked in (SSC CGL, MTS Steno and RRB (ALP & Group D) examinations.

Answer Figures

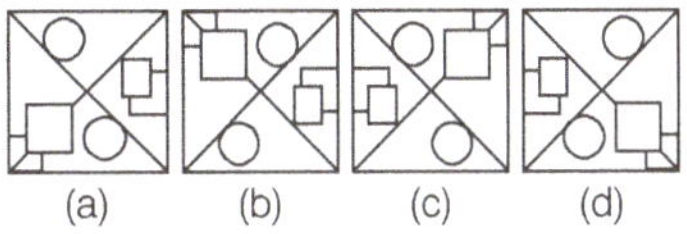

8. Question Figure Answer Figures

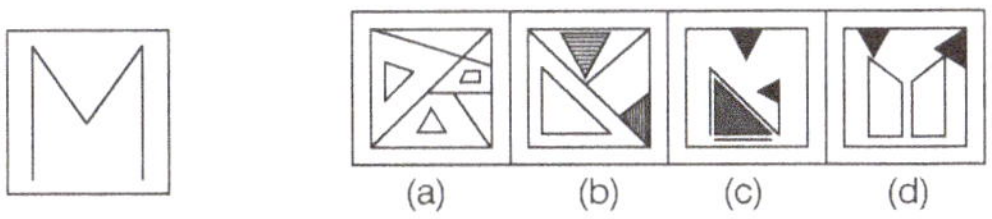

RRB ALP 2018

9. Question Figure Answer Figures

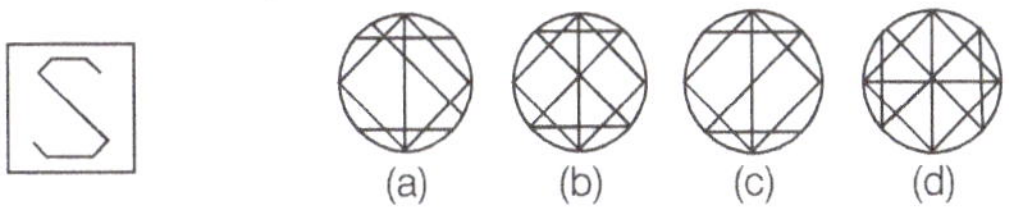

SSC CPO 2020

10. Question Figure Answer Figures

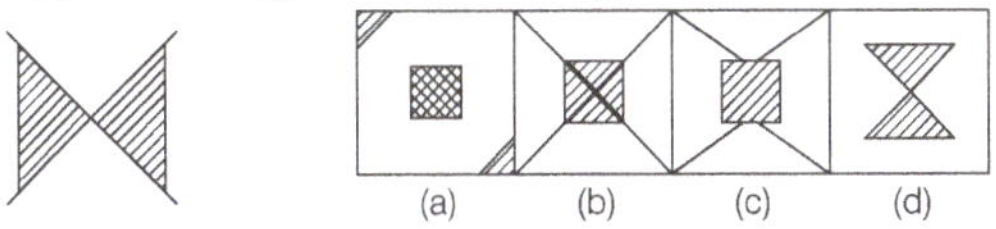

SSC Constable GD 2018

11. Question Figure Answer Figures

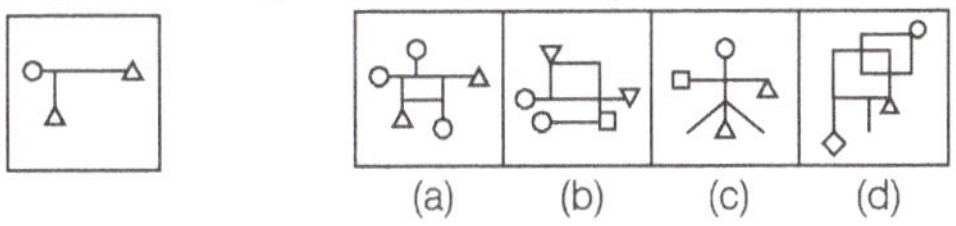

SSC CGL (Tier-II) 2025

12. Question Figure Answer Figures

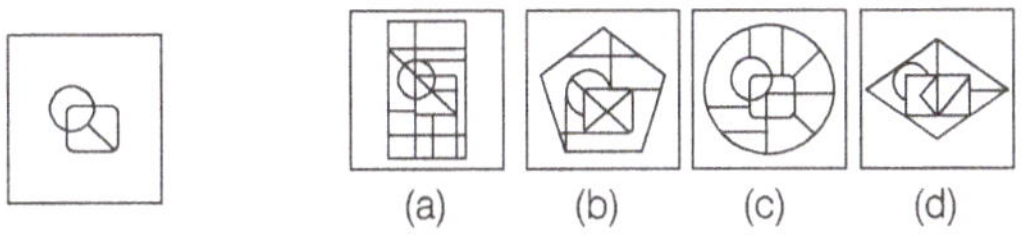

SSC Steno 2020

13. Question Figure Answer Figures

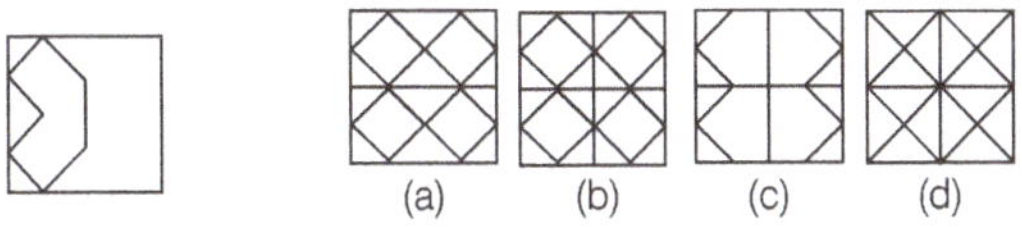

SSC MTS 2021

14. Question Figure Answer Figures

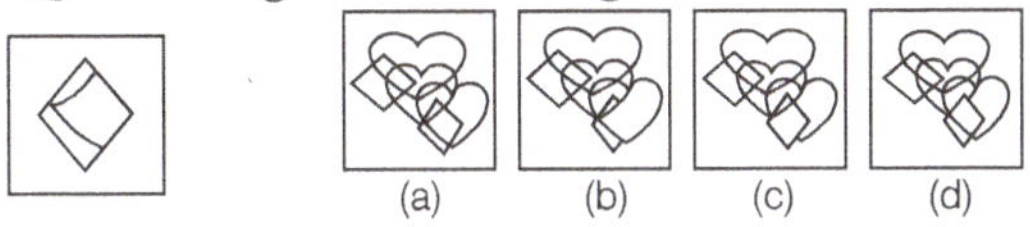

SSC CGL 2022

15. Question Figure Answer Figures

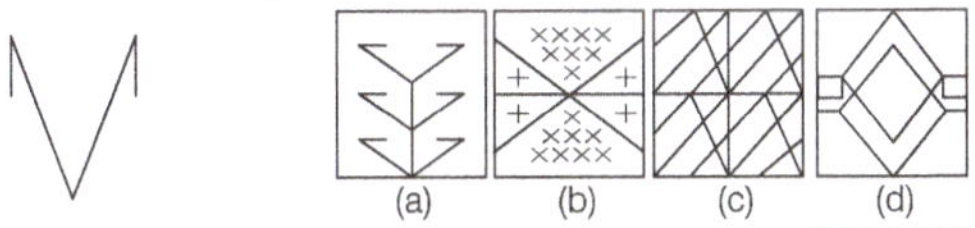

SSC CPO 2018

16. Question Figure Answer Figures

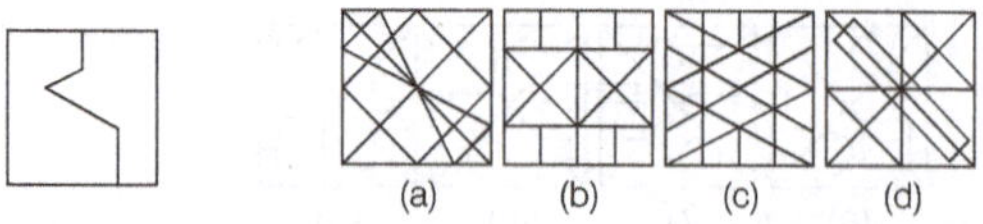

UP Police Constable 2018

17. Question Figure Answer Figures

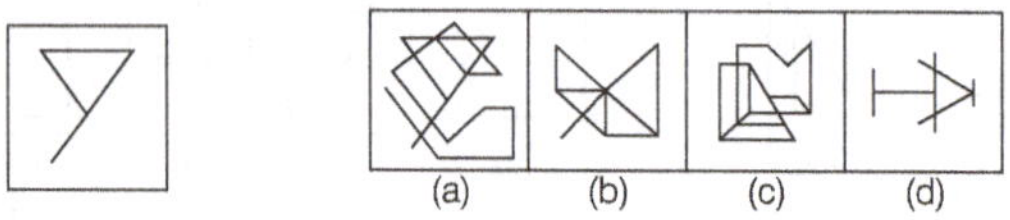

Rajasthan Police Constable 2018
RRB Group-D 2018

18. Question Figure Answer Figures

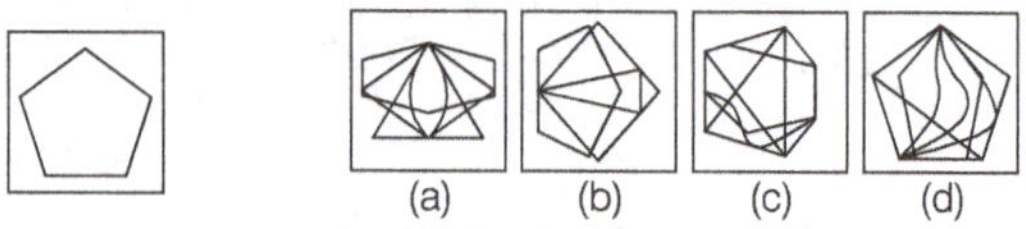

SSC (10+2) 2020

19. Question Figure Answer Figures

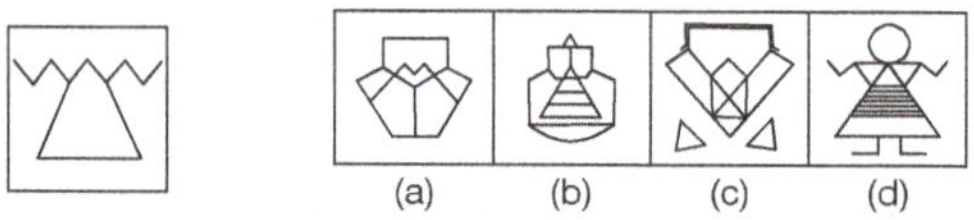

RRB ALP 2018

20. Question Figure Answer Figures

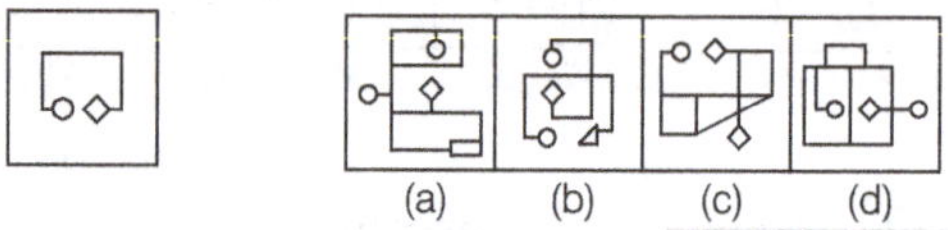

SSC CGL (Tier II) 2025

21. Question Figure Answer Figures

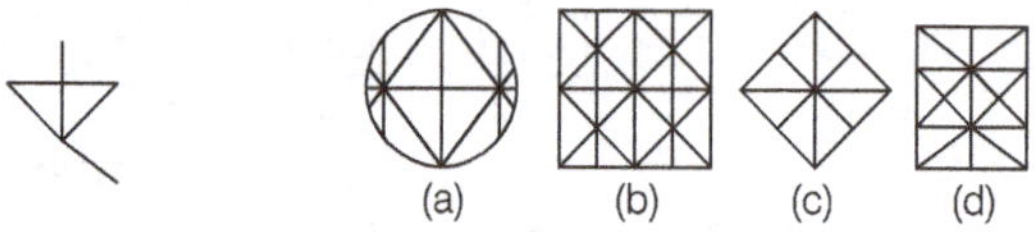

SSC CGL 2020

22. Question Figure Answer Figures

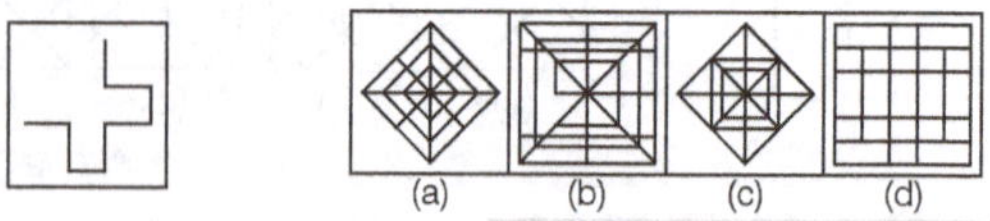

RRB Group-D 2018; UP B.Ed 2010

23. Question Figure Answer Figures

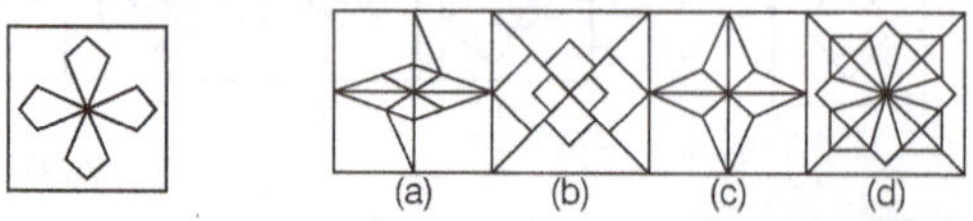

RRB ALP 2018

24. Question Figure

Answer Figures

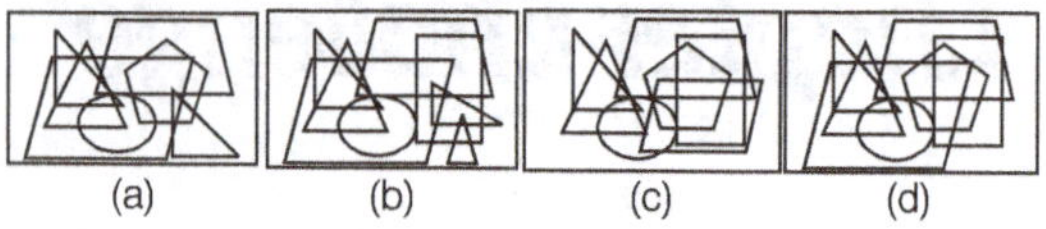

25. Question Figure Answer Figures

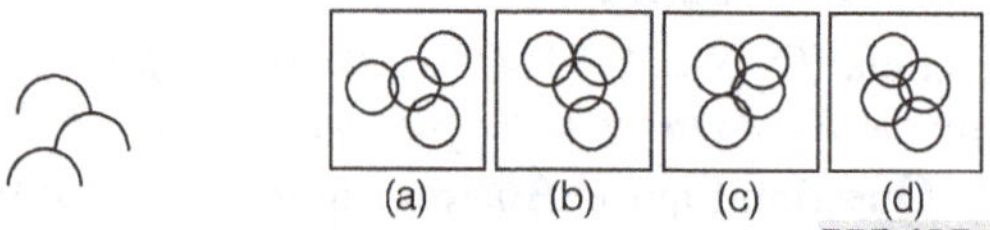

RRB ALP 2018

26. Question Figure Answer Figures

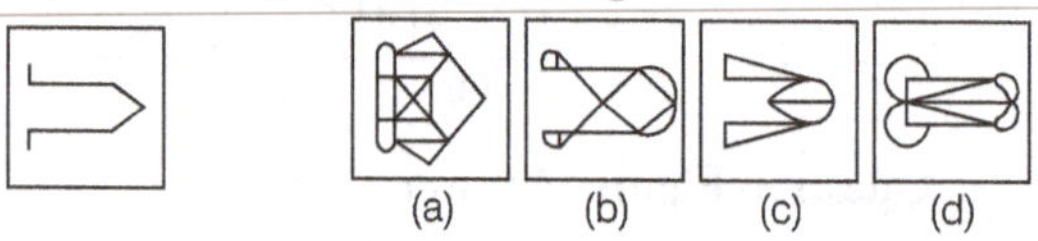

RRB ALP 2018

27. Question Figure Answer Figures

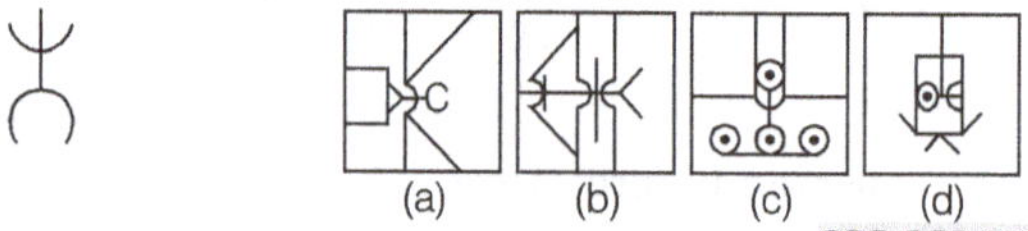

SSC CGL 2021

28. Question Figure Answer Figures

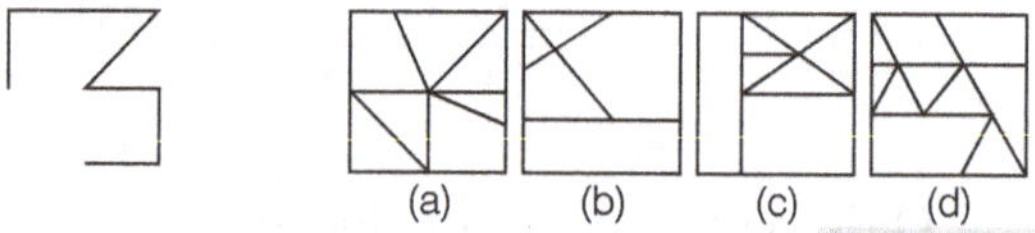

RRB ALP 2018

29. Question Figure Answer Figures

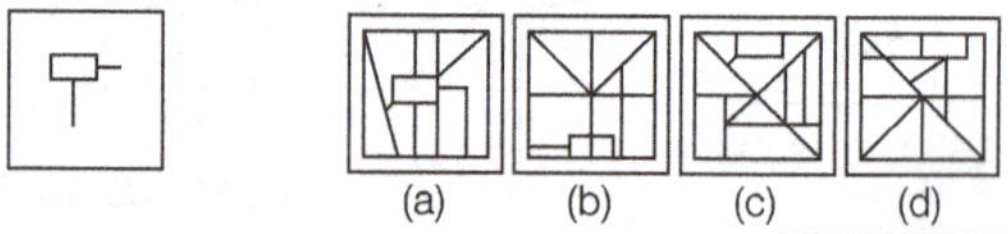

SSC (10+2) 2023

30. Question Figure Answer Figures

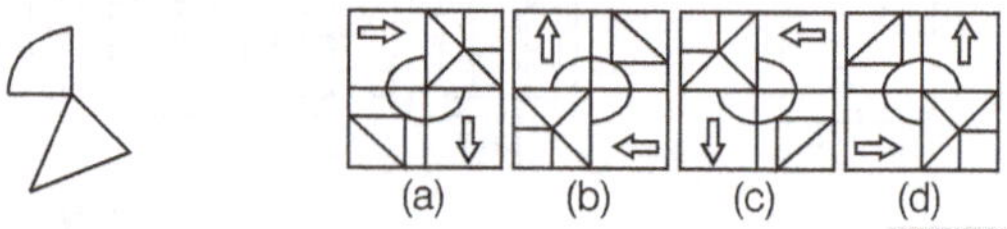

CISF 2023

31. Question Figure Answer Figures

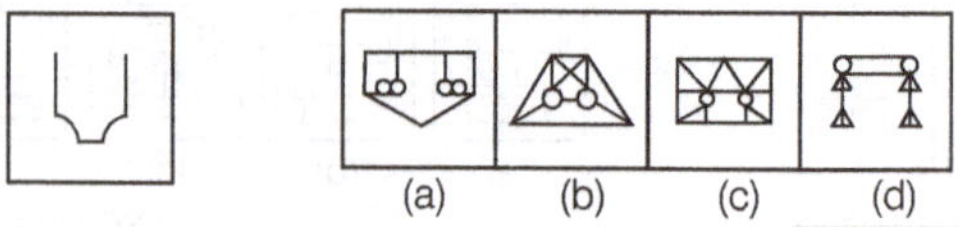

SSC Steno 2023

32. Question Figure Answer Figures

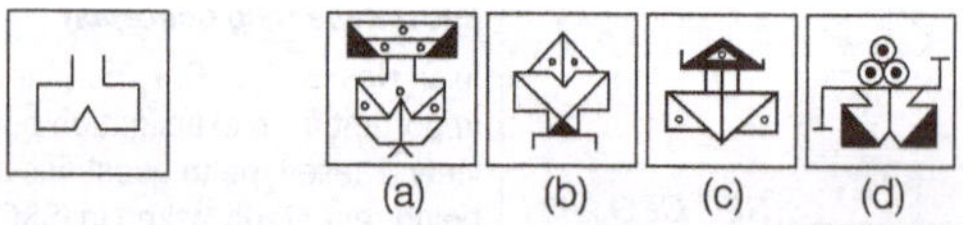

SSC CPO 2023

33. Question Figure Answer Figures

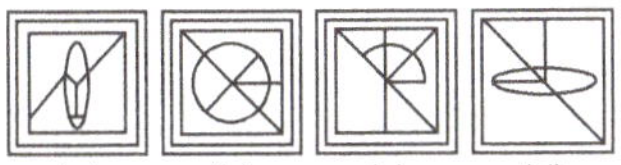

(a) (b) (c) (d)

SSC GD 2024

When Answer Figure is Embedded in Question Figure

Directions (Q. Nos. 34-40) *Find the answer figure out of the given options that is embedded in the question figure.*

34. Question Figure

SSC CGL (Tier I) 2023

Answer Figures

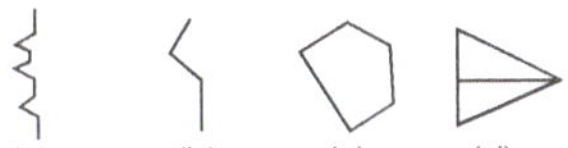

(a) (b) (c) (d)

35. Question Figure

SSC CGL (Tier I) 2023

Answer Figures

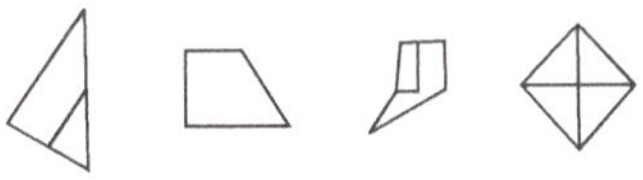

(a) (b) (c) (d)

36. Question Figure

CUET UG 2022

Answer Figures

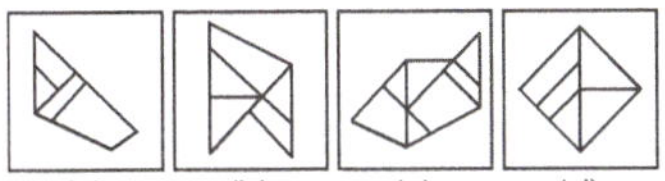

(a) (b) (c) (d)

37. Question Figure

SSC CGL (Tier-I) 2023

Answer Figures

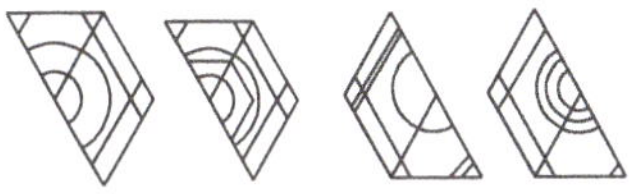

(a) (b) (c) (d)

38. Question Figure

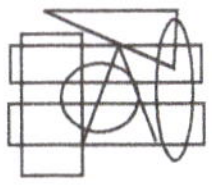

SSC CPO 2023

Answer Figures

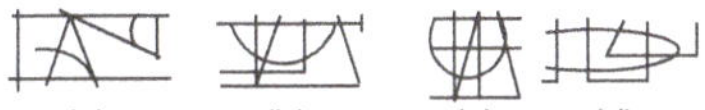

(a) (b) (c) (d)

39. Question Figure

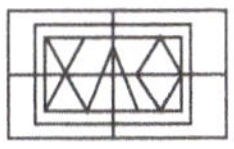

SSC CGL (Tier I) 2023

Answer Figures

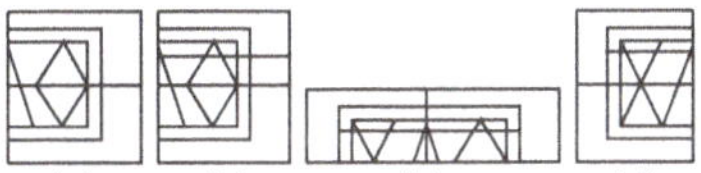

(a) (b) (c) (d)

40. Question Figure

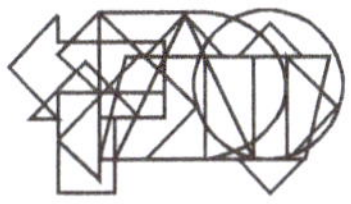

SSC GD 2023

Answer Figures

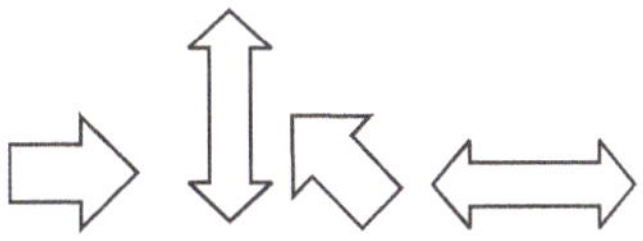

(a) (b) (c) (d)

Right Key

1. (c)	2. (a)	3. (b)	4. (c)	5. (b)	6. (b)	7. (a)	8. (b)	9. (b)	10. (b)
11. (a)	12. (a)	13. (b)	14. (a)	15. (d)	16. (c)	17. (a)	18. (d)	19. (d)	20. (d)
21. (d)	22. (d)	23. (d)	24. (d)	25. (c)	26. (b)	27. (c)	28. (a)	29. (a)	30. (d)
31. (b)	32. (a)	33. (a)	34. (b)	35. (a)	36. (b)	37. (b)	38. (a)	39. (a)	40. (b)

CHAPTER

07 Counting of Figures

Counting of Figures

Counting of figures can be explained as the realisation of simple geometrical figures from a complex figure.

The figure which are asked for counting can be straight lines, triangles, square, rectangles, circle etc. To find the accurate number of figure. Firstly, a candidate needs to find the required figures formed by individual section of the given figure and then find the figure formed by combination of two figures and so on.

Counting of Straight Lines

In this type of questions, a candidate is required to find out the number of straight lines in the given figure. A straight line is defined by its length but it has no breadth. There are three types of straight lines. (i) Horizontal line (ii) Vertical line (iii) Slant line

e.g. How many straight lines are there in the figure given below?

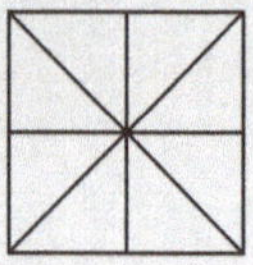

(a) 14 (b) 8 (c) 4 (d) 9

Sol. (b) Naming the figure,

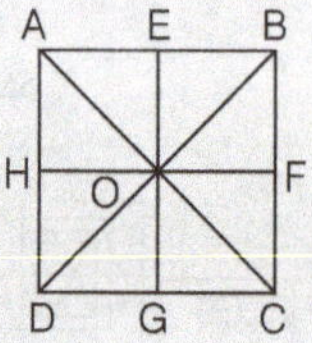

Horizontal lines = AB, HF, DC = 3

Vertical lines = AD, EG, BC = 3

Slant lines = AC, BD = 2

∴ Total number of lines = 3 + 3 + 2 = 8

Counting of Triangles

In this type of questions, candidates have to find out the total number of triangles in the given figure.

e.g. How many triangles are there in the given figure?

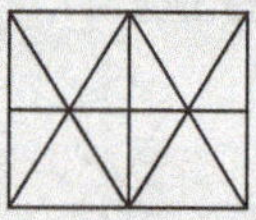

(a) 18 (b) 28 (c) 10 (d) 12

Sol. (b) Naming the figure,

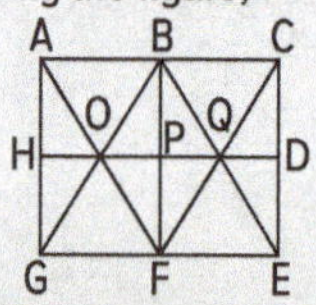

There are 28 triangles in the given figure namely,

ΔAHO, ΔAOB, ΔBOP, ΔBPQ, ΔBQC, ΔCQD, ΔHOG, ΔGOF, ΔFPO, ΔQPF, ΔFQE, ΔQDE, ΔAOG, ΔBOF, ΔBQF, ΔCQE, ΔBOQ, ΔFOQ, ΔAGF, ΔABF, ΔBAG, ΔBFG, ΔBFE, ΔBCE, ΔCBF, ΔCEF, ΔAFC and ΔGBE.

Counting of Squares/Rectangles

In this type of questions, candidates have to find out the total number of square/rectangle in the given figure.

e.g. Find the total number of squares in the figure.

(a) 10 (b) 8
(c) 6 (d) 12

Sol. (a) Naming the figure,

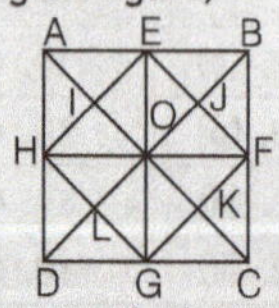

There are 10 squares in the given figure namely, □AEOH, □BEOF, □CFOG, □DHOG, □EJOI, □JOKF, □LOKG, □HIOL, □EFGH and □ABCD.

Counting of Circles

In this type of questions, a candidate is required to find the total number of circles in the given figure.

e.g. How many circles are there in the figure given below?

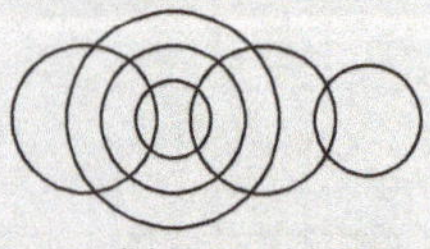

(a) 6 (b) 7 (c) 10 (d) 8

Sol. (a) While counting the circles,

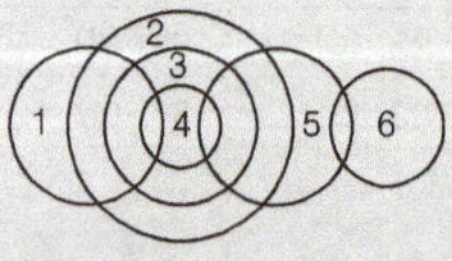

∴ Total number of circles = 6

Score Booster

To boost your score in counting figures questions, breakdown complex shapes into smaller shapes then systematically count each part and use formulas or pattern wherever possible. Do not forget to name the vertices given in the figure.

Exam Approach Examples

Counting of Straight Lines

Example 1 Find the minimum number of straight lines in the following figure. *RRB NTPC 2022*

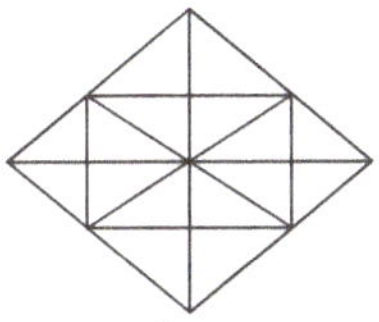

(a) 10 (b) 12
(c) 13 (d) 11

Sol. (*b*) Naming the figure,

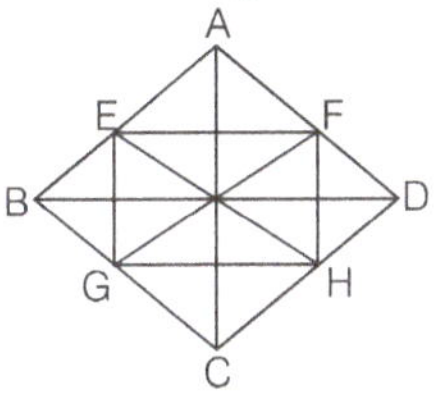

Horizontal lines = EF, BD, GH = 3
Vertical lines = AC, FH, EG = 3
Slant lines = BC, EH, AD, FG, AB, CD = 6
∴ Total numbers of straight lines
= 3 + 3 + 6 = 12

Counting of Triangles

Example 2 How many triangles are there in the given figure? *SSC CGL (Tier-I) 2024*

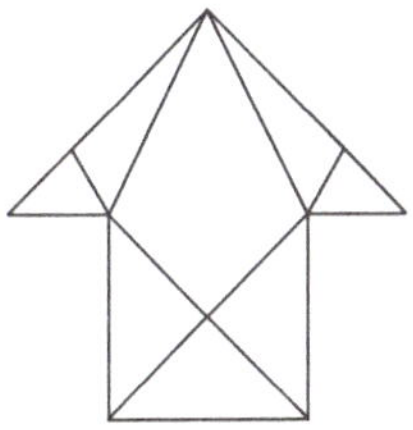

Trending Concept

Questions based on counting triangles are being frequently asked in the exams such as SSC CGL, CHSL and MTS. These questions are very important for these exams.

(a) 13 (b) 12 (c) 10 (d) 11

Sol. (*d*) Naming the figure,

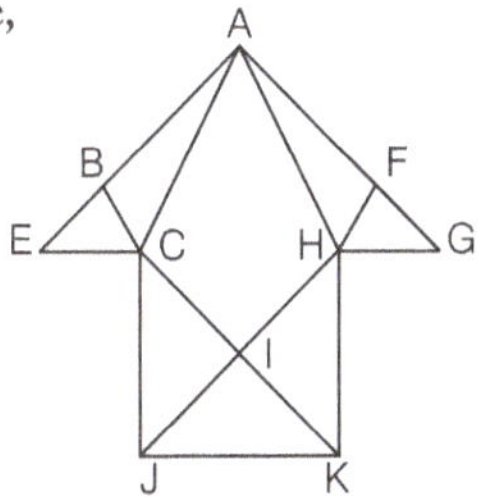

There are total 11 triangles in the given figure, namely
ΔBEC, ΔHFG, ΔABC, ΔAHF, ΔACE, ΔAHG, ΔCIJ, ΔJIK, ΔHIK, ΔHJK and ΔCJK.

Example 3 How many triangles are there in the given figure? *SSC (10+2) 2023*

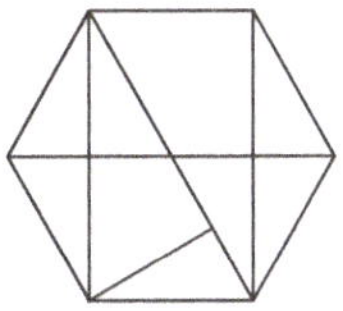

(a) 20 (b) 18
(c) 25 (d) 14

Sol. (*d*) Naming the figure,

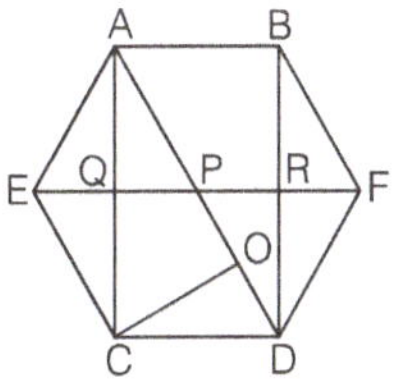

There are 14 triangles in the given figure namely,
ΔAEC, ΔAQE, ΔCQE, ΔACD, ΔBFD, ΔBFR, ΔDFR, ΔABD, ΔPRD, ΔCOD, ΔDFP, ΔAQP, ΔAEP and ΔAOC.

Counting of Squares and Rectangles

Example 4 How many maximum squares are there in the given figure? *RRB (JE) 2019*

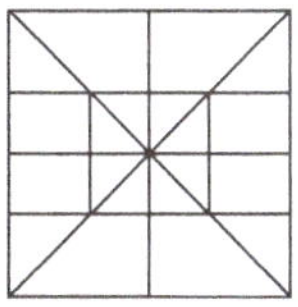

(a) 20 (b) 11
(c) 25 (d) 16

Sol. (*d*) Naming of the figure,

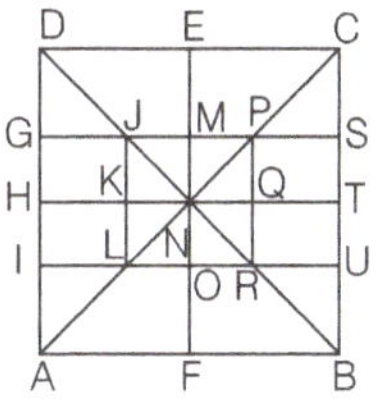

□GJKH, □HKLI, □JMNK, □KNOL, □MPQN, □NQRO, □PSTQ, □QTUR, □DENH, □ECTN, □NTBF, □HNFA, □GMOI, □JPRL, □MSUO, □ABCD

Hence, there are total '16' squares in the given figure.

Example 5 How many rectangles are there in the given figure? *UPSSSC (VDO) 2018*

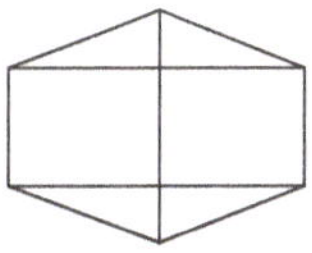

(a) 2 (b) 3 (c) 5 (d) 7

Sol. (*b*) Naming of the figure,

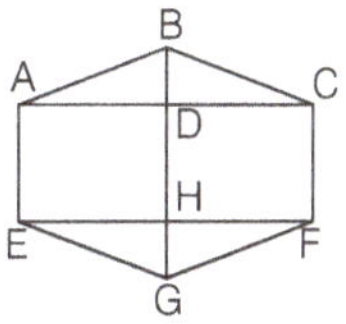

Helping Tips

All squares will be rectangle while all rectangles cannot be a square.

▭ADHE, ▭DCFH, ▭ACFE

Hence, there are total '3' rectangles given in the figure.

Counting of Circle

Example 6 How many circles are there in the given figure? *SSC (10+2) 2022*

(a) 11 (b) 9 (c) 12 (d) 10

Sol. (*d*) While counting the circles,

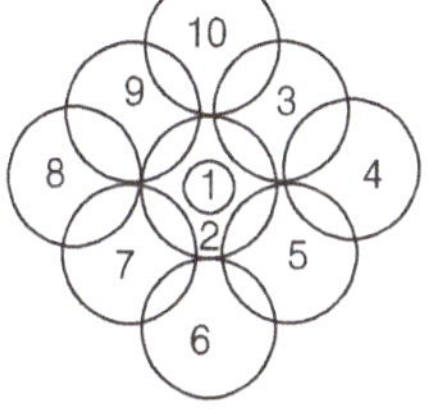

∴ Total number of circles = 10

Chapter Challenge

Counting of Straight Lines

1. How many straight lines are there in the given figure? ***RPF SI 2019***

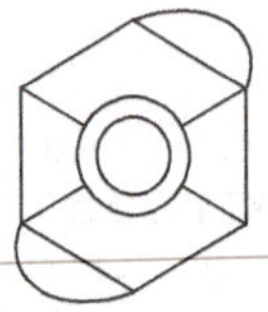

(a) 14 (b) 10 (c) 12 (d) 16

2. What is the minimum number of lines required to make the given image ? ***RRB ALP 2019***

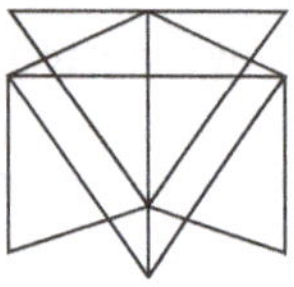

(a) 13 (b) 9 (c) 12 (d) 11

3. How many straight lines in the given figure ? ***CISF Head Constable 2018***

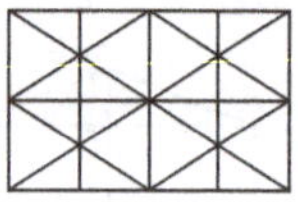

(a) 11 (b) 14 (c) 16 (d) 17

4. Find the minimum number of straight lines required to make the given figure. ***RRB Group D 2018***

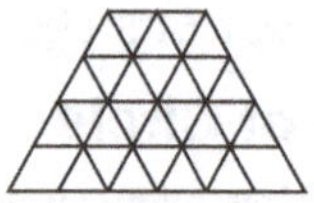

(a) 15 (b) 17 (c) 10 (d) 12

5. How many straight lines are there in the figure given below? ***CISF Head Constable 2023***

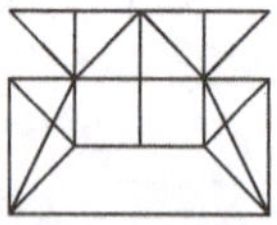

(a) 16 (b) 17 (c) 18 (d) 19

6. How many minimum number of straight lines are required to draw the following figure? ***RRB Group D 2018***

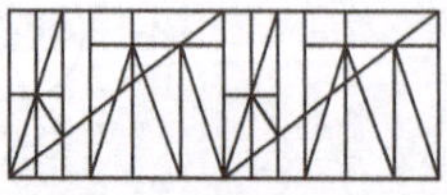

(a) 36 (b) 55 (c) 31 (d) 28

Counting of Triangles

7. How many triangles are there in the following figure? ***SSC (JE) 2023***

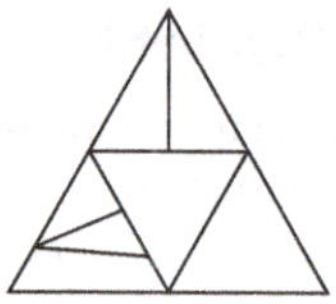

(a) 7 (b) 10 (c) 9 (d) 8

8. How many triangles are there in the following figure? ***UP Police Constable 2024***

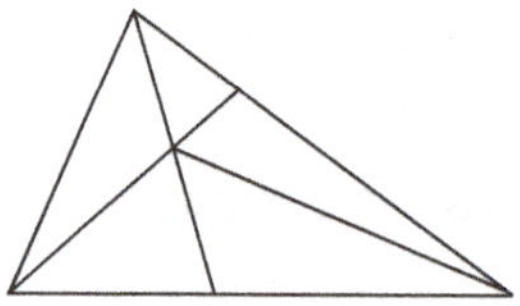

(a) 14 (b) 12 (c) 8 (d) 10

9. How many triangles are there in the following figure? ***RRB NTPC (Tier-I) 2021***

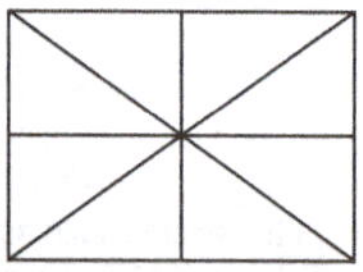

(a) 8 (b) 12
(c) 16 (d) 20

> **MRC*****
> ***(Most Repeating Concepts)***
> Question Nos. 5, 8, 9, 20, 23, 32 and 37 are frequently asked in RRB NTPC, RRB Group D, UP Police Constable and SSC CGL etc.

10. How many triangles are there in the given figure? ***SSC (10+2) 2023***

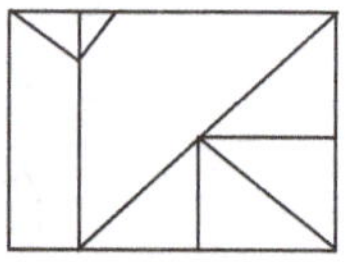

(a) 8 (b) 11 (c) 9 (d) 10

11. Identify the number of triangles in the given figure. ***SSC (10+2) 2023***

(a) 10 (b) 7 (c) 8 (d) 9

12. How many triangles are there in the given figure? ***BSSC (10+2) 2022***

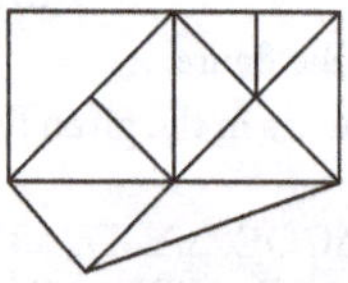

(a) 19 or more (b) 10
(c) 16 (d) 18

13. How many triangles are present in the following figure? ***SSC (10+2) 2022***

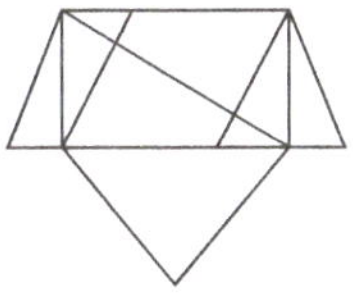

(a) 14 (b) 15 (c) 16 (d) 13

14. Find the number of triangles in the given figure. ***SSC (10+2) 2022***

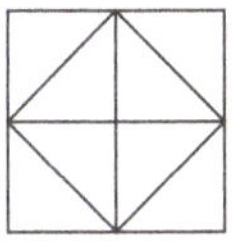

(a) 11 (b) 12 (c) 9 (d) 13

15. Find the number of triangles in the given figure.

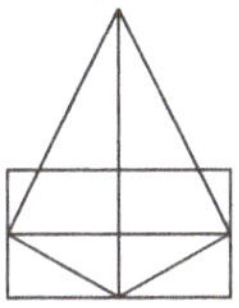

RRB ALP 2018

(a) 13 (b) 15 (c) 17 (d) 14

16. How many triangles are there in the given figure?

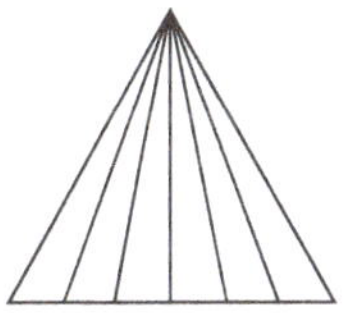

UP Police Constable 2024

(a) 23 (b) 21 (c) 22 (d) 20

17. How many triangles are present in the given figure? ***SSC CGL (Tier I) 2020***

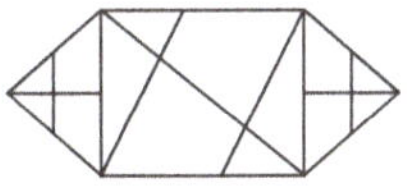

(a) 22 (b) 18 (c) 23 (d) 20

18. How many triangles are there in the following figure? ***MP Police Constable 2022***

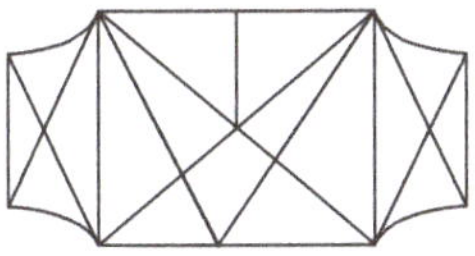

(a) 17 (b) 18 (c) 15 (d) 29

19. How many triangles are there in the given figure?

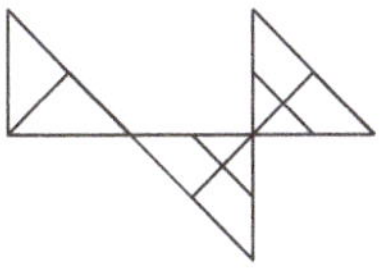

SSC (10+2) 2021

(a) 15 (b) 14 (c) 17 (d) 16

20. How many triangles are given in the given figure?

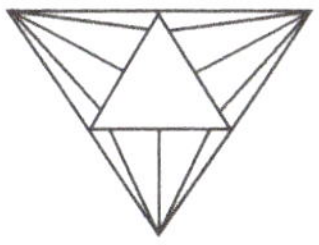

RRB NTPC 2020

(a) 31 (b) 30 (c) 29 (d) 32

21. How many triangles are there in the given figure?

SSC (10+2) 2022

(a) 22 (b) 24 (c) 20 (d) 18

22. How many triangles are there in the given figure?

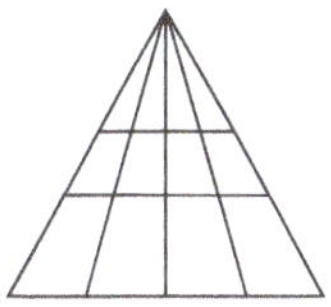

RRB JE 2019

(a) 21 (b) 26 (c) 30 (d) 34

23. How many triangles are there in the given figure?

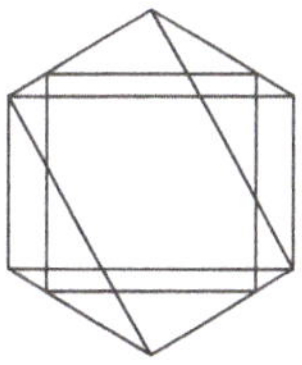

SSC CGL (Tier I) 2020

(a) 29 (b) 21 (c) 19 (d) 30

24. How many triangles are there in the given figure?

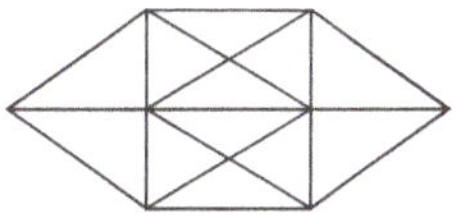

UPSSSC 2018

(a) 20 (b) 24 (c) 28 (d) 32

25. Find the number of triangles in the given figure.

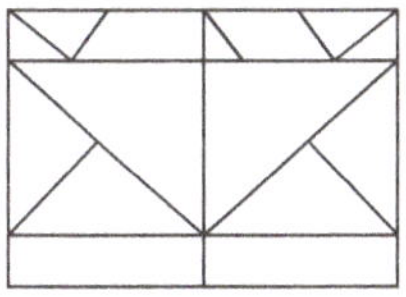

SSC (10+2) 2021

(a) 15 (b) 11 (c) 14 (d) 13

26. How many triangles are there in the given figure?

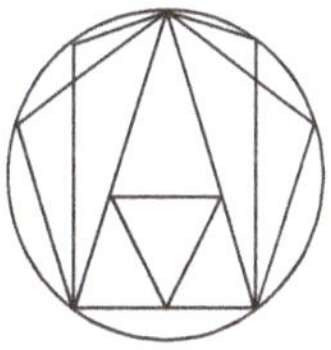

SSC (10+2) 2023

(a) 16 (b) 10 (c) 12 (d) 15

27. How many maximum triangles are there in the given figure?

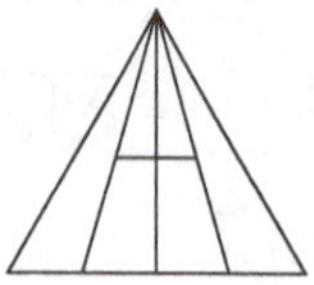

SSC (10+2) 2023

(a) 8 (b) 13 (c) 15 (d) 21

28. How many maximum triangles are there in the given figure? *RRB Group D 2018*

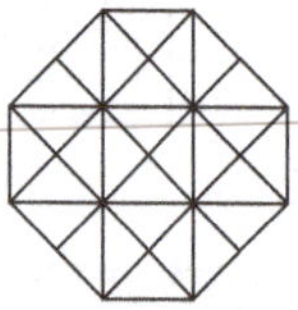

(a) 28 (b) 22 (c) 24 (d) 26

29. How many triangles are there in the given figure?

RRB Group D 2018

(a) 31 (b) 34 (c) 30 (d) 29

30. How many triangle are there in the given figure?

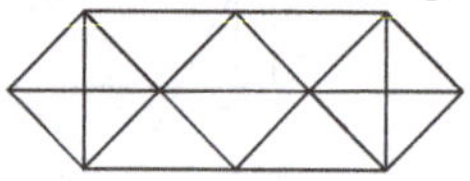

SSC CGL 2015

(a) 24 (b) 14 (c) 28 (d) 20

Counting of Squares and Rectangles

31. How many squares are given in following figure?

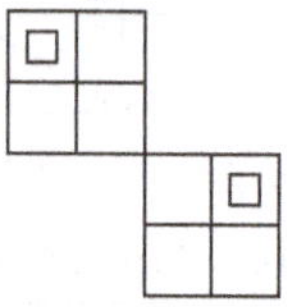

RPF Constable 2022

(a) 8 (b) 10 (c) 14 (d) 12

32. How many squares in the given figure?

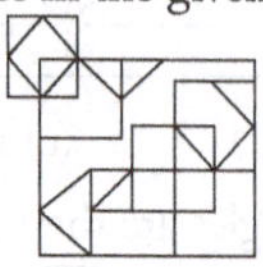

SSC CGL (Tier-I) 2024

(a) 14 (b) 13 (c) 15 (d) 12

33. How many rectangles are there in the given figure?

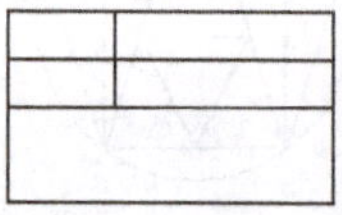

MP Police Constable 2024

(a) 6 (b) 8 (c) 7 (d) 10

34. How many rectangles are there in the given figure?

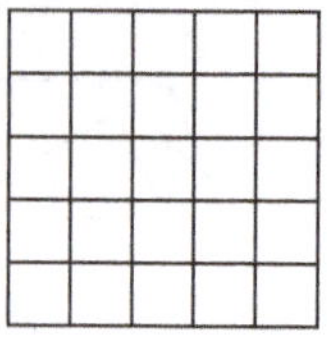

RRB JE 2019

(a) 23 (b) 36 (c) 55 (d) 45

35. Find the total number of squares in the given figure. *SSC CGL 2020*

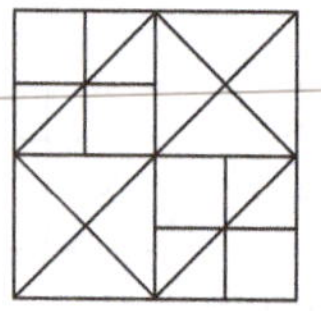

(a) 16 (b) 13 (c) 12 (d) 14

36. Find the total number of squares in the given figure. *RRB Group D 2018*

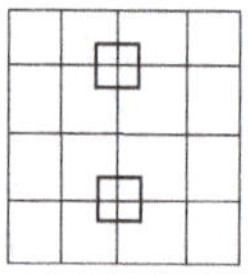

(a) 44 (b) 40 (c) 42 (d) 46

37. How many squares are there in the given figure?

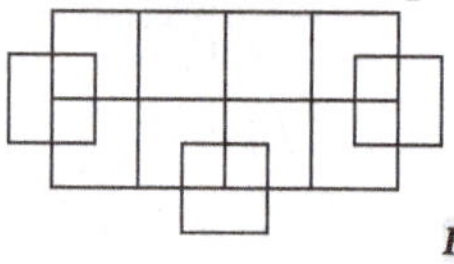

RRB Group D 2018

(a) 21 (b) 19 (c) 20 (d) 18

38. How many squares are there in the given figure?

UPSSSC 2018

(a) 11 (b) 21 (c) 24 (d) 26

Counting of Circle

39. How many circles are there in the given figure?

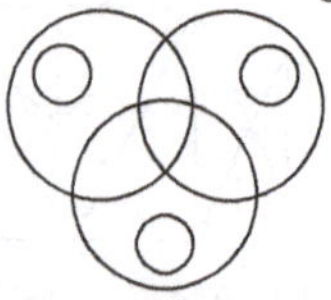

RRB Group D 2018

(a) 6 (b) 5 (c) 7 (d) 8

40. How many circles are there in the given figure?

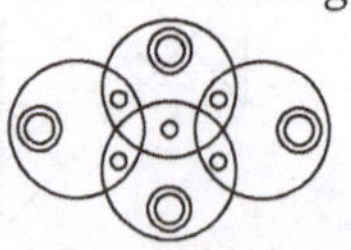

SSC CGL 2015

(a) 13 (b) 16 (c) 17 (d) 22

Right Key

1. (b)	2. (a)	3. (b)	4. (a)	5. (d)	6. (c)	7. (b)	8. (b)	9. (c)	10. (b)
11. (a)	12. (a)	13. (b)	14. (b)	15. (b)	16. (b)	17. (a)	18. (d)	19. (a)	20. (d)
21. (c)	22. (c)	23. (d)	24. (c)	25. (c)	26. (d)	27. (b)	28. (a)	29. (a)	30. (c)
31. (d)	32. (a)	33. (d)	34. (c)	35. (d)	36. (b)	37. (c)	38. (c)	39. (a)	40. (c)

Solutions

1. *(b)* Naming the figure,

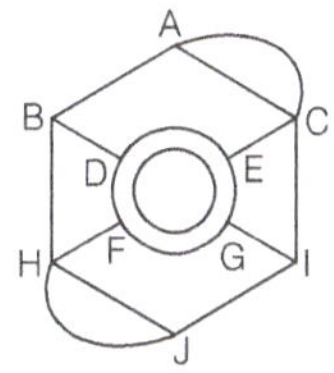

There are 10 straight lines in the given figure namely, AB, AC, BD, EC, HF, GI, JI, HJ, BH and CI.

2. *(a)* Naming the figure,

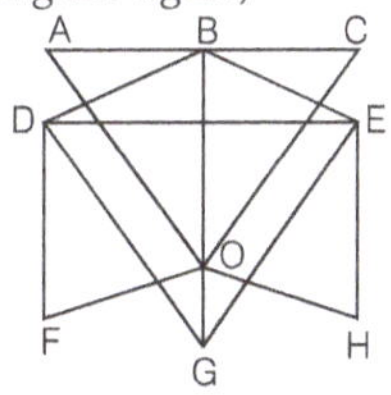

Horizontal lines = AC, DE = 2

Vertical lines = DF, BG, EH = 3

Slant lines = AO, CO, OH, OF, DG, EG, BD, BE = 8

∴ Total number of lines = 2 + 3 + 8 = 13

3. *(b)* Naming the figure,

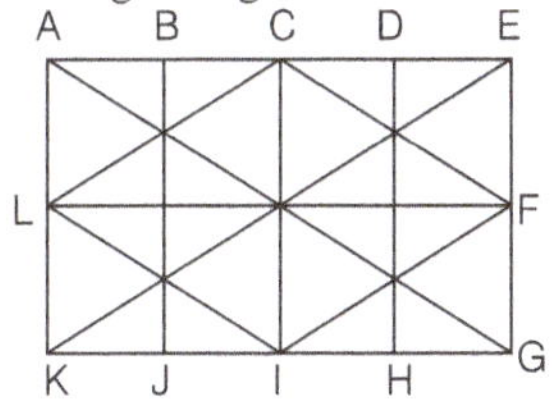

Horizontal lines = AE, LF, KG = 3

Vertical lines = AK, BJ, CI, DH, EG = 5

Slant lines = CL, CF, IL, IF, AG, EK = 6

∴ Total number of straight lines = 3 + 5 + 6 = 14

4. *(a)* Naming the figure,

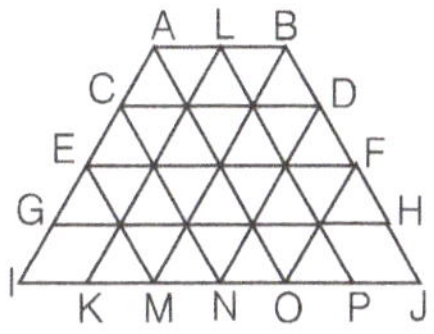

Horizontal lines = AB, CD, EF, GH, IJ = 5

Slant lines = AI, LK, BM, DN, FO, BJ, LP, AO, CN, EM = 10

∴ Total number of lines = 5 + 10 = 15

5. *(d)* Naming the figure,

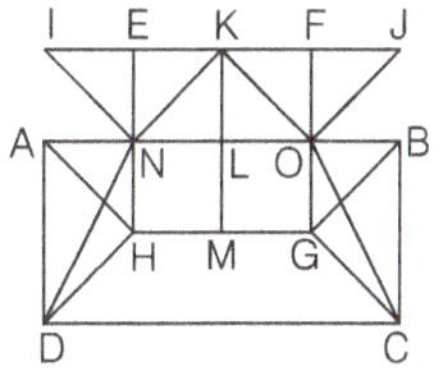

Horizontal lines = IJ, AB, DC, HG = 4

Vertical lines = AD, EH, KM, FG, BC = 5

Slant lines = IN, NK, KO, OJ, DH, CG, CO, DN, AH, BG = 10

∴ Total number of lines = 4 + 5 + 10 = 19

6. *(c)* Naming the figure,

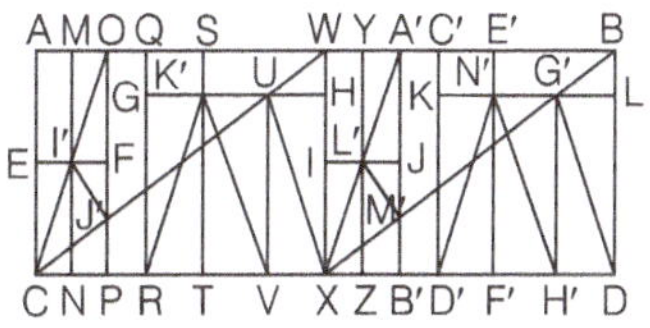

Horizontal lines = AB, CD, EF, GH, IJ, KL = 6

Vertical lines = AC, MN, OP, QR, ST, UV, WX, YZ, A'B', C'D', E'F', G'H', BD = 13

Slant lines = CO, I'J', CW, RK', K'V, UX, XA', XB, L'M', D'N', N'H', G'D = 12

∴ Total number of lines = 6 + 13 + 12 = 31

7. *(b)* Naming of the figure,

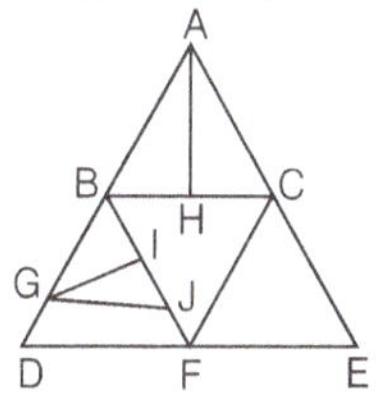

ΔAHC, ΔABH, ΔABC, ΔBGI, ΔGIJ, ΔBGJ, ΔBCF, ΔBDF, ΔFCE and ΔADE

Hence, total number of triangles = 10

8. *(b)* Naming of the figure,

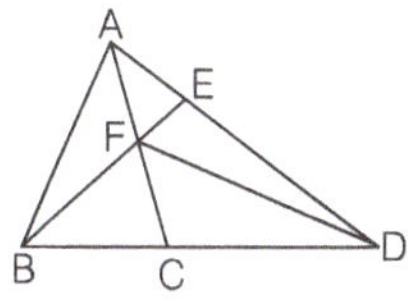

ΔABF, ΔAFE, ΔABE, Δ BFC, ΔFCD, ΔBFD, ΔFED, ΔABC, ΔACD, ΔABD, ΔBED, ΔAFD

Hence, total number of triangles = 12

9. *(c)* Naming of the figure,

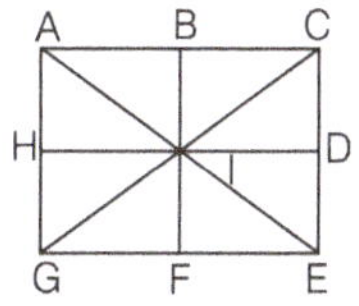

ΔABI, ΔBIC, ΔCID, ΔDIE, ΔEIF, ΔFIG, ΔGIH, ΔHIA, ΔAIC, ΔCIE, ΔGIE, ΔGIA, ΔAEG, ΔAEC, ΔGAC, ΔGCE

Hence, there are total '16' triangles.

Smart Approach

If a square is having two diagonals and having n blocks, then number of triangles = n (number of blocks) × 2

Here, number of triangles = 8 × 2 = 16

10. (*b*) Naming the figure,

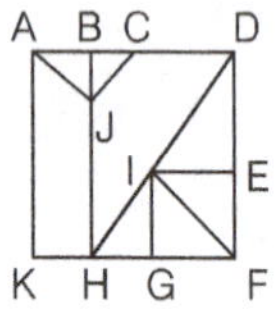

There are 11 triangles in the figure namely, ΔABJ, ΔBJC, ΔAJC, ΔGIF, ΔFIE, ΔIGH, ΔDIE, ΔBDH, ΔIHF, ΔFID and ΔDHF.

11. (*a*) Naming the figure,

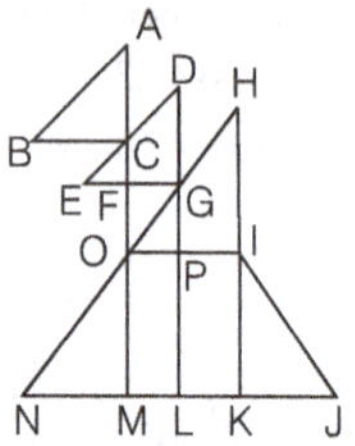

There are 10 triangles in the given figure namely, ΔABC, ΔCEF, ΔFGO, ΔOGP, ΔONM, ΔIKJ, ΔDEG, ΔHOI, ΔGLN and ΔHKN.

12. (*a*) Naming the figure,

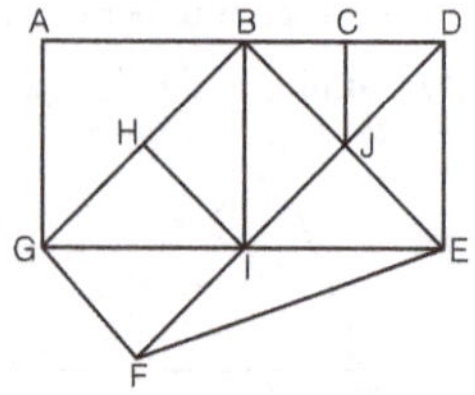

There are 20 triangles in the figure, ΔABG, ΔGHI, ΔHBI, ΔBIJ, ΔBJC, ΔCJD, ΔDJE, ΔIJE, ΔGIF, ΔFIE, ΔBGI, ΔBIE, ΔBJD, ΔDIE, ΔGEF, ΔFJE, ΔBID, ΔBDE, ΔBGE and ΔFDE.

13. (*b*) Naming the figure,

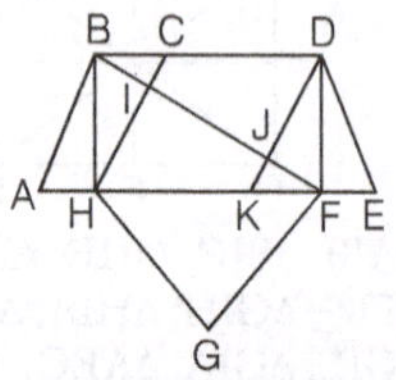

There are 15 triangles in the given figure namely,

ΔABH, ΔBHI, ΔBCI, ΔDFJ, ΔKJF, ΔDEF, ΔHFG, ΔBCH, ΔDKF, ΔBHF, ΔBDF, ΔHIF, ΔBJD, ΔABF and ΔKDE.

14. (*b*) Naming the figure,

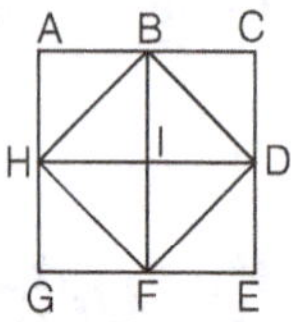

There are 12 triangles in the above figure namely,

ΔABH, ΔHIB, ΔBID, ΔBCD, ΔDEF, ΔDIF, ΔHGF, ΔHIF, ΔHBD, ΔHFD, ΔHBF and ΔBDF.

Smart Approach

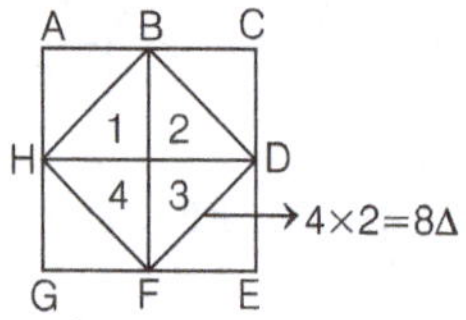

Total number of triangles

= 8Δ + ΔABH + ΔBCD + ΔFDE + ΔHGF

= 8Δ + 4Δ

= 12Δ

15. (*b*) Naming of the figure,

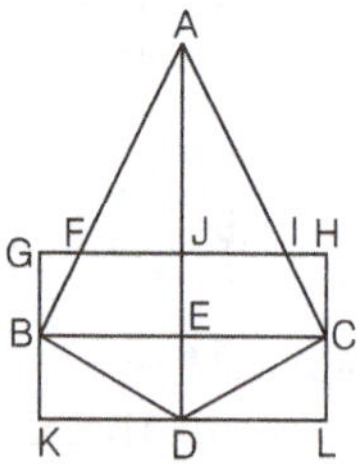

ΔAFJ, ΔAJI, ΔAFI, ΔABE, ΔAEC, ΔABC, ΔABD, ΔADC, ΔBCD, ΔBED, ΔDEC, ΔCDL, ΔBKD, ΔBGF, ΔCHI

Hence, there are total '15' triangles given in the figure.

16. (*b*) According to the question,

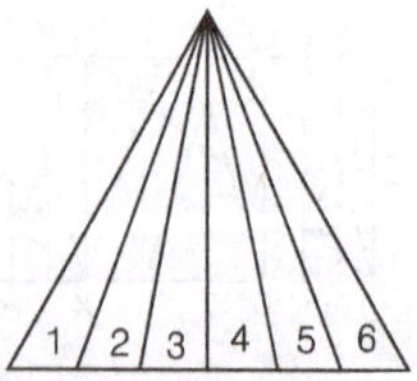

∴ Number of triangles in the given figure

= 6 + 5 + 4 + 3 + 2 + 1 = 21

17. (*a*) Naming the figure,

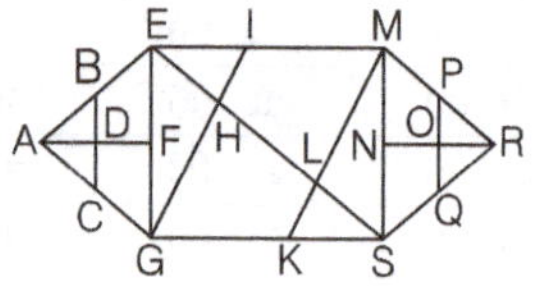

There are 22 triangles in the figure namely,

ΔABD, ΔADC, ΔABC, ΔAEF, ΔAFG, ΔAEG, ΔPOR, ΔROQ, ΔPRQ, ΔMNR, ΔRNS, ΔMRS, ΔMLS, ΔLKS, ΔMKS, ΔEIH, ΔEGH, ΔEIG, ΔEGS, ΔEMS, ΔEML and ΔGHS.

18. (*d*) Naming of the figure,

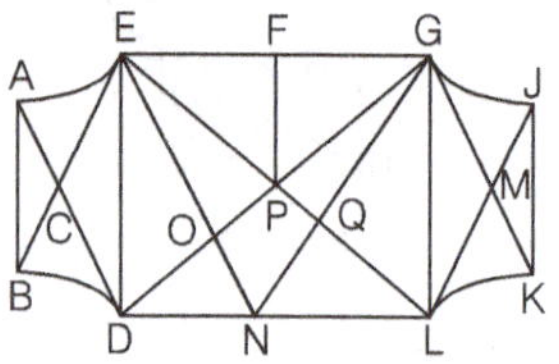

ΔABC, ΔCED, ΔGML, ΔJMK, ΔEOD, ΔEOP, ΔEDP, ΔEDN, ΔENQ, ΔENL, ΔEDL, ΔGPQ, ΔGQL, ΔGPL, ΔGON, ΔGDN, ΔGNL, ΔGDL, ΔODN, ΔQNL, ΔPDL, ΔEPF, ΔFPG, ΔEPG, ΔEOG, ΔEDG, ΔEQG, ΔELG and ΔENG

Hence, there are total 29 triangles given in the figure.

19. (*a*) Naming the figure,

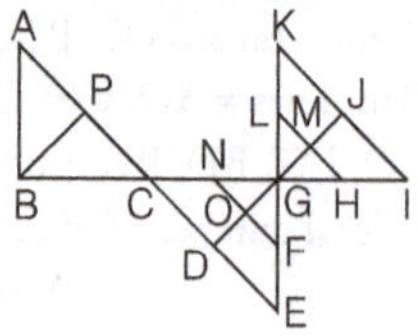

There are 15 triangles in the given figure namely,

ΔABP, ΔBPC, ΔABC, ΔNOG, ΔFOG, ΔNFG, ΔCGD, ΔEGD, ΔCEG, ΔLGM, ΔHGM, ΔLGH, ΔKGJ, ΔIGJ and ΔKGI.

20. (*d*) Naming of the figure,

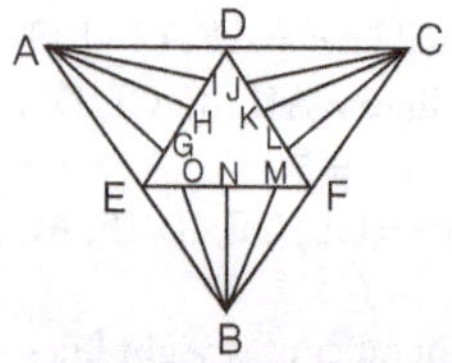

ΔAEG, ΔAGH, ΔAHI, ΔAID, ΔAEH, ΔAGI, ΔAHD, ΔAEI, ΔAGD, ΔAED, ΔBEO, ΔBON,

ΔBNM, ΔBMF, ΔBEN, ΔBOM, ΔBNF, ΔBEM, ΔBOF, ΔBEF, ΔCFL, ΔCLK, ΔCKJ, ΔCJD, ΔCFK, ΔCLJ, ΔCKD, ΔCFJ, ΔCLD, ΔCFD, ΔABC and ΔDEF

Hence, there are total '32' triangles.

Smart Approach

Total number of triangles
$= 3 \times (4 + 3 + 2 + 1) + \Delta DEF + \Delta ABC$
$= 3 \times 10 + 2 = 32$

21. *(c)* Naming the figure,

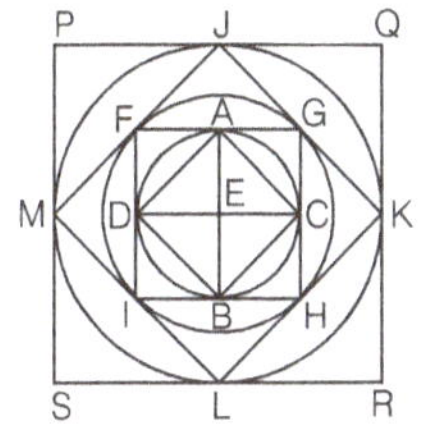

There are 20 triangles in the given figure,

ΔAEC, ΔBEC, ΔDEB, ΔDAE, ΔABC, ΔADB, ΔADC, ΔDBC, ΔAFD, ΔDIB, ΔBHC, ΔAGC, ΔJFG, ΔHKG, ΔIHL, ΔMFI, ΔPMJ, ΔQJK, ΔRKL and ΔSLM.

22. *(c)* Naming the figure,

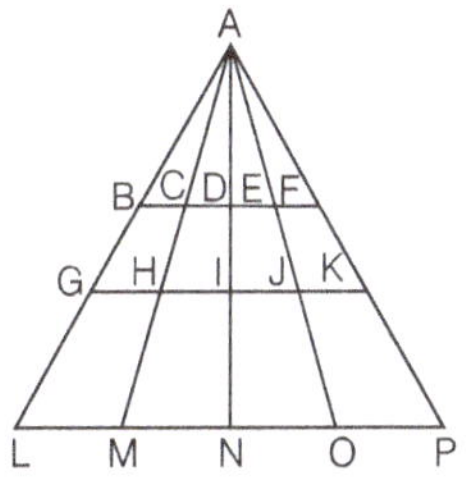

There are 30 triangles in the given figure namely,

ΔABC, ΔACD, ΔADE, ΔAEF, ΔABD, ΔACE, ΔADF, ΔABE, ΔAFC, ΔABF, ΔAGH, ΔAHI, ΔAIJ, ΔAJK, ΔAGI, ΔAHJ, ΔAIK, ΔAGJ, ΔAHK, ΔAGK, ΔALM, ΔAMN, ΔANO, ΔAOP, ΔALN, ΔAMO, ΔANP, ΔALO, ΔAMP and ΔALP.

Smart Approach

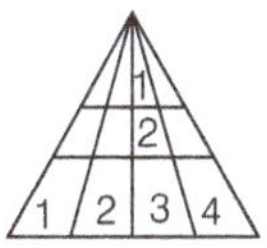

Total number of triangles
$= (4 + 3 + 2 + 1) \times 3$
$= 10 \times 3 = 30$

23. *(d)* Naming the figure,

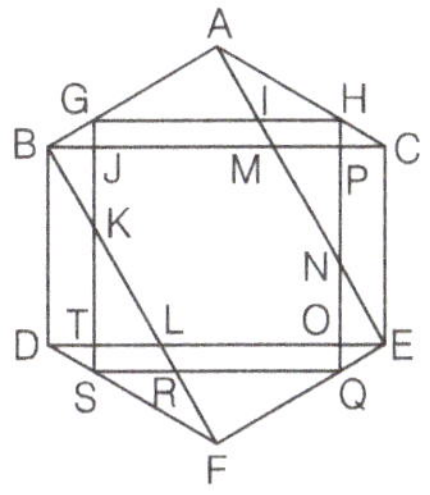

There are 30 triangles in the given figure namely,

ΔAGI, ΔAIH, ΔAGH, ΔABM, ΔAMC, ΔABC, ΔBGJ, ΔHCP, ΔFSR, ΔFRQ, ΔFSQ, ΔFDL, ΔFLE, ΔFDE, ΔDTS, ΔQOE, ΔBGK, ΔBJK, ΔKTL, ΔKSR, ΔQEN, ΔOEN, ΔNMP, ΔNIH, ΔBDL, ΔKSF, ΔBDF, ΔEMC, ΔNHA and ΔACE.

24. *(c)* Naming the figure,

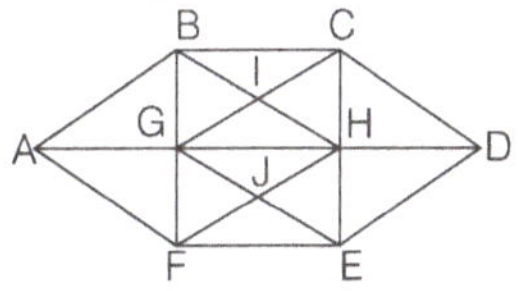

ΔAGB, ΔAGF, ΔBIC, ΔBIG, ΔIGH, ΔIHC, ΔCHD, ΔHDE, ΔEJH, ΔJHG, ΔJFG, ΔABF, ΔCDE, ΔABH, ΔAFH, ΔCDG, ΔDEG, ΔBCG, ΔBCH, ΔCHG, ΔHGB, ΔGHF, ΔGHE, ΔHEF, ΔEFG, ΔBHF, ΔCGE and ΔJFE.

Hence, there are total '28' triangles in the given figure.

25. *(c)* Naming the figure,

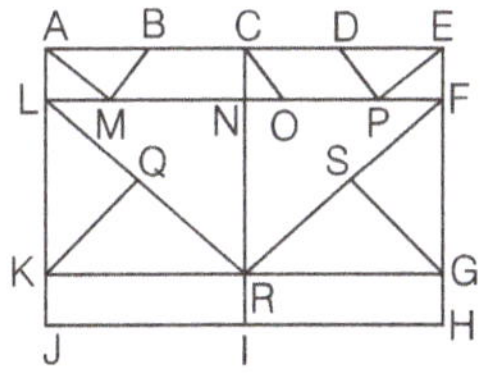

There are 14 triangles in the given figure namely,

ΔAMB, ΔLAM, ΔCNO, ΔDEP, ΔPEF, ΔLQK, ΔKQR, ΔLKR, ΔLRN, ΔNRF, ΔRSG, ΔFSG, ΔRFG and ΔLRF.

26. *(d)* Naming the figure,

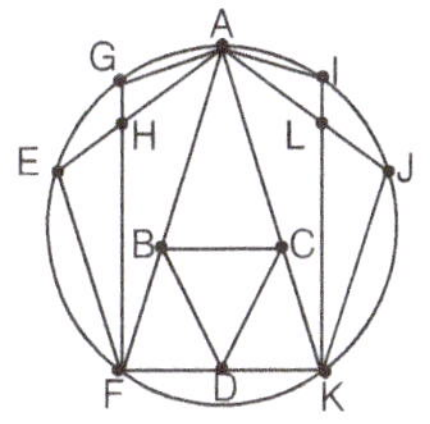

There are 15 triangles in the given figure namely,

ΔBFD, ΔDCK, ΔABC, ΔBCD, ΔAFK, ΔFHA, ΔEHF, ΔGAH, ΔFEA, ΔFGA, ΔALK, ΔAIL, ΔLJK, ΔAIK and ΔAJK.

27. *(b)* Naming the figure,

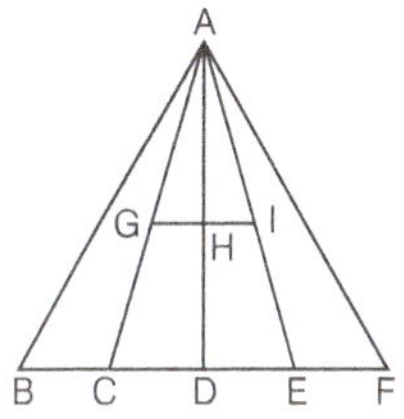

There are 13 triangles in the given figures namely,

ΔABC, ΔACD, ΔADE, ΔAEF, ΔAGH, ΔAHI, ΔAGI, ΔABD, ΔACE, ΔADF, ΔABE, ΔACF and ΔABF.

28. *(a)* Naming the figure,

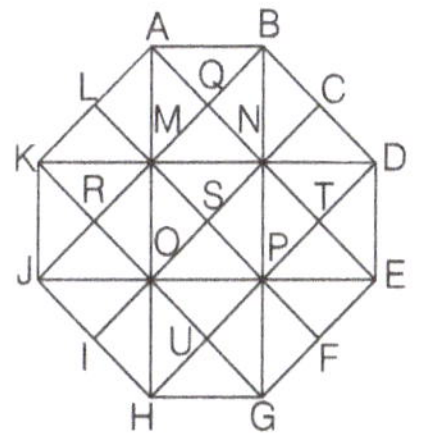

ΔLKM, ΔALM, ΔAQM, ΔABQ, ΔBQN, ΔMNQ, ΔBCN, ΔCDN, ΔKRM, ΔRMO, ΔROJ, ΔJRK, ΔMNS, ΔNSP, ΔPSO, ΔOSM, ΔNTD, ΔDTE, ΔETP, ΔPTN, ΔJOI, ΔOIH, ΔOPU, ΔPUG, ΔGUH, ΔHUO, ΔPGF, ΔPEF

Hence, there are total '28' triangles given in the figure.

29. *(a)* Naming of the figure,

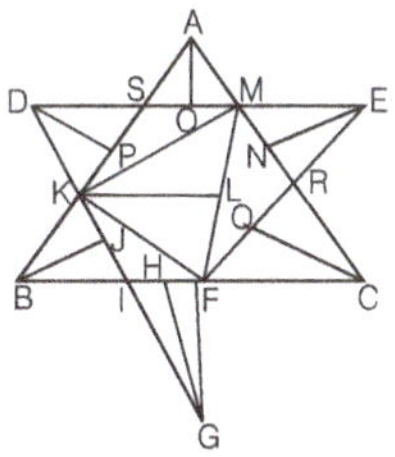

ΔABC, ΔDKS, ΔDPS, ΔDPK, ΔKFM, ΔKLF, ΔKLM, ΔASM, ΔAOS, ΔAOM, ΔEMR, ΔENM, ΔENR, ΔCRF, ΔCRQ, ΔCQF, ΔGIF, ΔGHF, ΔGHI, ΔBIK, ΔBIJ, ΔBJK, ΔKIF, ΔMRF, ΔKSM, ΔMEF, ΔDKM, ΔAKM, ΔGKF, ΔBFK, ΔFMC

∴ Total triangle = 31

30. *(c)* Naming of the figure,

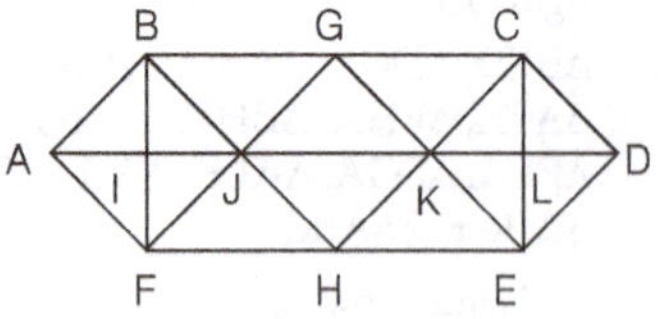

ΔABI, ΔBIJ, ΔIJF, ΔAIF, ΔBJG, ΔFJH, ΔGCK, ΔHKE, ΔKCL, ΔCLD, ΔLDE, ΔKLE, ΔGJK, ΔJKH, ΔABF, ΔABJ, ΔBJF, ΔAJF, ΔKCD, ΔCDE, ΔDEK, ΔEKC, ΔBGF, ΔBFH, ΔCEH, ΔGCE, ΔFGE, ΔBHC

∴ Total triangle = 28

31. *(d)* In the given figure,

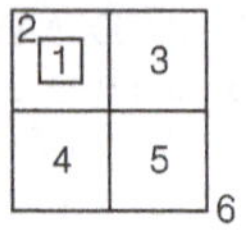

Number of square in the given figure = 6

∴ Total number of squares = 6 × 2 = 12

TOP TIPS

When the number of rows and column is equal. Then, assign consecutive number starting from 1 to each part. Then, sum of the number in square is equal to total number of square

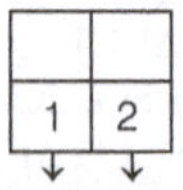

$(1)^2 + (2)^2 = 1 + 4 = 5$

32. *(a)* Naming of the figure,

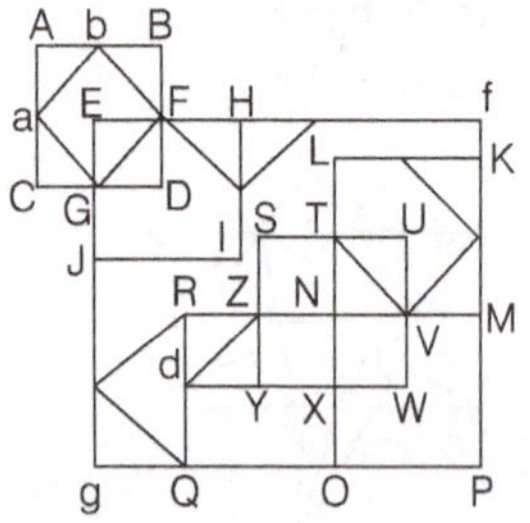

□ABDC, □abFG, □EFDG, □EHIJ, □LKMN, □NMPO, □RNOQ, □STNZ, □TUVN, □ZNXY, □NVWX, □SUWY, □RZYd and □EfPg

∴ Total number of squares = 14

33. *(d)* Naming of the figure,

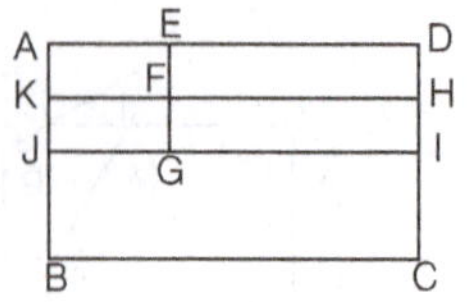

AEFK, EFHD, KFGJ, FGIH, JICB, AKHD, KJIH, AJID, KBCH and ABCD.

Hence, total number of rectangles is '10'.

34. *(c)* In the given row figure,

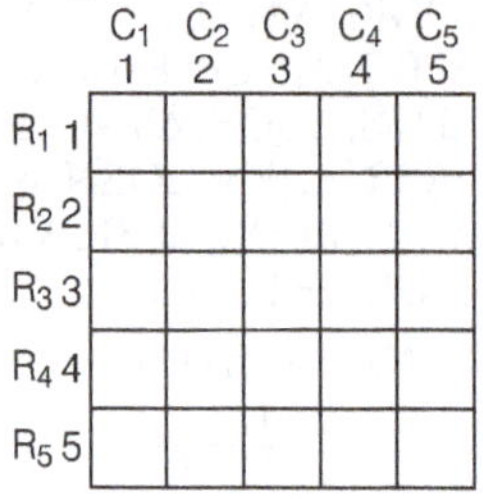

$(C_n \times R_n) + (C_{n-1} \times R_{n-1}) + \ldots .. (C_{n-n} \times R_{n-n})$

Row = 5, Column = 5

∴ Total square

$= (5 \times 5) + (4 \times 4) + (3 \times 3) + (2 \times 2) + (1 \times 1)$

$= 25 + 16 + 9 + 4 + 1 = 55$

35. *(d)* Naming of the figure,

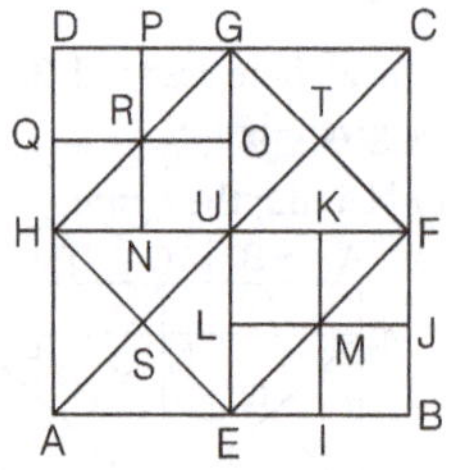

□HNRQ, □NUOR, □ROGP, □QRPD, □EIML, □IBJM, □MJFK, □LMKU, □HUGD, □EBFU, □AEUH, □UFCG, □EFGH, □ABCD

∴ Total number of squares = 14

36. *(b)* Small square = 8

Smallest square = 2

Second smallest square = 16

By combining four second smallest square = 9

Formed by combining nine second smallest square = 4

Largest square = 1

∴ Required number of square

= 8 + 2 + 16 + 9 + 4 + 1 = 40

37. *(c)* Naming of the figure,

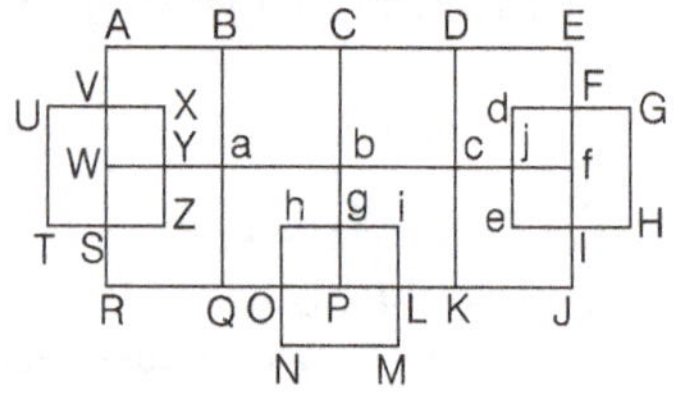

□ABaW, □BCba, □CDcb, □DEfc, □WaQR, □abPQ, □bcKP, □cfJK, □ACPR, □BDKQ, □CEJP, □UXZT, □VXYW, □WYZS, □hiMN, □hgPO, □giLP, □dGHe, □dFfj, □jfle

∴ Total number of squares = 20

38. *(c)* Naming of the figure,

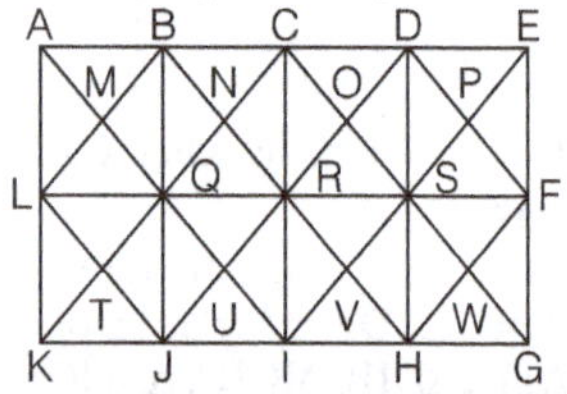

□BMQN, □LMQT, □TQUJ, □RNQU, □NCOR, □ROSV, □URVI, □ODPS, □PFWS, □SWHV, □ABQL, □BCRQ, □CDSR, □DEFS, □SFGH, □RSHI, □QRIJ, □LQJK, □LBRJ, □QCSI, □RDFH, □ACIK, □BDHJ, □CEGI

∴ Total number of squares = 24

39. *(a)* While counting the circles,

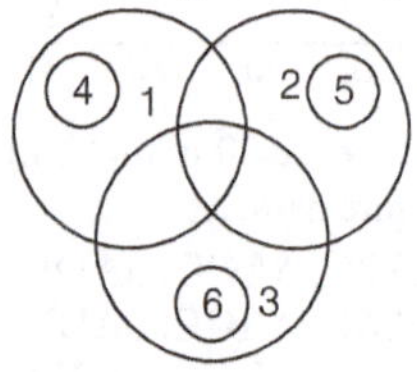

∴ Total circle = 6

40. *(c)* While counting the circles,

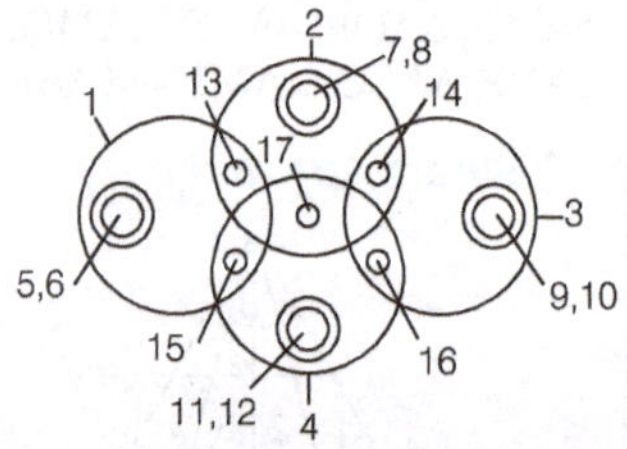

∴ Total circle = 17

CHAPTER

08 Mirror and Water Images

Image

An image is a visual representation of a picture or an object. When a person or an object is made to stand near a mirror or water, the shadow formed in the mirror or water is called the image of that person or object.
Questions based on images are generally of two types (i) Mirror Image (ii) Water Image.

Mirror Image

The figure obtained by putting a mirror in front of a real object is known as its mirror image or we can say that the reflection of an object in the mirror is called its mirror image.
In this type of questions the position of the mirror is on the right or left or above or below the object.

e.g. Choose the correct mirror image from the alternatives (a), (b), (c) and (d), when the mirror is placed along the line AB.

Question Figure

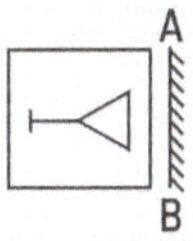

Answer Figures

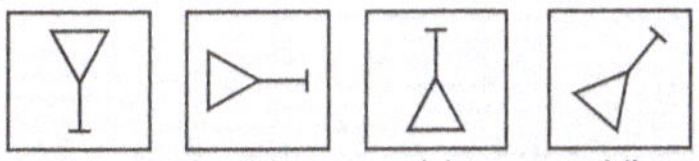

(a) (b) (c) (d)

Sol. (b) The figure given in option (b) is the correct mirror image of the given figure.

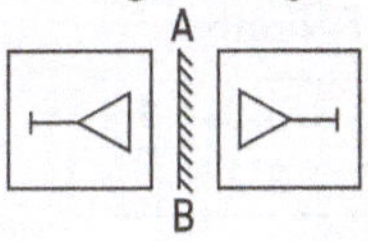

Score Booster

If the mirror in question is in front of the object, then in this case the candidate should look at the figure from the back side to find out the mirror image. The mirror image will be the same as the object seen from the back side.

Water Image

When an object is placed near a water source like a river, a pond or a water tub etc., then the image formed in the water is called the water image of that object.
The water image of the figure looks similar to the mirror image of the object when the mirror is placed horizontally below the object.

e.g. Choose the correct water image of the figure out of given alternatives.

Question Figure

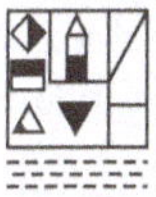

Answer Figures

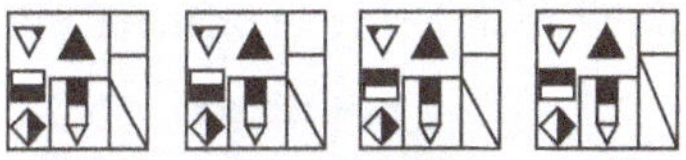

(a) (b) (c) (d)

Sol. (b) The figure given in option (b) is the correct water image of the given figure.

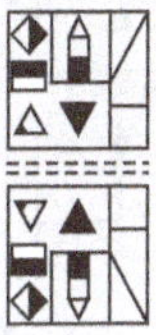

The image of an object can be obtained by keeping the mirror in following two positions.

I. When Mirror is Placed Vertically

When a mirror is placed vertically to the left or to the right of the object, then standard form of mirror image is formed. Here, the Left Hand Side (LHS) and Right Hand Side (RHS) of an object interchange their places while top and bottom remains at the same position.

The figure given below will help you to understand the formation of an image by a vertical mirror.

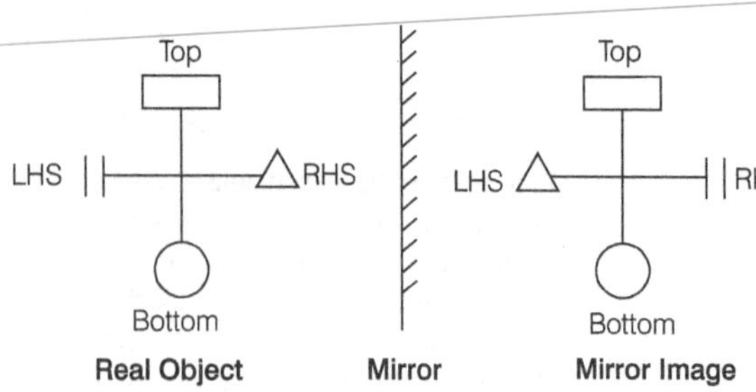

II. When Mirror is Placed Horizontally

When a mirror is placed at the top or at the bottom of the object, then the image, so obtained is as like its water image. Here, the top and bottom of an object interchange their places while LHS and RHS remains at the same position.

The figure given below will help you to understand the formation of an image by a horizontal mirror.

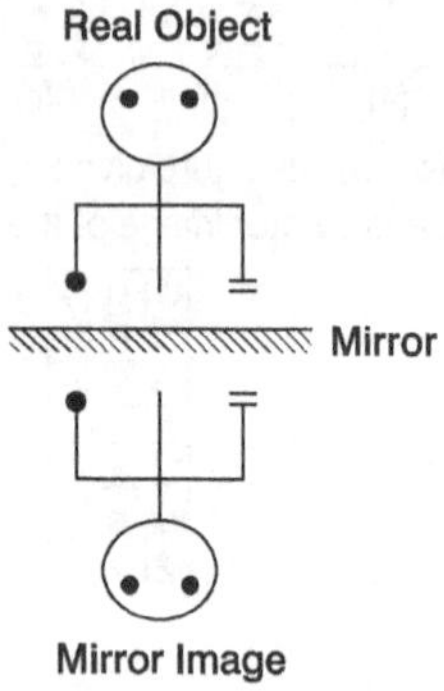

Mirror Image of English alphabets, Letters and Numbers

Mirror Images of Capital Letters

Real Image	A	B	C	D	E	F	G	H	I	J	K	L	M
Mirror Image	A	ᙠ	Ɔ	ᗡ	Ǝ	ꟻ	Ә	H	I	Ⴑ	ꓘ	⅃	M
Real Image	N	O	P	Q	R	S	T	U	V	W	X	Y	Z
Mirror Image	И	O	ꟼ	Ọ	Я	Ƨ	T	U	V	W	X	Y	Ƹ

Note The letters - A, H, I, M, O, T, U, V, W, X and Y have the same mirror images because of their symmetrical shape. Their left hand sides and right hand sides do not appear to change their positions.

Mirror Images of Small Letters

Real Image	a	b	c	d	e	f	g	h	i	j	k	l	m
Mirror Image	ɒ	d	ɔ	b	ɘ	ʇ	ϱ	ʜ	i	į	ʞ	l	m
Real Image	n	o	p	q	r	s	t	u	v	w	x	y	z
Mirror Image	n	o	q	p	ɿ	ƨ	ɟ	υ	v	w	x	ʏ	ƹ

Note The letters - i, l, o, v, w and x have the same mirror images i.e., their left hand sides and right hand sides do not appear to change their positions.

Mirror Images of Numbers

Real Image	1	2	3	4	5	6	7	8	9	0
Mirror Image	Ɩ	ς	Ɛ	ᔨ	ट	ə	٢	8	ɘ	0

Note Numbers 0 and 8 have the same mirror images.

Water Images of Letters

Letters	A B C D E F G H I
Water Image	∀ B C D E Ⅎ ⅁ H I
Letters	J K L M N O P Q R
Water Image	ſ K Γ W И O b Ọ ᴚ
Letters	S T U V W X Y Z
Water Image	S ⊥ ∩ Λ M X ⅄ Z

Note Water image of C, D, E, H, I, K, O and X is same.

Water Images of Numbers

Number	0 1 2 3 4 5 6 7 8 9
Water Image	0 ⇂ ᘔ 3 ᔭ ဌ 9 ㄥ 8 6

Note Water image of numbers, 0, 3 and 8 is same and the mirror and water images of letters H, I, O, and X are similar.

Exam Approach Examples

Based on Mirror Image

Directions (Ex. Nos. 1-5) *In each of the following questions. Choose the correct mirror image from alternatives* (a), (b), (c) *and* (d) *of the given figure.*

Example 1 Question Figure Answer Figures

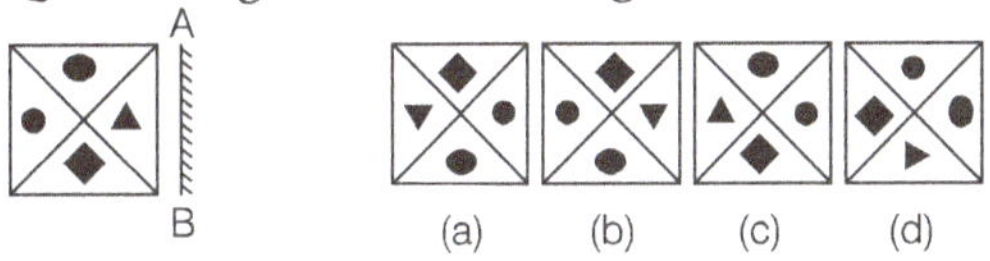

SSC (10+2) Tier-I 2024

Sol. *(c)* The figure given in option (c) is the correct mirror image of the given figure.

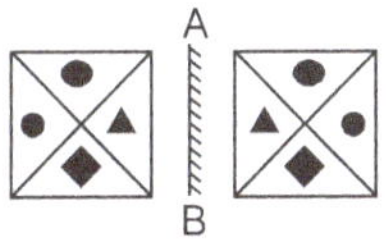

Example 2 Question Figure Answer Figures *SSC Steno 2021*

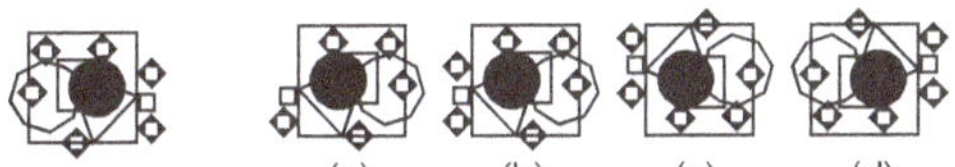

Sol. *(b)* The figure given in option (b) is the correct mirror image of the given figure.

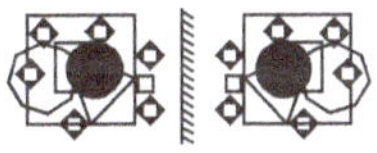

> ***Helping Tips***
> In the questions related to mirror image, if the position of mirror is not given, then always consider mirror to be placed on the right side of the object vertically.

Example 3

Question Figure Answer Figures

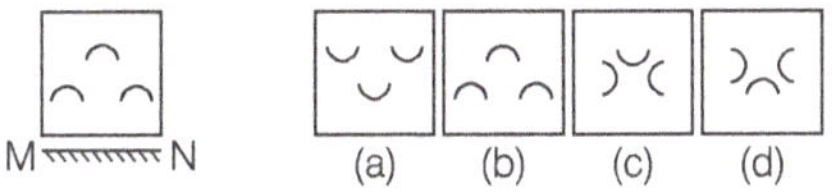

RRB Group-D 2018

Sol. *(a)* The figure given in option (a) is the correct mirror image of the given figure.

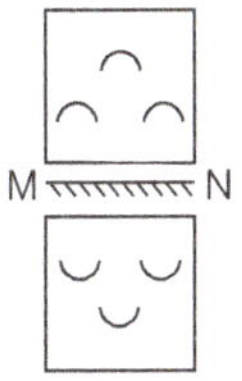

Example 4 Question Figure

ZVBCWP | P / Q (mirror)

SSC CGL (Tier-I) 2023

Answer Figures

(a) ƧΛBCMb (b) ꟼMƆBVƧ
(c) dWƆBVZ (d) ꟼWƆBVƧ

Sol. *(d)* The figure given in option (d) is the correct mirror image of the given figure.

ZVBCWP | ꟼWƆBVƧ (mirror PQ)

> ***Trending Concept***
> The questions on mirror and water images are asked in current examinations of SSC CGL, Steno, CHSL, MTS, UP Police constable, RRB Group-D, State Police exams and UPSSSC. This topic is very important for the upcoming examination.

Example 5 Wpa3z5 | M / N (mirror)

SSC MTS 2023

(a) 5ƨ3ɒpW (b) z5Ɛɒpʍ (c) ςz3ɘbʍ (d) ƼƨƐɒqW

Sol. *(d)* The figure given in option (d) is the correct mirror image of the given figure.

Wpa3z5 | ƼƨƐɒqW (mirror MN)

Based on Water Image

Directions (Ex. Nos. 6 and 7) *Choose the correct water image of the figure out of given four alternatives.*

Example 6 Question Figure Answer Figures

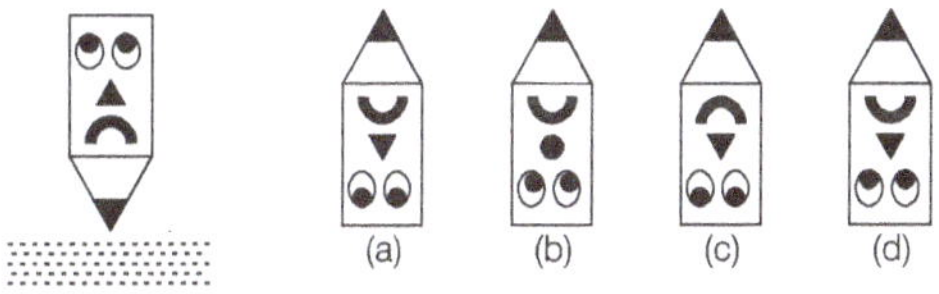

SSC MTS 2021

Sol. *(a)* The figure given in option (a) is the correct water image of the given figure.

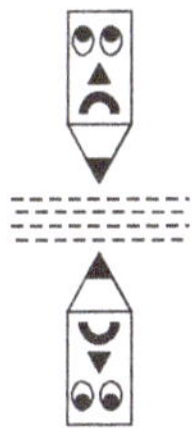

Example 7 CORDIAL *SSC Steno 2020*

(a) COꓤDIVL (b) COꓤDIVΓ (c) COꓤDIV⅃ (d) ⅃AIDЯOƆ

Sol. *(b)* The figure given in option (b) is the correct water image of the given figure,

CORDIAL
COꓤDIVΓ

Chapter Challenge

Based on Mirror Image

Directions (Q. Nos. 1-37) *In each of the following questions, choose the correct mirror image from alternatives* (a), (b), (c) *and* (d) *of the given figures.*

1. Question Figure Answer Figures

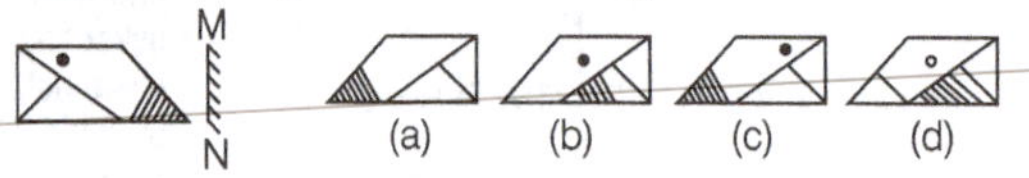

SSC CGL 2020

> **MRC*****
> ***(Most Repeating Concepts)***
> Questions Nos. 1, 3, 4, 5, 6, 7, 8, 17, 18, 23, 31, 33, 37, 38, 39, 43 and 44 are very important from exam point of view. The concept of mirror and water images are being asked in various examination such as SSC CGL, MTS, Steno, UP AO, CISF, RRB Group-D, UP police constable, ASI, CUET (UG), Rajasthan police constable.

2.

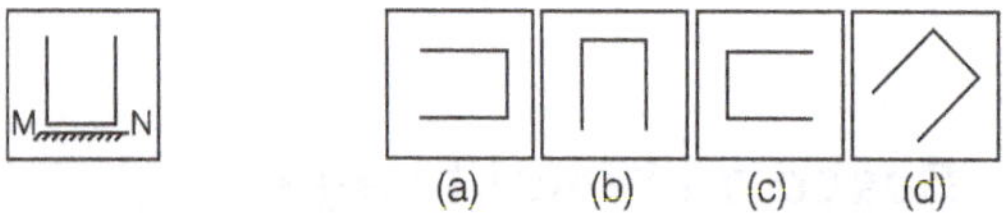

SSC Steno 2018

3.

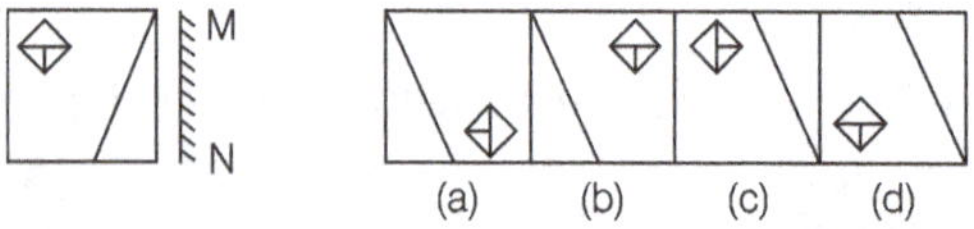

SSC (10+2) 2018

4.

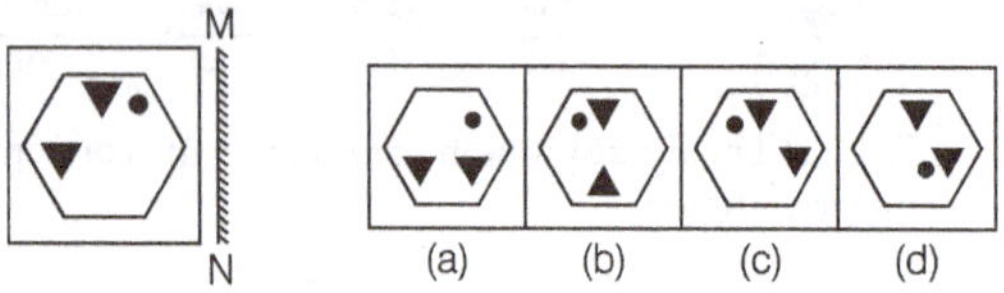

UP Police Constable 2024

5.

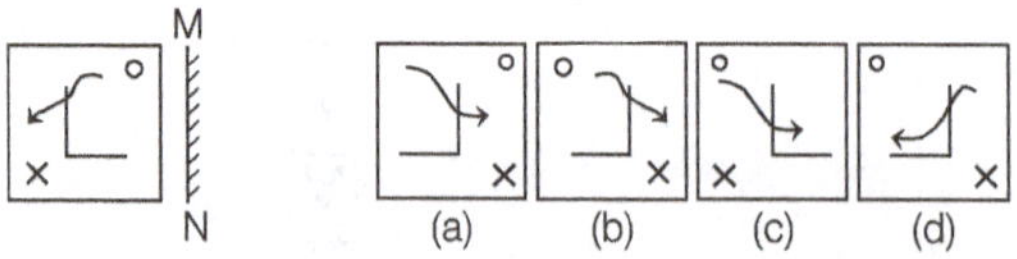

RRB Group-D 2018

6.

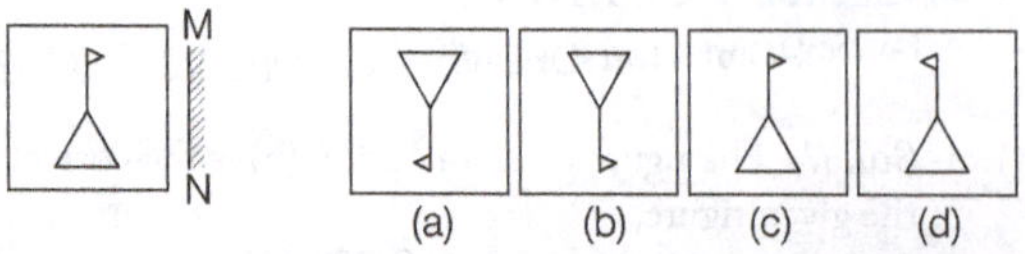

SSC CPO 2023

7. Question Figure Answer Figures

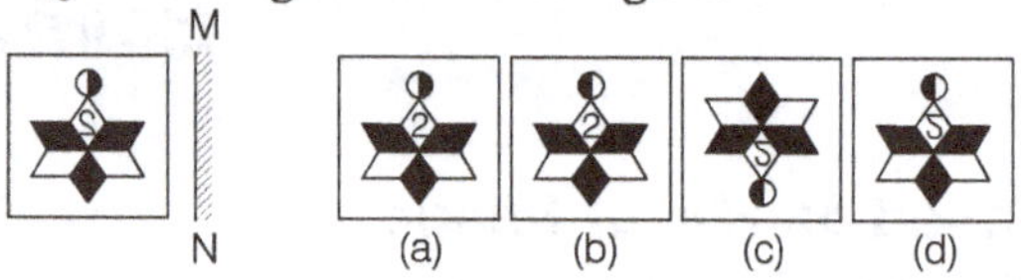

Rajasthan Police Constable 2022

8.

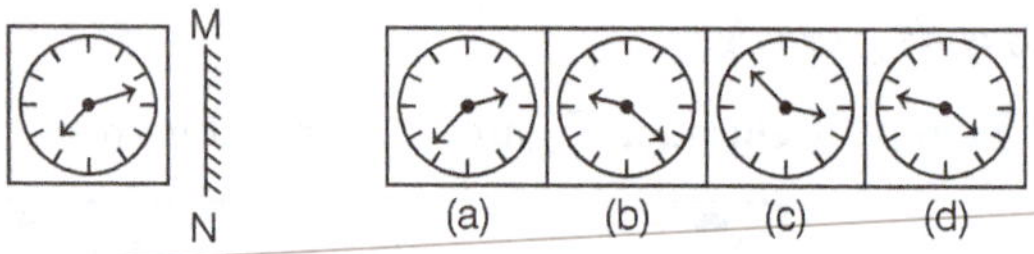

Delhi Police MTS 2018

9.

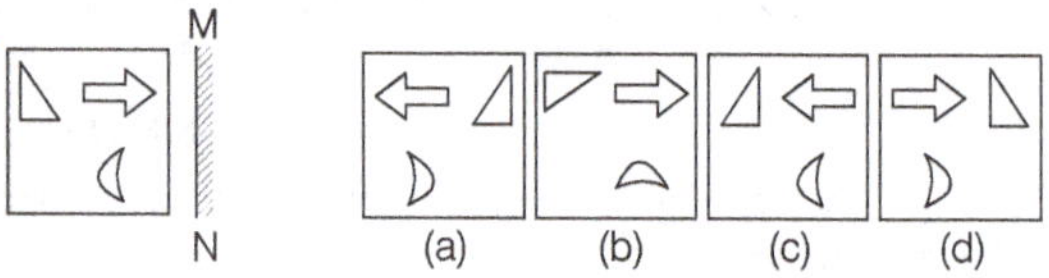

SSC (10+2) 2023

10.

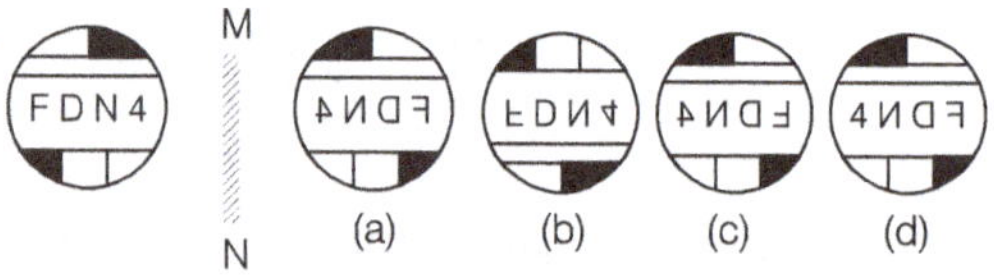

SSC (10+2) 2021

11.

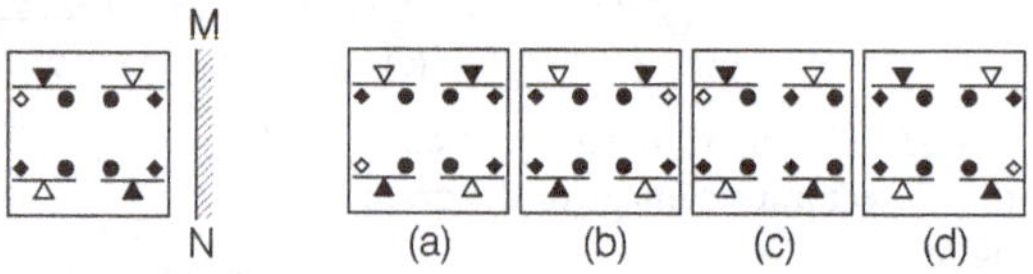

DP Constable 2023

12.

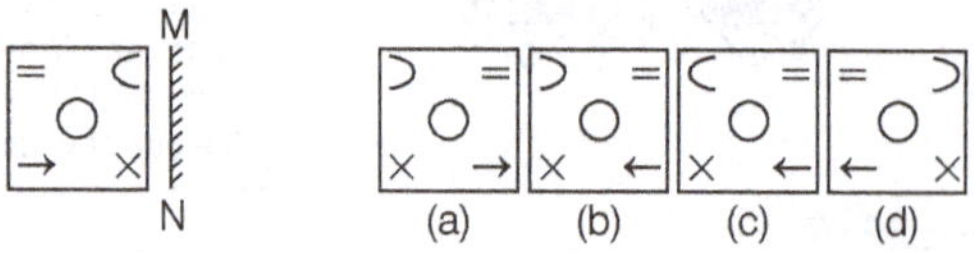

SSC CPO 2018

13.

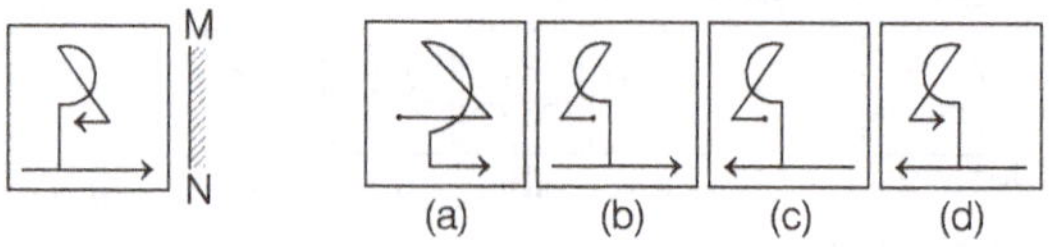

SSC (10+2) 2023

14.

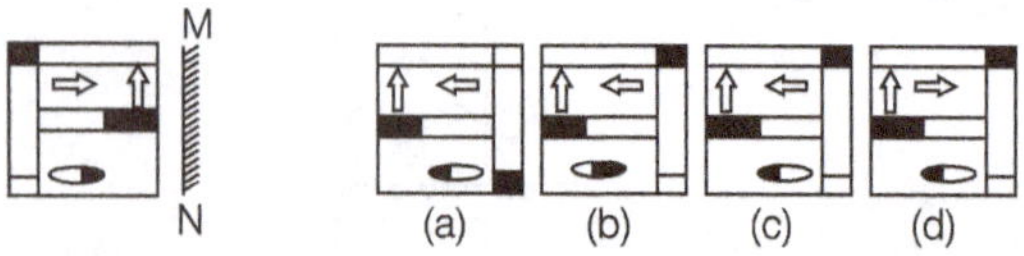

SSC CGL 2022

15.

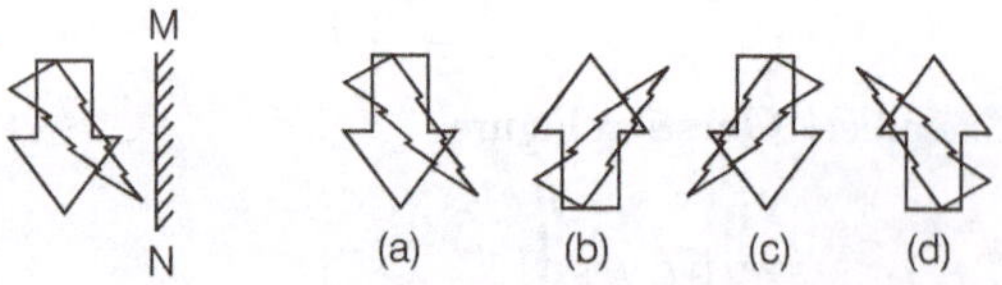

SSC (10+2) 2020

16. Question Figure Answer Figures

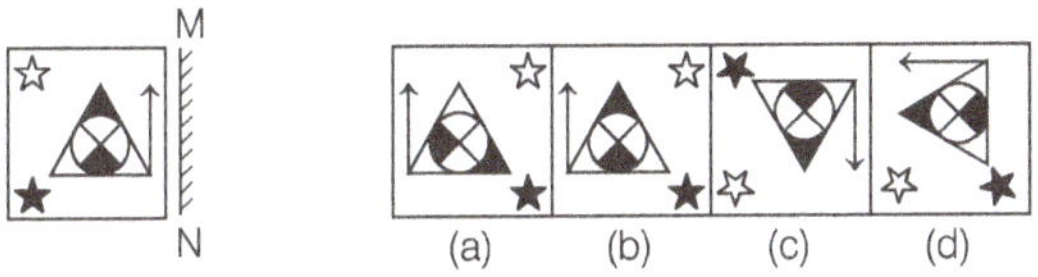

SSC Steno 2019

17.

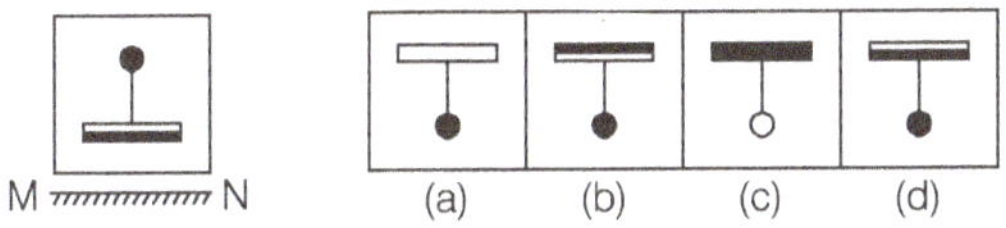

RRB Group-D 2018

18.

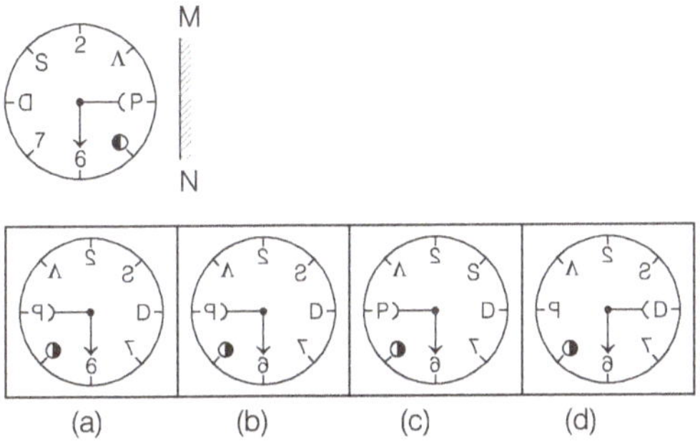

CISF 2023

19.

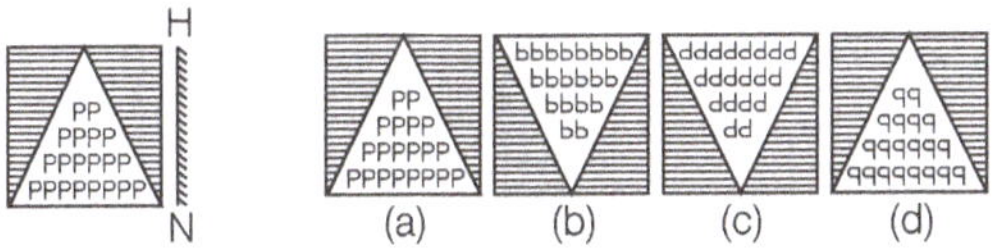

UPSSSC Forest Guard 2022

20. Y57nBe2 | M–N

(a) Ƨɘᗺuᒣ5Y (b) Ƨɘᗺnᒣ5Y

(c) Ƨɘᗺnᒣ5Y (d) 2eBnᒣ5Y

SSC CGL (Tier-II) 2025

21. c9v6n2 | M–N

(a) ƨuᑫʌ6ɔ (b) c9v6n2

(c) ɔ9ʌɘuƨ (d) ƨnǝʌǝɔ

SSC (10+2) Tier-I 2024

22. uP23AB | M–N

(a) ᗺAƐƧꟼu (b) ᗺAƐ29u

(c) BAƐƧꟼu (d) ᗺA23ꟼu

SSC CGL (Tier-I) 2024

23. Question Figure

REACH | M–N

Answer Figures

(a) HCAƎЯ (b) HCVƎЯ (c) EЯACH (d) ЯEACH

UP AO 2024

24. L27Aef | M–N

(a) ɟeA27⅃ (b) ɟeAᒣS⅃ (c) ɟeAᒧƧᒣ (d) ɟeAᒣS⅃

SSC CPO 2024

25. 47F29M8 | M–N

(a) 89MƧꟻᒣ4 (b) 8MeƧꟻᒣ4

(c) 8M29ꟻᒣ4 (d) 8WeƧꟻᒣ4

SSC CGL (Tier-II) 2025

26. bcFgl | M–N

(a) lgFɔb (b) lgꟻɔd (c) lgꟻcd (d) lgꟻcb

SSC CGL (Tier-I) 2024

27. yReA4kL | M–N

(a) Lʞ4AɘЯy (b) ⅃ʞ4AɘЯy

(c) ⅃ʞ4AɘЯy (d) ⅃ʞ4AɘЯʎ

SSC CGL (Tier-I) 2024

28. yTfr93n | M–N

(a) nƐeɿɟ⊥y (b) nƐeɿɟTy (c) nƐeɿɟTy (d) n93ɿɟTy

SSC CGL (Tier-I) 2024

29. zBNnGf | M–N

(a) ɟGuNBz (b) ɟGnИBƨ (c) ɟGnИBƨ (d) fGnИBƨ

SSC (10+2) Tier-II 2024

30. RkgEyw | M–N

(a) wʏƎɡʞЯ (b) wʎEɡʞЯ

(c) ʍʏEɡʞЯ (d) ywƎɡʞR

SSC CPO 2024

Chapter Challenge Mirror and Water Images

31.

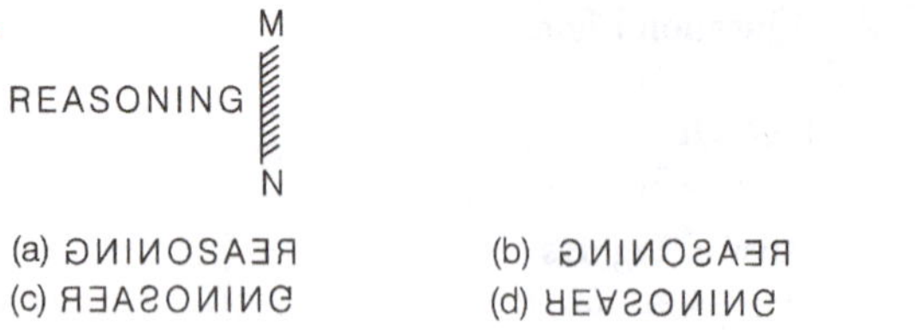

UP Police Constable 2024

32.

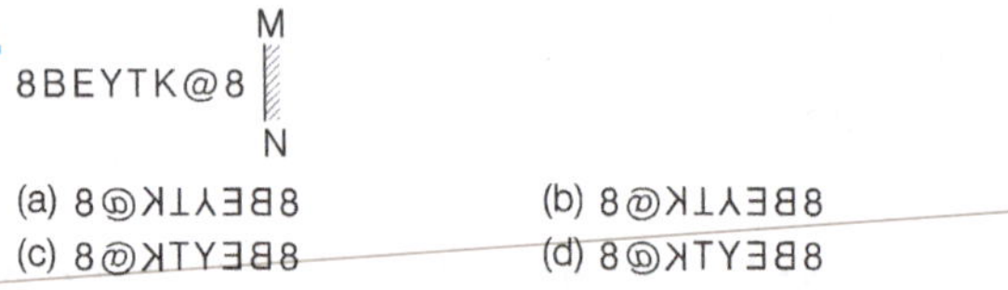

SSC CPO 2023

33.

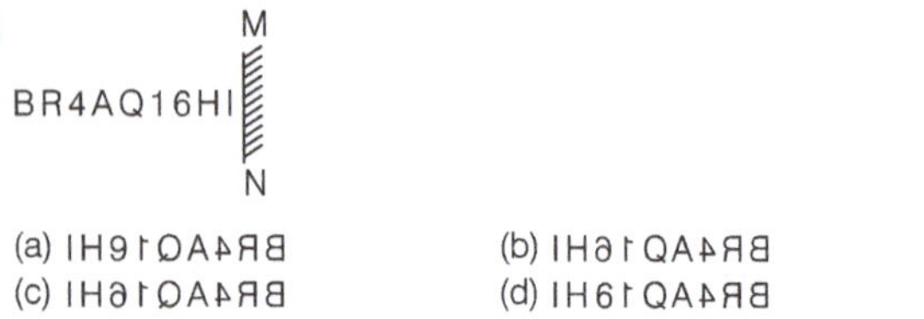

UP Police Constable 2024

34.

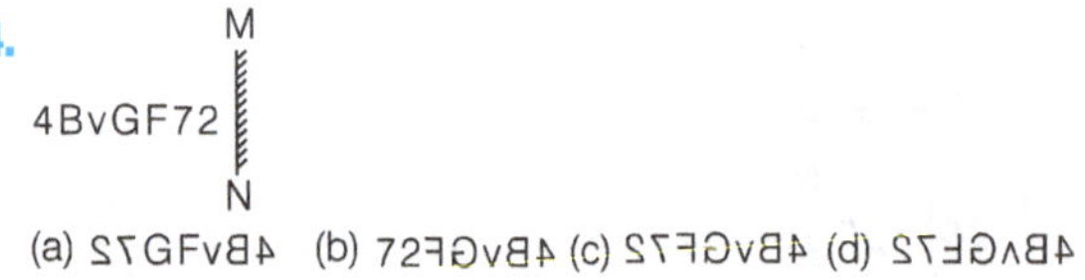

SSC CGL (Tier-II) 2025

35.

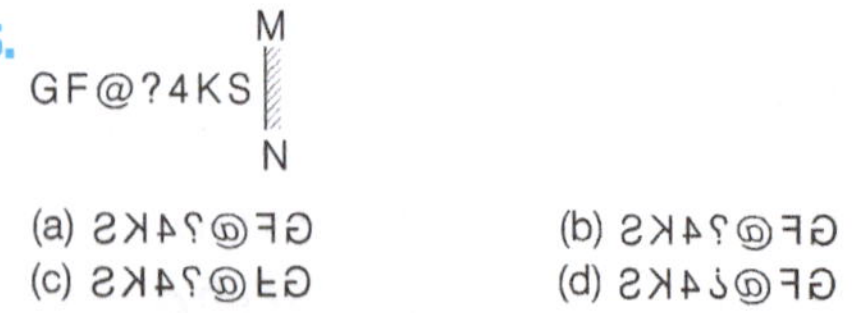

SSC JE 2023

36.

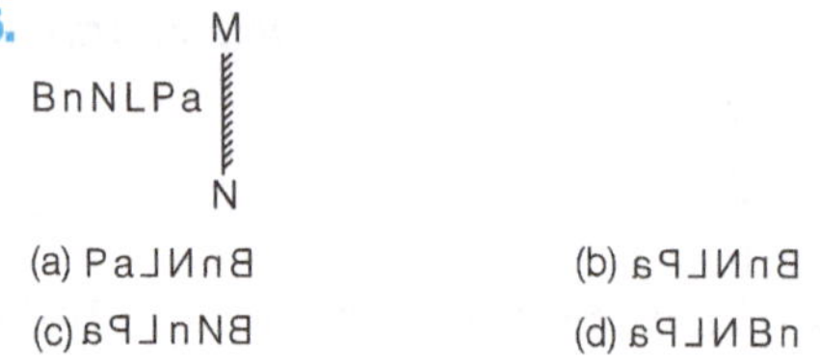

RPF SI 2024

37.

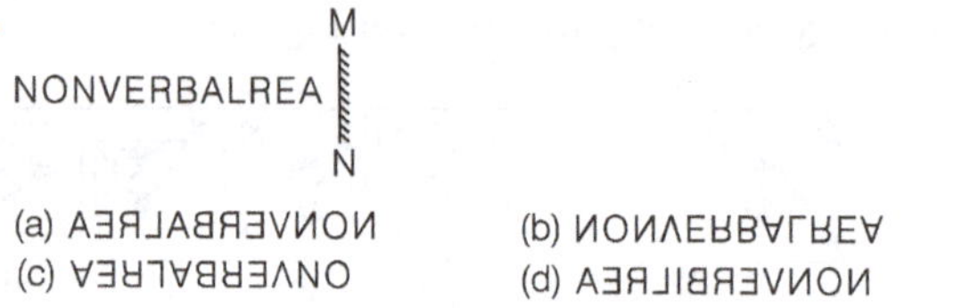

UPSSSC Forest Guard 2022

Based on Water Image

Directions (Q. Nos. 38-42) *In each of the following questions, a figure is given which is followed by four other figures* (a), (b), (c) *and* (d) *showing the possible water images of figure. Choose the correct water image of the figure out of the given four alternatives.*

38. Question Figure Answer Figures

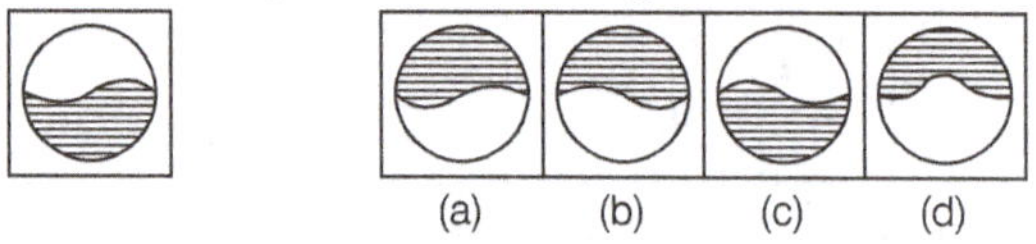

RRB ALP 2018

39.

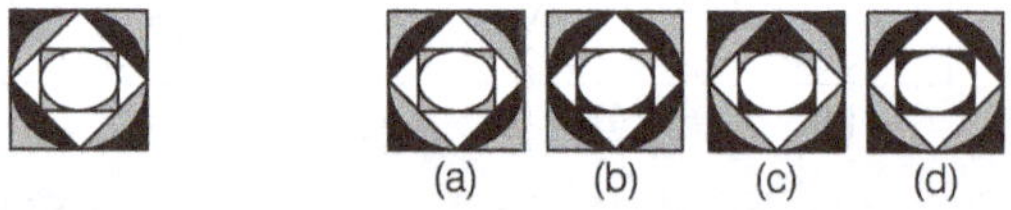

UPSSSC 2018

40.

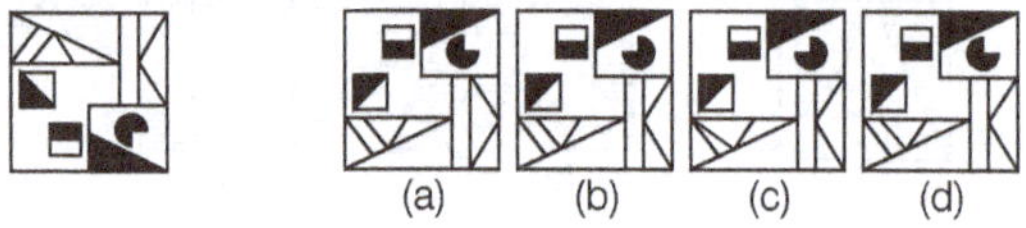

SSC (10+2) 2023

41. 59216Rgm

CUET (UG) 2022

42. PNe32YCA

SSC CGL (Tier-I) 2022

Right Key

1. (c)	2. (b)	3. (b)	4. (c)	5. (b)	6. (d)	7. (b)	8. (d)	9. (a)	10. (a)
11. (b)	12. (b)	13. (d)	14. (c)	15. (c)	16. (b)	17. (b)	18. (b)	19. (d)	20. (c)
21. (d)	22. (a)	23. (a)	24. (d)	25. (b)	26. (b)	27. (c)	28. (c)	29. (c)	30. (a)
31. (b)	32. (d)	33. (c)	34. (c)	35. (b)	36. (b)	37. (a)	38. (b)	39. (a)	40. (d)
41. (b)	42. (c)								

CHAPTER

09 Paper Folding and Cutting

Paper Folding

In this type of questions, a transparent sheet having a certain design and a dotted line on it is given. The candidates are required to identify the design/figure that would be formed when the sheet is folded along the dotted line.

e.g. Select the answer figure that will be formed when the question figure is folded along the dotted lines.

Question Figure

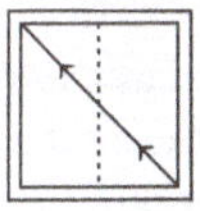

Answer Figures

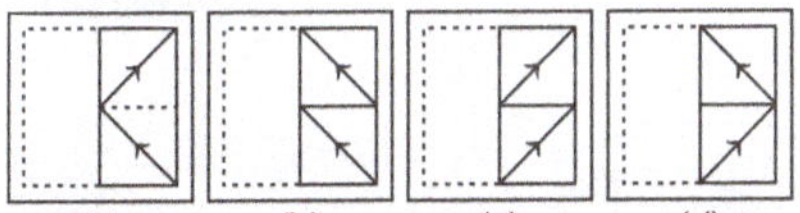

(a) (b) (c) (d)

Sol. (a) The left half of the question figure is being folded along the dotted line and placed on the right half of the figure.

Thus, the figure obtained resembles the answer figure (a).

Paper Folding and Cutting

When a square sheet of paper is folded along the dotted lines and specific punches or cuts are made on it as per the question, then the paper is unfolded and a particular shape/figure is formed. This process is known as paper folding and cutting.

In questions based on paper folding and cutting candidates can be asked to find either the folded or the unfolded pattern of the sheet.

Score Booster

To solve this type of questions, one should imagine a mirror placed on the dotted line which means that the other half of the paper will have the mirror image of the figure present in the first half. Then by folding half of the paper along the dotted lines the required figure/image is obtained.

Paper Cutting

In this type of questions, a sheet of paper is folded in certain given directions and cuts are made on it. Candidates have to determine how this sheet of paper will look like when it is unfolded.

e.g. A piece of paper is folded and a cut is made as shown below. How will it appear when unfolded?

Question Figures

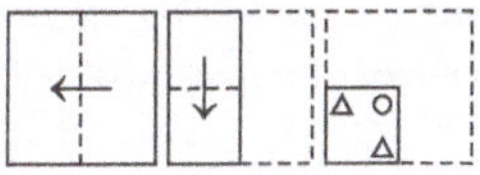

Answer Figures

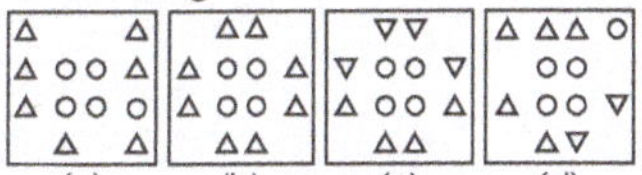

(a) (b) (c) (d)

Sol. (c) When we unfold the question figure, then it looks like as answer figure (c).

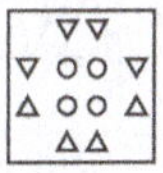

Exam Approach Examples

Based on Paper Folding

Example 1 Select the answer figure that will be formed when the given transparent sheet of paper is folded along the dotted lines. *SSC MTS 2021*

Question Figure

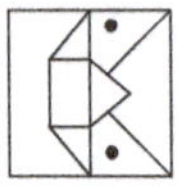

Answer Figures

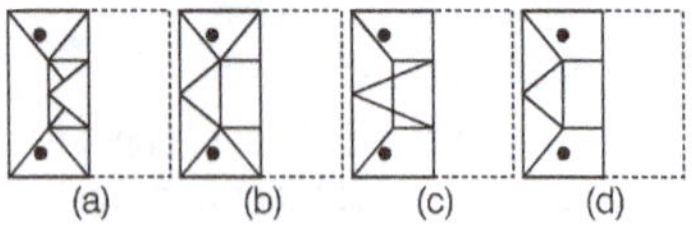

Sol. (*a*) When the given sheet of paper is folded along the dotted lines, the answer figure (a) will be formed.

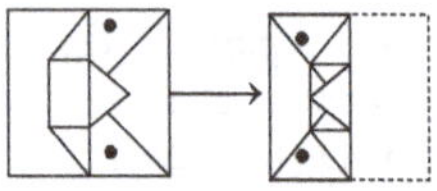

Example 2 Select the answer figure that will be formed when the given sheet of paper is folded along the dotted lines. *SSC Constable (GD) 2018*

Question Figure

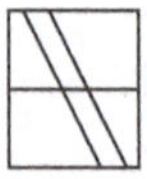

Helping Tips

In such questions, it is very important to have an understanding of folding the paper and images to convert as open figure into a closed figure.

Answer Figures

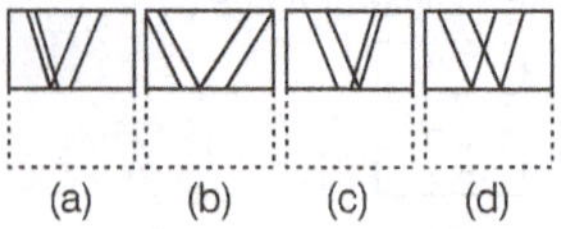

Sol. (*d*) When the given sheet of paper is folded along the dotted lines, then the answer figure (d) will be formed.

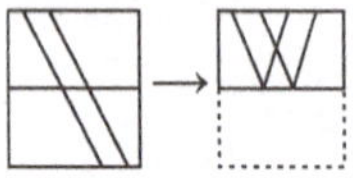

Based on Paper Cutting

Example 3 A transparent sheet of paper is folded as shown in the figure given below and several punches/cuts are made on it. Select the answer figure that will be formed when the paper is unfolded? *DP Constable 2023*

Question Figures

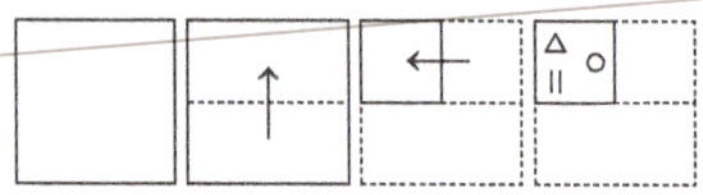

Trending Concept

Questions based on paper cutting are being continuously asked in current examinations such as SSC, MTS, CPO, CGL, DP Constable, DSSSB. They are important for upcoming examinations.

Answer Figures

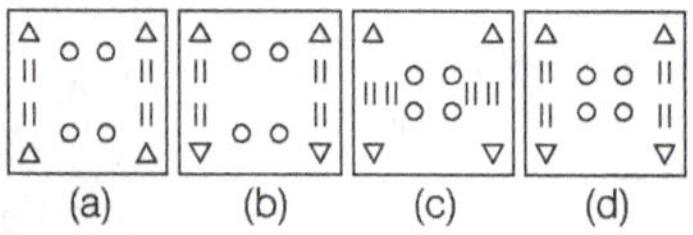

Sol. (*b*) The given figure when unfolded will look like the figure given in option (b).

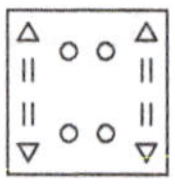

Example 4 A transparent sheet of paper is folded as shown below and several punches/cuts are made on it. Select the answer figure that will be formed when the paper is unfolded? *SSC CPO 2024*

Question Figures

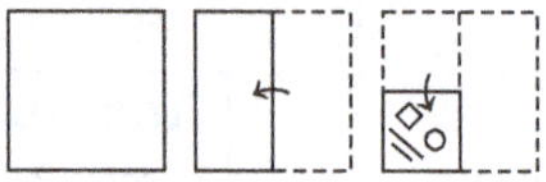

Answer Figures

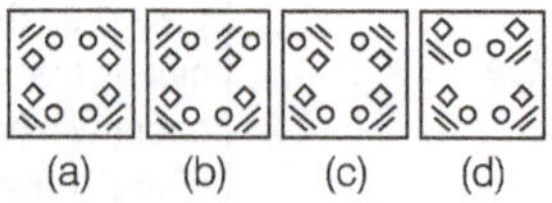

Sol. (*a*) The given figure when unfolded will look like the figure given in option (a).

Chapter Challenge

Based on Paper Folding

Directions (Q. Nos. 1-12) *In the following question a square transparent paper is given along with a sample figure. Find the figure from the four options which will be obtained when the transparent paper is folded along the dotted line.*

1. Question Figure

RRB ALP 2018

Answer Figures

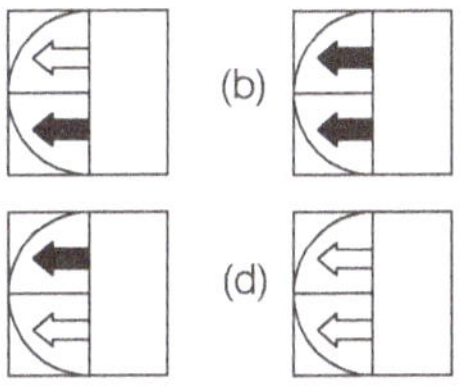

(a) (b) (c) (d)

> ***MRC******
> *(Most Repeating Concepts)*
> Q. Nos. 2, 3, 4, 5, 8, 10, 13, 14, 20, 22, 29 and 30 are important from examination point of view. These questions are being repeatedly asked in RRB ALP, UP Police Constable, SSC CHSL, CPO, Steno, DSSSB, CUET (UG) exams.

2. Question Figure

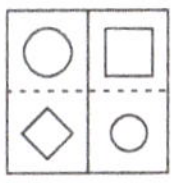

Answer Figures

RRB ALP 2018

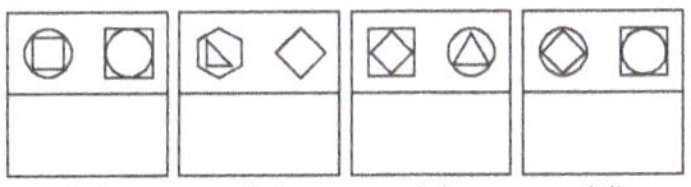

(a) (b) (c) (d)

3. Question Figure

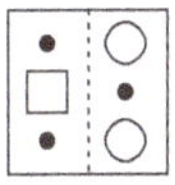

RRB ALP 2018

Answer Figures

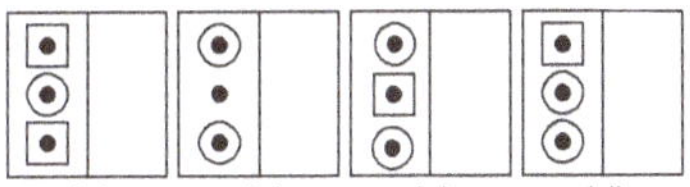

(a) (b) (c) (d)

4. Question Figure

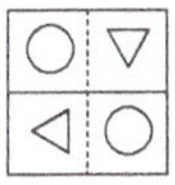

UP Police Constable 2024

Answer Figures

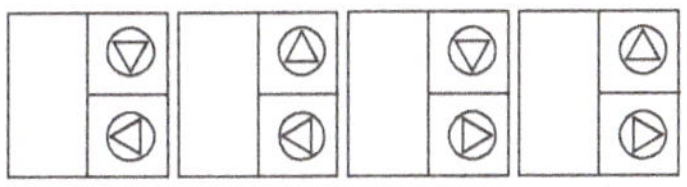

(a) (b) (c) (d)

5. Question Figure Answer Figures

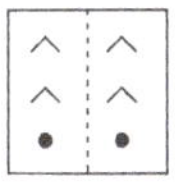

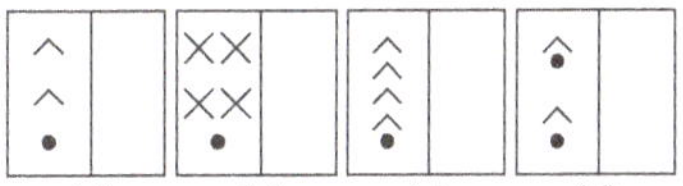

(a) (b) (c) (d)

UP Police Constable 2024

6. Question Figure

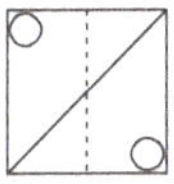

CRPF HC 2023

Answer Figures

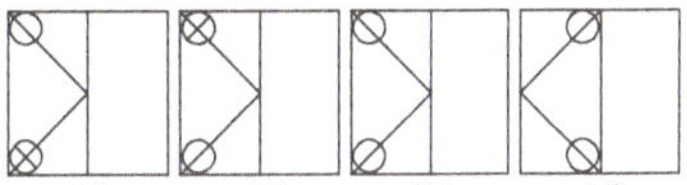

(a) (b) (c) (d)

7. Question Figure

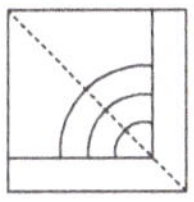

UP Police AO 2024

Answer Figures

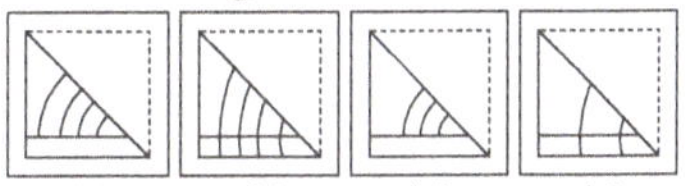

(a) (b) (c) (d)

8. Question Figure

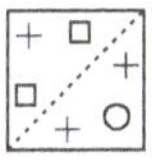

UP Police Constable 2024

Answer Figures

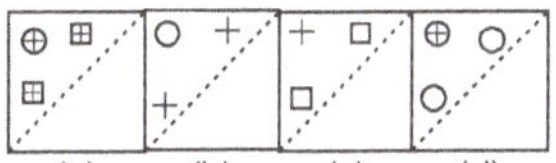

(a) (b) (c) (d)

9. Question Figure

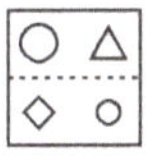

RRB ALP 2018

Answer Figures

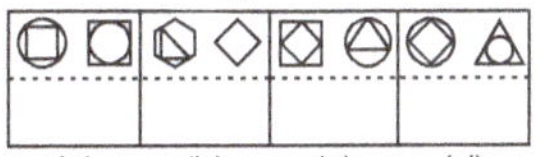

(a) (b) (c) (d)

10. Question Figure

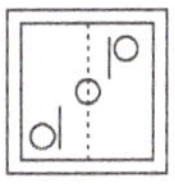

DSSSB 2020

Answer Figures

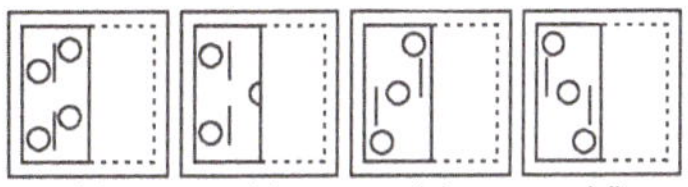

(a) (b) (c) (d)

11. Question Figure

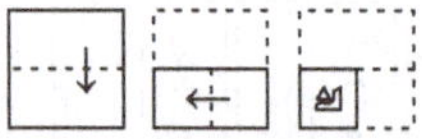

SSC CHSL (Tier II) 2024

Answer Figures

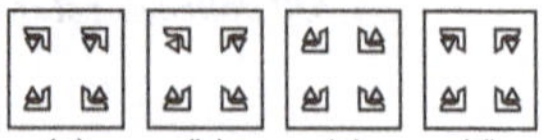

(a) (b) (c) (d)

12. Question Figure

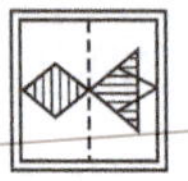

DSSSB 2020

Answer Figures

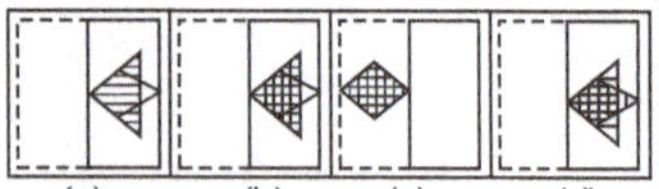

(a) (b) (c) (d)

Based on Paper Cutting

Directions (Q. Nos. 13-38) *A piece of paper is folded and a cut is made as shown below. From the given responses indicate how it will appear when opened? Choose the correct answer figure from the given answer figures* (a), (b), (c) *and* (d).

13. Question Figure

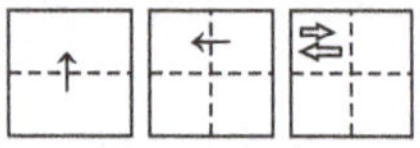

SSC (10+2) 2024

Answer Figures

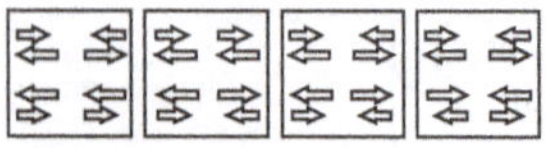

(a) (b) (c) (d)

14. Question Figure

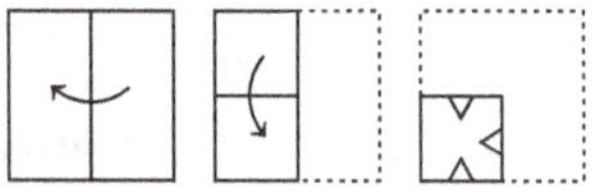

SSC Steno 2021

Answer Figures

(a) (b) (c) (d)

15. Question Figure

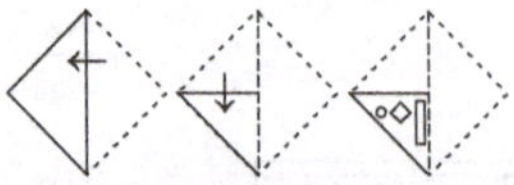

DP Constable 2023

Answer Figures

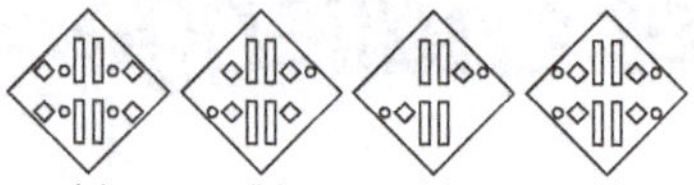

(a) (b) (c) (d)

16. Question Figure

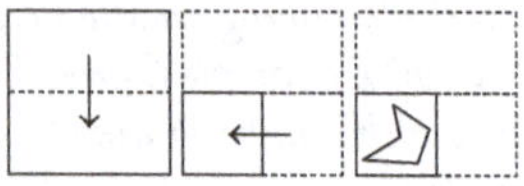

CISF HC (min) 2022

Answer Figures

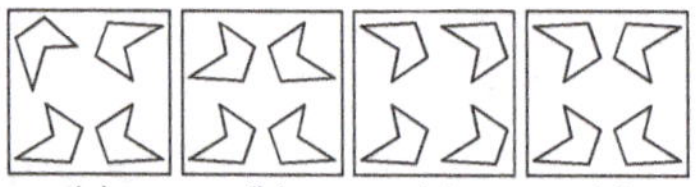

(a) (b) (c) (d)

17. Question Figure

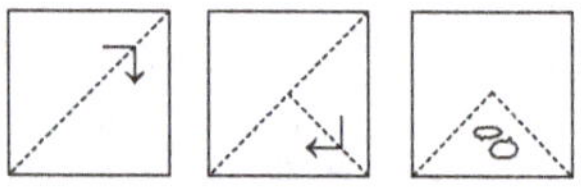

DP Constable 2023

Answer Figures

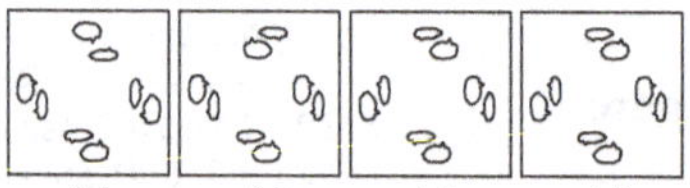

(a) (b) (c) (d)

18. Question Figure

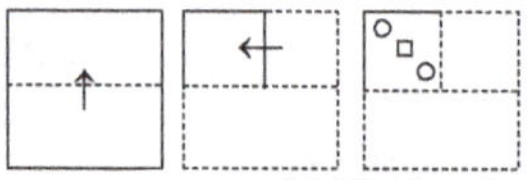

DP Constable 2023

Answer Figures

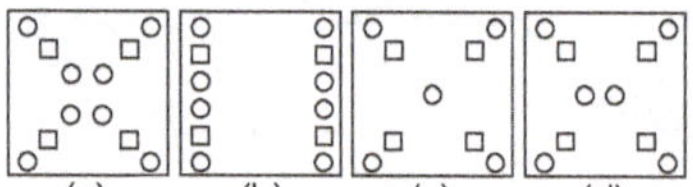

(a) (b) (c) (d)

19. Question Figure

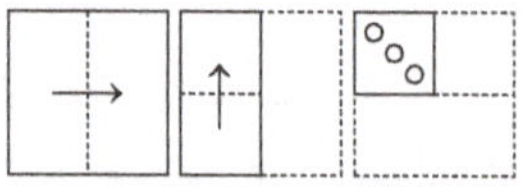

DSSSB Workshop 2024

Answer Figures

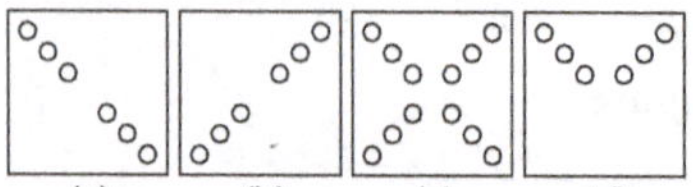

(a) (b) (c) (d)

20. Question Figure

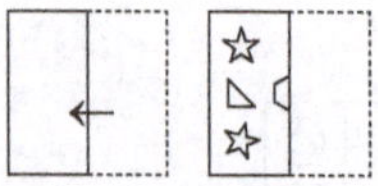

CUET (UG) 2022

Answer Figures

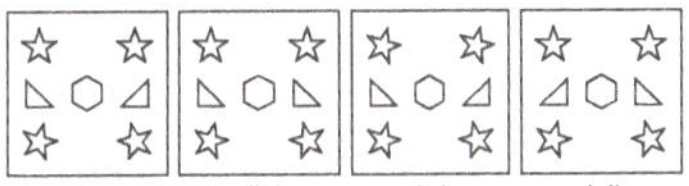

(a) (b) (c) (d)

21. Question Figure

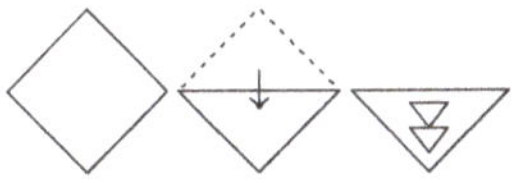

SSC (10+2) 2024

Answer Figures

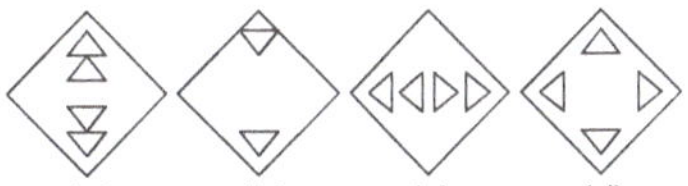

(a) (b) (c) (d)

22. Question Figure

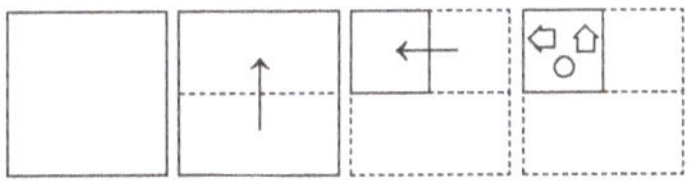

SSC CPO 2023

Answer Figures

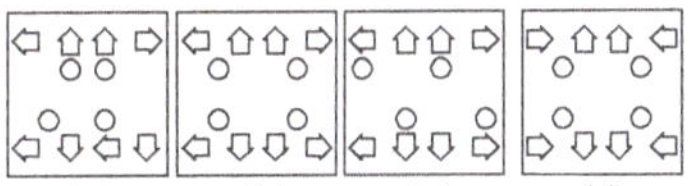

(a) (b) (c) (d)

23. Question Figure

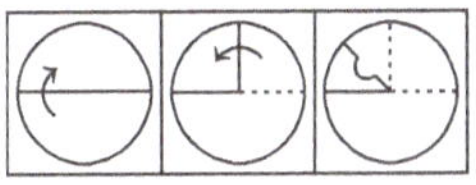

SSC CPO 2018

Answer Figures

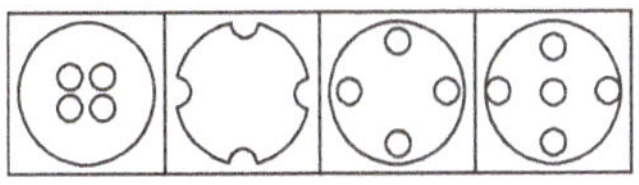

(a) (b) (c) (d)

24. Question Figure

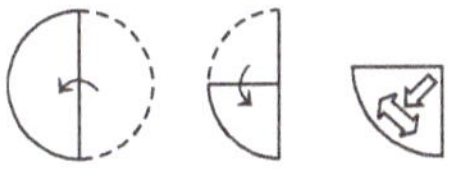

SSC CPO 2020

Answer Figures

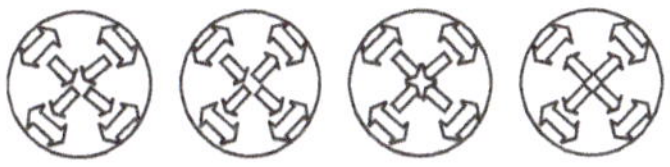

(a) (b) (c) (d)

25. Question Figure

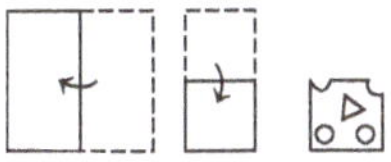

SSC CPO 2020

Answer Figures

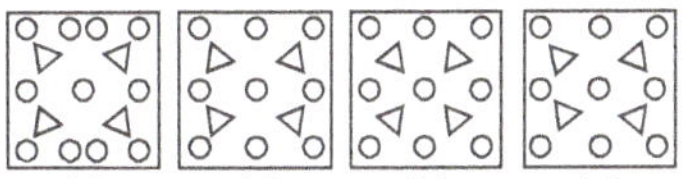

(a) (b) (c) (d)

26. Question Figure

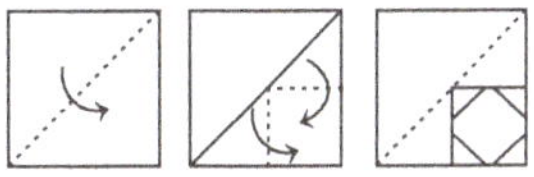

SSC CGL 2021

Answer Figures

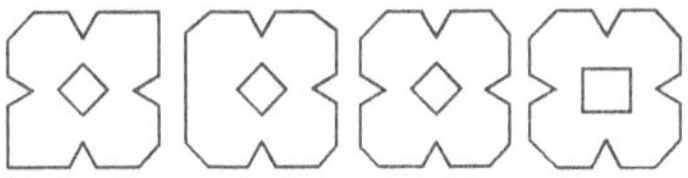

(a) (b) (c) (d)

27. Question Figure

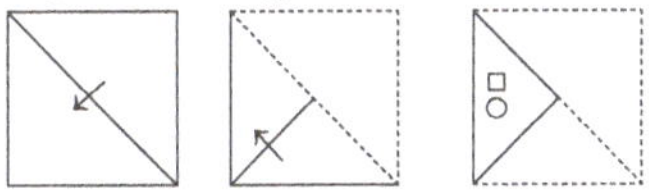

SSC Steno 2020

Answer Figures

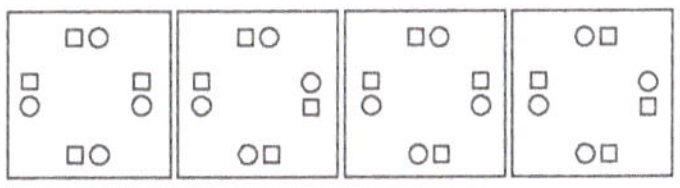

(a) (b) (c) (d)

28. Question Figure

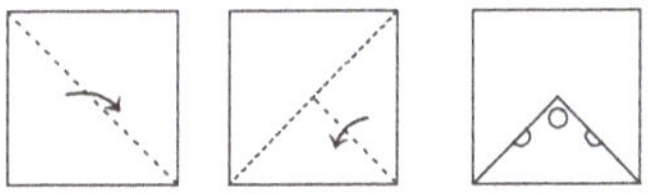

SSC (10+2) 2020

Answer Figures

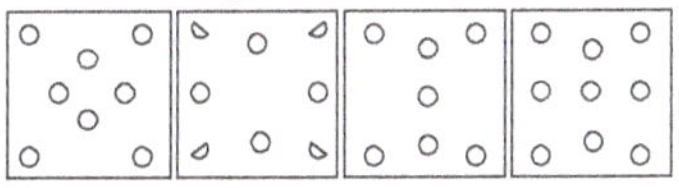

(a) (b) (c) (d)

29. Question Figure

SSC CGL 2022

Answer Figures

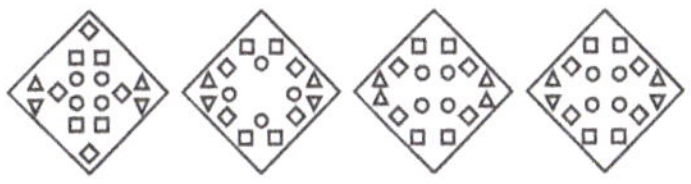

(a) (b) (c) (d)

30. Question Figure

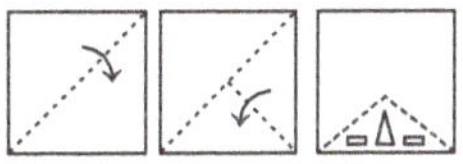

SSC (10+2) 2021

Answer Figures

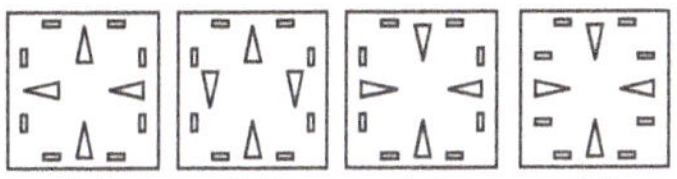

(a) (b) (c) (d)

31. Question Figure *SSC CGL (Tier-I) 2024*

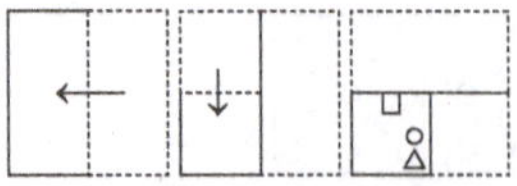

Answer Figures

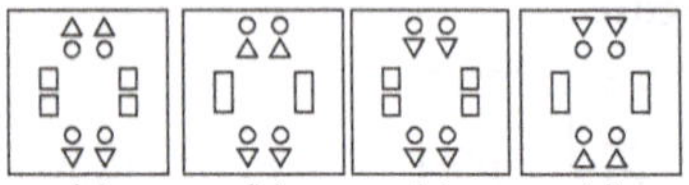

(a) (b) (c) (d)

32. Question Figure *CUET (UG) 2023*

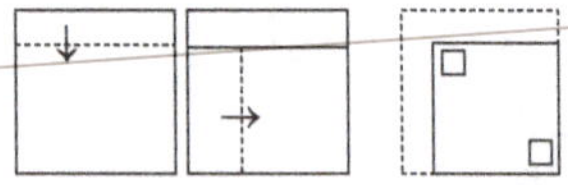

Answer Figures

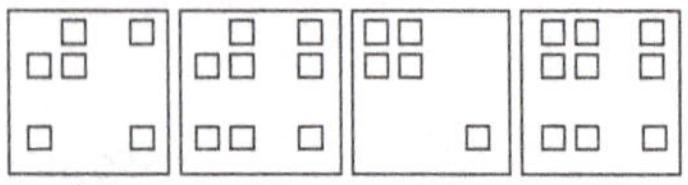

(a) (b) (c) (d)

33. Question Figure *SSC (10+2) 2022*

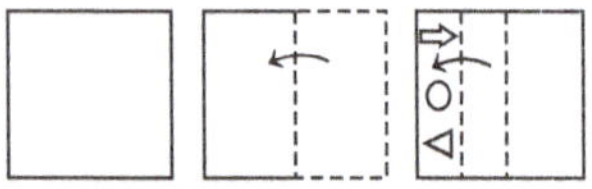

Answer Figures

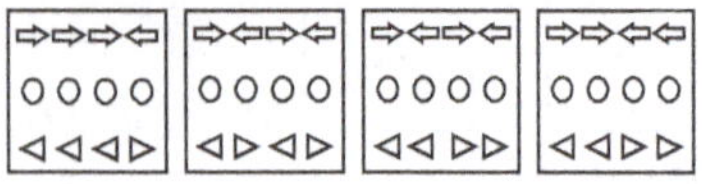

(a) (b) (c) (d)

34. Question Figure *SSC JE 2023*

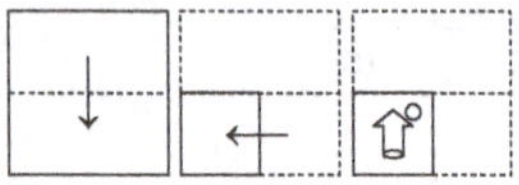

Answer Figures

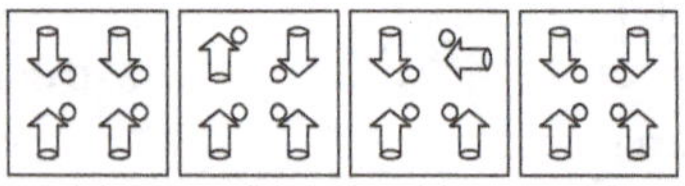

(a) (b) (c) (d)

35. Question Figure *DP Constable 2023*

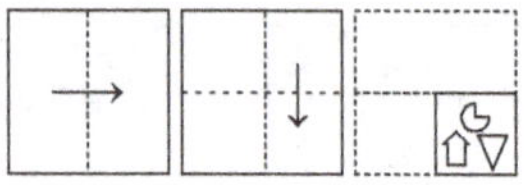

Answer Figures

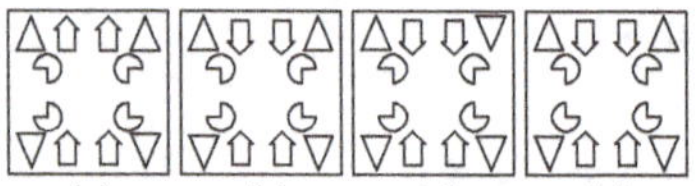

(a) (b) (c) (d)

36. Question Figure *SSC CGL (Tier-I) 2023*

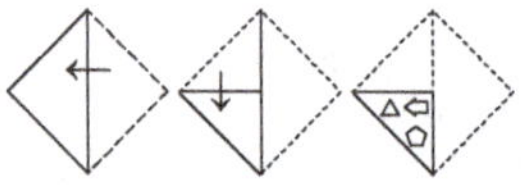

Answer Figures

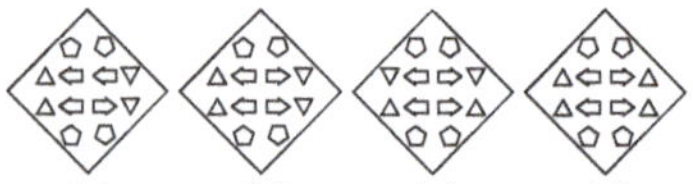

(a) (b) (c) (d)

37. Question Figure *SSC Constable (GD) 2024*

Answer Figures

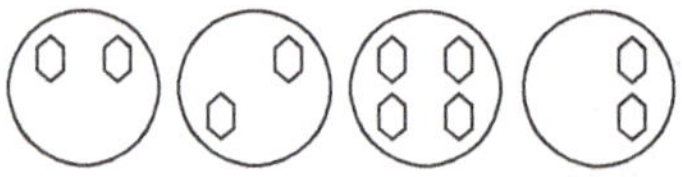

(a) (b) (c) (d)

38. Question Figure *SSC (10+2) 2023*

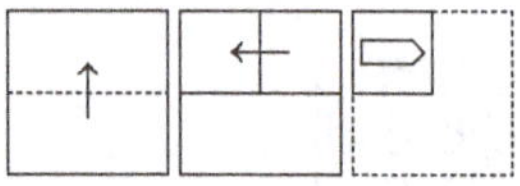

Answer Figures

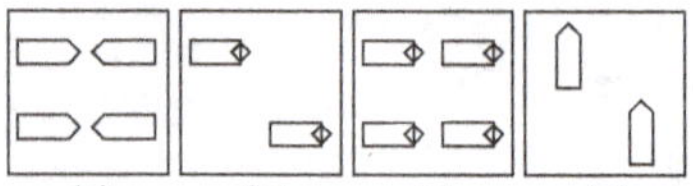

(a) (b) (c) (d)

Right Key

1. (c)	2. (d)	3. (c)	4. (c)	5. (a)	6. (c)	7. (c)	8. (a)	9. (d)	10. (b)
11. (d)	12. (d)	13. (c)	14. (b)	15. (d)	16. (d)	17. (a)	18. (a)	19. (c)	20. (a)
21. (a)	22. (b)	23. (a)	24. (d)	25. (a)	26. (c)	27. (b)	28. (a)	29. (d)	30. (c)
31. (d)	32. (c)	33. (b)	34. (d)	35. (b)	36. (c)	37. (c)	38. (a)		

CHAPTER

10 Figure Matrix

Based on 2 × 2 Matrix

In this type of questions, the figures are given in the form of a 2 × 2 matrix. In the matrix, except for one blank box, all the boxes contain some figure.

We have to find the figure according to the appropriate rule/pattern which will complete that figure matrix.

e.g. In the given question, find out the answer figure which completes the question figure matrix.

Question Figure

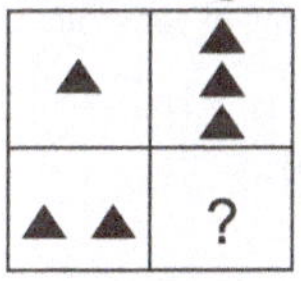

Answer Figures

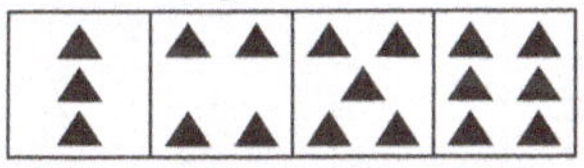

(a) (b) (c) (d)

Sol. (d) In each row moving from left to right, the number of triangles in the second part is thrice as in the first part.

So, in the missing figure there will be 2 × 3 = 6 triangles.

Figure Matrix

When the question figure is in the form of a matrix and the designs/elements/components given in the question figure follow a particular rule according to the row or column, then the matrix thus formed is called a figure matrix.

By analysing all the designs/elements/components given in the figure matrix, the rule or relation has to be found out on the basis of which the answer figure that comes at place of the question mark in the matrix has to be selected.

Score Booster

Solve problems of figure matrix by carefully analysing one of the complete rows/columns and deriving appropriate patters or rule.

Based on 3 × 3 Matrix

In this type of questions, the figures are given in the form of a 3 × 3 matrix. In the matrix, except for one blank box, all the boxes contain some figure. We have to find the figure according to the appropriate rule pattern which will complete the figure matrix.

e.g. In the given question, find out the answer figure which completes the question figure matrix.

Question Figure

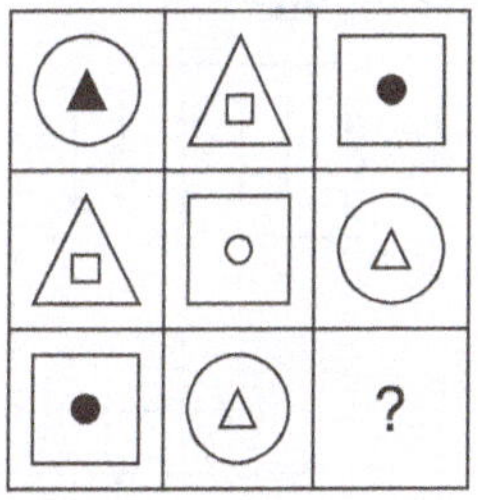

Answer Figures

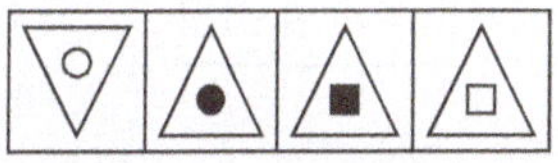

(a) (b) (c) (d)

Sol. (c) In each column and row, three types of figures , 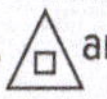 and  are used and in figures at each corner of the matrix the internal geometrical figure is shaded.
Hence, the figure given in option (c) will replace the question mark.

Exam Approach Examples

Based on 2 × 2 Matrix

Example 1 **In the given question, find out the answer figure which complete the question figure.**

Problem Figure

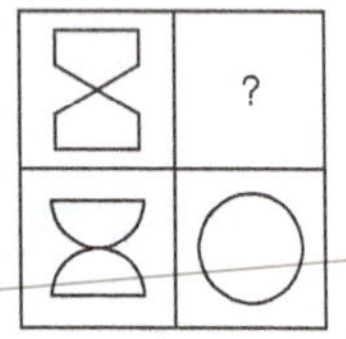

Answer Figures

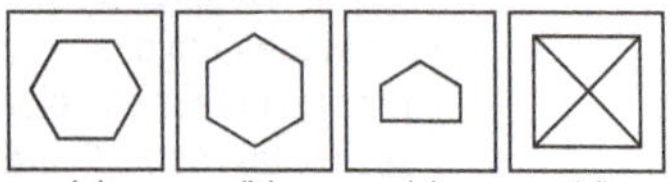

(a) (b) (c) (d)

Sol. (*b*) The second figure in each row from left is obtained by joining the inverted lower half of first figure with its inverted upper half.

Example 2 **In the given question, which answer figure will complete the given matrix?**

Problem Figure

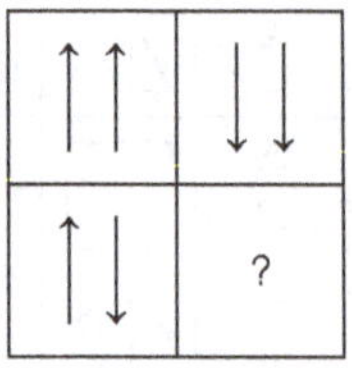

Answer Figures

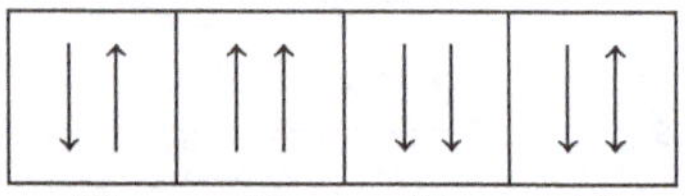

(a) (b) (c) (d)

Sol. (*a*) In each row, the second figure is obtained by rotating first figure by 180°. Similarly, in the second row, figure (a) will come at place of the question mark.

Based on 3 × 3 Matrix

Directions (Ex. Nos. 3-5) *In each of the following questions, find out the answer figure which completes the question figure matrix.*

Example 3 Problem Figure

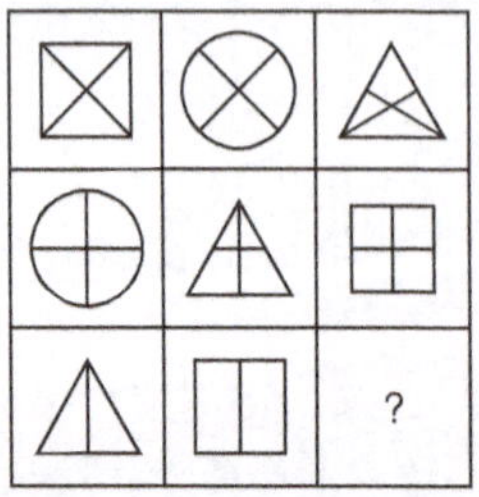

Helping Tips

While solving such questions, first of all we find out the appropriate rule or relation.

Answer Figures

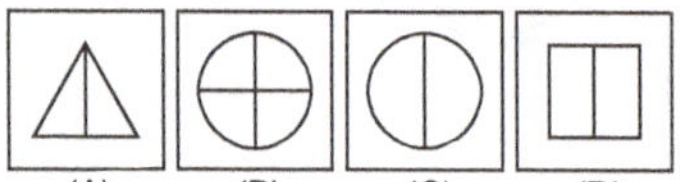

(A) (B) (C) (D)

RRB Group D 2018

(a) B (b) C
(c) A (d) D

Sol. (*b*) In the given matrix, in each column three types of geometrical figures i.e. square, circle and triangle are used. Moreover in first row '×', in second row '+' and in third row 'I' is used. Therefore, the figure (C) will replace the question mark.

Example 4 Problem Figure

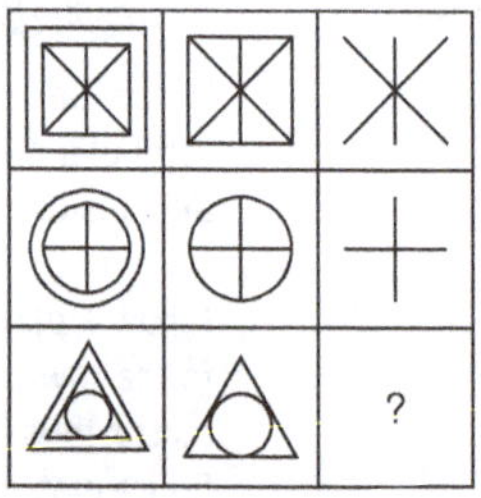

Trending Concept

Question based on 3 × 3 figure matrix are very important from the examination point of view. This type of questions is very important for RRB Group-D and RRB ALP exams etc.

Answer Figures

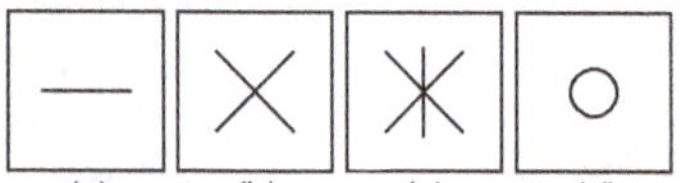

(a) (b) (c) (d)

Sol. (*d*) In each row moving from left to right, the second figure is obtained by removing the outermost element of the first figure and the third figure is obtained by removing the outermost element of the second figure.

Example 5 Problem Figure

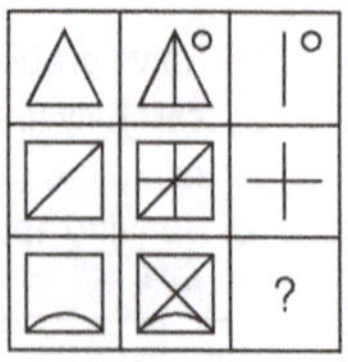

RRB ALP (Tier-I) 2018

Answer Figures

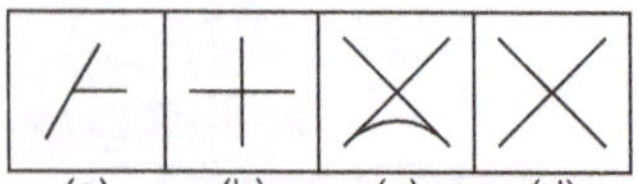

(a) (b) (c) (d)

Sol. (*d*) In each row the middle figure is formed by overlapping first figure over the last figure. Therefore figure given in option (d) will come at the place of '?'

Chapter Challenge

Based on 2 × 2 Matrix

Directions (Q. Nos. 1-4) *In each of the following questions, find out which of the answer figures* (a), (b), (c) *and* (d) *will complete the figure matrix.*

1. Problem Figure Answer Figures

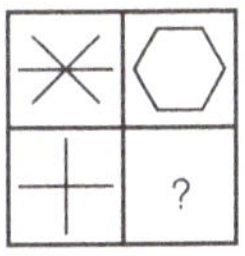

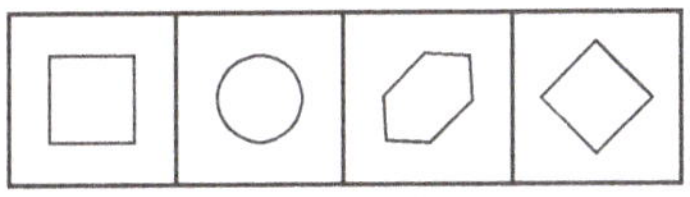

(a) (b) (c) (d)

2.

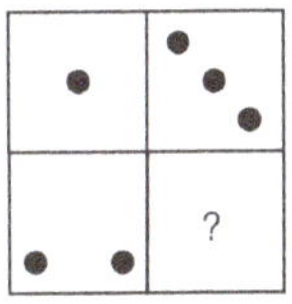

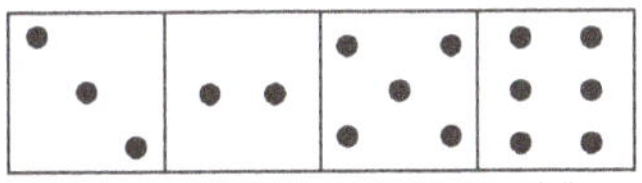

(a) (b) (c) (d)

3.

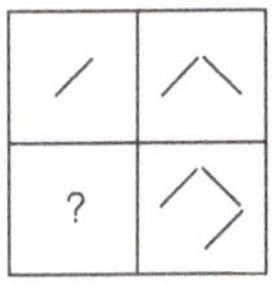

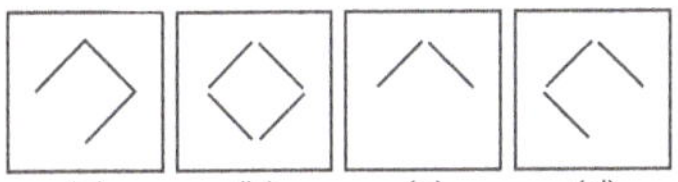

(a) (b) (c) (d)

4.

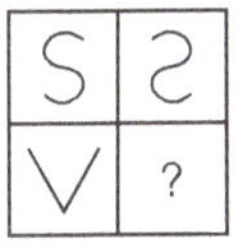

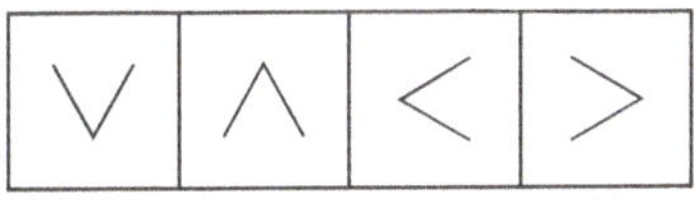

(a) (b) (c) (d)

Based on 3 × 3 Matrix

Directions (Q. Nos. 5-27) *In each of the following questions, analyze the figure and find out the rule which the given figures, follow and complete the missing figure in the matrix.*

5. Problem Figure Answer Figures

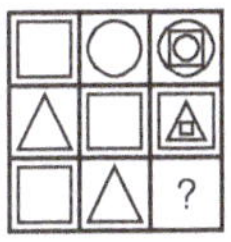

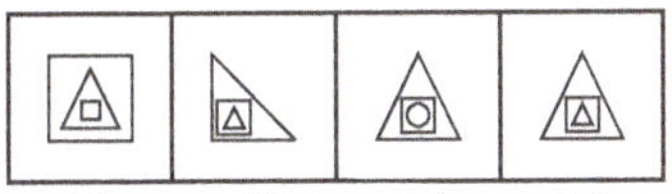

(a) (b) (c) (d)

DSSSB 2020

6.

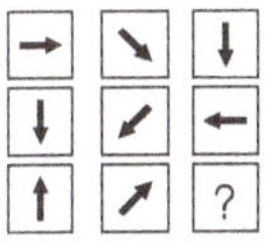

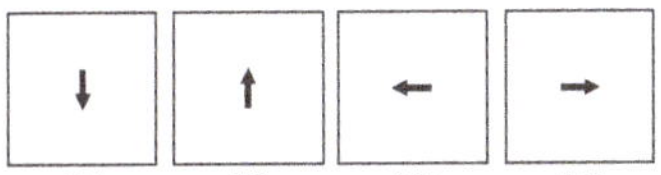

(A) (B) (C) (D)

UPSSSC 2019

(a) A (b) D (c) B (d) C

7.

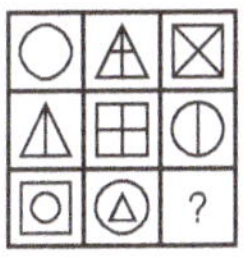

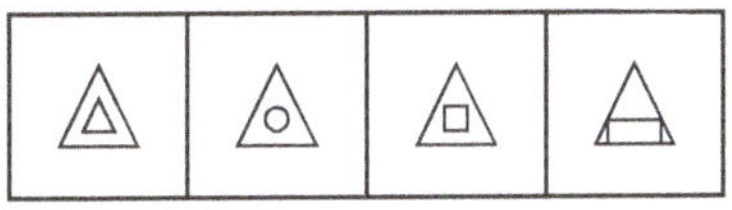

(a) (b) (c) (d)

Delhi Police MTS 2019

8. Problem Figure

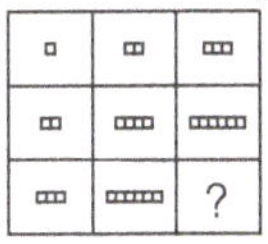

RRB ALP 2018

MRC***

(Most Repeating Concepts)

Q. Nos. 8, 10, 13 and 16 are very important for RRB ALP examination. Question on these concepts are being continuously asked in the exams.

Answer Figures

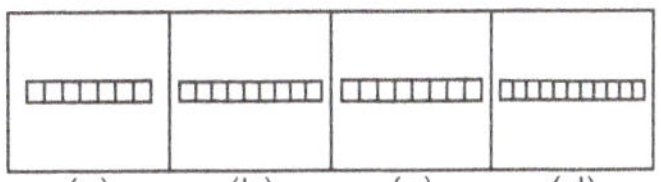

(a) (b) (c) (d)

9. Problem Figure Answer Figures

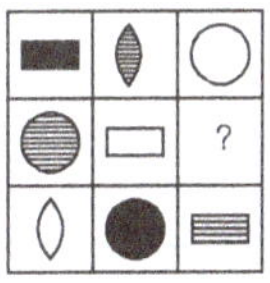

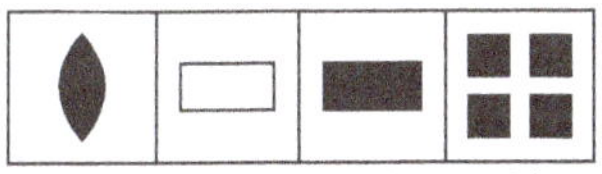

(a) (b) (c) (d)

Delhi Police MTS 2019

10.

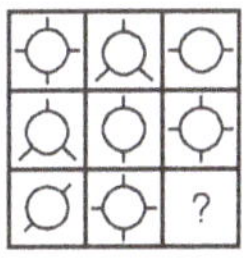

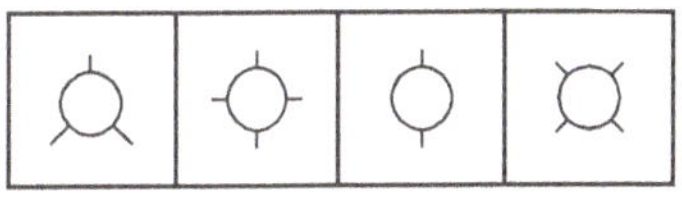

(a) (b) (c) (d)

RRB ALP 2018

11.

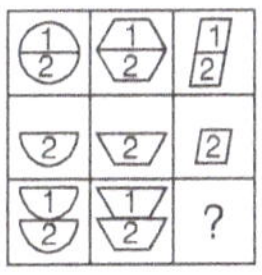

(a) (b) (c) (d)

12.

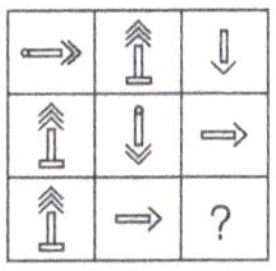

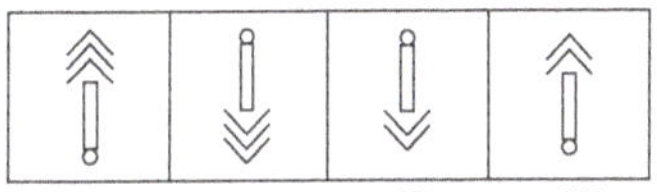

(A) (B) (C) (D)

RRB Group D 2018

(a) A (b) C
(c) B (d) D

13.

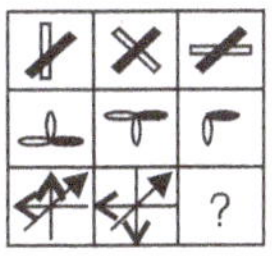

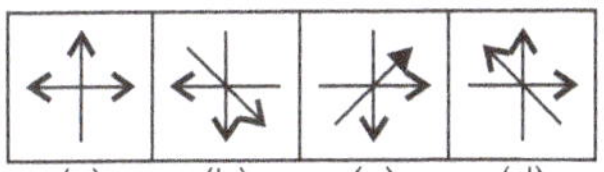

(a) (b) (c) (d)

RRB ALP 2018

14.

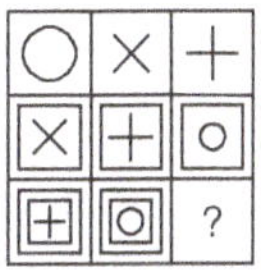

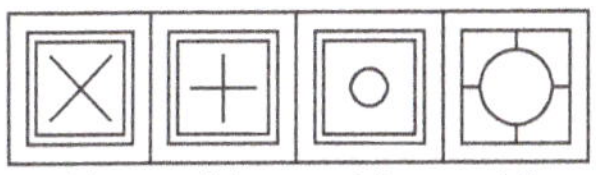

(a) (b) (c) (d)

15.

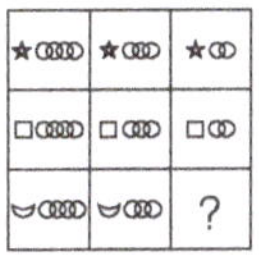

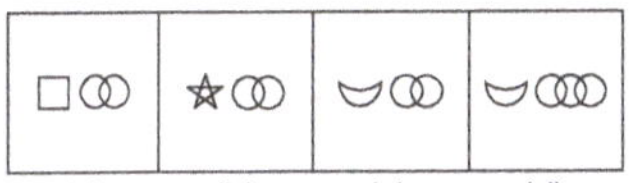

(a) (b) (c) (d)

RRB Group D 2018

16. Problem Figure Answer Figures

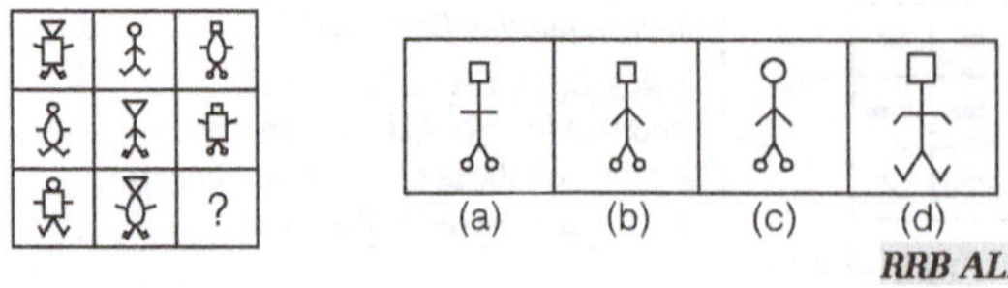

RRB ALP 2018

17.

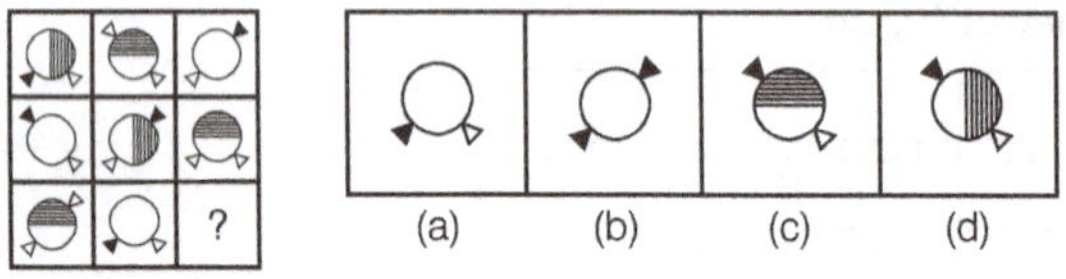

18.

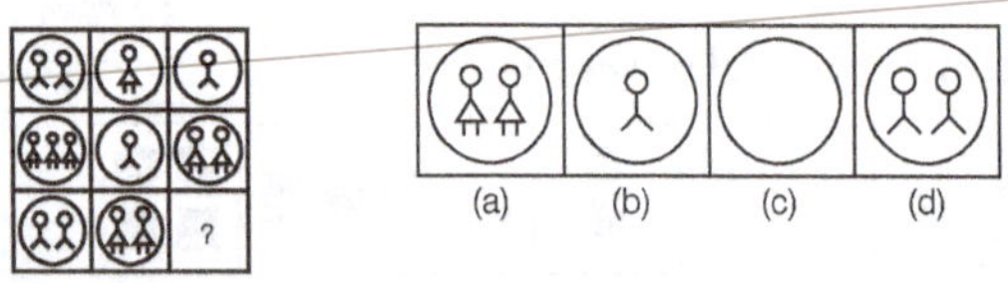

19.

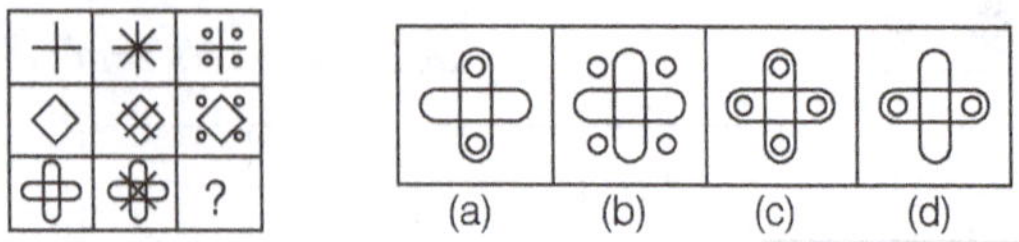

Delhi Police MTS 2019

20.

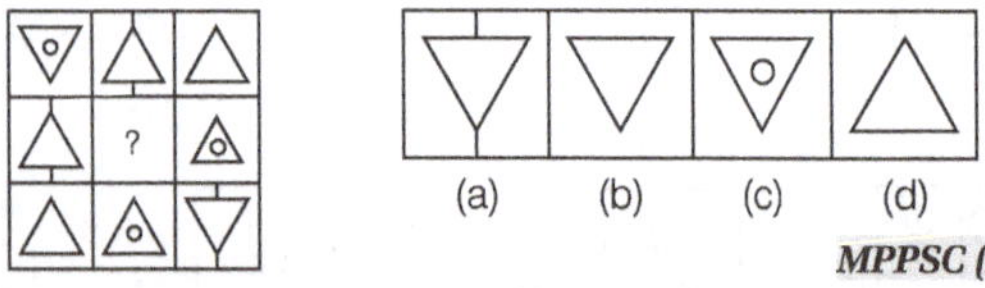

MPPSC (Pre) 2021

21.

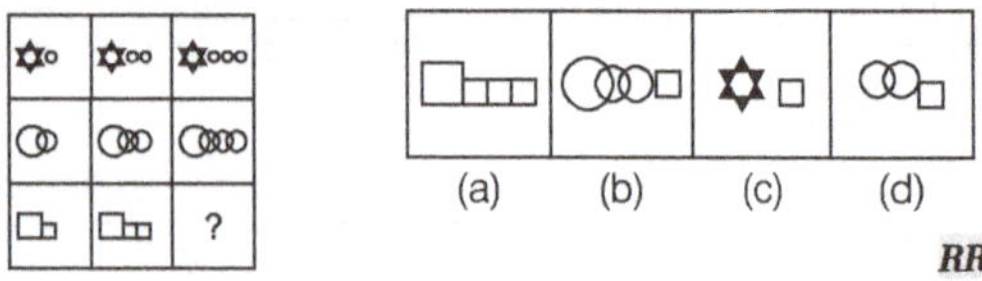

RRB JE 2019

22. Problem Figure Answer Figures

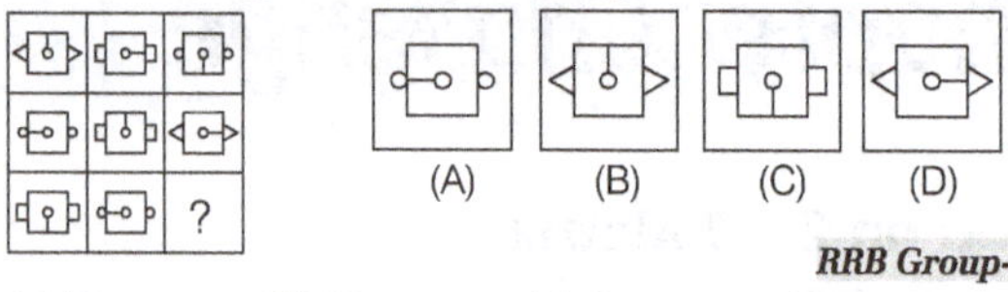

RRB Group-D 2018

(a) D (b) B (c) C (d) A

23.

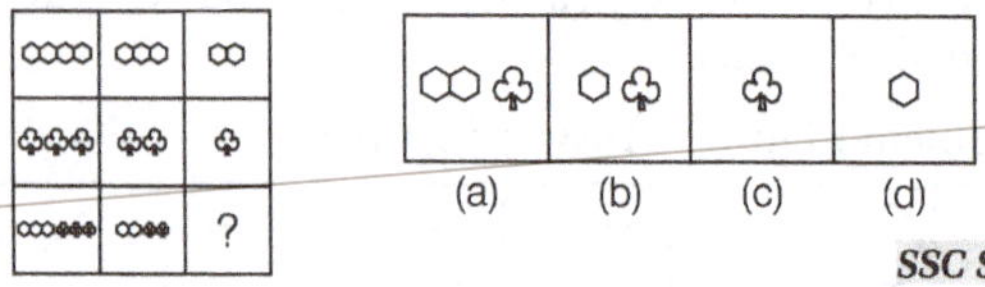

SSC Steno 2019

24.

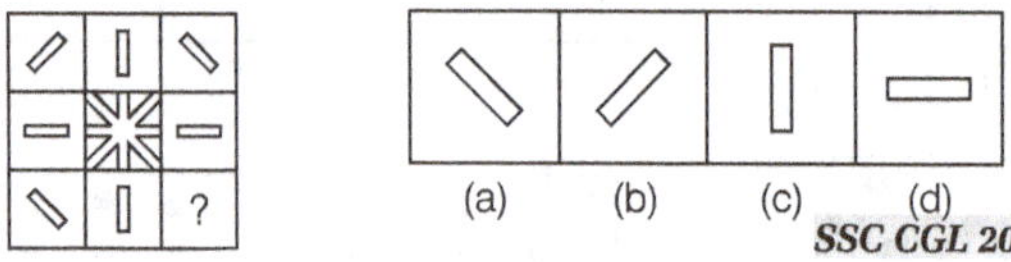

SSC CGL 2014, 2021

25.

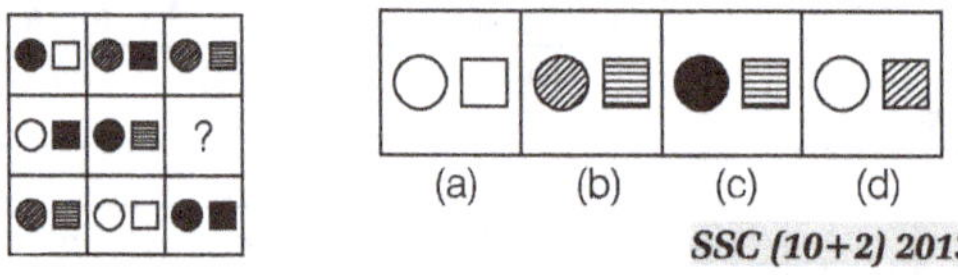

SSC (10+2) 2013, KVS 2020

26.

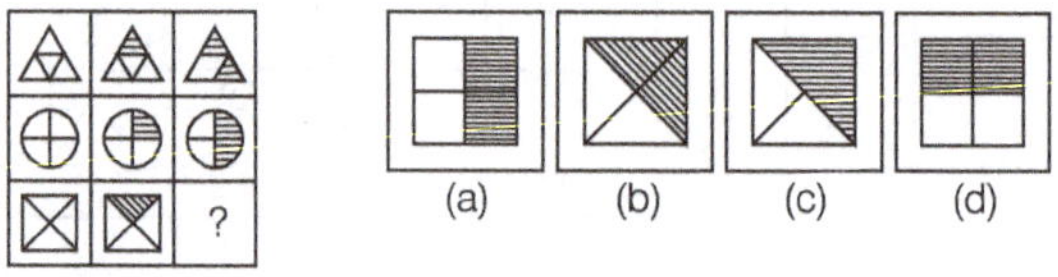

27.

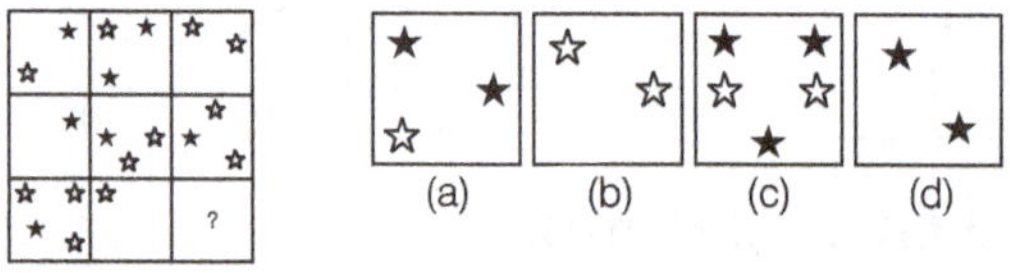

Right Key

1. (d)	2. (d)	3. (b)	4. (a)	5. (d)	6. (b)	7. (c)	8. (b)	9. (a)	10. (a)
11. (c)	12. (b)	13. (c)	14. (a)	15. (c)	16. (b)	17. (d)	18. (c)	19. (b)	20. (b)
21. (a)	22. (b)	23. (b)	24. (b)	25. (a)	26. (b)	27. (d)			

Solutions

1. *(d)* The pattern followed is

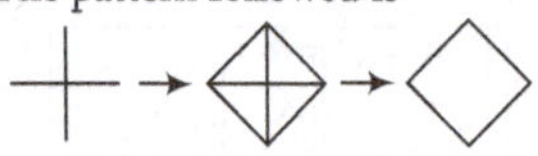

In each row the second figure is obtained by joining the adjacent end points of the intersecting lines.

2. *(d)* In each row the number of dots in the second figure is thrice the number of dots in the first figure.

3. *(b)* Starting with the top left figure, one line is increasing in each figure while moving in clockwise direction.

So, four lines will come in fourth part.

4. *(a)* The second figure in the first row is the mirror image of the first figure.

Hence, the second figure in the second row will also be the mirror image of the first figure.

> **TOP TIPS** While solving this type of question, it is very important to have knowledge of mirror images of figures.

5. *(d)* In each row, the third figure is obtained by placing second figure, inside and outside the first figure.

6. *(b)* In each row moving from left to right, the arrow is rotating 45° in clockwise direction with each step.

7. *(c)* In each row we have three figures, i.e. a square, a triangle and a circle.

In third row, we have a circle and a square present in outermost portion, so triangle is the outermost portion in missing figure.

We have also noticed that the figure enclosed in last figure of columns 1 and 2 is triangle and circle, so a square should be enclosed in last figure of column 3.

Hence, we can say that the missing part consist of a figure with triangle containing square.

8. *(b)* In first row, the number of squares is increasing by one.

In second row, the number of squares is increasing by two and in third row, the number of squares is increasing by three while moving from left to right.

Hence, option figure (b) will replace the question mark.

9. *(a)* In each row, figures ▭, ⬯, ○ are present only once. In which one figure is shaded, one is unshaded and one is lined. So, option figure (a) is the correct figure which will replace the question mark.

10. *(a)* In figure, each row consists of a circle attached with two, three and four line segments. So, in third row only the figure with three line segments is missing.

Hence, option figure (a) will replace the question mark (?).

Smart Approach

As per the figure given in the question, the number of small lines drawn around the circle follows a certain order.

11. *(c)* Each figure in third row comprises of figure marked as 1 of first row in inverted form and figure marked as 2 as it is.

12. *(b)* The given matrix is made by using only three figures.

These three figures are given in three directions i.e. ↑, →, ↓ in each row.

Hence, in the third row the third figure will be .

13. *(c)* In each row moving from left to right, the darkened part of each figure remains in the same direction while the remaining part of the figure rotates 45° anti-clockwise.

14. *(a)* Each column has one '+', one 'O' and one '×'. First figure of each column is without boundary and second one is in the square. Third figure is in two squares. As, there are '+' and 'O' in third column. So, figure '×' surrounded by two squares will come at the place of '?'.

15. *(c)* Moving from left to right in each row, the left most symbol remains same and the number of the intersecting circles is decreasing by one.

Hence, the figure (c) will replace the question mark.

16. *(b)* There are three types of faces, 3 types of bodies, 3 types of hands and 3 types of legs. Each of which is used only once in a row.

17. *(d)* Clearly, there are three types of circles in each row, one is unshaded, one has its right half shaded and one has its upper half shaded. Also, two of the figures in each row have one triangle shaded.

18. *(c)* Clearly, in each row, the number of elements in the third figure is equal to the difference in the number of elements in the first and second figures.

19. *(b)* In each row, first figure gets super imposed on second figure, then cross lines are replaced with four circles and this process is repeated in each row.

So, option figure (b) is the correct figure which replace the question mark.

20. *(b)* In each row we have three figures, i.e. a simple triangle, a triangle with a circle inside it and a triangle with two line segments. Also, in each row two triangles point upward while one triangle points downward.

21. *(a)* In each row, the number of smaller figures increases by one with each step from left to right.

22. *(b)* In each row, small squares, small circles and small triangles are getting attached to the bigger square. Each shape is used only once in each row. Moreover the line attached to a circle in the bigger square is rotating 90° clockwise with each step.

Hence, figure (B) will replace the question mark.

23. *(b)* Moving from left to right in each row, the number of each type of elements is decreasing by one with each step.

24. *(b)* Image in all boxes are part of the image that is in the center of the matrix and no part of image is repeating.

Image given in option (b) is the only part left to complete the middle figure.

25. *(a)* In each column there are three types of squares (shaded, unshaded and lined), each of which exists in pair with one of the three types of circles (shaded, unshaded and lined and each type of figure is used only once in each column).

So, option figure (a) is the correct figure which will come at the place of '?'.

26. *(b)* Moving from left to right, the first figure in each row is completely unshaded. The second one has one-fourth part shaded and the third one is half shaded, where the direction of shading for the last two figures in each row remains the same.

27. *(d)* In each column and row, the number (sum) of shaded and unshaded stars is three and four, respectively.